ADDISON-WESLEY

WORLD HISTORY

TRADITIONS AND NEW DIRECTIONS

Procession of the Magi (detail). Fresco. Benozzo Gozzoli, 1459.

ADDISON-WESLEY

WORLD HISTORY

TRADITIONS AND NEW DIRECTIONS

AUTHORS

PETER N. STEARNS

DONALD R. SCHWARTZ

BARRY K. BEYER

GEOGRAPHY CONSULTANT

CHRISTOPHER L. SALTER

ADDISON-WESLEY PUBLISHING COMPANY

Menlo Park, California · Reading, Massachusetts · New York · Don Mills, Ontario
Wokingham, England · Amsterdam · Bonn · Sydney · Singapore
Tokyo · Madrid · San Juan

AUTHORS

Peter N. Stearns, Heinz Professor, is head of the Department of History, Carnegie-Mellon University. He holds A.B., A.M., and Ph.D. degrees from Harvard University. In addition to being the founder and editor of the *Journal of Social History*, he has written 29 books and numerous articles, mainly on American and European social history. Peter Stearns has also been active in curriculum development, both on the college and high school level. Currently a member of the Council of the World History Association, he has taught world history and has participated in nationally funded teacher institutes.

Donald R. Schwartz is currently a member of the history department at California State University at Long Beach and is the Credential Coordinator for social science, history, and government. He holds a Ph.D. in diplomatic history from New York University. Donald Schwartz has had 15 years of experience teaching social studies in the New York City secondary schools. He has served as Chair of Social Studies at Sheepshead Bay High School and has acted as Coordinator of Social Studies for the White Plains, New York, public schools.

Barry K. Beyer is Professor of Education and director of a doctorate program at George Mason University, Fairfax, Virginia. He received an M.Ed. in Social Studies Education from Syracuse University and a Ph.D. in history from the University of Rochester. As a nationally recognized expert in the teaching of thinking, he has served as a consultant to school systems throughout the United States and Canada and has conducted numerous teacher training workshops and seminars. Prior to 1980, Barry Beyer was Professor of History at Carnegie-Mellon and, for eight years, was a high school history teacher. He has edited two special issues of the NCSS *Social Education*, one on writing in social studies and one on critical thinking. He is currently a consultant for the Association for Supervision and Curriculum Development and has contributed more than 100 articles to professional journals and other publications. Barry Beyer is the author of *Practical Strategies for the Teaching of Thinking* and of *Developing a Thinking Skills Program*.

GEOGRAPHY CONSULTANT

Christopher L. Salter is Professor and Chair of the Department of Geography at the University of Missouri-Columbia. He received a B.A. from Oberlin College and an M.A. and Ph.D. in geography from the University of California, Berkeley. Dr. Salter has served as the coordinator for the Geographic Alliance Network at the National Geographic Society. In 1984, Dr. Salter, with the help of Dean Juan Lara of UCLA's Center for Academic Interinstitutional Programs, founded the model California Geographic Alliance. Christopher Salter has conducted hundreds of workshops for secondary and college teachers of geography at the state, regional, and national levels. He has also published numerous articles in geography and social science journals.

ISBN 0-201-28684-X

3 4 5 6 7 8 9 10 - VH - 95 94 93 92

Area Specialists

Africa: Dr. Joseph Adjaye, African Studies Outreach Director, University of Wisconsin, Madison

Latin America: Dr. Susan Deans-Smith, Assistant Professor of History, University of Texas at Austin

Middle East: Dr. William J. Griswold, Professor of History, Colorado State University

East Asia: Professor Joyce K. Kallgren, Professor of Political Science, University of California, Davis; Chair of the Center for Chinese Studies and Associate Director of the Institute of East Asian Studies, University of California, Berkeley

South Asia: Dr. Barbara D. Metcalf, Professor of History, University of California, Davis

Review and Field Test

Curriculum Specialists

Mary Lynn Johnson, Program Director for Social Studies, Spring Independent School District, Houston, Texas

Evelyn Nash, Social Studies Supervisor, Detroit Public Schools, Detroit, Michigan

Classroom Teachers

Darlene Doull, World History Teacher, William Howard Taft High School, San Antonio, Texas

Joanne Lane, World History Teacher, Spring Woods High School, Houston, Texas

Diane Patin, Social Studies Teacher, Eisenhower High School, Houston, Texas

Thomas W. Reinsch, World History Team Leader, R. C. Clark High School, Plano, Texas

Jennifer Sullivan, World History Teacher, Carrollton Farmers' Branch Independent School District, Carrollton, Texas

Martha Allshouse, Social Studies Department Chair, Los Gatos High School, Los Gatos, California

Samuel Eigel, Social Studies Teacher, Southwestern High School, Detroit, Michigan

Mary Friel, Social Studies Teacher, Locust Valley High School, Locust Valley, New York

Contributing Writers

James T. Yenckel, an editor for *The Washington Post*, has published articles in *Historic Preservation* and other magazines and a book on travel.

Christopher Ward holds a Ph.D. in Latin American history. He has contributed articles to social science journals and has taught courses in American and European history.

Michael P. Plumpton, who holds an M.Ed., has been writing and developing educational materials for ten years. He has also taught social studies.

Diane Hart, a Woodrow Wilson Fellow, has authored a number of books in the social studies. She holds an M.A. in history from Stanford University.

Eric W. Engles has taught writing and has written educational materials in both social studies and science.

Author's Acknowledgment

Barry K. Beyer wishes to acknowledge Professor Jack Censer, Professor Marion Deshmukh, Professor Donald Holsinger, Assistant Vice-President for Academic Affairs James Fletcher, Jerry Thomas, and Sue Woodfine for their assistance in the development of the thinking skills manuscript.

Addison-Wesley Staff

Senior Editor: Diane G. Silver
Project Editor: Jan Alderson
Editor: Bobbi Watkinson
Associate Editor: John Burner
Production Coordinator: John F. Kelly

Cover: *Flying Horse*, Chinese bronze figure, Han Dynasty, second century A.D. Height: 9 1/2 inches (24.5 cm), length: 17 3/4 inches (45 cm).

This is the most impressive sculpture yet known of a tall Central Asian breed imported by the Chinese, who prized the animals as cavalry horses. These swift horses became status symbols in China, where artists and poets often called them "Horses of Heaven" and "Flying Dragons." Here the horse is depicted neighing and galloping while balanced on a flying swallow. The sculpture was excavated in 1969 in the northern Chinese province of Kansu.

AUTHORS' NOTE TO STUDENTS

In this book we deal with world history, a panorama of wonderful achievements and horrible cruelties, of human strengths and human frailties. We have compiled not just a series of facts, but a set of ideas about key civilizations, time periods, causes of change, and similarities and differences between peoples of the world.

We never intended to cover the whole vast human experience; in fact, we have had to omit more facts than we could include. However, what we have selected is information about most of the major cultures and civilizations that have developed over the past several thousand years.

World history, as a source of understanding where the world has been and what it has become, looks at the tensions between peoples that have arisen from their diversities. It also focuses on the various kinds of contacts between peoples that draw different groups together.

Though tensions are constant, both diversities and contacts change over time. World history charts the developments of major world civilizations and cultures and how, over time, they have repelled and attracted one another. With a grasp of such patterns of change and continuity, you will be able to understand the world around you as its diverse peoples and nations continue to follow their age-old traditions while moving forward in new directions.

Peter N. Stearns
Donald R. Schwartz
Barry K. Beyer

A WORD ABOUT GEOGRAPHY

Geography is an important part of the study of world history. Geography provides a method for asking the "where" and the "why there" questions of history. This in turn helps us understand the relationship between people and their environment, as well as the interaction between different groups of people over time. The *Understanding Geography and History* features in this text focus on five fundamental themes in geography.

Location: Position on the Earth's Surface. The first task in geography is to locate places. Location significantly shapes historical events. Knowing locations and their characteristics helps us understand these events.

Place: Physical and Human Characteristics. Places are described by physical and human characteristics. Physical processes and human activities shape these characteristics over time.

Relationships Within Places: Humans and Environments. People both modify and adapt to natural settings. The way people view their environment differs among societies and changes with time. Geography seeks to understand the interaction between humans and the environment.

Movement: Humans Interacting on Earth. Patterns of movement—trade, travel, and various forms of communication—have linked diverse peoples throughout history. Geographic studies can help trace the history of the spread of people, goods, ideas, and even disease. Because global interaction is increasing rapidly, understanding movement is especially helpful.

Regions: How They Form and Change. Regions are the basic units of geographic study. They may be defined by political boundaries, such as nations, or by other characteristics such as language or landform types. We can use the idea of regions as a tool to help us generalize about humans, the environment, and relationships between different areas of the world.

These five themes, developed by the National Council for Geographic Education and the Association of American Geographers, give us a picture of the role geography plays in understanding history. You will see these themes not only in geography features, but also throughout the text. This aspect of the study of history provides a way to better understand our relationship to earth and other peoples of the world.

CONTENTS

UNIT 4 GOLDEN AGES OF ASIA, AFRICA, AND THE MIDDLE EAST 250

MAPS

CHARTS, TABLES, AND GRAPHS

REFERENCE CENTER

THE ANCIENT WORLD

PREHISTORY–250 B.C.

Hail to thee, O Nile, That issues from the earth and comes to keep Egypt Alive . . . He that makes the desert to drink. All of thy children Jubilate for thee.

—Hymn to the Nile, Egyptian, about 1600 B.C.

Sky Goddess in the form of a cow. Egyptian papyrus, 1250 B.C.

GLOBAL TIMELINE

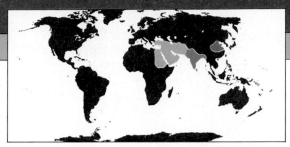

- ■ THE MIDDLE EAST
- ■ INDIA
- ■ CHINA

	POLITICAL	TECHNOLOGICAL	SOCIAL
		First stone tools (about 1.5 million B.C.)	
4000		Development of agriculture and domestication of animals (about 8000 B.C.)	Cro-Magnon cave paintings (about 25,000 B.C.)
3500	First cities	Invention of the wheel	Harps and flutes played in Egypt
3000	Sumerian civilization	Cuneiform writing / Hieroglyphic writing/ papyrus / Bronze tools	
2500	Sumerian city-states	First Egyptian pyramid / Legendary beginning of Chinese silk making	Wrestling becomes first highly developed sport
2000	Old Kingdom in Egypt / Height of Indus Valley civilization	Complex water system in Mohenjo-daro	Gilgamesh epic recorded
1500	Babylonian Empire / Middle Kingdom in Egypt	Obelisks used as sun dials in Egypt / Iron tools used in Mesopotamia	Code of Hammurabi
1000	New Kingdom in Egypt / Shang Dynasty / Vedic Age in India / Assyrian Empire	Early development of Chinese writing	Beginning of Judaism / Oral development of the *Vedas* and *Upanishads* in India
500	Hebrew kingdoms / Chou Dynasty		*I Ching* written
B.C.	Chaldean Empire / Height of Persian Empire		Founding of Zoroastrianism
A.D.			

ROOTS OF CIVILIZATION

PREHISTORY–3000 B.C.

Paleolithic hunters. Saharan rock painting.

The development of civilization was a long, slow process. Its beginnings are lost in the shadowy time before people invented writing. Although scientists have worked out many ways to unlock the secrets of that shadowy past, many questions remain unanswered.

What is known is that early human beings possessed such higher abilities as insight and thought. These abilities enabled people to conceive ideas and make changes that would affect human life for all time. Early people also gained the ability to work together in groups, which led to the development of civilizations. These early civilizations had some common features, but each also had its own special characteristics. Often, as different civilizations came into contact, ideas passed from one to another.

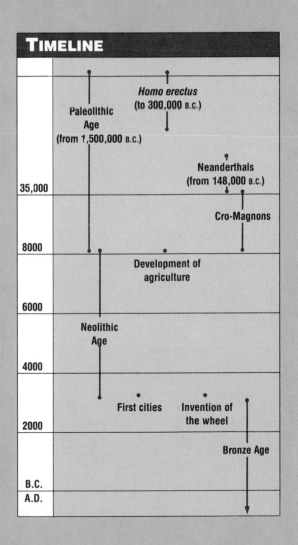

TIMELINE

1-1
PREHISTORY

READ TO FIND OUT

— what the terms *culture*, *prehistory*, *tundra*, *migrate*, *evolved*, *anthropologists*, *archaeologists*, *artifacts*, *society*, and *fossils* mean.
— how the Ice Age affected life on earth.
— what types of scientists study prehistoric times.
— what clues provide evidence of prehistoric life.

The ancestors of modern human beings began the slow development of human *culture* when they first made and used tools, perhaps as long as 2 million years ago. Human culture—the way of life of a people, including their arts, beliefs, inventions, traditions, and language—developed slowly over thousands of years.

Not until about 5,000 years ago did people begin to create written records of how they lived and what they believed. The extremely long period before writing was invented is called *prehistory*. If human history were compressed into the 12 hours of a clock-face, the period since writing has existed would take up only the last 14 minutes or so. The 11 hours and 46 minutes before then would represent prehistoric times.

THE ICE AGE

In the last 1.5 million years, the earth has experienced at least four cycles of warming and cooling. Together, these cycles are known as the Ice Age. Sometime after 20,000 B.C., the most recent warming trend began, and by 10,000 to 8,000 B.C., the earth's climate had become much like it is today.

When the earth's climate cooled 1.5 million years ago, more snow fell in the winter than could melt in the summer. Near the earth's North and South poles the snow began to pile up and turn to ice. Eventually, the ice became so thick that it began to move under the pressure of its own great weight. Huge masses of ice slowly flowed outward from the poles. These

Glaciers such as this one in British Columbia, Canada, powerfully shape the earth's surface. Prehistoric human and animal migrations were influenced by the flow of similar ice masses.

sheets of slow-moving ice, called glaciers, covered about one-third of the earth's land surface. In the Northern Hemisphere, large parts of Europe, Asia, and North America were buried in ice. In the Southern Hemisphere, where there is less land, ice spread over the sea.

Each time vast amounts of the earth's water turned to ice, the volume of water in the sea decreased. The sea level dropped as much as 500 feet (152 meters), exposing the shallower parts of the ocean bottom. In some places, lands that had once been buried under the sea now served as dry land bridges connecting islands and continents.

The ice affected the geography of the earth in other ways too. The glaciers gouged out deep valleys, and carved and polished mountain walls. As the glaciers crept slowly over the land, they pushed piles of soil and rock ahead of them. Some of the rock was ground into a fine soil called loess (LŌ-ehs). This soil was blown by the wind and deposited over large areas of the Northern Hemisphere. Later, when the

earth warmed and the glaciers began to melt, mounds of soil and rock were left behind. Lakes formed where the glaciers had gouged out basins. Meanwhile, streams fed by the melting glaciers carved the land.

Effects on living things. During the Ice Age, enormous changes took place in the climate. As the glaciers advanced, climate zones shifted and thereby affected plant life. For example, in the Northern Hemisphere, belts of thick, green forest became a frozen, treeless plain called *tundra*. In areas further south thick forests now grew. Around the world rains began to fall where there had once been deserts.

As the glaciers retreated, the zones of climate and vegetation shifted once again. To find suitable weather and plants for food, animals were forced to *migrate*, or move from one place to another, with the shifts in climate.

Scientists think that during the 1.5 million years of the Ice Age, modern human beings *evolved*, or developed by gradual changes. These

LOCATION: EARLY MAP PROJECTIONS

Over 2000 years ago, Greek scholars realized that our earth is a sphere. They knew that describing specific locations on the sphere would be a problem. A location is usually described by its *distance* and *direction* from another point. But on a sphere, every point is like every other point. With no beginning and no end, a sphere has no one place from which to begin measuring distance and direction.

To overcome this problem, the Greeks devised the network of latitude and longitude lines still in use today. They imagined a series of parallel lines—parallels of latitude—circling the earth between the North and South Poles. The circle that lays an equal distance from the poles is the equator. Locations from the equator to the North Pole are north latitude; from the equator to the South Pole, south latitude.

The Greeks imagined another series of lines crossing the parallels at right angles. These lines—the meridians of longitude—extend from pole to pole. By numbering the meridians from some starting point—today, the meridian that runs through the observatory in Greenwich, England—the Greeks could describe locations east and west of that point. With this network, or grid, of latitude and longitude lines, people could describe the location of any point on earth, even though they might not know what lands or seas lay there.

We know about these Greek scholars from the writings of Claudius Ptolemy, who lived in Alexandria, Egypt, about A.D. 150. Ptolemy also wrote about a problem cartographers, or mapmakers, have wrestled with ever since: how to project the grid system from a sphere onto a flat surface. Imagine peeling the earth's image off a globe, then laying it out flat on a sheet of paper. Ptolemy knew that no matter how you did this, part of the earth's image would have to be pulled and stretched into place. The pulling and stretching would distort distances, directions, shapes, and areas (sizes) on the map.

Ptolemy's greatest achievement was developing a reasonable way to project the latitude and longitude lines onto a flat surface. He drew a map of the world that he knew, from the Atlantic Ocean to China. Like the spokes of a fan, meridians of longitude radiated out from the North Pole. Parallels of latitude curved from left to right. Not for 1400 years did anyone find another solution to the problem.

In the 1500s, King Charles V of Spain, hired Gerhard Mercator to work out a map for navigators. Mercator stretched out the network of latitude and longitude lines to fit a rectangular map. All lines of latitude are parallel, just as they are on a globe. The meridians of longitude cross the latitude lines at right angles, just as on a globe. However, on Mercator's projection, the meridians do not meet at a single point like the poles on the globe.

Because stretching the meridians so far apart at the poles would greatly distort the shapes of land and water bodies there, Mercator also stretched apart the parallels of latitude closest to the poles. By stretching the polar regions both north-south and east-west, lands and seas can be shown in their proper shapes. However, the areas will be wrong; lands and seas in the polar regions will look much larger that they actually are in relation to places nearer the equator.

Still, because it is so easy to show directions on this map, the Mercator projection serves its purpose well. North and south are at the top and bottom; east and west are at the left and right. A navigator has only to draw a straight line to plot a course in any direction. This characteristic made the Mercator projection the most widely used map for 400 years.

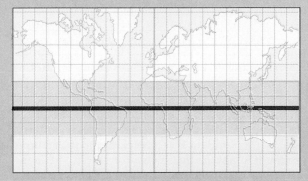

1. Explain the terms *parallels of latitude* and *meridians of longitude.*.

2. Where is the Mercator projection most distorted? For what is this map useful?

Excavation of this 2,200-year-old burial site of a child provided a recent American/Thai archaeological team with new information about early Southeast Asian culture.

early prehistoric people were hunters, who depended on migrating herds of animals, such as bison and woolly mammoths, for food. Some people followed their food supply from Asia to North America across a strip of ocean bottom exposed when the sea level dropped during the last glacial period. Other peoples crossed similar land bridges and reached Japan, Indonesia, and Australia. By 10,000 B.C., the sea level had risen again and submerged these bridges. By then, however, the descendants of the Ice Age hunters had spread to all the continents of the world except Antarctica.

As the weather warmed, the large animals of the tundra retreated north or became extinct. Human beings, however, were able to adapt to change, and they began to depend on smaller game animals and wild plants.

THE STUDY OF PREHISTORY

Because no written records exist to tell about the way early people lived, much of prehistoric life remains a mystery. However, human and animal bones, tools, pottery, and weapons provide clues to life in prehistoric times. Scientists study this evidence to develop theories about how early people lived.

Anthropologists (AN-thrō-PAHL-uh-jists) are scientists who study human beings and how they live in groups. Anthropologists who specialize in searching for clues to how human beings lived in the past are called *archaeologists* (AHR-kee-AHL-uh-jists). Among the clues that scientists study are *artifacts*, or small movable objects made by human hand, as well as remains of bones and teeth. Still other scientists investigate how people live together as a community. Such a community is called a *society*.

In addition to anthropologists, other kinds of scientists help to understand evidence of prehistoric life. For example, geologists provide information about the earth's history and *fossils*. Fossils are the remains or impressions of human, animal, or plant life preserved in rock. Botanists provide data about plants or animals that existed at a particular time in history. Working together, these scientists are able to piece together accounts of prehistoric life.

Searching for clues. In 1961, Dr. F. Clark Howell, an anthropologist from the University of Chicago, led a team of scientists to a site in Spain where people reported seeing old elephant bones. Dr. Howell's team dug up the site inch by inch, making a record of everything that they found. After analyzing the evidence, they reconstructed what they believed had taken place 400,000 years earlier. One writer described the conclusions of their study:

> What a spot. Bands of *Homo erectus* [a type of prehistoric human] would wait in the valleys between the hills for the big game herds. They drove the game into swamps by setting grass fires. They even trapped elephants that way. The elephants got mired [stuck in muddy ground] and

the hunters were able to kill them. It is all there to be seen: the stone tools the hunters left, the traces of burned grass, the animal fossils.

In addition to remains and small artifacts, archaeologists such as those on Howell's team also look for evidence of large structures. Clues to the past include large-scale remains such as buried tombs, ruins of buildings, and traces of irrigation canals. Finding and interpreting all of these remains and artifacts are long, delicate processes.

Determining the age of objects. To help them date—or estimate the age of—their findings, archaeologists use many methods. One method useful in estimating the age of objects that contain organic material is radiocarbon dating. Organic material is anything that was once living, such as bones and seeds.

All living things absorb radiocarbon from the atmosphere. This radiocarbon decays at a steady rate. When a plant or animal dies, it stops absorbing new radiocarbon although the radiocarbon already in it goes on decaying. By measuring the amount of radiocarbon remaining in an object, scientists can estimate its age. Other similar tests have been developed to measure the age of such material as clay pottery and volcanic rock.

After archaeological evidence has been discovered, gathered, and dated, scientists begin to draw conclusions about life in early times. New discoveries change old theories and raise even more questions. As archaeologists continue to make discoveries, their ideas and theories about prehistory will continue to change.

SECTION REVIEW

1. Define *culture*, *prehistory*, *tundra*, *migrate*, *evolved*, *anthropologists*, *archaeologists*, *artifacts*, *society*, and *fossils.*

2. How did the glaciers cause migrations of animals and people?

3. How do archaeologists learn about prehistoric people?

4. How do scientists determine the age of objects?

Evaluation. Agree or disagree with the following statement: The study of prehistory is important. Write at least three sentences that support your opinion.

1–2
THE STONE AGE

READ TO FIND OUT

—what the terms *nomads*, *technology*, *turning point*, *Agricultural Revolution*, *domesticate*, and *deities* mean.
—what paleolithic people achieved.
—how the Agricultural Revolution changed people's lives.
—what neolithic people achieved.

When archaeologists began searching for clues about early people, they discovered many axes, scrapers, knives, and other tools made of stone. Therefore, they began to call the period of time when these tools were used the Stone Age.

Scientists today have used the Greek word for stone, *lithus*, to form names for two parts of the Stone Age. The Paleolithic Age, or Old Stone Age, describes the period of time from 1.5 million years ago, when people first developed stone tools, to about 8000 B.C. The Neolithic Age, or New Stone Age, covers the years from about 8000 B.C. to about 3000 B.C., during which new ways of making tools were developed. After 3000 B.C., metal began to replace stone for tool making.

ORIGIN OF B.C. AND A.D.

About 1,500 years ago, there was a dispute within the Christian Church over how to date important events in church history. To settle the debate, the pope asked a monk to develop a standard method. The monk decided to start with what he believed was the year of Jesus Christ's birth. This became year 1. The years before Christ's birth later became known as *Before Christ*, abbreviated B.C. The monk called the years after Christ's birth *anno Domini*. These Latin words mean "in the year of the Lord" and are abbreviated A.D.

LIFE IN THE PALEOLITHIC AGE

Some of the earliest human remains yet found are those of people who lived 750,000 or more years ago on the island of Java in Indonesia. Similar remains of as many as 40 persons were found in a series of caves near Peking, China. Archaeologists estimate these remains to be about 500,000 years old.

Homo erectus. The Java and Peking remains are examples of an early type of people who scientists have called *Homo erectus*. *Homo* means "human." *Erectus* refers to the ability to walk upright. *Homo erectus* lived on the earth for about a million years, from 1.5 million years ago to about 300,000 years ago.

These prehistoric hunters made tools. At sites where *Homo erectus* once camped, scientists have found scrapers, choppers, and hammers chipped from stones. Thousands of stone hand axes have been found throughout Europe and Asia. These axes are carefully formed and follow a single design, indicating that *Homo erectus* had the ability to pass skills and learning from one group to another.

Remains of firepits at some sites are evidence that these early people knew how to control and use fire as long as 500,000 years ago. They probably first learned to capture fire started by lightning, volcanic activity, and other forces of nature and to carry it from place to place as live coals or slowly burning torches.

Once people controlled fire, they expanded their diet because by using fire for cooking, meats and other foods could be made more tender. Protecting humans by frightening away wild beasts, the campfire, with its warm glow, also became an important center of group life.

Neanderthals. In 1856, workers digging in a limestone quarry came upon an old skeleton buried in the floor of a small cave. Although most of the bones became scattered and lost, a few that had been given to a local science teacher survived. Eventually these were identified as a type of *Homo sapiens* (HŌ-mō SAY-pee-UHNS). *Sapiens* means "knowing" or "wise." All people living today belong to the scientific classification of *Homo sapiens*.

The paleolithic people found in the quarry were called the Neanderthals (nee-AN-der-THAWLS), after the Neander Gorge in Germany

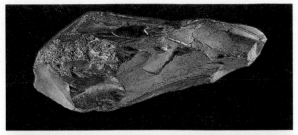

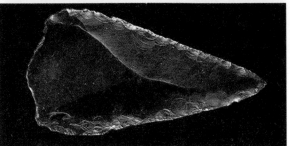

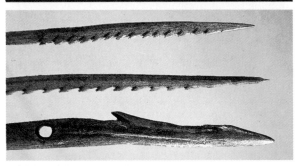

Paleolithic artifacts mainly consist of tools. Neanderthals replaced the hand-axe (top) with the point/scraper (center). Cro-Magnons carved these antler harpoons (bottom).

where the quarry was located. Since that first discovery of Neanderthal remains, other remains of a similar people have been found in Europe, Asia, and Africa.

The Neanderthal people lived from about 150,000 years ago to about 35,000 years ago. Remains at Neanderthal sites show that these people were **nomads**, people who move from place to place in search of food. Living in small groups, the Neanderthals hunted large game animals such as cave bears, woolly mammoths, and bison. They also fished and gathered nuts, seeds, and berries.

Neanderthals made advances in **technology**, methods for solving practical problems. One such advance was the development of better ways of making tools. Neanderthals also invented many different kinds of tools among which were stone scrapers for preparing hides, evidence that the Neanderthals fashioned clothing and shelters of animal skins.

At widely scattered sites, archaeologists have found evidence that may indicate that Neanderthals believed in life after death. Some excavations show that Neanderthals buried food and weapons with their dead. In at least one case, flowers were carefully placed in the grave.

Traces of the Neanderthals disappeared after about 34,000 B.C. No one is certain whether they vanished or intermingled with the people who came after them.

Cro-Magnons. In 1868, a group of workers digging a roadbed for a railway in southwestern France uncovered ancient tools and weapons along with five skeletons. These bones and artifacts were the remains of a paleolithic people who appeared in Europe about 35,000 B.C., about the same time that the Neanderthal people vanished. These paleolithic people, named *Cro-Magnons* after the hill where their remains were found, were a type of *Homo sapiens*. They closely resembled modern humans.

Little is known of how the Cro-Magnons replaced Neanderthals. The Cro-Magnons lived in much the same way as the people who came before them. They traveled in nomadic groups and survived by hunting. They camped in caves or built shelters of branches or small trees and covered their shelters with grasses or animal skins. Striking flint against rock or rubbing stick against stick, these hunters made fires for warmth, light, and cooking.

Group members cooperated to perform different tasks. Some members hunted in small bands while others gathered the fruits of wild plants. Some prepared animal hides for clothing and shelter.

Like the people before them, Cro-Magnons made advances in technology. Though gradual, these developments began to happen more rapidly than ever before. The Cro-Magnons manufactured more kinds of tools and finer tools than any people before them. They introduced sharp stone blades, chisels, barbed spear points, harpoons, and fish hooks. They also invented the needle, made of bone, which allowed them to make better fitting and warmer clothing. Toward the end of the Ice Age, Cro-Magnons developed a spear-thrower, a device that allowed them to throw weapons farther and harder. They also invented a bow and arrow. These long-distance weapons increased their ability to catch swiftly moving game.

Like the Neanderthals, Cro-Magnon people seem to have held ideas and beliefs about the unseen forces in their lives. With an awareness of their own impending death—an awareness no other species shares—these early humans may have believed in a life after death. Cro-Magnon people buried their dead with even greater care than the Neanderthals did, placing necklaces, richly carved weapons, and tools in the graves.

After about 25,000 B.C., prehistoric hunters began to create works of art. The earliest were small figurines of stone, ivory, bone, and clay. Some of the figurines represented animals and others represented female figures, perhaps to express the idea of motherhood.

The most startling works of art of the Paleolithic Age are the cave paintings of France, Spain, and Russia. Deep in the dark interiors of the caves, colored drawings of bison, horses, and other animals cover the walls and ceilings. Often, the cave paintings picture hunters and their prey. In one cave, outlines of human hands appear among the drawings. Although scientists have offered different explanations for cave art, many agree that these paintings may have been used in ceremonies.

The cave paintings of the Cro-Magnons as well as the burial practices of the Neanderthals hint that sometime during the Ice Age, paleolithic people had the power to think complicated thoughts. With that power, they also invented speech. With spoken language humans could share information, make plans, pass on knowledge to their children, and organize complex societies.

Paleolithic art often featured big game animals; they ensured human survival. This cave painting of a bison is from Altamira in northern Spain, a site discovered by a five-year-old child.

LIFE IN THE NEOLITHIC AGE

Scientists contrast the Paleolithic Age, when people chipped stone to make tools, with the Neolithic Age, beginning around 8000 B.C., when people began to grind and polish the stone to make better tools. Neolithic people also invented new tools—saws, chisels, wedges, axes, and drills. Along with advances in tool making came other developments that significantly changed life in prehistoric times.

The development of Agriculture. Until the Neolithic Age, people worldwide had survived by hunting and gathering. Some neolithic people, however, learned to grow their own food. As agriculture became widespread, it changed completely the way many people lived. This decisive change, or *turning point*, is called the *Agricultural Revolution*. It was probably the most important event of prehistoric times.

Agriculture began in the Middle East, a region that today includes Israel, Jordan, Lebanon, Syria, Turkey, Iran, and Iraq, as well as Egypt, Sudan, and the countries of the Arabian Peninsula. There, hunter-gatherers settled in the hill country where rain fell heavily, and golden fields of wild wheat grew high. Over time, the gatherers of wild wheat saw that they could save the seed and plant it later.

The cultivation of crops developed at different times in different parts of the world. The kinds of crops produced also varied from region to region with the soil and the climate. For example, a grain called millet was the first crop grown in China. Thousands of miles away in Mexico, beans and corn were two of the first crops tended.

Over time, farmers improved crop production with better tools and techniques. With the invention of the plow, about 6000 B.C., farmers were able to loosen the soil to help crops grow more easily. When farmers harnessed animals to pull the plow, they were able to cultivate larger fields. By about 5500 B.C., people had begun to dig simple irrigation systems, which gave them more abundant crops.

Unlike nomads, neolithic farmers could settle in permanent locations and produce a steady food supply for a growing population. At times, they even produced a surplus that could be stored or traded. These prehistoric farmers

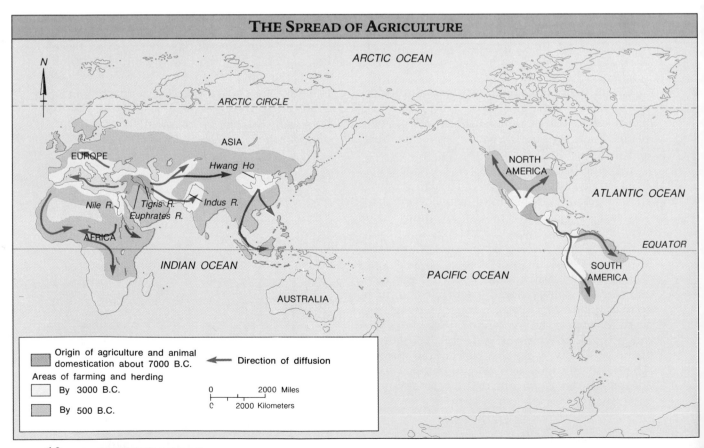

THE SPREAD OF AGRICULTURE

Origin of agriculture and animal domestication about 7000 B.C.

Direction of diffusion

Areas of farming and herding

By 3000 B.C.

By 500 B.C.

0   2000 Miles
0   2000 Kilometers

UNDERSTANDING MAP PROJECTIONS

Because the earth is a sphere, a globe is the truest representation of the earth. But carrying a globe around could be a nuisance. Think how big that globe would have to be to show each town and city in detail. For most purposes, maps are more convenient.

Like globes, maps show the *absolute location* of land masses and water bodies, that is, location on the network of latitude and longitude lines. When this network is transferred from a globe onto a map, the land masses and water bodies must go with it in their correct absolute locations. However, in projecting the network onto a flat surface, distances, directions, areas, and shapes become distorted.

Cartographers have devised thousands of projections. Most of these fall into three basic categories: *cylindrical, conic,* and *azimuthal.*

A. *Cylindrical.* Imagine that you have a translucent globe of the world with a light inside shining outward. Suppose you stand a cylinder of paper around the globe, with the paper touching the globe along a single line, for example, the equator. The light is projecting, or casting the shadows of, latitude and longitude lines, land masses, and water bodies onto the paper. If these shadows stick to the paper, when you unroll the paper you will have a cylindrical projection. World maps—such as the Mercator on page 360—are often cylindrical projections.

B. *Conic.* Imagine that you now place a paper cone somewhere on your lighted globe and project the shadows onto the cone. When you unroll the cone, you will have a fan-shaped map, like Ptolemy's. Conic projections are often used to show an entire hemisphere or just a slice of it. The map on page 448 is a conic projection known as Lambert Conic.

C. *Azimuthal.* Azimuth means distance measured from a single point. Imagine holding a flat sheet of paper against your lighted globe so that they touch at a single point. This could be the North Pole, the equator, or somewhere else. The map projected onto the paper will be focused on that point. The maps on pages 822 to 827 are all Lambert's Azimuthal projections, each focused on a different part of the globe.

With each kind of projection, the map would be truest where the paper had touched the globe—the line or point of *tangency,* which means "touching." Farther away, distances, directions, areas, and shapes would be distorted.

Cartographers have developed variations of each projection. For example, the Robinson projection on page 820 and the Homolosine projection at the beginning of each unit in your text are both related to cylindrical projections. However, all projections distort the earth in some way. The best method for judging a map's accuracy is to compare it with a globe.

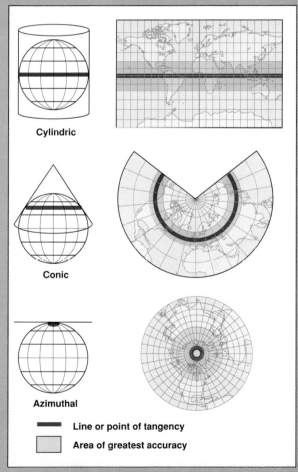

Cylindric

Conic

Azimuthal

▬▬▬ Line or point of tangency

▢ Area of greatest accuracy

1. Why do all maps distort the earth's image?

2. For each projection, explain what part of the map is most accurate.

had gained greater control over their environment than any people before them.

People also learned to **domesticate**, or tame, animals for human use by about 8000 B.C. Among the earliest animals tamed were sheep, dogs, and goats. By 1000 B.C., farmers in different parts of the world had domesticated at least 22 different kinds of animals, including cattle, honey bees, guinea pigs, and reindeer.

Other developments of the New Stone Age. To store grain and other foods, farmers developed clay pots, bowls, and jars. The earliest known clay vessel was made in India in 7000 B.C. The farmers used this pottery, which was too heavy for nomads to carry, to boil, steam, stew, and ferment their food.

Because neolithic farmers could live in settled communities, they began to build new kinds of dwellings. Instead of the temporary tents and huts of nomads, farmers constructed permanent dwellings made of wood, stone, or sunbaked mudbrick. As family groups built their permanent homes close to one another, villages developed.

As communities grew, the neolithic people faced new challenges in getting along together. They probably argued over such matters as land ownership, crops, and trading goods. In addition, they had to plan community projects, such as irrigation and defense. At first, family elders met to make decisions. Later, as the population increased, priests—who conducted religious ceremonies—or other community leaders took on these responsibilities. In this way, a few people made decisions about the lives of many people so that they all could live together as a community. This separation between decision-makers and others is one of the origins of society's division into social classes.

Religion played an important role in the community, and many religious practices were related to farming. Neolithic farmers believed in **deities**, or gods and goddesses, who controlled the forces of nature and, therefore, their lives. For example, the people thought that such disasters as floods and droughts were brought on by angry deities. Priests and priestesses were responsible for communicating with these powerful forces of nature. Over the years, these religious leaders developed rituals to try to win some control over the unseen forces and keep their world in order.

SECTION REVIEW

1. Define **nomads**, **technology**, **turning point**, **Agricultural Revolution**, **domesticate**, and **deities**.

2. Explain the terms *paleolithic* and *neolithic*.

3. List at least six accomplishments of paleolithic people.

4. Why is the Agricultural Revolution considered a major turning point?

5. Give three examples of technological advances made by neolithic people. Explain how each changed their lives.

Analysis. Make a chart comparing paleolithic and neolithic peoples. Consider tools, means of obtaining food, social organization, and other achievements.

1–3
FIRST CIVILIZATIONS

READ TO FIND OUT

—what the terms **civilization**, **artisans**, **urban**, **steppes**, and **cultural diffusion** mean.
—what features civilizations share.
—how early cities differed from farming villages.
—how ideas pass from one civilization to another.

Toward the end of the New Stone Age, around 4000 B.C., many groups of people throughout the world were settling in villages and towns. Most of these neolithic people were farmers. Because farming provided a plentiful, steady food supply, people were healthier and lived longer.

One result of this prosperity was a population explosion. Scientists estimate that at the beginning of the Agricultural Revolution around 8000 B.C., 5 million people were scattered across the world. By 4000 B.C., the world's population had reached 90 million. As the population grew, some towns and villages developed into cities.

THE BEGINNINGS OF CIVILIZATION

With the development of cities came the beginnings of **civilization**. A civilization is a society in which a high level of art, technology, and government has been achieved. The term *civilization* comes from the Latin word *civis*, meaning "citizens of a city."

Early civilization can be described in terms of special characteristics. These characteristics include a concentrated population in cities, complex governments and religions, specialization among workers, advanced technology, and some form of writing.

Early cities. The first cities probably arose in the Middle East after 3500 B.C. Within the next 2,000 years, cities also appeared to the east in India and China.

These early cities were located near fertile lands and a good water supply. They were usually separated from the surrounding lands by high walls with guarded gates. Toward the center of the city, public buildings soared above the homes of the city dwellers. These buildings included the temples of the city's deities and the palaces and tombs of the city's rulers. The temples and palaces often sat on the highest ground—a hill or an earthen platform. Other important public buildings, such as storehouses for grain, stood nearby.

Homes of reed, timber, and mudbrick lined streets leading away from the center of the city. In some cities, narrow streets twisted and turned as homes sprang up without plan. In other cities, the streets were systematically laid out in regular patterns.

Unlike farming villages, where the population was usually made up of a few large families, cities included numerous unrelated people. At first, these people shared the same background, religion, and way of life. Over time, however, cities included outsiders, such as prisoners of war or people from different regions searching for a better life.

With so many different people, the cities bustled with activity. Soon they became centers of trade for both farm products and craft items.

SPOTLIGHT: DAILY LIFE

ÇATAL HÜYÜK: AN EARLY NEOLITHIC TOWN

On the banks of a small stream that winds through the hilly plains of central Turkey, the mysterious town of Çatal Hüyük (chuh-TUL hoo-YOOK) was born about 8,000 years ago. Beneath the looming presence of three volcanoes, Çatal Hüyük prospered for more than 2,000 years. Then it was abandoned about 5600 B.C., for some still unknown reason. The winds of passing ages tried hard to bury any trace of this once busy community, where as many as 6,000 people may have lived. However, in 1961, archaeologists discovered the well-preserved remains of this prehistoric town.

The people of Çatal Hüyük left behind tools, beautiful wall paintings, and other objects that paint a vivid picture of how they lived. These neolithic people were hunters. They also farmed, growing wheat and barley, and they raised goats and sheep. With sharp flint tools to skin and cut, they made sandals from the leather, and they wove garments.

Curiously, the tightly packed, sundried brick houses of this neolithic metropolis had no doors. To enter, residents climbed down wooden ladders through a hole in the roof. Such a method of entry may have helped to keep out wild animals.

Each roof, made of woven reeds and mud, was connected on one or more sides to the houses next door. These roofs had to be strong enough to support the townspeople who walked across them to get from one house to another. On hot nights the roof even became a substitute bedroom.

Some members of the community found time to create works of art, such as stone and clay figurines. Colorful murals, often showing hunting scenes, have been found on the walls of a number of unearthed buildings where religious rites may have been practiced.

Life for the people of Çatal Hüyük was harsh, and it was short. By their late twenties, the people were nearing old age. At death, their bones were carefully wrapped and buried within their houses, where they remained through the centuries.

Government and religion. As communities grew, the task of governing became more demanding. The customs that guided villagers could not be applied to all of the new situations that arose in the cities, with their large, varied populations and diverse activities. There, more complex forms of government were needed.

Government and religion were usually closely linked. In some cities, the chief priest or priestess was also the ruler. In other cities, however, priests focused on their religious duties, and other leaders took on the duties of government, becoming princes, kings, or queens. Often people believed that the ruler had been given the right to rule by the city's chief god or goddess. The rulers made laws, supervised public works, and defended their cities from attack. Their authority gradually extended over the surrounding countryside.

Sometimes rulers were advised by a council of elder nobles. The rulers also appointed officials to carry out such tasks as collecting the taxes needed to support the government or the temple. Skilled workers, merchants, and farmers turned over part of their goods or crops as yearly tax payments. Sometimes, workers were required to contribute their labor, as well.

Specialization. As the need for food was met, some people had time to become skilled in performing other tasks. Many of these people became full-time *artisans*, skilled workers who made and sold tools, clothing, and other items. At first, these artisans wandered from village to village selling their own goods. However, as trade increased, a new kind of worker—the merchant—handled the exchange of goods.

The work that city people performed determined their social class. The rulers, priests, and wealthy landowners made up the upper class. Next came the government officials and wealthy merchants. Most people, however, belonged to the class made up of artisans, traders, and farmers. The outsiders—newcomers and slaves—formed the lowest class.

Technology. The inventions of neolithic farmers were related to agriculture. In contrast, the inventions of *urban*, or city, peoples were more often related to transportation and trade. For example, to transport goods across the Mediterranean and Arabian seas, large-scale shipbuilding developed.

By 2500 B.C. Chinese artisans, aided by the technology of the potter's wheel and ovens, produced elaborate vessels like this footed cup for use in permanent dwellings.

In the Middle East, the invention of the wheel about 3500 B.C. benefited trade. Once cattle-drawn carts were in use, farmers and merchants could move products great distances for trading.

Another invention, the potter's wheel, or turntable, enabled people to make finer pottery. At the same time, the development of new kinds of ovens for baking pottery made it possible to make stronger pots.

These ovens may have led to the discovery of bronze. By 5000 B.C., people had begun to hammer copper into beads. Later, metalworkers in the Middle East figured out how to smelt the copper, using heat to separate the ore from the rock. By 3000 B.C., people discovered that they could combine copper with tin to produce a new, harder metal—bronze.

Tools of bronze were stronger and more long-lasting than tools of copper. Bronze axes, knives, chisels, and hammers made it easier to shape wood and other materials. The period after 3000 B.C. is therefore known as the Bronze Age.

Writing. One of the most important inventions of early civilizations was writing. Writing may have begun sometime before 3000 B.C. as a way to keep track of the goods flowing into and out of the cities. With simple marks on wood, stone, or clay, merchants could record what they bought and sold. Tax collectors could note the products they collected. Over time, systems of writing were invented that could be used to record laws, family histories, and poetry.

Early systems of writing used pictographs—pictures that symbolized objects, such as jars of grain. Gradually, symbols that stood for ideas—ideograms—were added. The picture of a king, for example, might stand for the idea of government. However, some words or names cannot be easily represented with pictures. To solve this problem, symbols that represented sounds were developed. With such a system, any word in a language could be written down.

CONTACTS AMONG EARLY CIVILIZATIONS

Trade, warfare, and migration—the movement of groups from one region to another—brought different peoples into contact with each other thousands of years ago. The need for raw materials, such as tin and lumber, led to contacts among peoples along a network of trade routes throughout the Middle East and India. Nomads in search of pasture land came into contact with many peoples as they ranged across the *steppes*, the vast, nearly treeless plains of Central Asia. Sometimes such contact resulted in unfriendliness or warfare.

Whenever people from one group met people from another, they learned about each other's culture. Often, through trade, migration, or warfare, people discovered ideas, inventions, or customs unknown to their own culture. They then adapted these to their own way of life. This sharing and blending of ideas and customs is called *cultural diffusion*.

The use of the wheel is an example of cultural diffusion. The wheel had been invented about 3500 B.C. by people in the Middle East. By 2000 B.C., the idea had traveled westward as far as the North Sea and eastward into India and across the steppes of Asia. Meanwhile, Middle Eastern people had made a lighter, faster wheel, which enabled them to build swift horse-drawn chariots.

The chariot followed the path of the wheel. By 1600 B.C., the idea of the chariot had spread westward throughout the Mediterranean world and eastward to India and the Asian steppes. People in China learned of it later from the steppe nomads. Through such cultural diffusion, each new group borrowed ideas and modified them for its own purposes.

SECTION REVIEW

1. Define *civilization*, *artisans*, *urban*, *steppes*, and *cultural diffusion*.

2. What features do civilizations share?

3. How did the early cities differ from farming villages?

4. In what ways did ideas and customs pass from one group to another?

Analysis. What might you infer if, at an archaeological site, you found a clay jar containing seeds of grain dating from 2000 B.C., a bronze wire bracelet, a stone floor 200 by 75 feet (61 by 23 meters), and remnants of a thick brick wall nearly 1 mile (1.6 kilometers) long?

Data Search. The following plants and animals were eventually used in these areas: Africa—yams, bananas, dromedary camels; Middle East—olives, grapes, cattle; Europe—barley, rye, horses; Southeast Asia—rice, pigs, sweet potatoes. Refer to the appropriate chart on page 828 to identify the place of origin of each plant or animal introduced by diffusion.

HISTORY IN FOCUS

In their efforts to gain some measure of control over the world around them, early people took bold steps and made great discoveries that formed the basis of civilization. These developments did not happen quickly, and they did not happen in all parts of the world at once. Some discoveries, such as agriculture, seem to have occurred in different parts of the world at different times. Some inventions, such as the wheel, may have been discovered only once. Then, through contacts between groups of people, such knowledge spread.

Developed over thousands of years, tools, fire, warm clothing, long-distance weapons, and roofed dwellings enabled people to adapt to a wide variety of climates and terrains. The evolution of art and language, the stirrings of religious feeling, and the growth of communities gave people the ability to contend with the world. In working together to solve common problems, people tended to cluster in larger and larger groups, creating complex social patterns, governments, and religions. All of these immense achievements are what people today have inherited from the distant past.

SUMMARY

- During the Ice Age, starting 1.5 million years ago, glaciers moved outward from the poles. The sea level dropped and land bridges emerged between continents. Ice Age hunters followed animals in their migration, and by 8000 B.C., all the continents except Antarctica were populated.

- Without written records to rely on, archaeologists study artifacts, bones, and fossils and use various methods, like radiocarbon dating, to create a picture of prehistoric societies.

- The Stone Age, the period when stone tools were used, is divided into two parts: the Paleolithic Age, up to 8000 B.C., and the Neolithic Age, from 8000 B.C. to 3000 B.C.

- Paleolithic people—*Homo erectus*, Neanderthals, and Cro-Magnons—were nomadic hunter-gatherers. They used fire, developed tools, invented speech, created art, and organized complex societies.

- Neolithic people created new tools, replacing stone with metal. They developed agriculture, which allowed then to settle in permanent locations. Communities arose, animals were domesticated, and the first pottery was created. As the population increased, basic political organization evolved and religion was established.

- Toward the end of the Neolithic Age, the population exploded, and cities were formed. Civilizations arose with governments and religions, specialization, technology, and forms of writing. The wheel was invented and bronze was smelted. Social classes emerged, based on work roles. Trade increased and contacts were made between civilizations.

VOCABULARY REVIEW

Below are six vocabulary terms used in the chapter. Match each numbered term with the lettered term that is related to it. Then explain how each pair is related.

Example: The term *culture* is related to *society* because *culture* means the way of life of a people

and *society* refers to the community, or group of people.

1. urban	**(a)** migrate
2. nomads	**(b)** civilization
3. fossils	**(c)** artifacts

CHAPTER REVIEW

1. (a) What effect did Ice Age glaciers have on the landscape? **(b)** When did the climate become much like it is today?

2. (a) How is the work of archaeologists different from that of other anthropologists? **(b)** What are some objects archaeologists analyze in their work? **(c)** Explain radiocarbon dating.

3. (a) What is the importance of the remains found in Indonesia? In China? **(b)** Identify three characteristics of each of the following peoples: *Homo erectus*, Neanderthals, and Cro-Magnons. **(c)** How are the various types of paleolithic people similar? How are they different?

4. (a) Explain why scientists think Neanderthals made clothing and shelters. **(b)** What evidence is there that both Neanderthals and Cro-Magnons believed in life after death? **(c)** What art did Cro-Magnons create?

5. (a) Where did agriculture first evolve? **(b)** Describe two major effects of the Agricultural Revolution.

6. (a) Describe how dwellings changed in the Neolithic Age. **(b)** What effect did the creation of communities have on social and political organization?

7. List five characteristics of early civilizations. State which characteristics are identified with each of these groups: *Homo erectus*, Neanderthals, Cro-Magnons, neolithic people.

8. (a) How did the rise of cities affect government? **(b)** How were religion and government intertwined?

9. (a) Why did the work force become more specialized? **(b)** Describe the social classes of early cities.

10. (a) Give one reason why writing may have developed. **(b)** Describe the steps in the development of writing.

THINKING CRITICALLY: ACTIVITIES

1. With two or three other class members, assume that you are archaeologists. Make a list of the artifacts and fossils you might find if you were to uncover a neolithic village. Then prepare a report describing the ancient people and their way of life. Select a group member to present your list and your report to the class.

2. Devise your own ideograms for each of the following ideas: home, climate, agriculture, community, cultural diffusion. Each ideogram might be one or more symbols, standing for ideas, not sounds. Write a few sentences explaining why you chose those particular symbols.

3. Select a partner for a discussion of the following questions. In your experience, what are some examples of each of the characteristics of civilization? What are some advantages and disadvantages of living in a civilization? Make notes about your conclusions to use in a class discussion of these questions.

APPLYING SOCIAL STUDIES SKILLS

Understanding map projections. The Robinson projection, page 820, is related to cylindrical projections but with the meridians drawn closer together near the poles. This map's rounded shape gives a reasonable impression of the rounded earth. However, like others, this projection has some distortions.

1. Compare the Robinson projection with the Mercator projection, page 360, which shows land masses in their true shapes. On the Robinson projection, where are shapes most distorted? Most accurate?

2. South America is actually about eight times the area of Greenland. On which map is the area of Greenland depicted most accurately?

3. On the globe, latitudes 60°N and 60°S are actually half the length of the equator. How does the Robinson projection differ?

4. The Robinson projection is focused on the equator. The map scale shows that at the equator 1⁵⁄₁₆ inches on the map equals 2,000 miles on the earth. Can the scale also be true for latitudes 60°N and 60°S? For the poles? Explain.

APPLYING THINKING SKILLS

Organizing information. Each chapter in your textbook has been written according to an outline or plan that shows the relationships between ideas. Therefore, outlining a chapter helps you to review its main ideas.

An outline uses roman numerals, capital letters, arabic numerals, and lowercase letters to indicate how ideas are related to each other. For instance, roman numerals identify the most general ideas, while lowercase letters indicate specific supporting details.

Two common types of outlines are sentence outlines and topic outlines. Sentence outlines present information in complete sentences, while topic outlines present information in single words or phrases.

Below is a topic outline of the first section of Chapter 1. Copy this outline, adding information where indicated. Then outline the other two sections of the chapter. Note that a capital letter can be used to identify each subsection title. Each of these titles should have at least two numbers underneath it identifying the major topics in the subsection. The information related to each of these topics can usually be divided into subtopics. Use lowercase letters to identify each subtopic.

I. Prehistory
   A. The Ice Age
      1. Effects on geography
         a. Land bridges created
         b. _____
      2. Effects on living things
         a. Changes in vegetation as a result of changes in climate
         b. _____
         c. _____
   B. _____
      1. Types of scientists who study prehistory
         a. Archaeologists
         b. _____
         c. _____
      2. _____
         a. Careful digging at sites
         b. _____
         c. Estimating the age of objects

CHAPTER TWO

EARLY CIVILIZATIONS OF THE MIDDLE EAST

3500–300 B.C.

Assyrian officials. Mural detail, 750 B.C.

At the crossroads of three continents—Asia, Africa, and Europe—lies the region known as the Middle East. Although nomads in this area continued their wandering way of life, by 6000 B.C. small numbers of people began to settle. The story of the Middle East was partly shaped by conflict between settlers and nomads seeking wealth, and among settlers competing for land and power.

The story of the Middle East is also one of great achievement. Here, the earliest civilizations arose more than 5,000 years ago. One of these ancient civilizations developed in the valley of the Nile River in Egypt; another, in the valley between the Tigris and Euphrates (yoo-FRAY-teez) rivers in what today is the country of Iraq. Thousands of years ago, this "land between the rivers" was known as Mesopotamia.

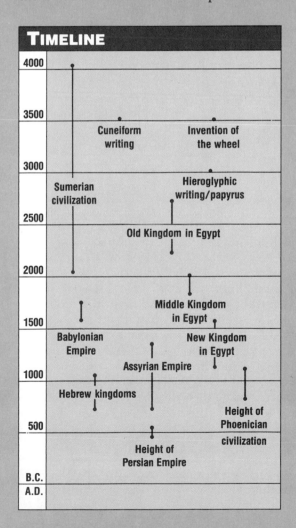

2-1
THE SUMERIANS

—what the terms *delta*, *silt*, *city-states*, *empire*, *polytheism*, *ziggurat*, *barter*, and *cuneiform* mean.
—what the city-states of Sumer were like.
—how Sargon shaped the world's first empire.
—what the first known code of law was.
—what roles religion played in Sumerian life.
—what ideas and inventions originated in Sumer.

Little is known of the earliest people who, with their herds of sheep, settled in Mesopotamia about 6000 B.C. Later, attracted by the area's rich soils and the waters of the rivers, other groups migrated to Mesopotamia. Early farmers came from the foothills of the Zagros Mountains in the northeast. Many Semitic nomads, the ancestors of modern-day Arabs and Hebrews, left the edges of the Saharan, Syrian, and Arabian deserts to make Mesopotamia their home.

About 4000 B.C., yet another group—the Sumerians—migrated from the north, probably from central Asia, to southeastern Mesopotamia. These people settled down to farm and blended with the earlier inhabitants of the region. The Sumerians, their language, and their ways dominated the southeastern end of the valley, which came to be called Sumer.

THE MIDDLE EAST: THE NATURAL SETTING

Vast expanses of the Middle East are desert. The Sahara Desert covers the part of the Middle East that lies in Africa. Other deserts take up most of the Arabian Peninsula. Together, all of the deserts of Arabia are called the Arabian Desert.

Through these dry lands of the Middle East flow two great river systems—the Nile River system and the Tigris-Euphrates river system. The Nile River, the longest in the world, arises in the highlands of central Africa and runs northward 4,187 miles (6,738 kilometers) to the

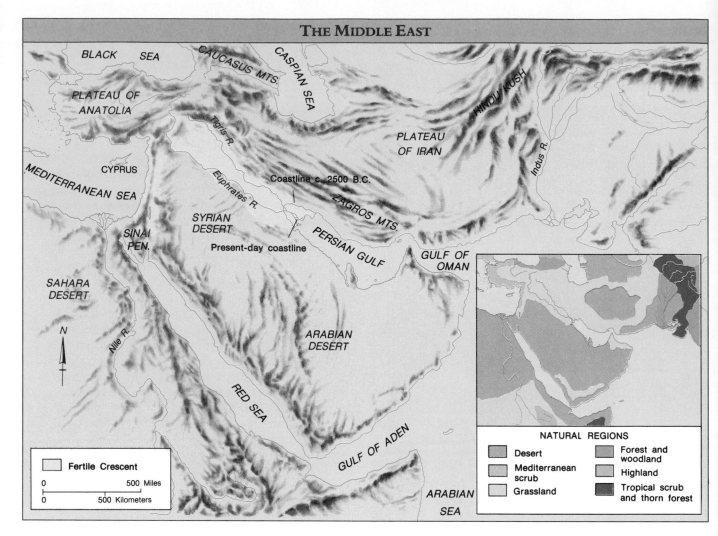

THE MIDDLE EAST

BLACK SEA
CAUCASUS MTS.
CASPIAN SEA
PLATEAU OF ANATOLIA
Tigris R.
PLATEAU OF IRAN
HINDU KUSH
MEDITERRANEAN SEA
CYPRUS
Euphrates R.
Indus R.
Coastline c. 2500 B.C.
ZAGROS MTS.
SYRIAN DESERT
SINAI PEN.
PERSIAN GULF
Present-day coastline
GULF OF OMAN
SAHARA DESERT
N
Nile R.
ARABIAN DESERT
RED SEA
GULF OF ADEN
ARABIAN SEA

NATURAL REGIONS
Desert
Mediterranean scrub
Grassland
Forest and woodland
Highland
Tropical scrub and thorn forest

Fertile Crescent
0   500 Miles
0   500 Kilometers

Mediterranean Sea. The Tigris and the Euphrates originate in the mountains of present-day Turkey and flow southeast for more than 1,000 miles (1,600 kilometers), emptying into the Persian Gulf.

In ancient times, the Tigris and the Euphrates poured separately into the Persian Gulf. However, over time these rivers carried tons of soil downstream and into the gulf, gradually building up a marshy *delta*. A delta is any area of land formed from sand and soil deposited by a river. In the delta, the Tigris and Euphrates now join, becoming one river for the last 120 miles (192 kilometers) of their journey.

Both the Tigris and Euphrates rivers flow through a region known as the Fertile Crescent. This area of land, shaped like a crescent, or quarter moon, stretches from the Persian Gulf to the Mediterranean Sea.

The western part of the Fertile Crescent has a mild climate, with hot, dry summers and moderate, rainy winters. However, little rain falls on the plains and valleys of the Tigris and the Euphrates in the eastern Fertile Crescent. In the spring, though, melting snow in the mountain ranges where the rivers begin swells the Tigris and the Euphrates. In ancient times, the two rivers often overflowed suddenly and unpredictably, flooding the land and causing great damage. However, the *silt*, or fine soil carried by water, made the valley between the rivers especially fertile.

THE SUMERIAN CITY-STATES

With the arrival of the Sumerians around 4000 B.C., the population grew and farms prospered. As the population of Mesopotamia continued to expand, some villages grew to become towns. By 3500 B.C., many early settlements such as Ur, Kish, Lagash, and Erech had grown into cities. With temples to honor the special deities of the region, the cities became religious centers. Each city also provided the people of the surrounding countryside a place to trade and to find protection from attacking nomads.

Sumerian cities developed intense rivalries over control of the fertile plains. Whenever open warfare broke out, in each city a council of leading citizens appointed a leader. At first this *lugal*, or "great man," ruled only as long as a crisis threatened, then gave up power and returned to civilian life. As rivalries between the cities continued, however, the "great men" kept their power and became kings.

By 3000 B.C., kings ruled the dozen or so Sumerian *city-states*. Each city-state was a political unit consisting of the city and its surrounding farmland dotted with villages. The city-states were independent of one another, and each had its own system of government. Sharing only a common language and culture, the city-states were in constant turmoil over territory, water rights, power, and prestige.

At times, however, some of the city-states united to fight others, to defend themselves against attacks by nomads, or to trade. The Sumerian system of loosely associated city-states continued for more than a thousand years. Then Sumerian control of the city-states was interrupted by outsiders.

SUMERIAN STRUGGLE FOR CONTROL

About 2340 B.C., Sargon, a descendant of Semitic nomads, claimed the throne of Kish. From there he launched a series of attacks against other city-states. With his conquests, Sargon had created the world's first *empire*, a form of government uniting a number of territories and peoples under one ruler. Sargon moved his capital to the city of Akkad. These peoples, united under his rule, became known as the Akkadians, and Akkadian became the language of the empire.

After Sargon died in 2305 B.C., his sons and grandsons ruled for nearly a century. However, the empire was weakened by revolts. Finally, in 2100 B.C., the people of Sumer drove out the invaders. The Sumerian city-state of Ur recovered control of Mesopotamia.

The Age of Ur. Ur-Nammu, the ruler of Ur, energetically began rebuilding the cities that had decayed under the northern invaders. Under Ur-Nammu and his descendants, the city-states regained much of their former glory. Agriculture, trade, and the arts flourished again throughout Sumer and Akkad.

Ur-Nammu also issued the first known code of law. The code was based on Sumerian traditions, but the laws were now organized and written on clay tablets for all the inhabitants of the kingdom to see.

Under this Code of Ur-Nammu, peasants and commoners as well as nobles received legal protection. However, the law was applied differently to different classes of people. For example, a noble who committed a crime was treated more harshly than a peasant because better behavior was expected of the noble. Penalties were usually fines or physical punishment based on the idea of "an eye for an eye, a tooth for a tooth."

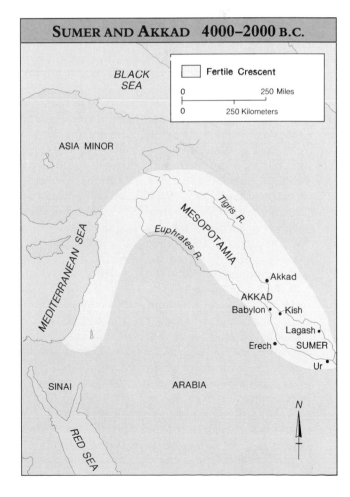

SUMER AND AKKAD 4000–2000 B.C.

Fertile Crescent

0   250 Miles
0   250 Kilometers

BLACK SEA

ASIA MINOR

MEDITERRANEAN SEA

Tigris R.

MESOPOTAMIA

Euphrates R.

Akkad

AKKAD

Babylon

Kish

Lagash

Erech

SUMER

Ur

SINAI

ARABIA

RED SEA

N

THINKING ABOUT HISTORY

"History doesn't have anything to do with my daily life—why do I have to study it?" This question probably sounds familiar because many people think that studying history just means remembering dates and events. Fortunately, it means more than that—much more.

One important reason for studying history is that it helps you improve at something you do every day: think! The thinking skills that you use in studying history are the same ones you use in your daily life. For example, when you think about how events today are caused by past events, you use the same skill you would in figuring out why your team lost a game. In both cases you identify causes. When you look for information that shows whether a certain king was a good ruler, you use the same skill as when checking whether a record store's prices are really the lowest in town. In both cases, you determine whether a statement is supported by facts.

THINKING ABOUT YOUR THINKING

To show how thinking about history involves the same skills as thinking about daily life, ten thinking problems appear on these pages. In problems 1 through 5, you will be thinking about everyday topics or situations. In problems A through E, you will be thinking about history. All of them involve doing something that perhaps you have never done before: think about your thinking. In other words, after you finish working on each problem you will be asking yourself, "How did I do it?"

Why is it so important to know *how* you did various thinking problems or tasks? The answer is that it makes you a more skillful thinker. You will be better prepared for a new problem or task because you will know which approach works best for you and why. Also, knowing exactly how you did a task helps you to change your approach if necessary.

Throughout this book you can review, learn, and practice important thinking skills, as well as improve your ability to think about your thinking. The thinking skills presented in the book

will help you improve your understanding of history and make you a better everyday thinker. Therefore, as you proceed with your study of world history, be ready to THINK!

TRYING SOME THINKING PROBLEMS

As you work on these problems, keep in mind that this is not a quiz. Getting the right answers is not as important as thinking about *how* you arrived at each answer.

1. Try to solve the problems one by one. After working on each one, do the following:

(a) On your own paper write down what you think is the answer.

(b) Write notes listing the steps you went through to arrive at your answer. Be prepared to explain these steps to another person.

(c) Write down what previous knowledge, if any, is needed in order to get the answer. Be prepared to tell another person what this knowledge is.

2. After you have completed the steps above, do the following:

(a) Write the number 1 on your paper, to stand for the first numbered problem. Next to the number write the letter of the history problem that required the same kind of thinking.

(b) Explain what was similar in the methods you used to try to solve the two problems.

(c) Follow steps (a) and (b) for the other numbered problems.

Thinking About Daily Life

1. Monday is to week as _____ is to year.

(a) month

(b) January

(c) Sunday

2. Two other students and a teacher saw Peter cheating on a semester exam. As a student at USA High, Peter had signed an honor pledge not to cheat. By signing this pledge, he agreed that anyone guilty of cheating was to be suspended from all extracurricular activities. Peter is captain and high scorer of the school's basketball team. Next Saturday the team plays for the state championship. Peter's father is president of the Board of Education and proud of the team's record.

What should the teacher and students do? Why?

3. **A.** Voice over school intercom: "Student Jamie Joyce, come to the principal's office immediately."

B. Students, after hearing the announcement: "Oh, oh! Jamie is in trouble."

If *A* is true, what must also be true if *B* is to be accepted as true?

4. Paula, José, and Tamile decided to work on the school play. Each picked one of these jobs to do: sell tickets, distribute programs, or operate the stage lights. Each completed the chosen task. Paula did not sell tickets. José did not operate the stage lights. Tamile did not distribute the programs or operate the stage lights.

Who did what?

5. The following items are sold at a local store. Examine this list. Then identify what type of store would sell such items. Also identify other items it might sell.

clipboards	chalk	sweatshirts
ski poles	baseball bats	field hockey
basketballs	snowshoes	sticks
boxing gloves	adhesive tape	footballs
rolls of	leather belts	parkas
elastic cloth	ski boots	sunglasses
sneakers	tee shirts	sweat suits
football	soccer shoes	softballs
jerseys	tennis balls	bike helmets
hockey pucks	ski wax	soccer balls

Thinking About World History

A. After World War I, Germany lost territory to France, Poland, and Great Britain. Each of these nations took a different territory, choosing from Danzig, Alsace, and Tanganyika.

France did not take Danzig. Great Britain did not take Alsace. Poland did not take Tanganyika or Alsace.

What territory did each nation take?

B. First Roman Senator: "I hear that Caesar has crossed the Rubicon River and is coming back to Rome."
Second Roman Senator: "_____
_____."
Third Roman Senator: "Our Republic is doomed!"

What statement by the second Roman Senator would lead to the third Roman Senator's response?

C. A sixteenth-century African king was converted to Christianity by Portuguese missionaries. Many of his people also became Christians. Later the king discovered that some Portuguese merchants were kidnapping his people and selling them as slaves. The king believed that all people should be treated with dignity as human beings.

What should he have done? Why?

D. What can you tell about the person who was buried in the Syrian tomb from which these items were recently recovered? The tomb dates from around 1750 B.C.

silver cups	gold bands on
oblong beads	leather
long bone mace with	bronze axes
gold and silver	bones of large grass-
decorations	eating animals
bronze coverings of a	bronze spears
chariot	gold leaf buttons
gold-covered bronze	two bronze goat
studs	heads
bronze incense	carved ivory plaques
burners	

E. Christianity is to Judaism as _____ is to Christianity.

(a) Buddhism

(b) Islam

(c) Shintoism

The fall of Sumer. The Sumerian emperors of Ur ruled Sumer and Akkad for about a hundred years. When desert nomads in the west and Sumer's old enemies in the east attacked, the empire began to disintegrate. Some of the city-states proclaimed their independence from Ur. Weakened, in 2000 B.C. Ur fell to the Elamites from a neighboring kingdom to the northeast. The Sumerians would never again rule Mesopotamia. Yet, many of their accomplishments lived on.

RELIGION AND GOVERNMENT

Through all the years the Sumerians ruled Mesopotamia, religion played an important role in their lives. According to Sumerian beliefs, the deities were all-powerful and immortal. They had human personalities and experienced human emotions. They also had created the universe and had written the laws that governed it.

The Sumerians believed in as many as 3,000 or 4,000 gods and goddesses. Belief in many deities is called *polytheism*. Among the many Sumerian deities, four were superior to all the others—the gods of heaven, air, and water, and the goddess of earth.

The deities could determine a person's days on earth. When humans died, their souls descended to an underworld somewhere beneath the earth, where they were judged. However, this shadowy underworld, the "Land of No Return," offered no rewards or joyous days after life.

Each city-state worshipped one particular god or goddess as its special protector. The city-state's well-being depended on the favor of its deity.

To honor their deities, the Sumerians built shrines and temples. A grand temple known as *ziggurat* (ZIG-er-raht), or "mountain of god," dominated the center of each city. Laboring for many years, more than a thousand workers built the largest ziggurats. These structures were terraced pyramids three or more stories high, each story smaller than the one beneath, like giant steps toward heaven.

In the city-states, religion and government were intertwined. In the eyes of the people, the ruler governed as the earthly representative of the city's deity. By looking after the well-being of the temple and the community, the king was carrying out the will of the deity.

Therefore, the king had obligations. As the city's defender, the ruler maintained the city's walls, raised an army, and expanded the city's territory. As the city's chief priest, the ruler saw to it that temples were built and maintained.

For advice the rulers often turned to the temple priests or a council of elders. Even when rulers were no longer appointed, the tradition of a council of elders remained.

SOCIETY AND THE ECONOMY

The ruler and the ruler's family were members of the highest social class, which also included the rich and powerful families with large land holdings. From these families came the priests of the temple, as well as army officers, high-ranking officials, and advisors to the king. The lowest class was made up of slaves, who were the property of the king, the temple, or the landowners. Slaves could own property, work for money if they could find the time to do so, and sometimes buy their freedom.

Between these two classes were the common people. Most commoners were farmers. Living in villages, they grew mainly wheat and barley, and raised sheep for the wool.

The class of commoners also included workers, artisans, traders, and lesser officials. Most of these people lived in the city. They worked in the temple, in the king's palace, or in their own workshops. The activities of such workers as carpenters, toolmakers, sailors, and architects contributed to the hustle and bustle of city life. Poets, storytellers, and musicians also entertained in the marketplace on market days.

Trade. Wealthy Sumerians enjoyed some of the luxuries that resulted from trade—the second most important economic activity after farming. Merchants sold Sumer's grain, wool, and manufactured articles to neighboring peoples. From Asia Minor and Egypt, merchant caravans brought back timber, ivory, and metals such as copper and gold, which Sumer lacked.

At first, business was conducted by *barter*, a system of payment in which goods or work of equal value are exchanged. For example, a temple worker was paid in food and clothing and perhaps a place to sleep at night. However, in time, some goods and work began to be exchanged for valuable objects such as shells or small bars of gold or silver.

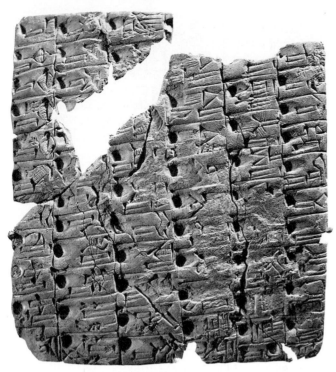

Mesopotamian scribes engraved cuneiform script on clay tablets such as this. Long forgotten, the secret of cuneiform was a mystery for centuries until it was deciphered in the mid-1800s.

Family life. In both the countryside and the city, family life was important. Children, who were highly prized, made valuable contributions to the family. For example, children on farms helped cultivate the fields.

Because men were at the head of the family, property was handed down from father to son. Although a man's wife and children were also legally his property, women were respected and had certain legal rights. For example, women were allowed to own property. Also, some women who became merchants or scribes gained wealth and power.

WRITING

Sometime between 3500 B.C. and 3000 B.C., writing developed in Mesopotamia. At first, such matters as property ownership and lists of goods were engraved on stone cylinders. These cylinder seals could be pressed into wet clay, leaving a symbol that served as a signature or trademark.

Gradually, Sumerian writing evolved into a form that communicated not only business contracts and tax or military records but also religious ideas, laws of astronomy and mathe-

matics, and poetry. The oldest known heroic tale was recorded in Sumer about 2000 B.C.

Sumerian writing was done with clay and reeds—both found in abundance in Mesopotamia. On wet clay tablets, the Sumerians made marks with a stylus, a pointed tool made from a reed. Once the clay hardened, the writing was permanently etched in the clay. The triangular tip of the stylus left wedge-shaped marks. Thus, Sumerian writing is known as **cuneiform** (kyoo-NEE-uh-FORM) writing, from the Latin word *cuneus*, meaning "wedge." Because few people could read and write, scribes—the men and the few women trained in writing—were highly valued.

OTHER SUMERIAN ACHIEVEMENTS

Many Sumerian achievements grew out of farming. Sumerian farmers drained swampland and constructed a complex system of dikes, dams, and canals to irrigate their fields. They also devised new methods and tools for farming, including the pickax and the plow.

Other achievements of the Sumerians grew out of their religion. To find signs of the deities' wishes, the priests studied the heavens and recorded the movements of the heavenly bodies. From these activities, the priests discovered the phases of the moon and the seasonal equinoxes, the times twice a year when day and night are of equal length all over the earth. With such knowledge, these priestly astronomers developed a 12-month calendar that was based on the moon's cycles.

The Sumerians also developed the earliest known system of mathematics. They divided the circle into 360 degrees. They based their mathematical system on the number 60. From this system comes the present practice of dividing the hour into 60 minutes and the minute into 60 seconds.

The Sumerians may have devised the first wheel about 3500 B.C. These wheels were made of sections cut from wooden planks and were attached to axles placed beneath wooden carts. Because ox-drawn carts could carry many times more than the animal alone could pack, the invention contributed to Sumer's brisk trade.

A related invention at about the same time was the potter's wheel. Turning the wet clay as the potter shaped it, the wheel made the work faster and smoother.

Sumerian artisans also made advances in techniques for working copper and gold. In addition, Sumerian metalsmiths discovered how best to combine copper and tin to make harder, more durable bronze.

SECTION REVIEW

1. Define **delta**, **silt**, **city-states**, **empire**, **polytheism**, **ziggurat**, **barter**, and **cuneiform**.

2. Briefly describe the Fertile Crescent.

3. List three issues that caused trouble among city-states. Under what circumstances did city-states unite?

4. Explain how Sargon's empire was governed.

5. How did the Code of Ur-Nammu apply differently to different classes of people?

6. List one new Sumerian idea or invention in each of the following areas: language, agriculture, mathematics, architecture, transportation.

Evaluation. Explain Sumerian contributions to civilization. Consider agriculture, government, and the economy.

ALMANAC

MESOPOTAMIA

Shelter: thick-walled mud-brick houses; thatch, mud, or wooden roofs; shoulder-high doors opening onto a central courtyard

Clothing: woolen skirts and tunics, leather sandals; variety of headdresses for women ranging from simple ribbon to a large helmetlike covering; gold and copper earrings and necklaces for both men and women

Food: barley (staple food, made into porridge or flat bread), wheat, rice, dates, cheese, onions, cucumbers, apples, fish, mutton, pork, duck

Some leisure activities: music (lyre, harp), storytelling, wrestling, games of chance

Research Activity: Make an almanac for one of the other civilizations discussed in this chapter. You may use whatever categories are appropriate.

2-2
ANCIENT EMPIRES OF THE FERTILE CRESCENT

READ TO FIND OUT

—what the term **tribute** means.
—how the Babylonians brought Mesopotamia under one rule.
—why the Hittites defeated the Babylonians.
—how the Assyrians built an empire.
—how the Chaldeans preserved Babylonian and Sumerian culture.

The flat, open lands of Sumer made it an easy target for invasion. With the fall of the last Sumerian kings, other peoples cast envious glances at the prosperous trade routes, rich cities, and fertile lands of Mesopotamia.

Wave after wave of invaders came into the river valley. Some ruled for a time, having little effect on the Mesopotamian way of life. Others—the Babylonians, the Assyrians, and the Chaldeans—left lasting effects. However, each new group adopted some Sumerian ideas and traditions, thus allowing much of the Sumerian way of life to continue with few changes.

THE BABYLONIANS

As the Sumerian city-states grew weak militarily from constant conflict, Amorites, Semitic tribes from the edge of the Arabian Desert, began to pour into Mesopotamia. The small Amorite town of Babylon (BAB-uh-lahn) on the Euphrates River grew to be a large city-state, ruled by Amorite kings. When Hammurabi (HAM-uh-RAH-bee) became the sixth Amorite ruler of Babylon in 1792 B.C., he was only one king among many who ruled the numerous city-states in Mesopotamia. However, Hammurabi began a campaign to unite the quarreling city-states into a single strong empire, as Sargon had done.

By 1759 B.C., Hammurabi had conquered the last city-state strong enough to oppose him. When Hammurabi had begun his campaign, Babylon ruled an area within a 50-mile (80-kilometer) radius of the city. By the time Hammurabi achieved his goal, his empire stretched along the Tigris and the Euphrates from the Persian Gulf on the east into present-day Turkey in the west. Because Babylon was its chief city, the empire became known as Babylonia, and its people, Babylonians.

The Code of Hammurabi. Like Ur-Nammu before him, Hammurabi revised the existing laws of various city-states, and then issued a single code of law for everyone in the empire to observe. The Code of Hammurabi was carved in cuneiform on a huge stone column.

One important result of the code was that it strengthened the central government. The list of crimes against the government was longer and the penalties for those crimes were more severe than under Sumerian law. In addition, although in the past it usually had been left to victims and their families to administer justice, now officials of the empire played a much stronger role in catching and punishing offenders.

The 282 laws in the Code of Hammurabi regulated almost every aspect of daily life. The code controlled trade, banking, business, and agriculture. It established working conditions, listed property rights, and gave the correct procedures for contracts, marriages, and divorces.

An important feature of the code was its concern for justice. "The strong shall not injure the weak," it proclaimed. False witnesses and corrupt judges were severely punished, and an individual was considered innocent until proven guilty.

Punishments, often harsh, depended on the social class of the victim. The most common punishments under the Code of Hammurabi were fines, mutilation, and death. There was no such penalty as imprisonment.

Hammurabi's code granted slaves and women rights that were denied them in most other ancient civilizations. A slave could own property, bring lawsuits against free people, and marry a free person. Although the code did not grant women equality with men, it did grant women some rights. For example, women were guaranteed the right to own, buy, and sell property, and to lend and borrow money.

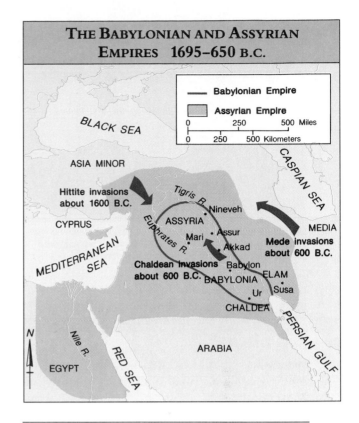

THE BABYLONIAN AND ASSYRIAN EMPIRES 1695–650 B.C.

THE FALL OF BABYLONIA

After Hammurabi's death about 1750 B.C., his heirs continued to rule for more than a century. However, old rivalries between city-states weakened the empire. About 1600 B.C. the Hittites from Asia Minor raided Babylonia. Earlier, the Hittites and other nomadic Indo-Europeans—ancestors of the people of modern Europe, Iran, and India—had migrated to Asia Minor from the north.

The Hittites used a light war chariot drawn by horses. The chariot had been invented before 1600 B.C. by Indo-Europeans in the western Fertile Crescent. As fleet horses drew the chariots across the plains, Hittite archers overwhelmed the Babylonian soldiers. The Hittite soldiers had another advantage over the Babylonians—iron. The Hittites had developed a way to make iron tools and weapons. Iron was so much stronger than bronze that for several hundred years the Hittites treated their new technology as a military secret.

After the Hittites raided Babylonia, they withdrew to their homeland in Asia Minor and the western Fertile Crescent. However, the Hittite invasion led to the collapse of Babylonian

New weapons like the battering ram on the right aided Assyrian conquest. Assyrian kings covered the walls of their immense palaces with carvings depicting their victories.

civilization. The Hittites had destroyed Babylonian power, and other invaders followed. The Kassites, from the mountains to the east, took control of Babylonia about 1550 B.C. and ruled it for more than four centuries. Eventually, Babylonia fell to the Assyrians (uh-SIHR-ee-uhnz), the most brutal of all the peoples to rule Mesopotamia.

THE ASSYRIANS

By 1600 B.C., peoples in the area north of Babylonia had established a few walled cities—Assur (AH-soor), Kalhu, and Nineveh. From the name Assur, the region was called Assyria (uh-SIHR-ee-uh) and the people, Assyrians.

Beginning about 1365 B.C., the Assyrians, who had become skilled warriors, set out on a path of conquest. They took over all of northern Mesopotamia and drove the Kassites out of Babylonia. Then they defeated the Hittites and other mountain people of Asia Minor and took over the cities and trade routes of the western Fertile Crescent.

After 700 B.C., the Assyrians began another series of conquests to extend their empire. By 650 B.C., the Assyrians had crushed nearly every group of people in the Middle East and created a mighty empire that extended from the Nile River to the plateaus of Anatolia and Iran.

Assyria's success was due in part to new techniques of warfare. While some of the elite soldiers still rode in war chariots, others fought from horseback. These mounted archers and lancers, who could maneuver quickly in difficult terrain, formed the first organized cavalry.

To smash opposing armies, the Assyrians developed new weapons of war, among them huge battering rams on wheeled wooden towers. In addition, Assyrian soldiers were clad in armor and carried swords of high-quality iron unmatched by the weapons of the people they subdued.

The Assyrians conquered with a policy of physical power and brutality. They made fear a weapon. For example, they sometimes nailed conquered leaders on the gates of their cities to intimidate the city's inhabitants.

Assyrian officials, responsible directly to the warrior-king, governed conquered cities. Revolts were put down without mercy. To transport armies and speed communication within the empire, the Assyrians established a system of roads and messengers.

Assyrian kings demanded **tribute** from the peoples they subdued. Tribute is wealth sent from one ruler or country to another as a sign that the other is supreme. Gold, precious stones, iron, timber, and other wealth poured into Assyrian cities from conquered lands.

Achievements. Throughout the Fertile Crescent the Assyrians built magnificent walled cities which included temples and ziggurats. To glorify the empire, their buildings were decorated with sculptures of fabulous beasts and stone carvings showing war and hunting.

The Assyrian empire reached its height under Assurbanipal (AH-shoor-BAH-neh-pahl), who ruled from about 669 B.C. to 633 B.C. Assurbanipal was a forceful general and an effective ruler. However, he had a particular interest in learning. He ordered scribes to travel throughout Mesopotamia, seeking Sumerian and Babylonian writings. As a result, more than 20,000 clay tablets were collected and placed in a library at Nineveh. Thus, knowledge of the Sumerian and Babylonian civilizations was preserved for the future.

The downfall of Assyria. Shortly after Assurbanipal's reign, the Assyrian empire came to a quick end. The Assyrian armies were worn down by continual war, and they had made many enemies. Throughout the empire, people began to revolt.

In 612 B.C., two groups living at the fringes of Assyria joined forces and easily smashed the empire. They destroyed Nineveh and killed the

This dragon, along with images of bulls, lions, and other animals, decorated the walls of Babylon, built by Nebuchadnezzar in the sixth century B.C. Dedicated to the goddess Ishtar, the gate spanned an 80-foot (24-meter) wide marble roadway used mainly for religious processions. The gate also played a role in the city's defense.

Assyrian king. These two groups, the Medes (MEEDS) from the Iranian plateau and the Chaldeans (kal-DEE-uhnz) from the western shores of the Persian Gulf, then divided the empire between them. The Medes took over the lands north of Mesopotamia that had been Elam, while the Chaldeans built their own empire in Babylonia.

THE CHALDEANS

After the breakup of the Assyrian empire, the Chaldeans ruled Mesopotamia for about 75 years. Under Nebuchadnezzar (NEB-uh-kud-NEZ-ur), who ruled from 605 B.C. to 562 B.C., the Chaldean empire encompassed nearly the entire Fertile Crescent.

Nebuchadnezzar called for new buildings and fortifications. With great splendor he rebuilt the city of Babylon, which the Assyrians had destroyed. The city's thick walls, palaces, and temples were decorated with glazed brick in brilliant red, blue, and yellow.

One of the most impressive buildings in the city was Nebuchadnezzar's palace. On the roof were the Hanging Gardens, which legend says were designed for his wife who was homesick for the green hills of her mountainous homeland. The lush gardens contained rare flowers, plants, and trees. Water pumped from the Euphrates gave life to this tropical wonder.

Chaldean culture was similar to that of the Sumerians and Babylonians. The Chaldeans returned to the Babylonian form of government and laws. Their economy relied on trade and farming, like the Sumerian and Babylonian economies. They read Babylonian books.

The Chaldeans also contributed to learning, especially in the fields of mathematics and astronomy. One major Chaldean accomplishment, which grew out of their interest in the heavens, was the accurate calculation of the length of the year to within 26 minutes.

After Nebuchadnezzar's death in 562 B.C., civil wars became common. In 538 B.C., the Chaldeans fell without a struggle to the mighty armies of the Persian empire.

SECTION REVIEW

1. Define *tribute*.

2. How did Hammurabi's Code strengthen the position of the central government?

3. Name two advantages Hittite armies had over Babylonian armies.

4. How did the Assyrians preserve the knowledge of the Sumerians and Babylonians?

5. Describe Chaldean culture.

Evaluation. Compare the strengths and weaknesses of Babylonian and Assyrian government.

2-3
THE EGYPTIANS

READ TO FIND OUT

— what the terms **cataracts**, **dynasty**, **pharaoh**, **monotheism**, **hieroglyphics**, and **papyrus** mean.
— why the pharaohs of the Old Kingdom had great power.
— how the Egyptians of the Middle Kingdom made contact with other civilizations.
— how strong pharaohs of the New Kingdom built an Egyptian empire.
— how religion and agriculture influenced patterns of living.
— what ideas and inventions originated in Egypt.

People began moving into the valley of the Nile River in search of food as early as 10,000 years ago. They found herds of wild animals, abundant plant life, and a good supply of water. These neolithic people gradually settled into farming villages along the banks of the Nile and laid the foundation of a thriving river valley civilization called Egypt.

THE NILE RIVER VALLEY: THE NATURAL SETTING

The Nile River flows out of the mountains of central Africa, rushes over a series of **cataracts**, or steep rapids, then winds its way through barren deserts north to the Mediterranean Sea. The Nile's journey is more than 4,000 miles (6,400 kilometers), making it the longest river in the world. Over countless years the Nile has cut a broad valley through the desert, leaving steep red limestone cliffs on either side. The river has filled the valley floor with rich black soil from the mountains. This strip of dark, fertile soil is never wider than 13 miles (10.8 kilometers).

Little rain falls in Egypt, and most of the country is desert. The Nile River valley is one of the few places in Egypt where crops can grow. The waters of the Nile provide both irrigation and transportation for the valley. For this reason, a Greek traveler who toured Egypt in

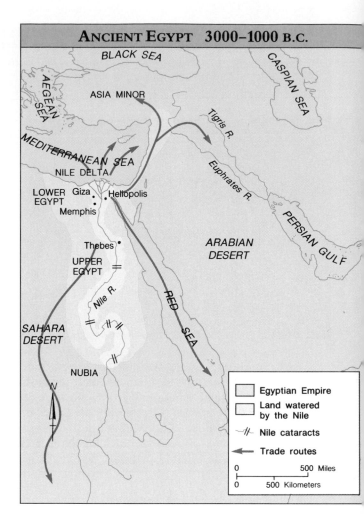

the 400s B.C., said "All Egypt is the gift of the Nile."

Each summer heavy rain in the mountains at the Nile's source caused the river to overflow its banks. As the water receded, it left behind a rich layer of silt. At the mouth of the river, silt deposits built up a marshy, fan-shaped delta. The deep delta soil provided especially rich farmland. The extent of the flooding could vary slightly from year to year. Usually, however, the Nile followed a regular pattern, unlike the Tigris and Euphrates rivers in Mesopotamia, whose flood waters were unpredictable, and often savage and destructive.

The Nile Valley enjoyed other natural advantages over Mesopotamia. The valley was almost completely surrounded by natural barriers that deterred invaders. The stark, barren deserts that lay to the east and west are some of the most forbidding in the world. The Mediterranean coast to the north had few harbors and could be easily defended. In the south, the cataracts made travel along the Nile difficult. Hindered by the difficulty of the surrounding lands, few outsiders came into the Nile Valley. The Egyptians felt secure in their homeland.

EARLY EGYPT

By about 5000 B.C., Egyptian farmers learned to time the planting and harvesting of their grains, mainly wheat and barley, to take advantage of the Nile's flooding. Working together, they built catch basins to trap the water and canals to carry it to land away from the river.

The efficiency and cooperative efforts of these early Egyptian farmers helped them produce bountiful crops, and as a result, the population grew in the peaceful valley. Scattered along the banks of the Nile, clusters of mud huts developed into villages and towns. The river served as a link between these centers of population.

The early villages along the Nile gradually united to form two kingdoms. The Kingdom of Lower Egypt, whose ruler wore a red crown, was located on the Nile delta. The Kingdom of Upper Egypt, symbolized by a white crown, was located to the south, along the banks of the Nile.

About 3100 B.C., Menes (MEE-neez), a ruler of Upper Egypt, conquered Lower Egypt and established a united kingdom in the Nile Valley. He built a capital, Memphis, where the two kingdoms met. Though united, the ancient Egyptians called their nation "the Kingdom of the Two Crowns."

Menes founded the first Egyptian *dynasty*, or series of rulers from the same family. In a dynasty, the right to rule is hereditary, or passed down from one family member to another. The dynasty continues until there are no more heirs or the dynasty is overthrown.

Over nearly 3,000 years, 30 dynasties ruled ancient Egypt. Little is known of the early period, which includes the dynasty founded by Menes and the one that followed. The history of the remaining Egyptian dynasties, however, can be divided into three periods—the Old, the Middle, and the New Kingdoms. The years between these periods were times of disruptive civil wars and invasions. After about 1100 B.C., outsiders established dynasties in Egypt.

THE OLD KINGDOM

During the early period and the 500 years of the Old Kingdom, the Egyptians established a strong government. Everyone, the rulers and the people alike, believed the rulers to be deities, the children of the sun god. One Egyptian said of his ruler, "He lights up the Two Lands [kingdoms] more than the sun. He makes the Two Lands more green than does a high Nile." To show respect for their divine rulers, the people were forbidden to call them by their personal names. Thus, the rulers came to be called *pharaoh* (FAIR-oh), meaning "royal house."

The pharaohs had great power, which they were expected to use for the good of the kingdom, not personal gain. The Egyptians had faith that their pharaohs would rule wisely.

To further the well-being of the kingdom, the pharaoh oversaw the construction of temples and irrigation systems, and regulated farming and trade. A *vizier* (vih-ZER), or prime minister, carried out the pharaoh's decisions. Other officials, including a chief architect and court judges, also served the pharaoh.

Under the pharaoh were local chieftains. These governors looked after the 42 local districts, or *nomes*, into which Egypt was divided. At first, the governors were appointed by the pharaoh. In time, however, the governors passed their power on to their heirs.

Government and religion were inseparable in Egypt. The pharaoh was both the ruler and the chief priest. Many of the officials who served the pharaoh were also priests.

The Age of Pyramids. In death, it was believed, the pharaoh would join the other deities. To house the body of the deceased pharaoh and the objects that would be needed in the afterlife, the Egyptians built nearly indestructible pyramids. The first known pyramid, designed by the architect Imhotep, was built near the city of Memphis about 2650 B.C. This structure was the world's first to be built entirely of stone.

During the years of the Old Kingdom, which is also known as The Age of Pyramids, barges plied the Nile carrying massive chunks of limestone from the hills east of the Nile. These blocks were dragged to construction sites on the west bank, where hundreds of thousands of laborers worked for as long as 20 years to build a single pyramid.

Situated along the Nile, these pyramids at Giza were constructed between 2650 B.C. and 2575 B.C. The monuments' grandeur was inspired by the belief that the pharaohs were divine.

The decline of the Old Kingdom. The Old Kingdom was generally a time of peace and prosperity. The pharaohs did not even keep a regular army, although each nome had soldiers that the pharaoh could call upon if invasion threatened.

About 2300 B.C., the power of the pharaohs began to weaken. Civil wars became common as local governors fought one another to increase their power. Egypt thus entered a period of disorder that lasted about 200 years.

THE MIDDLE KINGDOM

About 2000 B.C., a strong new ruler reorganized the government, established a new dynasty, and made Thebes (THEEBS) the capital. Egypt prospered once again.

The pharaohs of the Middle Kingdom did not quite achieve the absolute power of the royal rulers of the Old Kingdom. The local governors were not willing to give up all the powers they had gained. However, many of these local governors ruled badly, causing the people to side with the pharaohs against them.

To reward common people for their support, pharaohs began to award them government positions that before had been given only to priests and others close to the pharaoh. Additional privileges, such as the right to own land or to enter certain occupations, were awarded to common people, as well. Although pharaohs continued to build tombs and temples, they also increased the construction of public works, such as canals, to benefit the common people.

During the years of the Middle Kingdom, Egyptians began to look outward from their secluded homeland. Merchants sailed throughout the eastern Mediterranean region, south along the Nile to the African kingdom of Nubia, and along the western shore of the Red Sea. They traded Egyptian products for timber, precious stones, and other prized items. Such contact with other civilizations brought new ideas and culture into the Nile Valley.

Late in the period, Egypt was invaded by Amorites from the western Fertile Crescent. In 1730 B.C., Amorite warriors captured the Nile delta. The Egyptians called these people Hyksos (HIK-sōs), meaning "chief of the foreign hill country." The Hyksos used body armor, new types of bronze weapons, and horse-drawn chariots, which the Egyptians had never seen. After about 150 years of foreign rule, the Egyptians drove the Hyksos out of Egypt.

THE NEW KINGDOM

After the Hyksos were expelled in 1580 B.C., a new dynasty ruled Egypt from the city of Thebes. This marked the beginning of the New Kingdom. Determined to protect their country against future invasions, the pharaohs of the New Kingdom became military rulers with professional armies.

Ruling the New Kingdom from 1503 B.C. to 1482 B.C. was Hatshepsut (haht-SHEHP-soot), the first known female ruler in history. Daughter of a pharaoh, she was a popular and able ruler. Dedicating her rule to peace, she ordered the construction of temples, monuments, and other public buildings. She gained new markets for Egyptian merchants by sending trading expeditions throughout the Mediterranean and to other parts of Africa. During Hatshepsut's reign, Egypt prospered.

When Hatshepsut's successor, Thutmose III (thoot-MOH-suh), became ruler, he set out on a policy of conquest. After 16 military campaigns, he ruled an empire that extended from the Euphrates River in Mesopotamia to the farthest cataracts of the Nile, in modern-day Sudan. After the death of Thutmose in 1450 B.C., Egyptian pharaohs managed to hold together the empire through both military might and diplomacy for about a hundred years.

The reign of Amenhotep. In 1379 B.C., Amenhotep IV (AH-muhn-HŌ-tep) became the pharaoh of Egypt. He devoted his energies to bringing about a religious revolution in Egypt.

The Egyptians believed in many gods and goddesses. However, Amenhotep came to believe in only the sun god. Belief in one god rather than many deities is called **monotheism**.

Amenhotep called this god Aton, "the sole god beside whom there is no other." He even changed his name to Akhenaton (AH-kuh-NAH-tun), which means, "It goes well with Aton."

Akhenaton established a new capital called Akhetaton. Here temples to Aton were built. Unlike traditional temples, which were dimly lit, these were entirely unroofed so that the sun's rays could penetrate everywhere. Throughout Egypt, temples of other deities were shut down, and temple priests were dismissed. The names and images of other deities were removed from temples and tombs.

However, many Egyptians refused to give up their old beliefs, even in Akhenaton's capital. After the pharaoh died in 1358 B.C., Egypt's old religion was restored during the reign of Tutankhamen (TOOT-ahngk-AH-mun). Because Tutankhamen became pharaoh at nine years of age, his vizier served as co-ruler.

During Tutankhamen's reign of nine years, the capital was returned to Thebes. Old temples were reopened, and the priests were brought back. New statues of the deities were made, some in the likeness of Tutankhamen himself, who was called "beloved of the gods." Aton remained a god, but no longer the sole one.

While these religious changes were still in progress, Tutankhamen suddenly died. Thankful for the return of the old beliefs, Egyptians gave the "boy pharaoh" a burial that was remarkable for its richness.

The reign of Ramses. Ramses II (RAM-seez), the last great ruler of the New Kingdom, reigned from 1304 B.C. to 1237 B.C. During his reign, the Egyptians spent nearly 15 years battling the Hittites in the eastern part of the empire. Finally, in 1280 B.C., Ramses signed a treaty with the Hittites. For the rest of his reign, he concentrated on building colossal statues of himself and great temples throughout the empire. Ramses built so extensively that half the surviving buildings of Egypt can be traced to his reign.

After the death of Ramses, weak pharaohs lost the empire, and Egypt suffered invasion and conquest. From 715 B.C. to 656 B.C., Egypt was ruled first by desert nomads and then by the Assyrians. Egypt regained its independence for a time, but in 525 B.C. fell to the Persians, who ruled until 332 B.C.

SOCIETY

Throughout Egypt's 3,000-year history, Egyptian society and everyday life remained remarkably the same. Society was divided into four social classes. However, except for royalty, people could move from one class to another.

The royal family stood at the top of the Egyptian social structure. At the head of the royal family was the pharaoh. Below the pharaoh was a small ruling class of priests and nobles. Members of this class had great wealth, power, and influence. During the New Kingdom, a new social class of professional soldiers developed, ranking just below the nobles.

At the top of the middle class were the scribes. Since accurate records were necessary to keep the kingdom running efficiently, scribes were valued members of Egyptian society. Merchants and artisans who lived and worked in the cities were also part of the middle class. As trade increased from the time of the Middle Kingdom, the middle class grew in importance.

The largest group of people in ancient Egypt were peasants, most of whom were farmers.

Tomb walls were often covered with scenes of the deceased both in earthly life and afterlife. In this tomb portrait, dated 700 B.C., a Theban couple face the gods of the underworld.

Living in small villages along the river, these farmers planted barley and wheat, and fruits and vegetables. Other peasants, however, labored in cities, in the rock quarries, or in copper or turquoise mines.

Prisoners of war were brought back to Egypt to serve as slaves. They worked on temple lands or on the estates of the royal family or the nobles. These slaves were often better off than peasants were. However, other slaves were forced to work in government mines.

Family life. In ancient Egypt, family life was highly valued and children were treasured. Women in Egypt were equal to men in many ways. Women were allowed to own businesses, to buy and sell property, and to testify in court. Egyptian women were highly respected in their roles as mothers and wives.

Formal education was mostly for the sons of the wealthy. Often Egyptian schools were connected to a temple. In addition to studying religion, students learned reading, writing, and arithmetic.

Some Egyptian boys learned a trade or craft from their fathers or a local artisan. Girls usually received their training at home.

RELIGION

Religion was an essential part of Egyptian social, political, and economic life. Early Egyptians worshipped forces of nature, such as the wind. As towns evolved, the inhabitants worshipped their own gods and goddesses, the guardian deities of the community. After the kingdoms of Upper and Lower Egypt united, all of the guardian deities were united, as well, to become Re (RAY), the sun god. When the capital was moved to Thebes, the guardian god of Thebes, Amon, became the kingdom's chief deity. Eventually, the two gods were viewed as one, Amon-Re, the preserver of right and justice, the protector of order.

The Egyptians worshipped a multitude of other deities, as well. Because some animals, such as cats, crocodiles, and bulls, were thought to serve the deities in special ways, they also were considered sacred.

Belief in an afterlife. The Egyptians believed in life after death. People expected life after death to be much like their happiest moments

PAPYRUS

Before the ancient Egyptians invented a kind of paper, religious writings and records were often etched on bulky stone tablets. These were ponderous to carry and difficult to store. Then an unknown Egyptian living sometime after 3000 B.C. created the world's first paper, known as papyrus after the reed plants from which it was made.

Using thin sheets of papyrus, people could now send messages conveniently to distant places. Because of the fine qualities of papyrus, it became a major item of Egyptian trade. Papyrus was the most convenient writing material available until the invention of wood-pulp paper by the Chinese in about A.D. 100.

To make papyrus, stalks of the damp reeds were cut in foot-long strips. These strips were laid side by side lengthwise. Then a second layer was added, this one running at a right angle across the first. Next, the two layers were pounded together. After the papyrus dried, the final step was to smooth any lumps with a stone. Often many papyrus sheets were glued together side to side and rolled into a scroll that might, if stretched out, extend 40 yards (36 meters).

The Egyptians were a highly organized people, and to properly manage their society, they kept voluminous records, made possible by papyrus and hieroglyphics. Scribes were the record keepers, a highly prized job that could require 10 to 12 years of training to master. Students had to memorize as many as 600 hieroglyphic figures, and each had to be drawn with great skill. Often scribes worked for Egypt's rulers.

The many ancient writings left by Egyptian scribes were undecipherable until the early nineteenth century. Then scholars used the recently discovered Rosetta Stone, a tablet with the same inscription in both ancient Egyptian and Greek, to decode the hieroglyphics. From the "speech of the gods," as the Egyptians called their writing, many secrets of ancient Egyptian life have been revealed to modern scholars.

---

on earth. Originally, they thought that only the pharaoh was guaranteed life after death. In time, though, the Egyptians came to believe in an afterlife for all people.

Because they believed the soul would eventually return to the body, the Egyptians preserved the bodies of the dead through a process called mummification. The internal organs, except the heart and kidneys, were removed. The body was dried slowly in special salts, carefully wrapped in linen, and placed in a wood or stone coffin. Bodies so preserved are called mummies.

The Egyptian people prepared carefully for the afterlife. The wealthy built great stone tombs, called "houses of eternity." Tombs were also cut into rocky cliffs along the Nile. Egyptians stocked the tombs with food, jewelry, and other objects they would want or need in the afterlife. Most Egyptians could not afford elaborate burials. Yet even the poor buried food and a few simple articles with the deceased.

WRITING

By about 3000 B.C., the Egyptians had developed a system of writing called **hieroglyphics** (HĪ-ur-uh-GLIF-iks). The word *hieroglyphics* comes from the Greek words *hieros* and *glyphe,* meaning "sacred" and "carving." At first, the Egyptians carved their writing in stone. Later, they learned to make **papyrus**, a kind of paper, from reeds that grew along the Nile. They fashioned pens from sharpened reeds and used red and black ink made from soot and vegetable gum.

Hieroglyphics combined pictures or symbols for ideas and words with those for sounds. The Egyptians developed symbols for consonant sounds only, however. They never developed symbols for vowel sounds. Eventually, the Egyptians created more than 600 symbols, many of them representing more than one word or idea.

A ROYAL TOMB

In 1922, after ten years of dedicated searching, Howard Carter discovered the tomb of the pharaoh Tutankhamen. In the tomb, Carter found thousands of magnificent, priceless objects—including the pharaoh's solid gold coffin—that had lain buried for 3,200 years.

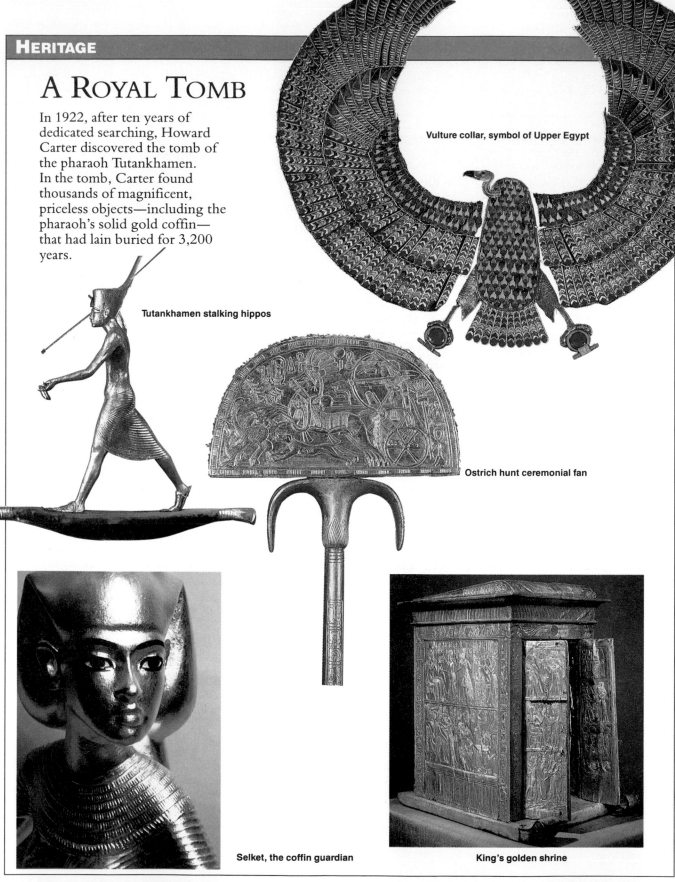

Vulture collar, symbol of Upper Egypt

Tutankhamen stalking hippos

Ostrich hunt ceremonial fan

Selket, the coffin guardian

King's golden shrine

Hieroglyphics were carved or painted on stone walls to proclaim the exploits of the pharaohs. However, most Egyptian writing was religious. The Egyptians wrote thousands of hymns glorifying their deities.

OTHER EGYPTIAN ACHIEVEMENTS

The Egyptians were skillful engineers. The Great Pyramid of the pharaoh Khufu, built during a period of 20 years around 2600 B.C., is over 450 feet (720 kilometers) high. Each side at the base is about the length of 2 city blocks. The Great Pyramid was made from more than 2 million huge stone blocks, each weighing about 2.5 tons (2.25 metric tons). An estimated 80,000 people worked on the monument.

In the process of building monumental structures, the Egyptians developed skills in arithmetic and geometry. They understood how to add, subtract, and divide. They learned how to determine accurately the volume of pyramids and cylinders. They also invented a decimal system although they did not have a symbol for zero.

Astronomy. The need to predict when the Nile would flood each year led to important discoveries in astronomy. The Egyptians observed that before the flood each year, the star Sirius rose in the eastern horizon just before dawn. Beginning with this event, the Egyptians counted the number of days—365—until Sirius rose again. Thus, they discovered the solar year, the length of time it takes the earth to make one complete journey around the sun. The Egyptians developed a calendar based on the solar year, which they divided into 12 thirty-day months. To each year, they added 5 additional days, which became feast days.

Medicine. Many Egyptian cures were designed to drive out evil spirits believed to cause disease. Nevertheless, Egyptian doctors made important progress in the field of medicine. Study of mummies shows that the Egyptians knew how to set bones. One ancient papyrus describes ways to recognize certain diseases and lists practical treatments, including surgery, for 48 different kinds of injuries. The knowledge of Egyptian doctors was highly valued and became the basis of medical treatment throughout the Mediterranean area.

SECTION REVIEW

1. Define **cataracts**, **dynasty**, **pharaoh**, **monotheism**, **hieroglyphics**, and **papyrus**.

2. How were the pharaohs expected to use their power?

3. What brought Egyptians into contact with other lands during the Middle Kingdom?

4. Describe the extent of the Egyptian empire.

5. Describe two practices that resulted from the Egyptian belief in afterlife.

Analysis. State three facts that support this claim: "Egypt is the gift of the Nile."

Data Search. Refer to the appropriate chart on page 829 to identify: **(a)** the building materials used in both Mesopotamia and Egypt during the period from 3000 to 2000 B.C., and **(b)** the differences in the use of building materials in these two regions.

2-4
PHOENICIA, PALESTINE, AND PERSIA

READ TO FIND OUT

—what the terms **tribe**, **covenant**, **prophets**, **ethics**, and **ethical monotheism** mean.
—how the Phoenicians spread the learning of Mesopotamia and Egypt.
—what enduring principles the Hebrews developed.
—how ideas circulated throughout the Persian empire.

While kingdoms and empires rose and fell in Mesopotamia and Egypt, other civilizations developed in the Middle East. These civilizations developed new, enduring ideas. Through trade and expansion, they also helped to spread the customs and beliefs of the various peoples living throughout the Middle East.

THE PHOENICIANS

As early as 3000 B.C., a Semitic people known as the Canaanites settled along the Mediterranean coast at the western edge of the Fertile Crescent. The region became known as Canaan. The northern coast of Canaan came to be called Phoenicia (fuh-NEE-shuh), and the people Phoenicians.

Phoenicia was ruled by Egypt for about 100 years during the New Kingdom. However, by the time of Akhenaton, about 1379 B.C., the Phoenician cities had again become self-ruling.

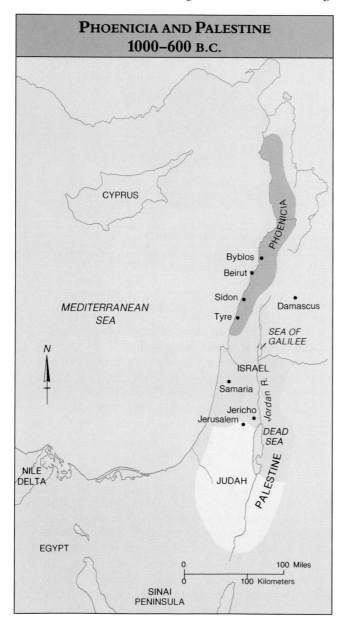

PHOENICIA AND PALESTINE 1000–600 B.C.

The Phoenicians lived by trade and built great port cities such as Byblos (BIB-lōs) and Beirut (bay-ROOT). By 1100 B.C., Phoenicia had developed as a great sea power. Phoenicians became skilled sailors, learning to navigate by the stars at night. Large sea-going vessels, powered by rowers, carried olive oil, glass, and other products throughout the Mediterranean. Merchant ships also sailed into the Atlantic Ocean, trading with settlements on the shores of Africa and Spain and possibly even Britain.

The Phoenicians were especially known for their purple-colored woolen and linen textiles. The Phoenicians had discovered how to extract the red-purple dye from a type of sea snail in the waters off the coast. Only the very wealthy could afford this expensive dyed cloth. Because it was so precious, purple became the color of clothing worn by monarchs.

At the height of their power, from about 1100 B.C. to 800 B.C., the Phoenicians established colonies on the shores of the Mediterranean in southern Spain, North Africa, and western Sicily. The most prosperous colony, Carthage, in North Africa, became a great manufacturing and trading center.

After 800 B.C., Phoenician power began to decline. By 700 B.C., the Assyrians extended control over Phoenicia. About 600 B.C., Phoenicia regained independence but was quickly subdued by the Chaldeans and then the Persians. During this time, Phoenician ships in search of trade made the first known voyage around the southern tip of Africa.

The spread of culture and learning. As the Phoenicians traded and colonized, they diffused the products, customs, and ideas of many peoples. Through the Phoenicians, the culture and learning of Mesopotamia and Egypt were carried throughout the Mediterranean world.

From the Egyptians the Phoenicians learned of writing. They adopted the Egyptian idea of using symbols for sounds but developed their own alphabet of 22 consonants. Under this system, people needed to learn only a few symbols in order to write all the words of their language.

Through trade, the Phoenician alphabet spread east to Babylonia and from there to Persia and eventually to India. The alphabet also went west to Greece, and from there versions of it went to both eastern and western Europe.

This Phoenician warship was employed about 700 B.C. by an Assyrian king. One row of oarsmen can be seen above deck; a second row of the oarsmen can be found inside the ship's hull.

THE HEBREWS

About 1800 B.C., a Semitic people, the Hebrews, left the Sumerian city-state of Ur and followed their leader Abraham into the area south of Phoenicia. This region was still known as Canaan. According to tradition, the god of Abraham had appeared to him and promised, "Leave your own country, your kinsmen, and your father's house, and go to a country that I will show you. I will make you [Abraham's people] into a great nation."

In Canaan, also according to tradition, Abraham's grandson Jacob had 12 sons, who each became the founder of a Hebrew *tribe*. A tribe is an organized group of people believed to descend from a common ancestor. Because Jacob was also known as Israel, the people were called the Israelites.

Also according to Hebrew tradition, sometime after 1600 B.C., a famine, or food shortage, caused Israelites to migrate west to Egypt, where food was more plentiful. The Hebrews lived in the Nile delta for several centuries. After a time, however, the pharaohs forced the Hebrews into slavery. About 1300 B.C., during the reign of Ramses II, Moses led the Hebrews in a great exodus out of Egypt.

The law of the Hebrews. Under Moses, the Hebrews had journeyed into the desert of the Sinai Peninsula, between Egypt and Palestine, where they lived for about 40 years. While the Hebrews were wandering in the Sinai Desert, Moses persuaded them to give up all other deities and worship only Yahweh (YAH-wuh), or God. Through Moses the Hebrews made a sacred *covenant*, or solemn agreement, with Yahweh, promising to worship only Yahweh and follow his laws.

According to tradition, God gave Moses a tablet containing the laws known as the Ten Commandments. The first several Commandments set forth the duties of individuals toward Yahweh. The rest forbid such crimes as false testimony, theft, and murder. The Commandments became the Hebrews' basic religious and moral laws.

Return to Palestine. Around 1250 B.C., the Hebrews returned to Canaan. At about the same time another group, the Philistines, settled there. Others had forced the Philistines out of their homeland, the Mediterranean island of Crete. From the Philistines, Canaan became known as Palestine. The Philistines, the Canaanites, and the Hebrews competed for land in Palestine.

The threat of war brought the several Hebrew tribes together. About 1025 B.C., for the first time, they chose one king, Saul, to rule over all the tribes. Discord continued to divide the tribes, however, until after Saul's death, when David became king. The armies of David drove out the Philistines and took over Canaanite cities.

Uniting the people under one strong government, David began to build a magnificent capital city at Jerusalem. When David died, his son Solomon became king. He completed the work of building the city, with its large stone temple.

Loss of independence. Even though Solomon expanded the influence of the Hebrews through both trade and war, high taxes and his policy of forced labor to build Jerusalem caused discontent among the people. After Solomon died, about 930 B.C., the kingdom split in two. The Hebrew tribes in the north refused to accept Solomon's son as king. The northern part became the kingdom of Israel, with its capital at Samaria. The southern part, with its capital at Jerusalem, became known as Judah.

In the centuries that followed, the Hebrew kingdoms suffered periodic warfare among the tribes and repeated invasions by outsiders. In 722 B.C., the Assyrians conquered Israel and carried away many Hebrews as slaves. In 586 B.C., the Chaldeans under Nebuchadnezzar conquered Judah, obliterated Solomon's magnificent temple in Jerusalem, and exiled the Hebrews to Babylon.

When the Persians conquered Babylon in 538 B.C., the Persian emperor freed the Hebrews and allowed them to return to their homeland. They then became known as Judeans, or Jews, from Judah, the name of their former kingdom. The Jews did not regain their political independence, however, for Palestine remained under Persian influence for about two hundred years.

JUDAISM

By the time of Moses, Judaism—the religion of the Hebrews—taught that Yahweh was the chief lawgiver and the only god of the He-

---

THE TEN COMMANDMENTS

Below is an excerpt from the Bible:

And Moses called unto all Israel, and said unto them:

"Hear, O Israel, the statutes and the ordinances which I speak in your ears this day that ye may learn them and observe to do them. The Lord spoke with you face to face in the mount out of the midst of the fire—I stood between the Lord and you at the time to declare unto you the word of the Lord, for ye were afraid because of the fire—saying:

I am the Lord thy God. . . . Thou shalt have no other gods before Me. . . .

Thou shalt not make unto thee a graven image. . . .

Thou shalt not take the name of the Lord thy God in vain. . . .

Observe the sabbath day, to keep it holy. . . . Six days shalt thou labor . . . but the seventh day is a sabbath unto the Lord. . . .

Honor thy father and thy mother. . . .

Thou shalt not murder.

Neither shalt thou commit adultery.

Neither shalt thou steal.

Neither shalt thou bear false witness against thy neighbor.

Neither shalt thou covet thy neighbor's wife; neither shalt thou desire . . . any thing that is thy neighbor's.

These words the Lord spoke unto all your assembly in the mount out of the midst of the fire . . . with a great voice. . . . And He wrote them upon two tables of stone, and gave them unto me.

For questions on Echoes of the Past, see "Analyzing Primary Sources" on page 67.

The town of Beersheba arose around a natural spring along the caravan route between Egypt and Palestine. Abraham is said to have owned the rights to one of the town's wells.

brews. By about 800 B.C., however, many Hebrews had adopted religious practices of the peoples around them. Hebrew religious leaders were determined to rid Judaism of these adopted practices. These religious thinkers, such as Amos, Isaiah, and Deborah, were accepted as *prophets*, or persons who speak with divine guidance.

The prophets wrote that the Hebrew god, or Yahweh, was the lord and creator of the universe. There was no other. In contrast to the deities of other ancient civilizations who had human qualities, Yahweh was considered to be pure spirit, all-powerful, and everywhere at all times.

The Hebrews, trusting that Yahweh was a god of goodness and justice, also believed that the main concern of religion is *ethics*, or a code of right and wrong conduct. According to this belief, people should follow God's example, heeding an inner voice of conscience to do only what is right and just. A doctrine that associates an emphasis on ethical behavior with the belief in one god is called *ethical monotheism*.

LITERATURE AND LAW

The history and beliefs of the Hebrews through the time of Moses are described in the first five books of the Hebrew Bible. These five books, which contain the laws laid down by Moses, are called the Torah, which means "The Law." The teachings of the prophets are contained in the next eight books of the Hebrew Bible, known as The Prophets. The remaining books, The Writings, contain prayers, hymns, discussion, and history. The Hebrew Bible is also known as the Old Testament.

Hebrew law stressed ethical conduct and concern for others. Other civilizations had codes of law listing crimes and punishments. Hebrew law, however, was the first to make wrongdoing a matter of personal conscience. The law emphasized the ability of the individual to choose between right and wrong.

Hebrew codes of law encouraged a more democratic society than other codes of the Middle East. Jewish rulers were not allowed to accumulate great wealth or consider themselves above the law. Members of the community participated in making and carrying out laws.

The beliefs of the Hebrews had a powerful impact. Hebrew ideas of social justice, respect for the law, and the worth of the individual had a lasting influence. Many of the teachings of Judaism became incorporated into the teachings of later civilizations.

THE PERSIANS

About 900 B.C., two Indo-European groups, the Medes and the Persians, migrated from the region north of the Black Sea into what is now Iran. The Medes established a strong state, controlling the Persians and other neighboring tribes. In 612 B.C., the Persians helped the Medes defeat the Assyrian empire.

About 550 B.C., Cyrus (SĪ-rehs), who had unified the Persian tribes under his rule, overthrew the Medes and founded the Persian empire. In just 20 years he went on to conquer all of the Fertile Crescent and Asia Minor. His son added Egypt to the empire. The next king,

Darius I (duh-RĪ-uhs), who reigned from 521 B.C. to 486 B.C., extended the empire until it reached from the Mediterranean Sea to the Indus River in India.

Governing the empire. The Persians adopted and improved upon the Assyrian system of governing an empire. They divided the empire into provinces, called *satrapies* (SAY-truh-pees). Each satrapy was governed by an official called a *satrap*. However, the Persians also created royal inspectors, known as the "Eyes" or the "Ears" of the king. These inspectors made unexpected visits to the provinces to examine official records and hear complaints from the local people against the satraps.

Persian rulers allowed the conquered people throughout the empire to worship their own gods and keep their own customs. This tolerant policy won the Persian rulers the loyalty of their subjects and fostered the exchange of ideas and customs throughout the empire. With their efficient system of government and the loyalty of the conquered people, the Persians ruled an

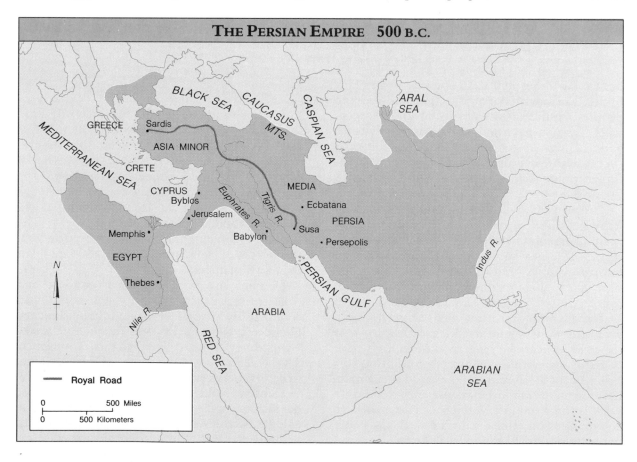

THE PERSIAN EMPIRE 500 B.C.

empire far more vast than any that had come before it.

The diffusion of ideas. Under Darius, the Persians improved and extended the system of roads built by the Assyrians. The main road was the Royal Road, extending more than 1,600 miles (2,500 kilometers), from the king's palace in Susa near the Persian Gulf to Sardis near the Mediterranean Sea in western Asia Minor.

Caravans carrying trade goods and ideas traveled the roadways. Ideas borrowed from Egypt, Greece, Asia Minor, Palestine, Phoenicia, and Mesopotamia made their way into Persian art and architecture. For example, the columns of Persian temples had palm tree designs at the base, as Egyptian temples did, and Greek designs at the top.

The Persians also borrowed an alphabet originally from Phoenicia, a solar calendar from Egypt, and a system of coins from the Lydians, who had ruled Asia Minor after the Hittites. Using coins, instead of barter, greatly simplified trading practices. With Persia's extensive trade, the new system spread quickly.

The Persians also spread a new religion called Zoroastrianism (ZŌ-rō-AS-tree-uhn-IHZ-uhm). The founder of this religion, Zoroaster (ZŌ-rō-AS-tur), lived in Persia about 600 B.C. Zoroaster, who preached a belief in one god, tried to eliminate his people's reliance on polytheism and magic.

Zoroaster was concerned with the universal struggle between good and evil. According to Zoroastrianism, human beings could choose by their conduct to follow either good or evil. The forces of good, however, would triumph in the end. Those who had chosen good would be rewarded in the afterlife with eternal paradise, while those who had chosen evil would be punished before they could enter paradise.

The decline of the empire. Darius's attempts to expand his empire brought him into conflict with the Greeks, a people who occupied a hilly peninsula west of Asia Minor. In 490 B.C., Persian armies led by Darius were defeated by the Greeks. Xerxes I (ZURK-seez), the son of Darius, also tried to conquer Greece, but he gave up after two crushing defeats.

When Xerxes died in 465 B.C., a series of weak rulers succeeded him. The ancient world's mightiest empire began a steady decline.

SECTION REVIEW

1. Define *tribe*, *covenant*, *prophets*, *ethics*, and *ethical monotheism*.

2. Explain the effect of Phoenicia's great seagoing power.

3. What religious beliefs were developed by the Hebrews?

Analysis. Explain why the Persians' policies toward conquered peoples would encourage the spread of ideas and customs.

Data Search. Refer to the appropriate chart on page 828 to identify which plants and animals were first domesticated in the Middle East.

HISTORY IN FOCUS

The two earliest civilizations—in Egypt and in the Fertile Crescent—were similar in many ways. The people of both regions developed agriculture on a large scale, large cities, monumental architecture, highly organized governments, and complex religions. In both regions, people made discoveries and produced inventions that are still in use today, including the 12-month calendar, the wheel, the alphabet, and a code of law.

However, in some ways Egypt differed from the Fertile Crescent. Because of the difficulty of crossing the harsh terrain that surrounds Egypt, few outsiders came into the Nile Valley. Those few who did trickle in adopted Egyptian ways. Left in peace, Egypt was united under the world's first strong central government. Despite short periods of unrest, the people of Egypt remained united for thousands of years, even under foreign rule.

In contrast to Egypt, the history of the Fertile Crescent was quite turbulent. Bounded by arid wastelands and rugged mountains, the Fertile Crescent formed a natural corridor from the Persian Gulf to the Mediterranean Sea. Many diverse peoples from surrounding areas entered the Fertile Crescent. While some groups blended with the people who came before them, others fought for their own places on these fruitful lands. Bloody warfare was often the result as one group after another came to power. In this turmoil, the ideas of the Sumerians and many other peoples were intermixed and eventually carried to many parts of the world.

SUMMARY

- The earliest civilizations arose more than 5000 years ago in the Middle East, along the Nile and the Tigris-Euphrates rivers.

- Around 4000 B.C., the Sumerians began to build a civilization in Mesopotamia. Sumerians developed writing, irrigation, astronomy, and mathematics.

- Babylonia succeeded Sumer in Mesopotamia. The Babylonians followed a code of law that emphasized justice and regulated daily life.

- Babylonia fell to the Assyrians, whose empire eventually stretched from the Nile to Anatolia and Iran. The Assyrians spread Sumerian and Babylonian culture.

- In Egypt, a civilization arose along the banks of the Nile River. The Egyptians established strong governments, constructed monuments, expanded trade, and made great advances in writing, engineering, astronomy, and medicine.

- Two important civilizations developed on the eastern shores of the Mediterranean. The Phoenicians created a trading and seafaring empire. The Hebrews developed ideas on ethics, social justice, and government that influenced later civilizations.

- In the 500s B.C., the Persians gained control of much of the Middle East, creating an empire that extended from Egypt to India.

VOCABULARY REVIEW

Think about the meaning of each vocabulary term below. Then group the terms with related meanings into categories and give each category a name.

Example: *Ziggurat* and *pyramid*, which are both structures, would fit into the category "ancient constructions."

hieroglyphics	city-states
cataracts	ethics
monotheism	delta
dynasty	cuneiform
papyrus	pharaoh

CHAPTER REVIEW

1. (a) Why was flooding of the Tigris-Euphrates important? **(b)** How did the flooding of this river differ from that of the Nile? **(c)** Explain how the Tigris-Euphrates and the Nile rivers affected the economies of civilizations in the Fertile Crescent and in Egypt.

2. (a) Describe the Sumerian city-states about 3000 B.C. **(b)** What was one major difference in the structure of the laws that governed Sumerians and Babylonians? **(c)** How did the Assyrians govern their empire? **(d)** In about 2500 B.C. how did Egypt's government differ from that of civilizations in the Fertile Crescent?

3. Sometimes one culture conquered another because of superior weapons. Compare the military advantages of the Amorites, Hittites, and Assyrians.

4. (a) Who was the most important Chaldean ruler? What was his main accomplishment? **(b)** In what ways were the Chaldeans similar to the Sumerians and Babylonians?

5. (a) Describe the position of women in Babylonia. In Egypt. **(b)** Explain whether Hatshepsut's position typified that of women in Egypt.

6. (a) What two geographic factors aided the development of Egyptian civilization? **(b)** Explain why Egypt was called "the Kingdom of the Two Crowns." **(c)** Describe how the role of the pharaoh changed from the Old Kingdom to the Middle Kingdom to the New Kingdom.

7. (a) Describe the four social classes in Egypt. **(b)** How were Egypt's social classes different from those of Sumer?

8. (a) Were each of the following peoples polytheistic or monotheistic: Sumerians, Egyptians, Hebrews, Persians? **(b)** What did Amenhotep and Zoroaster have in common? **(c)** How did Hebrew law differ from that of Mesopotamia? How was Hebrew law democratic?

9. (a) For what were the Phoenicians best known? **(b)** How did they aid cultural diffusion? **(c)** What was important about their writing?

10. (a) How did the Persians ensure the loyalty of their subjects? **(b)** Give two examples of cultural diffusion in Persia.

THINKING CRITICALLY: ACTIVITIES

1. Select a partner for a debate on the following statement: The rise and fall of empires is a consistent pattern in the ancient Middle East. Was this instability inevitable? Prepare an argument for one side of the debate. Have your partner prepare to argue the other side. Present your debate to the class.

2. Construct a chart that shows the technical and scientific achievements of the Sumerians, Chaldeans, and Egyptians. Compare your chart with that of another member of the class. Add to your list any achievements you may have omitted. Then make a generalization about the achievements of these civilizations.

APPLYING SOCIAL STUDIES SKILLS

Using tools of time and place. History makes more sense if you understand how geography influences human activities. Therefore, each chapter that introduces a particular region includes a map showing the region's geography. When you study the particular region again in a later chapter, you may want to refer to the appropriate map of physical features.

Now use the map on page 20 to answer the following questions. You may also need to look in the Atlas beginning on page 820 for a present-day map of the region.

1. What part of the world is shown on this map?

2. What two continents does this region span?

3. What seas border the Arabian Peninsula?

4. What land and sea routes would you expect traders to use when sending goods from the Arabian Sea to the Mediterranean?

5. Look at the smaller map titled "Natural Regions." What type of natural region is most common in this part of the world?

6. In which natural region would you expect people to settle and build cities? Why?

7. What present-day country contains most of the Tigris and Euphrates river valleys? The Arabian Peninsula? The Plateau of Anatolia? The Plateau of Iran?

APPLYING THINKING SKILLS

Thinking about history. Skillful thinking does not always happen automatically. Often you have to work carefully at it. This means thinking about how you think before, during, and after you have completed a complicated thinking task. But the effort is worth it. Skillful thinking pays off in helping you to learn history and other subjects. It also helps you in out-of-school activities, including any job you may have. The careful attention in this book to important thinking skills and to guided practice in applying these skills can help you improve your thinking.

To give you another opportunity to think about your thinking, here are four additional thinking problems. For each one, do the following:

(a) Write down what you think is the answer.

(b) Write notes listing the steps you went through to arrive at your answer. Be prepared to explain these steps to another person.

1. Luis's birthday is January 8, and he is just four days older than Melanie. This year New Year's Day is on a Tuesday. On what day of the week is Melanie's birthday?

2. Coded Message: dpnf up Mpoepo bu podf. Translated Message: Come to London at once. In this code, what would be the letter for *x*?

3. When you enter the house, you will find a window on the right-hand wall. When the sun sets, it shines straight through this window onto the opposite wall.

What direction are you facing when you stand in the doorway and look across the street?

4. Two kinds of people lived in the town of Nowhere: the Saffi and the Revels. The Saffi always lied. The Revels always told the truth. One day a visitor met three townspeople. The visitor asked the first one if he were a Saffi. The first townsperson answered the question. The second townsperson then reported that the first one had denied being a Saffi. The third townsperson then said that the first one really was a Saffi.

How many of these three townspeople were Saffi?

CHAPTER THREE

ANCIENT INDIA AND CHINA

3000–250 B.C.

The qilin, a legendary creature of good omen. Chinese silk.

Two of the earliest civilizations arose in Asia. As in the Middle East, these civilizations began in river valleys—the Indus River valley of India and the Hwang Ho valley in China.

In India, a complex civilization flourished by 2500 B.C. This civilization vanished at about the time that a new group entered India, about 1500 B.C. Over time, this new group also developed a civilization. Its language, government, social class system, and religion formed a basis for future Indian society.

In China, too, early civilizations established social and religious traditions. About 1500 B.C., a large area of China was brought under one rule for the first time. These early Chinese built cities, made technological advances, and developed the form of writing and cultural patterns found in China today.

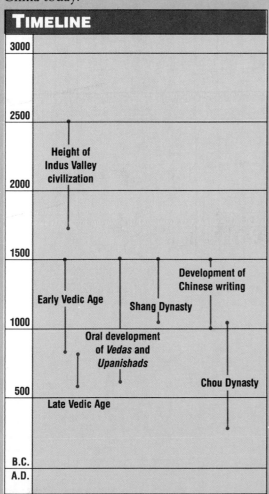

TIMELINE

3000	
2500	
2000	Height of Indus Valley civilization
1500	
1000	Development of Chinese writing / Early Vedic Age / Shang Dynasty
500	Oral development of *Vedas* and *Upanishads* / Chou Dynasty / Late Vedic Age
B.C.	
A.D.	

3–1
RISE OF CIVILIZATION IN INDIA

READ TO FIND OUT

—what the terms **subcontinent** and **monsoon** mean.
—what evidence indicates a strong central government in early India.
—what the Indus Valley people achieved.
—how the Indus Valley civilization came to an end.

In prehistoric times, early agricultural settlements were scattered throughout India. About 3000 B.C., the first Indian civilization arose in the Indus River valley in northwestern India. Over the next 500 years, many towns and cities sprang up in the valley, and trade among them flourished.

INDIA: THE NATURAL SETTING

India, located in southern Asia, is separated from the rest of the continent by mighty mountain ranges that include the world's loftiest peaks. The Himalaya mountain system lies to the northeast while the Hindu Kush and lower ranges lie to the northwest. Narrow passes such as the Khyber Pass provide age-old routes through these mountains. Being set off from the rest of the Asian continent by mountains, the large land mass of India is often referred to as a **subcontinent.**

Stretching across northern India is a vast fertile plain drained by two great river systems—the Ganges in the northeast and the Indus River in the northwest. A triangular plateau juts southward about 1,000 miles (1,600 kilometers) from the Indus-Ganges Plain. This hilly plateau is called the Deccan. A low mountain range, the Vindhya (VIND-yah), separates the Deccan from the northern plain. The Deccan is rimmed by mountains, the Western and Eastern Ghats, and narrow coastal plains.

India is a land of tropical climates. Most of India experiences three seasons—the cool, the hot, and the rainy season. Although it snows in the northern mountains, mild temperatures prevail throughout the rest of India during the cool season, October through February. During the hot season, March through June, temperatures may reach 120°F (49°C).

From June through September, the **monsoon**, or seasonal wind, blows from the southeast and the southwest. The monsoon picks up moisture from the ocean and brings almost all the rain that falls on India during the year. Throughout the other two seasons, dry monsoon winds blow from the north and northeast.

Over the centuries, Indian farmers have counted on the southern monsoons to irrigate their crops. If the rains arrive too late, crops may wither. However, if the monsoons bring too much rain, crops may wash away. Still, each year the southern monsoon is awaited as a relief from the long dry seasons.

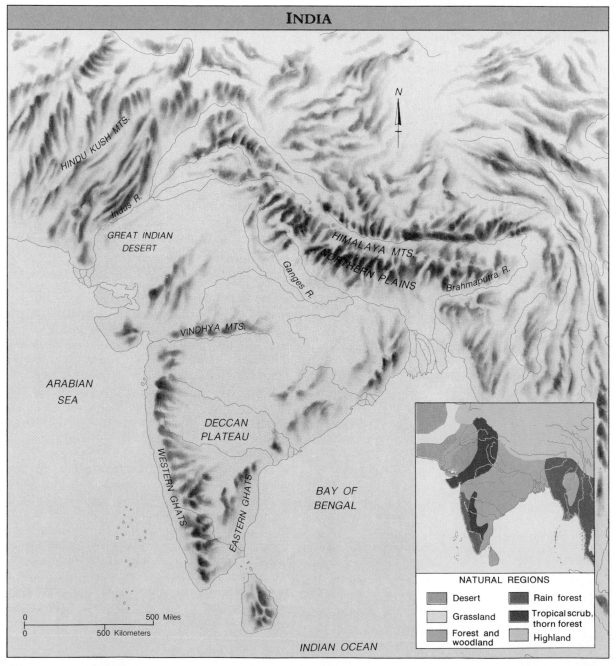

INDIA

HINDU KUSH MTS.

Indus R.

GREAT INDIAN DESERT

HIMALAYA MTS.

NORTHERN PLAINS

Ganges R.

Brahmaputra R.

VINDHYA MTS.

ARABIAN SEA

DECCAN PLATEAU

WESTERN GHATS

EASTERN GHATS

BAY OF BENGAL

0   500 Miles
0   500 Kilometers

INDIAN OCEAN

NATURAL REGIONS

- Desert
- Grassland
- Forest and woodland
- Rain forest
- Tropical scrub, thorn forest
- Highland

INDUS VALLEY CIVILIZATION

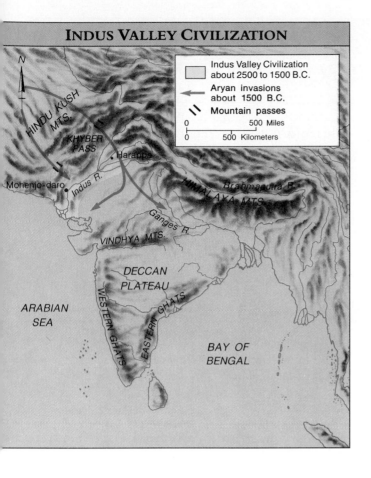

but also barley, rice, dates, and peas. These people may have been the first to cultivate cotton. They also domesticated animals, including cattle, water buffalo, and chickens.

HARAPPA AND MOHENJO-DARO

The two centers of the Indus Valley civilization were Harappa (huh-RAP-uh) and Mohenjo-daro (mō-HEN-jō-DAIR-ō). These two well-planned cities were laid out in orderly, rectangular city blocks. At Mohenjo-daro a broad avenue, 30 feet (9.1 meters) wide, ran through the city. Narrower streets crossed the main avenue at regular intervals. The houses and shops that lined the streets were built of mudbricks. These were strengthened to survive monsoon downpours by being baked in ovens rather than in the sun.

Throughout the city was a complex water system complete with drains and sewers. The system served individual homes, which had bathrooms of waterproof brick. The water system also served the Great Bath, a two-story structure that housed a large asphalt-lined bathing pool.

The Great Bath was on a large earthen platform 40 or more feet (12 meters) high. Surrounded by walls and towers, this platform was a fortress. On it stood other public buildings, including a ceremonial hall and a huge grain storehouse.

Life in Harappa and Mohenjo-daro centered on trade. Artisans crafted jewelry and other objects from gold, silver, ivory, copper, bronze, and a kind of reddish clay called terra cotta. Traders sailed the Indus River to trade such objects, as well as timber and ivory.

Traders also sailed along the coasts of the Arabian Sea to the Persian Gulf to trade with faraway cities in Sumer. Soapstone seals from the Indus Valley have been found in the ruins of these Mesopotamian cities. Like their counterparts in Sumer, Harappan merchants rolled carved soapstone seals across soft clay to identify property or sign contracts.

These seals provide evidence that the Indus Valley people had developed a form of pictographic writing. This writing has been found on other seals, which may have been used for religious purposes, and on other artifacts. However, overall, little writing has been found, and it has yet to be deciphered.

INDUS VALLEY CIVILIZATION

As early as 4000 B.C., agricultural settlements existed in the Indus River valley. Some time before 2500 B.C., a group of people came into the valley from the Iranian plateau. They brought with them bronze weapons and the idea of city life—developments they may have borrowed from Middle Eastern peoples. The invaders intermarried with the original inhabitants of the Indus Valley and adopted their language. Over time a new civilization emerged.

By 2500 B.C., about the time the Akkadians began to move into Sumer and the Egyptians were developing papyrus, this civilization was flourishing. Seventy or more settlements were sprinkled along the Indus River system in a 1,000-mile (1,600-kilometer) path from the foot of the Himalayas to the Arabian Sea. Some settlements were seaports or trading posts but most were agricultural villages.

The Indus Valley civilization was based on agriculture. The people mainly raised wheat,

CLASSIFYING

Classifying is sorting or categorizing. It consists of grouping similar objects or kinds of information together. Grocery stores and supermarkets, for example, classify the items they sell. As a result, the fresh meats are kept in one place, the fresh vegetables in another, and so on. Grouping these items together makes shopping easier.

People classify information so that they can understand it more easily. Classifying is especially useful when trying to make sense out of information that seems disorganized. This skill is also helpful in trying to handle what seems to be an overwhelming amount of information. By grouping together similar information, you can better determine what it means. Once you have classified information, you can work with the group labels rather than with all the individual items in each group.

EXPLAINING THE SKILL

Creating your own categories or groups can sometimes be difficult. The following steps show one way to invent your own groupings.

1. *State your purpose for classifying.* What are you trying to find out?

2. *Skim the information to get ideas about possible categories or groups.*

3. *Pick a piece of information and find another one that seems similar.* Put them together.

4. *Write a label for the group.* This label should identify the characteristic shared by these two pieces. For example, if a hammer and a saw were included in a list of objects, they could be placed in a group labeled *Tools*.

5. *Find all other pieces of information that fit this label and add them to the group.*

6. *Repeat steps 3 through 5 until all the pieces of information are in groups.*

7. *Combine or subdivide your groups as necessary to achieve your purpose.*

If at first you have difficulty classifying the information, you can put some items into a "don't know" category. Then classify these items after you have grouped the more familiar information.

APPLYING THE SKILL

Use the skill of classifying to make sense out of the following list of objects uncovered at the site of Mohenjo-daro. Your purpose in classifying them is to answer this question: What was life probably like in Mohenjo-daro 3,500 years ago? Follow the steps just described.

stone weights of various sizes
gold anklets
copper kettles
small clay containers
copper finger rings
gold necklaces
statue of a male wearing clothing similar to that of Ur around 2200 B.C.
soapstone figurines of bulls

bronze figurines
brick drain pipes
terracotta female figurines decorated with jewels
soapstone seals for stamping, decorated with carved rhinoceros, bulls, elephants
beads made in Mesopotamia
shell finger rings
ivory necklaces
clay drinking cups

MAKING MEANING

Classifying the ancient objects helps you to make the information meaningful. Use what you have learned to answer the questions that follow.

1. Which item does not match the other two? **(a)** copper finger rings **(b)** soapstone figurines of bulls **(c)** gold necklaces

2. In Mohenjo-daro around 3,500 years ago, people lived **(a)** a nomadic life, **(b)** a life on the sea, **(c)** in permanent settlements.

3. People in Mohenjo-daro **(a)** produced all they needed, **(b)** traded with other regions, **(c)** were mostly concerned about survival.

REVIEWING THE SKILL

4. Define the term *classify*.

5. When is it useful to classify?

6. What procedure can you follow to classify information efficiently?

Chess, a game for two players, originated in the Indus Valley. Its aim is to capture an enemy king by eliminating the king's forces. This crude stone board is from Harappa.

Although extensive written records of the Indus Valley people have never been found, the silent ruins show that these people had a highly organized civilization. To build the large cities, to unite the settlements scattered across the plain, and to carry out extensive trade, all required planning, cooperation, and peace. Thus, historians believe that the Indus Valley civilization must have had a strong, well-organized central government.

OTHER INDUS VALLEY ACHIEVEMENTS

The people of the Indus Valley developed many techniques similar to those developed by the peoples of the Middle East. They shaped items such as cups on potter's wheels and then decorated, glazed, and baked the pottery. Indus Valley smiths worked copper and bronze to make ornaments, fishhooks, and spears. Merchants and farmers transported goods in wheeled carts drawn by bullocks. In addition, Indus Valley artisans were known as far away as Sumer for their wooden furniture, often decorated with inlays of bone, shell, and ivory.

To ensure fair trade practices, Harappan artisans and merchants used a uniform system of weights and measures. The Harappans determined the weight of goods by using balance scales with weights of varying sizes. They measured with a ruler marked precisely each .264 inches (.66 centimeters).

THE END OF INDUS VALLEY CIVILIZATION

The Indus Valley civilization flourished for nearly a thousand years. Then, after about 1700 B.C., it died out. Although no one is certain what happened to the Indus Valley people, scientists believe a series of catastrophes struck their civilization.

According to this theory, a number of natural disasters occurred. Some time before 1700 B.C. movements of the earth's crust near the Arabian Sea forced a large section of coastline and sea floor upward. This change took place over many years. Cities that had once been on the coast were then miles inland.

Next, volcanoes may have erupted, spewing forth mud which blocked the flow of the Indus River. Over the years, water backed up in the valley, destroying some settlements and creating a marshy lake around Mohenjo-daro.

The residents of Mohenjo-daro struggled against the threatening waters. Although the people tried to rebuild the structures destroyed by flooding, the quality of the construction gradually declined with sun-dried brick being substituted for the sturdier oven-fired brick of earlier days. Eventually the city was abandoned.

In contrast to Mohenjo-daro, Harappa did not suffer flooding. However, the entire Indus Valley civilization was disrupted by the disasters. Then, around 1500 B.C., another catastrophe befell the Indus Valley people when a new group of people from the northwest began to move in and take over their valley. This event may have dealt the Indus Valley people a final blow.

SECTION REVIEW

1. Define **subcontinent** and **monsoon**.

2. Briefly describe Mohenjo-daro.

3. What evidence has been found that the Indus Valley people had developed writing?

4. What natural disasters weakened the Indus Valley civilization? What dealt this civilization a final blow?

Analysis. Give two statements of fact as evidence to support the following statement: The Indus Valley civilization must have had a strong central government.

3-2
THE VEDIC AGE

READ TO FIND OUT

—what the terms *patriarchal*, *extended family*, and *karma* mean.

—how the Aryans established an agricultural society during the Early Vedic Age.

—what changes took place in Aryan life during the Late Vedic Age.

—what social classes divided Aryan society.

—what religious beliefs the Aryans developed.

Some time around 1500 B.C. the Aryans, an Indo-European group living north of the Black and Caspian seas, began to migrate into India. Wave after wave of Aryan tribes pushed through the passes of the Hindu Kush and into the Indus Valley.

The history of these people for the next thousand years is called the Vedic Age, after their religious works, the *Vedas*. The period from 1500 B.C. to 800 B.C., when the Aryans established their culture in northwestern India, is called the Early Vedic Age. From 800 B.C. to 550 B.C., the Aryan people spread toward the south and east. This period is referred to as the Late Vedic Age. During the Vedic Age the Aryans built the foundation of some of India's most lasting traditions—strong family ties, village government, a firm social system, and some of the world's oldest religions.

THE EARLY VEDIC AGE

Nomadic herders, the Aryans wandered in tribes searching for fresh pastures for their cattle. These tribes were *patriarchal*, with the father or oldest male as the head of the family and male family elders at the head of the tribe.

The Ayrans developed excellent military skills. Their swift, horse-drawn chariots and heavy bronze battle-axes gave them an advantage over other peoples. As the Aryans moved south along the Indus River, they either conquered the people they met or drove them further south. These people, known as the Dravidians, were primarily traders. Possibly survivors of the Indus Valley civilization, they carried their traditions and language into the Deccan and the southern tip of India.

In time, the Aryans settled down to raise their cattle. The animals were prized as a sign of wealth. They were also used as the medium of exchange, or the measure of value in trading goods and services.

Gradually, the Aryans learned to farm, growing mainly barley and rice. Aryan farmers irrigated and fertilized their crops. They also plowed their fields with wooden plows and harvested the grains with metal sickles.

The Aryans settled in villages with houses of wood and bamboo. Some villages were laid out as a rectangle, with two roads crossing at the center. Many of these villages were surrounded, not by walls, but by hedges of thorns. Gates in the hedges allowed people in and out.

A system of local government gradually developed. In some villages the leaders, called headmen, inherited the position, while in others, they were elected. The headmen settled local issues, such as land disputes, and managed the irrigation systems. The strength and stability of village government made up for lack of a strong central government.

THE LATE VEDIC AGE

Some time between 1000 B.C. and 800 B.C., changes began to take place in Aryan India. From their foothold in the Indus River valley, the Aryan tribes steadily spread eastward into the Ganges River valley and south as far as the Vindhya Mountains.

Many Aryan tribes resettled in the east and formed several small states. Some states were led by a council of warrior nobles. Others were ruled by a *rajah*, or prince, who was advised by a council of nobles and elder relatives. Because the states were often at war with each other, the warrior chiefs began to maintain permanent armies. By 550 B.C., the kingdoms of Kosala (KŌ-suh-luh) and Magadha (MUG-ud-uh) in the eastern Ganges Valley emerged as the strongest of the warring Aryan states.

While the Aryan kingdoms in the northeast gained strength, Aryan power declined in the Indus Valley to the west. In 531 B.C., a Persian army crossed the Hindu Kush and invaded India. Darius of Persia soon conquered the Indus River valley, making it a province of Persia.

ARYAN SOCIETY

When the Aryans first came into India in about 1500 B.C., they were loosely divided into three social classes: nobles, including the tribal chiefs; priests; and commoners, who were the herders of cattle. Later, the people conquered by the Aryans became the fourth class. The Aryans considered these prisoners of war beneath them and forced them to live outside the villages, away from the Aryan people.

Over a thousand years, this separation of society into classes changed and became more complex. Rules and traditions governed class behavior, and each class had its own rights and duties.

The first distinct class was the Brahmans (BRAH-muhnz), the intellectual class of judges, teachers, and especially priests. The importance of religious ceremonies in Aryan society had helped to raise this priestly class above the others. "When a Brahman springs to light, he is born above the world, the chief of all creatures," says one ancient text.

Next were the Kshatriyas (KSHAT-ree-uhz), the warriors, nobles, and kings. The Vaisyas (VIS-yuhs), or the common people, comprised the third class, which included merchants, artisans, and landholding farmers. The fourth class was the Sudras (SOO-druhz), the descendants of the conquered peoples, who were slaves, servants, tenant farmers, and unskilled workers.

Aryan society remained patriarchal. The oldest married male headed the *extended family*, which played an important role in Aryan culture. An extended family consists of several generations of family members living in the same household, with other family members living nearby. Wives joined the families of their husbands.

Land was the property of the extended family rather than of individuals. However, the legal owner of the property was the man who was the head of the family. Women could not inherit or own land. Although women were treated with respect, they were expected to be obedient to their fathers and husbands.

THE RELIGION OF THE ARYANS

The early Aryans brought a polytheistic religion into India. Aryan deities represented such natural forces as the air, wind, and fire. The

The clay figures are copies of two found at an Indus Valley site. Indus Valley people domesticated many animals, but not the horse, which was probably introduced by foreign traders.

strongest god, Indra (IN-druh), for example, was the giver of rain. He was also a warrior god who brought victory in battle.

The Aryans believed in life after death. At death, the soul was supposed to enter either a dark pit of everlasting punishment or an endlessly joyful heaven, depending on whether or not a person had correctly practiced religious rituals.

The priests, or Brahmans, passed on their sacred knowledge from generation to generation by word of mouth. Only certain persons were allowed to learn this sacred knowledge. According to an observer, these students sat at the foot of a teacher, reciting the words "like the croaking of frogs." Not until much later was this knowledge written down in the four books known as the *Vedas*, which means "knowledge." The *Vedas* are still sacred to millions of people today, especially in India.

The oldest of the *Vedas*, the *Rig Veda*, contains hymns about the beginnings of the world and more than a thousand songs of praise to the gods. The other three *Vedas* contain magical formulas, rules for making sacrifices to please the deities, and rituals.

The Aryans believed that rituals were necessary to keep the world in order. By performing religious ceremonies, the Aryans hoped to ensure a plentiful harvest, peace at home, and victory over the enemy. At first, religious rituals were simple. Over time, however, the priests developed complex ceremonies. Sometimes many priests were required to conduct a single ceremony. In this way, the priests gained great position and power for themselves within the Aryan states.

Some religious thinkers of the time believed that the priests placed too great an emphasis on ritual. From about 800 B.C., the ideas of these thinkers were added to the *Vedas*. These additions were called the *Upanishads*.

The authors of the *Upanishads* praised the ancient deities of the *Rig Veda*. However, they also introduced new ideas. "Whence [from where] are we born, where do we live, and whither [where] do we go?" the writers of the *Upanishads* asked. In answering these questions, they taught that each person has an individual soul, but that all people, all deities, and all things are also part of a great universal spirit.

According to the teachings of the *Upanishads*, the individual soul is reborn when the body dies. *Karma*, which is the combined actions of a person in one life, determines how the soul will be born in the next life. According to this belief, the cycle of birth and death continues until the soul reaches perfection.

THE ARYAN HERITAGE

By the end of the Late Vedic Age, the Aryans had spread from the Indus Valley eastward to the shores of the Bay of Bengal, making northern India their home. In addition, Aryan culture gradually extended into the Deccan Plateau.

Wherever the Aryans settled, they established their customs and their language. They spoke Sanskrit, an Indo-European language related to the forerunners of modern Iranian and most modern European languages. Because by 600 B.C. the Aryans had not yet developed a written language, the Vedas were passed down orally from Brahman to Brahman in Sanskrit.

The Aryans had forced the Dravidians into the Deccan and the southern tip of India, where their languages, customs, and traditions took hold. Living apart from the Aryans, the Dravidians developed their own way of life. Differences between the Aryan north and the Dravidian south would remain for centuries.

Aryan language and literature, ideas about government and law, social classes, and especially religious traditions, became strong influences in Indian life. Aryan heritage would have far-reaching effects on India's future.

3-3
RISE OF CIVILIZATION IN CHINA

The fourth of the early civilizations arose in the hills and river valleys of north China, about one thousand years after civilization developed in the Indus Valley. Exactly how Chinese civilization came about is unknown. Archaeologists have found evidence that paleolithic people populated north China before 10,000 B.C. Over time, these people domesticated animals and learned to farm, planting millet crops in the soft, fertile soils. Gradually, small settlements grew into villages and towns protected by packed earthen walls.

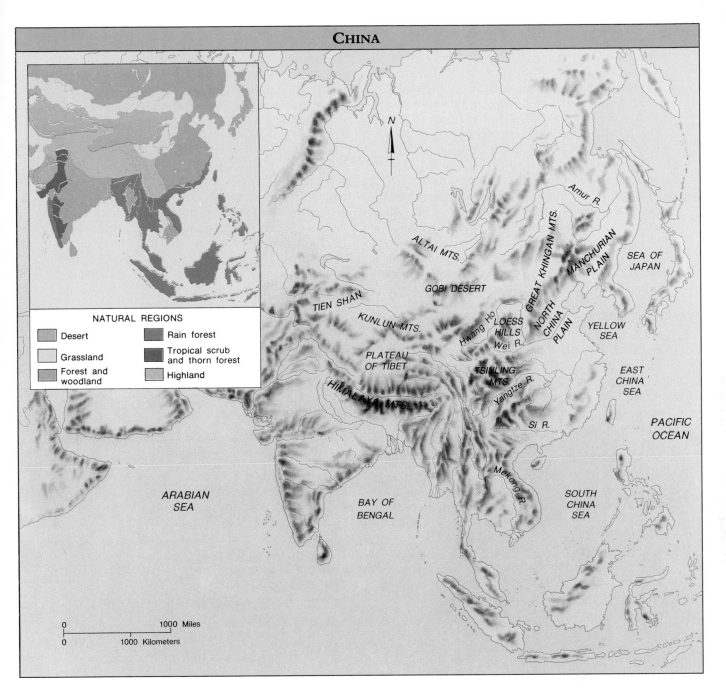

NATURAL REGIONS

- Desert
- Grassland
- Forest and woodland
- Rain forest
- Tropical scrub and thorn forest
- Highland

The Chinese have ancient legends about the Hsia (shee-YAH) people, who may have been the first to unite many of the farming settlements under one rule. According to these legends, Hsia kings gave many gifts to their people, including knowledge of fire, farming, the building of houses, medicine, the calendar, and writing. A Hsia dynasty may have existed, but no evidence of it has yet been discovered.

Chinese historians traditionally divide the history of their people according to ruling dynasties. The earliest known Chinese rulers were the Shang. Like the Hsia, the Shang were thought to be legendary until archaeologists found buried ruins of Shang cities. Therefore, Chinese history begins about 1500 B.C., when the Shang kings established rule in the valley of the Hwang Ho in north China.

CHINA: THE NATURAL SETTING

With 3.7 million square miles (9.6 million square kilometers), China is about the same size as the United States. China extends 2,500 miles (4,000 kilometers) from north to south and 3,000 miles (4,800 kilometers) from east to west. It encompasses a variety of climates from frigid to tropical, and contrasting landscapes from jagged mountains to rocky deserts. Only about 11 percent of the land can be farmed.

The country is separated from other Asian lands by forbidding landforms and harsh climates. For much of its history, China has been relatively isolated from the rest of the world. The heartland of China lies in the northeast, from the Loess Hills to the level North China Plain. The soils of the region are powdery, yellow loess, which provide rich farm land.

The fruitful North China Plain is irrigated by the waters of the Hwang Ho. Originating in the Plateau of Tibet, the Hwang Ho wanders a meandering course, cutting deep cliffs in the soft soil of the Loess Hills before it turns eastward and flows gently onto the North China Plain. Quantities of the fine yellow loess that are carried downstream give the river its name, *Hwang Ho*, which means "Yellow River."

Over the centuries great amounts of this fine silt have been deposited at the bottom of the river, building up the river's bed, as well as its banks. Because of its shallow bottom, most boats cannot navigate the river. In some places, however, the river and its banks are higher than the surrounding lands. As a result, if the banks give way or the volume of water in the river increases by only a small amount, flood waters spread over the land. Throughout the centuries, many floods have destroyed both life and property, giving the Hwang Ho yet another name—China's Sorrow.

South of the North China Plain, the steep slopes of the Tsinling (CHIN-LING) Mountains separate southeastern China from the northeast. South of the Tsinling Mountains lies the valley of the great Yangtze (YANG-see) River, over 3,000 miles (4,800 kilometers) long. The third longest river in the world, the Yangtze rises in the mountains of Tibet and eventually flows into the Yellow Sea. Broad and deep, the Yangtze is navigable for hundreds of miles.

The rest of southeastern China is made up of high hills, soaring peaks, deep gorges, and narrow mountain valleys. In early times a Chinese poet described the land:

> In winding valleys too tortuous to trace,
> On crags piled who knows how high,
> A thousand different grasses weep with dew
> And pines hum together in the wind.

China's climate is as varied as the landscape. In winter, monsoon winds carry dry air from the center of Asia toward the sea. In summer,

In China's southern regions limestone hills and pinnacles rise sharply from the plateau. For centuries this striking landscape has inspired a kind of Chinese painting called *shan shui*, meaning "mountain and water." These paintings usually feature steep-sided hills rising above a mist-cloaked plain.

THE SECRET OF SILK MAKING

The silkworm, really a caterpillar, is a finicky little creature. To thrive, it demands the kind of loving attention given an infant. It also requires a special diet—mulberry leaves. Such behavior is willingly tolerated because silkworms have been producing silk, considered the "queen of textiles," for more than 4,000 years.

No one knows who really first learned the silkworm's wonderful secret, but Chinese legend says it was the Empress Si-Ling-Chi, wife of a legendary Hsia king. While walking in her garden, she noticed strange cocoons in the twigs of the mulberry tree. Plucking one, she found she could unravel it into a long threadlike fiber. After gathering these fibers, the empress spun them into a radiant piece of cloth.

For ancient China, silk quickly became a prized item of trade. The strong, precious cloth was also used as ceremonial gifts to reward foreign neighbors. To keep up with the demand for the cloth, emperors set up silk factories, where work was done painstakingly by hand. Determined to keep other civilizations from discovering how to make silk, China's rulers threatened death to anyone who revealed how it was obtained. Thus, the Chinese held on to this secret for hundreds of years.

The secret of silk making begins when a female moth lays an egg. About 40 days after hatching, the silkworm begins to spin its cocoon, ejecting from its body a silken strand. Usually strands from five to eight cocoons are wound together to form a long thread of raw silk.

In the earliest days of raising silkworms, growers were warned that the delicate insect might be disturbed by the barking of a dog. Such concern continues. In China today people who work with the silkworms are not allowed to smoke or to wear makeup while in the presence of the insects.

Much of the work of silk making has always been done by hand in China, one reason the cloth is so expensive. It is estimated that to make one silk blouse, workers must gather the thread from 630 cocoons. Today, however, factory workers use machines to wind strands to the proper thicknesses. The silk factories of present-day China produce more than half of the world's fine silk.

---

the monsoon blows from the southeast, picking up moisture from the sea. As a result, southeastern China is tropical, moist and warm year round. In contrast, drier air and changing temperatures are characteristic of lands north of the Tsinling Mountains.

THE SHANG DYNASTY

By 1500 B.C., many villages and small towns in the valley of the Hwang Ho had been brought under the rule of one tribe—the Shang—by the legendary King T'ang. Exactly how the Shang came to power is unknown. However, they expanded their territory until it included most of the river valley. After learning to use the horse-drawn war chariot, possibly from nomads of the Asian steppes, the Shang extended their influence even farther.

The Shang built their first walled capital city amid the rich agricultural lands of the North China Plain and from there ruled the surrounding towns and farming villages. Assisted by priests and priestesses, advisors, and other officials, Shang kings provided the city-state with a strong government.

In 1300 B.C., the Shang Dynasty moved the capital to Anyang (AHN-YAHNG), on the North China Plain north of the Hwang Ho. Shang kings ruled there until about 1027 B.C., when this capital city was taken by the conquering armies of a neighboring tribe.

SHANG SOCIETY

At first, Shang society was divided into two classes—the nobles and the common people. Most of the common people were farmers, but a few were artisans, such as metalsmiths. After the Shang began to use the chariot, a warrior class developed, ranking just below the nobles.

Most of the population lived in small country villages. Many country people lived in pit houses, rooms dug into the earth protected by thatched roofs supported by wooden or bamboo poles. These farmers grew millet, wheat, and barley. They also raised sheep, goats, pigs, oxen, and chickens. To add to their food supply, they fished and hunted.

The products of the countryside also fed the city people, including the rulers. In addition, the farmers provided labor and military service for the rulers. In exchange, the rulers provided leadership, organization, and protection from wandering nomads.

In the kingdom's capital city stood the homes and temples of the ruling family, chief priests, nobles, and court advisors. These city dwellers lived in houses built above ground. The houses were constructed of packed earthern walls with thatched roofs.

Shang artisans also lived in the city or in the larger towns because most of the work they did was for the nobles. Some artisans made pottery with a fine white clay called kaolin. From threads spun by the silkworm, weavers made lustrous silk cloth for the nobles to wear.

In both the villages and the cities, the family was vitally important, especially the extended family. The Shang stressed the duties of children and treated the elderly with reverence.

SHANG RELIGION

Like many other agricultural peoples, the Shang worshipped spirits of nature, especially the spirits of earth and sky that could affect their crops. It was the chief duty of the king to communicate with these spirits. In the spring, the Shang held huge religious festivals to ask the spirits of nature to look with favor on the planting season. In autumn, the Shang held festivals of thanksgiving for the harvest.

Shang people also practiced *ancestor worship*, honoring the wisdom and guidance of their ancestors. For the Shang, the family was a union of both the living and the dead, one unbroken family circle. People made regular offerings of food and drink to their ancestors to ensure that the ancestors would be able to obtain the good will of the gods.

More than 100,000 Shang oracle bones and tortoise shells like the one shown above have been discovered. A few have not only the questions inscribed on them, but also the answers.

People of Shang China consulted their ancestors before making important decisions. A priest would scratch a question on the shoulder bone of an ox or deer, or on tortoise shell. The priest would then heat the bone or shell, causing it to crack, and would interpret the cracks as answers from dead ancestors. Such bones were known as oracle bones because they were meant to foretell the future.

SHANG ACHIEVEMENTS

Shang artisans laid the foundations for future Chinese arts and crafts. They made fine pottery and inlaid ivory carvings with turquoise, but they were especially skillful in the techniques of casting molten bronze. Shang metalsmiths created large, intricately designed objects. Many were magnificent vessels to be used in religious ceremonies. Such objects were highly decorated with dragons, animals, or geometric designs. The techniques of the Shang metalworkers were not surpassed for centuries anywhere in the world.

The Shang also laid the foundation for future Chinese achievements in the science of astronomy. To understand the natural order of the universe and to predict natural occurrences, the ancient Chinese searched the skies. The Shang believed that the knowledge a person gained from studying the heavens gave that person great powers over other people and nature. Therefore, only members of the noble class were allowed to become astronomers.

These ancient astronomers began to map the stars. They recorded all of the eclipses of the sun and moon, and they also devised a 12-month calendar. Shang astronomers correctly identified the first day of each of the 4 seasons. They also kept records of rainfall and drought and thus began to predict the weather.

Writing. The greatest accomplishment of the Shang was writing. Historians are not certain whether the Shang originated Chinese writing or improved a system begun by some earlier unknown people. However, the symbols that the Shang scratched on oracle bones, tortoise shells, and a few other objects are the earliest known Chinese writing. The system used by the Shang was the forerunner of modern Chinese. During Shang times, 5,000 characters were in use although only 1,500 of these have as yet been deciphered.

Like Egyptian writing, the system developed by the ancient Chinese is pictographic, with pictures representing objects. The symbols of Chinese writing are called characters. The Shang further developed writing with the use of ideographs, the combination of characters to express ideas. For example, the combination of the character showing a person kneeling and a symbol representing a deity meant "to pray." The character for "sun" written behind the character for "tree" meant "east." By adding special symbols, the Shang were able to use the pictographic symbol for one word to represent another word that they pronounced the same way, but that had a different meaning. Later, the Chinese added new characters and gradually altered the style of writing somewhat. However, the basic system of writing developed by the Shang has remained in use until modern times.

THE END OF THE SHANG

Historians do not know the reason for the decline of the Shang. However, what is known is that in 1027 B.C. the armies of a neighboring people, the Chou (JOE), swept through Shang territory. The Chou were related to the Shang, but had not yet developed either writing or bronze. The Chou destroyed much of the capital and established a new dynasty.

The Shang were not completely annihilated, however. The Chou allowed the Shang to keep a small area, including their ruined capital, so that they could continue to honor their ancestors. Adhering to an ancient Chinese belief, the Chou feared that neglected ancestors of the Shang might become troubled "hungry ghosts" and bring misfortune to the new rulers.

The Chou adopted many Shang ways. Thus, the Chou learned the skillful techniques of Shang artisans, especially those who made bronze or silk, or carved jade. In addition, the use of the horse-drawn war chariot, ideas about family and religion, and the Shang system of writing were passed down to future generations of Chinese.

Shaped as a tiger protecting a human, this bronze vessel was cast by Shang metalsmiths about the thirteenth century B.C. Such vessels were used for ritual offerings.

SECTION REVIEW

1. Define *ancestor worship*.

2. How has the Hwang Ho benefited China? How has it created problems?

3. What were the functions of Shang rulers?

4. Describe the two social classes into which Shang society was first divided.

5. Explain the Chinese system of writing.

Analysis. Why would identifying the first day of each season be important to a civilization?

Data Search. Refer to the appropriate chart on page 829 to identify: **(a)** the similarities in the types of tools used in Mesopotamia, Egypt, India, and China during the period from 2000 to 1000 B.C., and **(b)** the differences in the use of tools in these four regions.

3-4
THE CHOU DYNASTY

READ TO FIND OUT

— what the terms *mandate* and *principalities* mean.
— how the Chou explained the "Mandate of Heaven."
— how the Early Chou Dynasty governed.
— why the kings of the Late Chou Dynasty lost their power.
— how the Chou expanded Chinese writing.

After conquering the Shang, the Chou established a dynasty with its capital city in their homeland, which was west of Shang lands. The Chou Dynasty, lasting from 1027 B.C. to 256 B.C., proved to be the longest-ruling dynasty in Chinese history.

The Chou people came from the valley of the Wei (WAY) River, a tributary of the Hwang Ho. They built their capital along the river at Sian (SHE-ahn), from where Chou kings ruled until 771 B.C. The period from 1027 B.C. to 771 B.C. is referred to as the Western Chou or Early Chou Dynasty.

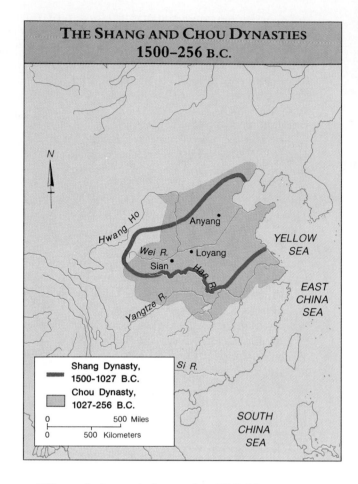

THE SHANG AND CHOU DYNASTIES
1500–256 B.C.

Shang Dynasty, 1500–1027 B.C.
Chou Dynasty, 1027–256 B.C.

When their capital on the Wei River was sacked by nomads in 771 B.C., the Chou shifted their chief residence east to Loyang (LŌ-YAHNG). Although the power of Chou kings dwindled after this time, they held the royal title for another 500 years, until about 256 B.C. The period from 771 B.C. to 256 B.C. is referred to as the Eastern Chou or Late Chou Dynasty.

THE MANDATE OF HEAVEN

Over the centuries, myths had grown up about China's earliest rulers, the Hsia and Shang kings, and how they came to rule. According to tradition, Yu the Great, the first Hsia king, was the son of an earthly mother and the sky god. He established the dynasty and passed the throne to his sons and grandsons, all of whom were called the Sons of Heaven. Similar stories grew up about the origins of the first Shang ruler, King T'ang. He and the Shang kings who followed were also known as Sons of Heaven.

During Chou times, a theory about government evolved from these myths—the principle of the Mandate of Heaven. A *mandate* is an order or command from a higher authority. The Chou people believed that their ruler received a mandate from T'ien (TYEN), a heavenly deity, to rule China. T'ien represented the highest spiritual power of the universe. The ruler was called the Son of Heaven not because he was thought to be a deity but because he ruled by permission of T'ien.

The dynasty kept this mandate, or spiritual authority to rule, as long as it was worthy and governed the country properly. If the dynasty failed to do so and allowed war, famine, disease, or other disorders to afflict the people, it lost the mandate. The mandate would then pass to a new dynasty.

According to the Chou, the last rulers of the Shang had become incompetent and corrupt. Their spiritual authority ran out. The Shang then lost the Mandate of Heaven, and T'ien passed it to the Chou.

THE WESTERN CHOU

The Chou Dynasty was established by King Wu (WOO). His brother, the Duke of Chou, recommended dividing the Chou homelands and the conquered Shang territory into many domains. Large blocks of land were ruled by the Chou king. Territories surrounding the king's lands were awarded to members of the royal family or to other loyal nobles. These nobles ruled the lands awarded to them, although the Chou king possessed the Mandate of Heaven and thus was the ceremonial ruler of all Chou territories.

In time, the territory ruled in the name of the Chou Dynasty grew. Some Chou *principalities* extended their territory by conquering neighboring lands. A principality is a territory governed by a ruler whose rank is less than king or queen. Land was also added when Chou people migrated to an unsettled area, which became part of a nearby Chou principality. Sometimes neighboring peoples who admired the Chou civilization asked to become part of the Chou system. Eventually, the Chou governed a territory that extended from the Hwang Ho and Yangtze valleys to the Pacific Coast.

Under the Western Chou, Chinese culture continued along the same course as under the Shang. To the Chou, their territory was "The Middle Kingdom," the very heart of the civilized world. To the north, northwest, and south lived people who were primarily nomadic. The Chinese regarded these people as uncivilized and dangerous. The Chinese called the most threatening of these groups "dog people."

THE EASTERN CHOU

Chou kings remained powerful figures for about 250 years. However, the Chou lost their homeland when the Wei Valley was invaded by surrounding nomadic tribes. In 770 B.C., the Chou Dynasty was forced to move its capital toward the east.

After the Chou ruling family fled to the east, the power of the Chou kings gradually weakened although the nobles still honored the Chou ruler as the Son of Heaven, the ruler of all China. The monarch retained his ceremonial duties, communicating with the spirit world to ensure the prosperity of the nation. However, the lands of the king were surrounded by those of the nobles. Therefore, the king could not expand the land under his control.

The high-ranking nobles who controlled large areas of land held great political and military power. These nobles raised armies, collected taxes, and acted as chief justices within their own territories. The Chou ruler depended on the loyalty of the nobles, who contributed money and warriors to support the king.

Over time, however, the landed nobles became increasingly independent of the king. As they struggled with each other for greater power, China entered a period of constant strife, intrigue, and, sometimes, open warfare. Boundaries shifted rapidly, and stronger states swallowed weaker ones. Where there had been over 200 separate principalities in the 700s B.C., by 500 B.C. there were about 20.

CHOU SOCIETY

At first, Chou society, like the Shang, was divided into two main social classes—nobles and commoners. However, just as Chinese political life changed over the centuries, so did Chinese society. As Chou civilization became more complex, the upper class became subdivided into several classes of nobles, ranked according to power, prestige, and wealth.

The nobles, along with the ruling family, had special privileges. Only they dressed in elaborate silks, often embroidered and trimmed with fur. Only they were allowed to study astronomy and learn to read and write.

In each principality, small cities grew up around the forts and living quarters of the noble families. Most of these cities consisted chiefly of nobles and their officials and servants. Their lives were mainly taken up with preparations for religious observances, hunting, and warfare. The community also included artisans who made objects of wood, bronze, clay, and silk for the nobility. Some artisans were slaves— prisoners of war or people being punished for breaking laws.

Despite political unrest and war, the common people continued to cluster in small country villages and tend the fields as they had under Shang rule. Chou farmers followed traditional ways. They continued to use stone tools— bronze was mainly for the nobles—and to plant millet, barley, wheat, and a new crop, soybeans. They began to increase farm land by cutting terraces out of the hillsides. Chinese farmers raised poultry, pigs, and silkworms. Some farmers even domesticated the elephant for agricultural chores.

The family. In each social class, family life was important, as it had been under the Shang. The family offered the individual security and support. On the other hand, the entire family was held responsible for the behavior of individuals. Therefore, family loyalty was highly valued, as was respect for parents.

Among the nobility it was common practice for parents to arrange their children's marriages. A wife was expected to live with her husband's family. Women held a lower position than men, but women had some rights. As head of the family, the father had authority over his sons, even the power of life and death. Similarly, the mother had complete authority over her daughters and daughters-in-law.

CHOU RELIGION

Like the Shang, the Chou worshipped deities of nature who, the Chinese thought, could help them raise enough crops to feed the growing population. The Chou ruler's most important duty was to communicate with the spirits of nature that could bring drought or rain.

Ancestor worship also continued. The king was responsible for communicating with the spirits of departed royal ancestors to ask for their guidance. The heads of families made offerings of food and drink to their ancestors and sought their advice. Properly treated ancestors, the people believed, would bring good fortune to the Middle Kingdom.

Animal themes found in bronzework influenced jade cutters. The animal most often portrayed was the dragon. This dragon pendant shows the skill with which Chou Dynasty artisans carved the precious, hard jade.

CHOU ACHIEVEMENTS

After the Chou conquered the Shang, they adopted many Shang ways. The Chou continued to make beautiful bronze ceremonial vessels as well as bronze weapons and armor. Because music had become an important part of religious services, metalsmiths cast sets of large bronze bells. The Chou also made many disk-shaped mirrors of highly polished bronze. The mirror was sometimes worn to protect its wearer from evil spirits.

Among the most important Chinese achievements during the Chou period was the continued development of writing and the creation of a body of literature. The Chou spoke a language related to the Shang's language, and they adopted the Shang system of writing. However, the Chou added hundreds of new characters. Some of these were partly phonetic—that is, they were symbols standing for sounds. Artisans often used written characters to decorate bronze, pottery, and jade objects.

The nobility, as well as some merchants, were expected to know how to write. Chou ruling families and other nobles began to write down the deeds of family members. They also composed essays and poems, which were written on wood or silk by using a brush dipped in ink made of soot.

One of the first Chinese books, written sometime before 600 B.C., was the *I Ching* (EE JING), or *Book of Changes*. It contains ancient beliefs about the nature of the universe as well as symbols used to foretell events. The *Book of Songs*, written at about the same time, is a collection of poems expressing thoughts about such topics as war, farming, and everyday life.

SECTION REVIEW

1. Define *mandate* and *principalities*.

2. What plan of government did the Duke of Chou devise?

3. How did the Chou kings gradually lose power?

4. Name the first Chinese books. What did they contain?

Analysis. Relate the theory of the Mandate of Heaven to developments that took place during the Chou Dynasty.

ALMANAC

ANCIENT CHINA

Shelter: wood-framed houses with plastered earthen walls and thatched or tiled roofs

Clothing: jacket, long tunic with belt or sash (hemp material for peasants, silk for upper class), straw sandals for peasants, cloth slippers for upper class

Food: millet, wheat, barley, turnips, melons, onions, peaches, plums, persimmons, small amounts of chicken or pork

Some leisure activities: hunting, board and table games, dancing, music (drums, bells, flutes)

Research Activity: Compare the above characteristics with those of life in modern China.

HISTORY IN FOCUS

Like the early civilizations of the Middle East, the two great civilizations that arose in Asia emerged in fertile river valleys—the valley of the Indus River in India and the Hwang Ho in China. Also like the other early civilizations, people in India and China conducted agriculture on a large scale, built cities, created systems of writing, and developed complex governments and religions.

The people of the Indus Valley created a remarkable civilization, but it was disrupted by disaster. No one knows exactly what influence the ideas of the Indus Valley people had on India's future. However, the social traditions and religious ideas of a new group of invaders—the Aryans—became a firm foundation for Indian society.

In China, strong social and religious traditions developed, too. However, theories of government also held an important place in Chinese thought. While India remained a collection of small states and kingdoms, the stage for political unity was being set in China. This unity has lasted for over two thousand years.

SUMMARY

- As in the Middle East, the early civilizations of India and China arose in river valleys: the Indus in India and the Hwang Ho in China.

- The first Indian civilization flourished in the Indus Valley by 2500 B.C. Its major cities, Harappa and Mohenjo-daro, were highly organized, with water systems, pottery, metalworking, and a system of weights and measures. This civilization ended by 1500 B.C., possibly as a result of natural disaster.

- During the Vedic Age, from 1500 B.C. to 550 B.C., the Aryans developed a civilization first in the Indus Valley, then around the Ganges. They established many of India's most lasting traditions, including rigid social classes and a complex polytheistic religion. Two important Aryan religious works were the *Vedas* and the *Upanishads*.

- The first Chinese civilization was the Shang Dynasty, established by 1500 B.C. It was characterized by a two-class system, ancestor worship, and achievements in art, astronomy, and writing.

- Ruling from 1027 B.C. to 256 B.C., the Chou Dynasty was the longest-ruling dynasty in Chinese history. Chou kings based their rule on a heavenly mandate. Their realm was divided into principalities governed by nobles, whose power eventually weakened the dynasty. The Chou expanded the Chinese written language and produced important books, such as the *I Ching*.

VOCABULARY REVIEW

The vocabulary terms in each pair listed below are related to each other. For each pair, explain what the two terms have in common. Also explain how they are different.

Example: *Pictographs* and *ideographs* both relate to writing. Pictographs are pictures that represent objects, and ideographs use combinations of characters to represent ideas.

1. mandate, principalities
2. subcontinent, monsoon
3. patriarchal, extended family

CHAPTER REVIEW

1. (a) How do the monsoons affect life in India? (b) Why is northern India especially suitable for agriculture? (c) How does the Deccan differ from the Indus-Ganges region?

2. (a) How do historians know that the Indus Valley civilization was not based solely on agriculture? (b) How was careful planning evident in the Indus Valley civilization? (c) How were Indus Valley and Middle Eastern civilizations similar?

3. (a) In what ways did the Aryans change their way of life after coming to India? (b) How did the Aryan civilization in India differ from the earlier Indus Valley civilization? (c) In what ways were the two civilizations similar?

4. (a) Compare the governments of the Early Vedic Age and the Late Vedic Age. (b) Why was military skill important among the Aryans? (c) How was this importance evident in the structure of Aryan government and society?

5. (a) State two purposes of religious ritual in Aryan society. (b) How did the social class structure reflect the importance of religion?

6. (a) Compare the land and climate of China and India. (b) How has China's geography affected its contact with the rest of the world? (c) How do southeastern and northeastern China differ in climate and geography?

7. (a) How were the Shang and Chou views on government authority similar? (b) How did Chou government organization differ from that of the Shang? (c) How did the relationship between the king and the nobles change during the Late Chou Dynasty? (d) Contrast political developments in China and India.

8. (a) How did religious beliefs influence the Chou's treatment of the Shang? (b) How did religion affect Chinese government? (c) How were Chinese and Aryan religion similar?

9. Compare each of the following in Aryan and Chinese society: role of women, family structure, and social class structure.

10. (a) What were the cultural achievements of the Indus Valley people? (b) How did the Aryans influence life in India? (c) What were the achievements of the Shang and Chou dynasties?

THINKING CRITICALLY: ACTIVITIES

1. Divide into groups of four or five to discuss the following question: Why did the Chinese consider themselves to be the most civilized people in the world?

2. Write an argument for or against the following statement: By 500 B.C., civilization in India was more advanced than civilization in China. Be sure to include supporting evidence.

3. Divide into groups of four or five to discuss the following question: Does an advanced civilization require a complex class structure? Support your responses with material from the chapter.

APPLYING SOCIAL STUDIES SKILLS

Using tools of time and place. When you have read all the chapters in a unit and are ready to begin your unit review, you may want to refer again to the unit introduction. The timeline and locator map found there will help you to compare developments within the various civilizations and cultures.

Use the Unit 1 introduction that begins on page XVIII to answer the following questions.

1. What regions of the world did you study in this unit? Where are they in relation to each other?

2. How many years did this unit cover?

3. What was the earliest civilization discussed in the unit?

4. Identify which of the following was developed first: **(a)** the wheel, **(b)** metal tools.

5. Which monotheistic religion developed first—Judaism or Zoroastrianism?

Now look at the introduction to Unit 2 on pages 68–69 to preview the next unit.

6. What regions will you be studying?

7. What period of time does the unit cover?

8. Name two of the social developments occurring during this period.

9. Name two political developments.

10. Name two of the key developments in technology.

APPLYING THINKING SKILLS

Classifying. The following burial sites are among the hundreds discovered near Anyang, the last of the Shang capitals. Classify these sites in order to identify characteristics of Shang customs and society. Then answer the questions that follow.

Site A: 1 large rectangular tomb measuring approximately 40 feet long by 30 feet wide and containing 9 human skeletons, chariot remains, leather armor, 100 bronze helmets, 360 bronze axeheaded spears, spearheads, and cauldrons

Site B: 209 graves, each containing between 3 and 39 skeletons

Site C: 58 graves, each measuring approximately 8 feet long by 3 feet wide and containing a single skeleton along with weapons, tools, and clay and bronze vessels

Site D: 1 large rectangular tomb measuring approximately 50 feet long by 40 feet wide and containing 7,000 cowrie shells, 400 bronze objects, 590 jade carvings, 560 bone objects, assorted ivory carvings, and shells

Site E: 191 graves containing a total of over 1,700 skeletons

Site F: 57 graves, each measuring approximately 20 feet long by 10 feet wide and containing between 2 and 11 skeletons along with pottery, bronze vessels, and ornaments

Site G: 1 large rectangular tomb measuring approximately 40 feet long by 30 feet wide and containing 11 skeletons, surrounded by 11 rows of 59 skeletons, with shields and leather armor

1. List the categories or groups you used to classify the burial sites.

2. Which burial sites seem to be most similar? Explain.

3. Which sites may contain the remains of wealthy people? What evidence indicates the people were wealthy?

4. What types of people were buried near the Shang capital?

5. Based on the above information, what were some general characteristics of Shang culture? Give evidence for each characteristic.

UNIT REVIEW

1. (a) Explain how the study of toolmaking sheds light on prehistory. **(b)** Explain what the following three inventions indicate about the periods or cultures in which they were used: pottery, the chariot, weights and measures.

2. (a) Explain why the Agricultural Revolution was important in the development of civilizations. **(b)** Describe how it stimulated trade. **(c)** Compare the relative importance of agriculture and trade in Egypt and Phoenicia.

3. (a) Explain how the development of early villages and cities might have provided opportunities for individuals to become leaders or rulers. **(b)** Explain the contribution of economic specialization to the growth of cities.

4. (a) Compare the type of art and its function during these periods: the Paleolithic Age; the height of the Indus Valley civilization; the Shang Dynasty. **(b)** Describe a common theme in the literature of the Chou, Aryans, Sumerians, and Egyptians.

5. (a) Describe the role of geography in the development of Egypt and the Fertile Crescent. **(b)** India and China were relatively isolated geographically. Explain how this isolation affected their development.

6. (a) List similarities among the religious beliefs of ancient Egyptians, Aryans, and Sumerians. **(b)** In what ways were Judaism and Zoroastrianism different from most ancient religions?

7. (a) Compare the writing systems of Egypt and China. **(b)** Explain why astronomy was the most developed science in ancient civilizations. **(c)** Compare the scientific achievements of the Sumerian, Egyptian, and Shang civilizations.

8. (a) Characterize each of the following civilizations in terms of whether it had a strong or a weak central government: Sumer around 3000 B.C.; Old Kingdom Egypt; Persia around 520 B.C.; Late Aryan India; Chou Dynasty China. **(b)** Briefly describe how each government was run. **(c)** Explain the differences between Babylonian and Hebrew systems of law.

9. (a) Does an aggressive military policy strengthen or weaken an empire? Cite examples to support your position. **(b)** Contrast the manner in which Assyria and Persia treated the peoples they had conquered.

10. (a) Compare the social classes of the Egyptian and the Aryan civilizations. **(b)** Describe the role and position of women in Egypt, India, and Babylonia.

RELATING PAST TO PRESENT

1. Pick two contributions from ancient civilizations and explain how the ideas or inventions influence people today: Sumerian wheel, 360-degree circle; Shang calculation of the first day of each season; Chou cultivation of soybeans, phonetic writing system; Babylonian code of law; Indus Valley cultivation of cotton; Egyptian paper, decimal system.

2. Since prehistoric times, people have migrated from place to place. Today, no country is untouched by the economic, social, and political impact of migration. Discuss the nature and some of the causes of migration, past and present. Have the reasons people migrate changed over time? Provide specific examples to support your ideas.

3. Ancient Egyptians believed that their rulers were enlightened and that they ruled in the best interest of the kingdom. Compare and contrast the Egyptian attitude with attitudes today.

4. Identify which of the following Hebrew beliefs have most influenced present-day political beliefs in the United States: social justice, limited powers of government, respect for law, and worth of the individual. Explain your answer.

PROJECTS AND ACTIVITIES

1. Prepare a timeline that shows important developments in prehistory and ancient civilizations. Include such events as the rise and fall of empires and dynasties, key conquests, and important technological changes. You may find it useful to divide your timeline into three parallel bands, showing the Middle East, India, and China.

2. Divide into small groups to research an ancient city such as Baghdad in Iraq. Each group member should investigate a different aspect:

government and politics, economy and resources, art and architecture, social structure and daily life, and so on. Prepare oral reports that, when presented as a group, provide an overview of that city's history. Use pictures and drawings if possible.

3. Write two statements about yourself that would define you as a member of one of the ancient cultures. Read your statements to the class and have the class members guess which culture you represent. Make sure that your statements can be correctly attributed to just one culture. Examples: I believe in Ra (Egypt). I sail to North Africa and Spain (Phoenicia).

ANALYZING PRIMARY SOURCES

Refer to the Ten Commandments on page 40 to answer the following questions:

1. To what does the name *Israel* refer: the people or the country? Support your answer with evidence from the excerpt.

2. Write the meanings of the following words after studying how each word is used in the excerpt: **(a)** statutes, **(b)** sabbath, **(c)** covet. Then use a dictionary to check your answers.

3. State the meaning of each commandment in your own words.

4. Some commandments refer to duties toward God. In general, to what do the others refer?

5. What is another way to divide the Ten Commandments into two groups based on their meanings?

6. What do you think is the general purpose of the Ten Commandments?

GEOGRAPHY REVIEW

Relationships within places. Today almost all human beings live in a cultural landscape—one that has been superimposed on the natural environment. A cultural landscape consists of fields, buildings, roads, and other human constructions. However, characteristics that give an area its sense of place and make it different from other areas also make up the cultural landscape. These characteristics include the sights, sounds, and smells associated with the activities of the people who live in a place.

Write a short three-part description of the natural environment and cultural landscape in which you live. You may want to describe a broad area, such as the Dallas–Fort Worth Area, a city or town such as Atlanta, or your specific neighborhood such as Flatbush in Brooklyn. You may decide to do some research to complete this activity.

In the first part of your description, portray your natural environment as it might have been before people entered the picture. Consider some of the following questions: What are the area's physical features? Are there mountains, valleys, plains, rivers, or lakes? What is the climate like? What is known about plants and animals native to the region?

In the second part of your description, explain what features in the natural environment attracted people to the area. Some possible answers might be mineral resources, location along a transportation route, or good soil for farming.

In the third part of your description, try to create for your readers a visual image of your cultural landscape. Also try to capture the character of your area by describing some of the sounds, smells, activities, and people.

SUGGESTED READINGS

Bronowski, Jacob. *The Ascent of Man.* Boston: Little, Brown, 1974. An overview of the origins and development of humankind.

Cottrell, Leonard. *Lost Pharaohs.* Westport, Conn: Greenwood Press, 1951. A 1980s' reprint of adventures in Egyptian archaeology.

Fairservis, Jr., Walter A. *Asia: Traditions and Treasures.* New York: Harry N. Abrams, Inc., 1981. A history of Asian civilizations, ancient to modern.

Renault, Mary. *The Persian Boy.* New York: Pantheon, 1972. A novel on the life of a slave boy in the Persian Empire.

Splendors of the Past: Lost Cities of the Ancient World. Washington, D.C.: National Geographic Society, 1981. An illustrated look at ancient cities.

GLOBAL TIMELINE

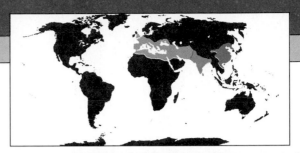

- ■ THE GREEK AND ROMAN WORLD
- ■ INDIA
- ■ CHINA

	POLITICAL	TECHNOLOGICAL	SOCIAL
2100			
1800		Minoan use of indoor plumbing	
1500	Mycenaean civilization Minoan civilization	Decimal system used in Crete	Religious dances developing in Crete
1200	Trojan War		Greek mythology develops
900	Dark Age of Greece	Silk looms invented in China	Caste system and Hinduism develop in India
600	First Greek city-states Etruscan civilization	Iron used in Greece Medical training in India using anatomical models	First recorded Olympic Games Homer's *Iliad* and *Odyssey* Confucius born
300	Beginnings of Athenian democracy Height of Alexander's empire Roman republic	Sun dial used in Greece and China Euclid's *Elements of Geometry*	Buddha born Library established at Alexandria
B.C.	Death of Julius Caesar Maurya Empire Ch'in Dynasty	Great Wall of China begun	Asoka's pillars Height of Greek philosophy and drama
A.D.	Pax Romana Han Dynasty	Levers and pulleys used by Romans Chinese invention of paper	Paul's missionary journeys Birth of Jesus Christ
300			
600	End of Roman Empire in the West Gupta Empire	Scrolls begin to be replaced by books	Emperor Theodosius ends Olympic Games Growth of Buddhism in China

ANCIENT GREEK CIVILIZATION

2000–334 B.C.

Horseman. Detail from Parthenon stone carving, about 440 B.C.

The rise of great civilizations in Greece, India, and China between about 1000 B.C. and 500 B.C. began what historians have called the Classical Age. The word *classical* describes anything that becomes a model or a standard. These civilizations are called classical because they produced ideas and cultural patterns that became models for civilizations that followed them.

Ancient Greeks built the first classical civilization in the Mediterranean region. They borrowed ideas from other civilizations, such as Egypt and Persia, and combined them with their own culture to create powerful, lasting traditions. Classical Greek civilization is called Hellenic after *Hellas*, an ancient word for Greece. Hellenic civilization flourished from about 750 B.C. to 431 B.C., although its roots lay deep in the past.

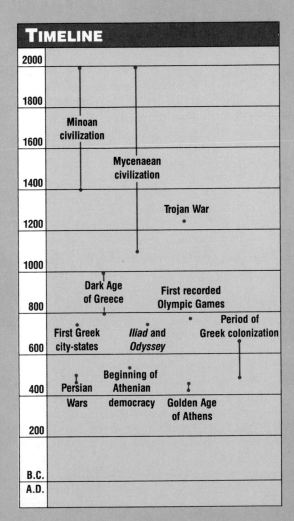

4-1
BEGINNINGS OF GREEK CIVILIZATION

READ TO FIND OUT

—what the terms *frescoes*, *cultural bridge*, and *epics* mean.
—how the geography of Greece influenced Greek civilization.
—how the Minoans affected the lives of the ancient Greeks.
—how the Mycenaeans came to be a major power in the Greek world.
—what caused the Dark Age of Greece.

About 6000 B.C., groups of people moved to the Greek mainland from the north, bringing with them different but related cultures. All these cultures together are called Aegean (uh-GEE-uhn) culture. The name *Aegean* comes from the sea around which these people lived. By 3000 B.C., Aegean culture had spread through the Aegean Islands off the east coast of the mainland and into parts of Asia Minor, the northwest corner of the Middle East.

GREECE: THE NATURAL SETTING

Greek civilization developed in what may seem an unlikely place. The Greek mainland is crisscrossed by low-lying but rugged mountain ranges, making travel and communication difficult. Unlike such centers of early civilization as the Fertile Crescent, the Indus Valley, and the Nile Valley, there are no major rivers.

In other ways, however, nature was kind to the Greeks. The mountains provided protection from invasion. Many small but fertile valleys lay between the ranges, and grapes and olives grew well in the mild climate of wet winters and dry summers.

Most of all, Greek civilization benefited from the sea. The Balkan Peninsula, home of Greek civilization, lies between the Aegean Sea to the east and the Ionian (ī-Ō-nee-uhn) Sea to the west. Both bodies of water are part of the Mediterranean, the largest inland sea in the world.

A temple dedicated to the Greek god of the sea stands atop Cape Sounion on Greece's Aegean coast. The cape was a landmark for early seafarers, guiding them safely toward Athens.

Easy access to the sea made Greece one of the first great maritime, or ocean-based, civilizations. Almost no point on the mainland is more than 50 miles (80 kilometers) from the Mediterranean. In many places, the sea cuts deep into the land, creating safe harbors.

The sea provided excellent opportunities for fishing and trade. Therefore, many Greeks could earn a living without having to farm the generally poor, rocky soil. The Greeks also enjoyed frequent contact with other peoples and cultures through their ocean-going activities.

The geography of the Balkan Peninsula influenced Greek politics in an important way, too. Because the mountains made travel slow and difficult, early Greek communities developed independently of one another. Although the people shared a similar background, language, and religion, they never became unified politically. From this political independence grew a Greek love of freedom.

THE MINOANS

On the island of Crete, which lies to the south of Greece, the first relatively advanced civilization in the Aegean region developed by about 2000 B.C. Scholars have called this civilization Minoan (mih-NŌ-uhn), after the legendary Cretan king Minos. Although it was influenced by Aegean culture, Minoan civilization borrowed ideas from Middle Eastern civilizations with which it had contact, such as Egypt and Phoenicia.

Much of what is known about the Minoans is based on the findings of the English archaeologist Sir Arthur Evans. In 1898, Evans uncovered the remains of an elaborate palace at Knossos (NAHS-uhs). This complex structure contained more than 800 rooms built around courtyards. A distinctive feature of the palace—and one that did not become common again for 3,600 years—was its indoor plumbing, including flush toilets and hot and cold running water.

The Minoan way of life. The walls in the palace's main rooms were decorated with *frescoes*—paintings done on wet plaster. These art works show the Minoans as a lively people, fond of animals, jewelry, dancing, and gardens. The Minoans also liked sports events, especially "bull leaping." In this activity, young athletes—girls as well as boys—would seize a bull by its horns and somersault across its back. The bull seems to have been sacred to the Minoans, and bull leaping may have begun as a religious ritual.

The Minoans worshipped the forces of nature. Their most important deity was the earth mother, or goddess of fertility. Like the Mesopotamians and the Egyptians, the Minoans built temples supervised by priests. However, the people seem to have performed many religious rituals themselves, sometimes in the home, and sometimes in caves or on mountaintops.

The Minoans were primarily traders, carrying olive oil, honey, wine, gold, grain, and linen by ship between Mesopotamia, Egypt, and settlements along the Black Sea. As a maritime civilization, Crete earned its living more from international sea trade than from farming.

Through trade, mainland Greeks came into contact with the Minoans and borrowed from their culture. Greek artisans imitated gold work, and Greek architects modeled fantastic palaces after those of their neighbors to the south. Greek scribes adapted Crete's system of writing, which Greeks used until they learned of the more efficient Phoenician alphabet, about 900 B.C. The Minoans had, in turn, borrowed ideas from their trading partners in the Fertile Crescent and Egypt. Thus, Minoan civilization served as a *cultural bridge*, or link through which ways of life pass, between the Middle East and Europe.

Minoan civilization reached its height about 1600 B.C. It collapsed 200 years later when its cities were mysteriously destroyed, perhaps by a volcano or by tidal waves created by an undersea earthquake. Control of the Mediterranean and of Crete itself then passed to the Greeks.

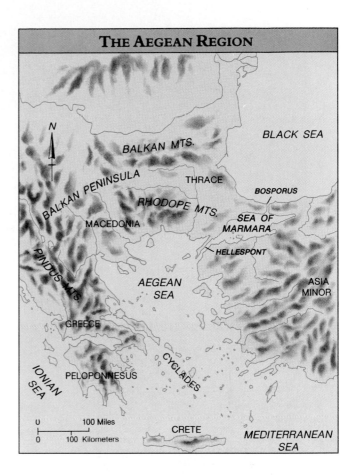

THE AEGEAN REGION

The portrait of the young woman adorns the walls of ruins at Knossos, a city of ancient Crete. Painted about 1500 B.C., the portrait is part of a fresco depicting a social gathering.

THE MYCENAEANS

Around 2000 B.C., a people called the Mycenaeans (mī-SEE-nee-uhns) made their way west from Central Asia into Europe. Like the Aryans who migrated into India, the Mycenaeans spoke an Indo-European language. They traveled south through the Balkan Peninsula until they came to the lowlands of Greece, where they settled and remained during the height of Minoan civilization. As they intermarried with the people who had come earlier, the Mycenaeans became the first true Greeks.

Throughout southern Greece, the Mycenaeans built strong fortresses, or citadels, on hilltops, bounded by great defensive walls made of stone. Mycenaean civilization is named for Mycenae (mī-SEE-nee), the most important of these fortified cities.

Greek myths, stories, and legends about the Greeks and their gods and goddesses portray the Mycenaeans as a very warlike people. Scenes of battle in their art and evidence of strong forts also suggest this characteristic.

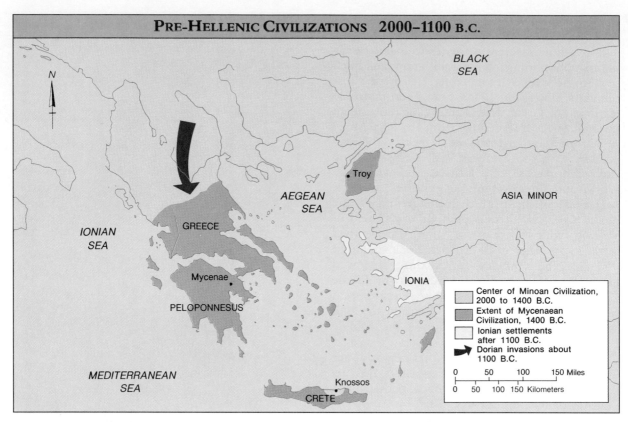

PRE-HELLENIC CIVILIZATIONS 2000–1100 B.C.

BLACK SEA

N

Troy

AEGEAN SEA

ASIA MINOR

IONIAN SEA

GREECE

IONIA

Mycenae

PELOPONNESUS

Center of Minoan Civilization, 2000 to 1400 B.C.

Extent of Mycenaean Civilization, 1400 B.C.

Ionian settlements after 1100 B.C.

Dorian invasions about 1100 B.C.

0   50   100   150 Miles

0   50   100 150 Kilometers

MEDITERRANEAN SEA

Knossos

CRETE

Scholars believe that, at first, the Mycenaeans fought each other. Then, as their knowledge of shipbuilding and navigation improved, they formed a loose confederation of kingdoms, outfitted raiding parties, and began plundering on land and sea. By about 1400 B.C., when Minoan civilization fell, they had replaced the Minoans as the major power of the Aegean world. The Mycenaeans maintained their position of power from about 1400 B.C. to 1200 B.C. This period is called the Heroic Age of Greece because later Greeks looked back to it as a time of heroic deeds.

THE TROJAN WAR

About 1250 B.C., the Mycenaeans launched a famous expedition against Troy, a city in Asia Minor that overlooked the important water passage between the Aegean and the Black seas called the Hellespont. Historians do not know why the Mycenaeans attacked Troy. They do know, however, that because of its location, Troy was able to tax the ships that carried grain and gold from settlements on the shores of the Black Sea to Greece. In what is called the Trojan

War, the Mycenaeans were said to have spent ten years attacking the city before they finally conquered the Trojans.

During the next 500 years, stories of the Trojan War were passed down from generation to generation. Around 750 B.C., the blind poet Homer used these stories when he composed the famous *epics*, or story length poems, called the *Iliad* and the *Odyssey*.

Mycenaean graves dating from 1600 to 1500 B.C. have yielded riches such as the bronze dagger with a lion hunt decoration crafted in silver and gold. *Mycenae* means ''rich in gold.''

READING MAPS

INTRODUCING THE SKILL

Maps are essential tools in the study of history. They show the location of important places and geographical features. They can also help you see how landforms played a part in shaping events. Maps can give you a clear picture of the size and extent of empires, civilizations, and countries, as well as any changes in their boundaries over time. In addition, maps can show movements of people, including armies, and goods from one region to another. Referring to the maps as you read will help you understand the material covered in the chapter.

EXPLAINING THE SKILL

Maps can present large amounts of information. To sort out the information, look for the following elements, which can be found on many of the maps in your textbook, as well as on maps in other sources.

A. *Title.* Look first at the map's title. It will give you an indication of the map's purpose.

B. *Directional Arrow.* Maps often use a directional arrow pointing toward an *N* to show where north is. If a map does not include such a directional arrow, then north is usually at the top of the page.

C. *Natural Features.* Natural features include hills, rivers, plains, coastlines, islands, and other landscape features that existed before humans arrived. Seas, lakes, and rivers are often shown in blue. The most important natural features on a map are usually named.

D. *Cultural Features.* Cultural features are created by people. Such features include empires, nations, cities, farmland, trade routes, roads, and railroads. Maps may use either symbols or colors, or both, to show cultural features. A map legend explains what each symbol and color represents.

E. *Scale.* Features on a map often look close together when in reality they are hundreds of miles apart. The scale on a map shows about how many miles or kilometers are covered by 1 inch. Using such information, you can estimate

distances on the map. On the scale shown on page 74, 1 inch equals 150 miles (240 kilometers).

APPLYING THE SKILL

Answer these questions about the map on page 74.

1. What is the purpose of this map?

2. Where is north?

3. What natural features are named on this map?

4. What kinds of cultural features are shown?

5. According to the legend, what is shown in pink? In green?

6. When the Dorians invaded, in what direction were they traveling?

7. Use the scale to estimate about how far the ships that left Mycenae had to travel to attack Troy during the Trojan War.

INTERPRETING THE INFORMATION

Imagine that you know nothing about early Greek civilizations beyond what the map on page 74 shows. Decide whether each statement below is **(a)** supported by the map, or **(b)** not supported by the map.

8. Greek civilizations expanded outward over time.

9. The Greeks were a seagoing people.

10. The invasion of the Dorians destroyed Greek culture.

11. The major Greek cities were seaports.

12. Troy was in a good position to control trade between the Greeks and the people around the Black Sea.

REVIEWING THE SKILL

13. What tells you the purpose of a map?

14. What two kinds of features are shown on maps? How do these features differ?

15. What is the purpose of a map legend? A map scale?

THE DARK AGE

Mycenaean supremacy came to an end between 1200 B.C. and 1100 B.C. when the Dorians (DOR-ee-uhns) invaded the Balkan Peninsula from the north. The iron weapons of the Dorians were stronger than the Mycenaeans' bronze weapons. With this advantage, the Dorians destroyed Mycenae and conquered the entire Peloponnesus (PEL-uh-puh-NEE-sus), which is the southernmost part of the Greek mainland.

Little is known about the conditions that led to these invasions. Many historians think that disputes among various groups of Mycenaeans may have weakened Mycenaean civilization. Others believe that a long drought may have brought famine to the Mycenaean people.

Whatever the cause, the Dorian invasion began a period of violence and instability that lasted from 1000 B.C. to 800 B.C. Farming was disrupted, and livestock were scattered. Overseas trade came almost to a standstill, and even the art of writing seemed to be lost. Historians refer to this period of cultural decline as the Dark Age of Greece.

The Dark Age was not completely bleak, however. Thousands of Mycenaean refugees fled the Greek mainland for the Aegean islands and the western shore of Asia Minor. These settlements were later called Ionia. Here the Mycenaeans preserved their traditions and developed ideas and ways of life that would later influence Greek civilization as a whole. On the Greek mainland, meanwhile, the Dorians mingled with the conquered Mycenaeans. Gradually, a new civilization began to develop. It drew from Mycenaean traditions but would eventually become very different.

SECTION REVIEW

1. Define *frescoes*, *cultural bridge*, and *epics*.

2. List five ways in which geography affected Greek society and politics.

3. What did the Greeks learn from the Minoans?

4. What evidence suggests that the Mycenaeans were warlike?

5. What was the effect of the Dorian invasion of the Balkan Peninsula?

Analysis. What are some possible reasons for the Greek attack on Troy?

4-2
GROWTH OF CITY-STATES

READ TO FIND OUT

—what the terms *polis*, *citizen*, *aristocrats*, *monarchy*, *oligarchy*, *democracy*, and *direct democracy* mean.

—how city-states developed out of villages.

—how colonization affected Greek society.

—how society in the city-states was divided into classes.

—how Athens differed from Sparta politically.

—what features of daily life were important to the Greeks.

—how the Greeks defeated the Persians.

Toward the end of the Dark Age, many of the small, isolated villages of the Greek mainland gradually grew into city-states. City-states were independent communities that became the only organized political structures of ancient Greece. Around 750 B.C., as Greece left the Dark Age behind, its city-states grew rapidly and prospered. Hellenic civilization began to develop the ideas, knowledge, and culture that would have a major influence on later civilization in Europe.

THE POLIS

The Greek city-state was called the *polis* (PŌ-lis), which meant simply "city." Originally, the polis consisted of a fortified point, around which were grouped several farming villages, together with the farmers' fields and orchards. The strong point was usually on a hill, or *acropolis*, on which the people built a temple for their local deity. At the foot of the acropolis was the *agora*, an open area that served as a marketplace and public meeting place.

Gradually, as population increased, artisans, traders, and nobles settled near the agora. By the 600s B.C. the core of the typical polis had developed into a city.

The concept of the *citizen* became basic to the workings of the polis. A citizen was not just a

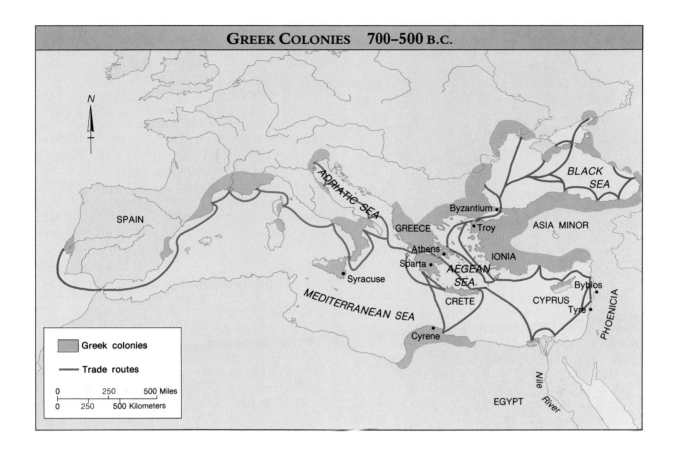

GREEK COLONIES   700–500 B.C.

Greek colonies

—— **Trade routes**

0   250   500 Miles

0   250   500 Kilometers

resident, but a person with rights and responsibilities. The Greeks believed that only certain people—men who owned property—deserved citizenship. Women, slaves, common people, and foreigners were excluded. Gradually, some city-states let men without property become citizens. Women were never granted the right to become citizens.

A citizen was expected to serve in the military and law courts, vote intelligently, and participate in political decision making. The small size of most city-states—5,000 to 10,000 citizens—enabled the polis to develop a political system in which many people were directly involved. The citizens often met together to take part in lively debates over the issues of the day and to vote on public policy. Many people became very skilled at oratory, or making speeches.

Between 750 B.C. and 500 B.C., economic growth and social changes led to important political developments in the Greek city-states. Each developed in its own unique way, and in several, a new and revolutionary form of government emerged.

ECONOMIC GROWTH AND COLONIZATION

After about 700 B.C., a shortage of farm land developed as the population grew. Local farms could not produce enough to feed all the cities' inhabitants. Many city-states began to set up colonies, or settlements in other lands, where grain could be grown and imported to Greece.

The period of colonization lasted about 200 years. About 250 Greek colonies were established along the shores of the Mediterranean, Aegean, and Black seas, from Asia Minor to North Africa to southern Europe. Among the most important were Byzantium, near the Bosporus—the narrow passage to the Black Sea—and Syracuse, on the island of Sicily. Each colony was independent but maintained close ties with the founding city-state.

Colonization brought about many economic changes. Supplied with imported grain, the city-states could use scarce land to grow crops that would be used for trade. The most important of these crops were olives and wine grapes.

Syracuse released this coin in 413 B.C. after defeating Athens in battle. Syracuse is symbolized as a charioteer being crowned by a winged Victory.

Because fewer workers were needed in the vineyards than in the grain fields, many farmers moved to the cities. There they learned metalworking, pottery making, and textile weaving. Now, with more goods to sell, Greek merchants could expand their overseas trade. They built larger ships, improved their harbors, and promoted banking. By 600 B.C., Greece was the leading commercial and maritime power in the Mediterranean.

SOCIAL CLASSES IN ANCIENT GREECE

By about this same time, clear-cut classes had developed in Greek society. The old, landowning families of nobles held great power in the polis, whether or not they ruled officially. The nobles had high standards of personal honor and excellent educations. Many people believed that because of these qualities, the nobles were the people best suited to owning land and being leaders. As a class, the nobles of Greece were called *aristocrats*, which meant "best people." No matter what form of government a city-state developed, aristocrats were always the most powerful class.

Merchants made up a second class. Often they were looked down upon because of their concern for building up wealth for its own sake. A third class was made up of farmers who owned small plots of land. A fourth class consisted of workers who did not own property. Farmers who worked on large estates, artisans, and sailors all belonged to this class. In most city-states, people in this class were not allowed to be citizens.

Slaves made up the lowest class. Most of them had been captured in war. People who could not pay their debts could also be sold into slavery. This system was called debt slavery. The Greeks relied on slaves to do most of the difficult labor in their society. They believed that slavery was inevitable in a civilized state. The Greek philosopher Aristotle said, "The lower sort of mankind are *by nature* slaves, and it is better for all inferiors that they should be under the rule of a master." The Greeks also believed that slaves were important to society. With slaves performing the labor, aristocratic citizens had the leisure time to devote to political discussion, learning, and art.

POLITICAL DEVELOPMENT

Important political changes occurred along with economic growth and the development of distinct classes. During the Dark Age, each Greek city-state had been ruled by a king. Such a system of government in which a king or queen has total power is known as a *monarchy*.

By 700 B.C., the nobles in all the city-states had seized political power from the kings. Decisions were now made by councils of landowning nobles—the aristocracy. The councils appointed officials for fixed terms to carry out special duties. This form of government is called *oligarchy*, or rule by a few.

Over time, tension arose between the nobles and the rest of the population. Because of the increase in trade, merchants gained wealth and began to challenge the nobles. Debt slavery and control of land by the aristocracy stirred discontent among the lower classes, too.

To end the unrest, military leaders, usually aristocrats, seized power. Such leaders became known as tyrants. Although the word *tyrant* today means a particularly cruel leader, the Greek word meant simply a person who had seized power rather than inherited it. Between 650 and 500 B.C., tyrants ruled many city-states during what has been called the Age of Tyrants. Most of these leaders were interested in improving their polis and the life of its citizens.

After 500 B.C., many city-states developed a form of government known as *democracy*, in which the people hold the power to rule. Often, however, leaders continued to be aristocrats. Although many city-states had democracies, that of Athens in the 400s B.C. is the best example.

RISE OF DEMOCRACY IN ATHENS

Athens, like all the city-states, was first a monarchy. In 682 B.C., the nobles replaced the king with an oligarchy of nine archons, or officials. The archons were elected for terms of one year by an Assembly composed of all the people who owned land.

Under oligarchic rule, population and trade increased, but so did discontent among the people. Crop failures caused farmers to fall heavily into debt. Many lost their land, and some were forced to sell themselves into slavery to repay their creditors.

The reformers. To avoid rebellion, Athenian leaders gradually moved in the direction of democratic government. One of the important ideas they had to work with in bringing about reform was the Greek concept of the citizen. This concept was based on the idea that the individual mattered. Over time, Athenian leaders began to place more importance on the views of individual citizens. During the next century, four reformers, all aristocrats, took important steps toward a more democratic government in which many individuals—not only the rulers—had more power.

The first reformer was Draco (DRAY-kō). In 621 B.C., he drew up a code of law. It called for harsh punishments, but it was set down in writing so that everyone knew what the laws were. A written code of law ensured that the laws would be applied equally to all people.

The second reformer was Solon (SŌ-luhn). In 594 B.C., he cancelled all debts for small farmers and outlawed debt slavery. He also placed a limit on the amount of land one person could own. Solon followed such economic reforms with political ones. He gave the Assembly the right to veto laws passed by the council of nobles. He also allowed foreign artisans to become citizens.

The third reformer was Pisistratus (pī-SIS-truh-tuhs), a wealthy relative of Solon who took over the government in 560 B.C. Pisistratus abolished the law that allowed only landowners to become citizens and to vote. This act greatly increased the number of Athenians who were considered citizens. He also broke up some large estates so as to distribute property to the landless, and he encouraged the development of trade and industry.

The Shrine of Delphi is located on Mt. Parnassus north of Athens. Here, early Greeks sought advice from an oracle, a priestess they believed spoke the words of Apollo.

Cleisthenes (KLĪS-thah-neez), who came to power in 508 B.C., was the fourth reformer. He introduced a series of laws that transformed Athens into the world's first democracy. Cleisthenes guaranteed freedom of speech and equality before the law to all citizens. He gave all citizens, regardless of whether or not they owned land, membership in the Assembly. The Assembly was given the power to pass laws instead of just approving them, to elect ten generals to run the armed forces, and to serve as a supreme court. The Assembly, which now included all 43,000 or so citizens, thus became the key part of democracy in Athens.

Matters such as finance, public works, shipping, and foreign affairs were turned over to a Council of Five Hundred. The 500 members of this Council were chosen each year by lot, a system in which names are selected randomly.

Political life. The Athenians preferred the lot to the ballot because it gave people equal opportunity to hold office. They felt that wealth, power, or the ability to speak well would give some people an advantage over others in an election. They also believed that every citizen was capable of holding public office. All citizens in Athens had the right to vote, hold office, own property, and defend themselves in court. In addition, they enjoyed freedom of speech and freedom of assembly.

The type of helmet, the cloak, and the bare feet identify the figure as a Spartan warrior. The statuette was cast in solid bronze during the sixth century B.C.

Athens was only one among many city-states, each with a varying form of government. In no polis were more than 40 percent of the adults citizens, and in most, this percentage was far lower. The belief that aristocrats made better leaders continued to be important in Athens. Most leaders were nobles who had great wealth and power.

Another important way in which Athenian democracy differed from democracy today is that it was direct, or participatory. In the *direct democracy* of Athens, all citizens could have a say in decisions by participating in face-to-face debate and discussion. Such a system differs from representative democracy, in which citizens elect representatives to make decisions. Citizens in the democracy of Athens were expected to participate in politics more directly than citizens in a modern-day representative democracy.

SPARTA

Each Greek city-state had its own history, political institutions, and ways of life. Often there were dramatic differences between them. Whereas Athens evolved a democratic system of government, the city-state of Sparta developed a system under which government had complete control over the people's lives.

Political development. About 750 B.C., Sparta began taking over neighboring city-states and enslaving their inhabitants. By 500 B.C., Sparta dominated the entire peninsula, called the Peloponnesus, on which the city lay.

The Spartan nobles lived off the labor of two lower classes. The *perioeci* (PER-ee-EE-see) were free persons who worked as artisans and merchants. The *helots* (HEHL-uhtz) were slaves owned by the polis rather than by individuals. Helots farmed the nobles' lands, turning over half of their crops to the nobles.

Eventually the nobles faced a dilemma, for the perioeci and helots outnumbered them by about 20 to 1. The Spartan nobles could either keep their subjects and slaves under control by force, or they could follow the Athenian example of allowing the lower classes to participate in the government. Unlike the Athenians, the Spartans chose to control through force, thus moving toward an authoritarian form of government in which many people obeyed the decisions of a few.

Every citizen also had political responsibilities. Participation in government was expected of every citizen. The Greek philosopher Aristotle once wrote, "If liberty and equality are chiefly to be found in democracy, they will be best attained when all persons share alike in the government to the utmost." Every citizen was likewise expected to support his polis on the field of battle.

Athenian democracy in perspective. By the time of Cleisthenes's reforms around 500 B.C., Athens had become the most democratic large-scale society known to that time. However, Athenian democracy was far different from democracy today. Women were not considered citizens and had no say in politics. Furthermore, Athenian democracy was made possible only through slavery. Because slaves did most of the hard work, citizens had the time to devote to the never-ending discussion, speech making, and debate that formed the heart of democracy in Athens.

By the early 400s B.C., political power was placed in the hands of a Council of Elders, made up of 28 nobles who were sixty years of age or older. The council served as a supreme court and also proposed laws to the Assembly, to which all citizens over twenty belonged. The members of the Assembly either accepted or rejected a proposed law by shouting their vote. Each year the Assembly also elected a board made up of five men to administer the affairs of the polis. This board had the power to veto any legislation.

The military. To maintain order and prevent revolts, the Spartans needed a strong, well-trained army. With this aim in mind, the government regulated every facet of Spartan life. Spartan babies were examined for physical fitness, and weak or deformed infants were left to die on a hillside. Healthy girls were trained to become wives and mothers of soldiers. Healthy boys were removed from their families at the age of seven and placed in barracks, where they were taught to become fierce and disciplined soldiers. By suffering public whippings, they learned how to bear pain without complaint. By going barefoot and dressing in the scantiest

The *Discus Thrower* is a Roman copy in marble of a life-size bronze sculpture created by the Greek artist Myron about 450 B.C. Modern Olympic Games still include this ancient Greek sport.

garments, even during the winter, they learned endurance. As a result of such training, Sparta had the finest army in Greece.

To preserve their traditions, the Spartans isolated themselves as much as possible. Industry and trade were limited, and foreigners were admitted only for short periods. Without trade, Sparta remained a society of mostly poor farmers. Also, since Sparta was dedicated to building a military state, the Spartans produced very little art, literature, philosophy, or science. They never valued the intellectual achievements of Athens, considering Athenians weak and badly disciplined.

LIFE IN ANCIENT GREECE

Despite the great contrasts between Athens and Sparta, a common culture connected all Greeks. Among the most important aspects of the Greek way of life were religious beliefs, love of sports, and family structure.

Religion. The Greeks believed in many gods and goddesses, a system called polytheism. Though immortal and more powerful than any humans, the Greek deities had human qualities. The Greeks believed that 12 powerful gods and goddesses lived on Mt. Olympus in northern Greece. The ruler of these deities was Zeus (ZOOS). Among the other gods were his brother Poseidon (pō-SI-duhn), who ruled the ocean, and Zeus's son, Apollo, who was god of the sun, music, and healing.

Among the goddesses were Hera, Athena, and Aphrodite (AHF-ruh-DIT-ee). Hera, wife of Zeus, was goddess of marriage. Athena was the goddess of wisdom, and Aphrodite, the goddess of love. Over the centuries, the Greeks developed a rich mythology, or set of stories, about the roles the gods and goddesses played in Greek life.

Honoring the gods and goddesses was an important state function and demonstrated loyalty to the polis. Ordinary peasants and townspeople, however, added beliefs from older traditions to the official religion. Many Greek farmers, for instance, celebrated the joy of the harvest and the mysteries of the earth every year. Often popular beliefs differed greatly from what the upper classes believed.

Sports. The Greeks believed in honoring their deities by striving for excellence in mind and body. They valued athletic ability and held sports contests. The most famous of these was the Olympic Games, which took place every four years. This contest became so important that the Greeks began dating events from 776 B.C., the first year the games were held.

Olympic contests included boxing, wrestling, foot and chariot races, discus and javelin throwing, and a ferocious free-for-all that sometimes resulted in death. Only citizens could compete. Foreigners could watch, but women were excluded altogether. Winners of contests became heroes in their native polis.

The family. The basic social unit of ancient Greece was a tightly organized family in which men had complete authority. Women were expected to obey husbands and fathers, raise children, and run the household. They were excluded from public life. Wealthy women rarely left the home, but poor women often had to work as dressmakers, wool-weavers, midwives, and so on to help support the family.

SPOTLIGHT: DAILY LIFE

GREEK SPORTS

Philip, like all of his friends in Athens, loves sports. A muscular young man of sixteen, he already has won fame in his city as an excellent wrestler. He practices almost every day, running races to build his wind. In two more years, he hopes to be good enough to represent Athens at the most important sports event in Greece, the Games at Olympia.

Philip knows he has a family reputation to uphold. At the last Olympic Games, his older brother Hector had entered the pentathlon and had almost won. In this event, Hector competed with champions from cities throughout Greece in five events—fast sprints, the javelin throw, the discus throw, the broad jump, and wrestling. Even after taking second place because he stumbled on the jump, Hector had been honored by the citizens of Athens.

Philip secretly hopes he can do better than his brother and wear home the winner's crown of laurel branches. Unlike Hector, he will only enter the wrestling competition. His good-natured brother is helping him train as other young men throughout Greece are training. In Greece, people work hard to build strong and healthy bodies, so the competition will be tough.

Because Athenians know they might have to fight a war some day, many of their sports are partly training for combat. Both Philip and Hector practice shooting with bow and arrow. They borrow their father's horse to enter chariot races. They learn to swim in case they have to fight at sea.

For fun, they play a game similar to hockey, choosing up teams to bat a leather ball up and down the field until someone scores a winning goal. As a youngster, Philip had become good at handball. Slapping the hard ball up against the wall with his hands helped him build stamina for wrestling. He will need to grow very strong for the challenge that faces him in two years. His parents, his brother, his sister and the city of Athens will be counting on him.

Hades with Persephone, king and queen of the underworld

Athena, born from the head of Zeus

Poseidon, protector of waters

Young musician playing cithera

The hero Heracles with the sea god Triton, a son of Poseidon

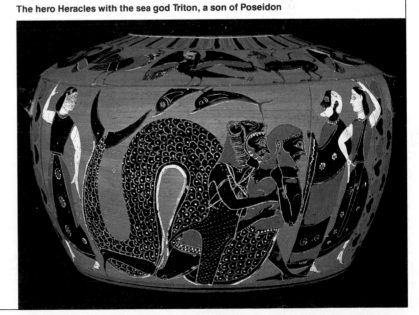

GREEK MYTHS

At religious festivals, the Greeks sang the praises of gods and goddesses and chanted tales of heroes and heroines. According to myth, the melodies and rhythms were inspired by Terpsichore, goddess of music and dance. Her symbol was the cithera, the stringed instrument being plucked by the youthful musician.

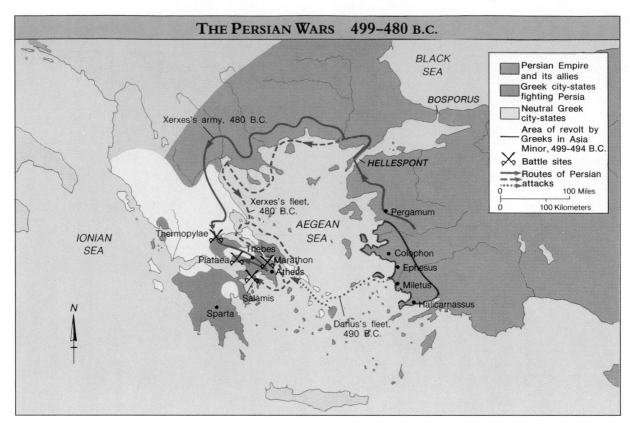

THE PERSIAN WARS 499–480 B.C.

Map Legend:
- Persian Empire and its allies
- Greek city-states fighting Persia
- Neutral Greek city-states
- Area of revolt by Greeks in Asia Minor, 499–494 B.C.
- ✕ Battle sites
- → Routes of Persian attacks

BLACK SEA

BOSPORUS

HELLESPONT

Xerxes's army, 480 B.C.

Xerxes's fleet, 480 B.C.

AEGEAN SEA

Pergamum

IONIAN SEA

Thermopylae

Thebes

Plataea

Marathon

Athens

Colophon

Ephesus

Miletus

Salamis

Halicarnassus

Sparta

Darius's fleet, 490 B.C.

N

THE PERSIAN WARS

As both Athens and Sparta reached their heights of power, Greece faced threats from a foreign enemy, Persia. The mightiest power of the time, the Persian Empire had been founded by the Persian king Cyrus in 550 B.C. Through a series of conquests, the king and his successor Darius I expanded the territory of the empire until it stretched from the Indus Valley to the Black Sea.

In 546 B.C., Persians had conquered the Greek colonies in Ionia on the coast of Asia Minor. In 499 B.C., the city-state of Miletus (mī-LEE-tis) revolted against Persian rule. Athens sent a fleet of ships to help, but Darius, the Persian ruler, crushed the uprising. He then set out to punish Athens for its interference and to conquer the Greek mainland.

Darius's first attempt to conquer Greece ended when a storm destroyed the Persian fleet. Two years later, in 490 B.C., Darius assembled a new fleet and set sail for Greece. The Persian force of 20,000 landed on the plain of Marathon, about 24 miles (34 kilometers) north of Athens.

Greek victory. The Athenians were outnumbered 2 to 1 at Marathon. Yet, under the leadership of Miltiades (mil-TĪ-uh-DEEZ), they succeeded in defeating the Persians. When the battle was over, the Greeks reportedly counted 192 dead; the Persians, 6,400!

According to legend, Miltiades sent a messenger named Pheidippides (fī-DIP-ih-DEEZ) to tell the citizens of Athens about the defeat of the Persians. The legend goes on to tell that Pheidippides ran the 26 miles from the battle site at Marathon to Athens, collapsed, and died after declaring: "Rejoice, we conquer!"

After the defeat at Marathon, Darius was more determined than ever to conquer Greece. He died, however, before he could complete his plans for another attack.

Xerxes' invasion. In 480 B.C., ten years after the battle at Marathon, Xerxes (ZUHRK-seez), Darius's son, launched another invasion of Greece. Within a few weeks the Persians—who this time numbered about 250,000—took over northern Greece.

As the Persians moved south, Themistocles (thuh-MIS-tuh-KLEEZ), the leader of Athens, convinced the Greeks that their best chance to win a victory would be in a sea battle. First, however, it was necessary to create a delaying action on land. At the narrow mountain pass of Thermopylae (thur-MAHP-ih-lee) north of Athens, a small force of Greeks—led by King Leonidas of Sparta—held back the Persian army for 3 days. On the third night, however, a traitor showed the Persians an unmarked trail by which they could go around the Greeks and attack them from the rear. Leonidas, realizing what was happening, ordered most of his men to retreat. Then he and 300 fellow Spartans hurled themselves into a fight to the death.

Meanwhile, Xerxes sent his fleet to attack the Greek ships waiting in the straits of Salamis. He mounted a golden throne set high above the strait to watch what he thought would be an easy victory. Instead, the Greek ships nearly wiped out the Persian fleet.

Xerxes withdrew to Persia, leaving behind part of his army to resume the campaign in the spring. In 479 B.C., a Greek army under Spartan command defeated the remaining Persian army at Plataea (pluh-TEE-uh), while Greek ships destroyed what was left of the Persian navy. The Persian threat to Greece was over, and the Greek city-states were free to develop their government and culture.

SECTION REVIEW

1. Define *polis*, *citizen*, *aristocrats*, *monarchy*, *oligarchy*, *democracy*, and *direct democracy*.

2. How did the city-states arise in Greece?

3. Describe the effects of colonization.

4. Describe the social classes in a Greek city-state.

5. How did Athens and Sparta differ in their political development?

6. What roles did religion, sports, and family life play in Greek life?

7. How did the Greeks defeat Xerxes?

Analysis. Why did the Greek city-states fight among themselves?

Data Search. Refer to the appropriate chart on page 829 to compare the average life expectancy for a citizen of ancient Greece with that of someone living in **(a)** ancient Rome, **(b)** the United States in 1850, and **(c)** the United States in 1980.

4–3
THE HEIGHT OF HELLENIC CIVILIZATION

READ TO FIND OUT

—what the term *philosophy* means.
—why the years between 461 B.C. and 429 B.C. are called the Golden Age of Athens.
—how Greek philosophy and religion differed.
—what basic beliefs were held by the Greek philosophers.
—what the famous Greek poets, playwrights, scientists, artists, and historians contributed to Hellenic civilization.

Between the 500s and 300s B.C., Greek civilization enjoyed a time of growing political and military power, economic development, and cultural achievement. The accomplishments of this age would have a marked influence in later European civilizations.

THE GOLDEN AGE OF ATHENS

After the Persian Wars, in which Athens played a leading part, Athens became the political and cultural center of Greece. Between 461 B.C. and 429 B.C., Greek accomplishments in thought, science, literature, and the arts peaked in what has been called the Golden Age of Athens. Although important scientists, artists, and philosophers lived outside of Athens before and after the Golden Age, these three decades are the most remarkable in Greek history.

Pericles. The Golden Age is also called the Age of Pericles (PER-uh-kleez), after the general who guided Athenian politics between 461 B.C. and 429 B.C. Like most leaders of Athens, Pericles came from a noble family. His calm and thoughtful personality and excellent skill at making speeches won him the respect of Athenian citizens.

Pericles had a deep faith in Athenian democracy and in the ordinary citizen. He carried out a number of reforms that advanced Athenian democracy. By paying salaries to public servants, for instance, he made it possible for poor, as well as rich, people to serve in the Assembly and as jurors.

Pericles set out to restore the splendor of Athens, which had been destroyed by the Persians before the Battle of Salamis in 480 B.C. Under his leadership, an ambitious building program transformed Athens into Greece's most beautiful and most admired city. At the same time, Athens attracted the best scholars and artists from all over Greece. Proud of Athenian achievements, Pericles called Athens "the school of Greece."

The Athenian empire. Under Pericles the Athenian empire was forged. In 478 B.C., Athens persuaded several city-states to unite to protect one another. The alliance, called the Delian (DEE-lee-uhn) League, received its name from the island of Delos, where the assembly of the League met and the funds contributed by each member were kept. The main weapon of the League was the Athenian navy.

The Delian League worked well for a number of years. It freed Ionia from Persian rule and cleared out pirate strongholds in the Aegean. Trade on the seas expanded. Gradually, however, Athens began to assume more and more control over other League members. Athenian soldiers were stationed in various city-states and were often used to support revolts against the ruling aristocracy. Criminal cases were tried in Athens rather than in the polis where the offense took place. Athenian coins became the common form of money.

In 454 B.C., Athens seized the treasury at Delos and demanded tribute from League members. This act transformed the Delian League into the Athenian empire. Dominant over much of Greece and the colonies it had established, Athens became the center of Greek civilization and its cultural achievements.

BEGINNINGS OF GREEK PHILOSOPHY

The ancient Greeks were one of the first societies to separate the study of ideas and knowledge from religion. In other cultures, religion had always been a source of both knowledge and a code of correct conduct, or ethics. The Greeks, however, believed that natural laws governed the world. One basic natural law, for instance, was that everything was made up of fire, light, earth, and water. Human beings, using reason, could come to understand these laws. The Greeks also believed that humans could create a code of ethics based on knowledge of natural laws.

In ancient Greece, this study of knowledge, ideas, and ethics became known as *philosophy*, which meant "love of knowledge." Greek philosophy, an important contribution of Hellenic civilization, forms the basis of much of the science, political theory, and beliefs that hold many present-day societies together.

Socrates. Considered one of the greatest philosophers of all time, Socrates (SOK-rah-teez), lived in Athens from 469 B.C. to 399 B.C. He was an inspiring teacher who devoted his life to the pursuit of truth, which he believed would lead to proper conduct. Socrates told people to "know yourself," because he thought that "the unexamined life is not worth living." Socrates wanted to force people to evaluate their deepest motives and beliefs. To help people understand ideas in this way, he developed a new method of gaining knowledge known as the Socratic method. It involved asking people a series of questions until they arrived on their own at a conclusion.

Socrates argued that striving for money and glory was less important than improving one's soul. He questioned basic assumptions in Greek religion, ethics, and politics. Because of his unconventional views, he was brought to trial on charges of teaching false religion and corrupting the young, and was condemned to death. Since Socrates believed that all citizens should honor and obey the laws of the polis, even when they were unjust, he refused to flee. He died in 399 B.C. after drinking poison made from the hemlock plant.

Plato. Socrates never wrote down any of his teachings. What is known about him comes from other sources, mainly from the writings of Plato (PLAY-tō), who was born about 427 B.C. Plato, a friend and pupil of Socrates, carried on and developed much of his teacher's thinking. Disturbed by the death of Socrates, Plato left Athens for many years. When he returned, he founded a school known as the Academy, where he taught mathematics and philosophy.

The mosaic wall panel portrays the philosopher Plato in discussion with his students at the Academy. Founded in 387 B.C., Plato's school was located in a public garden near Athens.

Plato presented his philosophical views in written dialogues, or conversations. He believed that society should be governed, not by the richest, the most powerful, or the most popular, but by the wisest. "Until philosophers are kings," wrote Plato, "or the kings and princes of this world have the spirit and power of philosophy, and political greatness and wisdom meet in one, cities will never rest from their evils." Plato set down his ideas in *The Republic*, the first book ever written on political science. It is still widely read today.

Aristotle. At the Academy, Plato recognized the brilliance of one of his students, calling him "the intelligence of the school." This student was Aristotle, who spent 20 years at the Academy. He became known as the most learned philosopher in Greece. In 334 B.C., he founded his own school in Athens, called the Lyceum.

Aristotle made impressive contributions to nearly every area of Greek thought. He wrote about such varied topics as art, ethics, biology, poetry, psychology, and the weather. He established the science of reasoning, called logic. He was the first to classify, or name, living things by a system of group names, called genera, and individual names, called species. His study of

Greek drama is still widely read today by people who study literature.

Aristotle was an excellent example of the Greek ideal of the well-educated man. Not just a scientist and philosopher, he was also involved in politics. In one of his most famous phrases, he claimed that "man is by nature a political animal."

SCIENCE AND MEDICINE

Aristotle was only one of many Greek scientists. The earliest of note was Thales (THAY-leez), who lived around 600 B.C. Thales tried to find a basic substance common to all matter. He concluded that this substance was water. Although his theory was incorrect, Thales arrived at his conclusion in a systematic, logical way that forms part of the basis for what is today called the scientific method. Thales developed the two-step method of collecting data and forming an hypothesis, or educated guess, about what happens in nature.

Several decades later, in the 500s B.C., the mathematician Pythagoras (pih-THAG-uhr-uhs) developed a theory of numbers and discovered that certain kinds of triangles have properties in common. Still in use in geometry today, the Pythagorean theorem is applied to find the length of a side of a right triangle if the lengths of the two other sides are known.

During Athens's Golden Age, Hippocrates (hip-PAHK-ruh-TEEZ) laid down the foundations of today's medical profession. Unlike other doctors of the times, Hippocrates did not believe that illness was punishment from the gods. Instead, he applied to medicine the Greek philosophers' use of reason. Every disease, he believed, had a natural cause and could be diagnosed and treated. He drew up a code of behavior for doctors known today as the Hippocratic oath. Today many graduating medical students still take the Hippocratic oath.

LITERATURE

Some of the greatest accomplishments of the Greeks were made in the field of literature. Like the works of Greek philosophers, much Greek literature is still read today.

Epic poetry. Greek literature begins with the *Iliad* and the *Odyssey*, two epic poems about the

A scene from the *Odyssey* decorates the vase made about 490 B.C. Lashed to the mast of his ship, the hero Odysseus resists the Sirens—part bird and part woman—who coax him to shipwreck.

Trojan War. Composed in the eighth century B.C., 500 years after the war, these poems are credited to the blind poet Homer. They probably began as folk songs and stories that were passed down orally from one generation to the next.

The *Iliad* describes the exploits of the Greek warrior Achilles (uh-KILL-eez) and the Trojan prince Hector during 40 days in the tenth year of the Trojan War. The *Odyssey* recounts the 10-year struggle of the Greek king Odysseus to return home after the war.

For more than 2,000 years, these poems were thought to be fiction. However, the archaeologist Heinrich Schliemann believed that they were based on real events, people, and places. In 1870, he used Homer's description of Troy to figure out where to dig and found an ancient city. Scholars concluded that Schliemann had found Troy and began to see the *Iliad* and the *Odyssey* as historical documents as well as poems.

The *Iliad* and the *Odyssey* had an enormous importance for the ancient Greeks. The style, language, and themes of these poems influenced much of later Greek literature. Children learned the legends of the many gods and goddesses from the epics.

The influence of the *Iliad* and the *Odyssey* reaches far beyond the ancient Greeks, however. These two masterpieces stand among the greatest works of literature. Their rich, subtle, beautiful language greatly influenced later literary works.

The poet Hesiod (HEE-see-uhd), who lived just after Homer, also wrote in the epic style. Hesiod was a poor peasant who lived on an isolated farm. In *Works and Days*, he detailed the daily life of the ancient Greek farmer. Hesiod also wrote the *Theogeny*, a Greek account of the creation of the universe and the history of the gods.

Lyric poetry. In contrast to the epic poets Homer and Hesiod, other Greeks produced lyric, or songlike, poetry. These poems were shorter, more personal than the epics, and dealt with feelings such as love instead of events such as wars. Lyric poems were sung or recited by an individual or chorus to the accompaniment of a lyre, a small, hand-held instrument belonging to the harp family.

One of the greatest Greek lyric poets was Pindar, who wrote in the 400s B.C. Many of his poems celebrate the victors in the Olympic Games and other athletic contests. Such poems were meant to be sung in a procession for the victors on their return to their home cities.

Another important Greek lyric poet was Sappho, a woman born sometime around 600 B.C. on an Ionian island. Sappho's poems won her great fame for their intense emotion and natural language. Many parents sent their daughters to the island to be taught by her. Unfortunately, few of her poems have survived. Yet, she is considered one of the greatest poets who ever lived.

Drama. The Greeks were perhaps the first people to write dramas, or plays. Drama was one of the few areas of intellectual life in which all classes of people could participate. The great Greek plays, which were performed in huge open-air theaters, were attended by thousands of common people.

The first Greek plays were tragedies. Tragedies focused on the suffering and ultimate downfall of a character. The Greeks believed that certain laws governed the universe and that people who broke these laws—even unknowingly—would be punished. The Greeks also believed that it was important for people to meet their fate with courage.

The great masters of Greek tragedy were Aeschylus (EHS-kuh-luhs), Sophocles (SOF-uh-KLEEZ), and Euripides (yoo-RIP-uh-DEEZ). All three lived in Athens during the 400s B.C.

HERODOTUS

People's ideas about the past came mostly from stories passed on by word-of-mouth. The few written records of the past were little more than lists of events. The first effort to write what is today called history was made in the fifth century B.C. by the Greek writer Herodotus.

Herodotus was born around 484 B.C. in Halicarnassus, a city in Asia Minor. Thirsty for knowledge, he eventually began to travel to Babylon, Syria, Egypt, northern Africa, the lands surrounding the Black Sea, Greece, and many of the Aegean islands. In every country Herodotus visited, he asked the local people questions about their customs, traditions, and religions. He then organized this information into a written study that he called *historia*, which in Greek means "inquiries."

Around 450 B.C., Herodotus decided to write a *historia* in which he attempted to explain the causes and outcomes of the Persian Wars. He checked information through his own observation and through interviews with people who had some knowledge of the wars.

Herodotus's writing style was both entertaining and readable. He further fired the interest of his readers by including quotations and lively stories, but he was usually careful to identify secondhand information. However, some people criticized his writings as being little more than a collection of charming stories.

The following excerpt from Herodotus's account of the Persian Wars typifies his writing style:

In this place they [the Greeks] defended themselves with swords—those of them who still had swords—or with their hands and teeth, until at last some of the barbarians [Persians] threw down the defensive wall. Then the Greeks were buried under a hail of missiles.

Such was the courage of those men from Sparta and Thespiai; there is nevertheless one man who is said to have been bravest of all—Dienekes, a Spartan. [A story] told by one of the local people [relates] that when the barbarians fired their arrows, the number of shafts was so vast that the sun was hidden. Dienekes was not at all perturbed at that, but made light of the Persian numbers, saying, "Our friend has brought us splendid news. If the Persians hide the sun, we shall be fighting in the shade."

The dead were buried just where they fell. There is an inscription on their tomb saying:

Here four thousand from the Peloponnese
fought against three millions.

Herodotus spent the last years of his life in southern Italy, writing and traveling to other lands. When he died around 430 B.C., his friends built a monument in his honor. However, the written word proved to be his enduring memorial.

Aeschylus's surviving works include *Prometheus Bound*, about a mythological character who angered the gods by bringing fire to humankind. Among Sophocles's best known works are *Antigone* and *Oedipus the King*. Euripides wrote *Medea* and *The Trojan Women*.

The second type of play to develop was the comedy. Comedies were humorous plays that mocked leaders, writers, philosophers, and other well-known figures of the time. The master of Greek comedy was Aristophanes (AR-uh-STAHF-uh-NEEZ) who wrote *The Birds, The Clouds*, and *The Frogs*. In his play *Lysistrata*, wives refuse to see their husbands until the men agree to end their war with an enemy.

HISTORY

The attempt to record, analyze, and explain past events in a systematic way began with the ancient Greeks. Herodotus (huh-ROD-uh-tuhs), who lived in the 400s B.C., wrote a history of the Persian Wars. He is often called the "father of history."

Another great historian was Thucydides (thoo-SID-uh-DEEZ), who lived about the same time as Herodotus. Thucydides was a scientific historian, who carefully sifted evidence in order to present an objective account of events. He analyzed political conflicts by looking at them from both sides.

THE ARTS

Greeks were active in all branches of the arts including architecture, sculpture, and painting. The Greeks saw perfection in nature and tried to reproduce its balance, order, and harmony in their work. "Nothing in excess, and everything in proportion" was the Greek principle of art.

In architecture the Greeks developed styles that set the standards for later architects. Probably the best example of Greek architecture is the Parthenon, a temple honoring the goddess Athena. It was built as part of Pericles's program for rebuilding Athens. Inside the Parthenon stood a gold and ivory statue of Athena by the sculptor Phidias (FID-ee-uhs). Phidias also created a statue of Zeus at the temple at Olympia, the site of the Olympic Games.

In keeping with the emphasis on excellence, classical Greek statues portrayed not specific people, but an ideal form, or what was imagined to be perfect. Because few Greek sculptures have survived intact, most of what is known today of Greek sculpture comes from fragments and copies made centuries later.

Even less is known of the painting of the Greeks. No original Greek paintings have survived, except for those on pottery. From later copies and descriptions in literary works of the time, historians do know that the Greeks created great mural paintings showing action and emotion. These murals often depicted scenes from the *Iliad* and the *Odyssey*.

The Greeks believed that beauty should be a part of daily life. They produced beautifully proportioned vases and other pottery painted with scenes from mythology and from Greek life. Often adorned with images of deities and heroes, even the everyday objects such as coins combined beauty with usefulness.

The Parthenon, or Temple of Athena, crowns the Acropolis, the highest point in Athens. Constructed of white marble, the temple was built over a period of nine years from 447 to 438 B.C.

Carved marble slabs designed by Phidias formed a decorative band around the top of the Parthenon above the pillars. The marble slabs picture the procession held every four years in honor of Athena.

SECTION REVIEW

1. Define *philosophy*.

2. How did Athens become the leading city-state in Greece?

3. Identify two ways in which the beliefs of Plato, Aristotle, and Socrates were similar.

4. What two works serve as the foundation of Greek literature? Why?

5. Explain how Greek scientists, historians, philosophers, and writers contributed to a lasting heritage.

Analysis. In what ways did Athens's democracy encourage cultural achievements?

HISTORY IN FOCUS

As the first classical civilization in Europe, Greece had a profound effect on the development of later European civilizations. Even after Greece's glory had faded, Europeans still looked back to ancient Greece as the beginning of advanced civilization in the western part of the world. To distinguish their heritage from the Asian, or Eastern, civilizations based on classical India and China, Europeans would call their culture Western civilization. Later, Western civilization would spread beyond Europe to North and South America, as well as Australia and New Zealand, to become the most influential civilization in the world.

Western civilization is based on many important ideas, beliefs, and artistic achievements created and developed by Hellenic civilization. Ancient Greeks were the first society to emphasize the rights of the individual and to value individual freedom. The Greek idea of democracy that flowed from this emphasis is at the heart of most political systems in present-day Western civilization. Greek sculpture and literature still stand as a standard of excellence today. Much of present-day science follows from the attempt of the Greek philosophers to find order in the natural world and from their confidence in human reason. These are only a few of the many ways Hellenic civilization, after more than 2,000 years, lives on in Western civilization.

SUMMARY

- Greek civilization began around 6000 B.C., with the gradual development of the Aegean culture on the Greek mainland.

- By 2000 B.C., Aegean culture was strongly influenced by the Minoans of Crete and by the Mycenaean migration into Greece. Another group, the Dorians, entered Greece about 1200 B.C.

- Around 750 B.C., Greek city-states began to prosper. The city-states founded colonies to grow food, which led to expanded trade.

- Social classes in the city-states became clearly defined. Generally, only property-owners were citizens, with the aristocracy holding most of the power.

- City-state governments gradually changed from monarchies to oligarchies. Athenian democracy grew, while Sparta developed an authoritarian government.

- In the 400s B.C., under Pericles, Athens emerged from the Persian Wars as Greece's most important political and cultural center.

- The ancient Greeks wrote many fine works of philosphy, science, history, poetry, and drama. Hellenic architects, sculptors, and painters accomplished harmony in their art. This rich Greek heritage is the basis for much of the culture of the Western world.

VOCABULARY REVIEW

Match each numbered vocabulary term with its origin. Then explain the connection between the origin and the vocabulary term.

Example: The origin of the word *frescoes* is the Italian word *fresco*, meaning "fresh." Frescoes are paintings done on wet, or fresh, plaster.

1. epics
2. aristocrats
3. oligarchy
4. democracy
5. philosophy

(a) Greek: *epos*, word, song
(b) Greek: *demos*, the people + *kratein*, to rule
(c) Greek: *philos*, loving + *sophia*, wisdom
(d) Greek: *oligos*, few + *archein*, to rule
(e) Greek: *aristos*, best + *kratein*, to rule

CHAPTER REVIEW

1. (a) Describe two ways in which the geography of the Greek mainland hindered the development of civilization. (b) Describe two ways in which the geography aided the development of civilization. (c) Explain the importance of the sea in the growth of Greek civilization.

2. (a) What did the Greeks on the mainland learn from the Minoans? (b) In what ways did the Mycenaeans affect the development of civilization on the Greek mainland? (c) What was the effect of the Dorian invasion?

3. (a) How did the Greek city-states arise? (b) Describe the role of the citizen in the city-states. (c) Why did the city-states set up colonies? (d) What economic changes resulted from colonization?

4. (a) Describe debt slavery. (b) Why did the Greeks believe that slavery was necessary? (c) Describe the four classes of free people in Greek society. (d) What was the typical requirement for citizenship in Greek society?

5. (a) How did the city-states replace monarchies with oligarchies? (b) Why did tyrants often replace oligarchies?

6. (a) What influenced Athens's movement toward democracy? (b) Explain how each of the following brought Athens closer to democracy: Draco, Solon, Pisistratus, Cleisthenes.

7. (a) Why did Sparta develop an authoritarian government? (b) What were the effects of Sparta's emphasis on isolation and military training?

8. (a) What was the Golden Age of Athens? (b) How did Pericles's reforms show his confidence in the ability of the ordinary citizen? (c) How did the Delian League develop into the Athenian Empire?

9. (a) What were the purposes of Greek philosophy? (b) How did Greek philosophy differ from Greek religion? (c) What was the Socratic method? (d) How did Plato's idea of the philosopher-king differ from the traditional Greek ideas about government?

10. (a) Why are the *Iliad* and the *Odyssey* now seen as historical documents? (b) Why were these epics important to ancient Greeks?

THINKING CRITICALLY: ACTIVITIES

1. You are an Athenian denied citizenship because you do not own land. Write a speech to all Athenians, arguing for extending citizenship to people who do not own land. Take into account how aristocrats would argue against you and to what Athenian values you could appeal.

2. Imagine you are one of the following people: Socrates, Plato, Aristotle, Thales, Hippocrates. Select four class members to play the others. Then have a discussion in which you each present the person's view of the world.

3. Make a list of the conditions that help a civilization to grow. Support your conditions with specific examples from the chapter. Compare your list with those of other class members.

APPLYING SOCIAL STUDIES SKILLS

Reading maps. Look at the map titled "The Aegean Region" on page 73. Then complete each of the following sentences.

1. The purpose of this map is to show
   (a) the spread of Greek civilization.
   (b) the geography of the Balkan Peninsula.
   (c) the routes used by Greek traders.

2. On this map north points
   (a) toward the right side of the page.
   (b) toward the left side of the page.
   (c) toward the top of the page.

3. The Balkan Peninsula lies
   (a) west of the Black Sea.
   (b) east of the Ionian Sea.
   (c) both of the above.

4. The Balkan Peninsula is mainly
   (a) rocky and mountainous.
   (b) a forested plain.
   (c) a flat plateau.

5. The peninsula's coastline suggests that
   (a) fishing is excellent in this region.
   (b) earthquakes are common in this area.
   (c) there are many fine natural harbors.

6. Measuring west to east, the peninsula is
   (a) about 50 miles (80 kilometers) wide.
   (b) about 100 miles (160 kilometers) wide.
   (c) about 500 miles (800 kilometers) wide.

APPLYING THINKING SKILLS

Classifying. Some of the items below are features of ancient Athens between 500 and 400 B.C. Others are features of Sparta during the same period. Some items are features of both Athens and Sparta. Based on the information in Chapter 4, classify these items. Your purpose in classifying them is to identify the main characteristics of life in Athens and Sparta during this period. After classifying the features, answer the questions that follow.

had a supreme court
allowed freedom of speech
nobles outnumbered by the lower classes
government control of all aspects of life
all citizens eligible for the Council
all able citizens required to serve as soldiers if necessary
Council members elected by drawing lots
placed most emphasis on military discipline
government authority preserved by force
policy of limited trade
strong navy
most political power held by nobles
women not considered citizens
valued intellectual achievements
most of the labor supplied by slaves
society composed mainly of farmers
most power held by the Assembly
strongest army in Greece

1. Define the term *classify*.

2. Why is it useful to classify information?

3. What features describe Athens?

4. What features describe Sparta?

5. What features could be grouped under the category of "democracy"?

6. What features could be grouped under the category of "social structure"?

7. Look closely at the similarities between Athens and Sparta. What were three major characteristics of life in these city-states between 500 and 400 B.C.?

CHAPTER FIVE

HELLENISTIC CIVILIZATION

431–30 B.C.

Detail from the "Alexander Sarcophagus," about 320 B.C.

Hellenic civilization began to crumble after the Golden Age of Athens, when a fateful civil war enveloped Greece in 431 B.C. Out of this decline, however, came rebirth. Less than a century later, a great general named Alexander brought Greek culture to a vast area of the world by building an empire that included Egypt, Persia, and parts of India. While Greek culture spread throughout Alexander's empire, cultural influences from the conquered lands changed Greek culture. Scholars have called the civilization that emerged Hellenistic—which means "Greek-like"—in order to show both its similarity to Hellenic civilization and its new, broader character. Hellenistic culture influenced the eastern Mediterranean and Middle Eastern worlds for nearly three centuries.

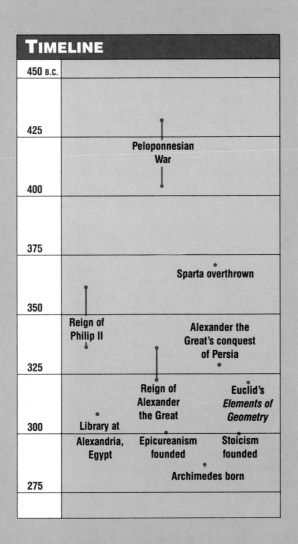

TIMELINE

450 B.C.	
425	Peloponnesian War
400	
375	
350	Sparta overthrown
325	Reign of Philip II — Alexander the Great's conquest of Persia
300	Reign of Alexander the Great — Euclid's *Elements of Geometry* — Library at Alexandria, Egypt — Epicureanism founded — Stoicism founded
275	Archimedes born

5-1
ALEXANDER'S EMPIRE

READ TO FIND OUT

—what the effects of the Peloponnesian War were.
—how the Greek city-states lost their independence.
—what Alexander's goals were.
—how Alexander the Great built his empire.

Even while Athens was enjoying its most democratic and creative period, Greece as a whole was becoming increasingly unstable politically. Toward the end of Pericles's rule, in 431 B.C., a long and devastating war broke out between Athens and Sparta, resulting in the rapid decline of Greek military power and Hellenic civilization.

As this age came to an end, however, the seeds of a new one were already sprouting. A strong ruler named Philip rose to power in Macedonia, a kingdom just north of Greece, in 359 B.C. Within 21 years, Philip had conquered most of Greece. He dreamed of spreading Greek culture throughout a world united under his rule. Philip's son Alexander carried on his father's dream, marching east and south to conquer great civilizations and rich cities from Egypt to the Indus River. In only 13 years, Alexander built the largest empire the Western world had yet known. This empire gave birth to Hellenistic civilization. Alexander died in 323 B.C., but Hellenistic civilization flourished long after his death.

THE PELOPONNESIAN WAR

In the 500s B.C., Sparta and several other city-states formed an alliance designed to balance Athenian power. As the wealth and power of Athens grew during its Golden Age, members of the alliance, called the Peloponnesian League, felt increasingly threatened. Old rivalries festered between many city-states, but the main line of conflict was drawn between Sparta and its allies on one side, and Athens and its allies on the other.

Finally, in 431 B.C., a dispute between Corinth, a member of the Peloponnesian League, and Athens set off a war that soon involved all of Greece. This war has become known as the Peloponnesian War. It raged, with only one interruption, for more than 27 years.

To strengthen its forces against Athens, Sparta obtained help from the Persians, who supplied gold that Sparta used to build ships. In exchange, Sparta agreed to return Ionia to the Persian Empire. In the fighting, Sparta relied on its army; Athens, on its navy. The Spartan army invaded Attica, the peninsula on which Athens is located, and the Athenians withdrew inside the walls of their city. In the crowded city, a plague spread uncontrollably. The disease killed Pericles in 429 B.C.

Despite these early setbacks, Athens was able to win several important victories during the war. Finally, however, after years of fighting, the Athenians could hold out no longer, and in 404 B.C. they surrendered.

Effects of the war. The Peloponnesian War was a disaster for Athens. It lost its empire, its confidence, and almost one-quarter of its population. Much of the land was devastated.

The war was also a disaster for Greece as a whole. Discouraged by the length and cost of the war, people became less interested in their city's common good and more interested in making money and looking out for themselves. Conflict among the residents of city-states arose as the poor grew more bitter about the wealth of the rich. In short, the polis as a political institution could no longer function.

For a time, after the end of the war, Greece was ruled by Sparta. The city-states, however, continued to fight each other. In 371 B.C., Sparta was overthrown by a group of city-states led by Thebes. The Thebans proved to be poor rulers and were themselves overthrown. Separated by mutual distrust and poisoned by disagreement, the city-states of Greece could be easily invaded.

THE MACEDONIAN CONQUEST

In 359 B.C., Philip II succeeded to the throne of Macedonia, a land on the northwest shores of the Ionian Sea. During his youth, Philip had spent three years as a hostage in Thebes. There, he had learned to admire Hellenic culture and,

at the same time, to despise the weaknesses of Greek government. When he became king, he set out to unify the quarreling Greek city-states under his rule and spread Greek culture. During his time as king, he thought of himself as Greek and believed that he was working in the best interests of Greece.

To achieve his goals, Philip bribed local Greek leaders with flattery and gold, and renewed quarrels between the city-states. To back up his strategy with force, he transformed the Macedonian army into a superb fighting unit. He made a powerful, professional, year-round army out of what had been a volunteer army that fought only in the summer. Soldiers were organized into a phalanx, or set of lines, and armed with a new, longer lance called a *sarissa*. With thorough training and support from cavalry, the Macedonian phalanx soon formed the heart of the finest military force existing at that time.

The Athenian orator Demosthenes (dih-MAHS-thuh-NEEZ) recognized the danger that Philip's goals and army posed to Greek independence. Demosthenes delivered eloquent speeches, calling on the Greeks to unite and resist. For 13 years he carried on this struggle. Meanwhile, Philip, who admired Athens, tried to make it his ally. However, Athenian leaders, seeing Philip's conquest of other kingdoms bordering Macedonia, distrusted him.

When a combined army from Athens and Thebes finally did challenge Philip's forces in 338 B.C., the Greeks were soundly defeated in the battle of Chaeronea (KEHR-uh-NEE-uh). This decisive battle marked the end of Greek independence. All the city-states except Sparta came under Macedonian rule. Then Philip made plans to attack Persia with united Greek and Macedonian forces. However, he was assassinated at his daughter's wedding in 336 B.C.

ALEXANDER THE GREAT

Philip's death did not halt Macedonian expansion. His son Alexander would prove himself an even more able leader.

Following his father's death, Alexander at once took steps to ensure that he would inherit the throne. He had his half-brother and cousin—two possible rivals—killed. Then he gained the support of the army and named himself king. He was only 20 years old.

COMPARING AND CONTRASTING

Comparing and contrasting mean determining how two or more things are alike and how they differ. In comparing, you look for similarities. In contrasting, you look for differences.

Comparing and contrasting are really two parts of the same skill. For example, when comparing your classmates, you might mention that they are in the same grade and have the same history teacher. However, while looking for similarities, you will also notice how your classmates differ in height, style of clothing, and so on. In fact, the word *compare* often means "to look for similarities or differences."

EXPLAINING THE SKILL

By looking for similarities and differences, you can learn more about the items you are examining. One way to compare and contrast items is to follow these steps:

1. *Identify the main features of each item.*

2. *Pick one feature in any item and determine whether it can be found in all the other items.*

3. *State as a similarity any feature found in all the items examined.*

4. *State as a difference any feature not found in all the items examined.*

5. *Repeat this process for each main feature.*

APPLYING THE SKILL

Follow the steps above to compare and contrast the military oath of ancient Athens with that of the United States today:

Oath A

I swear never to disgrace these sacred weapons,
Nor desert my comrades in the ranks;
I will protect the temples and public property
With others to help me, or alone if need be;
I will pass on my fatherland
Not less, but greater and better
Than it was handed down to me;
I will obey the magistrates
Who rule with reason;
I will observe the laws which have been
And those which are made by the people in the future

And I will oppose any man who will try to undo them;
I will honor the religion of my ancestors.
All this I swear by the gods Agraulos, Enyalios, Hestia, Enyo, Ares, Athena Areia, Zeus, Thallo, Auxo, Hegemone, and Heracles,
By the borders of my native land,
And by the wheat, barley, vines, and the trees of olive and fig that sustain us.

The Ephebic Oath, translated by James H. Hanscom.

Oath B

I do solemnly swear that I will support and defend the Constitution of the United States against all enemies, foreign and domestic; that I will bear true faith and allegiance to the same; and that I will obey the orders of the President of the United States and the orders of the officers appointed over me, according to regulations and the Uniform Code of Military Justice. So help me God.

MAKING MEANING

Use what you have learned by comparing and contrasting these oaths to complete the following sentences:

1. Both oaths include **(a)** promises to do certain things, **(b)** pledges to improve the nation, **(c)** references to benefits received by the soldier.

2. These oaths differ in how they treat **(a)** military defense, **(b)** religion, **(c)** respect for national leaders.

3. Both oaths **(a)** refer to valued objects as witnesses, **(b)** allow soldiers to choose how to carry out the oath, **(c)** stress the soldier's future duties.

4. In general, an oath is **(a)** a formal declaration, **(b)** a reference to sacred witnesses, **(c)** a description of the punishment for violating a promise.

REVIEWING THE SKILL

5. Why is it useful to compare and contrast items?

6. What is one way of comparing and contrasting items?

The mosaic panel depicts Alexander's victory at Issus. The youthful Alexander, left, charges at retreating Persian troops. Darius, center, turns back to face him in disbelief.

Alexander's father had trained him well for leadership. Alexander had spent three years learning about Greek culture and philosophy from Aristotle, the greatest scholar alive at the time. He had led a cavalry force in the battle of Chaeronea and had been ambassador to Athens. He had a strong will, a quick mind, and amazing fighting skill.

Early campaigns. Alexander's first step as ruler was to strengthen his control of Macedonia and Greece. With the army he had inherited from his father, he marched north to the Danube River and then south into Greece. During his absence, the city-state of Thebes had revolted. As punishment, and as an example to the rest of Greece, Alexander destroyed the city and sold its people into slavery.

With an army that had grown to about 40,000 Greek and Macedonian troops, Alexander marched east toward Persia in 334 B.C. to begin the attack that Philip had planned. Alexander's goal was to conquer the civilized world known to the Greeks. This area included Egypt, Persia, Asia Minor, and Arabia, lands known today as the Middle East. Alexander also wanted to reach further east to India and to China. His dream was to unify and rule this entire area, while creating for it a common culture based on a mixing of Greek and Persian ways of life.

Crossing the Hellespont, the strait between southern Europe and Asia Minor, Alexander challenged the Persian Empire. He met the Persian army for the first time in western Asia Minor and defeated it. Liberating Greek city-states from Persian rule as he marched down the coast of Asia Minor, Alexander prepared for another battle with the Persians. In 333 B.C., he defeated them at the battle of Issus in southern Asia Minor. Then he approached Phoenicia, on the far eastern shores of the Mediterranean.

At the Phoenician city of Tyre, Alexander met fierce resistance. Surrounding the city to cut off supplies, he defeated the people of Tyre and destroyed their city. He then moved into Egypt, where he founded the city of Alexandria in 332 B.C. near the mouth of the Nile River. The Egyptians, unhappy with Persian rule, welcomed him and called him pharaoh, a title given to Egyptian kings. Alexander, in turn, treated the Egyptians well.

The march east. The following year, Alexander marched into Mesopotamia to begin the next phase of his conquests. While Alexander was in Egypt, the Persian king Darius mustered his forces and prepared to face Alexander once again. As he had done so many times before, however, Alexander won a brilliant victory. He then went on to conquer the important Persian cities of Babylon, Susa, and Persepolis. In these cities, he captured tremendous riches, giving some to his troops and sending some home to Macedonia. Alexander estimated that the riches of Persepolis alone would require 5,000 camels and 20,000 mules to transport.

After making Babylon his capital, Alexander pursued Darius. When Darius was murdered by one of his own officers in 330 B.C., Alexander named himself King of Persia.

In 327 B.C., with the entire Persian Empire under his control, Alexander crossed the high mountain passes of northwestern India and conquered much of the Indus Valley. In 326 B.C., however, his men refused to go any further. They had marched more than 11,000 miles (17,600 kilometers), fighting many battles. Alexander tried to convince them to go on but faced the mutiny of all his troops. He gave in, and in 325 B.C. they began the long and difficult return to Persia, finally reaching Persepolis a year later.

In the short span of 13 years, without losing a single battle, Alexander had acquired the largest empire the world had ever seen. The lands he conquered extended some 3,000 miles (4,800 kilometers), from the Nile River to the Indus River.

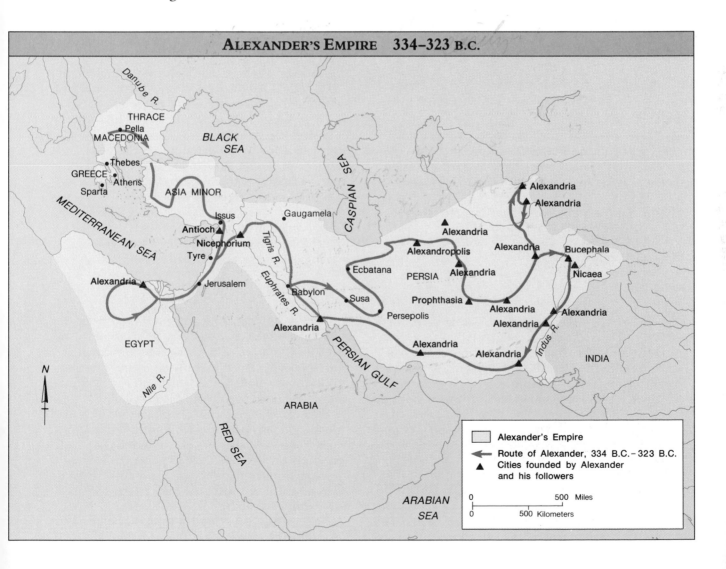

ALEXANDER'S EMPIRE 334–323 B.C.

Alexander's Empire
Route of Alexander, 334 B.C. – 323 B.C.
Cities founded by Alexander and his followers

SECTION REVIEW

1. How did the Peloponnesian War weaken Greece?

2. How did Philip gain control over Greece?

3. How did Macedonia's location in relation to Greece and the Middle East influence Alexander's goals?

4. Describe the major events of Alexander's conquests.

Synthesis. What strategies might Alexander have used to command the respect and loyalty of his troops for so many years and through such hardships?

5-2
THE CHANGING HELLENISTIC WORLD

READ TO FIND OUT

—what the term *hellenization* means.
—how Alexander stimulated cultural diffusion.
—how Alexander's empire was split up after his death.
—what form of government arose in most of the Hellenistic world.
—how economic growth occurred during Hellenistic times.

The political changes brought about by Alexander's conquests led to an economic and cultural transformation of the world known to the Greeks. Although many old ways of life remained unchanged, a great exchange of ideas took place among the various peoples in Alexander's empire. The blend of Greek ideas with those of other groups brought about a new culture in a large part of the ancient world during the Hellenistic Age.

A BLENDING OF CULTURES

A major result of Alexander's conquests and policies was a remarkable blending of Persian and Greek cultures. This sharing of ideas and traditions took place on a much larger scale and in a shorter time period than ever before. Scholars have called the process of spreading Greek influence **hellenization**. Similarly, Greek culture was influenced by the cultures of the East—Egypt, Persia, and India. Both of these processes are examples of cultural diffusion, or the exchange of ideas and ways of life between peoples of different regions.

To spread Greek influence, Alexander encouraged Greeks to settle in all parts of the empire. He established 70 new cities, many of which were named Alexandria or a variation of it. These cities had Greek constitutions and were settled by Greeks and Macedonians who followed the route of Alexander's conquests. Later on, these settlers married members of the local population and combined aspects of their different ways of life. Hellenization reached as far as India, where Greek sculpture styles influenced Indian art.

To help bring Persian culture to Greece and Macedonia, Alexander arranged the marriage of thousands of his men to Persian women at Susa. In a separate ceremony, eighty of his officers married the daughters of Persian nobles. He himself married the daughter of the dead Persian king Darius. Alexander also brought Persian soldiers into his army, wore Persian clothes, and followed many Persian customs. His officers, friends, and soldiers, however, were often disturbed to see him become so much like a Persian. Yet, Alexander was setting an important example for later rulers.

ALEXANDER AS RULER

In 324 B.C., when Alexander returned from India to the Persian royal city of Persepolis, he found his empire in disorder. He put down the revolts being staged in some cities and punished officials who had abused their power by stealing money and overtaxing the people.

His plan for ruling his large empire included a policy of maintaining local forms of government. He let the Greeks continue to rule through city-states. In Egypt, he ruled as a godlike king as the pharaohs had done. In Persia, he ruled through the control of the local governors, or satraps.

Rather than devoting his time to the business of ruling the empire, however, Alexander busied

The colossal sculptures from the tomb of a Seleucid ruler rest in present-day Turkey. These figures combine the naturalistic Greek style with Persian ideas of splendor.

himself with planning new explorations. On one expedition, which began only months after his return, his troops openly rebelled and demanded to be sent home. Alexander responded by executing the leaders and promising to let the veterans who had fought with him the longest return to Macedonia.

Alexander returned to Babylon in the spring of 323 B.C. There he organized an expedition to explore Arabia. Only a few days before he planned to leave, however, he caught a fever. Ten days later he could neither move nor speak. With no hope for his recovery, Alexander's soldiers filed through their leader's tent to say goodbye. The next day, just before his thirty-third birthday, Alexander died.

DIVIDING THE EMPIRE

After his death in 323 B.C., Alexander's generals fought among themselves for power. Eventually, after more than 20 years of conflict, the 3 rival generals divided the empire.

Seleucus (suh-LOO-kuhs) gained control of the huge provinces once making up the Persian Empire. He began what is called the Seleucid Dynasty. He and his descendants built many new cities, including the capital at Antioch in present-day Syria.

Ptolemy I (TAH-luh-mee) became ruler of Egypt, where he was considered a pharaoh. He established a great dynasty called the Ptolemaic, based in Alexandria. The last ruler of this dynasty was Cleopatra. When Cleopatra died in 30 B.C., the Ptolemaic Dynasty ended.

Antigonus I (an-TIHG-uh-nuhs) received the home territory of Greece and Macedonia, with its capital at Pella. He ruled Greece for a few years. Then most of the Greek city-states won their independence. The successors of Antigonus ruled Macedonia and influenced Greek politics until the 100s B.C.

In these new kingdoms, the democratic tradition of the Greek polis had little or no influence. Instead, the rulers governed with complete power over all their subjects, as the former kings and rulers had done in Persia and Egypt. The survival and spread of this form of government was one of the important ways in which Asia influenced the entire Hellenistic world.

In Egypt, the Ptolemaic rulers governed with the most complete authority over their subjects. They owned most of the land, controlled commerce, and taxed heavily. Seeing themselves as supreme rulers, the last Ptolemaic monarchs even began signing their laws with *theos*, the Greek word for "god."

During the Hellenistic Age, which lasted until the last century B.C., these kingdoms remained the most important political and military powers in the Hellenistic world. Boundaries shifted, smaller states acquired their independence, and wars were fought, but much of the Hellenistic world remained relatively stable. This stability was in part a result of the firm control the rulers had over their people.

ECONOMIC GROWTH DURING THE HELLENISTIC AGE

Alexander's conquests led to expanded trade between the Mediterranean world and East Africa, Arabia, India, and central Asia. For the first time, merchants from the Mediterranean traded with China for silk and spices. From throughout the Hellenistic world came a variety of resources that spurred economic growth. New industries grew up to process the newly available raw materials. New markets were opened up for food and craft products. Many merchants grew rich.

The enormous treasures of Persia captured by Alexander from such glittering cities as Persepolis were brought back to Macedonia and Greece. Once hoarded in palaces, the gold and jewels were now used in trade and commerce, exchanged like money. The increased wealth in circulation sparked an increase in investments. Governments, which controlled much of this great wealth, promoted trade and industry. Large tracts of agricultural land came under control of the state. Roads, harbors, and canals were built. Coins began to be used, replacing barter as a form of exchange. Banks became common in centers of commerce.

Although the Hellenistic Age was a period of prosperity, wealth was controlled by the rulers, the upper classes, and the merchants. Many peasants and workers in the cities lived in poverty as the gap between rich and poor widened. Wages dropped and the cost of living rose. Unemployment soared in major cities. Slavery declined partly because paying a free worker became cheaper than buying, feeding, and housing a slave.

African faces adorn this detail from a gold offering bowl made in the fourth century B.C. The bowl was fashioned northeast of Macedonia in Thrace, where Philip II leased gold mines. Bulgarian workers found the bowl in 1949. The faces may represent artisans or merchants. They are a reminder of the extensive economic and cultural links that existed between the Mediterranean world and Africa, Asia, and Europe in ancient times.

Cities grew faster in the Hellenistic Age than they ever had before. People flocked to the cities for entertainment and work as government and industry expanded. Antioch doubled its population twice in a century. The population of Alexandria swelled to perhaps one million. The economic center of the Hellenistic world shifted from Greece south and east to these two fast-growing commercial centers.

SECTION REVIEW

1. Define *hellenization*.

2. Give three examples of how cultures mixed in the Hellenistic world.

3. Describe the three dynasties established after Alexander's death.

4. Name three signs of economic growth in the Hellenistic world.

5. What form of government arose in lands once ruled by Alexander?

Analysis. Why did Alexander's empire break up after his death?

Data Search. Refer to the chart on page 828 to compare the roles of agriculture and trade in the following regions of Alexander's empire: Persia, Egypt, and Asia Minor. **(a)** In which region or regions was trade more important than agriculture? **(b)** In which region or regions was agriculture more important than trade?

5-3
CULTURAL ACHIEVEMENTS

READ TO FIND OUT

—what the terms *Epicureanism*, *Stoicism*, and *individualistic* mean.

—what the important characteristics of Hellenistic philosophy were.

—how Hellenistic achievements differed from those of Hellenic culture.

—how religious beliefs changed in the Hellenistic Age.

—what scientific developments occurred.

Political practices in the Hellenistic world had shifted away from the Greek democratic ideal. Economically, cities outside of Greece had become the centers of commerce and manufacturing. In areas of creative and intellectual achievement, however, the Greek tradition was still strong. As a result of hellenization, educated people throughout the Hellenistic world spoke Greek. Greek literature was taught in the schools, and styles of Greek architecture were used everywhere. In such a world of both Greek and non-Greek influences, philosophy, literature, art, and science developed differently than they had during Hellenic times.

PHILOSOPHY

Hellenic philosophers had concentrated on bringing order to the natural and human worlds. In contrast, most Hellenistic philosophers agreed that finding some way to get away from the evil and hardships of human life was most important. Two major philosophical beliefs emerged during this time.

Epicurus (EHP-uh-KYOOR-uhs), a philosopher who lived in Athens around 300 B.C., founded the philosophy called *Epicureanism* (EHP-ih-KYOOR-ee-uhn-izm). The basic belief of Epicureanism was that pleasure was the highest good. The goal of life was to avoid fear and pain. Epicureans believed that physical pleasures should be satisfied in moderation, and that mental pleasure and peace of mind were most important.

About the same time Epicurus lived in Athens, a philosopher named Zeno (ZEE-nō) founded a philosophy called *Stoicism* (STŌ-ih-sizm). Stoicism taught that human beings do not control what happens to them. Instead, fate, or destiny, controls the outcome of events in each person's life. People are free only to accept their fate or rebel against it. However, they cannot change it.

Stoics believed that happiness is achieved by accepting one's fate without bitterness or complaint. It was also important to Stoics to be tolerant and forgiving of other people. Slavery and war, they believed, were evil.

These philosophies had several important ideas in common. Both held that human problems could best be solved with reason instead of faith or belief in supernatural forces. This basic

In the first century B.C., a Hellenistic sculptor sought to capture in bronze the features and mood of an ordinary citizen from the Greek island of Delos. Hellenistic artists became interested in portraying human emotions realistically.

idea was inherited from the Hellenic philosophers. In addition, Stoicism and Epicureanism were both *individualistic*, which means they were concerned mainly with an individual's happiness, not the welfare or good of society. The individualism of these philosophies affected the art and literature of the time.

THE ARTS AND LITERATURE

Artists and writers had once been concerned with social issues such as politics, war, common hardships, and the deeds of heroes. Now their work often dealt with personal suffering and romance. Hellenistic artists began to portray people and things realistically, or as they were thought to actually be. Hellenistic realism replaced earlier Hellenic idealism, or love of perfection. Painting and sculpture became more detailed and were more apt to show emotion and drama.

Often even the unpleasant realities of everyday life were portrayed. Many art historians have pointed out that some of the works produced during this age tended to be exaggerated, grotesque, and overly sensational. Nevertheless, many great works, such as the famous statue of the winged goddess Victory, survive from this period.

In literature, many new authors produced a rapidly growing amount of material. Among the many outstanding Hellenistic writers was Theocritus (thee-AHK-rih-tuhs), who wrote poetry about rural life and country landscapes. Menander, who wrote comedies, was among the greatest writers of the time. His plays were very different from the plays of Aristophanes. Instead of satires critical of political figures, Menander wrote comedies that realistically portrayed romance, marriage, and other everyday experiences. Later poets and writers imitated the works of Menander and Theocritus.

GREEK THEATER

"The perfect day for theater!" exclaims a man dressed in a noble's robes, as he places his cushion on a stone seat already warm from the morning sun. Hundreds of people have already claimed the best seats in the huge, outdoor Theater of Dionysus, which stands below the Acropolis. For days Athenians rich and poor have been chattering excitedly about Menander's new comedy. It is one of five plays to be presented on this festival day.

More people file in, slowly filling the 14,000-seat stadium. They sit in circular rows set on the slopes of a bowl-shaped valley, looking down to a circular acting area called the orchestra. Behind the orchestra is a long building where the actors change costumes. The side of the building facing the audience is painted as background scenery for the plays.

As the comedy begins, the theatergoers cheer their favorites, hiss the actors who perform poorly, sip on beverages, and nibble on fruit and nuts. At the end of the day, the best actors and the best playwrights win prizes.

Greek drama gave birth to the theater as it is known today. At first, the performers only sang and danced to musical accompaniment. They were called the chorus. Then Thespis, a chorus director, had the idea of giving himself spoken lines, a very startling innovation to the Greeks.

From Thespis comes *thespian*, another word for actor often used today. Over time, actors who played speaking parts became more important in the performance, while the chorus became less important. By Menander's time, the chorus sang only during the parts of the play when actors left the stage to change costumes.

Only males appeared in Greek plays, taking the roles of both men and women. All actors wore masks, and these were often beautifully carved and painted to represent male and female deities. The mask might wear a scowl or a smile, depending on what character the actor was portraying. Because masks covered their faces, the actors had to be very skilled in the use of hand and arm gestures to convey the play's meaning. They also had to be sure to project their voices. The masks had brass mouthpieces that helped them do this. In the stadium theaters, however, the acoustics were so good that even the people sitting in the uppermost row are said to have been able to hear a performer's quiet sigh.

Out of the hundreds of plays that Greeks wrote and performed throughout the Hellenistic Age, only a few have survived. Those that have been passed down, however, have been translated into most modern languages. These plays continue to rank among the world's finest literary achievements.

RELIGION

Religious belief also changed during the Hellenistic Age. Many people began to give up their belief in the polytheism of the Greeks. Some people adopted one of the new philosophies as a sort of religion, using it as a source of guidelines for correct and moral behavior. Others began to practice religions, such as Zoroastrianism, that had come from Asia or the Middle East. The Egyptian mother-goddess, Isis, became the center of a rapidly growing religion at this time.

People began turning away from Greek polytheism for many reasons. One important reason was that they sought a more complete system of beliefs about right and wrong than the very humanlike Greek deities could offer. They also searched for comfort in a belief in life after death.

SCIENCE

In the Hellenic Age, philosophy and science had been closely related. Both had been ways of finding order in the natural world. Many leading thinkers, such as Aristotle, were both philosophers and scientists. In the Hellenistic Age, however, philosophy and science parted ways. Philosophy concerned itself with personal happiness, while science became more practical and technical. Building on past knowledge, Hellenistic scientists made discoveries that caused later scholars to call this period the "first great age of science."

Indirectly, Alexander the Great was responsible for much of the growth of science during this time. He had always had a love for science, acquired while being tutored by Aristotle. Because of this interest, Alexander made sure that botanists, historians, geographers, and surveyors accompanied him on his military exploits, which he considered scientific explorations as well. He ordered that scientific observations and objects of interest be reported to his former teacher, Aristotle. Alexander's interest in science set an example for later rulers.

After Alexander, scientific and intellectual pursuits were encouraged by other Hellenistic kings, who used some of their vast wealth to support scientists and libraries. The best examples of this effort were the libraries at Alexandria in Egypt and Pergamum in Asia Minor. The library at Alexandria, begun by Alexander's general Ptolemy, contained perhaps 750,000 papyrus scrolls, and became one of the major centers of Hellenistic learning.

In the Hellenistic Age, people also became more interested in new engineering and technology. They wanted to produce goods and foods more efficiently in order to increase wealth. Blending Greek learning with Egyptian and Persian science contributed to Hellenistic achievements in science and technology.

Astronomy. The first person to understand the enormous size of the universe was an astronomer named Aristarchus (AR-ihs-TAHR-kuhs), who was born on the Aegean island of Samos. His most notable theory rejected the accepted

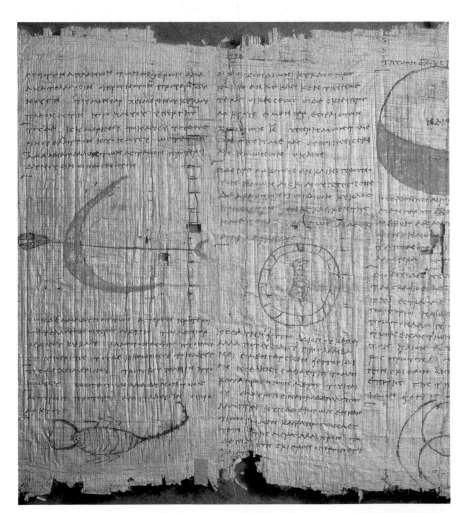

This fragment of a scroll is part of a treatise, or methodical study, of planetary movement about the sun. The scroll originated in ancient Alexandria about the third century B.C. Such works bear witness to early astronomical discoveries.

belief that the earth was the center of the universe and instead stated that the earth revolved around the sun. This theory was not generally accepted until nearly 2,000 years later. Eratosthenes (EHR-uh-TAHS-thuh-NEEZ), another astronomer, was the first to believe that the earth was spherical, not flat. He made an amazingly accurate estimate of the earth's circumference, with an error of only 1 percent. He also produced the most accurate world map made up to that time and suggested that a ship could reach India by sailing west.

Mathematics and physics. Euclid (YOO-klid), who taught in Alexandria during the rule of Ptolemy I, is the most famous of Hellenistic mathematicians. Although he made few original discoveries, his book *Elements of Geometry* pulled together existing ideas. It remained the basis of geometry for nearly 2,000 years after his death. Hipparchus (hih-PAHR-kuhs), another mathematician who worked in Alexandria, made many discoveries about trigonometry.

Perhaps the most famous of Hellenistic scientists was Archimedes (AR-kuh-MEE-deez), who was born about 287 B.C. in Syracuse, a former Greek colony on the island of Sicily. Exploring the principles of the lever, pulley, and screw, he invented a tubular screw for pumping water, lifting devices using more than one pulley, and the screw propeller for ships. Once, using a system of levers and pulleys, Archimedes single-handedly pulled a loaded ship from water onto land. He supposedly once said, "Give me a lever long enough, and a place to stand on, and I will move the world."

Although Archimedes was famous in his time for his inventions, he considered his theoretical works in mathematics and astronomy to be more important. One of the first scientists to base his ideas on experimentation, Archimedes made discoveries about the laws of physics and the principles of mathematics that still remain valid today.

Medicine. Herophilus (heh-RAHF-ih-luhs), who did his research in Alexandria in the 200s B.C., was probably the first physician to practice human dissection. Through this process he made discoveries about the blood, arteries, heart, and brain. His best-known successor was Erasistratus (AIR-a-SIHS-tra-tuhs), a Greek who also lived in Alexandria. Erasistratus established physiology, the study of the life processes and functions of living things, as a separate science. He discovered the valves of the heart, found two different kinds of nerves, and fought the common practice of bleeding people in order to heal them.

SECTION REVIEW

1. Define **Epicureanism**, **Stoicism**, and *individualistic*.

2. What basic ideas did the two major Hellenistic philosophies share?

3. How did Hellenistic art differ from Hellenic art?

4. How did religious beliefs change during the Hellenistic Age?

5. In what four areas of science did Hellenistic scientists make notable contributions?

Evaluation. Does cultural diffusion contribute to intellectual and scientific achievement? Give evidence to back up your answer.

HISTORY IN FOCUS

Alexander the Great's dream of uniting the known world under one rule and one culture was never realized. His attempt to do so, however, changed a large part of the world. Because of the expansion of trade and the exchange of ideas through cultural diffusion, many people in the eastern Mediterranean could, for the first time, experience a world larger than their own city-state.

With its economic growth and blending of cultures, Hellenistic civilization hinted at what would develop nearly 2,000 years later. Businesses grew, cities swelled, slums developed, and the divisions between rich and poor widened. Interest grew in technological development, material wealth, individualism, and realistic art.

These trends and developments molded the civilizations that followed. In the Mediterranean region, Hellenistic civilization carried on the achievements of Hellenic civilization and brought elements of Middle Eastern culture to the West. It also provided the environment in which a new and even more influential civilization arose and grew to power. That civilization was Rome.

CHAPTER SURVEY

SUMMARY

- In 404 B.C., Athens lost the Peloponnesian War to an alliance of city-states led by Sparta. Feuding among the city-states left Greece vulnerable to invasion.

- To the north in Macedonia, Philip II built a strong army and weakened the city-states. In 338 B.C., he took control of Greece.

- A great admirer of Hellenic culture, Philip's successor, Alexander, set out to build a great empire and spread Greek culture.

- After Alexander's death in 323 B.C., his empire split into three areas: the provinces that were once the Persian Empire, Egypt, and Greece and Macedonia.

- Alexander's conquests generated great wealth, but the gap between rich and poor widened. The state began to take a more active economic role, and cities grew rapidly. The center of the Mediterranean world shifted south and east from Greece.

- Two new forms of philosophy emerged—Epicureanism and Stoicism. These philosophies began to replace the traditional polytheism of Greece. They also infused art and literature with realism and an emphasis on the individual, rather than on society.

- Science became increasingly oriented toward practical and technical concerns. Great advances were made in astronomy, mathematics, physics, and medicine.

VOCABULARY REVIEW

Match each numbered vocabulary term with the lettered word or phrase most closely related to it. Then explain how the items in each pair are related.

Example: The term *phalanx* can be associated with *war* because *phalanx* was the name given to the Macedonian battle strategy of organizing soldiers in lines.

1. hellenization	(a) fatalistic
2. Epicureanism	(b) cultural diffusion
3. Stoicism	(c) pleasure
4. individualistic	(d) self-interest

CHAPTER REVIEW

1. (a) Explain what caused the Peloponnesian War. (b) What impact did the war have on Greek society? On politics?

2. (a) What two main effects did Philip II's years as a hostage in Thebes have on him? (b) What tactics did Philip use to weaken the city-states?

3. (a) What was Alexander's political goal? (b) What part did cultural diffusion play in that goal? (c) Why was Alexander's army welcomed in Egypt? (d) What prevented him from conquering all of India?

4. (a) How did the rule of Alexander differ in the various parts of his empire? (b) How did he ensure control and loyalty in the lands that he conquered?

5. (a) List three ways in which Alexander promoted hellenization. (b) List three ways in which Persian influence was brought to Greece and Macedonia.

6. (a) How were the three major divisions of the empire governed after Alexander's death? (b) How did these governments reflect Asian influence? (c) Which government was the most authoritarian? Explain.

7. (a) How did Alexander's conquests stimulate trade and industry? (b) Explain how economic developments widened the gap between rich and poor, yet discouraged slavery. (c) Give four examples of increasing state control of the economy. (d) How did the state's expanded role promote urbanization?

8. (a) How did the philosophies of Epicureanism and Stoicism represent a break with Hellenic thought? (b) Why did Epicureanism and Stoicism replace traditional polytheism for some Greeks?

9. (a) What two major trends were reflected in Hellenistic art and literature? (b) How did these trends mark a departure from the Hellenic period? Give examples.

10. (a) How did Alexander encourage scientific inquiry? (b) What effect did economic growth have on science? (c) Describe three achievements of Hellenistic scientists.

THINKING CRITICALLY: ACTIVITIES

1. The democratic tradition of the Greek polis had little or no influence in the territories divided by Alexander's generals after his death. Instead, Seleucus, Ptolemy, and Antigonus governed with complete power over their subjects, as the former kings and rulers had done. Divide into groups of four or five to discuss what conditions would have had to change for democratic rule to have prevailed in these lands.

2. One of the hallmarks of the Hellenistic Age was the blending of different cultures. Does the incorporation of different cultures and customs into a nation strengthen or weaken that society? Write a paragraph expressing an argument in favor of one side of the issue. Support your argument with material from the chapter.

APPLYING SOCIAL STUDIES SKILLS

Reading maps. The map titled "Alexander's Empire" on page 99 provides a visual record of Alexander's empire-building activities. Decide whether each statement below is **(a)** supported by the information provided on this map or **(b)** not supported by the map.

1. Alexander's empire stretched from the Black Sea south to the Red Sea.

2. The empire circled the Mediterranean Sea.

3. From west to east the empire extended about 9,000 miles (14,400 kilometers).

4. The empire included the Fertile Crescent, the Nile River valley, the Indus River valley, and the shores of the eastern Mediterranean.

5. Alexander's military campaign lasted more than ten years.

6. Alexander began his campaign of conquest in the city of Babylon.

7. Alexander and his followers founded many new cities named after him.

8. A large and powerful navy was an essential part of Alexander's military campaign.

9. Alexander died in 323 B.C.

10. After Alexander's death, his empire was divided among his generals.

APPLYING THINKING SKILLS

Comparing and contrasting. The following items were found in a Macedonian tomb that dates from Hellenistic times. The front of the tomb had a mural painting about 12 feet (3.6 meters) in length depicting a lion or boar hunt, showing hunting dogs, riders, and people on foot. Compare and contrast what was found in this tomb with the objects found in the Syrian tomb, which are listed on page 23. Then answer the questions that follow.

silver vessels with decorated handles

a gold and silver headband

iron javelin points

a gold box topped with a gold wreath and gold acorns

a long cylinder of bamboo wrapped in cloth and gold

an iron helmet decorated with figures of Athena

bronze vessels

a piece of iron body armor covered with gold strips

remains of a shield decorated with gold and silver, with silver handles

a sword in a wooden sheath decorated with gold and silver bands

an iron harness

1. What does it mean to compare items? What does it mean to contrast items?

2. Describe the procedure for comparing and contrasting items.

3. What kinds of objects were found in both the Syrian tomb and the Macedonian tomb?

4. What does the presence of these objects suggest about the social status of the people buried in these tombs?

5. What kinds of objects were found in one tomb and not in the other?

6. Based on the objects in the tombs, what seem to be the major similarities and major differences between the societies and times that they represent?

CHAPTER SIX

ROMAN CIVILIZATION

1000 B.C.–A.D. 180

A consul's parade. Roman hall of justice mural, about 340 B.C.

Beginning as a small farming village on the Italian peninsula around 1000 B.C., Rome had grown into a strong city-state by the time of Alexander's conquests. As Hellenistic civilization declined, Rome expanded. By A.D. 14, Rome had taken the lead in shaping the Mediterranean world.

The Romans conquered the western half of what had been Alexander's empire. They also pushed much farther west and north than the Greeks ever had, forging a vast empire. From the British Isles to North Africa to the Euphrates River, the proudest claim of many people was "I am a Roman citizen." In preserving Greek cultural achievements, and developing their own distinctive government, law, and culture, the Romans left a lasting imprint on Western civilization.

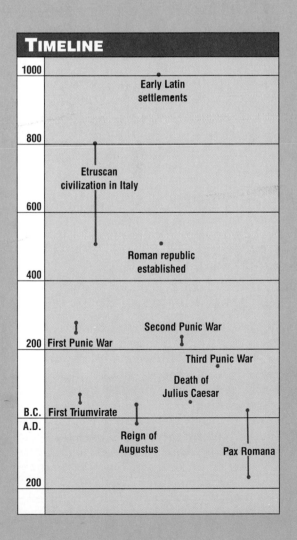

TIMELINE

1000	
	Early Latin settlements
800	
	Etruscan civilization in Italy
600	
	Roman republic established
400	
200	First Punic War / Second Punic War
	Third Punic War / Death of Julius Caesar
B.C.	First Triumvirate
A.D.	Reign of Augustus / Pax Romana
200	

6-1
RISE OF THE ROMAN REPUBLIC

READ TO FIND OUT

—what the terms *forum*, *republic*, *patricians*, and *plebeians* mean.
—how geography affected early Roman civilization.
—how the Etruscans and Greeks influenced the Romans.
—how the Roman republican form of government worked.
—what the different roles of men and women were in Roman society.
—how Roman religion was based on two different sets of deities.

As in Greece, several different groups of people, with different but related cultures, moved into Italy during its early history. By the 400s B.C., however, the Romans had emerged as a dominant group. During the next two centuries they developed the foundations of a system of law, a form of government, a military structure, and a distinctive way of life. These institutions later became influential forces in the growth of a Roman empire.

THE ITALIAN PENINSULA: THE NATURAL SETTING

The Italian peninsula juts far into the Mediterranean Sea. The island of Sicily, located off the southern tip of the peninsula, serves as a stepping-stone to the coast of North Africa, 80 miles (128 kilometers) away.

Most of the peninsula is hilly and mountainous. The Alps circle the northern end of Italy, while the Apennines (AP-uh-NEENZ) run like a backbone through the length of the peninsula. In the east, the Apennines drop sharply to the Mediterranean Sea. Because of the rugged landscape here, there are no good harbors. By contrast, in the west the mountains descend gently. Here a number of good harbors provide safety for sailing vessels.

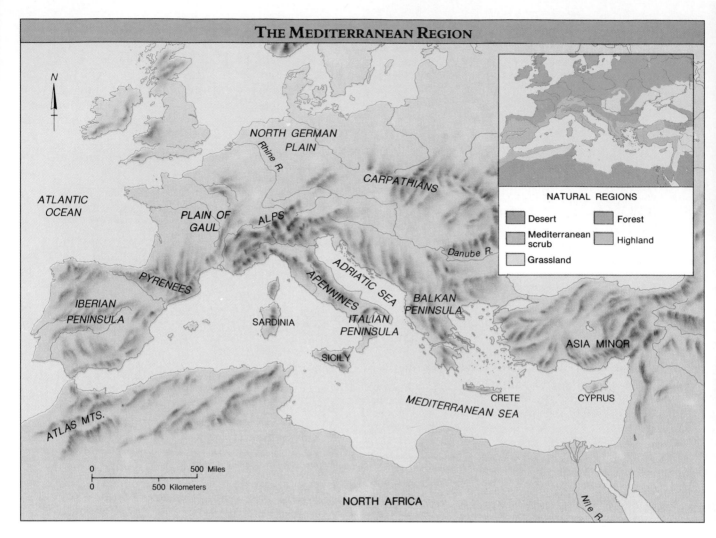

THE MEDITERRANEAN REGION

N

NORTH GERMAN PLAIN

Rhine R.

CARPATHIANS

ATLANTIC OCEAN

PLAIN OF GAUL

ALPS

Danube R.

PYRENEES

APENNINES

ADRIATIC SEA

BALKAN PENINSULA

IBERIAN PENINSULA

SARDINIA

ITALIAN PENINSULA

SICILY

ASIA MINOR

ATLAS MTS.

MEDITERRANEAN SEA

CRETE

CYPRUS

0   500 Miles

0   500 Kilometers

NORTH AFRICA

Nile R.

NATURAL REGIONS

Desert

Forest

Mediterranean scrub

Highland

Grassland

The Italian peninsula's location at the center of the Mediterranean region was ideal for establishing an empire. The Middle East, Greece, Spain, and North Africa were within easy reach of Rome by sea. Passes through the Alps gave Roman soldiers access to central and western Europe.

However, just as Rome could easily reach the world, so too could the world easily invade Rome. Foreign enemies could march through the mountain passes or land with no difficulty along the peninsula's unprotected west coast. For this reason, the inhabitants of Italy focused on building a strong military to protect themselves from attack. Domination by force was always more common than peaceful mixing of immigrants and early settlers.

Compared to Greece, Italy had more fertile land, most of it along the west coast. With fewer good harbors, the inhabitants of Italy relied more on farming than did the seafaring Greeks.

EARLY HISTORY OF ROME

About 1200 B.C., Indo-Europeans began invading the lands around the Mediterranean. One group, the Dorians, moved into the Balkan peninsula. Other groups entered the Italian peninsula. The Latins, the most important of these invaders, settled in Latium, the plains region of central Italy. About 1000 B.C., according to current archaeological evidence, the Latins founded settlements on seven hills overlooking the Tiber River. In time these settlements were united into the city of Rome.

Rome was located about 15 miles (24 kilometers) inland from the west coast. The Tiber

River provided access to the sea, while the city's inland location protected it from attack by sea. In the fertile plains surrounding Rome, the Latins created a society based on farming. Agriculture remained the basis of the Roman economy even after Rome became a great power.

The Etruscans. About the eighth century B.C., a new group of immigrants moved into the Italian peninsula, probably from Asia Minor. They are known as Etruscans (ih-TRUHS-kuhnz). At first, they lived north of the Tiber, in a group of strong city-states resembling those of Greece. Then, in the sixth century B.C., they moved south across the river and conquered Rome. The Etruscans set up a monarchy that lasted more than a century.

The Etruscans, whose way of life was similar to that of the Greeks, contributed a great deal to Roman civilization. They taught the Romans how to use the arch in building and how to drain the swamps at the banks of the Tiber. On the drained land, the Romans set up a *forum*, a public square similar to the agora in a Greek city-state. The forum contained law courts, government buildings, and a marketplace. In addition, the Romans learned the Phoenician alphabet from the Etruscans, who had adopted it from the Greeks. The Romans changed the alphabet to fit their own Latin language. The Roman alphabet later became a basis of many of the world's major languages, including modern-day English, French, and Spanish.

The Greek influence. During the period of Greek colonization between 750 B.C. and 500 B.C., Greek settlers established many towns in southern Italy and on the island of Sicily. The most important of these colonies were Syracuse on Sicily and Naples on the mainland. Each colony became an independent city-state. By 500 B.C., Greek civilization in Italy had become as advanced as that in Greece itself. Many famous Greeks, such as Pythagoras and Archimedes, lived in the Italian colonies, which became centers of trade, commerce, and learning. The Greek presence in Italy during the early development of Roman culture ensured that later Roman civilization would bear the stamp of Greece. Romans derived much of their art and mythology, and many of their religious ideas from the Greeks.

Tomb paintings recorded Etruscan customs. Entertainers at a lavish funeral banquet are shown in this fifth century B.C. wall decoration from Tarquinia, the chief Etruscan city-state.

ESTABLISHING THE REPUBLIC

In 509 B.C., the Romans overthrew the Etruscan monarchy and established a *republic*. In a republic, citizens elect representatives to run the government. The Roman Republic lasted almost 500 years. During this time, Rome became the leading power in the Mediterranean region. Though the republic of Rome was eventually replaced by a different form of government, the distinctive features of the republican system were largely responsible for Rome's success as a civilization.

The structure of government. To prevent one person from taking control, the Romans divided power among different branches of government. The first branch consisted of several magistrates, or ruling officials. The top two magistrates, called consuls, were elected for one year. The consuls administered the laws and controlled military affairs. Under the consuls

were judges called praetors (PREE-tuhrz), who defined and interpreted the law. Under the praetors were officials called censors, who collected taxes. In times of emergency, the consuls could choose a dictator, who held absolute power for six months.

The consuls were chosen by the second branch of government, the Senate. The Senate consisted of 300 wealthy landowners who served for life. It had the power to decide foreign policy, approve contracts for building temples and roads, propose laws, and handle the daily problems of government.

The third branch of government was the Assembly, which was much weaker than the Senate. It met infrequently and could not propose laws, only vote to approve or reject them.

Social structure. At first, the republic was completely controlled by an upper class called the *patricians*. Consuls, officials, senators, and most Assembly members were patricians. These wealthy landowners made up about 10 percent of Rome's population, not including slaves. The remaining 90 percent were nearly excluded from political life. This group, known as *plebeians* (plih-BEE-uhnz), consisted of farmers, merchants, laborers, and artisans.

Plebeians faced many restrictions. For example, they were forbidden to marry patricians, and they could be enslaved if they failed to pay their debts. In addition, because Roman laws were unwritten, plebeians were often punished for breaking rules they never knew existed.

THE PLEBEIAN STRUGGLE FOR REFORM

The plebeians, who had little power, had one advantage: numbers. As the republic expanded, the patricians began to rely more and more on plebeians to fill the ranks of the army. By threatening not to fight unless reforms were made, the plebeians gradually won many rights.

In about 494 B.C., the plebeians were able to force the creation of a new assembly called the Council of Plebeians to represent their interests in the government. The Council of Plebeians elected officials—at first two and then eventually ten—called tribunes. Tribunes could veto any acts of the Senate or of the consuls that directly affected the plebeians.

In response to plebeian demands, around 450 B.C., Roman laws were collected and written

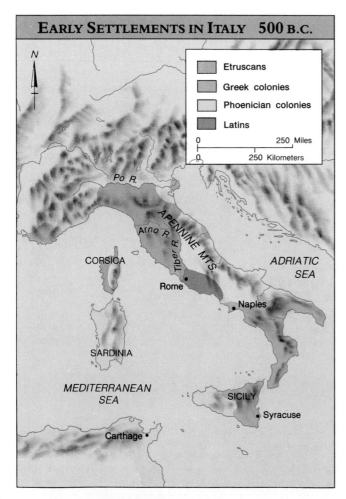

EARLY SETTLEMENTS IN ITALY 500 B.C.

N

Etruscans
Greek colonies
Phoenician colonies
Latins

0   250 Miles
0   250 Kilometers

Po R.

APENNINE MTS.

Arno R.

Tiber R.

CORSICA

Rome

ADRIATIC SEA

Naples

SARDINIA

MEDITERRANEAN SEA

SICILY

Syracuse

Carthage

RECOGNIZING RELEVANT INFORMATION

While information is important in understanding any subject, not just any information will do. To be useful, information must be relevant to the topic, problem, or issue being discussed or studied. Anything that is relevant to something applies, relates, or is connected to it in some way. Whatever does not apply or relate to it is said to be irrelevant. For example, a baseball player's batting average is relevant to determining how good the player is. The color of the player's uniform, however, is irrelevant to this topic. Distinguishing relevant information from irrelevant information is an important first step in understanding any topic.

EXPLAINING THE SKILL

One way to distinguish relevant information from irrelevant information is to follow these steps:

1. *Identify clearly the subject, problem, or issue you are focusing on.*

2. *Identify the general kinds of information that might be relevant to it—such as details about it, examples of it, explanations of it, evidence for or against it, or definitions of it.*

3. *Examine each piece of information to determine whether it is relevant.*

APPLYING THE SKILL

Use the above procedure to help you determine which of the following laws of the Twelve Tables are most relevant to this statement: "Early Romans did not believe in the equality of all people."

A. When a debt or court award is not paid within a given time, the debtor may be punished with death or sold across the Tiber.

B. Deformed offspring may be put to death by the father.

C. A father shall, during his whole life, have absolute power over his children. He may imprison or sell his son, or put him to death.

D. All women shall be under the authority of a guardian.

E. Length of possession by a non-citizen cannot give him title to property as against a Roman citizen.

F. Things sold and delivered shall not become the property of the buyer until he has paid or otherwise satisfied the seller.

G. Holders of property along a road shall maintain the road to keep it passable; but if it be impassable, anyone may drive his beast or cart where he wishes.

H. For breaking or bruising a freedman's bone with hand or club, the fine shall be 300 pieces [Roman coins]; if a slave's bone, 150 pieces.

I. Branches of a tree may be lopped off all round to a height of not more than 15 feet. Should a tree on a neighbor's farm be bent crooked by a wind and lean over your farm, action may be taken for removal of that tree.

J. If a person sings a song that insults another person, he shall be clubbed to death.

MAKING MEANING

Answer the following questions, using what you have learned through identifying the relevant laws.

1. Which group of laws is most relevant to the statement? **(a)** C-D-H, **(b)** B-E-G, **(c)** A-C-F.

2. Which group of laws is irrelevant to the statement? **(a)** A-B-C, **(b)** A-F-G, **(c)** C-G-H.

3. Which group of laws is most relevant to business dealings in early Rome?
(a) D-G-H, **(b)** C-F-H, **(c)** A-E-F.

4. According to the laws included here, Roman society **(a)** did not respect private property, **(b)** was generous and humane, **(c)** was male-dominated.

REVIEWING THE SKILL

5. What does the term *relevant* mean?

6. What kinds of information are usually relevant to a particular topic?

7. Why is it important to recognize relevant information?

LIFE IN ROMAN TIMES

Beneath the volcanic ash that buried the towns of Pompeii and Herculaneum when nearby Mount Vesuvius erupted in A.D. 79 lay artifacts and ruins that paint a colorful picture of everyday life in Roman times. The rock-strewn remains of other Roman cities have also provided reminders of the lives of the people who once lived there. These relics all tell us that city streets once stirred with a wide variety of activities as Romans went about their daily lives. Escaping from the concerns of republic and empire, the well-to-do retreated to elegant homes decorated with brightly painted or tiled scenes, realistically rendered.

Pompeiian boy, painted marble, A.D. 62

Hand-blown glass, A.D. 50-200

Dining room, Herculaneum, A.D. 79

Garden mural, Augustan villa

Baker's oven and corn mills, Pompeii

Pompeiian bread shop

Theatrical troupe mosaic, poet's house, Pompeii

Musicians, floor mosaic, 100 B.C.

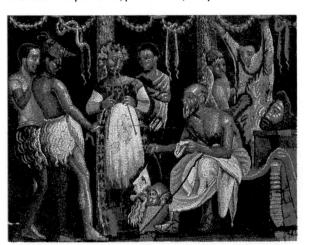

down on 12 bronze tablets displayed in the forum. The Twelve Tables, as these tablets were called, made it possible for all to know and understand the laws. Plebeians also won the right to marry patricians, and enslavement for debt was prohibited. Eventually, plebeians also won the right to hold any office, including that of consul.

Despite their gains, the plebeians did not change Roman government significantly. As in Greece, an aristocracy—the patricians—continued to exercise the most power. The Roman Republic also remained relatively undemocratic. Unlike politics in the Greek polis, Roman politics was not direct, or participatory, but representative. Most citizens had no direct say in political decisions. Unlike Athenians, Romans generally believed, according to one historian, that the people "were not to govern but to be governed." In practice, the Senate ruled with great authority, unchallenged even by the Council of Plebeians.

THE ROMAN FAMILY

While Roman government and political life were developing the patterns that would guide Rome's later history, the basic forms of social life had fallen into place as well. The most important social unit of the Roman Republic was the extended family. The Roman family usually included unmarried children, married sons and their families, and grandparents. Among patrician families, there were also servants, who were know as "familiars."

The father was the head of the household. Under Roman law, he had the power of life or death over all its members. The father taught his children to value hard work, and to be loyal, courageous, and disciplined. At the age of seven, wealthier boys went to school, where they studied such subjects as history and public speaking. When they reached the age of seventeen, boys were considered adults and had to serve in the army.

Women in Roman society. Girls were taught by their mothers to cook, spin, and weave. Girls from wealthier families also learned to paint, sing, dance, and play musical instruments such as the lyre and the flute. When they were six, they went to school to learn how to read and write.

The girl is using a marking device—a stylus—to write on a wax tablet. This fresco was likely a bridal portrait. In keeping with Roman custom, it adorned a wall in her home.

Whatever their economic background, Roman girls were usually engaged to be married at about the age of ten. The marriage was arranged by the father and took place when the bride was in her midteens.

Roman women of all social classes had the responsibility of managing the household and raising the children. In addition, many plebeian women worked. Inscriptions on old Roman tombstones show that women were employed as servants, weavers, seamstresses, merchants, and physicians.

As in Greece, women in Rome were legally subordinate to men—first to their fathers, then to their husbands. Women could neither vote nor hold public office. Despite the often good education many women received, few Roman women were allowed to act as the equals of men in politics, art, or philosophy. As a result, few achievements by Roman women were recorded in history.

Most astonishing, perhaps, is the fact that Roman women had no real names of their own. Instead, they were given family names, based on their fathers' name. A daughter in the Julian family, for instance, would be called "Julia." If a second daughter were born, she would be called "Julia the younger."

ROMAN RELIGIOUS LIFE

Religion was a vital part of both public and family life. The Romans originally worshipped spirits they believed existed in nature and in their homes. These spirits had to be kept friendly through ritual and sacrifice. The most important of these spirits were the lares (LAY-reez) and penates (pih-NAY-teez), the guardian spirits of the household. The lares watched over the land outside the house. Each household had one lar. The penates, which were the spirits of the storeroom, protected the food in the cupboards. There were always two penates in each household. The lares and penates were represented by statues, before which the Romans placed offerings.

Religious influences from other cultures. In time, contacts with other peoples added more layers to Roman beliefs. As a result of Etruscan influence, the Romans began to give human qualities to their spirits. Romans adopted new deities and imagined them to look and act like humans. Jupiter, originally an Etruscan god similar to the Greek god Zeus, became the pa-tron god of Rome. A great temple was built in his honor. Religious ideas and deities of the Persians and Egyptians also became part of the Romans' religious practices.

The state religion. Eventually, an official state religion emerged out of early Roman beliefs and the borrowed beliefs of other cultures, especially Greek culture. The Romans developed a pantheon, or set of deities, modeled after the Greek pantheon. It was made up of Roman gods, such as Janus, the god of doorways and gates, as well as many Greek deities. The Romans, for instance, borrowed Athena and called her Minerva. Likewise, Poseidon was named Neptune. Jupiter, whom the Romans had already adopted as a major deity, became the father of the gods, as Zeus had been for the Greeks.

Temples were built for individual gods and goddesses, and public festivals and games were held in their honor. As in Greece, honoring the deities demonstrated loyalty to the state. Still later, when emperors ruled Rome, their statues were publicly displayed, and people were expected to worship them as gods.

From left, the Roman hero Hercules and the state deities Minerva, Bacchus, Jupiter, Ceres, Juno, and Mercury gather to welcome an emperor's entourage in this detail from a triumphal arch.

1. Define *forum*, *republic*, *patricians*, and *plebeians*.

2. How did the geography of Italy help Rome become a great civilization?

3. What did the Romans learn from their contact with the Etruscans?

4. In what ways was power shared in the Roman Republic? What groups were excluded?

5. In what ways did the Roman family control the role of women in society?

6. How did Roman religious beliefs change over time?

Analysis. Provide examples from the chapter to support the following: The class division between patricians and plebeians was based on important Roman values and traditions.

6-2
FROM REPUBLIC TO EMPIRE

READ TO FIND OUT

—what the terms *mercenaries* and *latifundia* mean.
—why the Roman army was an effective force.
—what the causes and results of the Punic Wars were.
—how Roman citizens tried to reform society.
—what the effects of Roman expansion were.
—how Julius Caesar came to power.

During the first few centuries of the republic, Rome expanded its territory in a nearly endless series of wars. After taking over Italy in 264 B.C., Rome set its sights on the rest of the Mediterranean. When it defeated its major rival Carthage, Rome grew in power. In time, troubles at home weakened the political system, and an emperor took over. This change in rule set the stage for further growth of what became known as the Roman Empire.

CONQUEST OF THE ITALIAN PENINSULA

After defeating the Etruscans in 509 B.C., the Romans began to conquer territory beyond their city's boundaries. First they overran Etruscan cities north of the Tiber River. Then they conquered territories beyond the Etruscan lands. In southern Italy, Romans attacked the Greek city-states. At first, the Romans lost battles with the Greek general Pyrrhus (PIHR-uhs), but they killed so many Greek soldiers that the Greeks were eventually forced to flee. By 264 B.C., Rome controlled the entire Italian peninsula.

To strengthen their control over the conquered areas of Italy, the Romans used skillful diplomacy. Unlike the Egyptians, Assyrians, and Persians, they did not demand slaves or payments, called tribute, from the people they conquered. Instead, most conquered cities were allowed to keep their own governments, laws, and ways of life.

One of the Romans' most successful policies was to let many of the people they conquered become Roman citizens. This policy worked well in ensuring loyalty to Rome. In general, the Romans became known throughout Italy as mild rulers, and because of this good will, built up strong friendships and alliances with all the peoples of the Italian peninsula.

THE ROMAN ARMY

Rome's success depended not only on its diplomatic policies but on its well-organized and disciplined army. Eventually, every adult male citizen was required to serve in the Roman army. In fact, no man could be a candidate for public office until he had completed ten years of military service. Patricians and wealthy plebeians furnished their own equipment and served without pay. Other citizens who served as soldiers received a small salary.

The Roman army was divided into units known as legions, which contained from 4,500 to 6,000 men. Each legion was divided into smaller groups of 60 to 120 legionaries, as the soldiers were called. Because these smaller groups could separate and attack an enemy from the sides and rear as well as the front, the Roman army had much maneuverability.

Roman legionaries were highly trained and disciplined. Complete obedience to orders was

Legionaries on horseback and on foot do battle with invading barbarians in this marble coffin panel of about A.D. 250. Show of military power was a central theme of Roman art.

expected. Every day the legionaries went on forced marches, and every night they built a fortified camp in which to sleep. They spent many hours practicing the use of their double-edged iron swords. A soldier who was guilty of cowardice in battle was stoned to death, and it was taken for granted that a sentry never deserted his post.

THE WARS WITH CARTHAGE

While Roman armies moved through Italy, a large empire in North Africa, with its capital in Carthage, was building its military power, too. Carthage had been founded about 800 B.C. by the Phoenicians. The Carthaginians were excellent sailors, and by the third century B.C. they had replaced the Greeks as the leading traders of the Mediterranean.

The Carthaginians became Rome's major rivals. With the money that they earned from trade, the Carthaginians fielded large armies of **mercenaries**, or paid soldiers from other lands, commanded by Carthaginian generals. Car-

thage soon controlled large areas along the northern coast of Africa and the southern coast of Spain.

Rome and Carthage fought three wars between 264 and 146 B.C. These conflicts are known as the Punic Wars, after *Punici* (pyoo-NEE-chee), the Latin word for Phoenicians.

The First Punic War was set off by competition for the island of Sicily. Fighting broke out in 264 B.C. and lasted for 23 years. In 241 B.C., Rome was victorious and took over Sicily, which became Rome's first province, or territory, outside the Italian peninsula.

The Second Punic War began in 218 B.C. The Carthaginian general Hannibal led his army of 50,000 soldiers and 37 elephants across Spain and through the passes in the Alps to invade Italy from the north. Hannibal spent 15 years fighting in Italy, never losing a single battle. When a Roman army invaded North Africa in 203 B.C., however, Hannibal was forced to withdraw to defend Carthage. A year later, in a battle at Zama, near Carthage, Hannibal was defeated by forces led by the Roman general

THE ROMAN ARMY

Entrance requirements: 5'8" (172.72 cm) minimum height; physical examination

Training: swimming; marching with a 60-pound (27-kilogram) pack; lessons in use of the sword, in forming battle lines, and in pitching camp

Food: a few handfuls of grain daily, meat on occasion, and wine

Armor: curved, wooden shields (either round or oblong) covered with leather and canvas, and bordered with iron; brass helmets with neck guards and cheek flaps, and with high crests; leather jerkins with metal studs; sometimes armor, called greaves, for the legs

Weapons: short, double-edged swords, iron-headed ram, catapults used to throw iron darts, ballistae used to hurl heavy stones

Research Activity: Compare the Roman army with that of the Greeks.

Scipio. Rome took over all of Carthage's Spanish territory and forced Carthage to pay a huge tribute.

Despite their victory, many Romans were not satisfied. They believed that Carthage still represented a threat to Rome's expansion. Also, they wanted revenge for the destruction the war had brought to Italy. Their spokesperson was a Senator named Marcus Porcius Cato. For years he ended every speech with the declaration "Carthage must be destroyed!" Eventually, his call was heeded. The Third Punic War began in 149 B.C. with a surprise attack by Rome. Three years later, the Romans burned Carthage to the ground and plowed its soil with salt so that nothing could grow. The surviving inhabitants of the city were sold into slavery.

GROWTH OF ROMAN POWER IN THE HELLENISTIC EAST

After defeating Carthage in 202 B.C. in the Second Punic War, Rome turned its attention to the eastern Mediterranean region. At this time, descendants of Alexander the Great's top generals ruled Macedonia, Asia Minor, Egypt, Syria, and Persia. Recognizing that some of these kingdoms were not strong enough to resist them, the Romans readied their armies for new conquests. First they declared war on Macedonia, an ally of Carthage. After defeating the Macedonians in 197 B.C., the Romans went on to conquer other territories that had been part of Alexander's empire.

Some areas came under Roman rule without warfare. In Pergamum in Asia Minor, for instance, the king died without an heir and willed his kingdom to Rome. Although Egypt and Syria remained independent for a time, they were forced later to submit to Roman policies. By 133 B.C., most of the Hellenistic world had become Roman provinces. During the next two centuries, Hellenistic culture surviving in these areas had an increasingly important effect on the development of Roman civilization.

GOVERNING THE PROVINCES

As Roman power spread beyond Italy, Rome's treatment of the people it conquered changed. Instead of following the lenient policies set up during its early years of expansion, Rome now demanded tribute as well as slaves. Much of the tribute was paid in the form of grain, which could be produced more cheaply in the provinces than in Italy.

Rome maintained complete authority over the provinces, and the people were not given citizenship. To govern each province, the Senate appointed a Roman governor called a proconsul. The proconsuls served terms of one year and received no salaries. However, many proconsuls grew wealthy by extorting bribes from the people of the province.

To collect taxes in the provinces, the government employed officials called publicans. Publicans agreed to pay a fixed amount to the state, keeping anything above this amount for themselves. Some publicans became rich by placing an unjust tax burden on the people.

EFFECTS OF EXPANSION

As a result of Rome's wars of expansion, several problems arose at home. During Hannibal's invasion of Italy, the Romans and Carthaginians

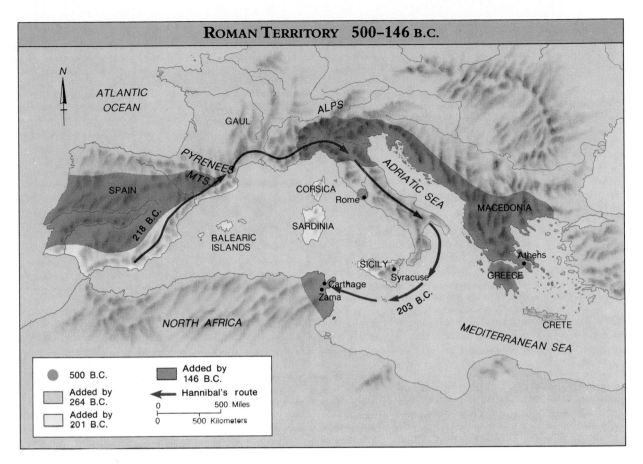

Added by 146 B.C.

500 B.C.

Added by 264 B.C.

Hannibal's route

Added by 201 B.C.

0   500 Miles

0   500 Kilometers

had fought up and down the peninsula. The Carthaginians had lived off the land, gathering food and supplies along the way, and destroying much of the countryside in the process. Restoring the devastated lands after the war required large sums of money.

Roman conquests also greatly increased the number of slaves in Rome. By the end of the Punic Wars, Rome was importing tens of thousands of war prisoners a year as slaves. The large slave population brought unrest and the danger of slave revolt.

Between 134 B.C. and 101 B.C., slaves in Sicily revolted twice. In 73 B.C., a slave named Spartacus led a revolt of some 90,000 slaves. For two years the revolt devastated much of central and southern Italy. Spartacus was eventually killed in battle, and the Roman army put down the uprising.

At the same time, the influx of grain as tribute from the provinces caused grain prices in Italy to fall, forcing many farmers into debt. Patricians and rich merchants bought up small farms from indebted farmers and combined the farms into large estates called *latifundia*. Latifundia owners, as well as the owners of medium-sized estates, used the cheap labor of slaves to work the land. The owners switched from growing grain to raising crops that promised greater profit. Most latifundia became sheep and cattle ranches. Olive groves and vineyards were also common.

As a result of all the changes that were taking place in the Italian countryside, more and more small farmers sold their land and moved to Rome. There they lived in crowded wooden tenements, each a block wide and six or more stories high. The buildings were so poorly constructed that they often collapsed, and fires raged almost every night. Rome's slums were probably as disease-ridden and dangerous as any the world has ever seen.

Many politicians became increasingly corrupt. They took advantage of their positions in the government to gain money dishonestly, spending little or no time on public affairs. At the same time, they developed a love for luxurious living.

Politicians competed for support among the poor in Rome by offering what was called "bread and circuses." Candidates for office would buy wheat and distribute it at low prices. The candidates would also sponsor free entertainment, such as chariot races and gladiatorial games. These games took place in an arena where bloody battles were fought between armed men, between wild animals, or between men and beasts.

While the numbers of poor and unemployed in Rome increased, many Romans prospered. Within Rome's vast territories, trade and commerce expanded. Businesspeople formed a new class, which had great wealth but little political power. As this group fought for more power, new political stresses and conflicts arose.

ATTEMPTS AT SOCIAL REFORM

Rome's growing pains after the Punic Wars caused bitter class conflict, wars, insurrections, and struggles between rival leaders. Many Romans came to believe that the old political system could not deal with the new problems caused by expansion. They began to call for reforms that would give land back to peasants and limit the power of the patricians. The reform movement was led by two brothers from the Gracchus (GRAK-uhs) family.

The first leader was Tiberius Gracchus, who was elected tribune in 133 B.C. Though a patrician, he was disturbed by the plight of Rome's poor. He proposed that latifundia be limited in size and that the surplus land be distributed to the landless. Large landowners, however, opposed his land reform proposals. Before he could pass these proposals as laws, a group of Senators stirred up riots in which a mob killed Tiberius and 300 of his followers.

In 123 B.C., Tiberius's younger brother Gaius was elected tribune. Although Tiberius's land reform proposal had since been passed by the Senate, Gaius wanted further reform. He proposed that people under Rome's rule outside of Italy be given citizenship, and that juries be set up to try provincial governors accused of taking advantage of their power. These and similar proposals angered many Senators. Again, a group of Senators stirred up riots, and these led to the death of 3,000 followers of Gaius. Rather than meet death at the hands of an angry mob, Gaius committed suicide.

The violent reactions to the proposals of Tiberius and Gaius Gracchus set a new tone for Roman politics. The attempts at reform had largely failed, if not backfired. Violence and force became the accepted route to political power. The upper classes, not wanting to deal with the underlying reasons for social conflict, resorted to repression of the lower classes and blocked most reform.

MILITARY RULE

After the deaths of Tiberius and Gaius, Roman politics turned in a new direction. The leaders who followed were military men rather than politicians.

The first military leader to come to power was a war hero named Gaius Marius. Marius rose to power because he had the support of the army and many plebeians. In contrast to the patrician Gracchus, Marius was the son of a laborer and the first plebeian to be elected consul.

Marius made a change in the Roman army that had far-reaching consequences. Until this time, Romans had been required to own at least a small plot of land in order to become legionaries. Marius opened the army's ranks to everyone. In addition to pay, he offered the soldiers pensions as well as spoils taken from the enemy in war.

Marius's policy had great appeal among the landless poor in Rome. However, it had serious effects that would eventually doom the republic. The legions gradually grew less loyal to the government and more loyal to the generals who hired and paid them. In addition, military leaders began to use their armies to put themselves in power.

In 88 B.C., Lucius Cornelius Sulla (SUH-luh), a rival of Marius, marched into Rome at the head of his army. In 82 B.C., after several years of bloody civil war between himself and Marius, Sulla assumed the emergency office of dictator. Although by law a dictator was supposed to hold office for only six months, Sulla refused to accept the time limit.

When Sulla did retire as dictator, in 79 B.C., a new group of generals began fighting for the control of Rome. The two leading rivals in the power struggle were Marcus Lucius Crassus (KRAS-uhs) and Gnaeus Pompey (NI-uhs PAHM-pih). Between 79 B.C. and 60 B.C., Crassus and Pompey shared power because

LOCATION: ALL ROADS LEAD TO ROME, CENTER OF THE EMPIRE

"All roads lead to Rome." That saying suggests the importance of Rome as the capital of the Roman Empire. However, how did a small village come to be the center of an empire encompassing millions of square miles?

Part of the answer lies in the location of Rome. Geographers describe location in two ways. First, location can be defined precisely using a mathematical grid system of latitude and longitude. This system allows geographers to specify the *absolute location*, or exact position, of any place on the earth's surface. Rome's absolute location is 41° 52′ north latitude and 12° 37′ east longitude.

Geographers can also define a place in terms of its *relative location*—its relationship to other places. Whether or not a particular place is said to have a favorable relative location depends upon the needs of the people there, as well as the purposes that the place serves. Many people consider places near resources or transportation routes to have the best relative locations. People, ideas, and goods can easily flow in and out of these areas. Other people sometimes view isolated places as favorable for their needs.

Lying on the Italian peninsula, Rome was in a good relative location to become the center of a great Mediterranean empire. The Italian peninsula juts into the middle of the Mediterranean Sea, where three continents meet. Unlike Greece, which was cut off from Europe by almost impassable mountains, Italy formed a pathway from the Mediterranean into western Europe. Rome was well-positioned to take control of ancient transportation routes on the Italian peninsula. The city lay on the major trade route between northern and southern Italy. It was also near the best east-west route across the Apennines.

The location of Rome had other advantages. The city was built on hills along the Tiber River, 15 miles (24 kilometers) from the coast. Its hilltop location made defense of the city relatively easy. While Roman ships could sail down the Tiber to the sea, Rome's inland location protected it from pirate raids.

As the Roman Empire grew, Rome's rulers improved the city's relative location by improving its *accessibility*—the degree of ease of travel to the city. An ambitious road-building program was begun that tied all of Italy to Rome and then linked Rome with other parts of the empire. Soon roads radiated out from Rome in every direction. In time, a Roman guidebook listed 300 major roads in the empire, many of which are still in use today.

Unlike earlier roads, which were often little more than winding dirt paths, Roman roads were wide and straight. They were also all-weather highways, paved with stone and raised in the middle so that water drained off quickly. Some roads ran for hundreds of miles, connecting Rome to new towns being built throughout the empire. For the soldiers and citizens of these farflung towns, the saying proved to be true. All roads did lead to Rome.

1. Compare absolute and relative location.

2. Describe the relative location of Rome in the early years of the Roman Republic.

3. How did Rome's leaders improve the relative location of their capital?

neither was powerful enough to be sole ruler. They soon joined forces with another military leader, Julius Caesar.

JULIUS CAESAR

Gaius Julius Caesar, a nephew of Marius, was well educated, a brilliant military leader, and a talented orator. Soon after entering politics, Caesar became a favorite with the public.

In 60 B.C. Caesar, Crassus, and Pompey established a partnership to rule Rome. This partnership was called a triumvirate, which means "rule of three." As agreed by this First Triumvirate, Pompey took power in Italy, while Crassus became governor of Rome's eastern provinces. Caesar became governor of Gaul, the Latin name for the territory that is today most of France and Belgium.

Caesar concentrated on using his army to expand Roman territory in Europe. Rome controlled part of Gaul, but the rest was held by warlike Germanic tribes. Over the next seven years, Caesar extended Rome's authority in Gaul to the Rhine River. He also invaded Britain twice.

After Crassus died in 53 B.C., Senators under Pompey's leadership grew uneasy about Caesar's rising popularity. They feared he might try to seize complete power over all of Rome and its provinces. In 49 B.C., the Senators ordered Caesar to disband his legions and return to Rome. Instead, Caesar defied the Senate and led his army into Italy.

Pompey fled Caesar's superior army, seeking more support in Greece. In 48 B.C., Caesar defeated Pompey and his forces. He then subdued several other opponents to become the sole leader of Rome. Two years later he had himself named dictator for ten years, and in 44 B.C., he was named dictator for life.

Caesar used his dictatorial power to bring about many reforms. He resettled thousands of landless veterans throughout Roman territory. He employed additional thousands on such public work projects as building roads and draining the marshes. He introduced a fairer system of taxation and tried to end corruption among government officials in the provinces. He reduced the debts of farmers.

One of his most important actions was to grant Roman citizenship to people outside of Italy—especially Greeks, Spaniards, and Gauls.

These new citizens became increasingly loyal to Rome.

Caesar's reforms were popular with most Romans. Many Senators, however, resented him for taking away their power. Before long about sixty men, most of them Senators, formed a conspiracy to kill the dictator. In 44 B.C., on the Ides of March—March 15—Caesar entered the Senate hall for a meeting. A group of men, led by Gaius Cassius Longinus and Caesar's long-time friend Marcus Junius Brutus, surrounded Caesar and stabbed him to death.

THE END OF THE REPUBLIC

After Caesar's assassination, civil war broke out. Caesar's co-consul, Mark Antony, and Caesar's grandnephew and adopted son, Octavian, defeated the forces of Brutus and Cassius. In 42 B.C., Mark Antony and Octavian joined with Marcus Lepidus, one of Caesar's generals, to form the Second Triumvirate.

This triumvirate ruled Rome for several years. When another power struggle broke out, Lepidus was forced into retirement. Antony, allied with the ruler of Egypt, Queen Cleopatra, tried to seize control from Octavian. In 31 B.C., Octavian defeated Antony and Cleopatra at the naval battle of Actium, off the coast of Greece. With this victory, Octavian became undisputed head of the Roman world. He remained in power for 45 years until A.D. 14. Although he never formally took the title, historians usually refer to Octavian as the first emperor of Rome.

SECTION REVIEW

1. Define **mercenaries** and **latifundia**.

2. Identify four reasons for Rome's success in building a large empire.

3. Why did Rome attack Carthage in the Third Punic War?

4. How did Rome expand its territory in the eastern Mediterranean region?

5. How did Rome's demand for tribute in the form of slaves and grain create problems for the republic?

6. What were the reforms proposed by Gaius and Tiberius Gracchus? Why did the proposals anger some Senators?

Analysis. What conditions in Rome enabled a dictator like Julius Caesar to come to power?

6-3
THE ROMAN EMPIRE

READ TO FIND OUT

—what the term *Romance languages* means.
—how Augustus strengthened the empire.
—what Roman emperors after Augustus accomplished.
—in what ways the Pax Romana benefited people in the empire.
—what factors were responsible for the stability and peace of the Pax Romana.

The reign of Octavian, which began in 31 B.C., marked the end of the Roman Republic and of 100 years of civil war and political upheaval. Beginning with Octavian, Rome—now an empire—entered a period of peace and greatness that lasted almost 200 years. This period is known as the *Pax Romana*, or "Roman peace." During the Pax Romana, Roman authority extended to all the lands surrounding the Mediterranean Sea, which then became known as a "Roman lake."

THE RULE OF AUGUSTUS

In 27 B.C., the Senate gave Octavian the title Augustus, meaning "honored," but he preferred to be known simply as Princeps, or "first citizen." After he was adopted by Julius Caesar, Octavian was also called Augustus Caesar. Following this practice, later Roman emperors also added Caesar to their titles.

Augustus was a skillful politician. Although he was sole ruler, he kept the framework of a republic and rejected all attempts to have himself crowned emperor. He retained the traditional assemblies and officials. He treated Senators with respect and made a great show of asking them for advice. In short, he let others have the appearance of power while he kept the real power for himself.

Augustus strengthened his authority by establishing control of the army. Every soldier had to swear an oath of allegiance directly to him. Although Augustus was not interested in expanding the empire, he did want borders that

could be easily defended. Therefore, he extended the empire to such natural boundaries as the Danube River in the north and the Sahara Desert in the south. To protect the empire against invasion, he assigned the legions to permanent duty along these frontiers. Only an elite troop of 3,000 men was left to serve as an imperial bodyguard in Rome. This troop was known as the Praetorian Guard.

Augustus's reform program. Augustus also carried on reforms in the provinces. He paid provincial governors large salaries so they would not be tempted to steal public funds. He also ordered a periodic census, or count of the population, to make certain that taxes were assessed properly. Augustus carried on Julius Caesar's policy of granting citizenship to many non-Romans in the provinces. He encouraged army veterans to settle in the provinces. These policies laid the foundation for much more stable government in the provinces, and for greater loyalty of their people to Rome.

In Rome, Augustus undertook a great building program. Temples, monuments, and other public buildings were erected or restored, many of them with his own money. New materials replaced the brick, wood, and stone of old Rome. "I found Rome built of sun-dried bricks," Augustus claimed. "I leave it clothed in marble."

AUGUSTUS'S SUCCESSORS

After 45 years of successful rule, Augustus died in A.D. 14. Rome then was ruled for over three-quarters of a century by a series of mostly weak emperors. A major reason why few able rulers rose to power was that the Romans had no formal law of succession. Each time an emperor died, Rome faced the problem of how to choose a new emperor.

Augustus had wisely chosen his stepson Tiberius as his successor before he died. Tiberius was an able ruler, but his successor, Caligula, was cruel and insane. He offended Senators and officials by such behavior as naming his favorite horse to the office of consul. Caligula was assassinated in A.D. 41 by a soldier of the Praetorian Guard, and his uncle Claudius was named emperor. During the reign of Claudius, Britain became a province of the Roman Empire. Claudius's successor was Nero. Many historians believe Nero was as insane as Caligula. During his reign, a disastrous fire swept Rome, destroying half the city. When the army revolted in A.D. 68, Nero committed suicide.

Despite this series of weak rulers, the Pax Romana continued. Augustus had created such a stable empire that even an unstable government could not weaken it.

When the throne again became vacant in A.D. 96, the Senate chose Nerva as emperor. Nerva adopted the Spanish general Trajan as his son and successor. This was an ingenious solution to the problem of succession. Each of the next three emperors followed Nerva's example and selected the ablest and hardest working man he knew as his son and successor. The result of this system was a long period of stable government between A.D. 96 and A.D. 180.

Trajan added Mesopotamia and other lands to the Roman Empire, bringing the empire to its greatest size. Hadrian, who succeeded Trajan

in A.D. 117, feared that too large a territory would strain the empire's resources. Consequently, he abandoned the lands that Trajan had conquered east of the Euphrates. Hadrian traveled throughout the remaining empire, including Britain, where he supervised the construction of a 73-mile (115-kilometer) defensive wall along the northern frontier.

Hadrian's successor was Antonius Pius, a capable emperor who ruled from A.D. 138 to A.D. 161. His reign was probably the most peaceful of any Roman emperor. Marcus Aurelius came to the throne in A.D. 161. Most of his reign was spent fighting off invaders along the empire's northern and eastern borders. Marcus Aurelius was also known as a scholar and a philosopher. Abandoning the adoptive system established by Nerva, Marcus Aurelius chose his son Commodus as his successor. Commodus was an unfit ruler, however, and his reign marked the beginning of the empire's decline.

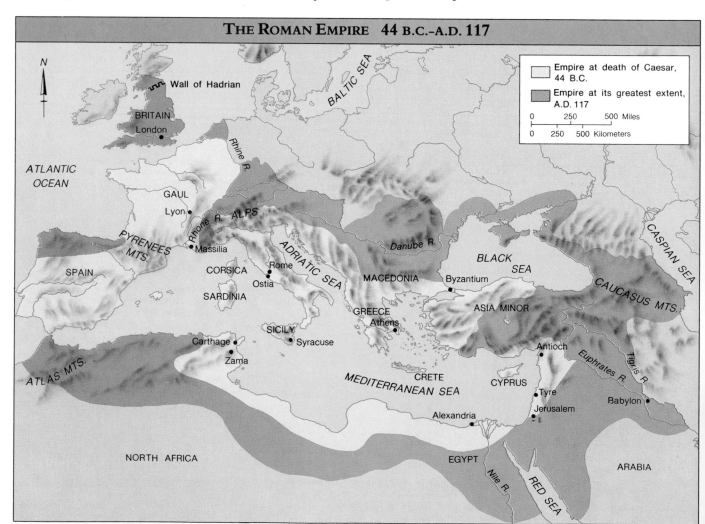

THE ROMAN EMPIRE 44 B.C.–A.D. 117

Empire at death of Caesar, 44 B.C.

Empire at its greatest extent, A.D. 117

0   250   500 Miles
0   250   500 Kilometers

Wall of Hadrian
BRITAIN
London
ATLANTIC OCEAN
GAUL
Lyon
Rhone R.
ALPS
Massilia
PYRENEES MTS.
SPAIN
CORSICA
SARDINIA
Rome
Ostia
ADRIATIC SEA
SICILY
Carthage
Zama
Syracuse
ATLAS MTS.
NORTH AFRICA
MEDITERRANEAN SEA
CRETE
GREECE
Athens
MACEDONIA
Byzantium
BALTIC SEA
Rhine R.
Danube R.
BLACK SEA
ASIA MINOR
CAUCASUS MTS.
CASPIAN SEA
Antioch
Euphrates R.
Tigris R.
Tyre
Jerusalem
Babylon
Alexandria
EGYPT
Nile R.
RED SEA
ARABIA
CYPRUS
N

This Roman mosaic shows the flood waters of the Nile as they transform the delta into an island community. Intrigued by Egypt, wealthy Romans often visited there during the Pax Romana.

THE EMPIRE DURING THE PAX ROMANA

In spite of a frequently unstable government in Rome, the Pax Romana lasted from 27 B.C. to A.D. 180, from the beginning of Augustus's reign to the death of Marcus Aurelius. During this period the majority of people within the vast Roman Empire lived without fear of war. Cities no longer needed walls for protection, and most legionaries completed their 20 years of military service without having to fight a single battle on land or at sea.

Economic growth and trade. Along with peace came increased trade. Goods came from every corner of the empire, and beyond. From the Germanic tribes of northern Europe came such products as animal furs, honey, and amber, which was used to make jewelry. A permanent trading route was opened up with China, from which came fine-silks and dyes. Emperors and nobles adorned themselves with clothes made

of this fabric, and merchants spread stories of the mysterious Orient where it was made. Pottery came from Spain and spices from India. To encourage trade, the government built a network of roads made with stone blocks or gravel paving. This system of roads linked Rome with the most distant provinces.

The Romans also established hundreds of cities, especially in western Europe, during the Pax Romana. Streets in these cities were laid out at right angles to each other, and a forum was built in the center of each city. Aqueducts, long pipelines carrying fresh water from nearby mountains, were built in many cities.

Roman law. Accompanying the growth in trade was an expansion of Roman law. A group of judges, elected annually, revised the Twelve Tables to take into consideration the laws of conquered peoples. Special lawyers called *juris prudentes*, or "those skilled in the law," helped these judges rewrite the laws and expand the

Roman legal system to include people in the provinces as well as citizens of Italy.

In their verdicts, judges gave opinions as well as specific rulings. Thus, legal interpretation became part of law. Also, judges' verdicts were often used as precedents, or examples, for other similar cases that followed. This practice made Roman law flexible, enabling the Romans to rule millions of people with very different cultural backgrounds.

Gradually Roman law developed principles that in later years were adopted by most Western nations. From these principles came the concept that the law should apply equally to all persons and that people should be punished only for their deeds and not their thoughts.

The spread of Latin. In addition to Roman law, the Latin language also spread throughout western Europe during the Pax Romana. Latin, along with Greek, became the language of commerce, learning, and government throughout the empire, helping to tie together people from different cultures. Today, hundreds of millions of people speak languages based on Latin. Because Latin was the language of Rome, these languages are known as *Romance languages*. They include French, Italian, Portuguese, Romanian, and Spanish. Over a third of the words

in English, which is basically a Germanic language, also come from Latin.

MAINTAINING UNITY WITHIN THE EMPIRE

The Romans relied heavily on the army and the threat of force to keep order in the empire. Maintaining peace and order throughout an empire so large, however, required more than an army. The Romans proved themselves to be good administrators, or managers. To a greater extent than the Greeks and the Persians, the Romans were able to secure the loyalty of most of the people within their empire, and to keep trade and commerce functioning smoothly through good administration.

Roman law played a major role in forging the Pax Romana. Because laws were written down, and offenses were dealt with in the same way everywhere, Roman law was widely thought to be fair. Roman citizens generally felt they could trust the legal system to protect them and treat everyone equally. The Romans extended the basic ideas of the legal system to tax collection and governing of the provinces. Citizens could trust that taxes were collected fairly and that governors were restrained from making arbitrary decisions.

A second important Roman policy was tolerance for local customs and religions. In most cases, as long as the local population showed its loyalty to the emperor through observance of the state religion, people were free to practice any other religion they wished. This same policy applied to local traditional ways of life and even sometimes to local forms of government. Thus, people throughout the empire could feel that the Romans were not always telling them how to run their lives.

The Romans balanced this tolerance for local customs and beliefs by granting citizenship to large numbers of people in the provinces. Sometimes, the people living in a city would all be granted citizenship at one time. Citizenship gave everyone a common identity. Therefore, many people became proud to say that they were Roman citizens. They also realized that the empire benefited them in many ways.

Overall, during the Pax Romana, Europe and the Middle East enjoyed greater peace and stability than at any time before or since. According to English historian Edward Gibbon, author

Petra, a city on the caravan route through present-day Jordan, came under Roman rule in A.D. 106. The people in Petra cut into the rocky cliffs to make many homes and civic buildings.

of a famous history of the Roman Empire, the Pax Romana was the period in history "during which the condition of the human race was most happy and prosperous."

SIGNS OF WEAKNESS

Though the Pax Romana was, in general, a prosperous time for the Roman Empire, many social and economic trends were threatening the foundations of the empire, even at its height. Slavery continued to be a basis of the economy. The reliance on slave labor put many small farmers and craftspeople out of work because they were unable to compete with the latifundias. As it had in the days of the republic, this displacement of farmers created growing numbers of poor in the cities.

The empire began to face another problem when it stopped expanding. No longer able to rely on the spoils of war, the government found it increasingly difficult to pay the large army and its officials. The government resorted to raising taxes and making more coins. At the same time, the upper classes became more and more accustomed to luxurious living. Rome imported great quantities of luxury goods from throughout the empire, but exported little to make money to pay for them. After the reign of Marcus Aurelius, these weaknesses began to show themselves as signs of decay.

SECTION REVIEW

1. Define *Romance languages*.

2. How did Augustus prepare the way for 200 years of peace?

3. How did Roman law contribute to the peace and prosperity of the Pax Romana?

4. How did Roman policy towards the provinces change during the Pax Romana? How was this change important?

5. What were the signs of weakness during the Pax Romana?

Synthesis. Form your own hypotheses about the relationship between social and political problems and times of peace and prosperity. Support your hypothesis with evidence from this chapter.

Data Search. Refer to the map titled "The Mediterranean Region" on page 112 to answer the following questions: How do the terrains of Egypt and the Italian Peninsula differ? How might this difference explain why Rome imported grain from Egypt?

HISTORY IN FOCUS

Roman civilization at first followed many patterns that had been established earlier by the Greeks. Rome, like Athens and Sparta, was organized as a city-state. Roman aristocrats, like Greek nobles, controlled politics and used the ceremonies of a polytheistic religion to encourage loyalty and unity among the people. In both Roman and Greek civilization, citizens actively participated in politics.

As it grew, however, Rome began developing very differently from the Greek city-states. Although the culture of Rome remained rooted in many Greek traditions, over time Roman civilization changed the Mediterranean world in ways the Greeks had probably never dreamed possible.

Roman civilization, first of all, was shifted west geographically. Whereas the Greeks had focused their trading, colonization, and later conquests in the eastern Mediterranean and the Middle East, the Romans first strove to dominate the western Mediterranean. Romans brought advanced civilization to Spain, Gaul, and Britain—to Iron Age peoples completely isolated from Greek influence. When the Romans conquered the Hellenistic East, in contrast, they never replaced the stronger Greek and Persian traditions rooted there. Rome's contribution as a classical civilization, therefore, was focused where Greek influence had not reached.

A large part of this contribution consisted of the creation of institutions unknown in Hellenic times. Rome was the first civilization in the Mediterranean region to unify the entire area under one rule and bring lasting peace to its diverse peoples. To achieve the amazing Pax Romana, the Romans relied heavily on a Roman innovation—a code of law based on principles of justice. Other civilizations had written law codes, but no other civilization made law both a science and a philosophy, and applied it fairly to all people. Through these and other achievements, the Romans built upon Greek traditions to fully develop the classical heritage passed on to Europe.

SUMMARY

- Rome was founded by the Latins around 1000 B.C. and was later influenced by the Etruscan and Greek civilizations. In 509 B.C., the Romans overthrew the Etruscans and established a republic.

- The Roman Republic lasted nearly 500 years. A government of three branches created a form of democracy, but power rested with the patricians, not the plebeian majority.

- The extended family was the basic unit of Roman society. The Roman state religion was based on the Greek model.

- Through military strength and diplomacy, Rome expanded its borders. By 264 B.C. it controlled Italy. Rome then defeated Carthage in the Punic Wars. By 133 B.C. Rome also controlled most of the Hellenistic world.

- As Rome expanded, its problems multiplied at home. A series of reforms only resulted in more violence and repression, and the beginning of military rule. Julius Caesar seized power and brought about many reforms. His assassination led to civil war and the end of the republic.

- Augustus founded the Roman Empire, which resulted in 200 years of peace and prosperity. During this Pax Romana, Rome extended and secured its borders, expanded trade, built cities, established a system of law, and spread the Latin language.

VOCABULARY REVIEW

Match each numbered vocabulary term with its origin. Then explain the connection between the origin and the vocabulary term.

1. mercenaries
2. Romance languages
3. patricians
4. republic

(a) Latin: *patres*, senators, fathers
(b) Latin: *merces*, pay, wages
(c) Latin: *Romanus*, Roman; *lingua*, tongue
(d) Latin: *res*, thing, affair, interest + *publicus*, public

CHAPTER REVIEW

1. (a) What was the basic purpose of dividing power among different branches of government? **(b)** List four government offices and describe their functions. **(c)** What was the significance of the Twelve Tables? **(d)** Explain why the plebeians' political gains did not result in real power for the majority.

2. (a) Name other cultures that influenced Roman religion. Give examples of this influence. **(b)** Explain how Roman religion was related to politics.

3. (a) How did the geography of Italy prompt the Romans to build a strong military? **(b)** Why was the military so effective?

4. (a) How did Carthage become Rome's major rival? **(b)** Describe the effects of the three Punic Wars. **(c)** Explain why Carthaginians were treated so harshly by the Romans.

5. (a) Give three reasons the Romans were initially regarded as mild rulers. **(b)** How did Rome's policy toward conquered peoples change outside Italy? **(c)** What can be implied about Roman treatment of conquered people from the actions of Spartacus?

6. (a) Why were there many poor in Rome? **(b)** What was meant by "bread and circuses"?

7. (a) Explain why the Gracchus reforms set a new tone for Roman politics. **(b)** What change did Gaius Marius make that had far-reaching consequences? **(c)** List four reforms enacted by Julius Caesar.

8. (a) Describe the improvements made in Rome by Augustus. **(b)** What change contributed to the stability of Roman government between A.D. 96 and A.D. 180? **(c)** How was trade encouraged during the Pax Romana?

9. How was the unity of the empire maintained during the Pax Romana?

10. (a) Describe Greek influence on each of the following: the development of city-states in Italy, Roman politics. **(b)** Explain how the Roman alphabet exemplifies the diffusion of an idea from culture to culture. **(c)** Describe an important Roman innovation that would influence later civilizations of Europe.

THINKING CRITICALLY: ACTIVITIES

1. Imagine that you are living during the early days of the Roman Republic and that you are involved in a movement for political rights for plebeians. Make a poster presenting your case. List specific rights.

2. Imagine that you are a member of the Council of Plebeians. Describe the reforms you would want the Senate to institute. Share your description with a partner.

3. Imagine that you are a recent migrant to Rome during the Pax Romana. Write a letter to your family who still live in the provinces. Using information from the text, discuss your daily activities and what you see around you.

APPLYING SOCIAL STUDIES SKILLS

Reading maps. Maps are often helpful in clarifying statements in a textbook. Look at the map on page 128 titled "The Roman Empire 44 B.C.–A.D. 117." Use that map to explain the following statements from this chapter.

1. ". . . the Mediterranean Sea then became known as a 'Roman lake.' "

2. "The island of Sicily . . . serves as a stepping stone to the coast of North Africa. . . ."

3. "The Italian peninsula's location . . . was ideal for establishing an empire."

Maps can also include information beyond what is discussed in the text. For example, the text explains that Augustus wanted to extend the Roman Empire to easily defended natural borders. The text, however, does not identify all the empire's natural borders. A natural border or boundary is a natural feature that tends to stop or block easy movement. Such a boundary might be an ocean or any other large body of water, a river, a mountain range, or a desert. Use the map to answer the following questions.

4. What natural feature marked the western boundary of the Roman Empire in A.D. 117? The northeastern boundary of Gaul?

5. Name two natural boundaries on the eastern edge of the empire.

APPLYING THINKING SKILLS

Recognizing relevant information. The following selection, written in the second century B.C., by the Roman Senator Marcus Porcius Cato, is titled *On Agriculture*. Which sentences contain information most directly relevant to the topic of agriculture?

It is true that to obtain money by trade is sometimes more profitable [than farming], were it not so hazardous; and likewise money-lending, if it were as honorable [as farming]. Our ancestors held this view and embodied it in their laws. And when they would praise a worthy man, their praise took this form: "good husbandman," "good farmer." The trader I consider to be an energetic man, but it is a dangerous career. On the other hand, it is from the farming class that the bravest men and the sturdiest soldiers come.

When acquiring a farm, notice how the neighbors keep up their places. The soil should be good and naturally strong. If possible, [the farm] should lie at the foot of a mountain and face south. It should be well-watered. Remember that a farm is like a man—however great the income, if there is extravagance little is left. If you ask me what is the best kind of farm, I should say: a hundred iugera [about 67 acres] of land comprising all sorts of soils, and in very good condition. A vineyard comes first; second, a watered garden; third, an osier-bed [a group of willow-like trees]; fourth, an oliveyard; fifth, a meadow; sixth, grainland; seventh, a wood lot; eighth, an orchard; ninth, a mast grove [plants providing livestock feed].

Abridged from *On Agriculture*, by Marcus Porcius Cato.

1. What is a procedure for determining whether information is relevant?

2. Which sentences in the above selection are most relevant to the topic of agriculture? Explain why each one is relevant.

3. Identify at least one sentence that is clearly irrelevant to the topic of agriculture. Explain why it is irrelevant.

4. In what way can the first paragraph be considered relevant to the topic of agriculture?

5. What other kinds of relevant information might the writer have provided? Explain your answer.

CHAPTER SEVEN

THE HERITAGE OF ROME

509 B.C.–A.D. 476

7-1 ROMAN ACHIEVEMENTS
7-2 BEGINNINGS OF CHRISTIANITY
7-3 DECLINE OF THE ROMAN EMPIRE

Emperor Constantine with family members. Cameo, fourth century A.D.

For more than eight centuries Roman civilization had an enormous effect on the lives of millions of people across much of Europe and the Mediterranean region. Today, that effect can still be felt throughout Western civilization. Rome borrowed heavily from the Greeks, helping to pass on to Europe such basic Greek concepts as freedom and belief in human reason as the best way to acquire knowledge. At the same time, distinctive styles and ideas in literature, art, architecture, and science arose from Roman culture.

Eventually, after about A.D. 180, the Roman Empire began to show signs of weakness. During its decline, however, Rome made its final contribution to Western civilization by helping to shape a major new religion growing up within its borders.

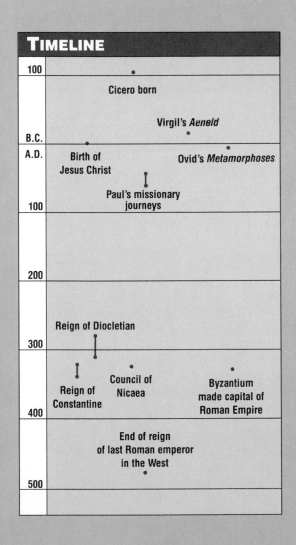

TIMELINE

100	
	Cicero born
	Virgil's *Aeneid*
B.C.	
A.D.	Birth of Jesus Christ • Ovid's *Metamorphoses*
	Paul's missionary journeys
100	
200	
300	Reign of Diocletian
400	Reign of Constantine • Council of Nicaea • Byzantium made capital of Roman Empire
500	End of reign of last Roman emperor in the West

7-1
ROMAN ACHIEVEMENTS

READ TO FIND OUT

—what innovations the Romans made in architecture and engineering.
—what kinds of sculpture the Romans were best known for.
—who the most well known Roman writers were.
—what two philosophies were most popular in Roman times.
—why many people's religious beliefs changed during Roman times.

Roman civilization was influenced by two equally strong outlooks on life, each pulling in a different direction. On the one hand, the Romans stubbornly held on to their old warlike traditions, their love of order, and a simple way of life based on farming. In many ways, they did not seek change.

On the other hand, the Romans were also strongly attracted to Greek culture and to the idea of improving the mind. By developing an advanced civilization, they hoped to be builders and empire makers, to change the world. The Romans were able to put together these two conflicting approaches to life and to create one of the greatest civilizations the world has ever known.

THE PRACTICAL ROMANS

Perhaps the most important result of combining these two outlooks was the remarkable talent of the Romans for organizing and practical problem solving. The ability to solve down-to-earth problems is one of the main characteristics differentiating the Romans from the more philosophical Greeks.

The Romans valued learning more for its practical uses than for its own sake. In science, for instance, Romans added little original work to the knowledge of the Greeks. Instead, the

This aqueduct was built during the reign of Claudius. Although where or when the first aqueducts were built is a mystery, it is known that they were used in ancient Jerusalem and Athens.

Romans applied scientific knowledge to problems such as how to move water over long distances. In solving such problems, they became the best engineers of the ancient world.

The Romans were at their best in what could be called the "practical arts"—military science, architecture, engineering, law, and government. Not surprisingly, Roman accomplishments in these practical arts make up a large part of the Roman cultural heritage passed on to Western civilizations.

ARCHITECTURE, ENGINEERING, AND TECHNOLOGY

Examples of Rome's engineering genius still exist nearly 2,000 years after their construction. Throughout Europe, buildings, walls, roads, stadiums, bridges, and aqueducts built by the Romans still stand, and many are still in use.

Roman roads linked the distant parts of the empire together in an extensive network. Built of stone over layers of gravel, these roads were for the use of the army and public officials, but private citizens used them too.

Rome's aqueducts, sewers, and roads were remarkable for their size and efficiency. In addition to using stone, as the Greeks did, the Romans introduced concrete as a new building material. It provided both strength and greater flexibility of style.

Architecture in Rome was closely connected to engineering as can be seen in the design of structures requiring great strength. The Romans based their architecture on Greek styles, such as rectangular forms and stately columns.

By the third century A.D., however, the Romans were using the arch and the vaulted dome extensively, which changed Roman architecture considerably. Both the arch and the dome were based on the same principle—that a curved structure could support its own weight better than a straight one. With these two innovations, the Romans were able to build much larger buildings than the Greeks. As Roman buildings became very massive, they moved away from the Greek style, which emphasized harmony and proportion. Roman buildings stood powerfully alone, representing the greatness of Rome.

The Romans also developed technology useful outside of architecture. One of their most important inventions was the waterwheel, or water-powered mill. This device was the first new way of harnessing a natural source of power since the invention of the sail.

The Romans tended to be uninterested in developing new technology to increase food production or to manufacture items more efficiently or quickly. Part of this lack of innovative spirit can be traced to the importance of slave labor. Since slaves did all the work, Romans were not motivated to make their work easier. Technology was seen as a way to strengthen the army or to provide the public with necessities such as water, but not to increase production. If the Romans needed to produce more food, they imported more slaves to work in the fields.

ART

Aside from architecture, Rome's greatest artistic achievements were in sculpture. At first, during Rome's early expansion in the 100s B.C., Romans simply brought home Hellenistic artworks as loot from conquests in Greece and Asia Minor. Then Roman sculptors copied the Greek statues.

In time, however, Romans developed their own style, which was much less idealized than the Greek but still similar to the Hellenistic style. Roman sculptors also used this more realistic style in creating elaborate reliefs, three-dimensional figures carved on flat surfaces. Roman portrait busts, especially of political figures, were extremely realistic. Another example of Roman practicality, they served to glorify the emperor and strengthen his authority.

SCIENCE AND MATHEMATICS

Most of the advances in science and mathematics that were made during Roman times were the work of Hellenistic scientists, not Romans. Galen, a Greek who lived in Rome during the second century A.D., was court physician to

ROMAN AQUEDUCTS

"Who will venture to compare these mighty aqueducts with the idle pyramids or the famous but useless works of the Greeks?" a Roman engineer once said proudly. Built to channel water into the cities from distant freshwater sources, Roman aqueducts were perhaps the greatest marvels of Roman engineering. Although the Romans were not the first aqueduct builders of the ancient world, they became the best.

Earlier civilizations had built aqueducts mainly for irrigation. The Romans, however, were the first to construct extensive water supply systems for cities. The first Roman aqueducts, like those of earlier civilizations, were stone channels running almost completely underground. By the second century B.C., the Romans began to build aqueducts with some sections high above the ground. Supported by impressive stone or concrete arches, these sections helped carry water gradually downhill from more distant sources.

Building the aqueducts, some of which were over 50 miles (80 kilometers) long, was a challenging job requiring the labor of hundreds of slaves. The arched sections sometimes towered over 100 feet (31 meters) above valley floors. Workers tunneled through hills too difficult to bypass. Around A.D. 100, the city of Rome had 9 aqueducts totaling about 260 miles (420 kilometers) in length, and for 30 of these miles (48 kilometers) the aqueducts were on arches.

Rome's aqueducts emptied millions of gallons daily into the city's elevated reservoirs. Small pipes, usually made of stone or clay, then carried the water throughout the city. About half the water went for public uses, such as public baths, water basins, and fountains. The rest was piped to the emperor's palace and private homes of the wealthy.

As the Roman empire declined, many aqueducts were abandoned, damaged, or destroyed. The remains of many may be seen today in Italy, Spain, and other areas once part of the Roman Empire. Some aqueducts are still in use—a tribute to the skilled people who designed and built them so long ago.

Roman doctors, who learned by observation, used crude metal tools like these. The brass cup was used in bloodletting, an ancient practice that was thought to rid the body of disease.

Marcus Aurelius. Galen learned about the body's organs by dissecting animals. He also compiled all the medical knowledge of his time in a huge encyclopedia.

Ptolemy (TAHL-uh-mee), an astronomer, mathematician, and geographer, worked in Alexandria in the second century A.D. He believed that the earth was at the center of the universe and that all other heavenly bodies revolved around it. Ptolemy's theory was accepted until the 1500s.

Pliny the Elder was one of the few outstanding Roman scientists. He wrote a 37-volume work called *Natural History* that contained information on astronomy, botany, geography, and medicine.

LITERATURE

The Romans produced many outstanding works of literature. Roman poets and writers adopted the forms and rhythms of Greek literature and adapted them to the Latin language.

Three of the greatest Roman poets lived during the Age of Augustus. Virgil, born in 70 B.C., is most famous for the epic poem *Aeneid* (ih-NEE-uhd). It describes the adventures of Aeneas, a Trojan who was rescued by the gods when Troy fell. According to the *Aeneid*, Aeneas finally landed in Italy, where his descendant Romulus founded the city of Rome. Horace, who lived in Rome, wrote odes, or poems writ-

ten for certain people or objects. Many of his odes praise Rome and the achievements of Augustus. Another Roman poet who lived during this time was Ovid. While Virgil and Horace wrote to inspire patriotism, Ovid wrote simply to entertain. His chief work is the *Metamorphoses*, a collection of legends.

One of the most influential Roman writers was Cicero, who lived during the late republic. Cicero was a statesman and a fine public speaker. His pure, eloquent writing style served as a model for many writers.

Cicero's style had a great influence on Roman historians, such as Tacitus. Tacitus was critical of the emperors, as well as the selfish and pleasure-seeking life of the Roman people. In his work *Germania*, Tacitus wrote about the history of the Germanic peoples on Rome's frontiers. He hoped he could shame the Romans into improving their behavior by praising the simplicity and endurance of the Germans.

PHILOSOPHY

To the Roman upper classes, the most appealing philosophies were the Hellenistic beliefs of Stoicism and Epicureanism. These philosophies heavily influenced Roman culture and thought in general, from science to literature to politics.

Stoicism. Stoicism changed from the days when Zeno and his followers first taught it in Greece. It became more concerned with politics and ethics, and developed a more religious character. In its new form, Stoicism fit Roman society well. It emphasized duty, self-discipline, and acceptance of the order of the universe—traditional Roman values.

Stoicism became very popular during the Pax Romana, even among many common people. The people's belief in this philosophy is probably one of the reasons the Roman system of administration worked so well during this time.

Epicureanism. Epicureanism was somewhat less popular than Stoicism. Like Stoicism, it was chiefly a belief of the upper classes. A leading Epicurean was Lucretius (loo-KREE-shee-uhs), who described the philosophy in a six-volume, beautifully written poem called *On the Order of Things*. Lucretius taught the basic Epicurean belief that one should seek pleasure of the mind and avoid pain and fear of the supernatural.

IDENTIFYING CAUSE-EFFECT RELATIONSHIPS

Studying history will often involve identifying cause-effect relationships. A cause makes something else happen. What happens is called an outcome, a result, or an effect. Any event, idea, or condition usually has several causes and produces several effects. *Underlying causes* are long-term ones, while *immediate causes* lead directly to an event. For example, months of studying may be an *underlying cause* of a student's receiving the Outstanding Sophomore Student award, while an *immediate cause* is the student's grade point average.

Immediate effects occur right away, in contrast with *long-range effects*. For example, an *immediate effect* of the student's award might be a present from his or her parents, while a *long-range effect* might be a college scholarship. *Direct effects* are clearly related to the cause, while *indirect effects* are side effects. Thus, the present and the scholarship are *direct effects*. An indirect effect might be that the student's award enables him or her to make new friends.

EXPLAINING THE SKILL

One way to identify cause-effect relationships is to follow these steps:

1. *Select an event, idea, or condition as the focus point.* Often your teacher will assign the focus point.
2. *Identify and sequence what occurred before the focus point (when looking for causes) or after the focus point (when looking for effects).*
3. *When looking for causes, look at each event that occurred before the focus point and ask, "How might this have brought about the focus point?"*
4. *When looking for effects, look at each event that occurred after the focus point and ask, "How might this have resulted from the focus point?"*
5. *Identify how each cause or effect is linked to the focus point.*

APPLYING THE SKILL

Use the above steps to examine the following information. Your purpose is to identify some

effects of Augustus Caesar's establishment of the Roman Empire by the end of his reign.

A. Ovid exiled, in part because he wrote poetry praising love instead of patriotism (A.D. 8).

B. Roman legions occupy most of Britain (A.D. 14–98).

C. Emperor Trajan conquers the Parthian empire in the East (A.D. 113–117).

D. The Roman army becomes a professional army (27 B.C.–A.D. 14).

E. Emperor Nero builds a palace (A.D. 54–68).

F. Augustus removes any Senators who were opposed to him (27–23 B.C.).

G. Augustus distributes grain to the Roman people (27 B.C.–A.D. 14).

H. Augustus's stepson Tiberius becomes ruler of Rome (A.D. 14).

MAKING MEANING

Review the events that you have identified from the above list as effects of Augustus Caesar's establishment of the empire. Then complete the following sentences:

1. The establishment of the empire resulted in: **(a)** more land ruled by Rome, **(b)** more freedom of speech, **(c)** a stronger Senate.
2. Examples of the above effect are: **(a)** A and E, **(b)** F and G, **(c)** B and C.
3. A direct effect of the rise of the empire was: **(a)** constant warfare, **(b)** increased trade, **(c)** increased power of the emperor.
4. Events providing evidence of or links to the above effect are: **(a)** A, B, and C; **(b)** E, F, and H; **(c)** D, F, and G.

REVIEWING THE SKILL

5. What is the difference between an underlying cause and an immediate cause? Between an immediate effect and a long-range effect? Between a direct effect and an indirect effect?
6. What is a useful way to identify cause-effect relationships?

Romans living in Egypt often adopted local customs and religion. These wax portraits were made to be placed on the faces of the mummified remains of this second-century Roman couple. The star on the man's forehead shows that he was a priest of the sun god.

CHANGES IN RELIGIOUS BELIEFS

The state religion of Rome, like that of Greece, did not offer people a deep ethical code or a belief in life after death. Rome's official religious beliefs were designed primarily to promote loyalty to the state. Even more than Greek religion, the Roman state religion was impersonal and was not at all concerned with creating a comfortable relationship between people and their world.

Many people did not find this state religion satisfactory. Thus, the upper classes turned mainly to the philosophies of Stoicism and Epicureanism for ethical and spiritual guidance. The common people, however, sought out religions that were more emotional. As in Greece, these religions were primarily older beliefs based on worship of nature gods, or religions from the Hellenistic East.

Religions from Egypt, Persia, and Asia Minor spread through much of the empire. The Romans did little to prevent the practice of other religions. Generally, they followed a policy of tolerating local beliefs. However, the Romans did suppress one religion, Christianity,

perhaps because they saw its power. This religion began among the Jews in Palestine at the beginning of the Pax Romana. It proved so appealing that nothing the Romans did could stop it. Eventually, the Romans would make it their official religion, but not before a long period of turmoil.

SECTION REVIEW

1. What three important innovations enabled the Romans to move beyond the Greek style of architecture?

2. How was the style of Roman sculpture similar to the Hellenistic style?

3. Name three leading Roman writers and their major works.

4. Why were Stoicism and Epicureanism popular with many upper-class Romans?

5. What were people in the Roman Empire looking for in a religion that they did not find in the Roman state religion?

Analysis. Why did Romans make few scientific achievements compared with the Greeks? In what areas did the Romans excel?

7-2
BEGINNINGS OF CHRISTIANITY

READ TO FIND OUT

—what the terms *apostles* and *martyrs* mean.
—what role Jews played in the development of Christianity.
—how Jesus' preachings led to his death.
—how Christianity spread after Jesus' death.
—why the Romans persecuted early Christians.

While the Romans were building the stable empire that began the Pax Romana, a new religion was beginning in the Middle East. This religion was called Christianity. Although it grew slowly at first, Christianity would become one of the most influential forces during the decline of the Roman Empire and throughout the later history of Western civilization.

THE JEWS AND THE ROMAN EMPIRE

By the beginning of the Roman Empire, Jewish people lived throughout the Middle East and the Mediterranean region. Since about 800 B.C., they had been spreading out from their homeland—Palestine—by choice or by force. Wherever they settled, Jews carefully protected their religious beliefs and customs from outside influence.

The Romans had conquered Palestine in 63 B.C., renaming the area Judea. As part of their policy of tolerating local religions, the Romans allowed the Jews to practice their own religion of Judaism. This religion, unlike the religion of the Romans, was based on monotheism, the belief in only one God.

Despite Roman tolerance, many Jews resented the rule of Rome. Opposition to Roman rule increased during the first century A.D. One group of Jews, known as Zealots, wanted to overthrow the Romans by force. They tried to organize armed resistance. Others who were not interested in political methods hoped that a messiah, or savior, would come and rescue them from their Roman oppressors.

JESUS AND THE ORIGIN OF CHRISTIANITY

Around A.D. 1, when religious fervor and political discontent were rising in Palestine, a Jew named Jesus was born in Bethlehem, near Jerusalem. Most of what is known of his life comes from the Gospels, the first four books of the New Testament of the Christian Bible. According to the Gospels, Jesus grew up in Nazareth, where he studied his religion in the synagogue and learned carpentry from his father.

Jesus began his public life of preaching when he was about 30 years old. His teachings were based on traditional Hebrew beliefs. For example, Jesus taught people to obey the Ten Commandments. He condensed the ten into two: People should love God with all their hearts, and they should love their neighbors as they love themselves.

Jesus also taught that God was loving and forgiving. He urged people to ignore wealth and fame and concentrate on helping others. To those who followed these teachings, Jesus promised eternal life.

Some people saw Jesus as a political leader—the King of the Jews who would free his people from the Romans. Jesus, however, claimed that his kingdom was a spiritual one—the Kingdom of God.

Jesus gathered around him a group of followers, 12 of whom he named as *apostles*. Jesus and his apostles spent three years traveling through Palestine, bringing his message to the people. According to the Gospels, Jesus attracted many followers and drew large crowds wherever he preached.

About A.D. 33 Jesus and the apostles arrived in Jerusalem to celebrate the Jewish holiday of Passover. The arrival of Jesus upset both the Roman authorities and the Jewish leaders in the city. The Romans were convinced that Jesus was a political agitator who wanted to start a rebellion. Some Jewish leaders were convinced that Jesus was attacking Judaism.

Jesus was arrested as a dangerous rebel, brought before Pontius Pilate, the Roman governor, and convicted of treason, or crimes against the state. He was executed in a customary Roman way called crucifixion, in which a prisoner was tied to a huge cross and left to die of suffocation. Sometimes, as in the case of Jesus, a prisoner was nailed to the cross in order to speed death.

Religious themes were popular in art for centuries. Ivory carvings like this fourth-century panel depicting the Ascension of Christ exemplify early European Christian art.

THE EARLY SPREAD OF CHRISTIANITY

With the death of Jesus, his followers at first lost hope. Then the word spread that Jesus had risen from the dead on the third day after his crucifixion and had been seen by some of his apostles. Jesus' followers now believed he was truly a divine being. With more enthusiasm than ever, they began preaching the teachings of their leader to Jews in Palestine. Jesus became a symbol and an inspiration to his followers because he had died for the cause. He also became identified with the Hebrew belief in a messiah. Because the Greek word for messiah was *Christos*, the followers of Jesus became known as Christians.

These first Christians had only limited success in converting Jews in Palestine to Christianity because most of them were looking for a political leader, not a religious one. Jesus' disciples were more successful in making converts, or people who change their religion, among the Jews who lived outside Palestine in such cities as Antioch, Corinth, and Rome.

The work of one person was particularly important in spreading Christianity. He was a Jew named Saul who was born in Asia Minor. Saul suddenly converted to Christianity, changed his name to Paul, and began preaching.

Paul made a very important decision—to preach Christianity not only to Jews but also to non-Jews. He believed that Jesus was sent by God to redeem, or save, not only Jews but all of humankind. He rejected many Jewish rituals and spoke of Christianity as a universal, or worldwide, religion.

From A.D. 47 to A.D. 65, Paul worked as a missionary, traveling throughout the Roman Empire preaching the beliefs of Christianity. Paul journeyed from city to city, establishing Christian communities called churches. Soon, Christianity was no longer identified as a form of Judaism, but became a separate religion. Most people who converted to Christianity after this time were non-Jews.

CHRISTIANITY AND ROME

For the first two centuries after the death of Jesus, Christianity grew slowly but steadily. Certain conditions within the Roman Empire helped Christianity to spread. For example, missionaries could travel quickly on the Roman roads and be relatively safe from harm because of the Pax Romana. In addition, the common languages of Latin and Greek allowed the missionaries to preach directly to most people throughout the empire.

At the same time, Christianity met resistance from the Romans, who saw its spread as dangerous. The Christians refused to worship the emperor as a god, or to serve in the Roman army. Other Romans, however, wished to tolerate Christianity as they did other religions. During the Pax Romana, therefore, Roman policy toward Christianity varied from official persecution to toleration.

The persecution of Christians did not stop the spread of Christianity, however. Some

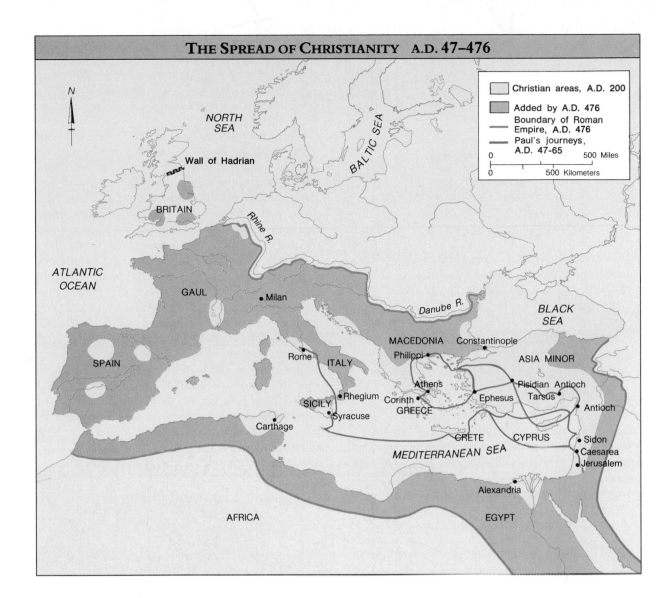

THE SPREAD OF CHRISTIANITY A.D. 47–476

Christian areas, A.D. 200
Added by A.D. 476
Boundary of Roman Empire, A.D. 476
Paul's journeys, A.D. 47–65

0   500 Miles
0   500 Kilometers

NORTH SEA
BALTIC SEA
Wall of Hadrian
BRITAIN
Rhine R.
ATLANTIC OCEAN
GAUL
Milan
Danube R.
BLACK SEA
MACEDONIA   Constantinople
Philippi
ASIA MINOR
SPAIN
Rome   ITALY
Athens
Pisidian Antioch
Tarsus
Rhegium   Corinth   Ephesus
SICILY   GREECE
Antioch
Syracuse
Carthage
CRETE   CYPRUS
Sidon
MEDITERRANEAN SEA
Caesarea
Jerusalem
Alexandria
AFRICA   EGYPT

Christians chose to die rather than give up their beliefs. These people, called **martyrs**, gained the admiration of many Romans. Numerous people were so inspired by the martyrs' bravery that they converted to the Christian faith. The new Christians also helped spread the religion.

Christianity was only one of many religions that offered emotional involvement and the promise of life after death. At the end of the Pax Romana, more than 90 percent of the people in the Roman Empire were still non-Christian. It was not until the third century A.D. that increasing hardship, poverty, and political turmoil made more people search for beliefs that offered hope. Under these conditions, Christianity spread quickly.

SECTION REVIEW

1. Define *apostles* and *martyrs*.

2. Why were the Jews important in the origins of Christianity?

3. Why was Jesus executed?

4. Why did Jesus' disciples continue to preach his teachings? What important role did Paul play in the early spread of Christianity?

5. How did the Romans respond to the early spread of Christianity?

Analysis. In what ways was Christianity different from the Roman state religion? Why might the Romans find it appealing?

7-3
DECLINE OF THE ROMAN EMPIRE

READ TO FIND OUT

—what the term *monasteries* means.
—what events contributed to the beginning of Rome's decline.
—why Christianity grew during the decline of Rome.
—how Diocletian and Constantine helped slow the decline of the empire for a time.
—how the Christian Church became an institution.
—what the major underlying causes of Rome's decline were.

When Marcus Aurelius, one of Rome's strongest and most popular emperors, died in A.D. 180, the Roman Empire entered a period of decline. The signs of weakness present during the Pax Romana finally began to surface and became real problems. While Rome declined during the next three centuries, the Christian Church grew stronger. By A.D. 476, the city of Rome had been captured by Germanic invaders, but Christianity was ready to become a leading force in the development of European civilization.

A CENTURY OF UPHEAVAL

During the Pax Romana, most Roman emperors had adopted the most able person they knew to be heir to the throne. Marcus Aurelius abandoned this system when he left the throne to his son Commodus (KAHM-ō-duhs). Unlike his father, who had been kind and thoughtful, Emperor Commodus was cruel and violent. He openly disregarded the Senate and did whatever he liked. In A.D. 192, his own bodyguard strangled him. With no one in line to rule as emperor, a power struggle followed. Several generals competed to gain control of the throne.

For the next hundred years, the empire was in turmoil. Legion fought against legion to in-stall the emperor of its choice. Between A.D. 193 and A.D. 284, twenty-six emperors took the throne, with the average reign lasting only two and one-half years. Most of these emperors, who lived in army camps, were assassinated by their own troops.

The years between A.D. 180 and A.D. 284 were a time of almost constant civil war. This internal political conflict nearly crippled the Roman economy as it disrupted farming and trade throughout the empire.

To help pay for running the empire, most emperors reduced the amount of gold and silver in coins. Because the money was worth less, this action only made prices go up. By the end of the third century A.D., the prices of most goods had increased by about 200 times. Emperors also took people's property in order to get money to support their armies and gain their soldiers' loyalty.

Economic problems hit the poor the hardest. Many people lived on the edge of starvation. Diseases swept through the weakened population, killing great numbers of people. With little hope for the future, many people stopped having children. The population declined rapidly in some places, reducing the number of badly needed soldiers, farmers, and taxpayers.

Caracalla and Geta succeeded their father, Septemius Severus, as emperors in 211 and became joint rulers. Caracalla soon had Geta killed and had his face erased from this family portrait.

At the same time, Rome faced renewed threats from external enemies. All along the northern and eastern borders of the empire, hostile tribes pressed at Roman defenses. Faced with bankruptcy and defended by small and unmotivated armies, Rome was not able to protect its former boundaries.

THE GERMANIC INVASIONS

Since the fifth century B.C., Germanic tribes had been living in the forests north of the Rhine and Danube rivers, where they had moved from the Baltic Sea area in northernmost Europe. During the Pax Romana, the Germans nearest the frontier had adopted much of Roman culture and many of them had settled peacefully in the empire.

The weaknesses of the empire, however, provided opportunities for other Germanic peoples to enter Roman territory. In large numbers, Germanic tribes swept into Greece and Gaul during the third century A.D. In 251, for instance, Germanic tribes crossed the Danube and defeated the Roman armies there. They killed the emperor leading the army and then marauded through the Balkan Peninsula.

In many of the empire's outlying areas, invaders disrupted trade and farming. Once again Roman cities were forced to surround themselves with walls for protection. The emperor Aurelian, for example, had a 12-mile (19-kilometer) brick wall built around Rome.

THE GROWTH OF CHRISTIANITY

During this period of political turmoil and economic hardship, Christianity, which had grown slowly up to this point, rapidly gained many converts. Most people, faced with dismal lives, sought hope and strength in a belief in an afterlife, or otherworldly salvation. Many religions in the Roman world offered a belief in life after death, but Christianity was more successful than others in drawing new converts.

Christianity had several important characteristics that made it appealing to people adrift in what they believed was an unfriendly world. First, Christianity prohibited its believers from practicing any other religion. The followers of Christianity preached that it was the one true belief, and people came to feel that they could trust in this one religion.

Second, Christianity had better developed ideas about the afterlife than did other religions. Christians preached that nonbelievers would burn in hell, whereas believers would enjoy eternal happiness in heaven. In an age of fear, this prospect probably won many converts to the new faith.

A third advantage of Christianity was its organization. By this time, priests with different levels of authority led worship and made religious decisions. Perhaps most importantly, Christian communities took care of their members, giving people a sense of belonging and purpose. Christianity also had the advantage of including women, unlike some other competing religions.

By A.D. 250, about 1 out of 10 persons in the Roman Empire was a Christian. Christians continued to be persecuted during the third century, but usually only for short periods of time and not very frequently. Most often the official policy of Rome was one of tolerance. When persecutions and executions did occur, they served only to create more martyrs, bring more converts to the faith, and reduce respect for Roman authority.

DIOCLETIAN AND STABILITY

Diocletian (dī-uh-KLEE-shun) was the first of two strong emperors who worked to save the empire from collapse. He reigned from A.D. 284 to A.D. 305. Diocletian instituted reforms that drastically changed the shape of the empire and its government. His policies stabilized the empire, but only slowed its decline.

Diocletian divided the empire into two parts. He ruled the eastern part of the empire himself, appointing another emperor, called an augustus, to rule the western part. Diocletian was careful, however, to retain absolute power for himself.

Diocletian rarely visited Rome, setting up his court in the city of Nicomedia, not far from the site of ancient Troy. He probably did so because the Greek-speaking eastern part of the empire contained more people, more cities, and more wealth than the Latin-speaking western part. Diocletian fortified the empire's frontiers and brought about many economic reforms. To end the rising of prices, he set maximum prices and wages. He reformed the coinage system by requiring a fixed relationship between the worth of a coin and its metal content.

The dome of the Pantheon symbolized the heavens. Built as a temple to Roman gods in A.D. 126 during the reign of Hadrian, the Pantheon was later used as a Christian church.

CONSTANTINE

When Diocletian retired, yet another civil war broke out over succession to the throne. A general named Constantine came to power in the western part of the empire in A.D. 312, and he became sole ruler of the entire empire 12 years later. Constantine made the shift of power from west to east official. In A.D. 330, he transferred the capital of the Roman Empire from Rome to the old Greek colony of Byzantium, in present-day Turkey. He rebuilt the city and called it New Rome. After his death, it was renamed Constantinople in his honor.

Constantine extended many of Diocletian's economic policies. To avoid the government regimentation that resulted, many powerful landowners fled the cities to live in country houses called estates or villas. Each villa and its surrounding fields formed a self-sufficient estate. Slaves farmed the estate's fields and produced the goods it needed, and private armies protected its inhabitants from attack. As time went on, these villas became more important, gradually replacing the empire as centers of social life and government. The growth of self-sufficient villas, which undermined central authority, was a sure sign that Constantine, like Diocletian, had only slowed Rome's decline.

Constantine's support of Christianity. One of Constantine's most important actions was to support Christianity in the empire. In A.D. 313, he issued the Edict of Milan, which granted re-ligious freedom to everyone in the Roman Empire. He encouraged Christianity, in particular, by building churches in Rome and Jerusalem and by exempting the clergy from taxes. Constantine hoped that by favoring Christianity he would bring spiritual unity to the empire. By the time he converted to Christianity—on his deathbed—about 2 out of 10 people in the empire were Christians.

Most of Constantine's successors continued his policies, and more and more people converted. In A.D. 392, Christianity became the official religion of the empire. Other religions were outlawed. Their temples and writings were taken over or destroyed, and their ceremonies—including the Olympic Games—were abolished. Soon, an overwhelming majority of the empire's inhabitants were Christian.

THE CHURCH AS AN INSTITUTION

After Constantine changed the official Roman policy toward Christianity, the organization and doctrines, or official beliefs, of the Christian Church went through important changes. During the first century A.D., Christians had lived together in groups called churches. Christians shared their possessions and took turns conducting religious services. By the time Christianity became the empire's official religion, the churches had changed drastically.

Church structure. Christians established a hierarchy of church officials—that is, officials were organized according to their rank. Each church covered an area called a parish, which was headed by a priest. Several parishes made up a diocese, which was governed by a bishop.

The bishops became important Church leaders. They supervised the preaching of the gospel and the performance of such rituals as baptism, the ceremony by which a person becomes a Christian. The bishops also managed church property. Some became archbishops, the highest ranking bishops, and administered a province made up of several dioceses.

Beginning in the third century A.D., bishops took part in councils to discuss questions about the Christian faith. Perhaps the most significant council was the Council of Nicaea (nī-SEE-uh). Three hundred bishops from all parts of the Roman Empire attended this council, called in A.D. 325 by Constantine. The bishops at Nicaea adopted the doctrine of the Trinity, which sees God as three entities—the Father, the Son, and the Holy Spirit—in one Supreme Being. The statement of this belief, an official doctrine of Christianity today, is known as the Nicene Creed.

The Church fathers. In addition to the Nicene Creed, the teachings of the Church were influenced by the writings of certain Christian scholars. These scholars, who wrote from the second to the fifth centuries A.D., are known as "fathers of the Church." Two of the most important were St. Jerome and St. Augustine. Both were born around A.D. 350.

St. Jerome's important work was the translation of the Old and New Testaments into Latin. St. Augustine wrote *City of God*. In it, he defended Christianity against its critics. He also claimed that all earthly cities were bound to fall sooner or later. The only city that could last forever was the City of God.

The Church fathers lived, worked, and practiced their faith in places that were isolated from the outside world. These residences are called *monasteries*. During the A.D. 300s, monasteries became centers of Christian thought. As the Roman Empire continued to decline, monks—as the Christians who lived in monasteries were called—collected and copied all the classical literature of Greece and Rome they could find. After the collapse of the empire, the monks helped to preserve the culture and achievements of the Romans.

THE FINAL INVASIONS

Despite the efforts of Diocletian and Constantine, the internal problems of the Roman Empire steadily worsened. At the same time, external pressure from the Germans continued to increase.

Toward the end of the fourth century A.D., large groups of Germans crossed the Danube. These Germans were desperate to enter Roman territory, for they were threatened from the east by the Huns, fierce nomads from the arid steppes of Asia.

SPOTLIGHT: PEOPLE

FABIOLA

As the Christian Church continued to grow during the fourth century A.D., bishops and priests often encouraged Christians to help people who were sick or poor. One of the people responding to this call was a Roman woman named Fabiola. She did not simply give poor people food, clothing, and medicine, though. She gave them hospitals.

A wealthy woman of noble birth, Fabiola was a major sponsor of what were probably the first public hospitals. Government-supported military hospitals were common in the Roman Empire. However, public hospitals supported by private citizens were a new development of the fourth century. Fabiola not only provided money for public hospitals but also worked tirelessly to improve the quality of nursing.

Little is known about Fabiola's early life, but it is believed that she converted to Christianity at the age of twenty. Later, after her husband's death, she devoted all her wealth and energy to providing decent health care for the poor. After establishing a public hospital in Rome in A.D. 380, she did not wait for the sick to come to her. Instead, she went out into the streets to search for them, often carrying the needy on her back to the hospital. All patients received her personal attention. This show of concern greatly impressed the poor people of Rome because rarely did someone of Fabiola's social standing have any dealings with the poor, let alone care for them.

Fabiola was an enthusiastic worker, but she was restless and never satisfied with her efforts. She constantly tried to improve her hospital's services. One practice she began was to send patients to her summer villa to complete their recovery.

When Fabiola died in A.D. 399, all Rome mourned her loss. As Jerome, a leader of the Christian Church in Rome, noted, "How great a marvel Fabiola had been to Rome while she lived is shown by the behavior of the people since her death. . . . I seem to hear even now the sound . . . of feet of the multitude who thronged in thousands to attend her funeral."

As the Huns pushed the Germans, the Germans pushed the Romans. In A.D. 378, a Germanic group inflicted a decisive defeat on Roman legions at the battle of Adrianople (AY-dree-uh-NŌ-puhl). When the Rhine froze in the winter of A.D. 406, other groups of Germans crossed the ice and entered Gaul. In A.D. 410, Germans led by the general Alaric attacked Rome. For the first time in eight centuries, a foreign army walked the streets of the city. The Senate sent a message to government officials throughout the empire telling them that Alaric and his soldiers had burned Rome's records and looted its treasury. "You can no longer rely on Rome for finance or direction," the message read. "You are on your own." Alaric fled the city after looting it, but Rome was seriously weakened.

THE FALL OF ROME

The invasions continued as nomadic tribes, often called barbarians, overran parts of the western empire. In A.D. 476, the last Roman emperor in the west, Romulus Augustulus, was forced to give up his throne when a German chief captured Rome. Because of this defeat, people sometimes refer to the year 476 as the date when the Roman Empire fell. In reality, the empire did not fall in a single year but had been gradually declining for a long time.

After 476, the western empire became a patchwork of Germanic kingdoms. Here the advanced level of civilization brought by the Romans nearly disappeared. The eastern part, with its capital in Constantinople, survived and eventually became the Byzantine Empire.

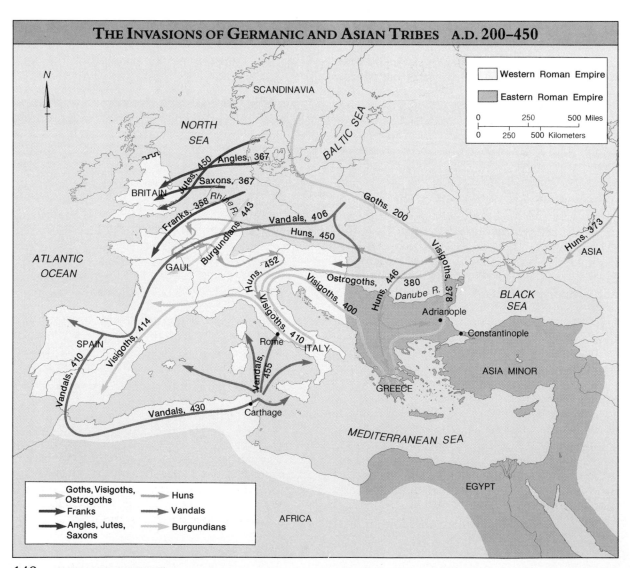

THE INVASIONS OF GERMANIC AND ASIAN TRIBES   A.D. 200–450

CAUSES OF ROME'S DECLINE

Historians have debated for centuries about the underlying causes of Rome's decline. Usually historians separate underlying causes from symptoms, or signs, of decline. Symptoms of Rome's decline were present from the days of the Pax Romana up to A.D 476. These signs included political conflict and disunity, a widening gap between rich and poor, declining population, weakening patriotism, and the growth of self-sufficient villas.

In contrast to such symptoms, underlying causes are basic characteristics of Roman civilization that caused these symptoms to develop. Historians often divide these causes into three kinds: political, economic, and social.

The political system had basic weaknesses. The government had been set up to rule a small city and could not adapt to meet the needs of an empire that had grown so vast in such a short time. Corruption and inefficiency were difficult to prevent. This weakness was made worse by the lack of a fixed way of choosing successors to the throne—a situation that led to rivalries, violence, and frequent civil war.

The empire's weak economy is often singled out as a major cause of Rome's decline. Roman practicality discouraged innovation for the purpose of increasing the production of food and goods. Furthermore, the Romans did not fully develop trade and commerce. Instead, the economy relied on the delicate foundations of slave labor and taxes. Slaves were difficult to control and expensive to house and feed. Taxes angered many people, and declining populations meant less tax money. The economy was thus always vulnerable to disruption and never had a strong foundation for growth.

Some historians believe social causes were most important in Rome's decline. These scholars claim that moral decay set in. The Roman upper classes, according to this theory, became too used to luxurious living. They wasted Rome's wealth on extravagant imports, ate too much, lost their sense of right and wrong, became greedy, and lost respect for Rome.

Most scholars agree that no one factor can be identified as the most important. Many causes, each one influencing all the rest, contributed to the weakening of the Roman Empire. After it weakened, the invading Germanic tribes could easily defeat and overrun the once great empire.

SECTION REVIEW

1. Define **monasteries**.

2. What major problems troubled the empire after the reign of Aurelius?

3. What conditions contributed to the growth of Christianity?

4. What did Diocletian and Constantine do to help stabilize the empire?

5. What changes in the Christian Church helped it become an institution?

6. Describe three underlying causes of Rome's decline.

Analysis. In what ways could the growth of self-sufficient estates be both a sign and an underlying cause of the empire's decline?

Data Search. Refer to the appropriate chart on page 829 to identify the regions in which people practiced **(a)** Christianity, **(b)** Judaism, and **(c)** Zoroastrianism.

HISTORY IN FOCUS

Roman culture did not die out with the collapse of the western empire. Roman civilization had lasted so long and spread so far from Italy that it was deeply imprinted throughout much of Europe and the Mediterranean area. The Latin language, for instance, gave birth to the Romance languages that include French, Italian, Spanish, and Portuguese. Roman law provided central ideas for later legal systems in Europe. Roman government served as a model for future constitutional governments. Roman literature, art, and architecture, moreover, helped to pass on Greek culture as they became part of

Rome's official recognition of Christianity helped shape the course of Western civilization. Under Roman influence, the Church became an institution. During the empire's last century, the Christian Church took advantage of Roman support to build up power, prestige, and huge numbers of followers.

Rome also lived on in the form of the Byzantine Empire, which grew out of the surviving eastern half of the Roman Empire. The eastern empire had developed its own form of Christianity and its own rich culture, with roots in both East and West. These unique characteristics shaped later Byzantine civilization.

SUMMARY

- The Romans combined the Greek love of intellect with their own practical nature to create one of the world's great civilizations.

- Rome excelled at architecture, engineering, and technology. Art was realistic, often glorifying the empire, and there were many outstanding writers. Stoicism and Epicureanism were popular philosophies among the upper classes.

- The state religion promoted loyalty to the empire, but was not popular. Thus, many Romans turned to philosophy or other religions. Jews were allowed to maintain their beliefs, but they still resented Roman rule.

- In just a few years, Jesus gained a following and laid the foundations for Christianity. Rome regarded him as a political threat and had him executed around A.D. 33. His disciple Paul helped spread the faith.

- The years from A.D. 180 to 284 were a period of turmoil for the empire, marked by civil war, economic disarray, population decline, and the threat of invasion. This instability facilitated the growth of Christianity.

- Two emperors—Diocletian and Constantine—tried to stabilize the empire through reforms but only postponed its collapse. Constantine encouraged Christianity, and the Christian Church became institutionalized, with a hierarchy, doctrines, and scholars who helped shape religious policy.

- The western part of the empire was overrun by Germanic tribes in the A.D. 400s. The eastern part became the Byzantine Empire.

VOCABULARY REVIEW

Match each vocabulary term below with its origin. Then explain the connection between the vocabulary term and its origin.

1. apostle
2. martyr
3. monastery

(a) Greek: *martus*, witness
(b) Greek: *monazein*, to live alone
(c) Greek: *apostulos*, a person sent forth

CHAPTER REVIEW

1. (a) Contrast the architecture of the Romans and the Greeks. **(b)** Explain how the building of aqueducts represents an important difference between the way Romans and Greeks thought.

2. (a) Describe Galen's contribution to science. **(b)** Explain how Ptolemy's theory might have affected people who lived long after him. **(c)** In what respect was Pliny the Elder different from most scientists in the Roman Empire?

3. (a) Explain the difference between Roman and Greek Stoicism. **(b)** Describe another Hellenistic philosophy adopted by the Romans.

4. (a) Point out ways in which the Romans showed religious tolerance. **(b)** Give an example of intolerance during the Pax Romana. **(c)** Describe the Jewish reaction to Roman rule during the first century A.D.

5. (a) How were the views of Roman and Jewish leaders toward Jesus similar? **(b)** Explain how Jesus' death helped foster his teachings.

6. (a) Describe conditions in the Roman Empire that helped Christianity spread in the first two centuries A.D. **(b)** Explain why some Romans regarded Christianity as dangerous.

7. (a) Describe the reasons for the population decline in some parts of the empire during the third century A.D. **(b)** In what ways did the population decline affect Rome's self-defense? **(c)** Explain actions by the German tribes that contributed to the decline of the Roman empire in the third to fifth centuries A.D.

8. (a) Why did Diocletian establish his rule in the eastern part of the empire? **(b)** In what way did Constantine's efforts to stabilize the Roman Empire through economic policies backfire? **(c)** Why did he encourage Christianity?

9. (a) Describe how other religions were affected when Christianity became the official religion of Rome. **(b)** Name two of the most important "fathers of the Church." **(c)** Why was the work of early monks important?

10. (a) Describe the Roman Empire after A.D. 476. **(b)** Describe six ways in which the Roman legacy has been significant.

THINKING CRITICALLY: ACTIVITIES

1. Although Jesus said that his goals were spiritual, not political, many Jews wanted him to lead a political movement. Imagine that you are living in Palestine under Roman rule and that you want to promote change. Prepare an argument with a partner, making a case for either a spiritual movement or a political one. Debate a team that has prepared the opposing argument.

2. Make a chart with two columns. Label one "Signs of Decline" and the other "Causes of Decline." Then, down the lefthand side of your paper, write the following five labels: "political," "military," "social," "economic," and "natural." Fill in the chart as completely as possible.

APPLYING SOCIAL STUDIES SKILLS

Reading maps. Maps sometimes suggest or reveal cause-and-effect relationships. Look at the map on page 143. Then answer these questions.

1. What is the purpose of this map?

2. Study the route followed by Paul on his journeys. What does this map suggest about the relationship between Paul's missionary activities and the early spread of Christianity?

3. What do you notice about the boundary of the Roman Empire in A.D. 476 and the spread of Christianity by that date?

4. What do you think the map suggests about the relationship between the Roman Empire and Christianity?

Maps can also show the movements of groups of people. Look at the map on page 148 and then answer the following questions.

5. What three groups invaded Britain?

6. What two groups crossed the Rhine to settle in Gaul?

7. Which group invaded first Greece and then Italy in the early 400s?

8. What route did the Vandals follow to Rome?

9. Where did the Huns come from?

10. How far west did the Huns go before invading Italy?

APPLYING THINKING SKILLS

Identifying cause-effect relationships. The following account of Augustus's rise to power was written by the Roman historian Tacitus, who was born about A.D. 56. As you read Tacitus's account, be aware of cause-effect relationships. Then answer the questions that follow the account.

My purpose is to relate a few facts about Augustus without either bitterness or partiality. . . . After the destruction of Brutus and Cassius there was no longer any army of the Commonwealth. Pompeius [had been] crushed in Sicily, Lepidus pushed aside and Antonius slain. Then, dropping the title of triumvir and [announcing] that he was a consul and [that he was] satisfied with a tribune's authority for protection of the people, Augustus won over soldiers with gifts and the populace with cheap corn, while he concentrated in himself the functions of the Senate, the magistrates, and the laws. He was wholly unopposed, for the boldest spirits had fallen in battle, while the remaining nobles he raised the higher by wealth and promotion, so that they preferred the safety of the present to the dangerous past. Nor did the provinces dislike that condition of affairs, for they distrusted the government of the Senate because of the rivalries between leading men and the rapacity [greediness] of the officials, [whose job performances were harmed] by violence, intrigue, and finally by corruption.

Abridged from Tacitus's *Annals.*

1. How does an underlying cause differ from an immediate cause?

2. Give your own examples of underlying and immediate causes, and of immediate, long-range, direct, and indirect effects.

3. What were two causes of Augustus's rise to power?

4. In what specific ways was each of these two causes linked to Augustus's rise to power?

5. Which of these two causes was an underlying cause, and which was an immediate cause? Explain your answer.

6. Explain in your own words how Augustus rose to power.

CHAPTER EIGHT

CLASSICAL INDIA AND CHINA

600 B.C.–A.D. 600

Noble as ''Great Boddhisatva.'' Ajanta wall painting, India, sixth century.

During the centuries when the civilizations of the Greeks and Romans rose to great heights, so, too, did the civilizations of India and China. The way of life in both India and China grew out of traditions established there in times past.

In India empires rose and fell, and no single dynasty could, for long, bind together the many Indian kingdoms and principalities. Yet, the Indian people were bound together by the ancient beliefs and customs woven into the patterns of their lives.

During these centuries, China became a unified domain. At times, political wars and popular revolts rocked China. Furthermore, powerful nomadic groups constantly threatened China's borders. However, the Chinese developed orderly social systems and stable political structures.

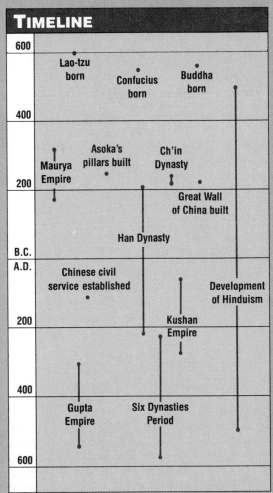

TIMELINE

600

Lao-tzu born

Confucius born

Buddha born

400

Maurya Empire

Asoka's pillars built

Ch'in Dynasty

200

Great Wall of China built

Han Dynasty

B.C.
A.D.

Chinese civil service established

Development of Hinduism

200

Kushan Empire

400

Gupta Empire

Six Dynasties Period

600

8-1
KINGDOMS AND EMPIRES OF INDIA

READ TO FIND OUT

—how the Maurya Empire was ruled.
—how the Kushan Empire was a bridge between cultures.
—how Gupta rule fostered a "Golden Age."

An ancient Indian tale tells of a time when greed and anger disrupted bonds among people. According to the tale, people had agreed to respect each other's lives and property, but each feared that the others would not keep their word. The people asked a deity to help them. The deity gave them a king.

To the Indian people, the king's duty was the protection of life, property, and tradition. To them, a strong ruler was necessary to keep peace and prosperity. In the centuries from about 550 B.C. to about A.D. 650, strong kings ruled small kingdoms and great empires, providing an atmosphere in which India's religious and social traditions thrived.

THE MAURYA EMPIRE

After Alexander the Great destroyed the Persian Empire, he led his armies into northwestern India. There, in 327 B.C., he seized Gandhara (gun-DAR-uh), a kingdom that had been under Persian control for 200 years. Battling both Persian and Indian troops, Alexander's forces then crossed the Indus River. When his soldiers refused to go further, however, Alexander was forced to turn back, leaving northwestern India without a strong ruler.

Meanwhile, in about 324 B.C. in northeastern India a young warrior, Chandragupta Maurya (CHUN-druh-GUP-tah MOR-yah), took possession of the throne of Magadha. Established earlier by the Aryans in a region rich in timber and minerals, Magadha had become a wealthy kingdom. It had also gradually expanded its boundaries until it had become the strongest kingdom on the Ganges plain.

Chandragupta dreamed of expanding the kingdom even further. Soon he added the Indus Valley and the Punjab, the region around the tributaries to the Indus River. Through both conquests and alliances he gained additional lands, thereby creating India's first empire.

Governing the empire. The empire was divided into provinces, made up of several local districts. Within each district were several villages. Village headmen reported to district governors who, in turn, reported to the viceroy, or ruler of the province. The viceroys were members of the Maurya family and answered to the emperor. This chain of command gave Maurya emperors firm control of affairs, even in the smallest districts.

From the capital at Pataliputra (PAH-tuh-lih-POO-truh), Chandragupta ruled his empire with an iron hand. He maintained an army of up to 700,000 soldiers. Chandragupta also maintained a secret service, whose members reported directly to him. Anyone suspected of disloyalty was assassinated. In this atmosphere of distrust, Chandragupta himself so feared assassination that he slept in a different bedroom each night.

Though Chandragupta ruled harshly, he fostered prosperity in his empire. He established a postal service, developed roads, and ordered extensive irrigation systems built. Under his reign business and trade flourished.

According to tradition, Chandragupta gave up his throne in 301 B.C. to become a monk. His son, Bindusara (BIHN-duh-SAHR-uh), pushed the boundaries of the Maurya Empire deep into the Deccan Plateau. However, the Maurya Empire reached its greatest size under Chandragupta's grandson Asoka (uh-SHŌ-kuh). Asoka's empire included all but the southern tip of India, Tamil (TAHM-uhl) Land, which was occupied by Dravidian peoples.

Asoka's reign. Asoka's campaign to expand the empire through the conquest of neighboring Kalinga was a bloody one. Soon after the conquest, Asoka became deeply religious. Sickened by the killing, he vowed to give up war and work for peace. He relaxed many of the harsh laws that Chandragupta had made and reduced punishments for crimes. He ordered that pillars be erected throughout India, engraved with instructions for virtuous conduct.

Asoka's columns were made of polished sandstone and stood over 35 feet (10.6 meters) high. Inscribed on rock walls as well as on pillars, about 30 of the emperor's messages have been found.

Asoka also sent "Officers of Righteousness" throughout the empire to see that local officials promoted the "welfare and happiness" of his subjects. These officers were also charged with preventing "wrongful imprisonment or punishment," especially in "cases where a man has a large family, has been struck by calamity, or is advanced in years."

After Asoka's death in 232 B.C., the Maurya empire began to weaken. While Asoka's sons squabbled over who was to follow him, the provincial viceroys became increasingly independent. In 184 B.C., the last Maurya ruler was assassinated.

AN AGE OF INVASIONS

With the fall of the Maurya Empire, India was plunged into centuries of unrest. Indians fought each other as well as invaders who came through passes in the Hindu Kush. Throughout India, kingdoms ruled by Indians and kingdoms ruled by outsiders rose and fell.

Only one of these groups was able to build an extensive kingdom. The Kushans, descendants of nomads of Central Asia, moved into the Punjab, and by A.D. 50, Kushan warrior kings had established control over a large part of northwestern India.

The Kushan Empire. The Kushan Empire was a melting pot where Asian, Indian, Greek, and Persian cultures blended. Because many trade routes passed through the empire, it served as a bridge linking the contrasting cultures. Indian spices, Chinese silks, Greek coins, and ideas and customs passed along this route.

The Kushan Empire survived for about 200 years. Exactly why it fell is not known. However, about A.D. 250 the Kushan kings lost control of their kingdom, and northwestern India was once again without a strong ruler.

THE GUPTA EMPIRE

In the A.D. 300s, another young leader named Chandragupta gained power in Magadha, and in A.D. 320, he established a new dynasty, the Gupta Dynasty. He has become known as Chandragupta I.

Chandragupta I set out to build a new empire. His son and grandson expanded the empire until it stretched across northern India from the Arabian Sea to the Bay of Bengal. These Gupta emperors even received tribute from neighboring territories.

The Guptas ruled through a system of viceroys and governors, as the Mauryas had, but with less rigorous control. The Gupta emperors allowed village and city councils to manage local affairs. Even though the empire was loosely organized, the Guptas gave India its longest period of unity, prosperity, and peace.

The emperors encouraged the arts and sciences. Such an outpouring of accomplishments in literature, sculpture, astronomy, mathematics, and medicine resulted, that the period of Gupta rule is known as India's "Golden Age."

Fall of the Guptas. During the reign of the fourth Gupta emperor, disaster struck. Beginning about A.D. 467, the Huns, nomadic peoples of Central Asia, crossed the mountains and spilled onto the Indian plains. The Guptas held back the Huns for a time, but the invaders finally gained control in the northwest. Though

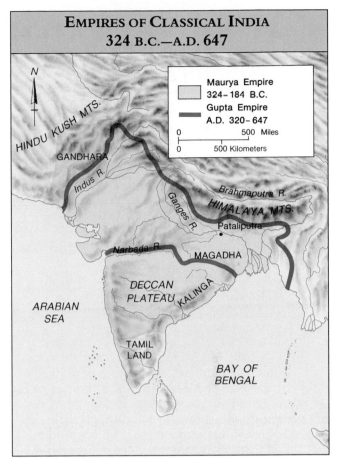

EMPIRES OF CLASSICAL INDIA 324 B.C.—A.D. 647

Maurya Empire 324–184 B.C.

Gupta Empire A.D. 320–647

0   500 Miles

0   500 Kilometers

they ruled briefly, the Huns succeeded in bringing down the Gupta Empire by A.D. 550.

In A.D. 606, at the age of sixteen, Harsha, a distant relation of the Gupta kings, ascended the throne of a small kingdom east of the Punjab. In the 41 years of his reign, he succeeded in rebuilding much of the former Gupta Empire. However, he left no heirs, and after his death in A.D. 647, the empire once more disintegrated.

SECTION REVIEW

1. With what empire is each associated: Chandragupta, Asoka, Chandragupta I, Harsha.

2. What did Asoka vow? Why? Describe at least two actions this vow caused him to take.

3. Why was the Kushan Empire a melting pot? How did ideas spread from the Kushan Empire?

4. Why is the Gupta Empire called India's "Golden Age"?

Analysis. Compare the organization of the Gupta and Maurya empires.

8-2
LIFE IN CLASSICAL INDIA

READ TO FIND OUT

—what the term *caste system* means.
—what the Buddha taught.
—how Hinduism developed.
—what ideals are represented in epic tales.
—how India became a link in international trade.
—what great invention Indian mathematicians made.
—what ideas were expressed in art and literature.

This second-century sculpture is one of the first portrayals of Buddha. The statue is from northwest India, where artists were influenced by the styles of Greek and Roman art.

Although they had no lasting, unified government, the people of India were united by their ideas and beliefs. Rooted in the Vedic faith of the Aryans, a complex body of religious ideas developed. Out of those ideas two religions took shape. These religions—Hinduism and Buddhism—still influence the lives of over a billion people worldwide.

The diverse people of India were increasingly bound by religious and social traditions. These traditions provided India with stability, enabling the Indian civilization to make remarkable achievements in such fields as mathematics, art, and literature.

INDIAN THOUGHT AND RELIGION

By 500 B.C., many religious teachers in India had begun to question the position of the Brahman priests and the effectiveness of their complex rituals. Several new schools of religious thought emerged, one of which gave rise to a new religion. It was called Buddhism, from the title Buddha, or "Enlightened One," that its followers gave to the founder, an Indian prince named Siddhartha Gautama (sihd-DAR-tuh GOWT-uh-muh).

Buddhism. According to tradition, Siddhartha was born in northeastern India about 563 B.C., where he grew up in wealth and luxury. Se-

cluded in the palace of his father, a warrior chief, the young prince was far from the daily burdens faced by most people. When Siddhartha was twenty-nine years old, however, he left the palace to ride through the streets in a chariot. For the first time he saw disease, old age, misery, and death. Shaken by what he had seen, he sorrowfully left his family and set out to find an answer to the question of why people must suffer.

For six years Gautama wandered. First he studied with leading Brahman priests. Then he tried a life of strict self-discipline. However, he did not find the answers he was seeking until he sat to meditate. After many days, he suddenly grasped the answer. From then on, Buddha spent his life teaching throughout the Ganges plain.

Buddha taught many traditional Indian beliefs. They included reincarnation, which is the belief that when the body dies, the soul is reborn in a different body, in a constant cycle of death and rebirth. He also taught the Four Noble Truths, which first state that as long as people remain within the cycle of death and rebirth, they cannot be free from suffering and sorrow. Second, this suffering is caused by a craving for individual satisfaction through things that have no lasting value. Third, people can break out of this cycle of suffering by giving up selfishness. Finally, the way to overcome this selfishness is to follow The Middle Way, a path between self-indulgence and rigid self-discipline.

Furthermore, according to the Buddha, when people rid themselves of their attachment to worldly things, they will achieve a state of peace called *nirvana*. Upon reaching nirvana, a person is released from the cycle of death and rebirth. To provide guidelines for following The Middle Way, the Buddha laid down the Noble Eightfold Path.

Buddha died about 483 B.C. at the age of eighty. After Buddha's death, his followers wandered throughout India spreading his teachings. They settled in monasteries, supported by contributions from the people to whom they preached. By 300 B.C., Buddhist temples and monasteries were scattered throughout India.

The spread of Buddhism. Traders and missionaries carried word of Buddhism beyond India. As Buddhism spread to China and to other areas, it developed two main branches: Theravada (ther-uh-VAH-duh), or the Way of the Elders, and Mahayana (mah-hah-YAH-nuh), or Great Vehicle.

According to Theravada Buddhism, individuals achieve understanding through their own efforts. The Buddha was seen only as a holy guide, not as a deity. Theravada Buddhism eventually spread to the lands of Ceylon, Burma, Thailand, Cambodia, Indonesia, and Malaysia.

In Mahayana Buddhism, however, the Buddha came to be worshipped as a deity and a savior of humankind. In addition, Mahayana Buddhists developed a belief in bodhisattvas (bō-dee-SUHT-vuhs), persons who have worked many lifetimes to achieve eternal peace, yet, instead of entering nirvana, choose instead to be reborn to help others achieve understanding. Mahayana Buddhists carried these ideas from India into China, Korea, Japan, Mongolia, and Tibet.

Although Buddhism spread from India to many other regions, it eventually nearly died out in the land of its birth. One reason was that Buddhism did not provide traditional rituals for birth, marriage, and death. Throughout India

ECHOES OF THE PAST

BUDDHA'S FIRST SERMON   528 B.C.

There are two ends *not* to be sought by a seeker of truth. What are those two? They are the pursuit of desires, which is base, common, and unprofitable; and the pursuit of hardship, which is grievous and unprofitable. The Middle Way avoids both these ends. It is enlightened. It brings clear vision and leads to peace, insight, full wisdom, and Nirvana. What is this Middle Way? It is the Noble Eightfold Path—Right Understanding, Right Purpose, Right Speech, Right Conduct, Right Means of Livelihood, Right Effort, Right Awareness, and Right Meditation. This is the Middle Way.

And this is the Noble Truth of Sorrow. Birth is sorrow, age is sorrow, disease is sorrow, death is sorrow, contact with the unpleasant is sor-

row, separation from the pleasant is sorrow, every wish unfulfilled is sorrow.

And this is the Noble Truth of the Arising of Sorrow. [It arises from] thirst, which leads to rebirth, which brings delight, and seeks pleasure now here, now there—the thirst for pleasure, the thirst for continued life, the thirst for power.

And this is the Noble Truth of the Stopping of Sorrow. It is the complete stopping of that thirst, so that no passion remains, leaving it, being emancipated from it, being released from it, giving no place to it.

And this is the Noble Truth of the Way which Leads to the Stopping of Sorrow. It is the Noble Eightfold Path.

For questions on Echoes of the Past, see "Analyzing Primary Sources" on page 173.

people relied on the Brahman priests for these ceremonies. Another reason was that Buddhist beliefs became absorbed into the Vedic religion of the Brahmans. By the time of the Guptas, the Brahmans had reestablished their authority.

Hinduism. Hinduism, which became the dominant religion of India, developed gradually out of the traditional beliefs and practices of the Brahman priests. For example, Hindu beliefs in reincarnation grew out of teachings found in the ancient *Vedas*. Closely related to this belief is the law of *karma*, which states that a person's behavior in one life will influence the next life into which that person will be born.

Hinduism embraces thousands of deities, although the majority of Hindus worship only one or two. Among the most widely revered deities are Vishnu, the preserver; Krishna, who is Vishnu in human form; Siva, the destroyer; Parvati, the goddess of motherhood; and Brahma, the creator. However, to many Hindus, all of these gods and goddesses are but various forms of the single universal spirit called Brahman, which is revealed in the *Upanishads*.

For many Hindus, the goal of life is to realize that the soul of the individual is part of a universal soul. To reach this understanding may take several lifetimes. When an individual's soul finally achieves oneness with the universal soul, or Brahman, the individual attains *moksha*, a release from the cycle of rebirths.

The great writings. The *Vedas*, including the *Upanishads*, are among the most important Hindu writings. These works are studied chiefly by the priests. However, over the centuries heroic tales that expressed Indian ideals were passed down by word of mouth. In time, they were written down as two great epics, the *Mahabharata* (ma-HAH-BAH-rah-tah) and the *Ramayana* (rah-mah-YAHN-uh).

Throughout India's history, these stories have been told and retold. They have been the subjects of painting, sculpture, and drama. The heroes and heroines of the tales have set examples of courage, virtue, and duty for others.

The longest poem known today, the *Mahabharata*, or "Great War," tells of a war fought for a kingdom in the most ancient of times. In

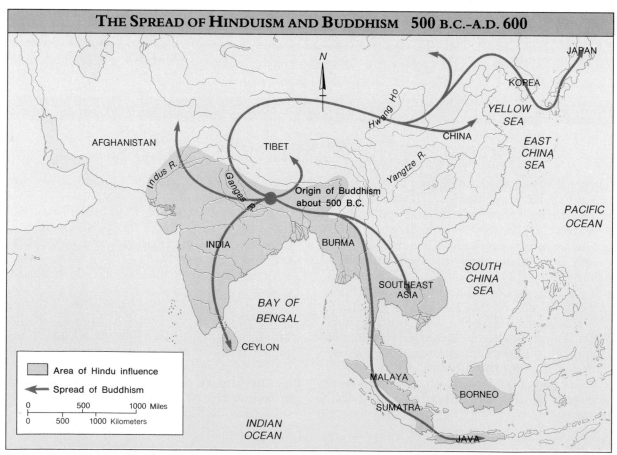

THE SPREAD OF HINDUISM AND BUDDHISM   500 B.C.–A.D. 600

Area of Hindu influence

Spread of Buddhism

As a god of both destruction and creativity, Siva is worshipped in many different forms. Here he is pictured as lord of dance. Siva is often shown with several arms to emphasize his powers.

this conflict, two branches of one family struggled against each other.

Considered the most sacred part of the *Mahabharata* is the *Bhagavad-Gita* (BAHG-uh-vud-GEE-tuh), or "Song of the Lord." In this story, the warrior Arjuna rides into battle with the god Krishna as his charioteer. Arjuna asks Krishna what he should do, for he does not want to kill his cousins.

Krishna replies that death is unimportant. "It [the spirit] is never born and never dies and will never cease to be; it is not slain when the body is slain." What is important, according to Krishna, is fulfilling the duties in your life.

In the *Ramayana*, or "Story of Rama," a hero named Rama helps to defend some forest dwellers against a demon army. With the aid of a monkey army, he also rescues his beloved wife Sita from the demons. Many historians believe the *Ramayana* is based on historic fact. The characters may represent an invasion force and the people who drove out the invaders. The importance of the *Ramayana*, however, lies in the emphasis it places on faithful and happy marriage. Rama and Sita have represented ideals of manhood and womanhood throughout India's history.

SOCIAL PATTERNS

India's traditional class system has also been passed down through history. Over many years, the social class system of the Aryans evolved into a fixed **caste system**, a way of organizing society with rigid distinctions between social classes.

In India's caste system an individual's social class was inherited, and the classes were kept separate by numerous rules of behavior. Some people were ranked below the lowest class and were not recognized as part of society. These people became *outcastes*.

Gradually the Brahman, Kshatriya, Vaisya, and Sudra castes became divided into smaller groups. These groups were divided once again, according to the occupations of the caste's members. Eventually about 3,000 castes developed in India.

In addition to occupations, the caste system determined the location of people's homes, their clothing, and their religious rituals. Complex rules governed cooking and eating. Marriages, usually arranged by families, followed the rules of the caste. Marriage between members of different castes was forbidden.

ALMANAC

HINDU IDEALS

Goals:
   artha: to acquire material wealth
   kama: to enjoy all the proper pleasures
   dharma: to perform one's proper duties
   moksha: to free one's soul from the cycle
      of reincarnation

Stages of Life:
   student: memorize Vedas, study subjects
      appropriate to one's caste
   householder: marry, have children
   hermit: retire from family responsibili-
      ties after becoming a grandparent,
      live simply and meditate
   wanderer: become completely detached
      from material possessions, become
      a homeless beggar

Research Activity: Write a report on how these Hindu ideals relate to the lives of Hindus today.

In spite of such restrictions, the caste system provided the Indian people with stability and a sense of security. The caste acted as an extended family, protecting its members and caring for its needy. At times when India was without a strong central government, the caste system served to provide guidelines for behavior. However, the caste system also kept people apart, thereby discouraging political unity.

ECONOMIC PATTERNS

Although most people lived in walled rural villages with huts clustered around a well or pond, more and more towns and cities began to dot both the Deccan and the northern plain. By A.D. 600, the populations of some cities reached as high as half a million. Temples and palaces dominated these cities. Schools, hospitals, and parks also lay within the city walls. The multi-storied homes of the wealthy, and the cottages and huts of poorer citizens lined the streets.

While agriculture provided a living for most people, there was also considerable manufacturing. Indian metal workers produced the best iron in the world at the time. A textile industry also developed. Using fine dyes and printing techniques, Indian weavers and dyers produced silk, cotton, and woolen cloth for export.

Trade. As early as 500 B.C., a network of roads crisscrossed the northern plains. By 200 B.C., the network extended throughout the Deccan. The roads not only connected Indian cities, but also made India a link in the chain of international trade. Merchants traveled in ox-drawn carts, carrying staples such as rice, salt, and sugar as well as luxury goods. Indian goods traveled overland to Persia and Mesopotamia in the west and to China in the east.

Trade was also carried on by sea. Port cities grew up at the mouths of the Ganges and the Indus rivers. Along the southern coasts, the Tamils developed harbors with lighthouses and wharves. Vessels carried Indian goods as far as Ceylon and Indonesia to the east, and westward to Egypt and Palestine.

Foreign vessels also frequented Indian harbors. For example, ships of the Roman Empire brought pottery, metals, glassware, slaves, and gold coins. The foreign traders took back spices, jewels, perfumes, and fine textiles, as well as sugar, rice, and ivory carvings.

THE ACHIEVEMENTS OF CLASSICAL INDIA

Through trade, Indian merchants spread a brilliant invention of Hindu mathematicians—the decimal system. Using only ten numerals and the idea of zero, which was unknown to other peoples at the time, the decimal system can be used to express any number, large or small.

Because it greatly simplified business dealings, Indian merchants adopted the decimal system. They then passed it on to Arab traders, who carried it into the Greek and Roman world. There it became known as the Arabic system. One of the world's most useful ways to express numbers, the decimal system is used today throughout much of the world.

Medicine. Medical science in classical India borrowed knowledge from the Greeks, as well as from the Arabs. Although medical research in India was limited by Hindu restrictions on contact with dead bodies, Indian doctors knew how to inoculate against smallpox with cowpox serum and, as early as the A.D. 300s, understood the importance of sterilizing wounds. Indian hospitals became known for their cleanliness.

The arts. Indian art showed both religious devotion and delight in everyday life. Indian artists excelled at sculpture, including tiny ornamental figures, large bronze statues, and elaborate carvings. Buddha's followers erected many dome-shaped shrines, called *stupas*, which were surrounded by walls ornately carved with scenes of Buddha's life.

The Buddha's followers also cut temples into rock walls. One temple cave, at Ajanta (uh-JAHN-tuh), south of the Vindhya range, reaches 68 feet (20.75 meters) into the mountainside. Decorated with murals, the walls depict Buddha and his followers, princes in chariots, jeweled noblewomen, acrobats, wrestlers, animals, birds, and flowers.

Literature. Writing had died out after the Aryan invasion. However, by the 500s B.C. a 39-letter alphabet—*Brahmi*—came into use. The origins of Brahmi are a mystery, but it may be a version of the Indus Valley writing that had disappeared a thousand years earlier. Nevertheless, now Brahmi was used to record such works as the *Vedas*.

Built about A.D. 1000, this large stupa is one of many still standing at Sanchi in central India. Celebrating the life of Buddha, pilgrims make ritual marches around the dome.

8-3
EMPIRES OF CHINA

READ TO FIND OUT

—what the terms **bureaucracy** and **civil service** mean.
—how the Ch'in Dynasty unified China.
—how the Han Dynasty expanded China's borders.
—why the Six Dynasties Period was a time of unrest in China.

Indian literature included other works besides the *Vedas*, the *Mahabharata*, and the *Ramayana*. Poems, for example, told of love, everyday life, and noble deeds. The greatest Sanskrit poet and playwright was Kalidasa (kah-lee-DAHS-uh), who lived from A.D. 375 to A.D. 455. He wrote many plays of love and adventure.

In addition, numerous fables and fairy tales were gathered into a collection called the *Panchatantra* (PUN-chuh-TUN-truh). Many of these tales traveled to Arabia and became part of the *Arabian Nights*. Others were known in Europe. Cinderella, for instance, was originally an Indian princess named Sumanadevi.

SECTION REVIEW

1. Define **caste system**.

2. How did Buddhism develop? What were the Four Noble Truths?

3. How did Hinduism originate? Explain two of its major beliefs.

4. With what nations did India carry on trade?

5. What was India's great mathematical gift to the world? Why was it important?

6. Give three examples of Indian literature.

Analysis. The people of classical India developed many ideas that were later adopted by people in other areas. Provide at least three examples of this cultural diffusion.

About 950 B.C., the Chou conquered the Shang and established the Chou Dynasty in China. However, after about 700 B.C., the many different Chinese principalities, or states ruled by princes, became more and more independent until the Chou king ruled in name only. Rivalries between the independent principalities grew so intense that the last years of the Chou Dynasty, from 403 B.C. to 221 B.C., are known as the Period of the Warring States.

During this long period some states began to expand. By the end of the 300s B.C., the states had merged into just three. One of these, the state of Ch'in (CHIN), deposed the Chou king in 256 B.C., and by 221 B.C. conquered the remaining two states.

THE CH'IN DYNASTY

The Ch'in Dynasty lasted only 15 years, until 206 B.C. Yet its political achievements were so important that China took its name from this dynasty. The Ch'in prince who led the conquest of the Chou adopted the name Shih Huang Ti (shee HWAHNG dee), meaning "first emperor." With a swift cavalry, Shih Huang Ti expanded China's territory. It now included the entire Yangtze River valley, as well as a narrow strip extending south to the Si River.

To seal out the nomad tribes along China's northern border, the emperor ordered a defensive wall to be built. Connecting existing smaller walls built during the Chou period, this Great Wall of China stretched for 1,400 miles (2,200 kilometers). In most places the Great

Over centuries, the Great Wall was lengthened and improved. By hand, millions of laborers placed the stones, bricks, and earth that form the wall. Today, the wall is being restored.

Wall was 25 feet (7.5 meters) high and 15 feet (4.5 meters) thick. A paved roadway along the top enabled troops to move quickly. Here and there along the wall were gateways through which trading caravans could pass.

Unification of China. Ruling from the city of Chang-an (CHAHNG-AHN), formerly called Sian, Shih Huang Ti unified China under a strong central government. He did not allow the lords of China's states to maintain their power. Instead, he divided China into districts and named governors who reported to him. Noble families from the states were resettled in the capital to keep them from regaining power.

Shih Huang Ti also took other steps to unify China. A national code of law replaced many local laws. Other laws created uniform systems of taxes, weights, measures, and money. In addition, new highways stretched from the capital to unite the nation.

Shih Huang Ti made China one of the world's great empires. Nevertheless, he was a most unpopular ruler. Many of his laws carried harsh penalties. For example, the death penalty was enforced for the crime of reading any books, except technical manuals, written before the Ch'in Dynasty.

When Shih Huang Ti died in 210 B.C., a revolt broke out, and a general of the army defeated the Ch'in. The general took the name Kao Tsu (GOW DZOO), meaning "chief ancestor," and founded a new dynasty in 202 B.C.

THE HAN DYNASTY

Kao Tsu called the new dynasty the Han, after the river where he had been stationed when he was in the army. The Han Dynasty ruled China from the city of Chang-an until A.D. 220. Accomplishments during those years were so numerous that many Chinese today still call themselves "Sons of Han."

Under Kao Tsu, China continued to be divided into provinces headed by governors who reported to the emperor. However, Kao Tsu abolished the harsh laws of the Ch'in. He was a just ruler. He understood the saying of one Chinese philosopher: "The prince is the boat. The common people are the water. The water can support the boat, or the water can capsize the boat."

After Kao Tsu's death in 195 B.C., Han rulers continued to expand the empire. Under the sixth emperor, Wu Ti (WOO DEE), who ruled from 140 B.C. to 87 B.C., China expanded to the northeast, the northwest, and the south.

Wu Ti sent his armies against the Huns, located northeast and northwest of China. As the Chinese gained ground, they populated these

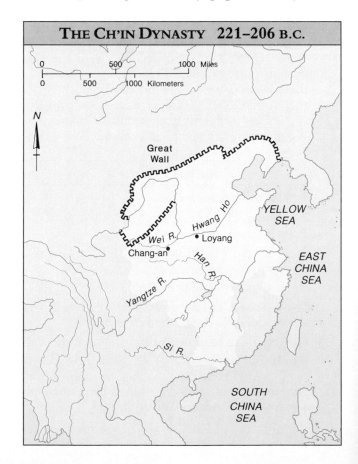

THE CH'IN DYNASTY 221–206 B.C.

areas with colonists to keep the Huns from returning. Soon the Chinese had taken over the desert basins of the northwest, and parts of Mongolia, Manchuria, and Korea. Meanwhile, Chinese armies also expanded the empire further south.

New trade routes. One result of Chinese expansion was the opening of new trade routes. One important route was discovered when General Chang Ch'ien set out in 139 B.C. with a bodyguard of 100 to secure an alliance with nomad rivals of the Huns. However, he was soon captured by the Huns. After 10 years, he escaped with only a few of his bodyguards.

Instead of returning to China, he turned westward, still seeking the rival nomads. The general finally caught up with them north of the Hindu Kush but could not persuade them to help the Chinese. The nomads instead went on to found the Kushan Empire in India. The general returned to China with one bodyguard and knowledge of lands as far west as Greece and Rome. With such knowledge, trade blossomed. The course that the general took became the trade route known as the Silk Road.

System of government. The Han ruled their empire with a vast **bureaucracy**, a system set up to carry out the affairs of government through various departments managed by appointed officials. The Chinese government had departments of agriculture, crime and justice, public works, finance, and the military, among others. Each department had a chief minister and numerous minor officials.

Under earlier dynasties, government officials had been selected from aristocratic families. Now, Han rulers vigorously recruited the best candidates both from the university at Changan and from recommendations made by local officials. After the candidates took examinations in such areas as literature, law, philosophy, and ethics, the emperor made appointments. The body of government workers hired according to such a system is called the **civil service**. The Chinese civil service system was the first such system in the world.

Civil service examinations helped to raise the quality of government officials. The examinations enabled a small number of people to rise in Chinese society. In addition, the bureaucracy limited the emperor's power. Because imperial

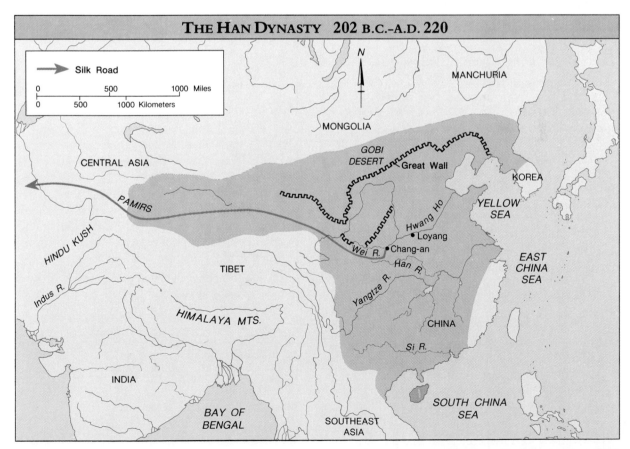

THE HAN DYNASTY 202 B.C.–A.D. 220

Silk Road

0   500   1000 Miles
0   500   1000 Kilometers

MANCHURIA

MONGOLIA

GOBI DESERT
Great Wall

CENTRAL ASIA

KOREA

PAMIRS

YELLOW SEA

HINDU KUSH

Hwang Ho
Loyang
Wei R. Chang-an

Indus R.

TIBET

EAST CHINA SEA

Han R.

HIMALAYA MTS.

Yangtze R.

CHINA

INDIA

Si R.

BAY OF BENGAL

SOUTHEAST ASIA

SOUTH CHINA SEA

ANALYZING PRIMARY SOURCES

INTRODUCING THE SKILL

Primary sources are historical records left by people who directly observed the events. Common types of primary sources include written accounts, paintings, and drawings. The more skilled you become at analyzing primary sources, the more they will reveal to you about the past.

EXPLAINING THE SKILL

Primary sources can mislead as well as reveal. The historian's first task, of course, is to understand the information given by the primary source. The next step is to analyze the primary source to try to determine whether it is an accurate account of events. When analyzing a primary source, a historian might ask the following questions:

A. Is this really a primary source? Did the person who created it participate in or observe the events described?

B. Was this account produced while the events were still fresh in the person's memory?

C. Is the person reliable? Did he or she have reason to leave out any facts or to exaggerate any of the facts?

D. Are there details in the account that can be checked against other sources?

E. Did the person indicate how he or she felt about the events being described?

APPLYING THE SKILL

The following poem—a primary source—was written by a Chinese princess named Hsi-ch'un (SHEE-JOON). She was sent by the emperor Wu Ti to be married to the chief of the Wu-sun, a nomadic tribe. The koumiss mentioned in the poem was a drink made of fermented horse's milk.

> My family has married me off,
> Alas! and sent me far,
> To the strange land of the Wu-sun.
> I'm now, woe is me, the king's wife.

> I live in a tent, and a house wall
> Have I exchanged for felt.
> My food is only meat;
> Koumiss they give to drink with it.
> O, my heart burns since they sent me here;
> I can only think of my home, over and over.
> Could I but be a yellow crane,
> Fast would I fly back to my own kingdom!

Use the information in the poem to answer these questions.

1. Why do you think this poem is regarded as a primary source? What is the poem about?

2. Do you think the poem was written while these events were still fresh in Hsi-ch'un's memory? Why or why not?

3. Do you think she was a reliable source of information? Why or why not?

4. What details did she include about her new life in the strange land that could be checked with other sources?

5. How did she feel about these events? What words or phrases in the poem reveal her feelings? Explain.

INTERPRETING THE INFORMATION

Read the poem again to determine what it tells you about Chinese society at the time Princess Hsi-ch'un lived.

6. What does the poem suggest about the education of Chinese noblewomen?

7. What does it suggest about Chinese attitudes toward the nomads on their borders? What does it reveal about the difference between the food and housing of Chinese nobility and that of the nomadic Wu-sun tribe?

8. What does the poem reveal about the rights of Chinese noblewomen?

REVIEWING THE SKILL

9. What is a primary source?

10. Explain why people need to analyze primary sources before accepting them as factual accounts.

orders had to pass through several levels of bureaucracy, unpopular orders could purposely be carried out inefficiently.

Wu Ti died in 87 B.C. The Han emperors who followed were not as able as he had been. For a brief time, from A.D. 9 to A.D. 23, a high government official, Wang Mang, seized the throne. He made plans for the government to take over private land and redistribute it to the peasants. However, a revolt that crossed class lines broke out. In A.D. 23, Wang Mang was killed, and the Han Dynasty was restored.

Moving the capital to Loyang, emperors of the later Han Dynasty ruled successfully for a time. With both military might and diplomacy, the Han succeeded in bringing some of the nomadic tribes along their northern borders under Chinese control. Many of the nomad groups were persuaded to settle and farm. However, eventually many of these former nomads rebelled. In addition, widespread flooding and other agricultural problems caused unrest. In A.D. 184, a peasant revolt led by a group known as the Yellow Turbans shook the empire. The Han crushed the revolt, but further uprisings ended Han rule in A.D. 220.

THE SIX DYNASTIES PERIOD

The period after the Han Dynasty is known as the Six Dynasties Period. From A.D. 220 to A.D. 589, no single leader or family could hold the great empire together, and China became a kaleidoscope of kingdoms.

Nevertheless, China endured the unrest of these four centuries. Conquering invaders were in time absorbed into the Chinese culture or forced out. Finally, in A.D. 589, the turmoil ended when a new dynasty, the Sui (SWEE), again united China.

SECTION REVIEW

1. Define *bureaucracy* and *civil service*.

2. How did Shih Huang Ti unify China?

3. How did the Han expand China's borders?

4. What caused unrest during the Six Dynasties Period?

Analysis. Explain the saying, "The prince is the boat. The common people are the water. The water can support the boat, or the water can capsize the boat."

8-4
LIFE IN CLASSICAL CHINA

READ TO FIND OUT

—what ideals Confucius and Lao-tzu taught.

—how Buddhism spread to China.

—how social patterns compared with those of earlier times.

—what the Chinese achieved in technology, science, art, and literature.

From the Period of the Warring States beginning about 400 B.C. through the Six Dynasties Period ending about A.D. 590, China expanded and the population grew. The first Chinese census, taken in A.D. 2, reported the Chinese population at 57 million. Within China's borders were people of many diverse backgrounds, including Chinese, descendants of steppe nomads, Koreans, and the farming peoples of Southeast Asia.

The Chinese created a vigorous culture based on tradition. Yet, many new schools of thought arose, concerned with questions about good government and good living. During the Han Dynasty, especially, Chinese achievements in thought, technology, science, the arts, and literature rivaled those of Greece and Rome.

CHINESE THOUGHT AND RELIGION

Sometime during the Period of the Warring States, K'ung Fu-Tze (kung FOO-dzee), or Confucius, developed ideas that were to have a great impact on Chinese society. Historians believe that Confucius lived from about 551 B.C. to 478 B.C., a time of great unrest. At the age of twenty-two, he began his career as a teacher. He then entered government service but gave up that post to resume teaching. Traveling from one Chinese state to another, Confucius taught ways of living and thinking that he believed would end the unrest of the time.

Confucianism. Confucius believed that in the past there had been a golden age. He believed

Life-sized terra cotta soldiers guard the tomb of Emperor Shih Huang Ti. Discovered in 1974, the underground army numbers 6,000 figures, each with distinctly different features.

that morality—acting according to principles of right conduct—was responsible for the golden age. According to Confucius, proper public and private behavior would recreate that time.

Confucius taught that human beings are by nature good. He said that in private life, a good person should know about traditions and try always to be loyal, courteous, kind, and hardworking. In public life, a good person should be honest and loyal to the group. In addition, a person should be obedient and respectful toward his or her superiors, just as children were to be obedient and respectful toward their elders. In turn, the emperor, like a father, was expected to set a good example by being just, not cruel. To Confucius, the basis of a stable society was not force but morality.

After Confucius died, his disciples passed on his teachings. Many of his sayings were eventually collected in a book called the *Analects* (AN-uh-lekts), and by the time of the Han Dynasty, Confucianism had had a strong impact on Chinese society. For example, candidates for the bureaucracy were expected to study the *Analects* and the works of Confucius's followers.

Taoism. The thought of Confucius centered on personal and public conduct. In contrast, Taoism, the philosophy of Lao-tzu (LOW-TSOO), was concerned with other aspects of life—the mysteries of nature and the role of the supernatural. Lao-tzu is thought to have lived from about 604 B.C. to 531 B.C. His thinking is collected in a book known as the Tao Te Ching (DOW duh JING), which means "The Classic of the Way and Its Power."

Taoism centered on the idea of the *tao* (DOW), or the "Way of the Universe." According to Lao-tzu, people should give up worldly pursuits, such as power and money, and instead live simply, in harmony with nature. In this way they would find immortality through achieving harmony with the *tao*.

Where Confucius stressed the importance of government, Lao-tzu took a different view. To Lao-tzu, harmony with the *tao* was more important than government and law. However, he did not teach that government should be abolished. He taught, instead, that if people were in harmony with the *tao*, little government would be necessary.

Many people who found little comfort in the Confucian view of the world were attracted to Taoism's mysticism. In addition, the Taoist reverence for all forms of life influenced many Chinese poets and landscape painters. Some individuals drew inspiration both from Confucianism's emphasis on duty to society and Taoism's concern with knowledge of nature.

Mo Ti. Living at about the same time as Confucius was the philosopher Mo Ti (MŌ DEE). His ideas had an important influence during his lifetime and for almost two centuries after.

Mo Ti taught that since "Heaven loves all people dearly," people should practice universal love. He expressed his idea with a golden rule: "One should take care of his friend as he does of himself, and take care of his friend's parents as he does of his own."

Mo Ti disapproved of all extravagance and waste. He considered war the worst form of waste. Although trained as warriors, he and his followers often went into combat to try to convince the opposing parties to settle their differences peacefully. When that effort failed, they joined the battle on the weaker side.

Legalism. After the fall of the Chou Dynasty, the ideas of Confucius seemed to be forgotten. The rulers of the Ch'in Dynasty followed a school of thought called Legalism. The Legalists believed that ideas about goodness and tradition were useless.

In contrast to Confucius's belief that human beings are by nature good, Legalism held that people are naturally greedy and fearful. Only the threat of harsh punishment would force people to be honest, loyal, and obedient.

The Legalists, therefore, favored a strict government with a clear code of law and a ruler with total power over the people. The Legalists also favored war as a means of strengthening the power of the state. Shih Huang Ti ran his dynasty on Legalist ideas after winning the Chinese throne in 221 B.C. Legalism died out with the dynasty, however.

Buddhism in China. Mahayana Buddhism probably entered China about the first century A.D. Missionaries from India may have accompanied the trading ships that sailed to south China or the overland caravans that had become common. By A.D. 148 Buddhist writings were being translated into Chinese.

At first, Buddhism appealed to the upper classes. However, as unrest swept China during the later Han Dynasty, Buddhism's appeal widened. The Buddha's words offered comfort and hope to many who suffered in these times. For this reason, the practice of Buddhism became widespread during the Six Dynasties Period. By the end of this period, the Chinese referred to Buddhism, Confucianism, and Taoism as the Three Doctrines.

Buddhism, which underwent some change in China, became an important part of Chinese culture. Buddhist convents and monasteries appeared throughout China, and some of them grew extremely wealthy. Buddhist ideas also influenced political thought.

SOCIAL PATTERNS

Social patterns in China did not change much from early Chou times. The emperor and the royal family were the highest class of Chinese society. Below them came the nobility. Many nobles owned large estates that they passed on through inheritance. The nobility spent much of their time conducting ceremonies or carrying on warfare. From this wealthy class came many members of the bureaucracy.

At the next level in the social structure were the commoners—peasants, artisans, and merchants. Some peasants owned land of their own and a few were wealthy. Most peasants, though, rented the land they tilled. They lived in poverty in small villages, paying heavy taxes to landlords and the state. They were also required to work on public projects such as building roads or canals for a month or so each year.

Artisans lived in cities near the palaces of the nobility for whom they provided services and luxury goods. Artisans' homes also served as shops and workplaces.

According to Confucian scholars, merchants contributed little to society. They were thus ranked just above slaves. However, many merchants did acquire great wealth, and with it, power. They could afford to send their children to schools where they could train to become scholars and bureaucrats. Merchants could also arrange marriage between their children and those of the nobility.

The lowest class was made up of entertainers and servants. A person of this class could not associate with people of other classes.

Confucius believed that a person's virtues and actions determined ranking in society. In fact, poor people did sometimes rise to positions of power and wealth in China. Most often, however, people stayed within the class into which they had been born.

ECONOMIC PATTERNS

The economy of classical China was chiefly agricultural. However, by the end of the Han Dynasty, China's technology had advanced far beyond that of any other civilization. The Chinese excelled at making practical items, such as the wheelbarrow, the bellows, and a folding umbrella, as well as fine steel. Chinese miners

A recently excavated Han site revealed this rare bronze horse poised on a flying swallow. The statue represents a fine, central Asian breed that the Chinese called "celestial horses."

introduced the pulley and winding gear to mine salt and other minerals. The Chinese were also the first to devise suspension bridges.

Perhaps the greatest Chinese invention of the time, however, was a type of paper. The first Chinese paper was made—by A.D. 100—from tree bark, hemp, old rags, and fishing net. Produced in various colors, paper quickly took the place of silk as the material on which the Chinese wrote important messages.

Trade. During the Period of the Warring States, Chinese trade expanded slowly. By river boat and by cart, merchants carried grains, salt, metals, furs, and leather throughout China.

International trade routes with the Middle East, India, and Southeast Asia were gradually established during the Han Dynasty. The two great empires of the world at the time—Rome and China—traded with each other. However, Chinese and Roman merchants did not ex-change goods with one another face to face. Instead they traded indirectly through merchants from other regions.

THE ACHIEVEMENTS OF CLASSICAL CHINA

The Chinese excelled at astronomy. Chinese records from 240 B.C. are the first to describe the appearance of Halley's Comet. Such records became the basis for an imperial almanac that gave the lengths of the months and first day of each of the seasons. The correct calculation of the first day of winter was extremely important, as this day was the beginning of the new year. By 444 B.C., the Chinese had a calendar based on a year of 365¼ days.

The Chinese also kept a careful record of earthquakes. A Chinese scientist living from A.D. 78 to A.D. 139 devised a seismograph, an instrument that records earthquakes. The Chi-

---

SPOTLIGHT: IDEAS AND DEVELOPMENTS

THE SILK ROAD

From the earliest of times, people exchanged goods with the people of neighboring towns or regions. A rough network of paths and roadways used by traders began to link the towns. As empires expanded, so did their trade routes.

One of the ancient world's trade routes was the nearly 4,000-mile (6,400-kilometer) Silk Road. A long slender thread connecting China with India, the Middle East, Persia, and the Roman Empire, the route was open from the second century B.C. to the seventh century A.D. From Chang-an in China, the road led through the Wei Valley, skirted the desert basins of western China, and climbed into the Pamirs, mountains so high they are called the "roof of the world." In the Pamirs, the route forked into the South Road, which led into India, and the North Road, which crossed Persia and ended at the Mediterranean Sea.

The road got its name because of the quantity of silk that was carried from China to India and the Mediterranean world along this route. Spices and other goods also flowed westward from China. At the Mediterranean's shores, Romans paid for the lustrous silks and pungent spices with products such as glass, metals, dyes, and especially gold. Other merchants—Greeks, Indians, and Arabs—traveled this route as well.

Merchants formed caravans to protect themselves from warfare or bands of thieves. Long trains of heavily laden pack animals and ox-drawn carts wore the trail ever deeper into the earth. Few traders traveled the entire route, however. Instead, goods changed hands at established points. A Chinese textile merchant might carry the silk from Chang-an as far as the desert. From there, the cloth might pass through the hands of several nomad traders, a Persian dealer, and a Roman merchant in the Middle East. The goods might then be loaded into the hold of a ship bound for Roman ports. Each exchange raised the price of the goods just a little bit.

Knowledge, like merchandise, also traveled. Through trade, Rome learned about India and China. In turn, India and China both came to know about Rome and other civilizations. Knowledge about the use of iron, wheat cultivation, and the domestication of poultry were just a few of the ideas to travel the Silk Road.

nese device not only indicated when an earthquake happened, but also from what direction.

Medicine was considered an honorable art, and the Chinese produced long texts filled with instructions for diagnosing diseases and for using herbs and minerals to cure them. Many of the ancient cures prescribed are found in modern medicine. Early Chinese also developed acupuncture, a method of treating disease and pain by pricking the skin with needles. This treatment is still in use in some parts of the world.

Arts and literature. Confucius believed that the most admirable achievement of a nation was not its wealth but the art its people produced. Painting, ceramics, architecture, and literature added to the quality of life.

Chinese artists painted landscapes and scenes of everyday life on paper and silk. Working with swift, delicate brush strokes, they attempted to portray not just the appearance of the subject, but "the spirit through the form." Classical Chinese art depicted nature in loving detail.

Beautiful brush strokes were so appreciated that the painting of characters used in Chinese writing became an art. This beautiful writing is called *calligraphy*. Painting, poetry, and calligraphy were the arts of nobility.

Other Chinese artists wove silk screens and tapestries, and carved figurines and jewelry from ivory and jade. Stone sculptures portrayed battles and scenes of court life with naturalness and a strong sense of movement.

To people living during the Han Dynasty, the most important literary works were the *Five Classics*. Although Confucius did not write them, these books expressed his ideas. It is not known who did write them, but they probably originated during the Chou Dynasty.

The *Five Classics* became the basis for civil service examinations. The *Classic of History* contains speeches and other materials on government. The *Classic of Poetry* contains more than 300 poems. The other three *Classics* deal with history, foretelling the future, and etiquette and ritual.

In addition to the *Five Classics*, Chinese writers produced many fine works of history, poetry, travel, and geography. For example, while traveling in India in search of Buddhist writings, Chinese monks wrote books describing

Indian life. Since Indians wrote little history, the Chinese writings are often the only records of the time.

SECTION REVIEW

1. State what each of the following taught about the purpose of government: Confucius, Lao-tzu, the Legalists.

2. Explain why the practice of Buddhism became widespread in China.

3. How did peasants, merchants and artisans fit into the Chinese social pattern?

4. List five major Chinese achievements in technology, science, and art.

Analysis. State which of the following were most likely influenced by Confucius and which by Lao-tzu: landscape painting, poetry reminiscing about the past, the *Classic* about etiquette and ritual. Explain your answer.

Data Search. Refer to the appropriate chart on page 830 to identify the major exports of India and China.

HISTORY IN FOCUS

In the A.D. 600s, the influence of Indian culture was felt over an even greater area than that influenced by Roman ways. Although some Indian ideas were adopted in places such as Persia or China, nowhere did Indian culture take root as strongly as in Southeast Asia. Royal courts in Indonesia, Thailand, and Vietnam adopted Indian styles of clothing and imported Indian works of art. Buddhist stupas were built throughout Indonesia, Ceylon, and other parts of Southeast Asia. In addition, the ancient tales of deities, and heroes and heroines were told and retold in Southeast Asia as well as India.

Chinese civilization spread gradually until it encompassed a large part of the continent of Asia. However, because so much rugged terrain separates China from other areas, Chinese civilization was relatively isolated from other cultures. The Chinese had less opportunity, therefore, to exchange ideas with others. Even so, with the opening of trade routes, ideas such as Buddhism were introduced into China from the outside. In addition, Chinese ideas, such as paper making, began to spread slowly to the rest of the world.

SUMMARY

- India's first empire, the Maurya, expanded from the Ganges plain to control most of India. Centuries of unrest followed its fall in 184 B.C., though the Kushans did establish an important kingdom in the northwest. In A.D. 320, the Gupta Dynasty brought in the "Golden Age" of India.

- India gave birth to two great religions. Buddhism spread to many other countries. Hinduism became the major religion of India.

- India's traditional class structure gave rise to a complex caste system. Manufacturing developed, and India became part of an international trade network. Indian civilization spread throughout Southeast Asia.

- In China, the Ch'in Dynasty brought unity through a strong central government. The Han Dynasty expanded the empire and created a civil service system. The Six Dynasties Period, from A.D. 220 to A.D. 589, marked a return to instability.

- The philosophies of Confucianism and Taoism provided much of the basis for Chinese thought. Buddhism also became an important part of Chinese culture.

- Chinese social structure changed little over the centuries. The economy remained rooted in agriculture, though technology and trade grew in importance. The Chinese excelled at astronomy, medicine, and the arts.

VOCABULARY REVIEW

Match each numbered vocabulary term with the lettered term most closely related to it. Then explain the relationship between the terms in each matched pair.

Example: The term *social responsibility* relates to the term *morality* because each concerns the proper conduct of people in society.

1. caste system
2. bureaucracy
3. civil service

   (a) governmental professionalism
   (b) class structure
   (c) governmental organization

CHAPTER REVIEW

1. (a) How was government organized in the Maurya Empire? **(b)** How did the Gupta system of government differ from that of the Maurya?

2. (a) How did Ch'in rule differ from the rule of previous dynasties in China? **(b)** Explain the measures taken by rulers of the Ch'in Dynasty to centralize the government. **(c)** In what ways was Han rule similar to Ch'in rule? How was it different?

3. Classical India and China each experienced a period that seemed to foster numerous accomplishments. **(a)** Identify this period in India and in China. **(b)** Which productive period came earlier, India's or China's?

4. (a) Compare the basic beliefs of Hinduism and Buddhism in India. **(b)** Describe the two main branches of Buddhism. **(c)** In general, what impact did religious beliefs have on the peoples of India?

5. (a) Why did Buddhism gain mass appeal in China? **(b)** Why did Buddhism lose appeal in India?

6. (a) List the important writings that developed from Hinduism. **(b)** What form of Indian literature spread to the rest of the world? **(c)** How did Chinese writers contribute to Indian history? **(d)** What were the customary themes of Chinese art?

7. (a) Describe Confucius's concept of the golden age. **(b)** According to Lao-tzu, how should people live their lives? **(c)** How did the Legalists react to Confucian teachings? **(d)** When these new schools of thought arose, was China in a state of stability or unrest?

8. (a) Describe the Indian and Chinese class systems. **(b)** What impact did the caste system have on Indians and their society?

9. (a) Describe how India carried out international trade. **(b)** Describe the extent of China's international trade.

10. (a) List three achievements of classical India. **(b)** List five practical Chinese inventions. **(c)** What two medical procedures did the Chinese use?

THINKING CRITICALLY: ACTIVITIES

1. Make a chart listing the major achievements and characteristics of classical China and India. At the top of the chart, write the labels "China" and "India." Then, down the lefthand side, list the following categories: Government, Economy, Social Structure, Philosophy and Religion, Art and Architecture, Literature, Science and Technology. Leave several lines between each category. Fill in the chart as completely as possible. Then write a short paragraph that summarizes the achievements and characteristics of each civilization.

2. With three other classmates, write a skit that takes place in classical China. Each person should assume the role of a follower of either Confucius, Lao-tzu, Mo Ti, or the Legalists. Create a story that allows each character to express ideas typical of his or her role model. Present the skit to the class. Then have the class guess who each actor was representing.

APPLYING SOCIAL STUDIES SKILLS

Analyzing primary sources. A eulogy (YOO-luh-jee) is a speech given to honor someone who has just died. At Confucius's death, his grandson gave the following eulogy.

> His fame overspreads the Middle Kingdom, and extends to all barbarous tribes. Wherever ships and carriages reach, wherever the strength of man penetrates, wherever the sun and moon shine, wherever frosts and dews fall—all who have blood and breath honor and love him. Hence it is said: "He is the equal of Heaven."

1. Summarize in your own words what the eulogy is saying.

2. What does this speech tell you about how the speaker viewed Confucius?

3. Do you think this is an accurate or an exaggerated account of Confucius's influence throughout the world? Why?

4. In general, do you think eulogies are likely to provide historians with an accurate picture of a person's life and importance? Why or why not?

APPLYING THINKING SKILLS

Classifying. The items below relate to classical India and China. Classify them for the purpose of understanding better the nature of these civilizations. Follow the procedure for classifying described on page 50. Then answer the questions below.

Officers of Righteousness
development of calligraphy
establishment of a civil service system
growth of Taoism
teaching of "the Enlightened One"
popularity of the *Five Classics*
development of suspension bridges
use of the decimal
stone pillars engraved with
   instructions for virtuous conduct
building of the Great Wall
trade with Rome
writing down of the epic *Ramayana*
invention of paper
development of a caste system
rise of Legalism
popularity of Confucianism
use of the Silk Road

1. What does it mean to classify information?

2. Describe one procedure for classifying.

3. Why do you think it might be useful to classify the same information in different ways?

4. Name and explain the categories you used to classify the above items.

5. Which of the items in the above list relate to India? Which relate to China? Which relate to both India and China?

6. Which items are governmental in nature?

7. Based on your classification of all the items, what generalizations can be made about the civilizations of classical India and China?

8. If you had to tell someone three years younger than you how to classify the above items, what instructions would you give?

UNIT REVIEW

1. (a) List the two basic activities that promoted cultural diffusion in the ancient world. **(b)** Describe the cultural diffusion that resulted from the conquests of Alexander. **(c)** Explain how the Minoan and Kushan civilizations were cultural bridges.

2. (a) Compare the structure of the government of the Roman Republic and Han China. **(b)** Explain some of the advantages of Roman law over Greek law.

3. (a) Compare classical Greece and Rome regarding the rights of the government versus the rights of the individual citizen. **(b)** How did the causes and effects of Athens's political reforms differ from those of the Gracchus brothers in Rome?

4. (a) How were conquered peoples ruled under the governments of each of the following: Alexander's empire, the Roman Republic, the Roman Empire? **(b)** What were at least four methods used by ancient governments to build and maintain unity in their empires?

5. (a) What role did geography play in the expansion of the Greek and Roman empires? **(b)** In what ways did geography affect the civilization of classical India? **(c)** Explain the circumstances that allowed China to break from its geographic isolation.

6. (a) What are similarities between the teachings of Jesus and the teachings of Siddhartha? Of Jesus and Mo Ti? **(b)** Compare the state religions of Greece and Rome with Hinduism. **(c)** Which philosophy was more similar to Buddhism: Stoicism or Epicureanism? Explain.

7. (a) Discuss in a paragraph similarities between the ideas of Plato and the ideas of Confucius. **(b)** Which Indian leader—Chandragupta or Asoka—would have appealed most to Confucius? Which, to Plato? Explain.

8. (a) List mathematical discoveries of Hellenic, Hellenistic, and Indian civilizations. **(b)** What contributions to medical science did each of the following civilizations make: Hellenic, Hellenistic, classical Indian, and classical Chinese?

9. (a) Explain how the purpose of science in Greece differed from the purpose of science in Rome, China, and the Hellenistic world. **(b)** What Chinese and Roman inventions demonstrate an inclination toward practical science?

10. (a) What basic attitude toward art did people in classical Greece and people in classical China share? **(b)** Describe the similarities and differences in the epic literature of Greece and India.

RELATING PAST TO PRESENT

1. Is the current political system of the United States more like Greek democracy or more like the government of the Roman Republic? Explain your answer.

2. The names of Greek and Roman deities, heroes, and heroines are often used today to identify products, objects, and other items. Select three of the following names: Poseidon, Ajax, Apollo, Nike, Hercules, Mt. Olympus, Atlas, Ares, Triton, Cupid, Mars, Jupiter, Vulcan, Saturn, Venus, Neptune. Explain how and why each is used today. Which names have been used in the United States space program? Why do you think the names were selected?

3. Confucius felt that the basis of a stable society is not force but morality. The Legalists thought just the opposite. Which position guides most political leaders today? Which position do you think political leaders should take? Explain.

4. Review the Roman idea of "bread and circuses." How does that idea relate to modern politics? Give examples.

PROJECTS AND ACTIVITIES

1. Pretend that you are a trader traveling one of the ancient trade routes. Write several diary entries giving details of your journey. Include your origin, destination, the goods you are trading, what you see, and so on.

2. Divide into groups of four to discuss issues from the ancient world, such as women's rights in Greece, the importance of Legalist and Confucian philosophies to Chinese society, or the possible impact in scientific thinking of the sun-centered and earth-centered theories of the universe.

3. Choose one of the following for research: Parthenon; Acropolis; Doric, Ionic, or Corinthian columns; Greek or Roman sculptures; Pantheon; Roman aqueducts; round arch, barrel vault; dome; Durga Temple; Ajanta cave temples; Indian stupas; Great Wall of China; Hadrian's Wall; Chinese bronze figures or bells; impact of dynamic symmetry on Greek art. Then organize a brief report for the class or prepare a poster or bulletin board display, using pictures and text.

ANALYZING PRIMARY SOURCES

Refer to Buddha's sermon on page 157 to answer the following questions.

1. What two pursuits does Buddha instruct people to avoid?

2. According to Buddha, how does one avoid these two pursuits?

3. Why is the Noble Eightfold Path called The Middle Way?

4. According to Buddha, how does one stop sorrow?

5. Give your own example of how thirst for power might lead to sorrow.

6. Is Buddha saying that it is wrong to experience pleasure? Explain.

7. Which do you think is the main purpose of the Noble Eightfold Path—to avoid sorrow or to acquire knowledge? Support your answer with material from the sermon.

GEOGRAPHY REVIEW

Location. The position of any place on the earth's surface can be defined in terms of both absolute and relative location. Cities and countries with favorable relative locations have good accessibility to people, ideas, trade, and resources. Generally such areas develop more rapidly than places with poor relative locations.

Areas with poor relative locations tend to be isolated, lacking access to transportation, trade, and resources.

Describe the location of your community. Begin by defining its absolute location in terms of latitude and longitude. You will probably have to consult an atlas to determine its position accurately.

Then describe your community's relative location in terms of the following:

(a) its location in the state

(b) links to the nearest major cities

(c) proximity, or closeness, to important natural resources such as farm land, mineral deposits, forests, fisheries, and hydroelectric power

(d) accessibility to centers of business, industry, and culture within the state by road, railroad, or waterways

(e) ease of transportation to other states by land, air, or water

(f) access to international trade routes

You may need to consult maps to gather information for your descriptions.

SUGGESTED READINGS

Bingham, Marjorie Wall, and Gross, Susan Hill. *Women in European History and Culture*, Vol I, *Ancient Greece and Rome*. St. Louis Park, Minn: Glenhurst, 1983. A description of the varying roles of women.

Cottrell, Leonard. *The Bull of Minos*. New York: Facts on File Publications, 1984. Archaeological discoveries at Mycenae and Knossos told as a travelog.

Renault, Mary. *The Bull from the Sea*. New York: Pantheon, 1962. A novel based on the story of Theseus' adventures in Crete.

Schafer, Edward H. *Ancient China*, Great Ages of Man. New York: Time-Life Books, 1967. A guided tour of the glories of ancient China.

Schulberg, Lucille. *Historic India*, Great Ages of Man. New York: Time-Life Books, 1969. The flowering of the Indian spirit and the story of the great ruler Asoka.

THE EUROPEAN MIDDLE AGES

A.D. 284–1505

To protect the Church, to fight against treachery, to reverence the priesthood . . . and, if need be, to lay down your life.

—John of Salisbury, on duties of a knight, twelfth century

Detail from the *Calendar of Charles d'Angoulême: February*. Manuscript illustration, 1400s.

CHAPTER NINE
THE BYZANTINE EMPIRE AND EARLY RUSSIA

CHAPTER TEN
THE EARLY MIDDLE AGES

CHAPTER ELEVEN
THE HIGH AND LATE MIDDLE AGES

GLOBAL TIMELINE

- ■ THE BYZANTINE EMPIRE
- ■ EARLY RUSSIA
- ■ MEDIEVAL EUROPE

	POLITICAL	TECHNOLOGICAL	SOCIAL
300	Diocletian officially splits Roman Empire		
	Reign of Constantine — Byzantium becomes capital of Roman Empire — Frankish kingdom established	Beginnings of alchemy	Constantine forbids gladiatorial combats and persecution of Christians
500	Fall of Roman Empire in the West — Reign of Justinian — Charles Martel defeats Muslims	Water wheels in use	Christianity spread by Benedictines in Europe
700	Reign of Charlemagne — Treaty of Verdun — First Russian kingdom	Crossbow in use — Heavy plow and padded horse collar in use — Early Viking shipbuilding	Greek replaces Latin as official language of Byzantine Empire — Christianity introduced to Russia
900			
	Battle of Hastings — Viking invasions of Europe	Early castles — Astrolabes in use — Linens and woolens manufactured in Flanders	Separation of Byzantine and Roman churches — Golden Age of Kiev
1100	Crusades — Magna Carta — Feudal monarchies established	Beginnings of Gothic architecture — Spectacles invented	Universities develop — Chivalry and secular music develop
1300	Hundred Years' War — Fall of Constantinople — Mongol rule in Russia	Longbow, gunpowder, and large cannon in use — Increasing use of armor	The Black Death — Chaucer's *Canterbury Tales* — Dante's *Divine Comedy*
1500			

CHAPTER NINE

THE BYZANTINE EMPIRE AND EARLY RUSSIA

A.D. 284–1505

9-1 DEVELOPMENT OF THE BYZANTINE EMPIRE
9-2 BYZANTINE CIVILIZATION
9-3 EARLY RUSSIA

Madonna on painted wood, with silver accents. Bulgarian icon, 1342.

The fall of Rome in A.D. 476 marked the end of the Classical Age and began what Europeans have called the Middle Ages, which lasted until about 1500. Rome's empire, achievements, and traditions passed on to three new civilizations that would shape the world of the Middle Ages. The first of these civilizations was the Byzantine Empire, made up of the eastern half of Rome's former empire.

With its capital Constantinople, the Byzantine Empire lay between the two worlds of Asia and Europe. Mixing traditions from these two continents, the Byzantines developed a vital culture and influenced the Mediterranean world and eastern Europe for nearly a thousand years. Before its power faded, the Byzantine Empire engraved a lasting imprint on a young civilization to the north, on the vast plains of Russia.

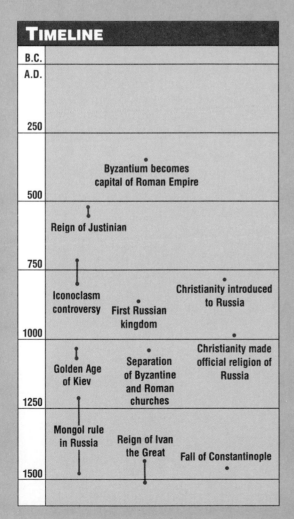

TIMELINE

B.C.	
A.D.	
250	
500	Byzantium becomes capital of Roman Empire
	Reign of Justinian
750	
1000	Iconoclasm controversy · First Russian kingdom · Christianity introduced to Russia
1250	Golden Age of Kiev · Separation of Byzantine and Roman churches · Christianity made official religion of Russia
1500	Mongol rule in Russia · Reign of Ivan the Great · Fall of Constantinople

READ TO FIND OUT

—what the terms *mosaics* and *icons* mean.
—how the Byzantine Empire's location between Europe and Asia influenced its culture and history.
—how Constantinople became the center of the Byzantine Empire.
—what important effects Justinian's rule had on the development of the Byzantine Empire.
—how the Byzantine Church differed from the Roman Church.

The beginnings of Byzantine civilization can be traced back as far as the reign of Emperor Diocletian, who officially split the Roman Empire in A.D. 284. Even before this division, however, the eastern part of the Roman Empire had followed its own political, cultural, and economic path. Built on the strong foundations of Hellenistic civilization, the eastern empire was always the most wealthy and populous part of Rome's empire. Nevertheless, Rome heavily influenced its eastern empire until Rome fell in A.D. 476. After the fall of Rome, the eastern empire continued in the Roman tradition, but Roman cultural influence slowly faded. Over the course of the next two centuries, the Eastern Roman Empire slowly became the Byzantine Empire.

CONSTANTINOPLE

About 660 B.C., a band of Greeks established a settlement called Byzantium on the European side of the Bosporous—the narrow strait connecting the Black Sea with the Mediterranean. Ten centuries later, Byzantium had developed into the center of a thriving civilization, with its memory preserved in the name Byzantine.

Until the time that the Roman emperor Constantine moved the capital of the Roman Empire to Byzantium in A.D. 330 and renamed the city Constantinople, the former Greek colony was a fairly unimportant small city whose residents made modest livings from trade. Constantinople was surrounded on three sides by water and had an excellent harbor. The port city provided safe anchorage for trading ships carrying goods between Europe and Asia. The overland trade route from India and China also passed through the city. During Roman times, Constantinople became a center of world trade and grew extremely rich.

Constantine completely rebuilt the city when it became the capital of the Roman Empire. He laid out the major streets and constructed a citadel and a forum. He built a huge defensive wall around the city. The new city resembled Rome in many ways. Roman styles of architecture were used in its government buildings and palaces. The city's roads, bridges, and sewers were modeled after those of Rome. The emperor observed Roman laws and was assisted by a Roman-style bureaucracy.

Constantinople differed from ancient Rome in several important ways, however. It was first of all a Christian city. Constantine and his successors filled it with magnificent Christian churches. Shrines containing the bodies of saints attracted thousands of people seeking cures for their illnesses and deformities. The cities differed, too, in the language people spoke. Unlike the Romans, the Byzantines spoke Greek in everyday life, although they did use Latin for government purposes.

Despite these differences, however, residents of Constantinople referred to themselves—even after the fall of Rome—as Romans. For many centuries after 476, in fact, they continued to call their city the Second Rome.

BETWEEN EAST AND WEST

With the decline of Roman power, Constantinople became the most important city in the Mediterranean region. It was at a crossroads between Asia and Europe, or East and West. Constantinople took advantage of its position to grow wealthy from trade and commerce and to combine ideas and ways of life from both East and West. Also because of its location, however, it suffered the nearly constant threat of invasion from growing military powers in Asia, the Middle East, and Europe.

The new empire centered in Constantinople always remained separate from most of Europe, even though it shared many European traditions. Whereas most of Christian Europe spoke Latin and Germanic languages, for example, the

Wealthy citizens often funded the decoration of Byzantine churches. This mosaic, created in Constantinople in about 1320, depicts Theodorus Methochites, an imperial official, presenting Christ with a model for the restoration of a sixth-century church. Now a world-famous museum named Kariye Camii, the small church is also known by the English name St. Savior in Chora.

major language of the Byzantine Empire was Greek. Most importantly, perhaps, the Byzantine Empire was very religious, and its religion was a form of Christianity that differed greatly from the western Christianity based in Rome. Because of such differences, the Byzantine Empire played an important role in helping much of eastern Europe establish its own political and cultural identity during the Middle Ages.

THE REIGN OF JUSTINIAN

Many historians mark the beginning of Byzantine history with the reign of its greatest emperor Justinian. Under Justinian, the Byzantine Empire began to develop the distinctive economic base, political systems, and way of life that would guide the rest of its history.

Justinian inherited the throne when his uncle, Emperor Justin, died in 527. Justinian dreamed of recapturing the Roman territory lost to the Germanic invaders and restoring Rome's glory. He began by making himself a powerful ruler.

Justinian controlled every branch of government. He made and issued laws, served as supreme judge, and appointed government officials. He led the army and navy, and had the sole right to declare war or make peace. Because the Byzantine Empire did not separate church and state, Justinian was the head of the Church as well as of the government. The Church reinforced the emperor's position by teaching the people that his acts were divinely inspired and therefore not to be questioned. Justinian, in the manner of Roman emperors, established a tradition of strong, central government that would last throughout Byzantine history.

The empress Theodora. Justinian's wife Theodora helped him rule. In 532, for instance, Justinian faced a revolt led by a group of senators protesting taxes. Justinian's advisors urged him to flee the city. Theodora, however, wanted him to stay and fight. "Caesar, you can leave," she said, grasping the purple robe that symbolized his leadership. "But I believe that those who put on the imperial purple must never take it off. I like the old saying that purple makes the finest shroud [for burial]." Justinian followed the empress's advice, crushed the revolt, and emerged stronger than ever.

Theodora was equally effective in persuading her husband to improve the legal position of women in the empire. As a result of Theodora's efforts, women received the right to own land equal in value to the wealth they possessed before their marriage. Widows also received the right to manage their late husbands' property and to raise their children without interference.

The Justinian Code. Justinian's first step toward restoring the Roman Empire was to ensure that Roman legal traditions were preserved. He had a group of scholars collect all the laws of his empire, as well as all the legal opinions of Roman judges and legal scholars. Justinian's scholars then organized the material according to legal principles. They also added the new laws that Justinian had issued. The resulting work was later known as Justinian's Code. It was through Justinian's Code that the basic ideas of Roman law passed into the legal system of almost every nation of western Europe.

Expansion of the empire. Before Justinian could begin to conquer former Roman territory, he faced threats from the Persian Empire in the east. Although the Persians succeeded in taking over some Byzantine territory, Byzantine armies pushed them back. For a while, Justinian controlled the threat of further invasions by paying tribute to the Persians.

In 533, Justinian's general Belisarius reorganized his army and began attacking the Germanic tribes in North Africa and southern Europe. After 20 years of difficult fighting, Byzantine armies were finally victorious, and Justinian controlled all the territory around the Mediterranean except the region controlled by the Franks, which is now France. This effort, however, emptied the treasury in Constantinople, and left the empire weak. Within a few years after Justinian's death in 565, most of the captured territory was lost, as the Byzantine armies were forced to leave these areas to face greater threats from Persia in the east.

Architectural achievements. Although Justinian's military campaigns weakened the Byzantine Empire more than they strengthened it, the emperor made lasting contributions to the empire in other ways—most importantly through architecture. Justinian was responsible for a vast program of public works construction that included bridges, churches, forts, forums, monasteries, and roads.

Justinian's outstanding architectural triumph was the church called Hagia Sophia, or "Holy Wisdom." Hagia Sophia featured a huge dome over a rectangular interior. Its marble walls were lined with elaborate *mosaics*—pictures made of bits of stone, glass, and enamel pieced together. Sunlight streamed through the dome's windows by day, illuminating the interior. At night, the glow of thousands of oil lamps and candles shining through the windows turned the church into a brilliant beacon. Sailors entering Constantinople's harbor at dusk steered their ships by the light from Hagia Sophia.

THE BYZANTINE CHURCH

Even as early as the reign of Constantine, the western and eastern branches of the Christian Church were growing apart. After 381, Byzantine Church leaders refused to accept the Bishop of Rome as the sole leader of the Christian faith. Instead, they looked upon the highest ranking church official in Constantinople, called the patriarch, as their leader.

By the time of Justinian, the Byzantine Church had its own doctrine, or set of accepted beliefs, its own organization, and its own rituals and art. The emperor of the Byzantine Empire also became the leader of the Byzantine Church. Unlike the Roman Church, the Byzantine Church was combined with the state. The emperor also appointed the patriarch of Constantinople, who was considered an official of the state. Under the patriarch were various ranks of clergy, including bishops and priests. In addition to appointing the patriarch and other high-ranking church officials, the emperor often made decisions on religious disputes and church doctrine.

Just as the Byzantine emperor was more involved in church affairs than Roman leaders had been, so too were the Byzantine people more involved in religion in general. Many Byzantine people were highly religious, and their faith meant a great deal to them. Often they were willing to fight or even die over the meaning of a few words of church doctrine.

The Byzantine Church stressed the separation between humanity and God. It taught that faith, or unquestioning belief, not human reason, was the path to finding God's truth. An important part of religious practice in the

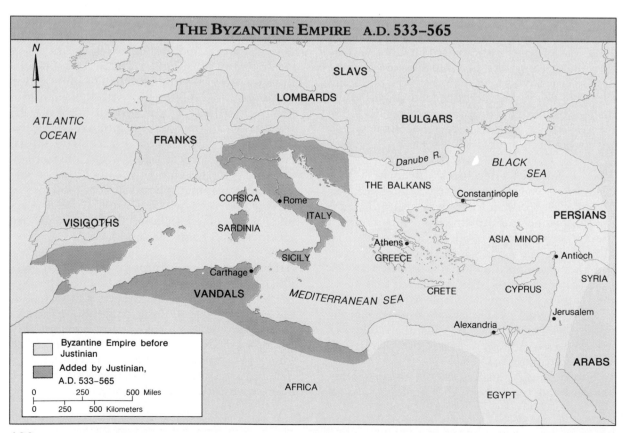

THE BYZANTINE EMPIRE A.D. 533–565

Byzantine Empire before Justinian

Added by Justinian, A.D. 533–565

0   250   500 Miles
0   250   500 Kilometers

DISTINGUISHING FACTS FROM VALUE JUDGMENTS

In your daily life and in your study of history, you hear or read different kinds of statements. Some are statements of fact, while others present opinions, often in the form of value judgments. Statements of fact give information that can be checked to see if it is true. Value judgments, however, present personal viewpoints that cannot be objectively tested. They reveal attitudes but often do not give accurate information about the subject. By distinguishing between statements of fact and value judgments, you can identify what information is useful for a given purpose.

A fact is an event or condition for which objective evidence exists. A statement of fact can be proved or disproved, but a value judgment always leaves room for disagreement. For example, the statement "Justinian was the Byzantine emperor from A.D. 527 to A.D. 565" is a statement of fact. These dates may be found in historical records. However, the statement "Justinian was the greatest Byzantine ruler" is a value judgment because people disagree about what makes a ruler "great."

Not all pieces of information are either statements of fact or value judgments. Some information includes both, such as the statement "Linda made an irresponsible decision to work two part-time jobs." It is a fact that she made a decision, but calling the decision irresponsible is a value judgment. Also, some opinions are theories that may be eventually proven.

EXPLAINING THE SKILL

Three basic steps may be followed to distinguish statements of fact from value judgments:

1. *Recall the definitions and criteria of a statement of fact and a value judgment.*

2. *Apply the definitions to each piece of information.* When in doubt about whether something is a statement of fact, ask: "Could it be proved or disproved to any reasonable person?"

3. *Determine the extent to which each piece of information is a statement of fact or a value judgment.*

Does it contain only facts? Is it only a value judgment? Or does it include both fact and value judgment?

APPLYING THE SKILL

Examine the following statements in order to distinguish statements of fact from statements that are value judgments.

A. Justinian's wife was named Theodora.

B. There can be little doubt about the greatness of Justinian.

C. Justinian was named emperor upon the death of his uncle, who was the previous Byzantine emperor.

D. Justinian did the right thing by having the empire's laws collected and written down by a group of scholars.

E. Justinian's armies conquered Italy.

F. Justinian wisely sought to restore the power of the old Roman Empire.

G. Rather than waste his resources on needless war, Justinian paid tribute to the Persians to guarantee peace.

H. Justinian made a wise choice in having Belisarius, one of his generals, attack the Germanic tribes.

MAKING MEANING

1. Which of the above are statements of fact? **(a)** D and B, **(b)** G and F, **(c)** E and A. Explain your answer

2. Which of the above statements include value judgments? **(a)** F and D, **(b)** E and C, **(c)** A and E. Explain your answer.

REVIEWING THE SKILL

3. What is the difference between a statement of fact and a value judgment?

4. Why is it important to distinguish between statements of fact and value judgments?

Hagia Sophia, completed in 537, was a monument to Justinian's lavish spending. Extravagant features, such as a gem-studded altar of solid gold, severely strained the treasury.

Byzantine Empire began to be the use of images or representations of religious figures, called *icons*. Some icons were statues, while others were paintings or mosaics.

FOUNDATIONS OF A STABLE SOCIETY

The strength of Christian belief among Byzantines was a source of unity in the Byzantine Empire. However, many other strengths help explain why the empire lasted so long in the face of outside military threats.

An efficient government. When weak emperors ruled, or several factions fought for power, the well-organized government kept the empire running smoothly. While in western Europe after the fall of Rome only priests and monks received educations, in the Byzantine Empire many people outside the church went to school. Such widespread education ensured a good supply of educated and well-trained government officials.

Byzantine officials regulated many aspects of life. They controlled education and religious practice. Government officials regulated trade and set prices and wages. They also organized the courts and the military. Under this supervision, Byzantine society functioned smoothly.

A strong economy. The Byzantine Empire also maintained a strong economy for much of its history. While cities declined in population and trade almost disappeared in the West, the cities of this eastern empire grew and prospered with a bustling trade. In time Constantinople became the center of trade between Europe, Asia, and the Middle East. Great quantities of raw materials from the West and luxury goods from the East passed through the city's port.

The empire also had industries of its own. It smuggled silkworms from China, for instance, and developed a thriving silk industry. Byzantine gold and silver coinage was respected as the most stable form of money in the Mediterranean region.

Farming, however, was perhaps the most important basis of the Byzantine economy. Compared with Rome, the empire relied less on imported grains and large estates worked by slaves. Instead, many Byzantines remained free peasants, growing food on the nearby plains of Asia Minor and the Balkan Peninsula.

SECTION REVIEW

1. Define *mosaics* and *icons*.

2. Name two ways that the Byzantine Empire was influenced by its position between Europe and Asia.

3. Why was Constantinople called the Second Rome?

4. In what ways did Justinian contribute to the development of the Byzantine Empire?

5. Describe three major differences between the Byzantine and Roman churches.

Analysis. Give three statements of fact that support the following claim: By the time of Justinian's rule, Constantinople's empire had become the Byzantine Empire and not just Rome's eastern empire.

9–2
BYZANTINE CIVILIZATION

READ TO FIND OUT

—what the terms *iconoclasts* and *heresy* mean.

—how Heraclius saved the Byzantine Empire from destruction.

—how Muslim Arabs threatened the Byzantine Empire.

—what the important Byzantine artistic and architectural achievements were.

—how Slavs and Russians were converted to Byzantine Christianity.

—what led to the decline of the Byzantine Empire.

Following Justinian's death in 565, the Byzantine Empire faced continual threats of invasion. Several times, foreign armies reached the walls of Constantinople itself. Each time, however, the Byzantines fought off the invaders. Despite these repeated attacks, the empire enjoyed five more centuries of prosperity and cultural development.

HERACLIUS

With a Persian army invading from the east, the Byzantine Empire stood at the edge of destruction in 610. Disgusted with the poor rule of the emperor Phocas, a Byzantine general named Heraclius (HER-uh-KLĪ-uhs) sailed from Carthage to seize the throne in Constantinople. As the new emperor, Heraclius reorganized the army and fought the Persians invading from the east.

In 626, the Persians threatened Constantinople from the Asian side of the Bosporus, while invaders from eastern Europe, called Slavs, pressed at the city from the European side. Heraclius, however, rallied his troops and beat back both armies. He went on to defeat the Persians and drive them from Asia Minor. He was even able to retake Palestine.

Heraclius strengthened the empire's armies just in time for them to be tested by still another enemy. Toward the end of Heraclius's reign, people called Muslims began to threaten the Byzantine Empire. Muslims were followers of a new religion called Islam, which had originated on the Arabian peninsula. As they took over more territory, the Muslims replaced the Persians as the Byzantines' major rivals in the eastern Mediterranean.

The years during which Heraclius ruled, from 610 to 641, were a turning point in Byzantine history. Before this time, Byzantine rulers had considered themselves Romans. Their major goal had been to restore the glory and power of the Roman Empire. The military challenges during Heraclius's reign, however, changed all this.

Because they were kept busy defending parts of Italy, the Balkan peninsula, and Asia Minor, the Byzantines were forced to give up their Roman dreams. After Heraclius's time, the Byzantines turned to defending their own modest territory, cutting ties to the Roman tradition and developing their own civilization.

Heraclius strengthened his armies to protect the empire. This soldier is part of a mosaic made in the 1200s for St. Mark's in Venice by artisans who copied images from Byzantine books.

Many icons were small enough to be carried by hand. This page from an illuminated manuscript depicts Empress Theodora, who ruled from 1042 to 1056, holding a sacred icon.

THE MUSLIM INVASIONS

Seeking both to spread their religion and gain wealth, Muslims conquered new territory quickly in the 630s and 640s. By 650, they had taken most of the Middle East, defeating the Persians and pushing the Byzantines out of Palestine and back to Asia Minor. The Muslims captured Egypt and then moved across North Africa, taking over lands once controlled by Constantinople.

Now rulers of large areas bordering the Mediterranean, the Muslims built a navy to better control their territory. In 717, they attacked Constantinople by land and sea, and once again the Byzantines came close to defeat.

Leo, the emperor, was a brilliant general. He repelled the Arab attack with the aid of a secret weapon called Greek fire. Byzantines mixed together chemicals that today remain a mystery and placed them in bronze tubes mounted on ships and on city walls. When lit, these tubes squirted liquid fire, burning ships and terrorizing soldiers. After this victory, the Byzantines were able to keep the Muslims from further advances although the empire still faced threats from Slavs and Asians from the north.

Historians have observed that Leo's victory was one of the most important in European history. Only Constantinople lay between the expanding Islamic Empire and Europe. If the Byzantines had not stopped the Muslims at Constantinople, the Muslims could have used the city as a jumping-off point to invade Europe, which at this time was too weak to resist.

RELIGIOUS DISPUTES

Soon after his successful campaign against the Muslims, Leo ignited a religious controversy that would have lasting effects on Byzantine civilization. In 726, Leo forbade the use of icons, religious images that had grown important in Byzantine worship. Leo and his supporters believed that the use of icons was non-Christian because icons were similar to the idols of non-Christians. People who were against the use of icons were called *iconoclasts*, which means "image-breakers."

The empire was split over the icon dispute. Throughout the empire, widespread rioting broke out in favor of icons. In the meantime, officials carried out Leo's order by force.

The controversy continued even after Leo's death. In 787, a council of bishops at Nicaea (nī-SEE-uh) declared that the use of icons was a *heresy*, or a belief opposed to church teachings. After more than 100 years of dispute, the controversy was finally settled in 843 by a compromise. It was agreed that people could use pictures in worship, but not statues.

The iconoclasm dispute had several lasting effects. The most significant was a split in Christianity. For a long time the patriarch of Constantinople had refused to accept the supremacy of the Bishop of Rome, who was now called the pope. The dispute over icons added fuel to the fire when the pope declared his opposition to the iconoclasts. Byzantine Church leaders felt that the pope was meddling in their affairs.

The disagreements between Rome and Constantinople led to a growing division between the Byzantine and Roman Churches. This split would grow in the coming centuries. In 1054, the Christian Church officially split into two parts—the Roman Catholic Church in western Europe and the Eastern Orthodox Church in eastern Europe.

The dispute over icons also led to a return to more traditional ways of religious thought. When the iconoclasts failed, their opponents led the way in suppressing any kind of religious experimentation. The old ways were thought to be best. Because of this return to tradition, the Eastern Orthodox Church became more devoted to contemplation, or pious thought. Contemplation was deemed to be the most important part of religious practice.

BYZANTINE ARCHITECTURE AND ART

Byzantine architecture and art were closely connected to the Church and religious practice. Church designs and decorations make up the bulk of Byzantine artistic achievements. In destroying icons, therefore, the iconoclasts destroyed much of the Byzantine cultural heritage. However, many icons survived outside the areas of iconoclast strength, such as in Italy, and architecture was not affected.

The domed church is the most notable contribution of Byzantine civilization to architecture. Until Byzantine architects figured out how to put a circular dome on rectangular walls, domes had been built only on circular walls. The Byzantine innovation enabled architects to be more flexible in their use of space. They could build rectangular or cross-shaped buildings of varying sizes, and create a sense of spaciousness by covering the building's central portion with a dome. Dome-shaped churches are found today in the Soviet Union, the Balkan countries, Italy, and Turkey.

Within the churches were beautiful mosaics of holy persons. These were arranged in the dome according to the importance of the figures and scenes. Thus, an image of Jesus always appeared in the highest part of the dome. Below came representations of angels, scenes from Jesus' life, the apostles, the prophets, and finally the saints. So they could be easily recognized from a distance, each figure had one or more distinguishing characteristics. For example, St. Peter was always shown with curly hair and a rounded white beard.

The mosaics were very skillfully made. Artists set the stones, enamel, and glass in curved lines and at different angles so that they would reflect light and glitter. Figures were slightly distorted and lengthened in order to make them look more majestic.

Byzantine artists also excelled in making jewelry covered with gems, embroidered tapestries, tableware of silver and gold, and carved ivory boxes. Artists also decorated their biblical manuscripts with brilliantly colored illustrations. This technique is called illumination.

In a move away from symbolic religious themes, many late Byzantine mosaics stressed natural imagery. This colorful mosaic depicts Noah taking pairs of birds into the ark before the flood.

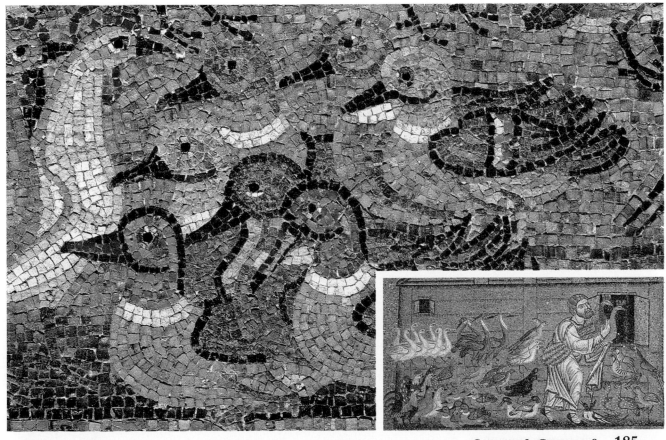

BYZANTINE ART

For a thousand years, highly skilled Byzantine artists fashioned countless splendid objects of luxurious materials such as glittering stones, creamy ivory, brightly colored enamels, golden thread, and sparkling jewels. The fame of these artisans spread far beyond the borders of the Byzantine Empire, influencing artists in both eastern and western Europe. Many Byzantine works glorified emperors and other leaders, but Christian symbols dominated this rich outpouring of art. The intricate sacred images and ornate holy objects helped inspire religious devotion.

Triumphal emperor, ivory carving, c. 500*

Angel and Christ, gilded icon

Gold pendant with enamel design

Cross with inlaid design and gems

Bronze cross with gold and lapis

*The abbreviation *c.* is used before a year or century when the exact date is unknown. The *c.* is a shortened form of the word *circa*, meaning "about."

Reliquary decorated with gold and gems

Carved chalice with gold base

Christ mosaic, c. 1200

THE CONVERSION OF THE SLAVS

During the two centuries beginning in the 850s, the Byzantine Empire entered its most prosperous, peaceful, and productive period. One of the most important events of this period was the conversion of the Slavic peoples to Byzantine Christianity.

The Slavs lived in eastern Europe, north of the Byzantine Empire. For centuries they had posed a problem to the empire, always threatening to invade Byzantine territory. In the 800s, however, the empire sent many missionaries, or church people who taught Christianity, into parts of eastern Europe inhabited by Slavs. The missionaries tried to convert the Slavs, who practiced polytheistic nature religions.

Two of the most famous of these missionaries were brothers named Cyril and Methodius. They knew the Slavic language and invented an alphabet in which it could be written. This alphabet, called the Cyrillic, after its inventor Cyril, is the one used today in the Soviet Union, Bulgaria, and parts of other eastern European countries.

The missionaries succeeded in converting to Byzantine Christianity the Bulgarians, who had forged a large kingdom north of Constantinople on the shores of the Black Sea. Among other groups, though, they were not as successful. Some eastern Europeans converted instead to Roman Christianity.

After converting the Bulgarians, the Byzantine missionaries concentrated their efforts in Russia, which lay further north. By the end of the tenth century, they had succeeded in converting the Russians to Byzantine Christianity. During the next few centuries, Russia and the Byzantine Empire established strong ties. Before the fall of Constantinople in 1453, Russia had absorbed much of Byzantine culture and religion.

THE DECLINE OF THE EMPIRE

In the eleventh century, after more than 200 years of relative prosperity and power, the Byzantine Empire began to weaken. As with the Roman Empire, there were many underlying reasons for this decay. Among these reasons were increasing taxes, the growth of large estates, and increased trade competition from rising European city-states such as Venice.

All in one year, however, military defeats sealed the fate of the Byzantine Empire. In the east, a group called the Seljuk Turks, who had been moving steadily westward from Central Asia for several centuries, gathered for battle. In the west, the Normans, warriors from northern Europe, moved south into Italy. In 1071, at the battle of Manzikert in Asia Minor, the Turks defeated the Byzantines and took the emperor prisoner, while the Normans seized Byzantine lands in southern Italy.

The Byzantine Empire appealed to western European kingdoms and the Roman Catholic Church for help. The pope responded by organizing a series of religious wars called the Crusades. Although one of their purposes was to "save" the Byzantine Empire from the Turks, members of both the First and Second Crusades took over Byzantine territories in their quest to take the holy land of Palestine back from the Seljuk Turks.

With each crusade, the westerners became more hostile to the Byzantine Empire. A German king who participated in the Third Crusade made preparations to attack Constantinople but agreed to hold back his army after accepting bribes from the Byzantine emperor. The Europeans in the Fourth Crusade not only attacked and captured Constantinople in 1204, they also burned the city, killed many of its inhabitants, and carried off its treasures to all parts of western Europe. With a complete lack of respect for their fellow Christians, the European crusaders even looted the Byzantine churches, an action the pope condemned.

The Byzantines recaptured Constantinople a little more than 50 years later, and the Byzantine Empire continued for another 200 years. Its territory, however, had shrunk to a small area around Constantinople, and its trade had been taken over by Italian city-states.

In 1347, Constantinople was devastated by the Black Death, or bubonic plague, which spread quickly and killed almost two-thirds of the city's inhabitants. In 1453, a new power in Asia Minor, the Ottoman Turks, attacked Constantinople with a powerful new weapon: the cannon. After seven weeks of siege, the Ottoman Turks captured the city and enslaved or killed many of its inhabitants. The Byzantine Empire ceased to exist. North of the Black Sea, however, Byzantine civilization had left its lasting mark on the vast land of Russia.

1. Define *iconoclasts* and *heresy*.

2. How did Heraclius strengthen the Byzantine Empire?

3. Why was Leo's victory over the Muslims in 717 an important event in European history?

4. Describe the most important features of Byzantine art and architecture.

5. Describe how the Byzantines converted Slavs and Russians to Christianity.

6. Name three major causes of decline of the Byzantine civilization.

Synthesis. Why would the Cyrillic alphabet be an important tool in the conversion of the Slavs to Christianity?

9–3
EARLY RUSSIA

READ TO FIND OUT

—what the term *boyars* means.
—how geography influenced Russian history.
—how Kievan Russia rose to power.
—what effects Vladimir's adoption of Byzantine Christianity had on Russia.
—who the Mongols were and how they controlled Russia.
—how Moscow rose to power.

During the early years of the Byzantine Empire, Constantinople established contact with the Slavic peoples living in the lands north of the Black Sea. At first, Byzantine merchants simply traded with the people of this vast land called Russia. After their military setbacks in the Mediterranean during Heraclius's reign, however, Byzantines eyed the north with thoughts of expansion.

Though the Byzantines never conquered Russia, they began to exert a heavy cultural and religious influence on it through increased trade and missionary activity. By 1453, when Constantinople fell, Russia had become the home of the Eastern Orthodox Church's leadership and the heir of Byzantine civilization. Like the Byzantine Empire, Russia never became fully European or Asian but lay caught between East and West.

RUSSIA: THE NATURAL SETTING

Much of Russia is a huge, treeless plain called the steppe. It stretches from the Black and Caspian seas eastward into Manchuria. North of the steppe lies a band of thick forests. North of these forests is the tundra, where only mosses and small shrubs grow in summer and where the ground is frozen most of the year. The major mountain range in Russia is the Ural Mountains. It runs north–south from the tundra to near the Caspian Sea. The Ural Mountains divide Europe and Asia.

The forests and steppes are drained by the most extensive river network in the world. Russia's major rivers flow south and empty into either the Black Sea or the Caspian Sea. Since early times these waterways have been a major means of transportation. Despite their navigability, however, they have one major limitation—they can be traveled only in summer.

Most of Russia is far away from the warm climate of the Mediterranean, and there are no east–west mountain chains to protect the land from the freezing winds that sweep down from the Arctic Ocean. Russia's rivers and most of its coastal harbors are frozen solid from early autumn to late spring, and winters are bitterly cold. As an English ambassador in the 1500s wrote: "It would breede a frost in a man to look abroad at that time and see the winter face of that country. Bears and wolves issue by troupes out of the woods. Rivers and all waters are frozen up a yarde or more thicke, however swifte or broade they may be."

Russia's environment has greatly affected its economy and history. Although the soil of the steppe is rich and black, rainfall is light. Growing enough grain and other crops has always been a problem. Because of the absence of natural defenses, the land has been subject to repeated invasions, both from the east and the west. However, the absence of geographic barriers also had some positive effects. It enabled language, art, and religion, for example, to spread quickly. Also a single political system could be established over the large area more easily.

STEPPE NOMADS

The fierce steppe nomads called no king their master and no kingdom their home. Since ancient times, nomadic groups had ridden freely across the steppes, changing the destiny of peoples and empires.

Although steppe nomads were skilled warriors, they spent much of their time in search of fresh grazing land for their livestock. Some of these livestock provided the nomads with a staple diet of goat's milk, beef, and mutton, as well as with wool and leather for clothing and tents.

The nomads' most important animal, however, was the one that kept them so mobile—the horse. Without horses, the nomads could not have controlled large herds of livestock or effectively hunted swift game such as elk. On horseback most of their waking hours, nomadic riders often ate their meals perched on a saddle.

A life of almost constant movement required appropriate clothing for riding, such as close-fitting trousers tucked into soft high boots. The nomadic life also required that each family's possessions be limited to what could be carried in a covered wagon. Perhaps the most important item transported from place to place was the collapsible felt tent. When the nomads set up camp, thick rugs made the tents comfortable inside, while colorfully dyed animal skins decorated the tent walls.

Typically, women supervised the daily activities of a nomad camp. In many tribes, the women's responsibilities also included hunting on horseback and joining the men in lightning raids on farming communities, cities, and trading caravans.

Although generally regarded by settled peoples as barbarians, many nomadic tribes had strong artistic traditions. Their small, carefully crafted gold and bronze sculptures often depicted animals, typically birds of prey, stags, and horses. These figures often show wild animals attacking tame animals. They reflect the harsh world of the nomads, where strength and movement were necessary for survival.

EARLY PEOPLES

The early Russians, like many eastern Europeans, were Slavs. Like the Aryans and Mycenaeans, the Slavs spoke an Indo-European language. However, historians are not certain about their place of origin.

Between 500 B.C. and A.D. 500, the Slavs lived in the river basins northeast of the Carpathian Mountains, in what is now eastern Poland and the western part of the Soviet Union. About the fourth century A.D., the Slavs began expanding. Some went west and south, following in the path of the Germanic peoples who were invading the Roman Empire. Many Slavs ended up in what is now western Poland and Czechoslovakia. Others settled in what is now Yugoslavia. Most Slavs pressed eastward, as far as the upper Volga River.

The Slavs were mostly farmers and hunters. After a while, they became traders as well. During the winter, they gathered honey, furs, timber, and other products from the forests. In late spring, after the ice on the rivers had melted, they sailed down the Dnieper (NEE-puhr) River and then across the Black Sea to Constantinople. There, they exchanged merchandise for textiles, weapons, spices, and wine. This and other north–south trade routes were important to their economy.

Slavs were not the only people who inhabited Russia. On the vast steppes lived many nomadic tribes. Throughout Russian history, different nomadic tribes, mostly from the steppes of Asia, invaded the areas where Slavs were settled. Some Asiatic invaders even reached as far west as Europe.

THE RISE OF KIEVAN RUSSIA

The first Russian kingdom was organized in the ninth century A.D., while the Byzantine Empire was at the height of its prosperity. The founders of this Russian state, however, were neither forest-dwelling Slavs nor steppe-dwelling nomads. Instead, they were warrior–traders from

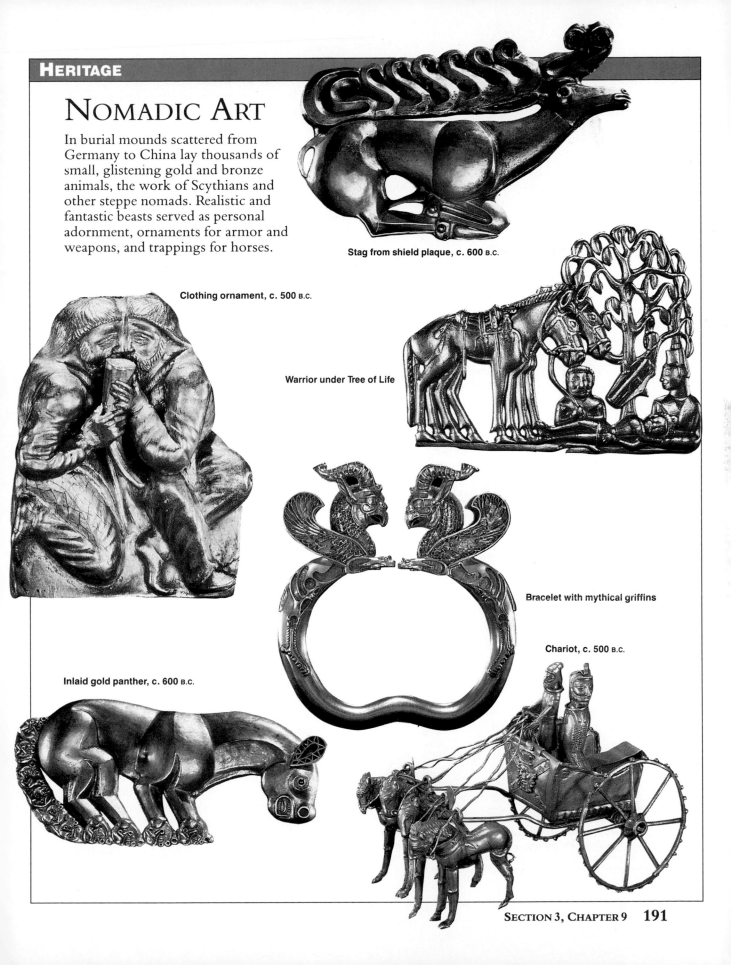

NOMADIC ART

In burial mounds scattered from Germany to China lay thousands of small, glistening gold and bronze animals, the work of Scythians and other steppe nomads. Realistic and fantastic beasts served as personal adornment, ornaments for armor and weapons, and trappings for horses.

Stag from shield plaque, c. 600 B.C.

Clothing ornament, c. 500 B.C.

Warrior under Tree of Life

Bracelet with mythical griffins

Chariot, c. 500 B.C.

Inlaid gold panther, c. 600 B.C.

Scandinavia, known in western Europe as the Vikings.

According to a Russian history written about 1100 called the *Primary Chronicle*, the Slavs asked the Vikings in 862 to help them protect their trade routes to Constantinople against outsiders. A Viking named Rurik supposedly accepted the invitation and established himself as ruler over Novgorod, the northernmost town along the Slavic trade route. Some historians question this story, however, believing that the Vikings invaded Russia.

After Rurik's death another Viking, named Oleg, seized control of Novgorod. In 882, Oleg captured the city of Kiev (KEE-ehv). Kiev lay several hundred miles to the south, on the Dnieper River, near the place where the forests met the steppe. All the Viking and Slavic trading vessels gathered at Kiev before making the run south to Constantinople. Kiev was thus in an excellent location to keep the north–south trade route open and to protect the merchant fleets from nomads seeking loot.

From his base in Kiev, Oleg took over the leadership of the Slavs. He called himself the Grand Prince of Kiev. The Kievan state he established, however, was really only a collection of small states, of which Kiev was simply the largest. The other states were forced to make payments, called tribute, to the grand prince. After Oleg, other grand princes ruled Kiev. The degree of loyalty shown to Kiev by the princes of the smaller states depended on how powerful the grand prince was.

During the late 800s, grand princes launched raids against Constantinople. They were attracted by the wealth of the Byzantine Empire. In 911, the rulers of Kiev and Constantinople signed a treaty and became trading partners instead of enemies. It was during this time that Byzantine missionaries were carrying the Cyrillic alphabet, Byzantine culture, and Byzantine Christianity to much of Russia. Many Russian merchants and travelers converted to Byzantine Christianity after spending time in Constantinople during the 800s and 900s.

VLADIMIR AND THE BYZANTINE CHURCH

Among the important rulers of Kievan Russia was Vladimir I, a great-grandson of Rurik. Vladimir reigned from 980 to 1015. His name is Slavic rather than Scandinavian, indicating that by this time the Vikings had been more or less absorbed by the Slavs through intermarriage.

Vladimir spent the first ten years of his reign on the field of battle. He pushed Russia's boundaries westward into Poland and northward along the Baltic coast. He also campaigned successfully against the nomads of the steppe.

Vladimir changed the history of Russia when he adopted Christianity as the country's official religion in 988. According to legend, he sent officials, called envoys, to examine various religions. He rejected Islam because the envoys said it forbade drinking alcohol. He turned away from Roman Christianity because according to the envoys it required fasting. However, after visiting a Byzantine church, his envoys reported, "We knew not whether we were in heaven or on earth, for on earth there is no such splendor or such beauty." Vladimir converted to Byzantine Christianity and, full of enthusiasm for his new faith, insisted that all Russians be baptized immediately.

Vladimir's order was not easily accepted by many Russians. Russians had long practiced a

The mother of Christ was considered an intermediary between people on earth and God. Icons like this twelfth-century Lady of Tenderness were common in villages throughout Russia.

St. Basil's in Moscow, completed about 1560, is one of Russia's most colorful churches. The czar supposedly had the architects blinded so they could never build a more beautiful church.

religion in which nature spirits, ancestors, and many gods and goddesses were important. They did not want to give up these old beliefs, which seemed to them to make more sense. Many were forced to convert. To symbolize the destruction of the old religion, Vladimir had a statue, or idol, of the thunder god Perun tied to a horse and pulled into the Dnieper River.

Effects of the new religion. The effects of adopting the Byzantine faith were mixed. On the one hand, Byzantine priests brought with them not only a colorful and impressive religious ritual but also an alphabet with which to write down their language. Russians today use a modified form of the Cyrillic alphabet.

Byzantine priests brought other elements of their culture to Russia, too. They brought the art of icon painting and the architectural style of domed churches. The Russians modified the domes to make them onion-shaped rather than round. Stone churches, which also served as storehouses and shelters against fire, began to be built in towns that had formerly consisted of buildings made entirely of wood. Monasteries sprang up in both towns and countryside. Byzantine priests also introduced a formal system of education.

On the other hand, Vladimir's choice of the Greek rather than the Latin branch of Christianity created a barrier between Russia and western Europe. Furthermore, the different alphabet meant that Russian scholars did not bother learning Latin. This language barrier cut them off from much of the Roman heritage of western Europe.

The overall effect, however, of Byzantine influence on Russia was positive. The combination of Byzantine culture, Slavic and Viking traditions, and wealth from trade quickly turned Russia into one of the greatest civilizations of the Middle Ages.

THE GOLDEN YEARS OF KIEVAN RUSSIA

Vladimir left behind 12 sons when he died in 1015. The brothers fought over the throne for 21 years. Finally, in 1036, Yaroslav became the grand prince. His reign, which lasted until 1054, marked a time of prosperity for Russia. This period is known as the Golden Age of Kiev.

In foreign affairs, Yaroslav defeated once and for all a group of warlike steppe nomads, called the Pechenegs, who had long disrupted Kievan trade. He then made important contacts with the royal families of western Europe. He arranged numerous marriages between members of his family and European royalty. He himself, for example, wed a Swedish princess. One sister married a Polish king, another a Byzantine prince. Three of Yaroslav's daughters were married to the kings of France, Hungary, and Norway. He also invited scholars from Constantinople to live and work in Kiev. These contacts helped Russia to overcome, for a time, some of the barriers between it and the rest of Europe.

Yaroslav was the first to codify, or write down in an organized way, Russian law. The code combined Slavic customs with Roman law as interpreted by the Byzantines. The code did not include the death penalty or torture. Criminals were fined. The code also reflected Kievan Russia's dependence on trade. Crimes against property were considered more serious than crimes against people.

By Yaroslav's time, social classes in Kievan Russia were distinct. At the top were the prince and his family. Next came the landed nobles and wealthy merchants, known as *boyars*, who served as advisors to the prince. The clergy formed a third class. At the bottom were the peasants, who made up the majority of the population. Compared to peasants in western Europe at this time, Russian peasants were relatively free.

During Kiev's Golden Age, Russian civilization reached a level that surpassed that of any kingdom in western Europe. Russia became a center of growing trade between Scandinavia and the Middle East, and between Europe and Asia.

The decline of Kiev. Yaroslav's death in 1054 opened the door to a struggle over the throne. The almost constant civil war among the princes undermined the strength of Kievan Russia. Raids by steppe nomads increased. The flow of goods along the north–south river route decreased, and with it, the basis of Kiev's wealth.

When the Fourth Crusade destroyed Constantinople as a center of international trade in 1204, economic conditions became even worse because Russia had lost its major trading partner. Gradually, many Russians fled from the dying towns and the dangers of the steppe to the forests along the upper Volga. Then, between 1237 and 1240, a new group of nomads swept out of central Asia. They captured Kiev and established control over Russia.

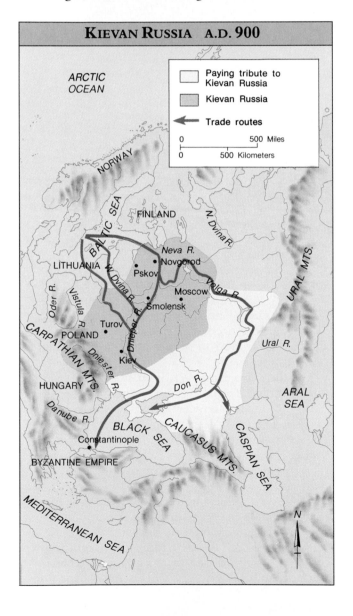

KIEVAN RUSSIA A.D. 900

☐ Paying tribute to Kievan Russia
▨ Kievan Russia
← Trade routes

0   500 Miles
0   500 Kilometers

ARCTIC OCEAN

NORWAY

BALTIC SEA

FINLAND

N. Dvina R.

Neva R.
Novgorod
Pskov

URAL MTS.

LITHUANIA

W. Dvina R.

Moscow
Volga R.
Smolensk
Dnieper R.

Oder R.

Vistula R.

Turov

POLAND

Dniester R.

Kiev

Ural R.

CARPATHIAN MTS.

HUNGARY

Don R.

ARAL SEA

Danube R.

BLACK SEA

CAUCASUS MTS.

CASPIAN SEA

Constantinople

BYZANTINE EMPIRE

MEDITERRANEAN SEA

N

THE MONGOL INVASION

The new invaders were Mongols, known in Russia as Tartars. Their empire had become the largest in the world up to that time. It stretched from the eastern edge of Asia to Poland and included, in addition to Russia, part of India and all of China. The empire had been founded by Genghis Khan (JEHNG-gihs KAHN) around 1220. His grandson, Batu Khan (BAH-too KAHN), conquered Russia.

The Mongols were expert riders and superb archers. Like the ancient Assyrians, they tortured and killed people in order to convince others not to resist. As they fought their way across southern Russia, it is said that they were so brutal that in many places "no eye was left open to weep for the dead."

Once the Mongols gained power, however, they were fairly mild rulers. They insisted only on tribute and soldiers for their armies. They allowed the Russians to keep their own language and customs, and to live under the rule of their own princes. Nevertheless, the Russians resented the presence of the Mongols. Occasional uprisings, though, were put down viciously by the Mongols.

NOVGOROD AND ALEXANDER NEVSKY

One Russian city escaped the Mongol invasions. This was the northern city of Novgorod. By the time of the invasions, Novgorod had become a wealthy center of trade. Its princes controlled territory from the Baltic Sea to the Ural Mountains. In 1238, Batu Khan led his cavalry against Novgorod, but the spring thaw turned the land into a swamp and forced him to turn back.

Now, however, Novgorod faced threats not from Asian nomads but from western Christians. Ever since the official split between the Roman Catholic and Eastern Orthodox churches in 1054, the pope in Rome had considered the eastern Christians to be heretics, or nonbelievers. Thus, he did not oppose efforts by other Catholics to attack the Russians for their beliefs. The first attack came from Swedish Catholics. The Prince of Novgorod, Alexander, met the Swedes and defeated them at the Neva River. Taking a name from the site of the victory, he became known as Alexander Nevsky (NEHV-skih).

Then, in 1242, a group of German warriors called the Teutonic Knights marched on Novgorod. They believed their mission was to bring western Christianity to Russia. Again, however, Nevsky defeated the invaders, this time on the frozen waters of a huge lake.

Shortly after this victory, Nevsky arranged an agreement with the Mongols. He realized he stood no chance against them in the long run, and so agreed to submit to their rule and pay them tribute in exchange for remaining Prince of Novgorod.

MONGOL RULE IN RUSSIA

Mongol rule, known as the Tartar Yoke, lasted in some parts of Russia for two centuries. During this time, the strongest unifying force in Russia was the Eastern Orthodox Church. Its priests encouraged the people's love for their country and continued to record important events.

At the same time, the Church grew inflexible and resistant to change, especially as its ties with Constantinople weakened. Following the rules of Church ritual became very important. Learning was frowned upon. The Church considered it sinful to study Greek writings and astronomy. Although the Church helped unify Russia, it also helped make the Russians suspicious of ideas that might change their way of life.

THE RISE OF MUSCOVY

The leading center of Russia's struggle for independence from the Mongols was the principality of Muscovy, whose capital was the city of Moscow. At the time of the Mongol conquest, Moscow was a small trading town at the edge of the northern forests. It was neither rich like Novgorod nor sophisticated like Kiev. Yet it had several advantages that enabled it to rise to power.

The first advantage was location. As refugees fleeing the Mongols moved to the northern forests, they passed through Moscow. Many decided to settle in or near the town instead of continuing farther north. Their numbers helped Moscow grow stronger, while their skills in business and the crafts helped the city grow richer. In addition, as the population moved to the north, Moscow became the geographic

This fifteenth-century painting depicts a victory by Novgorod over a rival city, Suzdal, in 1169. The people of Novgorod credited the victory to divine help, as seen in the winged figure.

center of Russia, rather than a town on the outskirts of settled areas.

The second advantage was the character of Moscow's princes. They were shrewd and determined individuals. For example, they decided to pass the throne only from father to eldest son instead of dividing territory among several sons. This method of transferring power avoided civil war and kept the principality large. In addition, the princes cooperated with the Mongols instead of rebelling against them. In return, the Mongols eventually gave the princes the power to collect taxes and to draft soldiers throughout all of Russia. As Muscovite princes gained power, Muscovy became the leading principality.

Ivan I. Among the most effective grand princes of Moscow was Ivan I, who ruled from 1325 to 1341. The Mongols gave him the title of Grand Prince of all Russia. Ivan I expanded Muscovy's territory by buying villages and forest land from boyars who were too poor to pay taxes.

Also during the reign of Ivan I, the Metropolitan, or head of the Eastern Orthodox Church, came to Moscow to live. The prestige of the Church greatly strengthened the city's power. The Russian people began to perceive the prince of Moscow the way the Byzantines perceived their emperor. The Russians believed that their ruler was selected by God and that it was the people's obligation to obey their leader without question.

While the power of Muscovy was increasing, that of the Mongols was declining. This weakening was mostly caused by quarrels among various nomadic chiefs. In 1378, the Muscovite prince Dimitry refused to pay the Mongols their usual tribute. Dimitry raised an army from the major Russian principalities and defeated the Mongols on the banks of the Don River. Although the Mongols did not leave Russia, they no longer had control over the lives of the Russian people.

MOSCOW AS THE THIRD ROME

With Mongol influence fading, the next Muscovite ruler, Ivan III, was able to greatly enlarge Moscow's territory. Becoming grand prince of

Moscow in 1462, he conquered or bought almost all of the existing Russian principalities.

In 1472, Ivan III married Sophia, the niece of the last Byzantine emperor. To the Russians, the marriage meant that Ivan III was now the heir of the Byzantine Empire. Since Constantinople had been the Second Rome, Russians began to consider Moscow as the Third Rome. To the Eastern Orthodox Church, Moscow had replaced Rome and Constantinople as headquarters of the true faith.

Because of his accomplishments, Ivan III became known as "Ivan the Great." He emphasized his power in many ways. He invited Italian architects to come to Moscow and build fine palaces and churches. He adopted the Byzantine coat of arms—the two-headed eagle. He built the huge walls that still surround Moscow's Kremlin, or fortress.

In 1480, Ivan informed the Mongol leaders that they no longer had any control over Russia or its people. By this time, the Mongols were so weak that they could not gather forces against Ivan.

Ivan the Great spent the rest of his reign strengthening his position and expanding Russia's borders. He died in 1505, after 43 years on the throne. He left behind a unified, independent nation. He also left behind the belief that the ruler of Russia should have absolute power over both church and state.

SECTION REVIEW

1. Define *boyars*.

2. Describe how geography has influenced Russia's development.

3. What role did Vikings have in Kiev's rise to power?

4. Describe three changes in Russia resulting from Vladimir's adoption of Christianity.

5. What were the effects of the Mongol invasions on Russia?

6. What did Ivan III do to help Moscow lay claim to being the Third Rome?

Synthesis. How might Russian history have changed if Vladimir had converted to Roman Christianity instead of Byzantine?

Data Search. After referring to the map on page 194, describe the major trade routes in Kievan Russia.

HISTORY IN FOCUS

The Byzantine Empire inherited much of Rome's greatness. The Byzantines followed Roman law and the tradition of strong rule by emperors. The Byzantines also preserved classical learning. As the Classical Age ended and the Middle Ages began, the existence of the Byzantine civilization ensured that at least in the eastern Mediterranean region, there would be little change in the level of civilization and the quality of life.

The development of Byzantine civilization, however, did lead to important and lasting changes in Europe and the Mediterranean region. The greatness and distinct character of Byzantine civilization helped divide West and East culturally and politically during the Middle Ages. The Greek-speaking Byzantine Empire remained wealthy and strong, while Latin-speaking western Europe became politically and economically weak and remained so for centuries. Learning and cultural achievement flourished in the East and stagnated in the West—an important difference with far-reaching consequences. Even Christianity developed differently in the two areas.

Western Europeans became jealous of the Byzantine Empire and set up a rivalry that eventually resulted in the crusaders' attack on Constantinople. Yet, while the West looked upon the Byzantine Empire as the exotic and wealthy East, Asians and Middle Easterners saw it as part of the Christian West. Caught between two unfriendly points of view, it seems remarkable today that the Byzantines were able to hold their empire together for as long as they did.

Russia inherited from the Byzantine Empire both its achievements and its rivalry with western Europe. The Byzantine heritage helped Russia achieve for a time a civilization more advanced than western Europe's. However, it also created hostility between Russia and western Europe.

The pattern of conflict between East and West that emerged with the rise of the Byzantine Empire continues to influence European politics even today. Outside of this conflict, however, lie the great Byzantine and Russian achievements that have contributed so much to the rich heritage of both western and eastern Europe.

SUMMARY

- Byzantine civilization can be traced back to the division of the Roman Empire in 284. The Byzantine Empire gradually emerged after the fall of Rome in 476.

- Justinian expanded the empire and created an efficient administration. Constantinople became a center of world trade, and the empire withstood numerous invasions.

- The Byzantine Church developed its own traditions, independent of Rome. The Church inspired much art and architecture. In the 800s, Byzantine missionaries spread their faith and culture to Slavic lands.

- Beginning around 1000, the empire gradually declined, in part because of invasions and increasing trade competition. In 1453, the Byzantine Empire was finally destroyed by the Ottoman Turks.

- Russia's first settlers were Slavs, who later opened trade routes to Constantinople. In the 800s, the Kievan kingdom was founded to protect this trade.

- Vladimir I expanded Kievan Russia and converted to Byzantine Christianity. Byzantine influence grew rapidly, dividing Russia from the rest of Europe.

- After Kiev's Golden Age under Yaroslav, the kingdom fell to the Mongols, who ruled for two centuries. During this time, the Church grew strong and Moscow became the center of Russia. By the 1400s, Russia had thrown off Mongol control and emerged as a unified state under Ivan the Great.

VOCABULARY REVIEW

The vocabulary terms in each pair listed below are related to each other. For each pair, explain what the terms have in common. Also explain how they differ.

Example: *Patriarch* and *metropolitan* both refer to leaders in the Eastern Orthodox Church. However, these leaders have different ranks.

1. icons, mosaics
2. iconoclasts, heresy

CHAPTER REVIEW

1. (a) Explain how location contributed to the growth of Constantinople, Kiev, and Moscow. (b) Which city had the best location for trade? Explain. (c) How did Russia's geography affect trade between the Slavic and Byzantine peoples? (d) How did geography affect the security of the Slavic and Byzantine peoples?

2. (a) What strengths of the Byzantine Empire helped it to endure invasions and weak emperors? Explain. (b) Why is Justinian considered the greatest Byzantine emperor? (c) In what ways did Theodora play an important role during Justinian's reign?

3. (a) In what ways were the Byzantines and Romans similar in their government and culture? (b) How did Byzantine culture differ from Roman culture?

4. (a) How was the importance of religion evident in Byzantine culture and society? (b) How did Byzantine religious beliefs strengthen the empire? (c) How did Byzantine religious beliefs affect the relationship between the Byzantine Empire and western Europe?

5. (a) How did the Byzantine Empire affect the stability of western Europe? (b) How did western Europe affect Byzantine stability?

6. (a) How did the Byzantines and Slavs come into contact? (b) How was Byzantine influence evident in early Russian culture? (c) Why was Moscow called the Third Rome?

7. (a) How did the Byzantine Empire affect the relationship between Russia and western Europe? (b) How were Byzantine and Russian contacts with western Europe similar?

8. (a) How did the Mongols help a unified Russia to develop? (b) What other factors contributed to the growth of the Russian nation? Explain your answer.

9. (a) What weaknesses in government contributed to Kiev's decline? (b) Why was Moscow's government more stable than Kiev's? (c) How was Byzantine influence evident in the governments of Kiev and Moscow?

10. Compare the economies of the Byzantine Empire and Russia.

THINKING CRITICALLY: ACTIVITIES

1. Imagine that you are a Byzantine Christian missionary traveling in Russia. Write a letter to your family describing the difference between everyday life in Russia and everyday life in Constantinople.

2. Imagine that you and another student in your class are two of the Byzantine emperor's advisors in 1453. Prepare arguments for and against surrendering Constantinople. Then debate your positions.

APPLYING SOCIAL STUDIES SKILLS

Analyzing primary sources. In 860, a fleet of ships attacked Constantinople. During the attack, the patriarch of Constantinople spoke to his people in a sermon:

> What is this? Why has this dreadful bolt fallen on us out of the farthest north? A people has crept down from the north [that] has no mercy. Woe is me, that I see a fierce and savage tribe fearlessly poured round the city, ravaging the suburbs, destroying everything, ruining everything—fields, houses, herds, horses, women, children, old men, youths—thrusting their swords through everything, taking pity on nothing.

1. Where did the invaders probably come from?
   (a) Russia
   (b) Italy
   (c) Egypt
   (d) Persia

2. Was the attack expected? What words in the sermon support your answer?

3. Was the attacking force large or small? What evidence supports your answer?

4. What was the attackers' main weapon?

5. Where was the fighting taking place?

6. How does the patriarch describe Constantinople's attackers?

7. With the exception of old men and youths, the list of victims cited by the patriarch does not include male residents of the city. How would you explain this omission?

APPLYING THINKING SKILLS

Distinguishing facts from value judgments. Sometime around 1050, a church official in Kiev delivered a tribute to Vladimir, the Russian ruler who made Christianity the official religion of Russia. The tribute was delivered in the church where Vladimir was buried. Examine this tribute in order to distinguish statements of fact from value judgments. Then answer the questions that follow.

> Let us lift our feeble voices to praise with all our might him who has done great and wonderful things, Vladimir, grandson of old Igor and son of the glorious Sviatoslav. Not in a poor or unknown land did they reign, but in Russia, which is known and heard of in every corner of the earth.
>
> Vladimir did the great deed of ordering all throughout this land to be baptized in the name of the Father and of the Son and of the Holy Ghost. Then the terrible heathen temples were destroyed. Churches were erected. Idols were cast down, and icons of the saints appeared.
>
> What great praise goes to you! You established the faith throughout this land. You equaled Constantine in the wisdom of your deeds. For Constantine prescribed the law for men, and you met with the bishops asking how to establish the law among men.
>
> Arise, revered ruler, from your grave. The city shines in majesty. The churches flourish. The city glitters, illumined by the icons and fragrant with incense. Having seen all these things, rejoice and be glad.

Adapted from Metropolitan Hilarion's eulogy of Prince Vladimir (c. 1050).

1. What is the difference between a statement of fact and a value judgment?

2. Are all statements either statements of fact or value judgments? Explain.

3. Identify four statements of fact in the above tribute. Explain how you identified them.

4. Identify three value judgments in the above tribute. Explain how you can tell that these are value judgments.

5. According to this tribute, why was Vladimir important in the history of Kiev?

CHAPTER TEN

THE EARLY MIDDLE AGES

A.D. 476–1050

Jesus Carrying the Cross. Stained glass from the Castle, Kreutzenstein, Austria.

Western Europe entered the Middle Ages in a much different condition than the wealthy and relatively stable eastern Mediterranean lands controlled by the Byzantines. The decline of Rome had disrupted the economy of western Europe. The invading Germanic tribes had divided up the lands, destroying the centralized rule of Rome. For about 600 years, western Europe remained in the shadow of Rome's other two heirs: the much more advanced Byzantine and Islamic civilizations flourishing at the eastern and southern edges of Europe.

During this time, however, western Europeans joined Christianity with Germanic and surviving Roman culture to build the foundations of a new civilization. This period, 500 to about 1050, is called the early Middle Ages, or early medieval times.

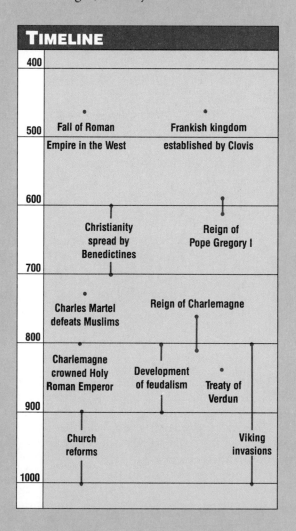

TIMELINE

400		
500	**Fall of Roman Empire in the West**	**Frankish kingdom established by Clovis**
600		**Reign of Pope Gregory I**
700	**Christianity spread by Benedictines**	
800	**Charles Martel defeats Muslims**	**Reign of Charlemagne**
900	**Charlemagne crowned Holy Roman Emperor**	**Development of feudalism** / **Treaty of Verdun**
1000	**Church reforms**	**Viking invasions**

10–1
GERMANIC KINGDOMS

READ TO FIND OUT

—what the terms **decentralized government** and **theology** mean.
—how most of Europe's land and climate differed from those of the Mediterranean region.
—how rival Germanic tribes controlled Europe after Rome's fall.
—how the Frankish kingdom became the most powerful of the Germanic kingdoms.

The prosperity and cultural development western Europe had enjoyed during the Pax Romana had all but disappeared by the beginning of the sixth century. Where Rome had controlled territory, rival Germanic warriors fought for power, and many Roman achievements were lost or forgotten. In other areas of Europe, people had yet to experience a settled way of life. For about 200 years, western Europeans lived with little centralized political rule, and almost no trade. During this time the Christian Church helped unify Europe spiritually, while one Germanic kingdom began to unify its territory politically.

EUROPE: THE NATURAL SETTING

Not until the Middle Ages did a civilization begin to grow up in the heart of Europe based on European land and resources. Though its southern edge borders the Mediterranean, most of Europe has climates and geographic features that are different from those of the Mediterranean region.

The continent of Europe can be thought of as a huge peninsula attached to Asia. The eastern boundary is formed by the Ural Mountains, the Ural River, and the Caspian Sea. The Black and Mediterranean seas separate Europe from Africa and Asia on the south. To the west lies the Atlantic Ocean, while the icy Arctic Ocean borders the continent on the north.

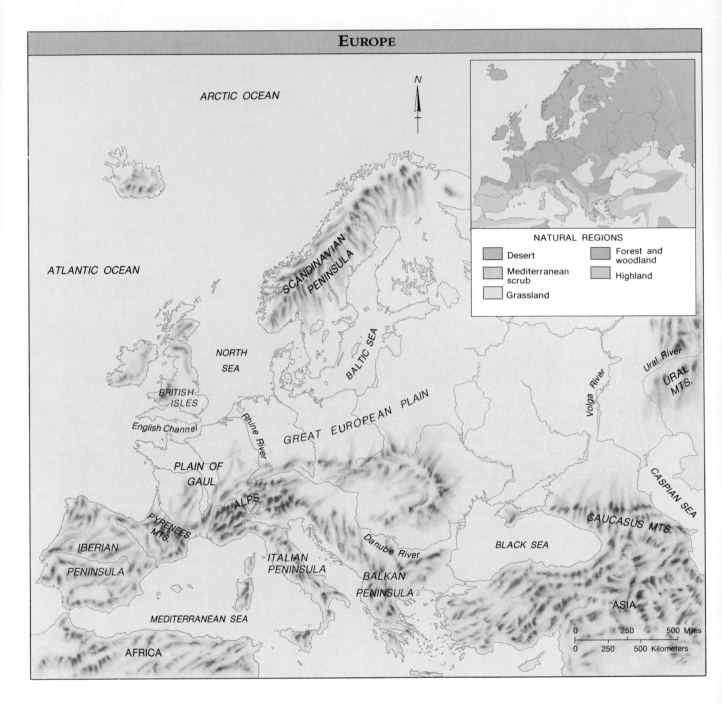

Four smaller peninsulas make up large portions of Europe. The Iberian Peninsula—present-day Spain and Portugal—lies in the southwest corner, separated from the the rest of Europe by the Pyrenees Mountains. The Scandinavian Peninsula curves over the top of Europe, enclosing the Baltic Sea. Jutting into the Mediterranean Sea are the Italian and Balkan peninsulas.

The British Isles lie off the northwest coast of the European mainland, halfway between the Iberian and Scandinavian peninsulas. The English Channel separates these islands from the mainland, and the North Sea lies between them and the Scandinavian Peninsula.

Stretching from Russia in the east to northwest Europe and parts of the British Isles is a large, fertile plain. Where this plain meets the sea in northwest Europe is a region called the Low Countries. South of this plain stretch several mountain ranges, the most important of which is the Alps.

Several large and important rivers flow through Europe. These waterways have always served as important trade routes. The busiest river is the Rhine, which flows north from the Alps to the North Sea. The Volga, Europe's longest river, flows from near the Scandinavian Peninsula in the north of Russia to the Caspian Sea. The Danube, nearly as long as the Volga, winds its way south and east from the Alps across the top of the Balkan Peninsula to the Black Sea.

Europe's diverse climates range from the year-round mild weather of Italy to the frigid weather of the far north. Grasslands and scrublands spread across the south, and broadleaf forests grow in the central lowlands. Conifer, or evergreen needleleaf, forests thrive in the north and in mountainous areas.

Unlike those of the Mediterranean region, Europe's geography and climate had, until the Middle Ages, acted as barriers to the development of an important civilization. Huge stretches of forest covered Europe in 500, and although the land was fertile, it could not be cultivated until the trees were removed. Even then, the more abundant rainfall made the soil heavier and more difficult to plow.

Many Europeans were also forced to develop ways of storing food in order to survive in the winter. Crops could not be grown year-round as in the Mediterranean region.

In general, the northern climate of Europe made farming more difficult than it was in the Mediterranean region. With the right methods and tools, however, European farmers could make their land produce even more food than most of the Mediterranean region.

EUROPE AFTER THE FALL OF ROME

During the 300s and 400s, Germanic tribes had invaded most of Europe. Slowly they gave up their nomadic ways and settled down. They mixed with the peoples they encountered, but maintained a fierce sense of independence and a love of freedom, hard work, and adventure. By the time Rome fell in 476, Germanic rulers had taken over Roman territories and divided the former empire into smaller kingdoms.

On the British Isles, the Germanic Angles and Saxons, who had crossed the English Channel in the middle of the 400s, were gaining more and more land from the native Celts. In the northern part of the former Roman province of Gaul, a Germanic tribe from northwest Europe called the Franks were creating a relatively powerful kingdom. On the Iberian Peninsula and in southern Gaul, the Visigoths ruled, while the Ostrogoths controlled Italy under King Theodoric.

The civilization that Rome had brought to much of Europe was already beginning to decline by about 200, and continued to decay after 476. Cities everywhere shrank in size and population, and workers stopped maintaining water supplies and sewage systems. The lack of maintenance allowed weeds to grow between the carefully set stones in Roman aqueducts, walls, and buildings, forcing the blocks apart. Many houses were left vacant or were torn down.

The once-thriving trade of the Roman world also declined and almost disappeared. What little trade did exist was mostly between neighboring towns. Therefore, most families and communities learned to be self-sufficient, growing barely enough to survive. The economic system was based almost entirely on local, small-scale agriculture.

The Germanic peoples, however, established a new kind of order in Europe. Rule became based on the power of local Germanic chiefs. This kind of local rule, without strong higher authority, is a form of *decentralized government*. The Germans contributed new ways of life, new ideas, and fresh energy to lands that had been ruled poorly for centuries.

THE FRANKISH KINGDOM

The most influential of the early Germanic kingdoms was created by the Franks. The way the Frankish kingdom was ruled established a pattern that would be followed in later European kingdoms.

In 481, a warrior named Clovis established the Frankish kingdom by invading Gaul and gradually taking control of the lands stretching from the North Sea to the Pyrenees and the Mediterranean Sea. His kingdom was the largest and most stable kingdom of the day because Clovis succeeded in gaining the loyalty of the local chiefs.

SEQUENCING EVENTS

INTRODUCING THE SKILL

Several organizational patterns have been used in writing history books. The most common pattern is based on sequence—the order in which events happen in time. This textbook is organized sequentially, moving through time from prehistory to the present.

There is a good reason for following this pattern. Once you know the order of events, you can then begin to explore why they occurred, understand how people solved various problems in the past, and recognize how long-term trends still shape people's lives today. As you become better at following the sequence of events, your understanding of history will expand.

EXPLAINING THE SKILL

Sequencing events means putting them into the order in which they happened. Sometimes this order is easy to see. Calendar markers—dates, centuries, numbers of years—locate events in time. The order of events is often indicated by signal words such as *first, last, before, after, soon, next*, and *meanwhile*. Calendar markers and signal words indicate the sequence of events in the following paragraph.

> Just *before* his death in *511*, Clovis divided his kingdom among his four sons. For the *next 200 years*, his descendants fought among themselves for power. *By the eighth century* certain royal officials, who were called mayors, had more power than the kings.

These events took place in the following order:
Clovis divided his kingdom.
Clovis died.
His descendants fought for power.
Mayors took power from the kings.

Sometimes the sequence of events is not well marked by dates and signal words. Instead, the sequence is implied, or shown by the order in which events are presented. In the following passage, the sequence is implied.

When Clovis died, his kingdom was divided among his four sons. The sons and their descendants fought among themselves for power. Gradually certain royal officials, who were called mayors, took over most of the powers once held by the kings.

The implied sequence of these events is as follows:
Clovis died.
His kingdom was divided.
His descendants fought for power.
Mayors took power from the kings.

APPLYING THE SKILL

Read the following paragraph. Then use calendar markers, signal words, and implied sequence to help you put the events in the order they occurred.

In 476, barbarians invaded Rome and sacked this once-proud city. Rome had fallen. Long before this event, Rome had been declining. The Roman Republic had given way to rule by power-hungry emperors. Constantine had moved the capital of the empire from Rome to Constantinople. By the time Rome fell, Germanic tribes had taken over most of the western empire and divided it into smaller kingdoms. After 476, Rome and the other cities of the empire fell into ruin.

1. The following events are discussed in the preceding paragraph. Place them in the order they occurred.
   (a) The capital was moved away from Rome.
   (b) Rome fell into ruin.
   (c) Barbarians sacked Rome.
   (d) The Roman Republic came to an end.
   (e) Emperors ruled the Roman Empire.
   (f) Germanic tribes divided up the western empire.

REVIEWING THE SKILL

2. How do writers use the sequence pattern to organize information?

3. What should you look for to help you follow the sequence of events?

This illumination from a twelfth-century French manuscript depicts Pope Gregory I dictating to his scribe. A lawyer by training, the pope wrote widely about the goals and beliefs of the Church. The dove on the pope's shoulder symbolizes divine inspiration.

During his rule, Clovis converted to Christianity, giving the Roman Church an important foothold in western Europe. Many of his subjects, following his example, also converted. Beginning with the early Frankish kingdom, Christianity became a foundation of developing western European civilization.

Just before he died in 511, Clovis divided the kingdom among his four sons, destroying his centralized rule. For the next 200 years, his descendants, called Merovingians, fought among themselves for power and land. Though the kingdom remained intact, its rulers lost most of their power to the local chiefs.

Eventually, the Merovingian kings lost even more power, as royal officials called "mayors of the palace" gained more authority than the kings. The Merovingian kings became known as the "do-nothing" kings.

Although the mayors of the palace were also relatively weak rulers, they managed to keep the Frankish kingdom the most powerful in Europe. The victories of Justinian, the emperor of the Byzantine Empire, over rivals of Frankish power in northern Africa and in Italy helped the Franks remain in control.

THE UNIFYING ROLE OF THE CHURCH

With political control decentralized, the Roman Church quickly became one of the most important forces holding together the medieval world. As more and more Europeans converted to Christianity, Christian beliefs became a major social and cultural tie between people. The Church was the only organization that touched a large territory, and the only institution in early medieval society where literacy and education survived.

Because an emperor no longer ruled in Rome, the bishop of Rome had become the most powerful political leader in Italy. He soon came to be called the pope. As pope he was also the leader of the Church throughout Europe.

Pope Gregory I. One of the most important popes during this time was Gregory I, who ruled from 590 to 604. Since the collapse of Rome's western empire, Roman popes had been under the influence and leadership of emperors and church leaders in Constantinople, the capital of the Byzantine Empire. Gregory, however, helped the Roman Church become different from the Byzantine, the first step in breaking away from its influence.

In order to establish a more independent church, he helped create a *theology*, or system of religious beliefs, separate from that of the Byzantine Church. For instance, he developed the idea of purgatory as a place one goes for purification before being admitted to heaven. The Byzantine Church had no such belief. Gregory also developed a new form of the Latin language that was closer to the language most people spoke. This new language began to be used in Church services. As the Roman Church became more independent from the Greek-speaking Byzantine Church, it became more powerful and exerted a stronger influence in western Europe.

Gregory also provided a more secure foundation for the Church by defending and strengthening the territories around Rome. These lands were called the Papal States. Run like small kingdoms, they provided resources and protection for the pope. The name "papal" comes from the Latin word for pope. Despite Gregory's efforts, however, the Roman Church remained under the influence of the Byzantine Church for another century and a half.

Monasteries and the spread of Christianity. During Gregory's reign as pope, the monasteries established during Roman times grew in power and influence. With support from Pope Gregory, they became centers of learning. The monks who lived in them were almost the only people in early medieval Europe who learned how to read and write.

By 600, monks called Benedictines controlled all the monasteries in western Europe. Benedictine monks were important in the spread of Christianity because they went out into the world to convert people to the religion. During the 600s, these monks, called missionaries, converted large numbers of people in Europe. The monks concentrated their efforts in northern Europe, where Scandinavian and Germanic people had not yet converted in large numbers. By about 700, missionaries had converted most of the Anglo-Saxon people living in England.

To make converts more comfortable with their new faith, missionaries often mixed Christian and pre-Christian ceremonies. Many Christian holidays were fixed at times when

This illustration is from the Book of Kells, a manuscript of the Gospels completed about 900. Created by Irish monks, this manuscript is thought to be the world's most beautiful.

people had formerly celebrated pre-Christian festivals. Christmas, for example, was celebrated at the same time as a Germanic winter festival, which was held near the solstice, or shortest day of the year. This festival had always featured feasting and the decoration of fir trees, ancient traditions that became part of the Christian holiday.

THE CHURCH'S INFLUENCE ON EUROPEAN IDEAS

During the early Middle Ages, the Church began to influence very basic European values and ideas. These values would become very important in later European civilization.

Classical thought had always stressed the importance of political loyalty. Western Christians, however, argued that loyalty to God and their faith was more important than loyalty to an earthly ruler or government. Both ideas of loyalty persisted in European thought, but they were often in conflict. In other societies, these two kinds of loyalty were not separate, and thus were not in conflict. This conflict, or tension, between ideas of loyalty has affected European civilization from the early Middle Ages to the present day, often in the form of rivalries between church and state.

Another development of the early Middle Ages was a growing intolerance of other religions. As Christianity became more powerful, Christians became more likely to carry out attacks on such groups as Muslims and Jews. The Christians, believing that their religion was the only true belief, felt that they were justified in using violence to punish nonbelievers. Such intolerance was a new development for the Christian faith.

Christianity also taught that all people had souls equal in the sight of God. This belief helped lead Europeans away from the inequalities of the ancient world. For instance, Christians held women in higher esteem than did Greek or Roman thinkers. Although women did not become fully equal in religious law, they could worship alongside men.

Largely because of Christianity, Europe became freer of the limitations of its Roman and Greek heritage. Unlike India and China, where the traditions of the classical civilizations remained strong, Europe developed new ways of life and thought that led to the building of a new civilization.

SECTION REVIEW

1. Define *decentralized government* and *theology*.

2. How did the land and climate of Europe affect European civilization?

3. Name the Germanic tribes that ruled Europe after Rome's fall. Describe the areas of Europe they controlled.

4. How did the Frankish rulers create the most influential Germanic kingdom? In what way did they help establish basic elements of western European civilization?

Analysis. Although Christian theology taught that all people had souls considered equal by God, many inequalities existed in medieval society. Give three examples showing how inequality was part of early medieval life in Europe.

10-2
AN EMERGING EUROPEAN CIVILIZATION

READ TO FIND OUT

—what the term *tithe* means.
—how the Roman Church and the Frankish kingdom built an alliance.
—what Charlemagne achieved.
—how invasions of Vikings from Scandinavia affected Europe's development.
—what reforms were made in the Church following the collapse of Charlemagne's empire.

About 700, the outlines of a distinctly European civilization began to take shape. Important changes occurred in politics and religion that set Europe apart from its classical origins. Under the leadership of a remarkable king named Charlemagne, the first large-scale, stable European empire arose and made important ties with the increasingly influential Roman Church.

THE RISE OF FRANKISH POWER

A line of strong rulers in the 700s helped the Frankish kingdom remain the most important political unit in early medieval Europe. The first of these rulers was named Pepin of Heristal. An ambitious mayor of the palace, he united all Frankish lands under his rule. Pepin's son, Charles Martel, was an even more effective ruler. He won fame and power through two major accomplishments.

First, Martel met an invading army of Muslims in the west of Gaul in 732. The Muslims had marched across North Africa and taken over Spain from the Visigoths. Now they were threatening the Frankish kingdom. Because the Muslims did not carefully maintain their supply lines, Martel won an easy victory. The Muslims never again reached that far into Europe. From this victory Martel achieved prestige and support.

Alliance with the Roman Church. Near the end of his rule, Martel took steps to build an alliance with the Roman Church. The Benedictine missionaries had just succeeded in converting England to Christianity and were turning their sights to the area of northern Europe known as Germany. Martel realized that he and the Benedictines had similar interests. In Germany, expansion of Frankish territory could go hand in hand with expansion of Christianity. Charles Martel and the Benedictine leader Boniface thus agreed to help each other accomplish their goals.

Although Martel died in 741, his son, Pepin the Short, continued the alliance with Boniface. In exchange for his promise to provide military protection for the Papal States, Pepin received from the pope the help he needed to overthrow the "do-nothing" king. Once he had the pope's support, Pepin became sole ruler of the Frankish kingdom in 751.

Once the increasingly powerful Franks could be relied on for protection, the Roman Church began to pull further away from the Byzantine Church. The iconoclasm controversy, at its height at this time, also contributed to the growing differences between the two churches. This conflict over the use of images in religious worship put the two branches of the Christian Church on opposite sides of an emotional issue. With the differences between the Roman and Byzantine churches growing, the Roman Church turned to Europe once and for all when it supported Pepin's rule.

This alliance between the Roman Church and the Frankish kingdom was one of the most important events in medieval history. The alliance strengthened both the Church and the Frankish state, and helped put Europe on a path of development and growth. Throughout the Middle Ages, the Roman Church would be closely tied to European politics.

THE AGE OF CHARLEMAGNE

Pepin the Short's son, Charles, inherited the throne in 768. He became one of the most important rulers of the Middle Ages. Charles founded a new dynasty called the Carolingian, from *Carolus*, the Latin version of Charles. His reign was so successful that people began to call him Charles the Great, or Charlemagne (SHAR-luh-mayn).

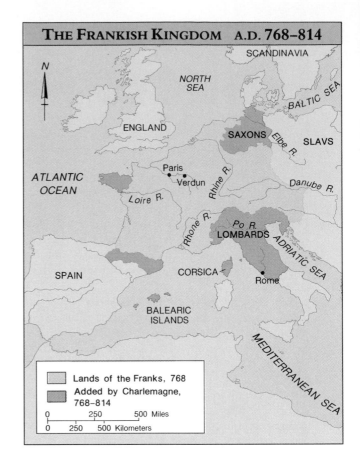

Charlemagne's greatest achievement was to greatly increase the size of the Frankish kingdom. He conquered northern Italy, northern Spain, and western Germany, thus creating the largest political unit in Europe since the Roman Empire. Controlling such an area required exceptional leadership ability. Despite the many people and lands it included, Charlemagne's empire enjoyed nearly constant peace during his reign.

Charlemagne retained the close ties to the pope begun by his grandfather Charles. He also encouraged Christianity in his kingdom. He divided Frankish lands into units called parishes, each with its own priest. Charlemagne ordered that all his subjects pay 10 percent of their income to their parish church. This payment, called a *tithe*, helped the Church become more powerful.

On Christmas Day in 800, the pope crowned Charlemagne emperor. Until that day, the only emperor since Roman times to rule in Europe had sat on the throne in Constantinople. Although neither Charlemagne nor the pope gained actual power from this coronation, the title of emperor symbolized the growing independence and confidence of Europe. By claiming its own emperor under church authority, Europe also gained a sense of unity and pride. In addition, Charlemagne's power helped Europe continue to build its own culture based on western Christianity and the Latin and Germanic languages.

THE CAROLINGIAN REVIVAL OF LEARNING

Charlemagne encouraged education during his reign, helping to bring literacy to Europe. His most important reasons for promoting education were political. To strengthen his rule, he needed to spread Christianity, which required educated monks. He also needed officials who could read and write to help govern the large kingdom. At the beginning of his reign, hardly anyone in the kingdom could read or write, and the Roman and Greek classics were almost completely unknown.

Charlemagne made a Benedictine monk named Alcuin (AL-kwin) responsible for founding new schools across the kingdom. Al-

cuin also saw to it that surviving examples of Roman and Greek literature were copied and preserved. Under Alcuin's direction, monks developed a new form of handwriting that was easier to read and write. It used both capital and lowercase letters, whereas the old Roman script had only used capitals. This handwriting became the basis of the "Roman" script used today for most European languages, including English, French, German, and Spanish.

THE COLLAPSE OF CHARLEMAGNE'S EMPIRE

Charlemagne's only surviving son, Louis the Pious, inherited the empire in 814. However, because he lacked the exceptional talent and energy of his father, the empire began to fall apart under his rule. Then Louis the Pious's three sons began to fight over who would inherit the kingdom. In 843, they agreed to the Treaty of Verdun. This agreement gave the western part of the empire, called West Frankland, to Charles the Bald; the eastern, called East Frankland, to Louis the German; and a middle section to Lothair. This division weakened the empire still further. Charlemagne's grandsons renewed the

Charlemagne was crowned by Pope Leo III at St. Peter's in Rome. In this French depiction of the coronation, the emperor Charlemagne is being handed the scepter of imperial Rome.

MEDIEVAL BOOKS

Books, both rare and expensive, were made completely by hand throughout the early Middle Ages. Secluded in monasteries, monks patiently copied old books and made new ones. A monk often worked for more than a year to copy a complete Bible.

The monks wrote in beautiful script on parchment and illuminated, or decorated, these manuscripts with miniature pictures and intricate patterns painted in gold, silver, and bold color. Most books were religious works, destined to become part of a church or royal treasury. The most prized works were bound with elaborately ornamented covers.

Scribe Ezra rewriting sacred records, c. 750

Jeweled Gospel cover, Ireland, c. 850

Chi-Rho page, Book of Kells, Ireland, c. 900

Medieval music notation

John the Baptist, ivory book cover cameo, c. 1100

Covers depicting "Fountain of Life," Godescalc Gospels, School of Charlemagne, 781-783

This eleventh-century tombstone was found in the cemetery of St. Paul's Cathedral in London. The mythical beast shown on the grave hints that it may be that of a Viking descendant.

conflict, fighting among themselves and plunging the Frankish kingdom into civil war.

At about the same time, new invaders threatened Europe. Thus, torn by internal conflicts and pressed by outside invaders, Charlemagne's empire declined quickly, breaking up into even smaller kingdoms.

These smaller kingdoms faced repeated invasions by several groups for the next 200 years. The invasions prevented Europe from building political unity. Muslims from North Africa attacked Italy, and nomads from Asia, called Magyars (MAG-yarz), raided the eastern lands of the former Frankish Empire. Later the Magyars settled in the valley of the Danube River and established a kingdom that would later become Hungary. People from far northeastern Europe, called Slavs, moved south and west. Most threatening of all to Europe, however, were the Vikings, Germanic peoples who came from Scandinavia.

THE VIKING INVASIONS

The Vikings attacked and harassed Europe during the 800s and 900s. Some of them sailed up the rivers of Russia, traveling as far south as Constantinople, while others attacked towns along the Atlantic coast of Europe. One group of Vikings, called the Danes, took control of some of England.

Many Vikings sailed up the rivers of the Frankish kingdom, devastating the countryside. Often they burned and looted towns. They also brutally killed many people in these raids. In 911, the Frankish king was forced to give a large area of northern France to Viking invaders called Normans. This region came to be called Normandy.

Although the Viking invaders generally converted to Christianity, settled down, and intermarried with the local populations, the violence they used when they arrived caused fear and uncertainty. The Vikings continued their attacks until about 1000.

Some historians think that overpopulation and a scarcity of farm land in Scandinavia may have led to the Viking invasions. With no land of their own, and no other means of support, many young men turned to raiding and looting as a way of gaining wealth.

CHANGES IN THE CHURCH

Following the collapse of Charlemagne's empire, the Church became increasingly corrupt and disorganized. Charlemagne had attempted to educate priests, organize the countryside into parishes, and give more central authority to bishops. Although these efforts worked for a time, the Church suffered a crisis in the 800s and 900s.

Powerful local nobles, called lords, took control of most churches and monasteries. They often sold or gave to relatives church offices, or positions of authority in the Church. As a result of this practice, many priests were unqualified, and few knew how to read or write. Many church leaders were also incompetent, and some even became pope mainly because of the power their families held in the Papal States around Rome.

Reforms in the Church. During the 900s, however, many church leaders and nobles pushed for reform. These changes began in the monasteries, which were more independent than the churches. In 910, a pious noble founded a new monastery at Cluny. The monks of the Cluniac monastery insisted that they would answer only to the pope and not be controlled by local lords or priests. Cluniac monasteries sprouted everywhere as others followed the Cluny model, igniting a movement called

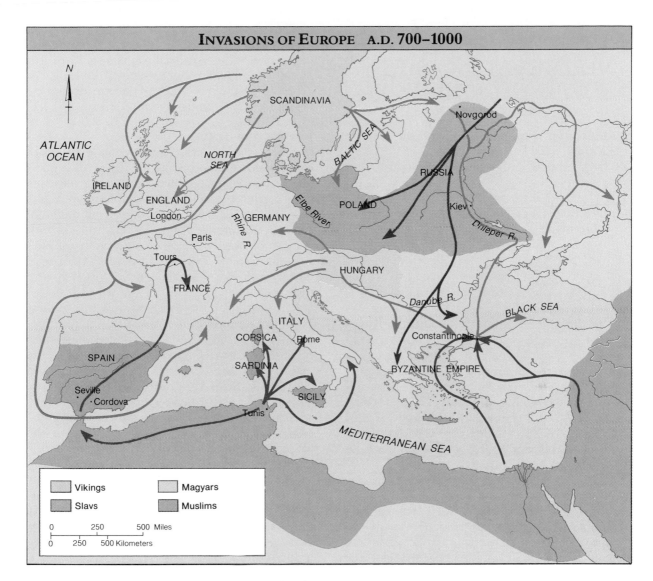

INVASIONS OF EUROPE A.D. 700–1000

N

ATLANTIC
OCEAN

IRELAND

ENGLAND
London

Paris

Tours

FRANCE

SPAIN

Seville
·Cordova

NORTH
SEA

Rhine R.

GERMANY

SCANDINAVIA

BALTIC SEA

Elbe River

POLAND

ITALY

CORSICA   Rome

SARDINIA

Tunis

SICILY

HUNGARY

Danube R.

Novgorod

RUSSIA

Kiev·

Dnieper R.

BYZANTINE EMPIRE

Constantinople

BLACK SEA

MEDITERRANEAN SEA

	Vikings		Magyars
	Slavs		Muslims

0   250   500 Miles

0   250   500 Kilometers

monastic reform. This movement spread religious fervor and created demands for reform in the Church itself.

Gradually the Church responded to these demands. Reformers pressed for a ban on the buying and selling of church offices. They also wanted to outlaw marriage for priests. Eventually, these reforms were made official church policy.

In the meantime, the powers and responsibilities of priests were clarified. By the tenth century, church law held that priests alone could administer the sacraments, or sacred Christian rituals such as baptism and holy Eucharist. Priests could be ordained, or given official priestly power, only through the sacrament of holy orders.

SECTION REVIEW

1. Define *tithe*.

2. Why was the alliance between the Church and the Frankish kingdom so important?

3. How did Charlemagne expand his empire?

4. How did the Viking invasions affect Europe?

5. Name four reforms made in the Church after the collapse of Charlemagne's empire.

Analysis. Why was it important that the Roman Church regain control of churches and monasteries from the local lords?

Data Search. Which chart on page 830 supports information on the above map about the extent of the area invaded by the Slavs? Explain.

10-3
MEDIEVAL SOCIETY

READ TO FIND OUT

—what the terms *manorialism*, *serfs*, *commons*, *feudalism*, *vassals*, and *fief* mean.
—what the rights and obligations of a serf were.
—how manors were organized.
—how feudalism created decentralized government.

As European civilization developed during the Age of Charlemagne, distinctive medieval economic and political systems began to emerge. Based on the decentralized rule and self-sufficient agriculture common in Europe since the fall of Rome's western empire, these systems became fully developed during the time of the Viking invasions. They provided the basis for the growth and change that led from the early Middle Ages into the next period of European history.

MANORIALISM

During the decline of the Roman Empire, self-sufficient estates, or villas, had become widespread. Small communities similar to these Roman estates survived into the early Middle Ages. Gradually, they changed and developed into the basis of a local food production and social system called *manorialism*. The manorial system spread throughout much of Europe during the early Middle Ages.

Under manorialism, nobles, called lords, owned scattered estates, called manors. The lands of a manor were worked by peasants called *serfs*. The serfs were tied to the land, meaning they were not free to leave the service of their lords.

Although their freedom was restricted, serfs had several advantages over the slaves that had worked the Roman estates. Most importantly, they controlled the land they worked on. Usually, the land could not be taken away from them, and they were free to use it as they wished.

The serfs' major responsibility to the lord was to work on his lands a fixed number of days per week or year, and pay taxes in the form of a share of the crops. In return, the lord was expected to protect the serfs from attacks by bandits and foreign invaders.

Life on the manor. The manor was a self-sufficient community. The peasants grew grain as the major food crop and tended small vegetable gardens. They paid fees to the lord to use his mill to grind the grain into flour. Some peasants raised sheep for wool, and others spun the wool and wove it into cloth for clothes. A blacksmith made tools. Only a few items came from outside the manor. The lord provided a form of government by running a court of justice to settle disputes.

The lord's house was built on the highest ground. Depending on his wealth, the dwelling could range from a modest wooden house to a huge stone castle. Clustered in the center of the many fields were the cottages of peasants, and beyond the fields lay grazing lands and forests. These lands were called *commons* because everyone on the manor shared them. Peasants gathered firewood, herbs, and mushrooms in the forests and shared with one another most farming tools and farm animals.

The sharing of property that was characteristic of manor life is an example of what is called communalism. The use of grazing and forestland as commons became a strong European peasant tradition that would last until modern times.

Communalism also helped make life bearable for peasants, who lived under very primitive conditions. Their cottages were often made of a few wooden beams, bundled twigs, straw, and mud, and they often slept on heaps of fern fronds. They ate mostly porridge and gruel, a few vegetables, and only a little meat. Crop failures often caused starvation in the winter.

WOMEN IN MEDIEVAL SOCIETY

European women during the Middle Ages had lower status than men and fewer rights. The role of women in society was influenced by the manorial system and Christian teachings.

As in most agricultural societies, the peasant family in early medieval Europe was an important economic unit. The entire family took part

This circular stained-glass window shows a serf planting seeds by hand. Boundaries of the field were often measured by the number of paces or the amount of plowing time.

in the production of food, and hard work was expected of husband, wife, and children.

Men and women, however, had different work roles. Men tended the main crops in the fields or worked as artisans. Although many women also worked as artisans, most women kept small garden plots near their homes, cooked, made clothing, and stored and preserved food. Men's work was given a higher value than that of women.

Noblewomen worked less than peasant women, but wealthy women were also considered subordinate to men. Women's marriages were usually arranged by their fathers to gain more wealth or land for the family. A noblewoman could own a manor but not run it. Her husband, son, or brother reserved this privilege.

The Church also influenced society's view of women. On the one hand, men held most of the power in the Church, and it taught that women were more easily tempted by evil than were men. This widespread belief often caused women to be treated as inferiors in everyday life. On the other hand, Christian beliefs held that women were the spiritual equals of men. Women active in the Church were respected, and many were named saints during the eighth and ninth centuries.

FEUDALISM

In the 800s, a new political system began to grow out of old Germanic customs and the economic system of manorialism. Under this new system, called *feudalism*, the manor lords gained full political control over their lands yet made oaths of loyalty to kings. Such oaths created kingdoms in name only, because the king could not challenge the local power of the lords.

Origins of feudalism. The invading German tribes in the later years of the Roman Empire had brought to Europe a system in which warriors swore oaths of loyalty to their chiefs. In Merovingian times, this system was carried on by lesser nobles, called knights, swearing loyalty to greater nobles, called lords or counts.

After the collapse of Charlemagne's empire, the Frankish kings were so weak they were unable to protect people from the invading Vikings. Local lords proved to be best able to provide this protection because they could raise armies of loyal knights and offer fortified buildings for protection. Feudalism arose as people began to rely more on the protection of their lords, and the lords began to acquire powers of government. They minted coins, made laws, and declared wars.

Government under feudalism thus became decentralized, or based on small, local units. Feudalism was much like the decentralized political system developed in the early Germanic kingdoms, except that it was much more organized, with formal titles and many unwritten rules of behavior, loyalty, and inheritance. By the 900s, feudalism was firmly established. It flourished mainly in the lands of the former Frankish Empire.

A system of mutual obligations. Under the feudal system, everyone had a well-defined place in society. There was a clear ranking of power and authority among the class of nobles. Powerful lords could grant part of their land to lesser lords, who were called *vassals*. The vassal built his estate on this land, called a *fief* (FEEF). The fief included all the peasants who lived there.

The vassal acted like a lord to his peasants, but still owed loyalty and military service to the greater lord. In theory, the powerful lords were vassals to the king. In practice, however, the kings never had the power to control any territory but their own local domain. The Frankish kings after Charlemagne had lands around Paris that they controlled as local lords, but the rest of France was controlled by lords called counts and dukes.

The feudal system held together through the interlocking obligations it placed on nobles. Lords were responsible for vassals, and vassals swore to serve their lords. Nobles were serious about these obligations because their social status depended on upholding them.

Vassals owed military service—usually about five weeks a year—to their lords. They also agreed to pay annual fees and to give the lord special payments when the lord's daughter was married. Vassals served in the lord's court of justice. An important feature of the feudal system was that vassals expected their lords to listen to their advice about matters affecting the lord's domains.

As time went on, the relationships between lords and vassals became more complex. Fiefs were divided with each new generation. It was possible, for instance, for a powerful lord to inherit through marriage a fief that made him the vassal of a lesser lord. It was also possible for a vassal to inherit several fiefs, each under a different lord. If these different lords were at war, the vassal, who had sworn to be loyal to all, found himself in a difficult position.

Feudalism at first contributed to political confusion and encouraged warfare. Wars thus became a common part of medieval life, often arising from conflicts between lords over boundaries, inheritance, or wealth. Often a lord's power was based simply on the strength of his knights and the size of his army.

At the end of the early Middle Ages, however, feudalism began to stabilize medieval society. By spreading the web of mutual obligations wider and wider, feudalism often served to prevent wars. Lords could preserve the peace, for example, by settling disputes between vassals. Slowly feudalism became the foundation of a new, more centralized political system.

SPOTLIGHT: DAILY LIFE

THE PEASANT FAMILY

The typical peasant family lived in a confined world. Life outside the manor was a mystery, while life within was governed by forces beyond the peasants' control. The sun determined how long they toiled, and the lord's assistants assigned their daily tasks. Since most peasants could neither read nor write, glimpses of their harsh life come mainly from medieval artists and the writings of medieval monks. Using this information, people today can picture what peasant family life might have been like during the early Middle Ages:

At dawn, the rooster crows and the church bell clangs, awakening the family to another demanding day. For father and son, there is plowing to be done. Leading an ox, they trudge toward the field. Throughout the day, the father strains behind a primitive plow, while his son goads the ox with a stick. Moving slowly along the furrows, they try to relieve the monotony by singing. The boy, who will almost certainly follow in his father's muddy footsteps, must become well-acquainted with the land. Meanwhile, his mother is teaching his sister how to shear sheep, weave woolen clothes, prepare meals, and tend the family's small vineyard and vegetable garden.

The children understand that the family survives by working together and that the manor will probably be their only home. Their marriages will be arranged by their parents, and their future spouses will probably come from within the small manor community.

Although manorial life revolves around work, Sundays, church feastdays, and occasional festivals provide some brief leisure time. Following Sunday services, the members of the community gather in the churchyard to sing and dance. On most days, though, the work stops only at dusk. Huddled around an open-hearth fire, the family eats a meager meal of black bread and barley-vegetable stew. Soon the last whisp of smoke escapes through the hole in their cottage's thatched roof. Shortly after sunset, the exhausted family is fast asleep. The morning will come early.

This illustration comes from a Book of Hours, a prayer book which included a calendar. The calendar was decorated with pictures depicting everyday life. Here a northern European family shares a meal beside a blazing fire during the harsh winter.

SECTION REVIEW

1. Define *manorialism*, *serfs*, *commons*, *feudalism*, *vassals*, and *fief*.

2. What were the differences and similarities between serfs and slaves?

3. Describe the typical manor and the work done by its inhabitants.

4. In what ways did feudalism bring about decentralization of government?

Analysis. How were manorialism and feudalism similar? How were they different?

Data Search. Which chart on page 830 relates to the subsection on page 214 titled "Women in Medieval Society"? Explain how the chart supports the information given in the subsection.

HISTORY IN FOCUS

Although it spanned more than five centuries, the period of the early Middle Ages is often forgotten in European history. Until recently, in fact, many historians referred to this period as the "Dark Ages." The achievements of the classical world—such as Greek democracy and Roman law—seem today to be more "modern" than any accomplishments attributed to the civilization of early medieval Europe.

Yet important foundations of Western civilization were established in Europe before 1050. One of the most important of these foundations was western Christianity. By the end of the early Middle Ages, most Europeans—from Spaniards to Scandinavians—had been converted to the Christian faith. European values and attitudes strongly reflected the Christian theology of the Roman Church.

The other important foundations of Western civilization were manorialism and feudalism. Although these decentralized systems seem simple, they eventually brought order and stability to Europe. Because they were flexible and decentralized, new, more centralized institutions could slowly develop out of them. Unlike Rome's rigid and centralized bureaucracy, they did not have to be destroyed to make room for change and growth.

SUMMARY

- Geography and climate limited the development of early European civilization. The decline of Rome's western empire thus left Europe in disarray.

- Germanic tribes that had settled in Europe in the 300s and 400s gradually established kingdoms. The Franks, under Clovis, created the largest and most stable kingdom of the time.

- The Roman Church became an important unifying force and began to influence basic European values and ideas. Pope Gregory I created a theology separate from that of the Byzantine Church. Monasteries became centers of learning.

- In the 700s, the Church and the Frankish kingdom forged an alliance. Charlemagne rose to power and created Europe's largest empire since Rome. He helped spread Christianity and promoted education.

- After Charlemagne's death, disunity and devastating Viking invasions caused the collapse of the Frankish kingdom. The Church then entered a period of crisis, which ultimately gave rise to reforms.

- Economic life in medieval Europe revolved around the manor, a self-sufficient community that depended on peasant labor. Out of manorialism came feudalism, a decentralized political system in which lords owed allegiance to a king.

VOCABULARY REVIEW

Match each numbered vocabulary term with the lettered word most closely related to it. Then explain how the words in each pair are related.

Example: The term *manor* is related to the word *community* because a manor in medieval Europe was a feudal community.

1. tithe	(a) decentralized
2. theology	(b) lord
3. vassal	(c) belief
4. feudalism	(d) tax

CHAPTER REVIEW

1. **(a)** Explain why European civilization lagged behind Mediterranean civilization. **(b)** How did the decline of Rome's western empire force European communities to rely on small-scale agriculture?

2. **(a)** Explain why decentralized government developed among the Franks. **(b)** What effect did decentralized government have on the role of the Church? Why?

3. **(a)** How did the Roman Church separate itself more from the Byzantine Church? **(b)** What effect did the Roman Church have on European ideas that were inherited from classical civilizations? **(c)** Explain how Christian monks played an important part in the development of European civilization.

4. **(a)** How did Charles Martel increase Frankish power? **(b)** How were both the Roman Church and the Frankish kingdom strengthened by their alliance?

5. **(a)** What was Charlemagne's greatest achievement? **(b)** What were three signs of the close relationship between Charlemagne and the Church? **(c)** Why did Charlemagne promote education?

6. **(a)** Why did Charlemagne's empire decline during the 800s and 900s? **(b)** Describe the church crisis of the 800s and 900s. **(c)** Explain how the church reformers responded to each of the following problems: the nobles' control of church offices, the large number of unqualified priests.

7. **(a)** Explain the mutual obligations between serfs and the lords. **(b)** Describe the life of the serfs.

8. **(a)** Why was shared property an important part of manorialism? **(b)** Why was the family an important part of manorial life?

9. **(a)** Explain how the Viking invasions helped lead to the development of feudalism. **(b)** Describe feudalism's effect on warfare.

10. **(a)** Compare the roles of medieval peasant women and noblewomen. **(b)** How did the Church influence the medieval attitude toward women?

THINKING CRITICALLY: ACTIVITIES

1. Imagine that you are a historian during medieval times. Write an evaluation of how your society compares with classical Greece and Rome.

2. Work with another student to present two views of manorialism. One of you should take the viewpoint of the lord while the other takes the viewpoint of the peasant. Compare and contrast views on everyday life as well as opinions on the overall system.

APPLYING SOCIAL STUDIES SKILLS

Sequencing events. The questions that follow are based on the section titled "An Emerging European Civilization," beginning on page 207. Use calendar markers, signal words, and implied sequence to help you answer each of the following questions.

1. Place the reigns of these Frankish kings in the correct order, from earliest to latest.
   (a) Louis the Pious
   (b) Pepin the Short
   (c) Charles Martel
   (d) Charlemagne
   (e) Charles the Bald
   (f) Pepin of Heristal

2. Which of the following were happening during the 900s?
   (a) Charlemagne was building an empire.
   (b) Cluniac monasteries were being built throughout Europe.
   (c) Church reforms were beginning to take effect.
   (d) Vikings from Scandinavia were invading parts of Europe.

3. What is the correct sequence of the following events?
   (a) Monastic reformers worked for church reforms.
   (b) Lords took control of churches and monasteries and sold church offices.
   (c) The Church banned selling offices.
   (d) Cluny founded a reform monastery that answered only to the pope.
   (e) Poorly qualified men became priests.

APPLYING THINKING SKILLS

Recognizing relevant information. Charlemagne sent special envoys called *missi dominici* throughout his kingdom. The following excerpt from a Frankish legal document of A.D. 802 describes the *missi dominici* and their duties. Determine what information in the excerpt is relevant to the duties of these envoys.

> The lord emperor Charlemagne has chosen from his nobles the wisest bishops, abbots, and pious laymen and has sent them throughout his whole kingdom. Through them he would have all persons live strictly in accordance with the law. Moreover, where anything that is not right has been made a law, he has ordered them to inform him of it. He desires, God granting, to reform it.
>
> Let the *missi* investigate any claim of injustice. They shall administer the law fully and justly in the case of the holy churches of God and of the poor, of wards and widows, and of the whole people.
>
> And if there shall be anything that the *missi* cannot correct, they shall, without reservations, refer it, together with their reports, to the judgment of the emperor. The straight path of justice shall not be impeded by anyone on account of flattery or gifts, or on account of any relationship, or from fear of the powerful.

Adapted from *Readings in European History*, Vol. 1, edited by James Robinson (Boston: Athenaeum).

1. What does the term *relevant* mean?

2. Why is it important to determine whether information is relevant?

3. Which sentences contain information that is relevant to the duties of the *missi dominici*?

4. Why is the information in each of these sentences relevant to the duties of the *missi dominici*?

5. Identify a sentence that contains information directly relevant to the topic of Charlemagne's role as leader. Explain your answer.

6. What ideas about Charlemagne or about life in his kingdom do you get from this document? Explain your answer.

7. How would you explain to a person two or three years younger than you how to recognize relevant information?

CHAPTER ELEVEN

THE HIGH AND LATE MIDDLE AGES

A.D. 1050–1450

Hearing, Thousand-flower Unicorn Series tapestry. Netherlands, c. 1450.

Around 1050, important changes began to sweep through Europe, beginning a period that people now call the high Middle Ages. Trade expanded, cities grew, and intellectual activity blossomed. By 1300, European civilization had entered a period of great achievement.

Between 1300 and 1450, a series of disasters destroyed much of Europe's prosperity, however. During this period, now referred to as the late Middle Ages, especially cold winters and heavy flooding were followed by the Black Death, a plague that eventually killed more than half of Europe's population. In addition, warfare again turned most of Europe into a battlefield. However, by the fifteenth century, another series of changes began to sweep through Europe, building the foundations of a new age to follow.

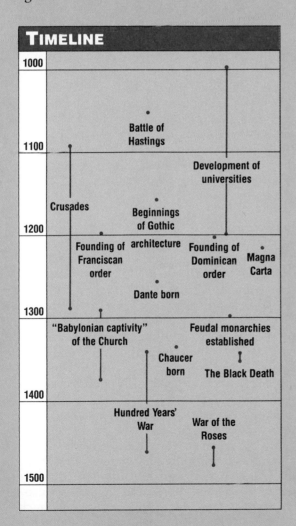

TIMELINE

1000	
1100	Battle of Hastings
	Development of universities
1200	Crusades / Beginnings of Gothic
	Founding of Franciscan order / architecture / Founding of Dominican order / Magna Carta
1300	Dante born
	"Babylonian captivity" of the Church / Feudal monarchies established
1400	Chaucer born / The Black Death
	Hundred Years' War / War of the Roses
1500	

11-1
THE CHANGING MEDIEVAL WORLD

READ TO FIND OUT

—what the terms **entrepreneurs** and **guild** mean.
—how food production increased between 1050 and 1300.
—what the effects of the Crusades were.
—what areas in Europe became trade centers.
—why cities were important in the development of medieval civilization.
—how the growth of an urban middle class affected European society.

The end of the Viking invasions around 1000 brought stability to Europe and opened the way for sweeping economic changes. These economic changes were important because they were the basis for social and political development. While farmers sharply increased their production of food, new industries arose, and growing trade exposed Europeans to luxury goods, ideas, and people from the world outside Europe. New attitudes about wealth and moneymaking began to challenge values established in the early Middle Ages, and a middle class developed in the growing cities.

THE REVOLUTION IN AGRICULTURE

About 1050, developments in farming began to provide the surplus food necessary for an expanding economy. Using agricultural innovations introduced at the end of the early Middle Ages, farmers took advantage of the growing political stability of the high Middle Ages to make enormous gains in productivity.

New farming tools. Europeans inherited farming methods and tools from the Romans. The Romans had not farmed much land in Europe because they had lacked the proper tools to till the heavy northern soils. The Roman plow, which just scratched the soil's surface, worked only in the light, dry soils of the Mediterranean region. The rain-soaked, heavy soil of most of

Europe needed to be dug deeply and turned over in order to get enough air into it for plant growth.

Because of such ineffective techniques and equipment, farmers in the early Middle Ages usually produced pitiful harvests. They could not support many nonfarmers, and so cities stayed small. At the end of the early Middle Ages, however, Europeans began to develop new techniques that were better suited to their rainy environment.

One of the most important innovations in farming was the heavy plow. Its plowshare, or cutting edge, was larger, longer, and heavier than the Roman plowshare. Therefore, it could cut deep enough into the northern soil to make the soil loose and airy for good plant growth. Besides helping plants grow better, the heavy plow reduced labor. The Roman plow had to be dragged twice across the field, each time in different directions. The heavy plow, however, needed only one pass.

Around 800, European peasants had borrowed from Asian nomads a device that helped the plow become even more useful. This invention was the padded horse collar. Up to this time, oxen, which had thick, fleshy necks, had been used to pull plows. Horses would have choked themselves to death if they pulled too hard on the plow's harness. The benefit of the padded collar was that it let horses pull with all their weight. Since horses were faster and longer-winded than oxen, the padded collar made plowing easier and faster.

New farming methods. While these new tools were being developed, advances were being made in farming methods, too. The most important medieval innovation was the three-field system. This system reduced the amount of land left unplanted, or fallow.

Under the three-field system, land was divided into thirds. In any one year, one-third would be allowed to lie fallow so it could regain its fertility. Another third was planted in the fall with a grain, usually wheat or rye, and harvested the following spring or summer. The final third was planted in the late spring with a summer crop of oats, barley, or beans, and harvested in the fall. Over the next two years, the fields were rotated so that each had a chance to lie fallow. Then the three-year cycle was begun anew.

This system had many advantages. The most important was that more land could be used in food production. Another benefit was that it spread a farmer's labor more evenly through the year. Also, two crops instead of one provided better insurance against starvation in case of a crop failure caused by a drought, insect attack, or plant disease.

Increases in the food supply. Even with these new tools and methods, early medieval farmers had not increased their production of food very much by 1000. Around 1050, however, this situation began to change.

First, peasants began clearing more land. In 1050, most of Europe was still forested. Only small islands of civilization dotted a green sea of forest. By 1200, the face of Europe had been transformed. Farm land spread everywhere. Now forests were islands in seas of wheat and oats.

As their lands became more productive, lords began to see farming as a way of gaining more wealth. Selling their surpluses to people in cities, the lords had more and more money available to buy better farm tools, which could be used to grow even more food. By 1300, European farmers were growing four times as much

In this fifteenth-century illustration, a woman carries wheat to a mill to be ground into flour. Known to the Romans, water-powered mills were not in general use in Europe until 1100.

grain as their ancestors had grown before Carolingian times. More land was also given over to new uses: raising sheep and growing cotton and grapes.

The increasing food supply could feed increasing numbers of people. Between 1050 and 1300, the population of Europe tripled. Not all these people could, or needed to, remain farmers. Cities, therefore, grew enormously during this time, stimulating further economic growth.

THE CRUSADES

The beginnings of rapid economic growth in Europe spurred greater confidence among Europeans. The Church had also grown stronger, having officially split with the Byzantine Church in 1054 to become the Roman Catholic Church. Many Europeans began to feel ready to test their military strength and promote their religious convictions outside Europe.

In 1095, Europeans banded together for a military campaign in the Middle East. Pope Urban II called upon nobles throughout Europe to join forces to free Palestine—the Christian Holy Land—from Islamic control. Islamic rulers had controlled Palestine for about four centuries. This campaign was the first of six military expeditions called the Crusades. Although the Crusades began as religious campaigns, their effect was to expand the economic horizons of Europe, spur trade, and make Europeans increasingly likely to seek wealth in lands outside of Europe.

A change of rulers in the Holy Land helped bring about the First Crusade. Followers of Islam called Seljuk Turks had taken over control of Palestine from the Arabs, also followers of Islam, in the early 1000s. The Turks closed Palestine to Christian pilgrims and threatened the Byzantine Empire.

When the emperor in Constantinople asked for aid to fight the invading Turks, Pope Urban II saw an opportunity to achieve several goals at once. The pope wanted to spread the Christian faith and also to inspire Europe's leaders with religious zeal in order to distract them from their constant warring. Instead of sending a small band of mercenary soldiers to aid Constantinople, as the emperor had requested, the pope decided to send a huge army to seize the Holy Land from Constantinople's attackers.

Results of the First Crusade. Although many crusaders lost their lives, the First Crusade, which took place from 1096 to 1099, was a great success from a European point of view. The defending Muslims were taken by surprise. The crusaders captured Antioch in 1098 and Jerusalem the next year. They established a thin strip of territories along the shores of the eastern Mediterranean called the Christian States. To defend these territories, crusaders built several immense castles.

The crusaders claimed this territory as their own property, and showed no mercy to its inhabitants. In Antioch, they killed all the Turks they could find. In Jerusalem, they murdered all the Muslim inhabitants. As they settled down, however, the Christians became less brutal and adopted some Middle Eastern ways. Meanwhile, Muslims began to recapture the territory they had lost to the Christians.

Later Crusades. During the twelfth century, two more Crusades were organized to win back the territory slowly being recaptured by the Muslims. Both of these Crusades, however, failed.

This manuscript illustration depicts the crusaders' assault on Jerusalem's north wall. The crusaders' weapons included moveable siege towers and apparatus for hurling heavy stones.

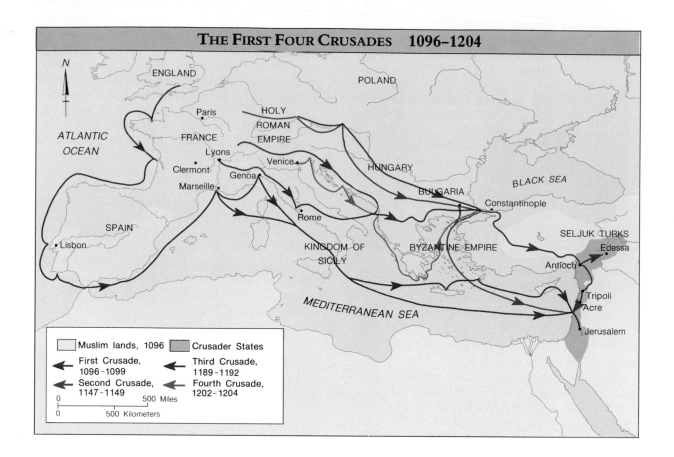

THE FIRST FOUR CRUSADES   1096–1204

Muslim lands, 1096   Crusader States

First Crusade, 1096–1099
Second Crusade, 1147–1149
Third Crusade, 1189–1192
Fourth Crusade, 1202–1204

0   500 Miles
0   500 Kilometers

In 1202, the pope organized a fourth Crusade to try to recapture Jerusalem. However, merchants from Venice took over control of the forces, promising rich booty to the Christian soldiers if they attacked Constantinople. The merchants from Venice wanted to eliminate their Byzantine competitors in Mediterranean trade.

Soldiers of the Fourth Crusade captured the Christian city of Constantinople in 1204 and looted its art treasures and rich churches. The attack fatally weakened the Byzantine Empire, which had long protected Europe from the Turks. The Venetians and the crusaders ruled the empire until 1261. Largely because of the diminished position of the Byzantine Empire, the Turks were later able to conquer it and invade southeast Europe.

In the 1200s, two more Crusades were launched, with mixed results. Then, in 1291, the Muslims captured the last Christian stronghold in Palestine, returning the Holy Land to Muslim control. The Crusades ended, having been only a temporary success for Europe.

THE DEVELOPING EUROPEAN ECONOMY

Despite the limited military success of the Crusades, they introduced Europe to a new world of exotic goods. Crusaders brought back sugar, rice, melons, fine cotton, perfumes, and spices from the Middle East. Demand for these products increased among the wealthy. Combined with growing agricultural production, this demand for imported goods provided the basis for a revival of trade and new developments in manufacturing.

Trade. By the twelfth century, merchants from Italian cities—especially Venice and Genoa—were carrying on a busy exchange with Constantinople and other Mediterranean ports. In return for Asian spices and fabrics, Italians traded woolen cloth, wine, and leather.

Trade also developed in the Baltic region. Baltic cities shipped mainly heavy goods such as timber, fur, fish, and grain to other parts of Europe. In the late 1200s, major Baltic cities joined together to form the Hanseatic League.

The league was an alliance that protected the commercial interests of these merchant cities.

Merchants transported goods overland as well as by water. Many cities and villages held periodic markets, where peasants sold surplus grain and products like eggs and vegetables. At great fairs held in Champagne, a region in northeastern France, merchants from all over Europe met to exchange goods and news.

Industry. Slowly, European manufacturing developed. A growing number of workshops, mills, and factories turned out such items as ships, tile, weapons, soap, paper, varnish, and metal tools. There were a few large centers of industry; these specialized in textiles, glassmaking, and metalwork.

One such center grew up around the cities of Ghent (GENT) and Bruges (BROOZH) in the Low Countries. In this area, certain businesspeople began to buy large quantities of raw wool, which was being produced more cheaply than ever before. Then they distributed it to workers, who worked in their homes spinning the wool and weaving it into cloth. The workers were paid a wage, while the owners took the profit. These businesspeople were *entrepreneurs*, or people who take the initial risk of organizing a business in order to make a profit.

Entrepreneurs in other cities also invested in new enterprises. By risking their money on mines, shipbuilding, warehouses, and shipments of goods, these entrepreneurs spurred the growth of a network of trade.

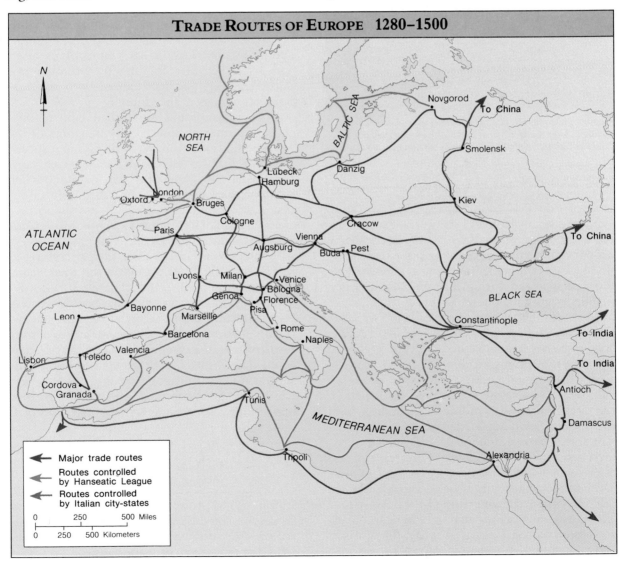

TRADE ROUTES OF EUROPE 1280–1500

Major trade routes

Routes controlled by Hanseatic League

Routes controlled by Italian city-states

0   250   500 Miles

0   250   500 Kilometers

A tray of silkworms stands nearby while the woman collects cocoons. After the secret of silk making was smuggled out of China by Byzantine monks, a European silk industry developed.

THE GROWTH OF CITIES

Growing population and rising trade made medieval cities important new centers of social and economic life. Urban growth in the high Middle Ages was remarkable because cities had almost disappeared during the early Middle Ages.

The largest cities—small by today's standards—were the trade centers of Italy. In 1200, Genoa and Milan had perhaps 100,000 inhabitants each. Average cities had between 5,000 and 10,000 people living in them.

A market square with a great church, a town hall, and a clock tower occupied the center of the city. In narrow, winding lanes leading from the square, shops and houses stood close together for protection. Most cities were dirty, crowded, and foul-smelling. Disease, fire, and crime were common.

In spite of these drawbacks, though, traders and traveling entertainers filled the busy streets. There was an atmosphere of freedom, and, consequently, cities became havens for escaped serfs. According to custom, if serfs lived in a city for a year and a day, they were free from their manor lord. Merchants, artisans, and shopkeepers were the most influential citizens of medieval cities.

Cities created their own courts of law, emphasizing regulations concerning trade and business. Most cities won special charters from the monarchy so they would be exempt from the manorial and feudal systems. Monarchs encouraged independent city governments, seeing them as a counterforce to balance the influence of feudal lords. Once a city was chartered, it formed its own government, usually under a mayor elected by the merchants.

GUILDS

The typical economic organization in the medieval city was the *guild*, an alliance of merchants or artisans. Guilds provided mutual support and protection. They also set limits on earnings and fixed penalties for shoddy production—both functions that harmonized with the economic teachings of the Church.

A merchant guild established control over commerce in each town. Only members of the guild could trade there without paying a special fee for a license. Merchant guilds set up controls on buying goods, too. For example, when a ship arrived carrying goods that were in demand, the guild gave each of its members a chance to share in buying so that no one member could control a desirable item.

Artisans developed craft guilds similar to merchant guilds. Craft guilds aided their members and gave them status. The guilds also developed rules to protect apprentices—young people learning a given trade. To ensure that apprentices were trained properly, artisans were restricted in the number of apprentices they could train. Finally, craft guilds protected consumers by ensuring good quality products and fair prices. Although most guilds were for men only, women sometimes formed their own craft guilds.

THE DECLINE OF THE MANORIAL SYSTEM

By the 1200s, growth in the economy began to be accompanied by changes in its basic organization. One of the most important changes occurred in the system of manorialism.

The freeing of serfs. As agriculture improved toward the end of the high Middle Ages, the manorial system became more flexible, and many serfs gained their freedom. This change had two major causes. The first was that new lands were constantly being opened to farming and settlement. Lords offered serfs their freedom in exchange for working on these new lands.

The second cause was that manors became less self-sufficient. As food became more plentiful and trade grew, nobles no longer relied solely on food grown on the manor, or tools or armor made by the village blacksmith. Instead, nobles began to desire money to buy more goods from outside the manor. In order to acquire more money, nobles began to charge rents instead of demanding crop payments and work obligations. Lords found that they could increase rents more easily than crop payments. In order to charge their serfs rent, however, lords had to free them.

Freed serfs often stayed on the manor as tenants. Others moved to towns. Still others were hired by the lord to work on his land. Serfs gained legal freedom, but they lost the security of controlling their own land and work. Peasants were increasingly forced to exchange their labor for wages in town or countryside.

Birth of the middle class. In the growing towns, the decline of manorialism was connected to other economic changes. The most important development was the rise of a town-dwelling, or urban, middle class made up of merchants and artisans. This class, composed of many former scrfs, grew in numbers and influence with the revival of trade and the growing use of money.

As the middle class grew, it helped change medieval attitudes toward wealth. In the early Middle Ages, medieval values had discouraged any interest in making profits. Christian leaders preached that other values were more important than money. In the 1200s, however, people in the new middle class who gained wealth through commerce or business began to be respected. Profit making was no longer considered shameful.

The growth of the middle class and its effect on medieval values threatened the nobles, whose prestige was based on birth. The new middle class valued achievement more than birth. Thus, the relationship between townspeople and land-owning lords often became tense. This tension was only the beginning of a long-term conflict that remained at the center of important political, social, and economic changes in Europe until modern times.

About 1338, an Italian artist adorned Siena's town hall with this fresco, *The Effects of Good Government*, the first realistic cityscape. Siena was a center of the Italian textile trade.

IDENTIFYING EVIDENCE

When authors make claims, they usually offer information that they regard as evidence for those claims. A claim is something someone says is true. Evidence is information that proves whether a claim *is* true. Any claim, no matter who makes it, is only as valid as the evidence that supports it. Therefore, it is important to identify evidence by analyzing a source—examining it part by part.

EXPLAINING THE SKILL

Evidence is often referred to as "the facts," pieces of information that can be checked out objectively by others. Evidence may consist of physical objects or documented (written down or otherwise recorded) actions, events, dates, statistics, and conditions. For example, the best evidence of a claim that you are a good student would be your grades or specific academic honors you have received. Your grades and honors can be objectively seen and judged.

To find evidence in a written source, you must search through the source to find what specific, objectively verifiable information it gives to support the claim or claims you are checking. One way to do this is to follow these steps:

1. *Identify and define clearly the claim for which you are trying to find evidence.* Make sure that you know the meanings of all the key terms in the claim so that you know what evidence to look for.

2. *Identify the general kinds of information that would be acceptable as evidence.* Will you be looking for statistics? Descriptions? Dates? Names? Events? Conditions?

3. *Examine the source line by line or sentence by sentence to locate any evidence that supports the claim.*

APPLYING THE SKILL

The following excerpt describes health conditions in London around the year 1350. Analyze the excerpt to identify its author's claim and the evidence that supports that claim.

The overall picture, therefore, is of a city squalid and unsanitary but aware of its deficiencies and doing its best, though with altogether inadequate tools, to put things right. By the early thirteenth century, Professor J.C. Russell has calculated, the population of London must have been about 30,000 and by 1348 had doubled to some 60,000.

Overcrowding was a major feature of life. One author writes of an earl and countess, their daughter, and their daughter's governess who all slept in the same room. In the houses of the poor, one could find a dozen people sleeping on the same floor of the same room. In many urban homes, pigs and chickens and perhaps ponies, cows, and sheep would share the common residence.

The lanes were barely wide enough to allow two ponies to pass between the steep walls of houses, which grew together at the top so as almost to blot out the light of day. The lanes themselves—they seem indeed to be more drains than lanes—were deep in mud and filth. It was a common practice to empty chamber pots directly into the streets from upper windows over these lanes.

Usually the privies of the aristocrats jutted out over the Thames River so their waste would fall directly into the river. The situation was worse when the privies projected not over a free-flowing river but above a shallow stream or ditch. According to a report in 1355, the ten-foot-wide Fleet Prison Ditch was choked by the filth from eleven latrines and sewers. So deep was the sludge that no water from Fleet Stream was flowing around the prison moat.

REFLECTING ON THE SKILL

In analyzing the above source for evidence, you should have identified and defined the claim to be checked. The claim here is that the city was squalid and unsanitary but was trying to improve. The key words or phrases in this claim are *squalid*, *unsanitary*, and *doing its best to put things right*.

Notice that analyzing a source to find evidence involves the use of other thinking skills. For example, identifying the appropriate kinds of evidence requires you to distinguish facts from value judgments because only facts will support this claim. This task also involves recognizing any information that is relevant to the claim. This enables you to identify the particular facts that directly support the claim you are checking.

Now that you have analyzed the source to find evidence, complete these questions:

1. Some evidence for the claim is provided in **(a)** paragraph 2, sentence 4; **(b)** paragraph 3, sentence 1; **(c)** paragraph 1, sentence 2. Explain your answer.

2. The evidence identified in the previous question consists of **(a)** statistics, **(b)** documented conditions, **(c)** documented events.

3. The excerpt does *not* provide evidence for the claim that **(a)** city conditions were squalid, **(b)** city conditions were unsanitary, **(c)** the city was trying to put things right.

APPLYING THE SKILL

Below is another excerpt from the same source. Continue your analysis to find evidence that supports the author's claim about the health conditions in medieval London.

> Butchers contributed to the filth. One royal instruction about these businesses complained that "by the killing of great beasts, from whose putrid blood running down the streets and the bowels cast into the Thames, the air in the city is very much corrupted and infected, whence abominable and most filthy stinks proceed. . . ."
>
> In the tenements of London, each story projected two or three feet beyond the one below. These buildings seemed designed for the emptying of slops and garbage into the streets. The gutters ran down the center of the narrower streets and both sides of the wider ones. They were generally inadequate to carry away the litter [which included] the dung of the innumerable domestic animals which lived in the center of the city. The open sewers which ran down to the river were better able to manage the load, but even these were often blocked and inadequate, especially in times of drought, to clear away all that was put in them.

To deal with these problems, the city council appointed scavengers or rakers to remove all filth from the streets. By 1345, the penalty for defiling a street had risen to two shillings and every householder was held responsible for any mess outside his house, unless he could prove his innocence. At least one city raker was appointed for each ward and there seem to have been between forty and fifty carts and horses. The householders, knowing that they would be the ones to suffer if a street was allowed to grow filthy, could generally be relied on to support the efforts of the authorities. Sometimes, indeed, their aid seemed overenthusiastic, as when a peddler threw some eel skins to the ground and was killed in the resulting struggle.

But improvement did not last long. In 1357, some years after these actions, the king still complained that his walks along the river were disturbed by the filth and dung piled up along its banks.

Adapted from *The Black Death*, by Philip Ziegler (New York: Penguin, 1969).

CHECKING YOUR UNDERSTANDING

Now that you have analyzed the second excerpt, complete the following items:

4. Some evidence for the claim that city conditions were unsanitary is provided in **(a)** paragraph 2, sentence 1; **(b)** paragraph 1, sentence 2; **(c)** paragraph 2, sentence 3. Explain your answer.

5. Some evidence that the city officials were trying to put things right is provided in **(a)** paragraph 3, sentence 5; **(b)** paragraph 3, sentence 2; **(c)** paragraph 2, sentence 2.

6. One of the sentences that does not provide evidence for any part of the claim is **(a)** paragraph 4, sentence 2; **(b)** paragraph 3, sentence 1; **(c)** paragraph 2, sentence 1.

REVIEWING THE SKILL

7. Define the term *evidence* and give examples of kinds of evidence.

8. What is one way to analyze a source for evidence in support of a claim?

1. Define *entrepreneurs* and *guild*.

2. How did farming change by the end of the high Middle Ages?

3. Describe how the Crusades affected Europe.

4. Where were the two centers of trade in Europe during the Middle Ages?

5. Describe the typical medieval city. How did the growth of cities affect medieval society?

6. How did the growth of an urban middle class cause a change in attitudes toward wealth?

Analysis. Why did the manorial system decline as Europe developed a more advanced economy?

11–2
FEUDAL MONARCHIES

READ TO FIND OUT

—what the term *feudal monarchies* means.

—what changes helped monarchs gain power.

—how William the Conqueror built a centralized government in England.

—how France's government gradually became more centralized.

—how the Holy Roman Empire was weakened through conflicts with the Church.

—how the Church and feudalism restrained the power of monarchs.

As Europe's economy became healthy and dynamic in the high Middle Ages, European monarchs grew in power. With larger armies and bureaucracies, kings began to gain authority over their vassals. The decentralized system of feudalism slowly gave way to more centralized rule. By 1300, the monarchs of several regions in Europe had built relatively centralized governments called *feudal monarchies*, in which monarchs ruled over kingdoms unified by feudal ties.

CONDITIONS LEADING TO POLITICAL CHANGE

In the early Middle Ages, monarchs had not been able to control territory outside their own feudal domain. There were several reasons for this. With almost no trade and an economy based on self-sufficient manors, monarchs could not gain wealth through taxes. Without money, they could not build large armies. Most of the peasants had little reason to give their loyalty to a king when it was their lord who gave them protection. Moreover, the Church jealously guarded its political power, thus limiting that of the monarchy. The Church owned much land, raised its own armies, and minted its own money. The Church also influenced people's ideas and behavior more than any other institution in Europe.

In order to build political power and solidify that power in centralized governments, mon-

Moneychangers like the one shown here were the first medieval bankers. At fairs along trade routes, bankers exchanged currency from different European countries and towns.

archs first had to acquire wealth, limit the power of both the feudal lords and the Church, and build a loyal following. Monarchs were not successful in meeting these challenges until economic changes in the high Middle Ages created the right conditions.

The increase in trade and use of money after about 1050 helped monarchs acquire wealth because they could tax wealthy trading cities. As towns grew, monarchs could gain the loyalty of more and more people not attached to a feudal lord. The rising middle class of merchants and artisans usually supported the monarchs because they could better maintain the stable and peaceful environment required for trade and business. Thus, monarchs established alliances with the middle-class townspeople. With this support and growing wealth, the rulers could build professional armies to challenge the feudal lords and the Church.

ENGLAND UNDER THE NORMANS

One of Europe's most centralized feudal monarchies came about in England. This feudal system was imposed by William, the duke of Normandy. Normandy lay within the old Frankish kingdom, a region later called France.

Though William was a vassal of the French king, he was also the closest adult heir of King Edward the Confessor of England. Edward had sent word to William that William would inherit the English throne. However, as Edward lay dying, he gave the throne instead to his brother-in-law, Harold. Harold had sworn allegiance to William, but now he accepted the throne.

William immediately invaded England. In 1066, he and his army of Normans defeated the English king Harold at the battle of Hastings and won control of England. This victory earned him the name of William the Conqueror.

In England, William created a carefully controlled feudal system in which he held centralized power. First, he put some land in his name, but he scattered the royal holdings rather than concentrating them in one spot. This made them less vulnerable to attack. Second, William rewarded his Norman warriors with fiefs of their own, thus making them the new English nobility. He also scattered the nobles' lands throughout England to make it difficult for them to unite against him. Third, he made all the lords swear loyalty to him as his vassals. In these ways, William built a base for direct centralized government.

William and his immediate successors also devised a central government that was partly separate from feudalism. William selected sheriffs in each district of the country as his own agents. His son, Henry I, who ruled from 1100 to 1134, created a special office, the exchequer (ehks-CHEHK-uhr). Through this office the government could tax the people directly.

Royal authority increased further under Henry II, king from 1154 to 1189. He allowed nobles to pay a fee instead of providing military service. The money from fees enabled the king to hire professional soldiers. Henry II also expanded the royal court system by instituting juries, or groups of people chosen to hear legal cases.

FRANCE UNDER THE CAPETIANS

A strong monarchy developed in France more gradually and with greater difficulty than in England. The Norman kings of England, with the advantage of conquest, could set up their own version of feudalism. In France, however, powerful regional lords dominated much of the kingdom, as they had for many centuries. One of these lords was the duke of Normandy, who retained that position after becoming king of England.

The building of a strong feudal monarchy in France mostly involved the gradual expansion of territory controlled by the monarch. The last king of the Carolingian Dynasty had been replaced in the late tenth century by a king named Hugh Capet (KAY-pet). The Capetian Dynasty established by Capet produced a line of effective rulers who, at first, built up their power through specialized government agencies. They strengthened their control over their own fief near Paris, while English lords controlled most of western France, and other French nobles ruled the rest of eastern France.

Philip II, who reigned from 1180 to 1223, was the first Capetian king to be successful in acquiring significantly more royal territory. He fought several wars with the English. By 1204, he had won Normandy, Main, Anjou, and other English-held territories for France. His successors continued this expansion. By 1328, the French monarchy controlled most of France.

THE HOLY ROMAN EMPIRE

In Germany, the lands northeast of France, political development progressed much differently than in England and France. Germany began, in the tenth century, with one of the most centralized governments in Europe. During the high Middle Ages, however, the power of its rulers began to fade.

The powerful monarch Otto I had gained control over the many lords ruling the hundreds of small states, or principalities, making up the region of Germany. In 962, he had claimed the title Charlemagne had held—Holy Roman Emperor. For centuries after Otto's reign, the lands that he had ruled, along with additional lands in France and Italy, were called the Holy Roman Empire.

The rule of the Holy Roman emperors over Germany had one basic weakness that began to show in the eleventh century. Although the emperors had prestige from their close ties with the Church in Rome, they failed to establish clear feudal links with powerful local lords. As a result, real power in Germany lay with local governments and cities.

When German emperors began to quarrel with the Church, what power they had over the local lords decreased. The most important of these quarrels began late in the eleventh century when a powerful new pope, Gregory VII, ordered an end to the power of Holy Roman em-

SPOTLIGHT: IDEAS AND DEVELOPMENTS

THE JURY SYSTEM

The Constitution of the United States provides that all citizens accused of a crime are entitled to a trial by a jury of their peers, or equals. The American jury system had its beginnings in the Middle Ages.

Before a jury system existed, trial by ordeal and trial by combat were often used to determine innocence or guilt. In a trial by ordeal, the accused underwent a torture such as carrying a red-hot iron a certain distance. Innocence was proven if the burned hand healed instead of becoming infected. In trial by combat, two people involved in a dispute fought each other until one of the two surrendered or was killed. Victory in the battle proved innocence.

To reform such unfair practices, King Henry II of England took important steps that eventually led to what are today known as the trial jury and the grand jury. Henry, who ruled from 1154 to 1189, hoped that reforming the English legal system would help him to govern properly his vast kingdom, which stretched from Scotland to France.

Under King Henry's reforms, the local sheriff served as a representative of the king in disputes over the ownership of land. Twelve trusted citizens who knew something about the case served as witnesses. The sheriff decided the case based on the men's testimony. Gradually, verdicts were entrusted to 12 jurors. In 1215, the Magna Carta established the principle that no person "shall be taken or imprisoned or in any way destroyed except by the lawful judgement of his peers."

Today, the trial jury is usually made up of 12 adults, men and women, who hear testimony by witnesses for both sides of a dispute. After considering all evidence, the jury decides whether the accused is innocent or guilty.

Through Henry's efforts, the method for identifying suspected murderers, arsonists, and robbers also changed. In 1166, Henry ordered that 12 men be present at every county court session. Their responsibility was to tell King Henry's officials about anyone they suspected of committing a major crime.

From this method of identifying suspected criminals came the grand jury. Today, the grand jury may have as many as 23 members, a majority of whom must agree on a decision. The prosecutor, or person who brings the legal proceedings, presents evidence, often by questioning witnesses. The grand jury then decides whether the evidence of wrongdoing is sufficient to make a formal accusation, called an indictment, against the accused. If indicted, the accused may be tried by a jury of peers.

King Henry's legacy is an important one. He opened the way for fair laws that gave the poor and the weak an equal voice with the strong and the powerful. Fair laws equally applied are foundation blocks of American democracy.

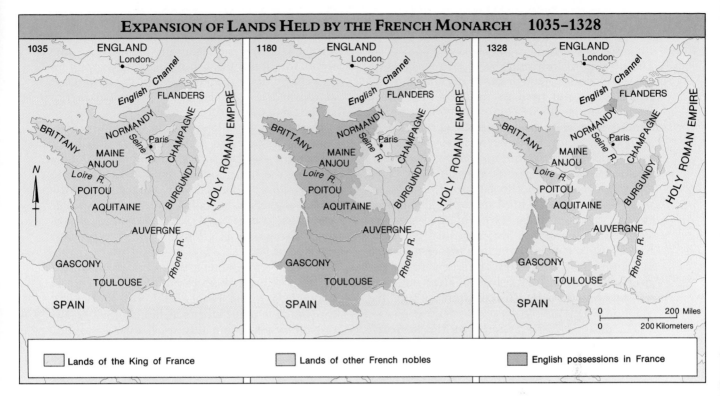

1035

1180

1328

☐ Lands of the King of France   ▨ Lands of other French nobles   ▨ English possessions in France

perors to choose German bishops. This power was called lay investiture.

When Emperor Henry IV refused to comply with Gregory's order, the pope expelled Henry from the Church. This action, called excommunication, prevented Henry from receiving the sacraments and released Henry's subjects from oaths of loyalty to him.

Opposed by German nobles as well as the pope, Henry had to give in. In the winter of 1077 he crossed the Alps to find the pope at the papal castle in Canossa, Italy. Barefoot in the snow, he begged for and received the pope's forgiveness.

This conflict between Henry and Gregory signaled the decline of the power of the German emperors. Germany remained a land of independent principalities throughout the Middle Ages, even though Holy Roman emperors continued to be elected by the most important German lords.

STRUGGLES BETWEEN MONARCHS AND THE CHURCH

As monarchs became more powerful, the Church acted to limit their power. Through its priests, the Church was in close contact with ordinary people. The Church taxed people directly and had its own system of courts to enforce religious law—for instance, regulations concerning marriage. Everyone owed loyalty to the Church as well as to the monarchy.

Pope Innocent III, who held office from 1198 to 1216, made the most sweeping claims for church power. He believed that as pope he was the supreme authority in Christian lands. To enforce his decisions and to provide examples for wavering monarchs, he replaced a disobedient Holy Roman emperor and excommunicated a defiant English king.

During Innocent's rule as pope, a new religious order, the Dominicans, sent preachers out among the people to strengthen their faith. The order was founded by Dominic, who began to preach among the people about 1205. In addition, the Church set up a special system of courts, the Inquisition, which investigated and punished heresy, or the belief in religious doctrines not accepted by the Church.

The period of Innocent's rule was the high point of the Church's political power in Europe. Later popes tended to focus their attention on revenues and attempts to rule central Italy. By 1300, the political power of the papacy had declined greatly.

STRUGGLES BETWEEN MONARCHS AND LORDS

The powers of monarchs were also checked by the institution of feudalism. Many disputes and crimes were still tried in feudal courts. Royal armies also depended heavily on feudal lords for military aid, especially in furnishing cavalry.

In England, the clash between royal and feudal claims produced an important document, the *Magna Carta*, or "Great Charter." The chain of events leading to the Magna Carta began around 1200, when King John of England made himself very unpopular. Not only had he lost a war in France, he was also punished by Innocent III for trying to name a worthless favorite to a high church office. His treasury empty, the king asked his lords for funds. They not only refused, but, in 1215, forced him to sign the Magna Carta.

The Magna Carta stated that the monarch could not collect any new taxes without consulting the leading nobles and church officials of England. The ruler had to promise to obey the laws and render justice fairly. The Magna

King Edward I presides over Parliament, with clergy at the left and nobles, right. In the center, judges sit on sacks of wool, tax payments received by the king from wool exporters.

Carta also guaranteed any accused person the right to a trial by a jury of peers—those equal in status. The Magna Carta thus spelled out some rights for all the English people, not just nobles and clergy. Its importance lies in the fact that it established the principle that the ruler is not above the law, but subject to it.

About 50 years later, a new institution, Parliament, was created in England to enforce the monarch's obligation to consult with feudal lords. In the 1260s, nobles revolted against King Henry III of England. To gain support, the leader of the nobles called a meeting of greater and lesser lords, knights, clergy, and representatives of townspeople. This meeting was the first Parliament.

In 1295, Parliament was divided into two parts, or houses. Nobles and clergy met in an upper house, the House of Lords. Following the principle that "what touches all must be approved by all," King Edward I invited knights, town representatives, and lesser clergy to meet in a lower house, the House of Commons. By going beyond the great lords to include other groups in society, Edward broadened the feudal idea of consultation.

As Parliament was being established, an important development was occurring in the English legal system. The decisions of the royal courts began to be written down. These decisions, based on interpretations of existing principles established by the Magna Carta and Parliament, formed the basis for later court decisions. This legal system, based on previous decisions rather than strict codes, became known as common law, because it was common to all of England.

Assemblies similar to the English Parliament developed in other countries in the later Middle Ages, especially in France. The French kings set up a parliament called the Estates-General in the 1300s as a means of winning approval for new taxes. In this parliament, nobles, clergy, and town representatives each met as a separate group, or estate.

An important effect of restraints on medieval monarchies was to limit their size. A ruler could control only relatively small units. No one could raise a large enough army to build a European empire. Therefore, Europe as a whole was disunited politically. Within each feudal monarchy, however, people began to develop a national identity and pride.

1. Define *feudal monarchies*.

2. How did the rise of the new urban middle class help the monarchs of Europe strengthen their power?

3. Name four ways in which William the Conqueror ensured that his government would remain centralized.

4. Why did France develop a centralized government more slowly than England?

5. What was the investiture controversy? How did it affect German politics?

6. What was the Magna Carta and what principles did it establish?

Analysis. If lords had not limited the power of monarchs, how might political systems have developed in Europe?

11–3
HIGH MEDIEVAL CIVILIZATION

READ TO FIND OUT

—what the terms *mystic*, *friars*, *scholasticism*, and *chivalry* mean.
—how Christian and Greek ideas combined to influence medieval thought and culture.
—how scientific experimentation developed.
—what kinds of literature, art, and architectural styles were common during the high Middle Ages.

With the expansion of the economy and the trend toward political unification in the high Middle Ages came a revival in intellectual and creative pursuits. More people received educations and towns became centers of cultural activity. Growing wealth encouraged more nobles to support the work of artists, philosophers, writers, and scientists. Works by the classical philosophers were rediscovered and formed the basis for new advances. By the end of the high Middle Ages, Europeans were justly proud of their beautiful cathedrals, fine paintings, musical compositions, and vivid poetry.

CHRISTIAN FAITH

The Church influenced medieval learning, thought, and artistic creation just as strongly as it affected political development. Since its beginning 1,000 years before, Christianity had developed many strong traditions that were deeply embedded in medieval society.

Many medieval religious leaders at this time held that faith alone made someone a good Christian. In order to be saved, they taught, it was necessary simply to believe in God, the Bible, and the teachings of the Church. Many important medieval scholars and thinkers accepted this point of view. Their ideas were strongly influenced by an emotional devotion to God.

Bernard of Clairvaux. An abbot of a monastery in France during the 1100s, Bernard of Clairvaux represented these beliefs. He stressed that the duty of people is to love God, arguing that people cannot love God adequately in comparison with God's great love for them, but nonetheless, they must try.

Bernard was a *mystic*, someone who believes that one learns spiritual truths through contemplation and faith, not through reason. He was one of many mystics in the Middle Ages who recorded their intimate contacts with God.

Francis of Assisi. A century later, the life of Francis of Assisi showed the continued power of deep faith. Son of a wealthy Italian merchant, Francis had little formal learning. He spent his time in rowdy pleasure-seeking until illness forced him to examine his life. At this time he decided to follow literally the teachings of Christ. Abandoning his riches, Francis lived in absolute poverty, preaching a joyful faith.

A new religious order, the Franciscans, resulted from the inspiration Francis generated in others. The order had spread throughout western Europe by the time Francis died in 1226, indicating the popularity of the emotional approach to religion. Unlike Benedictine monks, the Franciscans did not live in monasteries isolated from the world. Instead, they traveled from town to town preaching, much as Jesus had done. They came to be known as *friars*.

NEW CONFIDENCE IN HUMAN REASON

Despite the popularity of deep religious faith and mysticism, growing numbers of people both inside and outside the Church approached religion in a more intellectual way. These scholars pondered abstract religious ideas through reason instead of searching for emotional religious experiences.

With a growing appreciation for the power of human reason, scholars first began to consider the writings of Augustine and the Church Fathers. These thinkers of late Roman times had raised important problems by considering both Christianity and Greek philosophy.

Rediscovering Aristotle. Once they began to consider the intellectual achievements of the past, medieval thinkers took a renewed interest in the writings of Aristotle. Like other Greek thinkers, Aristotle had stressed the importance of human reason. By about 1250, Aristotle had become so completely accepted as the authority on philosophical questions that he was called "The Philosopher."

The interest in Aristotle's work stimulated wider intellectual contacts with Byzantine and Muslim scholars, who had translated Aristotle's writings from the Greek. Through these contacts western Europeans also became aware of other aspects of the Greek heritage, including science, and of Muslim achievements in philosophy, mathematics, and science.

EUROPEAN UNIVERSITIES

The growth of universities laid the foundation for the intellectual achievements of the Middle Ages. During the early Middle Ages, only some nobles and clergy had been educated, mainly through tutors. As prosperity increased, however, better education became available to more people.

The first schools developed around the churches of major towns. By 1100, more people were literate than had been a century before. More people were qualified to teach, and teachers began to attract their own students. They taught not only religious subjects but also medicine and law. Between 1000 and 1200, groups of teachers and students formed associations much like guilds. These academic guilds developed into universities in several cities—Paris in

St. Francis Preaching to the Birds is from *Little Flowers*, stories about the gentle monk published in 1452. One story tells of Francis taming wild animals by speaking to them.

France, Oxford and Cambridge in England, and Bologna and Salerno in Italy.

All the early universities established degrees to certify that students had successfully completed a course of study. A bachelor of arts degree indicated completion of basic courses. A master of arts degree qualified a person to teach at a university or go on to study a specialty such as law or medicine.

SCHOLASTICISM

In the universities, scholars began to rely more and more on the ideas and methods of the Greek philosophers. Seeking to categorize knowledge, or lay out everything humans knew in a systematic way, medieval thinkers came to completely accept Aristotle's confidence in human reason. At the same time, medieval thinkers were deeply religious. Because Christian ideas often seemed to conflict with Greek philosophy, scholars were confronted by a difficult problem: How could the Christian reliance on faith be balanced and combined, or reconciled, with the classical and Islamic stress on reason?

The attempt to solve this problem resulted in a kind of philosophy called **scholasticism**, because it arose in schools. Scholasticism, which taught that human reason and faith were compatible, became an influential philosophy in the high Middle Ages.

Peter Abelard, a monk who taught at the University of Paris in the 1100s, was one of the most important early scholastic philosophers. In his most famous work, *Yes and No*, he gathered opinions of Christian writers on major topics and showed how often they contradicted each other. Abelard justified his method with the motto: "By doubting we come to inquiry, and by inquiring we perceive the truth."

Scholasticism's effort to reconcile faith and reason found its most outstanding expression in the work of the greatest medieval thinker, Thomas Aquinas. Aquinas traveled and lectured widely. His major work is a summary of Christian thought called the *Summa Theologica*. Here he examined each major church teaching and showed how it could be proved by reasoning. The use of logic allowed Aquinas to include much that he had learned from Aristotle, the Islamic philosopher Averroës (uh-VER-ō-eez), and other thinkers, while preserving the idea that a true Christian also needed faith in order to be saved.

Unlike the political innovations of the Middle Ages, scholasticism is no longer part of mainstream Western civilization. Scholasticism, however, was important in that it helped bring classical and Arab learning into Western civilization. In addition, it led to an emphasis on strict logical method, which is still part of the Western intellectual tradition.

SCIENCE

The achievements of medieval scientists were generally less important than those of medieval philosophers. Like the scholastic thinkers, scientists of this time took an idea from a past authority and reasoned logically from it instead of experimenting. In medicine, for example, the ideas of the Greek physician Galen were treated as if they were proven statements of truth. No further proof or investigation seemed necessary.

By the 1200s, however, scientific progress was being made, especially in Italy and Britain. From the Arabs, Europeans had gained an interest in alchemy, the attempt to change other metals into gold. Of course, the efforts were unsuccessful, but alchemists' research did help launch the science of experimental chemistry in western Europe. European alchemists also discovered new drugs and chemicals. Some scientists experimented in optics, which helped bring about the invention of eyeglasses.

Some medieval research contradicted the findings of ancient authorities, even Aristotle. As a result, scholars like Roger Bacon at Oxford urged that conclusions by logical deduction should be tested through experimentation. This approach did not become dominant during the Middle Ages, but enough experimentation was undertaken to pave the way for further scientific discovery in later centuries.

ROMANESQUE AND GOTHIC ARCHITECTURE

The chief medieval art form was architecture. Medieval builders learned to make massive castles and designed impressive public buildings for cities. However, the builders' greatest achievements were their churches.

A church dominated every village and town. It was a sign that God's glory outshone everything else in life. The church was also an expression of local pride, and each locality tried to

Flying buttresses strengthen the walls of the magnificent cathedral at Bourges, France. Construction of the cathedral began in 1195 and took more than a century to complete.

The ceiling of Bourges Cathedral soars to a height of 118 feet (36 meters). Stained-glass windows pierce the walls, letting in the light. The windows depict scenes from Biblical stories.

PAINTING, SCULPTURE, AND MUSIC

Religious themes dominated the art of the Middle Ages. Painting and sculpture featured scenes from the Bible. The style of painting was flat and two-dimensional, but the works displayed a genuine depth of feeling.

Medieval artists showed great skill in stained glass. Religious scenes, rendered in brilliant colors, used figures from daily life, including peasants and farm animals. The use of natural likenesses foreshadowed the more realistic and lively styles in European painting that would emerge later.

Almost all medieval art was produced for display in churches. It was designed not only to please the eye but also to arouse emotion and teach illiterate people about the Bible.

Like painting and sculpture, medieval music was tied closely to the Church. Earlier music had consisted mostly of songs with one melody. The great musical invention of the high medieval period was polyphony (puh–LIH–fuh–nee), or the playing or singing of more than one melody at a time. Polyphony was used after 1170, when the mass in the Cathedral of Paris was sung by two voices delicately weaving together two harmonizing melodies.

At about the same time, musical notation was invented. This method of writing down music enabled singers and musicians to follow written music instead of relying on memory. The new technique also allowed composers to produce many more works and preserve them. These two medieval innovations laid the necessary foundation for all later developments in Western music.

MEDIEVAL LITERATURE

The high Middle Ages are noted for two quite different types of literature. The first type was written in Latin. and included works by scholars such as Abelard and Aquinas. The language of the Church, Latin was a useful way for philosophers, theologians, and scientists to communicate.

The other type of literature used vernacular languages, those actually spoken by ordinary people. These had begun to emerge during the late Roman Empire. Latin mixed with other languages and developed differently in different places to produce French, Spanish, and Italian.

outdo its neighbors. The most elaborate churches were cathedrals, which often took many years to build.

Medieval builders at first copied the round arches, domes, and straight lines of classical Roman architecture. The result was the style called Romanesque. To support the heavy domes, Romanesque churches needed thick, heavy walls with few windows. Many of the dark interiors were then brightened by frescoes.

Beginning about 1150, however, church builders developed a new style, later called Gothic, featuring towering spires. Masons developed a type of pointed arch and an outside support called a flying buttress. These innovations made it possible to construct high, vaulted ceilings and to design walls with many windows. Gothic architecture stressed the vertical, carrying the observer's eye upward toward God.

The cathedrals of Paris, such as Notre Dame, Reims (REEMZ), and Chartres (SHAHRT) are outstanding examples of Gothic architecture. The style is still used today for many churches and college buildings.

Vernacular languages that relied on Germanic roots included German and English. At first, most vernacular literature was spoken or sung; only later was it written down.

One form of vernacular literature was religious drama, portraying highly emotional scenes from the Bible or the lives of saints. Another was the epic that told the story of a national hero, such as England's King Arthur and the knights of the Round Table.

From southern France came a lyric style of vernacular poetry that was first sung by traveling minstrels called troubadours. Many of their poems celebrated the joys of battle or praised famous people. The troubadours were best known for love lyrics that glorified the romantic ideals of **chivalry** (SHIHV-uhl-ree).

Chivalry was a code of conduct for knights and nobles that developed at the beginning of the high Middle Ages. According to chivalric ideals, knights were supposed to protect women and fight honorably. They could fight only for noble causes and were careful to avoid unfair advantage. Although chivalry justified violence and made women seem powerless, it provided the basis for etiquette and table manners in Western societies today.

The two greatest medieval writers—both poets who wrote in vernacular languages—were Dante Alighieri of Italy and Geoffrey Chaucer of England. Dante, born in Florence in 1265, wrote poetry that helped standardize written Italian. His greatest work is the *Divine Comedy*. It tells of the poet's fictional journey through hell, purgatory, and heaven, guided by Virgil, the Roman poet. During this journey, Dante meets the souls of many famous people, both good and evil.

Chaucer's *Canterbury Tales*, written in the 1390s, is the first great work in the English language. It consists of stories told by pilgrims traveling to Canterbury Cathedral. They satirize human shortcomings and present a lively picture of medieval society.

Medieval literature demonstrates many prevailing medieval values. The epics, for instance,

SPOTLIGHT: PEOPLE

GEOFFREY CHAUCER

In fourteenth-century England, the languages of learning and literature were Latin and French. English was the language of everyday speech and was rarely written down. However, one person—the poet Geoffrey Chaucer (CHAW-sur)—changed this practice by producing a large body of work in English. Chaucer's poetry was of such high quality that he is considered to be the first great writer of English and the founder of English poetry.

Geoffrey Chaucer was born in London sometime between 1340 and 1343. His father held a minor position in the court of King Edward III. In the 1350s, Chaucer also entered royal service, as a page or servant. During the next four decades he served as a soldier, diplomat, and justice of the peace, or county judge. He also became a member of Parliament.

Chaucer spent his spare time studying languages, religion, and the sciences. Chaucer also broadened his knowledge by traveling throughout Europe. When he was in France in 1359 with King Edward's army, Chaucer was captured and held as a prisoner of war. He probably first thought of writing poetry while he was imprisoned in France.

Chaucer's early poetry did have a strong French flavor. However, another country—Italy—had far greater effect on his development as a poet. On his visits to Italy, Chaucer plunged into the poetry of the Italian poets Dante, Boccaccio, and Petrarch. The works of these writers greatly influenced Chaucer's later poetry, most notably his masterpiece, *The Canterbury Tales*.

Written toward the end of Chaucer's life, *The Canterbury Tales* describes the lives of English people of all classes, from ordinary peasants to wealthy adventurers. Chaucer intended his characters to represent the different segments of English society.

Unfortunately, ill health forced Chaucer to put the tales aside, and they were never finished. The poet died in 1400 and was buried in Westminster Abbey, a monastery in London. The section of the abbey that holds his grave became "Poets' Corner," the place where great English writers are buried and remembered.

show clearly the attitudes of medieval men toward women. Men are the major characters in these works. When women appear, they are always subservient to men. Husbands beat their wives, while brides were expected to be ready to die for their husbands. Warfare, a male activity, is usually highly praised, and vivid descriptions of heads being cut off are common.

SECTION REVIEW

1. Define **mystic, friars, scholasticism**, and **chivalry**.

2. How did the writings of Aristotle contribute to the development of scholasticism?

3. How did the use of experimentation in science begin during the high Middle Ages?

4. What did high medieval art, literature, architecture, and music all have in common?

Analysis. How did Christian values and beliefs, along with the power of the Christian Church, limit scientific advances during the high Middle Ages?

11–4
THE LATE MIDDLE AGES

READ TO FIND OUT

—what the effects of the Black Death were in Europe.

—why peasants revolted in many European countries after 1300.

—what crises in church leadership undermined the power of the Church.

—what happened during the Hundred Years' War.

Around 1300, the medieval economy began to weaken. The population grew more rapidly than food production, causing famine in many areas. Then, between 1347 and 1350, a devastating disease called the Black Death swept through Europe, killing over a third of the population. Wars, famine, economic disruption, despair, and recurrent outbreaks of plague followed the first terrible onslaught of the disease.

Soon, however, with fewer mouths to feed, Europeans began to overcome the difficult conditions. Instead of declining and collapsing like the Roman Empire had, Europe preserved what was most solid in medieval civilization and built the foundations for a great renewal.

THE BLACK DEATH

By 1300, Europeans had cleared immense tracts of land for farming. Even the best land, however, was by this time showing signs of having been overworked. Farmers found it difficult to grow enough food to feed the rapidly growing population.

In 1315, the worst floods in centuries struck most of Europe. The heavy rainfall washed away topsoil, ruined crops, rotted stored grain, and made the soil too wet to plow. Famine followed and lasted many years.

These events, however, only foreshadowed a worse natural disaster. In 1347, a disease called the Black Death or bubonic plague began spreading across Europe from Asia. By 1350, it had reached northern Europe. In some places, it killed over half the inhabitants. People did not know what caused it and so were powerless to stop its spread. Stricken people often died within five days. Some people went to bed healthy and were dead by morning.

In terror, people fled cities, leaving their jobs and abandoning shops. Food rotted in the fields with no one to harvest it. Prices rose and trade collapsed. The whole European economy was disrupted. Feelings of despair, gloom, and self-doubt overwhelmed the survivors.

Not knowing what caused the plague increased the sense of fear that gripped the continent. Many people believed God was punishing them for their sins. Ironically, the carriers of the plague were two of the creatures most familiar to medieval people—fleas and rats. Fleas carried the bacteria, infecting people with a bite while the rats' fur provided the home for the fleas. Scientists did not discover the bacteria causing the disease until 500 years later.

The plague killed about one-third of Europe's population. The wars and famine that

MOVEMENT: THE SPREAD OF THE BLACK PLAGUE THROUGHOUT EUROPE

Geographers identify patterns of movement of people, ideas, and goods from one place to another by studying trade and travel. In the 1300s, the movement of people and goods between Europe and Asia increased dramatically, hastening the growth of new towns across Europe. It also set the stage for perhaps the worst *pandemic*—an epidemic that knows no geographical bounds—in history. This pandemic was the bubonic plague, or Black Death.

The plague began in Asia and spread slowly westward along caravan routes. For Europeans, the pandemic began in 1347 in the city of Kaffa, now called Feodosiya, on the Black Sea in southern Russia. Kaffa, a busy Italian trading colony, had been under seige for a year by a Mongol army. Then, suddenly, the Mongols were struck down by the mysterious disease.

Hoping to spread the disease to his enemy, the Mongol commander loaded the corpses of his plague-stricken men onto catapults and hurled the bodies into the city. Although the Italians quickly dumped the bodies into the sea, the people inside Kaffa's walls were already dying as rapidly as the Mongols outside.

In January 1348, a few survivors from Kaffa sailed for Genoa and Venice, unknowingly carrying flea-infested rats with them. From these cities, the plague spread inland along trade routes into Italy and across the Alps into Switzerland. The plague reached the port of Messina, Sicily when 12 trading ships from Kaffa arrived. After the people of Messina learned of the dreadful illness, they drove the ships away, scattering them to other Mediterranean ports, including Marseilles in southern France.

Ships from Marseilles carried the plague to the Iberian peninsula. From Marseilles, the plague also moved north along well-traveled rivers and roads, reaching Paris in June of 1348. By August the plague had reached the French coast, where ships carried it across the English Channel. By October, Londoners were dying of the plague.

During 1349, the plague continued to spread throughout Europe, reaching Scandinavia by a ship that sailed from London. The entire crew died at sea and the ship ran aground in Bergen, Norway. Unsuspecting Norwegians boarded the ship and caught the plague. Norwegian ships then carried the Black Death as far west as Iceland and Greenland.

The plague finally reached northern Russia in 1351. It had moved in a great arc from southern Russia westward along trade routes to Italy, northward through Europe, and then back eastward into northern Russia. The only places to escape the pandemic were isolated pockets in eastern Europe where there was little trade.

The path of the plague is evidence of human interaction in the 1300s, as people and goods moved between Europe and Asia. Such interaction has sometimes had negative, as well as positive effects. The spread of the plague is an extreme example of human interaction leading to disastrous consequences.

1. What is a pandemic?

2. How did an epidemic originating in Asia spread throughout Asia and as far west as Greenland in four short years?

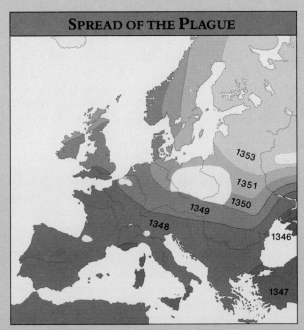

SPREAD OF THE PLAGUE

Owing to the grim realities of the plague and recurring war, medieval European artists often created powerful images of death. Here, death is personified as a triumphant skeleton.

followed on its heels killed thousands more, as did repeated outbreaks of the plague. Altogether, the plague and related events killed over one-half of Europe's people between 1300 and 1450. Some scholars estimate that this figure may have been as high as two-thirds. Europe did not fully recover from the economic disruption, social turmoil, and emotional trauma caused by the Black Death for about 100 years.

PEASANT AND WORKER REVOLTS

Peasants had extreme difficulty recovering from the economic turmoil caused by the Black Death. In the widespread warfare following the plague, invading armies burned and pillaged the peasants' homes and fields.

In both France and England, peasants felt they had suffered enough and revolted when rulers put additional burdens on them. In France, the peasants rose up in 1358 when they were heavily taxed to provide a ransom for their captured king. They burned the homes and castles of their lords, and often the lords with them. Soon, however, the lords fought back to protect their positions. They murdered the rebels and quickly restored order.

Another major peasant revolt occurred in England in 1381. English landlords tried to protect their wealth by passing laws to keep wages low. They also tried to force peasants to work their fields without pay as they had under the dying manorial system. Then the royal government demanded a head tax from everyone, regardless of income. Since peasants had to pay a much larger proportion of their incomes for this tax than wealthy lords, the peasants found the practice extremely unfair.

Anger built as head taxes were collected in 1377 and 1379. In 1381, an attempt to collect a third head tax caused peasants to resist. They burned local tax records and looted houses of the rich. They marched on London and killed two important royal officials. With his life seemingly threatened as well, King Richard II promised to meet the rebels' demands. The rebels dispersed, but the king later killed rebel leaders instead of keeping his promises.

Other revolts occurred in Germany and Italy during this time. Many took place in towns, among workers instead of peasants. One such uprising happened in Florence, Italy, in 1378, when wool workers revolted and took control of the town government for six weeks. Although landowners and aristocrats always gained the upper hand in these uprisings, they felt increasingly threatened by the lower classes.

CRISIS IN THE CHURCH

The Church had built its wealth and influence during the high Middle Ages, at the same time national monarchies had gained power. At the end of the thirteenth century, monarchs began to challenge the Church's power and authority. They resented that the Church did not pay taxes on its vast lands and that it interfered in politics. This challenge by monarchs, combined with other factors, undermined people's respect for the Church.

In 1294, the French king Philip IV tried to tax Church officials in France. Pope Boniface VIII ordered them not to pay. After a lengthy dispute, the king kidnapped the pope. He then used his influence to ensure that a new, French

COUNTESS JEANNE DE MONTFORT

Below are excerpts from an account written by the fourteenth-century historian Jean Froissart. In this account, he describes the heroics of Jeanne de Montfort, a countess who lived during that century. In one passage, Froissart notes how the countess rallies her husband's soldiers after he is captured and imprisoned by rival French lords:

> "Ah! sirs, be not cast down because of my lord, whom we have lost: he was but one man. I have riches in abundance, and I will provide you with such a captain that you shall all be comforted." When she had thus comforted her friends and soldiers in Rennes, she went to all her other fortresses and good towns, and did to them as she did at Rennes, and fortified all her garrisons.

Later, Froissart describes how the countess reacts when her town is under siege:

> The Countess herself, wearing armor, rode on a great war horse from street to street, desiring her people to make good defense, and she caused women to tear up the pavements of the streets and carry stones to the battlements to cast upon their enemies, and great pots full of quicklime.

In attacking the town, the enemy forces leave their own camp vulnerable. Froissart describes the countess's reaction to this opportunity:

> She caused three hundred men a-horseback to be ready, and went with them to another gate where there was no assault. She and her company dashed into the camp of the French lords, and cut down tents and fired huts. When the Lords of France looked behind them and saw their lodgings afire and heard the cry and noise there, they returned to camp crying "Treason! treason!" so that all the assault was left.

> When the Countess saw that, she drew together her company, and when she saw that she could not enter again into the town without great damage, she went straight away toward the castle of Brest, which is but three leagues [about nine miles] from there. When Sir Louis, who was marshal of the [enemy forces], was come to the field, and saw their lodgings burning and the Countess and her company going away, he followed after her with a great force of men at arms. But the Countess and the most part of her company rode so well that they came to Brest, where they were received with great joy by the townspeople.

For questions on Echoes of the Past, see "Analyzing Primary Sources" on page 249.

pope was elected. The new pope moved the papal government from Rome to Avignon (AH-vee-NYAWN) in southern France. Until 1378, French popes ruled the Church from Avignon and were under the control of the French king. This period is called the "Babylonian captivity," named after the time when the Hebrews were captives in Babylonia.

A new crisis developed in 1378, when the pope died and new popes were elected in both Avignon and Rome. France, Scotland, and parts of Spain recognized the French pope; the rest of Europe supported the Roman pope. The resulting division within the Church has been called the Great Schism (SIZ-m). During this time, the two rival popes, along with their followers, argued over who had divinely given authority. The Great Schism lasted until 1417, when church officials met, deposed both popes, and picked a new one acceptable to all.

These crises in the Church in part caused its followers to lose respect and loyalty. The Black Death caused even greater dissatisfaction with church leadership. At a time when people needed spiritual guidance the most, priests were at a loss as to how to help and often fled their churches when the plague struck their town. At the height of the plague, the pope retreated into his palace and refused to see anyone.

In the late 1300s, many people began attacking the corruption they saw in the Church. They believed that by amassing wealth, taxing people, and living luxuriously, church leaders were not fulfilling their duties. Several outspoken critics of the Church emerged. One was John Wycliffe, who claimed that priests and sacraments were not necessary for salvation.

The Church called such critics heretics. Some were killed and their followers persecuted. The spirit of criticism, however, remained. It

A German tapestry depicts Joan of Arc's arrival in 1429 at Chinon, the castle of Charles, king of France. According to accounts of the event, the king decided to test Joan's reputed God-given powers by placing a false king on the throne and disguising himself. Joan, who had never before seen King Charles, glanced only briefly at the false king. Then she immediately looked straight at the true king hidden among the courtiers and curtsied to him.

would resurface in the 1500s in a wave that would lead to profound changes in Christianity.

THE HUNDRED YEARS' WAR

Although much warfare occurred in the late Middle Ages, the most important war was the Hundred Years' War. A power struggle between France and England, this war was actually a series of conflicts from 1337 to 1453.

Even before the outbreak of fighting, war seemed unavoidable. English kings ruled territory in France that the French considered their own. The English also supported the Flemish people in the Low Countries in their rebellion against French rule. Other issues also arose, such as sailing and fishing rights in the English Channel.

Open warfare broke out when England invaded France in 1337. The English king, Edward III, had claimed the throne of France because his mother was sister to three French kings.

Even though France was wealthier than England and had more people, England won the most battles until late in the war. The English advantage came as a result of their tight discipline and use of the longbow, a new weapon in European warfare. With the light longbow, English archers on foot could knock the heavily-armored French knights off their horses. Unmounted knights were useless in battle. The French also suffered a blow when Burgundy, a French territory, allied with the English.

Joan of Arc. In 1429, when French fortunes were looking dim, a woman named Joan of Arc appeared in the court of Charles, the French king. She insisted she was sent by God to save France. She convinced Charles to put her at the head of the army.

Joan won victory after victory in battle against the English. Inspired by Joan's courage and sincerity, the French became optimistic. Within months, the French had cleared the English out of central France. In 1430, however, Joan of Arc was captured by the Burgundians and turned over to the English. The English accused her of being a witch and burned her publicly in a market square in France.

Still inspired by Joan, the French continued to win victories. By 1453, the French had captured all English territory except a small port town, and the war was over.

Effects of the war. The French monarchy emerged from the Hundred Years' War more powerful than ever. The French people had supported the king because his army seemed to provide the only defense against English rule.

The French also developed a sense of national pride and identity.

The war had much different results in England. The years of instability during the war had produced a rivalry between two noble families. On one side was the House of York, whose symbol was a white rose. On the other side was the House of Lancaster, who used a red rose as their badge. In 1455, a war for the throne broke out between these families. This civil war, called the Wars of the Roses, divided England for 30 years. Then Henry VII of the Lancasters defeated the Yorkist king in 1485 and married a prominent York noblewoman. Henry healed divided England and founded a new, strong dynasty called the Tudor Dynasty.

Military technology, developed toward the end of the Hundred Years' War and during the Wars of the Roses, changed the nature of warfare and signaled the end of the Middle Ages. The longbow made armored knights obsolete, and with gunpowder and cannons soldiers could break through castle walls. As knights and castles—two foundations of feudalism—became ineffective, feudalism declined more rapidly. Lords lost power to monarchs. After 1500, foot soldiers and national armies would decide the destinies of European countries.

ECONOMIC RECOVERY

After about 1400, when the worst effects of the Black Death had begun to disappear, some economic stability returned to much of Europe. The most important cause of this new stability was the drastically reduced population. With fewer mouths to feed, farmers could produce enough food to support the population.

With less grain needed, farmers now began to grow crops that were best suited to the soil and climate. Cities also became more important as more people moved to the cities because of the greater opportunities there.

The recovery of agriculture and the growth of cities helped stimulate more trade and commerce. Among cities in Germany, Scandinavia, and the Low Countries, the Hanseatic League helped revive trade in northern Europe. At the same time the wealthy city-states of northern Italy used their control of the Mediterranean to increase trade with Asia. Gradually, recovery spread through Europe and a strong foundation for further growth was established.

SECTION REVIEW

1. How did the Black Death affect the attitude of medieval people?

2. Describe two important peasant revolts and their causes.

3. What was the Great Schism?

4. How did warfare change after the Hundred Years' War? Why did this signal the end of the Middle Ages?

Evaluation. Some events, such as the Black Death, are caused by nature. Others, such as wars, are caused by people. Which type has a greater impact on history? Explain.

Data Search. Refer to the chart on the Black Death on page 830 to identify some medieval cities that **(a)** lost over half of their populations and **(b)** lost from one third to one half of their populations.

HISTORY IN FOCUS

After six centuries of slow change during the early Middle Ages, the high Middle Ages saw a burst of activity. Some historians have noted that revolutions occurred both in agriculture and in urban life. These revolutions stimulated changes in the systems of feudalism and manorialism that had developed earlier.

One of the most important developments of this period was the rising power of monarchs. For a time, the increase in royal power was somewhat limited by the Church and by feudal lords. The turmoil of the late Middle Ages, however, weakened the barriers to expansion of royal power as it undermined the power of both the Church and the feudal lords.

The building up of centralized European governments during the high and late Middle Ages began a new development in world history. Up to this time, centralized governments had always been created by very strong rulers, such as Alexander the Great, who formed large empires. Monarchs in high medieval Europe, however, began to control medium-sized land areas. The typical feudal monarchy linked together feudal domains to create regional units with a common language, culture, and identity. Unlike empires, feudal monarchies were united by shared ideas, not force. Feudal monarchies thus became the basis for the emergence of modern nations.

CHAPTER SURVEY

SUMMARY

- During the high Middle Ages, from 1050 to 1300, the European economy expanded, new political institutions evolved, and cultural activity flourished.

- Beginning in 1095, the Crusades introduced Europe to a larger world, stimulating trade. Increased food production provided the base for a growing economy. Cities developed with prosperous middle classes. Manorialism declined, and attitudes toward business and wealth began to change.

- Economic growth undermined feudalism and led to more centralized rule, especially in France and England. There, strong monarchs challenged the power of the Church, and were in turn limited by new political institutions. Germany, Italy, and Spain remained politically divided.

- Prosperity also stimulated intellectual and artistic activity. Universities were established, where scholars combined religious thought with classical learning. Music, art, and architecture were inspired by religious themes. Vernacular literature appeared, including the works of Dante and Chaucer.

- During the late Middle Ages, famine and plague ravaged the European population, and worker and peasant revolts followed. The Hundred Years' War broke out between France and England, and the Great Schism split the Church. By the end of the 1400s, however, Europe had begun to recover.

VOCABULARY REVIEW

The vocabulary terms in each pair listed below are related to each other. For each pair, explain what the two terms have in common. Also explain how they are different.

Example: *Polyphony* and *gothic* refer to innovations of the high Middle Ages. *Polyphony*, however, relates to music and *gothic* to architecture.

1. guild, entrepreneurs
2. mystic, friars
3. scholasticism, chivalry

CHAPTER REVIEW

1. (a) List four reasons why Pope Urban II called for the First Crusade. (b) Explain why the First and Fourth crusades were only a temporary success for Europe.

2. (a) How did the Crusades affect the spread of trade? (b) Describe how the Hanseatic League helped transform the European economy in the late 1200s. (c) Explain how medieval values toward wealth changed as the middle class profited from commerce.

3. (a) Discuss how the growth of cities affected medieval class structure. (b) Compare merchant and craft guilds. (c) What economic changes caused manorialism to decline?

4. (a) How did economic growth promote political centralization? (b) Why could England develop a strong monarchy more easily than France could? (c) How did the conflict between the Church and the Holy Roman emperors prevent unification in Germany and Italy?

5. Describe the political power of the Church under the reign of Pope Innocent III.

6. (a) How did the Magna Carta limit royal power? (b) Explain how Parliament and the Estates-General were alike. How were they different? (c) Discuss how restraints on royal power limited the size of monarchies.

7. (a) Discuss how the religious views of Bernard of Clairvaux and Francis of Assisi differ from those of Aristotle and Augustine. (b) Discuss how the attempts of scholars to reconcile faith and reason led to scholasticism.

8. (a) Explain Roger Bacon's views on experimentation in science. (b) Discuss how religion inspired Gothic architecture and medieval art and music. (c) Describe two forms of vernacular literature popular in the Middle Ages.

9. (a) Describe the impact of the Black Death on Europe. (b) Discuss the causes of peasant and worker revolts in the late 1300s.

10. (a) What were the causes of the Hundred Years' War? (b) Discuss the effects of the war on the monarchy in England and France. (c) Explain the significance of Joan of Arc to the French victory in the Hundred Years' War.

THINKING CRITICALLY: ACTIVITIES

1. Pair yourself with another student. From any one of the following pairs of people, each of you select a role to play: **(a)** monarch, pope; **(b)** monarch, lord; **(c)** monarch, peasant; **(d)** English king, French king; **(e)** merchant, noble; **(f)** mystic, scholar. Then write a dialogue that reveals how the people whose roles you are playing would have viewed each other on a particular issue. For example, the monarch and peasant could discuss the issue of taxation. Present your dialogue to the class.

2. Imagine that you are a reporter in Europe during the end of the Middle Ages. Write short articles about how each of the following affected the power and authority of the Church: **(a)** the "Babylonian captivity," **(b)** the Great Schism, **(c)** the Black Death, and **(d)** church corruption.

APPLYING SOCIAL STUDIES SKILLS

Analyzing primary sources. A painting can be a primary source if the artist actually observed the subject. After carefully studying the painting of Siena, Italy, on page 227, answer the following questions.

For items 1–3, identify whether each statement is **(a)** supported by the painting or **(b)** not supported by the painting.

1. A distinct boundary separated the city from the surrounding countryside.

2. Customers had to enter merchants' shops in order to buy goods.

3. Peasants were not allowed to bring their farm animals into the city.

4. State two general characteristics of the buildings in Siena.

5. How does the painting reveal that life in Siena involved both work and leisure?

6. How does the painting show that there were different social classes in Siena?

7. Does the artist show Siena in a positive way or a negative way? Explain.

8. Describe ways that goods were transported in Siena. How did people get around?

APPLYING THINKING SKILLS

Identifying evidence. People have made the claim that although the Magna Carta was secured by the efforts of the nobles and barons, it benefited all free men in England. Analyze the following excerpts from the Magna Carta to find evidence that supports this claim. Then answer the questions that follow.

A. We [King John] confirm that the English church shall be free and that the freedom of elections we shall observe and will be observed by our heirs forever.

B. If any earl or baron in our service shall die, his heir, if of age, shall have his inheritance.

C. No widow shall be compelled to marry as long as she prefers to live without a husband, provided she gives security that she will not marry without our consent, or without the consent of her lord.

D. No tax shall be imposed except by common council of our kingdom except for ransoming our body, for making our oldest son a knight and for once marrying our oldest daughter.

E. A free man shall not be fined for a small offense, except in proportion to the measure of the offense. No fines shall be imposed except by the oaths of honest men of the neighborhood.

F. Earls and barons shall be fined only by their peers, and only in proportion to their offense.

G. No free man shall be taken or imprisoned or dispossessed, or outlawed, or banished, or in any way destroyed, except by the legal judgment of his peers or by the law of the land.

Abridged from *Translations and Reprints from the Original Sources of European History*, edited by the Department of History of the University of Pennsylvania (Philadelphia, 1897).

1. Explain what is involved in identifying evidence related to a claim.

2. Why is it important to be able to identify evidence?

3. For what claim about the Magna Carta are you identifying evidence?

4. Which of the seven excerpts from the Magna Carta provide evidence for the given claim? Explain.

UNIT REVIEW

1. (a) Describe the geography and climate of the Byzantine Empire, Russia, and western Europe. **(b)** How did these conditions help give rise to distinct civilizations?

2. (a) List five institutions or other factors that had an important impact on the development of medieval civilization. **(b)** Why did the Byzantine Empire decline while the European civilizations grew stronger?

3. (a) Compare eastern and western Christianity. **(b)** What events or issues divided the two churches over time? **(c)** Why did the Roman Church experience various crises during the Middle Ages?

4. (a) Compare church-state relations in the Byzantine Empire, Russia, and medieval Europe. **(b)** How did those relations evolve in Europe? **(c)** What three governments identified themselves with Rome? Why?

5. (a) Describe the three main types of political systems during the Middle Ages and give examples of each. **(b)** Compare the rules of Justinian, Ivan the Great, and Charlemagne. **(c)** How did feudalism lead to more centralized government, yet prevent monarchs from taking absolute power?

6. (a) How did the Byzantine economy stimulate the growth of civilization in Russia and western Europe? **(b)** How did economic conditions help give rise to both feudalism and centralized government? **(c)** Explain the changing attitude toward business and wealth during the Middle Ages.

7. (a) Compare the differing effects of Mongol, Viking, and Muslim invasions during the Middle Ages. **(b)** How did these invasions compare with the Crusades? **(c)** How was the Hundred Years' War different from previous conflicts?

8. (a) Describe changes in the class structure of medieval Europe. **(b)** Why were the worker and peasant revolts of the 1300s a major turning point? **(c)** How were Christian and medieval values contradictory regarding the status of women? How did Joan of Arc symbolize this contradiction?

9. (a) What did much of the art, music, literature, and architecture of the Middle Ages have in common? **(b)** Trace the development of education during the Middle Ages. **(c)** How was scholasticism different from Russian Orthodox teachings?

10. (a) How did the activities of governments and the activities of the Christian Church promote cultural diffusion during the Middle Ages? **(b)** List three specific examples of cultural diffusion during the Middle Ages.

RELATING PAST TO PRESENT

1. Three characteristics of Christianity began to have an important impact on European thought during the early Middle Ages: the notion that loyalty to God was more important than political loyalty; a growing intolerance of other religions; and the idea that all people have souls equal in the sight of God. Discuss some of the ways these influences have affected Western civilization.

2. Our economic system, capitalism, has its roots in many of the economic institutions and practices of the medieval world. Also, some of the origins of modern labor movements can be found in the Middle Ages. Discuss those aspects of medieval economics and society that have given rise to modern capitalism and labor organization. Compare the current economic system of capitalist nations with the economic system of the Middle Ages. Also, compare modern labor movements with those of the Middle Ages.

3. Compare today's concept of the middle class with that of medieval times. Examine the factors that gave birth to and strengthened the medieval middle class, and whether those factors operate today. Consider the image, values, and characteristics of the middle class then and now.

4. Find out more about the place of women in medieval society. Compare the roles open to women then with the roles open to women in the second half of the twentieth century. Also, compare ideas about the ideal woman. Consider the position of women with regard to several of the following: politics, religion, economics, social status, education, and the arts.

PROJECTS AND ACTIVITIES

1. Choose an example of medieval art, architecture, literature, or music to research for an oral report. In your research, pay special attention to the way your subject embodied characteristics or values of life in the Middle Ages. Then present your report to the class, emphasizing those characteristics.

2. Imagine you are a journalist able to travel back in time. Choose an important event or issue of the Middle Ages, such as one of the Crusades, the Babylonian captivity, or a peasant revolt, and write a news story about it. Make sure your story covers the five Ws: Who? What? When? Where? Why?

3. With a group of classmates, pick one of the stories from Chaucer's *Canterbury Tales* to act out. Working together, create a short skit that conveys the story and its medieval flavor. Rehearse the skit and then present it in front of the class.

ANALYZING PRIMARY SOURCES

Refer to the account about Jeanne de Montfort on page 243 to answer the following questions.

1. What three reasons does the countess use to convince the soldiers to continue fighting?

2. How does the countess stop the siege?

3. Why do the countess and her soldiers ride to another town?

4. How does the historian's account reveal the countess's ability as a leader?

5. How is it evident that this account is written about people who lived in the Middle Ages?

GEOGRAPHY REVIEW

Movement. Today the movement of people, goods, and ideas takes place on a global scale. Lines of transportation and communication link human beings in many parts of the world so that people can easily interact to exchange information, negotiate agreements, and form trade partnerships. Evidence of this global interaction can be seen in the great number of products from all over the United States and many other countries that can be found in American homes.

To find out how important the movement of goods is in your life, conduct a product survey in your own home. Work from room to room, listing every item you find which has a label telling where it was made or grown. List each item and where it came from. Your list might include the following products:

    cars
    tools
    furniture and carpets
    appliances (refrigerators, stoves, toasters)
    electronics (TVs, stereos, computers)
    cameras
    canned, packaged, and frozen foods
    clothes and shoes
    accessories (watches, jewelry, wallets, belts)
    bikes and sporting equipment
    records, tapes, and compact disks
    toys
    books
    cosmetics and beauty aids

When you finish, count how many states and countries appear on your list and bring your list to class to share. Class members might use self-stick dots to mark on a large world map each state and nation that appears on their lists. The result will be surprising.

SUGGESTED READINGS

Cassin-Scott, Jack. *Costumes and Settings for Staging Historical Plays,* Vol. 2, *The Medieval Period.* Boston: Plays, Inc., 1979. Background information on historical costume.

Gies, Joseph and Frances. *Life in a Medieval Castle.* New York, Harper and Row, 1979. A study of the castle as the center of feudal life.

Macaulay, David. *Castles.* Boston: Houghton Mifflin, 1977. Castle architecture depicted through the history of an imaginary castle.

Power, Eileen. *Medieval People.* New York: Harper and Row, 1963. Sketches of the lives of six people who lived during the Middle Ages.

Tuchman, Barbara W. *A Distant Mirror.* New York: Ballantine, 1980. A discussion of great events and everyday life in the 1300s.

GOLDEN AGES OF ASIA, AFRICA, AND THE MIDDLE EAST

3000 B.C.–A.D. 1600

*God is most Great
There is no God but Allah
Muhammad is the
Messenger of Allah.
Come to Prayer!
Come to Salvation!
There is no God but Allah.*

—Muslim call to prayer

Wall painting, Chehel Sotun Palace. Isfahan, Iran, 1600s.

CHAPTER TWELVE
THE WORLD OF ISLAM

CHAPTER THIRTEEN
FLOWERING OF CHINA AND JAPAN

CHAPTER FOURTEEN
LIFE IN AFRICA AND THE AMERICAS

GLOBAL TIMELINE

- ■ THE ISLAMIC WORLD
- ■ CHINA, JAPAN, AND THE MONGOL EMPIRE
- ■ SUB-SAHARAN AFRICA
- ■ THE AMERICAS

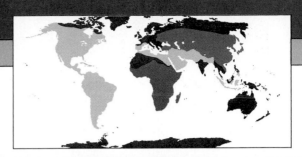

	POLITICAL	TECHNOLOGICAL	SOCIAL
250			
	Olmec civilization vanishes	Olmec calendar and hieroglyphics in use	
	Empire of the Kush	Kushite water reservoirs	
B.C.		and water tanks	
A.D.			Axum becomes a major trade center
	Bantu migrations begin	Technique of iron smelting spread by Kushites to sub-Saharan Africa	
250			
	Empire of Axum	Chinese writing introduced to Japan	Teotihuacán built: first large city in Middle America
	Beginnings of political unity in Japan	Mayan pyramids	Pre-Islamic poetry in Arabia
	Height of Mayan civilization		
500			
	Sui Dynasty	Chinese porcelain	Muhammad born / Early Chinese landscape painting / Buddhism introduced to Japan
		Invention of printing in China	
750	Umayyad Dynasty / T'ang Dynasty	First Arab coins	
	Ghana Empire	Mayan murals	Chinese cities develop into large trade centers
	Abbasid Dynasty	Machu Picchu built	
		Astrolabe perfected by Arabs	
1000			
	Toltec civilization	Mining and metal-casting techniques well-developed in Africa / Gunpowder perfected in China	Beginnings of arabesque style in Islamic art
	Sung Dynasty	Magnetic compass, sternpost rudder	Chinese introduce tea to Japan
1250			
	Aztec and Inca empires / Yuan Dynasty	Incas use *quipu* record-keeping system	Timbuktu established as a center of Muslim scholarship / Beginnings of Chinese and Japanese drama
	Mali Empire / Feudalism in Japan	Aztec city of Tenochtitlán completed	
1500	Ming Dynasty	Great Temple built at Zimbabwe	

CHAPTER TWELVE

THE WORLD OF ISLAM

A.D. 600–1566

Battle for the Persian throne. *Book of Kings*, early 1300s.

At the beginning of the seventh century, a new religion called Islam sprang up in the Middle East. Followers of this religion built a new civilization that outshone European civilization for more than six centuries. Islamic forces conquered Spain, North Africa, Syria, Persia, and large parts of India, uniting these areas in one vast empire.

Throughout this empire, people of different races, ethnic backgrounds, and cultures converted to the new faith while preserving many of their traditional ways of life. At its height, between 900 and 1100, Islamic civilization was one of the most advanced and dynamic the world had yet seen. Islam continues to exert a strong influence. Today, more than one-seventh of the world's people are Muslims, or followers of Islam.

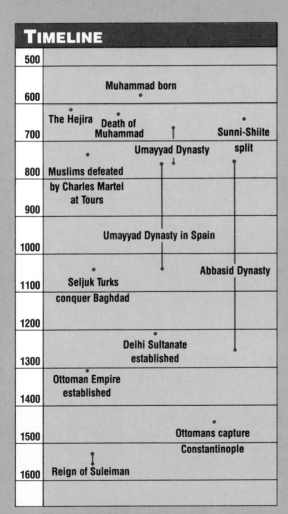

TIMELINE	
500	
600	Muhammad born
700	The Hejira Death of Muhammad Sunni-Shiite
800	Umayyad Dynasty split Muslims defeated
900	by Charles Martel at Tours
1000	Umayyad Dynasty in Spain
1100	Abbasid Dynasty Seljuk Turks
1200	conquer Baghdad
1300	Delhi Sultanate established
1400	Ottoman Empire established
1500	Ottomans capture
1600	Constantinople Reign of Suleiman

12-1
THE FOUNDING OF ISLAM

READ TO FIND OUT

—what the terms *Bedouins*, *jihad*, and *mosques* mean.
—how Muhammad began a new religion.
—what the teachings of Islam are.
—how Islam continued after Muhammad's death.
—how Muslims were able to build a large empire.
—how Shiite and Sunni Muslims became rivals.

The Arabian Peninsula, the birthplace of Islam, lies between Africa and Asia. Before the rise of Islam, the native people of the peninsula, called Arabs (AR-uhbz), lived mostly as desert nomads and traders. Located at the crossroads of the East and the West, Arab merchants carried ideas and goods among many civilizations.

With the emergence of Islam, however, Arab people adopted a new role as bearers of a new religion and a strong political organization. Islam's rise was a significant turning point in history because it set in motion a series of events that changed the rhythm of life in Africa, the Middle East, and large parts of Asia for centuries to come.

THE LAND AND PEOPLE OF ARABIA

Like the Phoenicians and the Hebrews, the Arabs are a Semitic people. They have lived in Arabia since before 900 B.C.

Much of the Arabs' land is sparsely inhabited desert. Good soil and rainfall along the coast of the Red Sea, however, allowed the development of villages, farming, trade, and cities. Cities on or near the coast, such as Medina, Mecca, and Jidda, were founded well before Islamic times.

The Arabs had always had some distaste for the settled life of their neighbors in Persia, in Egypt, and along the Mediterranean coast. Even after civilization on the peninsula advanced, many Arabs remained nomadic herders called **Bedouins** (BED-uh-wuhnz). Organized into tribes, the Bedouins were ruled by an elected *sheik* (SHEEK), or warrior chief. A tribe developed tight loyalties to its sheik.

By the time the Roman Empire was at its height, Arabia was known as a wealthy area, particularly because of its trade in perfumes and spices. Arabian cities developed an important merchant class. The merchants excelled in organizing trade between such distant places as India, China, Africa, and the cities along the Mediterranean.

Before Islam, the religion of most Arabs centered on the worship of many gods and spirits. In the cities, shrines to the gods were cared for by priests. Bedouins gave the same kind of strong loyalty to the spirits of particular places as they did to the sheiks.

MUHAMMAD

In about A.D. 570, a boy was born in the Arabian city of Mecca who would grow up to preach a much different religion to the Arabs. He was Muhammad (mō-HAM-uhd), the founder of Islam. Orphaned very young, Muhammad was raised by an uncle. Though he received no formal education, he thought seriously about religious matters. As a young man, he began to believe that there was only one God.

In A.D. 610, just before his fortieth birthday, Muhammad had a religious vision that changed his life. According to Muslim tradition, Muhammad was meditating on a mountaintop when the angel Gabriel spoke to him. Gabriel told Muhammad that he had been chosen to preach to the Arabs that there was only one God. The Arabic word meaning "God" is *Allah*.

According to Muslim tradition, Muhammad received regular revelations from God for the rest of his life. Muhammad began preaching what God told him to a small number of followers, who wrote down the revelations or memorized them. When he preached, Muhammad claimed no divine power of his own. Like Moses, he considered himself a teacher and a messenger of God, or prophet.

Having learned about Jewish and Christian teachings, Muhammad believed his mission was to bring to the Arabs the same belief in one God shared by Jews and Christians. Muhammad summed up the central belief of Islam in the words, "There is no God but Allah, and Muhammad is his prophet."

The Rub al Khali, a vast desert in southern Saudi Arabia, is inhabited only by a few Bedouin tribes. Large tents made of animal hides protect the nomads from heat and high winds.

Muslims believe that Muhammad was the last and greatest in a series of prophets that includes Abraham, Moses, and Jesus Christ. Although Muslims accept Jesus as a great prophet, they do not believe he is divine, as Christians do.

THE BEGINNING OF ISLAM

At the time that Muhammad began preaching the message of Islam, Mecca was a religious center to which many Arabs made a yearly pilgrimage. The pilgrims made the merchants of Mecca wealthy. The merchants feared that Muhammad's attacks against the polytheistic Arab religion would end the stream of pilgrims and the merchants' source of wealth. To prevent the poorer townsfolk's support of Muhammad from growing, the merchants forced Muhammad to flee.

With his uncle and a follower, Muhammad was welcomed in nearby Medina. Muhammad's flight from Mecca to Medina is called the *Hejira* (hih-JI-ruh). The Hejira occurred in 622, which was made the first year in the Muslim calendar.

Muhammad's message was well received in Medina, and Muhammad soon became the town's leader. He set about to shape the community according to what he believed was God's will. He taught that religious and political authority are one and the same, unlike Christianity, in which religious authority is usually separate from politics.

Soon, war between Medina and Mecca broke out. After a series of desert battles, Mecca surrendered to Muhammad's forces. Muhammad agreed to keep Mecca as a holy place for Arabs, however. He also decreed that his followers turn toward Mecca at times of prayer.

Once Islam became a respected religion and Muhammad enjoyed military and political success, he won converts in great numbers. The community of believers bound together by faith grew. By the time Muhammad died in 632, Islam had spread through most of the Arabian peninsula. Muhammad had brought a new and powerful religion to the Arabs. He also had established a political community that would come to dominate a large part of the world.

The idea of a single Muslim community spread with Islam. Jews, Christians, and Zoroastrians could practice their own religion, though. Muslims called followers of these other religions "People of the Book" because they also believed in a single God and had holy writings. However, Jews, Christians, and Zoroastrians had to pay a special tax as a sign of submission to the Muslim political community.

THE TEACHINGS OF ISLAM

Companions and followers of Muhammad helped Islam continue to grow after the prophet's death in 632. Their first step was to put Muhammad's teachings in writing. They brought together every record of what he had said because they believed his words were divinely inspired. From these memorized and written records, they assembled the Islamic holy book known as the Koran (kō-RAN). Muslims regard the Koran as the direct word of God as revealed to Muhammad.

An intricate set of laws emerged from the ideals set forth in the Koran. Also believed to be sacred, these laws affect all aspects of life, from politics to eating to marriage.

For centuries, Muslims would not translate the Koran into other languages. Converts were expected to learn Arabic. Thus, the Koran ensured that Islam would be not only a religion, but also a way of life, carrying with it a legal system and a language.

Major beliefs. The basic beliefs of Islam are simple and powerful. All of Islam flows from the idea of submission to Allah. The word *Islam* means "submission." As part of this submission, Muslims are obligated to follow five rules, called the Five Pillars. Muslims must publicly state their belief in Allah as the one God and Muhammad as his prophet. They must pray five times a day, kneeling in the direction of Mecca as they pray. They must fast from sunrise to sunset during the holy month of Ramadan (RAM-uh-DAHN). The faithful must give alms, or charity, to the poor. Finally, at least once in a lifetime, a Muslim who can afford it must make a pilgrimage to Mecca.

Muhammad urged his followers to practice temperance, generosity, justice, courage, and tolerance. All believers are thought to be equal. This belief discouraged racism among different peoples who embraced the faith.

Muhammad also encouraged his followers to undertake wars of conquest in order to spread Islam. A war either to spread Islam or in defense of Islam was called a **jihad** (jih-HAHD),

THE KORAN

Below are some excerpts from a translation of the Koran, the holy book of Islam.

In the Name of God, the Merciful, the
   Compassionate.
Praise be to God, the Lord of the Worlds,
The Merciful One, the Compassionate One,
Master of the Day of Doom.
Thee alone do we serve, to Thee alone we
   cry for help.
Guide us in the straight path
The path of them Thou hast blessed.
Not of those with whom Thou art angry
Nor of those who go astray.

God—
there is no god but He, the
Living, the Everlasting.
Slumber seizes Him not . . .
   to Him belongs
all that is in the heavens and the earth.
Who is there that shall intercede with Him
   save by His leave?
He knows what lies before them
   and what is after them,
and they comprehend not anything of His
   knowledge save such as He wills.
His Throne comprises the heavens and
   earth;
the preserving of them oppresses Him not;
He is the All-high, the All-glorious. . . .

It is not piety, that you turn your faces
   to the East and to the West.
   True piety is this:
to believe in God, and the Last Day,
the angels, the Book, and the Prophets,
to give of one's substance, however cherished, to kinsmen, and orphans,
the needy, the traveller, beggars,
   and to ransom the slave,
to perform the prayer, to pay the alms.
And they who fulfill their covenant . . .
   and endure with fortitude
   misfortune, hardship, and peril,
these are they who are true in their faith,
   these are the truly godfearing. . . .

For questions on Echoes of the Past, see "Analyzing Primary Sources" on page 323.

which means "righteous struggle." A jihad is sometimes called "a holy war." Not all warfare was considered righteous, however. In addition, a jihad may also be striving for Islam in some way other than warfare.

Islamic worship focused on individual prayer. Muhammad neither set up a church nor organized a priesthood to act as mediator between individuals and God. Muslims believe that each person is responsible for communicating directly with God through prayer.

The faithful built holy places called **mosques** (MAHSKS) where people could pray under the guidance of a prayer leader or *imam* (ih-MAHM). Scholars called *ulama* (OO-luh-MAH), educated in Islamic faith and laws, also became important in Islamic society. Their goal was to interpret the Koran, not to preach it.

Muslim women. Although according to the Koran "men are in charge of women," Muhammad improved the lot of Arab women over what it had been before. The long-time Arab practice of polygamy—having more than one wife—continued, but now a man was limited to four. The wives were to be kept well and treated equally.

Excluded from public life, a woman's role was limited to the family. Although considered equal in the sight of Allah, legally she was regarded as worth about half a man. Under Islam, though, women did gain property rights.

POLITICAL RULE AFTER MUHAMMAD

Because Muhammad left no heirs, a gathering of important followers selected abu-Bakr (ah-BOO BAK-uhr), Muhammad's father-in-law, to be Muhammad's successor. Abu-Bakr was named *caliph* (KAY-lihf), an Arabic word that means "successor."

As the new leader of Islam, abu-Bakr knew that for Islam to remain both a political and religious institution, the Muslims had to transfer to him the loyalty they had given to Muhammad. Abu-Bakr stated, "Whoever worships Muhammad, let him know that Muhammad is dead. But whoever worships God, let him know that God lives and dies not."

Abu-Bakr served as caliph for two years. During his reign, he strengthened the political power of Islam. Abu-Bakr sent troops against rebellious Bedouins and soon conquered the whole Arabian Peninsula for Islam.

The Koran acknowledges five major prophets before the time of Muhammad: Adam, Noah, Abraham, Moses, and Jesus. This picture of Noah and the flood is from a Koran made in the 1500s.

Expansion through conquests. When Abu-Bakr died in 634, he was succeeded by Omar, who was caliph until 644. Under Omar, Islamic armies quickly conquered a huge empire beyond the Arabian Peninsula. Arab armies were not particularly large. Neither did they have advantages in weapons or strategy. However, they did have religious zeal and a strong belief that God was with them in battle. The prospect of a blissful afterlife as a reward for death on the battlefield gave Islamic troops a fighting spirit that their enemies were unable to match.

Arabs conquered new lands for economic reasons as well as religious ones. As desert dwellers, many Arabs had always been relatively poor. Possessing new lands would bring wealth to the followers of Islam.

Muslim forces first turned to the north, where the Byzantine Empire held territory in the Middle East. Muslims easily defeated a larger but weaker Byzantine army. With the takeover of Syria and Palestine in 635, the Arab occupation of the Holy Land and of Jerusalem began.

In 636, after a three-day battle, a Muslim army defeated the Persians in what is present-day Iraq. A second Arab victory in 642 destroyed the Persian Empire and extended Islam's territory to the Caucasus Mountains on the north and to the borders of present-day Afghanistan and India on the east. Once Persia became part of the Islamic Empire, its art, literature, philosophy, and medicine began to strongly influence Islamic culture.

The Arabs also moved south and west, attacking Egypt, another part of the Byzantine Empire. The Arabs easily conquered Egypt in 642 because the Egyptians, dissatisfied with Byzantine rule, supported the Muslims. Near the southern part of the Nile Delta, the Arab conquerors established a military camp that became the city of Cairo and the Muslim capital of Egypt. In ten years, Islamic forces had created one of the greatest empires in the world.

THE SPLIT BETWEEN SHIITES AND SUNNIS

Omar's death in 644, brought the first of many divisions within the Islamic Empire. Different groups of Muslims argued over who should succeed Omar as leader of the Muslims.

A successor was chosen from the Umayyad (oo-MĪ-ad) family of Mecca. This new leader, named Othman, was unacceptable to many Muslims, who believed that only members of Muhammad's family should be caliphs. They favored Ali, Muhammad's cousin and son-in-law. Great struggles followed, in which both Othman and Ali were assassinated. An Umayyad ruler named Muawiyah (moo-AH-wih-ya) took over leadership in 661. Beginning with Muawiyah, the Umayyads would maintain control for almost 100 years, in what was called the Umayyad Dynasty.

Meanwhile, Ali's supporters claimed that Ali's son, Husayn (hoo-SAYN), was the rightful caliph. After more struggles, Umayyad troops killed Husayn and others of Ali's family. This action led to a permanent division among Muslims. Those who had supported Ali and believed that only members of Muhammad's

TAKING NOTES

INTRODUCING THE SKILL

Taking notes helps you concentrate on what you are reading or hearing. Notes provide a way to review main ideas and the facts that support them.

Some students take notes in outline form, while others use their own note-taking methods that work just as well. The more creative your notes are, the more you will enjoy taking notes and reviewing them later.

EXPLAINING THE SKILL

Your notetaking skills will improve rapidly if you follow these suggestions.

A. *Use the author's or speaker's outline.* An author's outline is often revealed in section and subsection headings. Some teachers also provide an outline of a lecture.

B. *Summarize, do not duplicate.* Identify and highlight the main points of a lecture or reading. Do not copy down every word. After you have written down the main ideas, you can add any details that seem important.

C. *Use abbreviations.* Save time by using abbreviations whenever you can. For example, when taking notes on this chapter, you might use *Is.* to stand for *Islam* or *Islamic*, and *Mus.* to stand for *Muslim.*

D. *Use symbols.* Symbols and pictures can replace words and show relationships in your notes. For example, arrows can show a cause-and-effect relationship, connect a problem to its solution, or show a sequence of events. Some other common symbols are listed here. You may also want to create some of your own.

Symbol	Meaning
=	the same, equals, equal to
≠	not the same, not equal to
+	plus, advantage, positive, good points about
–	minus, disadvantage, negative, bad points about
>	greater than, more than, better than
<	smaller than, less than, worse than
∴	therefore, because
↓	going down, under, decreasing
↑	going up, above, increasing
w/	with
w/o	without

E. *Make important ideas stand out.* Some notetakers use different colored pens to underline the most important ideas. OTHERS MAKE MAIN IDEAS OR HEADINGS STAND OUT BY WRITING THEM IN CAPITAL LETTERS. Then they add the details in smaller letters.

> Important ideas can be written in a box.

✔ They can also be marked by a check.
✔✔ Really important ideas deserve two checks.

Reread the subsection titled "The Beginning of Islam," which starts on page 255. Here are some sample notes on the first and second paragraphs:

Mecca = Ar. pil. ctr. → $ for mer.
Mer. worried that Muh. → pil. ↓
∴ mer. forced Muh. to leave
Muh. to Medina in 622 = Hejira
Muh.'s fortunes ↑
∴ yr. of Hejira = 1st yr. of Mus. cal.

APPLYING THE SKILL

Use these suggestions to take notes on section 12-1. Follow the general outline suggested by the section and subsection headings. Write down the main ideas and enough supporting details to help you remember those ideas. When you finish, compare your notes with those of another student.

family could be caliphs became known as Shi-ites (SHEE-īts), meaning "followers." Shiites were a minority of Muslims and continue to be so today. The majority of Muslims became known as Sunnis (SOON-ees), coming from the Arabic word for "tradition," and supported the Umayyad Dynasty and later rulers. Sunnis argued that the caliphs should be whomever God willed. Some Sunnis believed that political and religious leadership can and should be separate.

SECTION REVIEW

1. Define *Bedouins, jihad,* and *mosques.*

2. How was Muhammad inspired to begin a new religion?

3. What are the important teachings contained in the Koran?

4. How did abu-Bakr gain the loyalty of Muhammad's followers?

5. Give three reasons for the extraordinary success of Muslim conquests.

6. Describe the causes of the split between Shiites and Sunnis. Describe the basic difference in their beliefs.

Analysis. Why is the word *Islam* an appropriate name for the religion Muhammad founded?

12–2
THE ISLAMIC EMPIRE

READ TO FIND OUT

—how the Umayyad Dynasty expanded and strengthened the Islamic Empire.
—why non-Arabs began to convert to Islam.
—how the Islamic world became politically divided by 969.
—how Turks took over many Islamic lands after 1055.

Islam's ability to rule its huge territory was as impressive an achievement as its conquest. The process of organization begun under Omar, the second caliph, was continued by the Umayyad Dynasty. Umayyad caliphs governed using rules set by Muhammad as well as principles from the Koran. Even while Islamic leaders strengthened control over their empire, however, further conflicts within Islam politically divided the Muslim world.

THE UMAYYAD DYNASTY

As the first Umayyad caliph, Muawiyah began a new era of Islam. He replaced the election procedure with a simple system of inheritance and moved the central government to Damascus in Syria, where he ruled as a king from 661 to 680. He strengthened the Umayyad Dynasty by setting up a council of Arab chieftains and sheiks and by using them with great success to get the Arab tribes to do his bidding.

Umayyad expansion. Under Umayyad caliphs after Muawiyah, Muslim expansion continued into the eighth century. The Arabs moved west of Egypt and quickly conquered Africa's northern fringe all the way to the Atlantic. The chief fighting occurred against the Berbers (BUHR-burz), a nomadic people similar to the Bedouins. Many Berbers converted to Islam and practiced it with great zeal.

In 711, a small army made up mainly of Berbers moved across the Strait of Gibraltar to present-day Spain. The Arab army easily defeated an army of Visigoths—the Germanic people who had ruled the territory since the sixth century. In 732, the Muslims moved into France. At Tours, they were defeated by the Frankish army of Charles Martel. The Muslims had to settle for Spain, where Muslim civilization flourished for more than six centuries.

The end of expansion. In the meantime, Muslim armies had begun to meet costly resistance on the eastern borders of the Islamic Empire. Muslim forces that had pushed into central Asia and past the Indus River in northwestern India encountered a force of Turks. In 715, the Turks pushed the Arabs out of eastern Persia. In 717, an Umayyad attempt to take Constantinople, the Byzantine capital, failed. These defeats effectively stopped the military expansion of Islam. Muslims then settled into governing the empire. The Muslims added one final territory to their empire after 827, when they conquered the island of Sicily and part of southern Italy.

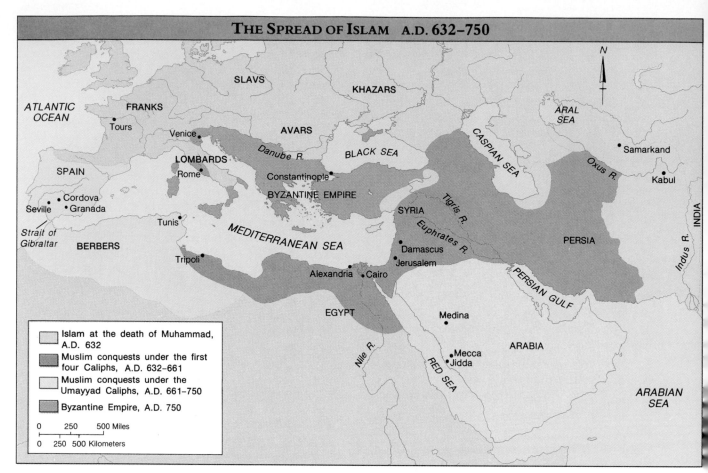

THE SPREAD OF ISLAM A.D. 632–750

Map legend:
- Islam at the death of Muhammad, A.D. 632
- Muslim conquests under the first four Caliphs, A.D. 632–661
- Muslim conquests under the Umayyad Caliphs, A.D. 661–750
- Byzantine Empire, A.D. 750

0   250   500 Miles
0   250 500 Kilometers

In 750, the Islamic world included a larger territory and more people than had the Roman Empire at its height. The orders of the caliph were obeyed all the way from the Atlantic shores of Spain to the western borders of China and India.

Umayyad rule. The Umayyads appointed loyal governors to rule the conquered provinces. The wealth amassed from the Islamic conquests and the taxes on non-Muslims allowed the Umayyads to build huge palaces and live in great luxury. Despite their political success, however, the Umayyads faced vexing problems of government, including feuds over succession.

THE SPREAD OF ISLAMIC CULTURE AND RELIGION

Following Islamic conquests came the spread of Islamic beliefs. During the 700s, the power of Islamic ideas became more important in spreading Islam than the jihad, or holy war. Once a majority of the people in the conquered lands converted to Islam, governing the territories often became much easier.

During the period of Arab expansion from 634 to 644, Islam remained chiefly an Arab religion. Many Arabs believed that Allah's truth was only for themselves. During the Umayyad Dynasty, however, Arabs converted an increasing number of non-Arab peoples. When Arabs entered North Africa, for instance, they converted many native Berbers to Islam.

Islam attracted many people. They saw in Islamic beliefs and laws the possibility of an orderly and well-organized life. Many of the people who converted to Islam learned Arabic in order to read the Koran. By reading the holy teachings, the converts learned Islamic ways and expanded the zone of Islamic culture.

Territories in North Africa, the Middle East, and parts of Asia became Islamic in culture and outlook. Groups that embraced Islam, however, did not entirely lose their own cultural identities. The Islamic world remained diverse because ways of life that did not conflict with Muslim teachings were preserved and because the Muslims tolerated Jewish and Christian minorities living in Islamic lands.

POLITICAL DIVISIONS IN THE ISLAMIC EMPIRE

The Umayyads were strong military leaders, which well suited them to ruling an expanding empire. When expansion halted in the mid-eighth century, however, people in the Muslim territories became dissatisfied with Umayyad rule. Non-Arabs were angry that the Umayyads treated them like second-class citizens. Some people wanted rulers who would help expand trade and improve agriculture.

This discontent set the stage for political divisions within the Islamic Empire. By 969, the Islamic Empire had split into three parts: one centered in Baghdad; another in Cordova; and the third in Cairo.

The Abbasid Dynasty. The Umayyad Dynasty ended in 750 when a rival family called the Abbasids (uh-BAS-uhdz) raised an army and defeated Umayyad forces in Persia and Iraq. The Abbasids began a new dynasty in the Middle East. They ruled this territory from the eighth to the thirteenth century. Under their rule, the capital of Islam was moved in 762 to Baghdad, a new city built along the banks of the Tigris River. Once in Baghdad, the Abbasids came under Persian influence. The Abbasids also began to employ Turks as mercenaries to strengthen their army.

The Abbasid caliphs surrounded themselves with great luxury and became famous for their splendid courts. During their rule, Islamic civilization flowered, enjoying the period of its greatest development. Under Abbasid rule, Arabic replaced Greek as the dominant language of the Middle East and North Africa.

Abbasid caliphs made important contacts with leaders in other parts of the world. Harun al-Rashid, who ruled from 786 to 809, was friendly with Charlemagne, the Frankish emperor. Another Abbasid caliph made an alliance with a ruler of the T'ang Dynasty in China.

The Muslims in Spain. When the Abbasids overthrew the Umayyads in 750, one Umayyad escaped to Spain. His name was Abdurrahman

Veiled women mourn their husbands who were killed defending Husayn, son of Ali. Long after the battle, this fresco was painted in a Shiite mosque in memory of Husayn.

(ab-DUHR-rah-MAHN). With followers devoted to his family's cause and line of succession, Abdurrahman declared himself leader of the Spanish Muslims in 756. Ruled from a capital at Cordova, the Spanish territory became the first part of the empire to break away. While Abbasids controlled the Middle East, Umayyads ruled in Spain. They presided over the development of an Islamic culture that rivaled the rest of the Muslim world.

The Fatimids. In the early tenth century, nearly two centuries after the beginning of the Abbasid Dynasty, the next major division occurred in the Islamic Empire. Shiites in North Africa gained power and set up a caliph who was a direct descendant of Muhammad's daughter Fatima (FAT-uh-muh). By the latter half of the tenth century, the Fatimid (FAT-uh-mihd) caliphs had added Egypt to their empire. Fatimid caliphs made Cairo the capital of their realm, which extended from Morocco in the west to Syria in the east. The rise of the Fatimids weakened Abbasid rule.

Despite the political divisions between the Umayyads in Spain, the Fatimids in Egypt, and the Abbasids, Islam continued to provide a common religion, language, legal system, and way of life throughout the Islamic world. In every area of Muslim rule, Islamic civilization continued to develop.

RULE UNDER THE TURKS

During the eleventh century, at the height of Islamic civilization, invaders began to push at Islamic borders in the Middle East. The first invaders were Turks from central Asia who had just recently converted to Islam. They were led by a chief named Seljuk (SEL-jook).

The Seljuk Turks. In 1055, the Seljuk Turks conquered Baghdad. They allowed the Abbasids to continue to hold the position of caliph.

The Seljuk leaders, however, who called themselves sultans, took over political power. The Abbasid caliphs were reduced to the role of religious leaders.

As Seljuks pushed northward in Asia Minor, they clashed with Byzantines, who were expanding their empire toward the south. When Seljuks soundly defeated a large Byzantine force, Byzantine leaders called upon western Christians for aid, thus prompting the Crusades. Eventually, both the Byzantine Empire and the Seljuk Dynasty were weakened by the Crusades.

The Mongols. In 1258, Asian warriors led by Hulagu, grandson of Genghis Khan, took Baghdad, deposed the Abbasid caliph, and ended Seljuk rule in much of the Middle East. The Mongols, as these Asian warriors were called, pushed south but were stopped in Egypt by Islamic troops in 1260.

Though stopped in their advance, for over a century the Mongols maintained control of

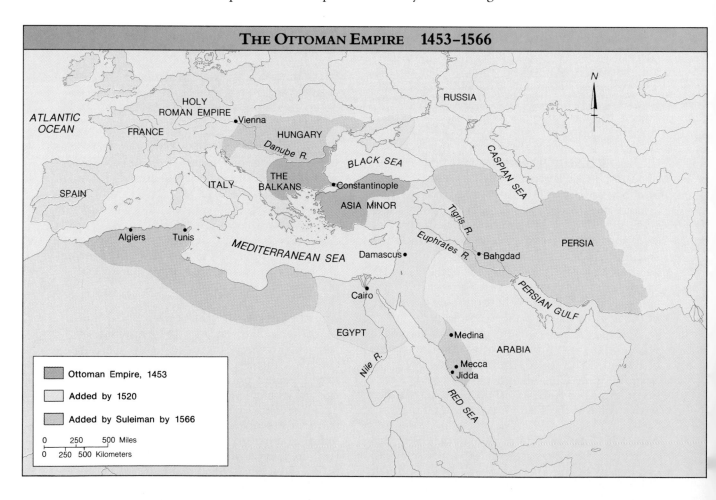

THE OTTOMAN EMPIRE 1453–1566

Ottoman Empire, 1453

Added by 1520

Added by Suleiman by 1566

0   250   500 Miles
0   250 500 Kilometers

parts of Persia that had once been held by Islamic rulers. As a result, Mongol rule in Persia marked a period of disunity in much of the Islamic world.

The Ottoman Turks. The defeat of the Seljuk Turks by the invading Mongols enabled another group of Muslim Turks from Asia Minor to rise to power in the Islamic Middle East. The first great leader of this tribe, called the Ottomans, was Osman, who ruled from 1290 to 1326. Osman conquered the northwestern portion of Asia Minor during his reign, paving the way for further Ottoman advances throughout the peninsula. In 1301, he established what came to be called the Ottoman Empire.

For two centuries, while Mongols and local Muslim sultans ruled other parts of the Islamic world, the Ottoman Empire grew slowly. In 1453, the Ottomans captured Constantinople and conquered former Byzantine lands. By 1520, the Ottoman Empire had grown to include Asia Minor, the Balkan Peninsula, Palestine, Egypt, and parts of North Africa and Syria.

Suleiman (soo-lay-MAHN), who ruled from 1520 to 1566, raised Ottoman power to its highest level. By the end of Suleiman's reign, Ottomans controlled not only much of the former Islamic Empire, but large sections of southeast Europe as well. The Ottoman Empire would influence politics in Europe until the twentieth century.

SECTION REVIEW

1. What was the greatest strength of the Umayyad caliphs?

2. Why did many non-Arabs convert to Islam after the first period of Muslim expansion? How did these conversions affect the Islamic world?

3. Describe how the Islamic world split into three factions by 969.

4. How did the Seljuk Turks give Europeans a reason to begin the Crusades?

Synthesis. Predict how the Islamic Empire might have developed if most of the people in its conquered territories had not converted to Islam. When making this prediction, what assumptions about the power of religious ideas must be made?

12–3
ISLAM BEYOND THE MIDDLE EAST

READ TO FIND OUT

—what characterized Muslim civilization in Spain.
—how Islam spread to Africa south of the Sahara Desert.
—how Islam influenced the history of India.

After Islamic forces created an empire in the Middle East and North Africa in the late 600s, Islam began to heavily influence other cultures, peoples, and places beyond the borders of this empire.

More and more people on three continents—Europe, Africa, and Asia—were exposed to Islamic ideas as Muslim merchants journeyed to new lands. In the 1200s, they were joined by religious mystics called *Sufis* (SOO-feez), who acted as Islamic missionaries. Through these peaceful contacts and further military expansion, Islam had an important impact in southern Europe, Africa south of the Sahara, Southeast Asia, and India.

MUSLIM SPAIN

Islam's main influence on western Europe occurred in Spain. Although Spain did not retain either the Arabic language or the Islamic faith, its culture and history were permanently affected by the Islamic conquest.

Muslims had invaded Spain in 711. There, the conquering Berbers from North Africa became known as Moors. Moorish civilization flourished in Spain between 756 and 1023, during the period of rule by independent Umayyad caliphs beginning with Abdurrahman. After 1023, Christian forces gradually reduced Moorish power and territory, and finally drove the Moors out of Spain by 1492.

Except for one or two brief periods, Muslim rulers in Spain practiced religious tolerance. As a result, Arabic, Jewish, and Christian influences combined to produce a vital civilization.

Cultural activity centered in the famous and beautiful cities of Cordova, Toledo, and Granada. Mosques and palaces filled the cities, which boasted public sewage systems and lighted streets. People enjoyed the feast days of both Islam and Christianity, and sang the romantic songs written by Moorish musicians. The universities of Seville, Granada, and Cordova became hubs of intellectual life.

Spanish Jews were especially active in science and learning during Muslim times. Skilled in languages, they translated Greek works on philosophy and medicine into Arabic. As Islamic scientific knowledge developed, the Jews translated information from Arabic into Latin and other European languages.

When Christians took over Muslim territory in Spain, they forced the Muslims and Jews to either convert to Christianity or to leave Spain. As educated Muslims and Jews left, they took with them a lively and productive tradition of cultural and religious diversity.

ISLAM IN AFRICA

The contact between Islam and sub-Saharan Africa—the part of Africa that lies south of the Sahara Desert—began in the early 700s. Attracted by the prospect of lucrative trade in gold and ivory, Muslim Arabs and Berbers pushed into Africa's interior. Bringing salt and European goods from ports in North Africa and the Middle East, Muslims set up trade routes across the desert and into the rest of Africa.

Muslim merchants developed an active trade throughout the huge Sahara Desert region and in areas farther to the west. These trade contacts brought numerous converts to Islam from among black African rulers and their people.

In Ghana (GAHN-uh), an ancient kingdom in western Africa that flourished from 400 to 1235, mosques were built as early as the seventh century to provide places of prayer for Muslim traders. The kingdom of Mali (MAHL-ee), which lasted from 1235 to 1468, flourished as a Muslim state. Following Muslim law and religious traditions, Mali's rulers created a well-organized bureaucracy. One of Mali's trading cities, Timbuktu, became a major center of Muslim scholarship.

Islam also spread down the east coast of Africa. Communities of Muslim traders occupied cities along the coast from the ninth century onward. By the thirteenth century, Muslim communities had formed in the major cities of present-day Tanzania (TAN-zuh-NEE-uh) and its island of Zanzibar (ZAN-zuh-BAHR). These trading communities included Arab traders and converted African people. The communities built mosques and cemeteries.

Although Islam did not penetrate into Africa's interior at this time, its influence in eastern Africa was substantial enough to give rise to a new language called Swahili (swah-HEE-lee).

Construction of Cordova's Great Mosque, now a cathedral, began in 756 and was finished 200 years later. The soaring arches of its great prayer hall are supported by 850 columns.

Written in the Arabic script and incorporating many Arab words and concepts, Swahili became more widespread than any of the local African languages.

ISLAM IN INDIA

In 711, the same year that Muslim rulers established themselves in Spain, Umayyad forces moved eastward into India. Halted by Indian opposition, Arabic and Persian Muslims ruled only northwestern India for the next 500 years.

As a result of Muslim rule, Islam began to gain converts in India. Many of these converts were tribal peoples who had not already become part of an established Hindu system. Other converts were groups who worked closely with their Muslim rulers. In addition, some Hindus along the southern coast became converts through their contact with Muslim traders.

The Islamic rulers set a policy of religious toleration. They treated Hindu subjects as protected people, just as these rulers also treated the Christians and Jews who lived there. The rulers sometimes hired Indian Hindus to serve as officials in the Muslim government.

Except for occasional periods of conflict, Muslims and Hindus lived side by side in peace. However, strong differences in religious beliefs and practices sometimes led to violent clashes between the two groups.

Beginning about 1000, new Muslim invaders appeared at India's frontiers. These were Turks from central Asia who had earlier converted to Islam. No permanent governments resulted from these eleventh-century invasions, which were looked on as holy wars by the Muslim troops.

The Delhi Sultanate. Early in the thirteenth century a Muslim ruling family of Turkish origin extended its rule over much of northern India, establishing a capital in the city of Delhi (DEL-ee) in 1206. This territory became known as the Delhi Sultanate. Five dynasties of Delhi sultans ruled much of India for 320 years.

This rule by Muslim Turks had important results. With more centralized rule, cities grew, agriculture spread, and trade flourished. The number of converts to Islam also increased as a result of the occupation.

Sufi missionaries concentrated their conversion efforts in the northwest and northeast,

where border peoples had not been fully integrated into Hindu culture. The converts came especially from the lower castes. While the converts to Islam were never numerous enough to be a majority of India's population, the Muslim influence produced a new language, Urdu (UR-doo). Blending Persian with an Indian language, Hindi, Urdu is written in Arabic script.

While Muslims ruled India, wars and political struggle between Muslims and Hindus broke out from time to time. During such conflicts, Muslims occasionally tore down Hindu temples, regarding them as houses of idol worship. Muslims also took over much land.

Although most Indians remained Hindus, the Muslims brought cultural change to India. For example, Muslim rulers encouraged the writing of poetry, not only in their language, Persian, but also in local languages. As a result, Hindu as well as Muslim poets began to write in local languages. This development reduced the role of Brahmans, traditionally the keepers of the Hindu literary language, Sanskrit.

Muslims also introduced new styles of art and architecture. Tall, slender mosques began to appear against the Indian sky. Muslim rulers

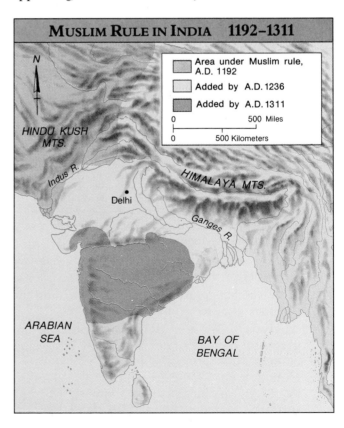

MUSLIM RULE IN INDIA   1192–1311

Area under Muslim rule, A.D. 1192

Added by A.D. 1236

Added by A.D. 1311

0   500 Miles

0   500 Kilometers

HINDU KUSH MTS.

Indus R.

Delhi

HIMALAYA MTS.

Ganges R.

ARABIAN SEA

BAY OF BENGAL

sometimes built whole cities. One ruler alone established 200 towns, 40 mosques, and 30 colleges, all in graceful Islamic styles.

The rule of the Delhi Sultans was interrupted for a short time in 1398, when a descendant of the famous Mongol Genghis Khan swept into northern India. This invader was Tamerlane, who was also called "the Prince of Destruction." With 90,000 soldiers on horseback, Tamerlane came seeking treasure. Though himself a Muslim, he destroyed Delhi and massacred the forces of the Delhi Sultanate. He also killed many Hindus. Tamerlane left India the next year, leaving behind great devastation. The Delhi sultans reestablished rule but were never again as powerful as they had once been. In 1526, new Muslim invaders called Moguls took control of India.

ISLAM IN SOUTHEAST ASIA

Islam had a strong impact as far away from Arabia as Southeast Asia. Arab merchants in several Indonesian cities had introduced Islam before 1300. After the Turkish conquests of India, Muslims took over more of India's trade with Southeast Asia, and more and more people in Southeast Asia were exposed to Islam.

Following the Muslim missionary influence of the times, Sufi holy men made many converts in the Southeast Asian lands of Malaya, the Philippines, and Indonesia. Islam became the dominant religion of Indonesia, where Hinduism lost most of its earlier influence. In Malaya, a mixture of local and Arabic influences created the Malay language and its Arabic script.

SECTION REVIEW

1. How did religious tolerance promote a lively civilization in Muslim Spain?

2. Where did Islam take hold in sub-Saharan Africa? How did it spread there?

3. What changes took place in India during the period of the Delhi Sultanate?

Analysis. List three different Muslim ruling groups in India from the 700s to the 1500s, and compare their different impacts.

Data Search. Refer to the appropriate chart on page 831 to identify which regions Islam had spread to: (a) before 800 and (b) after 800.

12-4
ISLAMIC CIVILIZATION

READ TO FIND OUT

—what Islamic beliefs and practices helped promote cultural diffusion.
—how Islamic trade spread ideas, ways of life, and goods all over the known world.
—why education and scholarship were important foundations of Islamic civilization.
—how religious beliefs influenced Islamic art and architecture.
—what important advances were made by Muslim scientists.

Before the rise of western European civilization, Islamic civilization was the major force spreading ideas, ways of life, and knowledge throughout the known world. Providing an important link between Africa, Europe, and Asia, Islamic traders not only brought the corners of the world closer together, but enriched their own lands and cultures with goods and customs from other lands. Muslims absorbed artistic styles and philosophical ideas from the Byzantines and the Persians. They learned mathematical concepts from India and new technology from China.

Just as importantly, Islam created a cultural umbrella, under which diverse peoples from lands stretching from Africa to India could share their ways of life united by a common religion and common language. The diverse origins of Islamic civilization are one of the major foundations of its greatness and worldwide influence. The people of the Islamic world grew intensely proud of their achievements. They felt superior to many other peoples, including the western Europeans.

CULTURAL DIFFUSION IN THE ISLAMIC WORLD

Islam was able to combine and spread cultures so remarkably well for two major reasons. First, its geographic location was ideal. After 700, the

Islamic rulers controlled much of the territory that separated Europe from Africa and Asia, giving Muslims a major role in the cultural exchange between the continents. Perhaps more important, however, was the character of the Islamic religion. Islamic beliefs led to at least four practices that enhanced cultural diffusion: Muslims tolerated other religions and cultures; they made pilgrimages to Mecca; they had to learn Arabic to read the Koran; and they valued trade as a livelihood.

Religious toleration. The Muslim policy of toleration contributed to the greatness of Islamic civilization. People of most other faiths lived without persecution throughout the Islamic world, contributing their different traditions to Islamic society. Christians remained an important minority in Egypt and along the shores of the eastern Mediterranean. Several caliphs employed educated Christians as secretaries or court poets. Jews lived all over the Islamic world and made notable contributions, especially in Spain. In India, Muslims and Hindus generally lived side by side in peace.

In the far-flung areas of Islamic influence, such as Indonesia, local customs and some traditional religions remained strong, combining with Islam to produce new and vital ways of life.

The pilgrimage. The Muslim idea of the pilgrimage to Mecca helped bring together peoples from different lands and cultures. Since the pilgrimage was one of the Five Pillars, Muslims from all over the world journeyed to Mecca every year. Particularly during the special pilgrimage month, thousands of Muslims from such widespread lands as Spain, Zanzibar, Asia Minor, Egypt, India, and Malaya converged on Mecca. There, they exchanged ideas and learned of each other's different ways of life. After making the pilgrimage, Muslims earned the title of *Hajji* (HAH-gee), a term of great respect. Hajjis carried news and ideas from other lands back to their own people.

The Arabic language. Because all Muslims had to learn Arabic in order to read the Koran, the Arabic language dominated the empire by the ninth century. It was the official language of religion and government, as well as the language used by scholars. Although many Mus-

This illustration depicts a caliph's pilgrimage caravan. Dated 1237, the colorful miniature decorated the travel commentaries of Al-Hariri, an Arabic scholar and merchant.

lims outside the Middle East spoke their native languages in everyday life, they knew Arabic or a related language such as Swahili or Urdu for religious purposes.

The existence of one common language throughout Islamic lands strongly aided cultural diffusion. Unlike Europeans, who spoke dozens of different languages, Muslims everywhere could understand each other. Merchants and travelers spread ideas more easily, and also better understood the customs and values of the people they met in other lands. Arabic ensured that the thousands of people from three continents meeting in Mecca at any one time could share ideas and views.

Muslim trade. A lively economy, centered on trade, was another important cause of cultural diffusion in the Islamic world. Seaports, market cities, and government centers all bustled with trading activities. Muhammad himself had been a merchant, and so trading was one of the most respected ways of making a living in the Islamic world.

Muslim ships controlled the Mediterranean Sea and the Indian Ocean until European merchants began to take over in Europe's late Middle Ages. From China, Muslims brought back spices, silk, and paper. From India came coconuts, tin, rubies, spices, and tropical woods. For centuries, most of the Asian imports prized in Europe passed through the hands of Muslim traders. Many important manufacturing techniques, such as paper making, also came to Europe from China by way of Muslim traders.

Muslim traders sailed north into the Black and Caspian seas and brought back furs and slaves from Russia and Scandinavia. From Africa, Islamic merchants imported gold and slaves by means of camel caravans that included as many as 4,000 animals.

The Islamic Empire learned about many fruits, spices, and grains from the lands it conquered and traded with. Through Muslims, these goods were later introduced into Europe and eventually into the Americas.

ISLAMIC SCHOLARSHIP

Muslims were not just good merchants. Many Muslims were excellent scholars who traded just as expertly in words and ideas. One of Muhammad's sayings was, "The ink of the scholar is holier than the blood of the martyr." This Muslim tradition established that intellectual activities were both important and based on Islamic faith. By recording, preserving, translating, and interpreting ideas from different cultures, Islamic scholars not only contributed to cultural diffusion, but also made many impressive intellectual achievements.

Education. Islamic scholarship was based on a strong program of formal education that was set up for some city-dwelling children. In Islamic lands, education began as soon as children were able to recite the basic prayers of the faith, usually at the age of six. Elementary schools were attached to mosques. There, many boys and some girls learned to read from the Koran and to write by copying poetry. Pupils also studied grammar, arithmetic, and the lives of the prophets. The Islamic system of education helped make a high percentage of Muslims literate at a time when only a handful of western Europeans could read and write.

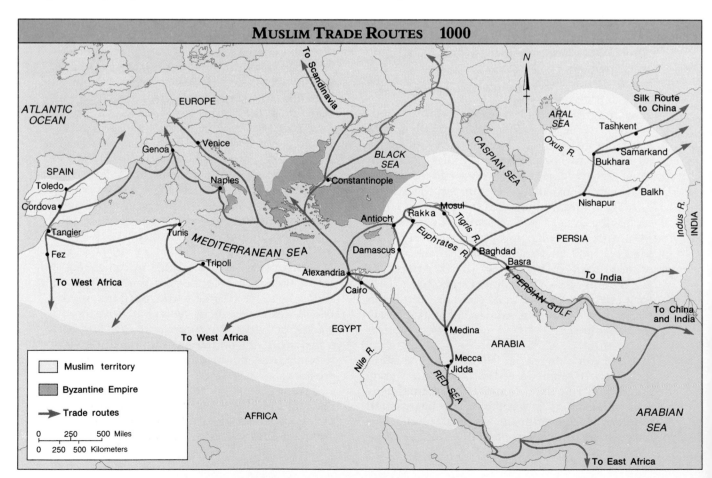

MUSLIM TRADE ROUTES   1000

After students finished their basic education, many went to universities. The oldest Islamic university was founded during the tenth century. By the twelfth century, several dozen great universities existed throughout the Middle East and Spain. University scholars taught law, philosophy, history, geography, and science as well as religion and poetry.

Books and libraries. In 704, when the Muslims captured Samarkand in Central Asia, they learned about the Chinese art of making paper. By 794, the first Islamic factory to manufacture paper was set up in Baghdad.

The invention of paper contributed to the establishment of public libraries throughout the Islamic world. Baghdad alone had 36 public libraries by the time of the Mongol invasions. In addition, most mosques contained excellent book collections.

Philosophy. One of the important results of excellent Islamic scholarship was the development of Islamic philosophy. From the ninth century on, Islamic scholars were busy translating works of philosophy and science from Greek, Persian, and Indian sources. A special school of translators—called the House of Wisdom—arose in Baghdad, with a library and a regular staff. Islamic scholars were familiar with classical Greek and Indian thinkers long before western Europeans were.

The translation of Greek philosophy, especially the writings of Aristotle, spurred a debate among Islamic scholars about the best path to truth. Islamic tradition held that the only truth was through faith in the revealed word of Allah. Greek tradition suggested, however, that human beings could gain truth through reason. Islamic philosophers tried to combine the two approaches long before Christian thinkers in medieval Europe tried to do the same. Indeed, the scholastic philosopher Thomas Aquinas borrowed many of his ideas from the Islamic philosopher ibn-Rushd, known in Europe as Averroës (uh-VEHR-ō-EEZ).

LITERATURE

Even before the Koran was written, Arabs had a strong tradition of storytelling. The Arabs were also particularly fond of poetry, which they used to recall past glories and to express religious ideas. These older traditions, as well as the influence of Persian verse and literature, survived into Islamic times.

The Koran itself was a major contribution to literature. Written in a highly polished style, it helped establish Arabic throughout the Islamic world as an expressive literary language. Skilled reciters of Koranic verse could move an entire audience to tears, to anger, or to laughter.

Written Arabic poetry began to appear during the Abbasid Dynasty. Many caliphs gathered poets at the court at Baghdad. By the eleventh century, a great deal of poetry was being written in Persian as well as Arabic. The most famous Persian poet was Omar Khayyam (kī-YAHM).

Fictional adventure stories also played an important part in Islamic literature. The most famous of these is a collection entitled *The Arabian Nights*. The wonderful tales of Ali Baba and Sinbad the Sailor are known today all over the world. These stories probably originated in India and were brought to Persia in the sixth century. By the eighth century they had become part of Arabic literature.

THE ARTS

Before the Arabs began their wars of expansion, they had little art or architecture. As they spread through Persia and Egypt, however, they borrowed elements of these cultures and blended them into a distinctive style.

Art and architecture. Early religious leaders prohibited the depiction of living beings in Islamic art. As a result, artists developed the decorative style called arabesque, which used detailed geometric patterns entwined with stars, leaves, and flowers. This rule was later relaxed.

Since architecture did not involve depicting humans or animals, it became the major Islamic art form. Mosques were the most important buildings in the Islamic world. They featured domes, towers called minarets, clusters of marble columns supporting vaulted ceilings, and pointed arches. Both interior and exterior walls were often gilded or decorated in brilliantly colored mosaics and tiles.

In other arts, the Muslims were especially noted for their textiles. The silk *taftah* created by the Persians became the taffeta worn by Europeans. Other fabrics such as damask linen from

Textile patterns often inspired Islamic tile arabesques. The elaborate vault shown here was built in an Iranian mosque as a *mihrab,* or prayer niche facing Mecca.

Damascus and cotton muslin from Mosul were also highly prized in Europe. So too were the magnificent wool carpets created by Persian, Egyptian, and Turkish weavers.

Music. Muhammad considered the use of musical instruments "the devil's call to damnation." Thus, music was not part of Islamic prayer services. However, it was an important part of ordinary life. The seventh-century singer Tways created the high-pitched nasal style that is characteristic of Arab singing. He also introduced rhythm into Muslim music and was the first to accompany his singing with a musical instrument—the tambourine. In time, musicians used other instruments such as castanets, cymbals, drums, flutes, guitars, and harps.

Arab instruments and rhythm influenced musical styles in Spain. These styles later spread to Latin America and influenced music in North America as well.

SCIENTIFIC ACHIEVEMENTS

Muslims excelled in science. Many inventions and ideas important to later European scientists, doctors, and navigators were developed by Islamic scientists.

As traders, Arabs had always been interested in using the stars to guide them in their travels across the desert. Although the Greeks are credited with the first astrolabe—an instrument through which time is measured and the position of stars computed—the Arabs perfected the astrolabe, which was used by European mariners until the seventeenth century. The Islamic scientist al-Biruni, who lived from 973 to 1048, accurately determined latitude and longitude. He also thought it likely that the earth rotated on an axis.

Muslims also studied geography and mapmaking, or cartography. With knowledge gained from centuries of trade and travel in India, China, Russia, Africa, and Europe, geographers developed a composite map of the earth. This map helped persuade European explorers of the fifteenth and sixteenth centuries that the world was round. During the 1300s, one of the world's greatest travelers, ibn-Batuta, spent 30 years visiting the Middle East, India, China, Southeast Asia, and Africa. Traveling over 75,000 miles (120,000 kilometers), he recorded the geography and culture of all the places he saw.

The scientific spirit extended, too, into the field of history. The Spanish Muslim ibn-Khaldun not only described past events, he also tried to discover laws that might explain why people and nations behaved the way they did. He was the first historian to examine climate, geography, and economics as factors that influence human behavior. Some consider ibn-Khaldun to be the founder of modern sociology.

Islamic scholars were also greatly interested in mathematics, which they adopted from Indian and Greek sources. It was from India that Islamic culture learned about the decimal system and the numerals Europeans were to call "Arabic numerals." This numeration system greatly assisted the spread of commerce. The study of geometry and trigonometry, which came from the Greeks, enabled Muslim scientists to determine such things as the speed of falling objects. Evidence of Islamic contributions to modern science exists in the English language. English contains many scientific and mathematical terms from Arabic including alchemy, algebra, cipher, zenith, and zero.

SECTION REVIEW

1. Name four Islamic practices or beliefs that helped make Islam a major force in spreading and combining different cultures.

2. Why was trade a respected profession among Muslims?

ISLAMIC MEDICINE

While doctors in medieval Europe still drained the blood of their patients to treat illness, Islamic physicians had developed such advanced techniques as performing successful surgery with anesthesia. At first, Muslim doctors borrowed medical knowledge passed on by the ancient Greeks, the Hindus of India, and others. However, through their own careful research and observation, Muslim physicians added greatly to this storehouse of information.

It was the Muslims who first discovered many of the healing drugs and ointments that are taken for granted today. The Muslims also opened the world's first school of pharmacy to train druggists. Likewise, a Muslim could not practice medicine without a diploma from a medical school.

A helpful treatment for the dreaded smallpox and measles was devised in the late ninth century by one of the greatest Muslim doctors, al-Razi, who was known in Europe as Rhazes (RAY-zeez). He studied infectious diseases carefully to find out how they differed from one another and how best to treat each one.

In surgery, Muslims introduced the use of animal gut to stitch incisions and bad wounds. The doctors were particularly good at treating diseases of the eyes, and they could remove cataracts, a clouding of the eye that prevents light from entering.

Many patients from Europe and the Muslim world flocked to Cordova in Muslim Spain, where the surgeons had a reputation for being the best. The most famous surgeon was Abulcasis. He wrote the first illustrated guide to surgery, which doctors used for centuries after.

Fortunately, much of the Muslim work in medicine was preserved in books written by scholarly physicians such as Abulcasis and ibn-Sina, known in Europe as Avicenna (AH-vih-SEHN-uh). Avicenna's gigantic medical book, summing up the accomplishments of Muslim medicine, touches on such diverse topics as the treatment of fevers, the benefits of bathing, the use of cosmetics, and skin care. So valuable was the book that 600 years after Avicenna died, students in European medical schools were still using it as a text.

3. Give three examples that indicate the advanced state of Islamic scholarship and education compared with that of medieval Europe.

4. Give two reasons why architecture became the major Islamic art form.

5. Describe the major achievements of Muslim scientists.

Analysis. Why did Muslim scientists excel mainly in astronomy, navigation, geography, and cartography?

HISTORY IN FOCUS

Before Islam, other cultures and civilizations had risen and fallen in the Middle East and North Africa. Many civilizations, such as those in Persia and Egypt, had achieved greatness but had fallen to foreign invaders. Overall, there had been little contact between distant peoples, and cultures had remained relatively independent from each other. The great achievement of Islam was to bring together many Middle Eastern traditions and diverse peoples to form a lasting civilization.

Islamic civilization endured because of its strong religious focus. Like Christianity, Islam's teachings of monotheism and devotion to the Supreme Being proved to be a force guiding its followers toward achievement and unity. Under Islam's spiritual focus, Muslims became the world's most active merchants, helping to spread ideas, values, and goods throughout the known world. Before the rise of Western civilization, Islam encouraged more cultural diffusion than any other civilization.

Islamic civilization began to decline in the thirteenth century, weakened by invaders from Asia. Yet, far from falling, Islam remained a dominant force in a large part of the world and continues to be a major religious and cultural influence in today's world.

CHAPTER SURVEY

SUMMARY

- Islam grew from its origins on the Arabian Peninsula to become one of the world's great religions and civilizations. Muhammad founded Islam around A.D. 610. By the time of his death in 632, Islam had spread through most of the Arabian Peninsula.

- Muhammad's followers wrote down his teachings in the Koran and continued to extend Islamic rule. Under Omar, from 634 to 644, Islam spread into Palestine, Persia, and Egypt, creating one of the greatest empires in the world.

- After Omar's death, Islam split into rival Sunni and Shiite factions. The Sunnis controlled most of the Islamic world under the Umayyad Dynasty, which continued to expand the empire from its capital at Damascus. Although many non-Arab peoples converted to Islam, the Muslim tolerance of other religions helped to maintain cultural diversity in the empire.

- By 969 the Islamic Empire had split into three dynasties: the Umayyad, the Abbasid, and the Fatimid. Later, invasions by the Seljuk Turks and the Mongols further divided the empire. In the 1200s the Ottomans took control of much of the Islamic world and ruled for many centuries thereafter.

- The spread of Islamic culture was aided by trade, religion, language, and geography. Islamic civilization flourished in Spain, sub-Saharan Africa, and Southeast Asia. Islam also influenced India where, in spite of occasional conflicts, Hindus and Muslims lived together peacefully. Muslims made great contributions in philosophy, literature, art, mathematics, science, and medicine.

VOCABULARY REVIEW

Match each numbered vocabulary term with the lettered word most closely related to it. Then explain how each pair is related.

1. Bedouin
2. mosques
3. jihad

    (a) worship
    (b) struggle
    (c) wanderer

CHAPTER REVIEW

1. (a) List two ways in which the geography of the Arabian Peninsula influenced early Arab culture. (b) How did those same geographic factors affect the development of Islamic civilization?

2. (a) Describe the typical lifestyle of people in pre-Islamic Arabia. (b) How did Islam affect traditional Arab life?

3. (a) How is Muhammad's position in Islam different from the place of Jesus in Christianity? (b) Explain both the cause and significance of the *Hejira*.

4. (a) List five beliefs of the Islamic religion. (b) What does Islam teach about the role of women? (c) How did Islamic teachings affect the growth of the Islamic Empire?

5. (a) What religious disagreements divided Muslims in the seventh century? (b) How was the division between the Umayyad and Abbasid dynasties different from the Abbasid-Fatimid split?

6. (a) Provide three examples of Islamic influence on other cultures and three examples of how other cultures influenced Islamic civilization. (b) Compare the impact of Islam in these areas: Spain, sub-Saharan Africa, Southeast Asia. (c) Describe the impact of the Delhi Sultanate on India.

7. (a) How did Moorish rule in Spain differ from that of the earlier Umayyad Dynasty in Syria? (b) How did Umayyad rule compare to Abbasid rule?

8. (a) Explain how the policy of tolerance influenced Muslim life. (b) Give two examples of Muslim intolerance. (c) How were Muslim and Christian rule in Spain different in dealing with other religions?

9. (a) Describe the relationship between religion and education in Islamic society. (b) Name three ways in which religion influenced Muslim art and scholarship.

10. (a) What contributions did Muslim geographers make that affected later civilizations? (b) How did Muslim interest in science affect their study of history?

THINKING CRITICALLY: ACTIVITIES

1. Draw a detailed timeline showing developments in the Islamic world from 600 to 1566. Include as many dates, periods, and reigns from the chapter as you can, using the timeline at the beginning of the chapter as a starting place. Then do research on a certain time period, place, person, or topic related to Islam, and add at least five dates to your timeline not mentioned in the chapter.

2. Consider this statement by Muhammad: "The ink of the scholar is holier than the blood of the martyr." Write a few paragraphs explaining what he meant.

APPLYING SOCIAL STUDIES SKILLS

Taking notes. Read these notes on the introduction to section 12-4 (page 266). Then answer the questions that follow.

> Before 1400s Is. civ. was the major force in spreading culture, ideas.

Reasons:

  1. link betw. Asia, Europe, Africa

  2. Mus. traded w/ known world.

  3. Is. cultural

language ⟶ ☂ ⟵ religion

Result: Mus. pride in Is. civ. ⟶ feelings of superiority over non-Mus.

1. Explain the following abbreviations:
  (a) Is.   **(d)** w/
  (b) civ.   **(e)** Mus.
  (c) betw.

2. What is the main idea in these notes?

3. How many reasons support this main idea?

4. What were the most important elements of Islam's cultural umbrella?

5. Were feelings of superiority a cause or an effect of Muslims' pride in their civilization?

APPLYING THINKING SKILLS

Classifying. The following items were among the possessions of the Abbasid caliph Harun al-Rashid, who died around A.D. 809. Classify these items to find out more about the life style, role, and status of this caliph. Then answer the questions that follow.

  1,000 Armenian carpets
  1,000 precious Chinese pitchers
  100,000 bows
  150,000 shields
  1,000 candlesticks
  1,500 silk carpets
  5,000 cushions
  10,000 decorated swords
  4,000 small tents
  4,000 embroidered robes
  1,000 jeweled rings
  30,000 saddles
  10,000 helmets
  500 pieces of velvet
  4,000 silk cloaks
  150,000 lances
  500 Tabari carpets
  100,000 ounces of musk
  1,000 cushions with silk brocade
  20,000 breastplates
  4,000 turbans
  5,000 pillows
  1,000 washbasins
  1,000 belts
  4,000 pairs of socks
  50,000 suits of armor

Abridged from *Islam from the Prophet Muhammad to the Capture of Constantinople*, edited and translated by Bernard Lewis (New York: Harper & Row, 1974).

1. Explain what the term *classify* means.

2. What is one procedure that can be used for classifying information?

3. List the categories you used to classify the information about the caliph.

4. What items could be placed in the same category as the 100,000 bows? Why?

5. Explain what the classified items suggest about each of the following aspects of the caliph's life: life style, role, status.

CHAPTER THIRTEEN

FLOWERING OF CHINA AND JAPAN

A.D. 50–1573

Emperor Ming Huang's Flight to Shu. Ink and colors on silk, T'ang Dynasty.

After the collapse of the Han Dynasty in the third century A.D., China endured nearly four centuries of chaos. Yet it reemerged as a powerful, centralized nation. Under three successive dynasties, China was stable and productive. It survived a century of foreign rule and rose again to magnificent heights. In the thousand-year period from the unification of China through the new dynasty that was established after the Mongols were driven out, the Chinese developed many of the customs and traditions that remain today.

The development of Japan during this era was equally dramatic. Although influenced by China, Japan formed its own institutions and created a feudal system resembling that of Europe. The Japanese blended foreign ideas with their own to produce a unique culture.

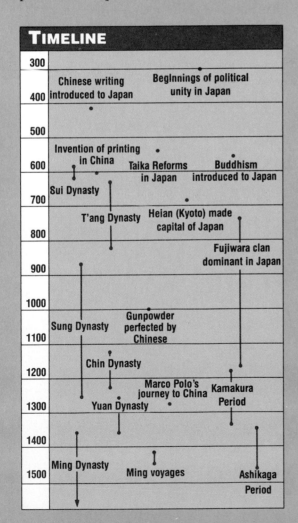

TIMELINE

300		
400	Chinese writing introduced to Japan	Beginnings of political unity in Japan
500		
600	Invention of printing in China	Taika Reforms in Japan — Buddhism introduced to Japan
700	Sui Dynasty	
800	T'ang Dynasty	Heian (Kyoto) made capital of Japan
900		Fujiwara clan dominant in Japan
1000		
1100	Sung Dynasty	Gunpowder perfected by Chinese
1200	Chin Dynasty	
1300	Yuan Dynasty	Marco Polo's journey to China — Kamakura Period
1400		
1500	Ming Dynasty	Ming voyages — Ashikaga Period

13-1
UNIFICATION AND DIVISION IN CHINA

READ TO FIND OUT

—how the Sui reunified China.
—how the T'ang organized a stable government.
—why the T'ang Dynasty fell.
—how the Sung Dynasty expanded the civil service system.
—how China became a divided country.

From A.D. 222 to the 580s, China was splintered into many kingdoms. Then, an official of one of these kingdoms formed an army, seized power, and founded the Sui (SWAY) Dynasty in 589. Only two emperors held power during the 30-year reign of the Sui. However, although their dynasty was short-lived, the Sui reunited China.

THE SUI DYNASTY

To control and defend their territory, the Sui rulers embarked on an ambitious program of public works. They fortified the Great Wall to increase protection from nomadic raiders. To prevent widespread famine, they ordered construction of the largest granaries ever known.

Perhaps the most ambitious project the Sui undertook, however, was the construction of a canal. Because the major rivers of China run from the west to the east, shipping goods between the heavily populated north and the food-producing south was difficult. By connecting a series of older, shorter canals to link the Yangtze River with the Hwang Ho, Sui rulers created the Grand Canal. Now goods could travel from Loyang on the Hwang Ho southeast to Hangchow on the coast.

Sui projects such as the Grand Canal exacted a terrible toll from the Chinese people. Yang Ti, the second Sui emperor, forced more than three million men and women to build the waterway. Children, women, and elders who refused to carry out tasks such as providing food for the workers were executed. The work schedule was so rigorous that thousands of laborers literally dropped dead from exhaustion.

More than one million other people were enrolled in the army as Yang Ti attempted to expand China's borders into Manchuria, Korea, and Tibet. These invasions failed miserably.

To finance both the military campaigns and the public works projects, Yang Ti ordered people to pay ten years' taxes in advance. Angered by the enormous tax burden, the Chinese people rebelled. Local officials and landowners raised their own troops, and for several years civil war raged in China. In 618, Yang Ti was assassinated, and a new dynasty, the T'ang (TAHNG), came to power.

THE T'ANG DYNASTY

In the confusion of the fall of the Sui Dynasty, Li Yuan established the T'ang Dynasty, with capitals at Chang-an and Loyang. The three centuries of T'ang rule—from 618 to 907—

have come to be regarded by many as China's greatest age.

Not only did the T'ang extend their rule over all the lands governed by the Sui, but they expanded China's boundaries as well. Their armies succeeded where the Sui had failed.

Under the rule of Li Yuan's successors, the emperors T'ai Tsung (TĪ ZONG) and Kao Tsung (KOW ZONG), T'ang armies defeated the Turks and took over their lands. The Turks, who wandered throughout the area north and west of China in the 600s, were related to the Huns and other nomadic peoples of Asia.

The T'ang also exerted control on weaker countries outside the borders of their empire, such as Tibet, northern Vietnam, and northern Korea. Additionally, Chinese culture strongly influenced Japan and the kingdoms of Southeast Asia. By the time the Empress Wu Chao (WOO JOW), wife of Kao Tsung, seized power in 690, the Chinese empire extended from Korea in the east to the borders of Persia in the west, where Arab power was expanding.

Painter Han Huang portrayed some of his friends at a scholarly gathering in the eighth century. At the left, two men study a scroll, while at the right another composes a poem.

Ruling the empire. T'ang rulers took steps to strengthen their control of the empire that they had established. T'ai Tsung, the second T'ang emperor, set about to reform land and tax laws. The T'ang restricted the amount of land a noble family could own and took control of the rest. Officials distributed land to peasant families based on the number of family members. The peasants were expected to pay taxes in grain as well as in silk or hemp and also to contribute 20 days of their labor to the government. These measures decreased the power and wealth of the nobles while strengthening the position of the government.

To strengthen the government further, the T'ang organized it into specialized departments, such as military, justice, and public works. Officials from these departments regularly checked on developments in the provinces.

The efficiency of the T'ang government depended on a large body of civil servants. Empress Wu Chao returned to the examination system for hiring public officials that was begun during the Han Dynasty. However, under the Han, examinations had been used only in addition to recommendations from persons of high rank. Now, taking an examination was the only way to obtain a government job, and the practice became firmly established.

The empress encouraged the development of new schools to train students for the civil service. The schools taught Confucian ideas of loyalty, respect, and family duty, as well as literature, mathematics, law, and calligraphy. The schools were not open to all. Merchants and women, for example, could not attend. However, the schools turned out many men with the skills needed to administer the vast Chinese empire. These people formed a new influential class, the scholar gentry.

As a result of the T'ang's firm control of China, trade routes that had fallen into disuse since Han times were reopened. Silk was once again transported along the Silk Road, and the treasures of Arabia, Persia, India, and Southeast Asia poured into China.

Chinese and foreign travelers came and went along these routes. Buddhist pilgrims made their way from China to holy shrines in India, while Christian and Zoroastrian missionaries traveled to China. Because of such travel, knowledge and ideas, along with goods, flowed into and out of China.

The T'ang golden age. The T'ang Dynasty reached its peak of riches and power during the long reign of Empress Wu's grandson, Hsuan Tsung (SHWAHN ZONG). Under his rule from 712 to 756, the government encouraged farming in lands south of the Yangtze River. With an increase in rice production, new wealth came to the empire.

Hsuan Tsung also encouraged technology, as well as calligraphy, astronomy, and music. Like the empress, he founded many schools. Hsuan Tsung's reign was a golden age of learning and the arts. Some of China's greatest artists and poets lived during this time.

FALL OF THE T'ANG

Although the T'ang raised China to new heights, the dynasty's power and influence began to ebb in the mid-700s. In trying to administer such a vast territory, the T'ang government had overextended itself.

In the 750s, Turkish and Arab warriors succeeded in driving the Chinese out of central Asia. Over the next century the Tibetans, Koreans, and the Thai (TĪ) in the south all threatened China's borders. The T'ang Dynasty entered a long period of decline.

Just 10 inches high (250 millimeters), this spirited ceramic figure represents a woman playing polo. Introduced into China from Persia, polo was a popular pastime during the T'ang Dynasty.

The high costs of war and the difficulties of keeping up the complicated records required by the tax system led to changes in the tax laws. However, the revised tax system, along with crop failures, increased the burden on peasant families. Nearly one million peasant families deserted the land.

A series of peasant revolts throughout the 800s further weakened the T'ang. Thus, disabled by military defeats, money problems, and rebellion, in 907 the T'ang Dynasty finally lost the Mandate of Heaven.

THE SUNG DYNASTY

Because warlords divided China when the T'ang Dynasty fell, the era from 907 to 960 is often called the Five Dynasties and the Ten Kingdoms. A hundred years later, one Chinese historian described the period: "Organized bandits numbering into the millions ran over the country, pillaging, burning, killing, and sacking cities."

In 960 one of the warlords, General Chao K'uang-yin (JOW KWAHNG-YIN), estab-

lished the Sung Dynasty. He gathered army chiefs from all over China and persuaded them to renounce their military commands. In exchange, Chao rewarded them with lands and riches. Chao reunited most of China south of the Great Wall.

North of the Great Wall, in Manchuria, a Mongolian tribe known as the Khitans (KEE-TAHNS) ruled their own large empire. The Khitans challenged Sung power. In 1004, the Sung emperor agreed to pay a yearly tribute to the Khitans of 100,000 ounces of silver and 200,000 pieces of silk. This agreement bought a short period of peace.

Prosperity under the Sung. Although the Sung Dynasty never gained great military strength, China prospered under its rule. Rice production increased, cities grew larger, and overseas trade expanded. To add to China's prosperity, the Sung undertook innumerable public works projects. One of their greatest accomplishments was a sea wall, 180 miles (288 kilometers) long. This giant barrier north of Hangchow protected the coast from storms.

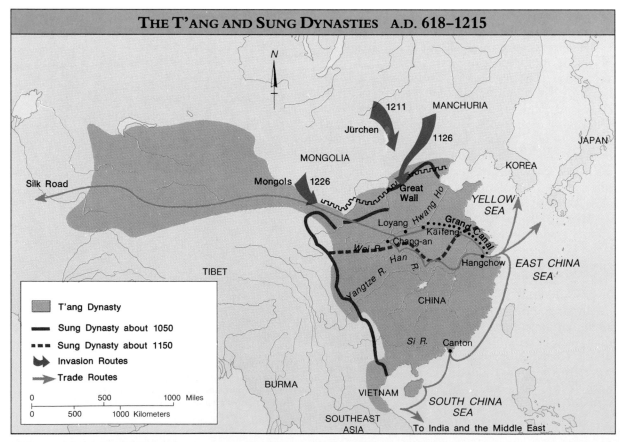

THE T'ANG AND SUNG DYNASTIES A.D. 618–1215

Legend:
- T'ang Dynasty
- Sung Dynasty about 1050
- Sung Dynasty about 1150
- Invasion Routes
- Trade Routes

After 1071, the Sung also made an important change in the civil service system, a change that would last down to the early 1900s. Based on recommendations from a high-ranking government official named Wang An-shih (WAHNG AHN-SHEE), schools now taught practical courses such as law, economics, and military affairs. These schools were public rather than private. Therefore, although most officials still came from the upper class, education for government service became available to a greater number of people than ever before.

Wang An-shih introduced other reforms. For example, the Green Sprouts policy allowed the government to grant loans to poor farmers in the spring that the farmers would repay in the fall after harvest. The government also agreed to purchase surplus goods and crops at a fair price, to be distributed in lean times. In addition, the tax burden was spread more reasonably among different groups.

In the 1100s, a nomadic people called the Jürchen (GER-kin) moved into Manchuria and conquered the Khitans. Pressing on to northern China, the Jürchen attacked Kaifeng, the Sung capital, and captured the emperor. Making Peking their capital, the Jürchen established a competing dynasty, the Chin. The remainder of the Sung court fled to the south, where in 1135 a Sung prince reestablished the dynasty with a capital at Hangchow. Once again, China was divided.

For more than a hundred years the Chin ruled the north and the Sung ruled the south. Then, in the 1200s, the Mongols invaded China and overwhelmed both dynasties. The Mongols went on to establish the largest empire the world has ever known.

SECTION REVIEW

1. What measures did the Sui Dynasty take to reunify China?

2. Explain three means T'ang rulers used to strengthen the central government.

3. What caused the fall of the T'ang Dynasty?

4. What changes did the Sung make in the civil service system?

5. Describe the division of China in the 1100s.

Evaluation. Review the fall of the Sui, T'ang, and Sung dynasties. What problems caused the greatest difficulty for Chinese rulers? Explain.

13–2
A NEW GOLDEN AGE FOR CHINA

READ TO FIND OUT

—how China became a rich agricultural nation.
—why China remained an agricultural nation.
—how the makeup of the aristocracy changed.
—what ideas were blended in Neo-Confucianism.
—what literature and art the T'ang and the Sung produced.
—what Chinese inventions had a worldwide impact.

Chinese civilization underwent great changes under the Sui, T'ang, and Sung dynasties. Agricultural production soared and new industries arose. During this period, from 589 to 1280, the Chinese also created magnificent works of art and literature, and produced some of the most important inventions in the world's history.

THE GROWTH OF AGRICULTURE AND INDUSTRY

During the T'ang and Sung dynasties, China became the most prosperous agricultural empire in the world. The Chinese made great strides in agricultural techniques, developing fertilizers and a variety of rice that enabled farmers to grow two crops a year rather than just one. The Sung also learned how to protect crops from insects.

Other changes occurred. When cotton became a major crop, China's textile industry expanded. Sugar quickly became a large industry when, during the 700s, Chinese travelers returning from India introduced techniques to refine sugar from sugarcane.

Industry and trade also prospered. Gold, silver, copper, and iron were mined on a large scale. Armies of workers extracted thousands of tons of iron ore every year to be made into iron tools and steel weapons. Metalwork, as well as many other objects such as musical instruments

The miniature paintings on Chinese porcelains that were made for export often depicted people at work. This detail from a decorated vase shows women weaving silk in a small workshop.

and pottery, were traded as far away as Japan and Persia.

The textile industry flourished, producing fabrics made of vegetable fibers such as hemp and banana, as well as cotton and silk. Dozens of spinners and weavers worked in every major city.

COMMERCIAL GROWTH

China also underwent a commercial revolution. Selling such goods as bronze, leather, cakes, and tea, marketplaces and shops multiplied. Cities serving as commercial centers developed for the first time. By 1100, China had five such cities with more than a million people each.

With the growth of commerce, the use of money increased rapidly and a shortage of coins developed. As a result, tea merchants issued their own paper money in A.D. 811. The government printed paper money for the first time in 1024.

Limits on commercial growth. Although manufacturing and trade boomed, China remained primarily an agricultural society, for several reasons. First, the Chinese had to concentrate on farming in order to feed the rapidly growing population. Second, the government favored farming over commerce, and official tax policies often interfered with trade.

Finally, Chinese society looked down on merchants as mere "movers of goods," and therefore many traders were foreigners. Often, as soon as Chinese merchants had earned enough money, they abandoned trade in the hope of gaining positions in government or purchasing land to farm. One result was that farming remained more important than trade.

CHANGES IN CHINESE SOCIETY

Despite economic growth, for many people life changed very little. Family life and family relationships remained the foundation of Chinese society. The population continued to be divided primarily into two main classes—the elite and the peasantry—with a small group of servants and slaves forming the lowest class.

However, from the middle of the T'ang Dynasty the makeup of the elite class began to change. As scholarship became more highly valued, members of the educated bureaucracy, the scholar gentry, rose to a higher social rank than the old landowning families. Further, as civil service examinations became more widely applied, this group even came to include some non-Chinese.

Another change in China was the growth of urban life. From T'ang times onward, many people flocked to the cities—merchants, artisans, landowning aristocrats, and peasants seeking a better life.

Colorfully garbed Indian and Persian merchants and fur-capped nomad traders passed each other in the streets. Into the cities from all parts of the empire came acrobats, dancers, and musicians. Restaurants and theaters sprang up. The smells of exotic foods and the strains of music that had originated in Southeast Asian jungles or northern deserts filled the marketplaces.

A third change in Chinese society was a decline in the status of women. This decline may have come about because women had a lesser role to play in city life than in country life.

PHILOSOPHY AND RELIGION

Confucianism, with its emphasis on duty and character, had become China's official philosophy during the Han Dynasty. However, during the early T'ang Dynasty, many people turned to Taoism or Buddhism. Yet, at the same time, they continued to carry out their duties according to Confucianism. The Chinese of early T'ang times also tolerated in their midst other religious groups, including Christians, Jews, Muslims, and Zoroastrians.

Later, however, many Confucian leaders began to see Buddhism as a threat. When a census of Buddhists in A.D. 845 showed "that there were approximately 4,600 temples, 40,000 shrines, and 260,500 monks and nuns" in the empire, a wave of alarm arose. Temples were destroyed, and monks and nuns were placed under government control. Buddhism survived in China but it never regained its former strength.

Although religious groups continued to follow their own separate paths, over time many people blended Taoist and Buddhist ideas with Confucianism. By the Sung Dynasty, this practice brought about a changed form of Confucianism, now referred to as Neo-Confucianism. The prefix *neo* means "new."

The ideas of Neo-Confucianism were written down by the philosopher Chu Hsi (JOO SHEE) in the 1100s. Chu Hsi wrote that through determined effort people could understand the patterns of nature and human life. He stressed the Confucian idea that people are basically good and only need education and a commitment to self-improvement to be worthy. He also emphasized the importance of family life. The philosopher saw the country, led by the emperor, simply as one large family. A good nation meant honorable leaders who would set aside their own private interests. These ideas expressed by Chu Hsi governed Chinese thinking for many centuries.

LITERATURE AND ART

Taoism, Buddhism, and Confucianism were all expressed in literature, art, and music. During the T'ang Dynasty, so much poetry was composed that the period has been called the golden age of Chinese poetry. One book contained nearly 50,000 poems by 2,300 poets.

Two of the greatest poets in Chinese history—Li Po (LEE BO) and Tu Fu (DOO FOO)—lived during the T'ang Dynasty. Li Po, a Taoist, yearned for a peaceful life. He wrote about nature, immortality, and the mysteries of life. Tu Fu wrote about the darker side of life in China. The poet denounced warfare, corrupt officials in government, and the inequalities of Chinese society.

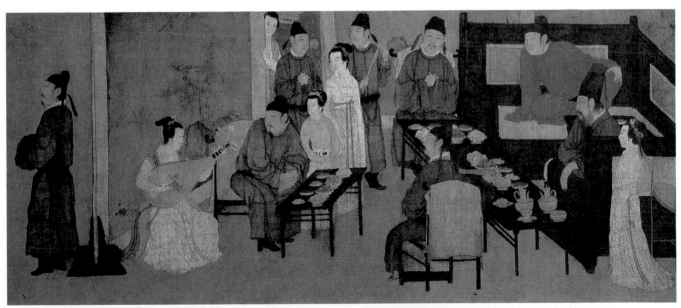

Han Xizai's Night Revelry was actually part of an intelligence report made to a T'ang Emperor. The ruler regarded the activities of Han, in the tall hat, as unworthy of a government official.

Like many of the poets, the artists of the time also portrayed scenes of nature. By the Sung Dynasty landscape painting was looked upon as the greatest of the arts. Artists painted monochromes, consisting of many shades of only one color. This technique tended to emphasize the shapes in nature—craggy, granite mountain peaks and sturdy, tall-standing timbers. Sung artists tried to capture a mood rather than copy a scene exactly.

TECHNOLOGY

The period of the T'ang and Sung could be called the age of inventions. During this period, the Chinese conceived a revolutionary development—the invention of printing.

Printing. Printing began some time in the 600s. Made possible by the earlier Chinese inventions of paper and ink, the first printing technique, blockprinting, used carved wooden blocks. The surface of the block was carved away, leaving raised characters to be inked, then stamped onto paper. The blocks could be used again and again.

Around 1050, a printer named Pi Sheng (BEE SHENG) invented movable type, placing several individual clay characters in a single wooden frame. This technique allowed printers to combine Chinese characters in order to make sentences. The pieces could be changed, rearranged, and used many times. With movable type, as well as wooden blocks, the Chinese printed thousands of books, including histories, encyclopedias, dictionaries, and travel books. Books became available to many, not just to a wealthy few.

Nautical improvements. Another Chinese invention that had far-reaching effects was the magnetic compass, developed sometime during the T'ang Dynasty. At first, the compass was used to help officials judge the most favorable sites for temples and tombs. However, by the early 1100s the compass was used in navigation. It enabled large seagoing vessels to sail out of sight of the shoreline with accuracy and safety.

Also by 1100, the Chinese had developed highly maneuverable sailing ships called *junks*. The largest junks had four decks and could carry a thousand people. Below deck were watertight compartments—not seen in European ships until later—that helped keep the ship afloat.

Another important Chinese innovation was the sternpost rudder, a flat piece of wood attached to the rear of the ship to enable the pilot to steer the ship more accurately. The rudder and the magnetic compass made Sung China a seagoing power and led to the establishment of China's first navy in 1127.

Other technological developments. Another Chinese invention with worldwide impact was gunpowder. Used first by the T'ang for fireworks, the Sung adapted it for hand grenades, missiles, and explosive rockets.

By the time of the T'ang Dynasty, Chinese potters had also developed a new product—porcelain. Made of a fine white clay, smooth porcelain ware was highly prized for its translucence, which means that it allows light to show through. Porcelain soon became one of China's chief exports. Today, fine quality porcelain is called china.

The spread of Chinese technology. Along busy highways and shipping lanes, Chinese ideas spread to the rest of the world. Arab sailors carried knowledge of the magnetic compass to the Mediterranean area. Gradually, inventions such as printing and gunpowder reached India, the Middle East, and Europe, where they were adopted with revolutionary effects.

SECTION REVIEW

1. Describe four improvements in agriculture during the T'ang and Sung dynasties.

2. Give two reasons why agriculture remained more important than trade.

3. How did the aristocracy change?

4. What was Neo-Confucianism? Explain.

5. At what kind of art did Sung painters excel?

6. List three Chinese inventions that eventually had an impact worldwide.

Evaluation. Japanese and Korean visitors to China were often dazzled by its wealth and accomplishments. As a foreign visitor, what would have impressed you the most? Explain.

Data Search. Refer to the appropriate chart on page 831 to compare China's populations during the T'ang Dynasty and in 1988.

13–3
MONGOL INVASION AND MING RESTORATION

READ TO FIND OUT

—how Genghis Khan conquered China.
—how the Mongols ruled China.
—what effect Marco Polo's book had.
—why the Chinese overthrew the Mongols.
—how the Ming Dynasty restored Chinese rule.
—what the effects of the Ming voyages were.

For years, a hardy nomadic people called the Mongols had roamed Mongolia, northwest of China. Each year the Mongols migrated throughout the region in small groups, seeking pasture for their herds of horses and flocks of sheep.

The Mongols were renowned for their riding skill and expert aim. They learned to shoot arrows with deadly accuracy while riding at full speed. Forming one vast army, with men taking the offense while women served as defense, the Mongols were always prepared for battle. As swift as lightning, Mongol riders instilled fear in other peoples for more than a century.

BUILDING THE MONGOL EMPIRE

At a great gathering of Mongol tribes in 1206, many tribal leaders swore allegiance to a nomad chieftain named Temujin (TEM-oo-jin). Thus united, the Mongols granted Temujin the name "Genghis Khan," meaning "Ruler of the Universe." Temujin was one of the fiercest warriors of all time.

About 1209, Genghis Khan and his nomad army galloped out of the north, intent on a course of conquest. By 1258 they had conquered much of Asia and parts of Europe. The fierce Mongol warriors left behind a grisly trail of corpses and smoke from burning cities.

In northern China, the Mongols overpowered the Chin Dynasty in 1234 and swept southward to attack the Sung. For the next 45 years, the Sung withstood Mongol attacks. Finally, in 1279, Sung resistance collapsed. When the Mongols killed the emperor, only a four-year-old descendant remained. A Sung minister grabbed the child emperor, and rather than submit to the Mongols, jumped into the sea and drowned. With their death the Sung Dynasty came to an end.

CHINA UNDER MONGOL RULE

Before Genghis Khan died in 1227, he arranged for all the land that the Mongols conquered to be divided into four parts called *khanates*

This page from a sixteenth-century Persian manuscript told of an ambush of Chinese troops by the forces of Genghis Khan. The warring Mongol forces often ate and slept on horseback.

(KAHN-ayts). The khanates were to be ruled by his sons and their descendants.

A grandson of Genghis Khan, Kublai Khan (KOO-blī KAHN) completed the conquest of China, which became included in the khanate of East Asia. There, in 1271, he established the Yuan (YOO-ahn) Dynasty and became emperor of China.

To strengthen his hold, Kublai Khan appointed only Mongols to chief government posts. Some foreigners were given secondary jobs, while Chinese usually held only the lowest positions.

To restore the country after years of warfare, Kublai Khan began a series of internal improvements. The "Great Khan," as he was called by the Mongols, repaired roads and built a new stone-paved highway 1,100 miles (1,770 kilometers) long between Hangchow and Peking. Eventually, roads linked China, Persia, and Russia.

Merchants, diplomats, and Mongol troops swarmed along the roads. The highway system spurred trade and allowed the Yuan Dynasty to expand the postal system. Kublai Khan also extended the Grand Canal to Peking.

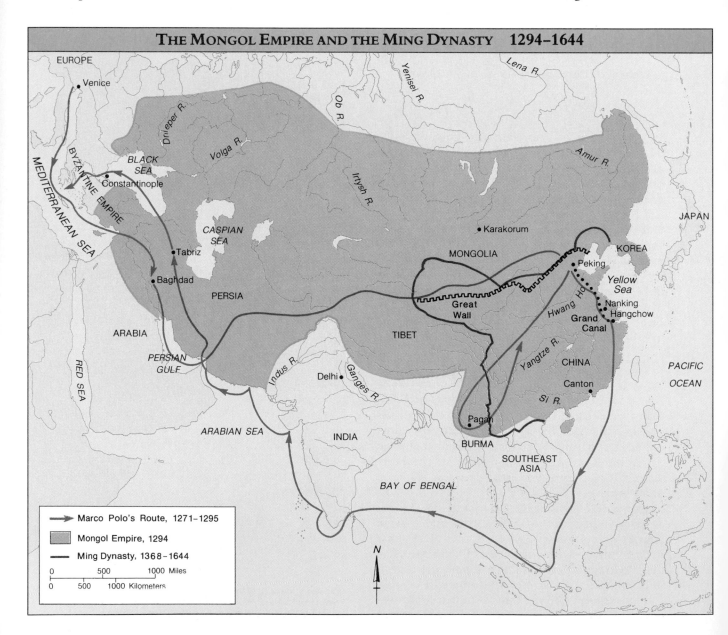

THE MONGOL EMPIRE AND THE MING DYNASTY 1294–1644

Marco Polo's Route, 1271–1295
Mongol Empire, 1294
Ming Dynasty, 1368–1644

The Great Khan ordered the building of hospitals. He also ordered local officials to assist aged scholars, the poor, and the sick.

Kublai Khan and many other Mongols adopted the type of Buddhism that had developed in Tibet as their religion. However, they also accepted Confucian ideas and maintained Confucian schools. They were tolerant of other religions, and Muslims, Christians, Buddhists, Taoists, and Confucians all served the Yuan court.

THE SPREAD OF IDEAS

Under Mongol rule, contact between China and Europe increased. Both King Louis IX of France and the pope in Rome sent ambassadors to China. The Mongols, in return, sent envoys to Europe.

One of the many European travelers to China was a young Italian merchant named Marco Polo. In 1271, with his father and his uncle, he journeyed by ship and then by camel from Venice to China. Polo learned the Mongol language and served for several years under Kublai Khan.

Returning to Europe in 1295, Polo wrote a book about his experiences, called *Description of the World*. The account became the most widely read book in Europe. Among other subjects, Marco Polo wrote about the use of coal for heat, paper money, public carriages, and street drains—all new ideas to Europeans at that time. Because of Polo's book, Europeans became more interested in China and its products.

THE DECLINE OF THE YUAN DYNASTY

The Yuan Dynasty followed a pattern similar to that of Chinese dynasties—a golden age followed by decline. After Kublai Khan's death in 1294, the Yuan began a long decline under a series of weak emperors. Simmering Chinese resentment of the Mongols, whom the Chinese considered to be "barbarian invaders," led to scattered revolts.

Mongol rulers retaliated with oppressive measures. They imposed a strict curfew and forbade Chinese to meet in groups or go hunting. They also forbade the Chinese to keep weapons.

During the 1300s, conditions worsened. In one year, the Yuan emperor confiscated more than 700,000 horses from the Chinese peasants. Taxes multiplied twentyfold, and many peasants were driven from the land.

As problems worsened, Mongol leaders quarreled. Public projects were abandoned. When dikes on the Hwang Ho fell into disrepair, floods engulfed the valleys. Famine spread, and revolts erupted throughout the countryside.

In 1356, a Buddhist monk named Chu Yuan-chang (JOO yoo-AHN-JAHNG) organized a band of peasants and captured Nanking. Twelve years of bitter warfare followed. Chu Yuan-chang finally succeeded in driving the Yuan armies north beyond Peking. In 1368, the Yuan Dynasty collapsed, and Chu Yuan-chang established the Ming Dynasty.

THE MING DYNASTY

Chu Yuan-chang restored the Chinese to power under the Ming Dynasty. As emperor, he took the name T'ai Tsu (TĪ SOO) and set about reorganizing the nation with Nanking as his capital.

The Ming emperor worked to reestablish agriculture. He gave peasants tools, animals, and seeds. Peasants who were willing to farm in lands ruined by warfare were exempted from taxation and government labor for three years. Because of the success of the emperor's program to rebuild China, the population boomed and the economy improved.

In addition to improving the economy, Ming emperors restored the nation's defenses. They strengthened the Great Wall. When pirates began raiding Chinese ships in the Yellow Sea, the Ming repaired and deepened the Grand Canal so that large ships could transport goods safely through the interior of China.

Five years after T'ai Tsu's death in 1398, Yung Lo came to power. A forceful leader, Yung Lo drove back Mongol armies attempting to reconquer China. Perhaps to keep an eye on the nomads to the north, the emperor moved his capital north to Peking. Within Peking, he constructed a private residence, which came to be known as the Forbidden City because this fantastic city within a city was forbidden to all but the emperor's household. The Forbidden City was filled with majestic palaces, marble terraces, magnificent statues, lakes, and gardens.

Rebirth of Chinese culture. Yung Lo sought to free the Chinese people from foreign ways.

DETERMINING THE CREDIBILITY OF A SOURCE

Often it is not possible to check the accuracy of every piece of information or every claim you hear or read. However, you can examine the source of the information or claim to determine whether that source is credible, or believable. A credible source is one that is generally regarded as providing accurate information. For example, a standard dictionary is considered a credible source for the meanings of words, whereas a small child is not. If a source has a general reputation for accuracy, you can feel fairly confident that the specific claims or pieces of information within it are accurate.

EXPLAINING THE SKILL

Whether or not a written source is to be believed depends greatly on who wrote it and how it was written. One way to determine the credibility of any written source is to:

1. *Check the qualifications of its authors.* Do the writers have particular training or expertise that qualifies them to write about the topic? Many sources include brief background information on the authors, which may help you in checking their qualifications.

2. *Check the reputations of the authors.* Do the authors have records of making accurate statements, either oral or written? Is there any reason to suspect that the authors might not be presenting an objective view of the topic?

3. *Check the methods used in preparing the source.* Did the authors cite their sources in footnotes or in a bibliography? Are these sources credible? Did the authors provide evidence to support their claims?

4. *Check to see if this source agrees with other sources known to be credible on the topic.*

As the above steps point out, determining credibility requires going beyond the source itself. However, once you have established that a certain source is credible, you can feel fairly confident in relying on it. You do not have to check the validity of every claim it makes. Remember, though, that no single source is likely to be completely accurate. Authors do make mistakes, which is why you should check several sources when trying to find accurate information on a topic.

APPLYING THE SKILL

Suppose you wanted to know more about the nature of the Ming sea voyages that took place between 1405 and 1433. Determine which of the following sources is likely to be the most credible on this topic.

A. A record of places seen and visited on three Ming voyages between 1413 and 1433, written by the official interpreter to the commander of the Chinese fleet. Immediately upon returning from each voyage, this Chinese interpreter, who was fluent in Arabic, wrote brief notes about the voyage in his diary. Seventeen years after the last voyage, he was asked to write a book on the voyages. Relying on his notes and his memory, he completed the book in 1451, when he was nearly eighty years old.

B. A heavily documented social and economic history of the Ming Dynasty, written by a Jesuit priest trained in Chinese history at Harvard University in Cambridge, Massachusetts. The study was based on more than twenty years of research in China, Japan, Hong Kong, Europe, and America. A Chinese reviewer called it "the most comprehensive study of the Ming Dynasty in Western languages."

C. A record of a Korean official who was cast ashore in China in the late fifteenth century. This official, who was mistaken for a pirate, was abused by the Chinese but was eventually freed and returned to Korea. While in China, the official had heard stories of the Ming voyages. By order of the king of Korea, the official recorded those stories in a diary.

REFLECTING ON THE SKILL

As you were considering the credibility of each source, you should have asked yourself questions such as the following: Did the author have access to detailed, accurate data on which to base the writing? Is it likely that the author might not have been objective in writing about the topic?

Now that you have considered the credibility of the three sources, answer these questions.

1. Which of the three sources is likely to be most credible on the topic of the Ming voyages? **(a)** source A, **(b)** source B, **(c)** source C. Explain your answer.

2. Which of the three sources is likely to be least credible on the topic of the Ming voyages? **(a)** source A, **(b)** source B, **(c)** source C. Explain your answer.

3. Which of the following would be the best source with which to check the accuracy of any of the above sources? **(a)** the official history of each emperor's rule prepared before the emperor's death by the heir to the throne, **(b)** the Ming fleet commander's private diary describing several of his voyages, **(c)** an account by an American historian who specialized in Chinese history. Explain your answer.

4. Of the following characteristics, which one is the best indication of credibility? **(a)** being written by a person who saw the events or conditions being described, **(b)** being written by a famous person, **(c)** being written by a person who has a reputation for being accurate. Explain your answer.

APPLYING THE SKILL

Determine the credibility of the following sources on the Ming voyages.

D. A completely rewritten and greatly shortened version of the official Chinese interpreter's account. The author of this shortened version was a prominent Chinese literary figure who disliked the style of the original account that was published in 1451. This shortened version was published in 1522.

E. An English translation of the Chinese interpreter's account. This translation has an introduction, background notes, and explanations comparing the account with other firsthand accounts of the voyages. The translation was written by a British historian who spent ten years researching Chinese history. The translation was published by Cambridge University Press in 1982.

F. A chronological history of the major events occurring during the reign of each Ming emperor. The history was completed by various anonymous scholars. These scholars worked under the direction of the heir to the Ming throne prior to the death of each emperor. The history was based on reports to the emperors from government ministers, petitions, and other records.

CHECKING YOUR UNDERSTANDING

Answer the following questions:

5. Which of the three sources is likely to be most credible on the topic of the Ming voyages? **(a)** source D, **(b)** source E, **(c)** source F. Explain your answer.

6. Which of the three sources is likely to be least credible on the topic of the Ming voyages? **(a)** source D, **(b)** source E, **(c)** source F. Explain your answer.

7. Which combination of sources would be best to consult if you wanted to prepare an accurate report on the nature of the Ming voyages? **(a)** B, D, F, **(b)** A, C, D, **(c)** A, E, B. Explain your answer.

8. Of the following characteristics, which one is the best indication of credibility? **(a)** being written by a person who is trained or experienced in the subject, **(b)** being written by a person who has written more than one book on the subject, **(c)** being published rather than unpublished. Explain your answer.

REVIEWING THE SKILL

9. Define *credibility*.

10. What can you do to determine the credibility of a written source?

11. Why is it important to determine the credibility of sources?

MING EXPORTS

The Chinese wares most in demand in Africa, the Middle East, and Europe were fine porcelains, cloisonné, and lacquerware. To make cloisonné, skilled artisans patiently applied slender wire designs to metal, then filled the spaces with brilliantly colored enamels. Durable lacquerware was created by painting up to 35 thin coats of varnish on a wooden object.

Man with Crane and Deer, porcelain

Lotus pattern lacquered box

Watering the Tea, detail, porcelain vase

Porcelain water pitcher

Prune blossom vase, cloisonné enamel

His goal was to restore Chinese culture. Looking back to the Neo-Confucianism of Chu Hsi, the emperor made Neo-Confucianism the official religion of the Ming Dynasty.

Yung Lo also gathered 2,000 scholars to compile a vast encyclopedia of Chinese knowledge. Five years in the making, the 11,095 volumes contained such subjects as history, science, art, and geography. Other books written during the Ming Dynasty set forth advances in medicine. One medical text, for example, described the practice of inoculation against smallpox and uses of iodine.

Chinese art and literature flourished again. Poetry continued to be the most admired type of literature among the scholarly class, but popular interest in fiction began to develop.

Ming artists carried on Sung tradition, but the Ming used new techniques and developed even greater skills than the Sung. Ming artists painted moody landscapes, some on long scrolls that made the viewer feel surrounded by the scene. Ming artisans crafted porcelains in pleasing shapes and in rich colors—violet, pale green, blue, and white. Their pottery is still considered among the finest ever made.

MING SEA VOYAGES

One of the greatest accomplishments of the Ming was their sea voyages. In 1405, Yung Lo appointed Cheng Ho (JUNG HŌ) to lead explorations of lands beyond Asia. Cheng Ho assembled a magnificent fleet of 63 vessels and 28,000 sailors. Between 1405 and 1433, he led seven expeditions to places as far away as Indonesia, India, Arabia, and Africa.

Cheng Ho returned after each voyage with tribute from foreign kings and new knowledge of sea routes. His voyages spread word of Chinese power and prestige throughout parts of Southeast Asia, the Middle East, and Africa. The Ming voyages stimulated an interest in trade with China. However, after Yung Lo's death the voyages abruptly stopped.

No one knows exactly why the Ming ships stopped sailing the seas. The voyages may have become too costly. The ruling classes may have feared that merchants would gain too much power. Whatever the reason, new Ming rulers forbade Chinese ships to sail outside of coastal waters. In addition, the government strictly regulated Chinese contacts with foreigners.

Whatever the causes, this change in policy had a profound impact on China. When the Chinese navy withdrew from the open seas, trade in the Pacific and Indian oceans was left to others. Chinese commerce declined.

The shift in Ming policies began a long period of decline in Chinese influence. Yet, China was not completely cut off from the rest of the world, for in the 1500s, European nations began to show an interest in trade with China.

SECTION REVIEW

1. How did Genghis Khan defeat the Chinese?

2. Describe two methods the Mongols used to control their empire.

3. What effect did Marco Polo's book have?

4. What led to the end of the Yuan Dynasty?

5. Explain three steps Ming rulers took to restore Chinese ways.

6. What were three results of the Ming sea voyages?

Synthesis. How might China's history have been altered if the sea voyages had continued?

13-4
THE DEVELOPMENT OF JAPAN

READ TO FIND OUT

—what the terms *animistic*, *samurai*, *shogun*, *bakufu*, and *shogunate* mean.
—what kind of terrain is found in Japan.
—what impact Chinese culture had on Japan.
—how people lived in early Kyoto.
—how feudalism came about.
—how Buddhism influenced Japanese art.

Records of early Japan are few. Chinese records show that the Japanese sent several ambassadors to China between A.D. 57 and 266. Korean records tell of an invasion about 360 led by a Japanese empress.

These contacts with China and with nearby Korea, which had itself been greatly influenced by Chinese culture, changed Japan dramatically. From them, the Japanese learned Chinese ways. The Japanese blended these ways with their own and created a distinct civilization.

JAPAN: THE NATURAL SETTING

Japan is made up of more than 3,000 islands, which form an arc almost 1,400 miles (2,240 kilometers) long. Most people live on four islands: Honshu (HAHN-shoo), Hokkaido (hō-KĪ-dō), Kyushu (kee-OO-shoo), and Shikoku (shih-KŌ-koo). These islands are the tops of volcanic mountains that rise from the ocean floor. The islands are so mountainous that only one-sixth of the land can be farmed.

In the center of Honshu, the largest island, rise Japan's loftiest peaks, the Japanese Alps. Nearby is Fujiyama, or Mount Fuji, the tallest mountain in Japan, rising 12,388 feet (3,776 meters). Other mountain chains make up the rest of the island, along with scattered inland valleys and narrow coastal plains.

Although the mountains of Hokkaido, Kyushu, and Shikoku are lower than those of Honshu, most of these islands are also craggy uplands rimmed by narrow coastal plains. The landscape includes volcanoes and fields of gray volcanic ash and gravel, as well as areas of dense, green forest.

No part of Japan is more than 100 miles (160 kilometers) from the ocean, which provides transportation between the islands. The jagged shoreline offers hundreds of safe harbors.

The climate of Japan varies from north to south. The south experiences hot summers and mild winters. In the north summers are cool, and heavy snows fall in the winter. All of Japan has abundant rainfall, with the heaviest rains falling between June and October. Occasionally, violent tropical storms called typhoons sweep over the islands, bringing gusty winds that can cause great damage.

EARLY JAPANESE SOCIETY

Thousands of years ago, people migrated from the Asian mainland to Japan. Because these people had no written language, early Japanese history remains shrouded in myth. According to legend, the Yamato (yuh-MAH-tō) clan es-

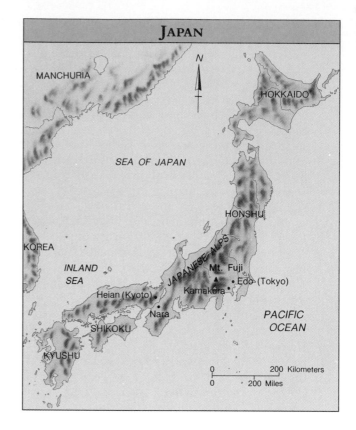

tablished rule in southern Honshu, and the Yamato leader, Jimmu-Tenno—said to be the grandson of Amaterasu (ah-MAH-ter-AH-soo), the sun goddess—became the first emperor.

By the first century A.D., the islands were occupied by warring clans, each headed by a hereditary chieftain. Settling along the coast of Honshu's Inland Sea, the Yamato emerged as the most powerful clan by the 300s. The Yamato chiefs traced their lineage to Jimmu-Tenno and, therefore, to the sun goddess.

During this early period, emperors and empresses became religious figureheads, worshipped as descendants of the sun goddess. The present-day emperor is also considered a member of the Yamato clan. Therefore, Jimmu-Tenno is said to have begun the longest uninterrupted reign in the history of the world.

Shinto religion. The religion that came to be called Shinto, "the way of the gods," also had its beginnings early in Japan's history. Shinto celebrates the mysteries and unseen forces of nature. It is *animistic*, which means it includes a belief that spirits or deities inhabit natural elements, such as sand, rocks, and plants.

PLACE: THE MOUNTAINOUS LANDSCAPE OF JAPAN'S VOLCANIC ISLANDS

Mount Fuji has long been a symbol of Japan. Each year, tens of thousands of Japanese make a trip up Mount Fuji, the tallest of Japan's lofty volcanic peaks. These travelers are following the footsteps of countless pilgrims who, in centuries past, hiked up this mountain which they considered Japan's most sacred place, "the beginning of heaven and earth."

Ancient Japanese also believed other high places to be sacred. Early legends described mountains as the homes of deities and saints. Many religious retreats and shrines were situated in remote high places.

The Japanese still cherish their craggy homeland, made up of a thousand islands formed by the 192 volcanoes that rise steeply from the ocean floor. Japan's physical characteristics—its mountainous landscape, along with its climate, soils, plants, and natural resources—distinguish it from all other places on earth. Japan's distinctive physical characteristics have had a strong effect on human activities—settlement patterns, transportation networks, styles of architecture, economic activities, and political systems, as well as the habits and religious beliefs of its people.

The tradition of going up Mount Fuji and other traditions associated with mountain peaks are examples of how the physical characteristics of a place have affected human activities. Physical characteristics—the towering mountains, the favorable climate, and the plentiful rainfall—have also had an impact on Japan's economic activities—for instance, agriculture.

The shortage of arable land has limited the size of a Japanese farm today to about two and a half acres (one hectare). To compensate for their tiny farms, Japanese farmers practice *intensive agriculture*—a system of farming that increases the quantity of food produced on each acre of land. Because under this system each plant is carefully nurtured, intensive agriculture requires the use of abundant resources such as water, fertilizer, and human labor for each acre of land. These practices are in sharp contrast to the *extensive agriculture* of ranches in Argentina, Australia, and the western United States, where farms are vast but little water and little human labor are used per acre.

Because Japan's mountainous terrain limits the amount of farm land, farmers have concentrated on increasing the quantity of food grown on each farm plot by using the same land to grow more than one crop in a single year. With thoughtful planning, farmers are able to grow two, and sometimes three, crops a year. In the summer, fields are flooded to grow rice. In the winter, the same fields are plowed and planted with grain. All year round, various vegetable crops are grown one after the other.

Under the system of intensive agriculture, no land is wasted. Land between the rows of one crop, between fields, and close to farm buildings is planted with special crops or with fruit trees. Wherever possible, farmers have carved additional fields out of hillsides, creating terraces that rise skyward like giant staircases.

Although only the coastal plains, a few upland basins, and the narrow river valleys of Japan can be farmed, the Japanese have reacted to their rugged land by developing their farms into some of the world's most efficient. Japanese farmers have even managed to produce more per acre of certain crops—rice, for example—than any other farmers in the world have been able to produce.

1. Describe the dominant physical characteristics of Japan.

2. How have these physical characteristics affected farming?

EARLY JAPAN

Shelter: thatched huts (lower class); windowless, wood-framed houses with rooms separated by movable screens (upper class); floors covered with woven-straw mats

Clothing: straw coat and conical hat (lower class); long, loose-fitting cloth or silk kimono (upper class); woven-straw slippers or wooden clogs

Food: rice, fish (tuna, salmon, shellfish), soybean curd, seaweed, tea, variety of fruits—including oranges, pears, pomegranates

Some leisure activities: music (drum, flute, stringed instruments), festivals, poetry contests, soccer

Research Activity: Write a short report on how early Japanese traditions are still evident in modern Japan.

According to Shinto beliefs, divine spirits, called *kami*, are associated with the awesome forces of nature, such as rushing rivers, thundering waterfalls, and ancient gnarled trees. The kami are respected rather than feared.

Shinto shrines still dot the Japanese landscape. Worshippers offer prayers and gifts, such as flowers, to the kami and call upon them to bring good crops, health, and peace.

CHINESE INFLUENCE IN JAPAN

Contact with nearby Korea changed Japan dramatically. Around 405, Chinese writing spread from Korea into Japan. Although Japanese and Chinese were very different languages, the Japanese were able to adapt Chinese symbols and begin keeping written records.

In 552, the emperor of Korea sent an envoy to Japan to ask the Japanese for help in fighting off an enemy. The Korean emperor also sent Buddhist priests and sacred Buddhist texts.

The Japanese became immensely interested in Buddhism. The Soga clan, an influential family in the Yamato court, welcomed this new religion. They saw it as a way to introduce Chinese ideas about strong central government. By organizing a strong government in Japan, the Soga clan could gain greater influence. Therefore, they urged the spread of Chinese ideas.

Prince Shotoku. Shotoku Taishi (shō-TŌ-koo TĪ-SHEE), whose father had been emperor and whose mother was from the Soga clan, ruled Japan from 592 to 621. He became a devout Buddhist. He also admired Confucian ethics and sent students, artists, and monks to the Sui and T'ang courts to bring back knowledge of Chinese philosophy, arts, law, and government. With China as a model, Shotoku strengthened his government, emphasizing the power of the emperor.

After Shotoku's death in 622, a bloody war ensued among rivals for power. The Soga clan lost its position of authority to the Fujiwara (FOO-gee-WAHR-uh) clan, who would play an important role in Japan's government for the next 500 years. Like the Soga, the Fujiwara continued to adopt Chinese ideas.

Government reform. In 645, the Fujiwara leader and the Yamato emperor issued the Taika (TĪ-kah) Reforms, laws intended to model the Japanese government more closely after that in China. This ambitious program declared all land to be the property of the government and provided for a census so that farm land could be assigned to peasants. Taxes would be collected in grain, textiles, and government service. Japanese rulers had only partial success in enforcing these laws, however.

Although it was patterned after the Chinese government, the Japanese government differed in two important ways. First, unlike the Chinese Mandate of Heaven, which passed from one dynasty to the next, the Japanese kept the same line of emperors and empresses as important religious symbols. Second, the Japanese did not develop a civil service system. Officials came from wealthy and important families.

THE HEIAN PERIOD

Before the 700s, Japan had no cities and few towns. The capital was wherever the ruler happened to be. In 710, however, Japan's rulers decided to build Nara, a city modeled after Chang-an, the T'ang capital. Buddhist influence increased rapidly in Nara, and Buddhist temples with tiled roofs soon lined the streets. When the power of the Buddhist monks in Nara grew too great, the emperor demanded that a capital be built away from the Buddhist temples and monasteries.

As a result, the great city of Heian (HAY-ahn), which was later renamed Kyoto (kee-Ō-TŌ), was erected in 794. Kyoto, which had tree-lined avenues, stately wooden houses, and imposing stone walls, would serve as Japan's capital for more than a thousand years.

Heian culture. Residence in Kyoto was reserved exclusively for the aristocracy. While life in the countryside was a constant struggle to survive amid wars over the best farm land, the elegant society of Kyoto followed such pursuits as art and poetry. The men also mastered the fine art of calligraphy.

Men tended to imitate the Chinese arts, which they considered superior, but women created a distinctly Japanese literature. For example, they devised the *tanka*, a five-line poem with a set pattern of syllables on such subjects as love, nature, and pride in their country. The greatest work of the period, however, was *The Tale of Genji*, considered the world's first novel. This long, sensitive tale of a legendary prince was written about 1008 by Lady Murasaki Shikibu (mur-uh-SAH-kee SHEE-kee-boo), a lady-in-waiting to an empress.

The government in Kyoto. Kammu had been a strong ruler. However, after his death in 806, the Fujiwara family became more powerful than before. Over time, many small landowners turned their land over to the Fujiwara in return for protection. This made the Fujiwara one of the leading families in Japan. Meanwhile, women of the Fujiwara family married into the royal family. In this way, the Fujiwara gained great influence over Japanese emperors. While the emperors ruled in name, the real rulers of Japan were the Fujiwara.

Gradually, however, problems arose. The government was never strong enough to collect all the taxes owed. Also, for a number of reasons, a growing number of privileged estate owners were not required to pay taxes. The government's income began to fall.

In addition, peasant farmers began to turn over their small plots of land to the estate owners in return for protection from the tax collec-

Scenes from *The Tale of Genji* decorate a rare handscroll made in the twelfth century. Delicate images provide a brief glimpse of polished manners and gracious living at the Heian court.

tor. As peasants turned to these landowners for leadership and protection, many of the landowners became quite powerful.

Gradually, the Fujiwara lost control of those who lived far from the capital city. Rival clans headed by landowning lords called daimyo (DĪ-myō) raised private armies. Political power gradually shifted from the court in Kyoto to the landowning families in the country. From 1180 to 1185, these clans fought a bitter civil war. After years of fighting, the Minamoto family emerged victorious over the Fujiwara and other rival warrior clans.

JAPAN'S FEUDAL SYSTEM

The society that arose during the 1100s was similar to the feudal society of Europe. Daimyo, warrior lords of the large landowning clans scattered across Japan, made agreements with small landowners, just as lords and their vassals

The saga of the Minamoto clan inspired artists of the Kamakura period. In this detail of the *Tale of the Heiji War Scroll*, nobles charge toward their emperor's palace during a Minamoto attack.

did in Europe. The daimyo protected the small landowner in return for land and loyalty.

A warrior class known as **samurai** (SAM-uh-RĪ) emerged. Samurai means "those who serve," and above all, they were bound to defend their daimyo, as well as the peasants who worked the daimyo's land. Awarded land in return for valiant service, some samurai themselves became wealthy feudal lords.

The samurai valued self-discipline, courage, and honor. Men and women of the samurai class were expected to commit *seppuku* (seh-POO-koo), or ritual suicide, rather than allow any stain on their honor. However, loyalty was considered the highest virtue. Loyalty to a lord and to the lord's clan came before religion or family, no matter what the personal cost. These ideals were embodied in a code called *Bushido* (BOO-shee-DŌ)—"the way of the warrior."

The Kamakura period. After the Minamoto clan defeated their rivals, they established the strongest government Japan had yet known. The emperor gave the head of the clan, Yoritomo, the new military title of **shogun** (SHŌ-gen), meaning "barbarian-subduing general." Not wishing to appear to compete with the em-

peror, Yoritomo set up headquarters at Kamakura (kahm-uh-KOOR-uh), away from the royal capital.

The shogun was not the official government of Japan. The official government consisted of the emperor, the nobles, and the ministers still in Kyoto. The emperor, who was much honored, carried out important ceremonies.

However, Japan was really governed by the **bakufu** (bah-KOO-foo), a group of military leaders headed by the shogun. *Bakufu* means "tent government" or "rule by the military." The bakufu consisted of officials who administered the government and a special bureau to manage samurai affairs. Through the bakufu, the shogun controlled both the government and the military.

After Yoritomo's death in 1199, members of his family struggled for the position of shogun. In 1219, however, the last of the Minamotos was assassinated, and a member of the Hojo clan established a **shogunate**, or government by a shogun. The Hojo shoguns ruled wisely and maintained peace.

In 1274, Mongols landed in Kyushu. Fearing a storm though, they soon turned back. In 1281, a mighty Mongol army landed again, and samurai rushed to meet them. The two enemies battled for nearly 60 days. Finally, a typhoon destroyed the Mongol fleet. Believing that the typhoon was sent by the gods, the Japanese called it *kamikaze* (KAH-mih-KAH-zee), the "divine wind."

The Ashikaga shogunate. The heavy costs of defense contributed to the fall of the Hojo shoguns. Rival clans again maneuvered for power, and full-scale civil war erupted among the feudal lords. In 1335, a new family of rulers, the Ashikaga (ah-shih-KAH-guh), came to power. They would hold the title of shogun for the next two hundred years.

Unlike Yoritomo, the Ashikaga shoguns were never powerful enough to rule the entire country. Consequently, throughout Japan daimyo challenged daimyo, and samurai fought fiercely. The last half of the Ashikaga reign was so torn by conflict that the central government practically collapsed and local daimyo ruled the land.

LIFE IN FEUDAL JAPAN

Despite the constant warfare during the feudal period, the Japanese economy thrived. Merchants and artisans were kept busy supplying the warring armies. Peasants became more prosperous as they began to use new farming techniques. In addition, a trade agreement in 1404 officially opened trade with Ming China. Japanese merchants imported such items as textiles, iron, books, and embroideries. In turn, they exported copper, fans, and the best swords in the world.

Buddhism spread rapidly. Along with the wealthy, farmers and artisans turned to Buddhism. These people frequently blended Shintoism with Buddhism.

Among the Buddhist sects that grew during the feudal period was Zen. Despite the nonviolent beliefs of Buddhism, Zen appealed to the samurai. They found the self-discipline and concentration required for Zen meditation ideal in preparing for battle.

Influenced by Buddhism, Japan experienced a golden age in art and literature. Landscaped gardens, flower arrangements, and miniature *bonsai* (BAHN-sī) trees reflected the Zen emphasis on tranquility. So, too, did the landscape paintings Japanese artists did in the Sung style.

The Japanese had borrowed much from the Chinese. However, by the beginning of the 1500s, the Japanese people had created their own unique culture.

SECTION REVIEW

1. Define *animistic*, *samurai*, *shogun*, *bakufu*, and *shogunate*.

2. What are Japan's main geographic features?

3. What are three practices the Japanese learned from China? What role did Korea play?

4. How did life in early Kyoto differ from life in the countryside?

5. Explain why power shifted from the government in Kyoto to the daimyo. What was the relationship between daimyo and samurai?

6. How was Buddhism expressed in Japanese art?

Analysis. Describe the parallel governments of Japan during the Kamakura period. How was this altered during the Ashikaga period?

HISTORY IN FOCUS

Relatively isolated from the rest of the world by geographic barriers, China developed a great civilization. Over the centuries the Chinese civilization experienced change, such as the rise and fall of dynasties and advancements in agriculture, technology, and the arts. Yet, in China, more than in most countries, lasting political and social traditions promoted continuity. Buddhism, Confucianism, and the development of the civil service system also contributed to the firm foundation that helped China withstand periods of political unrest.

Japan is also relatively isolated by geographic barriers. Nevertheless, Japan was greatly influenced by its contact with China, especially during the T'ang Dynasty. Chinese ideas about government, religion, and art all had an important impact on Japan. The Japanese, however, were able to adapt these borrowed ideas to their own needs, while still maintaining their particular views on such matters as the spirits of nature, the origin of the emperor, and the values of honor and loyalty. Consequently, the Japanese developed their own unique civilization with distinctive forms of government and original great works of art and literature.

SUMMARY

- In 589, the Sui Dynasty united China after nearly four centuries of chaos. Sui rule was harsh, however, and was overthrown in 618 by the T'ang, who began a golden age in China. Prosperity continued under the Sung Dynasty, beginning in 960, though invaders established a second dynasty, the Chin, in northern China.

- During the T'ang and Sung dynasties, Chinese agriculture, industry, trade, and the arts thrived. Cities grew. Neo-Confucianism gained favor over Buddhism.

- By 1279, the Mongols had conquered China, founding the Yuan Dynasty. The Yuan carried out public works and established contacts with Europe. In 1386, the Ming Dynasty took power and revived Chinese government and culture. The Ming sea voyages spread Chinese influence and trade.

- By the first century A.D., Japan was occupied by warring clans. The Yamato clan emerged as the ruling family. Chinese influence grew, bringing Buddhism, strong government, and written language.

- Over the centuries, the Japanese emperor became a figurehead. Rival clans fought for power, and a feudal system developed. Despite frequent warfare, the Japanese economy, the arts, and literature flourished.

VOCABULARY REVIEW

From the list below, select the four words or phrases whose meanings relate to the underlined vocabulary term and explain the relationships.

For example, the meaning of the word *dynasty* is related to the vocabulary term *mandate* because according to Chinese tradition, each *dynasty* received a *mandate*, or command, from heaven to rule.

animistic

(a) kami	**(d)** Shinto
(b) samurai	**(e)** Zen
(c) nature	**(f)** respect

CHAPTER REVIEW

1. (a) Compare public works in China under the Sui, Sung, and Yuan dynasties. **(b)** Why were such projects an important factor in Chinese history?

2. (a) Compare the T'ang and Sung dynasties in the following areas: civil service, land and tax laws, expansion. **(b)** Compare the reasons for taxation in China and Japan. For each country, explain some results of taxation.

3. (a) What contact did China have with other nations under the T'ang Dynasty? Under the Yuan Dynasty? **(b)** How did Chinese policy toward contact with foreign nations change under the Ming Dynasty? **(c)** How did Chinese influence change Japan?

4. (a) What enabled the Chinese economy to thrive during the T'ang and Sung dynasties? **(b)** Why did the Japanese economy thrive during the feudal period?

5. (a) What religions were often blended in China? In Japan? **(b)** Compare the position of Buddhism in the two countries. **(c)** How did religious ideas affect art in both China and Japan? **(d)** Explain the contradiction in the Zen practice of samurai.

6. (a) What subjects concerned Chinese poets? Japanese? **(b)** How did women influence Japanese literature? **(c)** How did Chinese literature change under the Ming?

7. (a) Describe two revolutionary technological developments in China. Then discuss their impact. **(b)** What technology did the Japanese develop that was highly prized?

8. (a) What two important differences distinguished the governments of China and Japan? **(b)** How was the role of the emperor often different in the two countries?

9. (a) Describe the role of the shogun in Japan. **(b)** Explain how the shogun's role changed during Japan's feudal period.

10. (a) Explain why the Mongols were more successful in attacking China than Japan. **(b)** Describe the effect that the Mongol invasions had on Japan. **(c)** How did the Mongols govern China?

THINKING CRITICALLY: ACTIVITIES

1. Make a chart listing the main characteristics and achievements of China and Japan from 57 to 1573. At the top of the chart, write the headings "China" and "Japan." Then, down the lefthand side, list the following categories: Government, Religion, Arts and Literature, Military, Technology. Leave several lines between each category. Using information in the chapter, fill in the chart as completely as possible. Then write a short paragraph that summarizes the characteristics and achievements of each civilization.

2. Assume that you are a thirteenth-century traveler, much like Marco Polo, and that you are visiting either China or Japan. Write a description of your experiences there, including what strikes you as new and unusual. Also include the problems you encounter.

APPLYING SOCIAL STUDIES SKILLS

Reading maps. Look at the map titled "The Mongol Empire and the Ming Dynasty 1294–1644" on page 284 to answer these questions.

1. What is the purpose of this map?

2. Where is north on the map?

3. Which of the following kinds of natural features are shown?

(a) rivers	**(d)** lakes
(b) coastlines	**(e)** oceans
(c) mountains	**(f)** deserts

4. What is the most prominent cultural feature shown on this map?

5. About how long was Marco Polo's journey? (To answer this question, lay a string or thread along the line marking Polo's route. Start at Venice and follow his route east across the Mongol Empire to Peking. From there follow his route southwest to Burma and back. Finally, follow his route home around Southeast Asia, across the Bay of Bengal and Arabian Sea, and back to Venice. When you have finished, measure the amount of string you laid out along the entire route. Using the scale in the legend, convert inches of string into thousands of miles or kilometers.)

APPLYING THINKING SKILLS

Determining the credibility of a source. Here are three sources you could consult about the Mongol rule of China. Determine which one of these sources would be most credible on this topic. Then answer the questions.

A. A record of the travels and experiences in China of an Italian who went there in 1271 and served the khan from 1275 to 1292. In 1298, while imprisoned in Italy, the Italian dictated in French an account of his time in China. The account was later published under the title of *The Book of Marco Polo*.

B. A document written in 1272 by a Chinese scholar employed at the court of Kublai Khan. The document announced a new dynastic name for the Mongol reign and justified Mongol rule by referring to many classical Chinese documents and traditions.

C. A detailed history of China beginning in A.D. 25, written by a number of anonymous Chinese historians appointed by royal edicts to write the history of their times. No one was allowed to look at what was written except the authors. Their collected history was translated into English by an English scholar. This translated version was published in 1897.

1. Define *credibility*.

2. What is one way to determine the credibility of a written source?

3. Why is it often useful to determine the credibility of a source?

4. Explain why each of the following characteristics does not necessarily indicate credibility: **(a)** being written by a person who has written many books on the subject and **(b)** being written by an eyewitness.

5. Which one of the above sources is likely to be most credible on Mongol rule in China? Explain your answer.

6. What might limit the credibility of the other two sources? Explain your answer.

7. What other kinds of sources would be useful in determining as accurately as possible what the Mongol rule in China was like? Explain your answer.

CHAPTER FOURTEEN

LIFE IN AFRICA AND THE AMERICAS

3000 B.C.–A.D. 1600

Mayan dignitaries. Reproduction of ancient mural, Mexico.

Until about 1500, North and South America and most of Africa south of the Sahara Desert had little direct contact with centers of civilization in Europe and Asia. Because they evolved separately, cultures on these three continents developed in unique ways.

Beginning in prehistoric times, groups of people organized in villages and clans created small-scale societies. Many of these cultures developed complex languages and religions, rich artistic traditions, and harmonious social organization. A second kind of society began to emerge about 700 B.C. Kingdoms and states similar to those in Asia and the Middle East established powerful armies, beautiful cities, and strong government. By A.D. 1200, these civilizations had equaled many achievements made elsewhere in the world.

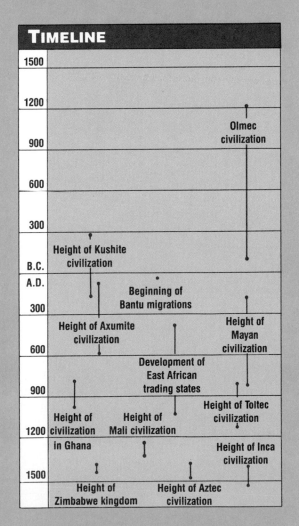

TIMELINE	
1500	
1200	Olmec civilization
900	
600	
300	
B.C.	Height of Kushite civilization
A.D.	
300	Beginning of Bantu migrations
600	Height of Axumite civilization · Height of Mayan civilization
900	Development of East African trading states
1200	Height of civilization in Ghana · Height of Mali civilization · Height of Toltec civilization
1500	Height of Inca civilization
	Height of Zimbabwe kingdom · Height of Aztec civilization

14-1
KINGDOMS OF ANCIENT AFRICA

READ TO FIND OUT

—what the term *savanna* means.
—how climate and geography affected African societies.
—how the empire of Kush developed.
—how the trade of gold and salt was important to the rise of empires in West Africa.
—how ancient Ghana was linked to areas outside sub-Saharan Africa.
—how Islam influenced East Africa.

The largest desert in the world, the Sahara, stretches across the northern end of Africa. An effective natural barrier, it divides the huge continent into two very different regions. North Africa, a strip of land north of the desert bordering the Mediterranean, had always been closely tied to Mediterranean civilizations such as ancient Greece and Rome.

South of the Sahara, however, in what is called sub-Saharan Africa, a variety of climates and vegetation zones gave rise to a rich diversity of cultures unlike any others in the world. By 750 B.C., some sub-Saharan cultures had developed into civilizations, with great cities and strong empires. Some of these African peoples—those living in present-day Sudan, Ethiopia, and Somalia—were already in contact with Egypt. Gradually, the people south of the Sahara also made contact with other civilizations around the Mediterranean and in the Middle East.

AFRICA: THE NATURAL SETTING

Africa is the world's second largest continent. It is three times larger than the United States. Bordered on the west by the Atlantic and on the east by the Indian Ocean, Africa is almost 5,000 miles (8,000 kilometers) wide. From north to south, Africa stretches more than 6,000 miles (9,600 kilometers). The Mediterranean Sea separates the continent from Europe, and the Red Sea separates it from Asia.

Some of the world's longest rivers, such as the Nile, the Congo, the Niger, and the Zambezi, drain this huge continent. Many parts of these rivers are unnavigable because of thick vegetation and long sections of rapids. Huge, spectacular waterfalls near the eastern coast hinder transportation into the interior of the continent. Few parts of the African coast have good natural harbors, a fact that contributed to Africa's isolation from the rest of the world.

Africa is a land of large valleys and basins ringed by mountains. One of the largest valleys is the Great Rift Valley, lying near the eastern coast. It extends more than 4,000 miles (6,400 kilometers) from north to south.

Africa has more desert and arid regions than any other continent. The northern third of Africa is covered by the Sahara Desert, which is bigger than the continental United States. Rain seldom falls in the Sahara, and fierce wind-

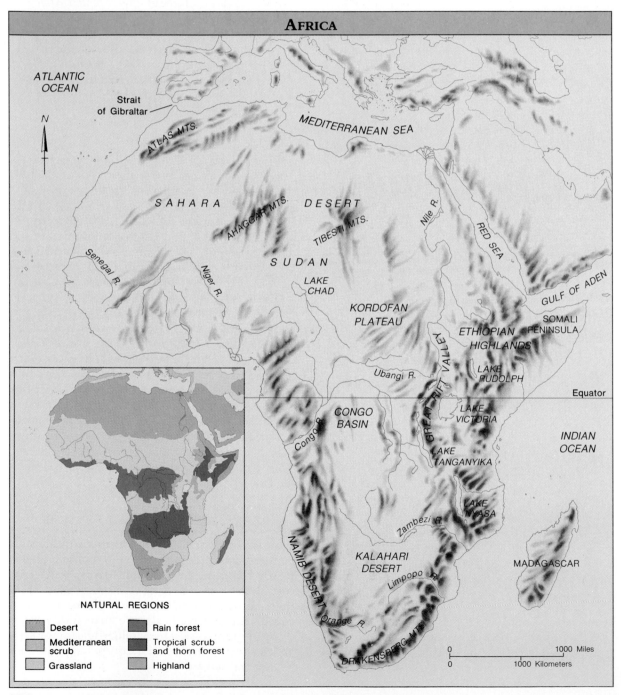

AFRICA

ATLANTIC OCEAN

Strait of Gibraltar

N

ATLAS MTS.

MEDITERRANEAN SEA

SAHARA DESERT

AHAGGAR MTS.

TIBESTI MTS.

Nile R.

RED SEA

Senegal R.

Niger R.

SUDAN

LAKE CHAD

GULF OF ADEN

KORDOFAN PLATEAU

SOMALI PENINSULA

ETHIOPIAN HIGHLANDS

LAKE RUDOLPH

Ubangi R.

Equator

Congo R.

CONGO BASIN

GREAT RIFT VALLEY

LAKE VICTORIA

INDIAN OCEAN

LAKE TANGANYIKA

LAKE NYASA

NAMIB DESERT

Zambezi R.

KALAHARI DESERT

MADAGASCAR

Limpopo R.

Orange R.

DRAKENSBERG MTS.

NATURAL REGIONS

Desert

Mediterranean scrub

Grassland

Rain forest

Tropical scrub and thorn forest

Highland

0   1000 Miles

0   1000 Kilometers

storms frequently whip sand across the barren landscape. Throughout history, the Sahara has been a natural barrier to human movement, much like an ocean.

South of the Sahara is a region of mostly flat grasslands dotted with trees. This type of tropical grassland is called *savanna*. The savanna is roughly similar to the prairies of the western United States. The African savanna supports herds of zebra, antelope, giraffe, and other wild animals.

Savanna extends over much of Africa. The savanna bordering the Sahara is often called the Sudan. Near the desert, the Sudan lacks trees completely. Farther south, trees become much more common. Other areas of savanna are found in regions called East Africa and South Africa. In these regions, savannas lie next to deserts, rain forests, and dry tropical forests called thorn forests.

South of the Sudan, near the equator, lie lush tropical rain forests, which cover about 10 percent of Africa. Huge trees grow densely in the hot, steamy valleys and vines tangle wildly around trees, making travel nearly impossible for humans unfamiliar with the rain forest. In some areas between forest and savanna, African sleeping sickness, carried by the tsetse fly, causes a major problem. Where this fly lives, domesticated animals cannot be kept because they become infected and die. The disease also affects humans.

THE EMPIRE OF THE KUSH

While Egyptian civilization emerged in the lower Nile Valley, another civilization, called Kush, was arising in the upper reaches of the Nile Valley. Kush developed a culture similar to that of ancient Egypt, and the two kingdoms actively traded with one another.

By 1000 B.C., Egyptian power had waned, and around 700 B.C., the Kushites gained control of Upper Egypt. About 70 years later, however, the Kushites were overthrown by invading Assyrians from the east. The Kushites, who used weapons of copper and bronze, could not withstand the superior iron weaponry of the Assyrians.

The Kushites retreated south. Although they had been defeated, they had gained a valuable skill from the Assyrians: the secret of smelting iron. Equipped with the iron hoe and iron

Built in Kush in the first century A.D., the pyramids of Meroë in the Sudan reflect Egyptian influence. The flat tops, however, were a distinctive characteristic of the Kushite style.

spear, the Kushites improved their agriculture, strengthened their army, and developed into a major commercial power. They began to trade not only in Africa but in Arabia, India, and possibly China as well. Among the first iron makers in Africa, the Kushites developed the first civilization in sub-Saharan Africa.

The Kushites built their capital city, Meroë (MER-ō-EE), between the Nile and Atbara rivers. This fertile region was rich with iron deposits and with thick forests that could provide wood to fuel the iron furnaces. As a result, Meroë became a crossroads for trade in northeastern Africa.

Between 250 B.C. and A.D. 200, Kush was the most powerful empire in Africa. Influenced by the Romans, the Kush built reservoirs and water tanks. Brick mansions with courtyards lined the streets, as did massive temples with carved pillars and giant stone rams.

THE EMPIRE OF AXUM

Around A.D. 100, a new empire called Axum arose southeast of Kush, near the Red Sea. Axum soon began to challenge Kush's power. The Axumite people were composed of both Africans and Arabs, many of whom practiced Judaism. The Axum Empire prospered from trade along the Red Sea. They traded such goods as ivory, gold, ebony, perfume, and even ostrich feathers.

In 325, Axum warriors under King Ezana attacked Meroë and destroyed the city, driving

Weights for measuring gold in ancient Ghana often depicted everyday activities. Here, a family pounds the starchy cassava root to make *fu-fu*, a staple in the African diet even today.

the Kushites west. This victory gave Axum control of valuable trade routes along the Nile north to Egypt and the Mediterranean.

King Ezana, who reigned from about 300 to 330, was the most powerful Axum ruler. After conquering Meroë, he took control of parts of Arabia. He then ordered masons to carve towering granite monuments called obelisks to commemorate his victories. Some of these obelisks still stand today.

Influenced by Egyptian missionaries and Byzantine traders, King Ezana converted to Christianity. The religion gradually spread throughout the Axum Empire and existed side by side with other faiths. The Axumites are known for the remarkable churches they carved into mountainsides. People today still use these churches for worship.

Axumite civilization endured for many centuries. In the 600s, however, Muslim Arabs took over the Red Sea trade. The spread of Islam in Arabia, Egypt, and North Africa cut off Axum's connections to the Christian world. The Christianity of Axum survived, however, in the rugged hills of present-day Ethiopia. Because of this isolation, Christianity, as well as Judaism, developed differently in Ethiopia than in other parts of the world.

TRADE IN WEST AFRICA

While Kush and Axum rose and fell in northeastern Africa, powerful empires began to develop in the west. These empires depended on the trade across the Sahara of two valuable commodities: gold and salt.

Vast deposits of gold lay in Wangara, a region of western Africa near the Senegal River. Wangara and other regions of Africa, however, had little salt, a substance vital to human existence. Salt was especially important in tropical zones, where people lost large amounts of the mineral through perspiration. In Wangara, and other places in the ancient world where it was not abundant, salt was considered so valuable that it could be exchanged for its weight in gold. To the north, however, near the city of Taghaza in the Sahara, salt was so common that people built houses of salt bricks mined from the earth.

By Roman times, or about the second century A.D., a trans-Saharan trade flourished in northern and western Africa. This trade increased after the Romans introduced a new beast of burden into Africa—the Arabian camel. Caravans from cities along the Mediterranean, with as many as a thousand camels, trekked across the Sahara, stopped at Taghaza to pick up salt, and passed through the Sudan to trade the salt and other products for the gold produced in Wangara.

Around the fourth century A.D., the people who lived in the part of the Sudan through which these caravans passed began regulating and taxing this trade. As trade increased, the power of these people grew. Their ruler became known as "the Ghana" (GAH-nuh), which means both "warrior king" and "king of the gold." The territory ruled by the Ghana ultimately took his name. By the ninth century, Ghana had become a powerful kingdom and dominated the western Sudan.

GHANA

Ghana's wealth rested on gold. When the king appeared in public or held court, he wore glistening robes made of silk from China, laced with fabulous gold ornaments. His attendants wove gold into the braids of their hair, and warriors guarded him with gold-mounted swords. Ghana's gold spanned continents. During the

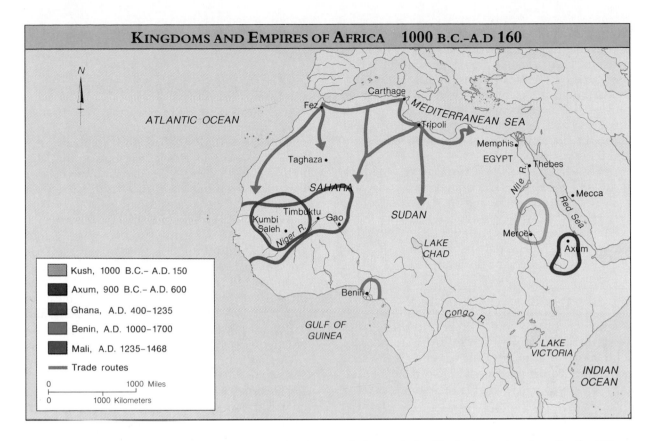

Map labels:

ATLANTIC OCEAN

Fez

Carthage

MEDITERRANEAN SEA

Tripoli

Memphis

EGYPT

Thebes

Mecca

Taghaza

SAHARA

Nile R.

Red Sea

Timbuktu

Kumbi Saleh

Gao

Niger R.

SUDAN

Meroë

Axum

LAKE CHAD

Benin

GULF OF GUINEA

Congo R.

LAKE VICTORIA

INDIAN OCEAN

Legend:

Kush, 1000 B.C.– A.D. 150

Axum, 900 B.C.– A.D. 600

Ghana, A.D. 400–1235

Benin, A.D. 1000–1700

Mali, A.D. 1235–1468

Trade routes

0   1000 Miles

0   1000 Kilometers

European Middle Ages, the kings of England, France, and Spain received most of their gold from Ghana.

The king of Ghana, like that of Kush, was considered to be a god. He delegated authority to many lesser rulers. He also hired educated Muslims as interpreters and advisors. Through trade with Muslim areas, Ghana was influenced by Islam, but the king and most of his subjects did not convert to that religion.

Ghana's power began to ebb in the eleventh century. Internal rivalries led to unrest, and the loyalties of many of the kingdom's diverse peoples began to waver. Muslim invaders from northern Africa attacked the empire several times, and finally captured the capital of Kumbi-Saleh (KOOM-bee-SAH-luh) in 1076. Ghana eventually repelled these invaders, but the kingdom never regained its former glory.

MALI

A new and larger empire founded by a people from a culture called the Mandingo gradually absorbed and replaced Ghana. These people named their empire Mali (MAH-lee) and built

their capital, Timbuktu, in the fertile Niger River valley. By 1240, Mali controlled the gold and salt trade and a larger territory than Ghana ever had.

Whereas Ghana had only been influenced by Islam, the Mandingo rulers fervently embraced Islam and spread the faith to many parts of their empire. Because its rulers were Muslims, Mali became the first Islamic empire south of the Sahara. Many of the common people of Mali, however, retained their original Mandingo beliefs. These traditional religions often included practices and beliefs that were not permitted by Islam.

Although most people in Mali were farmers and hunters, the empire's wealth—like that of Ghana—was based on gold. Mali became known for its efficient government, fair legal system, and law-abiding people. Ibn-Batuta, an Arab traveler who had journeyed to India and China, wrote in the fourteenth century that the people of Mali "have a greater horror of injustice than any other people. There is complete security in their country. Neither traveler nor inhabitant in it has anything to fear from robbers or men of violence."

Mansa Musa. Mali's greatest emperor, Mansa Musa, ruled from about 1312 to 1337. A devout Muslim, he made a stunning pilgrimage across the Sahara to Mecca. Mansa Musa built Timbuktu into a spectacular city renowned for its burnt-brick architecture and many mosques. A university was established, called Sankore, and Timbuktu became a great center of education and scholarship.

After Mansa Musa's death, Mali was led by a series of weak rulers. Foreign invasions and civil war further weakened the empire. During the 1400s, many provinces fought with each other to seize power. The province of Songhai (SAWNG-hī), centered in the city of Gao (GAH-ō), soon became the strongest.

THE BANTU MIGRATIONS

Beginning around 100, before the rise of any West African empires, West African peoples who spoke a language called Bantu (BAN-too) began migrating eastward. Historians believe they originated in a highland region between the Niger and Congo rivers. The Bantu-speakers first moved into central Africa, where many settled down to found new cultures, such as the Kongo. Others continued to move east and south.

The Bantu-speaking peoples were extremely adaptable. Some became herders and hunters, while others settled and became farmers. Having learned the technique of smelting iron, possibly from the Kush, they were able to make iron weapons that they used in conquering much of southern Africa.

Throughout this part of Africa, Bantu-speakers set up a network of kingdoms. The Luba, for example, established a Bantu kingdom in central Africa based on agriculture and copper mining.

The most powerful Bantu kingdom was Zimbabwe, which was established in the eleventh century. Located between the Zambezi and Limpopo rivers in the Great Rift Valley, Zimbabwe exported massive amounts of gold from local gold deposits it controlled. Zimbabwe reached its height during the 1400s, when it developed a healthy trade with Asia and greatly expanded its population.

Zimbabwe is remembered today by an enormous stone ruin called the "Great Zimbabwe." The stonework includes an oval-shaped fort with walls 30 feet (11 meters) high and nearly as thick.

EAST AFRICAN TRADING STATES

Some Bantu-speakers reached the east coast of Africa around 400 and settled in villages. These villages grew into seaports and gradually into large cities, such as Kilwa, Mombasa, and Malindi. By 1000, these cities had become centers of powerful trading states that rivaled the West African kingdoms in wealth.

Arab and Asian sailors traded goods with the Bantu and also settled in these regions. Bantu and Arabic cultures intermixed, some East Africans converted to Islam, and a new language called Swahili (swah-HEE-lee) developed. Swahili was written in Arabic script. The pleasing sounds of spoken Swahili encouraged songs and poetry, and Swahili remains to this day the major language of East Africa.

Trading with Zimbabwe, Arabia, India, and China, these Bantu cities prospered. Kilwa was considered one of the most beautiful cities in the world. Houses were built of stone and coral, and orchards and fruit gardens flourished everywhere. Kilwa had the first known mint, or coin-making operation, in Africa south of the Sahara, a sign of a complex economy. These East African trading states flourished during the fourteenth and fifteenth centuries.

SECTION REVIEW

1. Define *savanna*.

2. Explain how the natural setting of Africa influenced the development of African culture and society.

3. Why was the technique of iron smelting important to the development of Kush?

4. What made salt valuable enough to trade for gold?

5. Why was Ghana important to Europeans?

6. How did Islam influence the East African trading states?

Analysis. Islam existed alongside native religious beliefs more peacefully in Africa than in India. Why might this have been the case?

Data Search. Refer to the appropriate chart on page 831 to identify what percentage of Mali's population at the last census was Islamic.

14-2
DIVERSITY IN AFRICA

READ TO FIND OUT

—what the term *lineage* means.
—why many African cultures did not develop political units larger than links between villages.
—what roles women had in African societies.
—how religion formed a part of the daily lives of most Africans.
—in what ways artistic expression was an important part of African culture.

Ways of life in sub-Saharan Africa were based on traditional patterns that were established long before the rise of the first kingdoms and trading states. The different cultures that developed in Africa were extremely varied. In societies ranging from isolated forest villages to great empires, many diverse religions, languages, and social structures arose to shape daily life. What is known today of African societies and ways of life before the sixteenth century comes mostly from what has been preserved by Africans struggling to save their native cultures from changes brought by Western influence.

VARIED ECONOMIC SYSTEMS OF AFRICA

Before 1500, African people lived off the land in a variety of ways. Some cultures stressed farming, some favored herding, and others relied on hunting and gathering. Economic systems varied according to the land, climate, vegetation and other natural resources.

In the vast lands covered by savanna, people either farmed or herded animals. The farmers cleared the land and grew millet, a kind of grain, and a form of African rice adapted to dry climates. In areas where enough rain fell, farming peoples were able to support large populations. Other savanna dwellers were nomadic herders, who tended herds of sheep, goats, and cattle.

In the dense rain forests of the Congo River Basin, however, farming was difficult because of poor soil and thick vegetation. Herding was impossible because the tsetse fly threatened domesticated animals with disease. Forest people, therefore, learned to grow small plots of moisture-loving crops such as yams and plantains, to hunt the abundant game, and to gather forest roots and fruits.

Desert dwellers developed ingenious ways to survive in the dry, hot lands that covered much of Africa. In the Kalahari Desert of southern Africa, for example, people became expert hunters and gatherers. They provided enough food for their villages by hunting in bands for game and by collecting roots, berries, and desert plants to eat.

THE IMPORTANCE OF THE VILLAGE

Despite the great diversity of African culture, several common elements existed in most societies. The village, for instance, was the basis of political and social organization across much of Africa.

Villages were organized according to kinship ties, or relationships among family members. Authority developed within extended families, which sometimes included several hundred members. Family leaders enforced traditional laws and settled disputes. African families carefully preserved the memory of ancestors, remembering who was related to whom, because kinship ties were vital in establishing one's place in society.

Many village communities also organized themselves by age groupings. People in each age category were assigned special functions. This system helped villages that contained numerous families to work together because, in addition to having family loyalties, people felt bonds with others in their age group.

African community life fostered close relationships between people. Village councils led by chiefs and elders helped solve problems by discussing differences and enforcing local legal systems. Workers organized in cooperative groups and often labored in a festive atmosphere, with music and friendly competition. Cooperative groups also helped families build houses and harvest crops. Most African cultures encouraged their members to take responsibility for the well-being of everyone in the village—including the elderly and others who were unable to provide for themselves.

The tight local organization of African society and the strong loyalties created by village life enabled many Africans to live successfully without forming larger political units or formal states. Numerous African culture groups, some of which numbered up to a million people, lived in stateless societies with only loose bonds connecting villages. These societies often placed greater value on human relationships and personal honor than on developing large cities, armies, or great wealth.

POLITICAL AND SOCIAL LIFE IN THE KINGDOMS

In lands where kings created kingdoms and empires, such as Ghana and Mali, political organization was nearly always shaped by the system of local village governments. Kings ruled by extending kinship loyalties and creating ties with different family leaders.

In most of these kingdoms, whether large or small, most people believed rulers were divine. Kings and queens surrounded themselves with religious rituals and symbols and expected worship from their subjects.

Most African kingdoms, like those in all ancient civilizations, used slaves to perform some labor. Criminals, debtors, and especially prisoners of war were frequently forced into bondage. Slaves were sold in many parts of Africa, but slavery in Africa was seldom based on race. Anyone could be made a slave. Although every African empire used slave labor, the trading of slaves did not become a big business until Europeans became involved with it after 1500.

The flexibility of village life in Africa and its cooperative arrangement gave stability to society, even when kingdoms were in decline. In the communities that made up the kingdoms, village members saw to each other's needs and achieved both security and self-sufficiency.

FAMILY LIFE

Family life and organization in Africa varied according to the needs of the culture. In some societies, social groups were small, and the

AFRICAN STORYTELLING

Each separate African culture had its own traditions. However, one that all Africans shared was the art of storytelling. In addition to entertaining listeners, stories told the people about their history, taught lessons on good behavior, and brought news of happenings in other communities. Stories were passed down orally from generation to generation.

An African storyteller, usually the oldest person in the village, used many sound effects and voice patterns to bring a tale to life. The speaker might squeak like a mouse, imitate a powerful ruler's deep and lordly voice, race with the words to build excitement, or slow them down to create suspense. However, storytelling was not a one-person show—the audience also got involved. In addition to supplying sound effects, such as thunder claps, the listeners added details to the story, acted out parts, and sang accompanying songs.

Some stories were quite long, such as one account of the Earth's creation that took a week to recite. Others, such as some of the folktales, might be told in a few minutes. Folktales about animals or insects were favorites.

In one popular story, a Great Spider selfishly collects all of the world's wisdom, putting it in a gourd that he plans to hide at the top of a tall tree. Tying the gourd around his stomach, he begins climbing, but the gourd gets in his way. His son below teases him by saying, "Someone who is wise would have tied the gourd on his back." Knowing that his son is right, the Great Spider angrily flings the gourd at him. Upon hitting the ground, it breaks and scatters the wisdom everywhere, leaving each person with a small share.

Another popular type of tale was the "story without an ending." It challenged the audience to create a fitting lesson or conclusion.

The lively tradition of African storytelling continues to this day. It is really its own "story without an ending," one that keeps bringing to life the richness of African cultures and history.

BENIN BRONZE

By the 1400s, Benin sculptors were producing bronze statues and plaques for their kings by lost–wax casting. In this complex process, molds were shaped from soft wax, coated with damp clay, and heated. The heat hardened the clay mold and melted out, or "lost," the wax. Molten bronze, poured into the mold, hardened to form the plaques and statues.

Memorial head from ancestral shrine

Muslim emissary to Benin

Messengers from nearby Ife

Brass portrait of Benin queen mother

Warrior plaque for palace pillar

nuclear family—mother, father, and children—was important. In most other societies, the idea of a *lineage* became more important than the nuclear family. A lineage was a line of blood relationship to a particular ancestor, who was a man in some societies, and a woman in others. Villages were organized by lineages and large extended families. All the members of a lineage took care of each other as family members did in other societies.

From Mali, this sculpture shows two musicians playing an instrument similar to a xylophone. Often such sculptures were not purely decorative but were used for religious purposes.

African families stressed the careful nurture of children. Mothers typically carried young children with them as they worked so that the women could tend to the children's needs. Many African women, except in Islamic states, had considerable independence and power. They were active in trade, commerce, and the arts. In many kingdoms, succession to the throne was through the mother's side of the family. When the king died, he was succeeded by the son of his sister. In some African societies, the older women elected a new chief from among the eligible men when the presiding chief died.

RELIGION

Spiritual beliefs were basic to every African society. Although some people converted to Islam, Christianity, or Judaism before 1500, most Africans adhered to ancient beliefs that made no separation between religion and daily life. Many Africans believed in a great spirit who was creator of the world and humankind. Lesser deities, including spirits in nature and the spirits of ancestors, were also important parts of the spiritual world of Africans.

Specific beliefs and ceremonies varied greatly from culture to culture. Most Africans, however, practiced ceremonies to promote fertility and protect against illness. Africans emphasized communal ceremonies to mark the seasons, praise agricultural activities, and celebrate such family events as weddings, namings, and burials. Important religious rituals also surrounded the attainment of adulthood by young men and women. Such ceremonies helped reinforce kinship and community ties.

Africans saw their world and everything in it as one interconnected whole. Family life, village life, work, and nature were never separated. Religious practices and beliefs served mainly to preserve these connections in the world, and help all people feel a part of them. Today, many Africans feel their religious traditions place them in greater harmony with nature than people in Western civilizations.

THE ARTS

African society encouraged artistic expression. Music and dance were basic aspects of life and played a vital role in community festivals and religious practices. In forest societies, for instance, drums were sometimes used to pass information from one village to another, and to call meetings to order.

Traditional African music was based on intricate and complex patterns of rhythm. Probably the most rhythmically complicated music in the world, it has influenced modern forms of western music such as jazz.

Sculpture was the best-developed African visual art. Many African groups made pottery and earthenware, demonstrating the importance of linking art and the creation of useful objects. Some peoples, particularly in West Africa, worked in bronze, ivory, and wood. Bronze heads made in Benin in West Africa beginning in the fifteenth century are among the finest naturalistic figurines ever produced. African artists also made wooden masks that represented beliefs about creation and the rise of society. The artistic heritage of Africa had a profound impact on Europe in the development of the "modern" art movement in the twentieth century.

African religious beliefs were reflected in their art. For instance, the circle symbolized the indivisible wholeness of the world and the shape of time. Africans often emphasized the circle in their designs and in their architecture. Many African houses, often colorfully painted, were circular, unlike the square and angular Western style.

SECTION REVIEW

1. Define *lineage*.

2. Describe how common features of African village life and cultural traditions made larger political units unnecessary.

3. Give three examples of the power women had in some African societies.

4. What was the underlying purpose of most of the ancient African religious ceremonies and spiritual practices?

5. How were African art and music connected to religion?

Analysis. Describe how each of the following characteristics of African society before 1500 might be connected to the lack of a written language: the tradition of storytelling, the political system of local village governments, and the importance of music.

14-3
LAND AND PEOPLES OF THE AMERICAS

READ TO FIND OUT

—how geographic features and climates made North and South America environmentally diverse.

—how the first human beings entered North America.

—how the invention of agriculture changed life for many Native American groups.

Although Africa was relatively isolated, it was also the birthplace of the human species. In contrast, human beings came to North and South America relatively recently—probably between 25,000 and 35,000 years ago. Without contact from other places, people in the Americas developed cultures and languages unlike any in the rest of the world. Before 1500, when Europeans arrived, an amazing diversity of complex societies and civilizations developed in the Americas as its early inhabitants adapted to its richly varied geography and climate.

NORTH AND SOUTH AMERICA: THE NATURAL SETTING

The continents of North and South America stretch nearly 10,000 miles (16,000 kilometers) from north to south. Between them lies a narrow strip of land called Central America, usually considered part of North America. The Americas are bordered by two oceans, the Pacific on the west and the Atlantic on the east.

North and South America are lands of incredible natural diversity. The huge length of the two continents together places their ends close to the frigid poles and their middle near the steamy equator. A nearly unbroken chain of mountains rises in the far north and runs like a backbone down their entire western side. Called the Rocky Mountains in North America and the Andes Mountains in South America, this range affects the climate of much of the two continents.

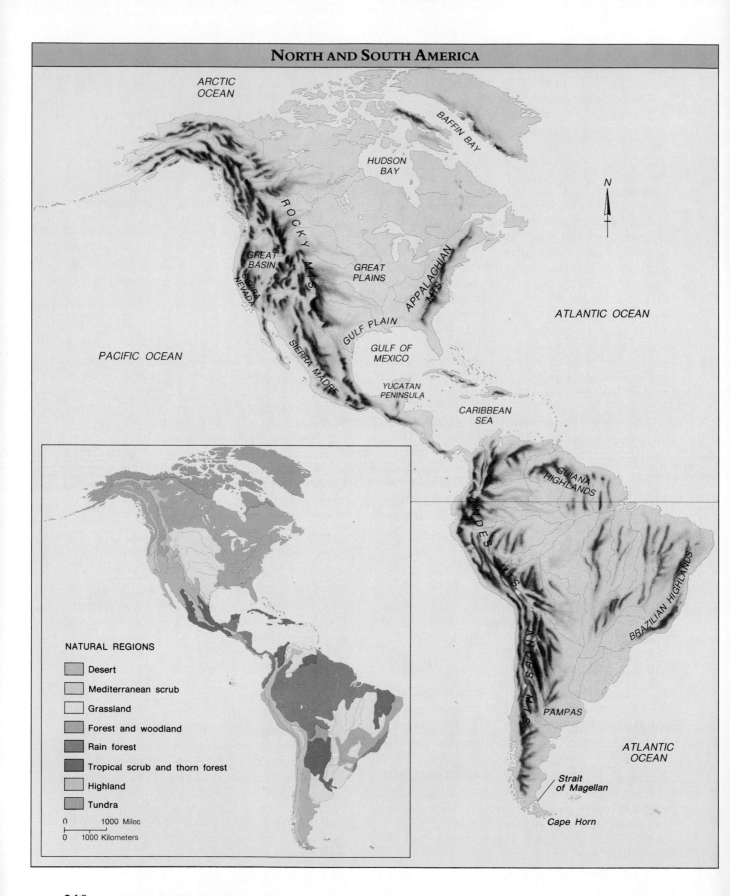

NORTH AND SOUTH AMERICA

ARCTIC OCEAN

BAFFIN BAY

HUDSON BAY

R O C K Y   M T S.

GREAT BASIN

SIERRA NEVADA

GREAT PLAINS

APPALACHIAN MTS.

ATLANTIC OCEAN

N

PACIFIC OCEAN

SIERRA MADRE

GULF PLAIN

GULF OF MEXICO

YUCATAN PENINSULA

CARIBBEAN SEA

GUIANA HIGHLANDS

A N D E S   M T S.

BRAZILIAN HIGHLANDS

PAMPAS

ATLANTIC OCEAN

Strait of Magellan

Cape Horn

NATURAL REGIONS

- Desert
- Mediterranean scrub
- Grassland
- Forest and woodland
- Rain forest
- Tropical scrub and thorn forest
- Highland
- Tundra

0   1000 Miles
0   1000 Kilometers

In the harsh desert environment of the American Southwest, some early Native Americans built dwellings into the sides of steep cliffs. This site is in what is now Canyon de Chelly National Monument, in northwestern Arizona.

In North America, a huge arid land, called the Great Basin, lies between the Rockies and another range to the west, called the Sierra Nevada. In South America, the Andes Mountains trap moisture from the Atlantic Ocean on their eastern side, creating lush tropical forests in the northern half of the continent.

Vast prairies cover much of both North and South America. East of the Rocky Mountains, in the center of North America, lie the Great Plains. This vast expanse of nearly treeless grassland stretches more than 1,000 miles (1,600 kilometers) west to east. Similar plains occur in the southeast corner of South America. These prairies are called the *pampas*. Like the Great Plains of North America, they provide rich soil for farming.

The northern and eastern parts of North America support large forested areas. These forests range from semitropical forests in the southeast to northern forests of evergreen needleleaf trees.

Both continents are carved by great networks of waterways. The Mississippi River, one of the world's longest rivers, unites many rivers draining the interior of North America. In South America, the major rivers of the north flow into the Amazon. Holding more water than any river in the world, the Amazon winds its way for more than 4,000 miles (6,400 kilometers). The Amazon Basin straddles the equator and is covered with thick, tropical rain forests, much like Africa near the equator.

THE FIRST AMERICANS

For millions of years, the Americas lay untouched by human beings. People had long since spread from Africa to Europe and Asia before the first human footprint was left on North or South American soil.

About 25,000 years ago, the glaciers of the Ice Age froze so much of the earth's water that ocean levels dropped as much as 500 feet (160 meters). Because of this drop in ocean level, a land bridge surfaced that connected Siberia, a region in northern Asia, and present-day Alaska. Archaeologists believe that Asiatic hunters migrated across this bridge to North America, perhaps in search of game. Some scientists believe that this migration occurred about 35,000 years ago, and others say that it occurred as far back as 70,000 years ago. However, when the earth warmed and the glaciers melted, the land bridge disappeared and the Americas became isolated.

The wandering hunters from Asia quickly spread south through North and South America and reached the tip of South America by about 10,000 B.C. People settled in practically every region of the two continents.

EARLY NOMADS AND FARMERS

Very little is known about the first people who spread throughout the Americas. Archaeologists believe that like their ancestors they had remained hunters and gatherers for many thousands of years. During this time, like Stone Age peoples in the rest of the world, these early Americans lived a nomadic life. They hunted the mammoth, the great bison, and other animals now extinct. Evidence of this way of life has been found in both Central and North America. Archaeologists have dug up the remains of extinct creatures and have found stone spear tips between their ribs.

About 5000 B.C., many groups of Native Americans began to grow crops. As in other parts of the world, the development of farming around this time—called the Agricultural Revolution—changed many people's way of life. Many groups settled down as farmers and began developing villages, more complex cultures, and new techniques for survival.

Corn became the most important crop in Central and North America. It formed the basis of the settled way of life that by 1200 B.C. had led to the growth of the first civilization in the Americas. In South America, people developed other crops from wild plants. Among the most important was the potato. Potatoes grew well in the Andes, where another civilization would eventually arise.

In other parts of the Americas, such as the Amazon jungles, the icy Arctic, and the southwest coast of North America, people remained hunter-gatherers. These people, however, developed a variety of rich cultures with complex languages, religions, art, and oral literature. By A.D. 1, at least 1,000 distinct languages had developed throughout the Americas. Some historians claim that Native Americans made up the most culturally diverse population on earth.

SECTION REVIEW

1. Describe the major geographic features of North and South America.

2. Where do scientists believe Native Americans originated? How did these people get to the Americas?

3. What plants were domesticated by Native Americans during the Agricultural Revolution?

Application. While excavating a cave in North America, an archaeologist finds fossilized corn cobs. Digging deeper, the archaeologist notices that the corn cobs are shorter the farther down they are. What might this mean?

14-4
CULTURES OF NORTH AMERICA

READ TO FIND OUT

—what the terms *culture areas* and *potlatches* mean.
—what beliefs most North American peoples shared.
—what the important characteristics of North American peoples in each of the nine culture areas were.

North American peoples inhabited a land with bountiful resources. Most groups remained hunter-gatherers or simple farmers. They did not develop the patterns characteristic of civilizations: cities, territorial expansion, social classes, and writing. Instead, the North Americans developed along a different path, evolving cultures that created remarkable harmony among people and between people and nature.

RESPECT FOR NATURE

Native North Americans shared a profound respect and reverence for nature. The oral literature of these peoples celebrated their connection to the natural world, as in this Yokut poem:

My words are tied in one
With the great mountains,
With the great rocks,
With the great trees,
In one with my body
And my heart.
Do you all help me
With supernatural power,
And you, day,
And you, night!
All of you see me
One with this world!

Most Native American cultures considered the land sacred. It was not a commodity that could be bought, sold, or owned. Reflecting these beliefs, many Native American languages

Totem poles are a vivid display of family pride and history among the Indians of the Northwest. Carved mainly of cedar, these markers represent family associations with specific animal spirits.

showed an advanced knowledge of the natural world, with different names for plants that only botanists can tell apart today.

The North Americans treasured valor, self-reliance, and independence. They governed themselves through councils of elders and warriors, not by absolute rulers. Typically, work was equally shared throughout the tribe. Rigid class divisions were rare, and large empires did not arise.

CULTURE AREAS

Hundreds of different Native American groups, with very different cultures, inhabited North America. Despite this cultural diversity, all of the groups living in a particular natural area, such as the Great Plains or the Southwest, showed similarities to each other. Noting these similarities, anthropologists have clustered the North American peoples into nine major groups called *culture areas*. In each culture area, ways of life were influenced in similar ways by the environment of the region.

Arctic and far north. Two similar culture areas developed where snow and ice covered the ground for much of the year in what is now Alaska and Canada. The harshest environment faced the people of the Arctic, who are often called Eskimos, a name that means "meat eaters." Eskimos are also called Inuit, which means simply "people."

Since only a few special plants can grow in the Arctic, Eskimos had to survive mostly as hunters. They depended on caribou, seals, whales, and fish for most of their food. These animals also provided the Eskimos with other products—harpoons, knives, skins for clothing, and blubber, which served as fuel for lamps.

For transportation the Eskimos built two kinds of skin-covered boats, the small *kayak* and the larger *umiak*. Eskimos used snow and ice to build houses called *igloos*. Many Eskimos were nomadic and lived in small, scattered villages in which people shared food and worked together in order to survive hunger and cold.

Northwest coast. On North America's northwestern coast grow lush evergreen forests. People here used timber to build houses and to carve their family emblems, called *totems*, onto giant wooden poles. Some people even used wood to make clothing by weaving tree bark into skirts.

In this plentiful environment near the sea, the people of the Northwest thrived on fishing and hunting. Social classes developed and chieftains became wealthy. Some peoples acquired slaves. One group, the Kwakiutl (KWAH-kee-OO-tuhl), were famous for their great feasts, called *potlatches*. At these gatherings, Kwakiutl hosts gave away food, furs, and jewelry to their guests. Potlatches provided a means of forming alliances and spreading wealth throughout the society.

California. South of the Northwest tribes, in what is today California, lived more than a hundred different groups. Though small in size, the California culture area contained the most diverse assortment of cultural groups. Many of the California groups spoke languages as different from each other as English and Chinese. Most California peoples lived in small groups called tribelets, which consisted of 3 to 30 neighboring villages. In the typical tribelet, people shared work and food equally, and the wisest man became a kind of leader.

Because food was usually plentiful in California's moderate climate, most California groups did no farming. Instead they lived each season where food was most plentiful, gathering nuts and seeds, hunting small game, and fishing. To store and carry food, California peoples made beautiful, strong baskets. Many were woven so well that they were watertight.

Great Basin and plateau. In the dry region between the Pacific Coast culture areas and the Rocky Mountains lived peoples of two similar culture areas who learned to cope with scarce food, little water, and bitterly cold winters. Scattered throughout this large area, they were organized in small bands. These peoples often wandered great distances to find food. They made use of every possible food source, including rabbits, insects, cactuses, seeds, pine nuts, and snakes.

Southwest. In the arid regions south of the Great Basin lived both nomadic groups and settled farmers. The farmers included the Pueblos, who lived in apartmentlike dwellings made of sun-dried brick called *adobe*.

The Pueblos and a similar tribe called the Hopis developed advanced farming methods. Using irrigation, they grew corn, squash, beans, and other crops. Pueblos and Hopis became known for their finely crafted pottery. Together, these groups developed the largest cities and

most complex societies in North America. Living in the same region were nomadic hunting and gathering tribes called the Navajo and the Apache.

The plains. The peoples of the plains were both farmers and hunters. Women, who usually did the farm work, cultivated corn, beans, and squash. These Indians depended greatly on the buffalo, which they followed and hunted across the plains during warm weather. The people of the plains used buffalo meat for food, skins for clothing and blankets, tendons for thread, and bones for tools. They lived in *tepees*, cone-shaped tents of buffalo skins draped over a wood frame. Few other cultures have relied so completely on a single animal.

Eastern woodlands. On the broad coastal plains and river valleys of eastern North America grew vast forests filled with wildlife. Most of the peoples living in this rich area had permanent villages and both hunted and farmed. Although most communities lived independently, five separate Native American groups—the Seneca, Cayuga, Onondaga, Oneida, and Mohawk—joined in the 1500s to form the Iroquois League.

Founded to promote peace, the Iroquois League exercised great power in what is present-day New York and New England. The tribes of the league governed themselves by holding councils in which *sachems*, or chiefs, of the five groups discussed issues and reached decisions. The sachems, all male, were chosen by women. Among the Iroquois League tribes, as among numerous other North American groups, women supervised the farming, controlled the distribution of food, and owned most of the property.

SECTION REVIEW

1. Define *culture areas* and *potlatches*.

2. How did most North American peoples view the land?

3. For each culture area in North America, describe the most common ways that peoples obtained food.

Analysis. Why did some North American groups become farmers while others remained hunters and gatherers?

14-5
CIVILIZATIONS OF CENTRAL AND SOUTH AMERICA

READ TO FIND OUT

—what achievements the Olmecs passed on to later Central American civilizations.
—what the Mayas achieved as a civilization.
—how the Aztecs created a large empire.
—how the Incas held their empire together.

In Central and South America about 2,000 years ago, several Native American groups began growing a surplus of food. Widespread farming enabled them to support growing populations. Soon they began to build cities, where social classes arose and writing, science, and architecture developed. These cultures became the first civilizations in the Americas.

THE OLMECS

About 1200 B.C., a people called the Olmecs built the first planned city in Central America. The Olmecs had developed a thriving civilization by 800 B.C. in the steamy forests and sunny swamplands along the southern coast of the Gulf of Mexico.

The people lived in farming villages surrounding religious centers that were built on hills made of mounded earth. These hills, shaped like the nearby volcanoes, were topped with pyramids that were used as temples. People had time to build these enormous structures because farming took up only about one-third of the year in the fertile Gulf region. However, the Olmecs had no metal tools, draft animals, or the wheel to help them. Instead, from quarries at least 60 miles (96 kilometers) away, they rolled the stone blocks for their pyramids on logs or dragged them through the jungle, and then floated them on rafts along rivers to the construction sites.

The Olmecs invented a hieroglyphic form of writing. They also developed a number system

with a zero. They used these advances to make amazingly accurate calendars.

Sometime around the first century B.C.—after flourishing for more than a thousand years—Olmec civilization vanished. Archaeologists have been unable to explain this disappearance. Many Olmec inventions and traditions, however, were adapted by later Central American cultures.

THE MAYAS

About the time the Romans were conquering territories around the Mediterranean, another civilization influenced by the Olmecs was arising in Central America. The people building this civilization were called the Mayas. They lived east of Olmec territory, on what is now called the Yucatán Peninsula.

The Mayan economy depended on trade and agriculture. Corn was the staple food, but farmers also raised many kinds of fruits and

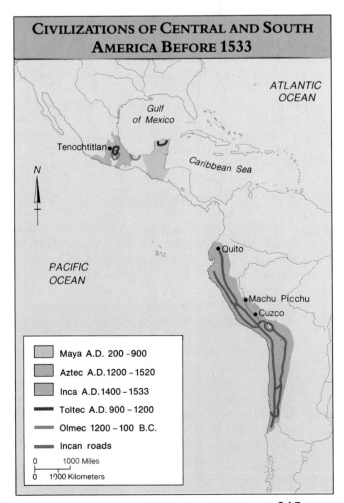

CIVILIZATIONS OF CENTRAL AND SOUTH AMERICA BEFORE 1533

ATLANTIC OCEAN

Gulf of Mexico

Tenochtitlan

Caribbean Sea

N

PACIFIC OCEAN

Quito

Machu Picchu

Cuzco

- Maya A.D. 200–900
- Aztec A.D. 1200–1520
- Inca A.D. 1400–1533
- Toltec A.D. 900–1200
- Olmec 1200–100 B.C.
- Incan roads

0   1000 Miles

0   1000 Kilometers

vegetables. Merchants traded salt, cloth, animal skins, and jewelry with other peoples in Central America.

The Mayas developed a writing system that, like the Olmec system, used pictograms. Later they developed characters called phonograms that represented sounds. Phonograms were inscribed on sheets of paper made from the bark of a tree, and the paper was folded to form pages. These were the first books ever made in the Western Hemisphere.

The Mayas also developed an advanced mathematics system that was based on units of 20 and included a zero. They combined their knowledge of mathematics and astronomy to create one of the world's most accurate calendars. One year consisted of 18 months of 20 days each, plus 5 extra days that were considered unlucky.

Mayan society was built on strict social class lines. Rulers and priests were at the top, followed by artisans, merchants, and peasants. Mayas depended heavily on the labor of slaves, most of whom had been captured in war. Slaves built great pyramids in Mayan cities, some of which stand today.

Mayan society prospered for about six hundred years. Then, around the ninth century A.D., Mayan population dropped sharply. Perhaps slaves revolted, invaders attacked, the soil wore out, or a natural disaster struck—no one knows. Although the Mayas stayed in the area, they abandoned their temples and their civilization declined.

THE TOLTECS

During the 800s, a people called the Toltecs (TAHL-tex) invaded northern Central America from the north. Little is known of their earlier culture, but they soon adopted the customs of the people they conquered. While Mayan civilization declined, the Toltecs became the most powerful society in Central America.

The Toltecs believed in many gods, including the mighty Quetzalcoatl (keht-SAHL-koh-AH-tuhl), who was portrayed in art as a feathered serpent. According to Toltec belief, this powerful god taught ancient peoples how to raise corn, how to govern, and how to write. Toltecs built temple-pyramids similar to those of the Mayas, and introduced sculptures of gold and silver into what is now Mexico.

At its height, Toltec society was supported by advanced farming and extensive trade. Toltec merchants may have traded with peoples in South America. By the 1100s, however, internal conflicts and droughts began to weaken the Toltec Empire. Then, about A.D. 1200, another group from the north, the Aztecs, invaded the empire.

THE AZTECS

Like the Toltecs, the Aztecs were probably nomadic hunters from the north. After a long period of warfare, they settled on an island in Lake Texcoco (tes-KŌ-kō) in the center of what is now Mexico. On this island they built a spectacular city called Tenochtitlán (teh-NOCH-tee-TLAHN). Now, more than six hundred years later, the site of Tenochtitlán is still inhabited: It is called Mexico City.

The building of Tenochtitlán, which was completed by 1325, was a marvel of Aztec technology. Several giant pyramids and dazzling palaces rose at the city's center. Three wide avenues with wooden drawbridges linked the city to the mainland. Two huge, brick aqueducts carried fresh water to the city. Canals served as streets, and large dug-out canoes carried passengers and goods from place to place.

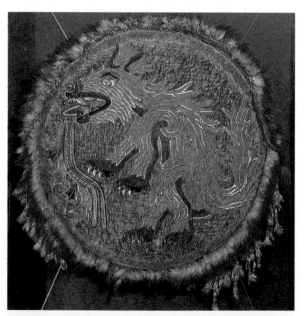

The blue coyote on this ceremonial shield was the emblem of Ahuitzotl, an Aztec king. A jaguar skin provides the undersurface for the elaborate feather work on the shield, which dates to about 1520.

TEST-TAKING TIPS

INTRODUCING THE SKILL

Preparing for a test means reading the assignments, taking good notes, and reviewing the material carefully. However, many well-prepared students still panic on test day because they do not really know how to *take* a test.

The following test-taking tips can help you use your time efficiently and respond effectively to some common types of test questions. If you have prepared well, they can help you improve your performance on test day.

EXPLAINING THE SKILL

The more relaxed you can be when taking a test, the better you will do. These tips can help you get through a test with confidence.

A. *Read through the entire test when you get it.* After reading all the test items, plan your time so that you can finish the test. Allow enough time for the major test items, such as essay questions. Also, make sure that you understand all the directions before beginning. If some directions are not clear, ask for an explanation.

B. *Start with what you know.* If you are unable to quickly answer certain questions, move on and come back to them later. Concentrate on showing what you do know, not on worrying about what you do not know.

C. *Try to complete multiple-choice questions without looking at the answers.* First read the question and then try to think of the answer. Next, read all the answers to find the one closest to your answer. Do not leave a question unanswered. An educated guess is better than no answer at all, unless the test penalizes you for guessing. When in doubt, it is usually best to trust your first impression. Studies have shown that your first answer is likely to be correct.

D. *Read essay questions carefully and then do exactly what is asked.* Different kinds of essay questions ask for different kinds of answers. If a question asks you to *identify* or to *list* examples or events, your answer should be short and to the point. If asked to *describe* or *discuss*, you should write a longer, more detailed answer. When asked to *trace* a development, write down the sequence of events in chronological order.

To *contrast* means to describe differences. To *compare* usually means to point out both similarities and differences. To *relate* means to show how one event or idea had an effect on another. If you are not sure what is being asked for, ask for an explanation.

E. *Organize your answers to essay questions before you write.* Use scratch paper to jot down a brief outline of your important points.

F. *Watch for qualifying words in true/false questions.* Read each statement carefully. Look for qualifying words such as *all, always, never, must, only, no,* or *not,* which suggest there can be no exception to the statement. Such statements are often false. Statements with indefinite terms such as *often, most, many, probably, sometimes, seldom,* or *usually* are more likely to be true.

G. *Reread your answers if you have time.* Eliminate careless errors. Make sure that your teacher can read what you have written.

REVIEWING THE SKILL

1. Identify what you should do first when you get a test.

2. True or false: Usually it is better to concentrate on what you know, not on what you do not know.

3. List five qualifying words that often make a statement false.

4. After reading a multiple-choice question,
   (a) first eliminate the incorrect answers.
   (b) try to answer the question before looking at the answers.
   (c) look for the longest answer because it is most likely the correct answer.
   (d) look for the shortest answer because it is most likely the correct answer.

5. When answering an essay question,
   (a) do exactly what is asked.
   (b) organize your thoughts before writing.
   (c) reread your answer if you have time.
   (d) all of the above.

INCA MESSENGERS

The Inca ruler must be warned of a possible uprising that might threaten the empire. A swift relay runner has memorized this important message and races along a steep, narrow road high in the Andes Mountains. Trained since boyhood as a royal messenger, he is conditioned to run at altitudes as high as 16,000 feet (5,600 meters).

The messenger is called a *chasqui* (CHAHS-kee), which means "to give and take." Typically, four to six messengers are stationed at each of the relay stations, which are spaced a mile apart. The Incas do not have horses, so they rely on the strong legs of their young men. Running at full speed, the chasqui carries a *quipu*. This slender rope has colored strings knotted to it. The strings represent additional information too complicated to memorize. In times of peace, the messenger might carry a basket of fresh fish from the sea for the table of an Inca lord in Cuzco. Now, however, his purpose is not simply to keep fish from spoiling.

He follows a narrow stone path that has been carved out of a cliffside by Inca engineers. Hundreds of feet below him, farmers grow crops on terraces that look like giant steps down the sides of slopes. Soon the path descends to a hanging bridge that crosses a deep mountain gorge cut by a rushing river. Made of braided *cabuya* plant fibers, the rope bridge bounces and sways under the messenger's weight but does not collapse. The local farmers have kept it in good condition.

Now the road climbs toward the next relay station, a small hut located at a high point for good visibility. However, the runner still shouts when approaching to make sure that the next messenger is ready. Quickly the next chasqui falls into step beside him to hear the vital message and receive the quipu. If the message is not accurately passed on, a battle could be lost. If necessary, these chasquis can relay a message 1,250 miles (2,000 kilometers) from Quito to Cuzco in only five days.

The Aztecs invented an ingenious method to increase the amount of land they could use for growing crops. In the lake, they built mounds of reeds and twigs and covered them with fertile mud from the lake bottom. There they sowed the seeds. These artificial islands, called *chinampas*, were extremely productive. The increased food supply boosted Tenochtitlán's population to near 300,000 in the 1400s, making it larger than any European city at the time.

The Aztecs were a fierce, warlike people. Soldiers and warriors ruled the empire and collected tribute from hundreds of surrounding states. The empire was held together through force. The Aztecs also took slaves and made human sacrifices. It has been reported that in one year alone, the Aztecs killed more than 20,000 people as human sacrifices to the gods. By the end of the fifteenth century, however, rebellions had begun to threaten the unity of the Aztec Empire. These rebellions were soon followed by the arrival of the Spaniards.

THE INCAS

While great civilizations emerged in Mexico and Central America, others developed in South America, beginning about A.D. 400. For a thousand years, several civilizations flourished in parts of the Andes Mountains, building large cities and creating beautiful art.

The last great civilization to emerge in South America was the Inca Empire. Between the 1200s and 1400s, the Incas overcame other peoples and created an empire stretching more than 2,000 miles (3,200 kilometers) in the Andes Mountains. It included about 12 million people speaking 20 different languages.

The Incas had originally been herders who raised llamas. Then they turned to farming. The Incas had learned from earlier Andean peoples how to cultivate the potato, which became one of their major crops.

At its height, about 1450, the Inca Empire was the largest unified territory in the Americas. A strong warrior class supported the Supreme Inca, who ruled with complete authority over his subjects. Like the Aztecs and many African peoples, the Incas considered their ruler divine. Unlike the Aztecs who used force to rule their empire, the Incas relied on absorbing other peoples into their culture. This method ensured the loyalty of their subjects because they came to share the same beliefs.

The Incas were master builders. They built stone-paved roads and rope bridges throughout their mountainous empire. The Inca roads enabled a team of runners to relay messages from one end of the continent to the other. Although the Incas never developed writing, they invented an ingenious device called the *quipu* (KEE-poo) to keep records. Quipus were knotted ropes of different lengths with which the Incas could make calculations. They used quipus to record tax payments, census figures, and crop yields.

The Incas made other notable achievements as well. They built great forts and monuments of stone without using mortar or cement. They fit the stones together so securely that many of the structures withstood centuries of earthquakes and some still stand today. The Incas studied medicine and learned to treat malaria victims with quinine, a substance made from bark. They even performed brain surgery and bone operations. The Incas were superb artisans, and their gold statues and ornaments are among the finest ever produced.

Machu Picchu in Peru was a walled city built by the Incas before 1500. Ruins of this remote fortress sanctuary high in the Andes were found by an American archaeologist in 1911.

SECTION REVIEW

1. Name three achievements of the Olmecs.

2. How did the Mayans improve on the Olmec system of writing?

3. How did the Aztecs support a large population in Tenochtitlán?

4. How were the Incas able to govern their large territory?

Analysis. Give three facts to support the claim that the Incas were skilled empire builders.

HISTORY IN FOCUS

The cultures and civilizations that developed on the relatively isolated continents of Africa and North and South America before 1500 represent some of the greatest of human achievements. Often these achievements of Africans and Native Americans are ignored or go unappreciated because they differ from those of Western civilization. Yet inventions, arts, ways of life, and ideas from Africa and the Americas continue to thrive and to influence human societies all over the world.

Among the most important contributions of Native American and African peoples were ideas and ways of life that enabled people to live peacefully among themselves and with nature. While Europeans developed instruments of war and commerce such as guns and ships, many Africans and Native Americans learned to avoid conflict and to work cooperatively.

Other cultures in Africa and the Americas did practice warfare, yet built empires that rank with the world's great civilizations. The huge empire of the Incas, for instance, was one of the world's greatest political accomplishments, and the Mayan calendar is far more accurate than that of any other civilization.

Many African and Native American innovations survive in today's world. For example, while Europeans were developing complex harmonies in their music, Africans had already developed the most rhythmically complex music in the world—music that has influenced jazz and other styles. Foods from the Americas—corn and the potato—now account for a large part of the world's food supply. Traditional art from Africa and the Americas is recognized as some of the world's finest.

SUMMARY

- Africa's varied geography gave rise to diverse cultures and peoples. The empire of Kush was followed by Axum, both in the northeast. Later, in the west, gold and trade with their Islamic neighbors brought prosperity to the kingdoms of Ghana and Mali. Bantu-speaking people migrated east, eventually forming the kingdom of Zimbabwe and the trading states of the east coast.

- Most Africans lived by farming, herding, or hunting. Village and kinship were the basis of political and social life. Religious beliefs emphasized community and nature, and inspired art. Sculpture, music, and dance were highly developed.

- The first Americans probably migrated from Asia to North America 25,000 years ago or more. Over time they developed agriculture and complex societies, with great regional differences.

- Most North American peoples did not develop large-scale societies with cities. Their societies were simpler, reflecting a respect for nature and a strong cooperative spirit. Culture areas arose based on geographic factors, with important regional variations.

- In Central and South America great civilizations arose with cities, social classes, and science. The Olmecs came first, around 1200 B.C., followed by the Mayas and Toltecs. The Aztecs then built a large empire in Mexico. All these groups developed mathematics, writing systems, and calendars. In South America the Incas controlled most of the Andes and were master builders, artisans, and artists.

VOCABULARY REVIEW

Match each numbered vocabulary term with the lettered word most closely related to it. Then explain how each pair is related.

1. savanna   **(a)** kinship
2. lineage   **(b)** wealth
3. culture area   **(c)** tropical
4. potlatch   **(d)** environment

CHAPTER REVIEW

1. (a) Compare the geographic factors that helped isolate Africa with those that isolated the Americas. **(b)** How did geography promote cultural diversity in the two regions? **(c)** Give five examples that show the influence of geography on the economies of the two regions.

2. (a) Describe the main features of the Kushite civilization. **(b)** Name one similarity and one difference between the civilizations of Kush and Axum.

3. (a) What were five characteristics of Mali? **(b)** How did the rulers of Mali differ from those of Ghana? **(c)** What was the economic foundation of both kingdoms?

4. (a) What were some basic similarities among most African kingdoms? **(b)** Explain why many African peoples did not form large political units. **(c)** Do those same reasons apply to North America?

5. (a) Name four elements common to most African religions. **(b)** What did the native religions of Africa and North America have in common? **(c)** How were religion and government intertwined in both Africa and Central and South America?

6. (a) How were African and North American societies similar? **(b)** What similar roles did women play in the two areas?

7. (a) How was the Iroquois League different from most other native North American groups? **(b)** How was the way of life in the Great Basin culture area like that of Africa's Kalahari Desert?

8. (a) List five differences between most North American cultures and those of Central and South America. **(b)** Explain the basic reason for those differences.

9. (a) What African technology did Central American cultures not have? **(b)** Name at least three technological achievements of Central and South American cultures.

10. (a) Compare the main features of the Aztec and Inca civilizations. **(b)** What did Mayan culture inherit from the Olmecs? **(c)** How did the Mayan calendar relate to mathematics?

THINKING CRITICALLY: ACTIVITIES

1. Write an argument for or against the following statement: The potlatch represented values and traditions common to most native North Americans. Support your argument with evidence from the chapter.

2. Decide in which kind of society you would rather have lived—a large-scale civilization like that of an Islamic empire or a small-scale society like those in North America and parts of Africa. Then discuss your decision and explain how your own values may affect the way you feel about this choice.

3. Divide into groups of four or five to discuss the following question: Did isolation from the rest of the world help or hinder the development of civilization in Africa and the Americas?

APPLYING SOCIAL STUDIES SKILLS

Test-taking tips. Read these essay questions carefully. Choose the answer that best describes what you should do to answer that question.

1. Discuss Mansa Musa's accomplishments.
(a) List a few examples of what he did.
(b) Write one page telling who he was and why he was important.

2. Compare the African savanna with the Great Plains.
(a) Tell how the savanna and plains are similar.
(b) Describe differences between the savanna and plains.
(c) Both of the above.

3. Describe African village life.
(a) Write several paragraphs on village government and the daily activities of villagers.
(b) Show how villages are different from the larger West African kingdoms.

4. Trace the development of early Americans from nomadic hunters to empire builders.
(a) Describe nomadic hunters and American civilizations in detail.
(b) Describe the sequence of changes that led from hunting to gathering, to farming, to villages, to cities, and to civilizations.

APPLYING THINKING SKILLS

Distinguishing facts from value judgments. This excerpt is from an eyewitness account of Mexico City around 1519. Study this account to distinguish statements of fact from value judgments. Then answer the questions below.

When we saw all those cities and villages built in the water, and other great towns on dry land, we were astounded. These great towns and buildings rising from the water, all made of stone, seemed like an enchanted vision.

So we stood there looking because that huge, accursed temple stood so high that it dominated everything. We saw the three causeways that led into Mexico [City]. We saw the bridges that were constructed at intervals on the causeways so that the water could flow in and out from one part of the lake to another.

We saw a great number of canoes, some coming with provisions and others returning with cargo and merchandise. We saw too that one could not pass from one house to another of that great city and the other cities that were built on the water except over wooden drawbridges or by canoe. We saw temples and shrines in these cities that looked like gleaming white towers and castles: a marvelous sight.

We turned back to the market and the swarm of people buying and selling. The mere murmur of their voices was loud enough to be heard more than three miles away. Some of us had never seen a market so well laid out, so large, so orderly, and so full of people.

Abridged from *The Conquest of New Spain*, by Bernal Díaz del Castillo (Aylesbury: Penguin, 1963).

1. What is the difference between a value judgment and a statement of fact?

2. Why is it important to distinguish between value judgments and statements of fact?

3. What are three value judgments contained in this excerpt? Explain.

4. What are three facts contained in this excerpt? Explain.

5. Suppose you had to explain to a person two or three years younger than you how to distinguish facts from value judgments. What procedure would you tell this person to follow?

UNIT REVIEW

1. List four factors that contributed to the decline of civilizations, dynasties, or empires in Africa, Asia, the Middle East, and the Americas.

2. (a) Name three general types of government that existed outside Europe between 57 and 1500. **(b)** What kinds of rule characterized the Incas, Ashikaga Japan, and the Iroquois League? **(c)** Compare government in China and the Islamic Empire.

3. (a) Which civilization showed the greatest ethnic and cultural diversity? **(b)** What factors explain that diversity? **(c)** How did diversity affect that civilization's development?

4. (a) Compare the impact of China and the Islamic Empire on cultural diffusion in the following areas: religion, government, science, and technology. **(b)** Name two ways in which Africa influenced Western art forms.

5. (a) How was Islam different from other religions in Asia, Africa, and the Americas? **(b)** What did Shinto have in common with African and North American religions? **(c)** Compare the role of religion in government in the Islamic Empire, China, Africa, and the Aztec Empire.

6. (a) Compare the status of women in Asia, the Islamic Empire, Africa, and North America. **(b)** What common factors characterized the societies in which women had higher status?

7. (a) What was the main difference between the economies of Arabia and T'ang China? **(b)** What accounts for that difference? **(c)** How did attitudes toward trade differ in the two areas?

8. (a) Was agriculture more developed in North America or in Central and South America? How do you know? **(b)** Name three agricultural innovations in China. **(c)** Which region had the most developed agricultural policy? What does this indicate about government and agriculture in this region?

9. (a) Compare the visual arts of Africa and the Islamic world. **(b)** In what way were African and Chinese art similar?

10. Compare the achievements of the Chinese, Muslims, Mayas, and Incas in mathematics, astronomy, engineering, and medicine.

RELATING PAST TO PRESENT

1. Ever since Muhammad led his followers in the first Islamic jihads, or "holy wars," Muslims have been inspired to political and military action by their religious beliefs. Militant Islam has been quite evident in the twentieth century. Investigate how Islamic beliefs have affected one of the following political or military developments in the 1970s and the 1980s. In your report, trace the origins of these developments back to issues that arose during the first century of Islam's existence.

   (a) Iran's "Islamic Revolution" under the Ayatollah Khomeini
   (b) Muammar Qadhafi's efforts to unite the Islamic world
   (c) the mujahidin's war against Soviet forces in Afghanistan

2. Do research on a city important in the history of the Middle East, Africa, Asia, or the Americas. Write a short report comparing past and present characteristics of the city.

PROJECTS AND ACTIVITIES

1. Create a timeline showing important human achievements throughout the world between 500 and 1500. Using information from the timelines of Units Three and Four, draw the timeline so that Europe and areas outside Europe can be easily compared. What do you learn when achievements of Europeans are compared with those of other peoples during this time period? Discuss your conclusions in class.

2. Form groups to prepare visual presentations on the art, architecture, and artisanry of Africa and the Americas. Each group should focus on one culture—the Mayas, Pueblos, Kushites, and so on. Each group member should be assigned a separate topic within that culture.

3. Pretend that you are either Cheng Ho or ibn-Batuta. Depending on your choice, imagine that you have traveled to either Arabia or to China. Write a letter home in which you compare the culture of the land you are visiting with that of your own land. Then discuss your letter with the class.

ANALYZING PRIMARY SOURCES

Refer to the excerpts from the Koran on page 256 to answer the following questions.

1. How does the first excerpt indicate human dependence on God?

2. According to the Koran, how do people learn about God? Give evidence to support your answer.

3. The first two excerpts both describe God. How are the two descriptions similar? How do they differ?

4. The Koran states that "it is not piety, that you turn your faces to the East and to the West." This statement refers to one of the Five Pillars, which are discussed on page 255. Identify the Pillar and explain the meaning of the statement.

5. Compare the ideas presented in these excerpts with those presented in the Ten Commandments on page 40.

GEOGRAPHY REVIEW

Place. The dominant physical characteristics of a place have an effect on the human activities that take place there. Describe the relationship between the physical characteristics of the county or parish in which you live and the activities of the people who live there. Answering the following questions will help you complete your description.

1. What are the dominant physical characteristics of the area? What are two or three physical characteristics that distinguish your county or parish from other places?

Consider such physical characteristics as landforms, waterways, year-round climate, types of soils, native plants and animals, and natural resources. Also consider such natural hazards as earthquakes, floods, tornadoes, or hurricanes.

2. What are two or three important human activities that are strongly affected by the distinctive physical characteristics of your county or parish?

Consider such human activities as settlement patterns (isolated farms, small towns, large cities, and so on), economic activities, transportation networks, styles of architecture, and recreation. Although you could probably name several activities, concentrate on only one or two. Try to include details about how the physical features of the place have affected the ways that people live and work.

3. In relation to the human activities you have described, what special efforts have people made to overcome the disadvantages of the place's particular physical characteristics? How have people taken advantage of the place's best physical characteristics?

Following is an example of notes a student might make in beginning a description of the relationship between physical and human characteristics in the place where he or she lives. Such notes would be expanded with details and explanations.

1. Physical characteristics: a navigable river; a sheltered bay on the coast

2. Related human activities: a large population center; a trading port

3. Response to advantages and disadvantages: dredging the harbor because of the silt; building modern port facilities to take advantage of the river and harbor

SUGGESTED READINGS

Bierhorst, John (ed.). *The Red Swan: Myths and Tales of the American Indians.* New York: Farrar, 1985. The folktales of native North Americans.

Cohen, Joan and Jerome. *China Today: And Her Ancient Treasures.* New York: Abrams, 1985. Chinese art and architecture.

Davidson, Basil. *The Lost Cities of Africa.* Boston: Little, 1970. Ancient African civilizations south of the Sahara.

Papadopoulo, Alexandre (trans. Robert Wolf). *Islam and Muslim Art.* New York: Abrams, 1979. The artistic life of Islam.

Piggott, Juliet. *Japanese Mythology.* Scranton, Pa.: P. Bedrick, 1983. The world of Japanese myths; photos of sacred places and artifacts.

CENTURIES OF TRANSITION

1300–1800

I gave the keys of those mighty barriers of ocean which were closed with such mighty chains.

—*Christopher Columbus*

Detail of *The Arrival of Silvius Aeneas Piccolomini* at the Harbor of Talamone, Italy. Fresco by Pinturicchio, 1502.

GLOBAL TIMELINE

Legend:
- EUROPE
- EUROPEAN EMPIRES
- RUSSIA
- CHINA AND JAPAN
- INDIA
- SUB-SAHARAN AFRICA

	POLITICAL	TECHNOLOGICAL	SOCIAL
1350			
		Triangular sails and sternpost rudders used in European ships	Boccaccio's *Decameron*
1400			
	Development of West African forest kingdoms	Caravels in use / Prince Henry's school of navigation	Card games become popular in Europe
1450	Spain unified under Ferdinand and Isabella	Compass and astrolabe improved / Gutenberg's movable-type printing press	Transatlantic slave trade begins / Beginnings of ballet
1500	Cortés conquers Mexico / Magellan's voyage / Columbus' first voyage / Mogul Empire established	Gunports in ships / Guns introduced to Japan / Musket invented	Protestant Reformation begins / Height of Timbuktu as a center of Muslim culture
1550	Height of Songhai Empire		
	Reign of Elizabeth I / Tokugawa shogunate established	Galleons in use / Mercator's map of the world	Height of the Renaissance / Shakespeare born
1600			
	Spanish Armada defeated / Height of Kanem-Bornu Empire	Guns introduced to sub-Saharan Africa / First British navy frigate	Wigs become fashionable in Europe / Growth of cities and money economy in Japan
1650			
	Asante confederation formed / Ch'ing Dynasty established	Postal services become well-established in Europe	Taj Mahal / Palace at Versailles
1700			
	Absolute monarchies become common in Europe	Sextant invented	Growth of mercantilism and middle class in Europe / 36,000-volume encyclopedia compiled in China
1750			
	Development of parliamentary government in England / Height of Ch'ing Dynasty under Ch'ien-lung	First nautical almanac	Dramatic population growth in China
1800			

RENAISSANCE AND REFORMATION

1300–1600

The Flagellation. Wall panel, Piero della Francesca, 1455.

Beginning in the 1300s, a renewed interest in the works of Greece and Rome led people to shift their attention away from the spiritual concerns of the Middle Ages to focus on human concerns. One result was a burst of creativity in art, literature, and learning, a movement that is called the Renaissance, which means "rebirth." The term also applies to the period of time during which this energetic spirit prevailed.

Beginning in the 1500s, a second movement, a religious reformation, came about that proceeded in two stages—a Protestant Reformation during which many groups broke away from the Roman Catholic Church, followed by a reform movement within the Catholic Church. The Renaissance and the Reformation marked the beginning of the transition from the Middle Ages to early modern times.

TIMELINE

1300	
	Petrarch born
1350	
	Boccaccio's *Decameron*
1400	
	Lorenzo de Medici born
1450	
	Leonardo da Vinci born — *Gutenberg Bible* published
1475	
	Michelangelo born
1500	
	Luther's *Ninety-Five Theses* — More's *Utopia*
	Erasmus's *Praise of Folly* — Machiavelli's *The Prince*
1525	
	Anglican church established — Calvin's *Institutes* — Jesuit order founded
1550	
	Peace of Augsburg — Shakespeare born — Council of Trent
1575	
	Edict of Nantes
1600	

15–1
THE RENAISSANCE

READ TO FIND OUT

—what the terms *humanism* and *patrons* mean.
—how the Renaissance came about in Italy.
—what Renaissance humanists believed about people.
—what works of literature express Renaissance ideas.
—how artists brought realism to their work.

> Now may every reflecting spirit thank God for being permitted to live in this new age, so full of hope and promise, which already rejoices in a greater array of nobly-gifted souls than the world has seen in a thousand years.

So wrote an Italian author, Matteo Palmieri (muh-TAY-yō palm-YEHR-ee), in the mid-1400s. Palmieri was referring to the Renaissance, which began in Italy in the 1300s. For many people, patterns of everyday life changed little from those of their ancestors. Yet many others, like Palmieri, who lived during the Renaissance, viewed their time as an enlightened period, in contrast to the years between the fall of Rome and the Renaissance, which they referred to as the "dark ages."

BEGINNINGS OF THE RENAISSANCE

In 1305, the popes of the Roman Catholic Church moved from Rome to France, and power in the Papal States was divided among the region's leading families. At the same time, the Holy Roman Empire lost control in northern Italy. Central and northern Italy became divided into a patchwork of city-states, while southern Italy remained a kingdom ruled from the city of Naples.

Italian merchants from these cities established new sea routes as Arab power in the Mediterranean declined. Through the port cities of Naples, Genoa, Pisa, and Venice, as well as through the inland distribution centers of Florence and Milan, flowed the merchandise of three continents. Into the banks and private treasuries of the Italian merchants flowed silver and gold. Situated at the heart of a trade network connecting Europe, Africa, the Middle East, and Asia, the Italian cities grew wealthy from trade, banking, and manufacturing.

The population of the Italian cities swelled as both peasant folk and nobles from the countryside moved into these trading centers to take advantage of the benefits of the flourishing commerce. Italian nobles built grand city palaces rather than country castles as nobles to the north did.

Although middle-class merchants had begun the profitable trade, the aristocrats also became involved. Many of the merchants grew wealthy and imitated the manners of the aristocracy—the powerful class of wealthy nobles—becoming themselves a new aristocracy. Distinguishing between the two classes became difficult.

Often, rivalries for power erupted within a city-state or between city-states. Feuds and warfare were frequent. Although the form of government varied from city-state to city-state, most were run by such rich and prominent families as the Medici (MED-uh-chee).

The Medici family was one of the most influential families of the Renaissance. Giovanni de Medici became wealthy both in banking and in woolens. The Medici were probably the wealthiest family in Italy when Cosimo de Medici came to power in Florence in the 1400s. The Medici kept a tight grip on the city's government for 60 years. They promoted the arts, beautified the city, and taxed the wealthy to provide programs for the poor.

The most famous of the Medici was Cosimo's grandson Lorenzo, called in his day "Lorenzo the Magnificent." He had a reputation for tolerance, charm, and wit. Under Lorenzo, Florence became one of the most powerful cities in Italy and one of the most beautiful cities in the world.

Rediscovery of Roman law and writing. The economic and political life of bustling centers such as Florence became increasingly complex. Agreements were made, companies were formed, contracts were written, and money changed hands. Questions of power, authority, and civic duty arose.

The laws and political writings of the Middle Ages did not provide solutions to the increas-

Rivals for civic power often hired mercenaries like Guidoriccio da Fogliano. After Fogliano helped Siena's leaders quash a rebellion, they had his portrait painted in the town hall.

ingly complex problems of Italian cities. Lawyers and scholars began to turn, therefore, to Roman law and political writings for answers. Out of their interest in Roman law came an interest in other writings, such as history and poetry. In turn, through their reading of classical Roman works, Italian scholars became more familiar with Greek works.

Knowledge of Greek and Roman thought had not died out completely during the Middle Ages. Many university students had studied Aristotle, and Byzantine and Muslim scholars had brought Greek learning to European universities. However, education during the Middle Ages was largely through the Church and was for religious purposes.

Now, scholars began to search in musty libraries for the forgotten writings of Greeks and Romans. A growing excitement accompanied the rediscovery of classical learning. Out of this excitement came pressure for a new kind of education—one that was more like that of ancient Rome. The scholars believed that this approach would suit the needs of the civic and commercial leaders of the Renaissance.

University courses of study were revised to include the reading of Greek and Roman classics, history, moral philosophy, and literary composition. An Italian thinker, Leonardo Bruni, labeled this course of study *studia humanitatis*, or "the humanities," and the people who followed such a course of study became known as humanists.

HUMANISM

Although not all Renaissance scholars thought alike, familiarity with Greek and Roman ideas gave them all a new outlook. They came to cherish the great thinkers and writers, the great ideas, and the great art of the pre-Christian Greeks and Romans. The Greeks had sought to develop body, mind, and spirit, and had found joy in living, whereas thinkers of the Middle Ages had emphasized that life on earth was preparation for life after death. Renaissance humanists did not abandon their belief in God, but, like the Greeks and Romans, they shifted their attention to the affairs of humankind. This way of thinking is called **humanism**.

Renaissance humanists believed in the worth of the individual human being. One Renaissance humanist expressed the view that humankind was God's greatest creation besides the angels. Others stressed the ability of humans to create great works of their own.

In keeping with this new outlook, Renaissance thinking was characterized by optimism and a spirit of adventure. Humanists developed great confidence in human powers. This confidence led some individuals to seek fame. Many people of the Renaissance, including poets, composers, and artists, focused on human problems and human emotions, even in their religious works.

Humanist thinkers also became concerned with such ethical issues as how people should behave to maintain an orderly society. Concentrating on this world rather than the next led to a renewed interest in nature. These currents of thought found expression in an outpouring of art and literature.

THE ITALIAN RENAISSANCE IN LITERATURE

The first great humanist author was Francisco Petrarch (fran-CHES-kō PEE-TRARK), a scholar of fourteenth-century Florence. Petrarch was a devoted Christian. However, he thought that the scholastics' concern with detail would discourage people from learning anything from their writings. Instead, he followed classical poetry as a model of good writing. This love of the classics sent Petrarch on a search through forgotten corners of monasteries and cathedrals for ancient Greek and Roman manuscripts. He regarded each discovery as a new and "welcomed companion," and he assembled a large private library.

Petrarch represented Renaissance thinking not only in his love for the classics, but also in his intense appreciation of the beauty of the world and his pride in his own accomplishments. He expressed both attitudes in an essay describing how he and his brother had climbed a mountain in southern France "to see what so great an elevation had to offer."

Petrarch hoped that his works on moral conduct, written in Latin, would bring him lasting fame. However, his fame as a writer rests on the more than 400 poems he wrote in Italian. A majority of these lovely, tender poems were written to a beloved woman named Laura, who died during the Black Death.

Widely admired for his scholarship, Petrarch was called upon by princes and popes for his knowledge of the classics. His love of learning, nature, and humanity had a great influence on other Renaissance figures.

Boccaccio. Petrarch's friend Giovanni Boccaccio (jō-VAHN-ee bō-KAH-chee-ō), a professor at the University of Florence, was also a humanist scholar. He helped Petrarch search for classical manuscripts and wrote scholarly works in Latin. The first writer of prose in a modern language, Boccaccio wrote entertaining, down-to-earth short stories in the colorful dialect of Florence.

After the death of Boccaccio in 1375, enthusiasm for literature in the vernacular, or everyday language of a people, waned for a time. Writing in Latin again became the fashion. In addition, scholars expended even greater energy looking for ancient manuscripts, ranging as far as Constantinople in their search.

Wealthy families throughout Italy built the first modern libraries, in which the newly found manuscripts could be preserved, copied, and studied. The Medici family alone supported three libraries in or near Rome.

Machiavelli. During the 1500s, Italian writers returned to use of the vernacular. One who wrote in a brilliant prose style was a political philosopher, Niccolò Machiavelli (NEEK-kō-LŌ MAH-kyah-VEL-lee).

In 1498, Machiavelli became an official in the government of Florence. His duties took him on a diplomatic mission to Rome. There he observed with admiration the workings of that unified city-state, which was the result of the efforts of Cesare Borgia (CHAY-zah-reh BOR-jah). Borgia's methods were shrewd and ruthless, but effective.

Machiavelli later wrote a handbook for rulers, called *The Prince*. The book described what Machiavelli considered to be political realities, not political ideals. He rejected medieval ideas about restraints on the power of government. To Machiavelli, the highest goal of any ruler was the maintainance of the state's power and prosperity. For Machiavelli this end justified any means. Wrote Machiavelli:

> A prince must be a fox so as to know the snares [traps], and a lion so as to frighten the wolves. For this reason a ruler cannot and should not keep his word if this would be against his interest. If human beings were all good, this teaching would not be fitting, but since they are bad, you do not have to keep [your word] with them.

Machiavelli's ideas inspired many political dictators, even down to the twentieth century.

Castiglione. In sharp contrast to Machiavelli's work about politics was *The Book of the Courtier* by Baldassare Castiglione (bahl-duhs-SAHR-eh kahs-tee-LYŌ-nee). In this guide to Renaissance manners, Castiglione described the desired qualities of a true "Renaissance man" as a noble person who could be witty, courteous, and brave. This ideal man would be educated, as well as accomplished in many pursuits, such as riding, fencing, dancing, musicianship, and conversation. Being able to discuss the classics was especially important. Castiglione also described the role of the high-born Renaissance woman. She was expected to be bright, witty, graceful, versatile, and accomplished in the art of intelligent conversation.

THE ITALIAN RENAISSANCE IN ART

Wealthy merchant princes, kings, and popes were often *patrons* of Renaissance art, sponsoring the artists whose work graced public buildings, palaces, private homes, and cathedrals. Patrons are people who support and encourage some person or institution. During the Middle Ages, most art had been created by anonymous artists for churches. Painters and sculptors had

been viewed as artisans, little different from carpenters or bricklayers. However, Renaissance artists often became well-known celebrities.

Renaissance art, like literature of the period, reflected an admiration of the Greeks and Romans. The art of the Middle Ages had been chiefly symbolic, decorative but flat. The figures in paintings reminded viewers of people they knew, but such representations did not look as if they could step out of the painting to speak. Renaissance artists, however, strived to portray lifelike figures and scenes of nature, just as the Greeks and Romans had.

Innovations in art. The movement toward realistic art began in Florence in the 1300s with a painter known as Giotto (JAH-tō). No one knows where he got the idea to use shades of light and dark to give his paintings the illusion of depth. However, his work electrified other Renaissance artists. Word of his accomplishments spread to other cities, and soon many artists were imitating his techniques.

The next Italian painter to discover techniques for making paintings more realistic was Tommaso Masaccio (mah-SAHT-chō). Painting biblical figures whose faces expressed human emotions, Masaccio managed to make the figures look more solid and real than painters before him had been able to do. He experimented with the rules of perspective, a mathematical system for arranging objects in a painting to give an illusion of depth.

Filippo Brunelleschi (BROO-nuh-LES-kee), the first important architect of the Italian Renaissance, pioneered perspective drawing. After studying the buildings of Greece and Rome, Brunelleschi designed magnificent new buildings combining classical styles with the construction techniques of the Middle Ages. He boldly capped the Cathedral of Florence with a large Roman dome. The Renaissance style architecture that he pioneered has been imitated many times over the centuries in the public buildings of countries throughout the world.

The masters. By the 1500s, three great artists stood out above all the rest. Perhaps the most versatile of the three was Leonardo da Vinci (duh VIN-chee). Leonardo once proclaimed, "I wish to work miracles." His endless talents and boundless energy seemed to make that feat almost possible.

FLORENTINE MASTERS

Florence—*Firenze* in Italian—was home to some of the greatest artists of the Renaissance. Giotto, Brunelleschi, della Robbia, Masaccio, Leonardo, and Michelangelo were all born in or near this city where the Renaissance dawned. In Florence today, cathedrals, palaces, and libraries still stand, adorned with the brilliant paintings and sculptures of these masters.

**Dome of Florence Cathedral.
Filippo Brunelleschi,
1420–1436**

**Cantoria (Choir). Florence
Cathedral. Luca della Robbia, 1438**

The Tribute Money. Brancacci Chapel, Florence.
Masaccio, c. 1427

Isabella d'Este, Patroness of the
arts. Leonardo da Vinci

Lamentation of the Dead Christ. Scrovegni
Chapel, Padua. Giotto, c. 1305

Moses. Tomb of Pope Julius II, Rome.
Michelangelo, 1513–1515

A gifted painter, engineer, and musician, Leonardo tackled many problems. On thousands of notebook pages, he sketched detailed designs for inventions such as a flying machine, a machine gun, and a submarine. He designed buildings, as well as a canal system for the city of Milan. He made a scientific study of the structure of plants, animals, and fossils.

Leonardo also studied human anatomy, making many accurate drawings of the structure of the human body. Based on his studies, Leonardo created such masterpieces as *The Last Supper* and the *Mona Lisa*.

Like Leonardo, Michelangelo Buonarroti (MĪ-kuhl-AN-juh-lō bahn-uh-RŌ-tee) was a man of many talents. Apprenticed as a painter at the age of twelve, he soon turned to sculpture. Of the two, he considered sculpture to have the greater power. "Each act," he said, "each limb, each bone [is] given life, and lo, man's body is raised breathing, alive, in wax or clay or stone." In both sculpture and painting Michelangelo created larger-than-life figures that seemed to possess great strength and energy.

Michelangelo's most famous work is probably the painting on the ceiling of the Sistine Chapel in the Vatican. A separate city within Rome, the Vatican is the home of the Roman Catholic Church. Employed by Pope Julius II, Michelangelo took four years to complete the nine expressive scenes inspired by the Old Testament of the Bible.

At the age of forty-five, Michelangelo added architecture to his list of achievements. Among other works he designed the dome atop Saint Peter's Church in the Vatican, as well as the square and surrounding buildings for the civic center of Rome.

RENAISSANCE MUSIC

Music provided a rich and varied accompaniment for many aspects of Renaissance life. The sound of trumpets announced religious and military processions, and colorfully costumed musicians played at the courtly dances and elaborate spectacles held by nobles. Street musicians performed in the marketplace in hopes of a penny or two for their efforts. During church services, choral music expressed both great rejoicing and deep solemnity.

Educated men and women of the Renaissance were expected to be able to read music, sing, and accompany themselves on a musical instrument. For both nobles and common folk, the most popular instrument was the lute, which resembles a plump, pear-shaped guitar. Other popular instruments were forerunners of the piano and the violin.

Just as in art and literature, many changes took place in music during the Renaissance. One such change was the development of harmony. In the earliest choral music, all of the people in the choir sang the same notes. During the late Middle Ages, singers began to combine different melodies, and by the Renaissance, each kind of voice in the choir, such as alto or soprano, sang a different part, all voices blending into luxurious chords. Madrigals became a popular type of secular music in which many voices sang different melodies to produce one harmonious song.

The sounds of instruments playing different melodies were also blended into single musical works. Concerts of instruments only, their tones combining, foreshadowed the performances of orchestras and bands today.

Many familiar musical forms originated with the Renaissance. Composers began to create songs by setting poems to music, especially love poems. These composers began to write their lyrics in the vernacular, rather than in Latin. Opera also had its beginnings during the Renaissance when composers began to set plays to music.

When a new printing method replaced the tedious copying of music notation by hand, for the first time books of songs and operas could be manufactured. As a result, great numbers of people in Renaissance Europe could enjoy the pleasures of music.

A fresco in a Vatican library, Raphael's *School of Athens* depicts the Greek philosophers who inspired the humanists. Raphael may have used faces of his friends to represent the Greeks.

Raphael Santi (RAF-ay-ehl san-TEE) was influenced by both Leonardo and Michelangelo. Raphael's paintings decorate the pope's private quarters in the Vatican. Serene in mood, Raphael's paintings made use of the new rules of perspective. Raphael portrayed humans with great dignity. He is best known for gentle portraits of the *Madonna*, the mother of Jesus.

The diffusion of ideas. In a burst of creativity, numerous other Italian painters, sculptors, architects, and writers created works that expressed the ideals of the Renaissance. An interest in ancient cultures, belief in human abilities, regard for the worth of the individual, concern with human affairs such as commerce and politics, and curiosity about the world characterized the Renaissance spirit that was born in Italy. Soon such Renaissance ideas began to spread to nearby nations.

SECTION REVIEW

1. Define **humanism** and **patrons**.

2. Explain what led Italian scholars to search for old manuscripts. What was one result of their acquaintance with classical manuscripts?

3. How did humanists view people?

4. What human qualities were praised by Renaissance writers?

5. Explain two ways Italian Renaissance art differed from the art of the Middle Ages.

Analysis. Renaissance writers and artists were optimistic about human ability to improve; critical of the Middle Ages; accomplished in many pursuits; inspired by Greek and Roman classics; and interested in creating realistic portrayals. List six of the Italian Renaissance artists and writers. For each one, tell which of these characteristics best describe his work.

15–2
SPREAD OF RENAISSANCE IDEAS

READ TO FIND OUT

—how Renaissance ideas spread.

—how the northern Renaissance differed from the Italian Renaissance.

—how the Renaissance spirit was expressed in Germany, France, Spain, and England.

—what impact Renaissance thinking had on the future.

As students from northern European countries such as France and England came to Italy to study in its universities, and as Italian writers and artists traveled to other countries to work for kings or aristocrats, Renaissance ideas spread throughout Europe. By the 1500s, the Renaissance had spread to Germany, France, Spain, and England. As in Italy, the Renaissance in the north first blossomed in busy commercial centers.

The door was opened for the spread of Renaissance ideas by the European development of movable type. Credit for this development is usually given to Johannes Gutenberg (yō-HAHN-uhs GOOT-ihn-BERG), a German printer. By 1456, Gutenberg had completed the publication of the first printed book in Europe. This work is known as the *Gutenberg Bible*. Whether Gutenberg invented movable type himself or perfected the work of others is not known. Neither do historians know whether European printers were aware of Chinese developments in printing. What is known, however, is that Gutenberg's use of movable type had a strong impact on Europe.

Within 50 years, more than 30,000 different books were in print. Because printed books were less costly than hand-copied manuscripts, religious works, Greek and Roman classics, and the writings of Renaissance thinkers became available to many people throughout Europe.

THE NORTHERN RENAISSANCE

In northern Europe the Renaissance took on a somewhat different character than in Italy. In the north, the strongest Renaissance movement was Christian humanism. Northern Christian humanists were concerned with blending their Christian outlook with Renaissance ideals, such as beliefs in the value of reason and the ability of individuals to determine their own good conduct.

Germany and the Low Countries. The Renaissance took root in German universities in the mid-1400s. There, humanist ideas about human worth and means for maintaining an orderly society became the basis of religious and political protests. Several German writers wrote works satirizing not the Christian faith, but the organization of the Church.

Desiderius Erasmus (ih-RAZ-muhs), a gentle Dutch priest, was the most influential figure of the northern Renaissance. A brilliant scholar, Erasmus studied the Bible and wrote works to help other scholars understand it. He urged the study of the Bible along with the texts of classical philosophers. Erasmus's hope was that

In the engraving *St. Jerome in His Study*, Albrecht Dürer portrayed the scholarly monk at work. Jerome had translated the Old Testament from Hebrew into Latin in the fourth century.

greater learning in both Christianity and humanism would improve humankind.

Erasmus stressed the importance of reason, tolerance, and noble conduct based on Christian ethics. He severely criticized ignorance and superstition both within the Church and without. In his witty essay, *The Praise of Folly*, he satirized stupidity and corruption among Christians, including the clergy.

Notable artists in the Netherlands and other Low Countries, and Germany were also concerned with the Christian faith. The German artist Albrecht Dürer (DYOO-rer), an admirer of Erasmus, often portrayed subjects from the Bible. Like other Renaissance artists, he was also interested in studying forms in nature and the proportions of the human body.

Hans Holbein (HŌL-BĪN) was another German artist who was influenced by the Italian Renaissance. He achieved renown for his realistic portraits of well-known people, such as Erasmus.

France. The Renaissance spirit reached France more than a century after it had originated in Italy. The monarchs of France became patrons of poets, writers, painters, and architects.

Two people who represent the French Renaissance are François Rabelais (frahn-SWAH RAB-uh-LAY) and Michel de Montaigne (mee-SHEL duh mahn-TAYN). Yet, these two writers were quite different from each other.

Rabelais, who lived in the early 1500s, gained a reputation as a merry man. He attacked the politics, education, and religious institutions of the Middle Ages with a comic story about two giants, *Gargantua and Pantagruel*.

Montaigne, who lived in the last half of the 1500s, was a quiet, contemplative man. He was skeptical about both faith and reason, feeling that too much of either one might lead people astray. In his *Essays* he encouraged people to live nobly in this world rather than spend time yearning for the next.

Spain. Spain remained more traditionally Catholic than other European nations. The study of ancient works was not as important in Spain as it was in Italy. However, during the 1500s, Spain also experienced a burst of creativity in art and literature.

Many Spaniards studied in Italy and by the late 1500s had brought Renaissance ideas home to Spain. Nevertheless, the painter who best represents the Spanish Renaissance was an immigrant from Crete who came to Spain after studying in Italy. His name was Doménikos Theotokópoulos (do-MEN-ih-kuhs THEE-ō-tuh-KAH-puh-lus), but he was called El Greco, which means "the Greek." El Greco painted realistic portraits of Spanish nobles and mystical portraits of biblical figures.

The most gifted writer of the Spanish Renaissance was Miguel de Cervantes (mee-GEL duh ser-VAHN-tees). Even in traditional Spain, as trade and commerce increased, social conditions began to change. Cervantes satirized the inappropriateness of medieval ideals of chivalry in this changing society. In his comic novel *Don Quixote* (dahn kee-HŌT-ee), a Spanish landowner who sees himself as a knight sets out to be a champion of honor and right. However, he is frustrated at every turn because his out-of-date actions do not fit reality. Don Quixote saves people who do not want to be saved and fights danger where there is none.

El Greco painted *Annunciation* about 1600. This work is one of several he completed on this subject: the angel Gabriel's announcement to Mary of the impending birth of Christ.

ASKING EFFECTIVE QUESTIONS

Much of what you know is a result of the questions you ask. If you do not ask questions about what you see or hear or read, you will probably know only what you are shown or told by others. However, if you ask good questions about the information presented to you, you can direct your own learning and come to learn more in the process.

EXPLAINING THE SKILL

To be effective, your questions should have two important features. First, they must be appropriate to your assigned task or chosen purpose. Different questions serve different purposes. For instance, if given an assignment to write a physical description of your classmates, you should ask questions that can be answered with facts, such as "What styles of clothing are most of my classmates wearing?" However, if your task is to identify the "best dressed" person in your class, your questions should lead you to state and support your opinions. For instance, you might ask, "What styles of clothing do I consider to be the best?"

Often your purpose will require asking questions that guide you in collecting and organizing information. For example, you might ask, "What is there about all these students that makes this class unique?" Questions like this do more than simply require you to identify facts. They lead to deeper insights by requiring you to organize information and see relationships between facts.

To be effective, questions must be appropriate not only to your purpose but also to the data or information you are examining. Suppose that you are asked to describe the abilities and interests of your classmates, based on a list of names, course grades, grade point averages, and hobbies. Your questions should lead you to identify the main abilities or interests evident from the list. Therefore, an effective question would be, "Which hobbies are the most popular with my classmates?" A question about their athletic or artistic awards, however, would not be effective because it cannot be answered with the information you are examining.

One procedure for inventing effective questions is to follow these steps:

1. *Identify and define clearly the topic or subject on which you are to focus.*

2. *Identify and define clearly your task or purpose in examining the information.*

3. *Determine what the given information might reveal to you.*

4. *Brainstorm specific questions that will provide answers directly related to your purpose and directly related to the given information.*

5. *Choose those questions most likely to help you accomplish your purpose and for which the given data appears best suited.*

APPLYING THE SKILL

Identify characteristics of Renaissance art by examining the works in the Heritage feature on page 331. Follow the previously described procedure for inventing effective questions.

REFLECTING ON THE SKILL

In following the procedure for inventing effective questions, you should have clearly identified the topic and your purpose. This means that you should have defined what is meant by "characteristics" of art. General characteristics would include such information as artistic styles, subject matter, and materials used by artists. After you determined how much of this information was available on page 331, your questions should have led you to identify some characteristics of the art. To check how well you followed the procedure, answer the questions below:

1. The purpose of examining the information was (a) to identify the most important Renaissance artists, (b) to identify the causes of the Renaissance, (c) to identify some characteristics of Renaissance art.

2. The information reveals (a) why Renaissance ideas spread from Italy to other parts of Europe, (b) some of the subject matter and

types of Renaissance art, **(c)** how Renaissance artists influenced each other's work.

3. Which of the following would be the most effective question for your purpose and the given information? **(a)** What are the similarities in the subject matter of these works of art? **(b)** Who were the artists who created these works of art? **(c)** How many of these works of art were displayed in churches? Explain why the question you chose is the most effective one.

APPLYING THE SKILL

Use the following information to help explain how Renaissance ideas spread outside of Italy. Follow the previously described procedure for inventing effective questions.

In the years 1530–1540 King Francois I set out to create in France an artistic center which would rival the great courts of Italy. Two Italian artists were called to France to decorate what was to become one of the most splendid palaces of Europe. One, Giovanni Battista Rosso (1494–1540), was from Florence. The other, Francesco Primaticcio (1504–1570), was trained in Bologna and Mantua. In their paintings these artists created novel variations on a style evolved in Italy by members of Raphael's studio.

During the first quarter of the sixteenth century, French soldiers and diplomats taking part in wars in Italy brought back sculptors and craftsmen capable of executing fine Italian decorations on buildings such as the church of Saint-Pierre at Caen. The first architect to bring a more consciously classical style of architecture into France was Sebastiano Serlio (1475-1554), an Italian architect who arrived in France in 1540 or 1541. Serlio exercised powerful influence through his *Treatise*, which appeared between 1537 and 1554. It was used as a textbook by French architects for the remainder of the sixteenth century.

This is all an example of a complete change of direction caused by the arrival of foreign artists in France. Till the early nineteenth century, Italy—and above all Rome—continued to be the goal of every French artist, and all those who were able went there to study. In this way they acquired a knowledge of Italian art which often exercised a

decisive influence on their style. If they went to Rome, their principal aim would be to see the works of ancient art—which they studied just as writers read the classics—but they were also influenced by the art of Raphael and other Italian Renaissance artists. They came back to France armed with drawings done of the works they particularly admired. Gradually French artists transformed what they learned in Italy into a national style.

Adapted from *French Art and Music Since 1500*, by Anthony Blunt and Edward Lockspeiser, (Suffolk: Methuen, 1972).

CHECKING YOUR UNDERSTANDING

To check how well you followed the procedure, answer the questions below:

4. The purpose of examining the information was **(a)** to identify Renaissance artists, **(b)** to explain how Renaissance ideas spread, **(c)** to determine the causes of the Renaissance.

5. The given information indicates **(a)** how Renaissance artistic ideas spread into France, **(b)** the major themes of Renaissance art, **(c)** the influence of France on Italian art.

6. Which of the following would be the most effective question, given your purpose and the given information? **(a)** Which Italian artists went to sixteenth-century France? **(b)** What kinds of Italian art had the greatest influence on French art? **(c)** How did Italian artistic ideas move into France? Explain why the question you chose is the most effective one.

REVIEWING THE SKILL

7. What are two important features of an effective question?

8. How can you tell whether a question is appropriate to the given information?

9. Why might it sometimes be ineffective to ask questions that require you to give only facts for answers?

10. What is a useful procedure for inventing effective questions?

11. Why is it important to ask effective questions about information presented to you?

England. When Erasmus wrote *The Praise of Folly*, he was visiting the home of his friend Sir Thomas More, a high official in the English government. More wrote prose and poetry in both English and Latin. He expressed his philosophy in *Utopia*, an account of an imagined ideal society based on justice and reason. Through his work, More criticized injustices of his time, such as poverty, unearned wealth, religious persecution, and war.

In England the Renaissance reached its peak during the reign of Elizabeth I, who encouraged English poets and writers. She enjoyed poetry that imitated the ancient classics, but she also supported the development of an English literature, free from the classical rules that governed the literature of Italy and France. Thus, literature flourished in England, as painting and sculpture had flourished in Italy.

The finest English literature was drama. English playwrights experimented with classical traditions until they created new forms of drama.

The first great dramatist of the English Renaissance was Christopher Marlowe, who wrote the tragedy *Doctor Faustus*. However, the master of English playwrights was William Shakespeare, a versatile writer whose works range from the fantasy of *A Midsummer Night's Dream* to the romance of *Romeo and Juliet* and the serious soul-searching of *Hamlet*. Shakespeare's plays, as well as his poems, are timeless studies of human character.

THE END OF THE RENAISSANCE

By the middle of the 1600s, the Renaissance was over. However, just as no single event marked its beginning, no one event can be identified as its end. Some Renaissance ideas, such as forms of humanism that made humankind nearly an object of worship, died out. Other Renaissance ideas and discoveries lived on by blending with new ones.

Many Renaissance achievements in literature, art, and music remained part of European life. Humanist views about a broad curriculum that includes languages, literature, history, and the arts, as well as religion and philosophy, have influenced education to this day. Furthermore, the Renaissance belief in the worth and dignity of the individual would have a great impact on future social and political affairs of Europe.

SECTION REVIEW

1. How did Renaissance ideas spread throughout Europe?

2. What was the major concern of northern European humanists?

3. Explain the major ideas of Erasmus. What did Rabelais and Cervantes have in common? What was the chief means by which Renaissance ideas were expressed in England?

4. What Renaissance attitudes remained after the Renaissance itself died away?

Analysis. Prove or disprove the following statement: In each country touched by the Renaissance spirit, humanist ideas spread, followed by a burst of creative achievement. Give some examples.

Data Search. In one of Shakespeare's plays, *Macbeth*, life is described as a "brief candle." Refer to the appropriate chart on page 829 to find out the average life expectancy in Renaissance England.

15–3
THE REFORMATION

READ TO FIND OUT

—what the terms *secular*, *canton*, *predestination*, and *dogma* mean.
—what Martin Luther believed.
—why the Protestant Reformation spread.
—how new churches formed.
—how the Catholic Church was reformed.
—what impact the Reformation had on Europe.

Pope and king, artist and writer, merchant and peasant—all western Europeans had one common link in 1500. All belonged to the Roman Catholic Church. Through the Church, western Europeans experienced a kind of unity.

However, the Church had never been completely without conflict, and starting in about the 1300s, demand for reform began to grow. By 1600, approximately half the Catholics in western Europe had left the Church to join one of the new religious groups founded by the reformers. The split in the Church shattered religious unity in western Europe. Because this revolution was led by religious "protesters," it became known as the Protestant Reformation, or Protestant Revolt.

LUTHER'S RELIGIOUS STRUGGLE

In 1501, a young German scholar, Martin Luther, enrolled in a university intending to study law. However, he found himself preoccupied by religious questions, and in 1505, the hard-working law student entered a monastery. There he tried to live a pious life. However, he could not rid himself of the feeling that he was a sinner.

Finally, a priest advised him to study the Bible. Soon, as Luther explained it, the Bible "took on a whole new meaning" to him. He concluded that the way to salvation—forgiveness for sin—was "justification by faith." According to this idea, good works—or the demonstration of faith by good deeds, sacred rites, and confession of sins—could not save a person. All that mattered was the inner faith of the believer.

This insight led Luther to challenge the Church's practice of granting indulgences. Indulgences were pardons that priests and monks granted to sinners in exchange for acts of repentance, or expressions of regret for wrongdoing. The practice of granting indulgences came from the belief that if sinners underwent earthly punishment for sins, they would be spared

SPOTLIGHT: PEOPLE

MARTIN LUTHER

On a July day in 1505, as Martin Luther walked toward the university where he was studying law, claps of thunder suddenly echoed all around, and flashes of lightning set the sky afire. Luther cried out, "St. Anne, help me! I will become a monk."

This event proved to have far-reaching effects. Luther gave up his study of law to become a priest. In 1511 he earned an advanced degree in theology. He was appointed a professor of religion at the University of Wittenberg, a position he held for the rest of his life. One aspect of university life that Luther loved was scholarly debate. When this soul-searching German priest and university professor posted his Ninety-Five Theses, he hoped it would stir debate. Instead, widely circulated, the theses created a storm of controversy over the practices and beliefs of the Roman Catholic Church.

Luther's translation of the Bible into German was also widely circulated. Before the Reformation, few people had read the Bible. When Luther's translation was published in 1522, 100,000 copies were quickly sold, and soon people were reading and interpreting the Bible for themselves.

The energetic Luther once said, "If I rest, I rust." Throughout his lifetime, Luther preached and wrote tirelessly, producing numerous works on such subjects as faith, rituals, and marriage. Published in their entirety for the first time in Germany in 1970, Luther's complete works totaled 80 volumes.

In addition to his devotion to his work, Luther loved good friends, good food, and music. A versatile man, Luther wrote hymns, including "A Mighty Fortress is Our God" and the Christmas Carol called "Cradle Hymn," or "Away in a Manger." "The devil doesn't stay where there is music," he observed.

Luther's marriage to Katherine von Bora, an ex-nun, brought him great happiness. During the many bouts of illness that plagued Luther, Katherine provided great comfort. Together he and Katherine had 6 children of their own and took in 11 orphaned children as well. Luther came to believe that "the most important vocation any man or woman can have is raising a family" and bringing them up well.

Sometimes dismayed at the tempest he had unleashed, Martin Luther was bothered that the Lutheran Church had been organized in his name, rather than in the name of Jesus Christ. However, at the time of his death on February 18, 1546, Luther was already recognized as a major influence on Christianity.

some punishment in the afterlife. Originally, indulgences had been awarded only for exceptionally religious acts, such as going on a crusade. In the early 1500s, Pope Julius II issued a decree stating that indulgences would be issued in return for donations to finance the dome that Michelangelo had designed for Saint Peter's Church in the Vatican.

In the view of the Church, any money given for indulgences was a voluntary offering. According to critics, however, some church figures were "selling" complete forgiveness as a way to raise money for the Church.

The Ninety-Five Theses. In 1517 Luther nailed a statement on the door of the church at Wittenberg, Germany. In this statement, known as the Ninety-Five Theses, or claims, Luther set forth an argument against the whole theory of indulgences. He hoped to provoke a debate that would lead to reform.

Martin Luther's Ninety-Five Theses were soon circulated throughout Europe. Meanwhile, Luther's attacks became bolder. Like early critics of the Church—John Wycliffe in England and Jan Hus in eastern Europe—Luther now claimed that the Bible was the ultimate source of religious authority. He called for a "priesthood of all believers"; that is, he argued that Christians with faith did not need priests. Instead, people could find salvation themselves through their own study of the Bible.

On June 15, 1520, Pope Leo X ordered Luther to renounce his beliefs or face excommunication. Luther responded by burning the pope's letter. In 1521, King Charles V, ruler of the Holy Roman Empire, summoned Luther to appear before a special diet, or committee, in the city of Worms, Germany. The diet, made up of both state and church officials, demanded that Luther change his views. Bound by his conscience, Luther refused their demands, saying: "My conscience is taken captive by God's word [the Bible]. I cannot and will not recant [take back] anything."

The diet declared Luther a heretic, for which he could be legally put to death. However, to protect Luther, a German prince hid him away in a mountain castle. While Luther remained there, his ideas gained a large following. Meanwhile, Luther translated the Bible from Latin into German, which allowed a greater number of people to read it for themselves.

After the Diet of Worms condemned Luther, the Church banned Lutheran doctrines. When a second Diet in 1529 reaffirmed the earlier decision, representatives of several German principalities and free cities protested. These protesters were called *Protestants*. From that time to the present, any Christian church that was not Eastern Orthodox or Roman Catholic has been called *Protestant*.

The Lutheran Church. Luther spent the rest of his life, until 1546, establishing the Lutheran Church. Although he kept many Catholic traditions, he also made important changes. For example, to make church services more understandable to people, he conducted them in German, not Latin. He insisted on the right of priests to marry, which made them more like other people. He eliminated most special rites and, instead, emphasized faith. Furthermore, instead of placing his church above the **secular**, or nonreligious, government, he organized his church under the government's supervision.

THE SPREAD OF THE REFORMATION

The impact of Luther's work was enormous. Along with the turmoil and conflict accompanying such a clash of deeply felt beliefs, the Reformation spread rapidly.

Several religious factors accounted for the widespread acceptance of Luther's ideas. First, some people's respect for the Roman Catholic Church had diminished during the Babylonian Captivity and the Great Schism. Second, early religious reformers such as John Wycliffe had already planted seeds of doubt about church practices. Third, Martin Luther's appeal to faith attracted many Christians who felt that the views of the scholastics and Thomas Aquinas were too unemotional. In addition, many of Luther's followers rejected any ideas or practices that were not mentioned in the Bible. By denying certain church practices, these followers believed they were returning to the purer form of Christianity that had existed before the Middle Ages.

Other reasons were political. The Great Schism had ended in 1417, and Rome had again become the center of the Church. Elsewhere, in countries such as England, Denmark, Sweden, and Germany, strong princes and national monarchs had gained power while feudalism de-

Martin Luther's friend Lucas Cranach the Elder often painted the religious reformer. A panel from Wittenburg's town church depicts Luther (right) preaching about the Crucifixion.

clined. These rulers no longer wished to be subjected to the authority of the Church. Feelings of national loyalty arose. People began to resent interference from outsiders, and the pope, away in Rome, began to be viewed as an outsider.

Still other reasons were economic. By the 1500s, the Church owned a great deal of land. In Germany, for example, the Church may have owned as much as one-third of the land, but paid no taxes on it. Thus, a heavier tax burden fell on other landowners. In addition, the Church itself had the power to collect taxes from every household. Many people felt that their lands were being drained of wealth, which was flowing to Rome. Said Luther, "Before long all the churches, palaces, walls, and bridges of Rome will be built out of our money."

Such a statement struck a responsive chord among European rulers eager to keep revenues within their own borders. A break with the Church afforded an opportunity to seize church lands and collect the taxes on them.

Germany. While arguments over Protestant ideas raged throughout Germany, that region was shaken by the largest mass uprising in its history. Long resentful of the heavy taxes and services demanded of them by their lords, German peasants rebelled in 1524. Although the war had not been started for religious reasons, the peasants believed that Luther would support them. However, they had misunderstood his writings about the freedom of Christians. Luther had been writing about freedom of spirit. Instead of siding with the peasants, Luther denounced their violence. More than one hundred thousand peasants lost their lives when the revolt was smashed.

Meanwhile Charles V, the Holy Roman Emperor, was embroiled in a series of wars with France. While Charles was so occupied, one German prince after another turned to the teachings of Martin Luther. The German principalities had little say in Rome, while the strong monarchies of France and Spain had great influence there. The German nobles were resentful that money from their principalities supported the church government they had little influence on. These princes saw Lutheranism as a way of freeing the German principalities from the domination of Rome.

Finally, in 1546, Charles threatened to crush the independent German princes. War loomed. However, the conflict was settled in 1555 with the Peace of Augsburg. In this agreement, the Holy Roman Emperor recognized the Lutheran Church. The Peace of Augsburg further stated that whoever ruled an area could decide the religion of that area. Most of northern Germany became Lutheran while most of southern and western Germany remained Catholic.

Switzerland. Lutheranism opened the way for other Protestant movements. In Zurich (ZUR-ihk), Switzerland, a priest named Ulrich

Zwingli (OOL-rihk ZWING-lee) established a new church that accepted most of Luther's teachings. By 1528, nearly all of northern Switzerland followed Zwingli's church. However, when Zwingli tried to establish his church in southern Switzerland, war broke out. To settle the conflict, Swiss leaders signed an agreement in 1531 that the government of each *canton*, or local district, would choose the religion for that canton.

Out of Zwingli's church arose a group who came to be called Anabaptists. These Protestants believed that church membership should be voluntary, not forced. Therefore, they believed in a complete separation of religion and government. Both Catholic and Protestant authorities in Switzerland saw this belief as a threat to their governments. In 1527, the Anabaptist leader was executed. Persecuted by both Protestants and Catholics, many Anabaptists left Switzerland and carried their views to Germany and the Low Countries.

Shortly after this time, John Calvin founded Calvinism. Born in France, Calvin was a law student when he became interested in Lutheranism. When the French government began an attack on suspected heretics, Calvin fled to Switzerland. There, in 1536, he published *The Institutes of the Christian Religion*, a book explaining his beliefs. Soon, he began preaching in Geneva, where he gained great influence.

Although he accepted the basic teachings of Lutheranism, Calvin set himself apart with his belief in *predestination*—the doctrine that God has already determined everything that will happen, including who will be saved and who will be condemned. Calvin said, "All are not created on equal terms but some are preordained [already ordered] to eternal life, others to eternal damnation." According to Calvinism, it was not always possible to know those who would be saved, "the elect," but one sign might be earthly success including wealth. Because no one could be certain who "the elect" were, everyone was expected to live according to the highest moral standards as if they were one of the chosen.

Calvinists were expected to follow rules of the Bible strictly, refrain from work and pleasure on the Sabbath, and pursue the virtues of thrift and hard work. Calvinism spread to other countries, such as France, the Low Countries, England, and Scotland.

France. In France, the followers of Calvin were known as Huguenots (HYOO-guh-NOTS). Their influence grew rapidly, until they formed a large minority. Occasional conflict between Huguenots and Catholics became bitter war in 1562.

To restore peace, the French royal family arranged a marriage in 1572 between one of their own and a Huguenot leader. However, the wedding bells set off a bloody massacre, as thousands of Parisians attacked the Huguenot leaders gathered for the wedding. The incident began another round of warfare. Finally, in 1598, King Henry IV ended the fighting by issuing the Edict of Nantes (NANTS). This ruling granted the Huguenots the right to practice their religion and gave them equal political rights with Catholic citizens.

ENGLAND'S BREAK WITH ROME

Another branch of Protestantism arose in England. There, the Reformation became intertwined with national politics. The English king, Henry VIII, desperately wanted a son to succeed him to the throne. He and his wife, Catherine of Aragon, had been unable to produce a male heir. To complicate the situation, Henry fell in love with sixteen-year-old Anne Boleyn. Henry finally asked Pope Clement VII to grant him a divorce from Catherine so that he could marry Anne.

After considering the request, the pope refused to grant Henry a divorce. Henry responded by breaking with the Church and decreeing his own divorce. In 1534, Parliament passed the Supremacy Act, making Henry the head of an independent Anglican, or English, church.

Henry could not have carried out these acts if the English people had been strongly opposed. However, because feelings of national pride had been growing, many people were ready to cut ties with the pope. Also, many people had been influenced by the criticisms of John Wycliffe and the Christian humanists, especially Thomas More.

The Anglican church did not make England a Protestant country, though, for it maintained mostly Catholic practices. However, the number of Protestants in England grew, and included two of Henry's children, Elizabeth and Edward.

A procession of Catholic faithful is shown marching through Paris streets in 1590. From 1562 to 1598, French Catholics and Protestants fought each other in eight separate wars.

After Henry died in 1547, Edward was king for just five years until his death at the age of fifteen. Following Edward VI as monarch was Henry and Catherine's daughter, Mary—who had remained a Catholic. Mary I attempted to restore Catholicism in England. This effort, however, led to bitter power struggles.

Upon Mary's death in 1558, Elizabeth, the daughter of Anne Boleyn, became the queen. She settled the matter of whether England was to be Catholic or Protestant once and for all. In 1570, a new Act of Supremacy made any English monarch the head of the Anglican church. The church would be Protestant.

Elizabeth I was a diplomat, however. She saw to it that church rules were broad enough so that people with either Lutheran or Catholic leanings could worship in different branches of the Anglican church.

THE CATHOLIC REFORMATION

The spirit of reform that produced the Protestant Revolt also produced a Catholic Reformation, or Counter Reformation. As early as the 1400s, concerned Catholics began to work at reforming the Church from within.

In part to counter the Protestant Revolt and in part to guide the reform movement within the Church, Pope Paul III called a meeting of leading clergy at Trent, Italy. This Council of Trent, which lasted from 1545 to 1563, tried to improve the church's organization and define church *dogma*, or the official teachings of the Church.

The Council reaffirmed basic Catholic teachings. It upheld the supremacy of the pope. Whereas Protestant churches held that the Bible was the only authority for beliefs, the Council said that both the teachings of the clergy and the word of the Bible were religious authorities. The Council also restated the need for both faith and good works. Finally, it openly rejected the idea of predestination, emphasizing instead free will, or the idea that the individual is free to choose between right and wrong.

In addition to redefining its doctrine, the Church took strong steps to deal with heresy. Church leaders revived the Inquisition—the church court that tried heretics in the Middle Ages. They also established the Index—a list of books forbidden to Catholics—which included many new humanist works.

Religious orders. Another development was the reformation of Catholic religious orders—societies of men or women devoted to serving the Church—and the rise of new ones. For example, Teresa de Cepeda (duh suh-PAY-duh), a Spanish noblewoman and Carmelite nun, had become dissatisfied with the Carmelite order, which had been founded in Syria in the 1100s. Her plan to restore stricter, more disciplined ways to the order met with strong opposition. However, after this strong-minded nun founded several new convents where she put her ideas into practice, she was invited by the pope to reform the existing Carmelite convents.

An important new religious order was the Society of Jesus, or the Jesuits. Founded in 1534 by a Spanish soldier named Ignatius Loyola, the Jesuits vowed to be soldiers of the Church. Whereas followers of other religious orders often lived quiet lives withdrawn from the world, the Jesuits lived active lives, broadcasting their faith throughout the world. Jesuit missionaries traveled as far as Southeast Asia, Japan, and the Americas. The Jesuits also established hundreds of schools and universities.

THE SOCIAL IMPACT OF THE PROTESTANT REFORMATION

The religious ferment that characterized the Reformation affected social attitudes, family relationships, and work habits, as well as other aspects of daily life. For example, virtues stressed by Calvinists, such as hard work, individual responsibility, and thrift, influenced the conduct of commerce.

The incessant strife over religion also added to an increasing obsession with witches. During the late Middle Ages, witches had been blamed for the plague. Later, they were blamed for nearly any misfortune.

To be accused of witchcraft nearly guaranteed that a person would be convicted, for any defense the accused person put forth was thought to be the work of the devil. In 1484,

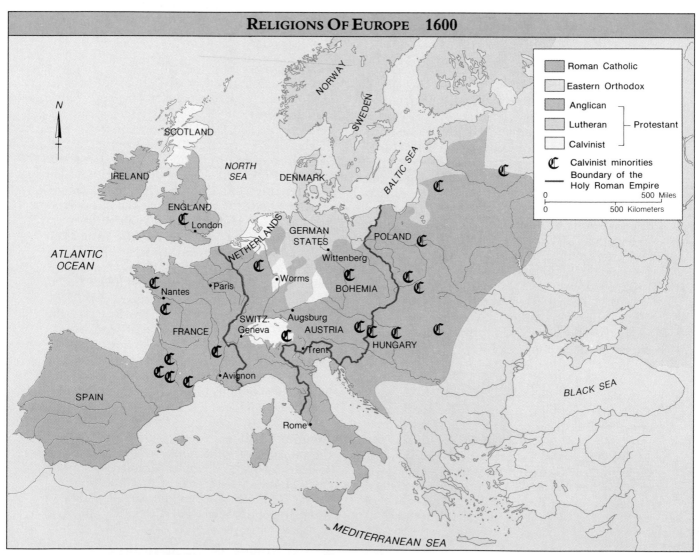

RELIGIONS OF EUROPE 1600

Roman Catholic
Eastern Orthodox
Anglican ⎤
Lutheran ⎟ Protestant
Calvinist ⎦
ℭ Calvinist minorities
Boundary of the Holy Roman Empire

0 — 500 Miles
0 — 500 Kilometers

In the marriage portrait *Giovanni Arnolfini and his Bride*, artist Jan van Eyck expresses the holiness of matrimony. The single candle symbolizes God's presence; the dog, fidelity.

Pope Innocent VIII had said, "Thou shalt not suffer a witch to live," and after that statement was issued, the penalty for witchcraft was death in Catholic and Protestant areas alike. Over the two hundred years that the witch craze raged, several hundred thousand people—most of them women—were burned, hanged, or tortured to death.

The Reformation had an effect on the role of women. In contrast to the Catholic Church, in which nuns played an important role, Protestant churches did not provide an environment in which women could devote themselves solely to a religious life. However, by encouraging all persons to read the Bible for themselves, Protestant churches encouraged education for women.

Women played an important role in the moral education of children, and the family was viewed as the best place to pass down Christian ideals. Protestant preachers praised the dignity of family life. They talked of husbands and wives as "helpmates." They also spoke of the importance of love in family life. Increasingly, marriage choices were made for personal rather than economic reasons.

SECTION REVIEW

1. Define **secular**, **canton**, **predestination**, and **dogma**.

2. Describe two basic issues on which Martin Luther disagreed with the Catholic Church.

3. Explain one religious, one political, and one economic reason that the Reformation spread.

4. How was a separate church established in Switzerland? In England?

5. What issues were decided by the Council of Trent?

6. List three permanent changes brought about in total or in part by the Reformation.

Analysis. Compare Catholic and Protestant beliefs at the time of the Reformation about the role of the clergy, true sources of religious authority, and the relationship between church and secular authority.

HISTORY IN FOCUS

The Renaissance and Reformation swept away many of the customs and attitudes of the Middle Ages. Both movements had an impact on European civilization that continues to this day.

Renewed curiosity about the world eventually contributed both to European exploration of the globe and a rapid increase in scientific discovery. The Renaissance emphasis on human affairs and the worth of the individual influenced later political thought, such as the development of democracy.

Perhaps the most undeniable impact of the Reformation was the formation of a new religious map of Europe. By the time the Reformation had run its course, the religious patterns of Europe had been altered for all time. In general, Protestant religions spread throughout northern Europe, while southern and eastern Europe remained Catholic. This division set the scene for a series of devastating religious wars, especially in France, the Netherlands, and Germany. For more than a century, Europe was rocked by both civil and international wars fought in the name of religion.

SUMMARY

- The Renaissance began in Italy in the 1300s and was marked by humanism and a blossoming of the arts. Renaissance ideas later spread to other parts of Europe.

- During the Italian Renaissance, art and literature were influenced by Greek and Roman classics. Writers produced works on law, civics, manners, and human experience. Artists brought new techniques and a greater sense of realism to painting and sculpture.

- The development of movable type in the 1400s helped the Renaissance to spread to the rest of Europe. In northern Europe, scholars followed the ideas of Christian humanism, a blend of faith and reason. Writers in England, France, and Spain produced literary masterpieces.

- In the early 1500s, Martin Luther opposed certain aspects of Catholic belief, like indulgences and the power of the priesthood. His ideas sparked the Reformation, a movement that split the Catholic Church.

- In addition to the Lutheran Church, the Reformation gave rise to other denominations and leaders: the churches of Calvin and Zwingli in Switzerland, the Huguenots in France, and the Anglican church in England. Meanwhile, the Catholic Church was reformed from within and traditional Catholic religious beliefs were reaffirmed.

VOCABULARY REVIEW

Match each numbered vocabulary term with the appropriate person. Then explain the connection between the person and the vocabulary term.

Example: *Dogma* could be associated with Pope Paul III because he, or any pope, was responsible for establishing and upholding Catholic dogma.

1. humanism   (a) Medici
2. patrons   (b) Calvin
3. predestination   (c) Erasmus

CHAPTER REVIEW

1. (a) Describe how political and economic conditions contributed to the birth of the Renaissance. (b) What political and economic factors contributed to the Reformation?

2. (a) What was the main inspiration for Renaissance thought? (b) How did changes in education provide a foundation for the Renaissance?

3. (a) What do the works of Boccaccio, Rabelais, and Cervantes have in common? (b) Compare the ideas of Erasmus, More, and Montaigne. (c) Summarize Renaissance literature by describing five subjects that concerned Renaissance writers. Also, list five literary forms through which they expressed their ideas.

4. (a) Describe the human qualities most admired during the Renaissance. (b) How did Michelangelo and Leonardo da Vinci embody these qualities?

5. (a) How was support for art different in the Renaissance than in the medieval period? (b) List four characteristics of Renaissance art. For each characteristic, name two artists whose work displayed that characteristic.

6. (a) Explain how Renaissance ideas differed from those of the Middle Ages. (b) How did the Reformation bring about a break with medieval ways?

7. (a) What was Martin Luther's intention when he wrote the Ninety-Five Theses? (b) What was Luther's basic religious belief? (c) Describe four ways in which the Lutheran Church differed from the Roman Catholic Church.

8. (a) Explain how the Reformation encouraged political revolt among both peasants and princes in Germany. (b) Compare the settlement of religious conflict in Germany, Switzerland, France, and England.

9. (a) How did the Reformation affect the position and role of women? (b) Compare this view of women with the Renaissance ideal.

10. (a) How were Christian humanism and the Protestant Reformation related? (b) Explain the difference between the Catholic and Protestant reformations.

THINKING CRITICALLY: ACTIVITIES

1. Write a paragraph from the point of view of Machiavelli on the following question: What responsibility does a government have to its people? Then, write a response from the point of view of Sir Thomas More.

2. Study three works of Renaissance art illustrating this chapter. For each work, write a short paragraph describing how the specific characteristics of the art represent Renaissance attitudes and ideas.

3. Pretend you are a printer working in the 1500s. Design a title page for one literary work mentioned in this chapter. Include the title, a brief description of the work, the place where the work was published, and a date of publication, if known. The title page might also contain a symbol, design, or illustration in keeping with the main ideas of the work.

APPLYING SOCIAL STUDIES SKILLS

Taking notes. The most familiar form used for taking notes is the outline. Copy the following outline for the beginning of section 15-2, which starts on page 334. Fill in the information called for in parentheses and add two supporting details for Dürer and Holbein. Complete your work by outlining the remainder of the section.

15-2 Spread of Renaissance Ideas
  I. Renaissance ideas moved across Europe
     A. (types of people who spread ideas)
     B. Gutenberg
        1. developed movable type
        2. printed Bible in 1456
        3. (importance of printed books)
  II. The Northern Renaissance
     A. Germany and the Low Countries
        1. Erasmus
           a. stressed reason, tolerance, ethics
           b. wrote *The Praise of Folly*
        2. Dürer
        3. Holbein

APPLYING THINKING SKILLS

Asking effective questions. Below is an excerpt from Niccolò Machiavelli's *The Prince*, written in 1513. Invent effective questions to help you understand Machiavelli's view of what enables a prince to govern. Then answer the questions that follow the excerpt.

To be a prince, it is necessary to know thoroughly the nature of the people. The populace should know the nature of princes. He who becomes prince by help of the nobility has greater difficulty in maintaining his power than he who is raised by the populace. For he is surrounded by those who think of themselves as his equals and he is thus unable to direct or command them as he pleases. But one who is raised to leadership by popular favor finds himself alone, and has no one, or very few, who are not ready to obey him.

It is very easy to satisfy the mass of the people. For, while the nobility desire to oppress, the people seek merely to avoid oppression. A wise prince will seek to have his subjects have need of his government so they will always be faithful.

It is much safer to be feared than loved. Men, in general, are ungrateful, anxious to avoid danger, and desirous of gain. As long as you benefit them, they are entirely yours. Love is held by a chain of obligation that is broken whenever it serves one's purpose to do so.

For men love at their own free will but fear at the will of the prince. A wise prince must rely on what is in his power and not what is in the power of others.

Abridged from *The Prince*, by Niccolò Machiavelli.

1. What are the characteristics of an effective question?

2. What is a useful procedure for inventing effective questions?

3. Why should you ask effective questions?

4. What is the purpose for inventing questions about the excerpt from *The Prince*?

5. What are two effective questions about the excerpt from *The Prince*? Explain.

6. Based on your answers to your questions, state Machiavelli's view regarding what enables a prince to govern.

CHAPTER SIXTEEN

EUROPE'S NEW HORIZONS

1400–1750

Allegory on the Art of Painting. Jan Vermeer, c. 1670.

From 1400 to about 1750, Europeans engaged in a series of daring sea voyages that changed the history of the world. Others had traveled great distances by sea. About a thousand years earlier, Polynesians migrated throughout the Pacific, sailing in large canoes. The Vikings are believed to have sailed from Europe to North America about A.D. 1000.

However, these earlier voyages did not establish permanent links among peoples. In just two and a half centuries, bold European seafarers, backed by governments and trading companies, transformed unknown seas into highways of commerce and conquest, and established a worldwide network of trade. People all over the globe began to feel the influence of European civilization.

TIMELINE

1400	
1420	School of navigation
1440	founded by Prince Henry
1480	Dias's voyage — Treaty of — Columbus's first voyage — Da Gama's
1500	Tordesillas — voyage — Balboa reaches
1520	Cabral's voyage — the Pacific
1540	Magellan's — Cortés conquers Mexico
1560	voyage — Portuguese — Pizarro conquers Peru
1580	reach Japan — Drake's voyage
1600	Dutch East India Co. founded — Hudson's — English East India Co. founded
1620	Jamestown — expedition — Quebec
1640	Plymouth — New Netherland
1660	
1680	
1700	La Salle's expedition

16-1
THE SEARCH FOR OCEAN PASSAGES

READ TO FIND OUT

—why Europeans in the 1400s embarked on voyages of exploration.
—why the age of exploration began with the Portuguese.
—how Europeans reacted at first to the discovery of a New World.

In 1400, Europe was just recovering from a century of famine, plague, unrest, and warfare. The wealth of European rulers did not match that of Indian rulers or the Chinese emperor. Europeans exhibited far less skill in sailing long distances than the Arabs or Chinese. Yet, as the century progressed, European ships began to sail further and further into the unknown, opening an age of European overseas expansion.

THE ROOTS OF EXPANSION

Europeans embarked on voyages of exploration for a variety of reasons. One reason was curiosity. The Renaissance had inspired a thirst for knowledge about the world. Religious fervor was another reason for European interest in foreign lands. The religious enthusiasm generated by the Crusades was still strong in the 1400s. This missionary spirit stimulated the desire to convert nonbelievers to Christianity, and the Reformation reinforced this spirit.

Perhaps the most compelling reason for overseas ventures, though, was the desire of Europeans to improve their economy. Europeans had been buying Asian goods since the time of the Crusades. However, these imports reached Europe by way of a long chain of Indian, Chinese, Arab, and Italian merchants. Each time the goods changed hands, the price of the merchandise rose. If European merchants outside Italy could trade directly with Asian countries, they could buy Asian goods at prices lower than

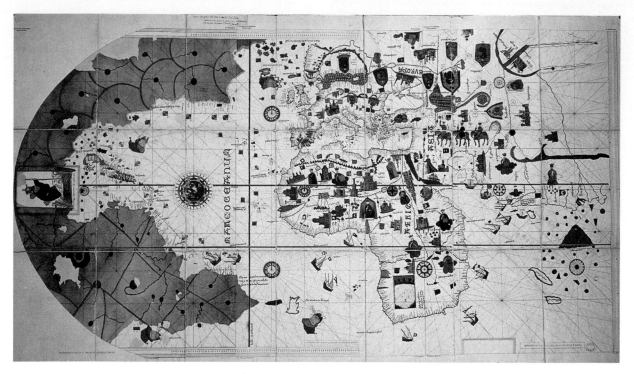

This map shows Columbus's first discoveries in the Caribbean. The original was made on oxhide by ship pilot Juan de la Cosa, who drew Asia and America as one continent, left.

those the Italians charged. Furthermore, Europeans had exhausted their deposits of precious metals for coins and needed to find new sources. To carry out trade with Asia, they needed to find a water passage to Asia that would bypass the Mediterranean.

Interest in finding other routes to the East increased after 1453. In that year, the Ottoman Turks overthrew the Byzantine Empire and threatened to cut off the east–west trade that passed through Constantinople.

Improvements in navigation. Several technological advances enabled Europeans to undertake the search for sea routes. Europeans had learned some of these improvements from Arab sailors, who may have learned them from the Chinese. One improvement was the triangular sail, which can be turned easily, thus making it possible to sail both with and against the wind. Earlier ships using rectangular sails could sail only in the direction the wind blew. Another new device, the sternpost rudder, made steering a ship easier. A third major improvement was the magnetic compass, which allowed navigators to gauge direction even in poor weather. Before the magnetic compass, sailors had to be

able to see the sun or the stars to determine their position. In addition, new shipbuilding techniques allowed Europeans to develop larger, roomier vessels capable of carrying more cargo, as well as heavier cannon.

THE EARLY VOYAGES

The search for an all-water passage to Asia began in Portugal, inspired by Prince Henry, often called Henry the Navigator. A deeply religious man, Prince Henry wanted to convert the peoples of distant lands to the Christian faith. He was also interested in promoting commerce. Prince Henry believed that ships could reach Asia by sailing south and east around Africa, giving Portugal direct access to the profitable Asian trade, as well as a share of the African trade then controlled by Muslims. To achieve his aims, in 1416 Prince Henry established a school of navigation. There he brought together some of the ablest sailors, astronomers, geographers, and shipbuilders of his day, including many Arabs, Italians, and Jews.

The knowledge of earlier sailors, such as the ancient Phoenicians, had been lost to Europeans. Overcoming this lack of knowledge, however, as well as their fear of the unknown, a series of Portuguese explorers worked their way south along the African coast, establishing trading posts as they went. Gradually, they opened up a thriving trade in gold, ivory, pepper, and slaves. Finally, in 1488, 28 years after Prince Henry's death, Bartholomeu Dias rounded the Cape of Good Hope at the southern tip of Africa, confirming Henry's idea of a sea route to India.

The voyage of Columbus. Meanwhile, Christopher Columbus, a young navigator from Genoa, Italy, believed that the shortest route to Asia lay westward across the Atlantic Ocean. When Columbus took his plans for a westward voyage to the Portuguese monarch, however, he was turned down. Disappointed, Columbus appealed to Portugal's old rival, Spain, and the Spanish rulers, King Ferdinand and Queen Isabella, eventually agreed to finance his venture across unknown waters.

On a summer day in 1492, Columbus set sail from Spain into the uncharted seas with three small ships. After more than a month at sea, crew members sighted land—one of the Bahama islands in the Caribbean. In honor of Christ, Columbus named the land San Salvador, which is Spanish for "holy savior." A recent study of Columbus's voyage places the landfall on the island known today as Samana Cay (suh-MAHN-uh KEE). Convinced that he had reached islands off the coast of India, Columbus called the natives "Indians." After three more Atlantic crossings, Columbus died in 1506, still believing that he had reached Asia.

The Treaty of Tordesillas. In the 1400s, Europeans assumed that Christian nations had a right to control any territory inhabited by non-Christians. After Columbus's first sea voyage, the Spanish government asked the pope to give Spain exclusive rights to all lands in the area where Columbus had landed. To protect its

ECHOES OF THE PAST

REPORT BY COLUMBUS: HIS FIRST VOYAGE

. . . I write you this letter, whereby you will learn how in thirty-three days' time I reached the Indies . . . I took possession [of the islands] without resistance for their Highnesses by proclamation made and with royal standard unfurled. . . . When I reached *Juana* [the fifth island], I thought it must be the mainland—the province of Cathay . . . [but] learned from some Indians that this land was an island. . . .

[On *Española*] there are lofty mountains . . . covered with trees of a thousand kinds of such great height that they seemed to reach the skies. Some were in bloom, others bearing fruit. . . . The nightingale was singing . . . and that, in November. . . . *Española* is a wonder. Its mountains and plains, and meadows, and fields are so beautiful and rich for planting and sowing, and rearing cattle of all kinds, and for building towns. The size of the rivers, most of them bearing gold, surpasses anything that would be believed by one who has not seen them. . . .

. . . The inhabitants have neither iron, nor steel, nor arms, nor are they competent to use them, not that they are not well-formed and of handsome stature, but because they are timid to a surprising degree. . . . They never refuse anything that they possess when it is asked of them; on the contrary, they offer it themselves . . . and they are firmly convinced that I came from heaven. . . .

. . . Finally, and speaking only of what has taken place in this voyage, . . . their Highnesses may see that I shall give them all the gold they require. . . . I think also I have found rhubarb and cinnamon, and I shall find a thousand other valuable things. . . . Much more I would have done if my vessels had been in as good a condition as by rights they ought to have been. . . . Our Redeemer hath granted this victory to our illustrious King and Queen, which have acquired great fame by an event of such high importance. . . .

Done on board the caravel, off the Canary Islands, on the fifteenth of February, fourteen hundred and ninety-three.

The Admiral

For questions on Echoes of the Past, see "Analyzing Primary Sources" on page 423.

African trade, Portugal had already asked for rights to lands south and west of the Atlantic Ocean.

After some heated negotiations, Spain and Portugal signed the Treaty of Tordesillas (TOR-day-SEE-yahs) in 1494. With the pope's approval they agreed to divide the southern portion of the world between them. Furthermore, the two nations finally agreed that the demarcation line should be about 1,000 miles (1,600 kilometers) west of the Azores, an island group in the Atlantic. Although they did not yet know what lands lay in each hemisphere, Portugal gained rights to lands lying southeast of the line while Spain obtained rights to lands lying toward the southwest.

In 1529, the two rival nations agreed to extend the line of demarcation around the globe into the Eastern Hemisphere. This new agreement gave Portugal the Molucca Islands in present-day Indonesia and most of the Philippine Islands. However, since the Portuguese never colonized the Philippines, Spain eventually claimed them.

While Spain looked westward, Portugal continued to seek a route to the east. Finally, in 1498, Vasco da Gama rounded the Cape of Good Hope and continued eastward across the Indian Ocean to India. He returned to Portugal with goods valued at 60 times the cost of his expedition. Da Gama's voyage, even longer and more dangerous than Columbus's bold journey, showed that Europeans no longer needed to rely on Muslim or Italian merchants.

The voyage of Cabot. Meanwhile, another Italian navigator, Giovanni Caboto (jo-VAHN-ee kah-BŌ-tō), known also as John Cabot, believed, like Columbus, that Asia could be reached by sailing westward. He convinced the English monarch, King Henry VII, to finance a westward voyage. In 1497, Cabot explored the coast of present-day Newfoundland, Nova Scotia, and New England, believing that he had reached Asia. Cabot's voyage later gave England a basis for claiming land in America.

THE NEW WORLD

Soon after Cabot's voyage, Europeans began to doubt that they had reached Asia. In 1499, a Florentine banker named Amerigo Vespucci (AH-meh-REE-gō veh-SPOO-chee) crossed

A Venetian nobleman who accompanied Magellan on his journey kept a journal of the global voyage. In this detailed drawing, Magellan appears in the red coat.

the Atlantic, sailing under the Portuguese flag. Vespucci was one of the first to realize that Columbus had discovered a continent unknown to Europeans, which "it is proper to call 'a new world.'" Mapmakers soon began to label the Western Hemisphere *America*, the Latin form of Vespucci's first name.

Portuguese claims to lands in the New World, however, were based on an expedition led by Pedro Cabral (kuh-BRAWL) in 1500. With a fleet of 13 ships, Cabral set off to follow da Gama's route around Africa. Whether winds blew his fleet far off course or whether he deliberately sailed west to explore lands near the line of demarcation is not known. Nevertheless, when members of his party sighted land, Cabral claimed the coast of present-day Brazil for Portugal and immediately sent one ship back to Portugal with the news.

Discovery of a western passage. In the early 1500s, numerous other adventurers explored the eastern coastline of the Americas, still seeking a route to Asia. Hopes were raised in 1513, when the Spanish adventurer Vasco Núñez de Balboa (VAHS-ko NOO-nyez duh bal-BO-uh) crossed the Isthmus (IHS-muhs) of Panama—the narrow strip of land linking North and South America—and sighted the Pacific Ocean. However, the way to Asia did not lie through Panama.

THE VOYAGE OF MAGELLAN

In September of 1519, Ferdinand Magellan set sail from Spain with a fleet of five worn vessels to seek a westward passage from Europe to Asia. Soon after reaching South America, one ship was lost in a storm. Further trouble arose when his Spanish officers mutinied, discontented with having a Portuguese commander. However, Magellan was able to put down the mutiny. He ordered that two of its leaders be executed and two be left behind on the bleak South American shore.

In October 1520, the expedition found a waterway from the Atlantic to the western ocean, a narrow strait, 350 miles (560 kilometers) long, separating a group of wind-swept islands from the tip of South America. Before the expedition entered the strait, one ship deserted and returned to Spain. It took more than a month for the other ships to navigate this stormy, rock-strewn passage, but Magellan's superb skills in navigation got them through.

On entering the western ocean, Magellan fell to his knees and wept joyful tears. Giving thanks to God for their deliverance, Magellan called this sea *Pacific,* which means "peaceful." Magellan could not have known the vastness of the Pacific. He expected to reach Asian lands in a matter of days. However, the expedition sailed on for three months without sighting land. One sailor described the hardships:

> The biscuit we were eating no longer deserved the name of bread; it was nothing but dust and worm. The water we were obliged to drink was putrid and offensive. We were even so far reduced to eat pieces of leather, sawdust, and even mice that sold for half a ducat [a coin] apiece.

Magellan drove the sailors on, forbidding them to speak any pessimistic words on pain of death. Finally, they made landfall on the island of Guam in March 1521 and replenished their supplies. A short time later, they arrived in the Philippines, where they were welcomed. Magellan made friends with one group of people there. He took their side in a local dispute and was killed in a skirmish.

Of the three remaining ships, one was abandoned because there were too few sailors left to sail it, and another was captured by the Portuguese. When the lone ship, the *Victoria,* returned to Spain, only 18 of the 280 sailors who began the voyage were on board.

Credit for finding a western sea route to Asia belongs to a Portuguese navigator named Ferdinand Magellan. Experienced in sailing the India and China seas, Magellan had long dreamed of sailing around the globe. When he presented his plan to the king of Portugal, however, he was rebuffed. Magellan then turned to the Spanish monarch, who quickly agreed to sponsor his voyage.

Magellan left Spain in 1519 with five ships. Crossing the Atlantic, the expedition eventually threaded its way through the straits at the southern tip of South America that now bear Magellan's name. After a difficult three-year journey, only one of the five ships returned, having circled the world by sea. This first circumnavigation of the globe was the crowning achievement of the sea journeys westward.

SECTION REVIEW

1. Explain three reasons why fifteenth-century Europeans set out to explore the seas.

2. How did Portugal come to lead other European nations in overseas exploration?

3. When Europeans realized that Columbus had reached lands formerly unknown to them, what did they seek in those lands at first?

Application. The Renaissance, the Reformation, and the voyages of discovery mark the end of the Middle Ages and the beginning of Early Modern times. How did Prince Henry, Christopher Columbus, and Ferdinand Magellan each display the spirit of the Renaissance? The Reformation? How did each contribute to a modern outlook?

16–2
OVERSEAS EMPIRES OF PORTUGAL AND SPAIN

READ TO FIND OUT

—what the terms *conquistadors, viceroy, creoles, mestizos*, and *mulattoes* mean.
—where the Portuguese established an overseas empire.
—how Spain ruled its New World lands.
—how a unique civilization developed in the New World.

Being the first to find sea routes to Africa and Asia, the Portuguese carefully guarded this knowledge and worked to keep other European nations out of the African and Asian trade. Portugal remained the strongest sea power on the Indian Ocean for most of the 1500s.

ESTABLISHING THE PORTUGUESE EMPIRE

To promote both commerce and Christianity, the Portuguese established a chain of 50 or more forts, trading posts, and small colonies from East Africa to Japan. Obtained by both diplomacy and conquest, few of these posts were larger than a small city. These Portuguese bases included Goa on the west coast of India and Malacca in the Malay Peninsula.

When the Portuguese established a trading post on the small Chinese peninsula of Macao (muh-COW) in 1513, the Chinese at first tried to drive them out. Since the early 1400s, Chinese laws had strictly limited contact with the outside world. In addition, the Chinese tended to look upon all foreigners as crude and uncivilized. However, the Portuguese eventually were able to establish trade with China through the port of Canton (can-TAHN).

From Macao, the Portuguese sailed on to become, in 1543, the first Europeans to reach Japan. Arriving six years after the traders, Francis

Xavier (ZAV-yer), a Spanish Jesuit missionary, introduced Christianity into Japan. However, by the early 1600s, Japan's rulers began to fear that European armies would follow the traders and missionaries. Thus, in 1614, the Japanese ordered all Christian priests to leave Japan and by the 1640s, Japan forbade foreign ships to enter its ports.

When a Portuguese expedition attempted to reopen trade with Japan in 1640, a Japanese military force killed almost the entire party. The few Portuguese who were spared were sent back to Europe to bear witness to Japan's resolve to remain free of foreign influence.

Portugal in the New World. Occupied with its posts in Africa and Asia, Portugal at first paid little attention to Brazil. When other European nations threatened Portuguese claims, however, the Portuguese decided to strengthen their hold by settling Brazil. The Portuguese established settlements along the coast beginning in 1530, introducing European cattle, grains, and fruits to the region. Because Brazil proved to be ideal for growing sugar cane, a sugar industry flourished and became Brazil's major source of wealth.

After 1629, Portuguese raiding parties began to penetrate Brazil's back country, rounding up numbers of Tupi (too-PEE), Guarani (GWAH-rah-NEE), and other Indians to labor on the sugar plantations. In their search for slave labor, raiding parties explored the interior of Brazil, thereby giving Portugal a claim to land west of the demarcation line. Toward the end of the 1600s, one of the raiding parties discovered gold. As a result, many Portuguese settlers streamed into Brazil's interior.

A small nation with limited resources, Portugal lacked the people and ships needed to expand the empire further. By the early 1600s, Portugal had lost to other European nations its place as the world's leading sea power. However, Portugal held much of its overseas empire down to the twentieth century.

THE SPANISH EMPIRE

Like the Portuguese, the Spanish carved out an empire in the New World. From settlements on Caribbean islands and the coast of Panama, the Spanish sent exploring parties into Central and South America. Leading the way were a few

REGIONS: FOUR REGIONS OF SOUTH AMERICA

This land is full of an infinity of trees, very green and very tall, and they yield a great many fruits. The fields bear abundant grass and flowers and very soft, good roots, so that at times the sweet scent of the grass and flowers and the taste of those fruits and roots is so wondrous that I could think myself close to paradise on earth.

With these words the Italian explorer Amerigo Vespucci began one of the first geographic descriptions of South America. Vespucci was describing the tropical rainforest of Brazil. The astonishing variety of birds and animals he saw there would, he wrote, "be able to enter Noah's Ark only with difficulty."

The early explorers of South America found a land of bewildering variety—vast tropical rainforests, broad plains, barren deserts, and towering peaks. Everywhere, they saw unfamiliar plants and animals, and a human landscape that seemed to be a jumble of cultures.

To make a large and varied area like South America easier to describe and study, people often divide the area into regions. A region is an area that displays homogeneity, or sameness, in terms of one or more characteristics. Regions can be defined according to physical characteristics such as climate or vegetation, and human characteristics such as languages spoken.

Using both kinds of characteristics, people often divide South America into four major regions. The first region is called Caribbean South America and includes Colombia, Venezuela, Guyana, French Guiana, and Surinam, former Dutch Guyana. Located on or near the equator, these nations share a hot, humid climate. They were colonized by Europeans who built plantations in the tropical lowlands along the Caribbean coast. The planters imported workers from Africa, India, and Indonesia, giving these nations racially mixed populations.

Peru, Ecuador, Bolivia, and Paraguay make up a second region known as the Andean West. While the low coastal areas have tropical climates, the mountains and inland plateaus are cooler. This region has the largest Indian population, ranging from about 50 percent in Peru, Bolivia, and Ecuador to more than 90 percent in Paraguay.

Chile, Argentina, and Uruguay make up a third region—Mid-Latitude South America. Because of their distance from the equator, these nations are cooler and drier than their northern neighbors. Millions of European immigrants have settled here, making this the most Europeanized South American region.

The fourth region, Brazil, contains nearly half of South America's land and people. Most of Brazil is highland bordered by the Amazon Basin in the north and the Rio de la Plata Basin in the south. Though a melting pot of Indians, Africans, and Europeans, Brazil has the largest African population in South America.

South America—or any continent—can also be divided into regions according to other characteristics, such as land forms and religions. Which characteristics people select to define a region will be determined by what they want to learn about a particular area.

1. What is a geographic region?

2. Name the physical and human characteristics commonly used to define four South American regions.

REGIONS OF SOUTH AMERICA

daring Spanish *conquistadors* (kahn-KEES-tuh-DORZ)—part discoverer, part adventurer, and part conqueror—who sought riches such as precious woods, pearls, and gold, as well as a route to the Pacific Ocean. These conquistadors claimed thousands of square miles for Spain.

The conquest of Mexico. The conquistadors' weapons, as well as their courage and ruthlessness, helped them to conquer the Aztecs in Mexico. In 1519, Hernan Cortés invaded Mexico with about 700 soldiers and 16 horses. After landing, Cortés ordered his crew to burn the fleet in order to show them that they must either conquer or die. On the march inland, Cortés made alliances with Indians who regarded the Aztecs as their enemies.

When the Spanish reached the central valley of Mexico, they saw a city of stone towers and temples rising from a glistening lake. The city was Tenochtitlán, the center of Aztec civiliza-

This illustration from a Spanish manuscript, dated about 1540, shows Mexican Indians escaping from conquistadors. The Indians are fleeing on foot and by boat with their possessions.

tion. According to Aztec legend, a bearded, fair-skinned god, Quetzalcoatl, had promised to return from the sunrise to Tenochtitlán. Moctezuma (MOK-tuh-ZOO-mah), the Aztec ruler believed that Cortés might be Quetzalcoatl and showered him with gifts of gold.

The Spanish, however, made Moctezuma their prisoner. He was killed in the bloody war that soon raged. By the time the Spanish defeated the Aztecs and reduced Tenochtitlán to rubble in 1521, more than 100,000 Aztecs had died from warfare and starvation. Engulfed by an epidemic of smallpox, a disease new to the Americas, thousands more Indians died.

A Spanish city, Mexico City, rose on the site of Tenochtitlán. This new city became the center of Spain's North American empire, called New Spain. From Mexico City new expeditions continued the search for riches and an all-water route to the Pacific.

The conquest of Peru. While Cortés was in Mexico, Francisco Pizarro, who had earlier crossed Panama with Balboa, set out from Panama to explore further south. In 1531, high in the Andes, he and his small army captured a city that proved to be part of the Inca empire and also Atahualpa (AH-tuh-WAHL-puh), the Inca ruler. Though Atahualpa gave Pizarro a treasure that made him and his army fabulously wealthy, Pizarro ordered that the emperor be executed.

Marching farther south, Pizarro captured the Inca capital of Cuzco (KOOS-kō) in 1533. The Inca empire fell, although angry Incas rebelled against Spanish rule for many more years. Meanwhile, in 1535, Pizarro established the city of Lima (LEE-muh) on the coast. Lima became a base for further Spanish explorations in South America.

North of Mexico. Many other European explorers helped to establish Spain's claims north of Mexico. In 1513, Juan Ponce de León (hwahn PAHNS duh lee-ON) explored a fertile land he named Florida. In 1527, Alvar Núñez Cabeza de Vaca (AHL-vahr NOO-nyez kah-BEH-zah duh VAH-kah) was shipwrecked along the coast of present-day Texas with several others including a black adventurer named Esteban. They trekked for eight years across the arid southwestern part of present-day United States before reaching Mexico City.

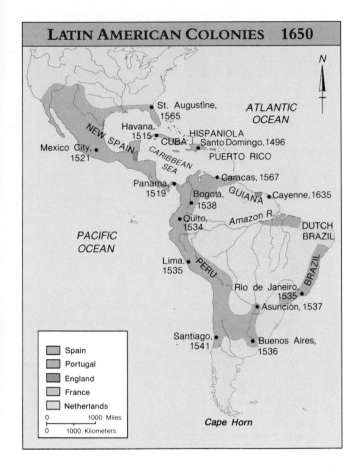

LATIN AMERICAN COLONIES 1650

ATLANTIC OCEAN

St. Augustine, 1565

NEW SPAIN

Havana, 1515
HISPANIOLA
CUBA
Santo Domingo, 1496
PUERTO RICO

Mexico City, 1521

CARIBBEAN SEA

Caracas, 1567

Panama, 1519

Bogota, 1538
GUIANA
Cayenne, 1635

Quito, 1534
Amazon R.

PACIFIC OCEAN

DUTCH BRAZIL

Lima, 1535
PERU
BRAZIL

Rio de Janeiro, 1535
Asunción, 1537

Santiago, 1541
Buenos Aires, 1536

Spain
Portugal
England
France
Netherlands

0   1000 Miles
0   1000 Kilometers

Cape Horn

Filled with stories of Cabeza de Vaca's trek, Hernando de Soto set out from Cuba to explore throughout the southeastern region of what is today the United States. In 1540, an expedition led by Francisco Vásquez de Coronado (VAS-kez duh KOR-uh-NAH-dō) attempted to find fabled cities of gold in the region where Cabeza de Vaca's party had traveled.

By 1600, Spain's empire included much of the West Indies, Central America, and South America, as well as the southern part of North America. These lands proved to contain great mineral and agricultural wealth. Products such as gold, silver, pearls, hides, and chocolate began to pour into Spain in amounts undreamed of before.

SPANISH SETTLEMENT IN THE AMERICAS

Prompted by hopes of sharing in the newfound wealth, Spanish settlers soon followed the explorers into the Americas. Spanish settlement began in the West Indies on the islands of Hispaniola (HIS-puhn-YO-luh), Cuba, and Puerto

Rico, and on the mainland in Panama in the early 1500s. The Spanish settlers brought their traditions and their language to the New World. Cities rose, dominated by European-style palaces and cathedrals. City homes had open patios and tiled roofs like houses in Spain. Nearby lay Spanish-style farms.

Colonial government. To govern Spain's settlements in the Americas, the Spanish ruler divided the land into four regions called viceroyalties. A *viceroy*, or governor, who represented the Spanish monarch, presided over each region. Under each viceroy were lesser officials, some appointed by the viceroy, others by the monarch. The Spanish ruler also appointed all Catholic bishops for Spanish America.

The role of the Church. The royal governments of both Spain and Portugal maintained close ties with the Catholic Church, ties that were carried to the Americas. Because the Church in Spanish America was under the direct control of the king, the spread of Christianity was one means of extending royal authority in the New World. In some areas the Church was the only authority, and priests served as royal officials.

The Church attempted to carry out Spain's official policy toward Native Americans—the people Columbus had called Indians. This policy was to convert them to Christianity and protect them from abuse. Church officials, as well as priests and monks, loudly criticized the treatment of Indians by their fellow Spaniards or Portuguese. As early as 1511 a Catholic priest in the West Indies, Antonio de Montesinos (duh MON-tuh-SEE-nos) preached: "Tell me, by what right or justice do you keep these Indians in such cruel and horrible servitude?" Other church figures echoed his voice.

Franciscans, Dominicans, and Jesuits organized mission villages, where they taught Christianity to the Indians while protecting them from slave raiders. The missionaries trained the Indians in agriculture and crafts, and taught many of them to read. However, although mission Indians gained an education, they lost their independence.

Native Americans. As Europeans transplanted their culture to the Americas, the traditional ways of life of the natives were threatened. The newcomers introduced diseases new to the Americas, such as smallpox, measles, typhus, and the common cold, against which the natives had no immunity. Epidemics caused the Indian population to fall from between 35 and 40 million to just 4 million by 1650.

The economic demands of the Spanish further destroyed Indian ways. Before the arrival of the Europeans, commoners in many Indian cultures paid tribute to their rulers in goods and labor. In return, the commoners received grants of farmland. Tradition regulated the obligations of both commoners and rulers.

With colonization, the Europeans easily became the new tribute collectors. Royal officials collected produce, livestock, manufactured goods, and silver as tribute from the Indians. However, because the Spaniards offered the Indians little in return, the tribute payments became a terrible burden.

The *encomienda* (en-KO-mee-EN-dah) system also disrupted Indian life. Under this system, the Spanish monarch entrusted a few wealthy and powerful Spaniards each with a number of Indians. The *encomendero* (en-KO-men-DER-o), or holder of this grant, expected the Indians to labor a certain number of days in fields or mines. In return, the encomendero would protect and Christianize the Indians.

The development of the *hacienda* system also disrupted Indian life. The growth of cities and large mining centers created a need for a steady food supply. To encourage food production, the Spanish crown began to distribute large estates, or haciendas, much like the European manors worked by landless peasants. At first, Indians were compelled to leave their traditional villages to work on the haciendas.

Eventually, the government allowed hacienda owners to attract more workers by advancing wages before the work was done. One result was that the Indian workers were in constant debt to the owners and therefore were bound to keep working on the haciendas. In addition, the Indians had to keep laboring on the haciendas to earn money for tribute payments.

BLACK SLAVERY

As the death rate among Indians soared, both the Portuguese and the Spanish imported black Africans as slaves. These unwilling colonists worked on sugar, rice, and cotton plantations.

The greatest number were imported into Brazil to work on the sugar plantations there.

The Spanish and Portuguese were not the only Europeans to bring African slaves to the New World. The English, French, Dutch, and Italians all took part in the profitable slave trade. Before the slave trade was ended in the 1800s, more than 10 million blacks had been shipped to the Americas.

A NEW BLEND OF PEOPLES

The culture of the Spaniards and the Portuguese—their forms of government, economic practices, and social patterns—took root in the New World. Spanish and Portuguese became the dominant languages. Because both languages are derived from Latin, the Americas from Mexico southward became known as Latin America.

The earliest known oil painting from Latin America is this portrait from Ecuador. The Spanish clothing and Indian-style gold ornaments exemplify the blending of cultures in the New World.

At first, distinct social classes divided society in Latin America. European-born nobles selected by the Spanish or Portuguese monarch to serve as officials in the New World ranked above everyone else there. These aristocrats usually returned to Europe after completing their service.

Other European-born settlers also ranked high on the social scale. People born in the colonies of European parents, *creoles* (KREE-ōlz), had a lower status than their parents. People tended to feel that anyone not born in Spain or Portugal was not a true Spaniard or Portuguese. However, many creoles gained great wealth and influence.

The offspring of Spanish or Portuguese and Native American marriages, called *mestizos* (mes-TEE-zōz), ranked below creoles on the social scale. *Mulattoes* (muh-LAT-ōz), born of marriages between Europeans and blacks, had less status than mestizos. Indians and black slaves were at the bottom of the social pyramid.

A new culture. Over time, a distinctive Latin American civilization began to emerge, characterized by its blending of peoples and their cultures. For example, the Christianity practiced in Latin America combined Indian customs with Catholic traditions. Catholic churches were often built on the sites of ruined Aztec, Mayan, or Inca temples, and Native Americans often performed their traditional ritual dances for Christian festivals. Furthermore, where Spanish or Portuguese was spoken, Indian and African words began to enter the language. In some places, people spoke both European languages and Indian dialects fluently.

Although the literature written in colonial Latin America followed Spanish styles and themes, in painting and sculpture Spanish and Indian styles began to blend. In music, Spanish sounds merged with Indian and African rhythms and sounds to create an entirely new style.

The population itself, although dominated by a European upper class, was mostly non-European. In many regions the population became an intermingling of peoples—white, Indian, and black. Although European colonization of the Americas destroyed the Indian civilizations there, these peoples—Europeans, Indians, and Africans—created a distinctively new culture.

SECTION REVIEW

1. Define *conquistadors, viceroy, creoles, mestizos,* and *mulattoes*.

2. Briefly describe Portugal's chain of trading posts and forts. In what ways did they differ from Spain's new territories?

3. How were Spain's New World territories governed? What role did the Church play in the new lands?

4. What is the chief characteristic of Latin American culture? Give three examples of how New World culture differed from that of Europe.

Synthesis. What qualities of character would the leader of a voyage of exploration in the 1500s and 1600s probably possess? Explain why you selected particular qualities.

16-3
OVERSEAS EMPIRES OF ENGLAND, FRANCE, AND THE NETHERLANDS

READ TO FIND OUT

—what the term *monopoly* means.
—why the English established colonies in America.
—why France claimed the heartland of North America.
—how the Dutch built a great trading empire.

During the 1500s, Portugal and Spain took the lead in world exploration and colonization. In the following century, however, England, France, and the Netherlands—the Dutch-speaking northern region of the Low Countries—entered the race for overseas trade and colonies. The competition for new territory was not completely peaceful. Armed force was often required to establish trading posts and protect them from rivals. Acts of piracy and skirmishes between ships occurred. Such rivalry over trade eventually led nations to war.

ENGLAND'S CLAIMS OVERSEAS

During much of the 1400s and 1500s, civil war and religious strife troubled England. By the late 1500s, when English merchants became interested in obtaining the spices of the Indies for themselves, they found the way blocked by the Spanish and the Portuguese.

The English challenged Spanish and Portuguese domination of the seas. With the approval of Queen Elizabeth I, adventurous sea captains raided Spanish and Portuguese treasure ships returning from the New World and Asia. The English called these raiders "sea dogs"; others called them pirates.

In 1577, one sea dog, Francis Drake, sailed from England, seeking a route to the Pacific. Along the way he raided Spanish ships and coastal settlements in the Americas. Drake rounded the tip of South America and sailed north. Wary of Spanish retaliation, he then sailed his treasure-laden ship home by way of the Pacific and Indian oceans rather than across the Atlantic. His three-year journey was the second voyage around the globe.

England's colonies in North America. Because Spain and Portugal controlled southern shipping lanes—those around Africa and South

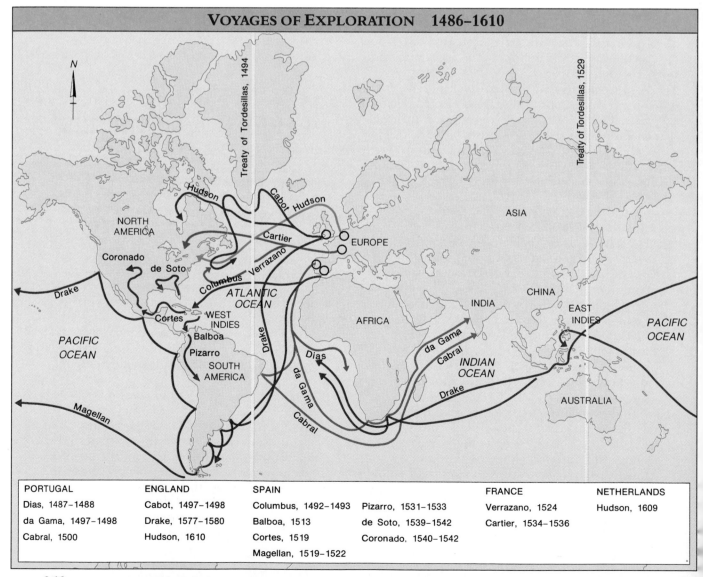

VOYAGES OF EXPLORATION   1486–1610

PORTUGAL	ENGLAND	SPAIN		FRANCE	NETHERLANDS
Dias, 1487–1488	Cabot, 1497–1498	Columbus, 1492–1493	Pizarro, 1531–1533	Verrazano, 1524	Hudson, 1609
da Gama, 1497–1498	Drake, 1577–1580	Balboa, 1513	de Soto, 1539–1542	Cartier, 1534–1536	
Cabral, 1500	Hudson, 1610	Cortes, 1519	Coronado, 1540–1542		
		Magellan, 1519–1522			

The English colony of Maryland, founded in 1632, purchased land for the city of Baltimore in 1729. This 1752 painting of the harbor shows tobacco warehouses and a merchant ship.

America—England began to search for a northern passage to Asia. Martin Frobisher in 1576, John Davis in 1586, and Henry Hudson in 1610 all led English expeditions in search of a northern passage around North America.

A fierce debate arose in England over whether such expeditions should sail northeast around Europe or northwest around or through North America. Sir Humphrey Gilbert, an English scholar and explorer, argued that colonies should be established in North America both as trading posts and as way stations for vessels sailing a northwest passage around North America. According to Gilbert, these colonies could also serve as a home for England's surplus population or for troublemakers. Gilbert's ideas eventually led the British to change their policy from that of raiding to one of colonizing.

Sir Walter Raleigh, Gilbert's half brother, made two attempts to establish colonies on the North American coast, but these early attempts failed. The first band of colonists returned to England, and the second vanished.

In 1607, a trading venture called the London Company successfully established Jamestown in present-day Virginia, the first permanent English settlement in North America. A few years later the Pilgrims, a Protestant group seeking a place to practice their religion without interference, negotiated an agreement with the London Company. In return for passage to the New World, they agreed to work for the company for seven years. However, their ship was blown off course, and they landed in present-day Massachusetts, outside of the London Company's lands. The Pilgrims established an independent colony in 1620.

By 1650, over 80,000 colonists had settled along the eastern coast of North America in 20 separate settlements and by 1700, the population of the English colonies had reached over 300,000, organized in 12 colonies. The thirteenth colony, Georgia, was added in 1733.

In addition, the English established trading stations in the West Indies on Barbados (bar-BAY-dos), the Bahamas, Bermuda, and Jamaica. There, cheap slave labor produced tobacco, coffee, and sugar.

Growth of the colonies. The English found a different situation in North America than the Spanish had in South America. No large native population existed that could be plundered or forced into labor. No gold and silver lay buried in the earth. Enterprising colonists soon turned from futile searches for easy riches to agriculture, commercial fishing, and fur trading. In so doing, they began gradually to push the Native Americans from their land.

At first, when the colonies did not seem to be particularly profitable, the English government paid little attention to them. By the mid-1600s, when it became apparent that the colonies could benefit England's economy, the government began to tighten its control over colonial trade. By then, however, the colonists had become accustomed to managing their own affairs.

Eventually most of the colonies came to be ruled by a governor and a legislative body, appointed either by the English monarch or the private owner to whom the monarch had granted the colony. Most colonies also had an elected assembly.

Each colony was unique, due in part to its particular geography. Further contributing to this uniqueness was the fact that different colonies were established for different reasons, from religious freedom to economic opportunity. Non-English colonists—including Scotch-Irish, Germans, Dutch, French, Scandinavians, Jews, and Africans brought as slaves—also helped shape the character of North American civilization. Although colonists came from all over Europe and Africa, they were predominately English. The English colonists established their language and their traditions, as well as their ideas about government.

DETECTING BIAS

A bias is a slanted, one-sided view or inclination. Often untested, it is either a preference for or a dislike of something. Many people have biases, which prevent them from making objective or impartial judgments. These people often prefer certain things or dislike other things without thoroughly examining them.

Some biases are relatively harmless. For instance, when given a choice of various types of candy, some people will always choose chocolate without even trying the other varieties of candy. Perhaps the only disadvantage of this bias is that these people will not find out whether they would like other candies.

In contrast, some biases can lead to serious misunderstandings or harmful actions. For example, a bias against a particular nationality can lead a person to ignore or misunderstand the special talents and qualities of individuals from that nation. The term *prejudice* refers to any bias that becomes a firm and unreasonable judgment about someone or something.

EXPLAINING THE SKILL

Any form of communication, such as a written report, a film, or a speech, might reflect a bias. Therefore, you need to be able to distinguish between an author's bias and the facts about the subject.

One way to detect bias in written material is to follow these steps:

1. *Recall the various clues to bias.*

One clue to bias is the repeated use of emotionally charged, or "loaded" words. For example, an author may state that "the servants toiled at the monstrous task imposed on them by their employer." This use of words such as *toiled*, *monstrous*, and *imposed* may indicate a bias against the employer. In contrast, an objective description might simply state that "the employees worked at the task assigned to them by their employer."

Another clue to bias is repeated use of exaggeration, which is frequently evident in the use of words like *every*, *never*, *none*, and *always*. Presenting only one side of an issue is also a clue.

Another clue is the statement of opinions as if they were obvious facts. A fifth clue is the use of "loaded" questions, those that already indicate how the author thinks they should be answered. For example, an author might ask, "Who could possibly doubt that Magellan was the greatest navigator of his time?" Use of devices such as these would indicate that the author might have a bias regarding the subject.

2. *Search the material sentence by sentence for specific examples of clues that may indicate bias.*

3. *Identify any patterns among the clues found.*

This process will help you determine whether there is enough evidence of bias. A few isolated clues may not indicate a bias. However, an author's bias may be indicated by repeated use of these clues to describe a topic in a positive or negative way.

4. *State any biases you find and give the evidence of those biases.*

APPLYING THE SKILL

By the mid-1700s, many Europeans had ventured into the tropical regions of Africa, South America, and Asia. Their descriptions of life in the tropics varied. Read Account A and use the procedure and clues just presented to help you determine whether this account presents a biased view of life in the tropics.

Account A

That tropical land is blessed with pleasant scenes of spring-like beauty, a tropical luxuriance, where fruits and flowers lavish their fragrance together in the same bough! There nature animates all life and reigns in vegetable and animal perfection. There nature perpetually glows in wild splendor and uncultivated maturity!

I contemplate the years I passed in that terrestrial Elysium. The simple food, which my solitude afforded, sweetened my rural life. My enjoyment was never broken by those corroding cares and perplexing fears which pride and folly create in the lives of populous communities.

The fertile soil produced all the food people need in abundance. Fish was in great plenty. The flocks and animals were numerous, the trees loaded with fruit. I never wanted for anything. Who but a fool would not be refreshed by such mildness of climate and land, such beauty and such luxury?

Adapted from *The Works of John Fothergill, M.D.*, (London, 1784).

REFLECTING ON THE SKILL

It should have been clear that the author of Account A seems to have a bias regarding life in the tropics. Now that you have examined the account, answer the following questions about evidence of the author's bias:

1. Which one of the following groups of words most likely reveals a bias? **(a)** *spring-like beauty, sweetened, wild splendor;* **(b)** *fruits, fertile soil, flocks and animals;* **(c)** *solitude, populous communities, rural life.* Explain your answer.

2. An example of exaggeration is the use of the words **(a)** *simple food,* **(b)** *perpetually glowing,* **(c)** *pleasant scenes.*

3. An example of an emotionally charged word that gives a positive impression is the word **(a)** *nature,* **(b)** *uncultivated,* **(c)** *sweetened.*

4. One group of emotionally charged words that give the same general impression is **(a)** *refreshed, populous, folly;* **(b)** *lavish, wild splendor, luxuriance;* **(c)** *mildness, perplexing, rural.* Explain your answer.

5. In general, this account **(a)** presents a balanced description of the good and bad aspects of living in the tropics, **(b)** shows a preference for a life of leisure, **(c)** expresses a preference for life in the tropics.

APPLYING THE SKILL

Now read Account B to determine whether it reflects any bias.

Account B

The tropical lands invite and repel. The fertile but often shallow soil produces fruits and spices, foods, and flowers in abundance. One can wander the land finding food aplenty as it is needed. Little need be done to cultivate what grows so naturally.

However, trying to grow indigo or rice or cotton in any quantity is difficult. If luxurious plants grow in abundance, weeds and grasses grow even more abundantly. Therefore, one is obliged to clear the fields continuously in order to allow one's own crops sunlight and space to grow. This work can be hard at times, especially in the heat and humidity. And this work is constant. If one neglects to weed even a week or two, a well-cultivated field becomes overgrown with dense vegetation.

The winds often blow gentle as spring breezes, bringing to all the fragrance of flowers. But they sometimes bring hurricanes, and therefore devastating rainstorms and floods. One cannot let the beautiful aspects of this region blind one to its imperfections.

Account B was written by Barry K. Beyer, one of the authors of this textbook.

CHECKING YOUR UNDERSTANDING

Answer the following questions:

6. Account A is **(a)** more biased than Account B, **(b)** less biased than Account B, **(c)** as biased as Account B.

7. After comparing the two accounts, one can state that **(a)** Account A has more emotionally charged words than Account B, **(b)** Account B contains more exaggeration than Account A, **(c)** Account B does not show both the advantages and disadvantages of living in the tropics.

8. Which of the following is most helpful in identifying bias? **(a)** Finding at least three of the same kinds of words. **(b)** Looking mainly for negative-sounding language. **(c)** Comparing one account with another account of the same topic.

REVIEWING THE SKILL

9. Define the term *bias*.

10. What are some clues to bias in a written source?

11. What is one procedure for detecting bias in a written source?

12. Why is it important to detect bias?

The English in Asia and Africa. The English challenged the Spanish and the Portuguese in Africa and Asia, as well as in the New World. As they had done in North America, the English established themselves in Asia by means of a trading company, the English East India Company, founded in 1600. Although the English East India Company eventually set up trading posts in West Africa and China, India proved to be its richest prize. Defeating a Portuguese fleet off the Indian coast in the early 1600s, the English acquired trading rights in India. Along the coast of India, they established many trading posts including Madras, Bombay, and Calcutta.

In return for trading rights, the English agreed not to acquire Indian territory. In the 1600s, the government of India was strong enough to keep all European traders along the coast. In the 1700s, however, India fell into political turmoil. To maintain their trading privileges, the English became involved in Indian politics.

FRENCH TERRITORIES OVERSEAS

Like England, France was troubled by unrest throughout the 1400s and 1500s. French explorers who did make voyages spent much of their time in a fruitless search for a northwest passage through North America. In 1524, France enlisted an Italian navigator, Giovanni da Verrazano (jō-VAHN-nee dah VER-rah-TSAH-nō), to seek such a passage. Verrazano, the first European to see New York Harbor, established French claims in North America. Ten years later, Jacques Cartier (car-tee-Ā) explored Labrador, Newfoundland, and the Gulf of St. Lawrence and claimed these regions for France.

France's colonies in North America. Not until the early 1600s did France establish permanent colonies in North America. Sieur Pierre du Guast de Monts (syehr pee-EHR doo GAHST duh MAWN), a Huguenot leader, obtained the French government's approval to carry on a fur trade. He asked Samuel de Champlain (sham-PLAYN), a French geographer, to help found a settlement to serve as a trading post and also a refuge for French Huguenots. In 1608, Champlain established Quebec (kwih-BEK), the first French colony in the New World. France's second colony was Mon-

treal, established as a Catholic mission in 1642. In 1663, King Louis XIV made the North American colonies—called New France—a province of France.

A series of explorations expanded French claims into the heartland of North America. In 1682, Sieur Robert Cavelier de La Salle (syehr rō-BER kahv-LYAY duh lah SAL) sailed down the Mississippi River to its mouth and claimed the entire Mississippi Valley for France. He named the territory Louisiana, in honor of Louis XIV. Louisiana became a royal colony, a colony under the king's direct control.

In North America the French traded with the Indians for furs, fish, and tobacco. By 1700, the French maintained trading posts, missions, and forts from Nova Scotia down the St. Lawrence River to the Great Lakes, and down the Mississippi to the Gulf of Mexico. Settlement throughout this vast territory remained sparse. Few French cared to migrate. Those who might have come, the Huguenots, were prohibited from doing so by new government policies excluding non-Catholics from the colonies. By 1700, French colonists in North America numbered only about 10,000.

Even more important to the French economy than their North American empire were their colonies in the Caribbean. There, on five islands, trading companies developed a thriving sugar industry.

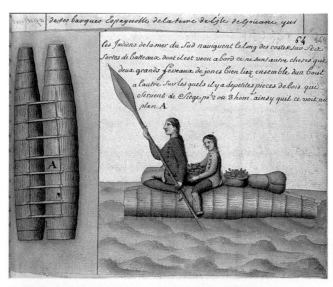

In this illustration from a travel book, European explorers experiment with a boat used by local Indians. Such documents recorded Indian customs and technologies, often in elaborate detail.

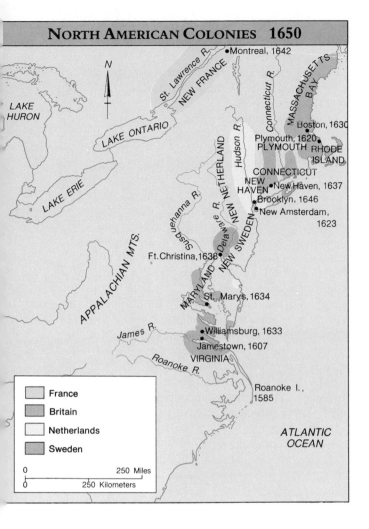

NORTH AMERICAN COLONIES 1650

LAKE HURON

LAKE ONTARIO

LAKE ERIE

St. Lawrence R.

NEW FRANCE

•Montreal, 1642

N

Connecticut R.

MASSACHUSETTS BAY

•Boston, 1630

Hudson R.

Plymouth, 1620•
PLYMOUTH

RHODE ISLAND

CONNECTICUT
NEW HAVEN •New Haven, 1637

•Brooklyn, 1646

•New Amsterdam, 1623

Susquehanna R.

Delaware R.

NEW NETHERLAND

NEW SWEDEN

APPALACHIAN MTS.

•Ft. Christina, 1638

MARYLAND

•St. Marys, 1634

James R.

•Williamsburg, 1633

•Jamestown, 1607

VIRGINIA

Roanoke R.

Roanoke I., 1585

ATLANTIC OCEAN

Legend:
- France
- Britain
- Netherlands
- Sweden

0   250 Miles
0   250 Kilometers

The French in Asia and Africa. France also formed an East India Company. The French traded in China and established posts along the coast of Africa and on the island of Madagascar, today the Malagasy Republic. Eventually, they took the island of Mauritius (maw-RISH-us) from the Dutch.

The French successfully competed with the English in India, establishing posts at Pondichéry (PON-dee-SHAY-ree), now Pondicherry, and other locations. Like the English, the French became involved in Indian politics in order to preserve their trade with India.

THE DUTCH TRADING EMPIRE

Located close to the sea, the Netherlands had long thrived on fishing, shipbuilding, and trade. Dutch merchants made a profit by reselling spices they had purchased from the Portuguese.

However, during the late 1500s, the Dutch determined to forge their own trade links with Asia. To carry out this trade, they formed the Dutch East India Company in 1602.

Like all the other nations engaged in exploration, the Dutch hoped to find an all-water passage through North America. Employed by the Dutch East India Company in 1609, the English sea captain Henry Hudson explored the North American coast and sailed up what is now called the Hudson River in search of such a northwest passage.

In the 1620s, the Dutch established a colony called New Netherland along the Hudson River. In 1655, New Netherland absorbed a nearby colony that had been established by Sweden. New Netherland was renamed New York in 1664, when the colony was seized by the English. However, the Dutch still retained all the colonies that they had founded in the West Indies and South America.

The Dutch East India Company achieved its greatest success in Asia. By establishing bases for trade in strategic locations and making agreements with local rulers, the Dutch forced other European traders out of some areas. For example, the Dutch succeeded in pushing the Portuguese out of Sri Lanka (SREE LAHN-kuh), also known as Ceylon, an island off the coast of India. They also became firmly established in the Spice Islands, now known as the Moluccas, which they held until the twentieth century. As a result of their control over these areas, the Dutch developed a *monopoly*, or exclusive control, of trade in such spices as pepper, cinnamon, nutmeg, and cloves. Because of this monopoly, the Dutch were able to control the supply and prices of the spices.

As a supply station for their ships, the Dutch established a post in South Africa, and they took additional posts from the Portuguese in West Africa. These posts enabled them to enter the valuable trade in ivory, gold, and slaves. Far to the east, the Dutch managed to obtain an agreement with the Japanese that gave them exclusive rights to trade in Japan. Two Dutch ships a year were allowed to call at the Japanese port of Nagasaki.

The vigorous competition of the Dutch East India Company made it the single largest trading company in Europe in the 1600s. Its headquarters, Amsterdam, became the world's leading commercial city.

1. Define *monopoly*.

2. At first, what value did the English think North American colonies might have? Of what value were they by the mid-1600s?

3. What did the French seek in North America? Did they achieve their goal?

4. Where was Dutch influence strongest? What trade did the Dutch control?

Application. What arguments might British, French, or Dutch traders have used to convince rulers in India, China, or Japan to grant them permission to carry on trade?

16–4
EFFECTS OF EXPANSION ON EUROPE

READ TO FIND OUT

—what the terms *capitalism, capital, joint-stock company, stock, shareholders, domestic system, mercantilism*, and *bourgeoisie* mean.
—how overseas expansion changed Europe's economic life.
—how European nations viewed their colonies.
—how patterns of power changed.
—how overseas expansion changed daily life and ideas in Europe.

In a relatively short time, Europe's expansion began to affect almost every part of the world. At the same time, this expansion led to economic and social changes within Europe itself.

THE COMMERCIAL REVOLUTION

Overseas expansion brought great changes to Europe's economic life. Between the 1300s and 1700s, European commerce grew from small-scale, local trade, where little money changed hands, to vigorous, worldwide trade involving great quantities of gold and silver. This turning point in economic affairs brought changes so sweeping that they are often called the Commercial Revolution.

Europe's overseas ventures changed economic relationships from local to global networks. For instance, gold and silver from mines in America, imported into Europe, might eventually enrich Chinese merchants who sold porcelain. On the other hand, European investments in Caribbean plantations impoverished Africa by stimulating the slave trade.

Europe's role in the world economy brought it prosperity. By 1650, precious metals from the New World had increased the European gold supply by 20 percent and tripled the supply of silver. With a larger amount of bullion—gold and silver—in circulation, suppliers of goods were able to raise their prices. As a result, Europeans experienced inflation, a period of constantly rising prices. In 1650, grain in Paris sold for 15 times its price in 1500. Meanwhile, consumers in sixteenth-century Spain had to cope with a 400 percent increase in the cost of finished goods.

Bankers, merchants, and others in business benefited from inflation because their profits rose along with prices. Most other Europeans, however, found that their wages did not keep up with inflation. Workers, farmers, and artisans experienced a lower standard of living because many goods were priced beyond their means.

Capitalism. Stimulated by increased trade, old companies grew and new companies arose. As European commerce expanded, a new economic system developed—*capitalism*, in which private persons invest money in the means of production or distribution and hope to gain a profit. Unlike the medieval economy in which guilds regulated production, prices, and wages, the capitalistic system allowed businesses to compete freely for markets and to work for unlimited profits. Workers, too, competed for jobs and were paid in wages.

The large pools of money available to invest in business ventures are called *capital*. The big government-sponsored trading companies as well as the private companies that ventured into Asia and the Americas needed unprecedented

The Forge, painted in the 1630s, depicts the workshop of a European metalworker. Blacksmiths, who made farm tools and weapons were often part of the domestic system of production.

amounts of capital. The need for capital led to the growth of banking.

During the Middle Ages, money lending had been frowned upon. However, originating in Italy in the mid-1300s, lending money for profit became a regular business. By the 1400s banks had been established in Spain, Germany, France, and the Low Countries. Along with banking, practices such as the extension of credit and payment by check came into use.

Although money had been in use in Europe for some time, no country had a standard currency. Monarchs, nobles, and cities all issued coins. Over time, however, to meet the needs of widespread trade, each country began to work out a simple and convenient standard system of money.

To meet the problems of conducting commerce on a large scale, people began to organize businesses in new ways. Usually one or two persons could not acquire the huge sums of money needed to carry on business on a large scale. Therefore, merchants and other business leaders began to raise capital through a new form of business organization called the *joint-stock company*. Such companies sold *stock*, or shares, in the company to individual investors.

The owners of the stock, or *shareholders*, became the company's joint owners. The various shareholders received a return on their investments in the form of dividends, or payments of a part of the company's profits. The percentage received by each shareholder depended on the number of shares of stock held.

One result of the formation of joint-stock companies was the stock exchange, where shares in trading companies could be bought and sold. One of the first exchanges was founded in Amsterdam in 1611, mainly for the buying and selling of shares in the Dutch East India Company.

The rise of manufacturing. Although the European economy remained primarily agricultural, the great expansion of business and trade stimulated a similar expansion of manufacturing. Shipbuilding increased greatly, for example. The invention of the printing press gave rise to an extensive printing industry. Metalworking also prospered—especially those companies that made cannons and other weapons of war.

Due to efforts to increase production, a system for organizing workers that had first developed in the woolen industry spread to other industries as well. This new organization became known as the *domestic system* because the workers hired by entrepreneurs did their work in their own homes instead of in the shops of master artisans. Under this system, individual workers specialized in a certain part of the manufacturing process, which made manufacturing more efficient.

The domestic system also avoided the craft guilds. Entrepreneurs did not have to submit the work for a guild's approval, and a guild had no power to limit the price entrepreneurs were able to charge. As a result, the medieval system of craft guilds began to decline.

MERCANTILISM

In the 1600s and 1700s, governments became involved in promoting trade and controlling the nation's economic affairs. The theory that government control of all the nation's economic interests strengthened the nation was called *mercantilism* (MUR-kun-til-ism).

Behind mercantilism was the belief that national wealth consisted of money in the form of gold and silver. Mercantilists said that a nation should aim to have as much gold and silver as possible. Money was easy to tax, bringing the monarch wealth which could then be used to build palaces, armies, and ships, all of which would bring the nation power and respect.

Under the mercantile system, nations with colonies strictly regulated colonial trade. Manufacturers in the founding country produced goods and services to sell in the colonies, while the government forbade the colonies to develop their own manufacturing. At the same time, the colonial merchants sold raw materials to the founding country. However, the value of the raw materials was always less than the value of the manufactured goods. Money also went into the treasury of the founding country from tariffs, or the taxes the government placed on exports to the colonies. Furthermore, each country severely limited trade between its colonies and other countries so that the colonies could bring wealth and power only to their founding country.

SHIFTING CENTERS OF POWER

As a result of overseas expansion, the centers of power in Europe and the Middle East began to shift. The Atlantic Ocean displaced the Mediterranean Sea as Europe's chief commercial highway. Political and economic power, therefore, moved from the Middle East and the Mediterranean to the countries of northern and western Europe. Venice and Genoa began to decline in the fifteenth century, while Lisbon, Antwerp, London, and Amsterdam grew as leading centers of commerce and finance.

Overseas expansion affected the power structure within Europe as well. The greater availability of money allowed monarchs to collect more taxes, which they could use to expand their armies and navies, increasing their authority.

As trade and manufacturing increased in importance, so did the role of the middle class, or the **bourgeoisie** (boor-ZHWAH-ZEE), who conducted such activities. The bourgeoisie began to have both political and social influence.

CHANGING HABITS

The most obvious impact of overseas expansion on Europe was the introduction of new prod-

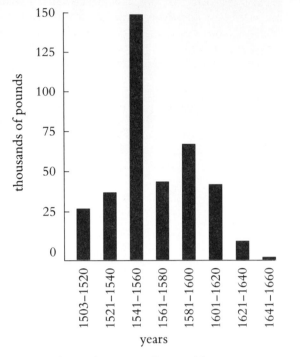

SPANISH IMPORTS OF GOLD FROM THE AMERICAS 1503–1660

Source: Earl J. Hamilton, *American Treasure and the Price Revolution in Spain*, 1982.

ucts, which changed diet and social habits, and raised the standard of living. Among the new products were foods from the New World. Europeans began adding corn, potatoes, squash, pumpkins, chili peppers, and turkey to their diet. Three new beverages also found a place on European tables. One was coffee from the Middle East and the Spice Islands. Another was cocoa from America, and the third was tea from China and India.

The introduction of coffee, cocoa, and tea changed social life. Enterprising merchants set up coffeehouses, chocolate shops, and tearooms where people met to gossip and exchange political and intellectual opinions.

Exotic products from abroad became increasingly available to upper-class Europeans in the 1500s and 1600s. From Asia came porcelain, spices, gems, silks, umbrellas, fans, embroideries, perfumes, and wallpaper. Africa supplied ivory, gold, and ostrich feathers. Furs from North America became a symbol of status and wealth. Precious woods such as mahogany and cedar from the West Indies improved the quality of housing and furniture.

The introduction of new foods, along with an increased supply of familiar foods, contributed to rapid population growth. Historians estimate that Europe's population in 1600 was about 50 percent greater than it had been a century earlier.

CHANGING ATTITUDES

Europeans of the age of exploration felt that they could learn nothing from non-Europeans. As a result, Europeans dismissed most of the foreign religious, philosophical, and ethical ideas that they encountered. Nevertheless, European culture and thought were affected by these ideas.

Exploration fired the imagination of many European thinkers and inspired many new literary themes. For example, Shakespeare and other poets wrote fantastic tales based on faraway places that explorers and traders described. Thomas More and Francis Bacon were among the writers who idealized the simpler societies of newly discovered regions, and in doing so, criticized their own. Portugal's greatest writer, Luiz Vaz de Camoëns (LWEES vash thuh KAM-ō-enz) wrote an epic poem in the 1500s, *The Lusitanians*, celebrating the voyage of Vasco da Gama.

News of faraway lands filled Europeans with curiosity. Travelers carefully observed and diligently recorded what they saw. They brought back journals, maps, drawings, and even specimens of plant and animal life providing detailed information about foreign landscapes, customs, plants, and animals. These world travelers laid the basis for development of modern geography, anthropology, and natural science.

SECTION REVIEW

1. Define *capitalism*, *capital*, *joint-stock company*, *stock*, *shareholders*, *domestic system*, *mercantilism*, and *bourgeoisie*.

2. List four major changes that were part of the Commercial Revolution. Explain why each came about.

3. Explain how the mercantile system affected the relationship between a nation and its overseas colonies.

4. Explain why Venice and Genoa became less powerful during this time, whereas London and Amsterdam became more so.

5. Briefly explain one way in which overseas expansion changed the habits and attitudes of many Europeans.

Application. If a person who lived in a seafaring nation of the 1600s wished to invest in trade, what steps could he or she have taken? In what could the person have invested? What would the risks have been?

Data Search. Refer to the appropriate chart on page 828 to identify which of the following plants and animals were introduced to the New World from other regions: rice, cattle, potatoes, horses, chickens, turkeys, sunflowers, maize, cocoa, and avocados.

HISTORY IN FOCUS

While Europeans embarked on their search for a route to Asian markets in the 1400s, other civilizations were more progressive and powerful. Chinese civilization, for example, was the most advanced in the world, and strong Muslim empires in the Middle East were expanding rapidly. Yet, by the 1700s, European influence was beginning to be felt around the globe.

In Central and South America native civilizations were destroyed for the most part and replaced with European civilizations. European civilization was also transplanted to North America, and the process began of forcing Native Americans off the land that Europeans or their descendants wished to use. In Asia and Africa, on the other hand, by the 1700s Europeans had established themselves mainly along the fringes of existing civilizations.

The movement of Europeans around the globe brought about the large-scale redistribution of plants and animals. This exchange led to an increase in the world's food supply. The expansion of Europe also led to a redistribution of the world's people. This movement of peoples resulted in widespread diffusion of languages, ideas, and religions.

Before 1500 contacts between regions of the world were few. Trade was limited to a few luxury items carried between Europe, Asia, and Africa. After 1500 all the continents of the globe gradually became linked by sea, and modern mass trade began to develop.

SUMMARY

- In the late 1400s, European nations began overseas explorations for political, economic, and religious reasons. Improvements in navigation allowed explorers to chart new sea routes and reach faraway lands.

- Portugal and Spain were the first European countries to establish overseas colonies and trading posts. Portugal focused on Africa, Asia, and Brazil, while most of Spain's attention was on the New World.

- The Spanish and Portuguese overcame native cultures and established their own customs in the Americas. They brought in African slaves and enslaved native Indians. A new blend of cultures and races emerged in what became known as Latin America.

- The British, Dutch, and French began exploration in the 1500s and 1600s. They founded colonies in North America and the Caribbean, and formed trading companies to expand commerce in Africa and Asia.

- Europe's overseas expansion sparked the Commercial Revolution, as increased trade brought greater wealth and new business practices to Europe. Mercantilist policies governed relations with the colonial empires. At the same time, overseas trade and contacts brought changes in European culture.

VOCABULARY REVIEW

The vocabulary terms in each pair listed below are related to each other. For each pair, explain what the two terms have in common. Also explain how they are different.

Example: *Capital* and *joint-stock company* are related in that a joint-stock company is formed for the purpose of raising capital. Capital is a large pool of money used for investment in a business enterprise, however, and a joint-stock company is a form of business organization.

1. viceroy, mercantilism
2. mestizos, mulattoes
3. capitalism, bourgeoisie
4. stock, shareholders

CHAPTER REVIEW

1. (a) How were European sea voyages of the 1500s different from earlier overseas voyages? **(b)** What regions were included in Europe's network of trade by 1600?

2. (a) For what did Prince Henry, Dias, and da Gama search? Explain the results. **(b)** For what did Columbus, Cabot, and Magellan search? With what results? **(c)** What did Frobisher, Davis, Hudson, and Verrazano seek? With what results?

3. Explain the origins of the following terms: **(a)** Indians; **(b)** America; **(c)** Straits of Magellan; **(d)** Latin America; **(e)** Louisiana.

4. Looking at the map on page 360, list the continents and island groups that lie southwest of the Treaty of Tordesillas line through the Atlantic Ocean. List the lands that lie toward the southeast.

5. (a) Compare the reasons why Portugal, Spain, England, France, and the Netherlands established overseas colonies. **(b)** Explain how mercantilism affected these nations and their colonies.

6. Compare the role of Christianity in Asia with its impact on the Americas.

7. (a) Describe the population of Spain's American colonies. What was the strongest cultural influence? **(b)** List four ways in which cultures blended in Latin America. **(c)** Describe the population of England's American colonies. What was the strongest cultural influence?

8. (a) Describe the encomienda system. Explain its purpose and its effect. **(b)** Very briefly, explain the treatment of Indians by each of the following groups: the Portuguese, the English, and the French. **(c)** Describe the origins of the slave trade to the Americas.

9. (a) Why did capitalism arise? **(b)** How did it undermine the guild system? **(c)** What other developments accompanied capitalism?

10. (a) Explain three ways expansion affected power in Europe. **(b)** Describe three effects of the introduction of new products to Europe. **(c)** How did Europeans react to foreign ideas? Explain your answer.

THINKING CRITICALLY: ACTIVITIES

1. In the 1400s, Europeans thought that there were four continents, possibly connected—Europe, Africa, Asia, and a huge land mass somewhere in the Southern Hemisphere, called *Terra Australis Incognita*, or "Unknown Southern Lands." They further thought that the earth contained more land than water; that Asia and Africa were connected and surrounded the Indian Ocean; and that the earth was about 18,000 miles (28,800 kilometers) in circumference. For each 10-year period from 1480 to 1520, write a note from a voyager to a mapmaker telling how to correct the world map.

2. Make a chart containing information on the colonial systems established by European nations. Down the left-hand side of your chart, write the nations—Spain, Portugal, England, France, the Netherlands. Across the top of the chart, write the categories "Colonies/Trading Posts," "How Obtained," "Type of Government," and "Chief Economic Activities." Fill in the chart as completely as possible.

APPLYING SOCIAL STUDIES SKILLS

Test-taking tips. Studying for tests is easier when you know what questions are likely to be asked. You can get a good idea by saving and studying earlier tests.

Answer these questions about your previous history tests. Use your answers to direct your studying for future tests.

1. Does your teacher include test items on vocabulary words introduced in the chapter?

2. Are there many questions on specific facts, such as dates, places, people, and events?

3. Are there essay questions that deal more with ideas and relationships than with facts?

4. Do some of the *Read to Find Out* items that begin each section show up on tests?

5. Does your teacher sometimes include test items about maps, pictures, graphs, cartoons, and information included in picture captions?

6. Are there test items on class lectures, discussions, films, or tapes?

APPLYING THINKING SKILLS

Detecting bias. The following account is abridged from the writings of an Englishman who visited Canton, China, in 1742. Examine this account for any indications of bias.

> Since we were the first British man-of-war ever to visit Canton, we might reasonably have been considered by the Chinese as a very uncommon and extraordinary sight. But though swarms of their boats passed close to us they did not appear at all interested in us. This insensibility, especially of maritime persons, is not at all to their credit.
>
> Their behavior in later instances gave more proof of that similar turn of mind. It may perhaps be doubted whether this behavior was the effect of nature or the effect of education, but in either case it is an incontestable symptom of a mean and contemptible disposition. This is alone sufficient argument against the extravagant praises which many prejudiced writers have bestowed on the ingenuity and capacity of this nation.
>
> While at anchor, tradesmen came daily on board. Their thieving and ingenious cheating were intolerable. In deception, falsehood, and attachment to all kinds of lucre [money], the Chinese are difficult to be paralleled by any other people. Their behavior exhibited a strange bias of the whole nation toward dishonesty. It would be endless to recount all the stealing, extortions, and frauds practiced upon us by this race.
>
> Chinese craftsmanship lacks originality. They labor under a poverty of genius which attends all servile imitators. Our experiences prove their magistrates are corrupt, their people all thieves and their tribunes unscrupulous.

Abridged from *A Voyage Round the World*, by Richard Walter (London: 1744).

1. Define the term *bias*.

2. What is one procedure for detecting bias in a written account?

3. Why is it important to detect bias?

4. Which clues to bias are evident in the author's account? Give two specific examples of each type of clue evident in the account.

5. Describe the author's bias and explain how the account provides evidence of that bias.

6. Why do you think the author had this bias regarding the Chinese?

CHAPTER SEVENTEEN
RISE OF NATION-STATES
1500–1800

The Battle of La Hogue. Benjamin West, 1778.

Between 1500 and 1800, the feudal monarchies of medieval Europe developed into modern centralized governments called nation-states. By the end of this period, most European nation-states had well-defined territories; unified rule; standing, or permanent, armies; and national identities.

These centuries were marked by war, conflict, and upheaval. Centralized governments attempted to unify their lands under one religion and to control the nation's economy. These attempts at greater state control led to uprisings, civil wars, and struggles between nations for the dominance of Europe. The struggles were especially intense before 1660. Then the nation-states began to establish more stable systems of government that would guide European politics until about 1800.

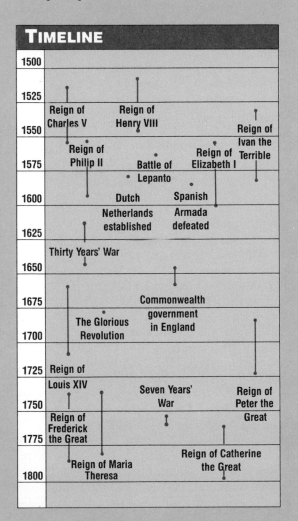

TIMELINE	
1500	
1525	
1550	Reign of Charles V — Reign of Henry VIII
1575	Reign of Philip II — Battle of Lepanto — Reign of Elizabeth I — Reign of Ivan the Terrible
1600	Dutch — Spanish
1625	Netherlands established — Armada defeated
1650	Thirty Years' War
1675	Commonwealth government in England
1700	The Glorious Revolution
1725	Reign of Louis XIV
1750	Seven Years' War — Reign of Peter the Great
1775	Reign of Frederick the Great
1800	Reign of Maria Theresa — Reign of Catherine the Great

17–1
SPAIN AND THE HAPSBURG EMPIRE

READ TO FIND OUT

—who the Hapsburgs were, and how they became powerful.
—how Charles V built an empire.
—how Philip II became Spain's most powerful monarch.
—why the Dutch declared independence from Spain.
—why Philip II assembled the "Invincible Armada" to attack England.

After the general economic collapse that occurred during the late Middle Ages, no one kingdom dominated Europe. Then, during the 1400s, several feudal monarchies grew in power, spurred by the Renaissance. England and France remained strong, while in the Low Countries, the Netherlands emerged as a new commercial power. However, overwhelming them all, in the 1500s, was Spain.

Disunified and weak during the Middle Ages, Spain in the 1500s took the lead in exploring the New World, building up an overseas empire and a strong navy. At the same time, members of a family called the Hapsburgs gained control of much of Europe—including Spain—through marriage, inheritance, and war.

THE RISE OF SPAIN

During the early Middle Ages, Spain was controlled by Muslims, and Spanish cities were thriving centers of Islamic culture. During the late Middle Ages, however, Christians began to recapture Muslim territory and create feudal kingdoms. By 1250, the only Muslim territory left in Spain was the small kingdom of Granada, in the south.

In 1479, the two largest kingdoms of Spain, Castille and Aragon, were united under the rule of Queen Isabella and King Ferdinand. Together they quickly built up Spain's power.

They captured Muslim Granada, sponsored exploration, and limited the power of feudal lords. They also made Spain exclusively Catholic by expelling all Jews and Muslims.

THE HAPSBURG FAMILY

At the same time, the power of the Hapsburgs was also increasing. Originally dukes of a small German state, they expanded their control of neighboring lands, soon ruling the region called Austria. The Hapsburgs had gained enough might in the German states by 1437 to ensure that a Hapsburg was always elected Holy Roman Emperor. Through the prestige of this title, they cleverly arranged marriages with powerful families in Europe. Because the emperor was elected and had no right to tax, he wielded little power over the independent German states. Nevertheless, by 1500 the Hapsburgs had used family ties to gain control or influence over many European lands. Together, these lands formed a vast Hapsburg Empire.

Charles V. The rising powers of both Spain and the Hapsburgs were joined in 1516, when the Hapsburg Charles I inherited the Spanish throne. This gave Charles control of not only Spain, but also Spanish territory in the New World and southern Italy, as well as Hapsburg family lands in Austria.

Three years later, Charles was also elected emperor of the Holy Roman Empire. With this title Charles acquired a new name—Emperor Charles V—and gained control of even more lands in Europe.

Charles had become one of the most powerful monarchs in Europe since Charlemagne, in the 700s. During his reign, Charles added still more territory to his domains. He inherited the Netherlands, and then acquired lands in eastern Europe. Like Charlemagne, he built a European empire.

Control of so much territory brought with it many problems and responsibilities. Charles ruled many peoples scattered across Europe. They included Dutch people in the Low Countries, Germans, Austrians, Hungarians, Italians, and Spaniards. As Holy Roman Emperor, Charles had to be concerned with the interests of all these people, as well as the protection of Europe from the Ottoman Turks occupying the Balkan Peninsula.

Despite these obstacles, Charles ruled his empire successfully for 37 years. During this time, he built up a large and powerful Spanish navy and shared with Portugal control of colonization in the New World. He also fought wars in France, Germany, and Italy, trying to advance the interests of both Spain and the Hapsburg family.

Charles faced a crisis early in his reign when the Ottoman Turks began marching toward Vienna, Austria, from their lands in the Balkans. Charles and his brother Ferdinand, the leader of Austria, succeeded in stopping the Turks at Vienna. However, Charles and Ferdinand were forced to accept a truce that left the Turks in control of most of Hungary—the lands east of Austria.

By 1556, Charles was tired of the responsibilities of ruling his empire. He retired to a monastery and gave Spain and its possessions in the New World, the Netherlands, and Italy to his son, Philip II. Philip II now became the leader of the branch of the family called the Spanish Hapsburgs. Charles's brother Ferdinand received the Hapsburg possessions in Austria and became the next Holy Roman Emperor. Ferdinand's branch of the family became known as the Austrian Hapsburgs. Austrian Hapsburgs would continue to be elected Holy Roman Emperors for another 250 years.

SPAIN UNDER PHILIP II

Philip built on the achievements of his father to become the most powerful monarch in Spanish history. Free of the responsibilities of being Holy Roman Emperor, Philip was able to concentrate on strengthening the Spanish government and achieving greater control of affairs within Spain. He made Spain one of Europe's first true nation-states.

Philip's strong commitment to Catholicism led him to try to stamp out Protestantism in Spain. Philip revived the Inquisition to try and sentence Protestants and others suspected of heresy. The Inquisition was so successful in suppressing Protestantism that Catholicism remained the only religion in Spain.

Philip's attempts to increase Hapsburg power and stamp out Protestantism in western Europe led Spain into wars with other countries. Spanish armies captured Portugal in 1580 and fought French troops over control of Italy. Under Philip's rule, Spain also attacked Turkish territory in the Mediterranean. In the battle of Lepanto in 1571, Philip's navy won a great victory over the Turkish fleet. The Turks, however, rebuilt their navy, and continued to control parts of the Mediterranean.

THE REVOLT IN THE NETHERLANDS

Philip faced a challenge to his power when his subjects in the Netherlands revolted. The Netherlands was composed of 17 provinces with a tradition of independent government. Since the Middle Ages, they had been major trading and manufacturing centers.

By the time of Philip's rule, the people of the Netherlands, called the Dutch, had begun to embrace Calvinism in greater and greater numbers, especially in the northern provinces. Philip created resentment among the Dutch when he ended self-rule in the Netherlands, taxed trade heavily, and persecuted Calvinists.

Led by William the Silent, the Dutch rose up in 1568. The Dutch fought bravely for their freedom. Although the Spaniards had a large

Jan Thomas's painting is titled *Marriage Banquet of Leopold I and Margaret Theresa*. Their wedding in 1666 united the Austrian and Spanish branches of the Hapsburg family.

army and killed thousands of Dutch people, the Dutch were able to prevent a military takeover of their lands.

In 1581, the northern provinces of the Netherlands declared their independence from Spain. The fighting continued until 1609, when the Spaniards finally agreed to a truce. The independent northern provinces then became the Dutch Netherlands.

During the 1600s, the Dutch Netherlands continued to prosper through trade. The city of Amsterdam grew into the financial capital of Europe. In contrast to the Spanish king, who had maintained authoritarian control over the country, the Dutch created one of the freest and most open societies in Europe. They guaranteed religious freedom and a voice in government to many people, and limited the power of rulers.

Meanwhile, the southern provinces of the Netherlands remained under Spanish control. The people of these provinces, who were mostly Catholic, were loyal to Catholic Spain. This area became known as the Spanish Netherlands and was ruled by the Spanish Hapsburgs until the early 1700s. A century later it would become Belgium.

THE SPANISH ARMADA

While the Dutch revolted, tensions were also growing between Spain and England. Elizabeth, Queen of England, feared that if Philip defeated the Dutch, he would next try to conquer England. Therefore, she gave support to the Dutch and allowed English pirates, such as Francis Drake, to raid Spanish treasure ships.

To punish England for its meddling, Philip resolved to invade the island nation. He assembled a huge fleet, called an armada, made up of about 130 ships. In 1588, the armada, with 24,000 soldiers and sailors aboard, sailed into the English Channel and met England's navy.

The English were outnumbered but had smaller, more maneuverable ships. By setting old ships on fire and sending them straight into the tight formation of Spanish ships, the English broke up the Spanish attack. As the Spanish ships retreated into the North Sea, a rising storm—called "Protestant winds" by the English—destroyed and sank many Spanish vessels. About 15,000 Spanish soldiers and sailors died, and only about half of the "Invincible Armada" returned home.

England's victory over Spain is symbolized in this portrait of Elizabeth I. On the left, the Spanish Armada sails toward England; on the right, it is wrecked on the coast of Scotland.

The defeat of the armada ended the Spanish threat to England and signaled a slow decline in Spanish power. In the meantime, increasing amounts of silver and gold from the Americas kept Spain wealthy and powerful through the early 1600s. By the mid-1600s, however, a decline in New World treasure, combined with the expense of many foreign wars, destroyed Spain's economy. Spanish power was further undermined when the Spanish territories in Italy revolted. War with France began in 1635, further draining the treasury. By the time Spain and France made peace in 1660, Spain was no longer Europe's major power.

SECTION REVIEW

1. How did the Hapsburg family gain control of much of Europe?

2. What extra responsibilities were placed on Charles V after he received the title of Holy Roman Emperor?

3. Why did Philip try to eliminate Protestantism from Spain?

4. What three policies, enforced by Philip, caused the Dutch to revolt?

5. Why did Philip assemble an armada to attack England?

Analysis. In what ways might the silver and gold from the New World have had a negative effect on Spain in the long run?

17–2
WARS AND REBELLIONS ACROSS EUROPE

READ TO FIND OUT

—how the Thirty Years' War affected political development throughout Europe.
—how centralized rule was resisted in France.
—how Parliament challenged royal power in England.
—what caused the English civil war of 1642.

Beginning in the late 1500s, religious struggles between Protestants and Catholics combined with political conflicts within the emerging nation-states of Europe to create a prolonged period of unrest. During the first half of the 1600s, Europe was torn by civil wars, peasant uprisings, and the first war to involve nearly all of Europe. Historians have called this period the "crisis of the 1600s." By 1660, Spain's power had declined, and new powers arose to compete for leadership of Europe as the political map of the continent was redrawn.

THE THIRTY YEARS' WAR

Although the Peace of Augsburg, signed in 1555, had for a time quieted religious controversy in the German states, conflicts arose again in the early 1600s. The struggle between Catholics and Protestants ignited a war, called the Thirty Years' War, that soon became more political than religious. The Thirty Years' War involved nearly every European nation.

The causes of the war can be traced back to the rivalries between German princes. Unlike most other European countries, the territory made up of the German states did not have a centralized government by the 1600s. Instead, about 300 princes controlled independent territories. Their rivalries grew more intense as one German prince after another converted to Protestantism. This both angered the Catholic princes and created greater pressure in the German states as a whole for independence from the Holy Roman Empire.

The war began in 1618 as a revolt of Protestants in Bohemia, a part of the Holy Roman Empire. When Ferdinand II, the Holy Roman Emperor, tried to suppress the revolt, angry Protestant princes, along with the king of the northern European nation of Denmark, declared war against the Holy Roman Empire. Soon, the Scandinavian nation of Sweden began fighting on the Protestant side, while Catholic Spain, ruled by Hapsburgs, supported the Holy Roman Emperor. France, though Catholic, joined the Protestant side because it wanted to reduce Hapsburg power.

The fighting raged for 30 years. It took place mostly in the German states, where the countryside was ravaged and towns were burned and looted many times over. Millions of people were killed by the fighting and by the famine and disease that followed.

The Peace of Westphalia. In 1648, the French and Protestant side finally emerged victorious. A treaty called the Peace of Westphalia redrew the political map of Europe, weakening some countries and strengthening others.

The Hapsburgs lost much of their power under the terms of the treaty. They could no longer hope to use the office of Holy Roman Emperor to control the German states. Their territories of Switzerland and the Dutch Netherlands were recognized as independent. To counter these losses in western Europe, the Hapsburgs worked to strengthen their power in

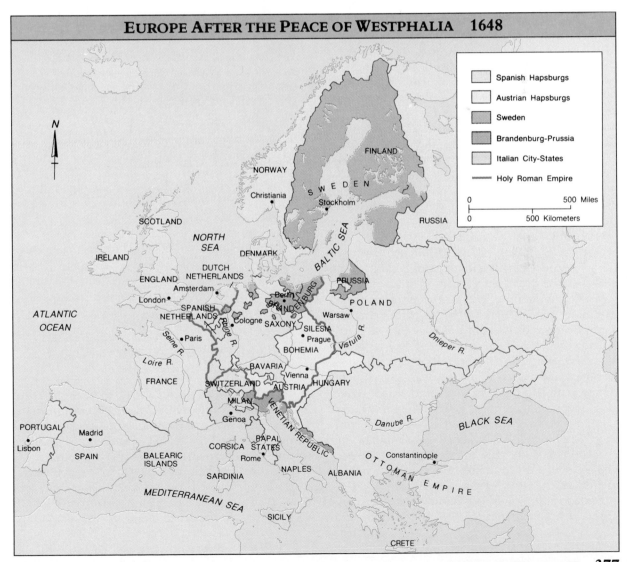

EUROPE AFTER THE PEACE OF WESTPHALIA 1648

eastern Europe, especially in Austria and the nearby states of Hungary and Bohemia.

Freed from domination by the Hapsburgs, the German states remained independent. The religious differences between the Protestant north and the Catholic south prevented any unification of the German states.

France and its allies made the biggest gains under the Peace of Westphalia. France and Sweden both received territory in former German lands. With France's growth, Spain's power was seriously weakened.

TURMOIL IN FRANCE

While the Thirty Years' War brought European nation-states into conflict with each other, religious and social unrest challenged centralized rule in France. Louis XIII had inherited the French throne in 1610. Because he was an ineffectual ruler, his chief advisor, Cardinal Richelieu, assumed power during most of Louis XIII's reign. Richelieu, a shrewd and ambitious man, took bold steps toward increasing the power of the French government. These steps led to conflict between the French state and many people in French society.

The first people to resist central control were the Huguenots. Although the French king Henry IV had quieted conflict between the Protestant Huguenot minority and Catholics by issuing the Edict of Nantes in 1598, this conflict erupted again in the early 1600s. The Huguenots rebelled against what they felt were unfair restrictions, and consequently they were attacked by Richelieu's army. Richelieu captured the Huguenots' fortified cities and then changed the Edict of Nantes. Under the new law, the Huguenots lost all the military rights originally given them by the edict, but retained some freedom of worship.

Meanwhile Richelieu involved France in the Thirty Years' War in an attempt to gain more territory and power for the royal government. Along with this aggressive foreign policy, he set up a new system of local government in France. Under this system, royal officials called *intendants* (an-tawn-DAWN) tried to eliminate any resistance to state rule in their regions. Richelieu's policies led to major revolts after his death in 1642.

Since 1500, uprisings had become increasingly common in France. By 1648, more than

Seventeenth-century French Catholics and Protestant Huguenots both stressed religious devotion. *Saying Grace* by Jean Chardin depicts children being led in prayer before a meal.

500 had broken out. Many of these uprisings were religious; others were led by peasants who were angry with new taxes imposed during times of hardship.

In 1648, these revolts culminated in an uprising called the *Fronde* (FROND). French aristocrats who had lost power under the centralized government were joined by peasants who were resisting rising taxes. The scattered rebellions of the Fronde continued for several years. Then, in 1653, the French government crushed its opposition and became even stronger than it had been before the revolt.

CHALLENGES TO ROYAL POWER IN ENGLAND

The early 1600s were also a time of political struggle in England. Unlike the conflicts in France, however, where resistance to central control proved ineffective, the struggles in England led to permanent limits on royal power.

At first English monarchs, like French kings, steadily increased their power. Two of England's most powerful rulers, both from a family called the Tudors, had ruled during the 1500s.

Henry VIII reigned from 1509 to 1547, and his daughter Elizabeth I held the throne from 1558 to 1603. Both Henry and Elizabeth strengthened the monarch's powers and contributed to economic growth in England.

Henry took the important step of splitting with the Roman Catholic Church to form the Anglican church, or Church of England. As leader of this new Protestant church, Henry took over the lands that had belonged to the Catholic Church. Henry also united Wales, a country bordering English lands, and England. Under Elizabeth's rule, the Spanish Armada was defeated, and England began to compete with Spain for wealth and colonies in the New World. National pride increased Elizabeth's power, as she brought England closer to absolute monarchy.

Religious opposition. During the 1500s, however, two major conflicts in English society developed. The first conflict was religious, and it involved Puritans and Catholics—two religious minorities that had grown in power. The Puritans thought the Anglican church should move further away from Catholicism. Most Puritans, for example, wanted to "purify" the English church of its elaborate ceremonies and simplify the method of church organization. Catholics, on the other hand, were still loyal to the Church in Rome. The Tudors persecuted both groups in an attempt to create religious unity in England. However, they succeeded only in creating dangerous enemies.

Opposition from Parliament. The second conflict was between the monarch and Parliament. This body had been created in the late 1200s by nobles seeking to limit the king's power. It was not then an official part of the English government. By the 1500s, however, Parliament had become a regular part of the government, with the power to pass tax laws. Because people of all classes saw it as their voice in government, the crown had difficulty governing without it. More and more, Parliament challenged the authority of the monarch.

Although Elizabeth had avoided major religious and political confrontations by shrewdly negotiating with Parliament, her successors from the Stuart family, which ruled Scotland, did not fare as well. James I came to the throne in 1603 with several disadvantages. First, the English regarded him as a foreigner because he was a Scot. Second, many people resented his insistence on the divine right of kings—the concept that monarchs, who "sit upon God's throne on earth," should rule without any restraints. Third, the new king inherited a large debt from Elizabeth's war with Spain.

James soon clashed with Parliament. Because the members of Parliament consistently refused to grant him enough money to run his government, he imposed new taxes without their consent. He also took a strong stand against the Puritans, who had much support in Parliament. Thus, the situation was already troubled when James's son, Charles I, came to the throne in 1625.

Charles had money difficulties, too. In 1628, Parliament refused to grant him funds unless he signed the Petition of Right. This document guaranteed that the monarch would not levy taxes without the consent of Parliament, nor would the king imprison anyone without cause. Charles, however, ignored the Petition of Right and dissolved Parliament.

In 1640, when he needed money to carry on a war against Scotland, Charles recalled Parliament. By this time, Puritans controlled the part of Parliament called the House of Commons. They were able to force Charles to agree that Parliament could no longer be dissolved unless it consented.

THE ENGLISH CIVIL WAR

When Charles tried to have opposition leaders from Parliament arrested in 1642, civil war broke out. The English civil war pitted the Cavaliers, or royalists—mainly Anglicans from the northwest of England supporting Charles—against the Roundheads, or parliamentarians and Puritans from the southwest. The parliamentarian forces, led by an outstanding general named Oliver Cromwell, were victorious in 1647. Two years later they abolished the monarchy and executed the king. Cromwell took control of the government, naming himself "Lord Protector" in 1653.

Although the government that ruled England from 1649 to 1660, called the Commonwealth, was essentially a dictatorship, the civil war that put it in control had broken the power of the monarchy. The way was opened for the development of a new kind of monarchy.

1. Describe the territorial changes brought about by the Peace of Westphalia.

2. What kinds of opposition did the French government face as it became more powerful and centralized?

3. What English traditions supported Parliament's attempt to limit royal power?

4. Describe the clashes leading to the English civil war. What was at stake in these conflicts?

Analysis. Name three major events that occurred in Europe during the years 1647-1649. Make educated guesses about how these events may have been related.

17-3
STRONG NATIONAL GOVERNMENT IN ENGLAND AND FRANCE

READ TO FIND OUT

—what the terms *limited constitutional monarchy* and *absolutism* mean.
—why the English monarchy was restored.
—how English royal power was limited after the Glorious Revolution.
—how Louis XIV weakened the power of the French aristocracy.
—how Louis XIV used a bureaucracy to strengthen his authority.

The conflicts of the early 1600s had been largely settled by 1660. The governments of the most powerful European nation-states were quickly breaking away from feudal patterns. Stronger central governments gave monarchs the power to enforce their policies without relying on the goodwill of nobles. In western Europe, France and England developed the strongest national governments. These governments, however, differed greatly in how much power they allowed the monarch.

THE BEGINNINGS OF PARLIAMENTARY GOVERNMENT IN ENGLAND

During the late 1600s, England gradually developed parliamentary government. Under this type of political system, the parliament, a body of representatives, holds the right to make laws and limit the power of the monarch. The first step toward parliamentary government had been taken in the English civil war; the second involved another change in rulers.

Cromwell's government became just as authoritarian as the monarchy that it had replaced. By the late 1650s, even many of the people who had supported Cromwell's takeover now felt that the Commonwealth government should be abolished.

Two years after Cromwell's death in 1658, one of his former generals seized power and called for the election of a new Parliament. Parliament then invited Charles I's son, Charles II, who was living in exile in France, to return to England to rule as king. Parliament was careful, however, to limit Charles's power.

The Restoration. Charles II's reign is called the Restoration, because the English monarchy had been brought back, or restored. Charles's rule, which lasted 25 years, was relatively peaceful. At first the king did not interfere with Parliament's newly won rights to conduct its own affairs and to control taxation. Then, however, Charles began to extend his power, alarming many people in Parliament. By the late 1670s, two factions had developed in Parliament. The supporters of the king were called "Tories" and his opponents, the "Whigs."

The Glorious Revolution. A crisis developed in England during the reign of Charles II's brother, James II. Many people in England resented James's rule because he was not only arrogant but also Catholic, and most English people were Anglican.

James reopened Catholic churches and chose Catholic advisors. Then James's Catholic wife gave birth to a son, who would inherit the throne. The English were strongly opposed to

Ten years after he began his exile in France, Charles II returned to England to be crowned king. Dutch painter Dirck Stoop depicted Charles's triumphal entry into London in 1661.

the idea of another Catholic ruler. James's opponents in Parliament, therefore, invited James's Protestant daughter, Mary, and her husband, the Dutch ruler William of Orange, to rule. They accepted, and James fled to France in 1688. This bloodless shift of power is known as the Glorious Revolution.

England's new rulers, William and Mary II, accepted important limitations on their power, such as the Declaration of Rights, or English Bill of Rights, which spelled out the limits on royal authority. The monarch could not suspend laws, levy taxes, or maintain a peacetime standing army without Parliament's consent. Parliament itself was to meet regularly, not simply when a monarch called it into session. An Act of Toleration, passed the same year, allowed more freedom to all Protestants.

A LIMITED MONARCHY

The passage of the Declaration of Rights and the Act of Toleration quieted political discontent, and so England avoided the kinds of rebellions and revolutions that many other nations faced. In a spirit of compromise, troublesome new issues were settled gradually and within the system. For example, Scotland was joined with England and Wales to form Great Britain in 1707, with no major difficulties.

Although Parliament had limited the powers of the monarchy, the ruler still appointed the ministers of state and conducted diplomacy. Parliament itself retained many medieval ideas and practices. Its upper house—the House of Lords—was composed of aristocrats and clergy.

Its lower house—the House of Commons—was elected by a small minority of people who owned a sizable amount of property.

Parliamentary government became more strongly established during the 1700s. In 1714, a new dynasty, the Hanoverians, came to the British throne with George I. He and his successor relied heavily on one minister, Sir Robert Walpole. As the most prominent member of the group that served as the monarch's advisors, called the Cabinet, he came to be called the prime minister. In time, this office would have more power in English politics than that of the monarch.

By the 1700s, the English government had become a *limited constitutional monarchy*. Under this system, a monarch rules, but his or her power is limited by a constitution. England's constitution was not one single document, but a collection of ideas, laws, and principles such as the Magna Carta, the Declaration of Rights, and the system of English common law.

THE RISE OF ABSOLUTISM IN FRANCE

While Parliament checked royal power in England after the crisis of the 1600s, French monarchs moved decisively to restore centralized, authoritarian government. The French king came to control all the functions of the state, becoming the only source of political power. This system of government is called absolute monarchy, or *absolutism*. By the late 1600s, France was the most fully developed example of an absolutist state in Europe. Many nations in Europe followed France's example.

Louis XIV. Louis XIV, who ruled France from 1661 to 1715, was the most powerful of all absolute monarchs. Louis inherited the throne in 1643, when only five years old. Between 1648 and 1653, during the time when his mother Anne and Cardinal Mazarin ruled France in his place, he saw the disruption and turmoil of the Fronde. Determined to avoid such turmoil in the future, he vowed to rule with absolute authority when he took over the government in 1661.

Louis XIV is said to have uttered a phrase which has become the classic slogan of absolute monarchy: "*L'etat, c'est moi*," meaning "I am the state." To signify his importance to France, Louis compared himself to the life-giving sun, which he made his personal symbol. The "Sun King," as Louis was called, had a huge, costly palace built at Versailles, outside of Paris. The royal court he maintained there was one of the most luxurious since the height of the Persian Empire.

Louis XIV appears on horseback amid nobles at Versailles in this painting based on a seventeenth-century engraving. The grilled windows display the symbol of the "Sun King."

LOUIS XIV'S PRINCIPLES OF ABSOLUTE RULE

Louis's absolutism was based on the doctrine of the divine right of kings. According to this belief, the monarch's right to rule came from God, and only God could punish the monarch for misrule. The king's power was supported by two strategies: weakening those elements that might compete with the state and strengthening government institutions.

Weakening competition. Like French rulers before him, Louis XIV worked to limit the power of both the Church and the aristocracy, the two authorities that had traditionally competed with the monarchy. To reduce church power, Louis XIV made sure he was seen as the head of the Catholic Church in France. He appointed bishops and often tried to tell the pope what to do.

Louis XIV also tried to reestablish religious unity in France by revoking the Edict of Nantes, thereby forcing the Protestant Huguenot minority to either convert to Catholicism or leave the country. Louis's policy drove thousands of Huguenots—many of them talented business leaders and artisans—to England, the Netherlands, the Protestant states of Germany and England's American colonies.

To attack the aristocracy, Louis XIV refused to call the Estates-General, the representative body similar to England's Parliament. This policy seriously weakened the parliamentary tradition in France. Louis drew the great landlords into his elaborate court, providing all sorts of rituals to keep them entertained and out of political trouble. Aristocrats competed for the privilege of attending the king while he ate, dressed, and bathed. By making the aristocrats' power dependent on his favor, Louis thus weakened the aristocracy without destroying it.

Strengthening the government. As another important part of his policy, Louis XIV built up the French bureaucracy. A bureaucracy is a system of administration made up of paid government officials working under a system of inflexible rules. Other civilizations, such as China, had also developed bureaucracies, but under Louis XIV, bureaucracy came close to its present-day form.

Louis chose bureaucrats, or officials in the bureaucracy, from the ranks of middle-class business and professional people rather than from the aristocracy. Because these officials owed their position to the king alone, they were more loyal than officials drawn from the aristocracy, who were born into their high place in society.

1. What are some words which typically signal that a claim is being made? **(a)** because, since, however; **(b)** so, therefore, thus; **(c)** probably, for, first.

2. What is an unstated assumption in the first two sentences of this account? **(a)** The best generals make a court brilliant. **(b)** Louis's officials were more capable than his generals. **(c)** Louis's generals were great because he trained them himself.

3. How does the assumption from question 2 relate to the claim in the second sentence of the account? **(a)** It explains why the generals should be considered "great." **(b)** It explains why Louis should be called a great king. **(c)** It explains why Louis's court was "brilliant."

4. In the second paragraph, the author claims that Louis's jealousy **(a)** prevented him from becoming a great ruler, **(b)** led to his great accomplishments, **(c)** kept him from recognizing that many officials were unqualified.

5. The claim referred to in question 4 is partly based on an unstated assumption that in order to become great a ruler must **(a)** appoint qualified officials, **(b)** be more qualified than the appointed officials, **(c)** rely only on the advice of other rulers.

6. The unstated assumption from question 5 supports the author's claim by explaining **(a)** why Louis chose unqualified officials, **(b)** why Louis could never reach greatness with unqualified officials, **(c)** why the new officials handled the important government matters.

APPLYING THE SKILL

The Duc de Saint-Simon's description of Louis XIV's reign continues below. Examine this description for any unstated assumptions.

> The new generals and officials sized the King up well: little common sense; an almost unbelievable ignorance; a love of admiration; and a thirst for grandeur, power, and glory which went so far as to tolerate no rivals. The generals and officials praised him and spoiled him. This flattery pleased him to a great extent. Thus, any people whom the king liked owed his affection for them to their flattery . . .
>
> . . . To keep control of the government, the officials overwhelmed Louis with little details. He went after these details eagerly and believed that he alone ruled. In the meantime, more important details remained in their hands.

CHECKING YOUR UNDERSTANDING

7. In the last two sentences of the first paragraph, the author seems to make an unstated assumption that **(a)** Louis disliked most of the government officials; **(b)** Louis's affection for people was never based on their personal qualities; **(c)** Louis knew that the people who flattered him were insincere.

8. The unstated assumption from question 7 supports the author's claim by explaining **(a)** why people had to flatter Louis in order to be liked by him, **(b)** why Louis loved admiration, **(c)** why Louis was not powerful.

9. In the second paragraph, the author claims that the officials **(a)** were overworked, **(b)** controlled the important details by keeping Louis busy with the little details, **(c)** were qualified to handle the important details.

10. The author's claim in the second paragraph is partly based on an unstated assumption that **(a)** the officials thought that Louis preferred handling minor details; **(b)** Louis trusted his officials with the important details; **(c)** Louis could not distinguish between important and unimportant details.

11. The unstated assumption from question 10 supports the author's claim by explaining **(a)** why Louis did not want to handle important details, **(b)** why Louis had a lot of details to handle, **(c)** why the officials could trick Louis into letting them handle important details.

REVIEWING THE SKILL

12. Explain what an unstated assumption is.

13. What can you do to identify unstated assumptions in a written source?

1. Define *limited constitutional monarchy* and *absolutism*.

2. Why did Parliament invite monarchs to come and rule England after the monarchy had been abolished?

3. What agreements limited English royal power after the Glorious Revolution?

4. How did Louis XIV weaken the power of the aristocracy in France?

5. How did Louis XIV's bureaucracy work to carry out his policies?

Analysis. Both France and England relied on old traditions when they established their different forms of government in the late 1600s. How were the English and French traditions similar? How were they different? What conclusions can you draw from this?

17–4
THE EUROPEAN BALANCE OF POWER

READ TO FIND OUT

—what the terms *balance of power* and *militarism* mean.
—how Prussia became a great power.
—how French–English rivalry led to the War of the Spanish Succession.
—which nations fought in the War of the Austrian Succession.
—how the Seven Years' War became a global war.

While the early 1600s saw an outbreak of civil wars, the 1700s became a century of conflict between nations. Like France and England, which developed strong national governments in the late 1600s, new nation-states all over Europe built up centralized rule and grew more powerful.

With many nations vying for power, alliances, treaties, and diplomacy became as important as warfare. Governments began to recognize that it was in their own interest to prevent any one nation from becoming too powerful. This idea—called *balance of power*—became a guiding principle of European politics. During the 1700s, the European balance of power shifted constantly as nation-states negotiated, threatened each other, and fought wars that for the first time spread around the globe.

MILITARISM IN PRUSSIA

The most powerful of the new nation-states outside of England and France arose in central Europe. One of these nations was Prussia.

The Prussian state began as two separate territories in northeastern Europe ruled by the Hohenzollern (HŌ-uhn-TSAHL-ern) family. The Hohenzollerns had ruled Brandenburg, which lay in Germany, since the 1400s. In the 1600s, they began to rule parts of Prussia, a land between Germany and Russia.

As a result of the Peace of Westphalia, the treaty ending the Thirty Years' War in 1648, the Hohenzollerns gained control of further territories. The first Hohenzollern leader to rule this expanded territory was Frederick William, who reigned from 1640 to 1688.

Frederick William was determined to make his territories dominant in northern Germany. To build up the economy, he encouraged agriculture and craft industries in the territories he ruled. His policy of religious toleration reduced friction between Protestants and Jews. Most importantly, he built up a professional standing army. A reliance on military power—a policy called *militarism*—guided Prussian politics.

Brandenburg and Prussia grew more powerful under Frederick William's son, who was given the title of king of Prussia, and the name of Frederick I. Under his rule, the Hohenzollern domains were called Prussia.

Frederick I and his son Frederick William I built up a hard-working, disciplined bureaucracy. Bureaucrats were required to attend training sessions and pass examinations—the first such measures ever known in Europe. Above all, the army continued to expand. By the mid-1700s, the Prussian army, consisting of 80,000 soldiers, was the third largest in Europe; only those of Russia and France were bigger.

Frederick the Great. The most notable of all Prussian rulers was the great-grandson of Frederick William, Frederick the Great. King from 1740 to 1786, Frederick built roads, canals, and drainage projects. To increase agricultural production, he introduced the potato, a crop domesticated in South America and brought to Europe by the Spanish. By abolishing torture and introducing a new code of laws, he strengthened the administration of justice. Frederick was also a witty intellectual, who entertained French thinkers and composed music for the flute.

Meanwhile, Frederick continued to expand the army. Under him, Prussia became a great European power.

THE AUSTRIAN HAPSBURGS

Prussian power in central Europe was challenged only by Austria. Although Austria—the Hapsburg homeland—was weakened by the Thirty Years' War, the Hapsburgs had made many territorial gains since that time. By the mid-1700s, Austria and Prussia had become major rivals.

In 1683, the Hapsburgs defeated an Ottoman Turk army that had besieged Vienna for two months. The Hapsburgs then counterattacked, winning further victories over the Turks in southeastern Europe. By 1700, the Hapsburg ruler of Austria was recognized as king of Hungary as well as king of Bohemia. The Austrian Empire, as it came to be known, also included what is now northern Yugoslavia.

RIVALRY BETWEEN GREAT BRITAIN AND FRANCE

While Prussia and Austria-Hungary grew powerful and became rivals in eastern Europe, France and Great Britain challenged each other in western Europe. These rivalries affected the emerging balance of power in the 1700s and led to wars involving most of Europe.

As England developed its parliamentary government, it also strengthened its navy and pursued a policy leading to rapid economic growth. By the 1700s, England had many overseas colonies in North America and in Asia. This island nation was developing its manufacturing technologies faster than any other country in the world. This economic and military

Frederick William I was an amateur painter. In this painting he placed himself (center) and his son, who became Frederick the Great, among some royal soldiers and servants.

expansion enabled England to challenge Europe's leading power—France.

The rivalry erupted in 1701 into a war called the War of the Spanish Succession. It began when Louis XIV of France attempted to place his grandson on the Spanish throne. Most European nations feared this action because it meant that one king might someday rule both France and Spain, and become immensely powerful. Great Britain, the Dutch Netherlands, and Austria therefore joined together to fight France.

In 1713, after France had lost most of the war's battles, Louis XIV was forced to agree never to combine France and Spain under one ruler. In return, his grandson, Philip V, was recognized as king of Spain. This agreement is called the Treaty of Utrecht.

Great Britain gained the most territory from the Treaty of Utrecht, including French territory in what is now Canada. This settlement made Great Britain and France even greater enemies than before.

THE GROWING POWER OF AUSTRIA

The Treaty of Utrecht also benefited Austria, which received the Spanish Netherlands, the island of Sardinia in the Mediterranean, and the kingdom of Naples in southern Italy. With this new territory, Austrian power continued to grow.

In this English engraving, Frederick the Great wins a major victory in his battle for the Austrian province of Silesia. By annexing Silesia, the kingdom of Prussia almost doubled its population and gained valuable industries.

Under Empress Maria Theresa, who came to power in 1740, the Hapsburg rulers of Austria began to adopt some of the policies of absolutism. For example, Maria Theresa limited the power of local aristocratic assemblies to regulate taxes. She also established more uniform law codes and strengthened the military.

Maria Theresa's son, Joseph II, was an absolutist like his mother but more interested in reform. He abolished serfdom and feudal dues, which had persisted in eastern Europe, but ran into serious opposition when he tried to institute tax and land reforms that would have benefited the peasantry.

The Hapsburgs were never able to create a full-fledged absolute monarchy like that of France. For one thing, they could not gain authority over the powerful lords. Another problem was the diversity of the empire. Although the Hapsburgs were staunch Catholics, large Protestant minorities existed in Hungary and Bohemia. The people of the empire included many different nationalities with many different languages. Under the circumstances, developing an efficient central administration proved to be impossible.

THE WAR OF THE AUSTRIAN SUCCESSION

The rivalry beween Prussia and Austria erupted into war in 1740, the first year of Maria Theresa's rule. Called the War of the Austrian Succession, it soon came to involve other European nation-states as well.

The fighting began when Frederick the Great of Prussia seized a province of Austria called Silesia (sī-LEE-zha), which was adjacent to Prussian territory. Then several other countries entered the war. France and two large German states fought on Prussia's side, while Great Britain, Russia, and the Dutch Netherlands became Austria's allies.

The fighting soon spread beyond Europe as France and England fought over colonies in the New World. Although the French won battles in Europe, England captured French territory in North America and the West Indies.

The war ended in 1748, when a peace treaty decreed that all captured territories should be returned to the nations that had held them before the war. The one exception was granted to Frederick the Great, who was allowed to keep Silesia.

THE SEVEN YEARS' WAR

Tensions between Austria and Prussia and France and England remained high after the war. Again in 1756, these rivals fought against each other in what was called the Seven Years' War.

In Europe, Russia and France allied with the Austrians to oppose Prussian expansion. Prussia, which was allied with England, was saved from crushing defeat only when Russia, under a new ruler, withdrew from the alliance and called off hostilities.

Meanwhile, France and England fought an overseas war. In North America, this war was called the French and Indian War. British troops captured the French capital of Quebec in what is now Canada and French holdings in the Caribbean. In this overseas war, the superior English navy proved the deciding force. In 1763, the treaty ending the Seven Years' War gave Canada and most French possessions east of the Mississippi River to the British.

This treaty also gave favorable terms to the Prussians, who were allowed to keep the territory they had taken from Austria before the war. Prussia could therefore remain a military power. In the late 1700s, Prussia took territory from neighboring Poland. Prussia remained a strong rival of Austria into the nineteenth century, continuing to influence the balance of power across Europe.

SECTION REVIEW

1. Define *balance of power* and *militarism*.

2. What policies did Prussian leaders pursue to make their nation powerful?

3. Explain what caused the War of the Spanish Succession.

4. Which nation-states fought on each side in the War of the Austrian Succession?

5. What did France and England fight over in the Seven Years' War?

Analysis. How were the wars in the 1700s different from the wars of the Middle Ages? Explain how the rise of nation-states accounts for this difference.

Data Search. Which chart on page 831 can be used to help explain the power of France in the 1600s and the growing power of Great Britain in the 1700s? Explain.

17–5
ABSOLUTISM IN RUSSIA

READ TO FIND OUT

—what the term *czar* means.
—how the first Romanov czars ruled as absolute monarchs.
—how Czar Peter the Great tried to westernize Russia.
—what Catherine the Great did to make Russia a major European power.

Although Russia influenced the balance of power in Europe and participated in the wars of the 1700s, it was isolated from most European politics by its location far to the east. Nevertheless, Russia developed into a major military power by 1700, expanding its territory across Asia to the Pacific Ocean. Although Russian monarchs ruled like French kings, Russian society remained distinct from that of western Europe.

IVAN THE TERRIBLE

Ever since the Russians had gained independence from the Mongols in 1480, Russian rulers, following the example of Ivan the Great, had worked to establish a tradition of strong monarchy and control of the nobility.

Ivan the Great's grandson, called Ivan the Terrible, increased the power of the Russian monarch during his rule between 1533 and 1584. As a symbol of absolutism, Ivan the Terrible began the practice of formally calling himself *czar*. Czar, a Russian word meaning "emperor," came directly from the Latin word *caesar*, the title given to Roman emperors.

EARLY ROMANOV CZARS

Absolutist policies continued to be practiced by other czars of the Rurik Dynasty and by the Romanov Dynasty that followed it in 1613. While most of Europe was leaving feudal economic practices behind, the Romanovs enacted new laws that gave serfs even less freedom than they had before. Other Romanov policies organized all of Russian society into rigid classes that served the czar.

The Romanovs also supported the Russian Orthodox Church in instituting reforms. When a group of traditional churchgoers called the Old Believers resisted these changes, the government exiled thousands of them to border areas in the south and east, where they served to extend Russian colonization.

Under the early Romanov czars, Russians explored northern lands between the Ural Mountains and the Pacific Ocean, called Siberia. There they discovered rich iron deposits and valuable fur-bearing animals and timber. In 1689, Russia signed a treaty with China recognizing Russia's claim to land north of China.

PETER THE GREAT

The third Romanov czar, Peter the Great, ruled Russia from 1689 to 1725. He used czarist power to westernize, or bring Western ideas and ways of life, to Russian society and to make Russia into a great European power. Disguised as an artisan, Peter traveled to western Europe, where he learned shipbuilding and other crafts and studied military techniques and science.

Back in Russia, Peter established a new capital at St. Petersburg because it was closer to the rest of Europe than the old capital of Moscow. Peter required Western dress and insisted that Russian men cut off their beards. More importantly, he hired European experts to improve his army and establish a navy.

Peter also strengthened government administration by following the methods of France's Louis XIV. He made the bureaucracy more specialized and divided Russia into districts, each administered by a governor he appointed. He required nobles to serve in the bureaucracy, and he also recruited a few bureaucrats from among nonnobles. To enforce his autocratic rule, Peter set up a secret police.

Peter the Great never succeeded in totally westernizing Russia. Many Russians resented the changes he introduced. The peasants, who made up the great bulk of the population, remained poor and uneducated. In addition, the Russian economy did not catch up with that of western Europe.

RUSSIAN EXPANSION 1598–1796

Legend:
- Russia, 1598
- Added by 1689
- Added by 1725
- Added by 1796

0 500 1000 Miles
0 500 1000 Kilometers

Russian text in woodcut:
РАСКОЛЬНИКЪ ГОВОРИТЪ СЛУШИ ЦЫРЮЛЬНИКЪ Я БОРОДЫ СТРИЧЬ НЕ ХОЧУ ВОТЪ ТЕБЯ НА ТЕБЯ СКОРО КАРАУЛЬ ЗАКРИЧУ

ЦЫРЮЛЬНИКЪ ХОЧЕТЪ РАСКОЛЬНИКУ БОРОДУ СТРИЧЬ.

Peter the Great forbade Russian men to wear beards because to him they symbolized the country's backwardness. In this woodcut, the artist mocks the czar's efforts at reform.

Peter did, however, create a more efficient state and military force. Using his army, he waged successful wars against Sweden and Poland, extending Russian territory to the Baltic Sea. The Russian victory over Sweden reduced this Scandinavian nation to the status of a second-rate power and made Russia an important actor in European affairs.

CATHERINE THE GREAT

Peter's immediate successors were comparatively weak rulers, but the framework of Russian absolutism remained intact. Catherine the Great—czarina, or empress, from 1762 to 1796—continued Peter's policies of westernization and military expansion. While Peter had extended Russian territories to the northwest, she extended them west and south.

One of Catherine's accomplishments was the defeat of the Ottoman Empire. Through this victory, Russia won Odessa, a warm-water port on the Black Sea—a goal of Russian rulers for centuries.

Together with the rulers of Prussia and Austria, Catherine played a role in the partitions of Poland. The three powers helped themselves to huge bites of Polish territory until, by 1795, that country no longer existed as an independent nation.

SECTION REVIEW

1. Define *czar*.

2. Give two examples that show how early Romanov rule was absolutist.

3. Give three examples of Peter the Great's admiration of the West.

4. What was Catherine the Great's most important military achievement?

Analysis. Why do you think Russian rulers desired a warm-water port?

HISTORY IN FOCUS

Between 1500 and 1800, many European countries became true nation-states. They replaced local, decentralized rule with centralized government; built large armies and navies; and sent professional diplomats to negotiate with other nations. At the same time, commercial and industrial growth and colonization of the Americas, Africa, and Asia created opportunities for increasing European wealth and power undreamed of only centuries before.

Together, these developments caused profound changes in Europe and in the world. Competition between nations for wealth and territory began to influence the economy and the ways of life of whole groups of people.

Before the rise of modern nation-states in Europe, cities were largely independent, territories were small, and ways of life developed differently in areas separated by only a mountain range or river. The most successful merchants were from small, independent territories in the Low Countries and Italy.

The establishment of centralized governments, however, ended forever the ability of towns and territories to act independently. The new commercial power belonged to merchants in the nations with the most centralized governments and the strongest navies.

As one historian stated, the world of the 1700s allowed "no profit without power and no security without war." After the 1700s, international politics became increasingly important, and Europe—the inventor of the nation-state—increasingly dominated the globe.

CHAPTER SURVEY

SUMMARY

- The period in Europe from 1500 to 1800 saw the rise of the nation-state. This process was accompanied by widespread war.

- In the early 1500s the Hapsburgs built an empire that ruled much of Europe. Under the Hapsburg Philip II, Spain emerged as the most powerful European kingdom, but it later lost the Netherlands and suffered defeat at the hands of England. By 1660 Spanish power had declined.

- In the 1600s the Thirty Years' War broke up the Hapsburg Empire and strengthened France. At the same time, growing state power in France and England sparked internal conflict. A civil war broke out in England in 1642, leading to the temporary abolition of the monarchy.

- In the late 1600s England evolved a parliamentary system, with controls on royal power. Under Louis XIV, France developed an absolutist state, which became a model for other European countries.

- The eighteenth century was a time of conflict between nations. Prussia and Austria became powerful rivals, as did England and France. Various wars broke out between these countries, at times spreading overseas.

- Russia, though isolated from the rest of Europe, took part in European conflicts and established a strong monarchy. Peter the Great and Catherine the Great used their power to westernize and modernize Russia.

VOCABULARY REVIEW

Match each numbered vocabulary term with the lettered term most closely related to it. Then explain how the terms in each pair are related.

1. limited constitutional monarchy
2. absolutism
3. balance of power
4. militarism
5. czar

(a) professional army
(b) Magna Carta
(c) emperor
(d) divine right
(e) diplomacy

CHAPTER REVIEW

1. (a) How did the Hapsburgs acquire a European empire? **(b)** Why was the position of Holy Roman Emperor both an advantage and a disadvantage to the holder of this title?

2. (a) How did Spain become the most powerful kingdom in Europe? **(b)** List four factors that led to Spain's decline.

3. (a) Why did England support Dutch independence? **(b)** What caused the division of the Netherlands? **(c)** How did Dutch and Spanish rule differ?

4. (a) Name three conflicts in the "crisis of the 1600s." What did these conflicts have in common? **(b)** Explain the cause and significance of the Thirty Years' War. **(c)** How were the revolts in England and France in the 1600s alike? How were they different?

5. (a) What was the Glorious Revolution and how did it come about? **(b)** Describe the two English documents that were designed to limit royal power. **(c)** Under England's parliamentary government in the 1700s, what powers did the monarch retain? Parliament?

6. (a) How were Sir Robert Walpole and Cardinal Richelieu alike? How were they different? **(b)** Compare these rulers: Ivan the Terrible, Frederick William, William and Mary.

7. (a) What were the two major principles of French absolutism? **(b)** How did Louis XIV deal with religious differences within France? **(c)** How and why did Louis XIV strengthen the French army?

8. (a) Compare the two types of government that emerged in France and in England in the late 1600s. **(b)** Were these types of political systems adopted elsewhere in Europe? Explain why or why not.

9. (a) How did the balance of power lead to wars and shifting alliances in the 1700s? **(b)** What were the two wars of succession? How did they differ?

10. (a) How did cultural diffusion contribute to Russia's political development in the late 1600s and 1700s? **(b)** What were the positive and negative results of that process?

THINKING CRITICALLY: ACTIVITIES

1. Choose a European country that became a nation-state by 1800 but was not discussed in the chapter. Do research and write a report on how government developed in that country, and how it was involved in European wars and the balance of power between 1500 and 1800. Then volunteer to present your report orally to the whole class. Possible choices include Sweden, Poland, Switzerland, and Portugal.

2. Divide into groups to discuss these questions: What effect did the rise of nation-states have on the lives of most Europeans? Were the results beneficial or harmful? Support your arguments with evidence from the chapter. Make sure you compare this period with the Middle Ages.

3. Choose the role of either Louis XIV or William of Orange, while a partner takes the other role. Debate whose form of government is best. During your debate, take positions that are consistent with historical fact.

APPLYING SOCIAL STUDIES SKILLS

Taking notes. The Cornell method, a commonly used style of notetaking, involves folding a notebook page lengthwise to make two columns. Notes on class reading assignments are written in one column. In the other column, you can list main topics, your questions on the reading, notes on related class discussions, and your own thoughts on the topics.

The following notes using the Cornell method are based on Section 17-5, which begins on page 389. Copy them in your notebook and then complete the notes by adding information on Russian rulers in the 1700s.

17-5 Absolutism in Russia

Ivan the Terrible (1533-1584)	—power of monarch —1st czar
	Q: Why "terrible"?
Early Romanovs (1613-)	—less freedom for serfs —rigid class system —Church reform

APPLYING THINKING SKILLS

Identifying unstated assumptions. Below are excerpts from letters to Parliament written by Oliver Cromwell in 1650. In these letters, Cromwell describes battles against the Scots. Cromwell sympathized with the Scots as fellow Puritans but fought them because they were loyal to Charles II rather than to the Commonwealth government.

Examine these excerpts to identify unstated assumptions. Then answer the questions.

> We drew up our cannon and did that day discharge two or three hundred great shot upon them; a considerable number they likewise returned to us. We had near twenty killed and wounded, but not one Commissioned Officer. The Enemy, as we are informed, had about eighty killed, including some considerable officers. So, we triumphed even in that skirmish. That night we quartered within a mile of Edinburgh and of the Enemy. The Enemy marched in the night to get between us and our food supplies. But the Lord shows mercy to those he favors. We got time enough to secure new supplies.
>
> Since we came into Scotland it has been our desire and longing to have avoided bloodshed, for God hath a people here fearing His name, though deceived. The Ministers of Scotland have prevented our intentions from reaching these people. And we now hear that not only some of these people but ministers, too, have fallen in this Battle. This is the great hand of the Lord that punishes all those who meddle with earthly power and neglect the Word of God.

Adapted from *Oliver Cromwell's Letters and Speeches*, (London: Chapman and Hall, 1897).

1. Explain what an unstated assumption is.

2. Why is it important to identify unstated assumptions in a written source?

3. What is an unstated assumption in the third and fourth sentences of the first paragraph? Explain your answer.

4. What is an unstated assumption in the last two sentences of the first paragraph?

5. Why do you think Cromwell believed that he and Parliament were doing the right thing by invading Scotland?

CHAPTER EIGHTEEN

CONTINUITY AND CHANGE IN ASIA AND AFRICA

1450–1800

Westerners Arrive in a Sailing Ship.
Painted screen, Kano Naigen Shigesto, Japan, seventeenth century.

Throughout most of the period from 1500 to 1800, powerful and capable rulers controlled empires and kingdoms in China, Japan, India, and Africa. Under strong, effective governments, many societies experienced long periods of peace that allowed steady cultural and economic growth.

A number of rulers in Asia, India, and Africa did not welcome the newly arrived European explorers and merchants. Some rulers strictly limited trade with the Europeans, regarding it as unnecessary for their economies and potentially threatening to their political power. Others tried to carefully regulate trade to their advantage. By the 1700s, however, increasing domestic pressures were gradually weakening the power of many of these rulers—and reducing their ability to control contacts with Europeans.

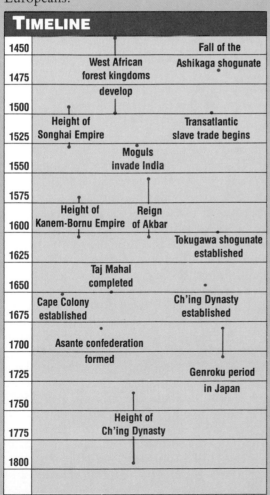

TIMELINE

1450	
	Fall of the
1475	West African forest kingdoms	Ashikaga shogunate
	develop
1500	
	Height of	Transatlantic
1525	Songhai Empire	slave trade begins
	Moguls
1550	invade India
1575	
	Height of	Reign
1600	Kanem-Bornu Empire	of Akbar
	Tokugawa shogunate
1625	established
	Taj Mahal
1650	completed
	Cape Colony	Ch'ing Dynasty
1675	established	established
	Asante confederation
1700	formed
1725	Genroku period
	in Japan
1750	
	Height of
1775	Ch'ing Dynasty
1800	

18-1
THE MING AND CH'ING DYNASTIES IN CHINA

READ TO FIND OUT

—what the term **kowtow** means.
—why the Ming Dynasty fell.
—how the Manchus controlled China.
—why the Chinese economy grew during the Ch'ing Dynasty.
—what Chinese cultural life was like under the Ch'ing Dynasty.
—what caused uprisings against the Ch'ing Dynasty.

After overthrowing the Mongols in the late 1300s, the Ming Dynasty had asserted its power through trading voyages to India, Africa, and other lands in the early 1400s. When the voyages stopped around 1433, China's overseas influence decreased. However, its economy remained healthy, as food, textile, and porcelain production increased.

Ming rulers faced challenges to their power during the 1500s and 1600s. Raids by pirates along the coast and nomads in the north posed a serious threat. More importantly, there was growing discontent among farmers and city dwellers, who were oppressed by an increasingly corrupt government. Weakened from within, the Ming Dynasty eventually succumbed to a foreign threat, the Manchus, who came from beyond the northern border. The new rulers became known as the Ch'ing.

MING RESPONSES TO THE EUROPEANS

The Ming rulers believed that agriculture, rather than trade, was the key to China's economic health. Therefore, they saw little benefit in trading with the Portuguese merchants who arrived in the early 1500s. Furthermore, the traditional Chinese view of foreigners as barbarians was not changed by the behavior of the

Europeans. Often acting more like pirates than merchants, the Portuguese were soon regarded as "Ocean Devils" and were expelled from the mainland ports of China in 1522.

After persistent efforts to resume this trade with China, the Portuguese were granted the right to establish a settlement on the island of Macao (muh-KOW) in 1557. However, their trading activities, as well as those of the Dutch and English who arrived later, were strictly controlled by the Chinese.

Despite the general policy of limiting contacts with foreigners, the government did allow Catholic missionaries from the new Jesuit order to enter China, beginning in 1582. The Ming rulers responded favorably to the Jesuits' respect for Chinese traditions. In addition, they admired the Jesuits as scholars and showed particular interest in the missionaries' knowledge of European science and mathematics.

The Chinese also showed an intense interest in a few European products, especially firearms. However, the Chinese usually accepted only silver or gold in exchange for their porcelains, silks, and teas. This control over trade with Europeans contributed to China's overall economic growth.

DECLINE OF THE MING DYNASTY

In the late 1500s and early 1600s, the Ming Dynasty was exhibiting the telltale signs that had accompanied the decline of earlier dynasties. Weak emperors were unable to prevent power struggles among their advisors, many of whom misused government funds. One official hoarded huge amounts of gold and silver, over 3,000 gold rings and pins, and over 4,000 jeweled belts.

The government was also weakened by a decline in income. Traditionally, the main source of government funds had been taxes on crops produced by small farmers. However, farm land was increasingly controlled by rich farmers, government officials, and local landlords. The previously independent farmers had to surrender most of their crops to the new landowners, many of whom avoided tax payments or were exempt from them.

With fewer taxpayers to support it, the government had difficulty maintaining its costly military campaigns against the northern nomadic tribes. A number of government services were also affected. For instance, emergency grain supplies were sold and the postal system was eliminated. Eventually, even the soldiers went for months without pay.

Discontent spread among the various people hurt most by these changes. Many tenant farmers were exploited by their landlords, while increasing taxes burdened city dwellers and the remaining independent farmers. Beginning in the late 1500s, tenant farmers, former postal employees, military deserters, overtaxed workers, and other oppressed people formed lawless bands. Their disorganized attacks on tax collectors and on the large landowners gradually turned into organized rebellion against the Ming government.

Eventually, a former government employee named Li Tzu-ch'eng (LEE ZOO-CHENG) formed a huge, well-disciplined army that seized Peking in 1644. However, he could not convince government officials that he had the Mandate of Heaven to rule. Without their support, he was unable to form an organized government. More importantly, he failed to gain the support of the generals commanding the northern Ming armies. Therefore, his control of the Imperial City was short-lived.

MANCHU CONQUEST

In the early 1600s, while revolts shook the Ming Dynasty, Ming forces guarding the northern border faced a powerful foreign threat. Before 1600, the Ming had prevented a major invasion by the nomadic Jürchen tribes of Manchuria, who were divided by rivalries. By 1616, however, a Jürchen chieftain named Nurhachi (NER-HAH-CHEE) had defeated rival chieftains and united the tribes into a single group, which became known as the Manchus.

The Manchus overcame Ming power in Manchuria and set up an independent state. Plans for further expansion were reflected in the Manchus' choice of the Chinese name Ch'ing for their dynasty. After gaining control of Manchuria, eastern Mongolia, and Korea, they turned south. Invited into China by a Ming general, and aided by key generals who defected from the Ming Dynasty, the Manchus took control of Peking in 1644. Eventually, they conquered the entire country. The Ming Dynasty collapsed as a result of corruption, revolts, and foreign conquest.

EXPANDING THE EMPIRE

For a number of years the Ch'ing, or Manchu, Dynasty faced serious resistance in southern China. However, under the great Ch'ing emperor K'ang-hsi (KAHNG-SHEE), who ruled from 1661 to 1722, all of China was conquered. To prevent outsiders from aiding any internal revolt, his armies extended China's frontiers. Pushing back the Mongol tribes to the north, the Manchus also extended their empire into Tibet and Muslim lands in Central Asia. After lengthy campaigns, the Ming forces in the south were defeated. The conquest of the island of Taiwan in 1683 crushed the last resistance to Manchu rule.

After gaining control of southern China, K'ang-hsi turned his attention to a frontier dispute with Russia. In 1689, the Manchus negotiated a treaty making the Amur River the border between China and Russia and establishing limited trading between the two countries. This agreement also removed the threat of a possible alliance between the Russians and the western Mongols. A secure northern border led to peace within China after the long period of unrest that marked the fall of the Ming and the rise of the Ch'ing Dynasty.

Under K'ang-hsi's grandson Ch'ien-lung (CHAY-EHN-LOONG), who reigned from 1736 to 1795, the empire reached its greatest extent. Through expensive military campaigns, Western Mongolia and Chinese Turkestan were conquered. Military expeditions also subdued peoples to the south, such as the Burmese and Vietnamese, forcing them to pay tribute. Their representatives to the Ch'ing court performed the **kowtow**, which was the act of kneeling and touching the ground with one's forehead to show submission.

CH'ING GOVERNMENT

Although they were in power, the Manchus were far outnumbered by the Chinese, most of whom regarded the conquerors as intruders.

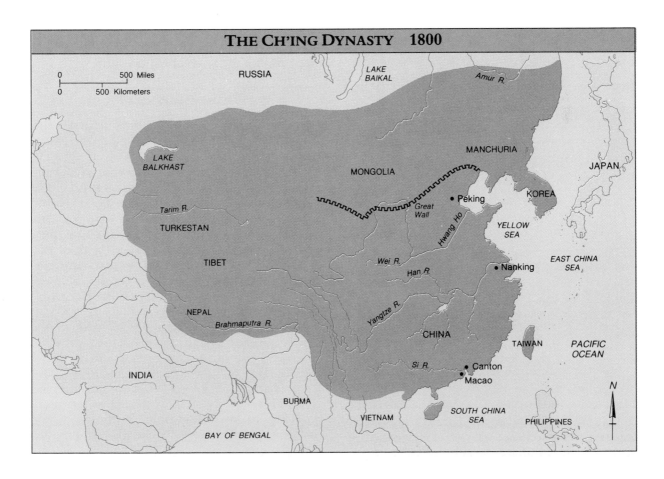

THE CH'ING DYNASTY   1800

An eighteenth-century scroll shows the Manchu emperor Ch'ien-lung, in the red robe, receiving English ambassadors bearing valuable gifts. The English were seeking trading rights.

Creating and establishing a new form of government would have been difficult, if not impossible. Therefore, in addition to adopting Chinese names, Ch'ing emperors, who treasured achievements of earlier dynasties, preserved the Chinese civil service system and generally followed the Confucian principles of honest government.

The Manchus took other steps that made many Chinese more tolerant of their rule. For example, taxes on farmers' crops were lowered and grain storehouses were filled with surplus crops, stored to provide food during times of crop failure. However, the conquerors did require a sign of submission from the Chinese. Each Chinese man had to shave the front of his head, leaving a long braid in back, called a queue (KYOO).

Supported by taxes paid by the Chinese, Manchu and Chinese soldiers lived in military garrisons and did no work other than protecting the state. After completion of the campaigns to expand the empire, Ch'ing power was not significantly challenged. Occasional revolts among minority peoples, such as the Muslims of Chinese Turkestan, were suppressed. Within China itself, peace and stability prevailed, especially during the reign of Ch'ien-lung.

ECONOMIC GROWTH

Under Ch'ing rule, the economy resumed the growth that had been evident before the Ming decline. Food production increased as agricultural techniques and crops introduced during the late Ming period spread throughout China. Among the most important were faster growing rice, improved irrigation and crop rotation methods, and better fertilizers. In addition, foreign trade had introduced new crops from the Americas. Two of these crops, corn and the sweet potato, were especially useful because they could be grown on land unsuitable for traditional Chinese crops.

The increase in agricultural production was a major cause of a dramatic population growth, an overall rise in life expectancy, and a rise in the standard of living during the early 1700s. Larger harvests enabled the Ch'ing government to lower land taxes on individual farms without reducing its overall income. With lower tax burdens, farmers were better able to support their families.

The journals of early European travelers often provide a glimpse into everyday life in China. This engraving of a street barber was made from a sketch in a British architect's travel diary.

Increased agricultural production also helped the growth of trade within China. For instance, cotton production expanded, contributing to the growth of the textile industry. Internal trade flourished during the 1700s, as various regions specialized in different goods, such as textiles in central China and porcelain in the southeast. Market towns grew and merchants, although still regarded as the lowest social class, prospered economically. They formed their own guilds, or trade associations, to regulate commerce within regions.

Before 1700, foreign trade was not a significant aspect of China's economic growth. Within the government, the traditional view prevailed that China had no need for foreign trade. However, any government effort to ban foreign trade would have required the unlikely cooperation of the Chinese merchants, who profited by trading Chinese products for European silver and gold.

Foreign trade expanded during the early 1700s, but beginning in 1760, the government restricted it to one port, Canton. Under this system, foreigners had to trade with a small group of Chinese merchants. Despite these limitations, a large volume of Chinese goods, such as porcelain and tea, were exported to Europe, where they stimulated a growing fascination with the Far East.

CH'ING CULTURE

The porcelains produced for the European market were crafted in styles that dated as far back as the T'ang Dynasty of the 600s. During the Ch'ing period, traditional Chinese culture blossomed again under peaceful conditions and the encouragement of the Ch'ing rulers. Chinese scholarship flourished, especially in the areas of history and philosophy. Scholars organized the histories of past dynasties into a 36,000-volume encyclopedia, which was larger than any previous collection of Chinese classics. Meanwhile, most artists followed the Sung Dynasty styles of nature painting and calligraphy. Architecture, especially in the grand palaces of Peking, also reproduced earlier Chinese styles.

The brushes of Chinese artists were given special care and were often kept in finely decorated pots. This carved boxwood brush pot is inscribed with a poem by Emperor Ch'ien-lung.

The cultural life of the Ch'ing period was not entirely tied to tradition. The novel and the short story had been traditionally despised by scholars as "low" forms of literature, inferior to the "classic" forms of poetry, essays, and history. However, stories and novels now found a growing audience among the general population. Economic growth during the Ming and Ch'ing periods made education more affordable, leading to a rise in literacy. Many new novels and stories vividly described, and often criticized, Chinese society. In modern times, Chinese scholars have finally acknowledged the masterpieces of the Ch'ing period, including what may be China's greatest novel, *The Dream of the Red Chamber.*

SIGNS OF INSTABILITY

Throughout the 1700s, China seemed prosperous and strong. However, economic growth created problems that gradually weakened the Ch'ing Dynasty.

The pressure of population growth. Between 1660 and 1800, the population rose from about 150 million to about 300 million, the most dramatic increase China had yet experienced. More people lived in China than in all of Europe. One cause of this staggering growth was the decline in war casualties as a result of the peace established under Ch'ing rule. Another cause was the expansion of agriculture.

However, agricultural resources were limited. The amount of farm land increased, but not enough to keep pace with the rapidly growing population. As the farm population increased, the amount of land owned by each farmer gradually decreased. By the late 1700s, many farmers were unable to make a living and often joined lawless bands, a pattern also evident during the decline of the Ming Dynasty.

Government inefficiency and corruption. Under K'ang-hsi, the government concentrated on securing its control over China and the surrounding territories. The government was run efficiently, and its funds were tightly managed. However, after the dynasty was firmly established, the behavior of officials was not closely regulated. Corruption gradually increased during the 1700s, as many officials spent government revenues on themselves rather than on the needs of the general population. The treasury was also drained by military campaigns that were prolonged by an inefficient army. In short, instead of serving the dynasty, government officials and soldiers had become a financial burden, a burden that was acutely felt by the common people who paid the taxes.

GROWING UNREST

Beginning in the 1770s, the economic pressures caused by population growth and overtaxation, coupled with anger at government corruption, led to large uprisings against the Manchus. The most threatening rebellion lasted from 1796 to 1804 and was led by members of the White Lotus Society, a rebel organization originally formed in the 1200s to oppose the Mongols. The Manchus crushed the uprisings. In one case they beheaded 20,000 people in four months. By 1804, China seemed quiet again. However, the brutal Manchu response had fueled, rather than weakened, Chinese opposition to the Manchus.

By 1800, the Ch'ing Dynasty was already showing signs of decay that paralleled the decline of earlier dynasties. Furthermore, as Ch'ing power continued to weaken during the 1800s, the growing strength of the Europeans would enter, and eventually play a part in ending, the Chinese dynastic cycle.

SECTION REVIEW

1. Define **kowtow**.

2. What led to the end of the Ming Dynasty?

3. How did the Manchus govern China?

4. Why did the economy grow during the Ch'ing Dynasty?

5. Describe Ch'ing cultural contributions.

6. Why did revolts break out against Ch'ing rule during the late 1700s?

Evaluation. Should the Ch'ing Dynasty be considered a period of cultural growth? Explain your opinion.

Data Search. Use data from the China population chart on page 831 to support the following statement: During the Ch'ing Dynasty, China's population grew more dramatically than ever before.

18–2
TOKUGAWA JAPAN

READ TO FIND OUT

—what the terms **kabuki** and **haiku** mean.
—how Japan became unified.
—how the Tokugawa shoguns controlled Japan.
—why Japan strictly limited contact with other nations.
—what new forms Japanese artists developed.
—how city life changed Japan's feudal society.

The Age of the Country at War, a bloody era of civil strife in Japan, lasted from 1467 until the end of the 1500s. Eager to increase their power and wealth, the daimyo, or great lords, warred with each other. Some also challenged the weakened Ashikaga shogunate. Meanwhile, many daimyo were themselves attacked by the joint forces of lesser landlords who had banded together.

Social unrest was also widespread. Bandits attacked traveling merchants, while peasants revolted against tax collectors and robbed storehouses for food. This period of turmoil was finally ended by three brilliant leaders who set the course Japan would follow for the next three hundred years.

THE PERIOD OF UNIFICATION

The first of these leaders was Oda Nobunaga (nō-boo-NAH-gah), who was originally a minor daimyo. A daring, innovative military leader, he quickly crushed the power of many rival daimyo. With armies composed largely of peasant foot soldiers armed with muskets, he defeated larger forces of mounted samurai swordsmen. Described by a Jesuit missionary as being "contemptuous of all other kings and nobles of Japan," Nobunaga defeated the forces of the Ashikaga shogun in 1573. However, before he could defeat his remaining rivals among the daimyo, he died in an attack by a rebellious general.

Toyotomi Hideyoshi (tō-yō-TŌ-mee hee-day-Ō-shee), one of Nobunaga's generals, killed Nobunaga's attacker and seized power for himself in 1582. Hideyoshi waged hard-fought campaigns in his effort to control Japan, but he also valued compromise. He gave Tokugawa Ieyasu (TŌ-koo-GAH-wah ee-ay-YAH-soo), a rival general, the eastern provinces of Japan to rule and made peace with several daimyo. Eventually, by 1590, all the daimyo had sworn oaths of loyalty to Hideyoshi, making Japan a united nation for the first time in more than a hundred years.

Hideyoshi's rise to power was truly remarkable because he came from a peasant family. In all of Japanese history, no person of such low birth had ever risen so high. However, hoping to prevent other commoners from challenging him, Hideyoshi issued strict laws designed to preserve Japan's rigid feudal class structure. In addition, he started a "sword hunt" policy, in which his soldiers searched all commoners for swords, firearms, and other weapons. He also

EVALUATING SECONDARY SOURCES

INTRODUCING THE SKILL

Most of the history books you read, including this textbook, are secondary sources. Authors of secondary sources get their information from other people, instead of from their own experiences and observations. Authors use eyewitness accounts and other primary sources, such as diaries, letters, firsthand newspaper accounts, and official records, to construct their historical accounts. They may also look at several secondary sources on the same topic for information and ideas. In this way, authors can build on the work of other historians.

Secondary sources, like primary sources, can be either informative or misleading. It is your job as a reader to evaluate each secondary source you use.

EXPLAINING THE SKILL

When you evaluate a secondary source, you are trying to determine how accurate and reliable it is. Here are four questions that will help you judge the usefulness of a secondary source.

A. *When was it written?* Newer works are not always better than older ones, but recent authors can take advantage of the newest research on their subject. On the copyright page you will find the first date the book was published, as well as the dates of more recent editions.

B. *What is the author's background?* Many books contain some information about the author on the cover or in the first few pages. What does this background information suggest about the author's qualifications to write on the subject?

C. *For whom was it written?* Authors write for a specific audience. Two books about the same subject may be intended for different audiences. Therefore, the books may present differing opinions about the subject. For example, a history of the Revolutionary War written for an American audience will differ from one written for British readers. The copyright page, introduction, preface, or foreword may provide information about the intended audience. The copyright page will tell you in what country a book was first published. In addition, the introduction, preface, or foreword may state the author's viewpoint.

D. *Why was it written?* Ask yourself whether the secondary source just presents facts, or whether it also tries to persuade you to accept the author's opinion. Authors sometimes explain their goals in a preface or introduction, but often the purpose becomes clear only as you read the main text itself.

APPLYING THE SKILL

In 1334, the Japanese historian Chikafusa Kitabatake wrote a book titled *History of the True Succession of the Divine Monarchs*. Kitabatake introduced his work in this way:

> Great Yamato [Japan] is a divine country. It is only our land whose foundations were first laid by the Divine Ancestor. It alone has been transmitted by the Sun Goddess to a long line of her descendants. There is nothing of this kind in foreign countries. Therefore it is called the Divine Land.

1. When was this account written?

2. What is the author's background?

3. How can you tell that this is a secondary source instead of a primary source?

4. For whom was it written? Explain.

5. Why was it written? Explain.

INTERPRETING THE INFORMATION

6. Based on Kitabatake's history, explain how the intended audience probably viewed: **(a)** the Japanese emperor, and **(b)** Japan's place among the world's nations.

REVIEWING THE SKILL

7. How does a primary source differ from a secondary source?

8. What four questions should you ask when evaluating a secondary source?

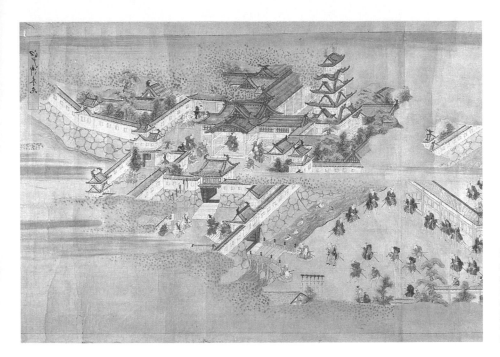

In this copy of an early handscroll, a daimyo and his samurai warriors approach the castle of Ieyasu. Such processions were a common sight along the Tokaido Road, the route joining Kyoto and Edo, as the daimyos made their required yearly visit to the shogun's court.

ensured sufficient income for his government. Since taxes were paid in rice, he had the productivity of each plot of land surveyed. In this way, he held farmers strictly accountable for their taxes.

Hideyoshi's laws were harder on the peasant farmers than on the townspeople. The growing towns and cities lay outside the traditional feudal system and therefore had fewer laws governing daily life. As Hideyoshi extended his control, however, both farmers and townspeople benefited. Food production increased as peasants no longer lost their rice crops to warring armies or roving bandits. Trade grew as merchants and artisans moved to cities and towns that had been rebuilt after being destroyed in wars.

After gaining firm control of Japan, Hideyoshi then attempted to conquer both Korea and China. His grand plans failed, however. Hideyoshi's attempt to establish a dynasty in Japan also failed, leading to a power struggle among the daimyo after his death in 1598. Eventually, Tokugawa Ieyasu, who had been ruling eastern Japan, defeated other rivals to become Hideyoshi's successor.

THE TOKUGAWA GOVERNMENT

Unlike Hideyoshi, Ieyasu concentrated completely on building a lasting dynasty at home. He saw no need for foreign conquests. After having the emperor declare him shogun in 1603, Ieyasu arranged for the position to be passed down within the Tokugawa family.

Ieyasu and his successors relied on two main methods to preserve their power. The first was a strict form of government known as the *baku-han* system. The second method they used was the adaptation of the rigid Confucian class structure to Japanese society.

The baku-han system. Ieyasu allowed local daimyo to rule their own territories, or *han*, as they had in the past. However, Ieyasu started a new system to ensure that the daimyo would not challenge the power of his central government, or *bakufu*. First, Ieyasu moved the government from Kyoto to a more easily defended city, Edo—known today as Tokyo. He then required the most powerful daimyo to spend every other year in Edo. When they went home to their own regions, the daimyo had to leave their wives and children in Edo as hostages who would be killed if the daimyo rose in revolt.

All roads leading to Edo had "sword and women" checkpoints. At these inspection points, armed guards examined all passing travelers to be sure that the families of the daimyo did not escape from the capital city of Edo. The guards also prevented weapons from being smuggled into the city.

The journeys of the daimyo to and from Edo, in the company of servants and followers, became colorful processions, but extremely expensive ones. In addition, each daimyo was required to maintain two elaborate households. These expenses reduced the funds the daimyo might have used in raising armies to challenge the shogun.

Tokugawa social structure. Tokugawa shoguns believed that their power would be best preserved in an unchanging society. Therefore, they adapted the four Confucian classes to Japanese society. The warriors, or samurai, were ranked first, in a position similar to scholar-officials in China. Peasants were ranked second because they produced food, and artisans third

The peasant farmer riding a water buffalo is a detail from *Buffaloes and Horses* by Hasegawa Sakon, c. 1650. Although often harshly treated, farmers were viewed as the backbone of Japan.

because they made less essential items. Last in the order were merchants, who were looked down upon in both Chinese and Japanese society because they lived off the goods produced by others.

However, this Confucian social structure, considered "ideal," did not reflect the realities of Japanese life. For example, under the Tokugawa shoguns, the proud samurai were no longer independent. They lived on salaries paid by the daimyo, and their weapons were provided for them. Laws restricted their travel and prohibited them from farming or going into business for themselves. Still, at least in the early Tokugawa period, they enjoyed many privileges and advantages over commoners. For example, they still had the right to execute any commoner who insulted them.

Under Tokugawa rule the peasants, who made up most of the Japanese population, lost almost all their rights. Tax collectors took half their crops and left them barely enough to survive. Therefore, many peasants defied the rules tying them to the land. They fled to towns and cities, trying the improve their lives.

In the cities, the artisans and merchants, although lowest in social rank, were prospering. Skilled artisans earned a fairly good living, while merchants and money lenders grew rich in spite of government efforts to limit their power by restricting their activities.

REACTIONS TO CHRISTIANITY

In the mid-1500s, the arrival of the Portuguese had brought two potential threats to Japan's feudal society. One was firearms. Although Nobunaga had used muskets effectively in rising to power, later Japanese rulers feared the power that the guns could give to the peasants. The other potential threat was the growth of Christianity among the peasants and local daimyo. Nobunaga had been friendly to the early Jesuit missionaries, in part because some Buddhist sects had opposed his efforts to gain power. Hideyoshi had also allowed the Jesuits to convert the Japanese. In 1586, however, he suddenly ordered the missionaries to leave the country. He did not strongly enforce this decree, but the missionaries worked as quietly as possible thereafter.

Tokugawa Ieyasu shared Hideyoshi's fears about the possibly unsettling effects of Christianity. Starting in 1606, Ieyasu issued a series of orders that were intended to stamp out the Christian religion in Japan. The later Tokugawa shoguns were also harsh in their enforcement of anti-Christian policies.

THE "CLOSED COUNTRY"

The Tokugawa shoguns, like China's rulers during the late Ming Dynasty and the Ch'ing Dynasty, saw foreign influences as a potential threat to their power. They came to fear all outside influences on Japanese society, including trade that might enrich the daimyo. The Japanese could no longer go abroad or build ocean-going ships. Portuguese traders were sent away, and contact with Europe was limited to one or two Dutch ships licensed to visit the port city of Nagasaki each year. The Japanese tolerated the Dutch because they did not attempt to spread Christianity.

For the next two hundred years, until the early 1800s, Japan kept foreign influences to a minimum, and the Japanese remained within their homeland. Some European techniques that had been introduced, such as the making and use of firearms, were almost eliminated. This policy of restricting contacts with foreigners was called the "Closed Country" by the Japanese. It kept Japan apart from the intellectual, social, and economic developments that changed the West during this time.

CHANGES IN JAPAN'S ECONOMY

Despite the efforts to cut off Japan from the world and keep it a feudal society, changes did creep in. Between 1600 and 1700, cities and towns grew along the routes to Edo, as merchants and artisans set up shops to serve the needs of the daimyo processions. These bustling centers of trade were a departure from the traditional feudal pattern of landlords and farmers. The fastest growing city was Edo, which was transformed from a village into a city of about 500,000. Daimyo competed with each other to build the most elaborate palaces there. Workers and artisans were needed to build these palaces and furnish them.

The growth of a money economy. With economic growth came changes in methods of trade. For centuries, the Japanese had used a barter system, exchanging rice for other goods. The unit of trade was the *koku*, the amount of rice that an average Japanese ate in a year. This system worked well enough in a feudal society, in which neighbors traded with each other or gave products to the local lord.

With the growth of cities like Edo, however, a new system was needed. The koku, which was about 5 bushels (141 liters), was too large and bulky for easy use in trade between cities and towns separated by great distances. A new medium of exchange, something that would be generally accepted in trade, was needed. Increasingly, the Japanese used coins, which were small and easily transportable. By the 1700s, gold, silver, and copper coins were circulating. With widespread use of such coins, the nation developed a full money economy.

TOKUGAWA CULTURE

Toward the end of the 1600s, a brilliant culture developed in the thriving cities of Japan. This time is known as the Genroku period and roughly covers the years from 1680 to 1709. Older forms of art and entertainment, such as the *No* plays and the elaborate tea ceremony, still pleased the nobles. The townspeople, though, now wanted new forms of theater and entertainment. Such amusements were found in the quarters of the city known as the Floating World.

Japanese artists captured the colorful life of this world in lovely wood-block prints. Romantic novels dealing with life and love in the society became popular. One of the major achievements of the Floating World was a new type of theater called **kabuki** (kuh-BOO-kee). Kabuki was a popular drama that mixed older traditions with stylized acting and dancing, music, and gorgeous costumes.

During this time, the Japanese also developed a new form of poetry known as **haiku** (HI-koo). A haiku contains just 17 syllables in 3 lines. Each poem is intended to present a sharp, striking image—usually from nature—that calls to mind deeper meanings.

Many of these new works were read and admired by the daimyo and samurai, who were well-educated. In addition, new schools helped spread knowledge more widely. Even small towns and villages had schools run by Buddhist monks or Shinto priests.

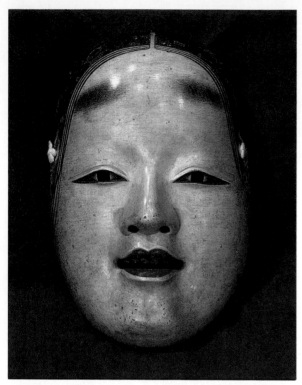

During the eighteenth century, families especially chosen for the task crafted *No* drama character masks of porcelain. Today, descendants of these same families make masks for the traditional plays.

CHANGES IN JAPANESE SOCIETY

In spite of their high social rank, many members of the daimyo-samurai class did not fare well during Tokugawa times. The daimyo had to pay salaries to their samurai and keep up two expensive homes, one in Edo and one in their own region. For their income, the daimyo depended on the labors of their peasants, who paid a portion of their crops to their lords. A poor or failed crop or a refusal by peasants to pay their taxes would drive the daimyo deeply into debt.

As for the samurai, peace had left them with no battles to fight, but Tokugawa laws kept them from going into money-making activities. They had to live on salaries based on the cost of living at the beginning of the Tokugawa period. Although prices rose during the 1600s, their salaries were not increased. Too proud to admit their poverty, many samurai sought loans.

Most daimyo and samurai did not understand money, credit, and finance. As experts in these areas, the city-dwelling merchants and bankers soon gained a large part of the nation's wealth. They grew rich by lending money to the daimyo and samurai. Around 1700, one writer estimated that daimyo and samurai owed a total sum that was one hundred times more than all the money then in Japan. Even members of the ruling Tokugawa family sometimes had to ask rich merchants for loans.

While the upper classes struggled with new burdens, the lower classes often advanced in society. Even in small villages, thrifty peasants set up businesses. In the towns, the more successful merchants and traders managed to buy their way into a higher class. They did this by agreeing to pay the debts of samurai. In return, the samurai would adopt them, thus giving them the privileges of the samurai class.

NEW FOREIGN CONTACTS

Some foreign influences crept into Japanese society in spite of the nation's policy of seclusion. Dutch traders were allowed to visit Edo once a year and give gifts to the shogun. A few of the educated samurai began to meet with the Dutch.

The samurai studied the Dutch language, European map making, military matters, and science. Some of them disagreed with the seclusion policy, arguing that it was keeping out useful knowledge. Although the Tokugawa rulers adhered to their policy, by 1800 there was growing pressure from within Japan to open up trade with the West.

SECTION REVIEW

1. Define *kabuki* and *haiku*.

2. How did Nobunaga, Hideyoshi, and Ieyasu unify Japan?

3. How did the Tokugawa shoguns govern Japanese society?

4. Why did the Tokugawa shoguns adopt a policy of seclusion?

5. How was art in the Genroku period characterized by both tradition and change?

6. Why did the merchants grow in importance during the Tokugawa shogunate?

Evaluation. Was the Tokugawa policy of seclusion beneficial or harmful to Japan? Explain your answer.

18-3
INDIA UNDER THE MOGULS

READ TO FIND OUT

—how a new empire came to power in India.
—what the characteristics of Mogul culture were.
—how Akbar furthered harmony among diverse peoples in the Mogul Empire.
—why the Mogul Empire began to decline.
—why European influence increased in India.

The Delhi sultans ruled India from 1206 to 1526. For a time, they reigned over a large part of India, from the plains of the north almost to the southern tip. However, their power was gradually weakened by Mongol raiders from Central Asia and wars between regional states. In addition, the sultans faced the constant threat of internal rebellion and conflict caused by rivalry among themselves.

During this time of unrest and confusion, new Muslim invaders from the north ended the empire of the Delhi sultans. Related to both the Turks and the Mongols, these conquerors were known as Moguls (or Mughals), another form of the word *Mongols*. The Moguls expanded their empire in India over a period of about two hundred years.

THE MOGUL INVASION

Babur, the leader of the Moguls, was a Muslim who descended from Genghis Khan on his mother's side and Tamerlane on his father's side. After leading his troops out of Central Asia into what is now Afghanistan, Babur invaded India in 1519.

The sultan's war elephants were terrified by Babur's cannon. Babur defeated the larger forces of the Delhi Sultanate, as well as a group of Hindu Rajput princes from northern India. By the time of his death in 1530, Babur had established a new Muslim empire in northern India.

CULTURE UNDER THE MOGULS

Under Babur and later Mogul rulers, Hindu and Muslim traditions continued to influence each other, blending into what became Mogul culture. However, these changes were mainly reflected in the lives of the Muslim rulers and the Hindu nobles who shared power with them. Although many common people converted to Islam, in most regions of India a majority of the people continued to practice their Hindu traditions. Ruled by Muslims, India remained primarily a Hindu nation.

However, during most of the years of Mogul rule, the most distinctive feature of Indian society was tolerance for an endless variety of beliefs and practices. As long as groups accepted the social rules of caste society, people could worship as they pleased. Although Muslims and Hindus occasionally divided along religious lines, they usually lived side by side in harmony, but with different places of worship and different customs.

Mogul literature and art. Although religious differences persisted in India, early Mogul rulers encouraged the combining of Muslim and Hindu traditions in literature and art. Classic Hindu literary works, such as the *Ramayana* and *Mahabharata*, were translated into the Mogul language, Persian. In addition, Urdu, a language made up of Indian words written in Arabic characters and dating back to the thirteenth century, became increasingly used in literature. Meanwhile, gifted court artists often featured both Indian and Persian traditions in their works. These artisans enriched the Persian style of miniature painting, at times using brushes with a single hair, and painted vivid portraits, court scenes, religious and literary subjects, and representations of nature.

The merging of artistic traditions was especially evident in Mogul architecture. Wall paintings combined elaborate Indian designs with passages from the Koran, the holy book of Islam. Mogul architects and workers covered Muslim spires and domes with rich Indian designs. Many beautiful Mogul palaces, forts, tombs, and mosques still stand today. The most famous example of Mogul architecture is the Taj Mahal. This tomb's white marble spires and domes are etched with delicate patterns and encrusted with gold, silver, and jewels.

THE MOGUL STYLE

Tuti-nama, or *Tales of a Parrot*, was produced in the court studios of Akbar from 1560 to 1567. These stories were illustrated with more than 200 miniature paintings, the work of at least 45 different artists. Akbar brought together illustrators from Persia, Central Asia, and all parts of India. Working side by side, these artists borrowed ideas from each other, resulting eventually in the Mogul style. Characterized by rich colors, realistically modeled figures, and lively detail, this style influenced Indian art for 300 years.

A woman with children coming upon a leopard in the woods

The parrot speaking with Khujasta, the heroine

A hunter offering the mother parrot to the king

Explaining that the merchant substituted gravel for sugar

"THE GREAT MOGUL"

The growth and blending of Muslim and Hindu culture was especially encouraged by Babur's grandson Akbar. Considered the greatest Mogul emperor, Akbar ruled from 1556 to 1605. As a skilled and daring military leader, he added much new territory to the Mogul Empire. However, he was also skilled at negotiating. Through the use of expert diplomacy, Akbar secured the allegiance of the diverse populations within his empire.

At the height of his political power, Akbar ended the taxes on non-Muslims and permitted Hindus to build new temples. He devised new codes of law meant to apply equally to all. In addition, he appointed Hindus to high government positions. In a further effort to secure Hindu support, Akbar negotiated peace treaties with the proud Rajput princes, Hindu rulers of western India.

Akbar believed that some truth could be found in every religion. To encourage unity among the various groups under his rule, Akbar held religious discussions, not only among Indians of different beliefs, but also with European Jesuits. "For an empire ruled by one head," he said, "it is a bad thing to have the members divided among themselves."

Akbar's system of government. A skilled administrator, Akbar divided his empire into provinces and districts, giving local governors salaries instead of land grants. Akbar believed that if the officials were dependent on the central government for income, they would probably not rebel.

The main source of government income was a tax on land. Akbar set up an efficient tax-collecting system and made an effort to ensure that it was applied fairly. Dishonest officials were severely punished.

JAHANGIR AND SHAH JAHAN

Akbar was succeeded by his son Jahangir (juh-HAN-GUHR), who reigned from 1605 to 1628, and by his grandson Shah Jahan (SHAH juh-HAHN), who reigned from 1628 to 1658. Neither emperor was able to carry out completely the unifying polices of Akbar. Reducing government salaries, Jahangir offered officials part of the income from farm land. Consequently,

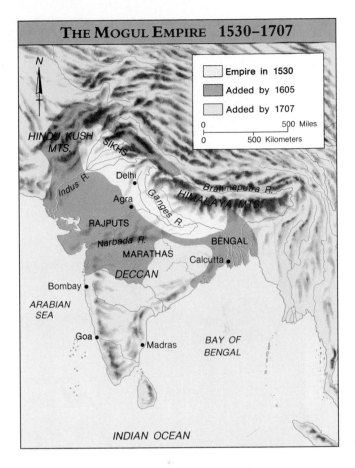

THE MOGUL EMPIRE 1530–1707

the officials pressured farmers to raise more crops, causing farmers hardships that sometimes brought on revolts.

Shah Jahan continued Jahangir's policy of reducing salaries. At the same time, he increased taxes to support military campaigns to expand the empire. Shah Jahan also spent heavily on costly building projects such as the Taj Mahal and the royal palace.

Both Jahangir and Shah Jahan supported beautiful art and architecture. Both men were also devoted to talented wives, who themselves encouraged Mogul art. Jahangir actually shared the responsibility of governing with his able wife, Nur Jahan. Shah Jahan built the magnificent Taj Mahal in memory of his beloved wife, Mumtaz-i-Mahal.

GROWING RELIGIOUS TENSIONS

The last strong Mogul ruler was Shah Jahan's son, Aurangzeb (or-AHNG-zehb), who ruled from 1658 until 1707. Although he expanded the empire to include almost all of India, his

For the last eight years of his life, Shah Jahan could only gaze at the Taj Mahal from his palace window. He was imprisoned there by his son Aurangzeb, who had seized the throne.

policies also contributed to the empire's downfall. Military expenses required heavier taxes, which increased the peasants' discontent with Mogul rule. Also, in his effort to cut nonmilitary expenses, Aurangzeb dismissed the court artists, architects, and historians. This policy stifled the growth of Mogul culture.

One result of Aurangzeb's policies was tension between Hindus and Muslims. This tension grew after Hindu rulers challenged Aurangzeb, and he reacted by reinstating a tax on non-Muslims and destroying many Hindu temples.

Viewing Aurangzeb's policies as a threat to their way of life, some local Hindu rulers and Muslim officials rebelled. Previously loyal Rajputs waged a war against Aurangzeb that dragged on for over 30 years. Two other groups—Marathas (muh-RAHT-uhs) and Sikhs (SEEKS)—also waged war against Aurangzeb.

The Marathas were a group of Hindu tribes in the western part of the Deccan. In the 1600s, a brilliant leader named Sivaji (sih-VAH-jee) formed them—along with some Muslim allies—into a successful fighting force. In 1717, the Moguls had to sign a treaty acknowledging the Marathas as rulers of the Deccan.

The Sikhs were followers of a religion started in northwest India in the early 1500s by Nanak Dev. With similarities to both Hinduism and Islam, the religion began as a peaceful reform movement. Akbar had maintained friendly relations with the Sikhs, but later Mogul rulers such as Aurangzeb came into conflict with them. To defend their faith, the Sikhs fought fiercely against Aurangzeb's armies.

Weakening of the empire. Under the burden of constant warfare, Aurangzeb's huge empire began to fall apart. Leaving Delhi in 1681 to wage war, he did not return until shortly before his death in 1707. During this long absence from the capital, the government began to crumble, its treasury drained by corrupt officials and costly wars. Many Indian states withdrew their support or declared independence from the empire.

Aurangzeb's descendants ruled the Mogul Empire until 1857. It was an empire greatly reduced in size and power, however. This weakening of Mogul rule made it easier for traders from European nations to gain control of parts of India.

EUROPEAN TRADE IN INDIA

European trade with India had begun with the arrival of Portuguese explorer Vasco da Gama in 1498, before the Moguls came to power. During the early 1500s, the Portuguese faced resistance from the Arab Muslim merchants, who wanted to control the trade with India, and local Hindu princes, who saw the Europeans as a threat to their rule. The Portuguese, however, with better guns and ships, seized several ports along India's western coast, making the port of Goa (GŌ-uh) their major trading center. They also took control of the Arab trade routes in the Indian Ocean.

The Portuguese were followed by traders from other European nations. In 1598, the Dutch established a few trading posts. However, their main interest lay further east, in the region now called Indonesia. During the 1600s, the English East India Company and French East India Company established trading posts along the coast and gradually squeezed the Portuguese out of most of the Indian trade.

India had many products that European traders wanted. It exported rice, sugar, pepper, and spices. In addition, Mogul rulers set up "factories" to produce artwork and fabrics, especially cottons and silks. One early European visitor

NUR JAHAN

Many of the women of the Mogul Empire lived under a system of *purdah,* or seclusion. When in public, they had to be veiled or hidden behind curtains. The emperor's wives were even more secluded, for they were rarely allowed to leave the harem. However, Nur Jahan—the wife of Jahangir—overcame these restrictions and actually became a real ruler of the Mogul Empire throughout much of her husband's reign.

Nur Jahan, whose given name was Mehrunissa, was the daughter of a Persian official in the Mogul court. In 1611, she came to the notice of Jahangir, and they were married two months later. Mehrunissa's beauty prompted the emperor to call her *Nur Mahal,* which means "Light of the Palace."

Mehrunissa was a gifted poet, artist, and architect, whose building designs were the first to use white marble and inlaid decoration—the hallmarks of Mogul architecture. As the emperor became increasingly enchanted with his talented and attractive wife, he selected her to be "the first among wives." With this new position came a new name: *Nur Jahan*—"Light of the World." She also gained new power, for Jahangir was content to let her run the empire. One observer noted that she "governs [Jahangir] at her pleasure."

For much of Jahangir's reign, Nur Jahan ruled fairly and efficiently. However, in the last years of Jahangir's life, she seemed more interested in keeping her power than in governing fairly. Becoming jealous of the popularity of one of Jahangir's sons, Prince Khurram, she tried unsuccessfully to prevent his ascent to the throne. After becoming emperor, the prince took the name *Shah Jahan,* which means "King of the World." Rather than oppose the new emperor, Nur Jahan quietly retired to the city of Lahore until her death in 1643.

Nur Jahan's rule lasted little more than a dozen years, but she had a tremendous impact on the empire. Not only did she encourage the adoption of Persian customs at the Mogul court, but she also influenced the flowering of Mogul art.

described these factories: "Large halls are seen in many places called *karkhanes*, or workshops. In one hall embroiderers are busily employed. In another you see goldsmiths, in a third painters, in a fourth varnishers in lacquer-work, in a fifth joiners, turners, tailors, shoemakers." European demand for Indian goods was high, but few European products were wanted in India. Therefore, the Europeans usually had to offer silver in exchange for Indian products.

The Mogul rulers were determined to restrict European trade and use it to their advantage. As long as the Moguls remained strong, British and French merchants patiently negotiated for trading rights. However, as European strength grew, the Moguls, as well as the local merchants and Hindu princes, gradually lost their control of the trade.

Throughout the 1600s, European merchants became firmly established in India. Fortified trading ports grew into settlements and then cities as the Europeans took advantage of the political unrest in India. In the 1700s, European traders and Indian princes tried to expand their influence at the expense of the weakening Mogul Empire. Often the princes offered trade privileges in exchange for European guns and assistance in training armies to fight the Moguls or other rivals for power.

THE GROWTH OF BRITISH CONTROL

As the French and English began to dominate European trade in India, each feared that the other might gain enough power to win a monopoly. Therefore, the directors of the trading companies instructed their agents to do whatever was needed to ensure continuing profits. The private companies had great powers, in some ways acting like independent governments. They acquired territory, made treaties, kept up armies, and took part in wars.

In 1740, the War of the Austrian Succession broke out in Europe, with Great Britain and France on opposing sides. This clash between the British and the French spilled over into In-

This eighteenth-century miniature painting in the Mogul style depicts a procession of Indians and Englishmen. An English dignitary rides atop the elephant, a position of honor.

dia as well and continued there for over 20 years. Under a military leader named Robert Clive, the British emerged from this struggle as the dominant European power in India.

Following the British victory, Clive was named the East India Company's governor in the state of Bengal. Seeking to enlarge the company's rule in India, he received from the Mogul emperor the power to collect taxes in Bengal and another wealthy state. Indians still managed the government, but the East India Company controlled government funds.

During the late 1700s, charges of corruption and poor business practices by the East India Company led the British government to play an ever-growing role in India. In 1773, Parliament began appointing a governor-general for the company and controlling company policies. Lord Cornwallis, who was named governor-general in the late 1780s, started a new civil service system. Company workers were now professionals receiving fixed salaries. Although reducing corruption, the system caused resentment among the Indians, who were barred from the most important positions.

During the 1780s and 1790s, governors expanded the company's territory, taking advantage of internal conflicts and rivalries between states. Company officials offered to protect individual states from attack. In return, the rulers of these states gave control of their foreign affairs to the company and allowed company troops to remain in their territory. As the eighteenth century drew to a close, the East India Company was gradually extending its power in India.

SECTION REVIEW

1. How did Babur, Akbar, and Aurangzeb shape the Mogul Empire in India?

2. What were the characteristics of Mogul culture?

3. How did Akbar promote unity?

4. How did Aurangzeb's policies weaken the empire?

5. How did Great Britain emerge as the dominant European power in India?

Analysis. Explain how Akbar and Aurangzeb would disagree regarding the best way to preserve political power.

18-4
EMPIRES AND KINGDOMS OF SUB-SAHARAN AFRICA

READ TO FIND OUT

—how the empires of Songhai and Kanem-Bornu rose and declined.
—how the forest kingdoms were established.
—how the African responses to Europeans varied.
—how the Europeans and Africans viewed slavery.
—how African societies were affected by expanding trade with Europeans.

By the late 1400s, new kingdoms and empires were emerging in sub-Saharan Africa. Like early Ghana and Mali, these states expanded by controlling trade routes and by collecting tribute from conquered communities. Military victories yielded war captives who became slaves, most of whom were absorbed into the conqueror's society as soldiers, agricultural workers, and artisans.

Although these expanding kingdoms had already developed strong economies and governments, a number of African rulers felt they could benefit from trade with the Europeans. However, in most of the kingdoms involvement with Europeans, especially through the slave trade, eventually led to political, economic, and social instability.

ISLAMIC EMPIRES

Strong rulers and powerful armies were key factors in the expansion of many African states from the 1400s through the 1700s. Military power was especially important in the growth of two Islamic empires during the 1500s—Songhai and Kanem-Bornu (KAH-nem BOR-new). As in Mali, the Islamic influence within

Built in the 1300s, the Sankore Mosque of Timbuktu was constructed of baked clay reinforced with wood. The ends of the timbers form a ladder, used when the building needs repairs.

The empire's glory, however, did not last more than a hundred years. Most of the Songhai people resisted Askia's efforts to convert them to Islam and resented his reliance on Muslim advisors. Without broad public support, he was unable to ensure an orderly succession to the throne and was overthrown by his son in 1528. Continuing power struggles further weakened the government, but its collapse was the result of a military weakness. In the 1590s, Songhai's proud force of mounted lancers was defeated by a small Moroccan army. Although greatly outnumbered, the Moroccans possessed a key weapon that dramatically changed sub-Saharan warfare—the musket.

Kanem-Bornu. The Kanem Empire emerged in the central Sudan region during the mid-800s, became an Islamic state by 1100, and eventually expanded to include the vast plain of Bornu. During the late 1500s, under Idris Alooma (EE-drees al-Ō-muh), the fierce cavalry acquired muskets, and the empire reached its height of military power. However, after Alooma's death, the empire gradually declined. During the 1600s and 1700s, ineffective rulers were unable to maintain peace among the conquered peoples. Meanwhile, the economy, which relied on slave raiding and taxation of trade, declined when expanding European trade routes moved west, beyond the range of the empire's armies.

FOREST KINGDOMS

Although Islam strongly influenced the governments of Songhai, Kanem-Bornu, and other states of the savanna, or grassland, region, it did not significantly affect the forest peoples south of the savanna. Within the forest communities, both the rulers and the general population continued to embrace traditional African beliefs.

Like most Africans, the forest peoples believed that social stability was rooted in traditions passed down through ancestors. The primary duty of the king was to communicate with the spirits of these ancestors. Regarded as having divine powers, the king performed religious rituals while nobles handled the daily affairs of government. Respect for ancestors and a belief in the spiritual authority of kings provided the forest peoples with strong foundations for their societies.

these empires was primarily limited to the government. Most of the general population remained loyal to their own religious traditions and felt no strong commitment to an Islamic government. Therefore, the stability of the Islamic empires in sub-Saharan Africa was largely based on the strength of their rulers and armies.

Songhai. In the early 1400s, as Mali declined under weak leadership, the province of Songhai broke away. Under its first great ruler, Sunni Ali (SOO-nee AH-lee), Songhai replaced Mali as the largest, most powerful West African trading empire. Sunni Ali kept Mali's system of provincial governors but established a civil service to ensure a stronger central government. At the empire's height under Askia (AHS-kee-uh) Muhammad in the early 1500s, its cavalry controlled the gold and salt trade in a region half the size of Europe. During Askia's reign, Timbuktu reached its height as a center of culture and learning, as students from many Muslim countries visited the Sankore mosque.

By the late 1400s, improvements in agriculture had led to increases in food production and therefore larger populations in a number of the forest communities. As growing populations created the need for expanded government and additional territory, some communities grew from small city-states into large kingdoms.

Benin, Oyo, and Asante. The most powerful forest kingdoms grew out of city-states established by peoples known as the Yoruba (YŌ-roo-bah) and the Akan (AH-kan). According to Yoruba oral history, the city-state of Ife (EE-fay) was founded about A.D. 1000. From Ife, groups of Yoruba settlers spread out, establishing a number of city-states, each with its own dynasty. Of these city-states, Benin (beh-NIN) and Oyo (ō-YŌ) had become the most powerful by the 1400s. The Akan, meanwhile, remained separated into many small states until

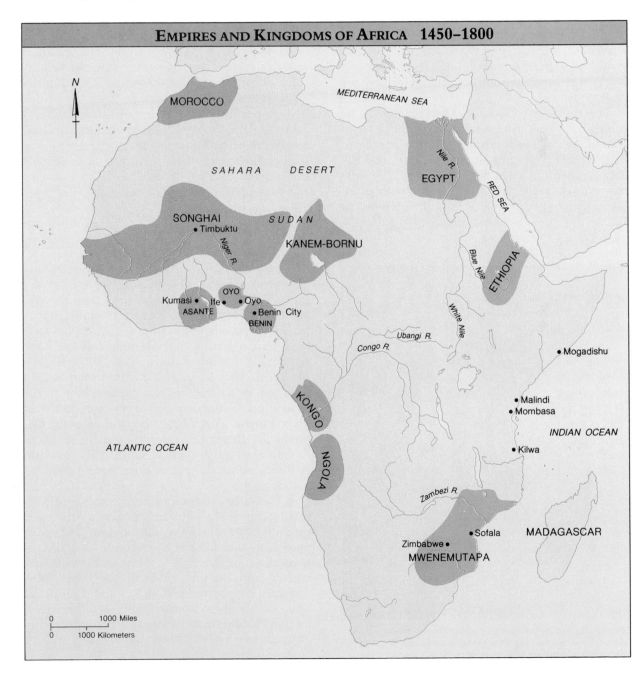

EMPIRES AND KINGDOMS OF AFRICA 1450–1800

about 1680, when they formed a powerful confederation that became known as Asante (uh-SAHNT-ee).

Benin was ruled by an *oba* (Ō-buh), or king, who resided in Benin City, a walled town containing about half the kingdom's population. This thriving trade center was one of the first cities in the world to be built according to a gridiron pattern, with broad avenues crossed by streets. Using cowrie shells and metal rings as currency, Benin merchants traded such items as ironwork, weapons, tools, and wood carvings. Benin's highly developed craft system included guilds for various types of artisans. An elite group of artisans served the oba, specializing in ivory and bronze sculptures that glorified the royal court.

The people of Oyo considered Benin to be somewhat of a "sister city" because both states recognized the spiritual authority of the king of Ife. Politically, the kingdom developed an elaborate system for balancing the power of hereditary officials with that of officials appointed by the *alafin* (ah-LAHF-in), or king. In addition, an alafin who was considered unworthy of the position could be dethroned by the governing council of nobles.

Oyo's growth had much to do with geography. Unlike the densely forested region around Benin, part of Oyo's territory bordered the savanna, where horses could be used effectively in warfare. With its fearsome cavalry, Oyo conquered the peoples of the nearby savanna north and west of Ife. Like Benin, Oyo had a strong military tradition. Generals were expected to return from battle only if victorious.

The unification of the small Akan states into the Asante confederation marked the birth of a powerful empire. The spiritual and political unity of Asante was represented by the beautiful Golden Stool, the throne of the empire's *asantehene* (uh-SAHN-tee-hee-nee), or ruler. The empire had an efficient hierarchy of government officials, a swift messenger system, and a network of well-maintained roads. Artisans in the bustling capital city of Kumasi (kuh-MAH-see) crafted dazzling bronze and gold jewelry and wove brilliant multicolored garments.

AFRICAN RESPONSES TO THE EUROPEANS

There were various African responses to the European traders who began arriving in the mid-1400s. The most common response was acceptance. Many African rulers wanted European guns and ammunition, while African artisans desired European tools and fabrics. As the slave trade developed during the 1500s, a number of African kingdoms became increasingly involved in it, trading war captives for European guns. Some African rulers were wary of involvement with Europeans and initially opposed the slave trade. However, many of these rulers eventually traded slaves for guns to strengthen their armies against threats from rival kingdoms.

While many African states became heavily involved in trade with Europeans, a few states carefully controlled the activities of European merchants and limited the volume of trade. In general, though, trade with Europeans increased from the mid-1400s through the 1700s, and relations between Africans and Europeans were essentially peaceful. Only in a few areas, notably southern and eastern Africa, did Africans have to resist violent European efforts to control territory.

Symbolic figures and teeth of gold embellish this antelope skin helmet, a ceremonial headpiece made for an Asante king. The golden bull's horns are an emblem of the king's power.

Figures such as the *nkisi* from the southwestern Kongo were carved out of wood. As part of a ritual, a figure was pierced with nails to tap its supernatural powers.

Acceptance. Many African rulers allowed the Europeans to increasingly influence the trade, and even the government, of their kingdoms. Two notable examples were the empires of Kongo (KAHN-gō) and Mwenemutapa (muh-WAY-nee-muh-TAH-puh).

When the Portuguese reached Kongo in the late 1400s, it was already the largest state in West Central Africa. Kongo had a strong economy, but its kings were still eager to learn about European culture, agriculture, and warfare. One of the kings, Nzinga Mbemba (uhn-ZEENG-guh muh-BEM-buh), welcomed Portuguese political advisors and missionaries and even tried unsuccessfully to transform Kongo into a Christian kingdom.

Internal power struggles enabled the Portuguese to gain influence within the Mwenemutapa empire. During the late 1400s, a series of weak rulers looked to the Portuguese for help in suppressing revolts. In return, the Portuguese gained increasing control over the trade until the people of the region eventually forced them to leave in the 1700s.

Control. The West African states of Benin and Asante were among the few kingdoms that chose to strictly control European trade. By usually restricting the Europeans to leased trading posts along the coast, these states prevented European merchants from significantly interfering with their traditional government, culture, and trade.

Benin and Asante had different reasons for controlling the slave trade within their territories. Being secure militarily, Benin often found slaves more valuable as members of society than as a means for acquiring additional guns. Asante, however, controlled its slave trade as a means of expanding its power. In contrast, most West African kingdoms were weakened by the constant slave raiding.

Resistance. Although most contacts between Africans and Europeans were peaceful up through the 1700s, some clashes did occur. The Portuguese, who were determined to seize control of the profitable trade between East Africa and India, attacked Kilwa, Mombasa, and other key cities along the East African coast. Although the cities' defenders fought fiercely, Portuguese muskets and cannon prevailed. The Africans and Arabs did not regain control of the eastern coast until Portuguese power declined in the 1700s.

In the 1600s and 1700s, peoples of southern Africa resisted Dutch colonization. In 1652, while competing for control of the Indian Ocean trade, the Dutch established a supply station at the Cape of Good Hope, which quickly grew into a colony. The settlers, known as Boers (BOHRZ), sought new grazing lands for their cattle. The small African communities of the Cape region tried unsuccessfully to stop the Boers from taking their land. However, by the late 1700s the Boers' steady eastward expansion was halted by the Bantu-speaking people of the southeast, who also desired grazing area for cattle and who proved to be a formidable foe.

DIFFERING VIEWS OF SLAVERY

Slavery had existed in Africa before the Muslims and Europeans had any impact on African society. However, the African view of slavery differed significantly from that of the Muslims and Europeans. In African communities, slaves were generally not regarded as mere property. Instead, most slaves gradually became members of the community. Slaves were usually respected and valued for the talents that they could contribute to society, and they could even earn freedom through work. Furthermore, mistreatment of slaves was considered immoral.

Muslims regarded slaves as property, but still treated them as members of the family or community and took care not to harm them. Also, Muslim masters frequently granted slaves their freedom. In contrast, the European view generally held that masters had complete and permanent ownership of their slaves, with no moral obligation to treat them kindly.

THE IMPACT OF THE SLAVE TRADE

Around the twelfth century, the slave trade began to grow significantly as a result of the increased presence of Muslim traders in North Africa, Ethiopia, East Africa, and the savanna region of West Africa. However the most extensive slave trading was the Atlantic slave trade conducted by the Europeans. One generally accepted estimate is that about 15 million Africans were transported to the Americas between 1500 and 1800.

Although the decline in Africa's population can be estimated, the extreme human suffering caused by the slave trade is immeasurable. Close social ties within small communities were destroyed as families were separated. One witness described the victims of a slave raid:

> Some [of the captured], grasping their feet with their hands, refused to rise. Others, bracing themselves against trees [would] resist with all the force of their muscles; or [entwine] themselves with their wives and children [in] knots which nothing short of a sword [could] untie. . . .

Millions of Africans died during the slave raids, on the way to the coast, and in the cramped, unsanitary slave ships. Only between one fifth and one half of the captured slaves survived to reach the Americas.

Conditions aboard a British slave ship, the *Albatross*, were recorded by Godfrey Meynall in this watercolor. Some slave ships were so crowded that people could neither stand nor sit up.

African societies, governments and economies survived the slave trade, but they were no longer as stable. Slave raiders took away community leaders, destroying traditional lines of authority within village governments. The slave trade also caused political instability in some of the large kingdoms. For instance, by allowing Portuguese advisors to control the trade, Nzinga Mbemba eventually lost political and economic control of Kongo. The slave trade rapidly expanded as the Portuguese traders dealt directly with Kongo's enemies, especially Ngola (un-GOH-luh), which the Portuguese called Angola. Eventually the slave trade led to war between Kongo and Ngola, hastening Kongo's decline. Angola later became a slave-trading colony controlled by the Portuguese.

In general, the slave trade hurt African economies because it did not encourage productive trade. Instead, it drained Africa of valued human resources while primarily supplying destructive weapons.

Other effects of expanding trade. As a result of the expanding trade with Europeans, an elite merchant class emerged in many African societies. These merchants were often slave traders who had become influential. Kings frequently had to depart from the tradition of hereditary status and appoint these merchants to government positions on the basis of merit.

Another development was the introduction of European and Islamic artistic styles, techniques, and materials to African artisans. Earlier African art was characterized by rock and body painting, ceramics, and stonework. However, after the 1500s, artisans increasingly experimented with textile design, metal casting, and wood sculpture. In exploring these techniques, they utilized the metals and yarns acquired through European trade. Changes in clothing design were also notable. Clothing became more elaborate, reflecting the status and wealth of the newly established merchant class.

SECTION REVIEW

1. How did Songhai and Kanem-Bornu become empires? Why did both empires eventually decline?

2. How did Benin, Oyo, and Asante become strong kingdoms?

3. Describe the three general African reactions to the Europeans.

4. How did the African and European views of slavery differ?

5. What were three effects of European trade on African societies?

Analysis. Why was there no significant conflict between the West African kingdoms and the Europeans?

Data Search. Refer to the slave imports chart on page 832. Explain how it illustrates: **(a)** the low survival rate of slaves transported to the Americas and **(b)** the dominance of the Brazil and West Indies slave trade.

HISTORY IN FOCUS

Developments between the mid-1400s and 1800 reflected some parallels among the European, Asian, and African societies. The most significant similarity among the three societies was the trend from decentralized government to centralized government. In addition, all three regions experienced economic growth and the emergence of an increasingly wealthy and influential merchant class.

However, there were significant differences in economic policies. European governments were earnestly competing with each other to expand their power through overseas exploration and trade. In contrast to this European mercantilism, Asian and African governments were essentially content with economic growth achieved primarily through internal trade and increased agricultural production. In addition, many Asian and African rulers saw foreign trade as a threat to their governments, not as a means of increasing political power. These rulers believed that their political security depended upon maintaining cultural traditions and a stable social structure.

The overall impact of European trade was stronger in Africa than in Asia. Many African societies allowed trade with Europeans to replace the traditional foundations of their economies. Meanwhile, the influence of the Europeans increased in China, Japan, and India, as domestic change and unrest weakened central governments. As the eighteenth century drew to a close, Asian and African states were gradually being drawn into a web of European commercial influence.

SUMMARY

- The Ming Dynasty collapsed as a result of corruption, declining income, rebellion, and the invasion of the Manchus. The Ch'ing Dynasty of the Manchus preserved Chinese government and culture and restricted European trade. In the 1700s, China experienced peace, economic growth, and a dramatic population increase. By the late 1700s, though, anger at overtaxation and corruption fueled rebellions against the Ch'ing Dynasty.

- Japan became unified under the Tokugawa shogunate, which controlled local daimyo, limited foreign contacts, and encouraged a rigid class structure. However, internal trade brought changes, such as a money economy, a wealthy merchant class, and a thriving urban culture.

- In India, the Moguls founded a new Muslim empire. The blending of the Muslim and Hindu cultures was mainly evident in the Mogul court. Akbar's religious tolerance and effective rule contrasted with his successors' policies of overspending and overtaxation. The resulting decline of the empire paved the way for British expansion.

- In sub-Saharan Africa, new kingdoms and empires arose in the 1400s. Stability in the Islamic states was based on military strength, while the forest kingdoms relied on shared cultural traditions. European trade centered in West Africa, and most African-European relations were characterized by trade, not conflict. However, involvement with the Europeans, especially in the Atlantic slave trade, eventually undermined African political, social, and economic stability.

VOCABULARY REVIEW

Match each numbered vocabulary term with the lettered word or phrase most closely related to it. Then explain how the items in each pair are related.

1. kowtow   (a) drama
2. haiku   (b) submission
3. kabuki   (c) poetry

CHAPTER REVIEW

1. (a) How was political stability established by the Ch'ing Dynasty? By the Tokugawa shogunate? **(b)** Explain how political stability aided economic growth in China and Japan.

2. (a) Why did the population of China grow rapidly between 1500 and 1800? **(b)** What effect did population growth have on China?

3. (a) Describe and explain the general economic growth in China, Japan, India, and sub-Saharan Africa. **(b)** Compare the social effects of economic growth in China, Japan, India, and sub-Saharan Africa. **(c)** Explain how economic growth affected political stability in China, Japan, India, and sub-Saharan Africa.

4. (a) In what way did the Manchus and the Moguls face a similar situation? **(b)** How did early Manchu and Mogul rulers respond to this situation?

5. Explain how China, Japan, India, and sub-Saharan Africa experienced both cultural continuity and cultural change.

6. (a) Give an example from the chapter of a ruler or government that showed tolerance of another culture. What was the political effect? **(b)** Give an example of a ruler or government that was intolerant of another culture. What was the political effect of this intolerance?

7. (a) Explain how Christianity was introduced to China and Japan. **(b)** Compare the way Chinese rulers reacted to Christianity with the way Japanese rulers reacted.

8. Compare the impact of Islam on India and sub-Saharan Africa.

9. (a) Compare Ming, Ch'ing, and Tokugawa policies regarding Europeans. **(b)** How did the Moguls react to European trade? **(c)** Why did the West African kingdoms trade with Europeans? **(d)** Give examples of the three types of African responses to Europeans.

10. (a) What weaknesses became apparent in both the Ming and the Ch'ing governments? **(b)** What weakened Mogul control over India? **(c)** Compare the political effects of European contacts with the following regions: China, Japan, India, sub-Saharan Africa.

THINKING CRITICALLY: ACTIVITIES

1. In an attempt to end Chinese restrictions on trade, the British government sent a representative to the court of Ch'ien-lung in 1793. The emperor refused to end the restrictions. In addition, he was shocked at the representative's refusal to kowtow. Imagine you are the emperor. Write a letter to the British king expressing your opinion about **(a)** the attempts to expand trade with China and **(b)** the behavior of the British representative.

2. With another student, discuss Japan's policy of seclusion. One of you can play the role of a samurai who advocates ending the seclusion, while the other can argue the viewpoint of the Tokugawa shogun.

3. Imagine that you are the ruler of a particular West African kingdom. Discuss your participation in the trade with the Europeans. Explain the benefits and drawbacks of this trade.

APPLYING SOCIAL STUDIES SKILLS

Evaluating secondary sources. Answer these questions about a secondary source you use every day—your history textbook.

1. When was it first published?

2. Has it been revised? If so, when?

3. How many authors wrote this textbook?

4. Which author is head of a history department and has published many history books?

5. Which author has both chaired and coordinated a social studies department?

6. Which author has written extensively about thinking skills?

7. For whom is this book written?

8. Which of the following goals do you think the authors had in writing this book? You may pick several goals. Then explain your answer.

   (a) to provide information

   (b) to promote patriotic feelings

   (c) to provide information on geography

   (d) to help students develop thinking skills

   (e) to state their own theories about history

APPLYING THINKING SKILLS

Determining the credibility of a source. Read these descriptions to determine which source is likely to be most credible on the topic of West Africa in the seventeenth century.

A. A book on West Africa written by a nineteenth-century French historian, who was an experienced writer but not a specialist in African history. The author spent six months researching his book. During this time, another historian gave him some diaries that he claimed were written by two Dutch merchants who visited West Africa in the early 1600s. These diaries became the author's most important sources.

B. A book on West Africa published in 1851. Its British author lived in West Africa for seven years and spent these years collecting information on West African peoples and cultures. For his sources, he used accounts written by Muslim merchants who had traveled and lived in West Africa during the 1600s. His book was frequently used as a source by other British historians during the early 1900s.

C. A five-volume account of West and Central Africa published in 1857 by a German explorer who spent eight years in West Africa. His research and his personal experience there provided what one African history specialist has called "the first scholarly and comprehensive understanding" of seventeeth-century West Africa. His main sources were oral historians of several West African peoples and accounts by seventeeth-century Muslim merchants who lived in West Africa.

1. Define the term *credibility*.

2. What is one way to determine the credibility of a written source?

3. What are the features of a credible source?

4. Why is it important to try to determine the credibility of your sources of information?

5. Which one of the above sources is likely to be most credible on the topic of West Africa in the seventeenth century? Explain your answer.

6. Which source is probably the least credible? Explain your answer.

UNIT REVIEW

1. (a) List two factors that promoted population growth and two that promoted urbanization in various parts of the world between 1500 and 1800. **(b)** In what two parts of the world did the population decline during this period? How were the declines related?

2. (a) How did the Renaissance and Reformation help create the conditions that would give rise to the nation-state? **(b)** In what sense did overseas expansion and the Commercial Revolution have both positive and negative effects on the nation-state?

3. Compare the following: **(a)** Ch'ing rule and the nation-state; **(b)** controls on nobles or officials in France and in Japan.

4. (a) How peaceful were Europe, China, and Japan in the 1700s? What explains the difference? **(b)** How did revolts in China and Europe differ?

5. (a) Compare how Charles V, Hideyoshi, and Akbar responded to religious issues. **(b)** What rulers in Spain and India tried to establish state religions, and with what results? **(c)** How was the influence of Islam in Africa different from that of Catholicism in Latin America?

6. (a) How did the Hapsburgs, the Manchus, and the British East India Company each gain control over large territories? **(b)** How did European empire-building change between 1500 and 1800? **(c)** How did European expansion differ from that of other world regions?

7. (a) How did the Chinese and European economies differ in the 1700s? **(b)** How was foreign trade regulated in Africa, China, Japan, and the Americas? **(c)** What capitalist traits did the Japanese economy have, and how did it differ from European capitalism?

8. (a) Compare the cultural diffusion in Latin America, Africa, and Mogul India. **(b)** How did Japan, China, and Europe react to foreign cultural influences?

9. (a) Compare the social structure of colonial Latin America and Tokugawa Japan. **(b)** How did the social positions of European, Chinese, and Japanese merchants differ?

10. (a) Compare the art and literature of the Ch'ing Dynasty and the Renaissance. **(b)** Compare support for art in India with that of Renaissance Italy. **(c)** What did art in Latin America and Mogul India have in common? **(d)** In what ways were African artisans influenced by contacts with Europeans and Muslims?

RELATING PAST TO PRESENT

1. Some Renaissance thinkers, like Machiavelli, believed that rulers should do whatever seemed necessary to strengthen the state. Others, like Erasmus and More, believed that leaders should be guided by ethics. Explain how modern politics reflect these opposing attitudes, referring to appropriate current events.

2. The Spanish and Portuguese colonization of the Americas produced an entirely new cultural blend. Research and write a report on how this blending is reflected in one of the following areas of Latin American culture: music, art, literature, politics, social class, religion, food, clothing, architecture, or medicine.

3. Select one city that played a role in the developments described in Unit 5. Some examples might be: Mombasa, Timbuktu, Nagasaki, Edo (Tokyo), Agra, Macao, Canton, Quebec, Amsterdam, Venice, Versailles, Mexico City, and Lima. Do research to describe the city between 1300 and 1800. Then describe the city today. Consider such topics as population, area, and economic and political activities.

PROJECTS AND ACTIVITIES

1. Divide into groups of four or five and prepare an oral report on an African kingdom or empire from the period 1450 to 1800. Each member of the group should choose a different aspect of the state's social, economic, political, or cultural life to investigate. Then present your report to the class.

2. Prepare a picture and text display on an artist of the Renaissance or a traditional style of art from China, Japan, India, Africa, or the Americas. Arrange your display on poster board or a bulletin board to share with the class.

3. Imagine that you are a Catholic missionary in colonial Latin America. Write a letter to your king in Spain or Portugal describing conditions for Native Americans and what should be done to protect their rights.

ANALYZING PRIMARY SOURCES

Refer to "Report by Columbus: His First Voyage" on page 351 to answer each of the following questions.

1. How does the letter reflect Columbus's belief that he had reached the Far East?

2. Who did Columbus think was mainly responsible for the success of his voyage—God or the king and queen of Spain? Support your answer with evidence from the letter.

3. What did Columbus find remarkable about the islands' natural features? About the weather?

4. According to Columbus, how could the islands be used by Spain? What did he seem to consider the most important benefit? Support your answer with evidence.

5. Why was Columbus able to take possession of the islands "without resistance"?

6. How does the letter indicate Columbus's plans for further voyages?

7. Do you think Columbus addressed this letter to the king and queen of Spain? Support your opinion with evidence.

GEOGRAPHY REVIEW

Regions. Dividing a large country like the United States into smaller regions such as the Southeast, the Midwest, the Great Plains, and the Rocky Mountain States helps geographers focus on the common characteristics within each region. The process of creating and analyzing regions also highlights differences between regions in terms of both human and physical characteristics. Answer these questions about your region of the country as a geographer might answer them.

1. What region of the country do you live in?

2. What other states, if any, are also considered to be part of this region?

3. What physical characteristics are generally used to define this region?

4. What human characteristics contribute to the region's special identity?

5. How is this region different from other regions within the United States?

6. What characteristics does your region share with most other regions of the United States?

7. Any area, small or large, can be divided into regions. Choose an area to divide into regions. The area might be your community, a large section of your community, or your neighborhood. Identify at least three regions within the area, using any characteristics that seem to you to show homogeneity, or sameness, within a region. An example might be a town divided into a business district, an industrial district, and a residential district.

Make a map of the area, showing the boundaries of the regions that you have defined. Label each region with a name that expresses its uniform characteristics.

SUGGESTED READINGS

An Age of Splendour: Islamic Art in India, ed. Saryu Doshi. Baltimore: Smithsonian Institution Press, 1986. A highly illustrated commentary on a rich variety of arts.

Cole, Bruce. *The Renaissance Artist at Work.* New York: Harper and Row, 1983. An illustrated study of how Renaissance artists worked.

Diaz del Castillo, Bernal. *The Conquest of New Spain.* New York: Penguin, 1963. An eyewitness account of the conquest of Mexico.

Franck, Irene M., and David Brownstone. *To the Ends of the Earth: The Great Travel and Trade Routes of History.* New York: Facts on File, 1984. Exciting accounts by contemporary travelers.

Trevino, Elizabeth (Borton). *I, Juan de Pareja.* New York: Farrar, 1965. Historical fiction about a black slave who becomes an artist at the Spanish court of Philip IV.

DAWN OF
THE MODERN AGE

1500-1914

*Here and today
begins a new age in
the history of the world . . .
I was present at its birth.*

—Goethe, c. 1792

Keelmen Heaving in Coals by Moonlight.
Joseph Mallord William Turner, England, c. 1935.

GLOBAL TIMELINE

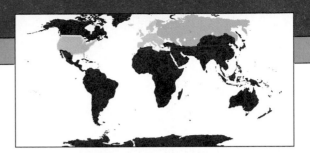

	POLITICAL	TECHNOLOGICAL	SOCIAL
1500	Hobbes's *Leviathan* 1651 — Locke's *Two Treatises of Government* 1690 — French and Indian War 1754-63	Copernicus's heliocentric theory 1543 — Vesalius's book on anatomy 1543 — Galileo's telescope; Kepler makes astronomy a science 1609 — Newton's laws of motion and gravitation 1687	Development of newspapers 1600s — Last witch execution in England 1721 — Baroque period 1600-1750
1760	Rousseau's *Social Contract* — American Revolution begins	Spinning jenny — Watt's steam engine	Diderot's *Encyclopédie* 1751 — "Classical" music develops
1780	French Revolution begins — U.S. Constitution ratified — France's first constitution	Cotton gin — Steam-powered textile mills	Adam Smith's *Wealth of Nations* — Height of Romanticism
1800	Napoleon becomes emperor — Congress of Vienna — Battle of Waterloo	First successful vaccination — Proof of existence of the atom — Steamboat and steam locomotive	First labor unions — Beethoven's Fifth Symphony
1820	Revolutions in France, Belgium, and Poland	First photographs — Mechanical reaper — Telegraph	Slavery abolished in Britain — Dickens' *Oliver Twist*
1840	Revolutions in France, Italy, and Austria — France's Second Republic formed — *Communist Manifesto*	First oil well — Bessemer process for making steel — Pasteur develops germ theory	Darwin's *Origin of Species* — First university degrees in U.S. for women
1860	France's Third Republic formed — Marx's *Das Kapital*	Telephone and phonograph — Electric lights	First department stores — Realism develops in art and literature — Impressionist period in painting
1880	Beginning of Progressive Era in U.S.	X-rays and radioactivity discovered — First airplane — Theory of Relativity	Bicycles become popular — Freud's *Interpretation of Dreams*
1900			

CHAPTER NINETEEN

A REVOLUTION IN THOUGHT

1500–1800

Young Woman Playing a Lute. Orazio Gentileschi, about 1610.

Between 1500 and 1800, revolutionary changes occurred in how Europeans viewed the world and their place in it. Overseas exploration, the Commercial Revolution, and the Renaissance all contributed to widespread questioning of traditional sources of authority and truth. By the 1700s, science had a key to understanding nature and society.

This shift in thinking began in the 1500s and continued into the 1600s, during a period of rapid change and discovery called the Scientific Revolution. In the 1700s, thinkers applied the new ideas of science to government, economics, education, and other areas of society during a period called the Enlightenment. Together, the Scientific Revolution and the Enlightenment reshaped European thought, signaling the beginning of the Modern Age.

TIMELINE

1525	
1550	Copernicus's *Revolution of the Heavenly Bodies* — Vesalius's book on anatomy
1575	Francis Bacon born — Kepler born
1600	
1625	Descartes born — Galileo's *Starry Messenger*
1650	Harvey's book on circulation — Leeuwenhoek born — Hooke born
1675	Hobbes's *Leviathan* — Royal Society of London founded
1700	Newton's *Mathematical Principles of Natural Philosophy* — Voltaire born
1725	
1750	Kant born — Swift's *Gulliver's Travels*
1775	Diderot's *Encyclopédie* — Mozart born — Rousseau's *Social Contract*
1800	Wollstonecraft's *Vindication of the Rights of Woman*

19-1
THE SCIENTIFIC REVOLUTION

READ TO FIND OUT

—what the terms *scientific method, rationality, objectivity*, and *mechanistic world view* mean.
—what beliefs made up the medieval view of the universe.
—how the view of the solar system changed.
—why the development of the scientific method was important.
—what Descartes contributed to science.
—how Newton built upon the ideas of others to make great discoveries.

While wars and economic crises dominated the lives of ordinary people in the 1500s and 1600s, a handful of scholars were looking at nature in new ways. Known as natural philosophers, these thinkers boldly explored both the heavens and the workings of the human body. Together these scholars helped shatter medieval ideas about nature and humankind.

THE MEDIEVAL WORLD VIEW

Until the 1500s, the western European world view, or way of seeing the universe, rested on two traditional foundations. The first was an accepted way of gaining knowledge based on the ideas of the ancient Greeks and the teachings of Christianity. The second was a certain way of seeing and understanding the world as a living organism.

Knowledge from reason and faith. From the Greeks, medieval scholars had inherited a way of discovering knowledge based on reasoning, or logic. Medieval thinkers, like the Greeks before them, had applied commonsense ideas based on everyday experience to understand everything they observed.

Medieval European scholars believed that a person needed only to think to gain true knowledge. For instance, they knew that heavy objects fell with greater force than light ones. From this knowledge, they reasoned that heavy objects such as cannonballs must fall faster than light objects such as apples. This conclusion was supported by Aristotle's laws of motion. In general, medieval thinkers did not test conclusions reached through reason.

Medieval thinkers usually began their reasoning with certain accepted assumptions and truths. While some of these truths had been established by the Greeks, others were matters of faith established by Christian theology. The Bible contained what God had chosen to tell humans and could not be doubted. Faith was the soundest foundation for finding truth.

The Church taught that people could know very little about the world compared to God, who was all-knowing. Many Europeans believed that much of nature would remain forever mysterious, controlled by the supernatural force of God.

At first, Christian faith and Greek reason often conflicted. Medieval thinkers such as Thomas Aquinas, however, had resolved the conflicts. Reason supported faith, according to the medieval scholastic philosophers, and faith explained what reason could not.

Nature as an organism. People use everyday objects as symbols to understand complicated ideas. Because most medieval people were farmers, plants and animals provided people with the symbols they used to understand such mysteries as life, death, the movement of the sun, and the organization of society.

To medieval people, everything in nature and society was connected, like the parts of a living thing, or organism. The earth was thought to be alive, with the soil as its skin. People compared society to a tree, with nobles in the top branches, clergy and merchants in the lower limbs, and peasants at the roots.

This way of looking at the world did not encourage change, and supported the power of the Church. It also gave people a distinct place in a world they could understand.

CHANGING PATTERNS OF THOUGHT

Although the medieval period was an age of faith, scholars made many important discoveries that helped pave the way for the major changes that occurred beginning in the 1500s. Some of

Georges de la Tour's *The Penitent Magdalene*, 1640, shows the biblical Mary Magdalene at the moment of conversion to Christianity. The painting reflects the medieval emphasis on religion.

these advances came from European contact with the Muslims, who had made many more scientific advancements than Europeans during the Middle Ages. Through these contacts, Europeans learned about the shape of the earth and gained new navigational instruments. They also began to use Arabic numerals and the concept of zero, both of which revolutionized European mathematics.

Other advances resulted from the rediscovery of the Greek classics. Acceptance of the ideas of Aristotle and other ancient Greeks forced scholars such as Thomas Aquinas to acknowledge the importance of reason, or logic.

When reason alone failed to explain natural phenomena, a few medieval scholars turned to experimentation. Among the earliest experimenters were people called alchemists who, searching for such knowledge as a way to change lead into gold, mixed magic and chemistry. They helped establish early methods of laboratory study.

As the Renaissance and the Reformation unfolded, the hold of medieval theology loosened. Gradually, philosophers and scientists began looking for new ways to study nature. At the same time, the voyages of exploration and the invention of the printing press broadened people's knowledge of the world. The discovery of new continents and new peoples did not fit well with the world described by the Bible and the Greek philosophers. Many people began challenging traditional assumptions.

A New View of the Solar System

The first major challenge to the medieval view of the world came as a result of a new understanding of the stars and the solar system. During the 1500s and early 1600s, discoveries in astronomy helped to create the basis of the Scientific Revolution.

The geocentric universe. To the ancient Greeks, the "universe" was everything they could see. They reasoned that the earth was the center of the universe because it did not seem to move. The planets, stars, and sun orbited about the earth in perfect circles because they could be seen making arcs, or portions of circles, in the night sky.

For more than a thousand years, most Europeans accepted this geocentric, or earth-centered, view of the universe. It seemed to fit what they could see. It also matched the ideas of people accustomed to viewing the earth as the most important organism they could imagine. Obviously, the earth must be at the center of the universe.

Moreover, a geocentric view conformed with medieval theology. If God had created the universe especially for humans, then logically, the earth would be at the center of the universe.

The new heliocentric solar system. A Polish astronomer and mathematician named Nicolaus Copernicus (kuh-PER-nih-kuhs) was the first to question the geocentric view. Born in 1473, Copernicus was educated as a doctor and lawyer and ordained as a member of the Catholic clergy. However, most of all he loved astronomy. Like the artists of his age, Copernicus dared to look at nature from a different perspective. Through more than thirty years of thought and study, he became convinced that the earth revolved around the sun. He envisioned a "solar system" instead of an earth-centered universe.

In describing his new heliocentric, or sun-centered, theory, Copernicus wrote, "In the middle of all sits the Sun enthroned. Could we place this luminary in any better position from which he can illuminate the whole at once?" Copernicus was one of the first to distinguish the solar system from the larger universe that included other stars.

Living in a period of religious upheaval, Copernicus realized the potential impact of his ideas. As a result, he delayed publication of his book, *The Revolution of the Heavenly Bodies*, until 1543. Finally, at almost 70 years of age, Copernicus braced himself and released his book.

As Copernicus had expected, his theory shocked European authorities. It upset the geocentric vision of Aristotle and Ptolemy. It challenged the traditional Christian view of humanity as the center of God's universe. It offended common sense and basic observation. Critics asked what made the earth revolve around the sun. They wanted to know why objects did not fly off the spinning earth, and why winds did not constantly blow on an earth moving through space. Catholic and Protestant theologians condemned the heliocentric theory, and most educated people rejected it.

The geocentric universe remained the accepted view for a century after Copernicus's death. His ideas, however, inspired two brilliant scientists, both born after Copernicus's lifetime. These scientists came forth with new evidence supporting the heliocentric view. Together, they helped create a turning point in the history of thought.

Kepler's Mathematical Universe

The first of these scientists was Johannes Kepler, a German astronomer born in 1571. Kepler accepted Copernicus's ideas and carried them one step further. A scientific genius and part-time astrologer, Kepler believed in the magical qualities of mathematics. As a result, he dedicated himself to revealing the secrets of nature

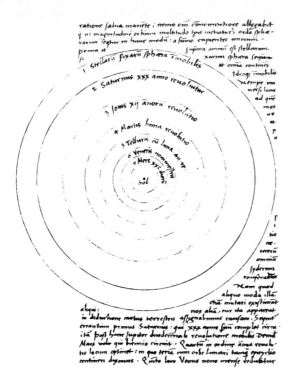

In this drawing from *The Revolution of the Heavenly Bodies*, Copernicus shows the orbits of eight planets around the sun. The ninth planet, Pluto, had not been discovered at that time.

Galileo, who advanced Copernicus's heliocentric theory, also made important discoveries about the measurement of time, specific gravity, and the laws of motion.

through numbers. In so doing, he turned Copernicus's general description of planetary motion into a precise mathematical formula.

Kepler's work rested upon three laws. The laws described the shape of the planets' orbits and their speed in relation to their distance from the sun. By revealing the mathematical logic of the universe, Kepler made it possible to chart the exact orbital paths of the planets. More importantly, he advanced the idea that heavenly bodies moved according to natural laws that people could discover and understand.

GALILEO'S CONFRONTATION WITH THE CHURCH

The other scientist influenced by Copernicus's ideas was Galileo (GAL-ih-LAY-ō), who lived at the same time as Kepler. In 1609, Galileo heard of the invention of a device that made distant objects seem near. With only the barest description in mind, Galileo set out to develop his own version of this instrument. The result was that he created a device with a much greater magnification than the one he tried to copy.

Using his new device—a forerunner to the modern telescope—Galileo turned his eyes toward the heavens. He observed the stars, recorded what he saw, and drew startling new conclusions.

In *The Starry Messenger*, published in 1610, Galileo reported his observations. He provided details on the four moons of Jupiter, spots on the sun, the stars of the Milky Way, and the rings of Saturn. He also vividly described the moon. From his observations, Galileo concluded that Copernicus had been correct in claiming that the earth revolved around the sun.

Galileo's findings caused an immediate sensation. The Catholic Church was deeply involved in struggles with Protestantism at this time. Galileo's theories eventually brought him before the Inquisition, the religious court established to pass judgement on heretics. Threatening Galileo, a sincere Catholic, with torture, church officials forced him to deny publicly that the earth moved around the sun. According to legend, as the 70-year-old Galileo left the courtroom, he whispered to himself, "And yet it does move!"

By the time of Galileo's death in 1642, many scientists had become convinced that the heliocentric theory of the universe was valid, even though the Catholic Church continued to oppose it. By gathering evidence supporting Copernicus's theory and boldly publishing their work, Galileo and Kepler had begun to overturn a basic assumption of the medieval view of the world. The doors to the Scientific Revolution were opened.

BACON AND THE SCIENTIFIC METHOD

While Kepler and Galileo struggled with the Church and their educated colleagues to gain acceptance of their radical ideas about the universe, a new method of gathering and interpreting information was emerging. This method is known today as the *scientific method*. Together with the heliocentric theory, the scientific method became the foundation of the Scientific Revolution.

During the 1500s, an Englishman named Sir Francis Bacon helped develop the scientific method. Bacon urged scientists to follow a fixed pattern of research. The first steps involved careful experimentation and observation. The next step called for the use of reason to interpret the experiment's results. From this point, scientists could draw valid conclusions, which in turn might be tested through further experimentation.

Bacon's scientific method differed from the ancient Greeks' method of acquiring knowledge. Bacon reasoned from specific observations to generalizations, a process called inductive reasoning. The Greeks, in contrast, had mainly started with accepted generalizations, using reason to arrive at specific details. This process, which is called deductive reasoning, avoided experimentation entirely.

Galileo was one of the first scientists to use the scientific method. In an attempt to disprove Aristotle's ideas about the motion of objects, Galileo conducted a variety of experiments. According to legend, he dropped balls of different weights from the Leaning Tower of Pisa to show that they traveled at the same rate of speed, or velocity, during their fall.

The impact of the scientific method. The scientific method became the basis of modern science. Its impact was felt in two major ways. First, it quickened the pace of scientific discovery because it provided a better way of finding out how nature actually worked. Second, and perhaps more importantly, it changed the way knowledge was judged and accepted. Gradually, most educated people no longer accepted explanations that were based on miracles, supernatural power, or magic. Instead, the scientific method, reason, and mathematical logic became the only ways to gather knowledge that were considered reliable.

DESCARTES'S CONTRIBUTION TO SCIENCE

The last great thinker to join with Kepler, Galileo, and Bacon in establishing the major ideas of the Scientific Revolution was the French philosopher René Descartes (reh-NAY day-KART). Descartes was born in 1596, when Francis Bacon was 35. He proposed several approaches to science that differed from Bacon's. Three of his ideas strongly influenced the development of science.

First, Descartes attacked the authority of ancient learning even more strongly than had Bacon. Vowing "never to accept anything for true which I did not clearly know to be such," Descartes emphasized the importance of doubting and questioning.

Second, unlike Bacon, Descartes did not think experimentation and inductive thinking were especially important. Instead, he believed that reason, or *rationality*, was the key to gaining knowledge. He promoted the deductive approach of the ancient Greeks. Descartes's strong belief in the importance of doubt, however, set him apart from the Greeks. Descartes became one of the foremost proponents of rationality during the 1600s.

Third, Descartes believed that outside of the human mind, all matter everywhere in the universe moved, changed, grew, and died according to natural laws. Because natural laws were themselves rational and orderly, scientists could discover these laws through rational thought alone.

As a result of Descartes's influence, the use of rationality—without emotion, intuition, or appeal to supernatural forces—gradually became the scientific ideal. This approach, later called *objectivity*, grew to become a key element in the quest for knowledge.

DISCOVERIES IN BIOLOGY AND MEDICINE

While astronomers and physicists helped change the way people gained knowledge and thought of the stars and planets, other scientists were making equally astonishing discoveries about plants, animals, and the human body. A Dutch scientist, Anton van Leeuwenhoek, (LAY-vuhn-HOOK), opened the way to new discoveries in the 1600s by greatly improving the device that today is called the microscope. Using this tool, he discovered one-celled microorganisms never seen before.

Robert Hooke of England expanded on Leeuwenhoek's early work with the microscope. Hooke became the first person to suggest that all plant and animal life was made up of cells. This discovery is one of the major foundations of modern-day biology.

Meanwhile, European scientists also made tremendous strides in medicine. For centuries, doctors had studied the medical teachings of the Hellenistic physician Galen. Following the Greek method, Galen had done little experi-

This painting by Poncet is strikingly similar to an engraving that appears in Vesalius's book, *Structure of the Human Body*. Here, Vesalius exhibits the tendons of a forearm.

mentation and actual examination of the human body. As a result, his work contained errors. Galen's ideas first began to be challenged in the early 1500s.

In 1543, the same year that Copernicus made public his theory, Andreas Vesalius, a doctor in what is now Belgium, published a book correcting some of Galen's faulty ideas. Instead of relying on Galen's generalizations, Vesalius himself had studied the human body through dissection. His research marked the beginning of modern anatomy.

A century later in England, another physician, William Harvey, built on Vesalius's findings. In 1628, Harvey discovered how blood circulated in the human body. Until this time, many people believed that blood remained stationary. Harvey, however, proved that the heart pumps blood throughout the entire body.

NEWTON'S GENIUS

In the last half of the seventeenth century, many young scientists inherited the ideas of Galileo, Kepler, Bacon, and Descartes and continued the Scientific Revolution. The most remarkable of these scientists was Isaac Newton, who was born in 1642, the year Galileo died.

While still in his twenties, Newton presented a ground-breaking study in optics, the study of light and its properties. Using a prism, he separated white light into the colors of the rainbow. Newton also invented a complex system of mathematics that he called "fluxions." This system, developed independently at about the same time by German mathematician Gottfried Leibniz, (LĪB-nits), is known today as calculus.

Newton's most important accomplishment, however, was his "law of universal gravitation," which was described in his *Mathematical Principles of Natural Philosophy*, published in 1687. According to this law, all objects in the universe are attracted to each other by a physical force called gravity. The degree of attraction between objects depends on their size and the distance that separates them.

Using the principle of gravity, Newton explained why the planets moved around the sun and why objects fell to earth. With a single theory, he pulled together the revolutionary ideas of Copernicus, Kepler, and Galileo. Said Newton modestly, "If I have seen farther, it is by standing on the shoulders of giants."

THE MECHANISTIC WORLD VIEW

Newton's achievements, combined with the work of scientists since Copernicus, helped forge a new world view. Instead of using the image of an organism to understand the social and natural worlds, scientists beginning in Newton's time began thinking of the universe as a giant mechanical clock. Like any machine, they believed, the universe was orderly and operated according to fixed rules, or natural laws. This comparison of the universe to a machine, or mechanism, began what has been called the *mechanistic world view*.

The mechanistic world view is one of the most important results of the Scientific Revolution. As it replaced the medieval world view, great changes began to occur in how people understood knowledge, God, and their place in the world.

In the mechanistic world view, God's role changed. Although God was still seen as having ultimate knowledge, humans were now considered capable of knowing many truths that only God had known before. Many scientists saw God as the "divine clockmaker," the Supreme Being who set the great clock of the universe in motion and then retired from worldly affairs. Now it was up to people to discover the rules that governed the machinelike workings of the universe.

SECTION REVIEW

1. Define *scientific method*, *rationality*, *objectivity*, and *mechanistic world view*.

2. How did Christian teachings contribute to the medieval view of the universe?

3. Compare the ancient Greek idea of a geocentric universe with Copernicus's theory of a solar system.

4. What were the two major effects of the scientific method?

5. How did Descartes's ideas differ from those of Bacon?

6. To whom was Newton referring when he said he stood "on the shoulders of giants" to formulate his new laws?

Analysis. What qualities does a clock have that make it an appropriate symbol for the mechanistic world view?

19–2 THE ENLIGHTENMENT

READ TO FIND OUT

—what basic ideas guided Enlightenment thinkers.
—what new theories about government emerged.
—what ideas about the economy were developed by economic philosophers.
—how education was linked to progress.

The accomplishments of the Scientific Revolution encouraged a spirit of confidence to spread across Europe. Many educated people strongly felt that they belonged to a new age in which ignorance and superstition were fast disappearing. Instead of looking to the past, European scholars looked optimistically to the future.

Because people believed that the "light" of science and reason would lead them forward, historians have called the 1700s the Age of Reason or the Enlightenment. During the Enlightenment, thinkers began to apply rationality, objectivity, and the model of an orderly, mechanistic universe—ideas that had developed in the 1600s—to the study and understanding of society.

CURRENTS OF THOUGHT

The leading thinkers of the Enlightenment called themselves *philosophes* (FEE-luh-ZAWFS), the French word for philosophers. Although the philosophes did not always hold the same views as one another, most agreed on certain basic principles. Key words or phrases appeared again and again in their writings.

Rationality. One of the most common words was *rational*. Inspired by the work of Isaac Newton and the ideas of Descartes, the philosophes upheld the authority of science. In their minds, reason and experimentation provided the surest routes to knowledge of the social as well as the natural world. Moreover, the mechanistic world view led philosophes to think more confidently than ever that it was possible to know and discover the laws that governed the universe. Thinkers promoted rationality as the secret to understanding society and to making it better, just as a clock might be redesigned to keep more accurate time.

Freedom of thought. This belief in rationality led the philosophes to attack what they saw as ignorance and superstition. It also encouraged them to challenge traditional authorities, including established Christian theology and the classical works of the Greeks.

The philosophes vigorously rejected strict obedience to religious doctrine. They felt that traditional Christian beliefs restricted freedom of inquiry and thought. The philosophes eagerly tackled the task of exploring new directions of thought. Immanuel Kant, a German thinker, perhaps best captured this feeling. "The motto of the Enlightenment," said Kant, is "Dare to Know! Have the courage to use your own intelligence!"

Progress. This release from a dependence on the past helped create great faith in human progress. The philosophes distinguished themselves from Renaissance scholars by believing that the "golden age" lay in the future, not in the past.

By 1700, Europeans had exploded cannons, seen other planets through telescopes, sailed to the Americas, and accomplished more than anyone had even dreamed of accomplishing before. Throughout the Enlightenment, the idea of progress gained ground steadily. Enlightenment thinkers optimistically pointed to the possibility of greater human comfort through improvements in life on earth.

Humanitarianism. This belief in progress sparked a new wave of humanitarianism, or belief in the importance of easing human suffering. The humanitarian impulse grew out of the feeling that cruelty and oppression were caused by irrational actions. Enlightenment thinkers lashed out against slavery, war, and religious persecution. They also suggested sweeping changes in existing political, social, and economic institutions.

ENLIGHTENMENT VIEWS OF GOVERNMENT

Enlightenment ideas gave rise to new political theories. Many educated people became concerned with politics during the widespread political upheavals that occurred during the 1600s and 1700s, such as the English civil war and peasant uprisings in France. In an age when powerful monarchs in Europe often ruled with strict authority, many political thinkers began to promote ideas of freedom and liberty.

Hobbes. One of the first important political thinkers of this age, Thomas Hobbes, lived in England during the troubled times of the middle seventeenth century. Hobbes's reaction to political turmoil differed from that of later thinkers. Although his voice did not represent Enlightenment ideas, it nevertheless influenced later thinkers of the Enlightenment.

In his major work, *Leviathan*, published in 1651, Hobbes introduced the idea of a "state of nature," an imagined stage of human development before civilization or culture existed.

These profiles of the philosophe Voltaire were drawn by Jacques Louis David. Voltaire, known for his critical wit, was once exiled to England for insulting a French nobleman.

Hobbes believed that in the state of nature, human life was "nasty, brutish, and short" because of natural human selfishness. Everyone fought in a "war of all against all."

In order to avoid returning to this chaotic existence, Hobbes argued, people made an agreement, or contract, with a ruler who promised to keep order. In exchange, the people lost the right to rebel against the monarch's absolute rule.

Locke. John Locke, who lived in England during the late seventeenth century, disagreed with Hobbes's pessimistic view of human nature. As one of the first thinkers to speak of individuals' "natural rights," he founded the tradition of Enlightenment political thought. Locke believed people were born into the world free and equal. They therefore had rights to life, liberty, and the ownership of property.

Locke claimed that governments should protect these natural rights. If governments failed to do so, he said, then the people had the right to rebel. Locke's book *Two Treatises of Government* had a strong influence on important political thinkers of the eighteenth century.

Voltaire. In France, François-Marie Arouet, better known as Voltaire (vōl-TARE), became one of the leading representatives of the Enlightenment. A brilliant and sarcastic writer, Voltaire ridiculed the superstitions and inequities of his age. He bitterly opposed religious persecution, especially when carried out by governments in the name of established religion. Wrote Voltaire, "I shall not cease to preach tolerance from the rooftops as long as persecution does not cease."

As a supporter of liberty, Voltaire endorsed Locke's idea of natural rights. As a French citizen living under a strict government, he also envied the freedoms enjoyed by the English.

Montesquieu. Another famous student of government was Baron de Montesquieu (MAHNT-uh-SKYEW), a French noble and judge. Montesquieu spent nearly 20 years comparing various forms of government from ancient times to his own day. In 1748, he published his findings in *The Spirit of Laws*. This book established Montesquieu as one of the founders of the systematic study of government called political science.

Montesquieu believed abuses of liberty occurred when power was concentrated in the hands of a single person or group of people. He therefore believed that power should be distributed among three branches of government—the legislative, the executive, and the judicial. The legislative branch would enact the laws, the executive branch would enforce them, while the judicial branch would interpret the laws and punish lawbreakers. Montesquieu's ideas about checks and balances and a separation of powers would later influence the authors of the United States Constitution.

Rousseau. Another major political thinker of the Enlightenment was Jean Jacques Rousseau (rew-SŌ). Rousseau had great faith in the common people, a faith not shared by either Voltaire or Montesquieu. Rousseau argued in favor of equality, calling for the abolition of all titles of rank and nobility. "Man is born free and everywhere is in chains," cried Rousseau.

In setting forth his views on society, Rousseau examined Thomas Hobbes's idea of the

By the 1800s, French art often served as a form of social comment. Jean Millet's *The Winnower*, which portrays a peasant husking wheat, reflects the period's respect for working people.

RECOGNIZING POINT OF VIEW

Different people often see and report the same event or situation differently. Sometimes this inconsistency is a result of people having different points of view. A point of view is the position from which a person observes or considers something.

A number of factors may be involved in the formation of a point of view, such as a person's age, personality, family background, culture, role in society, beliefs, attitudes, and concerns. When two people see an issue or event from different points of view, what they report is likely to differ and to be incomplete or inaccurate.

A point of view is somewhat like a telescope, serving as a lens through which a person sees the world. Like a telescope, a point of view can clarify some aspects of what is observed and distort others. A telescope focuses the viewer's attention on certain objects. However, objects outside the lens's direct field of vision are blurred or not visible at all. Similarly, a point of view can lead a person to focus on certain aspects of an issue or event and to ignore or pay less attention to other aspects.

EXPLAINING THE SKILL

An author's point of view can affect the way he or she writes about a subject. Sometimes the author's point of view is not evident to the reader. More often, however, it is reflected in the way the account is written. By being able to recognize an author's point of view, you can more easily determine how accurate the account is. This is especially important if the author is trying to persuade you to accept his or her account as being true.

One way to recognize the point of view expressed in a written source is to follow these steps:

1. *Identify the main topic or subject of the account.*

2. *Identify those aspects of the subject to which the author gives the most attention. To do this, look for what is repeated or emphasized.*

3. *Identify any aspects of the subject that the author ignores or mentions only briefly.*

4. *Identify words or phrases that suggest how the author feels about the subject.*

5. *Identify any unstated assumptions the author seems to make.*

6. *Based on what you have identified in steps 1 through 5, identify the author's point of view.*

If you have difficulty recognizing an author's point of view, examine another account on the same subject that is written by an author representing a different culture, family background, or beliefs.

APPLYING THE SKILL

The following account is from an essay written by a European author in the mid-1700s. Follow the previously described procedure to identify the author's point of view.

Account A

The type of Reason which leads men to know their duties is not very complex; that which leads a woman to understand hers is still simpler. The obedience and fidelity which she owes her husband are natural and obvious results of her position. As she is subject to men's judgment, she should deserve their esteem; she ought especially to obtain that of her husband, to justify his choice of her in the eyes of the public. Women, honor your state. In whatever station Providence [God] places you, you will always be respected. . . .

Works of genius are above women's comprehension; they have not enough accuracy and attention to succeed in the exact sciences. Being weak and having no resources outside themselves, women must supplement their weakness by understanding the emotions of men.

Men will philosophize better concerning the human heart; women will be much better able to read it. Men have more genius. Women observe, but men reason. . . .

In explaining women's duties, be clear and precise; do not let women believe their performance is a gloomy task. Give them an idea of an honest man and teach them to recognize him.

Adapted from one of Jean Jacques Rousseau's discourses on education, titled *Emile* (1762).

REFLECTING ON THE SKILL

Now that you have followed a specific procedure for recognizing point of view, answer the following. Be prepared to explain your answers to a classmate.

1. The main subject of Account A is **(a)** the abilities and roles of men and women, **(b)** the ways women should educate children, **(c)** the importance of marriage. Explain your answer.

2. Which words or phrases suggest how the author feels about women? **(a)** *honest, genius, reason;* **(b)** *husband, judgment, honor;* **(c)** *obedience and fidelity, subject to, weak.*

3. Which of the following assumptions seems to be made by the author? **(a)** Women should obey men. **(b)** Men are superior to women in every way. **(c)** Women are responsible for educating other women. Explain your answer.

4. The author's point of view is that of **(a)** a person who studies human behavior in a scientific manner, **(b)** a person who assumes that men are naturally smarter than women, **(c)** a person who has no respect for women. Explain your answer.

APPLYING THE SKILL

The following account is from a book written in the late 1700s about the same general subject as that of Account A. However, Account B was written by a different European author. Identify this author's point of view.

Account B

Let us examine the view that a woman should never, for a moment, feel herself independent, that she should be governed by fear to become a slave for man. It is argued that with respect to the female character obedience is the grand lesson which ought to be impressed with unrelenting rigor. What nonsense! When will a great man arise with sufficient strength of mind to puff away the fumes which pride has spread over the subject! Connected with man as daughters, wives and mothers, women's moral character may be estimated by their manner of fulfilling those simple duties. However, the end of their exertions should be to unfold their own faculties.

Probably the prevailing opinion that woman was created for man may have arisen from Moses's poetical story. Yet this only shows that man from the remotest antiquity found it convenient to exert his strength to subjugate his companion because he felt the whole creation was only made for his convenience and pleasure.

Adapted from *A Vindication of the Rights of Woman*, by Mary Wollstonecraft (1792).

CHECKING YOUR UNDERSTANDING

Now that you have examined Account B, answer the following:

5. The main subject of the account is **(a)** the ways women should serve men, **(b)** the superiority of women to men, **(c)** the view that women should obey men.

6. Which words or phrases indicate how the author feels about the subject? **(a)** *obedience, women's moral character, remotest antiquity;* **(b)** *what nonsense, should be to unfold their own faculties, a great man;* **(c)** *created for man, with respect to, unrelenting rigor.*

7. One of the author's concerns is that **(a)** women are not allowed to develop all their skills, **(b)** many women are illiterate, **(c)** most women prefer to be dependent on men.

8. The author's point of view is that of **(a)** a person who believes that the government should determine women's position in society, **(b)** a person who has no respect for men, **(c)** a person who believes that women are being denied their natural rights.

REVIEWING THE SKILL

9. Define the term *point of view* and state at least three factors that may be involved in a point of view.

10. What is one procedure for recognizing an author's point of view?

11. Why is it important to be able to recognize an author's point of view?

"state of nature." However, instead of seeing humans in this state as selfish and violent, Rousseau believed they were free and happy. He admired what he called the "noble savage," the person who lived free of the influences of civilization. Although Rousseau realized that people in the 1700s could not return to the natural state, he saw a noble savage living in every person. He believed human nature was basically good, and that society corrupted people.

Rousseau described the ideal society, based on this view of human nature, in his book *The Social Contract*. Rousseau saw a social contract as an agreement among the people of a society. In Rousseau's ideal society, the members of a community would agree among themselves to give up part of their freedom for the good of the group as a whole. The decisions of the majority, or the "general will," would apply to everyone.

NEW ECONOMIC IDEAS

Enlightenment thinkers also applied their ideas about natural laws and individual freedom to economics. Economic philosophers known as physiocrats opposed government regulation of business. Instead, they believed everyone should be free to make personal decisions in the marketplace so that the economy could function according to natural laws.

The physiocrats opposed mercantilism. In their opinion, agriculture, not gold and silver, formed the basis of a nation's wealth. Removing trade restrictions, reasoned the physiocrats, would allow farmers to sell their products at the highest price. The increased trade, they argued, would benefit the entire nation.

NEW IDEAS ABOUT EDUCATION

Education received growing attention. The belief in rationalism encouraged reformers to believe that they could eliminate superstition and ignorance through education. The school, which had formerly been only a minor force, expanded its role in society.

One of the leading educational thinkers was John Locke. He claimed that everyone enters the world with a blank mind, much like a slate on which nothing has been written. People are born neither good nor evil; rather, experience shapes their character and gives them knowledge. This view of human nature inspired a spirit of equality. It also led reformers to believe in progress through education.

SECTION REVIEW

1. Describe how the belief in rationality was a basis of the Enlightenment ideas of freedom of thought, progress, and humanitarianism.

2. Why did Montesquieu promote the idea of separation of powers and checks and balances?

3. What, according to the physiocrats, was the basis of a nation's wealth? How did this differ from what the mercantilists believed?

4. Why did Enlightenment thinkers believe that progress could be achieved through education?

Analysis. How could absolute monarchs maintain power in most European countries during the 1700s when the prominent political theorists were calling for liberty, separation of powers, and equality?

19–3
THE IMPACT OF SCIENTIFIC THOUGHT

READ TO FIND OUT

—what the term *enlightened despotism* means.
—how Enlightenment ideas were brought to broader segments of society.
—how women participated in the Enlightenment.
—how the arts began to reflect Enlightenment ideas during the 1700s.
—who in European society resisted the changes brought by the Enlightenment.

The philosophes traveled all over Europe, discussing their ideas with rulers and other thinkers. The philosophes saw themselves as more than citizens of a particular nation or social class. Believing that rationalism would eventually help everyone progress toward a better future, the philosophes tried to spread Enlightenment ideas to all classes of people throughout Europe.

As these ideas reached greater numbers of people, European culture began to change. Enlightenment ideas, however, did not completely replace existing ones. Instead, rationality, secular ideas, and demands for reform existed side by side with more traditional beliefs and ways of life. Although traditional culture gradually weakened, the differences between old and new would eventually produce great conflicts in European society.

ENLIGHTENED DESPOTISM

Some philosophes, such as Voltaire, had little confidence in the political abilities of the common people. At the same time, they opposed absolute monarchy as a form of government. They believed absolutism undermined liberty. These philosophes encouraged what they called *enlightened despotism*. Under this system, monarchs ruled "scientifically," basing decisions on rational thought rather than on tradition or whim. They also used their power to bring about reform.

The idea of enlightened despotism appealed to several powerful rulers in the 1700s. These rulers invited Voltaire and others to explain Enlightenment political ideas. As a result of the influence of the philosophes, the enlightened despots, as these monarchs came to be known, changed their method of rule. Although they retained many of the characteristics of absolute monarchs, they no longer justified their power in terms of a "divine right" to rule. Rather, they claimed their thrones on grounds of social usefulness, calling themselves by such names as "servants of the state."

Frederick the Great of Prussia, Catherine the Great of Russia, and Maria Theresa and her son, Joseph II, of Austria were good examples of enlightened despots. They codified laws, built roads and bridges, and granted or increased religious toleration. On the whole, however, they made only superficial attempts to restructure society. In eastern European nations, such as Russia, serfdom remained entrenched. In France and Spain, the nobility and clergy clung to power, thus limiting reform.

POPULARIZATION OF ENLIGHTENMENT IDEAS

The spread of Enlightenment ideas gradually extended beyond European royalty and intellectuals. Most Enlightenment thinkers wrote for a wide audience, not just for the monarchs and philosophers.

One French philosophe, Denis Diderot (DEE-duh-RŌ), undertook the ambitious task of compiling Enlightenment thought into one immense encyclopedia. Diderot's *Encyclopédie* (ehn-see-klō-pay-DEE) brought the ideas of the Enlightenment to thousands of readers outside the aristocracy.

Enlightenment ideas spread in many other ways, too. The first daily and weekly newspapers got their start in the 1700s as journalists began to write for the educated public. Scientific societies, such as the Royal Society of London, increased membership, promoted science among the public, and published written pamphlets on a variety of topics.

Lawyers, merchants, and other members of the middle class took an especially keen interest in the writings of the Enlightenment. As the reading public expanded, the demand for written materials increased. In addition to reading newspapers or pamphlets at home, people gathered in coffeehouses. There they debated politics or the latest scientific developments. In working-class neighborhoods, articles and popular verses were read aloud, further spreading Enlightenment attitudes.

Many Europeans, however, were not exposed to the new ideas. These people included the peasants, who still made up the majority of the population in most European nations.

WOMEN AND THE ENLIGHTENMENT

Because the monarchs and the intellectuals of the eighteenth century were mostly men, the Enlightenment largely excluded women. A few philosophes, including the Marquis de Condorcet (KŌN-dor-say), argued that women and men were equal by nature. Most philosophes, however, believed that women lacked the ability to make major contributions to the arts and sciences.

Despite the attitude of the philosophes, some women of the period did achieve prominence. In France, a number of wealthy, educated

DIDEROT'S ENCYCLOPÉDIE

Imagine the work needed to gather together in one place all the knowledge of the world. Denis Diderot (DEE-duh-RŌ), a French philosophe, spent almost 25 years at such a task. With the help of 160 of the greatest writers, philosophers, and scientists of his time, Diderot collected many articles on literature, religion, government, science, and technology, and created a great new encyclopedia.

When finished, Diderot's *Encyclopédie*, as it was called, filled 35 volumes. The volumes were printed one by one. The first volume appeared in 1751. The final work was published 21 years later, in 1772.

The major purpose of Diderot's amazing project was not to provide information, even though people used the *Encyclopédie* as a reference work. Diderot was a forward-looking scholar who wanted to change what he thought of as the backward thinking of his day. He urged the improvement of society through the use of reason. He strove to end superstition and intolerance by showing the public all the wonders of modern science.

Articles and beautifully drawn illustrations about new industrial processes and technology dominated the *Encyclopédie*. The article on the stocking-knitting machine, for instance, filled ten times more space than the article on cathedrals. The *Encyclopédie's* critical view of religion drew opposition from the Church, but most influential people were becoming tolerant enough of new ideas to support Diderot's work.

The *Encyclopédie* brought Europeans a new picture of the world. They saw nature described, classified, and seemingly brought under the control of people. The thousands of illustrations showed such techniques as how to perform surgery, mill grain into flour, or mine for minerals. Pictures of birds and animals unknown to most Europeans startled readers. Articles described the newly explored continents and their inhabitants.

Diderot, a much-honored man, lived in Paris for a dozen more years after he finished his encyclopedia. His work contributed to the spirit of the Enlightenment, showing people a remarkable and expanding new world.

---

women held informal meetings, or *salons* (sah-LŌN), in their homes. Here artists, writers, and musicians presented their works and exchanged ideas in an atmosphere promoting the frank discussion of issues.

The salons helped shape the manners and customs of the Enlightenment. They also did much to circulate many of the ideas that would ultimately bring about the downfall of the French monarchy. The salons, however, did relatively little to advance the rights of women as a whole.

Other women became famous in their own right. Emilie du Chatelet (shah-TLAY), for example, became a noted physicist and leading authority on Isaac Newton.

In England, a political theorist named Mary Wollstonecraft protested the lack of women's rights. In *Vindication of the Rights of Woman*, Wollstonecraft argued that women should have equal legal rights with men, including the right

to own property. Only then, said Wollstonecraft, could women realize their full human potential. In putting forth her arguments, Wollstonecraft expanded the idea of equality originally stated by John Locke and other Enlightenment thinkers. Her ideas became the basis for the later women's rights movement.

THE ARTS DURING THE ENLIGHTENMENT

Scientific discoveries and Enlightenment ideas influenced some artistic trends. However, artists and writers also responded to political and religious developments.

The visual arts. A highly ornamental style called baroque emerged and spread throughout much of Europe in the 1600s and early 1700s. The elaborate baroque architecture created a spacious, grand atmosphere that was intended

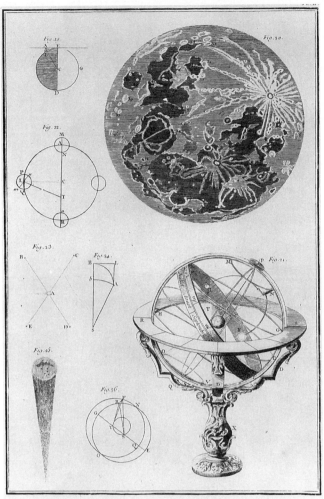

Astronomie.

This drawing from Diderot's *Encyclopédie* includes a sketch of the moon with oceans (top right) and astronomical measurements such as the cone-shaped shadow of a solar eclipse (bottom left).

A more distinct contrast to baroque art was the neoclassic movement that arose around 1750. Neoclassic artists imitated the "classic" simplicity, balance, and emotional restraint of ancient Greek and Roman art. The neoclassic emphasis on order and rationality reflected the Enlightenment spirit.

Music. The dominance of the baroque trend between 1600 and 1750 extended to the world of music. Like baroque art, baroque music was elaborate and emotional. Johann Sebastian Bach explored the keyboard's range of expression, while George Frederick Handel popularized large-scale instrumental accompaniment for singers. The opera, a new musical form developed by Italians, also reflected the elaborate baroque style.

During the late 1700s, a new musical style emerged. Although labeled "classical" music, it did not imitate Greek and Roman styles. However, it did stress the "classic" principles of order and control of emotion. The early masters of classical music, Franz Joseph Haydn and Wolfgang Amadeus Mozart, transformed the symphony into a long, carefully structured composition for a large orchestra.

Literature. Freed from the religious restraints of earlier years, writers embarked upon experiments that led to new literary forms. By the 1700s, prose had become more popular than poetry—that is, writers increasingly used language similar to everyday speech.

During the Enlightenment, writers searched for natural laws or literary rules to govern their work. They also used their talents to criticize the follies of the period. Satires, such as Jonathan Swift's *Gulliver's Travels* and the poems of Alexander Pope, became especially popular.

Other kinds of writing flourished during the Enlightenment as well. Dramatic writers, such as Jean Racine (rah-SEEN) and Jean-Baptiste Molière (mol-YAIR), presented classic tragedies and witty comedies about society.

The most successful innovation of the period, however, was the modern English novel. Novels offered readers adventure, romance, a plot, and believable characters. Well-known authors of the day included Daniel Defoe and Henry Fielding.

Neoclassicism influenced much of the literary work in the 1700s. However, its restraints

to evoke a strong emotional response from the observer. Many baroque sculptors, such as Gianlorenzo Bernini, and painters, such as Peter Paul Rubens, featured large figures in dynamic poses that contrasted with the generally static Renaissance styles. Baroque works frequently presented religious themes.

Following the death of Louis XIV in 1715, a new artistic style arose in France as a reaction against the pompous and formal art favored by the Sun King. Known as rococo, this style was rich and decorative like baroque but was done on a small, almost dainty, scale. The intricate designs and light colors of rococo interior design created a relaxed, intimate atmosphere.

A theatrical element is often seen in rococo art. In *Italian Comedians*, Jean Watteau depicts actors presenting the sad clown Pierrot to an audience.

provoked an outcry among writers, especially poets, who wanted freedom to express their emotions. This reaction later took shape in a movement called Romanticism.

RESISTANCE TO THE ENLIGHTENMENT

Not all elements of society accepted Enlightenment ideas readily. Enlightenment ideas tended to undermine the power of both monarchs and the church, and they threatened traditional ways of life.

The Catholic Church remained one of the Enlightenment's major critics during the 1700s. Although most Enlightenment thinkers still believed in the existence of God and attended church, they encouraged a movement away from religious ideas and a religious life. The Enlightenment thus contributed to the growing reliance on nonreligious, or secular, ideas begun during the Renaissance and Reformation. Threatened by the growing secularization of society, church leaders often criticized Enlightenment ideas and thinkers.

Many of the philosophes themselves challenged certain ideas of the Enlightenment. Among the most outspoken critics was Rousseau. Believing that reason often caused more evil than good, Rousseau encouraged more reliance on emotion. Other philosophers, such as Kant, joined Rousseau in questioning the great value the Enlightenment placed on reason.

Enlightenment ideas also helped cause changes that threatened many people indirectly. The acceptance of a mechanistic world view contributed to a change in the way some people thought about land. Landowners began to view their land not as a part of a living organism, but as a resource to use to gain more wealth. Under the old medieval world view, peasants were part of the land they lived on. Though poor, the peasants and their rights to the land were protected by the belief that together they formed an organic whole. The new ideas, however, made peasants seem expendable and separate from the land.

During the 1500s in England, landlords had begun fencing off land traditionally used as commons by peasants. As part of this process, called enclosure, landowners also drained swamps that the peasants used for fishing, and cut down forests used for hunting and wood gathering. By the 1700s, Enlightenment ideas had strongly reinforced the attitudes supporting enclosure.

As a result of enclosure, the lives of many people were completely disrupted. Great numbers of peasants were forced to move to cities, where they worked for low wages in the unsafe factories that were springing up throughout England. Similar changes gradually occurred across Europe, causing peasant uprisings and other forms of resistance to the transformation of European society.

SECTION REVIEW

1. Define *enlightened despotism*.

2. Name three ways Enlightenment ideas were popularized.

3. How did Mary Wollstonecraft use Enlightenment ideas to promote women's rights?

4. Explain ways in which neoclassicism reflected Enlightenment ideas. Use examples from art and music.

5. How did the shift from the medieval to a mechanistic world view affect attitudes toward land? How did this affect peasants?

Evaluation. Does "progress" always benefit everyone in a society? Give examples from this section that support your claim.

Data Search. Refer to the appropriate chart on page 832 to do the following: **(a)** compare the literacy rate of the English gentry and professionals with that of English laborers and servants for the period from 1754 to 1784, **(b)** identify which occupational groups had increasing literacy rates between 1754 and 1784, **(c)** identify which occupational groups had decreasing literacy rates between 1754 and 1784, and **(d)** identify the overall literacy rate in England for the period from 1754 to 1784.

HISTORY IN FOCUS

Changes in ideas often occur before changes in institutions and societies. Although the Scientific Revolution began during the 1500s, it and the Enlightenment of the 1700s heralded the Modern Age.

The changes in ideas and the shift in world view that occurred between 1500 and 1800 would, more than anything else, make later changes possible. The profoundly influential idea of "progress," for instance, was an invention of the Enlightenment. For the first time in history, people now dared turn their backs on the past to look forward optimistically to the future.

One of the most important effects of the Scientific Revolution was to change completely people's relationship to nature. Under the medieval world view, for instance, cutting the earth's skin to mine minerals from its flesh was considered violent and unethical. With the emergence of the mechanistic world view, however, people began to view the earth and its resources as nonliving and existing only for their own use. This shift in thinking opened the way for what would be the most significant change of the Modern Age: the growth of factories, manufacturing, and technology called the Industrial Revolution.

Similarly, the Enlightenment brought great changes and conflicts in society. At the same time the philosophes urged greater freedom and equality, monarchs held on to absolute power. While society's expectations for a better life rose, many people remained poor and powerless, and some even lost rights to the land guaranteed them under the manorial system of the Middle Ages. This difference between ideals and reality led to great struggles known as democratic revolutions in Europe and North America.

SUMMARY

- In the 1500s and 1600s, the Scientific Revolution gave rise to a new, more rational way to view the world. People began to regard the universe as an orderly system based on natural laws that could be understood through logic and experimentation.

- The Scientific Revolution began with the discoveries of Copernicus, Kepler, and Galileo on the nature of the solar system. Bacon and Descartes helped define a scientific approach to knowledge, which in turn led to a growing interest in sciences like biology and medicine. Newton pioneered important laws of physics.

- During the Enlightenment of the 1700s, this scientific spirit was applied to the study of society and government. Philosophes like Locke, Voltaire, Montesquieu, and Rousseau promoted the ideas of freedom of thought, progress, and humanitarianism. Education was seen as a way to improve society.

- Both the Scientific Revolution and the Enlightenment had a great impact on European life. Many new ideas were popularized, and enlightened despotism gained favor with some monarchs. Enlightenment ideas were reflected in the arts and began to affect the role of women.

- Not all elements of society accepted these new ideas. The Church and the peasantry, among others, felt threatened by the Enlightenment and clung to many of their traditional values.

VOCABULARY REVIEW

Match each numbered vocabulary term with the appropriate person. Then explain the connection between the person and the vocabulary term.

1. scientific method
2. rationality
3. mechanistic world view
4. enlightened despotism

(a) Voltaire
(b) Newton
(c) Bacon
(d) Descartes

CHAPTER REVIEW

1. (a) How did the medieval world view reinforce the social structure? Give an example. (b) How did Enlightenment ideas contribute to changes in the social structure?

2. For each of the following questions, answer from the perspective of both the medieval and the mechanistic world views. (a) What is the most reliable source of truth? (b) How should reason be used to arrive at the truth? (c) What is the relationship between nature and society?

3. (a) How was the Scientific Revolution of the 1500s and 1600s an outgrowth of the Renaissance? (b) Explain how the Scientific Revolution led to the Enlightenment.

4. (a) Compare the geocentric and heliocentric theories of the solar system. (b) Why did the Greek concept make sense to people? (c) Why was the heliocentric theory ridiculed?

5. (a) How did Kepler and Galileo contribute to an evolution in the history of thought? (b) Why did Galileo later deny his theory? (c) What did Newton contribute to earlier theories?

6. (a) What were the two basic steps toward gaining knowledge outlined in Bacon's scientific method? (b) How are deductive and inductive reasoning different? (c) How did Greek science differ from Descartes's approach to gaining knowledge?

7. (a) Describe two advances in biology and two in medicine. (b) What innovations led to these advances? (c) List three of Isaac Newton's discoveries.

8. (a) What ideas did most philosophes share? (b) How was their thought similar to and different from that of Renaissance thinkers?

9. (a) What was John Locke's most important contribution to political theory? (b) Describe Locke's "blank slate" theory and explain how it differed from Rousseau's ideas. (c) Compare the political thought of Voltaire, Montesquieu, and Rousseau.

10. (a) Why were salons important? (b) Contrast the baroque and neoclassic styles in art. (c) How did literature reflect changes during the Enlightenment?

THINKING CRITICALLY: ACTIVITIES

1. Leading thinkers of the Scientific Revolution and the Enlightenment placed a great value on skepticism. How valuable and important is a critical attitude toward authority? Is it necessary to accept some ideas without questioning? If so, when? Write a short essay expressing your ideas on skepticism.

2. Divide into groups of four or five to discuss the following questions: How does one's view of human nature affect one's ideas about politics and society? What kind of society is possible if people are basically good? If they are basically evil? Consider the ideas of the Enlightenment thinkers as examples.

3. The value of emotion to human society was an important issue among thinkers of the 1600s and 1700s. Choose a partner to discuss whether emotion contributes to or detracts from the pursuit of truth and achievements in society. One partner should play the role of Descartes; the other, Rousseau.

APPLYING SOCIAL STUDIES SKILLS

Taking notes. One form of notetaking is called mapping or diagramming. Its main advantage is flexibility. For example, it can be used to show the most important points of a small topic, a section of a chapter, or an entire chapter.

Here is how a student mapped the discussion of the heliocentric view of the solar system, which begins on page 429. The main idea is boxed. Supporting details are connected to it with lines. Copy this map and complete it by adding details on Kepler and Galileo. Then map another main idea from this chapter.

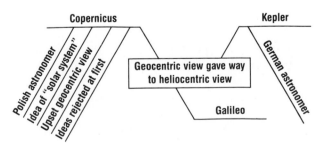

APPLYING THINKING SKILLS

Recognizing point of view. Read the following mid-seventeenth-century account. Then follow the procedure described on page 436 to identify the author's point of view. Next, answer the questions that follow the account.

He that willingly agrees to tolerate all religions, if he examines his heart by daylight, his conscience will tell him that he is either an Atheist or a Heretic or a Hypocrite. To tolerate more than indifference in matters of religious belief is not to deal indifferently with God. He that does it takes God's Scepter out of His hands and bids Him stand by.

Who has the right to establish religion, except for God? The power of all religion and laws is based on their purity, and their purity is a result of their simplicity. Mixtures of various religious beliefs cause great harm! I lived in a city where a papist [Roman Catholic] preached in one church, a Lutheran preached in another church, and a Calvinist preached in a third church. In one particular case, a Lutheran minister preached during one part of the day, and a Calvinist preached during another—in the same pulpit. The religion in the place was meager.

Suppose that all of humanity decided to do the Creator a mischief and to be very disrespectful toward Him. The worst signs of disrespect would be to proclaim untruths against His Truth and to undermine and corrupt His Truth with mixtures of various human ideas.

The removing of just one small word in Scripture may go against all of the Truth in the Bible. However, it is even worse for the government to tolerate untruths. This is like attacking the Walls of Heaven and battering God out of His Chair.

Adapted from a prominent Puritan's argument made in 1647.

1. Define *point of view*.

2. When you read an account, what should you look for in order to determine the author's point of view?

3. What is the main claim made by the author of the above account?

4. What is the author's point of view? What is a point of view that would differ from this author's? Explain your answer.

CHAPTER TWENTY

DEMOCRATIC REVOLUTIONS

1754–1821

The Fall of the Bastille, July 14, 1789. Unknown artist, late eighteenth century.

The eighteenth century was a time of sweeping change in the Western world. Revolutions in America and France changed political systems that had existed for centuries. In France, the social order also changed.

The notion that people had a right to determine how they would be governed was itself revolutionary in the 1700s. The Enlightenment ideas of personal freedom and equality were totally contrary to the way Western society functioned at the time. In this era of absolute monarchies the ideas of the Enlightenment were powerful sparks that ignited a revolutionary spirit, first in America and then in France. These upheavals changed the fundamental nature of politics, society, and culture in the Western world.

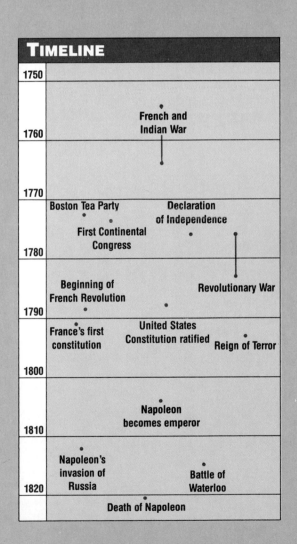

TIMELINE	
1750	
1760	French and Indian War
1770	
1780	Boston Tea Party · Declaration of Independence · First Continental Congress
1790	Beginning of French Revolution · Revolutionary War
1800	France's first constitution · United States Constitution ratified · Reign of Terror
1810	Napoleon becomes emperor
1820	Napoleon's invasion of Russia · Battle of Waterloo · Death of Napoleon

20-1
THE AMERICAN REVOLUTION

READ TO FIND OUT

—how self-government developed in America.
—what the causes and results of the French and Indian War were.
—how Britain's policies toward its American colonies led to the fight for independence.
—how the American Revolution led to changes in other parts of the world.

Although the American struggle for independence began in 1775, its seeds had been planted by policies and actions of the British Crown almost from the time the first colonists landed on American soil. As colonists began to develop their own identity—more American and less British with each passing year—they increasingly resented Britain's attempts at political and economic control. Disagreement over these controls and over the colonists' right to self-government led to armed conflict and ultimately to independence.

A BACKGROUND OF SELF-GOVERNMENT

From the time settlers established the first permanent British colony at Jamestown, Virginia, in 1607, colonists in America enjoyed a degree of liberty far above what they would have known in Europe. Self-government developed as a practical solution to the problem of being so far from the homeland. The colonists found it cumbersome to have to wait for decisions from Britain, 3,000 miles (4,800 kilometers) away. Besides, they believed that they knew best how to manage their own local affairs.

By the mid-1700s, each colony had an assembly chosen by the voters to make laws and represent the colony's interests in dealing with Britain. Although the vote was generally restricted to men who owned land—and most early colonists were landowners—these assemblies were the beginning of representative government in America.

Representative government was possible in the colonies because the rigid European social structure did not exist in the New World. There was a powerful landowning class but no true aristocracy. Colonists who made the most of the economic opportunities offered by the New World could usually improve their social as well as financial status. This freedom of individuals to control their own destiny was at the heart of the new society developing in Britain's American colonies. Unfortunately, this freedom only rarely extended to African slaves, although some were able to buy their freedom.

BRITAIN'S ATTITUDE TOWARD THE COLONIES

For more than 150 years the British government was fairly indifferent toward its faraway American colonies. Britain was too preoccupied with internal strife to pay much attention to colonial affairs. The power struggle between the king and Parliament, which led to civil war in 1642, left little time for the colonies.

Britain did not have a well-developed policy for managing its far-flung empire of colonies and trading posts in America, Asia, and Africa. Britain's major effort was directed at enforcing the mercantilist laws, which restricted colonial manufacturing and discouraged colonial trade with any partners outside the British Empire.

In addition to internal and colonial problems, Britain had wars with France and other European nations to contend with. These wars put a great strain on the British treasury, but it was not until the French and Indian War in North America that Britain began to look to its colonies for increased economic support.

THE FRENCH AND INDIAN WAR

Britain's indifference to its 13 colonies on the American mainland ended with the French and Indian War. This conflict, which lasted from 1754 to 1763, was the North American phase of a worldwide struggle between Europe's most powerful nations, Britain and France. It was a fight for political and commercial superiority, with vast colonial holdings at stake. British and French forces in North America fought for two years before the war in Europe was finally declared in 1756. In Europe and India the conflict was known as the Seven Years' War.

Both Britain and France had long-established claims in North America. The French had settled Quebec in 1608, claiming a vast territory to the north and west of Britain's 13 colonies. For decades the two nations fought for control of these lands.

The French objected when British settlers began moving west of the Appalachian Mountains into territory that the French claimed was theirs. This dispute over control of the upper Ohio River valley erupted into the French and Indian War. In this war, both sides relied on their Indian allies. France, however, had the advantage of friendly relations with more Indian tribes, who feared that the British wanted to continue moving westward by taking more Indian lands.

Ultimately, British forces were victorious, and the French and Indian War was formally ended in 1763. It was a decisive victory for Britain, which gained control of important French possessions, including Canada and all other French land east of the Mississippi River, except New Orleans. The war put an end to France's role as a colonial power in America and left Britain with an expanded empire—and a severely depleted treasury.

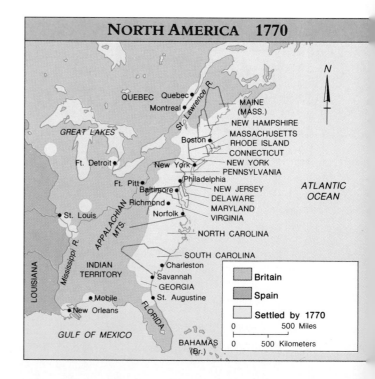

NORTH AMERICA 1770

Nathaniel Currier created this print of the Boston Tea Party in 1846. Here, crowds on the wharf watch disguised colonists dump chests of tea belonging to the British East India Company into Boston Harbor. Colonists in all American ports boycotted the company's tea.

BRITAIN'S NEW POLICIES

The French and Indian War was very costly for Britain, nearly doubling its national debt. British leaders thought that the colonists should bear part of the cost. Therefore, to increase revenues, Parliament decided to tighten economic and political control over the colonies and to enforce their mercantilist laws more strictly. Parliament also raised taxes and imposed new duties on imports.

The Sugar Act, Britain's first serious attempt to collect tax revenues in North America, led to the colonists' protests that they should not have to pay taxes they had not consented to. They declared that the colonial assemblies, which gave colonists direct representation, had the right to set taxes. However, the colonists did not elect representatives to Parliament, and a key rallying cry of protesters was "no taxation without representation."

The end of the French and Indian War lessened the colonies' dependence on Britain by eliminating the need for military protection from the French. When Britain began imposing taxes and exerting new controls, therefore, the colonists responded first with protests and boycotts, and finally with rebellion.

COLONIAL DEFIANCE

The colonists strongly objected to Britain's new policies. In defiance of mercantilist laws, they boycotted British products imported into the colonies and smuggled in other goods to avoid paying import duties. They were so violently opposed to the Stamp Act—which required the purchase of stamps for all official documents and for certain publications—that it was finally repealed by Parliament.

Throughout the 1760s and early 1770s, tensions increased. Each colonial protest provoked more punitive measures by Parliament. In a well-known incident, the Boston Tea Party of 1773, Massachusetts colonists dumped British tea into Boston Harbor to protest a tax on tea and a law giving a British company an unfair advantage in the colonial tea trade.

In retaliation against the colonists' actions in Boston, Parliament then passed a number of laws that the colonists called the Intolerable Acts. As punishment for the tea incident, Britain suspended self-government in Massachusetts and temporarily closed Boston Harbor. In a show of unity, the other colonies rallied to the aid of Massachusetts, providing food and other supplies as well as moral support.

The situation in the colonies had reached a crucial point. King George III and Parliament believed they had made enough concessions to the colonists and were determined to keep control. They refused to give up the tax on tea. The colonists, however, were just as determined that they would not buy English tea or pay the hateful tax. They would no longer tolerate what they termed acts of tyranny.

Surrender of Cornwallis at Yorktown by John Trumbull shows the official surrender of the British army, under General Charles Cornwallis, to American forces in October 1781. On the left, a white flag symbolizing the surrender floats over the scene. On the right, General George Washington, on horseback, is surrounded by his officers. Above them flies the flag of the new American nation.

FROM REBELLION TO INDEPENDENCE

Spurred to action by the events in Massachusetts and elsewhere, delegates from the colonies met at Philadelphia in 1774. They formed the First Continental Congress, which demanded repeal of the Intolerable Acts. Parliament refused, reluctant to yield in what was developing into a fight for control of the colonies.

In the spring of 1775, violence erupted. When British troops marched through Lexington on their way to Concord, where arms were stored, members of the Massachusetts militia stood ready to face the British. Suddenly, an exchange of gunfire pierced the air, leaving some colonists dead. The British troops then headed to Concord, where another battle erupted after the troops had destroyed the colonists' supplies. These battles rallied many colonists to the side of the Patriots, the anti-British faction. By the time the Second Continental Congress met a few weeks later, the colonists were prepared to fight. Formation of the Continental Army made that point clear.

The colonists did not formally sever their ties with Britain for more than a year, though. Many had hoped that Britain would give them the rights they asked for, such as representation in Parliament, and that the disagreements could be resolved peacefully. By 1776, however, many colonists considered themselves American rather than British. A growing spirit of independence was spurred by Thomas Paine, whose pamphlet *Common Sense*, published in January 1776, urged the colonies to separate from Britain. He said that the colonists had a clear choice: freedom or tyranny.

Declaration of Independence. Finally, on July 4, 1776, the Second Continental Congress launched the new United States of America by adopting the Declaration of Independence. Written chiefly by Thomas Jefferson, this document reflected Enlightenment philosopher John Locke's theory of natural rights. Locke believed that all people are endowed by nature with certain rights, chiefly life, liberty, and property. He also wrote that governments derive their power from the consent of the governed—from the people—and that consent carries with it the right of rebellion.

Revolutionary War. Winning independence was more difficult than declaring it. About a third of the colonists, the pro-British Loyalists, opposed the war and refused to fight; another third, the Patriots, favored it; and the rest simply did not care one way or the other. Even many Patriots were reluctant to leave their farms to go to war. Colonial neighbors in Canada, most of whom were French, declined an offer to join the American war.

The Continental Army was poorly equipped and easily outnumbered by the British forces. The colonists triumphed, however, for several reasons. One was the leadership of their commander in chief, General George Washington. Another was the aid they received from France, England's long-time enemy, and from Spain. These allies provided money, supplies, and arms. French naval support and soldiers, provided after 1777, were crucial, especially naval blockades of British fleets. A third reason for the American victory was the way that the war was conducted. The colonists were fighting on familiar ground, and their unconventional tactics confounded opponents trained in more traditional fighting techniques.

The last major battle of the war, in Yorktown, Virginia, in 1781, ended in defeat for the British. Separated from the colonies by the Atlantic, Britain had found it difficult to supply and communicate with its forces in North America. In the end, compared with its more profitable colonies in India and the West Indies, the 13 colonies that broke away in 1776 did not seem very important. Thus, unable to defeat the colonists, Britain signed the Treaty of Paris in 1783 and formally recognized American independence.

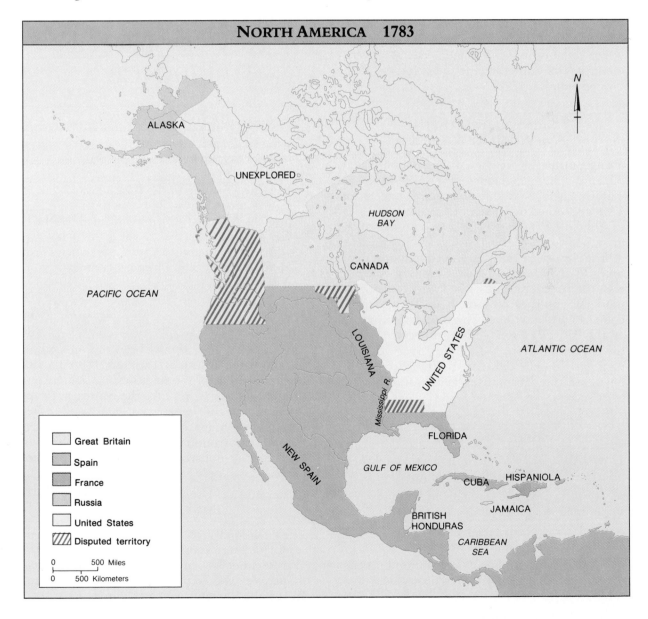

NORTH AMERICA 1783

Great Britain
Spain
France
Russia
United States
Disputed territory

0   500 Miles
0   500 Kilometers

New government. After declaring its independence from Britain, the new nation needed a new government. The nation would be a republic, run by representatives elected by voters in all 13 states. The Continental Congress decided on a federal system: The states would remain separate but would give certain powers to a central government to handle matters affecting all the states. The Articles of Confederation formed the constitution for this new federal government.

The Articles turned out to be relatively ineffective, however, because the states kept most of the important powers, such as taxation. For this reason, in 1787, delegates from 12 states met in Philadelphia to revise the Articles. Instead, the delegates wrote an entirely new document, which established a stronger federal government. It was ratified as the Constitution of the United States in 1788.

SIGNIFICANCE OF THE AMERICAN REVOLUTION

Many Europeans welcomed the American Revolution. They applauded the Americans for gaining liberty without descending into chaos. Victory seemed to offer proof that Locke's ideas of individual rights and rule by consent of the governed could be the basis of a successful state.

The American Revolution inspired other colonies to revolt against their European rulers. It also prompted Britain's leaders to adopt more moderate policies toward British colonies in Canada and elsewhere. The most direct impact of the American Revolution, however, was on the French. The success of the American colonists gave hope to those in France who had been resisting absolutism and working for a freer society.

SECTION REVIEW

1. What was the earliest form of self-government in the American colonies?

2. What caused the French and Indian War? What effects did it have?

3. How did Britain's change in attitude toward the colonies lead to the American Revolution?

4. How did the American Revolution influence people in other nations to rebel against their rulers?

Application. Explain how the Declaration of Independence embodies John Locke's theory of natural rights.

Data Search. Refer to the appropriate chart on page 831 to **(a)** compare the populations of Great Britain and the American colonies in 1750 and **(b)** describe the population growth in the United States from 1750 to 1800.

20-2
BEGINNINGS OF REVOLUTION IN FRANCE

READ TO FIND OUT

—what *landed aristocracy* means.
—how traditional French society was structured.
—why the storming of the Bastille was significant.
—how the National Assembly dismantled the Old Regime.
—what the characteristics were of the new form of government set up by the National Assembly.

The French Revolution, which began on the streets of Paris in 1789, attacked the foundations of the traditional social and political order in France. Like the American Revolution, its seeds were sown long before the eruption of violence. They were rooted in the growing opposition to the absolutist policies of the French monarchy and in Enlightenment ideas about people and government.

THE OLD REGIME

The traditional society of France in the seventeenth and eighteenth centuries is known as the Old Regime. Its central institution, an absolute monarchy, was supported by the aristocracy and by the Roman Catholic Church.

As an absolute monarch, the king of France ruled by divine right. Through ministers whom he could appoint and discharge as he pleased, he made the laws and enforced them. He controlled the courts and treasury, dispensing justice and levying taxes at will. He also directed foreign affairs.

The society of the Old Regime was divided into three groups called estates. Members of the clergy formed the First Estate. Aristocrats made up the Second Estate. Together, the clergy and aristocrats made up less than 3 percent of the total French population. The remaining 97 percent were commoners and belonged to the Third Estate.

The Third Estate was a diverse group. Its most influential members were the middle class, or bourgeoisie. The middle class included merchants, bankers, lawyers, and artisans. Many were educated and some were very rich. However, the Third Estate also included farmers and urban laborers.

The First and Second estates enjoyed many rights and privileges that were denied the Third Estate. The First and Second estates received preferential treatment in law courts and occupied the highest positions in government and the military. Although they owned most of the land and were the wealthiest people in France, they paid few taxes.

The Third Estate carried most of the tax burden in France and suffered most from the social and political inequities of the Old Regime. Each group within the Third Estate had grievances. Wealthy members of the middle class were bitter at being denied the status and prestige given the aristocracy. Merchants resented the numerous tariffs, especially since they had no voice in making laws. Business owners and workers were hampered by numerous guild restrictions and mercantilist regulations.

The peasants, the most numerous group in the Third Estate, were excessively burdened. In addition to the taxes they paid to the king, they had to help support the Church. The peasants also had to meet the obligations imposed by the **landed aristocracy**, the nobles who owned the land.

The system was unfair, but most people felt they had no power to change it. In time, however, major economic problems and bold new ideas embraced by the bourgeoisie led to abolition of the old ways.

A FAUT ESPERER Q'EU JEU LA FINIRA BEN TOT

L'auteur en Campagne Ap. 1789.

In this 1789 cartoon, the Third Estate, symbolized by a tired, troubled man, carries the burden of the First and Second estates. "One hopes this game ends soon," reads the caption.

MOVES TOWARD CHANGE

In 1789, France was a powerful nation with colonies throughout the world. The French people, however, were unhappy with the inequities of traditional society. A rapidly growing population put additional pressures on the deteriorating domestic economy.

As France's wealth had grown over the years, so had the size and wealth of the middle class. Colonial trade had spawned many new businesses and brought riches to merchants, bankers, and others. Although it now controlled much of the money in France, the bourgeoisie was largely denied aristocratic privileges. Some wealthy individuals did manage to elevate their status by buying aristocratic titles, but for the most part the middle class seemed destined to remain powerless.

The philosophes, who embraced Enlightenment ideas, envisioned an improved society in which people had control over their destiny rather than being at the mercy of others. Although thinkers like Rousseau, Voltaire, and Diderot called for reform rather than revolution, their writings stimulated the bourgeoisie to action by challenging the rights of traditional authorities. Also, the American Revolution convinced many people in France that revolution was an appropriate answer to tyranny.

The economy. The enormous debt of the monarchy, caused largely by expensive wars and lavish spending, had been draining the French treasury since the reign of Louis XIV. Helping the American colonists fight their war against the British only made the situation worse.

Matters might not have led to a crisis if the king had provided strong, competent leadership. However, Louis XVI, who came to the throne in 1774, was weak and indecisive. His marriage to Marie Antoinette of Austria, France's traditional rival, was unpopular. Louis made an attempt to improve finances by appointing an able minister, Jacques Turgot (tur-GŌ). However, when Turgot proposed to raise money by taxing the First and Second estates, Louis dismissed him.

By the mid-1780s, France was on the verge of bankruptcy. Even the king saw the need to make reforms, but the clergy and nobility stubbornly resisted any measures that would diminish their privileges. Finally, Louis summoned the Estates-General, hoping that it would approve a new tax system. This legislative body had not been convened for 175 years.

The Estates-General. When the Estates-General met at Versailles in May 1789, 300 delegates represented the First Estate, another 300

Jacques Louis David's *Oath of the Horatii*, painted in 1784, depicts three brothers who vowed to defend or die for ancient Rome. This picture inspired feelings of patriotism for France.

the Second Estate, and 600 the Third Estate. At the king's request, the voting was to be conducted as it had been centuries earlier, with the estates meeting separately and each estate having one vote. This meant that the First and Second estates could outvote the Third.

Delegates from the Third Estate, most of whom were lawyers, protested. They insisted that members of the Estates-General meet in a single National Assembly with each delegate casting one vote. Louis rejected the proposal. After weeks of argument, the Third Estate withdrew and declared itself the National Assembly of France. Some of the clergy and a few aristocrats joined the new assembly. Then the delegates vowed that they would not disband until they had provided France with a constitution. This rebellious act was the first step in changing the old system. The middle-class delegates were at last willing to seize the power they felt entitled to.

Aware of the degree of popular support for the National Assembly, the king agreed to recognize it as the single legislative body representing all three estates in France. Before that time, however, the king had nervously summoned troops to Versailles—a move that later proved to be a major blunder.

Outbreak of violence. Late June and early July was a tense time throughout the land, but especially in Paris. Widespread unemployment, high prices, food shortages, and general dissatisfaction with an unjust system had brought working-class people to the point of open defiance. Mobs formed in the streets of Paris, noisily protesting the high prices for bread and other staples. Rumors that the king had had a change of heart and was preparing to use troops to dissolve the new National Assembly spread throughout the city. Seeking arms for protection, and wanting to show their support for the National Assembly, Parisians stormed the Bastille (bas-TEEL) on July 14, 1789.

The attack on this fortress-prison, a hated symbol of the Old Regime, was a turning point in French history. The fall of the Bastille was a powerful demonstration of the strength of people united for a common goal—and the inability of a monarch to control them. The capture of the Bastille also prompted the king to recognize the National Assembly as the new governing body.

The violence that accompanied the storming of the Bastille had yet another impact. A wave of mass hysteria, called the Great Fear, swept Paris and much of France. Peasants in the countryside attacked the estates of nobles, destroying property and records of feudal obligations. Many aristocrats fled the country, and others renounced their special privileges. The French Revolution had begun, and for the rest of the summer, mob violence and destruction raged throughout the nation.

THE END OF THE OLD REGIME

Controlled by moderate members of the bourgeoisie, the National Assembly set about to dismantle the Old Regime, starting with its foundation. On the night of August 4, 1789, the Assembly abolished feudalism in France and eliminated the payment of church and manorial dues. It stripped the nobles of all their tax exemptions and special privileges, including their titles. It decreed that any citizen, regardless of birth, could apply for any position in government, the military, or the Church. These "August Decrees" also abolished the powerful manufacturing and commercial guilds.

A few weeks later, the National Assembly adopted the Declaration of the Rights of Man and Citizen. This document was clearly influenced by Enlightenment ideas and by the American Declaration of Independence. The French Declaration stated that people are "born free and equal in rights" and defined those rights as "liberty, property, security, and resistance to oppression." Asserting that law was "the expression of the will of the people," the declaration guaranteed freedom of the press, speech, and religion, as well as freedom from arbitrary arrest and punishment. It finally stated in official form the main principles of the revolution, popularized in the slogan "Liberty, equality, fraternity."

Later, the National Assembly further limited the privileges of the Roman Catholic Church and confiscated its lands. In 1790, the Civil Constitution of the Clergy placed the Church under state control. All of the church officials were elected by voters and received state salaries. None of the pope's decrees were enforced without government approval. However, these moves against the Church turned many of the peasants against the revolution.

RECOGNIZING STEREOTYPES

A stereotype is an overgeneralized and fixed image of an individual, group, or idea. Stereotypes can be formed about a variety of subjects, such as various nationalities, ethnic backgrounds, age groups, life styles, beliefs, and so on. A stereotype often makes it seem as if all members of a group are basically identical to each other. Stereotypes blur the many ways in which individuals within a group differ.

An example of a stereotype is the statement "All teenagers are irresponsible." This statement ignores and misrepresents the individual characteristics of teenagers, who vary in many different ways, including degrees of being responsible. To describe all teenagers in terms of one characteristic is simplistic and inaccurate.

Stereotypes may have positive, negative, or neutral meanings to those holding them. Stereotypes often shape how people think about and behave toward individual members of stereotyped groups. For example, people might respond to a teenager as being a supposedly "irresponsible" person rather than as a unique individual. The skill of recognizing stereotypes can help you avoid misunderstandings or problems that may arise from acting on such inaccurate images.

EXPLAINING THE SKILL

One way to recognize stereotypes in written accounts is to follow these steps:

1. *Skim the account to identify any characteristics that are attributed to whatever is being described.*

2. *Recall some of the clues that may indicate a stereotype:*

    a) Use of generalizations or exaggeration. Often generalizations contain words like *all*, *every*, *none*, *always*, and *never*.

    b) Use of vague words, such as *interesting* or *tricky*.

    c) Use of consistently positive- or negative-sounding words.

    d) Linking together features not logically connected to each other. One example of this is linking personal traits with possessions, as in the statement "All students who own computers are intelligent."

3. *Search line-by-line to determine what clues, if any, are evident in the account.*

4. *Recall what you know about any individual members or representatives of the group being described.* By doing this, you can identify whether there are exceptions to the stated characteristics.

5. *Determine the extent to which the stated description accurately describes individual examples or members of the group.*

6. *State any stereotype that is presented in the account.* For example, if you read an account that presents a stereotype of eighteenth-century European rulers, you might state, "This account presents a stereotype of all eighteenth-century monarchs as being cruel and unjust to the people they ruled."

If you cannot easily determine whether there is a stereotype in the account, you might want to study information about several members of the group to see how well they, as individuals, fit the given description.

APPLYING THE SKILL

The following account is about the failed attempt to involve nobles in the French government under Louis XV. Use the previously described procedure to determine whether the account presents any stereotype.

> The difficulty was the ignorance, the frivolity, and the lack of diligence of the nobility, who were accustomed to being good for nothing except getting killed, succeeding at war only by seniority, and romping around for the rest of the time in the most mortal uselessness. As a result they were devoted to idleness and disgusted with all knowledge outside of knowledge about war. They had a conditioned incapacity for being able to provide themselves with anything useful to do.
>
> Abridged from the memoirs of the Duke of Saint-Simon, who lived from 1675 to 1755.

REFLECTING ON THE SKILL

In searching for evidence of stereotyping in the previous account, you should have skimmed it to identify characteristics attributed to the nobility, reviewed the indicators of stereotyping, and then looked for any examples of these indicators in the account. To check how well you can recognize a stereotype, answer the following questions.

1. Which one of the following words or phrases in the account indicates a possible stereotype? **(a)** *good for nothing,* **(b)** *nobility,* **(c)** *seniority.* Explain your answer.

2. Some "loaded words" that give a negative impression of the nobility are found in **(a)** the first sentence only, **(b)** the second sentence only, **(c)** both the first and second sentences.

3. The best way to prove that this account presents a stereotype is to **(a)** list all clues to stereotyping present in the account, **(b)** research information on individual eighteenth-century French nobles, **(c)** determine the author's qualifications. Explain your answer.

4. This account presents a stereotype of French nobles as being **(a)** courageous people who were ignorant of the dangers of war, **(b)** incompetent and irresponsible people, **(c)** lazy but dignified people.

APPLYING THE SKILL

The following accounts are about the members of the Paris working class, who were known as *sans-culottes* ("without breeches"), because the men wore trousers instead of the knee breeches worn by the aristocrats. Examine each account to determine whether it presents a stereotype.

Account A

Claire Lacombe was one of the more famous *sans-culottes* in the early 1790s. A childless, single woman, she used her talents as an actress to actively promote the cause of the Revolution. She gave frequent patriotic speeches before the Legislative Assembly in Paris and helped stir up the Paris mob in its attack on the king's residence in August 1792.

In October 1793, she led her Paris women's revolutionary society in a series of often violent clashes with the market women of Paris over the wearing of the Revolutionary cockade [a ribbon worn on the hat as a badge] and over the controls on food prices. As a result, the Convention banned the society and barred women from political activity.

Abridged from the *Historical Dictionary of the French Revolution, 1789-1799.* Westport: Greenwood Press, 1985.

Account B

A *sans-culotte* always goes on foot. He has no millions as others might like to have, no chateau, no valets nor servants. He lives simply with his wife and children, if he has any, on the fourth or fifth story of a Paris tenement.

He is useful. He knows how to forge iron, to use a saw, to use a file, to roof a house, to make shoes, and to shed his last drop of blood for the Republic. Because he works, you are sure not to meet him in the cafes or in the gaming houses where others conspire and game.

Finally, a *sans-culotte* always has his sabre sharp, to cut off the ears of all enemies of the Revolution. At the first sound of the drum he is ready to leave for the army of the Alps or for the army of the North.

Abridged from a 1793 pamphlet written by an anonymous author.

CHECKING YOUR UNDERSTANDING

Now that you have analyzed Accounts A and B, answer the following:

5. One characteristic attributed to the subject of Account B is **(a)** dedication to the ideals of the French Revolution, **(b)** desire for money, **(c)** enjoyment of rural life.

6. Which one of the following phrases indicates a possible stereotype? **(a)** *one of the more famous,* **(b)** *always has his sabre sharp,* **(c)** *enemies of the Revolution.* Explain your answer.

7. A stereotype is presented in **(a)** Account A, **(b)** Account B, **(c)** both accounts. Explain your answer.

REVIEWING THE SKILL

8. What is a stereotype?

9. How might stereotyping be harmful?

10. What is one procedure you can follow in order to recognize a stereotype?

Revolutionary Parisian soldiers haul cannons to the heights of Montmartre on July 15, 1789. This move had sealed off the northern and eastern approaches to Paris from Louis XVI's troops.

LIMITING THE MONARCHY

In September 1791, the National Assembly issued France's first written constitution, establishing a limited constitutional monarchy. The king was to retain control over the military and foreign affairs, but he could exercise only a temporary veto over laws passed by the Legislative Assembly, France's new parliament.

The constitution included all the reforms adopted by the National Assembly during the previous two years. Voting rights were given to men who paid a certain sum in taxes, thus allowing about two-thirds of France's male population to vote. Women were not allowed to vote. Only property owners could be elected to the Legislative Assembly. The government established in 1791 was dominated by the male middle class. Although this government was not a democracy, it was the most broadly based political system in Europe at the time.

OPPONENTS WITHIN FRANCE

The limited monarchy established by the constitution of 1791 lasted less than a year. The new regime had many opponents, including those whom the revolution had deprived of power. The clergy and devout Catholics objected to the restrictions on the Church. *Émigrés* (EM-ee-gray), the nobles who had fled France, worked from outside the country to undo the changes introduced by the revolution. Even Louis XVI opposed the new constitution.

Other people opposed the new government because they wanted more radical, or extreme, changes, especially an end to the monarchy. Most of these opponents identified with one of two middle-class political factions, the Girondists (juh-RON-dists) and the Jacobins (JAK-uh-bins). Both groups wanted a republic, in which citizens elect people to represent their interests in running the country. Girondists wanted control by the middle class. The radical Jacobins were more sympathetic toward city laborers and the peasantry, groups whom the constitution of 1791 had passed over.

These differing attitudes were reflected in the Legislative Assembly. About a third of its members were conservatives, who favored traditional ways and supported the Old Regime. They thought that the revolution had gone far enough. A smaller number, consisting mainly of Jacobins and Girondists, wanted more drastic change. The largest group were moderate delegates, whose votes varied depending on the circumstances.

FOREIGN INVASION

The most immediate threat to France's new government came from outside the country. European monarchs feared that the revolutionary ideals of France might spread. In August 1791, the rulers of Austria and Prussia invited other European powers to join them in helping restore absolutism in France. The Legislative Assembly, fearing an invasion, acted first, and in April 1792, France declared war on Austria and Prussia. Then Austrian and Prussian troops began moving into France. By the end of summer they were only about 200 miles (320 kilometers) away from Paris.

As war hysteria gripped Paris, a radical group called the Commune took over the city government and challenged the Legislative Assembly. The Commune supported a mob that attacked the king's palace and then forced the Assembly to suspend the monarchy and imprison the royal family. The Commune then insisted that the Assembly call for a new legislature to be elected by a vote of all adult males.

Fearing invasion of Paris by Austrian and Prussian troops, and aware that Louis and his Austrian wife did not favor the revolution, mobs once again took to the streets. In September 1792, Parisian mobs stormed the jails, filled mainly with priests who had refused to abide by the Civil Constitution of the Clergy. In four days more than 1,200 prisoners, whom the mobs saw as opposing the revolution, were killed. Three weeks later the new governing body, the National Convention, took office. The French Revolution had entered a new and more radical phase.

SECTION REVIEW

1. Define **landed aristocracy**.

2. Describe the three groups that made up society in the Old Regime.

3. Discuss the significance of the storming of the Bastille.

4. Describe the actions taken by the National Assembly to dismantle the Old Regime.

5. Describe the new form of government set up by the National Assembly.

Application. How did new ideas in social and political thought in the 1700s help lead to the French Revolution?

20–3
FRANCE'S FIRST REPUBLIC

READ TO FIND OUT

—what **conscription, primogeniture**, and **nationalism** mean.
—how the more radical National Convention carried revolutionary ideas further than the Legislative Assembly had.
—what the Reign of Terror was.
—how modern nationalism emerged.

The hastily elected National Convention met at Paris in September 1792. It was more radical than the Legislative Assembly. At first, the Girondists, now considered a conservative faction, had a majority and assumed control. In less than a year, however, the radical Jacobins had won enough support to take over. The most powerful Jacobin leaders were Georges-Jacques Danton and Maximilien Robespierre (ROBES-pyair).

ACTS OF THE NATIONAL CONVENTION

The National Convention's first act was to abolish the monarchy and proclaim France a republic, a nation governed by elected representatives. After a trial and several days of voting, the Convention passed the death sentence on Louis XVI. The former monarch was beheaded on January 21, 1793.

On the military front, French armies finally forced the retreat of the Austrian and Prussian invaders. Full of confidence after this victory, the National Convention boldly declared that French armies would liberate everyone in Europe from absolutist rule.

The execution of Louis XVI had already alarmed the European monarchs, and the French threats to spread revolutionary ideals, by military conquest if necessary, alarmed them even further. The rulers formed an anti-French alliance called the First Coalition. It consisted of forces from Britain, Spain, the Netherlands, Austria, Prussia, and Sardinia. The alliance scored several victories over the French in the spring of 1793. The National Convention, deciding that extreme measures were necessary, appointed a dictatorial Committee of Public Safety to defend France against its enemies. The committee's Jacobin leaders included Danton and Robespierre.

THE JACOBINS IN CONTROL

By the spring of 1793, radicals, both in and outside the National Convention, regarded the conservative Girondists as enemies of the republic and had them expelled from the Convention. Now the Jacobins, working through the Committee of Public Safety, were in total control of the revolutionary government.

To protect France from foreign invaders, the Committee of Public Safety proceeded to raise the largest army in European history by subjecting men in France to military service. This first modern *conscription*, the drafting of eligible persons into military service, reflected the revolutionary belief that equal citizens owed equal duties to their state. In addition, officers were chosen for their talent, not their social status. Under the Old Regime, only aristocrats could become officers. France's army of almost a million patriotic citizen-soldiers proved far more effective than the armies of the First Coalition.

French revolutionaries used the guillotine to behead prisoners condemned to death. The machine was named for Joseph Guillotin, a doctor in the National Convention who urged its use.

In late 1793 and early 1794, the French repelled their enemies on all sides.

The fear of invasion and revolts against the government led the Committee of Public Safety to take more drastic steps. In September 1793, under the leadership of Robespierre, the Jacobins instituted the aptly named Reign of Terror. Robespierre, a fanatical idealist, believed that executions were necessary to preserve the republic. Anyone suspected of treason, no matter how flimsy the evidence, was arrested.

Among the first to be executed was the former queen and wife of Louis XVI, Marie Antoinette. Next came the Girondists who had not been able to flee Paris. During the bloodbath of the Terror, more than 20,000 real and imagined enemies of the revolution—mainly peasants and laborers—met their deaths. Thousands more were jailed. The toll was higher in the provinces than in Paris, for outlying areas had witnessed several revolts against the repub-

More than 2,500 people were executed in Paris from March 1793 to July 1794. These public executions were conducted by the Committee of Public Safety in the present-day Place de la Concorde.

lic. Fearing for their lives, tens of thousands of ordinary citizens fled the country.

In the spring of 1794, Robespierre turned on Danton, who believed that the Terror should be ended. After Danton's execution, moderates regained control of the Convention and in July overthrew Robespierre. He was sent to the guillotine, and the Terror finally ended.

ACCOMPLISHMENTS OF THE CONVENTION

The National Convention governed France for another year after the Terror. In spite of the hysteria and repression of its three-year rule, the Convention introduced a number of significant reforms. It ended slavery in the French colonies, abolished imprisonment for debt, and did away with *primogeniture*, a practice limiting the inheritance of family property to the oldest son.

Perhaps of greatest importance was the Convention's role in stimulating the birth of mod-

ern *nationalism*, the love of one's nation. By introducing conscription, the National Convention raised an army that was truly national in character, with members drawn from all parts of the country. Patriotism was stimulated by slogans, symbols, and songs. In time, the people of France developed feelings of attachment for their whole nation and began to identify with national goals.

THE DIRECTORY

After the Terror, the people of France experienced a wave of revulsion at the horrors of revolution. The National Convention, determined to set the nation on a more moderate course, drafted yet another constitution. This one returned government to the conservative middle class by limiting the vote to property owners. It provided for a two-house legislature, which would choose five directors as a joint executive body. The Directory, as this new government

Nine months after the execution of Louis XVI, Marie Antoinette met the same fate. David, the "Revolution's artist," drew this eyewitness sketch of the queen on her way to the guillotine.

was called, went into effect in October 1795 and ruled for four years.

The Directory proved even less effective than the Legislative Assembly and the National Convention in solving France's financial and military problems. Attacks on the republic by Catholics and other conservatives increased. Rising prices and disrupted production drove some groups in France to armed protests in 1795 and 1797.

Foreign hostility to France continued. The French military successes only made Europe's monarchs more eager to demolish the work of the revolution. All these pressures produced a more authoritarian government than the early revolutionary leaders had ever intended.

THE RISE OF NAPOLEON

In the decade after the attack on the Bastille, the people of France had endured three different governments, domestic turmoil, and foreign invasion. They were weary, and the weak Directory seemed unable to cope effectively with France's problems. The time was ripe for a strong leader who could restore stability while preserving the gains of the revolution. Napoleon Bonaparte, one of history's most dominating personalities, became that leader.

Napoleon Bonaparte was born of Italian parents on the island of Corsica in 1769, shortly before it was taken over by France. He enrolled in a French military school at the age of ten, graduated as an artillery officer, and became a general by the time he was twenty-four.

Napoleon served the revolution well. His loyalty was rewarded in 1796, when he was given command of the French armies fighting the Austrians in northern Italy. The Italian campaign offered Napoleon the first opportunity to demonstrate his genius for leadership. He led his troops into battle personally, thus winning their loyalty and admiration. He boosted their morale and inspired them to sacrifice by appealing to their sense of nationalism. Within a year, his superior tactical skills, particularly in the quick movement of troops and artillery, forced the Austrians to ask for peace.

After the defeat of Austria, only Britain was still fighting France. In 1798 Napoleon, determined to weaken the British by attacking their colonial interests, invaded Egypt as a step toward taking India. The campaign turned into a disaster when the British fleet sank the French fleet in the Battle of the Nile.

France was now in serious trouble. Britain, Austria, and Russia formed a Second Coalition to oppose the French. Their troops expelled French soldiers from Italy and threatened France itself. The Directory seemed incapable of handling the situation, and Napoleon joined others in a plot against the government. In November 1799, he forced the legislators to abolish the Directory. This was the first step in Napoleon's rise to power as a head of state.

SECTION REVIEW

1. Define **conscription, primogeniture**, and **nationalism**.

2. Explain how the actions of the National Convention differed from those of the Legislative Assembly.

3. Describe the Reign of Terror.

4. How did the National Convention promote feelings of nationalism?

Application. How do citizens today express feelings of nationalism? In what ways are these similar to and different from French nationalism after the revolution?

20-4
THE ERA OF NAPOLEON

READ TO FIND OUT

—what *Napoleonic Code* means.
—how Napoleon strengthened the power of the state.
—how Napoleon expanded the new French empire.
—what factors led to Napoleon's downfall.
—why the attempt to return to absolutism failed after the defeat of Napoleon.

The first government set up by Napoleon Bonaparte and his fellow conspirators was directed by three consuls. As First Consul, Napoleon dominated the others. A new constitution limited his rule to ten years, but in 1802 he maneuvered the legislature into appointing him First Consul for life. All pretense of maintaining a republic was dropped in 1804, when Napoleon became emperor.

THE NAPOLEONIC CODE

Napoleon was known chiefly for his military accomplishments. However, his domestic reforms had the most lasting impact on France. Napoleon's greatest achievement was a series of laws that were known collectively as the *Napoleonic Code*.

The code guaranteed the equality of all citizens before the law, confirmed the end of serfdom in France, and provided for freedom of occupation and freedom of religion. However, it fell short of the full equality envisioned by the leaders of the revolution. In fact, it reduced the rights of some groups, including women. In spite of its defects, however, the Napoleonic Code was more progressive than the laws of any other European power of the time. It was the foundation for present-day systems of law in France and several other nations.

OTHER REFORMS

Several other reforms instituted by Napoleon strengthened the power of the state. A new system of public education raised educational standards. Napoleon aided the financial recovery of France by instituting a fair system of taxation, balancing the budget, and repaying government debts.

Antoine Jean Gros's *Portrait of Bonaparte, First Consul*, shows the general just before he was named First Consul for life in 1802. Napoleon commissioned the portrait himself.

In an effort to heal the rift with the Roman Catholic Church, Napoleon returned to the papacy some power over selecting church officials in France. He also gained the support of many non-Catholics by guaranteeing Protestants and Jews the right to practice their religions.

BUILDING AN EMPIRE

Napoleon's principal goal was military conquest. His regime rose with military victory and fell with military defeat. In the process of creating an empire, however, Napoleon spread revolutionary change to a major part of Europe.

His first campaign was aimed at the Second Coalition. After an important French victory in 1800, most opposition to Napoleon ceased. Peace was not to last, though, for the spread of French influence seriously upset the European balance of power. In 1805, a Third Coalition united Britain, Austria, Russia, and Spain against France. In the decade that followed, the French were almost constantly at war.

Great Britain was Napoleon's most steadfast enemy. The British did not feel secure as long as one powerful nation dominated the European continent. For his part, Napoleon knew that his dream of a European empire would never be complete until Britain was defeated. His hopes of invading the British Isles were dashed in 1805 when the British fleet destroyed the French fleet off the coast of Spain.

French forces were more successful on land. Triumphs over the three strongest powers on the continent—Austria, Russia, and Prussia—made France the dominant land power from the Atlantic coast to Russia. Napoleon then set out to reorganize Europe. He abolished the Austrian-dominated Holy Roman Empire. He reduced the number of German states from 314 to 39 and unified most of them into the Confederation of the Rhine, a political unit dependent on France. In addition, he united several small northern Italian states into the Kingdom of Italy, also under French control. Southern Italy became the Kingdom of Naples.

SPOTLIGHT: PEOPLE

NAPOLEON BONAPARTE

The late 1700s and early 1800s were tumultuous times for Europe. For a time, the destiny of the continent lay in the hands of a short, unimpressive-looking soldier.

The character and abilities that enabled Napoleon to control much of Europe for ten years were forged at military schools in France. At Brienne, his first military school, Napoleon was mocked because of his size. He treated such attacks with arrogant scorn. This haughty attitude did not win Napoleon many friends, but he preferred to keep to himself anyway. He spent much of his time studying the great military campaigns of history and began to model himself on the Spartans of ancient Greece.

As a soldier, Napoleon had tremendous energy and was able to work 20 hours a day. He also seemed to be untouched by the hardships of military life. His willingness to share in these hardships won Napoleon the love of the rank-and-file soldiers.

On the battlefield, Napoleon was a general of intelligence, resourcefulness, and imagination who, in a matter of minutes, seemed to sense his opponent's mistakes and weaknesses. He rarely did the expected, and his unconventional approach to war won him a reputation as a gambler and a risk-taker. Napoleon answered critics by saying he preferred a glorious defeat to an ordinary victory. He suffered few defeats, yet in his success the seeds of his downfall were sown.

His victories on the battlefield convinced Napoleon that he was superior to other people and that fate held great things for him. His desire for glory began to take hold. "I am destined to change the face of the world," he said.

In the years after his coronation as emperor, it became clear that Napoleon intended to forge a worldwide French empire. This ambition, however, led to the disastrous invasion of Russia, his defeat at Waterloo, and his exile on St. Helena. He remarked, "If I had succeeded I should have been the greatest man known to history." In failure, Napoleon still commands history's attention.

British artist John Atkinson painted *The Battle of Waterloo* on site in 1815. The Duke of Wellington, commander of an allied force opposing Napoleon, is shown doffing his hat.

SECTION REVIEW

1. Define *Napoleonic Code*.

2. Describe some of the domestic reforms that Napoleon established.

3. Discuss how Napoleon expanded the new French empire.

4. What factors led to Napoleon's downfall?

5. Identify three characteristics of the French monarchy in 1815 which show that the revolutionary spirit survived.

Analysis. In what ways did Napoleon's reign embody and spread the ideals of the French Revolution?

HISTORY IN FOCUS

In the late eighteenth century, violent upheavals in America and France changed the very nature of politics, society, and culture in the modern world. The French Revolution attacked the tra-

ditions and institutions that had characterized Europe for centuries: absolutism, privilege, serfdom, and the economic monopoly of medieval guilds. The changes brought about by America's struggle for independence from Britain were not nearly as fundamental and widespread as those resulting from the French Revolution. However, the American example served as an inspiration to all people struggling against tyranny and proved that the ideas of the Enlightenment were workable.

In the 1800s, most of western Europe, influenced by the French Revolution and the positive contributions of Napoleon, entered a new, third stage of political and social development. Just as strong monarchies had replaced the feudal system, so now constitutional regimes began to replace traditional monarchies. This turbulent era ushered in middle-class domination, national awareness, and popular democracy—forces that have become familiar almost everywhere today. It also introduced the concept of revolution as a means of attaining social and political gains.

SUMMARY

- The American Revolution began in 1775 with the shots fired at Lexington and Concord, Massachusetts. The conflict grew out of the colonists' resentment over increasing British control.

- American troops defeated the larger British forces, and in 1783 Britain recognized American independence. A few years later the new nation adopted its Constitution. Many people in Europe were encouraged by the Americans' experiment with establishing a republican form of government.

- The French Revolution began with the storming of the Bastille in 1789. King Louis XVI was forced to recognize the National Assembly, which in turn established a limited monarchy.

- Violence and political turmoil swept France for ten years as various factions struggled for power and other European nations threatened to invade. Finally, in 1799, the French government was overthrown and a dictatorship was eventually established under Napoleon Bonaparte.

- Napoleon instituted various reforms, most notably the Napoleonic Code. Declaring himself emperor, he then set out to conquer Europe. Although a brilliant general, Napoleon was eventually defeated by a coalition of nations led by Britain.

- Napoleon escaped from exile, but was finally defeated at the Battle of Waterloo in 1815. The French monarchy was restored, but the revolutionary spirit, spread by Napoleon, had brought permanent changes to France and to Europe.

VOCABULARY REVIEW

Match each numbered vocabulary term with its origin. Then explain the connection between the origin and the vocabulary term.

1. primogeniture   **(a)** Latin: *conscriptus*, to enroll

2. conscription   **(b)** Latin: *primus*, first + *genitura*, birth

CHAPTER REVIEW

1. (a) Why was self-government possible in Britain's American colonies? **(b)** What factors allowed representative government to develop? **(c)** What gave rise to an American identity? How were the origins of French nationalism different?

2. (a) Why was Britain indifferent toward its American colonies? **(b)** In what ways did British policy toward the colonies change? Explain why British policy changed.

3. (a) Describe three specific causes of the American colonists' resentment toward Britain in the 1760s and 1770s. **(b)** Compare the grievances of the American colonists with those of the Third Estate in France.

4. (a) What American and French revolutionary documents were similar? Explain. **(b)** Compare the Articles of Confederation and the United States Constitution. **(c)** Compare the first two French constitutions.

5. (a) How were the American revolutionaries able to win? **(b)** How did France and Spain help the colonists? **(c)** Why did some Europeans applaud the American Revolution? **(d)** Why did the European powers that defeated Napoleon want to restore absolutism in France?

6. Compare the American and French revolutions in terms of: **(a)** causes; **(b)** fighting; **(c)** political and social change.

7. (a) What led to the storming of the Bastille? **(b)** Compare the Great Fear and the Reign of Terror. **(c)** What was the Commune?

8. (a) Compare the Girondists and the Jacobins. **(b)** Compare the actions and characteristics of the National Assembly, the National Convention, and the Directory.

9. (a) What factors were responsible for Napoleon's rise to power? **(b)** List Napoleon's principal reforms. **(c)** How did the Napoleonic Code both further and undermine revolutionary ideals?

10. (a) Why did Napoleon want to defeat Britain? Describe his strategy. **(b)** How did European feelings about Napoleonic rule change? Explain why.

THINKING CRITICALLY: ACTIVITIES

1. Divide into groups of four or five to discuss the following questions: What constitutes a successful revolution? Was the American Revolution more or less successful than the French Revolution? Support your arguments with material from the chapter.

2. Make a timeline of the French Revolution from the formation of the National Assembly to Napoleon's seizure of power. Include all important events in the course of the revolution. Then write a summary of those events, explaining how one change led to another.

APPLYING SOCIAL STUDIES SKILLS

Evaluating secondary sources. No one knows who fired the first shot at Lexington in April 1775. Below are two accounts of the battle. Each comes from a different source.

> The military governor of Massachusetts sent out . . . troops to take possession of military stores at Concord . . . . At Lexington, a handful of "embattled farmers," who had been tipped off by Paul Revere, barred the way. The "rebels" were ordered to disperse. They stood their ground. The English fired a volley of shots that killed eight patriots. Paul Revere spread the news of this new atrocity to the neighboring colonies.
>
> At five o'clock in the morning the local militia of Lexington, seventy strong, formed up on the village green. As the sun rose, the head of the British column . . . came into view. The leading officer, brandishing his sword, shouted, "Disperse you rebels, immediately!" The militia commander ordered his men to disperse . . . . But in the confusion someone fired. A volley was returned. The ranks of the militia were thinned . . . . The British column marched on to Concord.

Sources: Samuel Steinberg. *The United States: Story of a Free People.* (Boston: Allyn & Bacon, 1963). Winston Churchill. *History of the English Speaking Peoples*, Vol. 3. (New York: Dodd, Mead & Co., 1964).

1. Which account did American historian Samuel Steinberg write? Explain.

2. Which account did British historian Winston Churchill write? Explain.

APPLYING THINKING SKILLS

Recognizing stereotypes. Examine the following excerpt from a speech by Robespierre in 1792 to determine whether or not it presents a stereotype. Then answer the questions.

> But the enemies of our country, will they permit peace? No! As long as these tyrants live they will conspire against the French people. They will pour on us all the corrupt evils of their own hearts.
>
> Their armies consist of spies and traitors who keep coming without stopping. They use all the passions and methods, with great energy, to destroy us. Their mercenary writers try to excite the People to all the same disorders that the Girondists have tried.
>
> These enemies of ours and other agents of foreign powers agitate against us. Their intrigues seek to banish the People and the Patriots. They mingle with the defenders of the Revolution. They imitate our language. With false signs of patriotism they try to ridicule our cause. All our enemies apply unreflected zeal to their evil goals.

Abridged from a speech by Maximilien Robespierre.

1. What is a stereotype?

2. What are four types of clues that can indicate a stereotype? Explain how each type of clue can indicate stereotyping.

3. What is one procedure you can use to determine whether or not a written account presents a stereotype?

4. Why is it important to be able to recognize stereotypes?

5. In what ways might stereotyping be harmful to people?

6. Which clues to stereotyping are evident in Robespierre's speech? For each type of clue, give a specific example from the speech.

7. State the stereotype that is presented in the speech.

8. How would you prove that the description in this speech by Robespierre is overgeneralized and inaccurate?

9. Why do you think Robespierre presented a stereotype in this speech?

CHAPTER TWENTY-ONE

THE INDUSTRIAL REVOLUTION

1750–1914

Blue Morning. George Bellows, United States, 1909.

The Industrial Revolution—as important in human history as the Agricultural Revolution of neolithic times—had its beginnings in Great Britain in the mid-1700s, when machines began to replace hand labor. Britain's rapidly growing population, as well as its increased trade, created a need for manufactured goods—especially textiles—that could not be met by the old methods. Enterprising merchants, therefore, encouraged the development of ways to speed up the manufacturing process.

Already successful in commerce, entrepreneurs expanded into industry, where both the risks and the potential for profits were greater. Capitalism took on a new meaning as the face of business changed. As middle class entrepreneurs gained wealth and power, workers united to improve their lives.

TIMELINE

1760	
	Spinning jenny Watt's steam engine
1780	
	Steam-powered mills First textile Cotton gin
1800	
	machinery in the U.S. Steamboat
1820	
	Mechanical reaper Textile Factory Act Labor unions in Great Britain Telegraph
1840	
	Bessemer process
1860	
	Strikes legalized in Great Britain
1880	
	Sherman Antitrust Act
1900	
	Airplane
1920	

21-1
BEGINNINGS OF THE INDUSTRIAL REVOLUTION

READ TO FIND OUT

—what the terms *industrialization* and *enclosure movement* mean.
—why the Industrial Revolution began in Britain.
—how the factory system differed from the domestic system of production.
—why the invention of the steam engine was crucial to the onset of the Industrial Revolution.

The Industrial Revolution began in Great Britain in the 1700s, then spread to other nations in Europe and to the United States in the 1800s. A history of capitalism and commerical success created a favorable climate for its beginnings in Britain. *Industrialization*—the shift to production of goods using power-driven machines in factories—dramatically changed the economic and social systems of nations of Europe and North America. Advances in transportation, communication, science, and agriculture also contributed to widespread changes.

BEGINNINGS IN BRITAIN

Several factors favored Britain's taking the lead in industrial development. The nation's rapidly increasing population, which almost doubled between 1700 and 1800, provided a growing market for goods and a ready source of labor. Also, Britain had abundant natural resources such as coal and iron, as well as navigable rivers and seaports. Its vast colonial empire provided both raw materials—cotton, lumber, and dyes, for example—and markets for manufactured goods. Merchants who profited from this trade invested in shipping and other businesses.

The nation had a stable political system that was not susceptible to violent revolution like the one in France. Because of its naval strength and its location as an island nation, Britain did not experience the devastation of war that other European nations suffered from the 1600s to the 1800s. Although foreign wars strained the treasury, the land and the general population were spared.

Improvements in agriculture led to increased crop production, which provided a healthier diet for the growing population and increased profits for farmers. The textile industry's increasing demand for wool and the growing population's need for food in the 1700s prompted large landowners to expand both their crops and their flocks of sheep. Thus, in what was called the **enclosure movement**, these landowners enclosed, or fenced in, land that had formerly been used by small farmers, either for a fee or by custom. In so doing, the landowners left many people with land unsuitable for either cultivation or grazing—or with no land at all. Furthermore, the ability of rural areas to absorb the rapidly expanding population was reduced. As a result, many people drifted to towns and cities to find work, becoming a source of cheap labor.

By the mid-1700s, Britain was the world's leading colonial and commercial power. Merchants, bankers, and other capitalists profited from a thriving overseas trade. To make even more money, they reinvested the surplus in new and expanding businesses. Thus, the economy had ample capital for growth. In addition, people had the freedom to conduct business without excessive government regulation, unlike the French who worked under a strict mercantilist system.

The domestic system. Britain's continued success in commerce depended on its ability to meet growing market demands, especially for textiles. People in preindustrial Britain generally worked in their homes at their own pace to make cloth, clothing, and other goods. Many people were artisans who specialized in a single type of work. Others were farm families who made goods at home to earn additional money. Enterprising individuals known as entrepreneurs—people who organize, manage, and assume the risks of their own businesses—bought the raw materials, distributed them to the craftspeople, and often supplied the tools. This system was called the domestic, or cottage,

system. As Britain's market expanded, however, the domestic system was no longer adequate.

THE TEXTILE INDUSTRY

The textile industry was the first to benefit from an intensified interest in stepping up production. As demand increased for the new and popular cotton as well as the traditional woolen fabrics, so did efforts to expand the industry. The first invention to improve production in the textile industry was the flying shuttle, a weaving machine introduced in 1733. It was followed in 1764 by the spinning jenny, which could fill several spindles with thread at the same time. Then, in 1769, came the water frame, a water-powered spinning machine. A steam-powered loom introduced in the 1780's mechanized the weaving process. This invention was the forerunner of the modern power loom.

The invention of the cotton gin in 1793 led to even more growth in the textile industry. Removing the sticky seeds from cotton by hand was a slow process until an American, Eli Whitney, devised a machine that could do the work of 50 people.

THE GROWTH OF FACTORIES

Although the domestic system provided a livelihood for many families and resulted in profits for many entrepreneurs, they did not have much control over the quality of the goods or the scheduling of production. Some entrepreneurs, hoping to increase productivity by determining when and where people worked, provided shops where groups of craftspeople could work together.

New spinning and weaving machinery soon revolutionized the way cloth was made. Textile makers built large factories to house the huge new machines.

The new factory system changed the way of life for many people throughout Britain. For the first time, many workers now went to the new factories to do jobs for wages instead of making goods at home. Those who lived too far away for daily travel moved to the new towns that sprang up near the factories.

Many factory workers had done the same type of work under the domestic system. Others were unemployed people who just needed to

In *Landscape with Rainbow, Henley-on-Thames*, Dutch painter Jan Siberechts depicts a small British town in the late seventeenth century. With the coming of the Industrial Revolution, in many areas the peaceful countryside was soon filled with smoky factories and crowded worker housing.

work. Many were women and children who had to help support their families. This was the first time large numbers of women had gone to work for wages in other than domestic service. They soon formed a sizable component of the work force. Some other workers were artisans who could not compete with the lower prices of goods made in factories and were forced to give up their independence just to earn a living. Many factory workers were people from rural areas who found themselves without land, largely because of increasing competition from a rapidly growing population. Others had been displaced by the enclosure movement.

THE STEAM ENGINE

Although the first textile factories appeared in Britain in the 1740s, steam-powered mills were not built until 1785. The invention of the steam engine soon changed not only the textile industry and other types of manufacturing but transportation as well.

The steam engine is often called the most important invention of the Industrial Revolution. Production by the most advanced machines was limited by the amount of power available to drive them. Even waterwheels did not provide enough power.

Since the 1600s, inventors had been working to develop an efficient steam engine. However, such an engine eluded them until 1763, when James Watt began working to improve an engine designed earlier by Thomas Newcomen. Watt's new engine, patented in 1769, led directly to improvements in manufacturing, transportation, and mining.

Steam-powered machines improved productivity because they could do more work. Since they no longer relied on water power, factories were not limited to locations on rivers or swift streams. In addition, locating factories near coalfields reduced the cost of the fuel for the engines by eliminating transport fees.

ADVANCES IN IRON AND STEEL

Britain's growing industries required increasing amounts of iron and steel for new machinery and tools. Before the 1700s, iron production was primitive and expensive. It relied on enormous amounts of charcoal, made from increasingly scarce hardwoods, to provide the heat needed to separate the iron from the other elements in the ore, a process known as smelting. Because hardwood charcoal was so expensive, ironmakers needed a cheaper fuel. In 1709, an English iron maker successfully used coke, a fuel made from the cheaper and more abundant coal, in the smelting process. However, the iron made by the new process was more brittle and less workable than the charcoal-smelted metal.

QUEEN VICTORIA

"Quite charmed," exclaimed Queen Victoria, after journeying on the royal train from the palace in Windsor to London. When Queen Victoria, who reigned over Great Britain from 1837 to 1901, took this trip by steam train in 1842, the nation's industrial revolution was well under way. As the revolution moved into the twentieth century, the British people tended to credit the Queen of England with industrial progress—as if she in some way had inspired it.

British support of the queen was not constant, however. In 1837, when Queen Victoria became monarch after the death of her uncle William IV, the people at first rallied behind their new ruler. During the early 1830s, Great Britain had become a divided nation, politically and economically crippled by the Napoleonic Wars as well as by the lackluster reigns of William IV and George IV, who had ruled before William. Compared with these two kings, Victoria appeared a rather romantic and virtuous figure. This early popularity enjoyed by the queen was not long-lived. Many people soon became dismayed by the way the queen played party politics. Her fiery temper, willful nature,

and hasty judgments of people caused shock and outrage.

With the help of her husband, Prince Albert, Queen Victoria was able to regain her standing with the British people. The royal couple's obvious devotion to one another, and Victoria's image as a loving wife and mother as well as a dutiful and industrious sovereign, won the people's admiration.

Albert's views on the monarchy greatly influenced Victoria, and she soon came to depend on him for suggestions and advice. His death in 1861 was devastating to her. She spent the rest of her life in deep mourning for Albert and practically withdrew from public life.

During her 63-year reign, Victoria saw the nation through many changes on its path from division to prosperity. In doing so, she helped to establish the monarchy as the most enduring institution of British political life. The virtuous lady was the appropriate symbol of a good and great nation. By the time of her death in 1901, Victoria had invested the British monarchy with a dignity and authority that time has only slightly diminished.

By about 1760, the smelting process had been improved so that the iron was easier to work, and smelting with coke soon spread throughout the nation.

The developments in iron smelting led to new processes in the large-scale production of steel, a much stronger and more versatile metal that was in greater demand as machines—and machine parts—became more complex. Steel was five times stronger than iron and lasted longer.

A furnace invented by British engineer Henry Bessemer in the 1850s used a blast of air to burn off the impurities in molten iron, thereby refining it into steel. The open-hearth firing method, developed in England by William Siemans and later improved by Pierre Martin in France, used waste heat from the furnace to preheat the fuel and add more air to it. As a

result, refining steel was more efficient and more controllable. The Bessemer process and open-hearth firing revolutionized the steel-making industry. Soon steel had replaced iron in building not only machinery but also bridges, ships, and factories.

INNOVATIONS IN TRANSPORTATION AND COMMUNICATION

Barges and boats were widely used for carrying coal, iron ore, other raw materials, and manufactured goods. These vessels also carried passengers. Adding steam power made water transport faster and even more popular. In 1807, American inventor Robert Fulton built the first successful steamboat, and soon steam-powered boats and ships were traveling waterways throughout the world.

Railroads spread as a result of the development of steam locomotives. The first steam locomotive was built in the early 1800s, but building locomotives and rail systems was so expensive that railroads were not widely used in Britain until the 1830s. Investors saw railroads as a profit-making venture and poured vast amounts of capital into building rail systems throughout the nation.

New methods of road building were also an important development. Until the beginning of the nineteenth century, British roads were poor. They were badly rutted and became practically impassable in wet weather. Around the turn of the century, however, engineers Thomas Telford and John McAdam devised methods of building uniform, smooth, and durable roadbeds on which heavy goods could be carried in carts and wagons without destroying the roads.

The Industrial Revolution also brought major changes in communication. An understanding of how electricity worked began to develop in the late 1700s. In 1837, Samuel Morse, an American, patented the first telegraph. The new technology spread rapidly after the 1840s. In 1866, the first cable was laid between Great Britain and the United States, and eventually underwater telegraph cables connected all major nations.

CHANGES IN AGRICULTURE

In the early 1700s, farmers developed ways to improve crop yields. The invention of the seed drill by Jethro Tull in 1701 was one of the earliest steps in making agriculture more productive. This device placed seeds in the soil in rows at even intervals, thereby using far less seed and leaving fewer bare spots than the old method of scattering by hand.

New crop management techniques soon followed. Rotation of crops from season to season—alternating crops that took nutrients from the soil with crops that restored essential elements—maintained soil fertility even with continuous cultivation. The traditional method of letting the land rest for a season between crops was much less productive than rotation. Adding fertilizers to the soil also increased crop productivity.

Livestock improved in the 1700s as well. More available feed and new methods of selecting animals for breeding produced heavier

This 1799 engraving shows plans for cast-iron bridges. The stronger iron produced by new smelting methods enabled the spanning of greater distances than had been possible with other materials.

sheep and beef cattle and larger, stronger work horses. In addition, enclosure made more grazing land available for livestock.

Taking advantage of new technology and reinvestment of capital, farmers ran large farms like other businesses. With the invention of machinery to help with planting and harvesting, agriculture—like manufacturing—began to follow the same path toward increased production and greater profits.

SECTION REVIEW

1. Define *industrialization* and *enclosure movement*.

2. Give two reasons why the Industrial Revolution began in Britain.

3. Explain how the factory system changed the lives of many people in Britain.

4. Describe three uses for the steam engine.

Evaluation. Which was the more important factor in industrialization—the enclosure movement or the steam engine? Explain.

21-2
SPREAD OF INDUSTRIALIZATION

READ TO FIND OUT

—what the term **mass production** means.
—why industrialization in France developed slowly.
—how Samuel Slater helped establish the American textile industry.
—what factors helped the United States to become an industrialized nation.

Until 1850, the Industrial Revolution spread very slowly outside Britain, partly because of political and economic instability in other European nations and partly because of Britain's protective policies toward its new industries. Britain jealously guarded the technology of these new industries by enacting laws designed to protect its domestic interests. Until 1824, for example, skilled workers were not permitted to leave the country. The export of industrial machinery was prohibited until 1843. Despite the laws, people did leave the nation and spread technological information to other European and North American countries.

GROWTH OF EUROPEAN INDUSTRY

The Industrial Revolution moved slowly from Britain to the European continent until about the middle of the nineteenth century. Well into the 1800s, most European nations still suffered political and economic instability resulting from the French Revolution and the Napoleonic era. After mid-century, however, the pace of industrial growth quickened as Belgium, France, and the German states joined the ranks of industrialized nations.

The Industrial Revolution spread quickly in Belgium, aided by the development of an efficient railroad system. The major factors in Belgium's industrialization were large coal deposits, heavy financial assistance from the government, a large skilled labor force, and many

ambitious entrepreneurs who were willing to undertake the risk of building new factories. By 1870, most Belgians earned their living from industry or trade.

Industrialization in France first began in the mid-1700s. Like Britain, France at that time had a thriving colonial trade and many successful manufacturing businesses. The economy suffered, however, as a result of the French Revolution and the conquests of Napoleon, and industrialization almost came to an end. By 1815, the nation's foreign trade had diminished, its supply of capital had shrunk, and its transportation system was in chaos.

PRODUCTION OF CAST IRON IN FOUR INDUSTRIAL COUNTRIES   1800–1900

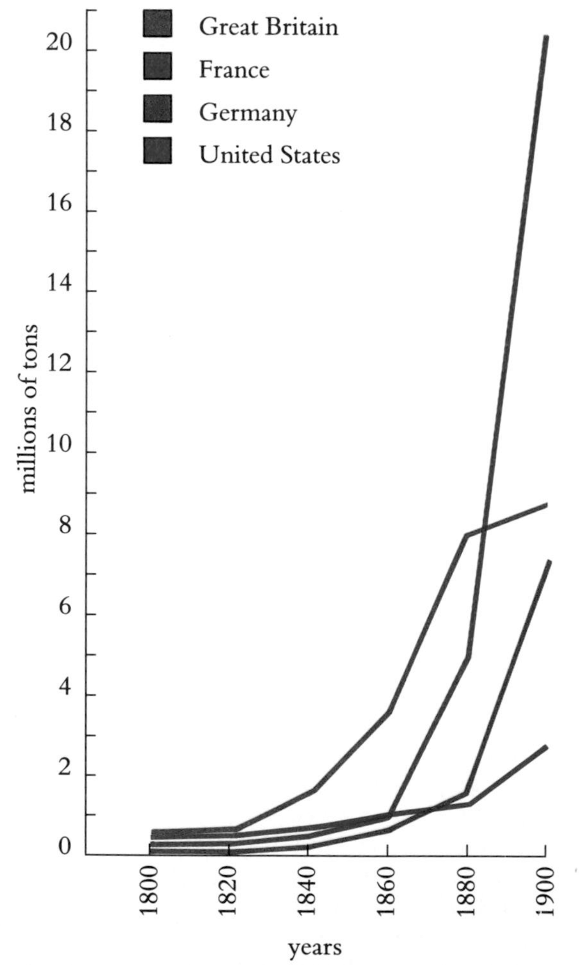

■ Great Britain
■ France
■ Germany
■ United States

millions of tons (y-axis: 0, 2, 4, 6, 8, 10, 12, 14, 16, 18, 20)

years (x-axis: 1800, 1820, 1840, 1860, 1880, 1900)

Source: Michel Beaud, *A History of Capitalism, 1500–1980.*

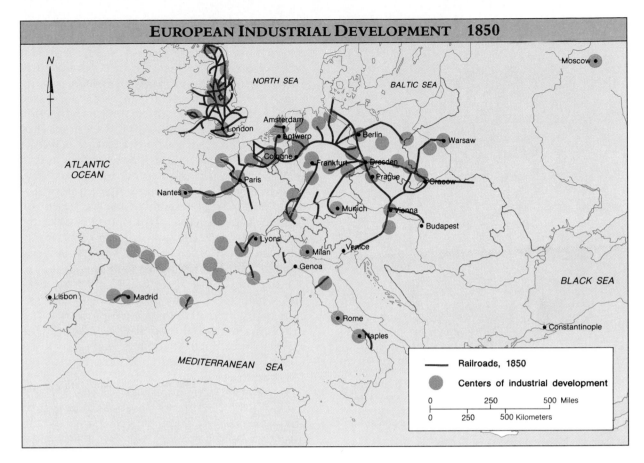

EUROPEAN INDUSTRIAL DEVELOPMENT 1850

Railroads, 1850

Centers of industrial development

0   250   500 Miles

0   250   500 Kilometers

In 1815, the Congress of Vienna—in which Europe's four major powers met to restore as much of the continent's absolutist system and territories as possible—gave much of France's best coal-mining region to Belgium. As a result, France lacked adequate coal for ironmaking and other heavy industries.

After a successful revolution in 1830 restored a republican form of government, France slowly began modernizing its industries. Establishing an effective transportation system was a top priority. Still, most French people earned their living through agriculture. Most entrepreneurs concentrated on commerce and small-scale manufacturing. The nation's history of political unrest had left investors wary of risking large sums of money.

A lack of national unity hampered the industrialization of the German states in the 1800s, since the states often refused to cooperate. Because of the wars with Napoleon's armies, treasuries were low and little capital was available for investment. Unification of the states in 1871 helped speed up progress. Germany had

ample coal and iron deposits, and with the help of money from foreign investors, these raw materials became the source of a thriving iron and steel industry. An extensive railroad system also aided industrial development. In time, Germany became a leading industrial power.

INDUSTRIALIZATION IN THE UNITED STATES

British-born Samuel Slater brought the new textile technology to the United States. While supervisor of a British textile mill, he memorized the workings of the spinning machines that were revolutionizing the textile industry. Disregarding Britain's law prohibiting skilled workers from leaving the country, the United States offered money to anyone bringing in information about the new technology.

Taking advantage of this offer, Slater disguised himself, slipped out of England, and landed in New York in 1789. The next year he formed a partnership with an American manufacturer in Providence, Rhode Island. Slater

This Jacquard loom, invented in 1801, used punched cards to automatically guide the threads in intricate weaving patterns. Flower designs or even pictures can be woven on this loom.

A new method of production. An invention by Eli Whitney, who also devised the cotton gin, aided manufacturers of many different types of products. What Whitney developed in 1800 was a method of *mass production*—making many copies of one item using standard parts. All the parts that performed the same function were exactly alike in all copies; therefore, they were interchangeable. Another feature of Whitney's method was the use of an assembly line, in which a series of workers added the standard parts in sequence to make a completed item. Today's automobile assembly line is based on Whitney's ideas. Gun manufacturers were the first to use the technique. By the early 1800s, other industries, such as textiles and shoes, had adapted it to their needs.

After the 1830s, coal mining and iron making, which were centered in Pennsylvania, increased to meet the growing demands of an expanding industrial economy. Gradually, with the help of federal loans and land grants, the United States developed an extensive system of canals and railroads.

Agriculture also improved. Cyrus McCormick's invention of the mechanical reaper in 1831 speeded the harvesting of grain, and the invention of the steel plow by John Deere in 1837 enabled farmers to cultivate soil deeper—for a bigger root system—and faster.

After the Civil War, the agricultural South devoted most of its resources to rebuilding. Industrial expansion in the North increased dramatically, however. Businesses became not only

reproduced from memory the blueprints for British spinning machines and installed the first textile machinery in the United States in 1790. A few years later, he established several textile mills of his own. By the 1820s, the New England states had a flourishing textile industry.

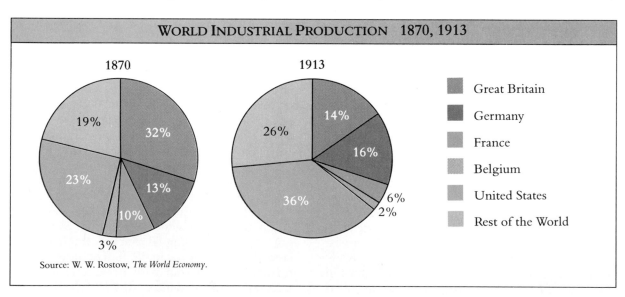

WORLD INDUSTRIAL PRODUCTION 1870, 1913

1870

1913

19%
32%
23%
13%
10%
3%

26%
14%
16%
36%
6%
2%

Great Britain
Germany
France
Belgium
United States
Rest of the World

Source: W. W. Rostow, *The World Economy.*

ANALYZING GRAPHS

INTRODUCING THE SKILL

History is the story of specific events, such as the invention of the steam engine, and broad developments, such as industrialization and urbanization. Historians rely on primary sources to reveal information about the specific events of history. However, the story of broad developments is often told best by statistics.

Statistics are collections of numerical data or information. For instance, statistics on the Industrial Revolution might include the number of factories in each industrialized country. Historians can use statistics for a number of purposes, such as measuring broad trends, making comparisons between groups, and showing patterns of change. In order to be easily understood, statistics are usually displayed in an organized manner. Frequently this display is in the form of a graph.

EXPLAINING THE SKILL

Graphs generally use lines, bars, or circles to display numerical information. A line graph is particularly useful for showing changes over a period of time. In a bar graph, horizontal or vertical bars make it easy to compare different amounts. A circle graph effectively displays percentages, showing them as "pie sections," or parts of a circle. When analyzing any type of graph, try following these steps:

A. *Read the title.* The title will give you a general idea of what the graph shows.

B. *Read all labels and legends.* Labels and legends will specify what the lines, bars, pie sections, colors, and numbers on a graph represent.

C. *Analyze the graph.* Scan all the lines, bars, pie sections, and numbers. Then look for interesting similarities, differences, increases, decreases, and sudden shifts.

D. *Make a general statement about what the graph shows.* Briefly state what general trends or patterns are shown in the graph. This will help you remember what the statistics revealed.

APPLYING THE SKILL

Use the circle graphs on the facing page to answer the following questions.

1. What is the general subject of these circle graphs?

2. What two years are compared in the graphs?

3. What do the numbers on the circle graphs represent?

4. What do the colors represent?

5. Which nation led the world in industrial production in 1870? In 1913?

6. Which nation had the greatest increase in its share of world production between 1870 and 1913?

7. Which nation saw the greatest drop?

8. Which nation's percentage of industrial production remained almost the same from 1870 to 1913?

9. Briefly state what general trend or pattern these graphs show.

INTERPRETING THE INFORMATION

Read each statement and tell whether it is **(a)** supported by the graphs, or **(b)** not supported by the graphs.

10. By 1913 the United States had become the world's leading industrial producer.

11. Great Britain produced fewer goods in 1913 than it did in 1870.

12. Germany's rise to second place was due to the unification of the German states.

13. The "Rest of the World" was increasing its industrial production during this period.

14. A nation's share of world industrial production is likely to change over time.

REVIEWING THE SKILL

15. What are statistics?

16. What four steps should be followed when reading graphs?

more numerous but larger, taking advantage of machines to make other machines and implementing Whitney's mass production techniques as never before.

An industrial giant. Once the Industrial Revolution reached the United States, the new nation took full advantage of its own resources and talents to become the world's leading industrial power by the beginning of the 1900s. Major factors in this success were the nation's abundant natural resources, ample capital for investment, a large labor pool, rapid advances in transportation and communication, a supportive government, and a wealth of creative and inventive people. The factory system, developed in Britain, grew and became more efficient in the United States.

As the Industrial Revolution spread, new technology developed rapidly. The internal combustion engine, developed in the late 1800s, was smaller, simpler and considerably more efficient than the steam engine. After the discovery of petroleum in Pennsylvania in the 1850s, the gasoline-powered internal combustion engine replaced the steam engine in early automobiles. This new engine also powered the first airplane in 1903.

Electricity, which came into use as a source of energy before 1850, made possible the invention of the telegraph, telephone, phonograph, incandescent light, and radio before the end of the century. The invention of the Linotype machine in 1884 speeded up printing by eliminating typesetting by hand. Books, magazines, and newspapers became cheaper and more numerous.

SECTION REVIEW

1. Define *mass production*.

2. Why did industrialization in France develop more slowly than in other European nations?

3. Explain Samuel Slater's role in the American textile industry.

4. What major factors contributed to the industrialization of the United States in the late 1700s and 1800s?

Analysis. Why was the British government anxious to keep industrial secrets away from other nations? Why was Britain not able to do so?

21-3
ECONOMIC AND SOCIAL CHANGES

READ TO FIND OUT

—what the terms *corporation*, *free enterprise*, *division of labor*, *unions*, and *strike* mean.
—how the growth of corporations led to regulation of American business.
—how industrialization changed cities.
—how reforms for workers came about.

Industrialization resulted in increased production, but not everyone benefited equally. Wealth gained from industry remained with relatively few owners and investors. As the middle class became more prosperous, the working class grew larger and poorer.

Industrialization required large amounts of money. People who provided the capital profited from their investments and reinvested those funds. This new kind of industrial capitalism stimulated business growth.

CHANGES IN BUSINESS

The Industrial Revolution broadened the concept of capitalism. Earlier, capitalism mainly involved individuals, such as the entrepreneurs in the domestic system. The growth of commerce produced so much wealth, however, that individuals sought larger enterprises for investment. Banks and individuals other than the business owner often provided the capital. The owner then repaid the investors out of the profits. Thus, a new class of capitalist—one who provides money but does not help operate the business—became increasingly important.

Also, manufacturing relied on the large-scale use of wage labor. Under the feudal system, people produced crops and goods to exchange for rent and things they needed. The domestic system involved work for wages, but on a small scale. With industrialization, however, large numbers of people were now being paid money for their labor.

A new form of business. The early part of the Industrial Revolution was characterized by many small businesses. As profits increased, however, so did the size of businesses. Industrialists needed large amounts of capital to expand existing factories and build new ones in other locations. With this expansion came an increase in the use of the **corporation**—a body formed and authorized by law to act as a single "person" whether consisting of one or many members—to provide capital and a pool of management talent. The individual investors, known as shareholders or stockholders, are not responsible for debts of the corporation, but they are entitled to share in the profits.

Maintaining a competitive market. An idea that is essential to capitalism is *free enterprise*, the freedom to do business in a competitive market with little regulation or interference by government. Businesses engaging in free enterprise are thus free to make as much profit as they can—*if* they can. In some cases, however, governments provided loans and other assistance—such as land for railroads—in order to encourage industrial expansion.

As industries grew, businesses began trying to eliminate competition and thereby ensure high profits. Through this practice, which is contradictory to the notion of free enterprise, a business tried to establish a monopoly—one company controlling the major means of production for an entire industry. The monopoly could then manipulate prices by regulating the supply of goods on the market.

Toward the end of the century, small business owners and consumers, particularly in the United States, complained so strongly about monopolistic practices that government regulation was inevitable. The Sherman Antitrust Act of 1890 was one example of prohibiting business practices that interfered with free trade.

CHANGES IN SOCIETY

Industrialization and the growth of capitalism created a small group of very wealthy business owners and financiers, an expanding middle class, and a mass of workers. Societies changed from rural to urban as people moved from the countryside to the rapidly growing cities. Also, many Europeans moved to distant countries in an effort to better their lives.

The Industrial Revolution changed the family as well. In preindustrial society, families were important cooperative units in which members worked together throughout the day. In the industrial age, the home and the workplace became separate, and family members spent most of their time apart. In middle-class families, the husband went to work while the wife remained at home to raise the children and care for the house.

In working-class families, often both husband and wife, and usually the children as well, had to work. Although most working-class wives were not employed in factories, many worked at home, sewing and doing other jobs to earn income.

The rise of the middle class. With industrialization, the middle class in Great Britain became larger and more influential as the number of factory owners, financiers, and capitalist farmers grew. The upper classes still had the land and titles, but the industrial middle class increasingly had the money. The landed aristocracy, which largely controlled Parliament, firmly resisted any attempts by the middle class to gain power.

In time, however, wealth also brought political influence. The new capitalists worked hard to eliminate government interference in business and to ensure a climate favorable for continued industrial expansion.

Just as the new industrialists had developed a new style of business, they also developed a new lifestyle. As their wealth grew, some imitated the aristocracy by buying country estates and taking up such sports as fox hunting and horse racing. Others began to develop a distinctive outlook and set of values. Many of these owners of factories, stores, and other property were relatively well educated. They considered hard work the key to a good life and to social success. They criticized poor people for not working hard enough and were reluctant to help the poor on the grounds that it encouraged bad habits among the needy.

At the time of the Industrial Revolution, the middle class valued leisure only when it promoted work skills and family life, and criticized aristocrats for idleness and their gambling. Also, many people in the middle class paid considerable attention to religion, believing it to be a good way to instill morality.

Annette's Soup, by Édouard Vuillard, captures a middle-class domestic scene. Unlike working-class children, most children of the middle class could look forward to getting an education.

The plight of the working class. The gains of the middle class were not shared by the working class. Most workers lived in desperate poverty, just barely surviving on the wages they earned. In cities, they paid high prices for both food and housing.

All family members who were able to work had to do so, even young children. Often 75 percent of the workers in early textile mills were single women and young children, since operating most machines did not require a great deal of physical strength. Conditions in underground mines were unhealthy and considerably more hazardous than elsewhere, but women and children worked there as well.

Life was difficult for the working class. These people had little or no education and little hope of bettering their lives. Because even young children had to work long hours, they generally did not attend school. Their future would be the same as their present—hard work and little time for leisure or personal pursuits. Several generations passed before conditions improved noticeably for most workers.

The growth of cities. With industrialization, new manufacturing and commercial cities sprang up near sources of raw materials, water power, coal, and transportation. Cities also grew rapidly in size. For example, Manchester, the center of Great Britain's cotton textile industry, had 25,000 people in 1772. By 1855, its population had soared to 455,000. Such rapid growth led to severe problems, such as high rates of crime and alcoholism.

Construction of new housing could not keep up with the influx of workers from rural areas. Entire families were often forced to live in a single room. Many rooms lacked windows, some were below ground and thus continually damp, and none had running water.

Sewage flowed in open trenches in the streets and emptied into rivers. Additional pollution came from the factories, which dumped their wastes into waterways and filled the air with thick black smoke.

Under such conditions, urban death rates rose dramatically. In some slums, 50 percent of all infants died before the age of two. Such diseases as cholera, typhoid, and tuberculosis reached epidemic proportions in Britain in the 1830s. Gradually, however, city governments—often with the aid of the national government—began to improve urban living conditions.

Emigration. At the same time that European cities were growing, many Europeans were emigrating, or moving to other countries or regions. Between 1846 and 1932, almost 60 million people emigrated from Europe. This mass movement of people, the largest in history, is often called the Atlantic Migration because the majority of the emigrants traveled to the Americas, particularly to the United States.

Europeans emigrated for a variety of reasons. Some were victims of crop failures, while others fled political turmoil or war within their countries. Still others left home to escape religious persecution. A large number of emigrants were urban workers seeking better jobs and improved living conditions.

Perhaps the most significant causes of the increased emigration were the conditions that made emigration easier. First, people were no longer restrained by laws that had required them to stay within their own communities or countries. Second, railroads and steamships made travel easier and cheaper. Third, throughout the 1800s European workers were generally welcomed by the United States and other countries in need of larger labor forces.

INDUSTRIAL WORKING CONDITIONS

Working in a factory was completely different from working at home and required new work habits. Factory work depended on a **division of labor**—the organization of the manufacturing process into separate tasks. Each worker or group of workers had a task and did only that job throughout the workday. Workers were closely supervised, with both schedules and production quotas strictly enforced. Factory owners spent a great deal of money on equipment, wages, and materials and wanted a maximum return on that investment.

Because the machines operated at a constant fast pace, the workers had to do the same. The work was monotonous and tiring, but workers had little relief during the day. During the early years of industrialization, factory workers labored 12 to 19 hours a day, 6 days a week. They had no paid vacation or sick leave.

With few safety regulations or safety devices on machinery, accidents happened often. Workers received no compensation for injuries. The factories also lacked heat, sanitary facilities, and adequate ventilation—especially important in textile mills where wool and cotton fibers clouded the air. Many workers suffered from lung diseases.

Most early factory owners kept workers' wages as low as possible. The entrepreneurs' goal was to produce the greatest amount of goods at the least cost. Their way to achieve that goal was to have workers labor as long as possible each day to meet production quotas. Workers who could not keep up the pace found themselves unemployed. A plentiful supply of labor meant that owners could easily replace a worker who was slow or sick.

This ample labor supply also kept wages low. Some people were willing to work for *any* wage, no matter how low. They dared not complain about wages or working conditions for fear of losing even the worst jobs. Poor planning of factory production often led to layoffs, but workers suffered through these times because they had no choice. Job security was nonexistent.

Many owners took full advantage of the labor situation and mercilessly exploited their workers. Others treated workers fairly, but they were the exception. In time, however, owners began to realize that workers were more productive when they were healthier and more content. Workers produced more when they were well rested and had ample food—the result of shorter workdays and increased wages. Most owners did not rush to this conclusion on their own, however. They were prodded by worker protests and the new labor movement.

German artist Käthe Kollwitz used her work to express her social concerns. This scene of a working-class mother and ill child includes a loom, which the family relied on for income.

THE LABOR MOVEMENT

As the Industrial Revolution spread and the number of workers increased, employees began to protest their low wages and poor working conditions by forming associations known as *unions*. Their main weapon was the *strike*, in which workers would refuse to work unless employers met certain demands. In 1800, after outbreaks of violence during protests, as well as sabotage in factories during strikes, Britain declared union activity illegal. Workers thereupon formed new societies, which they did not refer to as unions, and continued trying to improve their lot. They had found strength in unity.

Gradually, workers began to make progress. In 1824, Parliament repealed the law against unions. In 1845, workers formed a national labor organization. Beginning in 1859, the government permitted peaceful picketing. By 1871, Britain allowed workers to strike.

The labor movement progressed more slowly in other nations. Unions were not permitted in Belgium until 1866 and in France until 1884. German workers formed associations in the 1840s, but the government banned them from 1878 to 1890.

As early as the 1790s, skilled workers in the United States began organizing unions. Although a national trade union was formed in the 1830s, it did not survive for long. Because many state governments considered union members who went on strike to be criminal conspirators, union activity was curtailed. However, after the Massachusetts Supreme Court in 1842 affirmed that unions were legal, the labor movement gained momentum, and by the end of the 1850s, a national trade organization had been formed. The union movement grew even stronger after 1865.

Gains by unions. In both western Europe and the United States, some labor unions succeeded in establishing the right to negotiate with employers about such issues as working conditions, wages, and length of the workday. This

---

ECHOES OF THE PAST

MARY PAUL: LETTERS FROM THE FACTORY

Lowell Dec. 21st 1845

Dear Father,

I received your letter on Thursday the 14th with much pleasure. I am well, which is one comfort. My life and health are spared while others are cut off. Last Thursday a man was killed by the [railroad] cars [that transport cotton to the textile mill]. Another was nearly killed by falling down and having a bale of cotton fall on him. Last Tuesday we were paid. In all I had six dollars and sixty cents and paid $4.68 for board [room and meals]. . . .

Lowell April 12th 1846

Dear Father,

. . . I have a very good boarding place and enough to eat. The girls that I room with are all from Vermont. We have to go to bed about 10 o'clock. At half past 4 in the morning the bell rings for us to get up and at five for us to go to the mill. At seven we are called out to breakfast. We are allowed half an hour between bells and the same at noon. We have dinner at half past 12 and supper at seven. . . .

Lowell Nov. 5th 1848

Dear Father,

. . . It is *very* hard [work] indeed and sometimes I think I shall not be able to endure it. I presume you have heard that the wages are to be reduced on the 20th of this month. The [textile] companies pretend they are losing immense sums every *day* but this seems perfectly absurd to me, for they are constantly making repairs. . . .

It is very difficult for anyone to get [hired by a] mill. All seem to be very full of help. I expect to be paid about two dollars a week but it will be dearly earned. . . .

Write soon. Yours affectionately,

Mary S. Paul

For questions on Echoes of the Past, see "Analyzing Primary Sources" on page 531.

process is called collective bargaining. Although strikes were common, especially in the late 1800s, they often did not result in positive gains for workers. Workers sometimes lost their jobs, and occasionally workers and law enforcers died as a result of violence.

In some European nations, unions of skilled workers grew strong enough to wield some political power. As a result of pressure from unions, European governments sometimes enacted legislation favoring workers, such as state regulation of working conditions.

INDUSTRIAL REFORM

Before unions were able to achieve substantial economic improvements, however, government action brought about some changes in working conditions. Beginning in Britain in the 1830s, committees of Parliament investigated working conditions in mines and factories. The critical reports by the committees, which were publicized by journalists, led to demands for reform. Parliament responded by passing a series of acts to protect children and women. In 1833, the Textile Factory Act put restrictions on child labor. It forbade the employment in cotton mills of children under 9 years of age. Those between the ages of 9 and 13 could work no more than 9 hours a day, and teenagers between 13 and 18 could work no more than 12 hours a day.

Child labor abuses were worse in other industrial nations. In the United States, federal and state governments made attempts at regulation but did not succeed completely until 1938, when the federal Fair Labor Standards Act established a minimum age of 14 for nonmanufacturing work and 18 for hazardous work.

SECTION REVIEW

1. Define *corporation*, *free enterprise*, *division of labor*, *unions*, and *strike*.

2. Explain how the growth of corporations led to regulation of American business by government?

3. What effect did industrialization have on cities and city life?

4. Describe two ways in which changes in working conditions came about.

Analysis. How did capitalism change during the Industrial Revolution?

Data Search. Refer to the appropriate chart on page 832 to identify the following information about urbanization between 1800 and 1890: **(a)** the increase in urbanization in Great Britain, Prussia, and the United States; and **(b)** the difference between the urban populations of Great Britain and Russia in 1890.

HISTORY IN FOCUS

The Industrial Revolution that began in Britain in the 1700s spread to other European nations and to the United States in the 1800s. It ended the traditional rural way of life for many people and replaced it with a new urban existence. The vast amounts of money required by industry led to a major change in the way business was conducted. Large-scale capitalism dominated the economy, repaying risks with profits.

Power-driven machines replaced human labor in many kinds of jobs. The factory system further mechanized the process. Workers had less control over their jobs and their lives than ever before. They were forced to work for mere subsistence wages in boring jobs for long hours under poor conditions.

Workers flocked to cities and to new factory towns in search of work. High prices, inadequate housing, and unhealthy urban environments took their toll on the well-being of workers and their families. Most lived in desperate poverty with little hope of changing their situation.

The middle class had a completely different experience, for the most part. The owners of industry made up a significant portion of this group. Their desire to improve their lives—and the belief that it was their right to do so—led to wealth from the growing industries and to a successful move toward political power. Industrialists seemingly had few misgivings about exploiting workers for gain.

In time, as workers grew not only in number but in strength, the union movement and government reforms led to improvements in working conditions and to a better life in general for the working class.

Technological changes abounded, not only in industry but also in transportation and communication. As it spread throughout the world, the Industrial Revolution brought sweeping—and permanent—changes in the ways people worked and lived.

SUMMARY

- The Industrial Revolution began in Great Britain in the 1700s. The textile industry was the first to benefit from labor-saving machinery. Britain began to shift from the domestic system of production at home to a factory system marked by division of labor.

- The development of the steam engine was critical to industrialization, as were new processes for making iron and steel. New transportation and communication systems were developed, and agriculture also made great advances.

- Britain tried to protect its industrial secrets, but by the mid-1800s other countries were beginning to industrialize. The greatest strides were made in the United States, which by the early 1900s was the world's leading industrial nation.

- Industrialization brought many changes to business and society. Capitalism evolved as companies grew and corporations were founded. Cities sprang up and urban life became more difficult. The middle class gained increasing power.

- Life for workers worsened under industrialization, with long hours, low pay, no job security, and hazardous conditions. Eventually workers formed unions to fight for improvements. Governments also began to promote industrial reforms, but changes came slowly.

VOCABULARY REVIEW

The vocabulary terms in each pair listed below are related to each other. For each pair, explain what the two terms have in common. Also explain how they are different.

Example: *Free enterprise* and *entrepreneur* are both terms that relate to business. An entrepreneur is a person who takes business risks, however, while free enterprise is the concept of doing business with limited government interference.

1. industrialization, enclosure movement
2. division of labor, mass production
3. union, strike

CHAPTER REVIEW

1. (a) How did agriculture change in Great Britain during the 1700s? **(b)** Why did some people give up farming? **(c)** How did these changes contribute to the Industrial Revolution?

2. (a) Why was the domestic system inadequate for a growing economy? **(b)** Compare the factory system with the domestic system. **(c)** Who made up the new work force?

3. (a) Why was the steam engine so important to the Industrial Revolution? **(b)** How did this invention affect transport? **(c)** What replaced the steam engine? Explain why.

4. (a) Why were iron and steel critical to industrialization? **(b)** How did steel replace iron as a building material? Explain why.

5. Describe the following inventions or processes. Then explain their importance: **(a)** cotton gin, **(b)** Bessemer process, **(c)** seed drill, **(d)** crop rotation.

6. (a) How did Great Britain try to preserve its industrial advantage? **(b)** Why was Belgium among the first European countries to industrialize? **(c)** Compare industrialization in France and the German states.

7. (a) How did the textile industry begin in the United States? **(b)** What role did Eli Whitney play in industrialization? **(c)** Name two important inventors in American agriculture and explain why they were important.

8. (a) How did the use of the corporation spur industrial growth? **(b)** Why was the notion of free enterprise an important aspect of capitalism? **(c)** How did monopolies contradict free enterprise? What happened as a result?

9. (a) List three ways in which industrialization and the growth of capitalism affected society. **(b)** How did industrialization affect the middle class? The working class? **(c)** Give three reasons why Europeans emigrated during the Industrial Revolution.

10. (a) Why were working conditions and wages so poor for early factory workers? **(b)** How did working conditions slowly begin to improve? **(c)** What kind of opposition did unions encounter? Explain why.

THINKING CRITICALLY: ACTIVITIES

1. Imagine that it is 1769 and you are James Watt trying to patent a new steam engine design. Write a letter to the British authorities explaining why they should patent your new engine and how it will change industry.

2. Imagine that you are living during the early years of the Industrial Revolution. Choose a partner for a discussion of workers' rights. One of you should take the role of a union leader and the other take the role of a business owner. State your views on the following questions: Should unions be allowed to strike? What is the proper role for government in labor conflicts?

APPLYING SOCIAL STUDIES SKILLS

Analyzing graphs. Use the graph on page 476 to answer the following questions.

1. What is the general subject of this graph?

2. What period of time is covered by the graph?

3. What do the lines on the graph show?
   (a) tons of iron ore
   (b) tons of cast iron
   (c) tons of steel
   (d) tons of iron rails

4. What do the colors represent?
   (a) different time periods
   (b) types of iron
   (c) different countries

5. Which nation led world production in 1900?
   (a) Great Britain
   (b) France
   (c) Germany
   (d) the United States

6. Which two nations more than doubled their production between 1880 and 1900?
   (a) Great Britain
   (b) France
   (c) Germany
   (d) the United States

7. In 1900, production in the United States was
   (a) at least twice that of any other nation.
   (b) about as much as in Great Britain.
   (c) less than 20 million tons.
   (d) less than that in Great Britain.

APPLYING THINKING SKILLS

Identifying unstated assumptions. The account below is from a Scottish professor's discussion of child labor in British textile mills. It was first published in 1861. Examine it to identify any unstated assumptions.

I have visited many factories, and I never saw a single instance of physical punishment inflicted on a child. Nor, indeed, did I ever see children in ill-humor. They seemed to be always cheerful and alert, taking pleasure in the light play of their muscles—enjoying the mobility natural to their age. The scene of industry was always exhilarating.

It was delightful to observe the nimbleness with which the children pieced together the broken ends of the yarn as the spinning machine began to recede from the fixed roller, and to see them at leisure, after a few seconds' exercise of their tiny fingers, to amuse themselves in any manner they chose.

The work of these lively elves seemed to resemble a sport, in which habit gave them a pleasing dexterity. So, conscious of their skill, they were delighted to show it off to any stranger. As to exhaustion by the day's work, they evinced no trace of it on emerging from the mill in the evening; for they immediately began to skip about any neighborhood playground, and to commence their little amusements with the same alacrity as boys issuing from a school.

It is moreover my firm conviction that if children are not ill-used by bad parents or guardians, but receive in food and raiment the full benefit of what they earn, they would thrive better when employed in our modern factories than if left at home in apartments too often ill-aired, damp, and cold.

Abridged from *The Philosophy of Manufactures; or, an Exposition of the Scientific, Moral, and Commercial Economy of the Factory System in Great Britain*, by Andrew Ure. London: 1861.

1. Explain what an unstated assumption is.

2. Why is it important to be able to identify unstated assumptions?

3. What is one procedure for identifying unstated assumptions in a written account?

4. What is one unstated assumption in the above account? Explain your answer.

CHAPTER TWENTY-TWO

NEW IDEAS AND CREATIVE EXPRESSION

1790–1914

22-1 NEW IDEAS ABOUT SOCIETY
22-2 EXPLORATIONS IN THE CREATIVE ARTS
22-3 NEW PATHS IN SCIENCE

The City from Greenwich Village. John Sloan, United States, 1922.

The spread of industrialization and the growing influence of the middle class created economic problems and social tensions. Some political and economic theorists sought to justify the rise of the industrial middle class at the expense of the working class. Others protested what they saw as gross inequities of the system.

As people's lives changed in the new industrial age, so did their interests in art, music, and literature. Writers, thinkers, and artists began expressing their own responses to the new age. Their works reflected the growing spirit of nationalism and interest in the individual. A new creative movement, known as Romanticism, turned away from classical art forms and focused on personal expressions of emotion. Its proponents developed new styles that broke from tradition and forged a path into the Modern Age.

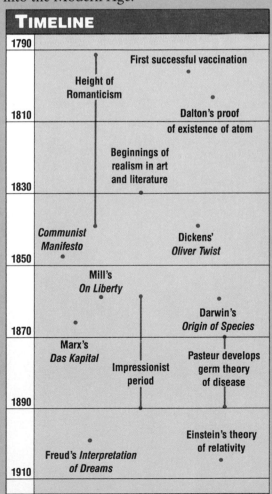

TIMELINE

1790	
	First successful vaccination
	Height of Romanticism
1810	Dalton's proof of existence of atom
	Beginnings of realism in art and literature
1830	
	Communist Manifesto · Dickens' Oliver Twist
1850	
	Mill's On Liberty
	Darwin's Origin of Species
1870	
	Marx's Das Kapital · Impressionist period · Pasteur develops germ theory of disease
1890	
	Einstein's theory of relativity
	Freud's Interpretation of Dreams
1910	

22–1
NEW IDEAS ABOUT SOCIETY

READ TO FIND OUT

—what the terms *laissez faire*, *socialism*, *proletariat*, *Marxism*, and *communism* mean.
—why some people believed that government should have no role in business.
—what the law of supply and demand is.
—what economic and social ideas Karl Marx developed.

The political and industrial revolutions of the 1700s brought profound social and economic changes to the Western world. Political and economic thinkers formed new theories to explain these changes. In Europe, the aristocracy lost power as the capitalist middle class grew larger, richer, and more influential. Members of the working class were not so fortunate. They were crowded into new industrial towns, worked long hours, and earned barely enough to survive.

LIBERALISM

Liberalism, a major philosophy of the industrial age, had its roots in the Enlightenment. Widely favored by the growing middle class, liberalism spread from Britain and France to the United States in the 1800s. Liberals believed in individual rights, especially the right to determine one's own future, and in representative government. However, most liberals preferred restricting the vote to property owners. They also felt that the middle class deserved a greater voice in government.

The most powerful liberals of the time were business owners, capitalists who believed that business should not be regulated—not by the government or by anyone else. This policy that business should be free from outside interference is known as *laissez faire* (LEHS-ay FEHR), a French term meaning "let people do as they choose."

MOVEMENT: TRANSPORT NETWORKS

"Hell is a city much like London—a populous and a smoky city," wrote British poet Percy Bysshe Shelley in 1819. By 1850 Shelley would have had even more cause for complaint. While Britain's population doubled between 1800 and 1850, London's population tripled. By then London had more than 2.4 million people, making it the largest urban area in the world.

The key to this rapid growth was a vast *transport network* linking London to raw materials and markets throughout Great Britain and its worldwide empire. A transport network is a system of transportation, including all forms of land, water, and air transport, and their connections.

From its earliest days, London was a trading city. Romans founded London along the banks of the Thames River where their oceangoing ships could find shelter from Atlantic storms. The Roman historian Tacitus described London as "filled with traders and a celebrated center of commerce." In the Middle Ages, London was called "the mart of many nations."

As Britain's empire expanded in the 1600s and 1700s, sailing ships from around the world unloaded their treasures on London's docks. However, while London was well connected to the world by sea, transportation to other places within Britain was difficult. Cities and towns remained isolated from one another.

In the 1800s, the British constructed an improved transport network that firmly linked London to the rest of the country. Many of the nation's roads were paved for the first time. Between 1780 and 1820, the time needed to travel by stagecoach from Manchester to London fell from 5 days to just a day and a half. Furthermore, a large system of canals was built to move heavy goods such as coal and iron ore.

Far more important than roads and canals, however, were the railroads. Between 1830 and 1850, more than 5,000 miles (8,045 kilometers) of track were laid in Britain. Travel time from London to Edinburgh fell from 4 days by coach to 12 hours by train. The main railroad lines all ended in London. People, food, and goods from all over England flowed into London along the twin ribbons of iron.

Curiously, London never built a central railroad station where all these rail lines could meet. Instead, each railroad company pushed its rails into London as far as possible and built a station at the end of its line. To travel between stations, passengers and freight had to cross London by horse-drawn coach or wagon.

During rush hours, clattering carts and carriages crowded London's streets. English poet Alfred, Lord Tennyson described the resulting noise as "streaming London's central roar." Furnishing the energy to move these noisy vehicles were a million horses—an average of two horses for every five persons in the city. The horses, carts, and people moving through the streets created tangled traffic jams.

Ironically, the transport network built to solve one problem had created a new problem. While railroads moved people and goods to London faster and more efficiently, movement within London became more difficult. This situation developed in many other cities of the world as the Industrial Revolution spread.

1. Define *transport network*.

2. How was Britain's transport network improved between 1800 and 1850?

3. What problem did the network create?

LAISSEZ-FAIRE ECONOMICS

People who believed in laissez faire also believed in free enterprise, or the freedom to conduct business with a minimum of government interference. The belief in free enterprise grew out of the Enlightenment, whose philosophers and writers believed in individual freedom and a natural law of progress. They thought that human life would improve as the years went on and that each generation would be better off than the last. Progress, they proclaimed, was inevitable. To many, government interference in business meant a slowing of the "natural" progress of society.

These beliefs contributed to the spread of capitalism and industrialization in Europe and the United States. Many people in the growing industrial middle class came from humble beginnings. Sharp, shrewd, and hard-working, they considered both the aristocracy above them and the poor below them to be people without energy or ambition.

Adam Smith. One of the leading defenders of laissez faire was a Scot, Adam Smith. His book *Wealth of Nations*, published in 1776, outlined the basic principles of free enterprise. Smith believed that business operated according to two natural laws: the law of supply and demand and the law of competition.

If a product fell into short supply or if demand increased, said Smith, the price for that product would rise. Higher prices would bring the manufacturer a greater profit, and more profit would allow the business to expand. With increased production, the amount of goods on the market would increase. Because people would be less willing to pay higher prices for the more plentiful goods, the manufacturer would be forced to reduce prices.

As prices dropped, Smith wrote, competition would increase among manufacturers. To attract buyers, competing manufacturers cut prices even more. Lower prices would lead to smaller profits. Some businesses would earn so little that they would be forced to close. Only the most efficient businesses would survive. With fewer competitors, and therefore fewer goods being produced, prices would rise again and the cycle would begin anew.

Smith believed that self-interest—a person's interest in making money—ran the laissez-faire

Many middle-class people invested in stocks. *Portraits at a Stock Exchange*, painted by Edgar Degas in 1897, shows French businessmen eagerly checking the current value of their stocks.

economy. Self-interest led people to do work their society would pay for, but something had to regulate the self-interest. Smith said that competition, not government, would keep the business community in control.

Other economic theorists. Differing from the general liberal optimism and commonly held belief in progress, British economist Thomas Malthus linked the size of the population with levels of poverty. In 1798, he published "An Essay on the Principle of Population as It Affects the Future Improvement of Society." Population, wrote Malthus, always grows at a faster rate than the food supply. People multiply, he pointed out, but the food supply does not grow as rapidly. If population continued to increase at the same rate, people would have less and less to eat. Eventually, there would be a food shortage. The poor, who could not afford food, would be the ones to go hungry.

David Ricardo, an English economist, was a close friend of Malthus. In his book *Principles of Political Economy and Taxation*, published in 1817, Ricardo described how, as population grew, the labor force grew. As more workers competed for jobs, wages would fall. People would be willing to work for less money, since even a small income was better than none. Faced with poverty, workers would have smaller families, eventually reducing the size of the labor force. As the labor supply decreased, employers would have to pay higher wages to attract workers from a smaller labor pool. In time, however, the cycle would be repeated. Ricardo called the cycle the "iron law of wages."

PROPOSALS FOR REFORM

Because of the ideas of Malthus and Ricardo, people in Britain began to realize that life did not necessarily treat everyone fairly. Life was not constantly improving for everyone, as Enlightenment writers had thought. Some people began to seek ways to improve society.

British philosopher Jeremy Bentham held what he called utilitarian views. According to these views, what made an action right or wrong—what gave it utility, or usefulness—was how much it added to the happiness of the world. He believed in striving for "the greatest happiness for the greatest number." People were free to do as they pleased so long as their actions did not conflict with the interests of the majority. Middle-class capitalists, most of whom believed that industrialization brought happiness for the general population, interpreted utilitarianism as supporting the continued expansion of business.

Many people who held utilitarian views were moral reformers who wished to change society. Their proposals included relief for the poor, public health and education, and more humane prisons. Among Bentham's followers was young John Stuart Mill. Mill's book *Principles of Political Economy*, published in 1848, brought up to date the ideas of Smith, Malthus, and Ricardo, and then went on to state a new economic theory.

According to Mill, society could simply change any part of the economy that it did not like. The government could tax some people and redistribute that wealth to others if necessary. This idea pitted Mill against the laissez-faire economists, who wanted government to stay out of commerce.

Although Mill believed that people had the intelligence to control their own lives, he also thought that government had a duty to protect each citizen's rights. He favored shortening work hours and giving workers a more favorable share of the profits from their labor.

Mill's 1859 essay "On Liberty" argued that individual freedom was essential to a society. Without freedom of thought and speech, individuals could not develop and the society would not improve. "If all mankind minus one were of one opinion," he wrote, "and only one person were of the contrary opinion, mankind would be no more justified in silencing that one person, than he, if he had the power, would be justified in silencing mankind."

Few could disagree with what Mill favored, even the middle class. His outlook was optimistic yet realistic. He urged gradual, not radical, changes.

Some reformers rejected completely the theories of Adam Smith and others who favored free enterprise. They looked at Britain in the 1820s and saw its dirty, crowded cities. They saw its labor force working long hours under difficult conditions. They could not believe the world was right as it was. Many of these people thought it unfair that industrialists became increasingly wealthy while workers suffered.

SOCIALISM

Some people wanted more than simple reform. They wanted to change the entire structure of society. One philosophy that called for such change was *socialism*, a social theory according to which the means of production—factories, machines, and land—are controlled or owned by a government or by the whole society, rather than by individuals.

Utopian socialism. The early socialists were usually known as utopian socialists. They got this name from the imaginary island of Utopia described in a book written by the Englishman Sir Thomas More in 1516. Utopia had a perfect system of government, law, and social justice.

In the 1800s, some of the utopian socialists set out to establish small ideal communities, which they hoped would set an example for their nations' leaders. The utopian communities would serve as models for changing society as a whole.

The leading utopian socialist was a British manufacturer named Robert Owen. In 1800, he bought several cotton mills in New Lanark,

This photograph from about 1900 shows two young girls sewing clothing in a Pennsylvania garment factory. Strong reform movements in Europe and the United States eventually put an end to child labor and other oppressive labor practices.

Scotland, and started a radical new factory system. Owen raised wages, shortened working hours, and provided housing for the workers and their families. He also started schools and did not allow children under the age of ten to work. To everyone's astonishment, the mill earned high profits.

Most of the other early socialists were French. In addition to the civil and legal equality established through the French Revolution, the socialists wanted social and economic equality. One such person was Charles Fourier (FOO-ree-ay), who drew up a plan by which society would be organized into small, self-sufficient groups called phalanxes. Fourier's new society was more radical than Owen's community. People would do the work that best suited them, and the phalanx members would share profits.

Utopian socialists wanted to persuade members of the upper and middle classes that social change was in their own self-interest, but the reformers never addressed themselves directly to workers. One school of thought that did encourage workers to take action had its roots in the scientific socialism of Karl Marx.

Scientific socialism. Karl Marx, a German thinker and writer, called his philosophy scientific socialism because he believed that history, like the world of nature, operated according to scientific laws. Marx disagreed with utopian socialism because it was based on morality and depended on the kindness of the rich toward the poor. He believed that a violent revolution would be necessary to overthrow capitalism.

The son of a liberal German lawyer, young Karl Marx read the works of such Enlightenment thinkers as Diderot and Voltaire. Marx studied law and earned degrees in history and philosophy. Marx also became involved in the philosophical and political debates of his day.

According to Marx, economics was the major force shaping society and all history was a story of class struggle. He believed that society did not remain the same but instead developed and changed through time. Eventually, he predicted, the working class would overthrow the factory-owning bourgeoisie and capitalism would collapse. Because of his radical political views, Marx was unable to find a teaching job in Germany. However, he did find a job as editor of a small newspaper. Marx used the paper to denounce the terrible living conditions of peasants and workers in Germany. After five months, though, the government closed down the newspaper.

Marx then moved to Paris to edit a radical journal, which did not last much longer than his newspaper. Later expelled from Paris for his radical writing, Marx lived briefly in Belgium and Germany before moving to London in 1849. There he wrote *Das Kapital*, his famous attack on free enterprise, first published in German in 1867. Throughout the rest of his life, Marx earned some money as a journalist, but for the most part he and his family were supported by his wealthy friend Friedrich Engels.

In this 1905 photograph, women workers push a heavily loaded coal cart. Socialists argued that low wages and harsh working conditions would soon lead workers to revolt against capitalism.

Marx and Engels met in Paris in 1844, the start of 40 years of friendship and work. Engels, the son of a wealthy German manufacturer, worked hard at his father's business. At the same time, he saw the injustices in German society and soon no longer believed in an economic system based on private property.

When he met Marx, Engels was on his way to manage his father's textile business in Manchester, England. There he was so horrified by living conditions in the industrial slums that he wrote *The Condition of the Working Class in England in 1844.*

Marx and Engels together wrote the *Communist Manifesto,* published in 1848, which urged workers to revolt. They used the term *communist* to refer to an ideal society in which property would be owned in common and the necessities of life would be shared by community members according to their needs. "Let the ruling classes tremble at a communistic revolution," they wrote. "The proletarians [working class] have nothing to lose but their chains. They have a world to win."

Marx believed that throughout history two groups had always been in conflict. One group controlled all the wealth, political power, and factors of production. The other group did all the work. In Marx's time, these two groups were the bourgeoisie, the capitalist middle class; and the ***proletariat***, the working class. Marx sided with the proletariat. He argued that labor is the most important factor in production and that the real value of goods or services is the amount of labor used in producing them. A worker should be paid the full value of the labor that goes into a job.

Marx felt the collapse of capitalism was inevitable. The working class would grow larger as more small producers were forced out of business by competition. The number of capitalists would thus decline. Frequent crises, such as unemployment, would cause widespread suffering, which would in turn lead to "class consciousness" among workers. They would then come to realize they could benefit from the overthrow of the bourgeoisie.

Marx predicted that if the proletarian majority were to overthrow the bourgeoisie minority, the leaders of the revolution would set up a "dictatorship of the proletariat," or rule by the working class. Under Marx's form of socialism—which soon came to be called ***Marxism***—land and all the means of production would be owned by the workers. Eventually, the state would "wither away." Everyone would work and earn equally, and people would live in true freedom in the new communist state. Since there would be only one class, there would be no class struggle. In this classless society, cooperation would replace competition, and everyone's needs would be met equally. Marx and Engels referred to this final stage of socialism as ***communism***.

Marx's doctrine led historians to pay more attention to economic forces in history. Marx also made people aware that societies do not stand still but are always changing. Ironically, Marx underestimated the ability of capitalistic society to change for the better. Marx believed that more and more people would become poor under capitalism. He did not, however, anticipate the enormous improvements in wages and working conditions that workers would achieve in industrialized, capitalist countries. As early as 1850, wages began to rise in Europe. By 1870, working men in most European countries usually had the right to vote. In addition, workers were allowed to organize labor unions and political parties.

SECTION REVIEW

1. Define *laissez faire*, *socialism*, *proletariat*, *Marxism*, and *communism*.

2. Why did some people believe that government should have no role in business?

3. Explain the law of supply and demand.

4. List Marx's main criticisms of capitalism.

Analysis. Explain how the theories of utopian socialism and communism have influenced modern society.

Data Search. Economic problems led many people to emigrate from Europe. Refer to the appropriate charts on page 832 to identify: **(a)** two countries from which over 9 million people emigrated between 1846 and 1932, and **(b)** two American nations, besides the United States, to which over 5 million people immigrated between 1821 and 1932.

22-2
EXPLORATIONS IN THE CREATIVE ARTS

READ TO FIND OUT

—what the terms **Romanticism** and **impressionism** mean.
—how Romantic writers reacted against the Enlightenment.
—what the major influences on the work of Romantic composers were.
—how impressionism differed from realism.

Along with revolution in industry and politics came changes in the arts. In the 1700s, art, literature, and music had stressed form and order. Artists had looked to ancient Greece and Rome for a simple, elegant style and had often chosen subjects from the classics. Daily life had not been considered important enough to be a subject for art.

Toward the end of the 1700s, European artists and writers began to challenge such ideas. A growing feeling of nationalism, especially in France and Germany, prompted artists to look to their own nations' histories for subjects. They also began to paint and write about nature and everyday life.

ROMANTICISM

The term *Romantic* refers to medieval stories known as romances. These simple, colorful stories were rejected by Enlightenment thinkers, who had seen the Middle Ages as a backward time. Romantic writers and artists, in contrast, found in them a spirit missing in their own time. The growth of nationalistic feelings led to a new interest in folk tales and legends, many of which began to appear in popular art, music, and literature.

Romanticism emphasized simplicity and naturalness, creativity, and freedom of expression. It rejected reason in favor of emotion and focused on the individual, encouraging creative growth in new directions. Contrary to the rigidly structured formality favored in the eighteenth century, Romantic styles were personal and innovative. The break from tradition was at first criticized by the public, especially the middle class, but in time the new styles gained wide acceptance.

Romantic literature. The French Revolution, with its stress on the freedom of the individual, inspired many French writers. The Romantic movement in France was led by Victor Hugo, who wrote poetry and plays in the new, more creative style. Popular French Romantic novels include Hugo's *Hunchback of Notre Dame*, a story about medieval Paris, and *The Three Musketeers*, a well-known adventure story by Alexander Dumas (du-MAH).

Germany's growing nationalism was reflected in the novels, poems, and plays of Johann Wolfgang von Goethe (GER-tuh). Goethe's best-known works are *Faust*, a play based on a German folk legend, and *The Sorrows of Young Werther*, a moving novel about love. *William Tell*, a play by Friedrich von Schiller, pleaded for the cause of individual freedom as it told the story of a Swiss hero.

In Britain, Sir Walter Scott wrote a series of historical novels, beginning with *Waverly* in

In the Romantic period, musicians gained great popularity and often performed at private gatherings. James Tissot's *Hush! The Concert* depicts a recital in a British home in about 1875. The musicians and partygoers in the painting were all real people from London society.

1814. In these books he created a new kind of fiction, mixing adventure and fantasy with keen observation. Other writers looked away from the crowded industrial cities shrouded in coal smoke and turned to nature. The poetry of William Wordsworth recorded the natural beauty he discovered everywhere. Wordsworth made the first break with the classical forms of Enlightenment poetry in *Lyrical Ballads*, published in 1798. The poetry in that collection was written in many different forms, including blank verse, a poem that does not rhyme.

Wordsworth's poetry spoke of common people and used everyday language. His simple style and emphasis on nature and feelings led to strong criticism by readers more accustomed to formal Enlightenment poetry.

Samuel Taylor Coleridge, who collaborated with Wordsworth on *Lyrical Ballads*, wrote the haunting poem "The Rime of the Ancient Mariner," which was included in that volume. Coleridge's *Biographia Literaria*, published in 1817, was the public declaration of British Romanticism. Other well-known British poets of the Romantic period were Percy Bysshe Shelley, John Keats, and Lord Byron.

Romantic music and art. Romantic composers, like writers, experimented with new forms in the 1800s. Their music expressed their feelings, personal experiences, and their love of nature. Nationalism also influenced the move-

ment, and composers used their countries' folk themes and melodies as the basis for their works.

In Germany, the music of Ludwig van Beethoven bridged classicism and Romanticism. Beethoven wrote in classical forms, such as symphonies with several different movements, or parts. Unlike the classicists, however, Beethoven expressed his feelings in his music with a power that touched the emotions of his listeners. The lyrical quality of Romantic poetry is heard in the songs of Austrian composer Franz Schubert and German composer Robert Schumann.

In Russia, Peter Ilyich Tchaikovsky (chī-KOF-skee) wrote Romantic symphonies, operas, and music for ballet, all filled with beautiful melodies. His best-known works include the *1812 Overture* and the ballets *Swan Lake* and *Nutcracker Suite*.

Romanticism in music reached its height in opera, with its emphasis on the emotion of characters and the drama of events. The two leading composers of Romantic opera were Richard Wagner of Germany and Giuseppe Verdi of Italy.

Romantic painters also emphasized feeling and emotion in their work, as writers and composers did. Color as an element of painting became more important than it had been in the 1700s. Working outdoors, painters concentrated on the effects of light and shadow rather than on line drawing and sculpturelike modeling. Real subjects and real life became more important to these painters than the ideal, classical models of the Enlightenment.

Many artists painted in glowing colors, often with visible brush strokes so that the viewer became aware of the painting as a painting, not just as a perfectly realistic rendering of a scene in the classical manner. In France, Eugène Delacroix (duh-lah-KRWAH) was a leading artist of the new style. John Constable and J. M. W. Turner were prominent British Romantic artists.

REALISM AND NATURALISM

Just as the classical style had been eclipsed by Romanticism, so Romanticism gave way to realism and then to naturalism. The term *realism*, which first appeared in France in 1826, referred to the detailed descriptions of costumes and

These sketches are from a journal kept by Eugène Delacroix on a trip to Morocco in 1832. Romantic artists often sought out exotic people and places as subjects for their work.

customs in historical novels. As the nineteenth century moved forward, however, with both its social problems and advances in science, artists and writers wanted a more "realistic" art, one that would tell the truth about the real world. They wanted first to study the world around them carefully and objectively, then to write or paint exactly what they saw. Many of their works were highly critical of the industrial middle class.

Realism in literature and art. In France, the new movement began in the 1830s with novelist Honoré de Balzac. His *Human Comedy* was critical of the middle class. The novels of French writer Gustave Flaubert also focused on the middle class. In his novel *Madame Bovary*, published in 1857, Flaubert developed a finely crafted work of art from a simple story about the unhappy life of an ordinary middle-class woman.

In Britain, realist literature often dealt with the social effects of the Industrial Revolution. In the mid-1800s, Charles Dickens criticized industrial society in many of his books. He wrote of debtors' prisons in *Pickwick Papers*, workhouses in *Oliver Twist*, and the misery of factory towns in *Hard Times*. The writings of Dickens and others of the Victorian era—so called because Victoria was monarch at the time—had an impact that went far beyond their value as art. The British government responded to this social criticism by gradually eliminating the most oppressive laws.

Another British writer, Marian Evans, wrote under the pen name of George Eliot. She examined the limits that society placed on women. Her eight-part novel *Middlemarch*, published in 1871 and 1872, is considered the masterpiece of British realism.

Writers in Germany and Italy had little interest in realism, but in Norway and Russia realist writers produced great literature. Henrik Ibsen, a Norwegian playwright, used drama for social criticism, as in *A Doll's House*. In Russia, Count Leon Tolstoy showed the grim reality of war in *War and Peace*. Another Russian novelist, Feodor Dostoevsky (DAHS-tuh-YEF-skee), explored emotional suffering in *Crime and Punishment*.

Painters had less interest in realism than writers. Yet in the second half of the 1800s, some painters did begin to observe nature and daily life. In France, realism in painting was usually

THE IMPRESSIONISTS

Shunning the somber hues and heavy shadows of earlier styles, the impressionists sought to paint on canvas what the eye sees in an instant. These artists believed that the secret of visual impressions is light. To emphasize the flickers of light reflected in ever-changing scenes, impressionist painters daubed brilliant patches of color on the canvas with quick brush strokes. Breaking with tradition, they portrayed unposed subjects from unexpected angles. Later "post-impressionist" painters such as Cézanne, van Gogh, and Gauguin, reflecting the impressionists' new attitude toward painting, continued to capture fleeting moments of everyday life.

The Folkestone Boat, Boulogne, Edouard Manet, 1869

Terrace at Sainte-Adresse, Claude Monet, 1867

The Artist's Sister at a Window, Berthe Morisot, 1869

The Swing, Auguste Renoir, 1876

Road with Cypresses, Vincent van Gogh, 1889

Portraits in an Office (The Cotton Exchange, New Orleans), Edgar Degas, 1873

The Gardener, Paul Cézanne, 1906

The Boating Party, Mary Cassatt, 1893–1894

Street in Tahiti, Paul Gauguin, 1891

associated with Gustave Courbet (KOOR-BEH), Jean Millet (MEE-LEH), and Honoré Daumier (dō-MYAY). French sculptor Auguste Rodin (rō-DAN) is best known for his portrayal of human subjects.

Naturalism. The naturalist movement in literature had much in common with realism. Like realism, naturalism began in France in the late 1800s. Both movements held that the most important part of literature, more important than technique or subject, was the relating of actual experience. Realism, however, tried only to present an objective report of an experience. Naturalism went beyond that and attempted to duplicate the style of scientific presentation. The advances in science in the 1800s, especially new understandings of how people were affected by environment and heredity, greatly influenced naturalist writers.

French writer Émile Zola first described the philosophy of naturalism in an 1880 essay called "The Experimental Novel." British writer Thomas Hardy used his novels to express his view that people were victims of their environment. The American novelist best known

Photography provided a means of objectively recording scenes from everyday life. This stark photograph captures the grim reality of life in a British slum in the late 1800s.

as a naturalist is Theodore Dreiser, whose characters are often victims of outside forces.

NEW STYLES IN PAINTING

In the 1860s, French painting moved beyond the realism of Courbet and Millet. Painters in the new style did not simply imitate nature by portraying exactly what they saw. Instead, they were concerned with capturing one fleeting moment in time, painting in rapid strokes with small dabs of color. These patches of color worked together to make figures and scenes.

The term *impressionism*, taken from the title of a painting, was applied to the entire movement by critics who disapproved of the technique of painting only an impression of an object or scene instead of a realistic representation. The new movement also provoked criticism from many people in the middle class, who disliked its departure from classical subjects and techniques.

The best-known French impressionists were Édouard Manet (mah-NEH), who bridged realism and impressionism; Auguste Renoir, who specialized in portraits of women and children; Edgar Degas (day-GAH), who often painted ballet dancers; Claude Monet (mō-NEH), who called his paintings impressions; and Berthe Morisot (mō-ree-ZŌ), a noted woman artist. Mary Cassatt, who lived in France, was the only American to be invited to exhibit with the French impressionists.

The end of the 1800s brought an end to impressionism. The change reflected the growing interest in science and the scientific method, and in subjects that were more abstract and less realistic. Artists continued the move, begun by the impressionists, away from seeking approval by the public and toward appreciation by their fellow artists. This emphasis on creating art for its own sake, rather than for the sake of popular appeal, was a further rejection of middle-class values.

Postimpressionist painters, those who came after the impressionists, tried to push beyond the limits of impressionism. Many of these artists were called expressionists because they saw their art as an expression of their own personal view of the world and their artistic individuality. Paul Cézanne (say-ZAN), a foremost French expressionist, was most concerned with form and mass, often distorting objects and

Auguste Rodin spent six years on this sculpture of Balzac, completed in 1898. Not content with just presenting an accurate likeness, Rodin struggled to capture the writer's creative energy.

perspective. Dutch artist Vincent van Gogh (van GŌ) used brilliant colors and had a forceful, intensely expressive technique. Paul Gauguin (gō-GAN), a French artist, is known for his paintings of Tahitian life.

The careful, rational style of the Enlightenment gave way to more creative forms of artistic expression in the 1800s, sparked by the new nationalism and Romanticism. Innovation was the key element of the period, not only in science and technology but also in art, music, and literature.

SECTION REVIEW

1. Define *Romanticism* and *impressionism*.

2. Why did Romantic writers use simple language and stress creativity?

3. Name four elements that influenced the work of Romantic composers.

4. How did impressionism in painting differ from realism?

Analysis. Describe ways in which the arts changed between the 1700s and 1800s.

22-3
NEW PATHS IN SCIENCE

READ TO FIND OUT

—what the terms *theory of relativity*, *evolution*, and *social Darwinism* mean.
—how Einstein expanded the laws of physics.
—why Darwin's theories caused controversy.
—how advances in medicine during the 1800s brought some deadly diseases under control.

During the Industrial Revolution, science seemed to mean progress, and progress meant a more comfortable life for the expanding middle class. At the same time, the industrial age brought problems that called for even more solutions from science. Crowded cities urgently needed better sanitation systems, and the growing population needed better health care.

EXPLORING THE WORLD OF THE ATOM

In the early 1800s the physical sciences, the study of nonliving things, continued to build on the work of Galileo and Newton. As the century progressed, however, scientists developed new ideas about the world around them.

An English chemistry teacher, John Dalton, made the first scientific proof of the existence of atoms in 1803 and developed a method for finding their weight. He discovered that each element—a simple substance that cannot be broken down any further by chemical means—contains atoms of different weights. Then, in 1869, Russian chemistry professor Dmitri Mendeleev (men-duh-LAY-uf) drew up a chart that he called the "Periodic Table of the Elements," listing elements in the order of their atomic weights. Realizing that scientists had not yet discovered all the elements, Mendeleev left blank spaces in his chart for future discoveries.

In 1898 and 1899 the chart gained two more elements with the discovery of polonium and radium by Pierre Curie, a French physicist, and Marie Curie, a Polish chemist. Their marriage made one of the most brilliant teams of modern science. They discovered the two new elements while studying the element uranium. All three of these elements are radioactive—that is, their atoms are not stable. These atoms are constantly breaking up and releasing energy, a process eventually harnessed to produce nuclear, or atomic, energy in the twentieth century—one of the most important scientific developments of all time.

In 1895, German physicist Wilhelm Roentgen (RENT-gen) discovered that certain energy rays—which he named X-rays, for unknown rays—could penetrate human skin and tissues and leave an image on a photographic plate. While studying the new X-rays, John Joseph Thomson, a British physics professor, noticed that they could conduct electricity. With further research, Thomson discovered the electron, a basic charge of negative electricity. This discovery showed that atoms were made up of even smaller particles. As a student of J. J. Thomson, Ernest Rutherford, a physicist from New Zealand, went on to describe the atom as being

Marie Curie, the first woman to win a Nobel Prize, shared the 1903 award for physics with her husband, who died in 1906. She went on to win an unprecedented second Nobel Prize in 1911.

like a miniature solar system. Each atom, he said, has a nucleus, or center, around which circle units of electrical energy called protons. Physicists have now discovered more than 30 different atomic particles.

ALBERT EINSTEIN AND THE THEORY OF RELATIVITY

One of the most important contributions to the current understanding of the physical universe was made by Albert Einstein. Born in Germany and trained as a physicist, Einstein investigated the relationship between matter and energy. In 1905, he began to present new laws of physics, the first change in Newton's basic laws in 200 years.

According to Newton, space and time were fixed, or constant. Therefore, Newton thought speed and motion could be measured. Einstein, however, believed that space and time were not fixed and that the speed of light was the only constant. Motion could not be measured because no single point existed from which to measure it. The only way to measure the motion of one object, said Einstein, was by relating it to the motion of another object. All measurements, therefore, were relative. This concept was the core of Einstein's *theory of relativity*.

CHARLES DARWIN AND THE THEORY OF EVOLUTION

Ideas about the natural world of plants and animals also changed in the 1800s. One of the most profound, and controversial, theories was proposed by naturalist Charles Darwin. In 1831, Darwin began a five-year voyage aboard the H.M.S. *Beagle*, sailing around the tip of South America to the Galapagos Islands in the Pacific. Darwin carefully observed the plants and animals he saw, collecting specimens and taking many notes.

After returning to England, Darwin began studying his collection and notes from the voyage. He saw that the same species of animals had developed different characteristics in different locations. Darwin reasoned that such changes must have been in response to changing environmental demands. Individuals that were able to adjust to environmental changes were the ones that survived.

In 1859 Darwin published his conclusions, titled *On the Origin of Species by Means of Natural Selection*, in which he provided a scientific basis for his ideas of **evolution**. He said that all forms of life have evolved, or developed, from earlier and simpler forms. People, animals, birds, and all other living things survive because of the biological process of natural selection. Recalling the population theory of Thomas Malthus, Darwin stated that all living things compete with one another for food. The ones that are successful in the competition—because of protective coloration or some other characteristic—are the ones that survive. The survivors pass their characteristics on to their offspring, and the process continues. Gradually, over thousands of years, new forms of life develop in the same way.

Darwin was not the first scientist to propose a theory of animal development. In 1809, French physician and botanist Jean Lamarck had tried to show that different parts of the body developed as they were needed for survival—or disappeared if they were not needed. If an animal needed to eat leaves off tall trees, for example, it developed a long neck, like a giraffe.

Darwin's ideas had a tremendous impact on people in the late 1800s. Like Copernicus and Galileo more than 300 years before him, Darwin was harshly criticized. Religious leaders accused him of contradicting the Bible, saying he denied the role of God in creation. In recent years biologists have challenged Darwin's ideas as to how evolution takes place, observing that some changes do not happen as Darwin said they did. Although most scientists today consider Darwin's central idea of evolution to be valid, the controversy persists.

CELL THEORY AND GENETICS

While Darwin and others were studying species and populations, some scientists were examining the most basic elements of life, cells and genes. One of the most important discoveries in biology was the cell theory, which says that all living things are made up of one or more simple units called cells. In order to create new cells—and therefore new tissues, organs, and even entire organisms—the existing cells divide. In 1838, botanist Matthias Schleiden (SHLĪ-den) published the results of his research showing that plants were made of cells. The next year a German physiologist named Theodor Schwann published a paper that extended Schleiden's ideas to animals.

Some years later, in a paper published in 1866, Gregor Mendel, an Austrian monk, explained how cells passed along information that determined what they would be like. In a series of experiments on plant breeding, Mendel had discovered that characteristics were passed from one generation to the next in a specific pattern. He called certain factors, or elements of inheritance, dominant because they dominated other factors, which he called recessive. Recessive factors could disappear at first and then reappear in later generations.

Mendel's observations were ignored during his lifetime. Darwin, although a contemporary of Mendel, probably never read the monk's findings. If he had, Darwin might have been able to explain how characteristics of living things are passed on from parent to offspring, a question Darwin never could answer.

This drawing is from Darwin's 1840 *Zoology of the Voyage of the Beagle*. Using details provided by Darwin, illustrator John Gould showed these Brazilian hummingbirds in their native habitat.

IDENTIFYING AN ARGUMENT

Language serves many purposes. For example, it is often used to describe, to explain, or to persuade. Accounts intended to persuade are often presented as arguments. Before you can determine how persuasive an argument is, you need to know what is included in an argument and how to recognize whether an author is presenting an argument.

An argument is what you present in order to prove that what you say is so. An argument contains two basic elements. One element is a claim. The claim is the main idea that the author wants you to believe. The other basic element is the reasons supporting the claim. For example, an argument for using a hall pass might be stated in the following way: "I should be allowed to use the hall pass. One of our classroom rules is that anyone who is finished with the work can use the hall pass. Sue, José, and Reggie already used it. I am the only other person in the class who is finished. So it is my turn to use the pass." This argument presents a number of reasons to support the claim "I should be allowed to use the hall pass."

EXPLAINING THE SKILL

To determine whether a written account presents an argument, you must be able to identify a claim and the reason or reasons supporting that claim. One way to do this is to follow these steps:

1. *Skim the entire account to get its general meaning.*

2. *Recall the basic elements of an argument: a claim and reasons supporting the claim.*

Frequently the author's claim appears in the first sentence or two. Sometimes it appears at the end of the account or in the middle of the account. For emphasis, the claim may be repeated in several places. Claims are often preceded by words like *thus, so, therefore,* and *it follows that.*

Reasons are often preceded by words like *for, since, because of,* and *for the reason that.* There are three common types of reasons that authors frequently use to support their claims: specific facts, rules, and generalizations.

a) *Specific facts.* These are accurate pieces of information, such as dates, statistics, quotations, and details about events or conditions.

b) *Rules.* Rules may be principles or guidelines, such as "all people are created equal." They may also be laws or regulations, such as the law that a driver must stop at a red light.

c) *Generalizations.* These are broad statements, such as "Factory workers were treated fairly." The author may explain a generalization by giving specific examples or may simply expect the reader to accept the generalization as valid.

3. *Search through the account sentence by sentence to determine whether the account contains a claim and any stated or unstated reasons.*

4. *If the account includes reasons, identify how each reason connects to the claim.* Also, try to determine how the reasons connect to each other.

APPLYING THE SKILL

Account A is from the writings of Andrew Carnegie, a nineteenth-century industrial leader in the United States. It presents an argument regarding free enterprise, the freedom of private businesses to compete with each other for profit. Examine the account to find the basic elements of an argument.

Account A

The advantages of the law of free competition are greater than its costs. It is to this law that we owe our wonderful material development. Today the poor enjoy what before even the rich could not afford. What were luxuries for some are now necessities for all.

The price we pay for this, no doubt, is great. We assemble thousands of workers in factory and mine. Rigid castes are formed. Mutual ignorance breeds mutual distrust.

While the law may be sometimes hard for the individual, it is best for the race, because it insures the survival of the fittest in every department. The law of competition is essential to the future progress of the race.

Abridged from Andrew Carnegie's essay titled "The Gospel of Wealth," which was published in 1889.

REFLECTING ON THE SKILL

In following the previously described procedure, you should have first skimmed Account A to get a general idea of what it is about. Then, as you reread the account, you may have asked yourself, "What does the author want me to believe is true?"

Now that you have followed a procedure for identifying an argument, answer the following questions:

1. The author's claim is that free competition **(a)** is difficult, **(b)** has more advantages than disadvantages, **(c)** is especially harmful to industrial workers.

2. The kinds of reasons included in the last two sentences of the first paragraph are **(a)** generalizations, **(b)** specific facts, **(c)** rules.

3. The third and fourth sentences in the first paragraph connect directly to **(a)** paragraph 1, sentence 2; **(b)** paragraph 2, sentence 1; **(c)** paragraph 1, sentence 1.

APPLYING THE SKILL

Use the previously described procedure to identify which one of the following accounts is an argument. Both accounts are from the writings of Friedrich Engels.

Account B

The failure of the gentry and merchants to improve the basic conditions of life for the workers condemns multitudes of our fellow creatures to destruction annually. In Liverpool and Manchester, says the *Report on the Sanitary Conditions of the Working Class*, more than 57 percent of all working class children die before their fifth year, while only 20 percent of the children of the higher classes perish by that age.

Because of unsanitary, overcrowded living conditions in these cities, diseases breed and spread. Inadequate food and putrid air makes city workers and children more susceptible to these diseases. According to an article in the *Citizen*, epidemics in Manchester are three times more fatal to children living in working class areas than to those living in other districts. Using city re-sources to eliminate unsanitary conditions and inadequate food would end this destruction. The gentry and merchants are aware of this but pay no heed.

Account C

In English cities and towns, many sick workers are doing nothing about their illnesses. Others are using ineffective remedies that are offered by people who claim to be doctors. An immense number of these quack doctors thrive in many English towns. They get their customers through advertisements, posters, and other such devices.

Vast quantities of medicines are sold for all sicknesses: Morrison's pills, Parr's Life pills, and a thousand other pills, each supposed to cure all the illnesses that people could possibly get. Since unwary purchasers are always recommended to take as much as possible, they swallow the pills whether they need them or not.

Adapted from *The Condition of the Working Class in England in 1844*, by Friedrich Engels (1887).

CHECKING YOUR UNDERSTANDING

Now that you have examined Accounts B and C, answer the following:

4. Account C is **(a)** a description, **(b)** an argument, **(c)** a request. Explain your answer.

5. The author of Account B states his claim in **(a)** paragraph 1, sentence 1; **(b)** paragraph 2, sentence 3; **(c)** paragraph 1, sentence 2.

6. In Account B, specific facts are given in **(a)** paragraph 1, sentence 2; **(b)** paragraph 2, sentence 1; **(c)** paragraph 2, sentence 4.

7. In Account B, a generalization is presented in **(a)** paragraph 2, sentence 3; **(b)** paragraph 2, sentence 5; **(c)** paragraph 1, sentence 2.

REVIEWING THE SKILL

8. What are the basic elements of an argument?

9. State three common types of reasons and explain how they differ.

10. What is one procedure for identifying an argument in a written account?

THE STUDY OF HUMAN SOCIETY

The growing interest in natural science in the 1800s led to scientific study of human society. One of the earliest of the new social sciences, as they were called, was sociology, the scientific study of the social behavior of human beings. Auguste Comte (KAWNT), a French philosopher, first used the term *sociology* and is considered the founder of the field. He believed that the history of society showed a clear path of development and could be understood by laws similar to those of the natural sciences.

English philosopher Herbert Spencer tried to apply the laws of natural science to human society, hoping to explain social and economic conditions. Recalling Darwin's process of natural selection, Spencer coined the phrase "survival of the fittest," a phrase often mistakenly credited to Darwin. Spencer's views, which became known as **social Darwinism**, appealed to the middle class. Social Darwinists opposed social reform, arguing that it would interfere with the natural law of the survival of the fittest.

The new interest in human beings, where they had come from and how they lived, led to the growth of another new social science—anthropology, the study of the origin of human beings, their development, and their customs. Continuing interest in the individual sparked the development of another kind of science in the 1800s. Psychology, the study of the human mind and its effects on behavior, was at first considered a type of philosophy. Psychologists, however, discovered that they could apply scientific methods and reason to the study of the human mind.

Ivan Pavlov, a Russian biologist, did some of the earliest psychological testing, beginning in the late 1890s. In a series of experiments, he proved that dogs would learn to associate the ringing of a bell with their mealtime. Pavlov described this behavior, in which a specific event triggered a predictable response, as a conditioned reflex. Pavlov later concluded that people exhibit similar behavior.

The theory of behaviorism developed from Pavlov's work. Behaviorists believe that the only way to study psychology is by observing the behavior and activity of people and animals.

Sigmund Freud, an Austrian physician, probed further into human thought and behavior. According to Freud, human behavior comes from unconscious mental processes—thoughts that people are not aware of. Freud developed the method of psychoanalysis, which involves

By the mid-1800s a growing interest in human history led to numerous archaeological expeditions. This photograph shows the excavation of an ancient Sumerian temple in what is now Iraq. The ruins date back to about 3000 B.C.

listening to patients talk and analyzing their statements and their dreams, to help people become more aware of the unconscious mind.

Freud believed that once patients understood the unconscious reasons for their behavior, they would be able to change it. Although some of Freud's specific ideas and methods have been challenged, his work remains very important in the treatment of mental illness.

ADVANCES IN MEDICINE

The impact of medical advances made in the 1800s, such as vaccinations, is still felt today. In 1850 the average life expectancy in industrialized nations was 42 years. By 1910 it had risen to almost 55 years. One factor increasing the lifespan was the discovery of how to prevent smallpox and other deadly diseases.

Edward Jenner, a British physician, was familiar with the popular belief that people who had been exposed to cowpox, a milder disease, were safe from smallpox. He theorized that intentional exposure might be an effective method of prevention. In 1796, Jenner performed the first successful vaccination, or inoculation—injecting a person with germs to prevent a serious attack of a disease.

Several decades later, French chemist Louis Pasteur applied Jenner's discoveries to help him develop vaccines against diseases such as rabies. In doing so, he determined that when weakened germs enter the human body, the body responds by building up a resistance to the germs. This response explained why vaccination worked. Pasteur also proved that bacteria reproduced like other living things and showed that some bacteria caused disease. This discovery became known as the germ theory of disease. To kill disease-carrying bacteria, Pasteur developed a heating process now called pasteurization, which is still used to destroy disease-producing bacteria in milk.

When Joseph Lister, a British surgeon, read of Pasteur's germ theory of disease, he immediately saw its importance in surgical procedures and insisted on cleanliness within the hospital. Before that time, death from infection following even the most minor surgery was common. Lister also did research on antiseptics, agents that kill germs, until he found one that could be used in the operating room. As a result, the death rate from surgery dropped dramatically.

A German doctor, Robert Koch, expanded the germ theory when he discovered the bacteria that caused several infectious diseases. He also developed techniques that are still used for growing bacteria in laboratories. Because of his work, Koch is credited with founding the science of bacteriology.

SECTION REVIEW

1. Define *theory of relativity*, *evolution*, and *social Darwinism*.

2. What was a major difference between Newton's and Einstein's ideas about measuring the physical world?

3. Why did many people in the 1800s find Darwin's theory of evolution shocking?

4. Discuss medical advances of the 1800s that helped bring a number of deadly diseases under control.

Evaluation. Why might Darwin's theories still be a source of controversy today?

HISTORY IN FOCUS

Changes brought by the industrial age went far beyond technological advances and rapid urbanization. The growing capitalist middle class embraced liberal economic and social theories that assured them their direction in life was proper. Profit making was more important than social reform, at least at first.

Some political thinkers, such as Karl Marx, disagreed with that philosophy and severely criticized the capitalist system. In time, social, economic, and political changes began to correct the inequities and make life easier for the working class.

The new industrial age was also an age of innovation and individual creativity. It brought the past into the present with a new spirit of nationalism. Artists, writers, and composers produced personal, emotional works, rejecting the formal classicism of the Enlightenment in favor of Romanticism. Much of the creative work in this period was also critical of middle-class values and life styles.

The quality of urban life improved as cities became cleaner. A new understanding of science and human behavior helped people to explore even further not only the physical universe but the nature of society.

CHAPTER SURVEY

SUMMARY

- The Industrial Revolution produced changes not only in ways goods were made and distributed but also in ways people saw and thought about the world.

- Some people, seeing great increases in manufactured goods and new wealth pouring into nations, felt that the new industrial systems would ultimately benefit most people and could regulate themselves without government interference. They spoke out strongly for free enterprise. Adam Smith and David Ricardo were among the leading exponents of free enterprise.

- Other people saw slums and poverty as products of capitalism and the Industrial Revolution. To control these abuses, they favored some form of socialism, or government control of the means of production.

- The Industrial Revolution produced differing reactions in artists as well. Some tried to escape from the effects of the industrial age through Romanticism, a movement that affected literature, music, and art. Other artists chose instead to look more sharply at the world around them and became part of movements known as realism and naturalism. Some painters focused their attention even more narrowly on their particular perceptions of the world and developed the styles known as impressionism and postimpressionism.

- Scientists' observations led to advances in the understanding of disease, of heredity, of physics and the nature of matter, and of the universe. The study of society began to emerge as the social sciences developed.

VOCABULARY REVIEW

Below are six vocabulary terms used in the chapter. Match each numbered term with the lettered term most closely related to it. Then explain how the terms in each pair are related.

1. socialism
2. social Darwinism
3. Romanticism

(a) impressionism
(b) Marxism
(c) evolution

CHAPTER REVIEW

1. (a) Why was Adam Smith an important figure in the field of economics? (b) In Smith's view, according to what laws did businesses operate? (c) What forces did he believe regulated business?

2. (a) Who were the utilitarians? (b) How did their views differ from those of laissez-faire economists? (c) How did John Stuart Mill's views fit in with those of the utilitarians?

3. (a) What is socialism? (b) Who were the utopian socialists, and what did some of them set out to do?

4. (a) Explain the basic idea behind Karl Marx's scientific socialism. (b) According to Marx, what role did the classes play in world history? (c) Why did Marx think that capitalism and the industrial system would change?

5. (a) What influenced the work of Romantic writers of the eighteenth and nineteenth centuries? (b) How did the ideas of realist writers differ from those of the Romantics? (c) What distinguished naturalism from realism?

6. What did Romantic composers have in common with Romantic writers?

7. (a) What elements were important in the work of Romantic painters? (b) How was realism a reaction to Romanticism? (c) What were impressionist and postimpressionist artists trying to do in their work?

8. (a) How did economic philosophy influence the scientific ideas of Charles Darwin? (b) How, according to Darwin, did the process of natural selection work? (c) How did Darwin's ideas affect the field of sociology?

9. (a) What is psychology? (b) How did Ivan Pavlov's work affect the field of psychology? (c) What did Freud contribute to psychology?

10. Explain the importance of the following scientists: (a) Dalton, (b) the Curies, (c) Roentgen, (d) Mendel.

THINKING CRITICALLY: ACTIVITIES

1. Pretend that you are one of the following people: Adam Smith, John Stuart Mill, Karl

Marx. Select class members to play the other roles. Prepare your positions. Then discuss, in character, the following issue: Should a government provide low-interest loans to enable poor workers to buy their own homes?

2. Some utopian socialists tried to start ideal societies. Select three partners and discuss your ideas for an ideal society, with special emphasis on the economy of the society. Prepare a written report on your society and present it to the class.

APPLYING SOCIAL STUDIES SKILLS

Analyzing graphs. Look carefully at this graph and answer the questions below.

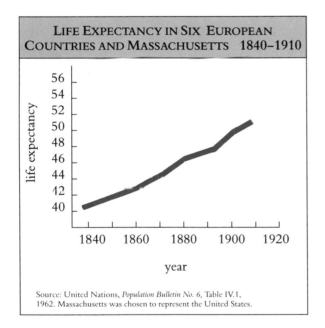

LIFE EXPECTANCY IN SIX EUROPEAN COUNTRIES AND MASSACHUSETTS 1840–1910

Source: United Nations, *Population Bulletin No. 6*, Table IV.1, 1962. Massachusetts was chosen to represent the United States.

1. What is the subject of the graph?

2. What span of time does it cover?

3. What do the numbers to the left of the graph represent?

4. What was the change in life expectancy between 1840 and 1910?

5. Briefly state what trend or pattern is shown for Europe and the United States.

6. Based on the trend shown in the graph, estimate the life expectancy in 1920.

APPLYING THINKING SKILLS

Identifying an argument. The following account was written in England in 1861. Use the procedure described on pages 504 and 505 to determine whether or not this account contains the basic elements of an argument. Then answer the questions that follow.

There is an abundant increase of intelligence and moral sentiment springing up among the factories as a result of Sunday Schools. These schools have been started and developed chiefly by the work-people themselves, unaided by wealth and unpatronized by power. It is a splendid spectacle to witness crowds of factory children arranged in a Sunday School. I would exhort the friends of humanity who may chance to pass through Cheshire or Lancashire, not to miss a Sunday's visit to the busy town of Stockport, which joins the two counties. It contains 67 factories, in which 21,489 workers of all ages are employed comfortably for their families.

The Sunday School of this place was erected by the voluntary contributions chiefly of millowners in the year 1805. When I visited this school a few months ago, there were 4,000 to 5,000 young people profiting by the instructions administered by 400 teachers, distributed into proper classes, and arranged in more than forty schoolrooms. I witnessed the very gratifying sight of about 1,500 boys, and as many girls, regularly seated upon separate benches, the one set on the right side, and the other on the left. They were attractively dressed, proper in their behavior, and of healthy, even blooming complexions. Their hymn-singing thrilled through the heart like the festival chorus of Westminster.

Adapted from *The Philosophy of Manufactures; or an Exposition of the Scientific, Moral, and Commercial Economy of the Factory System in Great Britain,* by Andrew Ure. London: 1861.

1. What are the basic elements of an argument?

2. What is one procedure for identifying an argument in a written account?

3. In the above account, what is the author's claim?

4. What types of reasons are used in this account? Give examples.

5. How does each of these reasons relate to the author's claim?

CHAPTER TWENTY-THREE

POLITICS AND SOCIAL CONFLICT

1814–1914

Public Funeral of the Victims of the March Revolution, 1848. Adolph von Menzel.

While industrialization and the rise of capitalism spawned new social theories, creative movements, and scientific progress, struggles were emerging between different groups in Western societies. After Napoleon's defeat in 1815, the aristocracy regained power across Europe and attempted to restore order through absolute rule. Soon, however, rulers met strong opposition from the growing middle and working classes.

These two new classes became a significant force of change. On the European continent, many middle- and working-class people, following the example of France's Third Estate, tried to cause drastic political change through revolutions. Meanwhile, in Great Britain and the United States, people from these same classes called for gradual, nonviolent change.

TIMELINE

1800	
1810	
1820	Congress of Vienna · Greek War of Independence · Concert of Europe formed
1830	
1840	Revolutions in France, Belgium, and Poland · Slavery banned in Great Britain
1850	
1860	Revolutions in France, Italy, and Austria · France's Second Republic established
1870	Abolition of slavery in the U.S.
1880	France's Third Republic established · Paris Commune
1890	
1900	
1910	Progressive Era in the U.S.
1920	Minimum wage law in Great Britain

23–1
THE RESTORATION OF ARISTOCRATIC RULE

READ TO FIND OUT

—what the term *conservatism* means.
—what goals the Congress of Vienna hoped to achieve.
—how the growth of the middle class challenged aristocratic power.
—why nationalism led to political struggle.
—how conservatives reacted to liberal demands.

During the 1700s, while much of European society began to be transformed through the growth of the middle class and the unfolding of the Industrial Revolution, the aristocracy held on to power and old forms of government. The aristocracy's resistance to change caused great conflicts in European society, beginning with the French Revolution.

Although the growing forces of change would fatally weaken the power of the aristocracy in the nineteenth century, the defeat of Napoleon in 1815 gave the ruling class of Europe an opportunity to restore the absolute rule that had existed before 1789. For a short time, the aristocracy succeeded in blocking the goals of middle-class liberals, forging a new balance of power in Europe, and preventing upheaval. The aristocracy did not succeed in actually restoring the Old Regime, however. Soon, reactions against aristocratic rule led to renewed disorder and revolt.

THE CONGRESS OF VIENNA

After Napoleon was exiled to Elba in 1814, several hundred representatives of the old ruling class met in Vienna for a conference known as the Congress of Vienna. The diplomats of the congress hoped to bring peace to Europe by acting quickly to settle disputes arising from the Napoleonic wars. They also hoped to maintain order by restoring the governments that had existed before 1789. The conference was interrupted when Napoleon returned from Elba but resumed its work when Napoleon was finally defeated at Waterloo in 1815.

The leading diplomats. The most important decisions at the Congress of Vienna were made by the diplomats representing the four great powers of Europe: Austria, Great Britain, Russia, and Prussia. Austria's chief minister, Prince Klemens von Metternich (MEHT-er-NIHK) hosted the congress. Metternich's strong belief in absolute rule and fear of liberalism influenced other delegates. The leading British delegate was Lord Castlereagh (KAS-ul-RAY), the foreign minister. The Russian delegation was headed by Czar Alexander I, and King Frederick William III and Prince Karl von Hardenberg decided matters for Prussia. France, the defeated nation, sent Prince Charles Maurice de Talleyrand (TAHL-ee-RAND), who managed to play a major role at the congress.

Maintaining international peace. A major aim of the delegates at the Congress of Vienna was to maintain order and peace. Twenty years of almost continuous fighting during the Napoleonic wars had left people weary of conflict. The way to achieve international peace, the congress leaders felt, was by establishing a balance of power. Napoleon's bid for a European empire had convinced everyone that no one nation should be allowed to become so powerful as to threaten the others.

To achieve their goal, the delegates reached important settlements that changed political boundaries in Europe. France was required to surrender all the territory it had conquered after 1790. Further, in an effort to discourage any future French expansion, the diplomats at Vienna strengthened the nations along France's borders. To the northeast of France, the Austrian territory, today called Belgium, became part of the kingdom of the Netherlands. To the southeast, Switzerland was reestablished as an independent neutral nation.

The congress formed a barrier to French expansion eastward by establishing a more stable confederation of 39 German states to replace the more than three hundred separate states of the old Holy Roman Empire. In addition, Prussia received the Rhineland, an important center of agriculture and industry.

Restoring absolute rule. Metternich convinced the delegates that the best way to maintain order within each nation was to strengthen central control over national affairs and oppose attempts by liberals and revolutionaries to gain a share of power. Believing in divine-right monarchy, the delegates agreed to restore to power those monarchs who had been deposed by the French Revolution and Napoleon.

In France, Louis XVIII was recognized as the legitimate, or legal, ruler in 1815. The French aristocracy, however, no longer had the complete power over French society it once enjoyed. Other hereditary rulers regained their thrones in Portugal, Spain, and several Italian states.

THE CONCERT OF EUROPE

Although the Congress of Vienna had achieved its goals, the leaders knew it would be hard to maintain order after the upheaval of war. Austria, Britain, Prussia, and Russia therefore agreed to meet periodically for "the purpose of consulting upon their common interests and for the maintenance of peace in Europe." This idea of cooperation between European powers came to be known as the Concert of Europe. "Concert" means mutual agreement.

In 1815, the four powers formed the Quadruple Alliance; in 1818, they allowed France to join, becoming the Quintuple Alliance. By setting up ways to resolve a crisis before it erupted into war, the Concert of Europe helped to preserve aristocratic rule and the balance of power.

Through the alliance, many European rulers helped each other put down revolts. In 1821, for instance, an Austrian army helped the king of Naples return to power after being ousted by liberals. An army from France helped the king of Spain suppress a liberal revolt in 1823.

CHALLENGES TO ARISTOCRATIC RULE

The Congress of Vienna and the Concert of Europe only partly succeeded in restoring absolutism and preventing war and revolution. It was growing more difficult to impose the absolutist institutions of the eighteenth century on the Europe of the early nineteenth century. The population boom, industrialization, and urbanization had begun to change society rapidly. Two major forces challenged Europe's aristocracy: liberalism and nationalism.

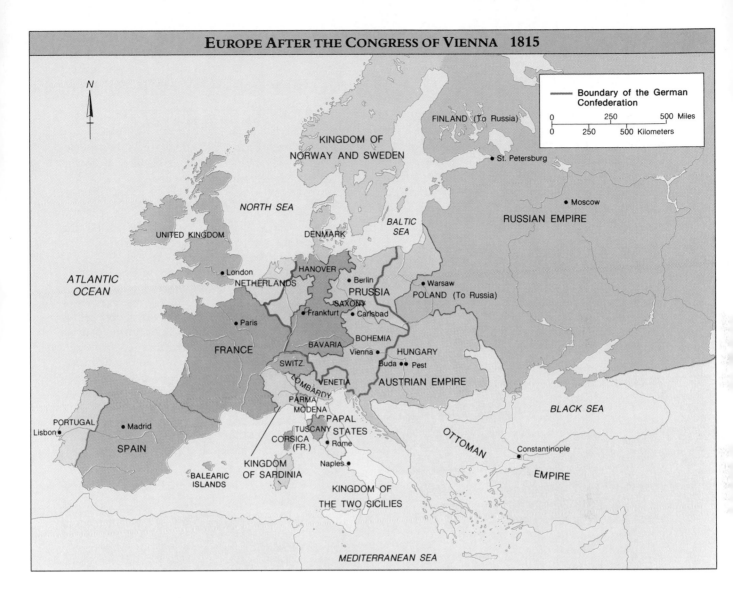

Boundary of the German
Confederation

The growth of liberalism.

The growth of liberalism. Since the 1700s, the ruling class, whose wealth depended on land, had been slowly losing power to the middle class, whose wealth depended on commerce. As commerce grew during the Industrial Revolution, so too did the wealth and power of the middle class. By the early 1800s, the middle class, or *bourgeoisie*, was seriously threatening the long tradition of aristocratic control of government, the economy, and society's values. The aristocracy, however, did not give up its power easily. The resulting struggles for political control shook Europe during most of the 1800s.

In these struggles, the political philosophy of liberalism guided most members of the middle class. Rooted in the ideas of the *philosophes* of the Enlightenment, liberalism gained strength in the early nineteenth century. As more and more people became educated and acquired the means to own some property—or at least hoped to achieve these goals—liberal ideas gained wide acceptance.

Liberals believed that governments should represent the interests of all educated people and guarantee them the right to gain wealth through commerce. Liberals supported freedom of speech and social reform, such as voting rights for more people, but did not necessarily believe in democracy. Although liberalism represented middle-class beliefs, people from all classes supported many liberal ideas.

DETERMINING THE STRENGTH OF AN ARGUMENT

Determining the strength of an argument means deciding the quality of the reasons given in support of a claim. An argument, as you will recall from pages 504-505, presents reasons supporting a claim. Judging the quality of reasons involves figuring out whether they are true. In a strong argument, the claim is based on accurate, relevant reasons.

EXPLAINING THE SKILL

Many of the other thinking skills presented earlier in the text are often involved in determining the strength of an argument. One procedure for determining the strength of an argument is to follow these steps:

1. *Identify and clarify the claim.*
To clarify the claim that is being made, be sure to define any vague terms.

2. *Identify any stated or unstated reasons given to support the claim, including specific facts, rules, and generalizations.*

3. *Distinguish reasons that are relevant to the claim from those that are irrelevant to the claim.*

4. *Identify any bias or use of language that affects the content of the given reasons.*

5. *Evaluate the reasons.*
  a) If possible, judge the *accuracy* of the reasons by checking the credibility of the sources cited or by determining how the reasons were developed.
  b) To judge the *consistency* of the reasons, check if they all logically support the claim.

6. *State a final judgment about the strength of the overall argument.*

Reasons have both content and a structure. You must look at what each reason says to see if it is generally accepted or has been proven true. You must also determine whether the reasons hang together so that they logically support the claim. As you analyze an argument, continue to ask yourself questions that lead you to evaluate the reasons, such as: How accurate and relevant are the reasons? What else must be true if I am to accept these reasons as true? To what degree do these reasons support the claim?

APPLYING THE SKILL

Use the previously described guidelines to determine which one of the following accounts presents the stronger argument.

Account A

In the rule of Napoleon was born the world's first modern dictatorship. It is a basic principle of democracy that sovereignty—supreme authority—comes from the people. The Revolution of 1789 firmly established this principle in France. As the historical record shows, the French people voted in the plebiscite [a direct vote on a political issue] of 1802 to make Napoleon consul for life. In 1804, they voted in another plebiscite for the empire with Napoleon as emperor. These votes vindicated this principle by giving Napoleon via popular vote the post of supreme power in the State. In this way arose in the modern world the idea that one man might himself represent the will of the people, and hold the authority of the most despotic rule, all in the name of democracy.

Adapted from *Dictatorship: Its History and Theory*, by Alfred Cobban. New York: Charles Scribner's Sons, 1939.

Account B

Napoleon Bonaparte sought only to create renown for himself. He hastened to enjoy and abuse his glory [as if it were] fleeting youth. In the manner of the gods of Homer, he wanted to reach the ends of the world in four strides. Rushing by, he threw crowns to his family and to his soldiers; he was hurried in establishing his monuments, his laws, his victories. Bonaparte could have enriched the nation. But, while promising to deliver men, he enchained them instead.

Adapted from Travels in America, by Francois René de Chateaubriand (1792).

REFLECTING ON THE SKILL

In order to determine which one of the above accounts presents the stronger argument, you had to first analyze each account to find and define the claim and any stated or unstated reasons relevant to the claim. Then you had to determine the accuracy of the content of the reasons and examine how the reasons link to the claim. Now that you have used the procedure to determine the strength of the arguments, answer the following questions:

1. What is the claim in Account A? **(a)** Napoleon kept the revolution alive. **(b)** The principle of the sovereignty of the people helped Napoleon to become the first modern dictator. **(c)** Napoleon firmly established the principle of democracy in France.

2. Which one of the following questions is helpful for checking the accuracy of reasons in Account A? **(a)** Did Napoleon give favors to his relatives? **(b)** Did Napoleon view himself as a dictator? **(c)** Were plebiscites held in France in 1802 and 1804?

3. A rule is stated in **(a)** Account A, sentence 7; **(b)** Account A, sentence 2; **(c)** Account B, sentence 1.

4. An unstated assumption in Account A is that the French people **(a)** did not realize their support of Napoleon would lead to a dictatorship, **(b)** pressured Napoleon into becoming a dictator, **(c)** opposed dictators. What statements in Account A support your answer?

5. Which account presents a stronger argument? **(a)** A, **(b)** B, **(c)** Both are equally strong. Explain your answer.

APPLYING THE SKILL

Determine the strength of the following argument.

Account C

Although often criticized as reactionary, the Congress of Vienna produced a constructive peace. Its leaders did not try to resurrect the Holy Roman Empire, though they did strengthen the German Confederation. They did not abolish France's constitutional charter, though they did restore the monarchy in the person of Louis XVIII. They did not take traditionally French land away from France, though they did create new kingdoms along France's eastern borders to prevent [France] from future expansion.

Metternich and his conservative allies acknowledged what they could not change. As a result, they created a remarkable balance, one that prevented any worldwide conflicts for almost a century.

Adapted from *The Political Collapse of Europe*, by Hajo Holborn. New York: Alfred A. Knopf, 1965.

CHECKING YOUR UNDERSTANDING

Now answer the following questions about Account C:

6. The author's claim is that the leaders of the Congress of Vienna **(a)** were reactionaries, **(b)** created a workable balance for world peace, **(c)** made decisions that were destructive.

7. What kind of reason does not appear in Account C? **(a)** facts, **(b)** generalizations, **(c)** rules, or guiding principles.

8. What is one reason that supports the author's claim? **(a)** Louis XVIII was made king of France. **(b)** The leaders of the Congress of Vienna were conservatives. **(c)** No worldwide war occurred for almost a century after the Congress of Vienna.

9. How would you rate Account C as an argument? **(a)** strong, **(b)** moderate, **(c)** weak. Explain how you evaluated the accuracy and consistency of the reasons for the claim.

REVIEWING THE SKILL
---

10. What is meant by determining the strength of an argument?

11. What are at least three things you can do to determine the strength of an argument?

12. Name at least three of the previously discussed thinking skills that may be involved in determining the strength of an argument. Explain how each skill is involved in determining an argument's strength.

13. Suppose that you had to explain to an eighth grader in your own words how to determine the strength of an argument. What specific directions would you give?

In the political struggles of the nineteenth century, liberals met the greatest resistance from people who followed the political philosophy of *conservatism*. Conservatives were mainly from the aristocracy and controlled most political power in the early 1800s. They wanted to maintain the old political and social order.

Nationalism. Another powerful force of change in the nineteenth century was nationalism. At this time, nationalism meant more than love of one's country. It also meant a desire for independence. Many groups, united by a common language and culture, did not have a country to call their own. Instead, like the Greeks under Ottoman rule, these Europeans were living within another country's borders.

Other cultural groups with a common heritage were scattered among several small independent states. Such a situation existed in the German states, where many wanted a unified German nation. Thus, nationalism was a movement for both national independence and national unification.

Nationalism, like liberalism, often led people to oppose aristocratic rule. However, nationalism also came into conflict with liberalism. Often liberals wanted a government that unified the entire nation, whereas ethnic minorities within a country desired their own independent nations. Depending on circumstances, liberalism became an important force in some countries, while nationalism dominated the politics of others.

LIBERAL REVOLTS AND CONSERVATIVE REACTION

Beginning in 1817 and continuing into the 1820s, liberals revolted against conservative governments. Although largely ineffective, these revolts widened the cracks in conservative power and the Concert of Europe.

In 1817, university students in the German states demonstrated for liberal reforms and unification. Metternich, the Austrian leader, responded by calling a conference of German state ministers at the town of Carlsbad. The ministers adopted a series of decrees that remained in force until 1848. These official orders, known as the Carlsbad Decrees, suppressed freedom of speech and provided for censorship of the press and the removal of university teachers who favored liberalism.

In 1820, uprisings erupted in other countries. Spanish liberals and army officers forced the Bourbon monarch, Ferdinand VII, to restore the constitution of 1812, which he had suspended when he returned to the throne in 1814. Liberals in Portugal then obtained a similar constitution from King John VI. Liberals in Naples, Italy, also forced their Bourbon monarch, Ferdinand I, to restore their constitution of 1812.

These revolts were all suppressed within a few years, however, by the conservative rulers of the various countries when they received aid from other monarchs. The constitutions were again revoked, and absolute rule was restored.

The Battle of Navarino took place off the coast of Greece in 1827. In support of Greek revolutionaries, combined British, French, and Russian squadrons sank most of a Turkish and Egyptian fleet. Although Europe's wooden ships withstood the intense attacks, this was the last major battle in which they were used; they were soon replaced by iron ships.

Metternich best expressed the attitude of the European aristocracy toward such liberal revolts when he said:

> There are always slogans and rallying cries for different groups. Sometimes the cry is "Constitution." Others want "Representation." Still others cry for "Reform." But everywhere, it means change and trouble. Society can no longer be saved unless governments deal with such dangerous ideas strongly. Therefore governments should see to it that the laws remain unchanged.

THE GREEK WAR OF INDEPENDENCE

The revolts in Spain, Portugal, and Naples against absolute rule had been motivated by liberalism. In Greece, meanwhile, a war was fought in the name of nationalism.

By the 1820s, the strength of the Ottoman Empire had declined in relation to that of European nations. Ottoman administration was corrupt and inefficient. Its armed forces had not recovered from the defeat inflicted by Napoleon in Egypt. In addition, the predominantly Christian population of the Balkans had long resented the rule of the Muslim Ottomans.

In 1821, the Greeks rose up against Ottoman domination. While the leaders of Austria and Prussia took their usual stand against revolution, the leaders of Britain and France supported the Greek cause. Russia likewise sided with the Greek rebels, for it had long awaited the collapse of the Ottoman Empire in order to gain access to the Mediterranean from the Black Sea. In 1830, after intervention by a combined British, French, and Russian naval force, Greece won its independence from the Ottomans.

SECTION REVIEW

1. Define *conservatism*.

2. Describe the two major goals of the delegates at the Congress of Vienna.

3. Why did the power of the middle class grow while that of the aristocracy declined?

4. Explain how nationalism could be in conflict with both liberalism and conservatism.

5. What was Metternich's attitude toward liberal reform?

Evaluation. Who did Metternich believe was his greatest enemy: foreign powers, such as France, or liberals? Use evidence from the chapter to support your position.

Data Search. Identify each of the following statements as being either *supported* or *not supported* by the chart titled "Balance of World Trade: 1860–1913" on page 833. **(a)** Of the four countries listed, Great Britain had the largest total volume of trade in 1913. **(b)** Of the four countries listed, only the United States exported more than it imported in 1913. **(c)** The United States, Great Britain, and France reduced their trade with South America, Asia, and Africa between 1860 and 1913.

23-2
DECADES OF REVOLUTION

READ TO FIND OUT

—what caused the 1830 uprising in France.

—what groups opposed the French monarch in the revolution of 1848.

—what happened as a result of the revolution of 1848 in Austria.

—how the causes and effects of the revolutions of 1848 differed in eastern and western Europe.

Except for the uprising in Greece, the first wave of revolutions after the restoration of absolute rule on the continent did not bring any lasting changes in European governments. Still inspired by the ideals of the French Revolution, however, liberals and nationalists continued to challenge aristocratic rule. As attempts at reform largely failed, a second wave of revolutions spread across the European continent.

THE 1830 UPRISING IN FRANCE

The first uprising broke out in France in 1830. The restored Bourbon monarch, Louis XVIII, had tried to steer a middle road between the conservative royalists, who supported a monarchy, and liberal republicans, who favored the creation of a republic. He tried to please the republicans while maintaining absolute rule.

In 1824, however, Louis XVIII was succeeded by his brother, Charles X. Charles hated the principles for which people had fought during the French Revolution. He angered liberals by paying large sums of money to aristocrats who had lost property during the revolution and by abolishing freedom of the press. He also decreed that only those who supported his position could have the right to vote.

In response to these repressive policies, the National Guard—a military group made up mostly of members of the middle class—took up arms against the king in July of 1830. Students and workers seized the city hall in Paris and barricades went up in the streets of the capital. In what is known as the July Revolution, liberals and republicans forced the king into exile in Great Britain.

Louis Philippe, the Duke of Orléans, was named the successor to Charles. Often called the "Bourgeois Monarch" because of his middle-class clothes and ideas, Louis Philippe restored the constitution. He extended the right to vote to more members of the middle class although voting rights were still determined by property ownership. Thus, the workers who had helped topple Charles X did not receive the right to vote. Because the interests of the working class were not considered, a large segment of French society remained dissatisfied.

Militant students raided a French arms depot in Paris during the July Revolution of 1830. This painting memorializes the brave death of Vaneau, a hero of the revolution.

OTHER REBELLIONS IN EUROPE

Various groups of people attempted other revolutions on the continent in 1830. The first occurred in the country today called Belgium, the territory of the Low Countries once ruled by Spain and then by Austria. Joined with the Dutch people to form the kingdom of the Netherlands by the Congress of Vienna, the Belgians complained that they were taxed more heavily than the Dutch. More importantly, they felt that the Protestant Church was hostile to their own Catholic religion.

When news of the July Revolution in France reached Brussels, the Belgians promptly revolted. They established a constitutional monarchy similar to that of France, with voting rights limited to well-to-do people. Austria, Prussia, and Russia each considered sending troops to help suppress the revolt, but their attention was distracted by a revolution that broke out in Poland. By 1833, the great powers of Europe agreed to recognize the independence of Belgium.

Perhaps the most violent struggle of 1830 was the one that took place in Poland. The Polish rebels were few in number and poorly organized. After a year of war, Czar Nicholas I of Russia put down the revolt and executed or imprisoned thousands of Poles. The University of Warsaw was closed, and Russia took over a large part of Polish land for its own use.

Other revolutions broke out in several of the Italian states. The rebels hoped for aid from France. Metternich, however, persuaded Louis Philippe, the new king of France, not to give support to the rebels. Austrian troops soon put down the revolts and restored the deposed monarchs.

THE REVOLUTION OF 1848 IN FRANCE

Revolutions again swept through Europe in 1848. The more than 50 separate rebellions of that year had the greatest impact of all the nineteenth-century revolutions.

As in earlier waves of revolutions, France was the location of the first and most important revolution of 1848. Commenting on France's revolutionary example, Metternich said, "Whenever France sneezes, Europe catches cold."

The revolution of 1848 in France had its roots in widespread discontent with Louis Philippe's rule. Although his domestic policies pleased some middle-class people, others felt they favored the wealthy at the expense of everyone else. Furthermore, the class with the least say in government—the working class—was growing rapidly and demanding economic and political reforms.

Opposition to Louis Philippe was led by two major groups, the republicans and the socialists. A new force in French politics, the socialists comprised workers and middle-class people sympathetic to the working-class cause. Although both republicans and socialists sought reforms, their goals differed. Republicans wanted voting rights and policies to benefit the middle class. Socialists also wanted voting rights extended but believed that ownership of private property should be abolished in order to make everyone in society more equal. This goal directly opposed middle-class interests.

Louis Philippe's response to republicans and socialists was to announce that "There will be no reform. I do not wish it." When workers tried to organize labor unions, he ordered the police to break up strikes. When reformers held meetings to discuss changing the constitution, he declared them illegal.

In 1848, a political meeting was scheduled to be held in Paris. Louis Philippe called out troops to prevent it. In the resulting confusion, the troops shot and killed several people. The people of Paris immediately put up barricades to restrict the movement of government troops. Crowds filled the street and shouted, "Down with Louis Philippe!"

The king called out the National Guard. However, siding with the rebels, as it had in 1830, the National Guard joined in fighting the regular French army. Three days later, the king fled to England.

The Second Republic. The leaders of the revolution now proclaimed France's Second Republic. During the three-month period before elections for the National Assembly were held, a temporary government was set up. Many of its members were socialists, who favored a system of "national workshops"—industries that would be owned and run by the workers. About 110,000 workers flocked to Paris, spending much of their time marching up and down the streets, threatening to get rid of bankers and to abolish private property.

LES POIRES,

Faites à la cour d'assises de Paris par le directeur de la CARICATURE

Vendues pour payer les 6,000 fr. d'amende du journal le *Charivari*.

(CHEZ AUBERT, GALERIE VERO-DODAT)

Caricatures by the publisher Charles Philipon transform King Louis Philippe into a pear, French slang for "simpleton." *Les Poires (The Pears)* ridicules the king's harsh censorship laws.

Soon conflict between the socialists and the republicans increased. Though they had been allies in fighting the king, they now disagreed on what course to pursue.

When elections for the National Assembly were held, more republicans than socialists were elected. The republicans organized a middle-class army that drove the workers out of Paris after 4 days of fighting and about 10,000 casualties. Then they drafted a new constitution. It provided for a president and a single Chamber of Representatives to be elected by all adult males.

THE REVOLUTIONS OF 1848 IN ITALY

Italy, too, was shaken by rebellions in 1848. They began in Sicily and spread north until most of the Italian states had obtained liberal constitutions. At the same time, rebels in two Italian states under Austrian control, Lombardy and Venetia, proclaimed their independence.

When nationalists seized Rome from Pope Pius IX in late 1848, the way seemed clear for the Italian states to unite, something many Italians had dreamed about since 1815. However, during the next months, the pope and aristocratic Italian rulers received aid from Austria and France. Rebels' gains throughout Italy were reversed. By 1849, the only change that remained as a result of the Italian revolutions was a liberal constitution in Piedmont, a state in northwest Italy.

THE REVOLUTION OF 1848 IN AUSTRIA

Although one of the great powers of Europe, Austria also succumbed to the spreading wave of revolutionary activity on the continent. One of Austria's great weaknesses was that it lacked cultural unity within its borders. It was a mixture of peoples, among them German, Czech, Magyar, Slovak, Polish, Croatian, and Italian. Instead of a government in which each group of people had a certain amount of self-government and cultural expression, the Austrian government remained predominantly German.

News of the French revolution of 1848 touched off an uprising in Vienna. The rebels demanded a liberal constitution and the abolition of feudalism. They also demanded the dismissal of Metternich. To everyone's surprise, the Austrian emperor, Ferdinand I, gave in. Metternich fled to England, the emperor moved to Innsbruck, and the citizens of Vienna wrote a constitution.

From Vienna, the revolution spread to other parts of the Hapsburg Empire. The Magyars in Hungary broke away from Austria and set up a liberal government, while the Czechs in Bohemia called for the unity of Slavic peoples against the Germans.

As in Italy, however, these revolts were soon suppressed. The Austrian government reestablished control over Bohemia and drove the liberals out of Vienna. The revolt in Hungary was then suppressed, when a Russian army joined forces with Austrian troops.

EFFECTS OF THE REVOLUTIONS OF 1848

Although most failed to achieve their goals, the revolutions of 1848 had important results in both eastern and western Europe. In order to defuse further revolutions, aristocratic leaders of Europe were forced to listen more often to the demands of middle-class liberals, the working class, and peasants.

In eastern Europe in particular, the revolutions turned many liberals and nationalists against each other. Nationalist sentiment overcame liberal demands for reform, often pitting middle-class urban liberals against nationalists from all classes.

In some parts of eastern Europe, nationalists themselves were divided. Because eastern Europeans were members of many different ethnic groups and had no history of unified government, nationalism had different meanings for different people. Arguments flared between ethnic groups. If one group achieved independence, members of another would become its enemies because they felt slighted.

As a result of these divisions among the opposition, the aristocracy was able to maintain a hold on political power across most of eastern Europe. Nationalist sentiment, however, remained high throughout the remainder of the nineteenth century, supporting continuing movements for national unification and national independence.

In France, the revolution of 1848 was somewhat more successful, in part because nationalism did not divide liberal opposition. Conflict between liberals and socialists, however, created a different kind of division.

Middle-class republicans had gained power in France, establishing the Second Republic. Although this republic was not to last long, its creation caused a permanent change in French politics. No longer could French rulers ignore middle-class interests. At the same time, the working class had learned to distrust the middle class, eliminating the possibility of another alliance against the aristocracy. As a result, great conflicts would continue among the aristocracy, the middle class, and the working class. With one exception, however, no outright revolutions would occur.

SECTION REVIEW

1. What policies of Charles X led to the 1830 uprising in France?

2. What groups opposed Louis Philippe in the revolution of 1848? How did they differ?

3. What caused Metternich to flee Austria in 1848?

4. Compare the revolutions of 1848 in Austria and Italy with that in France.

Evaluation. Did liberals, socialists, and nationalists help or hinder each other in their efforts to overthrow existing aristocratic governments in 1848? Explain your answer, and use evidence and examples from the chapter to support your claim.

23-3
REFORM IN SOCIETY

READ TO FIND OUT

—what the terms *solidarity*, *suffrage*, *minimum wage*, and *temperance* mean.
—how the middle class continued to grow and change.
—what values tied middle-class people together.
—how working-class demands were expressed through labor unions and socialist parties.
—what kinds of reform occurred in Great Britain and the United States.

While the increasing social conflict of the Industrial Age caused a wave of revolutions on the European continent, social change was being brought about with less upheaval in Great Britain and the United States. In these rapidly industrializing countries where political revolutions had already occurred, the middle class gained power with less conflict than on the European continent. In part, this lower level of conflict resulted from a stronger democratic tradition in Great Britain and the United States.

By the mid-nineteenth century, however, vast changes had occurred in the size, membership, values, and demands of both the middle and working classes in these industrialized nations. As elements of the middle class became very powerful, social conflict did not disappear but instead shifted its focus. Rather than arising from a middle-class challenge to aristocratic rule, social conflict in Great Britain and the

United States resulted more from the working class's growing demands for reform.

Although elements of the working class attempted to bring about revolutionary change in these countries, the middle class was able to curb working-class unrest by extending voting rights and raising workers' wages. Through such liberal reforms, Great Britain and the United States avoided revolution entirely and created a fertile environment for further industrial growth.

After 1850, other European nations such as France, recovering from revolutionary upheaval, began to follow the pattern established in the United States and Great Britain. Pressure from the middle and working classes throughout Europe began to result in reform and permanent limitations on aristocratic power.

A NEW MIDDLE CLASS

In Great Britain and the United States, and to a lesser extent in other countries, the middle class grew so large and strong during the nineteenth century that its role in society changed. While some members of the middle class became powerful as individuals, the class as a whole expanded rapidly to include a large segment of society in the industrialized countries. This expansion was a key element in the spread of reform and gradual social change.

With technological improvements in photography, family portraits became fashionable. A 1910 photograph depicts a middle-class family whose finery reflects their prosperity.

The most important change in the middle class was the growth of a new lower middle class, composed of people often called "white-collar" workers. White-collar workers—such as teachers, secretaries, salespeople, and telephone operators—served the new bureaucracies of the corporations and the state. In Great Britain, this group increased from 7 percent of the population in 1850 to more than 20 percent in 1900.

At the same time, the ranks of the professional middle class were growing. These people were mostly doctors, lawyers, accountants, and managers of corporations. They enjoyed greater wealth and higher social status than white-collar workers. Together, professionals and the lower middle class made up the segment of society commonly referred to as "middle class" today.

While the middle class expanded to include these new groups, many members of the original middle class of Renaissance merchants and business owners had grown so wealthy and powerful that they were no longer really "middle" class. In Great Britain, these people were the new factory owners and bankers. In many ways, they were beginning to have as much power in society as the aristocracy. In the United States, where no real aristocracy had existed, this small segment of the middle class consisted of leaders in government, industry, and commerce. By the end of the nineteenth century, the middle class had become the dominant class in many Western societies.

THE TRIUMPH OF MIDDLE-CLASS VALUES

As its composition changed, the middle class became a very diverse assortment of people with different levels of power and wealth. What tied the class together, however, was a common set of values. Middle-class values reflected the major ideas of liberalism: strong beliefs in individual freedom, personal achievement, and societal progress. As the middle class grew in numbers and power, these values were embraced by larger segments of society.

Even though most white-collar workers had jobs that were just as routine and low-paying as those of industrial workers, they adopted the middle-class values of their employers, the leaders of industry. These workers believed they would share in the growing prosperity created by industrialization. They supported the system that would give them the opportunity to rise in social status and gain more wealth.

As a whole, the new middle class embraced the idealism of the Enlightenment. Many middle-class people believed in fairness, justice, and equality of opportunity for all people. Some were ready to accept the idea that women and blacks deserved the vote, and that the suffering of poor people should be eased. Thus, the triumph of middle-class values became a major force behind the movement for democratic and social reform in the industrialized countries.

THE STRUGGLE OF THE WORKING CLASS

Although growing numbers of people acquired middle-class values, social conflict did not end in the industrialized countries. The aristocracy still clung to power in Great Britain—despite middle-class advances—resulting in continued political clashes. The most important source of social conflict, however, became the struggle between the working class and the middle-class owners of industry.

The growth of the urban working class, spawned by industrialization, was most dramatic in the United States and Great Britain. This class, composed of many former peasants and farmers, owned nothing that could be used to produce food, clothing, or manufactured goods. Members of the working class lacked the land, tools, and access to natural resources that many middle-class people had. To make a living, these workers had to work for wages in factories and workshops.

Like the working-class people who helped cause revolution in France and other European countries, the workers of Great Britain and the United States had reason to want drastic, even revolutionary, changes in the social and political structures. Often the workers lived in miserable conditions in the midst of plenty. Many had learned of Marx's theory that the working class would soon overthrow the capitalist owners and their supporters. As a result, growing numbers joined socialist political parties.

Yet, most workers in Great Britain and the United States did not rebel as workers had in France. Instead, British and American workers generally chose to fight for realistic goals that could be achieved without drastic change in government.

This decision to work for change "within the system" had two major causes. First, many workers felt that the only realistic goals to fight for were higher wages and shorter hours. Their status as wage workers seemed to be fixed, while the conditions and rewards of work, namely wages and hours, seemed negotiable.

Second, democracy in the United States and the parliamentary tradition in Great Britain gave workers confidence that their demands would be heard. There was no monarch—as in France—who flatly refused to reform the government.

THE GROWTH OF LABOR UNIONS

Workers' demands for reform found expression in the rise of labor unions. Labor unions brought together relatively powerless individuals into groups with the strength of numbers. Union members called the unity of purpose they had as a group *solidarity*. Although unions often fought bloody battles with employers and governments, they demanded reform more than revolutionary changes.

In the United States and Great Britain, the most intense union struggles occurred between 1880 and 1914, as workers called strikes against railroads, steel plants, and coal mines. In a strike, workers joined together in refusing to work, thereby shutting down factories and mines in an effort to force employers to meet their demands. Many strikes erupted into violent confrontations. In some cases, strikers were killed by police. Many union leaders were arrested, and a few were even executed under false charges.

Despite these clashes, worker protest focused mostly on making gains within the industrial system, rather than on challenging the foundations of industrial society. The demands for higher wages and shorter hours were nearly always the major issues in strikes in the industrialized nations after 1880.

THE SOCIALIST CHALLENGE

As unions grew in power during the last decades of the 1800s, so too did the new political force of socialism. While unions focused mostly on gaining higher wages and shorter hours, socialist political parties fought for greater political representation for the working class.

German workers storm a factory owner's home with cobblestones. The engraving by Käthe Kollwitz, who was inspired by a labor revolt, is from the series *Weavers' Rebellion*, 1893–1898.

Based on the ideas of Karl Marx and the utopian socialists, the socialist political platform called for revolution. Socialists believed that capitalism caused greater inequality in society by making some people very rich and others very poor. Their everyday experience as powerless workers confirmed this belief. The leaders of socialist parties hoped to gain enough political power to turn over the factories to the workers, so that workers could benefit from the wealth they created through their work.

During the 1860s and 1870s, socialist parties grew rapidly not just in the United States and Great Britain, but in most European countries. By 1914, the socialists had organized the largest political parties in Germany and Austria, winning millions of votes in each election. Socialist parties in other countries, including the United States, were also winning growing support.

Increasing electoral success helped move socialists away from demanding revolution, especially in the United States and Great Britain, where social change seemed possible without revolution. By 1900, many socialists were urging cooperation with moderate reforms. They also began to realize the necessity of working with liberals and labor unions to defend parliaments and worker rights. Although socialists, like unions, presented a serious challenge to established governments in many industrialized countries, they did not succeed in creating revolutionary change.

REFORM IN GREAT BRITAIN

Although the parliamentary tradition in Great Britain had limited the power of the monarch, members of the aristocracy controlled Parliament in the early 1800s. Throughout the century, British middle- and working-class people fought for representation and social reform within the parliamentary system. Although classes remained unequal in power, Britain had become a relatively democratic nation-state by 1914, with liberal ideas firmly established.

Electoral reform. In the early 1800s, only 6 percent of British men—mostly aristocratic landowners—could vote. Most middle class men, all working class men, and women of all social classes lacked political representation, as well as many of the basic rights that are taken for granted today.

In response to widespread pressure, however, Parliament passed the Reform Bill of 1832, which gave *suffrage*, or the right to vote, to all men who owned a certain amount of property. Election districts were also changed, giving more representation to the heavily populated urban centers. The number of men who could vote increased to about 20 percent. The Reform Bill of 1832 set an important precedent in Britain—that social change could be achieved through legislative action, without revolutionary violence.

Reformers pressed for more change. In 1838, a group called the Chartists circulated a document called the "People's Charter," which demanded a secret ballot and universal manhood suffrage, or the right to vote for all men. Although the Charter, which was signed by millions, produced no immediate results, most of its demands later became law. The Reform Bill of 1867 gave the vote to the urban working class, and the secret ballot became law in 1872. By 1885, when rural workers received the vote, most adult males in Britain could vote. Women, however, did not win the right to vote until 1918.

These electoral reforms were primarily responsible for an important shift that occurred in the distribution of political power among the British social classes. As the middle class received the right to vote, urban businesspeople grew more powerful than the rural landed aristocracy.

Political parties. As electoral reforms gave the middle class greater representation, political parties in Britain changed. The old Tory and Whig parties, both controlled by the aristocracy in the early 1800s, became the modern Liberal and Conservative parties by the mid-1800s. Although the Liberals were backed mostly by the middle class, and the Conservatives by the aristocracy, both parties tried to attract votes from the working class and the middle class.

Two men dominated British politics in the late 1800s: Benjamin Disraeli, a Conservative, and William Gladstone, a Liberal. Each served at least two terms as prime minister, the most powerful post in British government. Because both sought working-class votes, they both supported reform. Their major differences lay in how to achieve it. Disraeli wanted to preserve the aristocratic tradition and promote slow change, while Gladstone wanted more rapid and sweeping changes.

Social reform. British citizens gained additional freedoms through social reform. In the 1820s, the government lifted restrictions on the political activity of Catholics and non-Anglican Protestants. Parliament reformed the criminal code and reduced penalties for many crimes. It banned slavery in 1833. In 1909, Parliament passed a bill giving old-age pensions, or regular payments of money, to British subjects, and in 1912 established a *minimum wage*, or the lowest amount that a worker could be paid. These social reforms were accompanied by extensive industrial reforms that limited the length of the workweek and promoted safer working conditions in factories.

In the late 1800s and early 1900s, many women in Britain pressed for voting rights. The women here are being arrested for their suffrage demonstration at Buckingham Palace in 1914.

George Washington Carver is shown supervising students in the laboratory at Tuskegee Institute. Tuskegee had been founded in 1880 by Booker T. Washington, a former slave, to provide blacks with an opportunity to develop the industrial skills he believed necessary for economic advancement.

REFORM IN THE UNITED STATES

Efforts in the United States to extend the vote and introduce social reforms paralleled those of Great Britain. A spirit of reform spread through the nation between 1820 and 1850. The peaceful social change and expanding democracy of this period contrasted with the revolutionary upheaval occurring at the same time on the European continent.

One of the most important changes in the United States during these three decades was the extension of suffrage to greater numbers of people. By 1850, most states had dropped property ownership as a requirement for voting. Other states had acquired statehood with constitutions providing for white male suffrage.

Andrew Jackson, president from 1829 to 1837, encouraged such democratic reforms, becoming the hero of the people. Historians often recognize Jackson's role in reform by referring to this period as the Jacksonian Era.

Social reforms accompanied the expansion of suffrage. Many social reformers attacked drunkenness, calling for *temperance*, or moderation. Other people joined movements to improve public education, pushing for the establishment of free public schooling in all states.

By the 1840s, the major battles for reform focused on freedom for blacks and suffrage for women. The issue of slavery in the United States divided the North and South, resulting in the Civil War, which began in 1861. In 1865, Congress passed the Thirteenth Amendment to the Constitution, abolishing slavery. The Fifteenth Amendment, passed in 1870, said no citizen could be denied the right to vote on the basis of race or national origin.

The struggle to gain voting rights for women took longer. In the mid-1800s, women formed a movement for women's rights. They held their first conference in 1848 at Seneca Falls, New York. Led by Susan B. Anthony, Lucretia Mott, and Elizabeth Cady Stanton, middle-class women pushed for women's suffrage throughout the late 1800s. Finally, in 1920, the Nineteenth Amendment gave women the right to vote.

The Progressive Era. Large gains had been made during the 1800s in extending rights to all Americans and improving their quality of life. Another great age of reform in the United States began in 1900. This period of reform, which lasted until 1914, is called the Progressive Era.

Progressives, as the liberal reformers during this time were called, had three major aims: to help the poor, to curb what they saw as the greed of business owners, and to end widespread corruption in government. Writers and journalists called "muckrakers" helped gain support for the progressive cause by exposing poor working conditions, life in slums, bribery of government officials, and other evils.

By the end of the Progressive Era, many states and cities had passed an array of reforms. Some measures protected child workers; others saw that retired and injured workers would receive support. Voting was changed through the institution of secret ballots, and voters in many cities gained the right to recall, or remove from office, elected officials not performing their job adequately. In general, the Progressive Era resulted in people gaining greater control over government, and government gaining more control over business.

LIMITED REFORM IN FRANCE

While Great Britain and the United States moved toward greater democracy and equality, social change in France came with continued upheaval. The aristocracy remained powerful in France, while peasants still made up a large part of the population. Because of the conflict between these old forces and the new middle and working classes, continued political turmoil occurred in France after 1848, postponing lasting reform until the very late 1800s.

Louis Napoleon. The Second Republic, established as a result of the revolution of 1848, held elections for president in December of that year.

SPOTLIGHT: IDEAS AND DEVELOPMENTS

REUTERS NEWS SERVICE

When England's long-time enemy Napoleon died in 1821, almost two months passed before the news reached London. The information traveled slowly by horseback and carriage on land and by sailing ships at sea.

The communication of news remained slow until a man named Paul Julius Reuter (ROY-ter) created a way to send news between European capitals within hours of its occurrence. The new international news service, established in 1858, was called Reuters after its creator. Reuters revolutionized international politics, diplomacy, and war by reducing the length of time it took leaders and citizens to hear of such crucial events as invasions and assassinations.

Born in Germany in 1816, Reuter worked for a time as a reporter in France and in Germany. Then when Germany and France each built their first telegraph lines in the late 1840s, Reuter saw an opportunity to try something no one else had done. He arranged to send daily reports between Paris and Berlin on important financial matters such as the price of stocks. Fortunes could be won or lost depending on his reports.

Initially, Reuter had a problem. There was a 100-mile (160-kilometer) gap in the telegraph line. Reuter arranged for carrier pigeons to fly his messages across the gap until the lines were connected. A message was telegraphed from Paris to Brussels, Belgium. Then it was flown in two hours to Aachen, Germany, by pigeon.

From Aachen, it went again by telegraph to Berlin.

Reuter moved his financial reporting service from Berlin to London in 1850. In 1858, he began supplying political news to newspapers, thus creating the first real news service.

Reuter's news service made a dramatic impact on February 7, 1859, when the service telegraphed a major speech given in Paris by Emperor Napoleon III. In his speech Napoleon threatened to go to war with Austria, a possible event about which all of Europe would want to be informed.

To prepare for the transmission, a Reuters' reporter was given an advance copy of the speech. However, the news service agreed not to open the envelope until the emperor began to speak. Then the speech could be telegraphed. As a result, the people of London read the emperor's remarks in special afternoon editions of their papers later that same day.

Newspapers were sprouting up all over Europe. These papers relied on Reuters' service. In the past, the cost of gathering news from scattered, distant places made newspapers a luxury few could afford. Reuters, however, provided up-to-date news at low cost to newspapers, who passed on their savings to an expanding readership. Due in part to Paul Reuter, people began to receive more and more information about the world around them.

Louis Napoleon Bonaparte, nephew of Napoleon Bonaparte, was elected by a great majority of the voters, although most French people knew very little about him. However, they remembered the first Napoleon, who had made France the leading nation in Europe and had given the peasants land of their own. The people of France hoped the nephew would be as great as the uncle.

Louis Napoleon soon made himself popular with nearly every group in French society. Taking advantage of this popularity, he claimed greater powers, becoming a dictator in 1851. The next year he named himself Napoleon III, Emperor of the French, turning the Second French Republic into the Second Empire.

During the next two decades, Napoleon III ruled with absolute power, allowing no political opposition and establishing total control over the press. Despite such repressive policies, he became very popular with the middle class, having given them a welcome opportunity to make money.

Napoleon III also pursued an aggressive foreign policy, extending French colonial holdings and sending troops into Mexico. In 1870, however, after a defeat in a war with Prussia, Napoleon's government collapsed, and republicans declared the Third Republic.

The Paris Commune. With the establishment of the Third Republic, a National Assembly was elected. Many supporters of monarchy won seats, which angered both republicans and workers. In 1871, workers in Paris revolted and established a government called the Paris Commune. They called for reforms such as higher wages, lower prices, and shorter working hours.

When royalist forces attacked the supporters of the Commune, called Communards, a civil war erupted. Once again barricades were set up in the streets of Paris. During a week of fierce fighting, about 20,000 people were killed and the Communards were defeated. The conflict left the republicans and royalists even more bitterly divided than before.

The Third Republic survived this early crisis, however, and despite continued political clashes and scandals, gradually made some reforms. Restrictions on the press, labor unions, and public meetings were lifted, and the working day was reduced to 12 hours.

SECTION REVIEW

1. Define *solidarity*, *suffrage*, *minimum wage* and *temperance*.

2. Describe the composition of the middle class in the industrialized nations of the late nineteenth century.

3. What beliefs did most middle-class people share?

4. What kind of social change did labor unions generally demand?

5. Describe the most important reforms made in the United States between 1865 and 1914.

Analysis. Compare reform in the United States and Great Britain.

HISTORY IN FOCUS

The revolutions that swept the European continent in mid-century and the reform movement in Great Britain and the United States were the results of a profound change in Western society—a shifting of class relationships favoring the new middle class. As industrialization advanced, the middle class led in the destruction of the Old Regime, creating in the process new social conflicts.

At different times in different countries, the aristocracy lost much of its power, and the peasantry disappeared. In their place appeared an angry working class, a large lower middle class, and a new, powerful class of business owners, bankers, and politicians.

Unlike feudal society, no dramatic division now separated rich and poor, powerful and powerless. The middle class lay between the extremes, quieting conflict and making inequality less obvious. Greater democracy and freedom became possible because the guarantee of a political voice to everyone channeled discontent into reform instead of revolution.

The dominant values of society became those of the middle class. The liberal ideas and politics of the middle class reduced social conflict and encouraged industrial development. By 1914 in the industrialized countries, the values of the aristocracy had weakened and those of the peasantry had mostly died out. Through labor unions and socialist parties, the working class rose up to challenge the middle class but failed to stop its triumph.

SUMMARY

- After Napoleon's defeat in 1815, the aristocracy of Europe regained power for a time. Aristocrats sought to strengthen European monarchies and repress liberal ideas.

- Aristocratic power was challenged by the rising middle class and the ideas of liberalism and nationalism. Various uprisings took place in the early 1800s, including a successful nationalist revolt in Greece.

- Revolts broke out again in several European countries in 1830 and 1848. Although the French revolt of 1848 was the only one to establish a republic, these revolts did strengthen the position of the middle class.

- Great Britain and the United States were also going through a period of change and rising middle-class power. Liberal values of equality and progress fueled a number of political and social reforms.

- The working class gained strength in Britain and the United States, organizing through unions and socialist parties. Class tensions increased but were generally channeled into peaceful reform. In France social change continued to be marked by upheaval.

VOCABULARY REVIEW

Match each numbered vocabulary term with the lettered word or phrase most closely related to it. Then explain how the items in each pair are related.

1. conservatism   **(a)** voting
2. solidarity   **(b)** pay scale
3. suffrage   **(c)** aristocracy
4. minimum wage   **(d)** labor unions
5. temperance   **(e)** moderation

CHAPTER REVIEW

1. (a) What were the Congress of Vienna and the Concert of Europe? How were they related to each other? **(b)** How did the Congress of Vienna and the Concert of Europe represent both forward-thinking policies and a return to the past?

2. (a) Summarize the ideas of Metternich. **(b)** Who were Disraeli and Gladstone, and how did they differ from Metternich?

3. (a) Describe nineteenth-century liberalism. **(b)** Who supported liberalism and who opposed it? Explain why.

4. (a) What did nationalists struggle for in the nineteenth century? **(b)** What early successful revolt was inspired by nationalism? How was it different from other revolts of the time?

5. (a) Compare the revolts of the 1830s in France and Belgium. **(b)** Why did tensions remain after the French revolt? What would happen as a result?

6. (a) Describe the government established right after the revolution of 1848 in France. **(b)** What was the long-term effect of the revolt?

7. (a) How were the causes of the 1848 revolutions different in France and eastern Europe? **(b)** Compare the results of the revolutions of 1848 in eastern Europe and France.

8. (a) How did the nature of class conflict in Great Britain and the United States differ from that of Europe, and why? **(b)** How was worker unrest curbed in Britain and the United States?

9. (a) How did the middle class evolve in Britain and the United States during the nineteenth century? **(b)** How did the working class in these countries change? Why was it generally less radical than the working class on the European continent?

10. (a) What were the goals of the socialists? **(b)** How were progressives different from socialists? **(c)** How and why did socialists often join with progressives in the United States?

THINKING CRITICALLY: ACTIVITIES

1. Imagine that you are a member of the emerging French *bourgeoisie*, or middle class, in 1830. Write a short speech in which you argue that the French should overthrow Charles X and establish a new government.

2. Imagine that you are Metternich in 1848 and that you have just been dismissed from your job by Ferdinand I. Write a letter in reply, responding to the emperor's action and predicting the consequences. You may want to refer to other events in Europe at the time.

3. With a partner, plan a debate concerning worker rights in the United States in the late 1800s. One of you should take the role of a liberal reformer, the other of a socialist. In front of the class, debate the question of how best to improve conditions for American workers.

APPLYING SOCIAL STUDIES SKILLS

Sequencing events. Much of the organization of Chapter 23 is based on sequence, the order in which the events happened in time. However, the chapter is also organized according to major themes, particularly the themes of revolution and reform. In order to highlight these themes and compare the developments in various countries, the author does not place all the information on France in one section, all the information on Austria in another section, and so on. Therefore, you might have difficulty keeping track of the order of events in a particular country. One way to keep track of the sequence of events in a country is to make a timeline just for that country.

Make a timeline for France covering the 60 years from 1815 to 1875. Review the chapter to determine the year in which each event listed below occurred. Then place these events on your timeline in the correct sequence.

> Napoleon is defeated at Waterloo
> Workers form the Paris Commune
> Third Republic is formed
> Charles X becomes king
> Second Republic is formed
> Louis Philippe becomes king
> Louis Napoleon Bonaparte is elected president of France
> Louis Napoleon Bonaparte makes himself dictator
> Louis XVIII becomes king
> July Revolution
> Louis Napoleon Bonaparte becomes emperor of Second Empire
> Communards are defeated in civil war

APPLYING THINKING SKILLS

Determining the strength of an argument. The excerpt below is from a London newspaper published in 1851. Examine the account to determine how strong an argument its author makes. Then answer the questions that follow.

> Liberal lawyers, German literature, and German philosophy were the three main forces that caused the German middle class to unite against the absolute monarchy. The political movement of the middle class in Germany may be dated from 1840. However, this movement had been preceded by the influence of these three forces. As a result, in the 1830s the middle class of Germany was ripening into a state which would no longer allow it to continue apathetic and passive under the pressure of a half-feudal, half-bureaucratic government.
>
> The liberal lawyers were able to voice their ideas in the legislatures of the German states. These lawyers included the Rottecks, the Welckers, the Roemers, and other "popular men." By their speeches and writings, they made the language of Constitutionalism familiar to Germans.
>
> Meanwhile, a crude Constitutionalism was preached by almost all writers of the time. Poetry, novels, reviews, the drama, every literary production opposed absolute monarchy. They mixed French Socialism with German philosophy to promote liberal ideas of government.
>
> The influence of German philosophy was also evident, especially in Hegel's *Philosophy of Law*, which called Constitutional Monarchy the most perfect government. Followers of Hegel brought forward bold new political principles.
>
> Largely as a result of these three factors, the middle-class manufacturers and merchants gradually united against the absolute monarchy. The movement toward the 1848 revolution had begun.

Adapted from *Germany: Revolution and Counter-Revolution*, by Friedrich Engels (1851).

1. What is one procedure for determining the strength of an argument?

2. What is the claim in the above account?

3. What types of reasons are used in the account? For each type of reason, give a specific example from the account.

4. State and explain your judgment about the strength of the author's argument.

UNIT REVIEW

1. (a) Compare the three kinds of revolutions discussed in this unit. **(b)** How were these revolutions interrelated? **(c)** What elements of society resisted each kind of revolution?

2. (a) Which had a more direct impact on people at the time: the Scientific Revolution or the Industrial Revolution? Explain. **(b)** Discuss the relationship between the Scientific Revolution and the Enlightenment. **(c)** Compare the immediate impacts of the Enlightenment and the Industrial Revolution on women.

3. (a) What ideas did most Enlightenment thinkers share? **(b)** How did Enlightenment ideas lead to both liberalism and socialism?

4. (a) How did the French Revolution both reflect and go beyond the ideas of the Enlightenment? **(b)** Compare the French Revolution with subsequent European revolts of the 1800s.

5. (a) Discuss the Industrial Revolution's effect on political ideas and developments. How did industrialization contribute to political upheaval? **(b)** How did political revolutions both aid and hinder industrialization?

6. (a) Compare the views of Locke, Metternich, and Marx on the role of government. **(b)** Do you think Rousseau and Spencer would have agreed on social reform? Why or why not?

7. (a) What changes occurred in the class structure of Western societies from 1500 to 1900? **(b)** How did the values and influence of the middle class evolve? **(c)** What social and political changes occurred in the working class?

8. (a) Trace trends in economic philosophy from 1600 to 1900. **(b)** Was the notion of free enterprise crucial to the rise of capitalism? Explain. **(c)** How did mercantilism and laissez-faire policies contribute to industrialization?

9. (a) How did the scientists of the 1800s and early 1900s build on discoveries made during the Scientific Revolution? **(b)** How did the problems encountered by these later scientists compare with those of earlier scientists?

10. (a) Describe the evolution of artistic styles in the 1700s and 1800s. **(b)** How did art both reflect and contribute to social change?

RELATING PAST TO PRESENT

1. In the 1700s, physiocrats challenged the policy of mercantilism. Today a similar debate exists between those who support free market policies and those in favor of more government control of the economy. Find out more about this debate from newspapers and magazines, and then explain how the modern debate reflects the same issues that divided physiocrats and mercantilists.

2. The American and French revolutions unleashed forces of political and social change that still influence the world today. Investigate one of the following modern revolutions and consider how it reflects, and differs from, the French and American revolutions: **(a)** the Sandinista revolution in Nicaragua, **(b)** the revolution in Angola, and **(c)** the independence struggle in Zimbabwe.

PROJECTS AND ACTIVITIES

1. Imagine that you are preparing a museum exhibit to portray events in the Western world from 1780 to 1880. Select one 10-year period, and list 10 items that you would display to represent the decade you have chosen. Explain the significance of each item.

2. Divide into four groups, with each group choosing one of the following subjects: Scientific Revolution, Enlightenment, democratic revolutions, Industrial Revolution. One person in your group should prepare an oral report giving an overview of the subject, while the other students prepare reports on specific topics within the subject area. These reports might focus on an important individual, event, or issue. Present your reports as a group to the class, with the overview first.

3. Imagine that you are a member of the middle class in the 1700s. Write a paragraph describing the social, economic, and political ideas of the time that would have appealed most to you and explain why. Then imagine you are a member of the industrial working class of the 1800s and write a paragraph on the same ideas as the first. Compare the two positions and explain why they differ.

ANALYZING PRIMARY SOURCES

Refer to "Mary Paul: Letters from the Factory" on page 484 to answer the following questions.

1. What is revealed about factory working conditions in the first letter? In the second letter?

2. From these letters, one can infer that Mary Paul is probably **(a)** a young unmarried woman, **(b)** a married woman who has children, **(c)** a married woman who does not have children, **(d)** an elderly unmarried woman.

3. Where is the factory in which Mary Paul works located? Support your answer with evidence from the letters.

4. What positive comments does Mary make about her daily life?

5. How do the letters indicate that Mary Paul is not satisfied with her wages?

6. What is the company's explanation for reducing the wages? Why would the equipment repairs lead Mary to reject this explanation?

7. Based on the third letter, why do you think most workers tolerated reduced wages?

GEOGRAPHY REVIEW

Movement. The heavy lines on the map of the United States indicate the distance that a New Yorker could reasonably expect to travel in one week in 1800, 1830, and 1860. Boundary lines show present-day states. Use the map to answer the following questions.

1. Which of the following present-day states could a New Yorker reach in a week in 1800? 1830? 1860? Vermont, Texas, Florida, Oklahoma, Minnesota, Pennsylvania, Kentucky, Maine, Ohio

2. In 1800, New Yorkers traveled by foot or horse on a few poor roads, or they traveled by ship along the Atlantic Coast. Which mode of travel allowed them to travel farthest in a week?

3. By 1830 roads had improved, canals were being built, and steamboats were revolutionizing river transportation. Using the map scale, estimate the maximum distance a New Yorker could travel in a week that year.

4. By what year could a New Yorker travel beyond the Mississippi in less than a week? What form of transportation made this possible?

5. In one complete sentence, sum up what the map shows about the effect of improved transport networks.

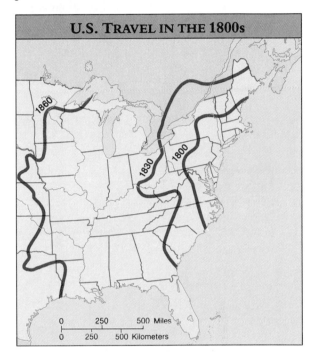

U.S. TRAVEL IN THE 1800s

SUGGESTED READINGS

Alic, Margaret. *Hypatia's Heritage*. Boston: Beacon Press, 1986. Women in science from antiquity through the nineteenth century.

Blunden, Maria and Godfrey. *Impressionists and Impressionism*. New York: Rizzoli, 1980. A lively, illustrated look at impressionist art.

Clark, Ronald W. *The Survival of Charles Darwin*. New York: Random House, 1984. The story of Charles Darwin and his theory of evolution.

Dickens, Charles. *A Tale of Two Cities*. New York: New American Library, 1980. A classic novel set during the French Revolution.

Voltaire. *Candide*, trans. Lowell Blair. New York: Bantam, 1981. The misadventures of Candide, satirizing the creed: "All is for the best in this best of all possible worlds."

THE AGE OF IMPERIALISM

1800-1914

*We want territory
even if it be inhabited
by foreign peoples,
so that we may shape their
future in accordance
with our needs.*

*—Ernst Hasse,
German expansionist, 1894*

Nagasaki Harbor. Artist unknown, Japan, 1800s.

GLOBAL TIMELINE

- ■ EUROPE
- ■ EUROPEAN EMPIRES
- ■ RUSSIA
- ■ OTTOMAN EMPIRE
- ■ CHINA AND JAPAN
- ■ THE AMERICAS

	POLITICAL	TECHNOLOGICAL	SOCIAL
1800			
	Louisiana Purchase — Early colonization of Australia	Volta's electric cell — First submarine; First canning factory	First accurate censuses in Europe and U.S.
1815	Mexican war of independence begins		
	Mexico gains independence	First iron steamship — Friction matches invented	Webster's dictionary — East India Company loses monopoly on trade with China
1830			
	Zollverein formed: economic pact between German states — First Opium War in China	Goodyear vulcanizes rubber — Colt's revolver	Braille developed — First kindergarten
1845			
	Crimean War; Sepoy Rebellion in India — Civil War in the U.S.	Elevator invented — Singer's sewing machine	London's Great Exhibition of 1851 — Potato famine in Ireland
1860			
	Germany unified; Italy unified — Tokugawa shogunate falls	Suez Canal completed — Internal combustion engine	Standard Oil Company founded — Rapid industrialization begins in Japan
1875			
	Triple Alliance formed — New Japanese constitution	First skyscrapers; Electric motor — Steam turbine engine	Health insurance introduced in Germany
1890			
	Spanish-American War — Growth of Indian nationalism	First automobiles and movies; Trenches first used in warfare — Diesel engine	First modern Olympic Games — First Nobel prizes
1905			
	Triple Entente formed — Republic of China established	Panama Canal completed — First plastics	Workdays in France limited to ten hours — First radio program
1920			

CHAPTER TWENTY-FOUR

IMPERIALISM AND EUROPEAN RIVALRY

1800–1914

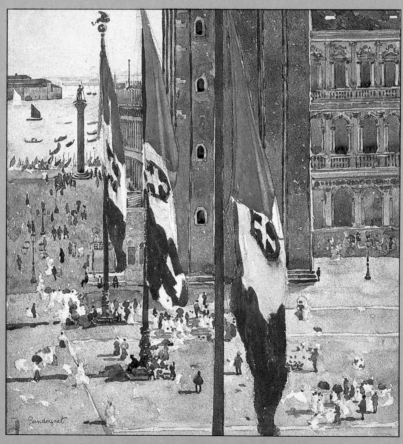

Piazza San Marco, Venice. Maurice Prendergast, 1898.

After the unsuccessful revolutions of 1848, Europe entered a period of intensified rivalry between nations. European leaders had largely cooperated with each other in stemming the liberal and nationalist challenges of the period between 1815 and 1848. However, they now began to find greater cause for competition and distrust. Social conflict and reform continued in Europe, but nations shifted their attention toward building national power. Meanwhile, Italy and Germany unified to become new European powers.

By 1880, economic and military competition between European powers began to spill over into the rest of the world. Great Britain, France, Italy, Germany, and Russia raced to build overseas empires, spreading conflict across a globe increasingly dominated by Europe.

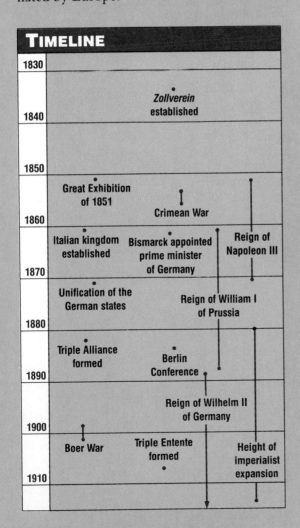

TIMELINE

1830	
1840	*Zollverein* established
1850	
1860	Great Exhibition of 1851 / Crimean War
1870	Italian kingdom established / Bismarck appointed prime minister of Germany / Reign of Napoleon III
1880	Unification of the German states / Reign of William I of Prussia
1890	Triple Alliance formed / Berlin Conference
1900	Reign of Wilhelm II of Germany
1910	Boer War / Triple Entente formed / Height of imperialist expansion

24-1
BEGINNINGS OF RIVALRY

READ TO FIND OUT

—why the British felt they were the center of the world during the Victorian Age.
—how the German states began to industrialize.
—which European powers fought in the Crimean War.

In 1850, European nations and states were in varying conditions and stages of development. Great Britain, the most industrialized country at the time, controlled an expanding overseas empire. Russia held vast territories in Asia. France was overcoming social upheaval and revolution, gaining strength under Napoleon III. Struggles for independence within its borders weakened the Austrian Empire, while the German and Italian states remained disunited.

Although European nations differed, common forces affected their development during the remainder of the century. Because European leaders saw the benefits brought by industrialization and colonial expansion, these became the goals that began to guide European growth and influence European politics. A new age was beginning, and every nation wanted its share of the benefits. A climate of competition developed that led to growing jealousy and distrust.

GREAT BRITAIN AS THE LEADER

By 1850, Great Britain was enjoying a great age of prosperity under the rule of Queen Victoria. Liberal reform had begun to quiet social conflict, and growing numbers of middle-class people began to enjoy the fruits of industrialization. This age, lasting until 1901, when Victoria died, has been called the Victorian Age.

Victorian Great Britain profited from its overseas empire. Goods flowed between Britain and its colonies, bringing wealth to merchants, while profits from investments in foreign lands filled English banks and the pockets of middle-

Queen Victoria, shown in this portrait (left) about 1850, ruled for 63 years. During this time, London became the center of international commerce. The rapid pace of London life is captured in this photograph (right) taken about 1900 of London Bridge and the financial district.

class entrepreneurs. With colonies and influence in Africa, Asia, the Middle East, and North America, Great Britain saw itself as the center of the world.

Nothing symbolized the central role of Great Britain as well as the Great Exhibition of 1851. Held in a huge glass and iron building called the Crystal Palace, the exhibition was the first world's fair. Exhibits from many of the world's countries filled the Crystal Palace, each demonstrating the fair's theme—progress.

To most of the exhibition's visitors, it seemed that Great Britain, the host, had achieved the most progress. Halls full of noisy, whirring British machines and such wonders as a huge steam engine amazed fairgoers. Compared with Britain's great industrial machines, the finely crafted items of India, Tunisia, and China seemed to be mere curiosities—exotic objects brought from the world's far corners. Londoners believed their country's machines heralded a new age in which Europe would lead the world into the future.

THE GROWTH OF GERMANY

Primarily agricultural in the early nineteenth century, the German states began to industrialize rapidly in the mid-1800s, trying to match Britain's prosperity. Their attempt to modernize, however, met with difficulties caused by their lack of political unity.

In 1834, an attempt to unify the economies of the German states had resulted in an economic union called the *Zollverein* (TSAWL-fer-ĭn), which helped create freer trade among the states. Industrial development was aided, too, by the rapid construction of railroads. By 1849, more than 3,000 miles (4,800 kilometers) of railroad had been laid in the German states.

The state of Prussia—having become a European power on its own in the eighteenth century—was the most powerful of the German states at this time. Many Germans began looking to Prussia for leadership in the process of political unification. At the same time, Austria opposed unification, fearing Prussia would dominate a unified Germany.

THE SECOND FRENCH EMPIRE

While the German states took their first steps toward unification, Louis Napoleon, elected president of France in 1848, quickly gained firm control of the country. In 1852, he named himself emperor Napoleon III, creating the second French Empire.

Under Napoleon III's rule, France, like Germany, began to promote industrial development in order to catch up with Britain. Jealous of Britain's overseas empire, Napoleon also sought to acquire more colonies and to restore France's position of power in Europe. These ambitions led France into international conflict.

THE GREAT EXHIBITION OF 1851

The streets of London were unusually busy the morning of May 1, 1851. On foot, by carriage, in crowded omnibuses, Londoners hurried to Hyde Park for the opening day of the first world's fair, the Great Exhibition of 1851. Soon, thousands filled the main hall of the glorious Crystal Palace, an imposing structure built of 30,000 panes of glass and 5,000 iron girders.

At noon, Queen Victoria arrived with a flourish of trumpets. The queen and her party traveled the length of the hall as a thousand-voice choir sang Handel's *Hallelujah Chorus*. Such a display was a fitting opening to a fair that would in six months attract more than six million visitors from all over the globe.

After watching the queen's entrance, opening-day visitors turned their attention to the exotic centerpieces that surrounded them. Ornamental carpets hung from the balconies, graceful palms decorated the display rooms, and a cut-glass fountain, three stories high, filled the hall with the sounds of waterfalls.

After visitors took in this astonishing splendor, they began to view the exhibits. These included some of the world's greatest treasures, its newest inventions, its finest manufactured products. There were fine cashmere shawls from India, laces from Belgium, beautifully made Spanish pistols, and a long birchbark Indian canoe from Canada—all items most people had never seen before, not even in pictures. The United States sent a statue that, to everyone's delight, could be spun around on its pedestal by turning a crank.

Although most of the world's countries had exhibits, half came from Britain and its empire. British industrial machines and products showed other nations how industrialized Britain had become. Inventions such as the high-speed printing press, tool-making devices, a knife with 80 blades, and a machine to shape railway wheels were all exhibited for visitors to inspect.

To most of its visitors, the Great Exhibition seemed to promise an age of progress. Transportation and communication were being revolutionized. Items once considered luxuries for the rich were being made for everyone. Soon, other nations would try to match Britain's industrial development, increasing economic growth around the world.

THE CRIMEAN WAR

Russia had ambitions similar to those of France. In 1853, Czar Nicholas I attempted to gain territory in the Balkans from the declining Ottoman Empire. The czar thus hoped to gain an outlet to the Mediterranean Sea. Fearing Russian expansion onto the Balkan Peninsula, Great Britain, France, and Austria joined the Ottomans in a war against the Russians in 1854. Fought primarily on the Crimean Peninsula in the Black Sea, this war was later called the Crimean War.

Bad planning and incompetent leadership on all sides characterized the war, leading to large numbers of casualties. In British field hospitals, a nurse named Florence Nightingale exposed the wretched and unsanitary conditions she found. As a result of her efforts to provide better medical care for wounded soldiers, she became renowned as the founder of modern nursing.

Overwhelmed by the western European powers, Russia admitted defeat in 1856. Under terms established at the peace conference, Russia lost its influence in the Balkans. Otherwise, few territorial changes resulted from the war.

SECTION REVIEW

1. Provide evidence supporting the claim of some British that Great Britain was the center of the world in 1851.

2. What role did the Zollverein play in the industrial growth of Germany?

3. Which powers fought against Russia in the Crimean War?

Analysis. How did the Great Exhibition of 1851 increase rivalry among European nations?

24-2
UNIFICATION OF GERMANY AND ITALY

READ TO FIND OUT

—what the terms *Realpolitik*, *reich*, and *guerrilla warfare* mean.
—why Bismarck provoked Austria into declaring war on Prussia.
—how Bismarck achieved the final unification of Germany.
—what was meant in Italy by *Risorgimento*.
—how Garibaldi helped complete the unification of Italy.

Strong leaders and patriots in the German and Italian states took advantage of growing nationalist feelings within their regions to make strides toward unification in the mid-1800s. As many people in these areas began to realize that national unity was the key to industrial development and imperial power, the forces of nationalism and liberalism combined. By 1871, both Germany and Italy had achieved unity. As new European powers, they sparked increasing competition for wealth and empire beyond Europe.

STEPS TOWARD UNIFICATION OF THE GERMAN STATES

Prussia grew in strength during the 1850s, taking a leading role among the 39 German states. King William I of Prussia, crowned in 1861, sought to further expand Prussian power by unifying the German states under his rule. To achieve this goal, he first built a stronger Prussian army.

Many Prussian liberals, however, opposed William's militarization, fearing that a strong army would be the first step toward a return to absolute rule, and that the cost of raising such an army would destroy the economy. Because of the liberals' political strength, William's ambitions were largely blocked until he chose a new prime minister in 1862.

The rise of Bismarck. William's choice for prime minister was Otto von Bismarck, a Prussian of the aristocratic landowning class called the *Junkers* (YOON-kerz). Bismarck became the major force behind German unification. Like William I, Bismarck desired German unification because it would bring power to Prussia, not because he believed in nationalism. A conservative, Bismarck opposed democratic rule because he had no faith in the ability of the people to govern themselves.

Bismarck's beliefs formed the basis of a political strategy called *Realpolitik* (ray-AHL-PO-lih-TEEK)—using whatever means are necessary to achieve practical goals. Bismarck believed that international politics in the age of growing competition between powers required strategies that were realistic, not idealistic. In a famous speech, he declared that "the great questions of the time are not to be solved by speeches . . . but by blood and iron."

Bismarck's first move as prime minister was to continue William's policy of building up Prussia's military might by enlarging and improving the army. Bismarck equipped Prussian forces with a new type of gun that could be loaded and fired very quickly. He also introduced steel cannons, a deadly addition to armaments. Under Bismarck's supervision, Prussia's coal and iron industries, which were vital in the production of weapons, grew rapidly. Soon railroads to move troops and equipment quickly stretched through Prussia and into other German states.

The unification of northern Germany. An obstacle in the way of a united Germany was Austria, the other major power among the 39 German states. Until now, Austria had succeeded in blocking all attempts at German unification. Austria, however, had lost both money and troops during the Crimean War between 1854 and 1856. Bismarck saw Austria's weakness and conceived a strategy to remove the state as an obstacle.

In 1864, Bismarck persuaded Austria to join Prussia in a war against Denmark in order to free the German-inhabited northern provinces of Schleswig and Holstein from Danish rule. After seizing the two provinces, Bismarck provoked Austria into declaring war on Prussia over the issue of which nation should annex Schleswig and Holstein. All the independent

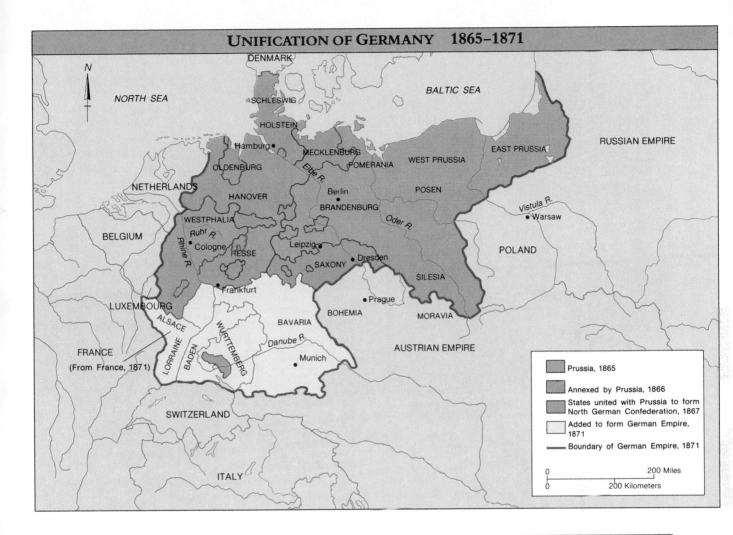

UNIFICATION OF GERMANY 1865–1871

N

NORTH SEA

DENMARK

BALTIC SEA

SCHLESWIG

HOLSTEIN

Hamburg

MECKLENBURG

OLDENBURG

POMERANIA

WEST PRUSSIA

EAST PRUSSIA

RUSSIAN EMPIRE

NETHERLANDS

HANOVER

Berlin

BRANDENBURG

POSEN

Elbe R.

Vistula R.

Warsaw

WESTPHALIA

Oder R.

BELGIUM

Ruhr R.

Rhine R.

Cologne

HESSE

Leipzig

POLAND

SAXONY

Dresden

SILESIA

Frankfurt

LUXEMBOURG

Prague

BOHEMIA

MORAVIA

ALSACE

BAVARIA

LORRAINE

WÜRTTEMBERG

Danube R.

AUSTRIAN EMPIRE

FRANCE
(From France, 1871)

BADEN

Munich

SWITZERLAND

ITALY

Legend:
- Prussia, 1865
- Annexed by Prussia, 1866
- States united with Prussia to form North German Confederation, 1867
- Added to form German Empire, 1871
- Boundary of German Empire, 1871

0 200 Miles
0 200 Kilometers

southern German states sided with Austria, partly because they were Catholic like Austria, whereas Prussia was Protestant. Napoleon III kept France neutral, believing the two German rivals would fatally weaken each other to France's benefit.

In only seven weeks, however, the Prussian army gained a resounding victory in what is called the Seven Weeks' War. Generously, Bismarck did not force Austria to give up any territory. He insisted, however, on establishing a new North German Confederation headed by Prussia. In 1866, Prussia annexed Schleswig and Holstein while several other, smaller northern German states joined with Prussia.

Through this acquisition of territory, Prussia became the largest German state. It was more powerful than all the other states put together and contained two-thirds of the German people.

THE FRANCO-PRUSSIAN WAR

The final step to German unification involved war with a foreign rival. In 1870, Bismarck provoked the French into declaring war against Prussia. He hoped the four southern German states remaining outside the North German Confederation would unite with Prussia in fighting France, a power these southern German states feared because they were close to the French border.

The superior Prussian troops moved quickly into France. They besieged Paris, captured Napoleon III, and forced France to surrender in 1871. Within a month, King William I of Prussia was crowned *Kaiser*, or emperor. In Germany, he was called Kaiser Wilhelm. Soon after, the southern German states, recognizing the strength of a unified Germany, joined in the new German Empire, or **reich** (RĪK). With the

During the Prussian siege of Paris, Parisians sent messages to the outside world via gas balloons. This photograph depicts a balloon ascent from Montmartre, the city's highest point.

addition of these remaining German states, Germany was finally unified politically.

The German Empire quickly became the most powerful nation on the European continent. William appointed Bismarck his chancellor. Bismarck, often called "the architect of German unification," continued his leadership role, promoting industrialization and military buildup.

Bismarck also made many liberal reforms in Germany. Despite his conservative views, he instituted a reform program that included accident, health, and old-age insurance for workers. In part, these reforms were designed to win worker support for the government and curb the power of the socialists. Whatever their reason, however, the reforms gave German workers one of the most generous social security programs in Europe.

ITALIAN NATIONALISM

Like Germany, Italy in the early 1800s was a collection of separate kingdoms and states. Some Italian states were ruled by Hapsburg dukes. Members of France's aristocratic House

of Bourbon ruled the Kingdom of Naples. The key northern states of Lombardy and Venetia were part of the Austrian Empire, while the Papal States around Rome were controlled by the Roman Catholic Church.

Nationalist sentiments began to grow in Italy after 1815. At first, only intellectuals supported the idea of unification. Gradually, however, this goal was taken up by other segments of Italian society, creating a movement called *Risorgimento* (ree-SOR-jee-MEN-tō), or the "reawakening" of Italian nationalism. One of the leaders of Risorgimento was Guiseppe Mazzini, who established a nationalist organization called Young Italy, and encouraged people in the various states to think of themselves as Italians.

In 1848, as part of the revolutionary movement that was sweeping Europe, Italian nationalists had attempted to end Austrian control over northern Italian states. Although these rebellions were put down, the nationalist spirit survived in the Kingdom of Sardinia, a territory that included the island of Sardinia and the northern province of Piedmont near France. Sardinia was the only Italian state to keep its liberal constitution after the aristocracy regained control following the rebellions of 1848.

In 1852, the king of Sardinia, Victor Emmanuel II, appointed Camillo di Cavour (kah-VOOR) prime minister. A staunch liberal and nationalist, Cavour led the struggle to unify the states of Italy.

UNITY IN NORTHERN ITALY

Cavour was convinced that a constitutional monarchy like that of Sardinia would be the best kind of government for the people of Italy. To establish such a government, he planned to unite the states of Italy under the Kingdom of Sardinia.

As his first step toward unity, Cavour strengthened and reformed Sardinia. He promoted business by establishing protective tariffs, building railroads and factories, and modernizing the seaport of Genoa. He also built up Sardinia's army.

Cavour then took steps to break Austria's hold on Italy. In 1858, he secured an alliance with Napoleon III by promising France the Italian provinces of Savoy (suh-VOY) and Nice (NEES) in exchange for French assistance in the event of war between Sardinia and Austria. The next year, Cavour provoked Austria into declaring war against Sardinia. With the help of French forces, Sardinia defeated Austria, gaining control of Lombardy.

Shortly after this victory, a series of successful nationalist revolutions furthered Cavour's plans. The states of Tuscany, Modena, and Parma declared independence from their Hapsburg rulers and then voted to unite with Sardinia. By 1860, Sardinia controlled nearly all of northern Italy.

THE CREATION OF AN ITALIAN NATION

The effort to bring the southern Italian states into a unified Italy was led by a great Italian patriot, Giuseppe Garibaldi. A participant in the uprisings of 1830, Garibaldi had been exiled and spent several years in South America. There he fought in a number of wars of independence, gaining experience in harassing enemy armies with hit-and-run tactics called *guerrilla warfare.*

In May 1860, Garibaldi and his "red shirt army," a force of a thousand middle-class volunteers wearing red shirts, helped free people on the island of Sicily from control by the Kingdom of Naples. Garibaldi then crossed from Sicily to Naples and helped overthrow its Bourbon ruler.

By late 1860, the people of the territories freed by Garibaldi had expressed their overwhelming support for a unified Italy. Garibaldi then surrendered southern Italy to the Kingdom of Sardinia. In March 1861, with most of the Italian peninsula controlled by Sardinia, Italy became a united kingdom under Victor Emmanuel II. Only Venetia, San Marino, and the city of Rome remained outside the rule of the new Italian government.

During the next decade, however, all these territories except tiny San Marino became part of the new nation. In 1866, Italian troops helped Prussia defeat Austria in the Seven Weeks' War. As a reward, Italy received Venetia, which had been ruled by Austria. Then in 1870, Italy seized Rome.

In 1870, the new Italian nation was still mostly agricultural, with high illiteracy rates and poverty. Yet it grew quickly, with industrialization and trade promoted by the new government, especially in the north. By the end of the nineteenth century, Italy had taken its place among the rival European powers. Together with the new nation of Germany, Italy helped make international politics in Europe more complicated and full of tension than they had ever been before.

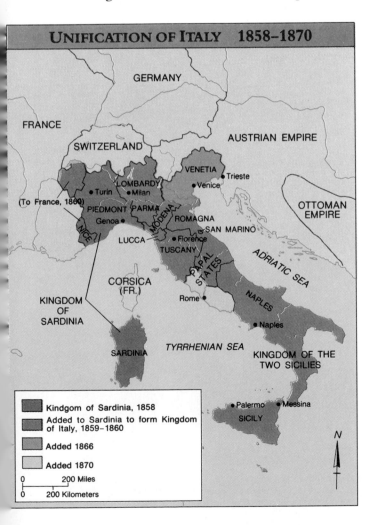

UNIFICATION OF ITALY 1858–1870

GERMANY
FRANCE
SWITZERLAND
AUSTRIAN EMPIRE
VENETIA
• Trieste
LOMBARDY
• Turin • Milan
• Venice
(To France, 1860)
PIEDMONT PARMA
OTTOMAN EMPIRE
NICE
Genoa •
MODENA
ROMAGNA
• SAN MARINO
LUCCA
• Florence
TUSCANY
ADRIATIC SEA
CORSICA (FR.)
PAPAL STATES
KINGDOM OF SARDINIA
Rome •
NAPLES
• Naples
TYRRHENIAN SEA
KINGDOM OF THE TWO SICILIES
SARDINIA
• Palermo • Messina
SICILY

Kingdom of Sardinia, 1858
Added to Sardinia to form Kingdom of Italy, 1859–1860
Added 1866
Added 1870
0   200 Miles
0   200 Kilometers
N

SECTION REVIEW

1. Define *Realpolitik*, *reich*, and *guerrilla warfare.*

2. Why did Bismarck want Austria to declare war on Prussia?

3. How did Bismarck bring the northern and southern German states together?

4. Describe the *Risorgimento*. Who was its major leader before 1848?

5. What role did Garibaldi play in the unification of Italy?

Analysis. In what ways were Cavour and Bismarck alike? In what ways were the two leaders different?

24–3
IMPERIALIST EXPANSION

READ TO FIND OUT

—what the terms *imperialism*, *spheres of influence*, and *protectorates* mean.
—how imperialism differed from earlier colonization.
—what caused the burst of imperialism occurring after 1880.
—which European nations participated in the competition for overseas colonies.

After the successful nation-building by Germany and Italy, rivalries intensified among European nations. At the same time, industrialization became so rapid in Europe that the decades after 1870 have been called the second Industrial Revolution. The European powers began to seek new sources of raw materials and new markets for manufactured goods.

About 1880, these pressures for expansion resulted in a sudden burst of competition for overseas colonies. European leaders believed colonies would not only ensure continued economic growth, but would also help them balance the growing power of rival nations.

The European powers began to pursue a policy called *imperialism*, in which strong countries gain social, political, and economic control over weaker countries. Between 1880 and 1914, European nations divided much of the globe among themselves during what has been called the Age of Imperialism.

THE ROOTS OF IMPERIALISM

The idea of building overseas empires was not new to nineteenth-century Europe. Spain, Portugal, France, Great Britain, and the Netherlands had all put down firm roots in the Americas beginning in the early 1500s. Some of these nations had built trading posts in Africa and Asia as well.

Yet Europe's empire-building did not move ahead on a steady course. In the seventeenth century, Spanish power declined. In the eighteenth century, the French and British empires in North America shrank as a result of the French and Indian War and the American Revolutionary War. With the Industrial Revolution, money once used in colonial ventures was channeled into the building of factories and railroads at home. By the end of the eighteenth century, some of Europe's zest for establishing overseas empires appeared to be withering away.

About 1880, however, most nations of Europe suddenly set out on a quest for empire once again. This nineteenth-century burst of imperialist conquest differed from earlier colonization. No longer was the object to settle thinly populated areas of "unknown" continents, or to set up trading posts and isolated military forts. Instead, imperialists chose to

In this photograph a young Asian worker cuts a diagonal groove in the bark of a rubber tree to release a milky white juice called latex. The latex is refined to produce crude rubber.

dominate overseas lands much more completely, to gain control over their economies and social structures. This phase of empire-building also saw former colonies, such as the United States, enter into the imperialist competition for overseas possessions.

CAUSES OF IMPERIALIST EXPANSION

The causes of this revival of empire-building are complex. Although it was part of the general process of European expansion, nineteenth-century imperialism was largely the result of particular economic, political, and social forces unleashed by the Industrial Revolution.

Economic causes. The Industrial Revolution created within Europe an immense need for raw materials. For instance, European industries used rubber in a large number of products ranging from waterproof rainwear to bicycle tires. Trees from which rubber was harvested grew wild in parts of Africa and Southeast Asia, but not in Europe. Some European nations, therefore, sought rubber-producing colonies in order to obtain a steady supply of this important raw material.

At the same time, the nations of Europe saw overseas possessions as important new markets for manufactured goods. The British, for instance, produced more cotton cloth than they could sell in Europe. If African and Asian buyers could be found for this product, British textile owners would be so much the wealthier. It was little wonder, then, that industrialists in European nations put pressure on their governments to obtain rights to sell their goods in overseas markets.

Political and social causes. In addition to business needs, political forces contributed to the growing competition for colonies. Among

The popularity of ''wellies'' contributed to British demand for rubber. These rubber boots were fashioned after leather ones favored by the Duke of Wellington, who defeated Napoleon.

the most important political forces was nationalism. At first, possession of foreign territories was an object of national pride. Soon, however, European nations began to see colonies as strategic necessities. With other nations building strong military forces and acquiring foreign territories, colonies became essential elements of national defense. This rivalry grew more intense when Germany and Italy became strong, unified nations and also sought colonies to build their power.

Imperialism also had religious causes. Missionaries, both Roman Catholic and Protestant, aroused European interest in foreign lands in their effort to spread the Christian gospel.

Just as the motive to spread Christianity to Africans and Asians was based on the idea that the Christian religion was superior, many Europeans justified imperialism on the grounds of the superiority of the white race. Other Europeans made a case for imperialism based on the ideas of social Darwinism. They argued that imperial conquests were but another example of the "survival of the fittest."

Such attitudes were expressed most vividly in the work of a British writer, Rudyard Kipling, who wrote extensively during the Age of Imperialism. Kipling believed that colonists had a duty to introduce Africans and Asians to the "civilizing" benefits of Western culture. He wrote of this responsibility as "the white man's burden."

THE COMPETITION FOR COLONIES

At the beginning of the nineteenth century, Great Britain had already amassed a huge empire. Private British companies controlled large parts of India and Canada, while the British flag flew over holdings in South Africa, Australia, New Zealand, and the Americas. During the 1830s, in what was a foreshadowing of the coming Age of Imperialism, Great Britain strengthened its control over India, and fought a war with China over trading rights.

Other European nations had also gained some colonial territory by the early 1800s. France moved into North Africa, Senegal in West Africa, and Indochina in Southeast Asia, while the Netherlands controlled parts of the East Indies. This early phase of imperialist expansion, however, was slow and moderate com-

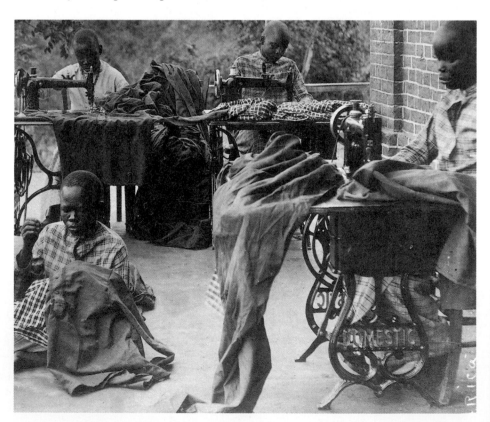

Demand for cotton led Europeans to establish large cotton plantations in the fertile lands of Belgian-held central Africa. Black Africans provided the labor for growing the cotton and later making it into cloth. In this photograph taken at the New Antwerp Mission in Congo, young African workers sew cotton clothing.

Christian missionaries in German Southwest Africa baptize an African child in this photograph taken about 1900. Diamond, copper, and other mineral deposits lured Europeans to this rugged desert and mountainous land which today is called Namibia.

pared with what would happen in the last decades of the nineteenth century.

About 1880, these early colonial powers—along with smaller and newer European nations—suddenly began carving up the globe into colonies. With technological developments such as machine guns, steamships, and the telegraph, European powers took over vast lands and controlled huge numbers of people.

Taking advantage of their early lead, the British not only strengthened their control of India and other colonies, but also began to move into Asia, Africa, and the Middle East. By the turn of the century, Great Britain's empire consisted of nearly 20 percent of the world's land mass. With colonies on every continent, British people boasted that the "sun never sets on the British Empire."

Cecil Rhodes typified the British enthusiasm for imperialism. As prime minister of Britain's colony in South Africa, he made a fortune in South African diamond mining. His dream was to create an unbroken chain of British colonies from North Africa to South Africa. "I would annex the planets if I could," he once said.

Striving to keep up with Britain, France also built a huge empire, second only to that of Britain. By 1914, France controlled much of North and West Africa, as well as chunks of Indochina twice as large as France itself.

Although Bismarck concentrated his efforts on building German power on the European continent, German merchants and industrialists wanted overseas colonies for Germany. By 1882, they had convinced Bismarck of the benefits of an imperialist policy, and Germany quickly seized colonies in East and West Africa. Then German imperialists gained control of several Pacific islands and Asian ports. By 1914, Germany had built the third largest overseas empire.

Italy, too, sought colonies, especially as a symbol of national honor. Although it lacked the military might to back up vast imperial claims, Italy succeeded in gaining control of territories in North and East Africa. By 1895, it had colonies in Somaliland (sō-MAH-lee-LAND) and Eritrea (AYR-uh-TREE-uh), both on the northeast "horn" of Africa. In 1911, Italy established control over Libya on the North African coast.

Smaller European nations were also active in the race for colonies. Belgium acquired lands in central Africa drained by the Congo River. Portugal annexed areas along the southeastern and southwestern coast of Africa, and the Netherlands expanded control of its long-held possession of the Dutch East Indies.

THE BERLIN CONFERENCE

In 1885, a few years after the race for colonies had begun, the imperialist powers met at a conference in Berlin to set the ground rules for the further partition of Africa. They agreed that to establish a colony, a nation had to formally announce its claim, and then actually occupy the territory. If these procedures were followed, the colony would be recognized as that nation's possession.

The Berlin Conference gave the green light to imperialist ventures in Africa. It also created a sense of urgency that speeded up the race for colonies in Asia and the Pacific as well. Before the conference, a nation had only to point to longstanding colonial claims. Now, however, a colonial power had to have its own citizens or troops actually holding the lands it claimed as colonies. Each European nation rushed troops, officials, and settlers to overseas lands before other nations did.

The conference also had the effect of encouraging imperial powers to make the legal status of their possessions clear to other nations. Three kinds of imperial control came to be recognized. In some instances, European powers set up colonies, possessions over which they had direct control. This situation was most common in Africa. In other situations, they obtained *spheres of influence*, areas in which they maintained sole investment or trading rights. In still other cases, European nations established *protectorates*, countries with their own rulers that were, in turn, controlled by the imperial powers.

SECTION REVIEW

1. Define *imperialism*, *spheres of influence*, and *protectorates*.

2. Describe how the imperialism that began about 1880 was different from earlier forms of colonization.

3. Give three causes of imperialist expansion occurring after 1880.

4. Which European nations were the major imperialist powers? In which parts of the world did they concentrate their efforts?

Analysis. Why did many Europeans believe that imperialism benefited the people they took over?

Data Search. Explain what the chart on world trade on page 833 reveals about French and British trade with Africa and Asia during the period of imperialist expansion.

24-4
TENSIONS AMONG IMPERIALIST POWERS

READ TO FIND OUT

—what the term *entente* means.
—how the Triple Alliance created a new balance of power in Europe.
—how Wilhelm II increased tensions in Europe.
—how imperialist competition led to confrontations in Africa.
—why the Balkans became a focus of tension in Europe.

While imperialist expansion continued overseas, tensions mounted in Europe itself, caused in part by this competition for colonies. Although leaders tried to maintain a balance of power through complex alliances, the possibility of violent confrontation loomed larger as the twentieth century began.

A NEW BALANCE OF POWER

When the new race for colonies began about 1880, relationships among European nations had changed drastically. France and Austria, once the most powerful countries on the European continent, had suffered serious military defeats. The unification of Italy and Germany, along with the decline of the Ottoman Empire, threatened to upset the delicate balance of power in Europe.

Although Britain remained a major power—largely because of its navy—Britain's chief interests still lay in managing and expanding its overseas empire rather than in gaining greater influence in Europe. Thus, the new unified German nation emerged as the dominant force on the European continent. Britain—an island nation—was not considered part of "the continent." The only threat to Germany's position came from France. Germans believed that France thirsted for revenge for its humiliating defeat in the Franco-Prussian War.

Bismarck dealt with the French threat by creating a new system of alliances that resulted

ART NOUVEAU

While European nations competed for colonies to benefit their growing industries, many artists turned against industrialization. These artists found beauty in objects made by hand rather than by machine. Inspired by flowing designs found in nature, artists used swirling lines and intricate patterns in paintings as well as to decorate common objects such as jewelry, books, home furnishings, dishes, and fabrics.

Portrait of Adele Bloch-Bauer,
Gustav Klimt, 1907

**Tiffany Studios leaded
glass lamp, 1910**

The Voice, Edvard Munch, 1893

Salome, the Peacock Skirt, Aubrey Beardsley, 1894

The Modern Poster, Will Bradley, 1898

Aristide Bruant in his Cabaret,
Toulouse-Lautrec, 1893

in a new balance of power. In 1882, Bismarck fashioned a defensive agreement among Germany, Italy, and Austria. Called the Triple Alliance, the agreement's purpose was to keep France isolated. Each party in the alliance promised to come to the aid of the others when any one of them was at war. Bismarck also forged a separate alliance with Russia in an effort to prevent that country from allying with France.

With the creation of the Triple Alliance, Bismarck seemed to have found the key to protecting Germany itself as well as European peace. Of the major powers other than France, only Britain was not allied with Germany, and Britain too saw France as its main rival. For the time being, this new balance of power kept Europe at peace. The growing competition for colonies, however, soon renewed tension, adding new strains that threatened Bismarck's diplomatic handiwork.

GROWING MILITARY RIVALRIES

In 1888, Wilhelm II, the first kaiser's grandson, became the new kaiser of Germany. Wilhelm II was young and ambitious. As leader of a powerful nation, he began to upset the tense yet workable balance of power developed in the early 1880s.

In 1890, Wilhelm II dismissed Bismarck, the master diplomat, and took control of diplomatic affairs himself. In Bismarck's hands, the Triple Alliance had been an aid to European stability. Under Wilhelm's policies, however, the alliance posed what seemed to France and England to be a growing threat.

At this point, Germany was already a strong industrial and military rival to Great Britain. Wilhelm II, however, promoted hostility by aggressively pursuing an imperialist policy. He declared that Germany must build an overseas empire to have its "place in the sun."

As Germany founded more colonies, its need grew for a powerful navy. Encouraged by Admiral Alfred von Tirpitz (TER-pits), Wilhelm II ordered the construction of a modern battle fleet. Because Great Britain was an island nation inaccessible by land routes, the English government could ignore a large German army, but once Great Britain saw Germany as a naval rival, friction between the two countries increased quickly.

MILITARY EXPENSES OF EUROPEAN POWERS 1890, 1914			
Nation	**Military Expenses** (in millions of dollars)		
	Army	*Navy*	*Total*
Germany			
1890	121	23	144
1914	442	112	554
Great Britain			
1890	88	69	157
1914	147	237	384
France			
1890	142	44	186
1914	197	90	287
Russia			
1890	123	22	145
1914	324	118	442

Since the mid-nineteenth century, Britain had followed a policy of maintaining a navy stronger than any other two nations' fleets combined. This program guaranteed British control of the oceans in wartime. Von Tirpitz's plan threatened to upset this program. To keep up with its rival, therefore, Great Britain built more and bigger ships, thus sparking a race for naval superiority.

France also saw Germany as a dangerous rival. Unlike Great Britain, however, France was more worried about a large German army than about the German navy. The humiliation of 1871, when German troops quickly destroyed France's army, could not be forgotten. France thus responded to Germany's militarization by building a larger army of its own.

Technological innovations that grew out of the Industrial Revolution also made Germany appear threatening to other European states, adding fuel to the growing rivalries. Since Germany's unification, German universities had been leaders in scientific research, providing German industry with up-to-date technology that could be used to develop new and better weapons. In many ways, Germany had overcome Britain's lead in industrial development. The steel Germany used to build ships, for example, was superior to that used by the British navy. Both Britain and France viewed German military expansion with growing unease.

ANALYZING STATISTICAL TABLES

INTRODUCING THE SKILL

As discussed in the lesson titled "Analyzing Graphs" on page 479, statistics are often presented in line graphs, bar graphs, and circle graphs. Another way of displaying statistics in an organized way is through statistical tables. A statistical table is an arrangement of numbers in rows and columns. It is a useful way of presenting large amounts of similar data, as in the table on military expenses on the facing page. In a statistical table, you can see all the organized data at a glance.

EXPLAINING THE SKILL

A table organizes statistics so that they are easier to read. However, you still must determine the significance of those statistics by analyzing the table—carefully examining each part of it. Follow these steps when analyzing a statistical table:

A. *Read the title.* The title will give you a general idea of what the table shows.

B. *Read all the labels.* The labels will tell you exactly what the numbers on a table represent. They may be percentages, precise figures, or rounded numbers.

C. *Analyze the statistics.* Look over the table quickly to get a sense of what it shows. Then study one part of the table at a time, looking for differences, similarities, increases, and decreases in the numbers. Finally, compare different parts of the table in order to find general trends and patterns of change that are indicated by the statistics.

D. *Make a general statement about what the table shows.* Briefly state what general patterns or trends are shown on the table. You will be able to remember these trends more easily than the specific statistics.

APPLYING THE SKILL

Use the statistical table on the facing page to answer the following questions.

1. What is the subject of the table?
2. What do the numbers represent?
   (a) hundreds of dollars
   (b) thousands of dollars
   (c) millions of dollars
3. Look at the army expenses. Did any nation spend less in 1914 than it did in 1890? Which nation spent the most in 1890? In 1914?
4. Look at the naval expenses. Which nation spent the least on its navy in 1890? In 1914?
5. Which nation spent more on its navy than on its army?
6. Which nation had the smallest increase in total military spending?
7. Which nation had the largest increase in total military spending?
8. Which nation had the largest military expenses in 1890? In 1914?
9. Briefly state what general trend or pattern this table shows.

INTERPRETING THE INFORMATION

Statistics may be used to support statements about history. Determine whether each of the following statements is supported by the statistics in the table. Explain your answers.

10. The European powers were creating overseas empires between 1890 and 1914.
11. Between 1890 and 1914, Germany was trying to become a major naval power.
12. In 1914, Russia's navy was larger than that of Germany.
13. Germany considered its army to be more important than its navy.
14. Great Britain was determined to maintain its naval superiority.

REVIEWING THE SKILL

15. What are statistics?
16. What four steps should be followed when reading statistical tables?

The Krupp Steelworks, which perfected a method of casting steel cannon, was the major manufacturer of German weapons. This vast complex, located in Essen, Germany, included more than eighty factories, power plants, and mills. In this photograph, workers use the mighty steam hammer "Fritz" to shape a beam of hot steel.

CONFRONTATIONS IN AFRICA

In an attempt to compete with Germany's military buildup, France and Great Britain not only expanded their own military forces, but also increased their efforts to establish larger overseas empires. In the race to gain strategic foreign colonies, Great Britain and France were far ahead of Germany, and they hoped to maintain this advantage in order to offset Germany's military strength.

France and Britain, however, were far from friendly as imperialist powers. In the late 1890s, as larger military forces claimed, protected, and explored territories all over Africa, this continent became the scene of tense confrontations between Britain, France, and Germany.

Showdown at Fashoda. The first confrontation occurred in the territory south of Egypt in the upper Nile Valley called the Sudan, a name taken from the larger natural region of savanna stretching across Africa south of the Sahara.

France, with its large holdings in the western bulge of Africa, hoped to create an empire that extended across the northern tier of the continent, from the Atlantic Ocean to the Red Sea. In the Sudan, however, French ambitions for an east-west empire in Africa collided with Britain's goal of an African empire stretching south from Egypt.

Anglo-French rivalry came to a head in 1898 when a small French force marched eastward from French territory to claim the southern part of the Sudan. Meanwhile, a larger British expedition marched southward from Egypt to hoist the British flag over the same territory.

The two imperialist powers confronted each other in a place called Fashoda in the Sudan. When neither side would yield to the other, war seemed inevitable. The outnumbered French, however, who regarded Germany as their chief European rival, wanted no quarrel with Great Britain. France decided to back down. As a result of the peaceful resolution of the Fashoda crisis, France recognized Britain's control over the Sudan in exchange for British recognition of French dominance in West Africa and Equatorial Africa.

The Boer War. In South Africa a year later, another crisis erupted into open warfare and increased diplomatic tensions in Europe. This crisis had roots in the early nineteenth century, before the race for colonies had begun.

South Africa had been transferred to British control by the Congress of Vienna in 1815, placing the earlier Dutch settlers, called the Afrikaners, or Boers, under British rule. In 1836, the Boers, resentful of British rule, had left Cape Colony, as South Africa was then called, on a great trek northward into territory where

British artillery forces fire at Boers in what proved to be a British victory in the Battle of Modder River in the Orange Free State in November 1899 (left). In May 1900, placards worn by London newsboys (right) announce the Boer surrender of the capital of Pretoria.

they hoped to be free of British interference. There, however, they met an African people called the Zulu, who had claimed the land before the Boers. After the rifle-equipped Boers defeated the spear-wielding Zulu warriors at the Battle of Blood River, the Boers established the independent republics of the Transvaal and the Orange Free State. Britain officially recognized the independence of these republics in 1852.

The British and the Boers remained uneasy but peaceful neighbors until the 1880s, when the discovery of gold and diamonds in the Transvaal attracted a rush of European and American miners. Tensions increased until finally Britain decided that control of all of South Africa was vital to its interests. At this point, Cecil Rhodes sent a small force to overthrow the Boer government, but the raid failed. When Kaiser Wilhelm II congratulated the Dutch farmers on their standoff, he further poisoned Anglo-German relations.

War between the British and the Boers broke out in 1899 and dragged on for three years. Britain eventually won the Boer War and in 1910 the British and Afrikaner territories were joined to form the Union of South Africa.

The Moroccan crisis. A third important confrontation occurred in Morocco, an Islamic nation in northwest Africa. France and Britain had quarreled over Morocco since the 1880s, while Morocco struggled to remain independent of European control.

In 1904, Britain and France finally agreed that in exchange for recognizing Britain's claim in Egypt, France would establish a sphere of influence in Morocco. In reaching this agreement with Britain, France made no attempt to gain German consent because Germany had no prior claims or direct interest in Morocco. Kaiser Wilhelm II, however, was determined not to allow France to have Morocco without obtaining something in return.

A crisis arose in 1905, when the kaiser objected to France's claim to special rights in Morocco and called for an international conference to settle the Moroccan question. Many believed France and Germany were on the brink of war. The crisis, however, was settled diplomatically in 1906, when representatives from the major imperialist powers agreed to place the administration of Morocco in French hands. The results of the conference represented a bitter diplomatic defeat for Germany.

NATIONALISM AND INSTABILITY IN EASTERN EUROPE

Like Africa, eastern Europe was a growing trouble spot and a center of rivalries affecting all of Europe. By 1905, every political development in eastern Europe—particularly in the Balkans—threatened to bring about a major war. The conflicts in this area, like those in South Africa, had their roots in the early nineteenth century.

Three old empires—the Austrian, Russian, and Ottoman—ruled eastern Europe. Many of the people living in these empires were still dominated by feudal practices and saw themselves as ethnic minorities ruled unfairly by other groups. As a result, social unrest and nationalist movements grew after 1848.

At the same time, Austria and the Ottoman Empire declined in strength, while Russia eyed their territories with imperialist interest. Russia, in particular, wanted access to the Mediterranean through the straits controlled by the Ottomans, called the Bosporus. The first result of Russian ambitions in the Balkans was the Crimean War.

Russia also saw itself as the leader of Slavic peoples struggling for independence in the Balkans. A movement supporting Slavic unity—called Pan-Slavism—gained strength in the late 1800s. Pan-Slavism fueled both nationalism and Russian expansionist plans in the Balkans.

The first major nationalist struggle after 1850, however, involved not Slavs but Magyars (MAG-yahrz), people who had inhabited an area known as Hungary since the 900s. Ruled by Austria, Hungary achieved partial independence in 1867 when it received its own parliament and constitution. However, one monarch—Francis Joseph I—continued to rule over both nations. Because of this arrangement, called the Dual Monarchy, Austria's name was changed to Austria-Hungary.

In 1875, nationalist revolts broke out in Slavic Balkan states ruled by the Ottomans. Russia, seeking greater influence in the area, decided to aid the rebels and declared war on the Ottoman Empire. The Ottomans were defeated, and under the terms of the Treaty of San Stefano, the Balkan states of Romania, Montenegro, and Serbia achieved independence. In addition, Russia gained the right to occupy Bulgaria and use its seaport on the Aegean Sea.

Again alarmed by Russia's expansion into the Balkans, other European nations forced Russia to participate in a conference in 1878 to rewrite the San Stefano treaty. The agreement reached at this meeting, called the Congress of Berlin, reduced Bulgaria's size—thus eliminating Russia's seaport—and gave control of the nearby island of Cyprus to Great Britain.

Growing tension in the Balkans. After 1880, the Balkan Peninsula became the focus of renewed Russian-Ottoman conflict which brought Austria-Hungary into the dispute. Austria-Hungary, even more than the Ottoman Empire, was an important force in the Balkans, and because it had lost control of many of its Slavic and Magyar populations, the Hapsburgs had the most to lose from the Russian policy of expansion.

Meanwhile, the now-independent Slavic nations sought to further unify Slavic peoples and take more territory from the Ottoman Empire and Austria-Hungary. Diplomatic tensions increased in the Balkans during the early 1900s, and many people began calling the area a "powder keg" ready to explode.

NEW ALIGNMENTS

As confrontations in Africa and the Balkans came closer to what seemed like actual war, diplomatic alignments shifted. Fearing German expansion more than ever, France and Britain sought allies.

Even before its confrontations with Germany and Britain in Africa, France had courted Russia's friendship. Through efforts that included a loan to Russia, France convinced Czar Nicholas II that it was in Russia's best interests to end its agreements with Germany and form an alliance with France. The two nations established an alliance in 1894.

Great Britain began to seek allies after 1900, ending its policy of "splendid isolation" because it felt increasingly threatened by Germany and its allies. In 1904, Great Britain and France entered into an agreement called an *entente*—a friendly understanding between nations not as formal as an alliance. By 1907, Britain had ironed out its differences with Russia, and the three nations formed the Triple Entente.

The two alliances—Triple Entente and the Triple Alliance—divided Europe into two

EUROPEAN ALLIANCES 1882–1915

N

NORWAY
SWEDEN
NORTH SEA
BALTIC SEA
GREAT BRITAIN
ATLANTIC OCEAN
NETHERLANDS
BELGIUM
GERMANY
RUSSIA
LUX.
FRANCE
SWITZ.
AUSTRIA-HUNGARY
ITALY
ROMANIA
BLACK SEA
SERBIA
BULGARIA
MONTENEGRO
PORTUGAL
SPAIN
ALBANIA
GREECE
OTTOMAN EMPIRE
MEDITERRANEAN SEA
CYPRUS

Triple Alliance, formed 1882
Triple Entente, formed 1904–1907
0   500 Miles
0   500 Kilometers

armed camps. Although the balance of power was maintained, with only two hostile sides it leaned more toward war than peace.

SECTION REVIEW

1. Define **entente**.

2. Why did the Triple Alliance create stability in Europe for a time?

3. What did Wilhelm II do to upset the balance of power?

4. Describe the events that led to the "showdown at Fashoda."

5. Why were the Balkans called a "powder keg"?

Analysis. Explain how imperialist expansion helped to increase conflict between the nations of Europe.

Data Search. Explain whether the chart on world trade on page 833 supports the following statement: Imperialist rivalry led to reduced trade between European nations.

HISTORY IN FOCUS

The rise of nation-states, the Industrial Revolution, the development of capitalism, and colonial expansion all propelled Europe into the Modern Age. By the last half of the nineteenth century, these four important forces had also transformed the nations of Europe into imperialist powers that dominated the globe.

Although imperialism was an outgrowth of the noble ideals of nationalism, liberalism, and progress, it forcefully changed the lives of millions of people across the globe who believed in very different ideals. Imperialism also had profound effects in Europe. By 1900, it had intensified conflicts brought about by efforts to build national power at any cost.

Europeans in 1914 found themselves enmeshed in a deep crisis. Internal social tensions—largely ignored while nations built up armaments, colonies, and expectations—had not been resolved. At the same time, the rising conflicts between powers seemed to have but one solution.

SUMMARY

- Europe's two strongest nations—Britain and France—continued to grow after 1850. Britain enjoyed prosperity and colonial expansion under Queen Victoria, and Napoleon III consolidated his power in France.

- Bismarck led efforts to unify Germany under Prussian rule, while a similar effort was underway in Italy. By the 1870s both Germany and Italy had become major European powers.

- Political, economic, and social factors gave rise to the Age of Imperialism, from about 1880 to 1914. During this period European powers rapidly expanded their overseas holdings and influence, especially on the African and Asian continents.

- Imperialism strengthened European nations but also fueled rivalries and tension. Germany became the strongest nation on the European continent and, with Italy and Austria, forged the Triple Alliance. In response, Britain, France, and Russia formed the Triple Entente.

- European conflicts spread to colonial areas as the major powers struggled for supremacy. Eastern Europe also had grown more volatile by the end of the 1800s.

VOCABULARY REVIEW

Match each numbered vocabulary term with the appropriate person. Then explain the connection between the person and the vocabulary term.

1. Realpolitik
2. reich
3. guerrilla warfare
4. imperialism
5. entente

(a) Rhodes
(b) Bismarck
(c) Czar Nicholas II
(d) Kaiser Wilhelm I
(e) Garibaldi

CHAPTER REVIEW

1. (a) How did cooperation among European nations change from the early 1800s to the late 1800s? (b) Why did this change occur, and how did it affect other parts of the world?

2. (a) What common goals did the main European countries have after 1850? (b) How were Britain and France different from Germany and Italy in 1850?

3. Explain the circumstances and results of: (a) the Crimean War, (b) the Franco-Prussian War, and (c) the Boer War.

4. (a) Describe Bismarck's political beliefs, goals, and strategy. (b) What liberal reforms did he support, and why? (c) Trace the steps in the unification of Germany.

5. (a) Compare the unification of Italy with that of Germany. (b) How was Cavour similar to, and different from, Bismarck? (c) Why did Garibaldi relinquish his power?

6. (a) Describe the decline of colonization in the 1700s. (b) Give five reasons for the resurgence of imperialism. (c) How did Europeans justify imperialism?

7. (a) Describe the three largest colonial empires. (b) How did the Berlin Conference affect imperialist expansion?

8. (a) Why was there a strong rivalry between France and Germany? (b) Why did tensions increase between Germany and Great Britain? What were the results?

9. (a) Describe the crisis over the Sudan. (b) What prompted the crisis in Morocco, and what happened?

10. (a) Why was eastern Europe so unstable? (b) How were Russian designs in the Balkans a combination of imperialism and nationalism?

THINKING CRITICALLY: ACTIVITIES

1. Imagine that you are a visitor to the Great Exhibition of 1851. Write a letter to your best friend back home, describing what you have seen and how it has affected you. Speculate about what the future may bring based on your impressions.

2. Imagine that you are Garibaldi and that you have decided to turn the newly freed lands of southern Italy over to the Kingdom of Sardinia. Write a speech to your soldiers explaining why they should support your decision. Give your speech in front of the class.

3. Choose a partner for a debate on imperialism between two leaders in a European country. One of you should take a role similar to that of Kipling, Rhodes, or another supporter of imperialism; the other should argue a position opposing imperialism. One way to argue the opposing position would be to take Bismarck's original opinion—that imperialism distracted from the more important task of building military power and influence in Europe. Another way would be to take the position of a native of a colonized area. Present your debate before the class.

APPLYING SOCIAL STUDIES SKILLS

Analyzing statistical tables. Look carefully at the table below and answer the questions that follow.

COLONIAL EXPANSION 1876, 1914		
Nation	**Area of Colonies** (in millions of square miles)	
	1876	*1914*
Germany	0	1.1
Great Britain	8.7	12.9
France	.3	4.1
Russia	6.6	6.7

1. What is the subject of this table?

2. What years does it compare?

3. What nations are compared?

4. What do the numbers represent?

5. Which nation controlled the largest colonial empire in 1876? In 1914?

6. Which nation had no colonies in 1876?

7. Which nation had the largest gain in colonial territory between 1876 and 1914? Which nation had the smallest gain?

8. About how much territory was colonized by the four nations listed in this table between 1876 and 1914?

9. Briefly state what general trend or pattern this table shows.

APPLYING THINKING SKILLS

Determining the credibility of a source. The following sources include information about the effects of nineteenth-century imperialism on the peoples of colonized areas. Using the procedure described on pages 286-287, decide which source is likely to be most credible on this topic. Then answer the questions below.

A. A book titled *Persia and the Persian Question*, published in 1892. It was written by Lord George Curzon, a British government official. He served as Governor General of India from 1899 to 1905 and held numerous other positions in the British government after 1905.

B. V.I. Lenin's *Imperialism as the Higher State of Capitalism*, which was published in 1916. In the book, Lenin criticized what he considered to be the capitalistic exploitation of Asia and Africa by European powers. Lenin was the leader who eventually brought the Communists to power in Russia.

C. Jamal Ad-Din Afghani's *The Refutation of the Materialists*, which was published in 1887. Born in Persia, Afghani wanted to be the religious leader of the Muslim world and agitated against European influence in the Middle East. He established groups of devoted followers in Egypt, Iraq, India, Turkey, Persia, and Afghanistan as a result of his preaching.

D. *Argonauts of the Western Pacific*, which was published in 1922. This book was written by Polish anthropologist Bronislaw Malinowski and was based on his years of experience living among and observing the peoples of Pacific islands. He was a professor at the University of London and Yale University, and established new approaches to anthropology.

1. Define the term *credibility*.

2. What is one procedure for determining the credibility of a source?

3. Why is it important to try to determine the credibility of a source?

4. Which one of the above sources is likely to be the most credible? Explain.

5. What might limit the credibility of each of the other three sources? Explain.

CHAPTER TWENTY-FIVE

NATION BUILDING IN THE AMERICAS

1800–1914

Revolutionists. José Clemente Orozco, Mexico, c. 1930.

During the early nineteenth century, before European powers began their imperialist expansion, Latin Americans began to throw off the colonial rule established in the 1500s and 1600s. The newly independent countries were faced with building stable societies and effective governments. After the mid-1800s, this challenge grew more formidable as imperialism brought a new form of foreign influence and created seemingly insurmountable economic problems for Latin Americans.

Meanwhile, in North America, industrialization made the United States a world power, and Canada gained self-rule from Britain. In the United States, however, conflict over the issue of slavery erupted into a civil war. After these issues had run their course, the United States, an emerging imperialist power, turned its attention to Latin America.

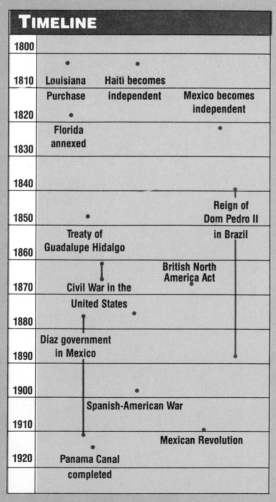

TIMELINE

1800	
1810	Louisiana Purchase • Haiti becomes independent •
1820	• Mexico becomes independent
1830	Florida annexed •
1840	
1850	• Reign of Dom Pedro II in Brazil
1860	Treaty of Guadalupe Hidalgo •
1870	Civil War in the United States • British North America Act •
1880	•
1890	Díaz government in Mexico •
1900	•
1910	Spanish-American War •
1920	Panama Canal completed • Mexican Revolution •

25-1
LATIN AMERICA AND INDEPENDENCE

READ TO FIND OUT

—what the terms *caudillismo* and *buffer state* mean.
—what developments pushed Latin America to break away from Spain and Portugal.
—who Simón Bolívar and José de San Martín were.
—what issues divided Latin American liberals from conservatives.

During the 1600s, Spain fell from the ranks of the major European political powers. Economic difficulties, military setbacks, and ineffective leadership contributed to its loss of power. As Spanish kings became less interested in the administration of the West Indies, creoles—upper-class but American-born Spaniards—began to fill government posts that had previously been tightly controlled by Spain. During the 1700s, desire for self-government grew among the creoles. By the early 1800s, this determination had evolved into bold struggles for independence.

IMPERIAL REFORM

In 1759, the Spanish crown fell to Carlos III, who had far greater administrative ability than his predecessors. He immediately began a program of reform aimed at reestablishing absolute Spanish authority in the New World. New ministers, all Spanish-born, were sent out to replace the creoles in important government positions. To help bring the colonies under more direct political control, King Carlos also redesigned the political divisions of the empire by creating the two new viceroyalties of Río de la Plata and New Granada.

The Enlightenment, in the meantime, was influencing the creole landowners and merchants in Latin America. Through the works of writers such as Locke and Rousseau, creoles read about equality and individual liberty. In the 1700s, creoles had become accustomed to running their own affairs with little interference from Spain. Now, it seemed, the Spanish government was taking away their ability to govern just at the moment when their desire to do so was growing strong.

THE WARS FOR INDEPENDENCE

The first organized effort to gain independence did not occur in a Spanish colony, however, but in the French colony of Saint Domingue, which was the western portion of the island of Hispaniola. Saint Domingue was the world's foremost producer of sugar, an industry that not only created a great amount of wealth for French landlords but also required the extensive use of slave labor.

When news of the French Revolution arrived, slaves on the island saw a chance to end years of harsh rule and cruel treatment by their owners. A 1791 uprising led by Toussaint L'Ouverture (TOO-SAHN LOO-vehr-TYOOR) marked the beginning of a long struggle for freedom. After a period of widespread bloodshed, Toussaint routed the French colonial forces and took control of the island. When Napoleon tried to take back the island in 1802, Toussaint resisted but was captured by the French. He died in prison in 1803.

After Toussaint's capture, Jean Jacques Dessalines (DAY-sa-LEEN) took up the fight and led the island to full independence in 1804, renaming it Haiti (HAY-tee). However, Haiti's economy never recovered from the devastation of the long revolution.

LATIN AMERICA 1790

Struggle in South America. A few years later, in 1808, Napoleon invaded Spain and captured Ferdinand VII, the Spanish king. With the occupation of Spain, many people in the colonies realized that their opportunity to break from Spain had arrived. Revolution erupted in several cities within a short time. At first, these conflicts were not true independence movements, since the creole leaders had pledged their loyalty to the king. However, as long as King Ferdinand was held captive in France, this formal pledge meant little.

After Napoleon's defeat, Ferdinand returned to the throne and made it clear that he had no intention of granting any privileges to the creoles. This policy rekindled the faltering independence movements. Able leaders such as Simón Bolívar and José de San Martín emerged.

Bolívar came from one of the wealthiest families in Latin America. His education was better than average, and his determination and military ability made him the most important figure of the Latin American independence movement. He quickly set himself up as leader of the struggle against Spain. Even after almost complete defeat in 1815, he was able to spring back and drive the Spanish from New Granada.

The military struggle for independence in northern South America ended in 1824, when one of Bolívar's followers defeated the Spanish in the battle of Ayacucho (AY-yah-KOO-chō). Bolívar became president of "Gran Colombia," the area now made up of Colombia, Venezuela, Ecuador, and Panama. Bolívar was also a great influence in Peru and the former colony of Upper Peru, renamed Bolivia in his honor.

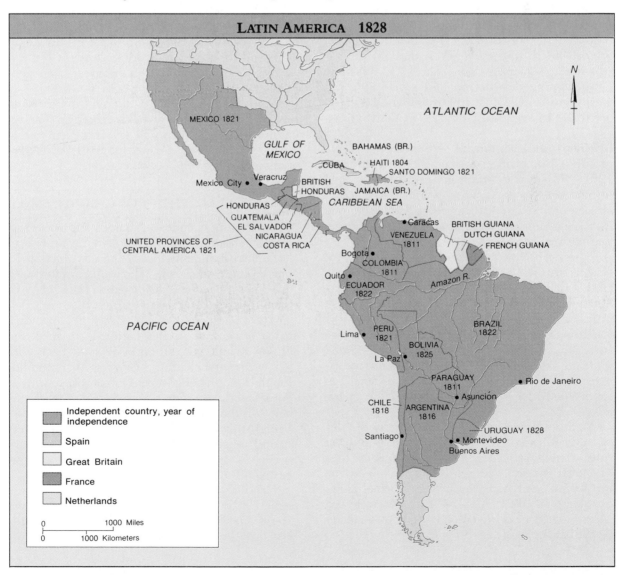

LATIN AMERICA 1828

Haiti's slave revolt succeeded largely because of Toussaint's guerrilla tactics, like this forest ambush. Latin American revolutionaries often used similar strategies against the Spanish.

In the southern part of the continent, the struggle was led by José de San Martín. Working from Argentina, which had gained independence in 1810, he liberated Chile and pressed north into Peru. Even though the war was not as violent in Río de la Plata as in New Granada, the destruction and social upheaval were significant. Most important, the great silver mines of Peru and Bolivia were destroyed.

Mexican independence. Independence came to Mexico in a different way. The revolution of 1810, unlike the creole-led insurrections of South America, was an uprising of the lower classes against creoles as well as Spaniards. Led by Father Hidalgo, a Catholic priest, the bloody war ravaged the Mexican countryside.

When Hidalgo's forces took the city of Guanajuato (GWAN-ah-WHAH-tō) and massacred several hundred whites, creoles remembered Haiti. Perhaps afraid of losing the Spanish military's protection, the creoles sided with the royalists and defeated Hidalgo's army. To be sure, the creoles in Latin America never wanted Hidalgo's type of social revolution. They recognized that with the destruction of the social and economic order would come the end to creole rule.

A creole-dominated revolt eventually did develop in Mexico. In 1820, the most important royalist military leader, Agustín de Iturbide (EE-TOOR-BEE-thay), himself a creole, joined the revolution, and Mexico achieved formal independence in 1821. Central America followed Mexico, gaining its independence with virtually no bloodshed at all.

SOCIAL AND ECONOMIC CONDITIONS AFTER INDEPENDENCE

After independence, Latin America continued to be divided along rather rigid racial and social lines. Creoles remained at the top of the social structure. Forming about 20 percent of the population, they held most of the land in large estates. As people of mixed European and Indian heritage, the mestizos ranked below the creoles in social standing. Just as during the colonial centuries, the mulattoes were below the mestizos, while Indians and blacks remained at the bottom of the social scale.

Many Indians lived in isolated regions where the soil was poor. They used inefficient farming methods that had changed little since the arrival of the conquistadors. Most blacks remained in slavery, although a few were freed because of service in the revolutionary armies. The freed blacks quickly became the poorest group. Lacking land, they had to work on estates for low wages or try to survive in villages where jobs were scarce.

Political independence did not dramatically change everyday life in Latin America. The region's social and economic systems ensured that many people never escaped poverty but always remained on the edge of starvation.

THE DEVELOPMENT OF CAUDILLISMO

Soon after independence, many Latin American countries came to be controlled by ambitious leaders who ruled by force. These tyrants developed a leadership style called *caudillismo* (KOW-dee-EES-mō) after *caudillo* (kow-DEE-yō), the Spanish word for "military leader."

The caudillo worked mainly for personal gain, often raiding the national treasury and killing anyone who stood in his way. Each with his own armed band of followers, rival caudillos fought one another for control of countries. Some of the caudillos seized power with the help of the military. The ties between these Latin American leaders and the military were strong. Many caudillos had been revolutionary war heroes, and they often gained the support of unemployed soldiers.

Caudillismo developed throughout South America. For example, during the 1830s and 1840s, Juan Manuel de Rosas (RŌ-sahs), a ruthless dictator, governed Argentina. Through the display of red armbands, his picture, and other symbols associated with his regime, Rosas created a sense of nationhood in a country divided between the export-oriented coastal areas near Buenos Aires and the isolated provinces of the interior. Along with this achievement, however, came corruption and the stifling of political rights.

Caudillos also became an important characteristic of Mexican politics soon after independence, when General Antonio López de Santa Anna emerged as a strong leader. Santa Anna dominated Mexican affairs for two decades until the mid-1850s. Unlike many other caudillos, Santa Anna gained wide popularity. His regime reached its high point after a victory against invading French troops in 1838. During the battle, the dictator lost his left leg. With due dignity, the severed member was interred in a cemetery in Mexico City. In attendance at the ceremony were the members of the Mexican Congress and the entire diplomatic corps. Mexico had a day of national celebration in honor of its popular leader.

In this Mexican painting, peasant women work in an upper-class home. After independence, wealthy creoles maintained their high standard of living and the poor remained landless.

Of the northern countries of South America, only Colombia was not ruled by a caudillo in the first years after independence. The major political figure in the region, Francisco de Paula Santander (SAN-TAN-DEHR), strongly supported constitutional government. He also was willing to compromise with his opponents.

Santander practiced compromise during the 1830s, when Catholics in Colombia revolted because they resented efforts by Santander's liberal government to free education from church control. However, cooperation rather than conflict prevailed, and though the state established schools as well as universities, it did not totally exclude the Church from higher education. In 1849, in contrast to a government run by a caudillo, the Colombian government established religious freedom, gave voting rights to all adult males, and liberated all remaining slaves in Colombia.

Although caudillismo endured well into the twentieth century in some countries, it had a major flaw. No clear means existed of passing power from one leader to the next. As a result, this form of leadership did not produce stability over the long term but instead guaranteed competition and the pitting of would-be leaders against existing rulers.

WARS AND POLITICAL DISUNITY

When the wars for Latin American independence ended in the 1820s, divisive forces caused the number of independent states to nearly double within a few years. In 1825, Uruguay was established in the area between Brazil and Argentina as a **buffer state**, or neutral zone, to put distance between opposing armies and bring stability to the southern part of South America. With Venezuela pulling away in 1829, and Ecuador in 1830, the Gran Colombia established by Bolívar disintegrated. Although Bolivia and Peru tried to unite in 1835, Chile opposed the rise of a possible rival and quickly destroyed what was a logical union by declaring war. By 1840, Central America had divided into the small states of Guatemala, El Salvador, Honduras, Nicaragua, and Costa Rica.

The pattern of wars and political instability created a bad reputation for the whole region in the eyes of European and North American leaders. As a result of this viewpoint, the new republics had difficulty attracting much-needed foreign investment because bankers and industrialists did not want to make risky investments in the unstable region.

STABILITY IN BRAZIL

Several countries stand as exceptions to the Latin American trend toward political instability—most notably, Brazil. After independence, Brazil remained relatively calm. Its emperor, Dom Pedro I, was the son of the Portuguese king and had ruled Brazil before independence. Thus, a political structure was already in place when independence came.

The new Brazilian constitutional monarchy, established in 1822, ruled successfully until 1889, and even when it fell, no major disorder resulted. Because Brazil avoided civil unrest for most of the nineteenth century, its government was able to sponsor the development of agriculture and transportation and to encourage industry. Coffee production soon came to dominate the national economy, providing a solid economic foundation for stability.

CLASH BETWEEN LIBERALS AND CONSERVATIVES

During the first decades after independence, most Latin American countries also witnessed the division of political opinion along conservative and liberal lines. Conservatives generally stood for the preservation of the Catholic religion and the traditional social order, while liberals usually wanted more democratic political institutions, less church power, and basic social reform. Coastal regions, with closer economic ties to Europe, were often dominated by liberals, while more remote areas remained conservative strongholds.

Conflict in Mexico. Conservatives in Mexico questioned liberal reforms, and many people openly yearned for a monarchy. Some conservatives praised Spain, while others suggested that independence may have been a mistake. At the same time, a liberal government led by Benito Juárez (beh-NEE-tō HWAH-rez) vowed major reform.

As a liberal, Juárez tried to force church officials to sell lands owned by the Church, and he ended the privileges of church courts, which had prevented priests from being tried in gov-

ernment courts for crimes. A new constitution adopted by the Juárez government in 1857 even provided for religious freedom and secular education. Conservative forces, meanwhile, with whom church officials were aligned, resisted any changes in the Church's privileges and status. The government finally responded to this opposition by seizing church treasuries and requiring the Church to sell most of its land. With such opposing forces contending for power, civil war broke out and the country was torn with strife.

In 1863, Mexican conservatives, inspired by Brazil's ability to maintain stability, called for the establishment of a new Mexican empire under the Austrian-born emperor Maximilian. Supported by troops sent by Napoleon III, who wanted to expand French influence in the Western Hemisphere, Maximilian hoped to build such an empire. However, Maximilian's ability failed to match his ambition. In addition, the majority of the Mexican people opposed living under a foreign prince.

Maximilian's hopes for an empire were shattered in 1865 when Napoleon III called his troops back to France in response to the rising militarism of Bismarck's Germany. Without French support, the fate of Maximilian and his conservative supporters was sealed. He was captured and executed by Juárez's forces in 1867, and Juárez was reelected president of

Caught up in conflict after independence, the Church remained a source of stability for Mexican people. *Village Church* by Leonard Sanchez captures a rural Sunday morning in the 1800s.

ASKING EFFECTIVE QUESTIONS

"A good question," it has been said, "is better than its own answer." Because the questions you ask shape what you learn, inventing effective questions is at least as important as being able to answer them.

EXPLAINING THE SKILL

To be most effective, questions must be appropriate to your task. To get details, you ask *what*, *where*, *when*, *how*, and *who* questions. To discover motives or causes, you ask *why* questions. *Why* questions can also help you see the significance of statements or events.

Effective questions must also fit the available data. If the data cannot produce the kinds of information you ask for, then the questions have not been very effective.

As stated on pages 336–337, inventing effective questions involves defining your topic and task, and clarifying what the data can tell you. Then you can brainstorm appropriate questions for your topic and task. Finally, you can choose the questions most likely to help you accomplish your task given the data available.

APPLYING THE SKILL

The procedure for inventing effective questions can also be used with data presented in charts and tables. Invent three effective questions about the following data to help you learn about Brazil's people and economy during the nineteenth century.

IMMIGRATION TO BRAZIL   1820–1883

	Average per year	Total
African	13,875	888,000
Portuguese	3,461	221,536
Italian	1,501	96,018
German	932	15,537
Spanish	243	59,674
Other European	535	34,281

BRAZIL'S POPULATION   1500–1873

	1500	1819	1873
Indian	2,341,000	800,000	215,000
Non-Indian			
Slave	0	1,107,389	1,510,806
Free	0	2,488,743	8,419,672

PRODUCTS AS PERCENTAGE OF TOTAL BRAZILIAN EXPORTS   1821–1870

Product	1821–1830	1841–1850	1861–1870
Coffee	18.6	41.3	45.2
Cotton	20	7.4	18.4
Hides	13.8	8.6	6.0
Rubber	.1	.4	6.2
Sugar	32.2	26.7	17.0

Source: *Brazil: A Handbook of Historical Statistics*, by Armin K. Ludwig. Boston: G. K. Hall and Co.

MAKING MEANING

1. The tables do not give information on (a) causes of European immigration to Brazil from 1820 to 1883, (b) ethnic backgrounds of Brazilians from 1820 to 1883, (c) major Brazilian exports from 1861 to 1870.

2. The three tables could be used to identify (a) Brazil's population in 1860, (b) ethnic groups producing particular products, (c) changes in Brazil's population during the 1800s.

3. Which one of these is a *why* question? (a) How many Indians lived in Brazil in 1819? (b) What was Brazil's largest export from 1861 to 1870? (c) Was the increase in Brazil's population mainly a result of immigration?

REVIEWING THE SKILL

4. Name the features of an effective question.

5. Explain how to invent effective questions.

Mexico. After almost 20 years of war, Mexico finally entered a period of peace.

Like Mexico, Colombia, Argentina, and several other countries experienced similar, though less violent, clashes between liberals and conservatives. Even though the liberals won in each instance, few aspects of society actually changed since the liberal governments did not institute lasting liberal reforms after all. One Latin American writer even remarked that there was nothing so conservative as a liberal in power.

SECTION REVIEW

1. Define *caudillismo* and *buffer state*.

2. Why did the creoles oppose the reforms of Carlos III?

3. What made Bolívar an important leader? What was the significance of the rebellion led by José de San Martín?

4. What role did the liberals play in Mexican politics?

Evaluation. Did most Latin Americans truly achieve independence? Explain your answer.

25–2
GROWTH OF THE UNITED STATES AND CANADA

READ TO FIND OUT

—what the terms *abolitionists* and *Reconstruction* mean.
—how the United States grew to its present size.
—why the Civil War broke out in the United States in the 1860s.
—how Canada, like the United States, grew westward.

Unlike the new Latin American republics, the United States did not go through a period of political instability and caudillismo.

Instead, during the first decades after 1800, territorial expansion toward the Pacific Ocean occupied the attention of the United States and Canada. By the 1830s, however, the divisive issue of slavery became the principal concern of Americans.

AMERICAN TERRITORIAL EXPANSION

The geographic expansion of the United States began in 1803 when Napoleon Bonaparte, needing money for his war against Great Britain, decided to sell Louisiana to the new republic. The Louisiana Purchase was the triumph of the administration of Thomas Jefferson. By this single act, he doubled the land size of the United States, adding more than 800,000 square miles (2,000,000 square kilometers). Now, with the United States stretching westward well beyond the Mississippi River, settlers headed in earnest toward the Pacific.

In 1819, the United States again stretched its borders, this time through the annexation of Florida. For some time, Florida had been a nagging problem for the United States. As a territory of Spain, a major European power, the peninsula represented a potential threat to national security. This threat became serious during the months leading up to the War of 1812, when the American government thought that Great Britain might seize the Spanish fortress at St. Augustine as a means of establishing a southern front. Although the United States occupied the western half of the territory during the War of 1812, eastern Florida remained Spanish for seven more years.

In 1818, the United States protested that Spain was unable to prevent bands of Seminole Indians from raiding across the border into Georgia. Andrew Jackson, who would later become president, was instructed to take the eastern part of the colony. Spain, faced with war against its rebellious colonies in Latin America, was unable to press its claim to Florida and so ceded the area to the United States in 1819.

THE MEXICAN WAR

By the 1830s, many expansionists—people who were in favor of expanding the nation's territory—believed in manifest destiny, claiming that the United States was destined to expand from the Atlantic Ocean to the Pacific. However,

RELATIONSHIPS WITHIN PLACES: CHANGING VIEWS OF THE AMERICAN WEST

Each society in each era perceives and interprets its physical surroundings through the prism of its own way of life.

With these words, geographer Jan Broek explained *environmental perception*, which is the way people see and use their surroundings. Environmental perception not only differs among societies, but it also changes over time.

The opening of the American West provides a good example of changing environmental perceptions. Americans knew next to nothing about lands west of the Mississippi when Napoleon offered to sell Louisiana in 1803. Wild rumors circulated about the wonders of the region. Somewhere out there, people said, was a huge mountain of salt worth far more than the $15 million Napoleon was demanding.

There was no salt mountain in the West. Instead, Louisiana was a broad plain stretching from the Mississippi to the Rocky Mountains. The western half was a region of semi-arid grasslands, known today as the Great Plains.

For centuries, the Great Plains had been the domain of the Commanche, Cheyenne, Sioux, and other Plains tribes. These Indians saw the plains chiefly as the home of the bison, or buffalo, on which the Indians' way of life depended. Millions of buffalo grazed from Texas to Canada, providing the Indians with food, shelter, clothing, and tools. The Indians may even have helped to create the grasslands on the plains by repeatedly burning forests to open up more grazing land for the buffalo.

The first Americans to explore the Great Plains had a perception of this region very different from that of the Indians. In 1820, an army explorer named Stephen Long labeled the plains the "Great American Desert" and described them as "almost wholly unfit for cultivation." Like most Americans at that time, Long believed that land without trees would not support crops.

Americans' perception of the Great Plains changed greatly after the first railroad crossed the West. Suddenly, cattle ranchers saw the grasslands as grazing land for their herds, which could be sent by rail to eastern cities and sold.

In 1883, "600,000 head of cattle" roamed the grasslands. One man recalled that only three years earlier "thousands of buffalo darkened the rolling plains" of Montana. The same displacement occurred everywhere else on the plains. To make room for cattle, the buffalo were destroyed and with them the way of life of the Plains Indians.

The Indians' way of life was also disrupted by the farmers who came west on the trains. These farmers were attracted by the fertile soil of the plains. Despite earlier perceptions that the plains were unfit for farming, plains soil proved to be good for growing wheat and other crops. New barbed wire fences protected crop land from grazing cattle, and fields of shimmering wheat quickly spread across the plains. By 1900, the "Great American Desert" had become America's breadbasket.

The various people who had inhabited the Great Plains had viewed the plains through the prisms of their own ways of life. Differing perceptions and technologies led people to use the plains in different ways, but in ways suited to their own culture and their times.

1. Define *environmental perception*.

2. Describe how perceptions of the Great Plains changed over time.

Mexico owned the vast territory southwest of the Louisiana Purchase.

In 1836, American settlers in the territory of Texas declared their independence from Mexico and established the Republic of Texas. Immediately, the United States began laying plans to annex the territory. Mexico, suspicious of its powerful northern neighbor, made it clear that any intervention in Texas would be considered an act of war.

For ten years no American president was willing to risk a confrontation. Then, in December 1845, a few months after President James Polk's term in office began, Texas was admitted to the Union. Five months later, when a boundary dispute could not be settled, Mexico declared war on the United States. The war lasted until Mexico City fell in 1847. In 1848 the Treaty of Guadalupe Hidalgo (gwah-dah-LOO-pay ee-DAHL-gō) formally ended the war and gave the United States an area that is today California, Nevada, Utah, and parts of Wyoming, Colorado, Arizona, and New Mexico. With the earlier addition of Oregon in 1846, then the Gadsden Purchase in 1853,

Alaska in 1867, and Hawaii in 1898, the growing nation had acquired all the territory that would form its 50 states.

THE CONTROVERSY OVER SLAVERY

For 30 years, expansion was overshadowed by another, more divisive issue. From the 1830s to the 1860s, the United States became sharply divided between supporters and opponents of slavery. Strong supporters of slavery included southern planters, who depended on slave labor. Opponents consisted mostly of small farmers, shopkeepers, and intellectuals, who lived in the North where slavery was not important to the industrial economy.

In contrast to the industrialized North, the South depended on its cotton and tobacco plantations for economic stability. The agricultural states of the South supported themselves by providing the North and Europe with raw materials such as cotton. From the industrial North, the South bought finished goods.

Although industrialization in the North progressed, the South did not advance beyond an

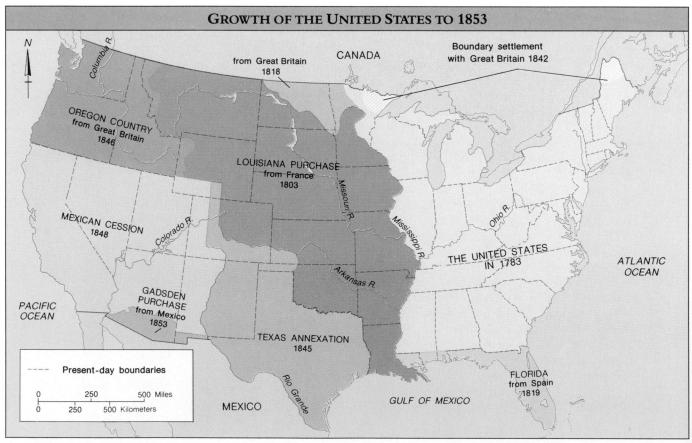

GROWTH OF THE UNITED STATES TO 1853

agricultural economy. Southern planters remained dependent on the slave labor system, while in the North, paid factory workers formed the backbone of the economy.

Abolitionists—or people calling for an end to slavery on moral grounds—strongly pressed the national government to force the southern states to abandon slavery. Slave owners in the meantime discovered that their best defense against antislavery sentiment was a strong stand supporting states' rights, a policy against interference from national authorities. Accordingly, they believed that each state had the right to make its own decision about issues such as slavery because, according to the Constitution, powers not given to the federal government belonged to the individual states.

Tensions grew as new areas applied for statehood. Southerners were opposed to the admission of any more free states for fear of strengthening the abolitionists in Congress. Compromises were usually worked out, however, whereby one slave state was admitted to the Union simultaneously with a free state, thus preserving the balance of power in Congress.

THE CIVIL WAR

In 1860, Abraham Lincoln, a strong opponent of slavery, was elected president. South Carolina, long the leader of the southern states, quickly seceded, or withdrew, from the Union, declaring itself independent. Ten other states followed by mid-1861. Together these states formed the Confederate States of America and elected Jefferson Davis of Mississippi, a former secretary of war, as their president. The North, however, was not prepared to let the United States disintegrate. War soon came when Confederate forces launched an attack on Fort Sumter in Charleston harbor.

While the South had the advantage of excellent generals, the North had most of the other advantages in the war. With a higher level of industrialization, a more efficient transportation system, and a larger population, the North could prepare for war quickly. In contrast, the South had to import most of its military hardware from Great Britain and other European countries. By 1863, a Union naval blockade cut off the Confederacy from its source of supplies. In spite of such disadvantages, southern commander Robert E. Lee was able to fight for four

Lincoln's decision to use black troops in combat against the South coincided with the Emancipation Proclamation. These black Union soldiers pause in a Tennessee camp between battles.

years against Union forces, led successfully by Ulysses S. Grant the last year of the war.

In 1863, President Lincoln issued the famous Emancipation Proclamation declaring that slaves in the South were free. Southerners, however, ignored the proclamation and continued fighting. By 1865, after much destruction and loss of life, the South was finally forced to surrender. Slavery, once the foundation of southern society, came to an end.

It is possible to see the Civil War as part of a trend toward the violent resolution of political problems that occurred throughout the Western Hemisphere in the mid-1800s. The war in Mexico, fought from 1853 to 1867 between conservatives and liberals, and wars in Paraguay, Uruguay, Argentina, Brazil, and Venezuela all demonstrate this trend. Although the controversy over slavery was the spark for violence in the United States, the Civil War was basically a conflict pitting traditional conservatives against reforming liberals.

The Civil War was followed by a period of federal military occupation of the South, called *Reconstruction*. As planned, Reconstruction was to be a program that would revitalize the southern states while readmitting them to the Union. Americans hoped that reconstructing the severed union, rebuilding the war-torn South, and securing a role for former slaves would take place quickly. However, the size of the task, as well as sharply opposing viewpoints, slowed the nation's recovery. Nevertheless, by the end of Reconstruction in 1877, the South had new schools, railroads, and factories, and a stronger economy.

INDUSTRIALIZATION IN THE UNITED STATES

During the Civil War, the production of war materials had required the expansion of northern factories. After the war, industries continued turning out goods and equipment. The United States became an important industrial power, second only to Great Britain, but it had a major advantage over all the European nations. Whereas Great Britain, France, and Germany had to establish empires in Africa and Asia to gain raw materials to supply their new industries, the United States had the American West at its doorstep. The construction of an extensive railroad system after the war further integrated the West—and its raw materials—into the American industrial economy.

Unlike the nations of Latin America, many of which were caught in the role of suppliers of raw materials to industries in Europe, the United States became the dominant power in the Western Hemisphere because of its industrialization. Economic independence provided the United States with considerable international influence.

CANADA IN THE NINETEENTH CENTURY

After the American Revolution in 1776, the only British territory in the Western Hemisphere, except for some small Caribbean possessions, was the large but rather unpopulated colony of Canada. The fur and timber trades dominated the economy of the colony.

Because Canada had been a French colony in the eighteenth century, there was also a large French-speaking population, in the province of Quebec. In the nineteenth century, tensions developed in Canada between the French population of Quebec and the rest of the country, which was dominated by the English language and British culture. Compromises, however, were worked out so that the French members of

SPOTLIGHT: PEOPLE

IDA TARBELL

As the United States was growing in size and military strength during the 1800s, its industries were also rapidly expanding. Among the dramatic success stories was the rise of the huge Standard Oil Company during the 1870s. By 1882, Standard Oil controlled almost 90 percent of the United States oil industry and much of the world oil trade. Many Americans praised this industrial giant as representing the growth and strength of American business, but others accused it of unfair practices. One of the most stinging attacks came from the pen of the journalist and historian Ida Tarbell.

By 1900, when she was asked by *McClure's* magazine to write about Standard Oil, Ida Tarbell was a well-established journalist who had been largely responsible for the magazine's success. However, she became most widely known for revealing how Standard Oil gained its grip on the oil industry.

After careful research, Tarbell concluded that Standard Oil president John D. Rockefeller squeezed out competitors by making secret agreements with railroads to transport his company's oil at lower rates. Tarbell worried that such practices represented a growing trend toward unfairness in business. She wrote:

> Very often people who admit that Mr. Rockefeller has employed force and fraud to secure his ends justify him by declaring, "It's business." That is, "it's business" has come to be a legitimate excuse for hard dealing, sly tricks, special privileges. [These practices are] employed by all sorts, from corner grocers up to bankers. There is something alarming that [many people] in this country are growing up with the idea that business is war and that morals have nothing to do with its practice.

Throughout her career Ida Tarbell emphasized that fair business competition was important for the welfare of the nation. She carried the hope that businesses would eventually embrace the belief that "a thing won by breaking the rules of the game is not worth the winning."

In this 1885 photograph, Canadian Pacific Railway officials drive the last spike to complete the transcontinental line that now connected ports on both coasts. Growth of Canada's western provinces increased rapidly as the railroad brought immigrants to settle the new land.

Canadian society could retain their own identity through the preservation of their religion, laws, and language.

Politically, Canada was very stable. British troops were only needed to suppress minor revolts in 1837 and 1838. However, to avoid future problems, the British government sent Lord Durham to the colony. He recommended that Canada be given home rule. Over the next 30 years, Great Britain carried out a program aimed at giving Canadians more control over their own affairs. This policy culminated in the 1867 British North America Act, which granted Canada self-government within the British Empire. A Scotsman, John A. MacDonald, became the first prime minister.

Expansionism. As in the United States, expansionism played a principal role in Canadian history. During the nineteenth century, joint-stock companies like the Hudson's Bay Company and the North West Company founded towns and brought settlers to the far north and west, but most of Canada's population remained in the south, usually within a few miles of the United States. The Klondike gold rush of 1896, however, provided incentive for settlers to move west. Manitoba, British Columbia, Alberta, and Saskatchewan became provinces between 1870 and 1905, paralleling the territorial expansion of the United States.

Though both nations expanded toward the Pacific, Canada differed from the United States in an important way. Whereas industrialization in the United States provided an economic foundation for imperialist expansion, Canada remained essentially an agricultural country. This difference in economic development is one of the reasons Canada never became an imperialist nation.

SECTION REVIEW

1. Define *abolitionists* and *Reconstruction*.

2. How did the Mexican War result in the territorial expansion of the United States?

3. Describe the economic differences between the northern and southern states before the beginning of the Civil War.

4. What brought settlers to the western portions of Canada?

Synthesis. What problems might Canada have encountered by having a large, expansionist nation like the United States on its southern border? Why do you think Canada fared better than Mexico in its relations with the United States?

Data Search. Refer to the appropriate charts on pages 831 and 832 to identify **(a)** the change in the population of the United States between 1800 and 1850, and **(b)** the change in the number of slave imports to British North America and the United States in the eighteenth and nineteenth centuries.

25-3
LATIN AMERICA'S SEARCH FOR STABILITY

READ TO FIND OUT

—what the term *dependency* means.
—how Latin America achieved political stability.
—how the United States became involved in Latin American politics.
—what caused the Mexican Revolution of 1910.

The problems facing Latin America between 1860 and 1914 were far different from those encountered in the decades after independence. After the 1860s, leaders tried to modernize their nations and bring economic progress to their people, who included thousands of European immigrants in such countries as Brazil, Uruguay, and Argentina. The greatest concern, however, was the preservation of independence and Latin American culture in the face of European and North American imperialism.

ORDER AND PROGRESS

Two words that define the political outlook of late nineteenth-century Latin American governments are *order* and *progress*. While order was seen in terms of political stability, progress was defined in terms of a country's ability to become more industrialized and Europeanized.

The Latin American republics did not have the financial resources to modernize on their own, and as a result they had to attract foreign capital. Before European and North American companies were willing to invest, however, the Latin American republics first had to achieve political stability. Hence, with the establishment of order came the opportunity for progress.

Mexico under Díaz. Soon after the victory in the war against Maximilian and his conservative backers in 1867, Mexico's liberal government under Juárez took a conservative turn. It was,

the liberals argued, impossible to bring peace to the countryside without taking strong actions against bandits and thieves.

In 1876, a new dictator, Porfirio Díaz (por-FIR-ee-ō DEE-ahz) seized power. Although Díaz restored order, he suppressed all political opposition, using paid assassins to eliminate his enemies and to achieve a measure of stability. He encouraged foreigners to invest in new mines, oil fields, and textile mills. The order, the clean streets of the cities, and the luxury of the rich that resulted from Díaz's dictatorship impressed foreigners, who soon began investing. Concentration of land ownership in the hands of a few wealthy landlords increased. By 1911, fewer than 3,000 families owned nearly half of Mexico, and about 95 percent of all people who earned a living in agriculture owned no land at all.

Colombia and Venezuela. In Colombia, Rafael Núñez (rah-fah-EL NOO-nyez) became president in 1880. During the 1880s and 1890s, he implemented a conservative program that came to be called the Colombian "regeneration." Núñez brought stable government to his country by strengthening the power of the state. Under his rule, rebels were severely punished, opposition newspapers were closed, and elections were rigged so that only Núñez's candidates were awarded office. Núñez was rewarded for his policies as European investors began to arrive.

In the 1880s, under Antonio Guzmán Blanco (gooz-MAHN BLAHN-kō), Venezuela also en-

Taken about 1910, this photograph shows Indians spinning yucca fibers. The many landless poor were generally not seen by foreign visitors seeking to make investments in Díaz's Mexico.

tered a period of order and progress. Caracas, the capital city, was completely rebuilt. Wide avenues and paved streets replaced dark alleys and muddy roads. Guzmán Blanco improved Venezuela's ports and railroads, and by the end of his administration in 1888, the people of Caracas strolled down lighted streets. Just as in Mexico, though, the government maintained order by jailing its opponents.

Brazil. Events took a different course in South America's largest country, Brazil. Fifty years of stability under the monarchy of Dom Pedro II, who ruled from 1840 to 1889, made it the most economically advanced nation in Latin America. However, it was divided between a predominantly conservative southeast, with a society based on slave labor, and a mainly liberal northeast, where free labor was more important.

Just as in the United States before the Civil War, friction between slave owners and abolitionists dominated Brazilian politics. In addition, Great Britain strongly pressured Brazil to end the slave trade, even seizing Brazilian slave ships. Gradually, the efforts of Brazilian abolitionists, as well as British threats, slowed the slave trade to a trickle. This trade was finally outlawed in 1850.

Then, some of Brazil's younger political and military leaders began to view both slavery and the monarchy as outdated. A movement arose to abolish slavery completely and at the same time to establish a republican form of government. While large landowners resisted these changes, the movement gained support from small property owners and city dwellers. Finally, the last slaves were freed in 1888. However, as a result, angry ex-slaveholders turned on Dom Pedro II, and one year after the slaves were freed, he was overthrown. Brazil was declared a republic.

DEPENDENCY AND DEVELOPMENT

Although foreign investment in Latin America continued in the late 1800s, the region was still chiefly a supplier of raw materials to the industrialized nations. Because of their greater economic power, Great Britain, France, Germany, and the United States were able to set the prices on Latin American products. With large loan payments to make to its foreign investors, Latin American countries could not refuse to sell their products at established prices. Latin America, therefore, had no control over its exports. Such a situation is called *dependency*.

Foreign investors were able to hold Latin America hostage with threats of loan foreclosures. In time, the investors gained key positions in Latin American society. Soon British and French merchants occupied the best houses and foreign engineers held the best jobs.

Secure in their new positions at the top of the Latin American economic structure, foreign investors were also able to dictate the terms of investment. For example, railroads were not built to connect important cities but rather to make it easier for the industrial nations to exploit the continent's natural resources. Likewise, ports were improved while hospitals and schools were left half-built. Foreign investment, originally seen as the quickest path to economic freedom, instead resulted in Latin America becoming part of European economic empires that were not so different from the imperialist empires established in Africa and Asia.

Other obstacles to industrialization. Dependency was only one side of the story. Latin America also faced other obstacles that prevented economic growth. Among these were geographic isolation, poor roads, poor communication, high rates of illiteracy, and perhaps most constricting, an uneven distribution of wealth. Little of the economic progress in the late 1800s helped the middle and lower classes but instead benefited only a few Latin Americans in addition to the foreign investors.

IMPERIALISM IN THE AMERICAS

The 1880s and 1890s saw an increase in foreign activity, especially in and around the Caribbean. France invested heavily in Panama between 1878 and 1890. Germany, thirsting for an empire, blockaded Venezuela's ports in the early twentieth century when the government of Cipriano Castro (sip-ṛee-AHN-nō KAHS-trō) defaulted on debts owed to German citizens. British Honduras, once part of the colony of Jamaica, was the only formal colony set up in Latin America at this time by a European power.

The Monroe Doctrine. One reason the European powers hesitated to establish colonies in the Americas was the Monroe Doctrine. The

Monroe Doctrine, declared in the 1820s by American president James Monroe, said that the United States would oppose any attempt by a European power to establish political control in the Western Hemisphere. Before 1900, however, the United States did not have the political or military strength to enforce this policy, and European troops often engaged in short interventions in Latin America. Nevertheless, no European state established formal control over a Latin American republic between the time of its independence and 1900.

As the United States became an industrial power, North American firms began investing in Latin America on a large scale. After 1900, the United States became the largest investor in Latin America, pushing Great Britain to second place.

The Spanish-American War. In 1898, Spain and the United States engaged in a war brought about by American imperialists. During the 1880s and 1890s, American activity in Spain's principal remaining colony, Cuba, had grown steadily. A strong Cuban independence movement gained American support. Spain resented this support, and tension between the two nations grew. When the American battleship *Maine* mysteriously exploded in the Havana harbor, expansionists seized the opportunity to pressure President McKinley into declaring war so that the United States could annex Cuba.

In battle, the new American navy easily outclassed Spain's weaker fleet in the Pacific and the Caribbean. Within a short time, the United States took control of Cuba, Puerto Rico, and the Philippines. Puerto Rico and the Philippines remained American possessions, but Cuba was given limited independence in 1901, after a few years of military occupation. The United States was concerned with controlling Cuba's economy, not in governing the island, but it reserved the right to intervene if conditions became unstable. The United States used this option from 1899 to 1902 and from 1906 to 1909.

Besides giving the United States new territories, the Spanish-American War generated interest for a canal between the Atlantic and the Pacific. Fighting a war in both the Caribbean and the Pacific had demonstrated the need for a quick route between the seas.

Both Nicaragua and Panama offered good sites for a canal, but Panama was the preferred

More than 250 Americans died in the explosion of the battleship *Maine* in Havana. "Remember the *Maine*" became the battle cry for Americans who urged support for a war with Spain.

location. In 1903, Panama still belonged to Colombia, and American negotiations with the Colombian government to build such a canal seemed to be getting nowhere. Finally, in exasperation, President Theodore Roosevelt secretly threw his support behind a Panamanian revolution led by Manuel Amador, a doctor on the Panama Railroad.

The revolution succeeded, and Panama became an independent state in 1903. The first act of the new Panamanian government was to sign a treaty giving the United States near total control over the canal and its adjacent territory. The United States began construction in 1904, and ten years later, in August 1914, the Panama Canal was opened.

The United States intervention in Panama began what would become several decades of active North American involvement in the region. Many of these interventions stemmed from an amendment to the Monroe Doctrine called the Roosevelt Corollary. Named after President Theodore Roosevelt, it stated that the United States had the right to intervene in Latin America to settle disputes—especially financial disputes—between the republics and the European powers. In keeping with the Roosevelt Corollary, the United States sent troops to Nicaragua, the Dominican Republic, Haiti, and Mexico during the first decades of the twentieth century. Intervention in Latin America was so frequent that the slogan "speak softly and carry a big stick" came to characterize American policy toward the region.

THE MEXICAN REVOLUTION

Eventually a backlash grew up against repressive government and foreign influence, including that of the United States. About 1900, a small group of Mexican intellectuals began to agitate against the Díaz dictatorship. These agitators advocated a return to the liberal principles of Benito Juárez. At first, the upper classes dominated the movement, but later workers and farmers joined the cause as reforms for the lower classes became part of the battle cry. A desire to return economic control to Mexican hands was an important part of the revolutionary movement. The movement had various kinds of grievances and different social groups, but the revolutionaries agreed on one goal: the overthrow of Díaz.

In late 1910, fighting broke out. A moderate leader, Francisco Madero (mah-DAY-rō), came to the fore and negotiated with Díaz, winning agreement on elections for a new president in 1911. Díaz resigned and left for France. Madero, who wanted only political change, was unable to contain the revolution. The peasants wanted changes such as land reform, and soon the country was again in the midst of civil war. In 1913, General Victoriano Huerta (HWER-tah), who supported the wealthy landowners, had Madero assassinated and took control of the country.

Because of Huerta's brutal tyranny, President Woodrow Wilson sent troops ashore at Veracruz in 1914 to aid Huerta's opposition, led by Venustiano Carranza (veh-noos-tee-AH-nō car-RAHN-zah). Soon after Huerta's resignation, Carranza became president. In 1917, a new constitution was adopted that laid the foundation for a new Mexican republic.

SECTION REVIEW

1. Define *dependency*.

2. How did strong dictators establish political stability in the Americas?

3. Why did the United States become an imperialist power in Latin America?

4. What caused the Mexican Revolution?

Synthesis. Why might a British banker hesitate to invest funds in an unstable Latin American country? How would a strong government in such a country make it easier to invest?

Data Search. Refer to the appropriate charts on page 833 to identify (a) two characteristics of trade between Latin America and the United States, Britain, and France from 1860 to 1913, and (b) major raw materials exported to Europe from Argentina, Brazil, Venezuela, Peru, and Mexico between 1880 and 1900.

HISTORY IN FOCUS

While some of the principal political issues in Latin America were solved by 1850, a huge gap remained between a white minority and an oppressed and impoverished mass of mestizo, Indian, and black workers. Despite independence, the basic social and economic structure of Latin America remained more difficult than ever to change. Latin American countries still produced raw materials and remained dependent on world markets they could not control. If anything, the economic and social situation, compounded by constant violence, left most Latin Americans worse off than they had been in 1700.

The order and progress policy of the various Latin American countries did not result in the new society envisioned by leaders in the principal countries. By 1900, dependency and imperialism made Latin America more impoverished and less independent than at any other time since 1825.

From the 1890s to 1914, growing discontent with the repressive governments caused the aging dictators to crack down still harder on civil liberties. Newspaper offices stayed closed, jails remained full, and people mysteriously disappeared. The economic distance between rich and poor grew larger, and the wealth of the continent was exported to factories in New York and Liverpool. After a century of independence, the vast majority of people in Latin America were no better off than they had been during the era of the Spanish monarchs. Life was still hard and still very short.

Only the United States and, to some extent, Canada, progressed in a material sense. As in Great Britain, France, and Germany, industrialization provided the United States with international economic independence which, in turn, led to imperialism. By the mid-twentieth century, the United States would even surpass the European powers, becoming one of the strongest nations on earth.

SUMMARY

- During the early 1800s, Latin Americans inspired by Enlightenment ideas began to seek greater independence from Spain. The first revolt, however, took place in Haiti, where slaves threw off French colonial rule and gained independence by 1804.

- The earliest independence movements in South America were led by Bolívar and San Martín, and in Mexico by Hidalgo and later by Iturbide.

- Independence did little to change social and economic conditions in Latin America. Politics were marked by caudillo rule and struggles between liberals and conservatives. Brazil was the exception, continuing its stability after independence under the monarchy of Dom Pedro II.

- During the 1800s, the United States expanded westward. The Civil War and Reconstruction weakened the nation for a time, but by the 1870s the country was industrializing rapidly. Canada also expanded, but with a smaller population, it experienced less conflict and less rapid industrial growth.

- After 1860, Latin American countries fell under the domination of the industrialized nations, which exploited the continent's resources at the expense of its people. The Mexican Revolution of 1910 was in part a response to such conditions.

- Following the Spanish-American War, the United States became the dominant imperialist power in the Western Hemisphere. Often the United States used the Monroe Doctrine to extend its influence.

VOCABULARY REVIEW

Match each numbered vocabulary term with the lettered word or phrase most closely related to it. Then explain how the items in each pair are related.

1. caudillismo
2. buffer state
3. abolitionists
4. dependency

    (a) domination
    (b) emancipate
    (c) dictator
    (d) neutral

CHAPTER REVIEW

1. **(a)** What developments led Latin Americans to seek their independence from Spain? **(b)** How were the circumstances of Haiti's revolt different? **(c)** Compare Mexico's independence movement with the Mexican Revolution.

2. **(a)** Describe social conditions in Latin America after independence. **(b)** Why did daily life not change much after independence?

3. **(a)** How did caudillo rule promote instability in Latin America? **(b)** Compare early caudillos with Latin American rulers of the late 1800s.

4. **(a)** How did the political map of Latin America change after independence? **(b)** What caused these changes?

5. **(a)** How did liberals and conservatives differ in Latin America? How were these differences linked to geography? **(b)** Compare Juárez and Santander. Contrast them with Rosas. **(c)** How were Maximilian and Dom Pedro II both alike and different?

6. **(a)** How was the period after independence in the United States different from that in Latin America? **(b)** Describe three ways in which the United States expanded, and give an example of each. **(c)** Compare the development of Canada with that of the United States.

7. **(a)** How did economic and political issues combine to provoke the American Civil War? **(b)** How was the situation in Brazil similar or different? **(c)** Compare the Civil War with political conflict in Latin America.

8. **(a)** How did the main concerns of Latin American governments change after 1860? **(b)** How did Latin American governments seek order and progress? What were the results?

9. **(a)** Why did dependency develop in Latin America? **(b)** What effect did foreign investment have on economic and social conditions in Latin America? **(c)** How did Old World and New World imperialism differ?

10. **(a)** How did the United States exert influence over Latin America? **(b)** Why was the Spanish-American War a turning point for the United States? **(c)** Explain how the United States obtained the Panama Canal.

THINKING CRITICALLY: ACTIVITIES

1. Simón Bolívar was a great Latin American hero, yet he died in poverty and despair in 1830, never having fulfilled his dream of a united Latin America. Imagine that you are Bolívar a few years before his death. Write a letter to a friend explaining your feelings about the course of Latin America since it gained independence from Spain.

2. Imagine that you are a member of the United States Congress in 1898, just prior to the Spanish-American War. With a partner, develop a pamphlet to either persuade others to go to war or to resist the war effort.

3. Divide into groups of four or five to discuss the following question: Why do many Latin Americans feel resentment and bitterness toward the United States? Are those feelings justified? Base your responses on material from the chapter.

APPLYING SOCIAL STUDIES SKILLS

Reading maps. Maps can show the impact of wars and revolutions. Compare the two maps on pages 558 and 559 in order to answer these questions.

1. What is the purpose of the two maps?

2. Which European nation lost all of its Latin American territory between 1790 and 1828?

3. Which European nation lost the most territory during this period?

4. Which European nation gained territory during this period? Where?

5. Name two nations that still had colonies in the Caribbean in 1828.

6. What six new nations were carved out of New Spain?

7. What three new nations were formed out of New Granada?

8. From what colony were Argentina, Paraguay, and Uruguay formed?

9. Bolivia was made up of territory from three colonies. Identify these colonies.

10. From what colony was Chile formed?

APPLYING THINKING SKILLS

Asking effective questions. The following observations were written in 1829 by Simón Bolívar. Determine the two or three most effective questions you could ask to help understand the early history of independence in Latin America. Then answer the questions that follow.

There is no good faith among the nations in America. Treaties are scraps of paper; constitutions, printed matter; elections, battles; freedom, anarchy; and life, a torment.

Elections were characterized by riots and intrigue. Many times armed soldiers marched to the polls in formation. And to what purpose?— momentary control amidst times of trouble, battle, and sacrifice. Virtually every government official has been replaced by a blood-stained victor. Rare are the elections that are free of terrible crimes. Rivadavia [a statesman who was active in Argentina's independence movement] was unable to stay in office half the legal term.

Nowhere do those elected come to office according to the law. Assassinations are being committed in Mexico, Bolivia, and Colombia. Is there any crime of which Guatemala is innocent? The lawful authorities have been removed, the provinces have rebelled against the capital; brother wars upon brother—and this war is to the death. Town fights town; city stands against city. Hapless Bolivia has had four different leaders in less than two weeks!

Recent events in Mexico dwarf everything. Horror and crime stalk that fair land. [Rebels] bathed the capital in blood and overran the finest city in America [Mexico City] with the scum of the earth. The New World is an abyss of abominations. We yearn for a stable government.

Abridged from *Selected Writings of Bolívar*, edited by Harold A. Bierck, Jr. New York: The Colonial Press Inc., 1951.

1. What are two important features of an effective question?

2. What is one procedure for inventing effective questions?

3. When would it be appropriate to ask a *so what* question? A *why* question? A *what* question? A *how* question?

4. What are two effective questions you could ask about Bolívar's account? Explain.

CHAPTER TWENTY-SIX

IMPERIALISM IN AFRICA AND THE MIDDLE EAST

1800–1914

26-1 IMPERIAL CONTROL IN SUB-SAHARAN AFRICA

26-2 IMPACT AND RESISTANCE

26-3 IMPERIALISM AND THE OTTOMAN EMPIRE

The Inauguration of the Suez Canal. Edouard Riou, nineteenth century.

Unlike Latin America, most of sub-Saharan Africa largely escaped the effects of European expansion until the late nineteenth century. Between the 1500s and the 1870s, the European presence in Africa was confined to coastal forts, trading posts, and only a few settlements. Beginning about 1880, however, rapid industrialization and increased competition among European powers caused a growing desire for colonial territory.

Between 1880 and 1914, Europeans established social, political, and economic control over nearly all of Africa. At the same time, they took advantage of the continuing decline of the Ottoman Empire to gain greater influence in North Africa and the Middle East. Although Africans and Middle Easterners resisted imperialism, European domination had far-reaching effects on their cultures and societies.

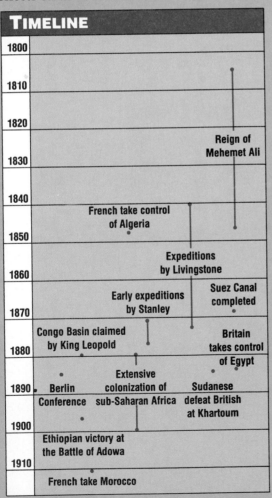

TIMELINE

1800		
1810		
1820		
1830		Reign of Mehemet Ali
1840		
1850	French take control of Algeria	
1860		Expeditions by Livingstone
1870	Early expeditions by Stanley	Suez Canal completed
1880	Congo Basin claimed by King Leopold	Britain takes control of Egypt
1890	Berlin Conference	Extensive colonization of sub-Saharan Africa	Sudanese defeat British at Khartoum
1900	Ethiopian victory at the Battle of Adowa	
1910	French take Morocco	

26–1
IMPERIAL CONTROL IN SUB-SAHARAN AFRICA

READ TO FIND OUT

—what the terms *paternalism* and *assimilation* mean.
—how African-European trade before 1880 affected Africa.
—where Europeans focused their first colonizing efforts.
—how Europeans gained political control over much of Africa.
—how Europeans gained economic control over their colonies.

Although Europeans held little territory in Africa before 1880, the demand Europeans created for slaves—especially before 1800—greatly affected African societies. Because of the slave trade, whole villages were destroyed and many traditional political systems were weakened.

By about 1880, when Europeans began entering Africa with the intention of taking over territory and establishing colonies, the disruption brought by the slave trade had weakened Africans' ability to resist. In addition, Western inventions aided European conquest. Deadly weapons such as machine guns and speedy transportation in the form of steamships enabled Europeans to create a new political order of their own in Africa.

While imperialism in Latin America took the form of economic dependency and military intervention, imperialism in Africa involved direct social, political, and economic control of African societies. Europeans obtained this complete control by setting up colonial administration, or a system of imperial rule designed to increase the power of Europeans and reduce that of Africans. The European domination of the African continent after 1880 became the most dramatic example of European expansion during the Age of Imperialism.

AFRICAN TRADE BETWEEN 1800 AND 1870

The slave trade that had flourished in Africa in the seventeenth and eighteenth centuries began to change after 1800. The demand for slaves in Western countries dropped because the new industrial economies ran on paid wage labor, not on slave labor. At the same time, antislavery movements in Europe and in the United States pushed to abolish slavery. By mid-century, the Atlantic slave trade had declined dramatically, although a slave trade continued within Africa, and Arab merchants still trafficked in human cargo along the East African coast.

While the slave trade declined, a new demand arose for palm oil. This oil, which was used in making soap and candles, could be produced in large quantities in parts of West Africa. Other African raw products, such as rubber and minerals, also became more valuable in the industrializing West. These new demands caused a great increase in Western trade with West and East Africa after 1800.

This new African trade had varying effects across Africa. While some coastal states rich in palm oil flourished, many other African kingdoms, dependent on slave trading before 1800, suffered crises. In the inland state of Oyo, for instance, the economy was crippled by the decline in the slave trade. As a result, the kingdom grew weak and was torn by social upheaval and eventually civil war in 1865.

Between 1800 and 1870, the slow transformation of African society originally caused by the slave trade continued. By 1880, African-

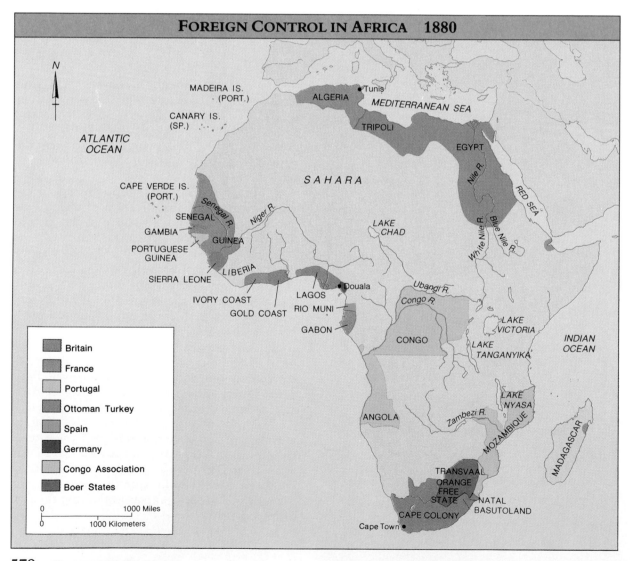

FOREIGN CONTROL IN AFRICA   1880

European trade had brought instability and conflict to many African societies. Small communities in the interior completely destroyed by the slave trade had not recovered. Coastal kingdoms had entered into rivalries that had not existed before the arrival of Europeans, and economies once self-sufficient became dependent on trade with foreigners. Traditional political authority was weakened as a new merchant class arose in Africa, challenging the power of hereditary chiefs.

EARLY SETTLERS, MISSIONARIES, AND EXPLORERS

Before 1879, Europeans had settled in significant numbers only in Algeria and South Africa. The British controlled mineral-rich South Africa, while Dutch settlers, the Boers, lived in independent republics to the north—Transvaal and Orange Free State. In Algeria, the French had established coastal settlements. Through these settlements, the French gained influence in Tunisia and Egypt.

Only a few Europeans journeyed outside these areas of settlement and beyond the coastal trading posts before 1879. Among these people were geographers and journalists who explored the continent's interior, and missionaries who tried to bring Christianity to its inhabitants.

Beginning in the early nineteenth century, European missionaries flocked to Africa and moved deep into the interior to introduce what they considered to be the benefits of European civilization. However, most Africans, adhering to their ancient beliefs, resisted efforts to Christianize them.

Missionary activity contributed to opening Africa to European imperialism. Picturesque accounts of missionary ventures that were published in the West aroused widespread interest in Africa. Governments sometimes sent troops into Africa to protect missionaries.

Explorers also sparked European interest in African territory. David Livingstone, who spent 30 years exploring sub-Saharan Africa in the middle of the nineteenth century, was a missionary-explorer from Scotland. Livingstone's reports on the land and people of Africa excited geographers and thrilled readers in Great Britain. His accounts convinced many people in Europe that Africa should be opened to Christianity and commerce.

The queen mother of the Banum stands beside her throne in the German colony of Cameroon. The Western-style umbrella reflects increasing European influence in Africa.

Henry M. Stanley, a British-born journalist, also wrote stories for the Western press about Africa. He explored the Congo River and became convinced of Africa's economic potential for Europe. In 1877, hearing Stanley's accounts of the wonders of Africa, Belgium's King Leopold II commissioned Stanley to make further explorations of the Congo River basin. As representative of the king's private company, the International Congo Association, Stanley signed more than 400 treaties with African chieftains, securing rights to their land in exchange for weapons.

THE RACE FOR COLONIES

Stanley's activities helped to generate new interest in African territory among European powers engaged in political rivalries. Between 1880 and 1885, nearly every European country began to compete not just for trading rights and isolated coastal forts, but for African land and direct control of African resources.

Based on Stanley's treaties, King Leopold established his personal claim to most of the Congo Basin in 1880. France responded by sending its own explorer, Savorgnan de Brazza (SAH-VOR-NEEAHN de BRAH-ZAH), to claim land to the north of the Congo River basin. Soon, France and Britain began expanding their scattered possessions on the coast of West Africa, sending well-equipped troops to claim and defend territory by force.

RESEARCHING INFORMATION IN PERIODICALS

INTRODUCING THE SKILL

Magazines and journals offer up-to-date information and varying viewpoints on almost any subject. These publications are called periodicals because they are issued at regular intervals, such as every week, month, or quarter of the year.

Most libraries have collections of periodicals that date back many years. Libraries also have resources indicating which magazines have articles on particular subjects. One resource increasingly being used is the computer database, a continually updated file of information and references. However, you should still be familiar with a standard resource known as the *Readers' Guide to Periodical Literature*, a series of volumes in the library's reference section. The *Readers' Guide to Periodical Literature* is an index to articles in about 200 commonly used periodicals published between 1900 and the present.

EXPLAINING THE SKILL

The *Readers' Guide to Periodical Literature* lists articles in alphabetical order by subject and author. Follow these steps when using the guide:

A. *Choose the volume or volumes with the appropriate dates.* The most recent guides are slim paperbacks. The older guides are thick books with listings for two years.

B. *Look up the subject of interest to you.* Most subject headings are followed by a list of entries on that topic. You may also find a list of related subjects to look at, such as these listed under the heading AFRICA:

AFRICA
   See also
   Agriculture—Africa
   Colonies in Africa
   Education—Africa

Broad subjects are often divided into subtopics, as in the following listing:

SLAVERY
   Africa
   Arabia
   United States

If there are no entries under a subject heading, you will usually be referred to another heading, as in this listing:

AFRICAN sculpture. See Sculpture, African

C. *Make a list of the articles you want to look at.* Include the following information:

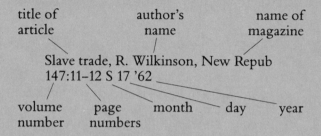

When writing down the information for each article, refer to the abbreviation keys at the front of the guide if necessary. One key lists abbreviations of the titles of the periodicals. Here are two examples:

U S News—*U. S. News and World Report*
New Repub—*New Republic*

The second key lists other abbreviations used in the *Readers' Guide to Periodical Literature*. Here are two examples:

il—illustrated
S—September

D. *Bring your list of articles to the librarian.* After referring to your list, the librarian can help you to get the magazines you need. For some articles, you may have to go to your community's main library or a nearby college library.

REVIEWING THE SKILL

1. What is the *Readers' Guide to Periodical Literature*, and how is it useful?

2. How are articles listed in the *Readers' Guide to Periodical Literature*?

3. Where will you find keys to the abbreviations used in the entries?

4. What information should you list about the articles you want to read?

Meanwhile, Portugal strengthened its control over its territories in Angola on the southwestern coast, and Mozambique on the southeastern. Germany entered the race in earnest in 1884, claiming West African lands in what became Togo and Cameroon, where German companies had trading posts. Germany also claimed lands in East Africa, now called Tanzania.

In 1885, the imperialist nations, meeting at the Berlin Conference, established rules for carving up Africa. This action helped quicken the pace of imperialist competition even more. By 1900, hardly a corner of Africa had escaped European conquest.

COLONIAL ADMINISTRATION

As soon as European powers established their claims to large tracts of land, they began to gain control over Africa and its people by setting up

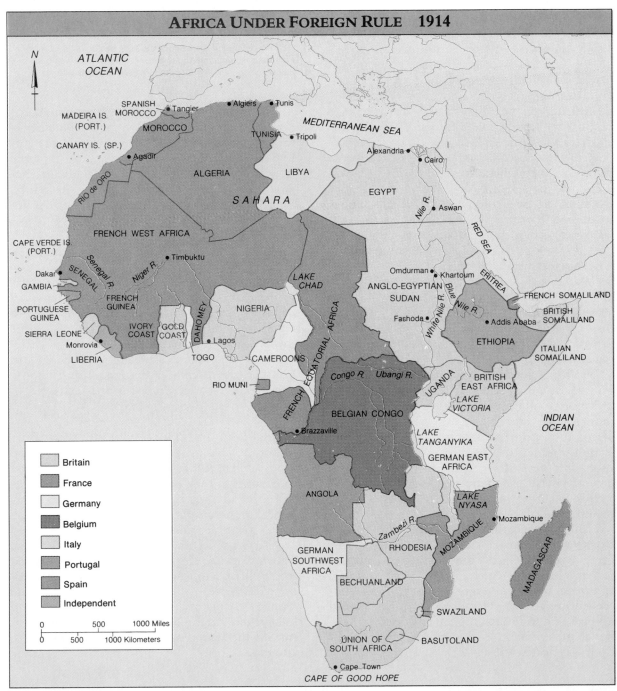

AFRICA UNDER FOREIGN RULE 1914

Legend:
- Britain
- France
- Germany
- Belgium
- Italy
- Portugal
- Spain
- Independent

0   500   1000 Miles
0   500   1000 Kilometers

colonial administration. Although the Africans did not quietly accept European rule, they were unable to effectively resist political control that was backed up by soldiers armed with sophisticated weapons.

In the typical colonial government, ultimate power lay with the European administrators, not with the village chiefs or elders. New boundaries were set up for colonial administration without considering traditional cultural boundaries or rivalries.

The administrators thought of themselves as parents and the Africans as children, an attitude called *paternalism*. When Europeans set up rules of behavior based on paternalism, the roles of parent and child were reinforced and strengthened through everyday activity. By seizing African land, disregarding traditional rule, and destroying traditional livelihoods, Europeans constantly reminded Africans of their lack of power. Thus, paternalism was a foundation of European imperialist control of Africa.

Systems of control. Each imperialist power developed its own style of political control over its African colonies. The British generally permitted local chieftains to maintain some authority. This system was not designed out of respect for traditional authority but rather to accomplish the practical goal of efficient rule. The British believed that by working with or through chiefs, colonial rule would seem more legitimate, or legal, to the people who were governed.

The local chieftains took orders from British officials on broad issues of taxation, commerce, and military matters. The chiefs were no longer the highest authority; however, they were forced to perform unpopular tasks such as collecting taxes. In this new role, they lost the respect they needed to maintain their traditional power. Instead of functioning as a spokesperson for his or her people, a chief became an agent of the imperialist power.

Other Europeans, most notably the French, attempted to replace traditional authority entirely by establishing a bureaucracy of paid European officials. Such systems of colonial administration, however, never entirely succeeded because they required too many trained officials and too much money to operate. Traditional government at the village level, moreover, was nearly impossible to destroy.

Workers toil beside the track of the Tanganyika Railroad as their numerous German overseers look on. The Germans built the railroad to connect Africa's eastern coast with the interior.

The French accompanied their system of colonial rule with a policy of *assimilation*— that is, the absorption of a people into the culture of another nation. The French expected Africans to exchange their own languages, beliefs, and ways of life for those of France. French colonies were to become French provinces when assimilation was complete.

METHODS OF ECONOMIC CONTROL

The primary goal of colonial administrators was to generate wealth for the imperialist country and for private business enterprises. In order to reach such a goal, many workers and large towns were required. Europeans used many methods to gather sufficient workers and to bring people to cities. Among the most important methods were forced labor, takeover of land, and head taxes.

Forced labor. Before the imposition of European rule, able men and women had no reason to leave their villages. When administrators first took control, they often had to use force to acquire the laborers needed to build roads, work mines, and transport goods. Usually, such laborers were provided by chiefs, who captured the necessary Africans ordered by Europeans. The Europeans then held the laborers against their will and did not pay them. The most extreme example of forced labor occurred in the Congo Basin, where Belgians tortured and killed their captured African workers, and terrorized the countryside in the search for more laborers.

Takeover of land. Eventually, forced labor was no longer necessary to create a labor force, because indirect means became effective for inducing some Africans to leave their villages. Throughout the Age of Imperialism in Africa, one of the most common and effective ways of achieving this goal was to appropriate, or take over, land.

Europeans appropriated land from Africans as part of early imperial claims in the 1800s. Explorers and colonial authorities deceived African chiefs, who believed their mark on a piece of paper would give them weapons and make the Europeans leave. Instead, it only brought more Europeans who claimed to have legal rights to the land.

Using similar methods, Europeans later appropriated the best farm land in many areas of Africa for themselves. As a result, many Africans who were forced onto less productive land chose to migrate to cities, where they often took low-paying jobs.

Head taxes. Another indirect method used by Europeans to develop a work force was the head tax or hut tax, levied throughout much of Africa. Such a tax was a yearly payment due for each individual or each dwelling in a village. A head tax—even a small one—created a demand for money, an item not available in the village. To get the tax money, many villages sent some of their young men to towns to earn the money the village needed. Some of these men stayed in the towns to work; others returned, often with stories that convinced other people to move to the city.

SECTION REVIEW

1. Define *paternalism* and *assimilation*.

2. In what ways were African societies weakened by trade with Europe before 1880?

3. Which areas of Africa were first colonized by Europeans?

4. Describe the goals and methods of colonial administration.

5. Describe three ways Europeans gained economic control of Africa.

Analysis. How did Europeans justify—to themselves and to Africans—their imperial control of Africa?

Data Search. Refer to the appropriate charts on page 833 to identify: **(a)** the major exports of South Africa and Belgian lands in the Congo to Europe in the late nineteenth century, **(b)** how Germany's trade with Africa in 1913 differed from that of France and Great Britain, **(c)** which of the following colonial powers had the greatest amount of trade with Africa in 1913: France, Great Britain, Germany.

26-2
IMPACT AND RESISTANCE

READ TO FIND OUT

—what the term *cash crops* means.
—how the African economy developed according to the European model.
—how traditional life in Africa changed as a result of European development.
—how some Africans met imperialism with armed resistance.

As Europeans established colonial administration, they began to introduce European transportation and communication systems, set up schools, and promote the growth of cities. This development of Africa according to the European model contributed to vast changes in much of African society.

Many Africans resisted these changes, and some took up arms to keep Europeans off their lands. Other Africans, who formed a new class in Africa, first welcomed many of the changes. This new class played a leading role in later African history.

COLONIAL DEVELOPMENT

To develop the African economy and make the colonies profitable, Europeans needed trained workers to mine diamonds and gold, staff offices, and drive vehicles. They wanted Africans to speak European languages and adopt Western values. Education, therefore, became an important part of colonial development. Europeans established schools all over Africa. Often Christian missionaries had a large role in creating and running these schools, which taught French, English, German, and other languages, and introduced ideas such as individualism, private property, and progress.

Western education undermined the beliefs and practices of traditional African cultures. It taught Africans that traditional ways were backward and should therefore be abandoned. By preaching individualism, for instance, Western education began to threaten the traditional African emphasis on cooperation and sharing. Such teachings also weakened the authority of traditional laws and rules based on the value of cooperation.

Not all Europeans, of course, promoted education for Africans out of self-interest. Many, especially the missionaries, believed education would benefit Africans and that Europeans were bringing the "light" of Western knowledge to Africa. This attitude, however, was paternalistic and based on the assumption that Western ways of life, races, and religions were superior to those of Africa.

In addition to educated workers, the colonial administrators needed modern transportation and communications systems to govern more efficiently and to maximize profit. The Europeans built railroads and roads mainly to bring raw materials from the interior to coastal ports, where the resources could be shipped to Europe. Administrators built telegraph lines to communicate with each other and with European businesspeople in the colonies.

CHANGES IN AFRICAN WAYS OF LIFE

In colonial Africa, growing towns became centers of social change. Meanwhile, new transportation enabled migration to these centers, and new political boundaries removed traditional barriers to movement that had existed between different or hostile cultures. Exposed to Western ideas, economic practices, and political rule, the values and ways of life of many Africans changed significantly.

Economic changes often had the strongest social impact. Among the most important economic changes was the introduction of *cash crops*—crops grown for sale on the world market and not for local consumption. In areas where agriculture was important, the growing of cash crops helped change traditional African economies and the ways of life and values based on them. Coffee, a common cash crop, was grown on plantations in Kenya. Cocoa was grown in the Gold Coast; cotton, in the Sudan. Cash crops involved villagers in an economy based on money, and often led to the appropriation of their land.

Even where Africans did not lose ownership of their land, growing crops for money still created important social changes. For example, this practice reinforced the idea of private property, a concept that was foreign to many societies in Africa.

In colonial Africa, land was divided into two types, depending on whether it was part of the money economy or the traditional economy. There was privately owned land on which cash crops were grown, and communal land on

Two Christian Kafir girls pose for the camera. While some Kafir people adopted Western dress and religion, others maintained their traditional ways.

AFRICAN RESPONSES TO IMPERIALISM

In 1890, the commander of German forces in Tanzania demanded the surrender of the Yao people. Below is the Yao ruler's reply:

> I have listened to your words but can find no reason why I should obey you—I would rather die first. If it should be friendship that you desire, then I am ready for it, today and always. If it should be war you desire, then I am ready, but never to be your subject. I do not fall at your feet, for you are God's creature just as I am. I am sultan here in my land. You are sultan there in yours. Yet listen, I do not say to you that you should obey me; for I know that you are a free man. As for me, I will not come to you, and if you are strong enough, then come and fetch me.

Below is a Kenya ruler's view of the impact of European culture on his people:

> Something has taken away the meaning of our lives; it has taken away the full days, the good work in the sunshine, the dancing, and the song. It has taken away laughter and the joy of living, the kinship and the love within a family. Above all it has taken from us the wise way of our living in which our lives from birth to death were dedicated to Ngai, supreme of all, and which, with our system of age groups and our councils, insured for all our people a life of responsibility and goodness. Something has taken away our belief in our Ngai and in the goodness of men. And there is not enough land on which to feed.
>
> These good things of the days when we were happy and strong have been taken. There is discontent and argument and violence and hate. Men seem to care more for disputes than for the fullness of life where all work and live for all.
>
> The children make marks which they call writing, but they forget their own language and customs. They know not the laws of their people and they do not pray to Ngai. They have no land and no food and they have lost laughter.

For questions on Echoes of the Past, see "Analyzing Primary Sources" on page 619.

which food was grown. Africans began to view the privately owned land as more valuable because it could bring in money, which was the key to higher status under European rule. Thus, the traditional belief in communal ownership of land was undermined.

In areas where Europeans had settled in greater numbers, such as South Africa and present day Kenya, most cash crops were grown on European-owned plantations. In these areas, Africans owned little land and earned a living working on the plantations. Tending the crops, however, was seasonal work, and plantation workers often had to migrate to different areas to get work. Such seasonal migration further disrupted family structure and village life.

Colonial rule also increased the influence of Christianity throughout Africa. Christian missionaries actively sought to alter African ways of life. They introduced the inhabitants of Africa to Western religions, medicine, and education. Where the Christian message was heeded, some Africans abandoned their belief in traditional religions.

THE LIMITS OF COLONIAL CHANGE

Despite the immense changes brought by European imperialism, European influence did not affect all of Africa the same way, nor did it completely destroy traditional cultures.

Africa's vast size created problems for European administration. For many Africans, especially those living deep in the interior, colonial administrators remained distant overlords. Despite European control, much of Africa south of the Sahara remained economically self-sufficient. Many Africans continued to go about their daily routines of hunting, herding, and farming.

Many Africans exposed to Western ways continued to prefer traditional rituals and religious beliefs. Few Muslims converted to Christianity, for example, and beliefs about the importance of ancestors and nature remained strong. In many areas, African family traditions were also largely preserved. Even today, large areas of the continent remain in many ways free of Western influences.

THE AFRICAN INSPIRATION

European artists found inspiration in African art, with its almost magical qualities. African artists did not portray features realistically; they conveyed the inner spirit of their subjects. In the geometric shapes, bold lines, and strong colors of African masks, the Europeans found stunning new ways to express their own ideas and thus revolutionized Western art.

Left, African beaded mask; right, portrait of Madame Matisse, Henri Matisse, 1905

Left, *Mother and Child*, Pablo Picasso, 1907; right, wood and clay mask from Gabon (west Africa), nineteenth or twentieth century

Left, Bakota funerary figure made of wood, brass, and copper from Gabon; right, *Actor's Mask*, Paul Klee, 1924

Armed Resistance to Colonial Rule

Many Africans resisted the changes brought by colonization. Other Africans sought to prevent European control of their lands through armed struggle. African armed resistance to imperialism dates back to the first European attempts to penetrate Africa's interior in the late 1800s.

The earliest opposition came from Muslim chieftains who had established their own empires in Africa. In West Africa, Ahmadu (AH-MAHDJ-oo), leader of the Tucolor Empire, raised armies to oppose the French advance from Senegal. In the nearby area of upper Guinea, Samori Touré, an outstanding Muslim leader, recruited Mandingo warriors to fight French troops during the 1880s. He built a small arms factory in a remote outpost and withstood French assaults for seven years. Until his capture by the French in 1898, many West Africans effectively resisted French colonial rule.

Widespread opposition. After 1895, defiance of European rule increased. The Hereros (huh-RAY-rōz) fought a brutal war against the Germans in southwest Africa. In Tanganyika—part of present-day Tanzania—Germany ruthlessly suppressed an uprising in which over 120,000 African warriors died.

Africans fought against the British, too. In the area south of Egypt now called the Sudan, an Islamic religious leader named Muhammad Ahmed (AH-med) claimed to be an agent of God appointed to expel the Europeans. The "Mahdi" (MAH-dee), as he was called, declared a *jihad*, or holy war, against the British and recruited a huge following of Africans and Arabs. He kept much of the area free of British control for many years.

In 1884, the British government ordered its soldiers and citizens to evacuate Khartoum, the Sudanese city they held, because of the Mahdi's strength. However, the British commander of the city, Charles Gordon, decided to defend it. In their attempt to keep control of Khartoum, Gordon and 11,000 British and Egyptian troops were killed by the Sudanese under the Mahdi.

Toward the turn of the century, the Matabele (mah-tah-BEHL-eh) and Mashona (mah-SHŌ-nuh) waged war in Rhodesia against the British. In West Africa, many chiefs revolted instead of paying taxes imposed by the British. The Ibo in eastern Nigeria and the Asante in the Gold Coast territory also offered stiff resistance to British rule.

Independence in Ethiopia and Liberia

In most uprisings, the Africans were no match for European armies equipped with advanced weapons, and Europeans eventually won military victories. In one uprising, however, African resistance permanently triumphed against an imperialist foe. This victory occurred in Ethiopia, a land in northeast Africa which was surrounded by the two Italian colonies of Eritrea and Somaliland.

Italy, like Germany, was a late entry in the European competition for African colonies. At the end of the nineteenth century, Eritrea and Somaliland were the only colonies that Italy had established in Africa.

In 1896 Italy, using Eritrea as a base, attacked Ethiopia, regarding it as a worthy prize. At the Battle of Adowa, however, a force of 80,000 Ethiopians destroyed a smaller Italian army. Ethiopia remained independent throughout the Age of Imperialism.

In 1914, the only African land besides Ethiopia free of imperialist control was Liberia. Located in West Africa, it had been settled by former slaves from the United States. Though free from colonial administration, Liberia was dependent on the United States for economic aid.

The Growth of a Local Elite

The 1800s saw an increase in the number of European-educated Africans, who usually lived in cities and were heavily influenced by Western culture. The members of this class were young, and unlike most Africans, they had risen in social status and economic position as a result of European control of Africa. Therefore, they were often called the local elite.

The local elite took advantage of both traditional and Western social systems. They found new positions within the colonial system as administrators or entrepreneurs. Although they were not allowed to gain as much power as Europeans, the authority they did have made colonial rule seem more legitimate to other Africans. The local elites seemed to identify

YAA ASANTEWA

Women often held positions of great power among the Asante, who lived in what is now part of Ghana. A woman leader called the queen mother played a major part in running the various Asante states. The mother, grandmother, aunt, or older sister of the king, the queen mother was among the king's chief advisors, and she ruled in his absence.

The greatest of the Asante queen mothers, Yaa Asantewa (yah ah-SAHN-teh-wuh), led her people in a war to halt the spread of British colonial power. The war began in March 1900, after the British had gained control of much Asante land, established forts, and banished the Asante king, Prempeh I.

During a conference at Kumasi (kuh-MAH-see), the capital of the Asante nation, the British governor met with Asante leaders, including queen mother Yaa Asantewa. The governor asked the Asante about their sacred Golden Stool, an object he thought would make a fitting throne for Britain's Queen Victoria. The Golden Stool, however, was more than just a throne to the Asante. It represented their independence, and not even an Asante king was allowed to sit on it. When the governor demanded, "Where is the Golden Stool? Why am I not sitting on the Golden Stool at this very moment?" the Asante were stunned into silence, and the conference broke up.

Soon the forests around Kumasi began to echo with the chant, "The Golden Stool shall be well washed with the blood of the white man," and the Asante took up arms to avenge the governor's insult. Their leader and inspiration was the queen mother, Yaa Asantewa.

The main exchange of the revolt took place at Kumasi, where the Asante besieged the governor and about 750 soldiers and civilians for more than eight weeks. However, the governor and a few troops were able to escape and go for reinforcements. From that time on, the Asante fought a defensive—and losing—war. They were no match for the British forces, who were armed with the latest rifles and machine guns. Under Yaa Asantewa, however, the Asante fought with courage and great zeal.

Yaa Asantewa, whom the British began to call "the fierce old African," evaded British forces until November 1900. Even then, about 2,000 troops were needed to capture the queen mother and her small band of followers.

Placed under arrest by the British, Yaa Asantewa was sent to join her son Prempeh I in exile on a distant island. She died there in 1921, never having returned to the land for which she fought so hard. However, her memory is preserved in the song that all Asante children learn: "Yaa Asantewa, the warrior woman who carries a gun and a sword of state into battle."

---

with Western values; however, they soon began to question the authority of the European powers in Africa.

Introduced to Western values of individualism, equality, and freedom, the local elites began to resent the fact that Europeans valued freedom but denied it to Africans. This new class thought that Africans should be equal to Europeans in every way. At the same time, they grew to better appreciate their own African identity and heritage. As a result, by 1914 the local elites had become the foundation of what would later become an important movement for African independence.

SECTION REVIEW

1. Define *cash crops*.

2. How did the colonial powers develop Africa in order to gain economic profit?

3. Describe two important cultural changes in Africa brought about by colonial rule.

4. Describe three instances of African armed resistance to European rule.

Analysis. Locate Ethiopia on the physical map of Africa on page 826. How might Ethiopia's geographic location have enabled its people to successfully resist foreign rule?

26-3
IMPERIALISM AND THE OTTOMAN EMPIRE

READ TO FIND OUT

—why European powers feared a collapse of the Ottoman Empire.

—how Mehemet Ali encouraged Western influence in Egypt.

—why Britain wanted control of the Suez Canal.

—how Tunisia and Algeria fell under French control.

—what two rival powers gained control of Persia.

Unlike most of Africa south of the Sahara Desert, North Africa and the Middle East had close contact with Europe well before the Age of Imperialism began in 1880. Technological development in this region surrounding the Mediterranean also matched—and for many centuries outpaced—that of nearby Europe. As a result, Europeans and Middle Easterners took turns, from ancient times to the 1800s, settling and conquering each other's territory. Despite this history of interaction, including the Crusades and the Muslim capture of Constantinople, European and Islamic civilizations had remained largely separate, neither threatening the culture or heartlands of the other.

During the 1800s, however, this standoff began to shift in favor of Europe. The Ottoman Empire—the ruling government of much of Islam since the sixteenth century—grew weaker in relation to Europe. Slowly the empire began to lose its lands in North Africa and the Balkans to European powers and nationalist movements. At the same time, Western cultural and economic influence grew in some parts of the Middle East. The Age of Imperialism brought further losses of territory until, by 1914, the Ottoman Empire consisted only of Turkey, Palestine, Syria, and the Arabian Peninsula.

DECLINE OF THE OTTOMAN EMPIRE

The Ottoman Empire was at the height of its power from 1520 to 1566, when under the rule of Suleiman the Magnificent. Ottoman possessions expanded to include much of North Africa and part of central Europe. After Suleiman, Ottoman strength declined gradually.

Once the economic and cultural center of the world, the region began to lose its vitality for several reasons. After the European explorations of the 1500s, the bulk of world trade shifted from the Mediterranean Sea to the Atlantic Ocean. Furthermore, the Islamic civilization, which once overshadowed Europe in its scientific and cultural achievement, ceased to keep pace with developments in Europe. Muslim societies now became more concerned with matters of faith and religious ritual.

The Ottoman Empire's first territorial losses were outside the Middle East. In 1699, the Ottomans lost a major territory when Austria acquired Hungary. Then, between 1730 and 1783, Russia took over Ottoman territory north of the Black Sea. In 1820, the Greeks began a revolt against Turkish rule. With assistance from Europe, the Greeks achieved independence in 1829.

By the mid-1800s, Europeans were calling the Ottoman Empire the "sick man of Europe" and looking at its territories with hopes of expansion. Each European power, however, feared that a collapse of the empire would enable another European nation to take over Ottoman lands and upset the balance of power in Europe.

Russia made the first major move toward expansion within Ottoman territory, seeking in particular control of the Bosporus—the straits connecting Russia's ports in the Black Sea with the Mediterranean. Russia's aggressive moves caused western European powers to ally with the Ottomans to stop the threat of Russian expansion. Britain and France thus sided with the Ottomans to stop the Russians during the Crimean War in 1854.

Similarly, after the Russo-Turkish War of 1877–1878, the western European powers prevented Russia from completely dismembering the Ottoman Empire. As a result of this war, however, the Ottoman Empire lost many of its possessions in the Balkans to independent rule or Russian control, and Great Britain gained its island territory of Cyprus.

GROWING TENSIONS WITHIN THE EMPIRE

In addition to external pressure from European powers, the Ottoman Empire was weakened by internal dissension. Each of the diverse ethnic and religious groups within the empire's borders sought more control over its own affairs. In the Balkans, for instance, many of the people were both non-Turkish and non-Muslim. Eastern Orthodox Christians formed a majority of the population, and different ethnic groups—such as Slavs and Magyars—voiced louder cries for independence.

In 1856, the Ottoman ruler, or sultan, Abdul-Mejid I (AHB-DOOL-meh-JEED), attempted to strengthen the empire with a decree promising extensive reform. He and his successors tried to reduce the power of local religious leaders, eliminate cultural divisions, and change tax laws.

These attempts at reform, however, only created more upheaval. Ottoman religious leaders and conservatives opposed the reform, while liberals demanded more. At the same time, nationalist groups thought the reforms neglected their demands.

In 1876, after an unsuccessful attempt to reform the monarchy, Abdul-Hamid II (hah-MEED) assumed leadership. The new sultan reversed all liberal reform, becoming an autocratic ruler who repressed all opposition to his government. His rule, though harsh, held the empire together while European influence in the Middle East increased.

WESTERN INFLUENCE IN EGYPT

The Western intrusion into the Middle Eastern world began with Napoleon's invasion of Egypt in 1798. Although the French were driven out of Egypt, European influence there grew stronger as a result of the changes brought about by this invasion.

From 1517, when it was added to the Ottoman Empire, Egypt had never been under the complete control of the Ottoman sultan. The Ottoman overlord, called a *pasha*, shared power with an Egyptian governor. In 1801, the pasha Mehemet Ali (meh-MEHT ah-LEE) helped drive the French out of Egypt. He used his victory to break away from Ottoman control and establish his own rule.

Modernization under Ali. Unlike earlier governors, Mehemet Ali was eager to westernize Egypt. He wanted to adopt certain Western practices and technologies to strengthen Egypt. Under his reign, which ended in 1848, Egypt became the focal point of European influence in the Middle East.

Mehemet Ali invited European experts to modernize Egypt's army and navy. He encouraged students to study abroad, and he opened Egyptian ports to foreign trade. To modernize Egyptian agriculture, he promoted irrigation projects and the cultivation of cotton, soon the country's leading cash crop.

Mehemet Ali dreamed of uniting all Arabs under his rule and restoring leadership within Islam to the Arabs. This idea, called Pan-Arabism, helped motivate Ali to take over territory outside Egypt. He captured Syria in 1833, but further expansion was blocked by the European powers, who feared a strong Pan-Arab state more than a weak Ottoman Empire.

THE SUEZ CANAL

European influence continued to grow in Egypt after Mehemet Ali's rule ended in 1848. At first, European powers had no need to invade or establish direct rule in order to reap benefits. Under Mehemet Ali's successors, Egypt's economy came under increasing control of Europe.

The first major step toward such control was the construction of the Suez Canal. Cut through the Isthmus of Suez by a French company between 1859 and 1869, the canal eliminated thousands of miles of sea travel between Europe and Asia by linking the Mediterranean with the Red Sea. Egypt suddenly became strategically important to trading nations. Britain, with its huge stake in India and commercial interests throughout the Far East, was very interested in safeguarding the new canal.

British foothold in Egypt. Britain gained a foothold in Egypt during the reign of Ismail I (ihs-MAH-EEL), the *khedive* (kuh-DEEV), or Ottoman overlord, who ruled from 1863 to 1879. Ismail, like Mehemet Ali, encouraged westernization of Egypt. He desired Western transportation systems, agriculture, and industry. Such development required great amounts of money, and European bankers encouraged Ismail to borrow from them.

While Egyptian cotton sold well on the world market, the khedive's borrowing strategy seemed sound. During the 1870s, however, competition lowered Egypt's profits on cotton. Soon, the treasury was bankrupt, and Ismail decided to sell Egypt's shares in the Suez Canal to pay his foreign debts. Britain, anxious to protect its vital trade route to the East, bought the stock and took control of the canal.

Egypt's financial troubles, however, continued, and misgovernment by the khedive prompted a rebellion in 1882. Britain sent troops to suppress the uprising, justifying the intervention by insisting that Britain had to protect the canal, which it considered a lifeline of the British Empire.

As a result of this intervention, Egypt came under British control. Although legally it remained a province within the Ottoman Empire and the khedive retained his position, the British consul-general became the real ruler of Egypt. In 1914, Egypt became a protectorate of Britain.

EUROPEAN INVASIONS OF NORTH AFRICA

Much land in North Africa came under direct European control before the British occupied Egypt. While Mehemet Ali encouraged westernization in Egypt, the city of Algiers and its surrounding territory, later called Algeria, fell to the French.

Algeria was inhabited by Berbers, North Africans who had converted to Islam in the 600s. Europeans called the area the Barbary Coast after these inhabitants. A part of the Ottoman Empire during the early 1800s, Algeria was the home of sailors who used fast-sailing ships to raid European and American merchant ships in the Mediterranean. The victims of these raids called the sailors "Barbary pirates."

In 1830, the French king Charles X invaded Algeria, claiming that he was retaliating for the raids of the Barbary pirates. The French, however, planned to stay. Despite heavy resistance lasting many years, France made Algeria the first European colony in North Africa.

For many years, Algeria was the only European colony in North Africa. Then in 1881, France used a border incident between Algeria and Tunisia—Algeria's neighbor to the east—as grounds for invading Tunisia and establishing control over the Tunisian government. Once the

The sign over this traditional shop in Tunis, the capital of Tunisia, beckons shoppers. After French occupation, the use of the French language became widespread in North Africa.

center of the great Carthaginian Empire, Tunisia became a French protectorate.

EUROPEAN ACQUISITIONS IN NORTH AFRICA AFTER 1900

The rest of North Africa came under European rule after 1900. As rivalries intensified between the European imperialist powers, France took control of Morocco, and Italy took Libya.

Morocco. Morocco's location at the gateway between the Atlantic Ocean and the Mediterranean Sea gave it great strategic and commercial importance. For this reason, the western European powers became intensely interested in Morocco during the late 1800s. Each imperialist power, however, was reluctant to annex Morocco for fear of antagonizing the other imperialist powers. As a result, Morocco retained its independence until relatively late in the Age of Imperialism.

In 1906, however, Morocco fell under a French sphere of influence, in which France gained political influence in the country but the ruler, or sultan, of Morocco retained his throne. Then in 1911, an uprising against the sultan gave France an excuse to invade the country and take complete control. Although the French colonial administrators built railways, roads, and harbors in Morocco and encouraged the growth of Moroccan industries, numerous nationalist uprisings occurred in Morocco between 1911 and 1914.

Libya. Italy's desire for an impressive African empire was largely frustrated by the other imperialist powers of western Europe. After suffering a humiliating defeat at the hands of the Ethiopians, Italy turned its attention to Libya, the Ottoman Empire's last remaining possession in North Africa.

Italy invaded Libya in 1911, but Italian troops met strong resistance from the defending Turkish forces. The war dragged on for over a year. It ended in 1912 when another war erupted in the Balkans, forcing the Ottomans to make peace and cede Libya to Italy.

THE PARTITION OF PERSIA

Persia was one of the few areas in the Middle East that remained independent of Ottoman control before 1800. Persia was ruled by a great dynasty, the Safawid (sah-FAH-wid), between 1502 and 1736. During this time, Persian civilization flourished, and its achievements rivaled Ottoman achievements. Throughout the remaining decades of the eighteenth century,

periods of unrest and assassinations of dynastic rulers weakened the country. Then, in the early 1800s, the Europeans began to gain greater influence in Persia.

Both Britain and Russia regarded Persia as vital to their respective strategic interests in the Middle East. Britain wanted Persia to serve as a buffer state against any other European encroachment upon India. For Russia, Persia represented a potential entry into India and, more important, a passageway to an ice-free port on the Persian Gulf.

Threatened with invasion, Persia signed treaties with Britain in 1814 and Russia in 1828, giving both countries some power in determining Persia's internal affairs. Then in 1907, Great Britain and Russia agreed to divide Persia into three zones. Russia obtained a sphere of influence in northern Persia, and Britain gained control over the southern part of Persia. These two spheres of influence were separated by a neutral zone.

Persia suffered more than most countries subjected to European rule because it was torn

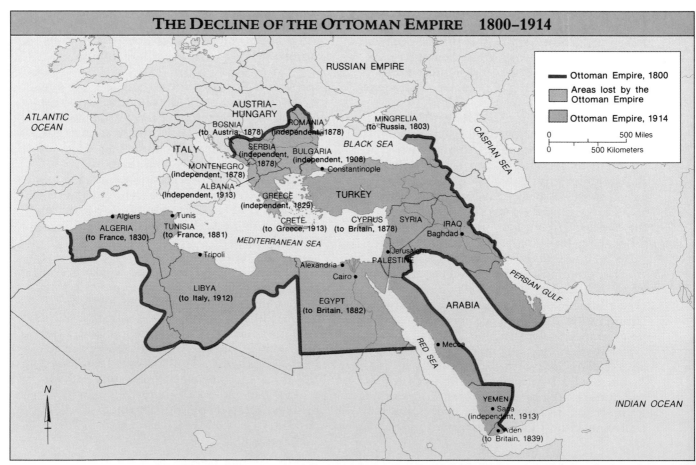

THE DECLINE OF THE OTTOMAN EMPIRE 1800–1914

between two powers that did not trust each other. Thus, while imperialist powers often introduced modern technology into their colonies, neither Britain nor Russia would allow one another to build railways or develop natural resources in Persia.

NATIONALISM AND RESISTANCE TO EUROPEAN RULE

Nationalism developed more slowly in North Africa and the Middle East than in India and other parts of Asia. Still, resentment against European domination ran high, and several Muslim revolts broke out against the Europeans.

In Egypt, many Egyptians charged that Britain deliberately kept the country in a subordinate position by discouraging the development of industry and by denying Egyptians their political rights. Egyptians particularly resented the arrogance of many of the British colonial administrators. As a result, nationalist groups arose in the early 1900s and began transforming anti-British feeling into a movement for Egyptian independence.

In North Africa, the native Berbers fought against European occupation. Although European powers controlled the governments in Morocco, Algeria, Tunisia, and Libya, Berbers resisted European penetration of most inland areas. Thus, they were able to confine European rule to the coast.

The Young Turks. An important nationalist movement arose in the Ottoman Empire. Although the empire's core in Turkey, Palestine, Syria, and Arabia remained free of European control, many Turks believed that the autocratic rule of the sultan restricted their freedom as much as rule by a foreign power. Although the sultan took on military advisors from Europe and allowed European nations to build railroads in Ottoman territory, he did not respond to demands for political change.

Around 1900, a new movement arose, composed of westernized bureaucrats and army officers, who were called "Young Turks." An attempt at revolution forced a new constitution, and the Young Turks gained some influence in government. While the Young Turks were unable to accomplish much change before 1914, they did prepare the way for a more far-reaching change in Turkish society.

SECTION REVIEW

1. Why did European powers fear the collapse of the Ottoman Empire?

2. How did Mehemet Ali attempt to westernize his country?

3. Who wanted to own the Suez Canal? Why?

4. How did France gain control of Algeria and Tunisia?

5. What countries partitioned Persia into spheres of influence? How did their rivalry affect Persia?

Analysis. What role did Islam play in the resistance to European imperialism in the Middle East and North Africa?

Data Search. Refer to the appropriate chart on page 833 to identify Egypt's major export to Europe in the late nineteenth century.

HISTORY IN FOCUS

In only a few decades, Africans lost their independence to Europeans intent on building world empires. Colonial rule thrust the people of Africa into a global web of international trade and political conflict that had permanent effects on their societies. Like Latin America, Africa became a supplier of raw materials to the industrial nations, which controlled the prices of African products. The development of cash-crop agriculture in some areas and extensive mining in others led in many colonies to unstable single-product economies and economic dependence on the Western world.

For most Africans, changes brought by colonial rule and dependency were dramatic and unwelcome. Europeans claimed they had brought the benefits of education, modern medicine, and agricultural innovation, but Africans felt wronged by the erosion of meaningful ways of life, the introduction of new diseases, and the loss of self-government.

The Middle East suffered less impact from European imperialism, in part because of its long history of competition and interaction with Europe. Islamic culture, too, contributed important strength and unity to Middle Eastern societies. Many of the important conflicts in this region today, however, can be traced back to the social and political changes that occurred between 1800 and 1914.

SUMMARY

- In the 1800s, Europeans began to see colonies as new markets, suppliers of raw materials, and strategic necessities. A race for African colonies began, and between 1880 and 1914 most of Africa fell under European control.

- European colonial administration established political control over African colonies. Colonial economies were dominated by European interests and the development of these colonies was geared to suit European needs.

- European imperialism caused deep changes in African societies, though many traditions still remained. Armed struggle against imperialism arose in many parts of Africa, but only Ethiopia and Liberia maintained their independence.

- The Ottoman Empire, which had ruled much of the Middle East, North Africa, and the Balkans since the 1500s, declined during the 1800s.

- As the Ottomans grew weaker, European powers moved into North Africa. France took Algeria, Tunisia, and Morocco; Britain occupied Egypt; and Italy took Libya. Persia was split between Britain and Russia. By the early 1900s nationalist groups were beginning to challenge European imperialism.

VOCABULARY REVIEW

Match each numbered vocabulary term with the lettered word or words most closely related to it. Then explain how the items in each pair are related.

1. paternalism	**(a)** money economy
2. cash crops	**(b)** westernization
3. assimilation	**(c)** superiority

CHAPTER REVIEW

1. (a) How and why did European economic motives in Africa change after 1800? **(b)** Give an example of how the decline in the slave trade affected some African kingdoms.

2. (a) Who were the first Europeans to explore Africa? What were their motives? **(b)** What impact did these contacts have on European countries?

3. (a) What methods did Europeans use to gain control over African lands? **(b)** How did colonial administration change African governments and societies? **(c)** Which European power tended to rule through local African chiefs? Explain why.

4. (a) Why did colonial rulers establish schools for Africans? **(b)** What effect did Western education have on African culture?

5. (a) In what two general ways did Africans resist changes brought by colonial rule? **(b)** Compare Ahmadu, Samori Touré, and the Mahdi. Contrast them with Mehemet Ali.

6. (a) How did the class of local elites develop? **(b)** How and why did their attitudes change over time?

7. (a) What caused the decline of the Ottoman Empire? **(b)** Describe the Ottomans' territorial losses. **(c)** Explain how and why some European countries sided with the Ottomans when the latter fought wars with Russia.

8. (a) How did Egypt's westernization plan backfire? **(b)** How did Britain gain control of the Suez Canal?

9. (a) Why were both Britain and Russia interested in Persia? **(b)** Compare imperialism in Persia and in Africa.

10. (a) Describe the resistance to European imperialism in the Middle East and North Africa, giving examples. **(b)** Compare those movements with the resistance in sub-Saharan Africa. **(c)** Compare the Young Turks with Africa's local elites.

THINKING CRITICALLY: ACTIVITIES

1. Imagine that you are an African chief. The lands of your village have been taken over by a British military force, and an administrator says he is now in charge. Write a letter to Queen Victoria in which you protest the British actions. In the letter show that you understand traditional African views of land and authority.

2. Choose a partner for a debate between Africans in the late 1800s. One of you should be a member of the local elite, while the other should be a member of a group resisting European rule. Debate the following question: What would be the best way to better the lives of most Africans?

3. Compare the map on page 581 of Africa in 1914 with the map of modern Africa in the Atlas on page 826. Divide into small groups to discuss how the European colonization of Africa has affected modern political boundaries. Make a table listing the names of former colonies and the names of roughly equivalent modern nations.

APPLYING SOCIAL STUDIES SKILLS

Researching information in periodicals. Use this key to help you write explanations of the numbered entries from the *Reader's Guide to Periodical Literature* that appear below.

Abbreviation Key

+	continued on later pages of same issue
bibliog	bibliography included
il	illustrated
Jl	July
Mr	March
N	November
S	September

Sample entry:

> Black cargoes, by D. P. Mannix. Review
> Time il 80:102 N 2 '62.

Sample explanation:
This is an illustrated review of the book *Black Cargoes* by D. P. Mannix in *Time* magazine, volume 80, page 102, the November 2, 1962 issue.

1. Africa. il Look 25:27–40 + Mr 28 '61.

2. African past. L. Bennett, jr. bibliog il Ebony 16:34–6 + Jl '61.

3. Africa in world affairs: address, July 28, 1961. M. Ngileruma. Vital Speeches 27:723–6 S 15 '61.

APPLYING THINKING SKILLS

Determining the strength of an argument. The following commentary was written in 1883 by an observer of events in Egypt between 1864 and 1880. Analyze the commentary to determine how strong an argument it is.

> There can be no doubt that the evils of foreign immigration made themselves immediately felt. In 1864 the price of cotton suddenly fell, and innumerable people were thrown out of employment. Taxes were raised to regain government income lost from a decline in cotton exports. The working population became distressed and uneasy.
>
> The Greeks and Syrians are born moneylenders. In every large village they gave loans to the distressed peasants. The fellah [Egyptian peasant] went into debt. He was threatened with the kurbash [whip] and was forced to pay interest rates of 30, 40, and 100 percent. I have myself known of interest as high as 200 percent. The gains of usury during this period helped build the modern cities of Alexandria and Cairo.
>
> Till the year 1876, however, usury was still in a certain measure regulated by Muslim laws. Muslims were generally not allowed to offer their land as payment for loans. Therefore, a lender usually had to settle for taking the personal belongings of a Muslim who was unable to repay a loan in cash. But in 1876 Nubar Pasha [an Egyptian diplomat] introduced his famous reform. This reform made it legal for a foreign moneylender to take a peasant's land if a debt was unpaid. The reform was a death blow to the Egyptian peasant. The courts made recovery of debts, real or pretended, against the Arab fellahin a matter of certainty for the foreign moneylender.

Adapted from *Origin of the National Party in Egypt*, by John Ninet (1883).

1. Explain what an argument is.

2. What is one procedure you can use to identify an argument?

3. According to the author of the above commentary, how did the presence of foreigners affect Egyptians?

4. How strong is the argument made by the author of the above commentary? Justify your answer.

CHAPTER TWENTY-SEVEN

ASIA AND WESTERN INFLUENCE

1800–1914

Sir David Ochterlony in Delhi. Painting, India, c. 1820.

By the nineteenth century, peoples throughout Asia had woven a rich tapestry of civilization. Although Asian cultures had undergone change over the centuries, many Asian peoples followed age-old patterns of life.

Into these traditional Eastern cultures came the Westerners, seeking raw materials and markets for their manufactured products. As the demand for Asian goods grew, Western nations became more and more likely to interfere in Asian politics to ensure that trade flowed freely.

In India, China, and most of Southeast Asia, the stress of Western demands contributed to the breakdown of governments, opening the way for European domination. Japan and Siam, on the other hand, made use of Western ways, maintaining their own political and social structures while becoming part of the network of world trade.

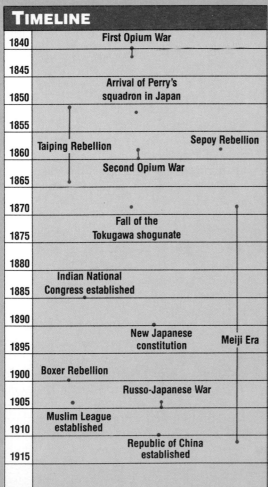

TIMELINE

1840	First Opium War
1845	
1850	Arrival of Perry's squadron in Japan
1855	
1860	Taiping Rebellion / Sepoy Rebellion
1865	Second Opium War
1870	
1875	Fall of the Tokugawa shogunate
1880	
1885	Indian National Congress established
1890	
1895	New Japanese constitution / Meiji Era
1900	Boxer Rebellion
1905	Russo-Japanese War
1910	Muslim League established
1915	Republic of China established

27–1
FOREIGN RULE IN INDIA

READ TO FIND OUT

—what the term *boycott* means.
—what changes the British East India Company brought to India.
—how Indians reacted to foreign rule.
—how expansion of trade affected India.
—what led Indians to demand self-rule.

During the first half of the nineteenth century, the British East India Company gained increasing control over India. The merchants of the East India Company had originally come to India to expand British commerce. To protect this trade, they became increasingly involved in Indian politics.

In the early nineteenth century, India was not one nation but a patchwork of small states that were often at odds with one another. The decline of the Mogul government and power struggles among local leaders contributed to the disunity among Indian states, giving the British East India Company opportunities to expand its influence. By 1850, the company had subdued the entire subcontinent.

INDIA UNDER THE EAST INDIA COMPANY

The company ruled three-fifths of India directly, with company agents taking on powers usually reserved for government officials, such as administering laws and collecting taxes. British troops and British-trained Indian recruits known as *sepoys* (SEE-poys) backed the company. The company indirectly influenced the other two-fifths of India by alliances with local rulers. While maintaining control of local matters, these Indian princes surrendered their authority over defense and foreign affairs to the British.

The East India Company brought many changes to India. The company began to establish uniform law courts, police agencies, and tax collection. A law commission was appointed to create a single criminal code and to standardize separate Hindu and Muslim civil codes.

To connect the territories under their rule, the East India Company improved transportation and communication. The company established the first public postal service and the first telegraph service. The British improved old roads, built new ones, and reconstructed canals. In addition, in the 1850s they began to construct a railroad network that was eventually larger than the one in Great Britain.

Social change. Despite the changes brought by the British, most Indians preserved their social and religious customs. However, the British eventually sought changes in Indian society. British officials, Christian missionaries, and influential Indian reformers such as Ram Mohan Roy (RAHM MŌ-hun ROY) all opposed customs practiced by some Indians. One such custom was the killing of unwanted female children. Another such custom practiced by a few was *suttee* (soo-TEE), in which widows committed suicide by throwing themselves on their husband's burning funeral pyres.

In the early 1800s, the British banned female infanticide and suttee, as well as slavery. Although many Indians had long worked to abolish these practices, this British interference in social and religious customs caused Hindus and Muslims alike to wonder whether the British would attack other customs.

Education. The most far-reaching changes that the British made were in education. In the early 1800s, centers of Hindu and Muslim learning were scattered across India. However, because English had replaced Persian—the language of the Moguls—as the official language of government and law and had become the unofficial language of trade, Indians hoping to enter government service or commerce wanted to learn English. Many Indians also hoped to study Western engineering or medicine.

In the 1850s, the British established a system of elementary and secondary schools throughout India, patterned after schools in Britain. In addition, Western-style universities that included scientific and technical courses were established. The first universities were located in Calcutta, Madras, and Bombay. Because no one language was spoken throughout India, university classes were taught in English.

Pilgrims gather at a Bombay dock in the 1870s before sailing to a Hindu shrine on nearby Elephanta Island. Even under British rule, Indians managed to keep most of their religious customs.

INDIAN RESPONSE TO BRITISH RULE

Indian reactions to changes brought by British rule were as varied as the groups of people living in India. As Mogul rule weakened, numerous gangs of robbers had plagued India. Gradually, the British stamped out these robber bands, and village farmers and townspeople alike welcomed the order brought by the British. In addition, some Indian people welcomed the chance to study Western technology. However, while Western-style education enabled many capable Indians to find employment in government service, it often left them torn between Indian traditions and Western ways.

Many Indians began to oppose British rule because they felt that their customs were under attack from East India Company policies and Christian missionaries. Muslims especially resented their loss of influence in the government and the replacement of Persian with English as an official language.

Opposition to British rule began to grow as British policies increasingly interfered with village life. For centuries, village officials had settled local disputes, kept the peace, and collected taxes based on the value of crops. The local tax collectors often made allowances for poor harvests. Even though the courts of law, police forces, and tax collection agencies established by the British included Indian officials, these officials were often outsiders who knew little about local conditions. Consequently, the settlement of disputes did not always follow local custom, and some landlords and farmers were heavily overtaxed.

Aggravating relations between the Indians and the British was the tendency of the British to set themselves apart as a new ruling class. Many Indians resented the British attitude of superiority. One Indian criticized British "aloofness, absorption in their own concerns."

The Sepoy Rebellion. Opposition to British rule suddenly erupted in 1857. Because the trouble began among sepoys in the East India Company's army, the uprising is known as the Sepoy Rebellion.

The spark that touched off the uprising came when the company issued the sepoys a new kind of rifle. To load the rifle, a soldier had to remove a tab from the end of a greased bullet with his teeth while pouring gunpowder into an attached pouch. Even though British officials maintained that only vegetable or mutton fat had been used, the sepoys became convinced that the fat came from cows, which Hindus regarded as sacred, or from pigs, which Muslims thought unclean. Both Hindus and Muslims believed that by using the bullets they would be breaking religious laws.

The rifles became a symbol for many Indian grievances against the British. The Indians, who had tolerated other offenses, now balked at breaking religious law. The sepoys mutinied, and many other Indians joined in. The mutineers captured the city of Delhi and much of north-central India as well. Many innocent people on both sides were massacred before the British, aided by other Indian troops, put down the rebellion in 1858.

INDIA UNDER THE BRITISH

That same year, believing that the East India Company had become ineffective, Parliament transferred rule of the company's territories to the British Crown. British rule of India under the Crown became known as the *Raj*, an Indian word meaning "rule." To ease some of the fears that had led to the rebellion, British Queen Victoria proclaimed, "We do strictly charge those in authority [to] abstain from interference with the religious belief of any of our subjects."

The territories under the Crown—"British India"—were governed by a viceroy, a five-member Executive Council, and a larger Legislative Council with limited power to pass laws. To give Indians some voice in government, a few were appointed to the Legislative Council. The 562 separate Indian territories allied with the British by treaties were called the "Indian States."

British rule was carried out by the Indian Civil Service, established by the East India Company in the late 1700s. When the British government took over, Queen Victoria proclaimed that "our subjects of whatever race and creed be freely admitted to offices in our service." However, because examinations for the service were conducted in London and required study of Western culture at a university level, only a few exceptional Indians could qualify.

Social changes brought about by the Sepoy Rebellion went even deeper than the political changes. Neither the British nor the Indians ever quite trusted the other again. Although the new British government of India continued to expand railways and canals, maintain law and order, and defend the country's frontiers, the British stopped trying to remake Indian society directly.

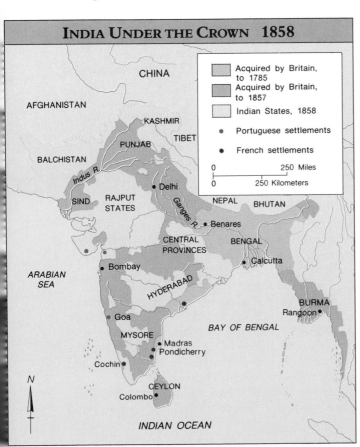

INDIA UNDER THE CROWN 1858

Acquired by Britain, to 1785
Acquired by Britain, to 1857
Indian States, 1858
• Portuguese settlements
• French settlements

0   250 Miles
0   250 Kilometers

CHINA
AFGHANISTAN
KASHMIR
PUNJAB
TIBET
BALCHISTAN
Indus R.
SIND
RAJPUT STATES
Delhi
Ganges R.
NEPAL
BHUTAN
Benares
CENTRAL PROVINCES
BENGAL
ARABIAN SEA
Bombay
Calcutta
HYDERABAD
BURMA
Rangoon
Goa
BAY OF BENGAL
MYSORE
Madras
Pondicherry
Cochin
N
CEYLON
Colombo
INDIAN OCEAN

The palanquin was used for city travel by people who could afford the fare. This 1870s photograph captures the haughty attitude of many Europeans toward Indians, especially those of the middle and lower classes.

Expansion of trade and industry. India continued to be vital to Britain's trade, however. The Suez Canal shortened voyages between India and Europe from more than 3 months to about 25 days, making large-scale trade with Europe possible for the first time.

At first, the expansion of trade disrupted Indian manufacturing. Most Indian wares were handmade and could not compete with the cheaper machine-made goods of industrialized Britain. However, from the 1860s on, factories and mines started to appear throughout India in increasing numbers.

In the 1800s, most factories were owned by Europeans. Over time, however, Indians invested in these factories and established new ones. The rapidly growing cotton industry was almost wholly developed by Indians. The number of cotton mills grew from just 10 in 1861 to 144 in 1895, and eventually India's cotton industry became one of the world's largest. The iron and steel industry was also developed mainly by Indians, while British industrialists developed tea plantations, jute mills, and coal mines.

___

THE RISE OF INDIAN NATIONALISM

Ironically, the changes introduced by the British contributed to a growing sense of unity among Indians. The postal service, telegraph, and railway brought the Indian people together as never before. Through education, upper-class Indians came to share a common language, as well as a knowledge of English history, law, and ideas of nationalism.

A few Indians educated in Western subjects but faithful to Indian traditions began to kindle a spark of Indian nationalism. The most influential of these Indian leaders were the Hindu scholar Ram Mohan Roy and the Muslim reformer Sayyid Ahmad Khan (SĪ-yihd AH-muhd KAHN). By emphasizing the people's Hindu and Muslim roots, these leaders reawakened pride in Indian traditions.

The Indian National Congress. By the late 1800s, many Indians were listening to the ideas of Indian journalist Surendranath Banerji (BA-nor-jee). Banerji applauded British principles of justice but realized that they were not always honored in practice. Other Indians, too, often found it difficult to reconcile British standards of justice with the injustices of daily life. They bristled at signs that read "Europeans Only" on trains or in private clubs. They were frustrated because they could not rise to high office in the civil service.

To discuss their grievances, Banerji and other influential Indians, along with some British supporters, organized the Indian National Congress in 1885. The congress demanded greater Indian participation in government and that civil service examinations be offered in India.

The congress directly influenced reforms, such as the Indian Councils Act of 1892, which broadened Indian representation in the Legislative Council, allowed Indians to vote for the first time for representatives to the council, and gave the council greater powers.

Sayyid Ahmad Khan believed that the congress mainly voiced Hindu opinion, and he urged Muslims not to participate in it. He claimed that any government favored by the congress would be dominated by Hindus.

Movement toward self-rule. The tide of nationalism swelled in 1905 in response to the unpopular British decision to partition, or divide, the large state of Bengal into two parts to govern it more efficiently. In dividing the state, the British overlooked the nationalistic feelings of Bengalis. A storm of protest followed, and Bengalis began to *boycott*, or refuse to buy, British goods. The protest movement spread to other states, and in 1911, the British government reversed the partition.

Although the British reunified Bengal, Indian nationalism continued to grow. However, Indian views varied, especially between Hindus and Muslims, who feared that Hindus would dominate an Indian government. The Muslims organized the Muslim League in 1906 to press for greater Muslim influence in politics. After 1907, the Indian National Congress split between those who wanted British rule with greater Indian representation and those who wanted complete independence.

Some Indians turned to violence. One leader incited students, factory workers, and farmers to terrorist tactics, for which he was jailed. Other Indians opposed violence and urged the viceroy to control it.

Although early in the twentieth century Indians differed in their visions of India's future, they all expressed their hopes with growing confidence that their voice would be heard. They had learned that they could achieve much by organizing. Meanwhile, a new slogan—*swaraj*, meaning "self-rule"—was beginning to be heard across India.

SECTION REVIEW

---

1. Define *boycott*.

2. Describe one major change introduced by the British East India Company in transportation, social customs, and education.

3. Explain both the long-term and the immediate causes of the Sepoy Rebellion.

4. What were the effects of the expansion of Indian trade?

5. Describe some of the factors that prompted Indian leaders to demand self-rule.

Synthesis. From the point of view of an Indian nationalist, argue that Indians should have a greater role in their government.

27–2
THE COLLAPSE
OF CHINA

READ TO FIND OUT

—what the terms *treaty port* and *extraterritoriality* mean.
—how Britain increased China's trade with foreign nations.
—how rebellion disrupted China.
—what losses China suffered to foreign nations as a result of war and internal strife.
—how revolution ended the Ch'ing Dynasty.

At the turn of the nineteenth century, China was still under the rule of the Ch'ing Dynasty established in the 1600s by the conquering Manchus. The Ch'ing Dynasty had brought stability and extended Chinese influence to nearby countries. Over their 156-year reign, the Manchus had adopted Chinese traditions and attitudes, including negative attitudes toward foreigners.

Like Chinese dynasties before them, the Ch'ing Dynasty expected tribute from foreign countries as a sign of respect. The Ch'ing rulers also expected foreign merchants to abide by strict regulations. These merchants could carry on their commerce at only one port, Canton, and they could deal only with Chinese firms selected by the government. Once their ships were loaded, the foreign traders had to leave China or confine themselves solely to the port of Macao.

Throughout the nineteenth century, the Manchus' desire to maintain tradition clashed with the desire of European nations to trade freely. Each side was firmly convinced that it represented a superior civilization, and each side made little attempt to understand the customs of the other.

THE OPIUM WARS

Despite Manchu regulations, by the early 1800s, trade between the Chinese and the British began to change. To pay for the thousands of chests of tea that the British East India Company bought each year, the British had been selling some cloth and tin to the Chinese. However, the Chinese wanted little that the British had to trade, so the British paid for most of the tea with silver. To prevent Britain from being drained of its silver, the British East India Company searched for a product that the Chinese would buy. The British settled on opium, a habit-forming drug.

Like other peoples, the Chinese used opium as a painkiller for the seriously ill. At the same time, they recognized the dangers of the addictive drug for idle users, and thus China banned the importing of opium for sale to the general public.

In spite of the ban, small numbers of Chinese used the drug. British merchants found they could ship opium from India, sell the opium for silver, and use the silver to buy Chinese goods. As increasing numbers of people became addicted, British and Chinese smugglers brought tons of opium into China. The British began to take in more silver than they paid out.

In 1839, the Chinese government appointed a special commissioner, Lin Tsehsu (LEEN ZEH-SHOO), to smash the illegal trade. Lin successfully stopped many Chinese smugglers. However, in 1840, when he ordered that 20,000 chests of British opium be seized and burned, war broke out.

Unequal treaties. During the Opium War, as this conflict was called, armed British steamships captured ports from Canton to Shanghai. While the Manchu government fought back, small groups of Chinese cooperated with the British to keep the opium trade alive. This Opium War ended in 1842, when, to restore order, the Manchu government gave in to the British invaders' demands.

The Treaty of Nanking, which ended the war, made the island of Hong Kong a *treaty port*, a port that must be kept open for foreign trade, and turned over the island to Britain. Shanghai and three other cities were made treaty ports, as well. The Manchus also agreed to pay the British for the cost of the war and the loss of the opium that had been destroyed. In addition, the treaty abolished the system of trading only through government selected firms. However, the treaty did not ban the opium trade, and it continued.

A year later the British forced the Chinese to sign another treaty acknowledging the principle of *extraterritoriality*, or the exemption of foreigners from the authority of local officials. Criminal, and later civil, cases involving foreigners were to be tried by foreign officials in buildings rented from the Chinese but considered to be outside the territory of China. With

French Catholics built this cathedral in Canton in 1861, a year after China signed a treaty permitting the practice of Christianity. A bold reminder of Western victories in the Opium Wars, the European architecture stands in sharp contrast to the simple structures of the Chinese waterfront.

these treaties, the British had forced Western ways of conducting trade, law, and diplomacy on China.

Other nations benefited from Britain's actions. France, Russia, the United States, and others soon negotiated similar treaties. Each treaty contained a "most favored nation clause," a statement that gave to the signers of the treaty any privileges the Chinese had granted to any other nation.

The second Opium War. A second war broke out in 1858 between the Chinese and the British, this time with France as a British ally. For the Europeans, important issues causing conflict were whether or not foreigners would be allowed to live in Chinese cities and whether diplomats would be received in Peking. For their part, the Chinese were angered by the kidnapping of Chinese laborers by Western traders.

After British and French forces defeated the Chinese armies, the Manchus agreed that China would once again pay the cost of war. The treaty ending this second Opium War in 1860 named ten more treaty ports, guaranteed that foreign merchants and missionaries could travel throughout China, and recognized diplomats. The treaty also legalized the opium trade.

DECADES OF REBELLION

The Manchus also faced grave internal problems. From 1750 to 1850, China's population more than doubled, putting a burden on the country's farmers to produce more food. When floods or droughts occurred, severe famines swept the land. Many people grew desperate when they lost their jobs or their farms, and, to avoid starvation, roamed the countryside as bandits.

The Taiping Rebellion. Economic crisis in the 1840s prompted many Chinese to join a society called *Taiping Tienguo* (TĪ-PING TEEIN-GWŌ), meaning "Heavenly Kingdom of Great Peace." This society based its ideas on a combination of ancient Chinese teachings and Christian beliefs. The society gained the support of peasants by calling for equal distribution of land and attracted women with its goal of equality for the sexes. Taiping leaders also outlawed the use of drugs, liquor, and tobacco among their followers.

The Manchu government tried to suppress the society but touched off a rebellion instead. In 1851, Taiping leaders organized their followers, both men and women, into an army and began a march down the Yangtze. Totally disrupting shipping along the river, the rebel army took control of central China, and in 1853 captured Nanking.

When Manchu armies failed to put down the rebellion, local Chinese officials organized armies to fight the rebels. These Chinese civilian armies used Western guns, ships, and methods of warfare against the Taiping. Fearful that the disorder might threaten trade, Europeans eventually joined the battle on the side of the Manchu government. With Western help, the civilian armies and the Manchu government finally crushed the Taiping revolt in 1864.

The Taiping Rebellion was not the only rebellion the Manchu government faced. Between 1850 and 1873 several other revolts broke out. These rebellions cost China untold suffering and more than 25 million lives. The cost of putting down these rebellions also weighed heavily on the government.

In the mid-1800s, many Chinese died during times of famine. The government treasury, depleted by war, could provide no aid for people like these homeless peasants in Hunan province.

INCREASING FOREIGN INFLUENCE

The reliance of the Manchus on Chinese armies to put down rebellion signaled the beginning of a gradual collapse of Manchu authority. The Manchu rulers tried to restore their power by turning to ancient Chinese traditions. In the meantime, while millions of Chinese followed age-old patterns of life, Western influence began to spread.

Some scholar gentry began to think that China could maintain its traditional way of life and still accept Western technology. Their ideas were expressed by the saying, "Chinese learning for being; Western learning for use." Slowly, the Chinese adopted modern weapons, machinery, steamships, and telegraph lines.

War with Japan. In 1894, Japan dealt China a crushing blow. When an uprising took place in Korea that year, the Korean monarch asked for Chinese aid and China sent troops. Backing the rebels, Japan also sent in troops, leading to the Sino-Japanese War. *Sino* is a word form used in combinations and means "Chinese." When the two sides met in combat, Japanese forces proved far better equipped and more efficiently trained. Therefore, Japan won the war in less than nine months.

China had to sign a peace treaty yielding to Japan the island of Taiwan and a sphere of influence on the Liaotung (LYOW-DOONG) peninsula, directly south of Manchuria. China also agreed to independence for Korea. In addition, China agreed to open more treaty ports and to pay Japan some of the costs of war.

Attempts at reform. The loss to Japan shocked both the Chinese who favored traditional ways and those who favored modernization. Many Chinese felt that the nation could not regain its power and prestige without far-reaching change.

In 1898, the young Manchu emperor Kuang Hsu (KWANG SHOO) proposed to reorganize the military, put an end to corruption in government, and modernize education. However, some of the officials who would be affected by his program plotted against him. As a result, the emperor was imprisoned and his idealistic program set aside. Empress Tz'u Hsi (TSOO SHEE), his aunt, now became the real power at the Manchu court.

During such upheavals, Britain, France, Germany, Russia, and Japan scrambled to divide China into spheres of influence. To protect American trade, in September 1899, United States Secretary of State John Hay sent messages to several nations asking that Chinese ports be kept open to all nations. The Europeans agreed to this Open Door Policy, which may have helped to keep China independent.

The Boxer Rebellion. Meanwhile, new secret societies sprang up, many seeking to end Western influence in China. One of these societies went by the name of "Righteousness and Harmony." Its members practiced ceremonial martial arts exercises that resembled shadowboxing, and so the society became known in English as Boxers.

The Boxers blamed China's troubles on Chinese Christians as well as outsiders, and they sought to rid their country of "foreign devils." The rebellion centered in the north, where the Boxers burned houses, schools, and churches.

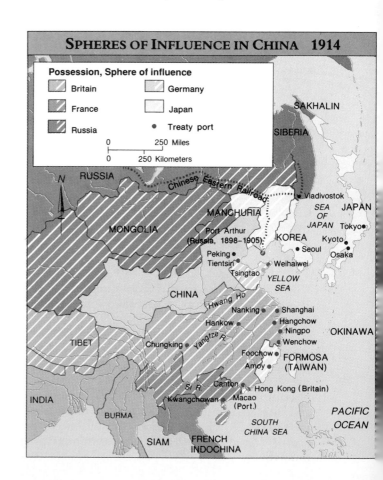

SPHERES OF INFLUENCE IN CHINA 1914

Boxers parading through Peking (left) carry banners symbolizing their identification with traditional Chinese values. The Boxers' attempt to rid the city of foreigners began just hours later. This 1904 photograph (right) captures the strength of Empress Tz'u Hsi, who sympathized with the Boxers. She sent imperial troops to support the Boxer attack on foreign embassies.

At first, government troops opposed the Boxers, but the society had touched strong antiforeign sentiment among members of the Manchu court. The Empress Tz'u Hsi, beginning to believe that the Boxers might in fact be able to drive the Europeans from China, allowed the rebels to enter the capital of Peking in June 1900.

For 55 days, the Boxers laid siege to European sections of the city. Then, in August 1900, an international relief force made up of 18,000 troops from several nations including the United States and Japan fought its way into Peking. The besieged Europeans were rescued just as food was running out.

When the rebellion was crushed, the empress was forced to agree to European terms. China had to pay Western governments more than $300 million to make up for their losses. China also agreed to allow Western nations to station armed guards in Peking. Many Chinese felt shame at the sight of foreign troops parading in their capital.

The Boxer Rebellion emphasized the urgent need for economic and political reforms in order to solve China's ills. Between 1901 and 1910, Chinese reformers reorganized government offices, abolished the civil service exami-

nations, and modernized the education system. Nevertheless, the Manchu government continued to decline. When the Empress Tz'u Hsi died in 1908, the last strong force holding the dynasty together died too.

THE REVOLUTION OF 1911

Many groups made plans to overthrow the Manchu government. One of these groups was led by Dr. Sun Yat-sen. In contrast to the Boxers, who had believed that China could become independent by driving Europeans away, Sun thought China could free itself of foreign domination by learning as much as possible from the West. Sun built his movement around his Three People's Principles: national unity, democracy, and economic self-help.

The end of the Manchus. Events soon gave Sun a chance to put his ideas into action. In October 1911, revolt broke out among soldiers and students. With little fighting, one area after another declared independence. Dr. Sun was in the United States at the time but immediately returned to his homeland. In January 1912, he became temporary president of a new Republic of China, and later that year he founded the

Kuomintang (KWŌ-MIN-TAHNG), or National People's party.

China seemed at last to have set out on a promising path. Yet, in northern China, fragments of the imperial army threatened civil war. To avert turmoil Sun tried to build an alliance with Yuan Shih-kai (yoo-AHN SHIH-KĪ), the commander of that army.

Yuan agreed to accept the republic in return for being made its president. In February, Sun stepped down as leader and Yuan took office. Meanwhile, the six-year-old boy who had become emperor on the death of the Empress Tz'u Hsi was forced to give up the throne. With his abdication, two thousand years of dynastic rule in China ended. New power struggles were soon to begin.

An uncertain future. Within two years Yuan became a virtual dictator. He tried to declare himself emperor but met opposition. In 1913, Sun organized another revolt. When that failed, Sun was forced to flee to Japan, his dreams of democracy and stability shattered. In 1915, Yuan became "president for life." Ironically, he died a year later. Despite the hopes that had been raised by the new republic, China's future remained uncertain.

SECTION REVIEW

1. Define *treaty port* and *extraterritoriality*.

2. Describe four actions that Britain took to increase its trade with China.

3. What was the chief cause of the Taiping Rebellion? The results?

4. What were the results of the war with Japan? The Boxer Rebellion?

5. What were the goals of Sun Yat-sen? Of Yuan Shih-kai?

Analysis. Sun Yat-sen placed blame both on foreign nations and on China itself for the nation's downfall. Write a brief paragraph supporting his opinion.

Data Search. Refer to the appropriate charts on pages 831 and 833 to: **(a)** compare the change in China's population between 1776 and 1851 with the change in China's population between 1851 and 1912, and **(b)** identify the major raw materials that the Chinese exported to Europe from 1880 to 1900.

27–3
THE TRANSFORMATION OF JAPAN

READ TO FIND OUT

—what the term *consul* means.
—what led to the downfall of the shoguns.
—how the Japanese ended the feudal system and modernized their nation.
—what events made Japan a world power.

At the turn of the nineteenth century, the Tokugawa shoguns still ruled Japan. Like the Chinese, the Tokugawa government remained wary of foreigners. Since 1639, only China and the Netherlands had been allowed to trade in Japan.

In spite of trade restrictions, Japanese scholars showed interest in the knowledge of the West. Through the Dutch, they had obtained writings on such subjects as astronomy, medicine, botany, and mathematics, and translated these works into Japanese.

Still, the Tokugawa shogunate, determined to keep Japan a "closed country," continued to prevent foreign ships from entering Japanese harbors to take on food and water. Shipwrecked sailors who washed up on Japan's shores were often harshly treated. From the late 1700s to the mid-1800s, some Russian and American missions tried to approach the Japanese to discuss shipping and trade, but these efforts came to nothing.

SOURCES OF CHANGE

In the early 1850s, the president of the United States, Millard Fillmore, was seeking markets for the goods produced by America's new factories. He was also concerned about the protection of American ships and sailors in Japanese waters. To impress the Japanese with the seriousness of American interest in trade agreements, as well as agreements concerning the treatment of ships and their crews, the American president sent a squadron of ships commanded by Commodore Matthew C. Perry to Japan.

When Perry's squadron appeared in Tokyo Bay in July 1853, it aroused both great alarm and curiosity on shore. Perry gave Japanese officials a letter from President Fillmore urging a treaty. Perry promised to return for negotiations the following spring, and he made it clear that when he returned, it would be with an even greater force.

Perry's visit left the Japanese government with a dilemma—whether to keep up the policy of isolation and risk the use of force by the United States or give in to Perry's demands and antagonize patriotic Japanese. The shogun consulted the emperor and the daimyo throughout the country. Most of those consulted urged a show of force against Perry. Others, worrying that in a test of strength with the West, Japan could not win, argued for a treaty. The shogun agreed.

The commercial treaties. As promised, Perry returned to Japan in 1854 and negotiations began. In March, the United States and Japan signed a treaty opening two small Japanese harbors to American ships and assuring better treatment for shipwrecked sailors. The Japanese also agreed to accept an American *consul*, a person who looks after a nation's citizens and commercial interests in a foreign country.

In 1858, the new American consul to Japan concluded another treaty, opening additional ports. The new treaty also established tariff rules, gave Americans the rights of extraterritoriality, and granted them permission to live in Japan. The United States promised to supply Japan with ships and weapons as well as experts to train the Japanese in the use of these armaments.

Before long, the British, Russians, French, and Dutch won similar agreements. Soon, the Japanese went to work to have the extraterritoriality provisions erased from the treaties. Japan achieved that goal by 1900.

The downfall of the Tokugawa. The treaties stirred controversy within Japan. Many Japanese criticized the shogun for not being able to resist the foreign powers. Meanwhile, a group of Japanese scholars were also criticizing the Confucian practices of the Tokugawa govern-

Many Japanese artists interpreted Western culture in their own way. Titled *Views of Savage Countries*, these scenes of a French port depict Western-clad women with Japanese features.

ment, which had been weakened by economic and social turmoil. Research into early Japanese history had led the scholars to believe that the true ruler of Japan should be the emperor, not the shogun.

From 1858 to 1868, several groups struggled against one another to determine Japan's future. Finally, in 1868, two powerful clans joined forces in support of the emperor and defeated the Tokugawa. The clan of the shogun was allowed to keep large plots of land, but nearly seven hundred years of rule by shogun was at an end.

THE MEIJI ERA

In 1868, Crown Prince Mutsuhito (MOO-tsoo-HEE-tō), only sixteen years of age, became the emperor. Because the new emperor adopted the title Meiji (MAY-JEE), meaning "enlightened peace," his reign became known as the Meiji Era. The young Emperor Meiji was installed in the shogun's palace in Edo, now renamed Tokyo, meaning "Eastern Capital."

The emperor and the young samurai who served as his advisors vigorously set out to modernize Japan to keep it from falling victim to European imperialism as China had already done. From 1868 to 1900, the new leaders introduced sweeping reforms.

The end of feudalism. The reformers first replaced the old feudal system of land ownership. They directed the daimyo to turn over land to the emperor in return for cash payments and income from taxes on the land. The country was divided into local regions called prefectures, and most daimyo were rewarded by being made governors of the prefectures.

The samurai did not fare as well as the daimyo under the new system. The government reduced the incomes of the samurai and banned the swords they wore as evidence of their rank. The Meiji reformers also reorganized the army and the navy. In 1873, the government issued a new draft law making all men, regardless of their social class, subject to service in the new armed forces. This policy spelled an end for the samurai, once the only Japanese allowed to carry weapons.

The former feudal domains became the property of the peasant farmers who occupied them. Once taxed on crops, small farmers were now taxed on the worth of their land. This method of taxation provided the government with a steadier income.

Learning from the West. Rather than looking to the past, the Japanese now looked outward. "Knowledge shall be sought throughout the world," the emperor pledged, "in order to strengthen imperial rule." Before long, groups of Japanese were traveling throughout Europe and the United States, seeking knowledge in many fields.

Knowledge thus gathered was used to develop Japanese industry and commerce. Western ideas could be seen in Japanese-built railroads and telegraph lines, in the seagoing vessels cruising into Japanese harbors from recently opened shipyards, and in the ways Japanese merchants marketed their products.

Economic measures. Industrial development, along with payments to the samurai and the daimyo, proved costly. To raise cash without borrowing from foreign nations, the Japanese government introduced capitalism by selling to private buyers some of the enterprises it had developed. From these sales emerged large firms—the *zaibatsu* (ZĪ-baht-SOO), meaning "financial clan"—owned by single families who came to control several enterprises. The most powerful of the zaibatsu were Mitsui (mit-SOO-ee), Mitsubishi (MIT-soo-BEE-shee), and Sumitomo (SOO-mee-TŌ-mo), all still active in Japan today.

SPOTLIGHT: PEOPLE

YOSHIDA SHOIN

On November 21, 1859—the day of his execution—Yoshida Shoin (yō-SHEE-duh shō-EEN) wrote, "Today I am to die. But if my companions take over my task, the seed of the future will not die." Yoshida was barely thirty years of age.

Only nine years earlier, as an eager young teacher, Yoshida had traveled throughout Japan. In his travels, he met members of the growing movement to restore the power of the emperor. Yoshida listened to the talk of inefficiency, corruption, and weakness in the shogun's government. Yoshida also heard the ideas of a well-known teacher, Sakuma Shozan, who set forth the idea that Japan could become strong enough to stand up to the West only if the Japanese adopted Western science.

Blending the views of the antishogunate movement and Sakuma with his own fervent patriotism, Yoshida became an outspoken force for change. At the same time, he nourished a fierce pride in the traditional spirit of Japan.

Voices such as Yoshida's grew louder and angrier when, in 1858, the shogun signed foreign treaties unfavorable to Japan. To silence the opposition, the shogunate commenced a reign of terror, imprisoning or executing hundreds of people. Irate, Yoshida and a small band of students plotted to assassinate the shogunate official responsible for the repression. However, the plan was discovered, and Yoshida was quickly arrested and sentenced to death.

Still devoted to strengthening Japan before it could be devoured by Western powers, Yoshida continued to teach. In prison, he converted several of the guards to his way of thinking.

After his death, Yoshida's fiery spirit lived on, for his companions did take over his task. Many of his students were among those who fought and died to restore the power of the emperor. Other students became high officials in the service of the Emperor Meiji, and soon they put into practice many of the changes that Yoshida had advocated.

THE JAPANESE STYLE

In 1888, the Dutch painter Vincent van Gogh wrote, "We like Japanese painting, we have felt its influence, all the impressionists have that in common." Japanese prints, such as the one shown here by Chōki, offered informal glimpses of everyday life depicted from unusual points of view. The Japanese worked with unshaded colors, graceful lines, outlined silhouettes, and patches of decorative pattern. Instead of emphasizing depth, Japanese artists divided the picture into large flat surfaces. As Western artists adopted these techniques, new styles of Western art emerged.

Catching Fireflies,
Eishōsai Chōki, Japan, 1790s

The Letter, Mary Cassatt, United States, 1891

The Dance Lesson,
Edgar Degas,
France, 1879

Variations in Flesh Color and Green,
J. Whistler, United States, 1865

The Elder Tanguy, Vincent
van Gogh, Netherlands, 1887

The government. To the Japanese, some form of democracy seemed to be the key to the success of Western nations. In 1884, the Meiji emperor sent abroad one of his top advisors, Hirobumi Ito (HIHR-ō-BOO-mee EE-tō), to study how Western governments worked. Ito's findings influenced a new constitution that took effect in 1889.

Under this constitution, the emperor remained the head of state. A cabinet headed by a prime minister would carry out the nation's affairs. The constitution established a parliament known as the Diet, with two houses—an upper house composed of nobles and imperial appointees, and a lower house chosen by the nation's voters.

Japan's leaders proceeded cautiously in introducing a democratic form of government. The Japanese constitution limited voting rights to males over the age of twenty-five who paid a specified amount in taxes. At first, the number of eligible voters equalled only about 1 percent of the population.

Education. To provide a solid foundation for modernization, the government introduced a national system of elementary education, influenced in part by American practices. The Japanese government also established new universities, in which Confucian ideals of public service and European ideas of nationalism blended with Japanese patriotism. This blend created a new emphasis on education for the good of the nation.

This photograph shows Yokohama's busy theater district in the early 1900s. One of the few cities where foreigners were allowed to live, Yokohama became a major Japanese trading port.

JAPANESE EXPANSION

The national pride that produced the buildup of industry and the military also contributed to a new policy of expansion as the nineteenth century ended. Adopting Western practices in foreign affairs, the Japanese claimed that their economy required foreign trade, especially access to raw materials their homeland could not supply.

The policy of expansion led the Japanese to challenge Chinese influence in Korea in the Sino-Japanese War. The treaty that ended the war gave Japan control of Taiwan and a sphere of influence in China. Although the treaty proclaimed Korean independence, Japan and Russia continued to compete for control of Korea.

War with Russia. Japan's new sphere of influence on the Asian mainland caused concern in Russia. The Russians had obtained permission from the Chinese to build a railroad across Manchuria to the Russian port of Vladivostok (VLAD-ih-VAHS-tahk). Russian and Japanese negotiations for areas of influence in Manchuria broke down in 1904, resulting in the Russo-Japanese War. The Japanese drove the Russian army from Manchuria and then, in May 1905, won a decisive victory over the Russian navy in the waters between Korea and Japan.

In September 1905, Russian and Japanese diplomats met in Portsmouth, New Hampshire, in the United States to work out a treaty. The Russians agreed to give up most of their rights in Manchuria, as well as the southern half of Sakhalin (sah-kah-LEEN) Island. Japan continued its expansion in Manchuria, and in 1910 annexed Korea.

With the assassination of Ito in 1909 and the death of the Emperor Meiji in 1912, the Meiji Era came to a close. During this remarkable period in Japan's history, Japan had developed from an isolated nation to a world power.

SECTION REVIEW

1. Define *consul*.

2. What were two issues that led to the downfall of the Tokugawa?

3. Summarize the basic changes in each of the following in Japan: land ownership, economic structure, government, and education.

4. Explain Japan's reasons for pursuing a policy of overseas expansion.

Evaluation. A Japanese slogan often heard during the Meiji Era was, "Eastern ethics and Western knowledge." Was this idea evident in Japanese life? Explain your answer.

Data Search. Refer to the appropriate charts on pages 831 and 832 to identify: **(a)** the number of people who emigrated from Japan between the years 1846 and 1932, and **(b)** the difference between the populations of Japan and Korea in 1850.

27–4
WESTERN EXPANSION IN SOUTHEAST ASIA AND THE PACIFIC

READ TO FIND OUT

—how Western nations gained control of Southeast Asia.
—how the people of Southeast Asia reacted to Western control.
—why Western nations expanded into the Pacific.

Impelled by the desire for raw materials to feed their growing industries, Western nations sought trade in lands beyond India, China, and Japan. The search carried the Westerners as far as Southeast Asia, which consists of a large peninsula jutting southward from the Asian mainland and a number of archipelagoes, or island chains, stretching between the Indian and Pacific oceans. Today, the countries of Burma, Thailand (TĪ-land), Laos (LAH-ōs), Cambodia, and Vietnam cover the mountainous peninsula. Nearby, Brunei (broo-NĪ), Singapore, Indonesia, and the Philippines occupy more than 20,000 densely forested islands. The nation of Malaysia lies partly on the peninsula and partly on the island of Borneo, which it shares with Indonesia.

Before the Europeans arrived, three strong influences—Chinese, Indian, and Arab—helped to shape the character of Southeast Asia. From the 100s B.C. to the A.D. 900s, China ruled northern Vietnam, introducing Chinese traditions and Confucian ideals.

Elsewhere in Southeast Asia, Indian traders and missionaries introduced their customs along with Hinduism and Buddhism. Southeast Asian peoples blended Indian ways with their own. These peoples erected gold-clad Buddhas or stone temples richly carved with Hindu gods in jungle clearings and on river deltas. In the 1200s, Arab traders and missionaries introduced Islam, which spread rapidly in Malaysia, Indonesia, and the Philippines.

THE ARRIVAL OF THE EUROPEANS

During the Middle Ages in Europe, the small number of Europeans who traveled to Asia returned home with intriguing tales of kingdoms "where grows pepper, silk, and sandalwood," and cities "with good houses and palaces built of stone." In 1511, a Portuguese expedition reached Malacca, one of the cities near the southern tip of the peninsula. Malacca was the busiest trading port in Southeast Asia.

Shwe Dagon Pagoda is a Buddhist shrine surrounded by smaller shrines in Rangoon, Burma's capital. Here, in 1824, the Burmese successfully resisted an attack by invading British forces.

Soon the Portuguese captured the city and, to monopolize the spice trade, drove out Arab, Persian, and Indian traders. From Malacca, the Portuguese voyaged to part of the Indonesian island chain, the Moluccas, which they called the "Spice Islands" because of the cloves and nutmeg that grew there.

Southeast Asian islands. Throughout the 1500s, Portugal dominated the commerce of the Southeast Asian islands, but Spain determined to share the trade. Spain concentrated on the Philippine Islands, where Magellan had been killed in 1521. After several unsuccessful attempts to plant settlements, the Spanish finally succeeded in founding San Miguel and Manila by 1571.

By the end of the 1500s, the Spaniards had gained control of all the Philippines, where they introduced Spanish forms of government and Spanish customs. Spanish missionaries converted many Filipinos to Catholicism, and as a result the Catholic Church gained great influence in the Philippines.

By the 1600s, the English and the Dutch were challenging both Portugal and Spain in Southeast Asia. The Dutch East India Company, formed in 1602, set about to take over the spice trade. Soon the Dutch took Malacca from the Portuguese and won control of a large part of the Indonesian islands, which became known as the Dutch East Indies.

Because their main interest was trade, not colonization or religious conversion, the Dutch allowed the island's peoples self-rule in local affairs. However, the Dutch created great discontent when they forced farmers to grow crops such as coffee, sugar, tea, and cinnamon, which Europeans desired, instead of food crops such as rice for Indonesians.

The peninsula. In the 1600s, many Europeans saw Vietnam as an important link in trade with China. However, because of Vietnam's agricultural economy and the lack of cooperation from Vietnamese rulers, European merchants were not successful in establishing profitable trade with Vietnam.

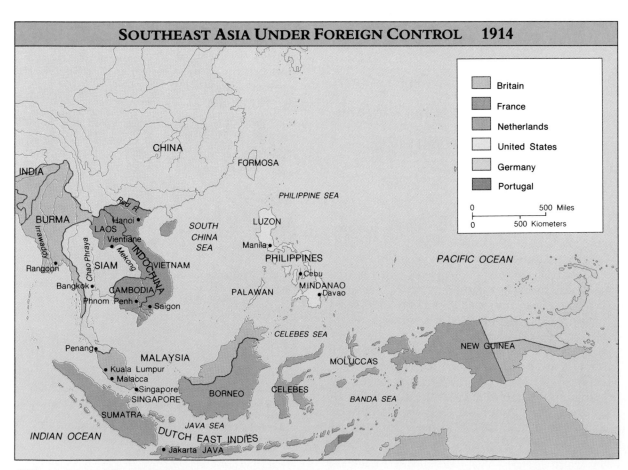

SOUTHEAST ASIA UNDER FOREIGN CONTROL   1914

Britain
France
Netherlands
United States
Germany
Portugal

0   500 Miles
0   500 Kiometers

CHINA
FORMOSA
INDIA
PHILIPPINE SEA
BURMA
Red R.
Hanoi
LAOS
Vientiane
SOUTH CHINA SEA
LUZON
Irrawaddy
Chao Phraya
Mekong
INDOCHINA
VIETNAM
Manila
PHILIPPINES
PACIFIC OCEAN
Rangoon
SIAM
Bangkok
CAMBODIA
Phnom Penh
Saigon
Cebu
MINDANAO
Davao
PALAWAN
CELEBES SEA
NEW GUINEA
Penang
MALAYSIA
MOLUCCAS
Kuala Lumpur
Malacca
Singapore
SINGAPORE
BORNEO
CELEBES
BANDA SEA
SUMATRA
INDIAN OCEAN
JAVA SEA
DUTCH EAST INDIES
Jakarta JAVA

DETECTING BIAS

A bias is an inclination for or against something, which prevents you from making an impartial judgment. A bias is a one-sided or slanted view, usually untested. Most people have biases. Some biases, such as those regarding certain sports or foods or music, are not likely to hurt anyone, but others, such as biases for or against certain types of people, may lead to harmful actions. Biases distort or misrepresent the way things really are. Being able to detect bias can help you avoid believing and acting on an inaccurate account.

EXPLAINING THE SKILL

As noted in the procedure described on pages 362-363, one of the clues to bias is the repeated use of emotionally charged, or "loaded," words. Another clue is repeated exaggerations. A third common clue is the use of "loaded" questions that tell you the answer you should give, such as the question: "You don't want people to think you're stupid, do you?" Presentation of only one side of an issue or situation is also a clue. A fifth clue is the statement of opinions as if they were obvious facts.

If an account has repeated examples of all or most of these clues in reference to a particular subject, the account may be biased. To detect bias, you can search a written account sentence by sentence to find clues. If you find any clues, note whether they give a favorable or unfavorable impression of the subject.

APPLYING THE SKILL

The excerpt that follows is from a poem written in 1899 by British author Rudyard Kipling in praise of the American annexation of the Philippine Islands. Use the procedure outlined above and on pages 362-363 to decide whether the excerpt shows any bias.

Take up the White Man's burden—
    Send forth the best ye breed—
Go, bind your sons to exile
    To serve your captives' need;
To wait, in heavy harness,

On fluttered folk and wild—
Your new-caught sullen peoples,
    Half devil and half child.

Take up the White Man's burden—
    In patience to abide,
To veil the threat of terror
    And check the show of pride;
By open speech and simple,
    An hundred times made plain,
To seek another's profit
    And work another's gain.

Take up the White Man's burden—
    The savage wars of peace—
Fill full the mouth of Famine,
    And bid the sickness cease;
And when your goal is nearest
    (The end for others sought)
Watch sloth and heathen folly
    Bring all your hope to nought.

Abridged from *The White Man's Burden*, by Rudyard Kipling (1899).

MAKING MEANING

Answer the following questions:

1. What words does the author use to describe the Filipinos? **(a)** *savage, heavy, best, warlike;* **(b)** *fluttered, wild, half devil, sullen;* **(c)** *exiled, plain, open, simple.*

2. The poem portrays the Filipinos as being **(a)** patient, but warlike, **(b)** sullen and untamed, **(c)** grateful and humble.

3. The author believes that Americans are **(a)** generous people who are committed to helping others, **(b)** people who are warlike and wild, **(c)** people who are unwilling to share their possessions with others.

4. In what way is the poem one-sided? **(a)** It gives only negative aspects of imperialism. **(b)** It gives a detailed description of the Americans only. **(c)** It describes the Filipinos negatively and the Americans positively.

REVIEWING THE SKILL

5. Define the term *bias*.

6. What are five clues to the existence of bias in a written account?

European missionaries tried to preach Catholicism in Vietnam but were harassed by Vietnamese rulers. In the mid-1800s, France sent in troops to free some of its missionaries from jail. The French, under the leadership of Napoleon III, soon acquired their first Asian colony. Despite Vietnamese resistance, France gained control of Vietnam in 1884. Later, when France took Laos and Cambodia, these two countries, together with Vietnam, became known as French Indochina.

Meanwhile, Britain took over part of Burma after Burma tried to invade India in the early 1800s. The British then pressured the Burmese to open trade and diplomatic relations. When the British were rebuffed after lengthy negotiations, they marched on the Burmese capital in frustration. By 1897, Great Britain had brought the country of Burma under its rule as a province of India.

To the south of Burma, the British established a naval station at Penang, near the tip of the peninsula. They also established a port on the uninhabited island of Singapore, located along the route between the Pacific and Indian oceans. In time, Singapore became the major trading center of Southeast Asia. After the British traded a settlement in Indonesia to the Dutch in exchange for Malacca, the cities of Penang, Singapore, and Malacca became one colony. From there, Great Britain eventually took control of Malaya, which is the area of present-day Malaysia.

By the end of the 1800s, only Siam, now called Thailand, remained free of European domination. Siamese rulers used clever diplomacy to convince the two rival European powers that it was in their best interest to leave Siam as a free state separating French and British territories. The Siamese also quickly modernized their government, freely allowed foreign missionaries to enter, and opened the country to foreign trade. These measures removed the reasons European nations might have had for taking control of Siam.

INDEPENDENCE MOVEMENTS

By the late 1800s, open revolts against foreign rule broke out in the Philippine Islands. During the Spanish-American War in 1898, an army of Filipino revolutionaries, led by Emilio Aguinaldo (eh-MEEL-yō AH-gee-NAHL-dō), fought along with the Americans to free the Philippines from Spain. Although Filipinos proclaimed independence when the war ended, the United States took over the Philippines. Disappointed to have exchanged one foreign ruler for another, Filipinos continued to agitate for self-rule. Gradually the United States in-

The Maoris, New Zealand's original inhabitants, often gathered at meeting houses like the one in this 1870s photograph. The decorations, which have spiritual meanings, cannot be used on private homes. Today, many modern Maoris still attend traditional social gatherings in their villages.

creased Filipino participation in the government, but to many Filipinos, progress seemed all too slow.

Meanwhile, people in Indonesia also agitated for independence. As a result, the Dutch organized a council through which Indonesians could express their opinions. However, because the Indonesians felt they had no real role in decision making, they began to organize revolutionary groups. In Burma, Malaya, and Indochina, feelings of nationalism stirred, but by the early 1900s the seeds of discontent had not yet grown into organized national movements toward independence.

THE PACIFIC ISLANDS

Throughout the 1800s, European nations and the United States continued to expand their worldwide trade networks. To provide bases for the steamships as well as the whaling ships that sailed the long overseas routes, these nations began to stake claims to the thousands of islands that dot the vast Pacific.

Australia and New Zealand. Although most of the Pacific islands are tiny, one is so large that many consider it to be the world's smallest continent—Australia. A British expedition explored the coastline of Australia and nearby New Zealand in 1769 and 1770. Eighteen years later, Britain began to colonize Australia with convicts from overcrowded British prisons. As the century wore on, other British settlers sought opportunities in Australia. When gold was discovered in 1851, fortune seekers from all over the world poured in, and by 1861 the colony's population surged to 1,145,000.

Settlement of New Zealand followed that of Australia. The original inhabitants of New Zealand, the Maoris (MOW-rees), fought hard to keep British settlers from taking over their lands. In the end, however, the Maoris were defeated. Both Australia and New Zealand became self-governing states within the British Empire in the early 1900s.

By the dawn of the twentieth century, European and American influence extended from the Indian Ocean across the waters of the Pacific. From the smallest islands to the island continent of Australia, these Pacific possessions played a significant role in the extensive system of world trade.

SECTION REVIEW

1. Describe how Western nations took control of the Southeast Asian peninsula.

2. How did Southeast Asian people respond to European control?

3. What led Western nations to take Australia and New Zealand?

Analysis. Compare the responses of the Burmese, the Vietnamese, and the Siamese to European demands for trade.

Data Search. Refer to the appropriate charts on pages 832 and 833 to identify: **(a)** the major raw materials exported to Europe from China, India, Ceylon, and New Zealand in the late 1800s, and **(b)** the number of people who immigrated to Australia between 1861 and 1932.

HISTORY IN FOCUS

The impact of the West on Asia was enormous. Whether Asian nations fell to Western control or maintained their independence by adapting Western knowledge, all Asian nations were forced to find a way to deal with Western ideas. Ironically, it was the Westerners who planted the ideas of justice and nationalism that would eventually bring an end to Western imperialism in Asia.

Sometimes, Westerners made improvements that benefited Asian societies, such as irrigation systems, railroads, universities, and hospitals. However, Western ideas brought rapid change that contributed to the breakdown of established ways. This change often caused severe discontent among Asian peoples.

Westerners were not completely untouched by their experiences in Asia, and some Asian ideas did enter Western culture. Some Western thinkers and artists began to incorporate Asian ideas into their works. For example, Asian designs were often used in Western decorative arts such as porcelains, wallpaper, and furniture.

Gradually, some Westerners began to become concerned with the plight of Asian peoples dominated by Western rule. In the West, societies began to spring up to work for self-rule for Asians. For the first time, the people of the conquering nations began to experience pangs of conscience regarding the people whom they had conquered.

SUMMARY

- In the nineteenth century, trade brought the European powers into increasing contact with the countries of Asia and the Pacific. Although many of these lands fell under European control, a few of them managed to adapt to Western ways and to maintain their independence.

- By 1850, all of India was controlled by the British East India Company, which brought major changes to Indian society. After the Sepoy Rebellion, the British government took over the rule of India. Indian nationalism grew to become an important force by the early 1900s.

- In China, European pressure and rebellions by the Chinese undermined Manchu rule and left the country open to foreign influence. Reforms failed to stabilize the Ch'ing Dynasty, and it was overthrown in 1911. Although a republic was established, instability continued.

- The Tokugawa government of Japan finally gave in to American pressure in 1854 and opened the country to Western trade and influence. The Meiji rulers who followed the Tokugawa shogunate enacted sweeping reforms and modernized Japan, making the nation a world power by the early part of the twentieth century.

- The lands of Southeast Asia, long influenced by Chinese, Indian, and Arab cultures, gradually came under European control after the 1500s. European colonies were established in the South Pacific by the 1800s, including Australia and New Zealand.

VOCABULARY REVIEW

Match each numbered vocabulary term with the lettered word or phrase most closely related to it. Then explain how the items in each pair are related.

1. boycott   (a) representative
2. treaty port   (b) refusal
3. extraterritoriality (c) foreign trade
4. consul   (d) legal system

CHAPTER REVIEW

1. (a) How did the British gain political control of India? (b) Compare the extent of foreign political influence in India, China, and Japan.

2. Compare the changes that came about during the nineteenth century in India, China, and Japan in the following areas: (a) education, (b) the economy, (c) government.

3. (a) Explain Hindu and Muslim reactions to British rule. (b) Compare Chinese and Indian reactions to European imperialism. (c) How did the Japanese response to foreign influence differ from that of other Asian nations?

4. (a) Describe changes resulting from the Sepoy Rebellion. (b) Compare causes and results of the Sepoy, Taiping, and Boxer rebellions.

5. (a) Explain how the Opium Wars came about. What were the results? (b) In what way was the cause of the Russo–Japanese War similar to the causes of the Opium Wars?

6. (a) Describe European trade with India, China, and Japan around 1800. (b) What caused changes to be made in the trade policies of China and Japan? Explain.

7. Give an example of cultural diffusion or blending in India, China, Japan, and Southeast Asia.

8. (a) Describe the early cultural development of Southeast Asia. (b) When and why did Europeans arrive in the area?

9. (a) Describe the French colonization of Indochina. (b) How did the British take over Burma and Malaya? (c) How did Siam remain independent?

10. (a) What were some signs of the growth of nationalism in India, China, Japan, and Southeast Asia by the early 1900s? (b) Where were nationalist movements most successful?

THINKING CRITICALLY: ACTIVITIES

1. Imagine that you are one of the leaders of the Indian National Congress. Prepare a pamphlet outlining the changes you are advocating in India and setting forth a plan to carry them out.

2. Prepare a response to the following questions as if you were a Japanese citizen around 1860: Should Japan open itself up to Western influence? If so, why and to what degree? If not, why not? Some students may wish to present their answers as a debate before the class.

3. Divide into groups of four or five and discuss the following question: What combination of factors made some Asian countries more subject to European imperialism than others? Support your responses with material from the chapter. Report your group's conclusions to the class.

APPLYING SOCIAL STUDIES SKILLS

Analyzing primary sources. Below is an excerpt from a letter written to Queen Victoria in 1839 by the Chinese trade commissioner, Lin Tsehsu.

> It appears that this particular form of poison [opium] is illegally prepared by scoundrels in the tributary tribes of your honorable country. You do not allow your own people to smoke [opium], evidently knowing what a curse it is. But would it not be better still to forbid the sale and preparation of opium? Not to smoke yourselves, but yet to dare to prepare and sell to and beguile the foolish masses of [China]—this is to protect one's own life while leading others to death, to gather profit for oneself while bringing injury to others. Such behavior is repugnant to the feelings of human beings, and is not tolerated by the ways of God. On receipt of this letter, make haste to reply, stating the measures adopted at all seaports for cutting off the supply.

Abridged from *Gems of Chinese Literature*, translated by Herbert A Giles. Shanghai: Kelly & Walsh, 1923.

1. What evidence in the letter indicates that it is a primary source?

2. What words in the letter reveal Lin Tsehsu's feelings about opium and the smuggling of opium?

3. What reasons did Lin Tsehsu give in support of his request to end opium trading?

4. What did Lin Tsehsu assume about Queen Victoria's reaction to the letter? How can you tell that he made this assumption?

APPLYING THINKING SKILLS

Detecting bias. The British poet and diplomat Wilfred Scawen Blunt wrote the following entry in his diary on December 22, 1899. Analyze his diary entry carefully to determine whether he shows any bias toward the topic he is writing about. Then answer the questions that follow the diary entry.

> The old century is very nearly out, and the British Empire is playing the devil in it as never an empire before has done on so large a scale. We may live to see the British Empire's fall.
>
> All the nations of Europe are making the same hell upon earth in China, massacring and pillaging in the captured cities as outrageously as in the Middle Ages. The Emperor of Germany gives the word for slaughter and the Pope looks on and approves. In South Africa our troops are burning farms under Kitchener's command, as the Queen and the two Houses of Parliament and the bishops thank God publicly and vote money for the work.
>
> The Americans are spending fifty million a year on slaughtering the Filipinos; the King of the Belgians has invested his whole fortune on the Congo, where he is brutalizing the negroes to fill his pockets. The French and Italians for the moment are playing a less prominent part in the slaughter, but their inactivity grieves them. The whole white race is reveling openly in violence, as though it had never pretended to be Christian. God's equal curse be on them all! So ends the famous nineteenth century into which we were so proud to have been born.

Abridged from *My Diaries*, by Wilfred Scawen Blunt. London: Martin Secker, 1919-1920.

1. What is one procedure for detecting bias in a written source?

2. Explain why it is important to be able to detect bias.

3. What is the bias that is evident in the above account?

4. What clues to bias can be found in this account? For each type of clue you found, give a specific example from the account.

5. What is one common clue to bias that is *not* found in the above account?

UNIT REVIEW

1. (a) Compare nation building in Europe and Latin America in the 1800s. **(b)** How did *caudillos* differ from European leaders of the time?

2. (a) Describe American and European expansion in the nineteenth century. **(b)** How did American and European imperialism differ? **(c)** How were the Monroe Doctrine and the Berlin Conference similar? How were they different?

3. (a) Compare European and Japanese imperialism. **(b)** What was similar about Kaiser Wilhelm and Emperor Meiji? How were Bismarck and Ito similar?

4. In general terms, how was the political and economic development of Latin America different from the development of Asia and Africa in the nineteenth and early twentieth centuries?

5. (a) What countries in Africa and Southeast Asia remained independent? Did they do it in the same way? Explain. **(b)** Name a buffer state in Latin America and one in Southeast Asia. How did each function as a buffer state?

6. (a) Explain the circumstances and results of both the Mexican and Chinese revolutions of the early 1900s. **(b)** How was the American Civil War different from these other wars?

7. (a) Describe the goals of each of the following groups: Indian National Congress, Taiping Society, Young Turks. **(b)** What did the Pan-Arab movement have in common with efforts to unify Latin America? How were they different?

8. (a) Compare the effects of nineteenth-century trade with Europe on Latin America, Africa, and Japan. **(b)** Compare industrialization in India, Latin America, and the United States. **(c)** How were changes in agriculture similar and different in Africa and Indonesia?

9. (a) How did leaders of Egypt, Japan, and Latin America view progress? How did they achieve it? **(b)** Compare the situations of Ismail, Porfirio Díaz, and Sun Yat-sen.

10. Compare the Suez and Panama canals in the following respects: **(a)** reasons for construction, **(b)** how imperial powers gained control over them, and **(c)** overall impact.

RELATING PAST TO PRESENT

1. The nineteenth-century Pan-Arab and Pan-American movements were efforts to forge regional unity in the Arab world and Latin America. Today similar efforts are underway in those regions and in other parts of the world. Investigate one of the following movements or organizations and write a report on how it has evolved from historical circumstances: **(a)** Arab unity, as expressed through the League of Arab Nations; **(b)** the Organization for African Unity (OAU); **(c)** efforts to unify Latin America, including the Organization of American States (OAS).

2. Select any modern nation that was a colonial possession of the United States or a European power during the nineteenth and early twentieth centuries. Learn what effects of colonialism can still be seen today in that country. Present your findings in a brochure intended for a tour group studying the effects of imperialism. Point out signs of the country's former status as a colony, such as language, religion, architecture, education, industry, and medicine. Also consider problems resulting from colonial economic and political policies, such as border disputes due to poorly drawn borders, the depletion of resources, and instability due to lack of experience with self-government.

3. In about 1910, nearly 25 percent of the earth's people and 20 percent of the earth's land were within the British Empire. On an outline map of the world, identify the territories of the British Empire in the early twentieth century. Find out what the British Commonwealth is and indicate on your map the regions associated with the British Commonwealth today.

PROJECTS AND ACTIVITIES

1. Create a set of four parallel timelines about imperialism in Africa, the Middle East, the Americas, and Asia and the Pacific. Begin each timeline with the date of the area's first contact with Europeans. Next add the main events occurring since then, including those covered in this unit. Finally, write a summary analyzing the information the timelines contain.

2. Find out more about one historical figure referred to in this unit—such as Queen Victoria, Bolívar, Banerji, or Sun Yat-sen. Then write a speech expressing that person's hopes for the future of his or her nation, but do not give that person's name. Instead, include hints about your historical figure's identity. Give your speech and have your classmates guess who you are.

3. Divide into three groups and choose a region, either Latin America, Africa, or Southeast Asia and the Pacific. Prepare a group report on that region around 1900, with each student taking an individual country or colony. Each individual report should cover such topics as government, the economy, and key aspects of the society, such as social structure, arts, and urban and rural life. Present your report as a group, using visual aids if possible.

ANALYZING PRIMARY SOURCES

Refer to "African Responses to Imperialism" on page 585 to answer the following questions.

1. What is the Yao ruler's attitude toward the German commander? Support your answer with evidence from the letter.

2. Review the discussion on pages 583–588 concerning the impact of colonialism on African life. Then explain how the Kenyan ruler's comments reflect colonialism's effect on each of the following: **(a)** African religious beliefs, **(b)** African emphasis on cooperation and sharing, **(c)** African government and law, and **(d)** the African economy.

3. Explain the Kenyan ruler's statement that "something has taken away the meaning of our lives."

4. Why do you think that Kenya's ruler and his people lost their belief in human goodness?

5. How do the letters of the two rulers differ?

GEOGRAPHY REVIEW

Relationships within places. Today, as in the past, people perceive and change their environments according to their cultural values, economic priorities, and technological capabilities.

As you answer these questions, think about the area in which you live in terms of changing environmental perceptions. While you may not be sure of each response, base your answers on what you already know about your area and its history. You might decide to do research to answer the questions.

1. What physical features do you think attracted Indians to the area?

2. What resources did the Indians use to maintain their way of life?

3. What attracted the first European or American settlers to your area?

4. What resources did these settlers use to maintain their way of life?

5. How did the early settlers alter the environment they found?

6. How has industrialization affected the environment of your area?

7. Which aspects of your environment are most important to you? How do you take advantage of them? Consider such matters as the work that you do or plan to do, your leisure time activities, local foods that you enjoy, and transportation routes that you use.

8. In the next century, what do you think people will value about your area's environment?

SUGGESTED READINGS

Achebe, Chinua. *Things Fall Apart.* New York: Aston-Honor, 1959. A story of Ibo tribal life in a remote Nigerian village in the late 1800s.

Azuela, Mariano. *The Underdogs.* New York: Signet Classics, 1962. A classic novel of the Mexican Revolution.

Bence-Jones, Mark. *Viceroys of India.* New York: St. Martin, 1984. Sketches of the British rulers of India during the Raj.

O'Connor, Richard. *Pacific Destiny.* Boston: Little Brown, 1969. Stories of high-spirited American adventurers in the Pacific.

Robinson, Francis. *Atlas of the Islamic World Since 1500.* New York: Facts on File, 1982. A political and social history of Islam, with colorful maps and illustrations.

CRISES IN THE TWENTIETH CENTURY

1912-1946

*I have seen war. . . .
I have seen blood running
from the wounded. . . .
I have seen the agony of
mothers and wives.
I hate war.*

—*Franklin Roosevelt, 1936*

Guernica. Pablo Picasso, Spain, 1937.

CHAPTER TWENTY-EIGHT
THE FIRST WORLD WAR

CHAPTER TWENTY-NINE
AFTERMATH OF THE WAR

CHAPTER THIRTY
TOTALITARIANISM: THE CHALLENGE TO LIBERTY

CHAPTER THIRTY-ONE
THE SECOND WORLD WAR

GLOBAL TIMELINE

	POLITICAL	TECHNOLOGICAL	SOCIAL
1914			
1918	World War I Russian Revolution	Ford's assembly line Fighter airplanes Military tanks Sonar developed	First Charlie Chaplin movies Jazz becomes popular in U.S. Beginnings of functionalist architecture
1922	Treaty of Versailles Mussolini founds Fascist movement	Radio becomes widely used First helicopter	Woman suffrage in U.S.
1926	Mussolini comes to power Gandhi made leader of India's National Congress Party	Refrigerators used widely Insecticides first used	Surrealist art develops in Europe; muralist art develops in Mexico
1930	Stalin comes to power Five-Year Plan introduced in USSR	First televisions and sound movies Liquid-fuel rocket invented	General strike in Great Britain Modernization reforms in Turkey Woman suffrage in Great Britain
1934	Hitler comes to power Roosevelt begins New Deal Military government formed in Japan	Fluorescent lights invented	Stock market crash Great Depression
1938	Spanish Civil War Mao Zedong leads the "Long March"	Radar Electron microscope Jet engine	Nuremberg laws deny citizenship to Jews Beginning of mass emigration of artists from Germany
1942	Fall of France Japan attacks Pearl Harbor	Penicillin used widely First nuclear reactor	Forty-hour work week in U.S.
1946	World War II D-Day United Nations established	Magnetic tape First atomic bomb exploded	"Black markets" for food and clothing develop in Europe

THE FIRST WORLD WAR

1912–1920

Assault on Verdun. Henri J. C. C. de Groux, Belgium, 1916.

A war engulfed Europe in 1914, shattering nearly a century of relative peace. Called either the Great War or World War I, it was one of the most dramatic turning points in world history. In four short years, the Europe that had existed since the sixteenth century came crashing down, destroyed by social and political revolutions.

The destruction of war greatly disrupted the European economy, and the loss of life was enormous. The forces of nationalism brought about the breakup of formerly great empires and the formation of many new countries. However, perhaps the most significant changes were the rise of the United States as the dominant world power and the creation of a new government in Russia. When World War I ended in 1918, the world was very different than it had been before 1914.

TIMELINE

1914		
	Assassination of Archduke Ferdinand	Austria-Hungary declares war on Serbia
1915	Germany declares war on Russia and France	Great Britain declares war on Germany
		Sinking of the *Lusitania*
1916		
	Battle of Jutland	
1917		
	United States declares war on the Central Powers	American troops arrive in France
1918		
		Treaty of Brest-Litovsk
1919	Armistice signed	
	Treaty of Versailles	First meeting of the League of Nations
1920		

28–1
THE ROAD TO WAR

READ TO FIND OUT

—what the term *mobilize* means.
—why tension existed between France and Germany.
—how Pan-Slavism was a threat to the Austro-Hungarian Empire.
—how a small conflict between Austria-Hungary and Serbia became a world war.

World War I was rooted in the century of imperialism that came before it. As European nations competed around the globe, they clashed constantly. With feelings of intense national pride, the competing powers became increasingly suspicious of each other. These nations formed a complex system of alliances intended to keep the peace. Britain, France, and Russia formed the Triple Entente, and Germany, Austria–Hungary, and Italy, the Triple Alliance. The many secret provisions of their treaties, however, provoked distrust instead of peace.

Suspicions also led to vast military buildups, and some Europeans came to believe that war was the only solution to their conflicts. Winston Churchill, Britain's lord of the admiralty, described the atmosphere of the early 1900s: "Almost one might think the world wished to suffer. Certainly men were everywhere eager to dare." Tensions grew, until by 1914 Europe was a powder keg ready to explode.

FOREIGN POLICIES

Fervent nationalism led each European power to pursue its own goals. At the same time, the spirit of nationalism also bred unrest within some nations, as various ethnic groups clamored to form their own separate countries.

Germany. In the early twentieth century, the key word in German foreign policy was *militarism*. Because Germany had the largest population in western Europe and because its industrial output was among the largest in the world, its leaders argued that their country

Frank Wood depicted the strength of the British navy in *H.M.S. Dreadnought*, which means "fear nothing." This armor-plated battleship made earlier models obsolete when launched in 1906.

should be the dominant military power on the continent. Therefore, between 1890 and 1914, the German army had been expanded, and as a result, the rival states, especially France and Russia, began to fear for their national security. German dreams of imperial power, however, were not limited to the continent of Europe itself, and as German influence in Africa and Asia grew, the German navy was expanded. This development made Great Britain apprehensive about German intentions.

The German military buildup was also motivated by the fear of increased Russian–French cooperation. German leaders did not want to be faced with enemies in both the east and the west at the same time. Fear of an alliance between France and Russia not only led to still larger military buildups, but it also made Germany fearful of a general war.

France. France, on the other hand, wanted a chance to go to war with Germany to get revenge for the military humiliation of 1870, when German troops had destroyed the French army. French leaders also wanted to regain the territories of Alsace and Lorraine, lands seized by Germany as the price of peace in 1871. To this end, France strengthened its military ties to Russia and built a larger army to keep up with Germany's growing strength. French hatred for Germany was one of the strongest forces influencing international politics in the first years of the twentieth century.

Great Britain. In London, the aggressive German naval growth caused strained relations between Germany and Great Britain. British officials refused to permit Germany to become a threat to the British overseas empire in Africa and Asia. Accordingly, Britain, with the goal of maintaining its position as the strongest colonial power, devoted more and more resources to expanding its already powerful navy.

Italy. Even though Italy was a member of the Triple Alliance, Italian leaders were not strong allies of Austria-Hungary and Germany. Indeed, Italy's principal goal was to take several Italian-speaking provinces from Austria-Hungary, an act which Austria-Hungary was unwilling to permit. Knowing that Italy was not closely tied to Germany and Austria-Hungary, both France and Russia frequently attempted to get Italian leaders to withdraw from the Triple Alliance with promises of Austrian territory.

Austria-Hungary. Of all the nations of Europe, Austria-Hungary stood to lose the most from a European war. The House of Hapsburg had ruled in Vienna since the thirteenth century, and the Austro-Hungarian state more closely resembled an eighteenth-century absolutist state than a twentieth-century nation. Austria-Hungary also had a major weakness not shared by the other European powers. A tiny minority of Germans ruled over millions of Croats, Bohemians, and other Slavic peoples, many of whom wanted political freedom and, eventually, independence.

Austria-Hungary's attempts to maintain imperial rule over its minority populations were thwarted by countries like Russia and Serbia. The leaders of these nations tried to destabilize eastern Europe so as to end Austro-Hungarian domination of the region. Austria-Hungary's main foreign policy goal, therefore, was to maintain the most influential position in eastern Europe at the expense of Russia and smaller neighboring states like Serbia which had nationalist ambitions.

Russia. Although Czar Nicholas II had essentially peaceful intentions, Russian foreign policy was actually being run by a group of militarist officials who hoped to bring about a war in Europe. The Russians felt that a war would bring glory to the Russian military, and victory would result in expanded Russian influence in eastern Europe and the Balkans at the expense of Austria-Hungary. A war would also distract the Russian people from problems such as political repression and food shortages.

One of Russia's main concerns—the one that explains Russian interest in the Balkans—was to acquire a warm-water port so that Russian ships could operate during winter, when Russian ports in the north were frozen shut for several months. To gain a warm-water port—which would have to be on the Black Sea—Russia needed to establish either direct control or, at the very least, great influence over the straits at Constantinople. In 1914, this strategic waterway was still controlled by the Ottoman Empire. Russia knew that Austria-Hungary and the Ottoman Empire would never peacefully allow Russian control of these straits. Thus, the Russians believed that their aims could be achieved only through war.

THE BALKANS 1913

Serbia. Although not a major power, Serbia was a strong force in international diplomacy in the first decade of the twentieth century. In Serbia, officials assumed for themselves the role of leaders in the Pan-Slavic movement. The main goal of the movement, and thus the main goal of Serbia, was to unite the southern European Slavs into a Slavic nation. This aim, of course, meant the liberation of the Slavic peoples living under Austro-Hungarian rule. Like Russia and France, Serbia knew its goals could be achieved only through war.

CRISES IN THE BALKANS

The five small independent states of Greece, Romania, Bulgaria, Montenegro, and Serbia made up the Balkan region. Of the five, Serbia, as the leader of the Pan-Slavic movement, was the most important. Serbia's goal of uniting the Slavic people into a single nation had suffered a setback in 1908 when Bosnia and Herzegovina, two areas with large Slavic populations, were annexed by Austria-Hungary.

The Slavic peoples in Bosnia and Herzegovina bitterly resented the annexation, as did the people of Serbia, who angrily denounced the move because they had wanted to unite the two provinces with Serbia. Hoping to make further inroads into the Balkans, the Russians joined the Serbians in protest. Austria-Hungary, however, relied on German support and forced Russia and Serbia to back down. Even though the crisis passed, both Serbia and Russia sat back to await the next crisis in the region, vowing to be more forceful next time.

Further trouble erupted in the Balkan region in 1912. Encouraged by Russian support, Serbia—together with Bulgaria, Greece, and Montenegro—formed what was called the Balkan League and declared war on the Ottoman Empire. The league hoped to take the province of Macedonia away from the sultan and end Ottoman control of the straits to the Black Sea. This conflict came to be known as the First Balkan War. In 1913, the Balkan League easily defeated the Ottomans, dividing up Macedonia among its victorious members. The sultan, however, did retain some land in Europe as well as the strategically significant straits.

At the same time Serbia, which wanted to gain an outlet to the Adriatic Sea, annexed the

Ottoman province of Albania. Not wanting Serbia to grow stronger, Austria-Hungary—backed by Germany and Italy—demanded that Serbia give up Albania so that the province could be made into an independent state. Without significant international support, Serbia was forced to give up its claims. Once again, general conflict was narrowly avoided.

In June 1913, still another Balkan crisis occurred when Bulgaria suddenly attacked Serbia and Greece. Bulgaria argued that the other Balkan nations had cheated it out of territory during the peace settlements that ended the First Balkan War. With the support of Austria-Hungary and Germany, Bulgaria attempted to gain territory by taking the parts of Macedonia that Serbia and Greece had been given. In just one month, however, Bulgaria's army was soundly defeated. As a result of this conflict, called the Second Balkan War, Serbia doubled its territory. Meanwhile, Austria-Hungary looked on in anger, uncertain of what the Serbians would do next.

BEGINNING OF A WORLD WAR

As Austria-Hungary had feared, Serbian expansion inflamed Slavic nationalists within the Hapsburg Empire. Throughout Serbia and Austria-Hungary, secret societies formed to unite Bosnia and Herzegovina with Serbia to form a greater Slavic state. One of these groups, called the Black Hand, adopted the threatening slogan, "Union or Death."

During the reign of the Austrian emperor Francis Joseph II, the Slavic minorities in Austria-Hungary were given few political or economic rights, and leaders of the Slavic independence movement were dealt with harshly. Instead of eliminating the problem, however, this harsh policy made the Slavic nationalists more determined than ever. Indeed, the uncompromising approach of the crown was their greatest source of strength.

As Francis Joseph grew old, supporters of a Slavic state became worried because the heir to the throne, Archduke Francis Ferdinand, promised to bring a policy of moderation. It was his intention to give the Slavic minorities more say in their own affairs. Because Francis Ferdinand was perceived as a friend of the Slavs, he became the greatest enemy of the militant Slavic nationalists, who did not want the Slavic peo-

Archduke Francis Ferdinand and his wife, Sophie, ride through Sarajevo one hour before their death. Ironically, they made their trip to show Austria's concern for Serbian interests.

ples to remain under the rule of Austria-Hungary. The militant nationalists wanted a violent revolution out of which could be forged a new Slavic state.

The assassination. On June 28, 1914—while on a visit to Sarajevo (SAHR-ah-yeh-vō), the capital of Bosnia—Archduke Francis Ferdinand and his wife, Sophie, were assassinated by a member of the Black Hand. Although the assassin had acted on his own, some Serbian military officers had not only known of the plot but had also provided weapons and undercover assistance.

Outraged, Austria-Hungary decided to use the incident to crush Serbia once and for all, thus destroying the center of Slavic nationalism. Before taking any action, however, Austria-Hungary contacted its ally, Germany. Kaiser Wilhelm II advised Austria-Hungary to be firm. Confident of German support and feeling the kaiser's words to be a "blank check," leaders in Vienna were encouraged to do whatever seemed necessary to solve the Serbian problem.

Meanwhile, France and Russia saw the growing crisis in the Balkans as a threat to their interests. Russia, wanting to further its influence in the Balkans, was opposed to any Austro-Hungarian solution to the problem of the Slavic minorities. France did not want the Triple Alliance to have still another diplomatic victory that would strengthen Germany's international position. Accordingly, during July 1914, France encouraged Russia to stand firm in support of Serbia against any impending Austro-Hungarian action. Just as Germany had given Austria-Hungary a "blank check," now France told the czar's ministers that it would support any Russian action, up to and including war.

The ultimatum. On July 23, Austria-Hungary sent an ultimatum, or final set of demands, to Serbia. This ultimatum called for an end to all activities against Austria-Hungary and insisted that Austrian officials be involved in the investigation of the assassination.

Counting on Russian support, Serbia gave in to all demands except one: it would not agree to allow Austrian officials to participate in the investigation. The Serbians declared that allowing Austrian officials across the border would be an infringement on Serbia's national rights. However, the Serbian government had a much more important reason for refusing Austrian participation in the investigation. The Serbian government was afraid that the Austrians might find some evidence of official involvement in the assassination plot. Confident of German support, Austria-Hungary answered Serbia's refusal by declaring war on its neighbor on July 28, 1914.

Mobilization. The outbreak of fighting brought the alliance system into operation. Russia, Serbia's ally, was the first to *mobilize*, or organize its resources for combat. With the Russian mobilization, the situation became more serious. Thinking Germany was the real force behind the Austro-Hungarian action against Serbia, the czar's troops mobilized against Germany rather than Austria-Hungary. With Russia prepared to strike against Germany, the Balkan affair became a European crisis. Suddenly, nations began to scramble for the best military position.

Germany demanded that Russia cancel its mobilization immediately or face war. By now, however, the Russian military leaders, encouraged by the French leaders, who smelled revenge in the air, had decided in favor of a military confrontation. After waiting two days for the Russians to cancel the mobilization order, Germany declared war on Russia on August 1, 1914. Two days later, convinced that France would support Russia, Germany also declared war against its neighbor to the west. Italy, the third member of the Triple Alliance, decided to stay neutral, while the Ottoman Em-pire, influenced by Germany, joined the war against Russia.

Because Austria-Hungary, Germany, and the Ottoman Empire were centrally located in Europe, they became known as the Central Powers in what was now an all-out war in Europe. France, Russia, and Serbia—later joined by Great Britain—became known as the Allied Powers, or Allies.

SECTION REVIEW

1. Define *mobilize*.

2. How did the foreign policy goals of France and Germany conflict?

3. Why did Austria-Hungary feel threatened by Pan-Slavism?

4. How did the Serbian conflict become a major war?

Evaluation. Given the various foreign policy goals of the European powers, how might resolutions to the conflicting aims have been made, short of war? In the end, did the system of alliances make Europe more stable?

28–2
THE COURSE OF CONFLICT

READ TO FIND OUT

—what the term *propaganda* means.

—what strategy the Germans used during the war.

—how technological innovations changed the way wars were fought.

—why the United States entered the war on the side of the Allies.

—how the Allies defeated the Central Powers.

Initially, leaders of both the Allies and Central Powers thought that the war would be a short one, lasting six to eight weeks. By 1915, however, it became apparent that this war

RECOGNIZING STEREOTYPES

A stereotype is an unvarying, overgeneralized description or concept of a group or individual. Stereotyping inaccurately depicts the individual members of a group as being all generally alike. For example, a common stereotype is that all used-car salespersons are dishonest and overly persistent. People who form this stereotype ignore the unique traits of the many used-car salespersons who do not fit this description.

Your view of individuals or groups shapes how you usually behave toward them. Therefore, recognizing stereotyped descriptions can enable you to keep an open mind about other people and to avoid acting inappropriately toward them.

EXPLAINING THE SKILL

As you learned on pages 456 and 457, to recognize a stereotype you need to know some clues to stereotyping as well as something about the subject being described. Stereotyped descriptions often use words such as *every, all, any,* and *always.* In addition, they frequently use overgeneralizations or vague words, as well as many positive- or negative-sounding words. Stereotyped descriptions may also link together features that are not logically connected to each other, as in linking a person's physical traits with his or her mental skills.

In order to identify a stereotype, you can search line by line to determine whether a description contains any of the clues mentioned above. You can also recall what you know about the characteristics of individual members of any group being described.

Stereotypes can be communicated through pictures as well as by words. The clues to stereotypes in pictures include the use of symbols, labels, names, phrases, and physical appearances or activities commonly associated with a particular group. For example, a stereotype of cowhands has often been presented in movies and paintings. Clues to this stereotype include symbols such as ten-gallon hats, phrases such as "Howdy, pardner," and activities such as twirling a lasso or riding a bucking horse. Such devices associate a general image with particular cowhands who may not fit that image.

APPLYING THE SKILL

Identify the stereotype in this poster:

MAKING MEANING

Answer the following questions:

1. This poster emphasizes the stereotype of **(a)** the tough British Army, **(b)** frightened children, **(c)** supportive, determined British women.

2. What stereotyping technique is used in this poster? **(a)** overgeneralization, **(b)** loaded language, **(c)** vague words.

3. What visual clues does the poster use to stereotype? **(a)** clothing and hairstyles, **(b)** facial expressions and body positions, **(c)** colors and scenery.

REVIEWING THE SKILL

4. Define the term *stereotype.*

5. What are some of the clues to stereotypes in pictures?

6. Why is it important to be able to identify stereotypes?

would be fought like no other. As British prime minister Sir Edward Grey commented, "The lamps are going out all over Europe; we shall not see them lit again in our lifetime."

In its horror and destruction, World War I—often described as the first total war, because of both civilian and military participation—demonstrated a darker side of modern civilization and technology. Like the factories of the new industrial societies that mass-produced goods for consumers, twentieth-century warfare delivered mass death in proportions that shocked the world. Europeans, encouraged by *propaganda*—the spreading of ideas to promote a given cause or damage an opposing one—turned all their energies toward self-destruction. By 1918, the achievements of centuries of civilization lay in smoldering heaps, bombed and burned almost beyond human recognition.

THE FIRST MONTHS OF WAR

As early as 1905, the German generals had devised a plan for a possible war against an allied France and Russia. Named the Schlieffen (SHLEE-fen) plan after its creator, Alfred von Schlieffen who was chief of the German General Staff, it called for a quick strike against France in the first weeks of the war. The Germans thought that because Russia was such a large country, more time would be needed to mobilize the czar's army than the French forces. Therefore, if Germany could knock France out of the war fast enough, Germany could then put its major forces in the east well before Russia could attack. The quick destruction of France, however, required that German troops march through Belgium, which had declared neutrality. Once through Belgium, the Germans could encircle French troops who were heading east, and attack from the rear, cutting off any means of escape.

The Schlieffen plan was put into operation, and by the first week of August, German troops were marching across the Belgian border. Great Britain, however, had pledged to defend Belgian neutrality. Therefore, only a few days after the war began, Great Britain joined the Allies by declaring war against Germany. The Schlieffen plan had not taken into account Great Britain's defense of Belgium. British and French troops slowed the German march through Belgium.

Because of stiff Belgian and French resistance, the German army did not advance as fast as had been planned. Although the Germans pushed to within one day's march of Paris, Allied defenses stopped the advance at the Marne River in September of 1914 in the First Battle of the Marne. Retreating to the Aisne River, the Germans lost hope of a quick victory.

By now, the Russians were mobilized and on the move. To defend Germany against Russia in the east, the German generals had to pull large numbers of troops out of France. Although the Russians advanced into Austria-Hungary and Germany with alarming speed, the German forces were strengthened with reinforcements from the French battlefield. The Germans stopped the Russian invasion at Tannenburg, near the German–Russian border.

Divided to fight enemies in both the east and the west, the large German army no longer had the strength to achieve a quick lasting victory against either France or Russia. At the end of

This military recruiting poster shows Great Britain as a powerful lion with parts of its empire as lion cubs. By the end of the war, the British Empire had suffered 2,384,860 casualties.

1914, the Germans recognized that the Schlieffen plan had failed. They had checked the Russian invasion, but the German army in France was stalled on the Marne River. The war was a stalemate, or deadlock, and Europe settled in for a long fight.

AN EXPANDING WAR

In southern Europe, some significant events occurred during 1915 and 1916, the most important of which was Italy's entry into the war on the side of the Allies. Promises of Austrian territory made by French and British leaders had been enough to entice Italy away from the Triple Alliance. Austro-Hungarian troops that would have served in battle on the eastern front against Russia now had to be sent to the Italian frontier.

The war also raged in the Ottoman Empire, which had joined the Central Powers. In 1915, British forces and troops sent from British colonies such as India and Australia, attempted to take control of the straits into the Black Sea. However, the Allied forces were defeated by Turks at the battle of Gallipoli.

Throughout southern Africa, German forces operating out of German East Africa harassed British settlers. Led by General von Lettow-Vorbeck, 2,000 guerrilla fighters made up of both Germans and Africans from the German colonies held out against tens of thousands of British troops until the end of the war. The war also extended to Asia, where Japanese forces occupied German possessions.

CHANGES IN WARFARE

Technological innovations in warfare made survival in combat difficult. Airplanes were originally used mainly for reconnaissance missions, but within a short time many planes were carrying bombs and machine guns, adding a new dimension to the war.

A few daring pilots engaged in air duels known as dogfights. Any pilot who successfully shot down five or more enemy planes won the nickname "flying ace." One of the most famous aces was Germany's Baron Manfred von Richthofen (RISH-tō-fen), who became known as the "Red Baron." Another well-known ace was Eddie Rickenbacker, an American volunteer in the French Air Force.

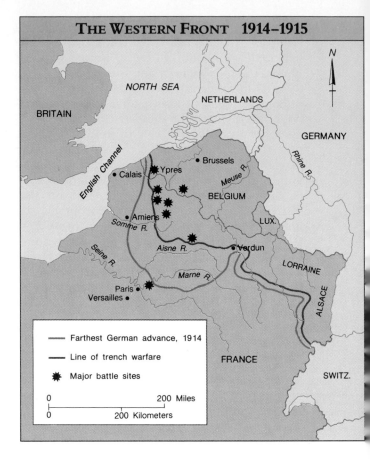

THE WESTERN FRONT 1914–1915

— Farthest German advance, 1914
— Line of trench warfare
✸ Major battle sites

0   200 Miles
0   200 Kilometers

Tanks and long-range artillery made their first appearance during World War I. On the oceans, submarines and bigger and better battleships revolutionized naval strategy.

Trench warfare. By mid-1915, both sides had dug extensive networks of trenches that stretched from the English Channel to the Alps. Only a few hundred yards apart, the trenches marked the combat area, or front line, in the war. They provided a measure of protection against heavy artillery and machine-gun fire. Terror, sickness, and death, however, were the hallmarks of life in these trenches. Soldiers lived knee-deep in stagnant pools of mud and filth, while rats and insects devoured the half-rotted bodies of the dead and wounded.

The most horrible aspect of trench fighting came in the form of chemical warfare. Each side developed poison gases to kill enemy soldiers. One chemical, mustard gas, caused huge sores to develop upon contact with the skin. In the filthy trenches, these sores invariably became infected.

Official war artist John Nash showed a 1917 British assault in France in *Over the Top at Marcoing*. This trench battle took 1,500 lives but gained the Allies little ground.

Fighting raged from trench to trench, one army charging across "no man's land"—the very dangerous space between the enemy lines—while the other fought to hold its position. During some major battles such as Verdun and the Somme in France, hundreds of thousands of soldiers were killed each week. However, as the death toll grew higher and the financial cost of war greater, neither side had any gains to show for its efforts.

THE WAR AT SEA

With the failure of the Schlieffen plan, the German General Staff began devising a new strategy for winning the war. Nothing the German army could do in France seemed to tip the balance in its favor. Worse still, from Germany's point of view, the island nation of Great Britain was unravaged by the war. Although many English soldiers were dying in the trenches in France, England itself was untouched. The Germans realized that the only way they could strike at their island foe was at sea.

The German navy, however, was outnumbered. Despite the active naval construction program put into effect by Germany in the years before the war, Great Britain still had a great advantage over its foe. German ships were technologically superior to vessels in the British

ECHOES OF THE PAST

FROM THE TRENCHES

The following poignant descriptions of trench warfare are from diaries kept by soldiers who fought in France during World War I. During the Battle of the Somme in 1916, many came face to face with their enemies in the terrifying "no man's land."

> I told my comrades, "We must be prepared; the English will attack soon." We got our machine-gun ready on the top step of the dug-out and we put all our equipment on; then we waited. We all expected to die. We thought of God. We prayed. Then someone shouted, "They're coming! They're coming!" We rushed up and got our machine-gun in position. We could see the English soldiers pouring out at us, thousands and thousands of them. We opened fire.
>
> —Grenadier Emil Kury, 109th Reserve Regiment

> Eventually I took shelter in a shell hole with two other men from the battalion; we were all wounded. I looked over the edge and could see the Germans in their trench again. I suddenly became very angry. I had seen my battalion mowed down by machine-guns and one of them trapped in the wire. I thought of my particular pal who had been killed a few days before by a shell. I thought we were all doomed; I just couldn't see how any of us would get out of it alive and, so far, I hadn't done anything to the Germans. I made up my mind to get one of them, at least, before I was killed.
>
> —Private H. C. Bloor, Accrington Pals

> I then went on to the second-line trench and jumped in, to see a German soldier lying on the parapet. With fixed bayonet I approached, then I saw his putty-colored face which convinced me he was mortally wounded. The German brought up an arm and actually saluted me. I understood no German language but the poor chap kept muttering two words *"Wasser, Wasser,"* and *"Mutter, Mutter"* ["Mother, Mother"]. It took me a minute or so to realize he wanted a drink of water. The second word I could not cotton on to. I am glad to this day that I gave him a drink of my precious water.
>
> —Private G. R. S. Mayne, 11th Royal Fusiliers

For questions on Echoes of the Past, see "Analyzing Primary Sources" on page 713.

navy, but being outnumbered by almost two to one, German warships had little chance of winning the war at sea.

U-boats. Technology, however, provided the German navy with an alternative to conventional naval warfare—the submarine. Known as U-boats, from the German word *unterseeboot*, submarines could hide from the large British navy by staying underwater. They could sneak up on their victims, launch torpedo attacks, and then slide silently into the safety of the ocean depths.

There was, however, one problem with submarine warfare. U-boat commanders found it difficult to determine if the ship under attack belonged to the Allied nations or if it flew the flag of a neutral power. This problem was serious because submarines usually gave no warning before an attack, and passengers and crews—neutral or otherwise—were often unable to abandon the ships before they sank.

Q-ships. The obvious solution to the problem, the Germans argued, was to have the submarines surface to check the target's nationality and to give crews a chance to abandon ship. This plan worked for a few months, but in early 1915, Britain began sending out Q-ships. Designed to look like merchant ships, the Q-ships were heavily armed. Thus, when the German U-boats surfaced to give warning, the Q-ships could suddenly open fire.

After Germany lost several submarines to the Q-ships, the German high command decided to resume U-boat attacks without warning. To safeguard against sinking neutral ships, the German government drew a "war zone" in the waters around Britain, declaring that all ships found in this zone would be considered enemy vessels and sunk.

American neutrality. The German declaration of the war zone caused a flurry of protests from neutral countries, especially the United States. As Great Britain's largest trading partner, the United States saw submarine warfare as a threat to its own economy, as well as to the British economy. Although relations between Germany and the United States had been poor since the turn of the century, the disagreement over U-boats brought about the first real crisis between the two countries.

From the beginning of the war, President Woodrow Wilson proclaimed the neutrality of the United States. Wilson hoped that by remaining neutral, the United States would be in a position to help European countries negotiate a peace. He called for the European powers to accept a "peace without victory." Wilson's policy reflected the feelings of Americans in 1914 that this was a European war.

Neutrality also permitted Americans to trade with all of the countries at war. However, even though Wilson had said that the United States "must be neutral in fact as well as in name," private companies and individuals sent money and military supplies. Because of the close economic and cultural ties between the United States and Great Britain, as well as the fact that Britain controlled the seas, most of this support went to the Allies.

The *Lusitania* affair. Relations between the United States and Germany reached a crisis point in May 1915, when a German U-boat sank the *Lusitania*, a British passenger ship. Claiming the British were transporting ammunition on the ship, the German embassy in Washington, D.C., had published a warning in American newspapers against traveling on the *Lusitania*. No one, however, took seriously the threat of sinking a passenger ship. On May 7, 1915, when a German U-boat did sink the ship, more than 1,200 people died, many of them American citizens.

Believing that Germany had viciously attacked a passenger ship, more and more Americans began to favor American involvement in the war. Wilson, nevertheless, was able to hold to his policy of neutrality. A few weeks after the *Lusitania* went down, however, a second British ship, the *Arabic*, was attacked by a U-boat, resulting in the loss of two more American lives. Secretary of State Robert Lansing then felt obliged to threaten war unless Germany abandoned its submarine war against Great Britain. Because Germany could not afford to add the powerful United States to its list of enemies, it brought the submarine war to a temporary halt.

The German High Seas Fleet. With their submarine force now useless, the German admirals became restless. They decided that their powerful battleships, the High Seas Fleet, should no longer remain contained in German

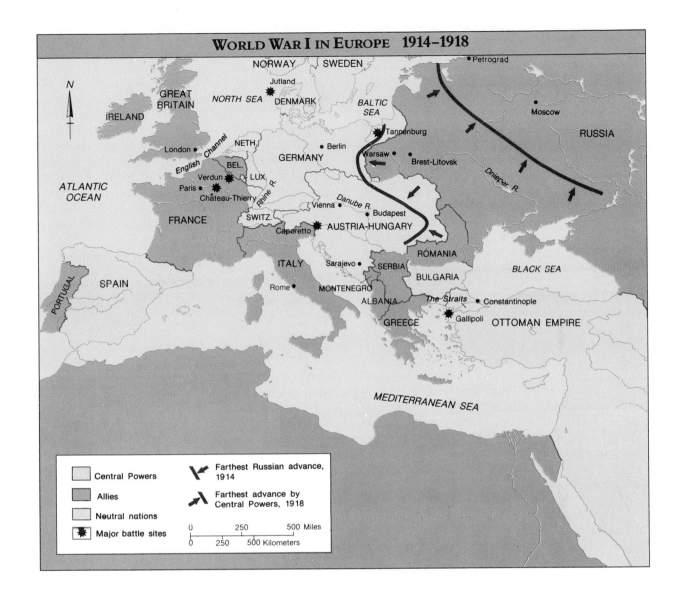

WORLD WAR I IN EUROPE 1914–1918

Central Powers

Allies

Neutral nations

✳ **Major battle sites**

↘ **Farthest Russian advance, 1914**

↗ **Farthest advance by Central Powers, 1918**

0   250   500 Miles
0 250   500 Kilometers

---

ports. In the spring of 1916, therefore, the German fleet tried to slip into the North Sea. There the Germans hoped to sink British warships.

Before the German fleet reached the North Sea, however, the British launched a surprise attack off the coast of Denmark. The two navies engaged in a furious battle for several hours. Even though the Germans sank more ships than the British, the Germans retreated rather than risk major losses, and the battle was a draw. Nevertheless, after the so-called Battle of Jutland, German warships were again largely confined to their bases because the German admirals were afraid to risk losses. With the High Seas Fleet ordered off the seas, the Allies retained control of the Atlantic.

A CHANGE OF DIRECTION

Unlike the two previous years, 1917 held some dramatic events that altered the direction of the war. Political events in Russia gave the German General Staff new hope that the war might be brought to a successful conclusion.

Revolution in Russia. The war on the eastern front had gone badly for the Russians after their initial advances in 1914 and 1915. With neither enough supplies nor enough soldiers, the Russian army was pushed farther and farther back by the superior German and Austro-Hungarian forces. Under the strains of a failing war effort, the political and economic situation in Russia deteriorated quickly after 1916. People flocked to the streets in "bread riots" to protest food shortages. By spring of 1917, the government had lost control, and on March 15, Czar Nicholas II abdicated the throne as revolution swept the countryside.

A new Russian government—this time a republican one—formed in the wake of the fall of the Romanov Dynasty. Although Germany hoped that the new government—led by Alexander Kerensky—would take Russia out of the war, Russia decided to stay with the Allies.

The Russian people, meanwhile, felt that peace would bring an end to the food shortages, while continuing the war could only bring additional defeats by the Germans. Because the new government refused to deal with Russia's problems by bowing out of the war, the regime never gained the people's loyalty.

In mid-1917 Germany, taking advantage of dissension in Russia, permitted a communist agitator named Vladimir Ilich Ulyanov—known as Lenin—to travel by train from Switzerland to Russia. The German government hoped Lenin would stir up unrest that would result in Russia's withdrawal from the war. Once Lenin arrived in Russia, he organized his followers, and in October, only seven months after the overthrow of the czar, he led a second revolt called the October Revolution.

One of Lenin's first acts as leader was to sign a treaty with the Central Powers. With the

SPOTLIGHT: DAILY LIFE

AMERICAN WOMEN IN WORLD WAR I

A war, a dramatic event in the history of a nation, can bring about unforeseen changes in society. World War I greatly changed the role of women in the American work force. Because women were needed to support the war effort, they gained opportunities to perform jobs that before 1917 had generally been open only to men.

Prior to the war, women had worked outside the home, often as servants in other people's homes and laborers in textile mills. However, before the United States entered the war, women made up only one-fifth of the wage earners in the nation. In 1917, when the government drafted thousands of men into the army and thousands of others enlisted, the number of women workers increased as women filled the jobs left behind by soldiers.

Women entered many new fields during the war. They worked as streetcar conductors in the United States and ambulance drivers at the battlefronts in Europe. As American factories geared up to produce clothing and weapons for the war effort, women took the new jobs that became available in the quickly expanding war industries.

Many women became skilled craftsworkers in heavy industry. They welded bombs, assembled airplanes, operated drill presses, and built railway locomotives. According to many Americans, these were the kinds of jobs that were "inappropriate" for women. The war, however, was teaching people that women were fully capable of handling difficult tasks. As an American labor leader said, "Many operations in the manufacture of munitions can not only be as well done by women as men, but are better done by female help." New opportunities for women opened in other fields as well, and women became bank tellers, department managers, and executives. Black women who had been shut out of industrial jobs also got a foothold in the labor force.

Meanwhile, the government was attempting to reform the work environment by reducing the number of work hours in a day and by improving wages, which often were well below those of men in similar jobs. Shorter work days made it less difficult for women to be away from their homes and children, and women who performed a hard day's labor gained the confidence to take up the fight for satisfactory wages.

When the soldiers returned at the war's end, many women gave up their new jobs, some willingly, others regretfully. American society, however, had been changed. The success of the nation's working women could not be ignored. Women realized that they had employment opportunities outside the home if they chose to take advantage of them.

Treaty of Brest-Litovsk, Russia pulled out of the war, giving Germany control over much of eastern Europe. More importantly, the treaty freed up several million German soldiers who could be used against France and England on the western front. Suddenly, the prospects of a German victory looked better than at any time since 1914.

A new German strategy. In early 1917, even before Lenin's October Revolution, it was apparent that Russia would soon withdraw from the war. The German General Staff, therefore, attempted to find some solution to the stalemate in France.

With the prospect of gaining millions of soldiers from the eastern front, Germany now felt that it was in a position to rekindle the submarine war against Britain, even if such action increased the risk of bringing the United States into the war. German generals argued that even if the United States were to enter the war, a submarine blockade could starve Britain out of the war before American troops could arrive on the scene. Furthermore, the Germans reasoned, by the time the United States could make its presence felt, German troops from Russia would have already defeated France. The strategy was a gamble, but in 1917, after three terrible years of trench warfare, no other alternative seemed viable. The submarine war was renewed on January 31, 1917.

American declaration of war. German diplomatic blunders further strained relations between Germany and the United States. Arthur Zimmermann, the German foreign secretary, was sure that the new U-boat campaign would bring the United States into the war. Accordingly, he devised a plan to preoccupy the United States with a war on its own border.

In early 1917, Zimmermann sent a telegram to the German minister in Mexico. In it, he directed that if the United States went to war against Germany, the minister was to offer Mexico its "lost territory in New Mexico, Texas, and Arizona" on the condition that Mexico declare war on the United States. The British, however, intercepted the message. When they revealed its contents, the American people were outraged.

President Wilson responded to the public pressure, British propaganda, and renewed

Here a young woman welds war equipment in a makeshift factory. During the war more than 595,000 women in Britain and France manufactured munitions, many laboring under unsafe conditions.

submarine warfare. Saying "the world must be made safe for democracy," Wilson asked Congress to declare war on the Central Powers on April 6, 1917. However, the United States' entry into the war did not immediately affect the strength of its embattled allies. The U-boat campaign began to take a large toll, and by the end of 1917, the Germans paralyzed British shipping. With great shortages of food and supplies, the Allies feared that Britain was within six weeks of mass starvation.

Meanwhile, across the English Channel in France, troops from the eastern front began to swell the German forces. The Central Powers prepared for a final offensive. The attack was set for spring 1918.

THE FINAL THRUST

In June 1917, the first American soldiers landed on French soil. Called the American Expeditionary Force and commanded by General John Pershing, its arrival boosted the morale of the Allied forces. Before long, the new American troops were put to the test. Just as planned, in the spring of 1918, the Germans crashed through the Allied lines. By this time, however, 250,000 American soldiers were pouring into

Allies Day, May 1917 was painted by American impressionist Childe Hassam. After the United States entered the war, American and Allied flags often decked New York City's Fifth Avenue.

France each month. Along with these "dough-boys," as they were called, came American tanks, guns, and heavy artillery.

In June 1918, the Allies stopped the German advance at Château-Thierry (shah-tō tyeh-REE) on the Marne River, only a few miles from where the Germans had been turned back in 1914. The next month, the combined British, French, and American forces launched a counterattack. The German army fell into retreat. The Allied troops pushed the Germans eastward and broke their main supply line.

As the Germans fell back, the Central Powers crumbled. In October, the Ottoman Empire surrendered, and successful revolts by Czechs, Hungarians, Slavs, and Poles brought down the Austro-Hungarian government. By November 1918, Germany stood alone. On November 9, Kaiser Wilhelm gave up the throne, and Germany declared itself a republic. At 11:00 A.M. on November 11, 1918, the war officially ended when generals from the Allied and Central Powers signed an armistice, or truce.

SECTION REVIEW

1. Define *propaganda*.

2. What was the Schlieffen plan?

3. Describe the technological innovations that modernized war.

4. How did the controversy over the U-boats affect German-American relations?

5. What strategy did the Allies use to achieve victory?

Analysis. Why did the Central Powers lose the war?

28–3
THE PRICE OF PEACE

READ TO FIND OUT

—what the terms *reparations* and *isolationism* mean.
—what the provisions of the Treaty of Versailles were.
—how the League of Nations was created.

World War I took the highest toll of any war yet fought, claiming the lives of between 10 and 13 million people, approximately one-third of them civilians. For every person who died, another two or three were wounded. Billions of dollars of property was destroyed, and national economies were ruined.

Against this troubling background, Allied leaders prepared to debate the terms of peace. Neither Russia nor any of the defeated nations of the Central Powers were to have a voice in the discussions. Instead, the task fell to the Big Four—Great Britain, France, Italy, and the United States.

WILSON'S FOURTEEN POINTS

Before the war ended, President Wilson had talked of a "peace without victory." He set forth his ideas in a list of proposals known as the Fourteen Points, which outlined the conditions he believed necessary for a lasting peace. These proposals included preserving freedom of the seas in times of both peace and war, settling all colonial claims with respect for the interests and rights of national groups, agreeing to mutual reductions in arms, and establishing a "general association of nations"—a League of Nations—to guarantee future peace.

Because of the immense destruction of World War I, however, other Allied leaders resisted the idea of a generous peace, and they regarded Wilson's proposals as unrealistic. French premier Georges Clemenceau (KLEH-mon-SŌ), for example, was outraged by the Fourteen Points. Almost all of the fighting along the western front had been done on French soil, and France had lost 50 percent of its male population between the ages of twenty and thirty-two. Embittered, he wanted to avenge French losses and to protect his nation from future wars. The best protection, reasoned Clemenceau, was the destruction of Germany.

Italy's prime minister, Vittorio Orlando, also disagreed with Wilson. Orlando's main goal was not to secure a generous peace but rather to gain the Austrian lands promised to Italy at the start of the war. In 1919, Orlando stormed out of the Paris peace conference when Wilson insisted on applying the principle of self-determination to Europe. According to this principle, any territorial changes were to reflect the rights of national groups rather than the demands of the imperialist nations. The placing of Austrians under Italian control simply to satisfy Orlando's ambitions went against Wilson's policy. Because of such opposition from Allied leaders, President Wilson gave up some proposals, hoping that the negotiated peace would include the League of Nations.

THE PEACE SETTLEMENTS

At the peace conference in 1919, separate treaties were drawn up for each of the defeated nations. Each peace treaty included provisions giving a League of Nations responsibility for enforcing the treaty.

The treaty with Germany—the Treaty of Versailles—proved harsh. Under the terms of this treaty, Germany lost much of its territory. It returned Alsace-Lorraine to France and was forced to agree to French occupation of the coal-rich Saar Basin for 15 years. To help create

an independent Poland, Germany also had to give up West Prussia. In addition, Poland gained access to the Baltic Sea through the possession of a strip of land called the Polish Corridor, which divided Germany in two. The treaty further stripped Germany of all its overseas colonies in Africa and the Pacific.

The treaty went on to restrict German military power. It limited the German army to a reserve force of 100,000 and banned the draft. The treaty also forbade Germany from manufacturing armaments, fortifying its territory along the French border, building submarines, and developing an air force. The Germans were also required to scrap the High Seas Fleet.

Of all the treaty's provisions, however, the German people most hated what became known as the "war-guilt" clause. This clause blamed Germany for the war and made the German government financially responsible for all war damages. ***Reparations***, or payment for war damages, were then levied against Germany. A commission fixed the sum at $33 billion.

Because many Germans believed that the Allies had also helped cause the war, the German people deeply resented the Versailles settlement. Even so, German leaders had little choice but to sign the agreement because the alternative was an Allied occupation of Germany.

Here British Prime Minister Lloyd George, left, strolls with Clemenceau and Wilson, on the right, at Versailles in 1919.

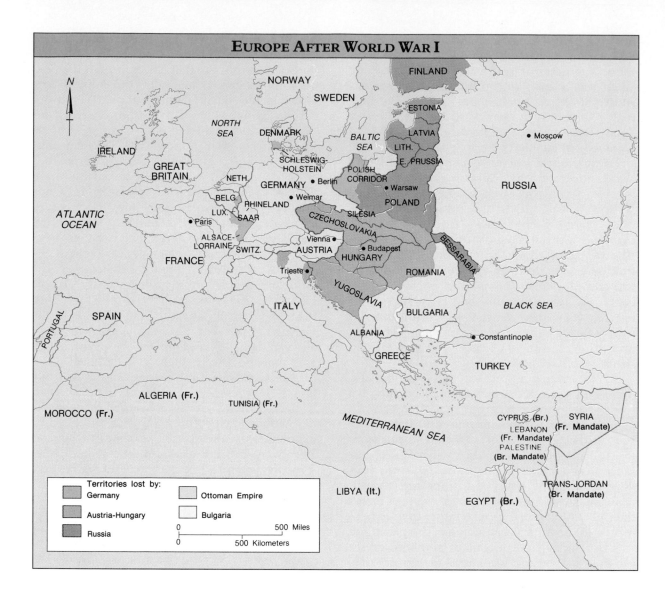

EUROPE AFTER WORLD WAR I

Territories lost by:
Germany
Austria-Hungary
Russia
Ottoman Empire
Bulgaria

0   500 Miles
0   500 Kilometers

Other treaties. The treaties with the other Central Powers changed the map of both eastern Europe and the Middle East. The Hapsburg Empire was reduced to one-tenth of its former size. Hungary became a separate nation, while various minority groups from Germany, Russia, and Austria-Hungary were combined to create the new nation of Czechoslovakia. In the south, Serbia's prewar ambitions were realized when Bosnia, Herzegovina, and Montenegro were added to Serbia to form the new nation of Yugoslavia. Four other new nations, Finland, Estonia, Latvia, and Lithuania, also were created out of former Russian territory.

The breakup of the Ottoman Empire resulted in the formation of Turkey and a number of new colonies. Great Britain gained the territories of Palestine, Trans-Jordan, and Iraq, and France received Syria and Lebanon.

REACTION TO THE TREATIES

When Europeans learned the details of the treaties, they hotly debated the terms of peace. Defenders of the treaties argued that the aggressors needed to be taught a lesson. Some people, especially in Belgium and France, thought the treaties were in fact too easy on the Central Powers. Many wanted to divide Germany even further to end its power forever.

Critics of the treaties believed that a "peace of vengeance" would lead to another war. They charged that the treaties left both Austria and Hungary with insufficient raw materials and farm lands. As a result, both nations would have great difficulty recovering economically. Critics further claimed that the treaty doomed the new democratic government of Germany by burdening the German people with staggering reparations payments.

THE LEAGUE OF NATIONS

In the United States, debate over the treaties was especially intense. Many Americans were shocked to learn that President Wilson had negotiated away many of the Fourteen Points. A large number also worried that American membership in a League of Nations would drag the United States into other wars. Public opinion favored a policy of *isolationism*, through which the nation would be kept out of foreign agreements. Americans wanted less government involvement in world affairs. As a result, the United States Senate narrowly rejected the Treaty of Versailles and, thereby, American membership in the league.

The league thus began without the support of the United States, by then the strongest nation in the world. Member nations held their first meeting in 1920 at Geneva, Switzerland. The organization consisted of three main agencies: the General Assembly, the Council, and the Secretariat. Delegates from all member nations sat in the General Assembly in which each, regardless of size, received one vote. The Council decided all important issues. Great powers such as Great Britain, France, Italy, and Japan held permanent seats on the Council. A number of smaller nations occupied nonpermanent seats on a rotating basis. The league's day-to-day administrative affairs were handled by the Secretariat, staffed by civil employees.

The league's two major goals were to promote global cooperation and to settle international disputes peacefully by bringing all nations together. The league, however, had little power to enforce its decisions. It could advise member nations to sever diplomatic ties or to suspend trade with an aggressor nation, but without an international police force of its own, the organization could take no military action.

The league, however, did establish one policy that had important effects in many areas of the world. Former colonial territories, considered by the Europeans to be unprepared for self-rule, were placed under the protection of league members. These territories, called mandates, were administered by the member nation but not fully owned by them. France and Britain, for instance, managed the governments of former German territories in Africa and former Ottoman territories in the Middle East.

SECTION REVIEW

1. Define *reparations* and *isolationism*.

2. How did the Treaty of Versailles affect Germany?

3. How did the League of Nations come into being?

Analysis. Why was Woodrow Wilson more willing than European leaders to give Germany a "generous peace"?

Data Search. After referring to the appropriate chart on page 833, list the following countries in order according to how heavy their casualties were: Great Britain, Russia, France, Germany, the United States. Begin with the country that had the heaviest casualties.

HISTORY IN FOCUS

Between the sixteenth and the nineteenth centuries, Europe was able to expand its influence so that countries like France, Great Britain, and Germany were at the "center of the world." The events that occurred between 1914 and 1918, however, marked the beginning of the decline of Europe. World War I left the United States as the strongest nation, while leading to a revolution in Russia that would have far-reaching effects. Within a generation after the war, European leaders found themselves to be followers, rather than directors, in world affairs.

World War I also made Europeans look at themselves in a new light. For the first time, many thinkers began to wonder how nations could inflict such death and destruction upon themselves. Also, the realization of the national ambitions of the eastern European minorities inspired the populations in the European overseas colonies to reassess their relationships with the imperialist powers. In general, the war loosened the European hold on these colonies and led to increasing pressure for independence.

SUMMARY

- By the early 1900s, militarism and national rivalries had created great tensions in Europe. On one side stood the Triple Alliance of Germany, Austria-Hungary, and Italy; on the other, the Triple Entente of Britain, France, and Russia.

- Slavic nationalism set off several Balkan crises in the early 1900s. After the assassination of Archduke Francis Ferdinand, war broke out between Austria-Hungary and Serbia. The system of alliances quickly escalated the conflict into World War I.

- Germany, the leader of the Central Powers, planned to defeat France quickly, then concentrate German forces on Russia. Britain soon joined the Allies, however, and both sides became bogged down in trench warfare on the western front. Germany began U-boat attacks, but tried to avoid provoking the United States.

- Russia withdrew from the war after the 1917 revolution, leaving Germany free to focus on the western front. The United States soon entered the war, however, and renewed Allied strength brought victory in 1918.

- Despite President Wilson's efforts to secure a fair peace, the peace treaties dealt harshly with the Central Powers. The map of Europe was redrawn and the League of Nations was formed, though it was too weak to ensure a lasting peace.

VOCABULARY REVIEW

Match each numbered vocabulary term with its origin. Then explain the connection between the origin and the vocabulary term.

Example: The origin of the term *U-boat* is the German word *unterseeboot*, meaning "undersea boat." U-boats could travel underwater.

1. mobilize
2. reparations
3. isolationism

    (a) Latin: *insula*, island
    (b) Old French: *mobile*, mobile
    (c) Latin: *reparare*, to repair

CHAPTER REVIEW

1. (a) List one major goal of each of the six European powers at the turn of the century. **(b)** Why was Serbia important? **(c)** Explain the reasons behind the European alliances.

2. (a) Why were the Balkans so unstable? **(b)** What was the Balkan League? Why did it go to war? **(c)** Describe three Balkan crises between 1908 and 1913. **(d)** What was the Black Hand?

3. (a) How did Austria-Hungary treat Slavs, and what were the results? **(b)** Explain the Slavic reaction to Francis Ferdinand's ideas.

4. (a) Why did Britain enter the war? What advantage did it have? **(b)** Why was Italy's entry into the war important? **(c)** Describe the factors that led to Russia's withdrawal from the war.

5. (a) Why did the Schlieffen plan fail? **(b)** Describe and explain Germany's use of a new strategy in 1915. **(c)** What was the key element in that new strategy? How did its advantage also create a problem?

6. (a) Describe trench warfare. **(b)** Explain the various developments in the sea war.

7. Discuss the significance of the battles at the following locations: **(a)** Marne, **(b)** Tannenburg, **(c)** Jutland.

8. (a) Why did President Wilson favor American neutrality? Why was that policy hard to maintain? **(b)** Describe the *Lusitania* affair and its importance. **(c)** What was the significance of the Zimmermann telegram?

9. (a) State the general proposals in the Fourteen Points and explain the opposition to them. **(b)** How did the peace treaties rearrange Europe? **(c)** Describe the reactions to the peace treaties.

10. Discuss the following aspects of the League of Nations: **(a)** organization, **(b)** goals, **(c)** problems.

THINKING CRITICALLY: ACTIVITIES

1. Work with a partner to create an imaginary correspondence between Archduke Francis Ferdinand and the leaders of the Pan-Slavic movement. Take the role of Ferdinand and write a letter explaining your position on the Slavic question and why Slavs should be patient and support you. Have your partner write a reply from a militant Slavic leader. Base your positions on material from the chapter.

2. Divide into groups of four or five to discuss the following questions: What ideological or strategic questions might have played a part in Lenin's decision in 1917 to withdraw from World War I? Was it a wise decision?

3. President Wilson and many other Americans believed that World War I should be a "war to end all wars," one that would make the world "safe for democracy." Imagine that you are Wilson. Write a speech promoting your Fourteen Points as the best way to bring lasting peace. Present your speech to the class.

APPLYING SOCIAL STUDIES SKILLS

Analyzing statistical tables. Look carefully at the table below. Then answer the questions that follow.

STRENGTH OF THE GREAT POWERS 1914			
	Army (millions of soldiers)	Battleships	Airplanes
Germany	4.5	37	500
Austria-Hungary	2.5	14	100
Russia	5.5	8	500
France	4.0	24	500
Britain	0.8	69	250
Italy	2.0	9	150

1. Which nation had the largest army? The smallest army?

2. Which nation had the largest battleship fleet?

3. Compare the Central Powers and the Allies. Which alliance had the greatest number of soldiers—the Central Powers or the Allies? The most battleships? The most airplanes?

4. Briefly state any conclusions you can draw from these statistics.

APPLYING THINKING SKILLS

Recognizing stereotypes. The following account is an excerpt from a book originally published in 1917. The book describes France in the early days of World War I. Examine the account to see if its author presents a stereotype of the French people. Then answer the questions that follow the account.

There has not been a Frenchman or a Frenchwoman—outside a few harmless and perhaps nervous theorizers—who has wavered about the military policy of the country. There have been some to whom it was harder than they imagined to give up a certain way of living, or a certain kind of breakfast roll. [However] the French, being fundamentally temperate, are far less the slaves of the luxuries they have invented than are the other races who have adopted these luxuries. All have had the strength to hide their despair and to say of the great national effort which has lost most of its meaning to them, "Though it slay me, yet will I trust in it." That is probably the finest triumph of the tone of France.

This does not in the least imply that resignation is the prevailing note in the tone of France. The attitude of the French people, after fourteen months of trial, is not one of submission to unparalleled calamity. It is one of exaltation, energy, the hot resolve to dominate the disaster. In all classes the feeling is the same: every word and every act is based on the resolute ignoring of any alternative to victory. The French people no more think of a compromise than people would think of facing a flood or an earthquake with a white flag.

Abridged from Edith Wharton, *Fighting France*. Westport: Greenwood Press, 1974.

1. Explain what a stereotype is.

2. What is one procedure you can use in order to recognize a stereotype?

3. Why is it important to be able to recognize a stereotype?

4. What stereotype of the French people is presented in the above excerpt?

5. Explain how you identified this description as a stereotype.

CHAPTER TWENTY-NINE

AFTERMATH OF THE WAR

1917–1939

Detroit Industry (detail). Diego Rivera, Mexico, 1932–1933.

The effects of World War I were enormous and far-reaching. They could be measured in the millions of lives lost or in the billions of dollars spent. In Russia, the human costs of the war led the Russian people to overthrow czarist rule. The impact of world war could also be seen on maps as the boundaries of new nations were drawn. Changes in the balance of power led to new international alliances and relationships. Also, the treaties that ended the war called for new forms of government in nations like Germany and Austria. These governments gave many people their first taste of democracy. Meanwhile, nationalism became a major force as European colonies in Africa and Asia began a quest for political independence.

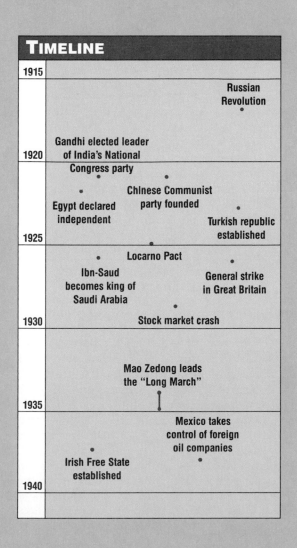

TIMELINE

1915	
	Russian Revolution
1920	Gandhi elected leader of India's National Congress party
	Chinese Communist party founded
	Egypt declared independent
	Turkish republic established
1925	
	Locarno Pact
	Ibn-Saud becomes king of Saudi Arabia
	General strike in Great Britain
1930	Stock market crash
	Mao Zedong leads the "Long March"
1935	
	Mexico takes control of foreign oil companies
	Irish Free State established
1940	

29–1
THE RUSSIAN REVOLUTION

READ TO FIND OUT

—what the terms *soviets* and *war communism* mean.
—who the Bolsheviks were.
—the role Lenin played in the Russian Revolution.
—how a civil war divided Russia.

Out of the destruction and discontent of World War I grew the most important revolution of the twentieth century. At the turn of the century, Russian peasants and workers led miserable lives, toiling on the margins of survival. World War I deepened their discontent. The middle class suggested reforms that would help the government's war effort, but Czar Nicholas II did not permit any kind of political reform that would lessen his absolute authority. During the war, Nicholas II ended even those few democratic reforms that had been made, further propelling the nation toward revolution.

THE FALL OF CZARIST RUSSIA

Although he was devoted to his family and his country, Nicholas II was an indecisive ruler. His vision rooted in the traditions of imperial Russia, the czar was unprepared to deal with the new political and economic forces developing in his country.

With the nation moving toward open revolt during a brief war with Japan in 1905, however, Nicholas II agreed to make some changes. Although he permitted the calling of an elected parliament—the *Duma*—Nicholas II believed that all government power should rest in his hands. Whenever the Duma opposed him, he dissolved the assembly, calling it back into session only when he thought he could control it.

When World War I first broke out, the Russian people supported the effort out of a sense

On January 22, 1905, thousands of striking workers marched on Czar Nicholas II's palace to ask for reforms. Government troops fired on the crowd, killing hundreds of people. Known as Bloody Sunday, this massacre sparked a wave of strikes across the country and political activity against the government.

of patriotism. However, this early enthusiasm faded quickly, as badly trained and poorly led Russian troops suffered defeat after defeat at the hands of the German army. In the first year alone, almost 4 million Russian soldiers were killed, wounded, or taken prisoner.

By March 1917, Russia seethed with discontent. Thousands of soldiers deserted the army, and in Russian cities, labor strikes protesting food and fuel shortages paralyzed the economy. Once again the workers of Petrograd—the new name given to St. Petersburg in 1914—moved into the streets demanding bread and fuel and an end to the war. The czar tried to maintain order, but soldiers sent against the rioters turned on their officers and joined the revolt. Realizing he was powerless, Nicholas II abdicated, or gave up his throne. Imperial Russia came to an end on March 15, 1917.

The provisional government. A provisional government was hastily put together to administer the nation. The new government proclaimed freedom of speech, of the press, and of religion. It also released political prisoners from the czar's dungeons. Yet the educated middle-class liberals who controlled the provisional government were out of touch with Russian peasants and workers who demanded even more radical reforms. Most important of all, the new government did not end the hated war with Germany.

In the cities, angry workers began to form *soviets*, or small councils, to discuss Russia's political and economic problems. Influenced by Marxism, many soviets moved beyond discussion and openly agitated for a restructuring of Russian society according to Marx's vision of a communist society. For the most part, however, the soviets were run by moderate socialists called *Mensheviks*, after the Russian word meaning "minority." More radical soviets were headed by *Bolsheviks*, which meant "majority." The Bolsheviks grew steadily in power under the leadership of Vladimir Ilich Ulyanov, known by his revolutionary name, Lenin.

LENIN AND THE BOLSHEVIK REVOLUTION

Lenin, born in Russia in 1870, grew up in a middle-class family. When he was sixteen, his older brother was hanged for his part in a plot to kill Czar Alexander III. The execution made Lenin a relentless enemy of czarist Russia, a viewpoint that found expression through Marxism. Arrested for revolutionary activity in 1897, Lenin spent three years in exile in Siberia, after which he went to western Europe, where he remained until his return to Russia in 1917.

Though faced by great difficulties, Lenin never stopped working for a revolution of the proletariat to replace rule by the upper and middle classes with rule by the working class.

Lenin was a socialist revolutionary whose genius lay in his ability to adapt the ideas of Marx to the conditions of twentieth-century Russia. Marx had predicted that as a capitalist industrial society continued to exploit its workers, inevitably the workers would rise up in violent revolution. Lenin, however, believed that a Marxist revolution was also possible in a nonindustrial nation like Russia. Workers could not carry out such a revolution by themselves but would have to be led by a small group of full-time revolutionaries.

The revolution. As soon as Lenin arrived in Russia, he organized the Bolsheviks to lead a revolution. Winning the support of the disgruntled masses with promises of "peace, land, and bread," Lenin's powerful appeal could not be matched by the provisional government or the Mensheviks. On the night of October 25, 1917, Bolshevik forces seized the Petrograd railway station, banks, power stations, and other strategic points in the city. The following day they surrounded the Winter Palace, where the provisional government held out. As its leaders were arrested, the provisional government crumbled.

A new government. To attract popular support, Lenin quickly proclaimed that a democratically elected legislative assembly would determine the future course of the nation. In late November 1917, Russia held its first and last free election. Because the Bolsheviks won only a quarter of the seats, a dissatisfied Lenin sent an armed force to disband the legislature after its first session.

Since Lenin could not trust an elected government, he proclaimed a new constitution in July 1918 that set up a pyramid structure of government. According to Lenin's constitution, soviets of workers and peasants formed the base of local governments. The soviets also elected a national congress, but the administrative affairs of state were to be handled by a select committee. Only one political party was permitted, and all government officials had to be members. Because of the structure of Lenin's government, real power in Russia was held by the Politburo, or the high officials of the Communist party, a group made up of Bolsheviks. Because Lenin made himself general secretary of the party, his word became law.

Russian artist I. Vladimirov shows soldiers preparing to burn a portrait of Czar Nicholas II. Such destruction became routine after army units joined the revolution in March, 1917.

CIVIL WAR

Lenin had won his revolution, but he ruled over a country exhausted by war and torn by civil strife. Lenin's new policies proved unpopular with groups such as landowners and industrialists because the restructuring of Russian society reduced upper class and wealthy citizens to the same level as everyone else. In addition, many czarist army officers wanted to restore the old order. These anti-Bolshevik forces became known as the "Whites," in contrast to the communist "Reds," so named for the red color of the flag of Marxist revolution.

Additional opposition to Russia came in the form of foreign intervention: not only were the the Allies bitter that Lenin had taken Russia out of the war, but Western leaders also perceived soviet communism as an international threat. Lenin's calls for worldwide revolution did not calm these fears. By 1919, British, French, and American troops had landed in Russia to support the White cause. Great Britain and France especially wanted a White victory because Lenin had announced his government would not repay loans that had been made to czarist Russia during World War I.

With the support of Allied troops, the Whites launched a civil war that raged for three years. The struggle was marked by extreme brutality on both sides. Soldiers leveled villages and stole or destroyed crops, and thousands of people were tortured or killed. Among the casualties of the war were Nicholas II and the royal family, who were executed by Red forces.

Lenin addresses Russian soldiers and civilians in this speech in 1919. In addition to defeating the White armies, Lenin also wanted to destroy capitalism worldwide.

29–2
EUROPE IN THE 1920s

READ TO FIND OUT

—how France tried to protect itself against the threat of future wars.
—how the new Weimar government of Germany tried to cope with its debts.
—what economic difficulties Great Britain faced after the war.
—what situations led to social unrest in southern and eastern Europe.

In an effort not to lose power, Lenin adopted a drastic policy called *war communism*, in which the government took over all factories and outlawed labor strikes. Lenin's government seized all the farm land and prohibited most private ownership. Factories and farms were run by administrators who reported directly to the Communist party. In addition, a secret police force called the *Cheka*, or *NKVD*, was formed that suppressed all dissent.

Political terror became an important part of Lenin's Communist rule in Russia. The harsh measures imposed by Lenin, however, did keep control of the Russian government in Communist hands. Allied help to the White armies failed to turn the tide against the Reds. The Red Army was far more effective than the scattered and poorly organized White armies. Thus, by 1921, the foreign armies had withdrawn from Russia in the wake of White defeat.

SECTION REVIEW

1. Define *soviets* and *war communism*.

2. What changes in Russian society did the Bolsheviks favor?

3. What role did Lenin play in the Russian Revolution of 1917?

4. Who opposed the Red forces in Russia's civil war?

Analysis. How did the Bolshevik Revolution of 1917 show that Marx's ideas about revolution were too rigid?

A map of Europe drawn in 1920 looked very different from one drawn in 1914. Some nations, like Austria-Hungary, had been greatly reduced in size, and new nations, like Czechoslovakia, appeared for the first time. Different peoples now lived together within new boundaries and were expected to work together. The map, however, did not show the enormous cost of the recent war on the lives of Europe's people or the difficulties they would face in trying to rebuild destroyed economies and shattered expectations.

FRANCE IN THE 1920s

In 1918, the French people looked out on a country ruined by war. Almost 1 million buildings—including about 9,000 factories—had been destroyed, six thousand bridges were down, and many railroads were out of service. While factories and bridges could be rebuilt, the 1.5 million young French soldiers who died in the war could never be replaced.

Economic difficulties, though, were not the only problems French leaders faced in the 1920s. Another overriding concern was national defense against Germany. Twice within a generation—in 1870 and 1914—German troops had marched across the French countryside, and French leaders vowed not to let this happen again. To this end, the French government took steps to protect France from its long-time foe.

The foremost defensive measure was the construction of the Maginot (MAZH-uh-NŌ) Line, more than 200 miles (320 kilometers) of steel and concrete fortifications along the French–German border. Because French military strategists looked to the Maginot Line as a cure-all for France's defensive problems, the French government put most of its military resources into constructing the defense. Consequently, other areas of the armed forces suffered, and by the mid-1930s, the French army, navy, and air force lagged behind those of the other major European powers.

French fear of German aggression also translated into international diplomacy. Just as before World War I, France looked to other European countries to form defensive alliances. During the 1920s, France signed agreements with Belgium, Poland, Czechoslovakia, and Yugoslavia, all countries that bordered Germany. Like the Maginot Line on Germany's western frontier, these alliances in eastern Europe gave France a sense of security.

The question of French economic reconstruction also centered on Germany. The French held the Germans responsible for the destruction of the war and insisted that Germany keep up the huge reparations payments called for in the Treaty of Versailles. The French counted on these payments to rebuild their nation. In 1923, when Germany defaulted, or failed to make the payments, French Premier Raymond Poincaré (PWAN-CAH-RAY) sent troops to occupy the steel factories and mines of Germany's Ruhr Valley. With this move, France struck both an economic blow against its enemy and gained the industrial resources of Germany's most heavily industrialized area. The French tried to run these industries for their own benefit, but gained little from the occupation because German workers went on strike.

GERMANY AFTER THE WAR

After a year of political chaos in Germany following World War I, elections were held to establish a new democratic government. Meetings during which a new constitution was written were held in the city of Weimar (VĪ-mar). Germany's new government was called the Weimar Republic.

The Weimar Republic faced many problems, among the worst of which was a faltering economy. After the war, Germany faced reparations payments on a war debt of $35 billion. Payments to France and Great Britain drained Germany of most of its wealth and left little money for economic reconstruction. When Germany failed to make its reparations payment causing France to occupy the Ruhr—Germany's main source of economic vitality—the German economy collapsed.

World War I ravaged the French countryside, where 673,000 civilians lost their lives. Towns such as Houplines (oo-PLEEN)—shown after its capture by the British in 1918—suffered severe damage. Surviving farmers were not able to achieve levels of prewar crop production until 1930.

This Berlin woman literally has money to burn in 1923, when German marks were as useful for fuel as for currency. Banking reforms later slowed down Germany's terrible rate of inflation.

To pay its mounting debts, the German government began to print more and more paper money. This flood of money decreased its value and thus aggravated the inflation already set off by the war. By the end of 1923, the value of the German mark was decreasing by the hour. One trillion marks were needed to equal the value of 25 American cents, and sums of money that once had fit into a wallet now had to be carried in wheelbarrows. As German salaries, pensions, and savings became worthless, middle-class Germans suddenly had no more financial security than the poorest citizens. The desperate plight of many Germans paved the way for the emergence of an authoritarian government in the 1930s.

The Locarno Pact. In late 1925, the tension between Germany and France was eased as the Great Powers met at Locarno, a Swiss town. Delegates from Germany, France, Belgium, Great Britain, and Italy tried to settle differences and construct a solid foundation for a peaceful future in Europe. Most important of all, the Locarno Pact, as the agreements came to be called, provided that each nation respect each other's borders and try to solve problems through negotiations rather than war. As a result of what became known as the "Locarno Spirit," Germany was allowed to join the League of Nations in 1926. Germany once more was a full member of the international community.

ECONOMIC AND POLITICAL CHANGE IN GREAT BRITAIN

Although Great Britain did not suffer extensive damage as France and Germany had during the war, it did lose more than 40 percent of its merchant fleet. The United States and Japan were competing in textile markets previously dominated by Great Britain. In addition, other countries in Asia were developing their own textile industries, further cutting into Great Britain's markets. To protect their manufacturing industries from foreign competition after the war, many nations raised the prices of foreign goods by imposing tariffs, or taxes levied on exports and imports. Such tariffs were especially hard on Great Britain because they made British exports too expensive to compete with industries in other countries. As a result, British trade steadily declined.

In addition to a decline in its overseas trade, Great Britain also faced tremendous war debts. It had financed its war effort by borrowing from foreign governments, especially the United States. As in Germany, the large repayments being made to these foreign governments was draining the British economy of capital, or financial resources.

All these issues combined to cause a slowdown in the British economy that greatly affected the working classes. Labor unions grew in size as more and more workers banded together to protect themselves from layoffs and wage cuts. Anger and frustration over lack of jobs reached a climax in 1926 when coal miners went on strike to protest massive wage cuts. Because a threat to workers in one industry was perceived as a threat to workers in other areas of the economy, labor unions in textile and steel mills and other industries joined the coal miners in a general strike, a strike against all industries. This work stoppage paralyzed Great Britain for ten days. Violent protests occurred in many cities, and in some areas people feared for their own safety. Finally, the British government declared a state of emergency and called out the army to restore order.

In the wake of the general strike, British workers found a leader in Ramsay MacDonald, head of the Labour party. Between 1924 and 1930, under MacDonald's direction Parliament enacted reform measures that helped reduce political unrest in Britain. The Labour party, working with the Liberal party, put some people back to work building housing and public structures such as bridges and streets. MacDonald's government also introduced unemployment insurance.

Irish independence. After the war, a political crisis occurred over the question of Irish independence. Ireland had been under British control since the Middle Ages, and in 1801 the British and Irish parliaments had formed the United Kingdom of Great Britain and Ireland. The British government maintained that Ireland should remain part of the United Kingdom, but many Irish would only accept complete independence. In 1916, hoping to take advantage of British involvement in World War I, people in southern Ireland revolted. British troops, however, swiftly put down the rebellion.

The violence of the revolt embittered both the Irish and the British, but in 1921, the British government and the Irish rebels agreed to a treaty that established the Irish Free State as a self-governing British dominion. However, some northern counties which had been settled by Scottish Presbyterians and had strong ties to British Protestant traditions, decided to remain under direct British rule. The southern part of the island, where Roman Catholics were in the majority, formally organized itself into a "sovereign, independent, democratic state" in 1937. In 1949, all ties to Britain were cut and the Free State became the Republic of Ireland. Trouble between the northern and southern parts of Ireland continues to this day as Irish nationalists seek Irish unity.

SOUTHERN AND EASTERN EUROPE

For Italy in southern Europe and the new nations of eastern Europe, the years immediately after World War I were very difficult in both an economic and a political sense. Many people in these nations came to believe that democratic government was unable to solve the problems of unemployment and high prices that had left people starving and homeless.

Italy. The key problem for Italy in the 1920s was a lack of jobs for millions of workers. Inflation kept prices high, while wages stayed low. Moreover, the war had cost Italy $15 billion, most of which had been borrowed. Although this debt was no greater than that of Great Britain or France, Italy—much poorer than either of these two nations—faced greater difficulty in repaying it.

For these reasons, social unrest grew. Italian factory workers went on strike, and some even demanded that they be allowed to take control of the factories. Tenant farmers refused to pay rents. The peasants demanded the land for themselves and urged the breakup of large estates into smaller plots of land.

The Italian parliamentary system, which functioned under a constitutional monarchy, did little to solve Italy's severe problems. The government, which had never been highly respected, lost support. In postwar elections in 1919 and 1921, socialists and radicals began to win seats in Parliament, and by the mid-1920s, a new authoritarian government had taken the reigns of power.

Eastern Europe in the 1920s. Life in eastern European nations such as Hungary, Poland, and Czechoslovakia had traditionally centered around agriculture on large estates. After the war, however, peasants who had always worked as tenant farmers were given land and told to go into business for themselves, although few of them had the money to buy seeds, equipment, or livestock.

Tension over nationalism, however, was the most significant problem in eastern Europe after World War I. In forming some of the new countries, the postwar treaties had established national boundaries that brought together different national groups. People who had never felt any friendship or common culture with one another were suddenly declared to be citizens of the same nation. Germans found themselves living in lands given to Czechoslovakia or Poland, and Russian minority groups now lived in other Slavic states, such as Romania.

Alphonse Mucha's 1928 poster hails the tenth anniversary of Czechoslovakia's independence. After the war, Mucha designed currency, stamps, and a coat of arms for the new country.

Economic difficulties also plagued the new countries of eastern Europe. Greatly reduced in size, both Austria and Hungary were no longer self-sufficient. Czechoslovakia, having no outlet to the sea, was unable to establish a strong economy based on international trade. Perhaps because the peoples of eastern Europe had had little experience with democratic government, the economic crises facing them gave rise to strong dictatorships in Hungary, Poland, and Austria. Czechoslovakia, however, remained democratic although there was little economic progress throughout the 1920s and 1930s.

SECTION REVIEW

1. What was the Maginot Line? Why was it built?

2. What economic problems did Germany face after World War I? How did the government try to solve them?

3. How were economic and political problems in Great Britain similar to those of Germany and France after World War I?

4. Explain the key problems in Italy that led to social unrest. What situations caused tension in Eastern Europe?

Evaluation. Explain why French leaders were justified in fearing future German aggression.

29–3
WORLDWIDE DEPRESSION

READ TO FIND OUT

—what the term *depression* means.
—why the American stock market crashed.
—how Franklin Roosevelt worked to end the Great Depression.
—how the depression spread from the United States to Europe.

The United States had been spared the destruction so many European nations had suffered during World War I. After the war, those nations turned to the United States to buy products their devastated economies could not produce. They also turned to the United States for loans to help them rebuild and pay their war debts. By the early 1920s, the Allies owed the United States about $10 billion. In addition, American businesses were exporting more than $7 billion in goods each year. To be sure, one of the major postwar effects was the tying together of the world economy.

Throughout the 1920s, the United States prospered. Many businesses boomed. Electrical and telephone service spread around the country. Factories produced cars, radios, and other new goods. What was less visible to Europeans and Americans alike was the fact that this bustling economy rested on a shaky foundation. By the end of the decade, the great American economic boom would collapse, and the shock of that collapse would be felt around the world.

THE UNITED STATES IN THE 1920S

As Woodrow Wilson negotiated with European leaders, Americans at home welcomed their returning soldiers and looked forward to a return to a normal way of life. The presidents elected after Wilson in the 1920s supported the laissez-faire economic policies in effect since the Industrial Revolution. This meant that such leaders as Warren G. Harding and Calvin Coolidge actively sought the growth of industry by allowing businesses to be run without government interference.

Economic expansion. Soon after the war, modern production methods yielded a flood of goods from American factories. By 1925, Henry Ford's assembly lines in Detroit, Michigan, were churning out automobiles at the rate of 9,000 a day. This huge volume of production allowed Ford to sell cars cheaply. Low prices spurred car sales, and as a result, the sales of steel, glass, and rubber also rose. The boom in the automobile industry bolstered America's entire economy during the 1920s.

As families eagerly bought up new refrigerators, washing machines, vacuum cleaners, and radios, the nation's economy seemed healthier than ever. In the 1920s Americans had the highest standard of living yet known.

Despite the rosy economic picture, though, some basic problems threatened to bring an end to the prosperity. Farmers, for instance, did not always benefit from commercial expansion. Prices for agricultural goods, especially wheat, fell dramatically just after the war when Europe once again began to grow its own food. Unable to sell crops overseas, farmers in the United States had to dump thousands of tons of wheat on American consumers. Because supply exceeded demand, wheat prices fell further. With the price of wheat extremely low, many farmers were unable to stay in business.

Another problem was that too many people began to borrow money to buy consumer goods. Called buying on credit, borrowing money to buy goods such as a car or radio soon left millions of people with debts that eventually had to be paid off. Few people, though—including government leaders—recognized that extensive borrowing weakened the foundation of the economy. A harsh lesson in economics was to come at the end of the 1920s.

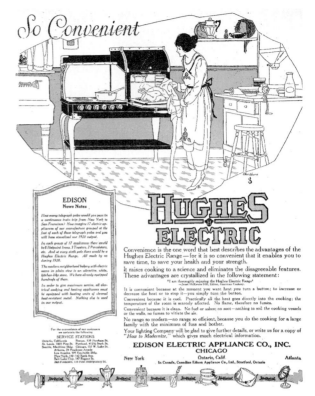

This 1920 advertisement for the Hughes Electric Range reflects post-World War I prosperity in the United States. Demand for new products turned advertising itself into a big business.

THE STOCK MARKET CRASH

The summer of 1929 saw the highpoint of the postwar American boom years. More stocks—or shares of ownership in corporations—were bought and sold on the New York Stock Exchange than ever before. Everyone wanted to be part of the business boom, and with a little extra money from savings—or with a loan—middle-class workers could buy stocks in hopes of selling later at a great profit.

A fever of speculation, or buying to sell soon at great profit, gripped the United States. Stock prices soared higher and higher. As with consumer goods, however, much of the money invested in the stocks was borrowed. Many were bought "on margin," or with loans raised by pledging the value of the stocks themselves as security, or a guarantee that the loan would be repaid. Each investor was gambling that stock prices would continue rising.

Such confidence in the stock market could not last forever. Speculators began to worry that their stocks were overpriced. When these investors began to sell their stock in the fall of 1929,

INTERPRETING POLITICAL CARTOONS

INTRODUCING THE SKILL

A political cartoon is a form of visual communication about a current event. Political cartoonists both simplify and exaggerate in order to make some point about people and events in the news. While cartoons are often humorous, they can also communicate serious messages.

Cartoonists are able to simplify complex issues into images that can be easily understood. Boss Tweed, a corrupt nineteenth-century American politician, knew the power of the biting political cartoons created about him by Thomas Nast. "I don't care what they write about me," Tweed said. "But those damn pictures—people understand them."

EXPLAINING THE SKILL

Cartoonists use both words and pictures to communicate their ideas. If you follow these steps, you can increase your appreciation of political cartoons.

A. *Identify the main characters, issues, or events to which the cartoon refers.* Cartoonists use both caricatures and symbols in their cartoons. Caricatures are drawings of real people that exaggerate their most prominent physical features. Such exaggeration helps readers to recognize characters easily. Symbols are drawings of people, animals, or objects that stand for something else. For example, the figure of "Uncle Sam" stands for the United States or the American people; a dove represents peace; and a globe stands for the entire earth.

B. *If characters are shown, study their actions and facial expressions.* Decide what the main characters are doing and look at their faces to see how they feel about what is going on.

C. *Read the captions, labels, and word balloons.* Captions often reveal what the cartoonist thinks about the topic of the cartoon. Labels identify the characters and actions. Word balloons tell you what the characters are saying.

D. *Summarize the message of the cartoon in your own words.*

APPLYING THE SKILL

The following cartoon by Ted Gale appeared in 1929 in the *Los Angeles Times*. Shortly before the cartoon appeared, the Federal Reserve Board had raised interest rates, making bank loans for stock purchases more difficult to obtain.

SOMEBODY HAD TO SAVE HIM FROM HIMSELF!

1. Are the two characters in this cartoon caricatures of real people or symbols? Who are they, or what do they stand for?

2. Describe what each character is doing.

3. How has the shape of the character on the left been distorted? Why do you think the cartoonist drew him this way?

4. What does each character say or seem to feel about what is going on?

5. Explain what the caption means.

6. Summarize the message of this cartoon in your own words.

REVIEWING THE SKILL

7. What is a political cartoon?

8. What four steps can be followed in order to interpret a political cartoon?

they did not find other buyers. Realizing that their riches existed only in credit instead of in real money, the investors began to panic. By the end of October 1929, thousands of shares owned by corporations and banks, as well as by small investors, were being put up for sale. With everyone trying to sell stocks, prices plummeted. The stock market fell so quickly that the term *great crash* began to be used in describing the event.

THE GREAT DEPRESSION

The stock market crash of 1929 set off a decline in economic activity, or a ***depression***, that was worse than any the United States or the world had ever seen. Those who owned much of the wealth in the United States lost it as businesses in which they had invested failed and stocks became worthless. The business failures hurt not only investors but also thousands of workers, who suddenly lost their jobs as entire industries shut down.

Factories were not the only businesses to go under as the economic crises spread from the New York Stock Exchange to the rest of the country. Some banks that had made large in-

vestments in the stock market went totally bankrupt. People who had money in bank accounts began to fear that the banks had lost their savings, and so they went to the banks and demanded to withdraw their money. Thus began a cycle of panic that led to withdrawals of bank deposits, which led to more bank failures and more panic.

Because they had lost their savings, people around the country began to cut back on purchases of all kinds, which led to still more factory layoffs as the demand for products fell sharply. By 1933, at the worst point of what became known as the Great Depression, almost 13 million people in the United States were unemployed, about one fourth of the entire work force. The period of prosperity had come to an abrupt end.

THE NEW DEAL

Franklin D. Roosevelt, elected president over Herbert Hoover in 1932, called for government action to bring the nation back to economic health. In stark contrast to Hoover's economic policy—one of government noninvolvement in the economy—Roosevelt's program called the

Unemployment made soup kitchens and food distribution lines common in American cities in the early 1930s, as seen in Reginald Marsh's 1932 etching, *Breadline—No One Has Starved.*

New Deal was a series of relief, recovery, and reform measures spearheaded by the government.

At Roosevelt's direction, government took a more active role in the nation's economy, acting as banker, employer, and insurer. The federal government loaned money to states for unemployment insurance and put people to work building bridges, roads, and schools. During the Roosevelt years, government took on the new role of providing relief to the poor.

In 1933, the government also passed a law that provided for the federal government to insure bank deposits. This measure renewed Americans' confidence in the banking system. Assured that the government would back up the banks, people again began to put what savings they had into bank accounts.

The federal government, however, could not perform all of these functions and keep a balanced budget. Accordingly, the government borrowed money and ran up its debts. Roosevelt looked on such actions as "priming the pump": spending money in order to start up business activity again and get people back to work. Between 1932 and 1940, federal spending remained high, and the debt of the United States doubled. New Deal programs, however, provided essential emergency support for workers and farmers.

THE DEPRESSION IN EUROPE

The depression had a great effect on Europe as well as the United States. By the 1920s, intricate networks of transportation, communication, and trade linked the nations of the world, knitting their economies into a single worldwide pattern. Economic trouble in one part of the world—in this case the United States—had devastating effects everywhere else. International commerce fell by 65 percent between 1929 and 1933.

The depression spread quickly to Europe when soon after the stock market crash many American bankers asked the European Allies to pay back their outstanding loans. Because Europe was still recovering from the effects of World War I, the Allies could not afford to make loan payments on time. When the Allies refused to repay the loans, the United States stopped loaning and investing money in Europe. Without the economic support of the United States, Europe too began to suffer from the depression. By 1932, 30 percent of all German working men were unemployed.

As in the United States, unemployment in Great Britain and France soared as their respective economies slowed down in the wake of the American depression. Great Britain and France, however, were better prepared to face the crisis than the United States had been. By 1929, both countries already had unemployment insurance and other programs of poor relief to assist the many people hurt by the depression.

On the whole, the depression in Great Britain and France was not nearly as severe as in the United States. Even so, economic difficulties in Europe lasted well into the 1930s.

In other European countries such as Germany, Italy, Austria, and Poland, the depression hit very hard. In these countries—especially Germany—economic recovery from the war had been slow. When worldwide depression brought an end to the little economic prosperity that had developed in the late 1920s, many people became embittered against their governments, which were seen as weak and ineffective. In Poland, Germany, and Austria, people turned to strong central governments that promised economic relief.

SECTION REVIEW

1. Define *depression*.

2. What economic problems led to the American stock market crash of 1929?

3. Identify the principal aspects of Franklin Roosevelt's policy to end the Great Depression.

4. How did the spread of the depression affect the economy of Europe?

Analysis. One reason the depression spread from the United States to Europe was that the economies of nations around the world were closely tied to each other, and all were linked to the United States. How had the United States gained such economic power and influence?

Data Search. Refer to the appropriate chart on page 833 to identify when the sharpest increase in unemployment occurred in the following countries between 1923 and 1938: Germany, the United Kingdom, the United States.

29-4
NEW FORCES OF NATIONALISM

In 1928, Mustapha Kemal, later called Ataturk, teaches the use of the Latin alphabet to replace Arabic letters. He considered this change essential for modern education in Turkey.

After World War I, Europe was no longer the center of world power, either economically or politically. People outside Europe noted this shift and began, with great confidence, to resist European imperial rule. European nations, however, aware of their postwar weakness, tried to preserve their empires by asserting tighter control over their colonies. Strong national movements grew, nevertheless, seeking both economic and political independence from Europe, and in some cases colonies of European powers became new nations.

INDEPENDENT STATES IN THE MIDDLE EAST

Nowhere was the nationalist spirit clearer than in the Middle East, where the final collapse of the Ottoman Empire in 1919 destroyed political unity. The new states of Iran, Turkey, and Arabia emerged, while other areas formerly controlled by the Ottoman sultan—Syria, Lebanon, Palestine, Iraq, and Trans-Jordan—were given to France and Britain as mandates.

The Islamic religion remained a strong force in Turkey, but new secular, or nonreligious, loyalties developed as well. Of these, a spirit of nationalism was most important.

During World War I, Turkey had allied itself with the Central Powers. In October of 1918, the Ottoman sultan surrendered to the Allies, and the Ottoman government agreed to terms of peace. However, Turkish resistance flared over the Allies' plans to divide up much of Turkey's territory among themselves.

Dismayed by the sultan's inability to defend Turkey, patriots rallied behind General Mustapha Kemal (kuh-MAHL), a war hero, as he worked to form a new Turkish government rivaling the sultan's. In 1922, Kemal's troops drove off invading Greek and Allied forces, and then took Constantinople proclaiming a republican government for Turkey.

The new government renegotiated a peace treaty with the Allies. The 1923 Treaty of Lausanne allowed Turkey to keep Asia Minor and also a bit of European territory across the straits joining the Black Sea to the Aegean Sea.

Once in power, Kemal set out to make Turkey a vigorous modern nation. He proclaimed a democracy, and in 1935, he extended the right to vote to women. He also introduced modern laws based on secular European tradition rather than Islamic law. In 1935, the Turkish Assembly honored him with the name Ataturk, which means "father of the Turks."

Kemal pushed for economic growth, too. Turkish engineers and technical experts were trained to replace foreign advisors. By 1939, the Turkish economy was strong enough for the government to buy out the foreign companies that owned the Turkish railroads. Kemal died in 1938, but his successors continued to stress Turkish national development.

Saudi Arabia. The family of Abdul ibn-Saud had ruled the kingdom of Nejd (NEZHD) in the Arabian peninsula since the mid-1700s. In the 1920s, Abdul ibn-Saud defeated a neighboring leader and took control of the kingdom of Hejaz. Combining Hejaz with Nejd, he formed Saudi Arabia and made himself king.

Ibn-Saud ruled as a traditional despot under the laws of Islam. In contrast to Ataturk, ibn-Saud enforced traditional styles of dress and demanded traditional Muslim penalties for criminals. Yet he knew that his nation could not survive as an independent state without some adaptations to the times. The discovery of vast oil reserves in the Arabian desert in the 1930s helped ibn-Saud modernize his land.

ARAB-JEWISH TENSION IN PALESTINE

While Islamic nationalists were forging new nations in Turkey and Saudi Arabia, Jews in Europe, Asia, and North America joined a movement called *Zionism*, which represented a belief in establishing an independent Jewish state in Palestine. The Zionist movement gained strength in the late 1800s after waves of anti-Semitic, or anti-Jewish, hatred and violence swept through Europe and Russia. Zionists sought to restore the Jewish state that had been destroyed by the Roman Empire in A.D. 70. The Zionists argued that Jews could escape persecution only by having a state of their own.

Jews emigrating to Palestine created a new element in the balance of power in the Middle East. During World War I, the Zionists won support from Great Britain which, in 1917, issued the Balfour Declaration, stating that Britain "viewed with favor the establishment of a national home for the Jewish people." Meanwhile, persecution of the Jews in central and eastern Europe during the 1920s and 1930s led to increased immigration in Palestine. In 1932, 83,790 Jews lived in Palestine; by 1940, the number had grown to 463,535. Although Arabs in Palestine still greatly outnumbered the Jews, Jewish power was growing.

Arab nationalists vigorously opposed Zionist plans. Arabs pressed Great Britain, which ruled Palestine under a mandate from the League of Nations, to restrict Jewish immigration there. When the British cut off Jewish immigration, Jewish Palestinians rioted, putting pressure on the British to end immigration restrictions. However, violent Arab protests continued throughout the 1930s.

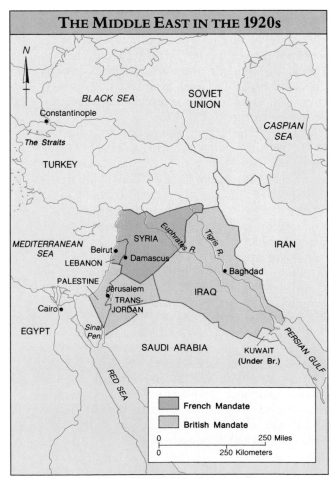

THE MIDDLE EAST IN THE 1920s

French Mandate

British Mandate

0   250 Miles
0   250 Kilometers

GROWING NATIONALISM IN COLONIAL AFRICA

Nationalistic movements in sub-Saharan Africa provided the foundation for later independence movements. In Egypt and French North Africa, however, strong nationalist movements developed in the 1920s, resulting in change.

After the First World War, the European powers expressed new concern about the well-being of their African subjects. This outlook led to the building of new schools, hospitals, and libraries in the African colonies. For the most part, however, changes in Africa in the 1920s were made with business interests in mind, and the continent's natural resources were developed at the expense of African society.

Political reform. After 1918, nationalist movements in several African nations began to agitate for self-rule. In many French and British colonies, black Africans gained some forms of political expression during the 1920s. In French Senegal, for example, some members of a government council were elected by Africans rather than appointed by the French. In Morocco and Tunisia, France offered various political concessions, but they all fell short of full independence.

The British formed legislative councils in most of their colonies. These councils gave Africans a measure of self-rule. Egypt, however, gained full independence from Great Britain in 1922, after a long and bloody campaign carried out by an Egyptian nationalist group known as the Wafd.

POLITICAL DEVELOPMENTS IN INDIA

During World War I, 3 million Indian soldiers had fought for Great Britain, and Indian factories had stepped up their production to send arms and ammunition to the Allies. The Indian people cooperated with Britain's war effort because they counted on independence as the reward for their support.

The postwar period, however, brought great disappointment to Indians when Great Britain refused to give up its Indian empire. The Government of India Act, passed by the British Parliament in 1919, fell far short of Indian expectations. Instead of granting independence, the act provided for India to remain a British colony and restricted the right to vote to a tiny minority of Indians.

Political protest against British rule was set off by a serious economic problem that hit India during the 1920s. An influenza epidemic, combined with a major crop failure, killed 5 million people. These disasters led to waves of rural uprisings, as Indians vented their frustrations on unpopular landlords and moneylenders. Later in the 1920s, as poverty and hunger became more widespread, protest in the cities grew, with strikes among textile and railroad workers.

At first, the British took very strong measures against these uprisings, a policy that slowly eroded Indian support. Reacting to the harsh repression, many Indians who had earlier favored British rule joined the nationalist movement. Among these nationalists was Mohandas K. Gandhi.

Gandhi. Gandhi had studied law in England and practiced as a lawyer in South Africa. After he returned to India and built up a following, Gandhi was elected leader of India's National Congress party in 1921. Over the next ten years, he became the universally respected symbol of India's political awakening. He appealed

At a village industries fair in Faizpur, India, in 1937, Gandhi (right) chats with Jawaharlal Nehru, the newly elected president of the India National Congress. To help India gain economic as well as political independence from Great Britain, Gandhi promoted cottage industries such as hand spinning and weaving, on display at this fair.

both to discontented peasants and to committed nationalist leaders, and he worked to discourage Western influence by strengthening India's traditional culture and religion.

Indians called Gandhi *Mahatma*, which means "great soul," though he discouraged any effort to make him a religious symbol. Gandhi was a shrewd man, skillful in working out compromises among the various Indian groups. He insisted on the rights of all Indian citizens, which won him the support of the untouchables and the Muslims. Gandhi criticized the caste system but praised other Hindu traditions.

While practicing law in South Africa, Gandhi developed his philosophy and technique of passive resistance, or "nonviolent noncooperation" in which protesters engaged in sit-ins and other nonviolent actions. Passive resistance, which appealed to the religious, worked as a shrewd military tactic as well, for the British could justify firing on an armed uprising but not on an unarmed one. Another tenet of Gandhi's beliefs was civil disobedience, which included the refusal to obey unjust laws or to pay taxes.

Gandhi and his followers organized a series of campaigns aimed at forcing the British to grant India independence. The Indians refused to buy British goods, pay taxes, vote, or hold office. They blocked trains by lying down on the tracks, and thousands of silent demonstrators surrounded government buildings so that officials had to climb over their bodies to get to work. Gandhi went to jail many times for practicing civil disobedience.

Although Gandhi insisted that Hindus and Muslims must work together toward a unified independent India, friction between the two groups increased during the 1930s. The British used the friction between Hindus and Muslims as a reason not to give India complete independence, claiming that independence would bring violent clashes between the two groups. Instead of independence, the British offered further reforms and a new constitution.

The new constitution, enacted in 1935, divided the country into 11 provinces, each with an elected assembly. A British governor, however, was appointed administrator of each province, and India as a whole was still ruled by a British viceroy. The new constitution disappointed Indian nationalists who wanted full self-government, but with British troops in every province, there was little they could do.

THE STRUGGLE TO UNIFY CHINA

In 1911, after one hundred years of weak, ineffective rule, the Ch'ing Dynasty in China was overthrown. Dr. Sun Yat-sen's faction formed a nationalist party, the Kuomintang, and named him the republic's first president.

In an effort to promote harmony among competing factions, Dr. Sun stepped down and recommended that Yuan Shih-kai, a military commander from the north, be made president. In 1912, however, Yuan took all power for himself and ruled as a military dictator until his death in 1916.

After Yuan's death, a number of warlords, military rulers who commanded personal armies, held power in different sections of China. No political party or individual was powerful enough to stop the warlords and unite the nation. Chaos and turmoil at the hands of armed bands led to destruction of the countryside. Armed with the latest weapons, the warlords collected taxes in their provinces, maintained armies, and negotiated with other nations.

Economic growth. During World War I, European manufactured goods were scarce in China because European factories were busy making munitions. As prices rose, Chinese industrialists saw the value of building factories at home. The Chinese economy boomed as new textile mills, banks, and steel mills sprang up.

In 1917, China joined the war against the Central Powers in hopes of gaining territory in the north at the expense of Russia. At the Paris Peace Conference, however, all of China's requests were ignored. This Allied action angered the Chinese. On May 4, 1919, students and workers joined in a huge demonstration against the Western powers. The "May Fourth Movement," as it became known, signaled the start of a new outburst of Chinese nationalism.

The Chinese Communist party. Inspired by the success of the Russian Revolution in toppling the czar, some Chinese thought communism could end the domination of China by Western powers. These Chinese founded the Chinese Communist party in 1921.

While the Chinese Communist party took shape, Sun Yat-sen revived the Kuomintang and sought a democratic parliamentary system. Under his leadership, the Kuomintang grew into a strong, well-disciplined party. It ruled from Canton, working to defeat the warlords and promising an honest government. Sun Yat-sen died in 1925, but through his writings and speeches—which had developed the principles of nationalism, self-government, and a higher standard of living—his memory remained to inspire the Kuomintang.

The Kuomintang dictatorship. In 1926, the Kuomintang felt strong enough to move beyond Canton and take on the warlords' armies. Under the command of General Chiang Kai-shek (KĪ-SHEK) the Kuomintang forces took over half the provinces of China in less than six months and set up a dictatorship.

Chiang deeply distrusted the Communists, however. His goal of unity for China did not include a role for the Communist party. As early as 1928 many Chinese Communists were either driven from the Kuomintang or killed. Many left urban areas and moved to the country, where Chiang's power was weak.

Focused on crushing his opponents, Chiang did little to aid the Chinese economy. He made no efforts at land reform, and as the population increased, rural poverty grew steadily.

The Chinese government was also unable to stop Japan from invading. The Japanese, eager to acquire new territory in a quest for imperial greatness, had taken over some German territory in Asia after World War I, and in 1931, a Japanese army invaded the Chinese province of Manchuria. China asked the League of Nations to condemn the invasion, but the league took no effective action. Japan then set up a Japanese dominated state named Manchukuo and stood poised to move deeper into China.

Mao Zedong. The Chinese Communist party had for the most part moved out of the cities into the rural areas. In the provinces of Kiangsi (kee-AHNG-SEE) a young library assistant of peasant background named Mao Zedong (MOW DZUH-DOONG) emerged as a new leader. Mao used guerrilla tactics against the Kuomintang armies and slowly rebuilt the party's strength.

In 1934, Chiang Kai-shek decided to launch a massive attack on the Communists. The Communists saw that they could not win over the nearly one million Kuomintang troops, so they decided to retreat. In October 1934, the

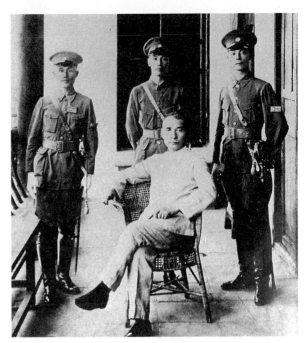

The young officer Chiang Kai-shek stands directly behind Sun Yat-sen in this 1920 photograph. Sun reorganized the Kuomintang along military lines to consolidate his power.

Communists began their "Long March" north across the Chinese countryside. For one year, the Communists marched across 6,000 miles (9,600 kilometers) of desert, swampland, and mountain ranges, all the while being pursued by Kuomintang forces. Although 90,000 started on the march in southern China, only about 30,000 survived to reach the northern province of Shensi. On the march, Mao took over as the unquestioned head of the party.

In Shensi, Mao once again strengthened the communist forces. The Japanese invasion of China in 1937 diverted Chiang Kai-shek's troops and gave the Communists time to regroup. The question of who would rule China, however, could be resolved only after the defeat of the Japanese.

CHANGES IN LATIN AMERICA

Major change in Latin America came about when the economies of European nations faltered after the war. These nations could no longer make large investments in Latin America, as they had before the war. As the United States' economy expanded during the 1920s, it gradually replaced Great Britain as the leading trade partner of the Latin American republics.

To make up for the slowdown in foreign investment, by the beginning of the 1920s, many Latin American nations were attempting to diversify their economies. They tried to manufacture basic products that could be sold at home, thus reducing the need to import such products from abroad at high cost. Despite some success in industrializing, however, the economies of Latin American nations remained basically agricultural.

When foreign investment stopped during the worldwide depression, the Latin American nations suffered greatly. The value of Latin American exports decreased by two-thirds, and every nation except Argentina and Haiti defaulted on, or failed to repay its foreign loans.

Political reaction to the depression came quickly. In Brazil, for instance, Getúlio Vargas (VAHR-gahs) became dictator in 1930 and vowed economic reform. He wanted to industrialize the Brazilian economy. Because Vargas's program was largely successful, by the time he left office in 1945, Brazil was producing many of its own consumer goods.

In Mexico, Lázaro Cárdenas (CAHR-day-NAHS) ruled from 1934 to 1940. Like Vargas, Cárdenas undertook major economic reforms. Siding with peasants and workers, Cárdenas's support for the lower classes was strong. In 1938, this support was demonstrated when his government took over all foreign oil companies during a wage dispute involving Mexican workers.

State ownership of Mexican industries—similar to Lenin's economic order in Communist Russia—was a cause for concern in the United States. Some Americans who had lost money when the Mexican government took over the oil companies called for American military intervention to prevent a "communist revolution" in Mexico. President Franklin Roosevelt, however, refused. Instead of confrontation with Mexico—and the rest of Latin America—Roosevelt developed his "Good Neighbor" policy for Latin America in which he offered Mexico long-term loans so that the Mexican government could pay American companies for the oil fields it had taken. Through the Good Neighbor policy, the United States recognized Mexico as a sovereign state with the same international rights as any other power.

In the 1930s, as the Good Neighbor policy was applied to other Latin American countries, relations between the United States and the region became friendlier. The memory of American imperialism in Latin America was temporarily put aside as each Latin American country competed for American economic aid.

SECTION REVIEW

1. Define *Zionism*.

2. What effect did Mustapha Kemal's modernizing reforms have on Turkey?

3. How did Gandhi influence the Indian nationalist movement?

4. Discuss the rise of the Communist party in China.

5. Describe three measures that different Latin American nations took in an attempt to overcome economic problems. What were the results of each?

Evaluation. If you were in Gandhi's position, what actions would you have taken to end British domination of India? When explaining your response, tell why you would or would not have used passive resistance.

29–5
CULTURAL TRENDS

READ TO FIND OUT

—what *surrealism* and *cubism* mean.
—how World War I changed some women's lives.
—how World War I affected literature and art.

World War I shocked the world deeply. The war transformed not only European borders but also the way many people thought. Just when more and more people were becoming literate, newspapers brought reports of inhuman cruelty and photographs of extreme suffering. This picture of the state of the world made many people reconsider the value of scientific and technological "progress." Writers and painters tried to face the challenge of a new world, one where established beliefs and traditions seemed to have vanished.

CHANGES IN DOMESTIC LIFE

Even far from its battlefields, the First World War created profound changes in society. As men went off to war, women filled their jobs and showed that they could do work that many people considered inappropriate for them. The new economic roles resulted in new political roles for women. Women were granted the right to vote in several nations, including the United States, Great Britain, and Germany shortly after the war. Although suffrage did not bring immediate political equality, it did give women a new sense of freedom.

Popular culture. Popular culture in the 1920s—especially in the United States—was full of new fads and fashions, from flagpole sitting to bobbed hair. Movies and sports events drew huge crowds of men and women who sought entertainment and relaxation. The movies that people flocked to see became the models for many people's lives. Film stars such as Charlie Chaplin and Greta Garbo were known around the world.

Cars and radios became the visible symbols of success. The United States, the most prosperous industrial country, often adopted with enthusiasm the latest fads, including new forms of music such as jazz and popular dances such as the Charleston.

LITERATURE IN THE 1920S AND 1930S

Not all of the culture of the 1920s was based on fads, however. Writers were profoundly affected by the war and its aftermath. Their works expressed the confusion of the time.

Many American writers, disillusioned by war, came to Paris in the 1920s and mixed there with French and British writers. One of these Americans was Ernest Hemingway, who had been severely wounded in the war. The simple, clear prose style of his short stories and novels, which he had learned as a newspaper reporter, was new in fiction. Gertrude Stein was another American writer living in Paris. She made her Paris home into an informal salon visited by painters, musicians, and writers.

With the installation of dial telephones in 1922, New Yorkers could make local calls themselves. However, switchboard operators like these still had to place long-distance calls.

Another writer, James Joyce, also lived outside his homeland, having left Ireland for France. Joyce created a new prose style called "stream of consciousness," which makes the reader aware of what is spontaneously going on in the mind of a character, often moving quickly from one thought or experience to another. This style reflected the influence of Sigmund Freud and his "free association" technique of psychoanalysis. Using this technique in *Ulysses*, published in 1922, Joyce severely criticized Ireland and Western culture. At the same time his work was strong and energetic, and its new and lively form was itself an expression of hope.

In the United States, John Steinbeck used fiction for social protest, speaking out for the victims of the Great Depression. His novel *The Grapes of Wrath*, published in 1939, told the story of poverty-stricken Oklahoma farmers looking for a better life in California. In France, on the other hand, the interests and concerns of André Malraux went beyond the borders of his own nation. He wrote about French imperialism in Indochina and about civil war in Spain. His 1934 novel, *Man's Fate*, told the story of the Chinese revolution from the point of view of a small group of Chinese Communists.

In Germany, the playwright Bertolt Brecht wrote with compassion and biting humor. A poet who had studied Marxism, he sought to awaken his audience rather than entertain them.

THE ARMORY SHOW

On February 15, 1913, the International Exhibition of Modern Art opened at the 69th Infantry Regiment Armory in New York City. With more than 1,100 paintings and sculptures, the Armory Show was the first major exhibition in North America of nontraditional works by European and a few American artists. The visitors who flooded the armory halls were stunned by the works of the new European art movements, and their responses ranged from ridicule to enthusiasm. As a result of the Armory Show, many American artists turned to the new styles, while many patrons of art supported this new spirit.

Poster for the Armory Show, 1913

Horse, **Raymond Duchamp-Villon, 1914 (cast 1954–1963)**

Garden of Love, Improvisation No. 27, **Wassily Kandinsky, 1912**

Mademoiselle Pogany,
Constantin Brancusi, 1913

The Red Studio, Henri Matisse, 1911

Woman with Mustard Pot, Pablo Picasso, 1910

Portrait of Chess Players, Marcel Duchamp, 1911

The lively jazz of the "Roaring Twenties" is anticipated by Charles Demuth's 1918 watercolor, *In Vaudeville*. Spirited dances were part of America's prosperous postwar culture.

In musicals such as *The Threepenny Opera*, first performed in 1928, Brecht developed his own special language, a blend of the common and the philosophical, mixed with wit and satire. In other areas of the world, especially in Latin America, writers and poets gained international fame. In 1945, Gabriela Mistral of Chile, for instance, was the first woman to receive the Nobel Prize for literature.

ART AND ARCHITECTURE AFTER THE WAR

As in the case of writers, the trauma of World War I affected artists around the world. Many artists and architects were also influenced by technological developments. The style of the French painter Marcel Duchamp (DOO-shahn), for example, satirized the modern glorification of machines by exhibiting a bicycle wheel as if it were art. In 1916, Duchamp broke with the impressionist school when he and several other artists in Paris founded the Dada movement in art. The French word *dada* means "hobbyhorse." The artists supposedly picked a word at random from a dictionary. Dada artists embraced *dada* as a nonsense word to reflect their feeling that World War I had made meaningless all earlier moral and artistic values. Some critics found dadaism completely negative, not considering it to be "art" at all. Others, however, saw dadaism as a way for artists to free themselves from the traditions of the past and to shock viewers into new ways of seeing and understanding.

Surrealism, which combined art and an attempt to harness the subconscious, grew out of dadaism and, like literature in the 1920s, was greatly influenced by Sigmund Freud's theory of psychoanalysis. Many of the paintings of Salvador Dali, one of the most important surrealists, look like dreams or hallucinations. Surrealists sought to make art based on feeling, not reason. They believed art did not need a moral purpose in order to exist.

Some of the paintings of Pablo Picasso, born in 1881, are similar to the surrealists' work. Picasso, a Spaniard who lived in France, is more closely associated with the cubist school of art, however. *Cubism* is a complicated, careful way of looking at objects that showed the influence of the new arts of photography and filmmaking. Picasso and other cubists were also influenced by African art. Cubists broke up their paintings into sharp, angular pieces.

In the 1920s in Mexico, the styles and themes of ancient Mexican art—particularly those of the Aztecs and Mayas—were incorporated into modern sculpture and painting. Diego Rivera and José Orozco were the most important of the new Latin American painters. Each is famous for the huge murals he painted on the walls of schools and public buildings. In their paintings they developed an original, authentic Latin American art form.

In architecture, the postwar period saw the spread of "functionalism," the idea that buildings should be designed simply to fit their function, not in order to appear "beautiful." Originating in the 1880s and 1890s with the early work of such architects as Louis Sullivan, Frank Lloyd Wright, and Otto Wagner, functionalism stressed that architecture should re-

GABRIELA MISTRAL

During the twentieth century, the works of many Latin American authors have become recognized as some of the most original and exciting in world literature. Worldwide recognition of Latin American literature can be said to date from 1945, when the Nobel Prize for literature was awarded to Gabriela Mistral. Born Lucila Godoy Alcayaga in 1889, she grew up in a small village in northern Chile. Because Lucila was a dreamy child, other students made fun of her, and her teachers thought she was a slow learner. As an escape from her unhappy school life, Lucila began to write. By her early teens, Lucila's poems were being published in local newspapers.

Although Lucila had decided to become a teacher, she was denied entry to the local teacher's college because the principal thought she had revolutionary ideas. Undaunted, Lucila completed a course of study in education with the help of her mother, and in 1904 she took a job as a teacher in a small rural school. Her personal life, though, was unhappy. She had a stormy relationship with a young man who committed suicide in 1909. Devastated, Lucila turned to her writing, pouring her despair into a series of poems she called "Sonnets to Death." These poems were so forthright and emotional that she was afraid to put her own name to them. Instead, she published them as Gabriela Mistral, a name she took from the names of two of her favorite writers.

In 1914, these poems won her first prize in the Chilean national poetry competition. In the next few years, Lucila's fame as Gabriela Mistral the poet grew throughout Latin America. Even after she had gained an international reputation as a poet, Gabriela still considered herself a teacher. In 1925, she entered the Chilean diplomatic service. Eventually she also worked at the League of Nations and later at the United Nations, where she helped to start the United Nations International Children's Emergency Fund (UNICEF). While a diplomat, Gabriela continued to write and teach. She died in New York in 1957.

flect an increasingly technological world. Postwar architecture and interior design were especially influenced by the Bauhaus design school, which was established by the German architect Walter Gropius in 1919. Bauhaus functionalism, which by the 1930s had become known as the "international style," is especially evident in the typical glass-and-steel skyscrapers of the twentieth century.

SECTION REVIEW

1. Define *surrealism* and *cubism*.

2. How did the war change the lives of some women?

3. How did the work of painters and writers reflect the spirit of the postwar world?

Application. Gertrude Stein called Ernest Hemingway and other young writers of the postwar period a "lost generation." Explain what she meant.

HISTORY IN FOCUS

The rise of the United States to a position of world stature and the establishment of a communist regime in Russia were two momentous consequences of World War I. Western capitalism and Russian communism eventually would compete for world power. American wealth was pitted against Russian ideology.

While many countries looked to the American financial empire for economic aid in the 1920s and 1930s, most countries viewed the communist revolution in Russia as a grave threat to the established world order, in much the same way as the French Revolution had been seen as a threat in the 1790s. Lenin, calling for widespread social and economic reform, was perceived as a modern-day Robespierre. From the great capitals of the Western world, leaders looked at Communist Russia with fear and apprehension, but the real enemy turned out to be closer to home.

SUMMARY

- Hard times followed World War I in Europe. The destruction of war and unsettled economic conditions contributed to this unrest. Germany and Italy were hit especially hard, but all over Europe democratic governments seemed unable to solve basic problems.

- In Russia a revolution deposed Czar Nicholas II and led to the establishment of a communist government. After the revolution, a civil war raged for a number of years.

- Only the United States seemed to prosper after the war, but questionable business practices led to a stock market crash in 1929. A great economic depression that quickly spread around the world followed the crash. Economic relief measures were undertaken in a number of countries to help people live through the hard times.

- In the wake of economic unrest, many countries began to shake off Western domination. In the Middle East new nations and new political movements emerged. A huge movement to free India from British rule developed, and in China a civil war to determine control of that nation's fate.

- Throughout this period, modern technology was changing the ways in which people did their jobs and lived their lives. However, after the horror of World War I, many writers and artists questioned the nature of the modern world in their works.

VOCABULARY REVIEW

Below are four vocabulary terms used in the chapter. Match each numbered term with the lettered term most closely related to it. Then explain how the terms in each pair are related.

Example: The term *duma* is related to the term *parliament* because the *duma* was Russia's legislative assembly.

1. soviet	(a) Jews
2. Zionism	(b) economy
3. depression	(c) psychology
4. surrealism	(d) workers

CHAPTER REVIEW

1. (a) What role did World War I play in the fall of the czar? (b) Why did Lenin implement war communism in Russia after the revolution?

2. How did France attempt try to defend itself against Germany after World War I?

3. What forces combined to weaken democratic governments in Germany and Italy in the 1920s?

4. (a) Describe two economic factors that affected the stock market crash of 1929. (b) How did President Roosevelt attempt to deal with the Great Depression?

5. (a) What goals did Mustapha Kemal have for Turkey? (b) What led to increased tensions in Palestine after the war?

6. (a) Why did the Government of India Act of 1919 disappoint many Indians? (b) What role did Mohandas Gandhi play in India's independence movement?

7. (a) Why did the May Fourth Movement occur in China? (b) Why did Chinese communists oppose the Kuomintang?

8. (a) What reforms did Lázaro Cárdenas introduce in Mexico? (b) How did the Good Neighbor policy help to improve relations between the United States and the Latin American countries?

9. (a) How did World War I change the lives of many women? (b) What effects did the changing roles of women have on society?

10. (a) Why did many writers and artists move to Paris in the 1920s? (b) What were some of the influences behind Picasso's paintings?

THINKING CRITICALLY: ACTIVITIES

1. Select three members of your class to be an interview team. Find at least four family members, friends, teachers, or others who lived through the Great Depression. Ask them to share their most significant memories. Present your written or taped interviews to the class.

2. Although individual artists of the early twentieth century painted in different styles,

they all tended to reject traditional methods of showing reality. Instead, they used color, shapes, and lines to produce sensations and emotions. The painter Henri Matisse said, "Composition is the art of arranging in a decorative manner various elements for the expression of [the painter's] feelings." Study the paintings on pages 662 and 663. What moods or sensations do you think each artist was attempting to convey? Explain.

APPLYING SOCIAL STUDIES SKILLS

Interpreting political cartoons. The following cartoon by Clifford Berryman appeared in an American newspaper in 1938. At the time it appeared, the United States was experiencing a decline in business activity and a sharp increase in unemployment.

OLD RELIABLE!

1. Who is the main character in this cartoon? How is he dressed?

2. What is he doing in the cartoon?

3. What is the rabbit a symbol for?

4. What does the main character say? What do you think he means by this statement?

5. Explain the caption of the cartoon.

6. Summarize the message of the cartoon.

7. What seems to be the cartoonist's attitude toward the action being illustrated? Explain.

APPLYING THINKING SKILLS

Identifying unstated assumptions. In March 1927, Mao Zedong wrote an account of the conflict between peasants and landlords in the Hunan province of China. Analyze the following excerpt from the account to find any unstated assumptions. Then answer the questions.

During my recent visit to Hunan, I made a first-hand investigation of conditions in five counties. In the thirty-two days from January 4 to February 5, I called together fact-finding conferences in villages and county towns which were attended by experienced peasants and by comrades working in the peasant movement. I listened attentively to their reports and collected a great deal of material. Many of the hows and whys of the peasant movement were the exact opposite of what the gentry are saying. Thus, all talk directed against the peasant movement must be speedily set right. Only thus can the future of the revolution be benefited.

The great peasant masses have risen to fulfill their historic mission. And so, the forces of rural democracy have risen to overthrow the forces of rural feudalism. The feudal class of local tyrants, evil gentry, and lawless landlords is the cornerstone of imperialism, warlordism, and corrupt officialdom. The national revolution is accomplishing one of its real objectives. In a few months the peasants have done what Dr. Sun Yat-sen wanted, but failed, to accomplish in the forty years he devoted to the National Revolution. This is a marvelous feat. The National Revolution requires a great change in the countryside. The Revolution of 1911 did not bring about this change. But this change is now taking place. What the peasants are doing is absolutely right.

From Mao Zedong, "Report on an Investigation of the Peasant Movement in Hunan." Peking: Foreign Languages Press, 1965.

1. Why is it important to be able to identify unstated assumptions?

2. What are two unstated assumptions in the excerpt from Mao Zedong's account?

3. What did you do to identify each of the assumptions in the excerpt?

4. According to Mao, how were the peasants helping the National Revolution?

CHAPTER THIRTY

TOTALITARIANISM: THE CHALLENGE TO LIBERTY

1919–1939

30–1 COMMUNIST RULE IN RUSSIA
30–2 FASCISM IN ITALY
30–3 NAZI GERMANY
30–4 MILITARISM IN JAPAN

Rally of the National Socialist Party Congress, Nuremberg, Germany, September 6, 1934.

While struggling to carry on World War I, governments had been forced to play an expanded role in the lives of their citizens. In the period of instability and uncertainty following the war, many governments took a similarly expanded role in dealing with economic hardships, political upheaval, and social changes.

During the 1920s and 1930s, strong leaders rose to power in Russia, Italy, Germany, and Japan. Their supporters saw strong government and nationalist expansion as the solutions to their problems. By the end of the 1930s, these strong leaders, using new technologies of communication, had begun to gain almost complete control over the lives of their citizens. The leaders created a new form of authoritarian government that would have a major impact on world history.

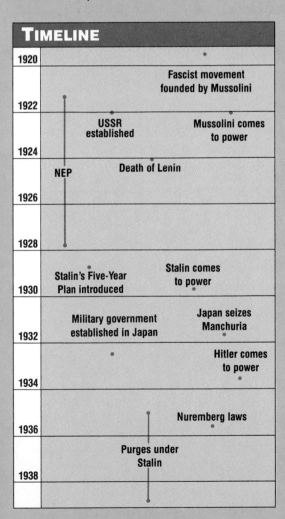

TIMELINE	
1920	
1922	**Fascist movement founded by Mussolini**
1924	**USSR established** **Mussolini comes to power**
1926	**NEP** **Death of Lenin**
1928	
1930	**Stalin's Five-Year Plan introduced** **Stalin comes to power**
1932	**Military government established in Japan** **Japan seizes Manchuria**
1934	**Hitler comes to power**
1936	**Nuremberg laws**
1938	**Purges under Stalin**

30–1
COMMUNIST RULE IN RUSSIA

READ TO FIND OUT

—what the terms *totalitarianism*, *mass communication*, and *ideology* mean.
—what was planned under Lenin's New Economic Policy.
—what goals Stalin hoped to achieve by instituting five-year plans.
—how Stalin's government differed from the Marxist vision of an ideal society.
—what Stalin hoped to accomplish with the purges.

During the civil war that raged from 1918 to 1920, Lenin and his followers had made the Russian government increasingly authoritarian, instituting the policy of war communism and creating a secret police, the *Cheka*, or *NKVD*. After the defeat of the Whites, these policies of repression continued.

When Lenin died in 1924, a struggle for power arose between two top Communist party leaders. Finally, in 1929, Joseph Stalin emerged as the sole leader of Russia. Under Stalin's rule, the Soviet government began to exert even more control over its citizens. It became the first government to impose a system of rule called *totalitarianism*, in which the state completely controls individuals' lives by demanding that they give up their own interests and goals to serve those of the state.

Totalitarianism differs from earlier forms of absolute rule in that it achieves greater power over people's daily activities, work, and thoughts. This greater degree of control became possible only with the development of *mass communication*—methods of communication, such as newspapers, radio, and magazines, designed to reach large numbers of people at once. Mass communication enabled the state to control the sources of information people used to make choices and form opinions.

PRESERVING THE COMMUNIST STATE

The defeat of the White armies in 1920 left the Communists undisputed rulers of a country on the verge of economic collapse. Peasants were farming only 62 percent as much land as they had been in 1914. The nation's transportation system had broken down. Little food was reaching the cities, and a drought produced widespread famine that killed 4 to 5 million people. Lenin realized that new government policies were needed.

Economic policies. In order to revive the economy, Lenin abandoned war communism in 1921 and announced a New Economic Policy, or NEP. Under the NEP, heavy industry, banking, and transportation remained under government control. Private ownership of small factories and stores was permitted, however, and farmers were allowed to sell their surplus crops for a profit on the open market. Lenin encouraged economic experimentation and worker initiative.

Although Russia made no real economic progress under the NEP, industrial and farm production did return to prewar levels. In 1928, when the NEP ended, the nation was producing as much grain, coal, and oil as it had in 1913, a great achievement under the circumstances.

The USSR. Once the civil war had ended in 1920, Lenin could reorganize the new Russian state. The Union of Soviet Socialist Republics, or USSR, was established in 1922, and the name "Russia" was no longer officially used. The Soviet Union, as the USSR was also called, was divided into separate republics joined under a federal government. Eventually, 15 republics would make up the Soviet Union. Although each republic had elected representatives in the federal government in Moscow, the Communist party effectively controlled politics throughout the Soviet Union.

STRUGGLE OVER LEADERSHIP

Lenin never saw the new Soviet Union that he thought would develop after the NEP. Partly disabled by an assassination attempt in 1918, he died early in 1924 after a series of strokes. The city of Petrograd was renamed Leningrad in his honor.

Because the Communist regime had no plan for choosing a successor to Lenin, a long struggle for leadership among top Communist officials emerged. The contest finally narrowed to Leon Trotsky, Lenin's second-in-command, and Joseph Stalin, whom Lenin did not trust. Shortly before his death, Lenin wrote that "Comrade Stalin has concentrated enormous

Communist party leaders from Europe and Asia stand beneath Stalin's portrait at a celebration of his seventieth birthday in 1949. By this time, Stalin had been dictator for 20 years.

REGIONS: SOVIET SIBERIA, THE SLEEPING LAND

The region of Russia known as Siberia stretches from the Ural Mountains to the Pacific, spanning nine time zones. Long, frozen winters have given this region its name, which comes from an old Tartar word meaning "Sleeping Land."

A forbidding climate has made Siberia remote, despite the flatness of most of the land. Much of Siberia lies within or near the Arctic Circle. Winters last for eight months, during which temperatures in the northernmost towns such as Verkhoyansk—one of the coldest spots in the northern hemisphere—may occasionally drop below -90°F (-68°C). Icy winds howl across the densely forested plains and plateaus, trees stoop under their burden of snow, and all the rivers freeze over.

Although Siberia has been inhabited since ancient times, the population remained sparse and the region largely undeveloped for centuries. After the revolution, however, the new Soviet government sent scientific expeditions to survey Siberia's resources. The scientists discovered enormous reserves of coal and rich deposits of iron, copper, gold, silver, and other minerals. Natural gas and diamonds were also added to the list of Siberia's treasures. The Russians later found that Siberia holds more untapped reserves of oil than even Saudi Arabia.

By 1930, an ambitious program to develop and industrialize Siberia was underway. However, Russian pioneers in Siberia faced unusual challenges resulting from the harsh climate. Learning how to live and work through the long Siberian winter was, perhaps, the greatest challenge. Temperatures routinely drop below -40°F in winter, making frostbite a constant danger. Siberians have learned to be watchful for signs of freezing flesh. If passersby point to their nose, it means that another person's nose has turned white and could freeze in seconds unless rubbed vigorously.

Because of *permafrost*, the permanently frozen earth which covers two-thirds of Siberia, the pioneers had to devise new methods to carry out such routine activities as farming or building. To farm or build in ground that is frozen to a depth of 5,000 feet (1,524 meters) in some areas required ingenuity. Resourceful pioneers learned to raise cabbages, potatoes, cucumbers, wheat, and tomatoes—which never turn red—during the brief summer, when the top layer of soil thaws. The settlers developed a new kind of apple tree to survive in the frozen soil. The tree's roots spread out on the surface, while the branches rise only an inch or two above the ground. In bloom, the trees look like baskets of flowers strewn across a field.

Building on permafrost proved to be even more difficult than farming. Early buildings sank into the ground at odd angles as heat from within them unevenly melted the frozen earth beneath. To avoid this problem, buildings now stand above the ground on pillars sunk into the permafrost. The air space beneath the structures prevents the ground from thawing. Thus, Siberia's unique physical features have led to distinctive, regional cultural characteristics.

Although Siberia is still sparsely populated, in just the past few decades, thousands of Russians have migrated east to develop Siberia's rich resources. Separated by miles of empty wilderness, old towns have been transformed into industrial centers. New towns and cities have sprung up, each with its forest of factory smokestacks. Siberians now boast that "Siber, the sleeping land, has awakened."

1. Describe the region of Siberia.
2. Define *permafrost*. Why do buildings have to be built off the ground in parts of Siberia?
3. Today, Soviet citizens working in Siberia receive larger salaries and longer vacations than other Soviet workers. Explain why.

power in his hands, and I am not sure that he always knows how to use that power."

Trotsky and Stalin disagreed about the future path of the revolution. Trotsky believed in the Marxist doctrine of world revolution. He did not think communism could survive in Russia unless the rest of the world adopted it also. In contrast, Stalin advocated a doctrine of "socialism in one country." Only when socialism had triumphed in the Soviet Union, he said, would that nation be able to spread world revolution.

Although Trotsky was popular within the Communist party, Stalin managed to win more power. After 1924, Stalin began to force his rivals out of the party. Trotsky and his supporters slowly lost their government and party offices. By 1929, Stalin was able to force Trotsky into exile and gain firm control of the Soviet Union.

THE FIVE-YEAR PLANS

As he took the reins of power, Stalin set out to build the Soviet Union into an industrial and military giant that could defend itself and spread communism throughout the world. The Soviet economy was then a mixture of socialism and private enterprise. Peasants outnumbered workers, and Soviet industry lagged far behind that of the West. Stalin realized that radical changes were needed to achieve his goals, and beginning in 1928, he introduced the First Five-Year Plan, which was designed to develop the Soviet economy.

Under Stalin's First Five-Year Plan, a staff of economists and technical experts set production schedules for industry and agriculture. Every trace of the NEP was ended, and every aspect of the Soviet economy was organized by the central government. The First Five-Year Plan created for the Soviet Union a planned economy—an economy in which the central government decides which factories will use which raw materials to produce which goods.

Stalin's program aimed at tripling the output of heavy industries such as coal, oil, and steel in only five years. Such an ambitious project required enormous sacrifices from the Soviet people. Stalin appealed to their nationalist and socialist feelings as if in wartime. "We are 50 or 100 years behind the advanced countries," he said. "We must make good this lag in 10 years. Either we do it or they crush us."

In order to industrialize the Soviet Union rapidly, the government forced hundreds of thousands of peasants off their land and moved them to factories or mines or construction sites, where they worked long days for very low wages. The population of the cities in the Soviet Union mushroomed, with most workers living in dreary, crowded conditions.

Communist party leaders realized that for the First Five-Year Plan to succeed, the Soviet Union also had to grow enough crops, especially grain, to export and sell abroad. Such sales would supply money to purchase new industrial equipment. To make sure that farmers grew enough of the needed crops, Stalin placed agriculture under tight government control.

The First Five-Year Plan called for the pooling of agricultural land into large farms on which people would work together to produce food. Such lands were called collective farms. In theory the peasants who lived on the collective farms owned them jointly. However, the state, not the peasants, decided what was to be produced and owned most of what was grown.

RUSSIAN STEEL AND AUTO PRODUCTION 1913–1938

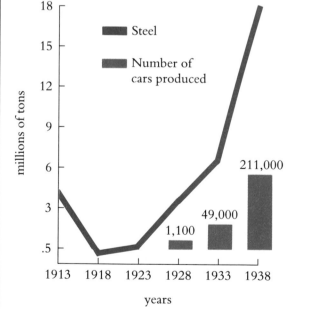

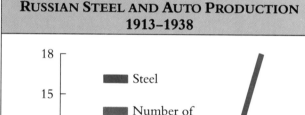

Data source: B. R. Mitchell, *European Historical Statistics 1750–1975*.

Soviet farmers drive rented tractors back to their collective farm from the Betjetzk Machine and Tractor Station in Moscow Province. These tractors were designed in the United States but manufactured in the Soviet Union, which depended on foreign technology to advance its own industries during the 1930s.

Wealthy peasants, called *kulaks*, reacted strongly to Stalin's order in 1929 to give up their land to the collective farms. Rather than submit, the kulaks destroyed livestock and food crops, which resulted in a temporary food shortage. Stalin, in retaliation, had millions of kulaks killed or exiled.

By 1939, in spite of farmers' resistance, approximately 95 percent of Soviet farms had become part of a larger collective farm. These farms could grow food more efficiently than the smaller farms because scarce tractors and technical advice could be shared.

Results of the plans. Although the First Five-Year Plan did not achieve all its goals, the results were impressive. Building on its success, the Second Five-Year Plan was instituted in 1933. By the end of this plan in 1938, the Soviet Union had become a major industrial power, ranking behind only the United States and Germany in overall industrial production. In 1936, the Soviet Union produced 16 times more electricity, 3 times more iron and oil, and 4 times more steel than it had in 1913.

The Soviet Union's achievements occurred at a time when the rest of the world was experiencing the worst economic depression in history. Many Westerners who traveled to the Soviet Union in the 1930s marveled at what the country had accomplished. In addition to creating industrial growth, the Soviet Union had dramatically raised literacy through free public education and had raised the standard of living for many peasants.

TOTALITARIANISM UNDER STALIN

Although Stalin achieved remarkable success in industrializing the Soviet Union, he carried out his goals through repression, force, and absolute rule. As a result of his use of increasingly totalitarian methods, Stalin moved the Soviet Union farther away from the ideal society envisioned by Marx—the vision that had inspired the Russian Revolution.

Marx had not described his idea of a new society in great detail. He said only that classes would cease to exist, exploitation of workers would end, and people would for the first time in history be able to develop their human potential fully.

Communism did not require totalitarian rule. Marx's idea of communism, in fact, called for what was in many ways the opposite of totalitarianism. Yet Stalin and Communist party leaders effectively combined the idea of communism with the practice of totalitarian rule, making them appear, in the Soviet Union, to be one and the same.

Even though the Soviet Union drifted away from Marx's original vision, the state continued to use the appeal of Marxist ideas to justify its rule. It claimed, for instance, to be building a classless society, when in fact a few leaders had much more power than most Soviet people. Communism became the ***ideology***, or official political philosophy, of the Soviet state. The state promoted communist ideology through education, public posters and broadcasts, and control of art and creative expression.

IDENTIFYING AN ARGUMENT

An argument is an account that presents reasons in support of a claim. The statement "We should be allowed more freedom in school" is only a claim, not an argument. To make an argument of this statement, a student might say, "We are now seniors. The records show we have had a B average ever since we entered this school. Seniors with good grades should be allowed more freedom than other students. So let us have more freedom in school." When you have reasons in support of a claim, you have an argument. Being able to identify an argument is a first step in deciding whether or not you can accept a given claim as valid.

EXPLAINING THE SKILL

As explained on pages 504 and 505 of your text, an argument consists of two basic elements: a claim and reasons that link together to support that claim. These reasons may provide specific facts, rules, or generalizations. An argument may also include unstated reasons or assumptions supporting the claim.

Sometimes an account may consist of more than one argument. When these arguments together support a broader claim, the account is sometimes called a complex argument.

To identify an argument, first identify and define the claim that the author makes. Then search for the various kinds of reasons. Finally, determine how these reasons connect to the claim and to each other.

APPLYING THE SKILL

The following paragraphs are from a 1929 speech by Joseph Stalin. Identify the paragraph that presents an argument.

How are our agricultural units to be enlarged? There are two ways of doing this. There is the *capitalist* way, which is to enlarge the agricultural units by introducing capitalism in agriculture. There is a second way: the *Socialist* way, which is to set up collective farms and state farms . . . .

Can we permit the expropriation of the kulaks [the taking of the kulaks' land] in the regions of solid collectivization? This is a ridiculous question! Earlier we could not expropriate the kulaks. We were pursuing a policy of [merely] restricting the kulaks, and we were unable to launch a determined offensive against them. We were unable to substitute for kulak output the output of the collective farms. But now the situation is different. We are able to carry on a determined offensive against the kulaks, to break their resistance, to eliminate them as a class and substitute for their output the output of the collective farms. Now the masses of peasants are putting solid collectivization into practice. Now the expropriation of the kulaks is an integral part of the development of collective farms. That is why it is ridiculous to discuss the expropriation of the kulaks.

Abridged from Joseph Stalin, "Problems of Agrarian Policy in the USSR." Moscow: Foreign Languages, 1940.

MAKING MEANING

Answer the following questions:

1. What is the main topic of these paragraphs? **(a)** the disadvantages of capitalism, **(b)** the establishment of collective farms, **(c)** the creation of new private farms.

2. The first paragraph's purpose is to **(a)** explain, **(b)** request, **(c)** persuade.

3. The second paragraph is **(a)** one claim supported by reasons, **(b)** a complex argument that includes two related claims and their supporting reasons, **(c)** an explanation of how a collective farm operates.

4. Claims that are supported by reasons are stated in **(a)** paragraph 2, sentences 3 and 6; **(b)** paragraph 1, sentences 1 and 3; **(c)** paragraph 2, sentences 4 and 7.

5. Reasons supporting the same claim are stated in **(a)** paragraph 1, sentences 2 and 3; **(b)** paragraph 2, sentences 4 and 5; **(c)** paragraph 2, sentences 6 and 10.

REVIEWING THE SKILL

6. What is an argument?

7. What is the difference between an argument and an explanation?

Marc Chagall's 1924 painting *I and the Village* recalls his rural childhood. It reflects a modern trend in Russian art, which the government tolerated during the NEP but suppressed under Stalin.

THE PURGES

Among the most dramatic examples of Stalin's totalitarian rule were the series of trials and murders called purges that occurred between 1935 and 1939. *Purge* means "to remove," and Stalin's purges were designed to remove from the Communist party and Soviet society anyone who opposed his control.

Stalin's secret police, the NKVD, searched out any sign of disagreement or dissent at all levels of society. Those who seemed critical of Stalin were accused of treason, sabotage, or conspiracy. Once arrested by the NKVD, a person was either deported, imprisoned, or executed. Even top-ranking party officials and military leaders were purged in this way.

Some important figures were tried in public in what were called "show trials," where the accused were forced to "confess" to their crimes through psychological torture. Although exact figures are not known, it is estimated that during the purges, about 8 to 10 million people were jailed, exiled, sent to labor camps, or killed. The purges helped Stalin increase his power over Soviet society.

SECTION REVIEW

1. Define *totalitarianism*, *mass communication*, and *ideology*.

2. Describe Lenin's New Economic Policy and its goals.

3. What did Stalin hope to accomplish with his five-year plans?

4. Compare Marx's idea of communist society with Communist party rule under Stalin.

5. Why did Stalin begin the purges of the late 1930s?

Analysis. How was Stalin similar to the Russian czars? How was he different?

30-2
FASCISM IN ITALY

READ TO FIND OUT

—what the term *fascism* means.
—how the Fascists changed their platform to gain broader support.
—what Fascists believed about the role of the state in a society.
—how Mussolini reorganized the economy and government in Italy.

Although the Italians had helped the Allies to victory in World War I, the postwar era found Italy feeling beaten rather than victorious. The treaties ending World War I awarded Italy little of the territory its people had expected in return for their war effort. Instead, Italians were burdened with a tremendous war debt. Millions of soldiers returned home to face unemployment, while inflation made prices soar. A series of weak governments seemed helpless in the face of these problems.

In this postwar environment, many people began to desire a strong government that would bring law and order, and rekindle nationalist pride. Soon Benito Mussolini, who promised such a government, emerged as a new leader. Mussolini's plan for ruling Italy led to a new

In October 1932, Mussolini addressed 25,000 followers on the tenth anniversary of the Fascists' "March on Rome." Between 1922 and 1932, Mussolini established a dictatorship.

form of totalitarianism called *fascism*, in which one political party assumes supreme power through the rule of a nationalist dictator.

THE RISE OF MUSSOLINI

Benito Mussolini, born in 1883, was the son of a blacksmith and a school teacher. He became a journalist and edited *Avanti!*, a socialist newspaper. After several years as a socialist, Mussolini left the party, joined the army, and became an extreme nationalist.

After the war, Mussolini developed a political philosophy he called fascism, after the Latin word *fasces*, the ax surrounded by a bundle of sticks that was the symbol of authority in the ancient Roman Empire. Fascism, which called for the unity of all social classes under a strong state, became the guiding philosophy of a movement agitating for political change.

The first platform of the fascist movement, drafted in 1919 by Mussolini, was similar to that of the socialists, who had strong support from discontented workers. Even though this platform advocated voting rights for all men, an eight-hour workday, and heavy taxes on the rich, it did not draw as much support as had been hoped and was soon modified.

In the early 1920s, in part to appeal to broader segments of Italian society, Mussolini and the Fascists changed many of their earlier positions. They became strong supporters of the Roman Catholic Church, capitalism, and the monarch. They began to emphasize anti-communism and to stand for law and order and the protection of private property. The movement drew increased support from industrialists and members of the middle class, who feared communist-inspired unrest. Mussolini also promised jobs to the unemployed.

In 1921, the Fascist party was officially recognized. Mussolini's followers—called Black Shirts, for the way they dressed—began to break up socialist meetings, burn down union halls, and torture and kill Communist party members. The Italian king and parliament, who wanted the communist influence suppressed, did little to stop the Fascists.

In October 1922, about 50,000 Fascists marched into Rome from all directions, claiming they were preventing a communist revolution. The Italian parliament wanted to proclaim martial law, or the suspension of normal laws due to war, but King Victor Emmanuel III refused. When the prime minister resigned in protest, the king made Mussolini the new prime minister. Mussolini formed a new government, and the Italian parliament, expecting government as usual, gave the Fascist party full power for a year. Unlike the Communists in the Soviet Union, the Fascists had risen to power instead of overthrowing the existing government through revolution.

THE CREATION OF A TOTALITARIAN STATE

After a 1924 election in which Fascists won a majority of the seats, Mussolini moved to gain complete control of Italy and create a totalitarian government. He abolished the Italian cabinet and all opposition parties, and limited voting rights. Those allowed to vote had to choose from a list of candidates supplied by the Fascist party. Italians began to call Mussolini *Il Duce* (EEL DOO-chay), which in Italian means "the leader."

Although the beliefs and goals of fascism had changed drastically since Mussolini founded the movement in 1919, one element of the original philosophy still remained—the belief in a strong state. This belief became the most important element in fascist doctrine. "Nothing above the state, nothing outside the state, nothing against the state," declared Mussolini.

Like communist rule in Russia, Italian fascism gave supreme power to the state, and the only political party allowed made up the government. The philosophies upon which these two totalitarian systems were based, however, had many differences. Whereas the philosophy of communism did not require totalitarian rule, fascism was based on the belief in a strong state. Fascism urged Italians to concentrate on their own nation, while Marxist communism ignored national borders and was meant to inspire a worldwide movement.

The two philosophies also differed strongly in what they advocated for the economy. Communism opposed capitalism and promised a classless society. Fascism, on the other hand, supported capitalism and private ownership of factories and land—the means of production. Fascism promised economic security by maintaining the existing class structure.

POLITICAL AND ECONOMIC REORGANIZATION

When the Fascists came to power, the Italian economy was in poor condition. Inflation, unemployment, and government debt had created great hardships for most Italians. The Fascists believed that in order to revitalize the economy, a new system of political representation had to be created. The old system of representation by geographic region, they argued, was outdated in an industrial society.

In place of geographic representation, the Fascists instituted representation based on economic activity. Each major industry was organized into a syndicate, or corporation. Each of the 22 syndicates included workers, labor unions, and employers in a particular industry such as agriculture or transportation, as well as representatives from the government. These syndicates then sent representatives to a legislature in Rome that set wage and production policies. The syndicates, therefore, took the place of political parties.

In theory, this system was democratic. Under Mussolini, however, the central government controlled the syndicates' decisions and policies. Employers were favored over workers, and no opposition was allowed.

As a result of Mussolini's reorganization, economic conditions improved somewhat in Italy in the late 1920s, as they did all over Europe. The syndicate system had little success, however, in solving Italy's troubles during the depression of the 1930s. The government did, however, begin a series of public works projects, such as the building of schools and libraries. Mussolini also declared a "battle of wheat" to increase food production. Overall, however, Italian peasants and workers remained poor.

Although Italians did not get the economic security promised them in return for the individual freedoms they gave up, they did seem to feel that someone had taken charge of their nation. As the depression wore on after 1935, Mussolini turned to foreign military adventures in an effort to keep the people's hope alive.

1. Define *fascism*.

2. How did Mussolini's political and economic ideas change by the early 1920s?

3. Describe the most important element in Fascist doctrine.

4. How did Mussolini organize his government and the Italian economy?

Analysis. Why were the Fascists able to achieve such success in Italy after World War I?

30–3
NAZI GERMANY

READ TO FIND OUT

—why the Weimar government was unpopular.
—what major beliefs guided Hitler's actions.
—how Hitler gained control of Germany.
—how persecution of such minorities as Jews spread during Hitler's rule.

Germany after World War I suffered much the same unrest and confusion as did Italy. However, the Germans bore the additional burden of having lost the war. In 1920, the Treaty of Versailles changed German borders and government, forbade the nation to rearm, and ordered it to pay reparations to the Allies. The Germans found the treaty humiliating and deeply unfair.

During the 1920s, as inflation, hunger, and unemployment increased, Germans longed for the days when their nation had been a world power with a strong army. Nationalism grew in strength while confidence in the postwar government decreased. Many Germans were ready to listen to radical new ideas and leaders who promised to restore Germany's greatness.

By the 1930s, Germany was controlled by a fascist government much like that in Italy. As fascism spread beyond Italy, the term came to be associated not simply with the policies of one particular political party, but rather with

any government ruled by a dictator who stresses nationalism and who enforces strong government control over individuals and the economy.

DISCONTENT IN THE WEIMAR REPUBLIC

Germany's new democratic government, the Weimar Republic, never achieved widespread popularity or support. Although officials of the Weimar Republic did not negotiate the Treaty of Versailles, they signed it, and Germans came to associate the harsh terms of the treaty with the new government.

By 1923, Germans also associated the Weimar Republic with the soaring inflation that wiped out their savings and made salaries and pensions almost worthless. German socialist parties began to gain some political power, while military leaders and rich industrialists remained suspicious of the new democratic government. The German middle class—shop owners, office workers, artisans—grew increasingly fearful of socialists and communists. They worried that the inexperienced Weimar government could neither stop the growth of these parties nor restore order to Germany's chaotic economy.

HITLER AND THE NAZI PARTY

Along with many other new political parties, the National Socialist German Workers' party appeared in Germany after World War I. It was also called the Nazi party, a short name taken from the German pronunciation of the first two syllables of *National*. The Nazis were both anticommunist and ardently nationalistic. In 1921, party membership stood at only 6,000. That year Adolf Hitler became the party's leader.

Adolf Hitler was born in Austria in 1889, the son of a customs officer. A poor student and rebellious youth, he yearned to study art. At 19, he moved to Vienna, but he failed the entrance examination to the Art Academy there. For a few years he made a living doing odd jobs, but he did not like the life in Vienna. He disapproved of almost everyone—the aristocracy, capitalists, Marxists, and above all, Jews, many of whom had risen to influential positions in the city.

Considering himself a "true German," Hitler moved to Munich in 1913. When World War I

Hitler (center) attracts a crowd as he walks down the street with military leaders in Munich, Germany. Carefully planned public appearances such as this one helped Hitler gain support. Local business owners provided strong financial backing for the Nazi party.

broke out, he joined the German army. He reached the rank of corporal during the war and was decorated for bravery. After the war, he returned to Munich and with a few other soldiers founded the party which in 1920 became the Nazi party.

The Nazi party grew by appealing to Germans who disagreed with the Weimar government. In 1923, attempting to imitate the "March on Rome" by Mussolini's Fascist Black Shirts, Hitler and Nazi followers—called Brown Shirts—tried to start a revolution in Munich. This attempt to overthrow the government was quickly ended by the police. Hitler was arrested, tried for his part in the uprising, and served one year of a five-year prison sentence.

While in jail, Hitler wrote *Mein Kampf*, or "My Struggle," an account of his hatred for democracy, communism, and Jews. In it, he also described his belief that the German people were superior and that Germany needed a strong government to bring the nation back to its rightful place in the world.

When Hitler was released from prison in 1924, he found that the Nazi party had lost what little strength it had. During the next four years, he struggled to rebuild the party, while Germans regained some confidence in the government of the Weimar Republic.

HITLER'S RISE TO POWER

In 1929, when depression hit the United States and Europe, foreign loans to Germany dried up. Without financial aid, building and manufacturing ground to a halt. By 1932, about one third of Germany's work force—6 million people—was unemployed.

Votes for political parties promising radical solutions to Germany's problems increased rapidly. By 1932, the Communists held 100 seats in the Reichstag, the lower house of the German parliament. Votes for the Nazi party grew even more dramatically. In 1932, the Nazis won 196 seats in the Reichstag—more than any single party. The Nazis had suddenly become the most powerful political force in Germany.

Nazi power reflected the growing appeal of the party's doctrines to discontented German voters. Hitler was also a powerful and hypnotic speaker whose carefully staged rallies appealed to the emotions of his audience.

What Germany needed, Hitler said, was a new form of true democracy under a strong leader. Hitler blamed factors outside German control such as the Treaty of Versailles and communism for Germany's problems. Above all, he appealed to those he considered true Germans, whom he called Aryans, to return to traditions such as the small shop, the peasant farm, classic styles of dress, and women staying home to care for the family.

Hitler as chancellor. The seats the Nazis held in the Reichstag in 1932 were enough to halt the workings of the German parliament. The Nazis would not support any government that did not include Hitler as chancellor. Another party, the Nationalists, also worked to make Hitler chancellor. They assumed that once Hitler was in office, the Nazis would form a coalition government with the Nationalists.

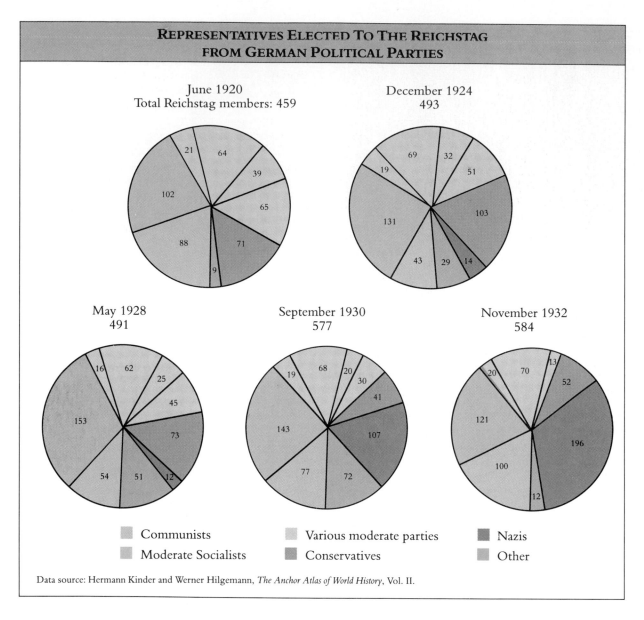

REPRESENTATIVES ELECTED TO THE REICHSTAG FROM GERMAN POLITICAL PARTIES

June 1920
Total Reichstag members: 459

December 1924
493

May 1928
491

September 1930
577

November 1932
584

- Communists
- Moderate Socialists
- Various moderate parties
- Conservatives
- Nazis
- Other

Data source: Hermann Kinder and Werner Hilgemann, *The Anchor Atlas of World History*, Vol. II.

In January 1933, Hitler was named chancellor by Paul von Hindenburg, the president of the republic. The Nazis and Nationalists shared power within the cabinet. Like Mussolini, however, Hitler had no intention of sharing power, and thus called for another election.

Shortly before election day, the Reichstag building caught fire. The incident gave Hitler an excuse to create an atmosphere of crisis. Without proof, the Nazis blamed the Communists for setting the fire. Hitler censored the press and banned public meetings. Brown Shirts harassed the voters. The Nazis won only 44 percent of the vote, but with the National-

ists, the Nazi party held a slight majority. Declaring a national state of emergency, Hitler kept the Communists out of the Reichstag and had that body give him full powers. Totalitarian dictatorship had come to Germany.

THE THIRD REICH

According to Hitler's view of history, in the past there had been two great German empires, or reichs. The first was the Holy Roman Empire and the second was Germany under the rule of the kaisers, from 1871 to 1918. Hitler announced that the coming to power of the Nazis

Jewish physicist Albert Einstein found personal and political liberty in the United States after leaving Nazi Germany. Successful American research on the atomic bomb owed much to Einstein.

Military buildup. Hitler's goals for the Third Reich included returning Germany to the status of a great power. In order to realize this goal, he began an extensive program of rearmament and military expansion. In secret, Germany began to manufacture arms and ammunition, an illegal act under the Treaty of Versailles. The German armed forces also grew larger.

Hitler's military buildup helped the German economy recover by fueling industrial growth and creating jobs. A larger military also prepared Germany for expansion. Hitler believed Germany needed more "living space," a goal he called *lebensraum* (LAY-buhns-ROWM). He promoted the Nazi slogan, "Today Germany, tomorrow the world." By the mid-1930s, Hitler was ready to bring new territory under Nazi rule.

PERSECUTION OF JEWS

As dictator of Germany, Hitler persecuted many different groups of people, such as intellectuals, Communists, and gypsies. He reserved a special hatred, however, for Jews, whom he considered to be an "inferior race."

Jews had long been discriminated against in Europe. In Germany, anti-Semitism, or hatred

Hitler singled out Jews for public abuse by making them wear yellow Star of David badges. With only a few belongings, this family leaves Germany to escape persecution.

marked the beginning of the Third Reich, an empire he claimed would last 1,000 years.

Hitler called himself "The Leader," or *Der Führer* in German. He was both head of state and leader of the nation's only political party. Within a year of taking office as chancellor, Hitler abolished the constitution of the Weimar Republic. He also saw to it that all information that went out through newspapers, magazines, radio, and movies was carefully controlled. Hitler used such mass media to spread propaganda—information designed to convince people to support a particular ideology or doctrine by appealing to their emotions.

To keep order and maintain control, Hitler relied on Nazi "storm troopers," a special group of Brown Shirts who used violence and intimidation to suppress dissent. As many as 500,000 members of opposition parties were imprisoned in concentration camps, prisons to which all those considered enemies of the reich were sent.

NAZI PROPAGANDA

"The intelligence of the masses is small," wrote Adolf Hitler. "Their forgetfulness is great. They must be told the same thing a thousand times." With this belief in mind, Hitler created a propaganda program well known for its effectiveness. Repeating phrases that stirred feelings of national pride, and gaining control of radio, movies, and newspapers, Hitler convinced most Germans to support the Nazi regime.

Hitler's success, however, was not due to what he considered the small intelligence of Germans, but to the power of Nazi propaganda. Forms of propaganda occur today in all nations, often used when organizations, governments, or businesses wish to persuade people to act or believe in a certain way. Advertising, for instance, is considered propaganda by many experts. Hitler's propaganda, however, went beyond persuasion to include deliberate lying, distortion, and concealment.

Propaganda was very important to Hitler in his rise to power. Following Germany's defeat in World War I, the morale of the German people was very low. Taking advantage of this situation, Hitler told the people that they had lost the war because of traitors in the government. He repeated this charge so often people believed him.

After Hitler became head of the government, he named Joseph Goebbels (GUB-uhlz), one of his faithful followers, minister of propaganda and enlightenment. Under Goebbels's direction, posters, movies, radio programs, and newspapers constantly told the Germans they were a master race and that other races, such as Jews of German birth, were inferior.

In addition to controlling the media, the Nazis staged giant party rallies. In the historic city of Nuremberg, they built a vast arena where tens of thousands of party members gathered to hear Hitler speak. There, torchlight parades, brilliant fireworks, and thousands of flags and banners with the swastika, the Nazi symbol, inspired people to rally behind Hitler. Nazi propaganda was so successful that Hitler was able to unite much of the German nation behind him.

of Jews, had grown during the late 1800s, when Jews began to enter the mainstream of economic and professional life. Anti-Semites blamed Jews for all the evils in German society, especially the economic disasters of inflation and depression.

Hitler played on the hatred many Germans already had for Jews, portraying them as national enemies. He insisted that they could never be truly German. The Nuremberg laws of 1935 denied German citizenship to Jews, took away their jobs, and forbade them to marry non-Jews. Jews were also required to wear a yellow Star of David in public. Mobs beat and killed Jews, destroyed their places of worship, looted their shops, and wrecked their homes.

Thousands of Jews fled Germany during the 1930s. Prominent among them were many scientists and mathematicians, such as Albert Einstein, who emigrated to the United States. Many other Jews, however, remained trapped in Germany because most nations, including the United States, would not ease their restrictive immigration policies and accepted only some of the refugees.

SECTION REVIEW

1. Why did many Germans lack confidence in the Weimar government?

2. Describe four of the most important beliefs that Hitler preached.

3. How did Hitler gain control of Germany?

4. What were the Nuremberg laws?

Analysis. Find evidence in the section to support the following conclusion: The Weimar government would probably have fallen during the 1930s, even if Hitler had not taken power.

Data Search. Explain how the unemployment chart on page 833 reflects Germany's economic recovery under Hitler.

30–4
MILITARISM IN JAPAN

READ TO FIND OUT

—what democratic practices were introduced in Japan after World War I.
—how the structure of Japanese government enabled military influence to grow.
—how economic problems further increased military influence.
—how the seizure of Manchuria led to military control of the government.

During the reign of the Meiji emperor from 1868 to 1912, Japan was being transformed from a feudal farming society into a modern industrial state. Japan then sided with the Allies during World War I, hoping to win territory in China that was held by Germany. By the end of the war, Japan had become the most powerful nation in East Asia. Japanese delegates participated in the peace treaty negotiations along with Great Britain, France, Italy, and the United States. In addition, Japan joined the League of Nations.

Postwar developments in Japan, however, followed a somewhat similar course to those in Germany and Italy. Once again a fragile democratic system subject to economic and political stress gave way to authoritarian, militarist forces.

LIBERAL DEMOCRACY IN THE 1920s

The postwar period saw a new liberal spirit in Japan. Political changes introduced before the war during the Meiji Restoration seemed to be leading toward a broader democracy. Most Japanese had become literate under new education programs. New technologies led to the greatly increased spread of information through radio, movies, and high-circulation newspapers and magazines. Increasingly, the Japanese saw, heard, and read about the political ideas and fashions of the West. The Japanese also formed new political parties—democratic, socialist, communist, and anarchist—modeled on those of the West.

In 1918, Hara Kei (hah-rah kī) became prime minister. He was the first Japanese head of government who did not come from the military or the noble class, a sign that democracy was advancing in Japan. In 1925, most men received the right to vote, increasing Japan's voting population from 3.5 million to 14 million.

Young people in cities began to adopt Western styles of dress and music. Baseball became popular, as did movies. More important, young Japanese began to resist centuries-old traditions of family authority, such as marriages arranged by their parents.

Even Japan's foreign relations in the early 1920s seemed marked by a spirit of liberal, international cooperation. This attitude was demonstrated by Japan's participation in the Washington Naval Conference and by its respect for the "Open Door" policy that the conference supported in China. Japan also agreed to withdraw its troops from China's Shantung province.

SIGNS OF REACTION

Despite the signs of liberal change in the 1920s, many Japanese were not content with the new shape their nation was taking. Industrialization and Western influence had produced rising expectations for improved standards of living, yet few Japanese felt that the changes of the past few decades had benefited them directly. Discontent among workers, youths, and intellectuals increased during the 1920s, fueling tensions between those who wanted broader social changes and those who embraced traditional ways.

Many Japanese leaders reacted to this unrest with alarm. They believed social conflict within Japan would weaken the country and threaten its security.

Gradually, Japan began to turn away from liberal reform. Leaders emphasized tradition as a source of national strength. They suppressed protest by promoting traditional Japanese respect for authority and strengthening feelings of nationalism.

THE RISE OF MILITARISM

As the Japanese government became more conservative, the military gained increased influence over the country and its civilian rulers.

Japan moved toward a policy of militarism, and the liberalism of the early 1920s gave way to increasingly authoritarian rule.

The structure of Japanese government, with its roots in tradition, helped encourage military influence. Japanese government was set up as an oligarchy, in which power was in practice shared by an emperor, his unelected advisors, a prime minister, and military leaders.

Among these military leaders were cabinet ministers for the army and the navy, who could consult with the emperor directly rather than reporting to the prime minister. This practice, in some cases, let the military set government policy without the knowledge or approval of the prime minister.

Members of the government had close ties to the *zaibatsu*—the huge corporations that ran most of Japan's industry and business. Zaibatsu families were often active in politics and regularly contributed large sums to political leaders. In the 1930s, these business leaders also generally agreed with the policies of military leaders and often worked to increase the power of the latter.

Economic problems in the late 1920s also brought the country closer to military rule. A financial panic gripped the nation in 1927, followed by the depression in 1929. By 1930, one million Japanese were out of work. Many of them returned to their home villages, only to face famine as crops failed. Many Japanese threw their support behind the military because military leaders made clear their sympathy with suffering peasants and because military ideas for territorial expansion seemed to offer a solution to economic problems.

Changes in foreign policy. While military leaders gained more power within Japan, increasing discrimination against Asians by Western nations in the 1920s fed the fires of militarism and turned the Japanese away from international cooperation. For instance, the United States Congress had passed the Immigration Act of 1924, which forbade Japanese immigration to the United States. After the worldwide depression began in 1929, the Japanese lost Western markets for silk and other goods, as many nations imposed high tariffs to protect their own industries.

In the face of such policies, the Japanese felt less obligation to cooperate internationally. Expansionist and militarist groups inside and outside of government began to have stronger voices. If the Japanese could not emigrate and if other nations' tariffs limited Japanese export income, they said, then the nation had only one alternative: territorial expansion.

THE SEIZURE OF MANCHURIA

Those in Japan who favored territorial expansion looked first to Manchuria, a province of northern China. Manchuria had mineral resources Japan lacked, as well as rich farm land and new markets for Japanese products.

In September 1931, a group of Japanese officers stationed in a part of Manchuria under lease to Japan blew up a section of railroad near the city of Mukden, then blamed the act on troops of the Chinese warlord who controlled the area. Using this "Mukden Incident" as an excuse, the Japanese officers directed their soldiers to attack the warlord's army and "restore order." Japanese forces quickly took over much of Manchuria.

When the League of Nations condemned Japan's seizure of Manchuria, Japan withdrew from the organization. Within Japan, extreme nationalists began to call moderate leaders who disapproved of the army's action "enemies of the state." In 1932, these nationalists began a campaign of terror at home. Moderate political and business leaders were wounded or killed. Press censorship was imposed. Socialists and Communists were suppressed.

Political unrest and violence at home caused even more Japanese to support strong military rule, while protests from other countries increased nationalist fervor. Military leaders quickly gained effective control over the government, setting up an authoritarian rule. Although the government was neither fascist nor fully totalitarian, its leaders expected citizens to commit themselves to the state.

Meanwhile, expansionism seemed to pay off economically. The production of arms for military expansion and an increase in production of export materials helped bring Japan out of the depression and put people back to work.

To many Japanese, nationalism took on an almost spiritual quality. Radical nationalists believed the use of force was necessary to return Japan to its former glory. "Heaven," they said, had "chosen Japan as champion of the East."

Japanese soldiers pause for a moment during the fighting at Mukden in 1931. After taking Manchuria, the Japanese used its coal and iron resources to support Japan's industrialization.

SECTION REVIEW

1. What signs of liberal reforms could be found in Japanese society after World War I?

2. How did the structure of Japanese government encourage military influence?

3. How did economic crises strengthen the power and influence of the military?

4. Explain the effects of the seizure of Manchuria on Japanese politics.

Evaluation. How could the liberal democratic trends of the 1920s have been preserved in Japan? What events or factors would have had to be different?

HISTORY IN FOCUS

During the 1920s and 1930s, forms of totalitarian rule arose in four separate nations with very different histories, cultures, and circumstances. The root causes of totalitarian rule, therefore, seem to lie not in these individual nations, but in worldwide forces. Industrialized nations all over the globe were subject to the same forces of social conflict, economic crisis, and political instability. Democracy in nations such as the United States and Great Britain survived only because of the strength of their democratic traditions.

Where totalitarianism did take root, it was not brought on single-handedly by unusually strong, evil leaders, nor by the characteristics of a particular culture or people. The complete domination of individuals by powerful states would not have been possible without the development of mass communications technology, without the international rivalry caused by imperialist expansion, and without the social conflict caused by both industrialization and rapid social change.

Totalitarian rule arose in nations most dissatisfied with the results of World War I, and where governments were least successful in dealing with the pressures and strains that followed the war. In Germany, Italy, Russia, and Japan, those who preached the destruction of their nations' unsuccessful governments rose to power. These leaders' methods of dealing with internal and global crises gained them support; however, they would bring the world to the point of violent confrontation once again.

SUMMARY

- In the years after World War I, three nations developed totalitarian governments, and Japan moved in a similar direction. These regimes put the interests of the state ahead of the rights of individuals. The governments eliminated or completely controlled any political opposition and watched over almost all aspects of the daily lives of their citizens.

- In the Soviet Union, totalitarianism grew under the rule of Joseph Stalin, who replaced Lenin as leader of the Communist party. The Soviet Union, with its planned economy, became a major industrial power. Stalin's purges of suspected opponents terrified the nation and helped him keep all power firmly in his hands.

- In Italy and Germany, totalitarian regimes arose from the economic instability and political unrest that followed the war. Benito Mussolini's Fascist rule promised a return to the glories of the Roman Empire. Adolf Hitler put Germans back to work by rebuilding Germany's military forces and made plans to extend Germany's borders. He used storm troopers and concentration camps to crush any opposition.

- In Japan, a weak democratic government that experimented with liberalism in the 1920s gave way, in the face of economic hardship in the 1930s, to a military government. Although full totalitarianism did not develop in Japan, authoritarian rule, nationalism, and military expansion made this Asian nation similar to Germany and Italy.

VOCABULARY REVIEW

Match each numbered vocabulary term with the lettered word or phrase most closely related to it. Then explain how the items in each pair are related.

1. totalitarianism
2. mass communication
3. ideology
4. fascism

(a) state control
(b) Nazi
(c) propaganda
(d) Marxism

CHAPTER REVIEW

1. (a) How did Lenin alter economic policies after 1921? (b) What changes did Stalin make in the Soviet economy?

2. (a) What major changes were made in Russian society between 1913 and 1936? (b) Compare the scope of these changes to those in Italy and Germany. (c) How did the method by which the Communist party came to power differ from the way fascist rule was established in Italy and Germany?

3. (a) How did Stalin and Trotsky differ in their attitudes regarding the extension of communist revolution to other nations? (b) How did Hitler and Mussolini differ in their plans to extend fascist rule?

4. (a) What effects did postwar economic conditions have on Italy? (b) How did these effects compare to the effects on Germany? (c) What effect did the postwar economic conditions have on Japan?

5. (a) How did Hitler use anti-Jewish feeling in his attempt to gain political power? (b) What anti-Jewish measures did he take as ruler of Germany?

6. (a) Compare Nazi ideology with Communist ideology. (b) Which society came closer to accomplishing the goals of its ideology—Nazi Germany or the Soviet Union? Explain.

7. (a) Compare the rise to power of Hitler and Mussolini. (b) Compare the ways in which the two leaders established totalitarian rule in their nations.

8. (a) How did the zaibatsu influence government in postwar Japan? (b) Why did the trend toward liberalism there die out? (c) How did Japan's military come to play a growing role in government affairs?

9. (a) Why did some Japanese favor a policy of expansion in Asia? (b) What steps did Japan take to realize this policy?

10. (a) What were the common features of totalitarian rule in Germany, Italy, and the Soviet Union? (b) Compare the Japanese government of the 1930s with the governments of Nazi Germany, Fascist Italy, and the Soviet Union.

THINKING CRITICALLY: ACTIVITIES

1. Write a brief essay in which you agree or disagree with the following statement: The Soviet Union would not have developed into a totalitarian state if Stalin had not won control of the Communist party.

2. Make parallel timelines covering the years 1919 to 1939 for the Soviet Union, Italy, Germany, and Japan. On these timelines chart events indicating the growth of totalitarianism in each of these nations.

APPLYING SOCIAL STUDIES SKILLS

Analyzing primary sources. The following primary sources are from Nazi Germany during the 1930s. The first is a kindergarten recitation that students said each day before lunch.

> Führer, my Führer, bequeathed to me by God.
> Protect and preserve me as long as I live!
> You have rescued Germany from deep despair.
> I thank you for my daily bread.
> Abide long with me.
> Forsake me not.
> Führer, my Führer, my faith and my light.
> Heil, my Führer.

German schoolchildren sang the following song to celebrate Hitler's fiftieth birthday.

> Adolf Hitler is our savior, our hero.
> He is the noblest being in the whole wide world.
> For Hitler we live.
> For Hitler we die.
> Our Hitler is our Lord,
> Who rules a brave New World.

From James D. Forman, *Nazism*. New York: Franklin Watts, 1978.

1. Whom were the children addressing in the kindergarten recitation?

2. For what were the children giving thanks in the kindergarten recitation?

3. How is Hitler portrayed in the song?

4. In what ways is the kindergarten recitation similar to the song?

5. What do the song and the recitation indicate about the role of schools in Nazi Germany?

APPLYING THINKING SKILLS

Identifying an argument. Below is an excerpt from an article written by political scientist Michael Curtis in 1969. Analyze it to determine whether it presents any argument.

> Enormously different purposes [were] sought by the ideologies [of Nazism and Marxism]. To offer brief lists of the major characteristics of the belief systems is to illustrate their different purposes.
>
> Nazism was characterized by nationalism, racism, anti-Semitism, and stress on violence and force. The precapitalist, feudal aspects of Nazism are illustrated by Teutonic imagery; elitist decision-making; and the stress on honor, blood, and soil. The Nazis drew their main strength from the lower-middle class, military desperados, and those who had suffered by greater industrialization. For Hitler, "force was the first law" and war the normal condition. The Nazi movement had no fixed aims. Its strength lay in incessant activity [and] its lust for power and adventure.
>
> Contrasted with these characteristics are the ends of Marxism. It seeks a society based on equality and humanitarianism, the end of political coercion, an industrialized economy, and a higher form of democracy. It is internationalist in nature. Traditional elite groups have no place in such a society. That the Communist regime distorted these high expectations and ended political liberty is not to deny the loftiness of the ideas. There is no inherent insistence on violence in the Communist system. In Communist systems, violence is an incidental factor, a means to achieve a desired end.

Abridged from Michael Curtis, "Retreat from Totalitarianism," in Carl J. Friedrich, ed., *Totalitarianism in Perspective*. New York: Holt, Rinehart, and Winston, 1969.

1. Explain what an argument is.

2. Why is identifying an argument important?

3. What claim does the author of the above excerpt make?

4. What kinds of reasons does the author use? For each kind of reason you identify, give a specific example from the excerpt.

5. In what ways do the reasons support the author's claim?

6. Write a set of directions to an eighth grader explaining how to determine whether an account is an argument.

CHAPTER THIRTY-ONE

THE SECOND WORLD WAR

1935–1946

Liberation. Ben Shahn, United States, 1945.

World War II had its roots in conflicts left unresolved in the Treaty of Versailles that ended World War I. In the 1930s, totalitarian rulers in many nations challenged the treaty's provisions.

Preoccupied with domestic economic difficulties, the Western democracies at first seemed unwilling to thwart German and Italian expansion. At all costs, France and Great Britain wanted to avoid involvement in another bloody European power struggle. They also did not have any desire to interfere in the Asian territorial conflict between China and Japan.

As Italian, German, and Japanese expansion continued, however, the democratic nations refused to stand back and watch smaller nations be gobbled up by militarist regimes. The war which they so desperately tried to avoid was suddenly thrust upon them.

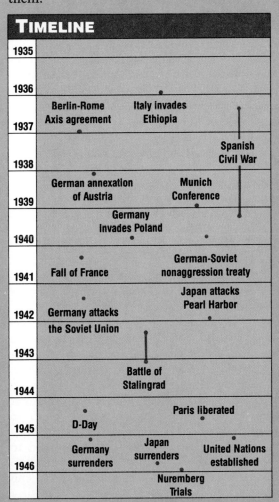

TIMELINE

1935		
1936		
1937	Berlin-Rome Axis agreement	Italy invades Ethiopia
1938		Spanish Civil War
1939	German annexation of Austria	Munich Conference
1940	Germany invades Poland	
1941	Fall of France	German-Soviet nonaggression treaty
1942	Germany attacks the Soviet Union	Japan attacks Pearl Harbor
1943		
1944	Battle of Stalingrad	
1945	D-Day	Paris liberated
1946	Germany surrenders	Japan surrenders / United Nations established / Nuremberg Trials

31–1
THE FAILURE OF PEACE

READ TO FIND OUT

—what the terms *economic sanctions* and *appeasement* mean.
—why the Japanese waged war with China.
—how the League of Nations responded to Italy's invasion of Ethiopia.
—how the Spanish Civil War led European nations to form new alliances.
—why Stalin signed a treaty with Hitler.

The totalitarian nations grew stronger in the 1930s. Under Hitler, Germany began to rearm openly, in direct violation of the 1919 Treaty of Versailles. By 1935 the German army numbered 550,000, even though the treaty allowed no more than 100,000. Great Britain and France protested the illegal increase but made no effort to end it.

The new League of Nations was ineffective in its attempts to keep peace because the league had no way to enforce its authority. Members such as Great Britain hoped that world opinion alone would prevent conflict. However, nations that disagreed with the league's position simply withdrew from the body to pursue their own goals. By the end of the 1930s, the league had lost a quarter of its members.

JAPANESE EXPANSION

The ineffectiveness of the League of Nations was evident in its response to the 1931 Japanese invasion of Manchuria, a region in northeastern China. The league protested but took no other actions, and in 1933 Japan left the organization. Chiang Kai-shek, China's leader, had let Manchuria go with little resistance. His Nationalist party was engaged in a civil war with the Chinese Communists, and he knew his troops were no match for Japanese forces. China's weakness, combined with the lack of condemnation from the rest of the world, encouraged Japan to take even more Chinese territory. Fear of having a

Throughout China, civilians were pressed into service to resist the Japanese invasion. This 1937 photograph shows farmers practicing with spears as part of their Communist army training. In contrast, the Nationalist army had rifles and other modern weapons. Despite the brief collaboration of Communists and Nationalists, and the limited success of the Communists' guerrilla tactics, Chinese troops were no match for Japan's highly trained, well-equipped forces.

Communist government in China gave the Japanese another reason for wanting to bring China under their control.

Japan also had visions of expanding its sphere of influence in Asia by establishing a group of nations with Japan as leader. Under this plan, Japan would expand its empire by using conquered territories as colonies to provide farm products and raw materials for industry.

In July 1937, Chinese troops fired on Japanese troops outside Peking. This act gave Japanese expansionists the excuse they needed for full-scale war. They responded by sending more troops into China, where Chinese forces resisted fiercely.

Many historians consider this conflict to be the beginning of World War II. By November 1938, Japan controlled about a third of China, including all its major cities and most of its railroads. The conflict continued until 1945.

ITALIAN EXPANSION

Meanwhile, in Europe, Benito Mussolini, Italy's premier and head of the nation's Fascist party, began a push for more territory. He wanted Italy to regain the glory of the Roman Empire. To distract his people from economic problems at home and to revive sagging industries, Musso-

lini looked for new lands to colonize. He set his sights on Ethiopia, an independent nation in Africa. When Ethiopian troops clashed with an Italian-backed Somali force on their border in December 1934, Mussolini found a reason to move against Ethiopia. Haile Selassie (hī-LEE seh-LAHS-ee), Ethiopia's emperor, desperately appealed to the League of Nations. The league debated what to do about the problem for almost a year. Meanwhile, Mussolini had prepared his army and in October 1935 invaded Ethiopia.

The League of Nations immediately labeled Italy an aggressor, the first time the league had taken such an action. The league, however, did not take any meaningful action that would have ended the war.

Soon the League of Nations outlined *economic sanctions*—rules forbidding trade with a nation—against Italy. League members were ordered to stop selling arms and certain goods to Italy. Because league members, especially France and Great Britain, feared that stronger measures would provoke Mussolini to go to war in Europe, they voted for limited sanctions.

In March 1936, Ethiopia fell. It seemed to the world that the League of Nations wanted to avoid war in Europe more than it wanted to end war elsewhere.

THE SPANISH CIVIL WAR

In Europe, as forces favoring conflict grew stronger, peace became less certain. Internal struggles for control in Spain soon erupted into a full-scale civil war that eventually involved other nations.

In 1923, General Miguel Primo de Rivera led a revolt and established a military dictatorship that lasted until 1930. Established in 1931, the new government of the Republic of Spain immediately began drastic reforms in many areas. The republican government advocated the separation of church and state. It broke up large estates, gave land to peasants, and began a program of social insurance.

The new government was not strong enough to maintain control, however, and angry peasants burned churches, and workers went on strike. Conservatives, shocked by the sudden changes and afraid that the nation would collapse, formed a fascist party called the Falange (FAY-lanj). The conservative Falange won elections in 1933. The republicans now feared the nation would return to a monarchy or become a fascist state.

By this time, the people of Spain had become divided. On one side, the Falange included the army, monarchists, landowners, and many Roman Catholics. On the republican side, communists, socialists, trade unionists, and some liberals joined together to form the Popular Front party.

The Popular Front won elections held in February 1936, but the Falange rebelled. Led by General Francisco Franco, these rebels, called Nationalists, sought to overthrow the Loyalists—those republicans loyal to the state.

The Nationalists versus the Loyalists. Both Mussolini and Hitler backed the fascist Nationalist rebels by providing soldiers and equipment. When the Soviet Union saw Germany and Italy helping the fascist side—the Nationalists—it sent aid to the Loyalists. The United States, Great Britain, and France stayed out of the conflict for fear of broadening the war, although France had briefly aided the Loyalists at the beginning of the rebellion.

In spite of the official policies of the United States, Britain, and many other Western governments, individual volunteers from Europe, the United States, and Canada went to Spain to fight for the Loyalists. Outnumbered and lacking the technical support that had been given to the Nationalists, the Loyalists slowly lost ground. In March 1939, Francisco Franco took over as dictator of Spain.

With Franco's victory, another totalitarian regime was established in Europe. France now found itself surrounded by fascist governments: Franco's Spain, Hitler's Germany, and Mussolini's Italy.

GERMAN EXPANSION

Hitler had strongly objected to the provision in the Versailles treaty that demilitarized the Rhineland, and he vowed to reassert German military rights in this territory along the Rhine River. When German troops marched into the Rhineland in the spring of 1936, European leaders in the League of Nations could not decide how to respond to this treaty violation. Not believing Hitler wanted war, they thought he was only trying to correct injustices in the Versailles treaty. The British would not risk war to keep Germany from its own territory, and

Two years after sending troops into the Rhineland, Hitler moved into Austria. Many Austrians, like these residents of Salzburg, favored union with Germany and welcomed the German soldiers.

the French did not want to act against Hitler without British help.

The British, however, were very mistaken about Hitler's intentions. The Europe that Hitler planned would be a single political and economic system, ruled from Berlin. One of Hitler's first steps toward this end was to annex Austria, an action forbidden by the Versailles treaty. Political unrest in Austria stirred up by the Austrian Nazi party gave Hitler the excuse he needed to invade. Claiming that German troops were needed to restore order in Austria, in March 1938 Hitler took Austria without firing a shot. Once again other European nations and the United States were shocked, yet they did nothing but send letters of protest. The League of Nations remained silent.

Carving up Czechoslovakia. Hitler's next target was Czechoslovakia, which in the 1930s seemed to be a strong nation. It had mutual defense treaties with France and the Soviet Union,

and had its own army. However, 3 million Germans, including many Nazis, lived in the Sudetenland of western Czechoslovakia, a well-fortified, mountainous area on the German border. In 1938, on the pretext of protecting the "oppressed" Germans in Czechoslovakia, Hitler announced his intention to annex the Sudetenland—by force if necessary. Some of his military advisors warned that such aggression could lead to another world war, but Hitler was more than willing to take the risk.

In an effort to avoid war, British Prime Minister Neville Chamberlain held a series of meetings with Hitler. In September 1938, Hitler's ally Mussolini arranged a meeting in Munich of European leaders, including Chamberlain and French Prime Minister Daladier (DAH-LAH-DYAY). He did not invite a representative from the Soviet Union—perhaps an attempt to isolate it from the West—nor were representatives from Czechoslovakia allowed to attend. Instead, after the meeting, the Czech government

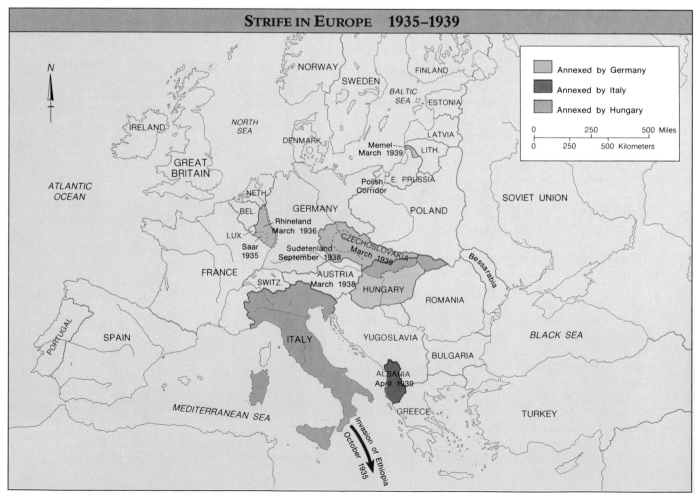

STRIFE IN EUROPE   1935–1939

received maps of the territories that the leaders had agreed should be given to Hitler. Chamberlain went home convinced that by this policy of *appeasement*—giving in to the demands of the aggressor—he had avoided war.

Hitler, however, wasn't satisfied with just the Sudetenland. In early 1939, he broke his promise to Chamberlain and Daladier by sending German troops to annex the rest of Czechoslovakia. France and Britain had once again failed to check German expansion.

Reactions to expansion. Events in Czechoslovakia led the British and French governments to change their policy toward Hitler. It was clear that Hitler was no longer simply protecting the rights of Germans living in other nations. He had caused an entire nation to disappear from the map.

As Hitler gained more power and territory in the 1930s, Stalin began to fear invasion from the west. Stalin's own purges during the 1930s had weakened his Red Army. By the end of the decade, a treaty with his strongest enemy seemed to be the most strategic move. Hitler, on the other hand, sought a treaty so that he could move into Poland without opposition from the Soviets.

In August 1939, Hitler and Stalin signed a nonaggression pact in which the two nations agreed to respect each other's borders. Secret provisions of the pact divided Poland between the Nazis and the Soviets and allowed the Soviets to move into the Baltic states and the Romanian province of Bessarabia. Seeing that Stalin could not be trusted and that Hitler's appetite for territory could not be appeased, Britain and France prepared for war.

SECTION REVIEW

1. Define *economic sanctions* and *appeasement*.

2. Why did Japan go to war with China?

3. What measures did the League of Nations take to condemn Italy's invasion of Ethiopia?

4. Why did the Nationalists win the Spanish Civil War?

5. Describe the provisions of the German-Soviet nonaggression pact.

Analysis. The German-Soviet pact of 1939 shocked other nations. Explain why.

31-2
WAR IN EUROPE

READ TO FIND OUT

—what the terms *blitzkrieg*, *partisans*, *genocide*, and *Holocaust* mean.
—why Hitler invaded Poland.
—why Hitler's plans to invade Great Britain failed.
—what stopped the advance of the German army in the Soviet Union.

For Germans, one of the most unpopular provisions of the Treaty of Versailles had been the creation of a Polish Corridor through Germany. This corridor, which allowed Poland access to the Baltic Sea, also isolated the German region of East Prussia from the rest of the nation. In the same provision, the German port city of Danzig (DAN-sig) had been designated to serve as a port for both Germany and Poland. Hitler demanded that Danzig be returned to Germany and that he be allowed to build a railway and a highway across the Polish Corridor to East Prussia. Hitler also began a propaganda campaign accusing Poles of mistreating Germans in Poland.

ATTACK ON POLAND

On September 1, 1939, German forces invaded Poland. In two days they had taken over the Polish Corridor, and in a week, they had moved to just outside the capital city of Warsaw. The Poles were unprepared for this *blitzkrieg* (BLIHTZ-KREEG), or "lightning war"—so named because it struck rapidly and with great force. German dive bombers struck far behind battle lines, destroying vital materials, disrupting communications, and preparing the way for tanks and infantry. This pattern would be repeated many times by Hitler's war machine.

For a day, the Allied powers—Great Britain and France—which had pledged to stand by Poland, tried in vain to negotiate with Hitler. Then, on September 3, they declared war on Germany. World War II had begun.

DETERMINING THE STRENGTH OF AN ARGUMENT

People often present arguments to support their claims. Since claims are often controversial, it is important to be able to judge the strength of an argument. The first step in making such a judgment is to determine whether a given account presents an argument, a skill you practiced on page 674. If an argument exists, you can then examine it to determine its strength.

EXPLAINING THE SKILL

Determining the strength of an argument involves figuring out if the reasons are relevant to the claim. It also involves deciding whether the reasons are accurate.

As explained in the procedure outlined on pages 514 and 515, you begin by identifying the meaning of the claim or claims presented by the author. Then you can identify the stated and unstated reasons offered in support of each claim. You must also distinguish reasons relevant to a claim from those that are irrelevant, identify any unstated assumptions, and identify any biases evident in the argument. Then you can examine the reasons carefully to judge whether they are accurate and determine how they are connected to a claim.

In addition, you should check for the sufficiency and significance of the reasons. A claim should be supported by more than just one or two reasons, and the reasons should deal with important points.

APPLYING THE SKILL

Examine the following excerpt to determine the strength of any argument presented.

> The war that came to Europe in 1939 came because the only alternative for Hitler, when faced with a country [Poland] that would not succumb to threats, was war. Hitler had promised to restore Germany to its rightful place in the world. Poland had received German territory through the Treaty of Versailles. Therefore, Hitler could not back down from Poland; he had to proceed with his objectives.

Many political commentators since 1939 have claimed that, if nations had acted earlier, there would have been no war. But neither the people nor the governments of [Britain and France] were conditioned to the idea of war. The only way they could accept war after 1918 was for it to be thrust upon them. Arguments over when and where Hitler should have been halted, then, are purely academic. Before September 1, 1939, Hitler had done nothing that any major power considered dangerous enough to warrant [starting] a major European war. Nor was there any existing coalition that could have opposed Hitler's massive forces. For Britain sought to appease Hitler [and] the French feared a repetition of the bloody sacrifices of 1914–1918. Stalin wanted an agreement with Hitler on partitioning Europe, and the United States rejected all responsibility for Europe.

Abridged from Keith Eubank, *The Origins of World War II*. New York: Thomas Y. Crowell, 1969.

MAKING MEANING

1. The author's claims are stated in **(a)** paragraph 1, sentence 2 and paragraph 2, sentence 1; **(b)** paragraph 1, sentence 1 and paragraph 2, sentence 4; **(c)** paragraph 2, sentence 2 and paragraph 2, sentence 8.

2. Two sentences that support one claim are **(a)** paragraph 1, sentences 2 and 3; **(b)** paragraph 1, sentences 1 and 4; **(c)** paragraph 2, sentences 1 and 4.

3. Specific facts are given in **(a)** paragraph 2, sentences 3 and 4; **(b)** paragraph 1, sentences 2 and 3; **(c)** paragraph 1, sentences 1 and 4.

4. The arguments presented in the above account are **(a)** strong, **(b)** weak. Support your opinion.

REVIEWING THE SKILL

5. Identify three characteristics of a strong argument.

6. What is one procedure you could use to determine the strength of an argument?

Stalin's Soviet armies invaded Poland from the east, and by the end of September, it had fallen. As agreed in the German-Soviet pact, Germany and the Soviet Union divided Poland and the Soviets took over Lithuania, Latvia, and Estonia on the Baltic Sea. Stalin, taking further advantage of the pact, invaded Finland in December 1939. Finland, however, held out against the Red Army until March 1940.

BLITZKRIEG IN WESTERN EUROPE

During World War I, the Allies had trapped the Germans in the Baltic Sea, preventing their access to the Atlantic. Hitler, determined not to let this happen again, invaded Denmark and Norway in April 1940, thereby ensuring access to the vital waterway.

On May 10, 1940, Hitler began the conquest of France as 4,000 paratroopers invaded the Netherlands, Belgium, and Luxembourg. Hitler's purpose in invading these nations was to gain access to France through Belgium, and on May 14, 1940, he succeeded.

The invasion cut off thousands of British and French troops in the north of France. These Allied soldiers had gone to Belgium's aid but were no match for German air power. British leaders ordered an evacuation from Dunkirk, a French port on the English Channel.

Hitler used air power to try to destroy the Allied forces trapped in Dunkirk. The Luftwaffe, the German air force, bombed Dunkirk and the English Channel, but Britain's Royal Air Force was able to fight back so the evacuation could proceed.

On June 10, when France was about to fall to Hitler, Mussolini declared war on France and announced that Italy would invade from the south. On June 14 Paris fell, and a week later, on June 22, 1940, France surrendered. German troops occupied the northern half of France, including the Atlantic coast, and a fascist-type regime ruled southern France from the city of Vichy (VISH-ee).

In just six weeks Hitler's troops had smashed five nations in western Europe. In less than a year, beginning with the invasion of Poland in September 1939, German and Soviet forces had overrun more than 10 countries. Spain remained neutral in the conflict but was sympathetic to Germany and Italy, which became known as the Axis powers. This term reflected what Mussolini described as an imaginary "axis" running through Berlin and Rome, around which the fascist world would spin.

THE BATTLE OF BRITAIN

On May 10, 1940, Winston Churchill became British prime minister, replacing Neville Chamberlain, who was responsible for the appeasement policy toward Hitler. After France fell, Hitler offered Churchill peace in return for recognition of Nazi rule in western Europe. Churchill refused. Hitler then made plans to invade Great Britain by sea, but his troops needed time to prepare. Meanwhile, Hitler tried to cripple the Royal Air Force and break the British spirit through daily bombing attacks.

Bombing of merchant ships in the English Channel began in July 1940. In August, what became known as the Battle of Britain started. In this effort to soften up Britain for invasion, German bombers at first aimed at airfields and radar stations. However, the new technology of radar—named for *r*adio *d*etection *a*nd *r*anging—served the British well, allowing them to detect German planes in advance. British fighter planes then met German bombers and fought

The German air raids on Britain caused widespread suffering. Many families were permanently separated when children were sent to live with relatives in the safety of the countryside.

them back before they could unload their bombs.

After German bombs began to fall on London, the British bombed Berlin in retaliation. Furious, Hitler ordered the Luftwaffe to concentrate on London and other cities, rather than airfields. During what the British called "the Blitz," Britain was bombed night and day with firebombs and conventional explosives. Damage to London was heavy, with entire city blocks reduced to rubble. However, people soon learned to protect themselves in underground railway stations, and daily life continued. Although the hardship to British civilians was severe, Churchill's fiery speeches boosted their spirits. During the Blitz, he encouraged the people with these words: "We shall defend our island, whatever the cost may be, . . . we shall never surrender!"

Hitler's change in tactics—bombing cities instead of military bases—saved the Royal Air Force from almost certain destruction. While German bombers were attacking London, British airplane factories rebuilt. Before long, German planes were again being challenged by British fighters. The moment for an invasion was lost. Island Britain had survived.

AMERICAN INVOLVEMENT

The United States watched the bombing of Great Britain with horror. Throughout the late 1930s, the United States had tried to stay neutral and would not ship military supplies to any warring nation. As Axis aggression increased, however, American sentiment began to swing away from isolationism and toward aid to the Allies. The United States began a buildup of military strength. A change in American neutrality laws allowed Britain to buy American military goods and arm itself against the threat of Nazi invasion.

At the end of 1940, President Franklin Roosevelt proposed a lend-lease program under which the United States could sell, lend, or lease military goods to the Allies for any kind of payment the president thought satisfactory. Despite fears that the plan would pull the United States into the war, Congress passed the Lend-Lease Act in March 1941.

As the United States drew closer to entering the war, Roosevelt and Churchill met in August 1941. Out of the conference came both a strong friendship and the Atlantic Charter, a document outlining the democratic principles for which the war was being fought. The charter included statements that neither nation sought to increase its territory and that any territorial changes must be approved by the people in the areas involved.

WAR IN EASTERN EUROPE

In 1940, as France fell and Hitler bombed Great Britain, Stalin invaded the Baltic states and Bessarabia. Seeing the Soviets move westward, Hitler resolved to take the remaining independent nations in eastern Europe. Having these eastern European nations in his power would clear the way for German troops to move on the Soviet Union—one of Hitler's longstanding goals. Early in 1941, he forced Hungary, Romania, and Bulgaria into an alliance dominated by Germany.

Mussolini, who had taken over Albania in 1939, used that nation as a base from which to invade Greece in October 1940. He expected an easy victory, but the Greeks fought hard—with the aid of British planes and troops.

Encouraged by the British presence in Greece, Yugoslavia resisted signing a treaty with Hitler. An angry Hitler invaded Yugoslavia, assisted the Italian war effort in Greece, and ordered a massive bombing and invasion of the island of Crete. German troops, under the leadership of General Erwin Rommel, also aided the Italian invasion of North Africa. Mussolini was trying to capture Egypt, with its important Suez Canal, so that he could take India. By the end of May 1941, most Mediterranean nations were under Axis control.

Attack on the Soviets. In spite of his 1939 treaty with Stalin, on June 22, 1941, Hitler launched a surprise attack on the Soviet Union in one of the largest campaigns of World War II. Nazi troops numbered 3 million, including many from German-occupied lands. Now Stalin's Red Army joined the Allied forces.

At first, the blitzkrieg moved with its usual speed, but the Soviet Union proved difficult to defeat. In a strategy like that used against Napoleon's invasion more than a century earlier, Soviet troops left nothing behind for the Germans. Stalin's "scorched-earth" policy required that Soviets burn crops and kill livestock as they retreated. The Germans were conquering a dead land.

Still, the Nazis moved on. By October, Hitler's forces were near Moscow, the capital. Stalin stayed behind when most of the officials of the Soviet government moved out of Moscow. In stirring speeches, Stalin urged his people not to give up.

When winter brought an end to German advances in the Soviet Union, the Germans still had not taken Moscow. Fierce resistance combined with brutal winter weather ended Hitler's plans for a quick victory over the Soviet Union. Ironically, the 1941 winter was the harshest in a hundred years, just as the 1812 winter that decimated Napoleon's troops had been the coldest of the nineteenth century.

EUROPE UNDER NAZI RULE

Germany used its new territories to support its war effort, taking food, raw materials, oil, and machinery from conquered areas. The Nazis also made use of conquered peoples, who were forced to work for the German war effort or were drafted into the Nazi army. By war's end, about 4 million foreigners were working for Germany.

The Nazis used brutality to maintain control over captured territories. People who resisted Nazi control were tortured, killed, or imprisoned in concentration camps.

Nevertheless, resistance movements grew in the conquered nations. Resistance fighters, called *partisans*, could not form armies and wage open war against the Germans, but they aided the Allies with information and rescue efforts that saved thousands of people from the Nazis. They also sabotaged the German war machine, leading strikes and damaging factories, roads, and railway lines. Even in Germany and Italy, people worked secretly against fascist rule.

THE HOLOCAUST

Hitler convinced many Germans that they, the Aryan German people, were of a master race and were destined to rule all "lesser" peoples. The Nazis considered a number of other peoples—such as Slavs, gypsies, and Jews—to be inferior. Hitler planned to clear parts of the conquered lands of these "inferiors" and open the territory to colonization by Germans. A major effort of Hitler's "New Order" was directed at persecution of the people he consid-

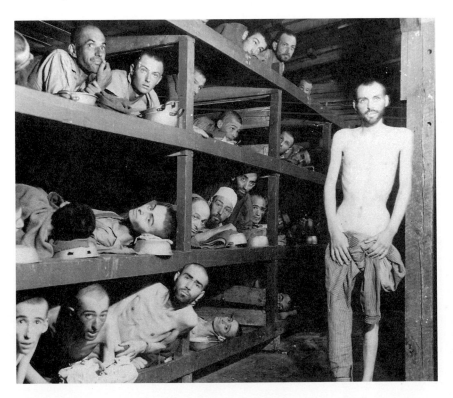

Although millions died in Nazi concentration camps, like this one at Buchenwald in Germany, some people survived to tell the world of the horrors they experienced. Shown in this photograph taken in 1945, the year the war ended, is Elie Wiesel (*middle row, center cubicle, right*). Wiesel was awarded the 1986 Nobel Peace Prize in recognition of his life's work as a chronicler of the Holocaust.

ered inferior. "The final solution to the Jewish problem," as it was called in Germany, was *genocide*—the attempt to destroy an entire ethnic group.

As soon as the Nazis conquered Poland in 1939, they began building concentration camps there with the idea of isolating the people they considered "undesirable." In early 1942, upon approval of a plan to wipe out Europe's Jews, the Nazis built new death camps. In many cases, the prisoners—including small children—were tortured or starved. Among the worst of the camps was Auschwitz (OWSH-vitz), where almost 12,000 prisoners a day were shot or killed by poison gas. Approximately 6 million Jews died at Auschwitz and other camps such as Dachau (DAHK-ow), Buchenwald (BOO-ken-vald), and Treblinka.

The mass killing of the Jews by the Nazis has become known as the *Holocaust*. In addition to Jews, about 6 million others—Slavs, gypsies, and partisans from all nations—died in the camps.

SECTION REVIEW

1. Define *blitzkrieg*, *partisans*, *genocide*, and *Holocaust*.

2. What reasons did Hitler give for invading Poland?

3. What caused Hitler to change his plans to invade Great Britain?

4. What factors helped halt the German invasion of the Soviet Union?

Evaluation. Why was Hitler able to convince many Germans of their alleged superiority?

31–3
WAR IN THE PACIFIC

READ TO FIND OUT

—how Japan planned to expand its empire.
—what the results of Japan's surprise attack on Pearl Harbor were.
—how the Japanese treated their new possessions.

The Japanese had gained territory as a result of World War I, and now, with Europe in flames, they saw another chance to do so. While American and British attention was concentrated on the war in Europe, Japan could move against their possessions throughout the Pacific.

JAPANESE AGGRESSION

For years, much of eastern Asia had been controlled by Western nations. In 1940, however, France and the Netherlands had been defeated

This American battleship, the U.S.S. *Arizona*, was only one of many vessels that were sunk or severely damaged when the Japanese attacked the American naval base at Pearl Harbor in Hawaii. The attack was intended not to start a war with the United States but merely to eliminate the American threat to Japan's aggressive expansionism. When the United States responded swiftly with a declaration of war against Japan, World War II escalated from a battle for dominance in Europe to a global conflict.

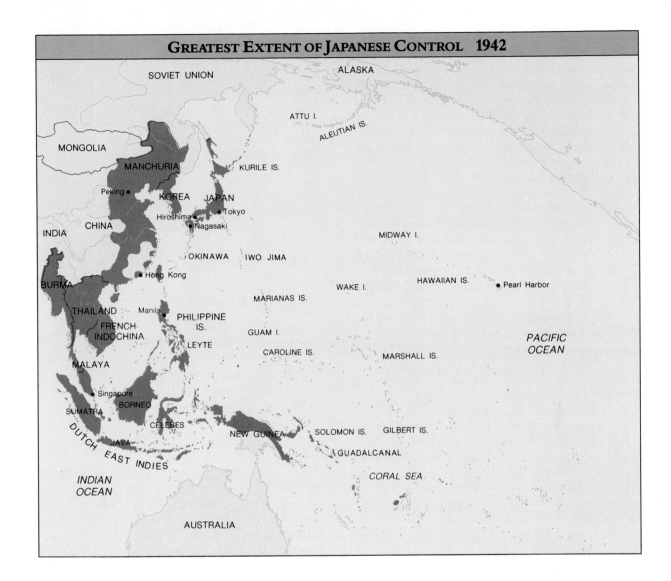

by Germany, and Great Britain was fighting to stay alive. Only the United States stood between Japan and its plans to expand its Asian empire.

Fearing the spread of Soviet communism—the leaders of which had threatened to overthrow governments throughout the world—Japan and Germany had signed an agreement in 1936 to help prevent such takeovers. Italy endorsed the treaty, and Japan formally joined Germany and Italy as an Axis power in September 1940. President Roosevelt responded to the new alliance by ending the export of steel, scrap metal, and oil to Japan.

Relations with the United States and the Allies continued to worsen throughout 1941, as Japan took over new territories from weakened Western powers. The Japanese signed a nonaggression treaty with the Soviet Union in an attempt to prevent Stalin from offering aid to other Asian nations. In October, General Hideki Tojo (HEE-dee-kee TŌ-jō) became prime minister of Japan. Committed to war if necessary to achieve Japanese goals, Tojo also wanted to remove all Western influences in Asia.

PEARL HARBOR

To prevent interference with its expansion into new areas, the Japanese needed to cripple the American naval forces stationed in Hawaii. The Japanese aimed their first attack at the United States naval base at Pearl Harbor on the island of Oahu. On December 7, 1941, in the darkness of early morning, 350 Japanese planes screamed down on the naval base at Pearl Harbor and a nearby army airfield, destroying ships in the harbor and planes on the ground. However, the aircraft carriers, the main targets of the attack, survived because they were at sea.

Completely unprepared, most of the American troops were asleep or eating breakfast on that Sunday morning. Japan had issued no formal declaration of war, and this surprise attack was a military success.

Calling December 7, 1941, "a day which will live in infamy," President Roosevelt asked Congress to declare war. Debates over the American policy of isolationism ended, and on December 8 the United States entered the war. The conflicts in Europe and Asia now became a true world war. In keeping with their pledges of alliance to Japan, on December 11, Germany and Italy declared war on the United States.

EARLY JAPANESE VICTORIES

The next several months were a dark time for the Allies. In eastern Asia, Japan struck one quick blow after another. By the end of March 1942, the Japanese had taken most of the Philippine Islands, which had been under American control since 1898. Thousands of American and Filipino soldiers died on a forced "death march" to railway cars waiting to take the troops to prisoner-of-war camps.

The United States and Great Britain had underestimated the strength and ability of the Japanese war machine, and for six months the Japanese maintained the advantage. In addition, relatively few Asians within the former colonies of European nations wanted to oppose the Japanese. In fact, at first the other Asians welcomed the Japanese troops and the end of Western control, but these Asians soon found the Japanese occupation to be harsh.

The Japanese ruthlessly exploited their new possessions for food, tin, oil, and rubber, and had little respect for the ancient traditions of the people. Angered by the treatment they received, Asians in conquered territories began to work for independence.

SECTION REVIEW

1. How did Japan set about expanding its empire in Asia?

2. Why did the Japanese attack Pearl Harbor? What were the results of that attack?

3. How did the Japanese treat the people in their new possessions?

Analysis. Japanese culture differs from the cultures of Germany and Italy. What, then, may account for the similarities in the actions of these nations during World War II?

31-4
ALLIED OFFENSIVES

READ TO FIND OUT

—how the Allies used a victory in North Africa to launch an invasion of Italy.
—why the battles of the Coral Sea and Midway were important to the Allied cause.
—what Operation Overlord was.
—how the Allies defeated Japan.

The winter of 1941 was bleak for the Allies. German submarines patrolled the Atlantic Ocean, making impossible the safe transport of troops and supplies from the United States to Great Britain. Also, the Germans invaded North Africa. Japan ruled the Asian mainland and most of the Pacific, snapping up one nation after another.

ALLIED STRATEGIES

A war of such worldwide scale required careful strategy, and Allied leaders met several times to coordinate plans. In their August 1941 meeting—which yielded the Atlantic Charter—Roosevelt and Churchill had agreed that the top priority of the war was defeating Hitler.

Stalingrad. The harsh winter of 1941 had halted the Germans before they reached Moscow. Hitler then decided not to try to take Moscow but instead to attack Stalingrad—called Volgograd today—on the Volga River. Control of this city would aid the Nazi effort to seize the Soviet oilfields in the Caucasus.

This American political cartoon, which appeared in the *St. Louis Post-Dispatch* on November 25, 1942, offers a grim comment on the desperate position of the Nazi army in Stalingrad.

The German blitzkrieg began in August and by September had destroyed much of the city. Finally, 300,000 Nazi troops gained control of the city, but only briefly. In November the Soviets surrounded Stalingrad, trapping the Germans. The battle continued through the bleak winter months, until fewer than half the Germans survived to surrender in February 1943.

The battle of Stalingrad proved to be a crucial turning point in the war. Not only did it break the German offensive in the Soviet Union, it also demonstrated the strength and staying power of the Soviet Red Army.

North Africa. German forces soon suffered another major defeat, this time in North Africa. In September 1940, Italian troops had invaded Egypt from Libya in a quest for control of the Suez Canal. After a small British force turned back the Italians, Hitler sent aid in February 1941. By the summer of 1942, Allied troops had chased the Germans out of Egypt.

In November 1942, the Allies, led by American General Dwight D. Eisenhower, landed in North Africa and moved in from the west on the fleeing Germans. Finally, in May 1943, Axis forces made a final retreat. With North Africa

liberated from the Axis orbit, the Allies now held a base from which to invade Italy.

Invasion of Italy. In January of 1943, Roosevelt and Churchill had decided to attack Italy, whose ports and air bases would be strategically important for the bombing campaign they were planning against Germany. Moreover, eliminating Mussolini's Fascist forces from the war would raise the morale of Allied soldiers and civilians alike.

The loss of North Africa had already shaken Mussolini's rule, and in July 1943 he was overthrown and imprisoned. However, German troops stationed in Italy freed Mussolini and set him up in a puppet state in northern Italy. In this state, Mussolini's government appeared to be independent but was controlled by Germany. Meanwhile, the Allies moved slowly up the boot of Italy, in the face of fierce German resistance, and liberated Rome in June 1944. As the Allies approached Milan in April 1945, Mussolini tried to escape but was recognized and executed by partisans.

Turning the tide in the Pacific. As Allied forces gained ground in Europe and North Africa, the war in the Pacific also took a favorable turn for the Allies. In May 1942, after their string of successes in the Pacific, the Japanese sent a huge fleet into the Coral Sea north of New Guinea in an attempt to take both that island and Australia, the last Allied stronghold in the Pacific. After two days, however, American naval forces succeeded in turning back the Japanese fleet.

Next, the Japanese tried to establish a base within reach of Hawaii by taking the Midway Islands, just northwest of the Hawaiian Islands. Again the Japanese were turned back and were now clearly on the defensive.

These key naval battles took place as the Soviets pushed the Germans back from Stalingrad and Allied forces secured North Africa. Just eight months after Pearl Harbor, on August 8, 1942, the United States Marines invaded Guadalcanal in the Solomon Islands, where the Japanese had begun to build air bases. This assault was the first American offensive in the Pacific. Fierce jungle fighting continued on Guadalcanal until February 1943, when the Japanese retreated from the island in their first land defeat of the war.

By 1944, the United States had the strongest navy in the world. In an October battle of the Leyte (LAYT-ee) Gulf in the Philippines, the Japanese first used the kamikaze, or suicide attack, in which a pilot crashed a bomb-laden plane into an Allied ship. From that battle until the end of the war, young Japanese airmen considered the kamikaze attack an honored duty to their nation.

By the end of 1944, the Allies had reclaimed all of the islands in the Philippines. Japan had suffered tremendous losses and now lay open to Allied attack.

Normandy. In November, 1943, Roosevelt, Churchill, and Stalin had all met together for the first time. Meeting at Tehran, Iran, they agreed on a major assault the following spring, an invasion of Europe through northern France.

Planning for this offensive, whose code name was Operation Overlord, had begun a year before. American General Dwight D. Eisenhower, who had led the Allied forces in North Africa, would be supreme commander of all the Allied troops in this invasion. The troops would invade from England, crossing the English Channel. By early June 1944, southern England was filled with troops, tanks, and aircraft.

June 6, 1944, was set as D-Day, the date of the invasion along the coast of Normandy. Three million troops were ready, but fewer than 200,000 made the first assault. Four thousand ships carried the troops, and 12,000 planes protected them.

Paratroopers began the invasion, dropping behind German lines before dawn. Within a month, a million troops had landed in France, and by August, Allied forces had reached Paris.

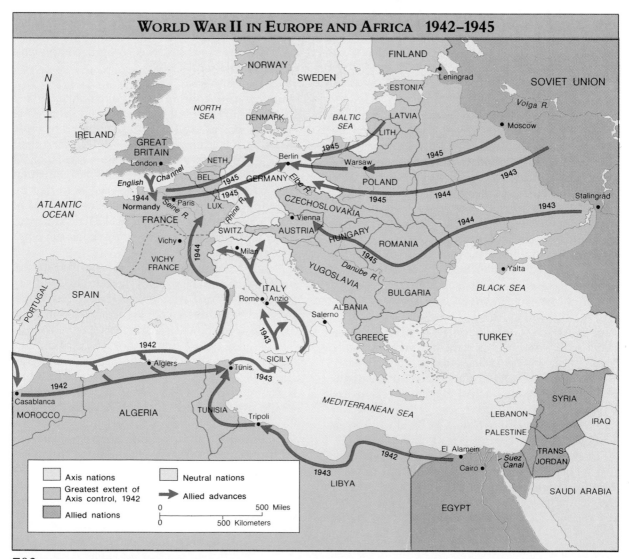

WORLD WAR II IN EUROPE AND AFRICA 1942–1945

American troops wade ashore at Normandy on D-Day. Hitler was tricked into believing that this landing was a decoy and that the real Allied invasion would take place at Calais, farther to the east along the French coast and closer to Britain.

After 4 years of humiliating occupation, Paris was liberated on August 25, 1944, with the help of French resistance groups. General Charles de Gaulle, leader of the Free French resistance movement, marched through the city to loud cheers. By the end of the summer, the Allies had driven the Germans out of both France and Belgium.

VICTORY IN EUROPE

As the American, British, and Free French troops invaded France in June 1944, Stalin's Red Army began a drive on Germany from the east. Meeting in Yalta in the southern part of the Soviet Union on the Black Sea, Roosevelt, Churchill, and Stalin agreed in February 1945 to coordinate their last attacks on Germany. They also made plans for dividing up control of postwar Europe.

In January 1945, Hungary had already surrendered to the Soviets. The Soviets next marched through Poland, Yugoslavia, and the Slovakian part of Czechoslovakia in pursuit of the German army. In April, the Soviets took control of Vienna, and on April 21, Soviet forces arrived just outside Berlin.

On April 25, the Americans and British met up with the Soviets at the Elbe River. As Soviet forces pushed into Berlin, Hitler committed suicide on April 30. By May 8, 1945, all the German armies had surrendered and the Allies celebrated V-E Day—Victory in Europe.

VICTORY OVER JAPAN

Even as Allied forces fought their last battles with Germany, American forces began to move on Japan. Following a policy that became known as "island hopping," American forces bypassed strongly defended islands and concentrated their attention on islands that could be captured more easily. These islands then served as bases for air raids on Japan and Japanese ships. By June 1945, Allied troops had taken the small island of Okinawa, from which a land invasion of Japan could be launched. However, Allied military leaders estimated that such an invasion would cost the lives of as many as a million Allied soldiers.

Meeting in Potsdam, just outside Berlin, in July 1945, the Big Three—as the leaders of Great Britain, the Soviet Union, and the United States were called—all agreed to demand that

THE FRENCH RESISTANCE FIGHTERS

The French surrender to German forces in 1940 had demoralized the French people. Within months, however, an underground guerrilla army sprang up, dedicated to driving the Germans out of France and restoring the French government. The underground movement, which became known as the French resistance, did much to help French people regain their pride. From outside France, General Charles de Gaulle, the leader of the Free French resistance forces, urged his people to fight on.

An early attempt to organize the underground fighters into a centralized army was broken up by the Nazis. Through much of the war, therefore, local guerrilla groups acted on their own. They sabotaged Nazi-managed weapons factories, destroyed railway lines and bridges, cut telephone and telegraph wires to interrupt enemy communications, and sometimes attacked troop convoys.

As the Allied landing in France approached in 1944, the resistance fighters transmitted important information about German military activities. They also rescued downed British and American bomber crews and helped them return safely to their bases in Britain.

Throughout the war, the underground was aided by the British, who parachuted small weapons, radios, explosives, and other essential supplies such as flashlights. When the United States entered the war, it also helped supply the French. Both the United States and Britain dropped special agents and radio operators behind enemy lines to coordinate resistance efforts with the Allied military moves. Many French citizens who did not actually join the underground provided food, clothing, and a safe hiding place when needed.

As many as 500,000 people aided in the cause. An estimated 24,000 died in skirmishes with the enemy. The Nazis discovered and executed another 25,000 and sent countless thousands to concentration camps.

Perhaps the underground's most important contribution was to give the French people the hope they needed that France would be free again someday. The people's refusal to admit defeat ultimately led to victory.

Japan surrender. At this meeting, American President Harry Truman and British Prime Minister Clement Atlee—successors to Roosevelt and Churchill—also discussed the postwar division of Europe and the question of punishment for Germany.

The Japanese did not respond to the Allied demand for surrender. On August 6, 1945, the United States dropped the atomic bomb on Hiroshima, a Japanese city of 330,000. The bomb destroyed 60 percent of the city and killed 80,000 people immediately. Many others died later from radiation poisoning, a sickness still suffered by some survivors alive today.

After Japan still refused to surrender, on August 9 the United States dropped another atomic weapon, a plutonium bomb, this time on Nagasaki. The following day Emperor Hirohito addressed the nation by radio and told the Japanese people that the long, brutal war was over. On August 14, 1945, Japan surrendered unconditionally. The following day the world celebrated V-J Day—Victory over Japan.

SECTION REVIEW

1. Why was victory in North Africa important for the Allies?

2. Why were the battles of the Coral Sea and Midway important to the Allies?

3. How did the invasion of Normandy lead to Allied victory over Germany?

4. How did the Allies finally defeat Japan?

Evaluation. What factors do you think convinced President Truman to drop the atomic bomb on Japan? If he had today's knowledge of the destructive potential of atomic weapons, would he be as likely to make the same decision? Why or why not?

31-5
GLOBAL IMPACT OF THE WAR

READ TO FIND OUT

—what *veto power* means.
—why civilian war casualties were so high.
—what the Nuremberg trials were.
—how the Allies arranged for the occupation of Germany.
—what impact the war had on European influence in the world.

While fighting together to defeat the Axis powers, the United States, Great Britain, and the Soviet Union had put aside their differences. When the battles finally ended, nations needed to repair devastating damage, but unresolved problems of the past complicated the rebuilding effort.

Decisions about which Allies would control the occupied territory, particularly in Germany, Austria, and Eastern Europe, were difficult because of the distrust that had begun 30 years earlier, when Western allies had aided the White Armies against the Communists in the Russian Revolution.

CASUALTIES AND DAMAGE

World War II was a shattering end to a difficult period in European history. As many as 50 million people, both soldiers and civilians, may have died as a result of the war. About 15 million died in battle. Many of the wounded would have also died without medical advances, such as blood transfusions and penicillin, achieved before and during the war.

The Soviet Union suffered the greatest losses—an estimated 7 million soldiers and 13 million civilians. One out of every 22 Soviets, one out of every 25 Germans, and one out of every 46 Japanese were dead or missing at the end of the war. The high civilian death rate resulted from the intense bombing of cities, Hitler's concentration camps, the forced deportation of thousands, and the famines and epidemics during and after the war.

Property damage was also immense. In monetary terms, the cost of the war is estimated at more than two trillion dollars. Entire cities such as Stalingrad, Warsaw, and Hamburg lay in ruins. In Japan, atomic bombs had leveled much of Hiroshima and Nagasaki. Many cities in both Europe and Asia that had little or no military significance were totally destroyed or severely damaged.

Nazi murder of the Jews and other groups was the foremost atrocity of the war, but the Allies also acted harshly. The Soviet army burned and looted many German cities. In

Hiroshima stands in ruins a few days after the atomic bomb exploded there in August 1945. Two days before the attack, American planes dropped more than 700,000 leaflets warning Hiroshima's residents of impending disaster. Japanese authorities had no idea of the destruction that lay ahead and did not evacuate the city.

an act of revenge for earlier German bombings, the British—with American aid—deliberately destroyed Dresden with bombs, killing 135,000 people. The city had little military importance and was filled with refugees.

Such tactics ended the traditional wartime distinction between soldier and civilian. In addition, World War II saw the invention and use of the most destructive weapons in history. As scientists in the United States worked to develop the atomic bomb, so did those in Germany, each side driven by the fear that the other would develop and use the weapon first. Later in the war, Germany began to concentrate on the development of "pilotless bombers," the rockets called V–1s and V–2s, which caused extensive damage in London and Belgium.

EFFECTS OF THE HOLOCAUST

The devastation of entire cities by the new weapons was easy to see, but many people had never heard of Hitler's concentration camps. As the Allied forces moved into Germany in 1945, they discovered the horrors of those Nazi death camps. They found survivors who had been starved and tortured, as well as proof of the extermination of millions. The revelation of the Holocaust stunned the world.

The pain of those who had survived the camps did not end with the war. Freed from the camps, many found themselves homeless, their cities destroyed, and their families and friends either dead or in distant lands, having sought refuge in other nations. Their dislocation added to the instability of the postwar period.

The Nuremberg trials. The Allies, having learned of the vicious Nazi atrocities, believed that the surviving German leaders should be tried as war criminals, and the United States, Great Britain, France, and the Soviet Union formed a tribunal. Twenty-two of the most important Nazi leaders went on trial in November 1945 in Nuremberg, Germany, charged with "crimes against humanity" and "crimes against

---

SPOTLIGHT: IDEAS AND DEVELOPMENTS

THE RACE TO BE FIRST

At the outset of the Second World War, scientists in the United States, Great Britain, the Soviet Union, Japan, and Nazi Germany all had ideas about how to build the atomic bomb. The problem facing the United States and Great Britain was how to build the bomb first, before the Nazis did.

To win the race, two goals became especially important to the Allies. First, they had to destroy the Axis-controlled manufacturing plant in Norway that produced a substance called "heavy water." The hydrogen in heavy water has an atomic weight of 2 instead of the usual 1 and is thus a "heavy" isotope that can be used to produce a nuclear reaction, which releases enormous amounts of energy.

Early in the war, when the Nazis occupied Norway, they seized control of the only heavy-water plant in Europe. The Allies' first attempts to bomb the plant were unsuccessful because of its location deep in a mountain canyon. They then trained a small band of agents who were to gain entry to the plant and destroy it. With the help of the Norwegian workers, the agents succeeded.

Although this was a setback for the Nazis' bomb-building plans, a few months later the Nazis partially rebuilt the plant and began sending heavy water to Germany. This time Allied agents blew up the ship carrying the material.

The second Allied goal was to rescue the brilliant Danish physicist Niels Bohr—a Nobel Prize winner and an expert on atomic energy—who was trapped inside Nazi-occupied Denmark. Bohr escaped from Denmark to neighboring Sweden, a neutral country, but he still had to get to Britain. In a daring rescue mission, a British pilot flew to Sweden and brought Bohr out of the country.

The United States, with the aid of Great Britain, won the race to build an atomic bomb. Much is owed to the genius of scientists such as Bohr, but much is also owed to the courage of individuals such as the pilot who flew Bohr out of Sweden and the agents who blew up the heavy-water plant in Norway.

the peace." Their testimony went on for 10 months, revealing slave labor, medical experiments on human beings, forced starvation, and mass murder. Trials of less important Nazi figures—guards at concentration camps, German military officers, doctors who engaged in the medical experiments—continue to this day. Similar trials took place in Japan.

POLITICAL ISSUES AND TENSIONS

Meetings among the Allied leaders during the war had tended to downplay political tensions in order to achieve unity on war strategy. Meeting in February 1945 in Yalta, Roosevelt, Stalin, and Churchill knew that the imminent Allied victory meant that plans had to be made for the postwar world.

Stalin wanted the return of territory lost to Japan in 1905, as well as territory in Europe. His position at the meeting was strong, since Soviet troops had already driven the Nazis out of Poland and part of Czechoslovakia and stood ready to invade Germany. Roosevelt feared the spread of communism but believed he had to make concessions to Stalin in return for Soviet aid against Japan.

At the Yalta meeting, the leaders agreed to rearrange the borders of Poland, with a new frontier that gave the Soviet Union some Polish territory and compensated Poland with German territory. They also designated Allied occupation zones in Germany and Austria and established a policy of German reparations. The payments were to be made in goods rather than in cash. The leaders also called for "free elections of governments responsive to the will of the people" in postwar Europe.

Stalin, Churchill, and Roosevelt also agreed to establish a new international organization after the war to ensure peace. With that agreement, a date was set for the first meeting of the United Nations, at which a charter for the organization could be adopted.

At the next meeting of Allied leaders, held in Potsdam in July 1945—after the war in Europe had ended—Germany was divided into four zones to be occupied by the United States, Great Britain, the Soviet Union, and France. Instead of taking reparations from Germany as a whole, the Allies agreed to structure separate payments for each zone. This decision reflected the lack of trust that the Soviet Union and the

Seated from left to right, Churchill, Roosevelt, and Stalin—the Big Three— meet in Yalta to discuss forcing Hitler to surrender. At the meeting, they also made plans for postwar Europe.

Western Allies had for each other and forecast growing East-West tensions.

Moreover, though Stalin had agreed to democratic governments in Poland and other nations under Soviet control, it was not at all clear whether he would follow through on this plan. Western leaders at the conference did not press the question, however, hoping to keep good relations with Stalin.

THE UNITED NATIONS

In 1942 the Allies had agreed to act as "united nations," in President Roosevelt's phrase, in the war against the Axis powers. Despite their political differences, Roosevelt, Stalin, and Churchill always agreed on the need for an international organization. In April 1945, delegates from 50 nations met in San Francisco, California, to write the charter of the United Nations. The organization's goals were to preserve peace and to "save succeeding generations from the scourge of war." Although the League of Nations had failed—it was formally dissolved in 1946—the world held out hope for the new organization. The United States was the first nation to ratify the United Nations charter, followed soon afterward by the Soviet Union.

The organization has six divisions: General Assembly, Security Council, the International Court of Justice, Secretariat, Trusteeship Council, and Economic and Social Council. All member nations belong to the General Assem-

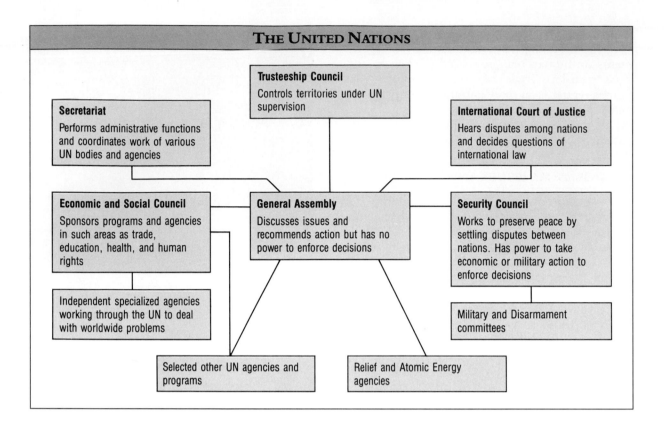

THE UNITED NATIONS

Trusteeship Council
Controls territories under UN supervision

Secretariat
Performs administrative functions and coordinates work of various UN bodies and agencies

International Court of Justice
Hears disputes among nations and decides questions of international law

Economic and Social Council
Sponsors programs and agencies in such areas as trade, education, health, and human rights

General Assembly
Discusses issues and recommends action but has no power to enforce decisions

Security Council
Works to preserve peace by settling disputes between nations. Has power to take economic or military action to enforce decisions

Independent specialized agencies working through the UN to deal with worldwide problems

Military and Disarmament committees

Selected other UN agencies and programs

Relief and Atomic Energy agencies

bly, each nation having one vote. The Security Council, the peacekeeping division, has five permanent members: the United States, Great Britain, France, the Soviet Union, and China. Each permanent member has *veto power*, the right to cast a vote prohibiting action, on issues taken up by the Security Council.

EFFECTS OF THE WAR

World War II weakened both Europe's economic power and its claim to superiority over nonindustrial nations. The Japanese invasion of European colonies in Asia served eventually to strengthen Asian resistance to imperialism. Exhausted by the war, Europe had difficulty holding onto colonies elsewhere in the world.

Not only had the United States been spared physical damage during the war, it had actually improved its manufacturing capability. Women in the United States and elsewhere played an important role in keeping industries running. They filled jobs vacated by men who went to war and extra jobs created by the round-the-clock shifts of the defense industry. Many women remained in the work force after the war.

American leaders saw that they could no more succeed in peacetime by acting in isolation than they could in war. The postwar period brought an expanded American influence that has continued to this day.

The horrors of the war stimulated a desire for a new beginning in Western Europe. Leaders called for an end to selfish interests and for the removal of the people and institutions that had brought failure to Europe. World War II had reduced Europe's role in the world, but at the same time it helped start a period of dramatic economic and political revival.

SECTION REVIEW

1. Define *veto power*.

2. Why were there so many civilian casualties?

3. What was the goal of the Nuremberg trials?

4. What happened to Germany after the war?

5. How did Europe's position in the world change after World War II?

Analysis. What are some problems that would be faced by any international organization such as the United Nations?

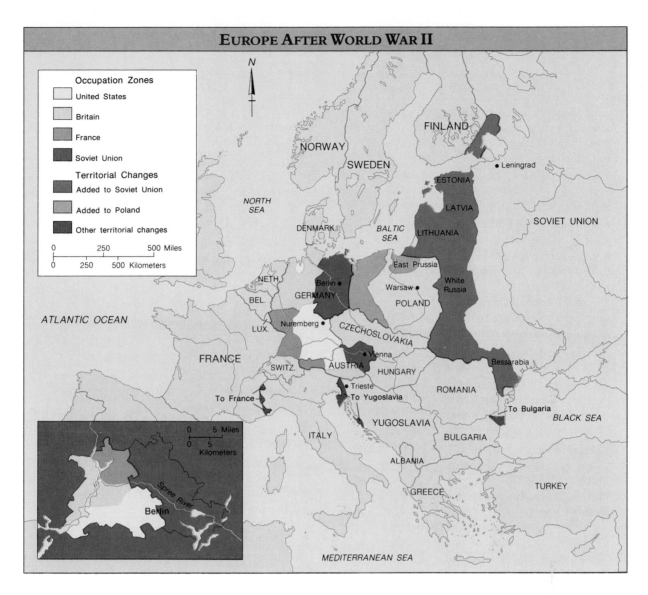

EUROPE AFTER WORLD WAR II

Occupation Zones
- United States
- Britain
- France
- Soviet Union

Territorial Changes
- Added to Soviet Union
- Added to Poland
- Other territorial changes

0   250   500 Miles
0   250   500 Kilometers

NORWAY
SWEDEN
FINLAND
• Leningrad
ESTONIA
LATVIA
LITHUANIA
East Prussia
NORTH SEA
DENMARK
BALTIC SEA
NETH.
Berlin •
GERMANY
BEL.
Warsaw •
White Russia
POLAND
SOVIET UNION
ATLANTIC OCEAN
LUX.
Nuremberg •
CZECHOSLOVAKIA
FRANCE
SWITZ.
AUSTRIA
Vienna •
HUNGARY
Bessarabia
To France
• Trieste
To Yugoslavia
ROMANIA
To Bulgaria
BLACK SEA
YUGOSLAVIA
ITALY
BULGARIA
ALBANIA
GREECE
TURKEY
MEDITERRANEAN SEA

0   5 Miles
0   5 Kilometers
Spree River
Berlin

Data Search. Identify the countries listed in the war casualties chart on page 833 that had **(a)** greater casualties in World War II than in World War I, and **(b)** fewer casualties in World War II than in World War I.

HISTORY IN FOCUS

The atomic age, which began with Hiroshima, vastly increased the destructive potential of any future world war. The reality of atomic weapons and the new fear they aroused have been part of world history since 1945.

The development of the formidable atomic bomb also made the United States the leading power in the world—a power less willing to compromise on political issues. Europe's dominance in world affairs, which had weakened after World War I, now ended.

In place of European dominance, the war had created two superpowers: the Soviet Union and the United States. The successful Red Army advance through eastern Germany gave the Soviet Union new territory and power in Europe. The United States, the only major industrial nation not damaged by the war, changed from a reluctant world power to an eager one. In the years following the war, it controlled Japan and heavily influenced Western Europe. How the United States and the Soviet Union handled their new power had a strong effect on the world for years to come.

SUMMARY

- The aggressions of totalitarian nations led to another world war, larger and more destructive than World War I. In 1936, Italy took over Ethiopia. Japan began a full-scale war with China in 1937. In Spain, a brutal civil war led to fascist rule and served as a rehearsal for later conflict in Europe.

- Hitler put troops back in the Rhineland and gained control of Austria and Czechoslovakia. Germany made a treaty with the Soviets, then invaded Poland in 1939. Britain and France declared war but were unable to stop Germany from overrunning most of Europe. Germany also invaded the Soviet Union and assisted Italian expansion in North Africa.

- The United States supported Britain and its allies but did not enter the war until a surprise attack by the Japanese in 1941 on an American base at Pearl Harbor. The Japanese quickly went on to seize control of most of Southeast Asia and the South Pacific.

- The tide turned against the Axis powers when the Soviets defeated the Germans at Stalingrad in 1942. After the Allies reclaimed North Africa, they invaded Italy and staged a massive landing in France in 1944. Advancing from east and west, the Allies forced the German surrender in 1945. After fierce fighting in the Pacific, the United States dropped two atomic bombs on Japan in August 1945, and Japan surrendered.

- Millions died in the war and trillions of dollars in damage had been done. Yet even as the Allies dedicated the new United Nations to keeping the peace, East-West tensions were mounting.

VOCABULARY REVIEW

Match each numbered vocabulary term with the lettered term most closely related to it. Then explain how the terms in each pair are related.

1. economic sanctions   (a) giving in
2. appeasement   (b) prohibition
3. blitzkrieg   (c) genocide
4. Holocaust   (d) forceful attack

CHAPTER REVIEW

1. (a) Who were the opposing forces in the Spanish Civil War? (b) Why did other European nations aid them?

2. (a) How did the League of Nations respond to Japanese aggression in China? (b) How did European nations react to Hitler's pressure on Czechoslovakia? (c) Why did Britain and France react as they did to Hitler's invasion of Poland?

3. (a) Describe the foreign policy the United States attempted to follow during the 1930s. (b) What change in policy did President Roosevelt call for in 1941? (c) Why did he make this move?

4. (a) What was the German-Soviet pact of 1939? (b) Why did Hitler violate the pact? (c) What were the results of Hitler's action?

5. (a) What was Japan's plan for Asia? (b) How did it differ from Hitler's New Order?

6. (a) Why did Japan attack Pearl Harbor? (b) How was Japan able to make such rapid military advances in 1941 and 1942?

7. (a) Why was the battle of Stalingrad important? (b) What did the Allies hope to accomplish by invading Italy? (c) Why did Stalin press for the invasion of France?

8. (a) Why did the Allies not invade Japan? (b) Why did the Japanese surrender?

9. (a) What was Hitler's policy of genocide? (b) How did he implement it? (c) What was the Allied reaction to this policy after the war?

10. (a) How did World War II shift the world balance of power? (b) How did the treatment of Germany after the war reflect tensions among the Allies?

THINKING CRITICALLY: ACTIVITIES

1. Talk to a person who was an adult during World War II. What was the attitude of the people during that time? How did life change? Record the interview on tape, or write a brief report of your findings.

2. Divide into groups of four or five to discuss the following question: Could the Holocaust happen today?

3. Select one of the photographs of war in this chapter. Write a brief report describing how the aspect of war depicted differs from fighting both in World War I and in the present.

APPLYING SOCIAL STUDIES SKILLS

Interpreting political cartoons. The following cartoon by Albert Hirschfeld appeared in 1938 in the American magazine *New Masses*.

© Al Hirschfeld

1. Is the main character a real person or a symbol? Who or what does he represent?

2. What action has he just completed?

3. Judging from his facial expression and the position of his body, how does he feel about what he has done?

4. What does the globe symbolize? Which half of the globe remains in the cartoon? Which half of the globe is missing?

5. Why has this half of the world been cut off?

6. Do you think the cartoonist agrees with the attitude of the character pictured in the cartoon? Support your opinion with reasons.

APPLYING THINKING SKILLS

Determining the strength of an argument. In 1979, historian Charles W. Sydnor, Jr., reviewed a new book on Hitler. Its author claimed that Hitler neither ordered the annihilation of Europe's Jews nor knew about the killings that took place. Sydnor disagreed with this claim. Examine this excerpt from Sydnor's review to determine the strength of his argument.

> [The] book seems, at first glance, a work whose conclusions appear massively documented. A closer analysis, however, reveals something a bit different. [The author] uses several techniques. The first is omission. That Hitler was both interested in and consistently informed about the mass murder of Jews is clearly documented in reports Himmler [chief of the Nazi secret police] sent him in the fall of 1942. [Hitler read] report number 51, as evidenced by the annotation on it. For the period August–November 1942, the report lists 363,211 "Jews executed."
>
> More alarming than his failure to mention this significant document is [his] effort to manipulate or alter evidence. He contends that a notation in Himmler's telephone pad resulted from a general order by Hitler that no Jews were to be liquidated. [This] interpretation has been convincingly refuted by Professor Broszat, [who] has shown that Himmler's call was prompted by the uproar over semipublic massacres of Jews in Riga [a town in the USSR]. Hence, Himmler's call was almost certainly intended to prevent the on-arrival massacre of a single transport [of Jews] that had left Berlin for Riga. [The] attempt to make this document what it was not raises an additional interesting point. If Hitler was totally unaware [of] these liquidations, as the author claims, then how could he order that there be no liquidations?

From Charles W. Sydnor, Jr., "The Selling of Adolf Hitler: David Irving's *Hitler's War*." *Central European History*, Vol. XII (June 1979).

1. Explain what is involved in determining the strength of an argument.

2. What is Sydnor's claim?

3. What kinds of reasons does Sydnor give to support his claim? For each kind of reason you identify, give an example from the excerpt.

4. How strong is Sydnor's argument? Support your opinion with reasons.

UNIT REVIEW

1. (a) How did official French, German, and American attitudes toward involvement in war differ before World War I? Before World War II? **(b)** Discuss the impacts of these two wars on France, Britain, and the United States.

2. (a) Compare Japan's motives for expansion with the motives of Germany and Italy. **(b)** How did the motives for Japanese militarism in the 1930s differ from the motives for German militarism between 1890 and 1914?

3. Explain the degree to which each of the following factors was a cause of World War I and World War II: **(a)** nationalism, **(b)** alliances between nations, **(c)** military aggression, **(d)** the failure of diplomacy.

4. Compare the world wars in these respects: **(a)** types of warfare, **(b)** role and effect of technology, **(c)** strategies, **(d)** global impact.

5. Discuss the effects of the two world wars on the following: **(a)** economies of nations, **(b)** balance of power, and **(c)** colonialism.

6. (a) Describe and contrast the following Soviet policies: war communism, New Economic Policy, Five-Year Plans. **(b)** Compare the origins and strategies of the New Deal with those of the Five-Year Plans.

7. (a) How did the Treaty of Versailles and the depression contribute to European dictatorships? **(b)** Compare the treaty and the Yalta meeting.

8. (a) How were the Locarno Pact and the Atlantic Charter similar? **(b)** Give two examples of the failure of the League of Nations to resolve conflict. **(c)** Compare the League of Nations with the United Nations.

9. (a) Discuss how these governments were similar and different: the Spanish Republic, Kemal's Turkey, Sun Yat-sen's China, and Cárdenas's Mexico. **(b)** Compare the Spanish Civil War with the struggle between the Communists and the Kuomintang in China.

10. (a) Explain how social and political unrest, and the response to it, differed in Great Britain, India, and Japan in the 1920s, and the Soviet Union in the 1930s. **(b)** Contrast discrimination against Slavs in the Balkans, Jews in Europe, and the Japanese by Western nations.

RELATING PAST TO PRESENT

1. Economic and social developments in the United States between the two world wars—especially the Great Depression and the New Deal—had an important impact on later American life. Consider how the Great Depression and the New Deal have influenced the development of the modern American economy and the welfare system.

2. Compare the nonviolent tactics pioneered by Mahatma Gandhi with the nonviolent protests today. Be sure to discuss the methods and degree of effectiveness of recent nonviolent protests.

3. Two important developments in World War II were the dropping of the atomic bomb and the emergence of the Soviet Union as a world power. Discuss the political and social impact of these developments on the modern world.

PROJECTS AND ACTIVITIES

1. In a group with two or three classmates, research an area of art and culture from the 1920s and 1930s. Examples include the "lost generation" of American writers, American popular culture and fads, Dadism, surrealism, cubism, and the Mexican muralists. Organize a chart or bulletin board display, using pictures, captions, and short explanations to provide an overview of your subject.

2. Imagine that you are a follower of either Mao Zedong or Mahatma Gandhi. If you choose Mao, write a journal entry during the Long March. If you choose Gandhi, write an entry about the Indian resistance to British colonialism. In either case, describe your activities, what you are struggling for, and why you think your method of struggle is the right one.

3. With a group of classmates, prepare an oral report on one of the following subjects: the Russian Revolution, Irish independence, the Spanish Civil War, Latin American politics between the two world wars, the Holocaust, or another topic covered in this unit.

4. With two or three other students, prepare an oral presentation on the role of propaganda during World War I and World War II. Describe types of propaganda, such as posters, political cartoons, speeches, and patriotic songs. Where appropriate, show examples of some of these types of propaganda, explaining what techniques were used and why they were effective. Also, compare the propaganda of various nations during World War I and World II.

ANALYZING PRIMARY SOURCES

Refer to the soldiers' accounts on page 631 to answer the following questions.

1. For each diary excerpt, identify whether the soldier who wrote it fought for one of the Allies or for one of the Central Powers.

2. Based on the descriptions in the three diary excerpts, why do you think the area between enemy lines was called "no man's land"?

3. What do the three diary excerpts reveal about trench warfare during World War I?

4. What feeling is expressed by both the writer of the first excerpt and the writer of the second excerpt? What words or phrases in each of these excerpts reflect this feeling?

5. What feeling expressed by the writer of the third excerpt is not expressed by the other two writers? How is this feeling evident in the third excerpt?

6. Why do you think the writer of the third excerpt was glad he gave the German soldier some water?

7. Based on these diary excerpts, what can be said about the soldiers' attitudes toward the war and about the effect that the war had upon them? Support your answer with evidence.

GEOGRAPHY REVIEW

Regions. Siberia is defined as a region according to several characteristics, including its history and landforms. However, climate—the average weather over a long period of time—plays an important role in defining Siberia as a region.

For some purposes, people divide areas into regions according to just a single characteristic, such as climate. Following is a list of the major climate regions of the United States.

Tundra: Very severe winter; no warm season; light precipitation (rain and snow).
Subarctic: Severe winter; short summer; light to moderate year-round precipitation.
Continental: Cold winter; cool to warm summer; moderate year-round precipitation.
Marine West Coast: Mild winter; cool summer; rainy year-round.
Mediterranean: Mild, wet winter; warm, dry summer.
Subtropical: Mild winter; warm or hot summer; rainy year-round.
Desert: Cool winter; warm or hot summer; very dry year-round.
Steppe: Cool or cold winter; warm summer; little rain, much of it from summer thunderstorms.
Tropical Rainforest: Warm year-round, no winter; very rainy year-round.
Highland: Climate varies with elevation.

1. Describe the year-round climate of your area. Then, match it to one of the climate regions on the list.

2. Whether people live in the extreme cold of a Siberian winter or in the unvarying warmth of an Amazon rainforest, climate shapes how they live. Write a paragraph explaining how climate affects life in your area. Consider the climate's effects on economic activities such as farming, construction, and tourism, as well as on energy needs, dress, eating habits, and recreation.

SUGGESTED READINGS

Hemingway, Ernest. *For Whom the Bell Tolls.* New York: Charles Scribner's Sons, 1983. A novel set during the Spanish Civil War.

Hersey, John. *Hiroshima.* New York: Knopf, 1985. An account of the bombing of Hiroshima, as related by survivors.

Mehta, Ved. *Mahatma Gandhi and His Apostles.* New York: Penguin, 1977. An engaging, detailed biography of the Indian leader.

Sim, Kevin. *Women at War.* New York: Morrow, 1982. Stories of five women who defied the Nazis and survived.

This Fabulous Century, Vols. II-V (1910-1950). Alexandria, Va.: Time-Life Books, 1969. Lively popular history of the twentieth century.

GLOBAL CHALLENGES

1945-PRESENT

*What we call
results,
are beginnings.*

—Ralph Waldo Emerson

Mahoning. Franz Kline, United States, 1956.

GLOBAL TIMELINE

	POLITICAL	TECHNOLOGICAL	SOCIAL
1945			
1950	League of Arab Nations formed • Communists come to power in China • State of Israel proclaimed	First electronic computer • Xerography • Transistor invented	Apartheid policy established in South Africa
1955	NATO formed • Korean War	First hydrogen bomb • DNA structure discovered	TV sets common in U.S. • Beginnings of rock-and-roll music
1960	Warsaw Pact • Suez Crisis • Cuban Revolution • Common Market established	Microwave oven • Solar battery • Videotape recorder • Sputnik I launched	Modernization programs in Saudi Arabia and Iran • Great Leap Forward in China
1965	OPEC formed • Split between USSR and China • Berlin Wall built	First human spaceflight • Laser • Japanese "bullet train"	Latin American novelists gain worldwide attention
1970	PLO formed • Cultural Revolution in China • Six-Day War	Integrated circuit (microchip) • First heart transplant	Color TV becomes popular
1975	SALT I • OPEC oil embargo	U.S. astronauts land on moon	Inflation strikes worldwide • Energy crisis in U.S., Europe, and Japan
1980	Helsinki Accords • Islamic Revolution in Iran • Vietnam War ends	First space shuttle flight • CAT scanner developed	VCR's become popular
1985	Iran-Iraq War begins • U.S. and China establish diplomatic relations	Smallpox eliminated • Compact disc players	Strikes in Poland • Wole Soyinka becomes first African to win Nobel prize for literature
1990	Gorbachev introduces *glasnost* in USSR • End of Marcos government in Philippines		

EMERGENCE OF TWO WORLD VIEWS

1945–PRESENT

The Berlin Wall, symbol of a divided Germany.

Shortly after the end of World War II, the world became politically polarized between two opposing camps. One group of nations—the West—included the United States, Great Britain, France, and most of the other democracies of Western Europe. The other group—the Eastern bloc—included the Soviet Union and the nations of Eastern Europe that came under Soviet control in the last year of the war. The ideological struggle between capitalism and communism has dominated the global political scene since the late 1940s.

The postwar years also saw rapid social and cultural changes. In many Western countries, women became a larger part of the work force and organized to win equality. In the Soviet Union and Eastern Europe, repression gradually gave way to a more open society.

TIMELINE

1945	
	Berlin airlift — Marshall Plan Established
1950	
	NATO formed — First Soviet atomic bomb tested
1955	Warsaw Pact formed
	Sputnik launched — Revolts in Hungary and Poland — Common Market established
1960	
	Fifth French Republic established — Berlin Wall built — Cuban missile crisis — Limited Test Ban Treaty
1965	
	Soviets invade Czechoslovakia
1970	
	U.S. astronauts walk on moon — SALT I
1975	
	Helsinki Accords — SALT II
1980	
	Strikes in Poland — Thatcher elected for third term
1985	

32–1
RELATIONS BETWEEN THE SUPERPOWERS

READ TO FIND OUT

—what the terms *cold war*, *containment*, *domino theory*, *peaceful coexistence*, *détente*, and *dissidents* mean.
—how the nuclear arms race began.
—how relations between the United States and the Soviet Union changed in the 1950s.
—what led to a lessening of Soviet-American tensions in the late 1980s.

The military, economic, and social strains of war removed Great Britain, France, and Germany from the center of world power. Instead, the Soviet Union and the United States, the two superpowers, emerged as the dominant players on the twentieth-century world stage.

After the war, the Soviet Union had the world's largest armies and was able to gain control of much of Eastern Europe, an area that provided the Soviet economy with both markets and resources to expand well beyond its prewar capacity. The United States, on the other hand, had essentially been spared the destruction of war. No mainland American property was damaged as a result of enemy attack. Moreover, the United States was the only nation that possessed the atomic bomb.

Soon after World War II ended, East–West relations became strained as it grew apparent that the Soviets did not intend to relinquish control over the Eastern European lands they had liberated from the Nazis. Hostility continued in what came to be called the *cold war*, a state of tension and hostility between the non-Communist nations of the West and the Eastern bloc.

DEVELOPMENT OF THE COLD WAR

The cold war grew out of long-held distrust between East and West. Soviet leaders had never forgotten that Western nations helped anti-Bolshevik forces in the Russian Revolution. The

Soviets also resented the Allies' prewar policy toward Hitler, which had allowed him to gain control of lands within striking distance of the Soviet Union. After the Germans invaded the Soviet Union, the Soviets felt that the Allies' refusal to open a second front had left the Soviet people bearing most of the burden of war.

Western leaders, on the other hand, believed that the Soviet Union's 1939 treaty with Germany had made possible Hitler's invasion of Poland and touched off the war. Moreover, Western powers saw the Soviets as leaders of a worldwide Communist movement to spread revolution and destroy democracy. Soviet-backed Communist parties had already taken control of Poland, Hungary, Romania, Bulgaria, and Czechoslovakia, and the Soviet Union had made these nations its satellites—nations dominated by another nation. Yugoslavia and Albania also had Communist governments. However, both nations, which had been liberated from the Nazis by their own leaders and not by the Red Army, remained somewhat independent of the Soviet Union.

In March 1946, Winston Churchill described the separation of Eastern and Western Europe: "An iron curtain has descended across the continent." The Soviet Union controlled almost every nation to the east of that "iron curtain."

American response to Soviet expansion. Beginning in 1946, several events alarmed American leaders and convinced them that the Soviet Union planned to expand its influence beyond Eastern Europe. In the Mediterranean, both Greece and Turkey came under Soviet pressure. George F. Kennan, an American diplomat who had served in the Soviet Union, urged a policy to halt the spread of Communist influence. This policy became known as ***containment***.

In March 1947, President Truman stated, in what became the Truman Doctrine, that the United States must "support free peoples who are resisting attempted subjugation [conquest] by armed minorities or by outside pressure." He asked Congress for $400 million in aid for Greece and Turkey. Congress agreed, and the American assistance enabled both nations to resist Communist takeovers. Thus began a long-running commitment to fight Communist aggression throughout the world.

American leaders saw that economic aid was an important way of combating Communist influence, since a nation with a strong economy would be less likely to yield to outside pressures. Further, the Americans felt that helping other nations rebuild would improve the worldwide economy and ward off another depression.

In June 1947, Secretary of State George Marshall proposed a program of massive American financial aid to help European nations recover from the devastation of war. The Marshall Plan—formally titled the European Recovery Program—was offered to all European nations, but the Soviets would not allow Eastern European nations to participate in the program. In Western Europe, where the plan was used, industry was revived and living standards grew to exceed prewar levels.

The Berlin airlift. Meanwhile, in June 1948, world attention turned to a crisis in Germany. The United States, Great Britain, and France planned to merge their three occupation zones in Germany and turn over control of the territory to a new government run by Germans. Fearful of German resurgence, the Soviet Union objected and the four-power council could come to no agreement. Seeking to force the Western Allies to change their policy on Germany, the Soviets blocked all land routes across their zone of Germany to Berlin, effectively isolating the city within Soviet-held territory. Like Germany, Berlin was also divided into four sectors, and the Western Allies had to find a way to supply their sectors of the city.

In response to the plight of the Berliners, the United States and Britain organized a massive airlift to bring food, coal, and other supplies to the city of 2.5 million. A year later, having failed to achieve their goals, the Soviets lifted the blockade, but Germany and Berlin remained split between East and West. West Berlin continued to be isolated inside Communist territory. Almost immediately, a new constitution created a democratic government for the Federal Republic of Germany, or West Germany, the former Western Allied zones. A few months later, the Soviet-held territory became the German Democratic Republic.

NATO. In April 1949, before the Berlin airlift had ended, the Western powers formed a military alliance as a shield against Communist aggression. The alliance was called the North

Children perch on a fence to watch American planes during the Berlin airlift. In little over a year, more than 2 million tons of supplies—including fuel for factories—were brought in.

Atlantic Treaty Organization, or NATO. Its 12 original members were the United States, Canada, Great Britain, France, Italy, Norway, Denmark, Iceland, Belgium, Luxembourg, Portugal, and the Netherlands. Greece and Turkey joined in 1952, West Germany became a member in 1955, and Spain joined in 1982. Member nations provide troops and arms for NATO's own military forces, which are stationed in Europe.

In the meantime, the Soviet Union took countermeasures to stabilize its influence in Eastern Europe. The Soviets set up an organization to promote economic cooperation among Europe's Communist nations—the Council for Mutual Economic Assistance, (COMECON). Nations within the Communist bloc also formed their own military alliance, formalized in 1955 in the Warsaw Treaty Organization, known as the Warsaw Pact. The pact allowed Soviet troops to be stationed in Albania, Bulgaria, Czechoslovakia, Hungary, Poland, Romania, and East Germany. Yugoslavia never joined, and Albania dropped out in 1968.

BEGINNING OF THE ARMS RACE

Western distrust of the Soviets continued to grow in the late 1940s. Then, in 1949—years earlier than American leaders had expected—the Soviet Union tested its first atomic bomb. This event marked the beginning of the Soviet-American arms race, in which each nation tried to develop superior military strength.

Under President Dwight D. Eisenhower, the United States built up its nuclear aresenal. In

1952, the United States exploded its first hydrogen bomb, but less than a year later, the Soviet Union did the same. Along with new types of bombs, both superpowers also developed new rockets able to carry their destructive loads thousands of miles in a matter of minutes.

The goal behind these new weapons was to be able to respond with devastating force if the enemy attacked first. According to this strategy, if a nation knew that its own destruction by nuclear weapons was certain to follow any attack it started, that nation would be discouraged from striking first.

Asian conflicts. Support for the arms buildup was in part a response to conflicts in Asia. American leaders saw the invasion of South Korea by North Korean Communists in 1950 as proof that Communists intended to continue an aggressive policy of expansion. The United States, through the United Nations, sent thousands of troops to aid the South Koreans in a bloody war that lasted until 1953.

Some American troops also went to Vietnam in the early 1950s to help the French fight an independence movement led by Ho Chi Minh (HŌ CHEE MIN), a Communist rebel. Ho Chi Minh had set up a Communist government in northern Vietnam. American leaders feared that the non-Communist government in the south would fall to the Communists and that a united Communist Vietnam would serve as a base for the export of revolution. According to the **domino theory**, neighboring countries' governments would then topple—like a row of dominoes—until the Communists controlled all of eastern Asia.

The French were defeated by Ho Chi Minh's forces in 1954. Three years later, fighting broke out between the non-Communist government in South Vietnam and Communist-led rebels. To keep South Vietnam from falling to communism, the United States sent more and more troops and became deeply involved in the Vietnam War.

Peaceful coexistence. A slight thaw in the chill of the cold war followed the death of Soviet dictator Joseph Stalin in 1953. After a power struggle within the Communist party, a new Soviet leader emerged—Nikita Khrushchev (kroosh-CHAWF). He called for **peaceful coexistence**—a policy of maintaining peaceful relations with the West and not interfering in each other's affairs. American, Soviet, British, and French leaders agreed to a summit meeting—a meeting of top government leaders—in Geneva, Switzerland, in 1955. Later, in 1958, Soviets and Americans began to exchange scientific information and cultural programs.

While touring an American cultural exhibition in Moscow in July 1959, American Vice-President Richard Nixon (*center, dark suit*) engages Soviet Premier Nikita Khrushchev in a spirited discussion of the relative merits of the two superpowers' economic systems and ways of life. At Nixon's right is future Soviet Premier Leonid Brezhnev. Nixon, who later became president, referred to the encounter as the "kitchen debate." Khrushchev's policy of peaceful coexistence led to more frequent meetings between Soviet and American officials.

IDENTIFYING EVIDENCE

A claim, which is something someone says is true, is no stronger that the evidence on which it is based. Evidence is information that is relevant to a claim and that can be objectively checked. For example, the best evidence for the claim that "the Morris is the fastest car made" would be information from speed trials showing that the car is faster than all other cars. Searching for evidence will help you determine whether a claim is acceptable.

EXPLAINING THE SKILL

As you read on pages 228 and 229, identifying evidence first involves clearly defining the claim itself. Then ask yourself, "If this claim is true, what types of information exist to prove it is true?" Finally, search through the account to identify examples of these types of relevant information. In examining any account, look also for evidence that contradicts or casts doubt on the claim. Ask yourself, "What should *not* exist if this claim is true?"

APPLYING THE SKILL

Read the following excerpt from a speech delivered in 1956 by Soviet Premier Nikita Khrushchev. Determine what evidence in the account supports his claim. Then answer the questions.

The desire of the United States, Britain, and France to enforce their will on other countries reflects the aspiration to win world supremacy and their plans for military adventures against the socialist camp. Many big U.S. military bases designed for use against the USSR and the People's Democracies were built thousands of miles from the borders of the United States. "Cold war" was begun against the socialist camp. International distrust was artificially kindled, and nations set against one another. A bloody war was launched in Korea. The war in Indochina dragged on for years.

The inspirers of the "cold war" began to establish military blocs—the North Atlantic bloc, SEATO, and the Baghdad pact. [They claim] they have united for defense against the "communist threat." But that is sheer hypocrisy! We know

from history that when planning a redivision of the world, the imperialist powers have always lined up military blocs. Today the "anti-communism" slogan is being used as a smoke-screen to cover up the claims of one power for world domination. The United States wants, by means of blocs and pacts, to secure a dominant position in the capitalist world.

The inspirers of the "positions of strength" policy assert that it makes another war impossible because it ensures a "balance of power" in the world. [They] offer the arms race as their main recipe for the preservation of peace! It is perfectly obvious that when nations compete to increase their military might, the danger of war becomes greater, not lesser. Capitalism will find its grave in another world war, should it unleash it.

Abridged from Nikita S. Khrushchev, *Report of the Central Committee of the Communist Party of the Soviet Union to the 20th Party Congress.* Moscow, 1956.

MAKING MEANING

Now that you have analyzed the speech, answer the following questions:

1. The main claim is stated in **(a)** paragraph 2, sentence 1; **(b)** paragraph 1, sentence 1; **(c)** paragraph 3, sentence 1.

2. Of the following statements, which can be most easily checked for accuracy? **(a)** paragraph 1, sentences 2 and 5; **(b)** paragraph 2, sentences 5 and 6; **(c)** paragraph 1, sentence 3 and paragraph 2, sentence 5.

3. Of the following statements, which one would be most difficult to check for accuracy? **(a)** paragraph 1, sentence 2; **(b)** paragraph 2, sentence 1; **(c)** paragraph 2, sentence 5.

4. The sentences that link most directly to Khrushchev's main claim include **(a)** paragraph 3, sentences 1 and 3; **(b)** paragraph 3, sentences 2 and 4; **(c)** paragraph 1, sentence 2 and paragraph 2, sentence 1.

REVIEWING THE SKILL

5. Define the term *evidence*.

6. What is one procedure for finding evidence that is relevant to a claim?

This 1960 photograph captures Fidel Castro addressing his people. An idealistic young lawyer from a wealthy family, Castro made his first attempt to overthrow dictator Batista in 1953.

At Eisenhower's invitation, Khrushchev visited the United States in 1959. Eisenhower planned to return the visit, but in May 1960 the Soviets shot down an American U-2 spy plane flying high above Soviet territory. Khrushchev angrily withdrew his invitation, accusing the United States of treachery.

Khrushchev also opposed the Western presence in Berlin. Every month thousands of East Germans, including many skilled workers needed by Communist industries, came to Berlin and from that city escaped to West Germany. Then, in August 1961, East German officials built a wall between East and West Berlin. The Berlin Wall was heavily guarded to prevent unauthorized travel between the two sectors. After the wall was built, Khrushchev dropped his demand that the Western powers leave Berlin. The wall, however, stood as a constant reminder of the bitter division between Communist and non-Communist countries.

Showdown over Cuba. Also in 1961, trouble developed closer to home and American leaders turned their attention to the Caribbean island of Cuba, 90 miles (144 kilometers) south of Florida. A revolution there had ended a right-wing dictatorship in 1959. The new leader, Fidel Castro, in a move toward communism, made sweeping social reforms. He also nationalized, or took control of, private industry, much of which was owned by American companies. In response, the United States cut off trade with Cuba and ended diplomatic relations. Khrushchev then promised Soviet aid for Cuba.

Believing that Castro's government threatened the United States, Americans supported Cuban exiles who wanted to overthrow Castro. In April 1961, with President John F. Kennedy's reluctant approval, about 1,300 exiles invaded southern Cuba at the Bay of Pigs, but Castro's forces easily overcame the invasion. This victory strengthened Castro's position, and Khrushchev promised more support.

Kennedy ordered high-flying U-2 planes to keep a close watch on Cuba. In October 1962, photographs revealed that launch pads for missiles were being built on the island. Soviet missiles based at such sites could strike far inside the United States.

Kennedy responded to this threat, called the Cuban missile crisis, with a naval and air blockade of Cuba. Then he demanded that the Soviets remove their launch pads and missiles from Cuba. For a week, the threat of nuclear war loomed over the world. Finally, the Soviets agreed to remove the missiles, ending the crisis.

RESTRAINING THE ARMS RACE

The Cuban missile crisis, coming right after the confrontation over Berlin, alarmed American and Soviet leaders. Twice the world had been on the brink of nuclear destruction. Leaders from both countries began to explore ways of restraining the arms race.

Although disputes continued, the superpower leaders signed important agreements in the 1960s. By the end of the decade, tensions between the two nations had eased in what was called **détente** (day-TAHNT), a French word meaning "a lessening of tension." A series of treaties put limits on the arms race. In the 1970s the superpowers agreed to limit strategic weapons, those nuclear weapons capable of attacking bases or cities in the United States or the Soviet Union. The Strategic Arms Limitations Talks of 1972, known as SALT I, put strict limits on various types of missiles, and in 1979, SALT II further limited the weapons.

ARMS TREATIES 1963–1987			
Year	**Treaty**	**Purpose**	**Signers**
1963	Limited Test Ban Treaty	Ban all but underground testing of nuclear devices	United States, Great Britain, Soviet Union
1967	Outer Space Treaty	Prohibit installation of nuclear weapons in space	United States, Great Britain, Soviet Union
1968	Nonproliferation Treaty	Halt the spread of nuclear arms to nations that did not yet have them	All members of United Nations except France and China
1972	Strategic Arms Limitation Talks (SALT I)	Limit types of offensive and defensive weapons held by the superpowers	United States, Soviet Union
1979	Strategic Arms Limitation Talks (SALT II)	Limit long-range bombers and missiles	United States (unratified by Senate), Soviet Union
1987	Intermediate-Range Nuclear Forces (INF) Treaty	Eliminate all short- and medium-range nuclear weapons	United States, Soviet Union

In another move toward cooperation, representatives from the United States, the Soviet Union, and 35 other nations met in Helsinki, Finland, in 1975 to sign what were called the Helsinki Accords. The signers formally accepted Europe's existing borders, promised to respect one another's independence, and pledged to protect basic human rights such as freedom from government repression.

TENSIONS AND HOPE

Détente suffered major setbacks in the late 1970s and early 1980s, as each superpower accused the other of stepping up the arms race. Although American President Jimmy Carter had signed the SALT II treaty, the Senate was still debating it late in 1979 when Soviet troops invaded Afghanistan, an Islamic nation that borders the Soviet Union. American leaders denounced the Soviet intervention in Afghanistan and withdrew the SALT II treaty from Senate consideration. Carter temporarily halted trade with the Soviets and prohibited American participation in the 1980 Olympics in Moscow. Nevertheless, Americans and Soviets pledged to observe the terms of SALT II.

In the 1980s, American leaders suggested that new technology might finally make defense against a nuclear attack possible. American scientists stepped up work on new defensive weapons, including various types of lasers. President Ronald Reagan revealed the new plan in 1983, two years after he took office, calling it the Strategic Defense Initiative (SDI). Others dubbed it the Star Wars program, from a popular movie series.

Following Reagan's proposal, tensions between the superpowers increased. President Reagan, describing the Soviet Union as an "evil empire," took a hard line against the Soviet Union, and the Soviets returned the denunciations. Now led by Mikhail Gorbachev (MEE-kah-EEL gor-bah-CHOFF), who took over in 1985, the Soviets opposed the placement of cruise missiles—low-flying, guided missiles with acute accuracy—in Europe and bitterly condemned the Star Wars program.

In 1986, however, relations between the superpowers showed some signs of warming. In a human rights gesture, the Soviets permitted a number of *dissidents*—outspoken critics of the Soviet system—to leave the country. Representatives of the two nations resumed Strategic Arms Reduction Talks (START) begun in 1982. Reagan and Gorbachev also met in November 1986 in Iceland. Although the talks ended with no formal agreements, for the first time the leaders of the superpowers had discussed face to face the idea of removing missiles from Europe and doing away with nuclear forces.

In December 1987, Reagan and Gorbachev signed a treaty to ban all short- and medium-range nuclear weapons. This was the first agreement to eliminate an entire class of weapons. A year later, the two leaders met again, this time with Vice-President and President-elect George Bush. Bush and Gorbachev were hopeful that further progress could be made on arms control.

SECTION REVIEW

1. Define **cold war**, **containment**, **domino theory**, **peaceful coexistence**, **détente**, and **dissidents**.

2. What started the nuclear arms race?

3. In what ways did Soviet-American relations change in the 1950s?

4. What caused Soviet-American tensions to decrease in the late 1980s?

Analysis. Compare the cold war and détente. How did the attitudes of Soviet and American leaders influence the change in relations?

32–2
STABILITY IN THE WEST

READ TO FIND OUT

—what the terms **welfare state** and **civil rights** mean.
—how the nations of Western Europe developed means of economic cooperation.
—how cheaper imported goods affected the American economy in the 1970s and 1980s.
—why some Canadians disagree over language.

After World War II, superpower disputes had centered on Europe. By the 1970s, however, the superpowers were competing for dominance around the globe in Asia, Africa, and Latin America. European leaders decided to work together to solve their own economic and political problems.

ECONOMIC COOPERATION IN WESTERN EUROPE

The greatest cooperation among the nations of Western Europe developed on the economic front. By pooling their resources and breaking down economic barriers, these nations could better compete for world markets.

First, Belgium, the Netherlands, and Luxembourg signed an agreement of mutual cooperation, forming the Benelux Economic Union. In 1952 France, West Germany, Italy, and the three Benelux nations formed the European Coal and Steel Community (ECSC). This body ended tariffs on coal and steel, which benefited each nation's industry and made the nations more competitive in world markets.

In 1957, the same six nations created the European Economic Community, known as the Common Market. By 1968, the three organizations had merged, and member nations had eliminated all tariffs on all goods traded within the Common Market community.

Great Britain hesitated to join the Common Market because of its trade commitments to the British Commonwealth of Nations. The Commonwealth, formed in 1931, is a group of nations that once belonged to Britain and have cooperative agreements with the British government. When Britain tried to join the Common Market in the 1960s, France blocked its membership. French President Charles de Gaulle feared that Britain's ties to the United States would bring American influence into the Common Market. Britain, however, was able to join in 1973. Denmark, Ireland, Greece, Spain, and Portugal also became members.

The 12-member organization has come to be known as the European Communities (EC). In recent years these 12 nations have agreed to remove all barriers to the movement of people and goods by 1992, for instance, by using a common currency. The nations of the EC are also working together to foster technological developments, improve working conditions, and restore the environment. In 1989, EC members agreed to ban by the year 2000 production of particular chemicals harmful to the earth's ozone layer.

POSTWAR POLICIES IN WESTERN EUROPE

Europe embraced a wide range of political ideologies, from conservatism to communism. In time, however, many governments and political parties modified their approaches. Some democratic governments, for example, developed a **welfare state**, in which the government took responsibility for the needs of citizens. Some governments also nationalized major industries such as coal and steel, utilities, and transportation. The term *democratic socialism* is sometimes applied to this form of government.

By taking such steps as building public housing and providing free health care, European governments sought to avoid the worker discontent that occurred after World War I. To pay for these programs, nations imposed high taxes, with industry carrying the heaviest burden.

Weaknesses of welfare states. In the increasingly healthy economies of postwar Europe, high taxes for social programs met little opposition. By the 1970s, however, economic growth had slowed and unemployment had increased. As a result, people began protesting the high cost of social programs as well as rising prices.

People also complained that the socialistic policies had not provided for the welfare of all citizens. In Great Britain and other Western European countries, voters expressed their dissatisfaction with expensive social programs by electing conservative leaders who pledged to reduce government spending.

Meanwhile, socialists and communists used more peaceful tactics, as gains by the working class made Marxist revolution unlikely. Socialist parties in France and Italy worked within existing democratic systems and soon began to play an important role in government.

The 1970s saw the rise of conservative Christian Democratic parties in several nations, such as West Germany. These parties supported democracy but opposed broad social programs. Economic crises in the 1970s—especially the tremendous rise in the cost of oil, which led to inflation and a slowdown of business—increased votes for moderates and conservatives throughout the Western world.

Great Britain. The government of Britain changed after World War II largely as a result of

Prime Minister Margaret Thatcher, the first woman in Great Britain's history to hold that office, celebrates her reelection in 1983. Her policies stimulated a strong economic recovery.

economics. Political power shifted back and forth between the Labour party and the Conservative party, but Britain remained a stable and democratic nation.

Although Britain's economy improved, nagging problems continued. Unable to pay the costs of maintaining an empire, Britain gave up its overseas possessions, beginning in 1947 with India and Pakistan. As Britain's exports dropped, its taxes rose and the value of its currency fell. To pay for the imported food and raw materials the nation required, as well as its social programs, Britain needed rapid industrial growth. However, it could not compete with other industrial nations. As a result, businesses closed and unemployment soared. The burden of supporting the welfare state now fell on the middle class.

The civil strife in Northern Ireland continued as well. Northern Ireland, with a largely Protestant population, had remained in the United

FOUR KINDS OF ECONOMIC SYSTEMS*

	Capitalism	Socialism	Communism	Fascism
Who owns resources for production?	Mainly privately owned and operated.	Mixed. Many major resources government owned and operated; others privately owned.	Nearly all government owned and operated.	Mainly privately owned and operated.
Who decides production, wages, and prices?	Mainly private individuals and businesses; limited government regulation.	Mainly the government; to a degree, private individuals and businesses.	Mainly the government.	The government alone.
What are economic decisions based on?	Available supplies and demands of consumers.	Mixed. Government plans for nation; available supplies and demands of consumers.	Government plans for nation.	Government plans for nation.
What is the role of individuals?	Free to engage in any economic activity, buy any available goods and services, join labor unions.	Free to engage in many economic activities, buy any available goods and services, join labor unions.	Some individual choice of work; free to buy government goods and services. Labor unions exist to help meet production goals.	May be some individual choice of work; free to buy goods and services permitted by government. Labor unions banned.
Examples	United States, Canada, Japan	Britain, Sweden, India	Soviet Union, China, Cuba	World-War-II Germany, Italy; Argentina, 1943–1955; Niger

* The economies of most countries include some features from more than one economic system.

Kingdom when the rest of Ireland gained independence in 1921. Catholics in Northern Ireland began violent demonstrations in 1969, demanding that the two Irelands be reunited. Protestants responded with violence, and the British government stationed troops in Northern Ireland. Acts of terrorism continue today, with seemingly little hope for peace.

Under Conservative Prime Minister Margaret Thatcher, the British government's control over the economy was reduced after 1979. Thatcher argued that Britain's economy was suffering because the government was burdened by too many social programs, and the nation's state-owned industries were crippled by bureaucratic management. She also argued that citizens were hurt by high income taxes. Thatcher advocated more free enterprise and a reduction in public spending. As her changes began to take effect, the economy improved,

taxes were lowered, and many government programs were reduced or eliminated.

In 1983, despite unemployment that reached depression-era levels, British voters gave Thatcher and the Conservatives a second term of office, and in 1987 she was voted in for an unprecedented third consecutive term. By the end of her second term, about 40 percent of the country's state-owned industries had been sold, mainly to first-time shareholders, creating a whole new class of capitalists. She also made possible the sale of public housing to its tenants and encouraged a record number of new business starts. Such socialistic programs as national health care and poor relief, however, have remained untouched by the Conservative agenda.

France. France emerged from the war with so many political parties that governments could be formed only by coalition—a temporary alliance of parties. As a result, the governments tended to be indecisive and slow to act.

Nevertheless, the new government formed in 1946, known as the Fourth Republic, brought about great improvements in French business and social welfare policies in the 1950s. Aided by the Marshall Plan, France invested heavily in factories and equipment, establishing a strong industrial base for restoring prosperity. Postwar governments nationalized major businesses and increased government aid to citizens.

When General Charles de Gaulle, the resistance hero of World War II, took over temporary leadership of France in 1958, he changed the entire governmental structure. A new constitution, limiting parliamentary powers and increasing presidential powers, created the Fifth Republic in 1958.

By 1968, economic and social problems prompted widespread protests, and de Gaulle resigned in 1969. Throughout the 1970s, right-wing parties dominated French politics. At the same time, opposition parties grew in strength and number, and the Socialists formed a coalition with the Communists.

In 1981 the French elected a Socialist president, François Mitterrand (MEE-ter-AHN). Mitterrand began to nationalize more industries and proposed new social reforms. He dropped many of his plans, however, when an economic slump reduced his popularity and caused a tightening of France's budget in the mid-1980s.

West Germany. West Germany made a rapid recovery from the ravages of war. After the founding of the German Federal Republic in 1949, West Germany developed a multiparty political system in which two large parties—the Christian Democratic Union and the Social Democrats—and a number of small parties competed for votes. The conservative Christian Democrats dominated the government in the 1960s. Between 1949 and 1963, under Chancellor Konrad Adenauer, West Germany restored its industries and regained economic stability.

By the 1980s, the West German economy was strong, and West Germans enjoyed one of the highest standards of living in the world. The economy was capitalistic yet carefully guided by the government.

Soon after World War II had ended, both West and East German leaders had hoped eventually to reunify Germany. The postwar years saw each Germany become the strongest industrial nation of its respective bloc. To reunite West Germany with East Germany would have meant another shift in the world balance of power. In the meantime, the people had also progressed on different paths until each nation considered the other "foreign." Since the 1970s, most Germans have been content to think of themselves as "one nation, two states."

Italy. Following World War II, Italian leaders ended the Savoy monarchy, which was associated with Fascist party rule. They wrote a new constitution and in 1946 declared Italy a republic. Although many different political parties existed, two stood out: the moderate-conservative Christian Democrats and the Communists, who gained respect because of their work with the wartime resistance.

With help from the Marshall Plan and the Common Market, Italy had become a world industrial power by the 1960s. In the 1970s, however, Italy suffered more than any other industrial nation from high unemployment and inflation. As voters began to blame the Christian Democrats, who had been in office since the 1960s, both the Socialist and Communist parties gained strength. By the mid-1980s, Italy's government was run by a coalition of political parties, with the Christian Democrats as the majority and the Socialists second. By the late 1980s, the Communist party had gained enough support to influence the coalition government even though not a part of it.

The Italians had the strongest Communist party in the West. They sharply criticized the Soviet Union and followed their own brand of politics, which became known as Eurocommunism. Eurocommunism formalized the Western Communists' trend toward moderation and working within the democratic system.

CHALLENGES AND OPPORTUNITIES IN THE UNITED STATES

After World War II, the United States federal government expanded dramatically in both size and role, although not to the extent of the socialized nations of Western Europe. Programs to help citizens began even before the war, with aid to the needy during the Great Depression, and grew rapidly in the 1940s. By the 1960s, these programs included free health care for the elderly and federal aid to schools. Increased federal spending for such programs led to higher personal income taxes.

As the economy slowed in the 1970s, people began calling for cuts in federal spending, especially in assistance programs. They also called for tax cuts to ease the burden on individual incomes already weakened by inflation. Like voters in European welfare states, Americans began electing more conservative candidates who promised to cut federal spending. Ronald Reagan was elected president largely as a result of such promises, and in the 1980s he dramatically cut social programs. Critics pointed out, however, that his cuts in domestic programs were more than offset by increases in defense expenditures. During his years in office, the federal debt continued to skyrocket.

The American economy. As the United States increased its exports to other nations after World War II, business boomed. Recessions—temporary slowdowns of business—occurred from time to time in the 1950s and 1960s, but the nation avoided the sort of depression that had darkened the 1930s.

In the 1970s, dramatic price increases for oil—from about $3 to $20 per barrel—combined with increasing social and military spending to begin a period of economic turbulence. Price hikes that began with oil rippled throughout the economy to increase the entire cost of living. This inflation bit into workers' paychecks. In addition, skyrocketing production costs and interest rates caused thousands of farmers to lose their businesses when they could not repay loans.

By the 1980s, oil prices dropped and inflation eased, yet economic troubles persisted. The federal budget grew increasingly unbalanced. In order to support a military buildup and ongoing social programs, the government was forced to borrow money and operate at a greater deficit—that is, spending more than it took in—than ever before.

Problems also arose as Americans increasingly bought cheaper foreign products. Soon an unfavorable balance of trade developed—more money was leaving the country to pay for these imports than was coming in. As Americans bought fewer domestic products, unemployment soared in industries such as auto manufacturing, and so, many businesses closed.

Struggle for rights. In the 1960s, President Lyndon B. Johnson called for a "Great Society" that would bring equal opportunities for education, jobs, and *civil rights* to all citizens. Civil rights are the rights guaranteed to all people by their nation's laws and constitution. Many social programs in the 1960s were designed to right the wrongs caused by the nation's tradition of segregation—the practice of separating whites from blacks and other minorities. World War II changed the situation somewhat as the armed forces moved toward integration—the inclusion of all people on an equal basis—and as blacks filled jobs that formerly were held only by whites.

A 1954 Supreme Court decision put civil rights into the center of public attention. In the case *Brown v. Board of Education of Topeka*, the Court overturned an 1896 decision that had allowed "separate but equal" schools for blacks and whites and ordered schools to integrate.

The civil rights movement grew rapidly in the late 1950s and the 1960s. Among its many leaders, Martin Luther King, Jr., a Baptist minister, stood out. His philosophy of nonviolent protest, which was influenced by Indian nationalist Mohandas Gandhi, was widely adopted in the civil rights movement. Boycotts and other forms of peaceful protest spread throughout the South and won support. Blacks gained equal access to public education and to public facilities such as restaurants. They also gained guarantees for their rights to vote and to have equal opportunities in employment.

The successes of blacks encouraged other minority groups to seek broader rights and equal opportunities. Women activists founded the National Organization for Women (NOW) in 1966. Women helped gain the passage of laws barring discrimination on the basis of sex and proposed a constitutional amendment to formalize those rights. Other groups seeking new guarantees of their rights included American Indians, homosexuals, Hispanics, the elderly, and the disabled.

Antiwar movement. American participation in the Vietnam War led to a bitter debate in the 1960s and early 1970s between its supporters and its critics, who did not believe Vietnam was vital to American security. The divisions in American society brought on by the war troubled the nation for many years after

The Reverend Martin Luther King, Jr. (*seventh from right*), and other American civil rights leaders join hands and stride up Constitution Avenue in the historic 1963 March on Washington. More than 200,000 people from throughout the United States participated in the march, the purpose of which was to protest segregation and job discrimination. It was on this occasion that Dr. King gave his stirring "I Have a Dream" speech.

1973, when the United States pulled its troops out of Vietnam. Many Americans questioned the nation's self-proclaimed role as leader of the free world. They feared that attempts by the United States to impose its policies on other nations, such as those in Central America, might lead to more situations like Vietnam.

Changing foreign policy. Even as the United States was freeing itself from the Vietnam War, its relations with Communist powers were improving. The alliance between Communist China and the neighboring Soviet Union had been strained since the 1950s. Border skirmishes between these nations flared up in the 1960s, and China began to seek friends elsewhere. President Nixon's visit in 1972 led to the reestablishment of Chinese-American trade and to scientific and cultural exchanges between China and the United States.

President Nixon also visited the Soviet Union in 1972 to sign SALT I. These events marked a new era of cooperation and negotiation with the Communist nations and an easing of international tensions.

CANADA: AN INDEPENDENT PARTNER

Canada has played major roles in the political and economic affairs of the world since World War II. It took an active part in the founding of both the United Nations and NATO and has

cooperated with the United States in the defense of North America.

Canada's economy grew rapidly after World War II, aided by abundant natural resources. Manufacturers built new plants to turn out goods for a growing population, swelled by immigrants from many parts of the world.

Much of the money for Canada's expansion came from American investors and from American companies with Canadian branches. Canadians welcomed these investments but worried that the United States would gain too much control over Canada's economy. In the 1960s and 1970s, Canada adopted laws requiring a large measure of Canadian ownership in key industries such as oil and gas.

Government. Once a British colony, Canada has been self-governing since 1867. It is democratic and has a parliamentary system of government. In 1982, Queen Elizabeth approved the Constitution Act, formally ending Canada's governmental ties to Great Britain. However, Canada has remained within the Commonwealth of Nations.

Canada's ten provinces have more powers than American states, and regional divisions are much stronger. Language is a major point of debate among many people in Canada. Part of the nation was originally a French colony, and many Canadians still speak only French. The French-speaking minority demanded more civil rights in the 1960s and 1970s. The 1969

Official Languages Act made Canada a bilingual country, giving French equal status with English in government.

In the province of Quebec, where 80 percent of the people speak only French or are bilingual, some French-Canadians have long sought independence, and Quebec refused to sign the 1982 constitution. Amendments in 1987 acknowledging Quebec as a "distinct society" within Canada finally gained approval by the largely French-speaking province.

SECTION REVIEW

1. Define *welfare state* and *civil rights*.

2. Describe two groups that promote economic unity in Europe.

3. Describe how imported goods affected the American economy in the 1970s and 1980s.

4. Why is language a matter for debate in Canada today?

Evaluation. Should the United States become a welfare state? State your opinion and give reasons to support it.

32–3
THE SOVIET UNION AND EASTERN EUROPE

READ TO FIND OUT

—how the Communist world changed after Stalin's death.

—why the "classless" Communist society has distinct social classes.

—how the Brezhnev Doctrine affected the Soviet Union's satellite nations.

—what caused discontent in the Soviet satellites.

By the end of 1947, Hungary, Poland, Bulgaria, and Romania had Soviet-backed governments. In the next two years,

Czechoslovakia and East Germany also became Soviet satellites, with their foreign and domestic policies directed by Stalin. Yugoslavia and Albania remained the only independent Communist nations in Eastern Europe.

In some cases, nations in Eastern Europe did not submit to permanent Soviet control without resistance. Revolts against Soviet domination occurred in Hungary, Czechoslovakia, and Poland. However, in each case, Soviet military might proved more than sufficient to maintain the authority of Moscow well beyond the Soviet frontier.

CHANGING SOVIET POLICIES

After World War II, Stalin put the Soviet Union back on five-year plans and resumed tight control of the nation's political and cultural affairs. Repression continued to be a way of life in the Soviet Union after Stalin's death in 1953. The government controlled all information, and artists and political commentators had to follow a strict Communist party line or risk being labeled as dissidents. Many dissidents were exiled, sent to labor camps, or declared insane and then institutionalized.

Loyalty to the Communist party was essential for success in any field. The classless society, one of the original Marxist goals, did not exist. Soviet scientists and other highly trained professionals, party officers, and military leaders enjoyed a privileged status in the upper class.

Instead of a middle class of business people, like that in the West, Eastern European nations developed a new middle class of Communist party officials. Members of this class held positions of power and received financial rewards for their service to the party. Consequently, they had a higher standard of living than the average citizen.

Below this class were the urban workers, and at the lowest rung of society were the many people who still worked on farms. Because a family's standard of living was tied to its status in the Communist party, most workers had little hope for gaining a better life.

Khrushchev. Nikita Khrushchev gained power within a few years of Stalin's death. Khrushchev then began to change some economic goals and to institute mild political reforms. In 1956, he shocked Communist party members by denouncing Stalin as a tyrant. In what became known as de-Stalinization, Khrushchev released some people from labor camps and resumed cultural contact with the West.

De-Stalinization caused a serious rift in the Communist world. The Chinese objected to this policy and to Khrushchev's talk of peaceful coexistence with the West. In 1961, they walked out of the Communist party conference, and Albania took their side. Khrushchev, however, continued his new policies and cut off aid to the Chinese.

Khrushchev began to lose power after backing down to the United States during the Cuban missile crisis of 1962. Other Soviet leaders blamed Khrushchev for the Soviet Union's declining agricultural and industrial production. They also felt that Khrushchev had amassed far too much power. As a result, Khrushchev was forced out of office in 1964.

Brezhnev. Leonid I. Brezhnev (BREZH-nef), secretary of the Communist party, at first shared power with Aleksei Kosygin (kō-SEE-gin), premier of the Soviet Union. By the 1970s, however, Brezhnev was in full control and expanded relations with the West. The Soviets bought computers and machinery from the United States and hired American firms to help them build factories. Slowly, Soviet industrial output and living standards rose.

The collective farms, however, still remained the weakest part of the Soviet economy. Harvest failures in 1972 and 1975 caused severe food shortages and led the Soviet Union to buy grain from the United States and Canada.

Although Brezhnev worked at détente with the United States throughout the 1970s, he continued repression at home. Dissidents, including those who favored nuclear disarmament, were not allowed to leave the country. Others were jailed or hospitalized as "politically insane." Many Soviet Jews who were seeking permission to emigrate to Israel were forbidden to do so on grounds that they had access to government secrets.

Brezhnev also did not permit dissent in the European satellite nations. Under what was called the Brezhnev Doctrine, the Soviet Union reserved the right to intervene wherever it believed communism to be threatened. So great was the threat of this doctrine that when Polish dissidents sought more freedom in the early 1980s, the Polish government cracked down rather than risk invasion by Soviet troops.

Outside Europe, Soviet hostility toward China continued until the 1980s. Then officials from the two nations began meeting again, and relations improved.

Brezhnev died in 1982. His immediate successors, first Yuri Andropov and then Konstantin Chernenko, were elderly men who died after brief terms.

Gorbachev. Mikhail Gorbachev came to power in 1985. Only fourteen years old when World War II ended, Gorbachev represented a younger Soviet generation—one that had not experienced the worst years of Stalin's rule.

Gorbachev brought far-reaching reforms to the Soviet Union. In his economic program of *perestroika*, or "restructuring," he used limited forms of free enterprise in an attempt to speed up the sluggish Soviet economy. State-owned businesses were encouraged to become more independent and competitive, and government control of the distribution and prices of goods was reduced.

In addition, private enterprise was encouraged by the government in small-scale service businesses, such as carpentry and plumbing, which can be run by an individual or a family. Small-scale private farming was also encouraged. Gorbachev hoped that such farms would

Mikhail and Raisa Gorbachev arrive in Iceland for Soviet-American arms-control talks. In addition to easing world tensions, the Soviet leader seeks to modernize the Soviet Union's economy.

supplement the inadequate output of collective farms.

Gorbachev also established a policy of *glasnost*, or "openness." Under *Glasnost*, the Soviet media could report events and problems more freely. Books that were once banned were now published, and Western movies and rock music, once forbidden, were now permitted.

As the Soviet Union entered the 1990s, Gorbachev and other leaders struggled with urgent problems: a failing economy and serious threats to national unity. Despite the nation's position as a leading producer of oil, steel, machinery, and technical equipment, its system for producing and distributing consumer goods was desperately inefficient. The people faced severe food shortages. One worker declared, "Where is *perestroika* when the supply of goods in shops is as poor as ever, sugar is bought with ration cards, and there is no meat?" By February 1990, pressures led Gorbachev to call for a multi-party political system.

Dissent threatened Soviet unity. Although Russians are in the majority, over 100 national groups live in the Soviet Union. Encouraged by *glasnost*, some of these groups began to speak freely, voicing long-standing resentment of Soviet rule. For example, in January 1990, leaders of once-independent Lithuania, on the Baltic Sea, sent shock waves through the nation by calling for complete independence.

Meanwhile, in Azerbaijan (A-zhur-bī-ZHON) and Armenia—bordering Iran and Turkey—an old rivalry flared into bloody warfare. This conflict between the Muslim Azerbaijanis and the Christian Armenians forced Soviet officials to "take the measure of last resort" by sending troops to keep order. Some Azerbaijanis then turned their rage against the Soviets and began to demand separation from the Soviet Union and unification with Iran. One Soviet official worried that if one republic seceded, it would be "the beginning of the end."

CHANGE IN EASTERN EUROPE

After 1947, when the Soviet Union would not let the satellites participate in the Marshall Plan, those nations were bound to the Soviet Union economically and politically. The Soviets introduced five-year plans, forcing industrialization and the collectivization of farms. Dissenters fled in the face of jail or death.

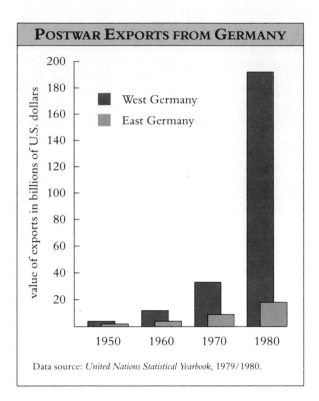

POSTWAR EXPORTS FROM GERMANY

value of exports in billions of U.S. dollars

West Germany
East Germany

1950   1960   1970   1980

Data source: *United Nations Statistical Yearbook,* 1979/1980.

The five-year plans emphasized machinery and heavy equipment rather than consumer goods, and much of what the satellites produced was exported to the Soviet Union. Collective farms proved no more successful in the satellites than in the Soviet Union. Farmers in Poland resisted so strongly that the Soviets finally gave up the effort in that country.

Discontent grew during Stalin's last years. People in satellite nations wanted fewer economic and political controls and improved living standards. In East Germany, severe economic policies and a low standard of living led to strikes and riots in 1953, but Soviet troops quickly crushed the revolt. Living conditions gradually improved, but thousands of East Germans fled to West Germany in pursuit of a democratic and prosperous way of life.

Although Khrushchev and Brezhnev generally kept tight political control of the satellites, they eventually allowed more flexible economic policies. Hungary, for example, introduced some features of a free market system into its economy in the late 1960s. Government control of state-owned factories and farms was reduced, and managers were given some freedom to make decisions. Hungary also increased production of consumer goods and traded with nations outside the Eastern bloc, including the United States.

Struggle for more freedom. Khrushchev's denunciation of Stalin in 1956 gave some of the satellites hope for greater independence from Moscow. Khrushchev allowed Poland to make some national reforms, as long as it remained a member of the Warsaw Pact.

In 1956, encouraged by reforms allowed to the Poles, Hungarian students and workers began demanding an end to the Communist regime and withdrawal from the Warsaw Pact. Khrushchev sent troops and tanks to Budapest, the capital, to put down the uprising.

In Czechoslovakia in 1968, Soviet-backed leaders lost control of the government, and a new leader, Alexander Dubcek (DOOB-chek), came to power. Vowing to bring about "communism with a human face," Dubcek introduced major reforms such as a free press. Soviet leaders saw Dubcek's reforms as a threat. After all, if one satellite state was permitted political freedom from Moscow, soon the rest would demand similar privileges. Citing the Brezhnev Doctrine, the Soviets sent troops into Czechoslovakia and reestablished control.

In Poland, worsening economic conditions led to strikes by workers in 1980. The government gave workers permission to form a new labor union controlled by its members, not by the state. In a drive for economic and political reforms, the union—called Solidarity—staged strikes and demonstrations and at first seemed to make headway. After the Polish army took control of the country in 1981, the new government leader promised reforms. Then, fearing that Soviet troops would step in, he banned the union in 1982 and arrested many of its leaders. Demonstrations dropped dramatically.

SPOTLIGHT: DAILY LIFE

THE SOVIET UNION AND WORLD TRADE

The Soviet Union produces about 20 percent of the world's total industrial output. Yet, it accounts for less than 3 percent of the world's trade. Why does such an industrial giant play so small a role in international trade? The answer, in part, lies in the nature of the Soviet currency—the ruble.

When traders sell goods, they expect to be paid in money that they can use. Therefore, most world trade is carried out in the currencies of highly-industrialized nations because this money can be used easily to buy the products industrial nations have to sell. For example, if Costa Rica sells its farm products for American dollars, it can use those dollars to buy needed manufactured goods from the United States. Other widely-used currencies are the Japanese yen, the British pound, the West German mark, and the Swiss franc.

The Soviet ruble is not part of this system of world trade. To maintain control over its economy, the Soviet government has greatly restricted the use of the ruble. It is illegal to bring rubles into or take them out of the Soviet Union. Therefore, if a foreign trader sells a product in the Soviet Union in return for rubles, the trader must spend the rubles in the Soviet Union. However, the Soviets have concentrated on producing military hardware and heavy machinery for use in their own country rather than on consumer goods a trader might want to buy.

The nature of the ruble has also hampered recent Soviet efforts at *perestroika*. The Soviet Union has tried to attract investments from foreign companies. However, these companies have had trouble taking their profits out of the Soviet Union. Because they cannot exchange the ruble for other currencies, foreign companies have to find other ways to take their profits.

Some companies take their profits in goods and then sell these goods for a more useful currency. For example, Roma Food, a New Jersey pizza company with plans to open a chain of pizzerias with Soviet partners, has agreed to take its profits in mushrooms, champagne, and cut glass. For other companies, profits come in the form of gasoline, furs, caviar, sugar, and even T-shirts.

Many foreign companies are willing to accept this barter arrangement. However, economists on both sides of the Iron Curtain agree that foreign investment in the Soviet economy will not expand until the Soviet ruble becomes freely-exchangeable currency.

Tearing down the iron curtain. In 1988, with the Polish economy tottering, workers once again went on strike. Finally, public pressure led the failing Communist government to legalize Solidarity, led by Lech Walesa. An election was held in June 1989, and Solidarity members won nearly half the seats in the legislature. By August, Poland had a non-Communist prime minister, creating the first non-Communist government in Eastern Europe since World War II.

Hungary also began to move away from Communism. Seeking to improve its ties with the West, Hungary startled the Communist world by tearing down the 150-mile barbed wire barrier separating it from Austria.

As a result, East Germans began to flee their country through Hungary. First thousands, then tens of thousands, made their way west. Meanwhile, influenced by Gorbachev's ideas of openness and reform and by Poland's success, those who remained behind flooded the streets of cities, chanting for democratic reforms.

On November 10, the East German government made an historic announcement: "Today, the decision was taken that makes it possible for all citizens to leave the country through East German border crossing points." Within 2 days, more than 1 million East Germans streamed into West Berlin through the gates of the Berlin Wall, symbol of the cold war. Soon, Germans even began to speak openly of reuniting the two Germanies—East and West—into one nation.

Change came swiftly. By spring 1990, in the first free elections since before World War II, East Germans chose a non-Communist government. The new government moved quickly to develop closer ties with West Germany. By June 1990, the two Germanies had worked out a plan to unify the economies of the two nations—by having a single currency, for example.

Change came swiftly to other nations, as well. In fall 1989, in Czechoslovakia the first anti-government demonstration in 20 years took place, with throngs of people parading the streets of Prague. By New Year's Day 1990, a non-Communist president took the oath of office.

In December 1989, thousands rallied in Sofia, Bulgaria, in support of reform, and in January 1990, the national legislature voted to end one-party rule. Pushed to the limit by harsh rule, the Romanian people also took to the streets. The hardline Communist government was toppled and its leader executed. In January 1990, Romania outlawed the Communist party.

Crowds of East and West Germans celebrated the end of the Berlin Wall with cheering, singing, and dancing in the streets of Berlin. Thousands rejoiced by climbing atop the wall.

Changes in Yugoslavia. After World War II, Yugoslavia had followed a different course than the Eastern European satellites. Yugoslavia was freed from the Nazis largely by Yugoslav forces led by Josip Broz, known as Tito (TEE-toh), who took control of the country. Tito was a Communist, but he refused to let the Soviet Union dictate to Yugoslavia. He allowed profit making, worker control of industry, and some private land ownership. Yugoslavia traded with the West and received Western foreign aid. In 1989, the Communist party of Yugoslavia voted to allow greater political expression and more individual freedom.

1. How did the Soviet Union and other Communist nations change after the death of Stalin?

2. What factors determine class status in the Communist countries?

3. Describe one instance in which the Soviets acted on the Brezhnev Doctrine.

4. Describe the major reasons for discontent in the Soviet satellites.

Analysis. Compare the Soviet economic system with that of a free-enterprise nation. In what important ways are they different?

32–4
CULTURE AND SOCIETY: EAST AND WEST

READ TO FIND OUT

—what the terms *high-tech* and *popular culture* mean.

—who the new immigrants to Western societies in the 1970s were.

—how the roles of women changed after World War II.

—how influences on artists and writers in the West and in Eastern Europe differed.

Rapid advances in technology had a major impact on culture and the arts. Songs and movies that once might have been popular in only one nation now gained worldwide audiences. Even so, vast differences have remained between the cultures of the East and the West, despite some common elements.

CHANGES IN WESTERN SOCIETY

By the 1950s, many people in the West began to enjoy a level of affluence, or high standard of living, such as had never been seen before. In this time of prosperity, people gained more education and the middle class grew rapidly. The new affluence and increasing technological advances brought an increase in service jobs, such as white-collar office jobs, many of them held by women.

Work in manufacturing, or blue-collar jobs, began to decline after the 1950s. In the United States and several other industrialized nations, this change signaled the beginning of a major shift in the economy—from manufacturing and heavy industry, such as steel and auto production, to service and *high-tech* industries. High-tech, which is short for high-technology, refers to very specialized, complex technology. Beginning in the 1960s, production of computers and sophisticated electronic equipment formed an entirely new segment of Western industry and required highly skilled workers.

The rising affluence of Western societies attracted immigrants, most of whom took unskilled and low-paying jobs that native-born workers no longer wished to fill. Beginning in the 1970s, these immigrants included political refugees from Asia and Latin America. Many of these immigrants had been professionals or business owners in their homelands and within a few years regained their former economic status. Other immigrants, however, were unskilled and uneducated. Many observers worried about a permanent split between an affluent majority and a poorly educated, low-paid minority.

Opportunities for women. The booming Western economies in the 1950s and 1960s also helped to open new opportunities for women in the labor force. By the 1970s, women made up more than 40 percent of the work force in Western nations. However, even though women now had more education than ever before, they found many jobs closed to them. They also discovered that they generally received less pay than men for doing the same work.

Women soon began a vigorous protest against these inequities. The women's rights movement that began in the United States in the 1960s among middle-class women soon spread to other Western countries and to all social classes.

Women also made significant political advances. Some, such as Margaret Thatcher, won key political offices, and in 1984, Geraldine Ferraro ran for vice-president of the United

ABSTRACT EXPRESSIONISM

By the mid-twentieth century, many artists were working in abstract styles that depended upon shapes, colors, and textures to provoke strong feelings. Little interested in representing events or objects, these artists cared about the expression of inner spirit in their work. One artist voiced the views of many: "Are not the children who construct directly from the secrets of their emotions more creative than the imitators of Greek form?"

Marilyn Monroe, Willem de Kooning, 1954

Black Widow, Alexander Calder, 1959

Magenta, Black, Green on Orange, Mark Rothko, 1949

Convergence Number 10, 1952, Jackson Pollock, 1952

States. The mere fact of her nomination was revolutionary, since a woman had never before been selected by a major American political party to run for such a high office.

Literature and the arts. Postwar literature reflected the complexity and variety of modern life. Many writers tried to understand the war that had just taken place. Others reacted to what they felt was the futility of living in a world under the threat of nuclear holocaust, or total destruction of life. Some writers used their work to protest the conditions of modern life.

One of the major influences on postwar literature and thought was a philosophy called existentialism. The existentialists rejected scientific methods and ideals as inappropriate to philosophy. They emphasized the importance of the individual, arguing that human beings create meaning through their actions and choices.

In art and architecture, a lively period of experimentation began after the war. The most influential school of art in the 1950s and early 1960s was abstract expressionism. Painters who used this style, such as American Mark Rothko, born Marcus Rothkovich in Russia, experimented with color and forms. Sculpture also went through a period of abstraction.

In the late 1960s, "pop" artists such as Andy Warhol, also from the United States, used everyday objects like soup cans and comic strips in their work. These large, hard-edged images became another kind of abstract expression. "Op" art took abstraction one step further by creating optical effects, such as the illusion of movement. Representational art, which sought to show people and objects as they were, returned to favor in the 1970s and 1980s.

In architecture, the international style, which had its roots in prewar Germany, dominated the postwar period. This style featured unadorned exteriors and extensive use of glass and concrete. The 1970s saw the rise of a style called postmodernism, which combined elements of old and new, such as the use of classical figures on sleek skyscrapers.

Entertainment. Affluence produced an explosion of *popular culture*—entertainment that appeals to a mass audience. Television became an especially powerful agent of this mass culture, uniting people within the country and tying nations more closely together. Television also pro-

Television brought the Vietnam War into millions of American homes. The conflict has been called the first to be fought on TV. Here, TV crews film South Vietnamese Communist leaders.

vided an easy escape from daily life, with an unending stream of comedies, police shows, westerns, sports events, and newscasts. Television played an important role in shaping people's perceptions of events and their response to those events.

Technological advances revolutionized the way music was made and recorded, and electronic devices called synthesizers created completely new sounds. Social developments also changed the music scene, with the influence of black musicians showing in the popularity of rhythm and blues, reggae, and rap. Popular music became an important means of cross-cultural communication.

Rock music served as a major form of expression for young people in the 1960s and 1970s. In the late 1970s, punk rockers in Western countries began protesting conformity and complacency in society.

After World War II, most movies continued to be a way to escape from everyday life, as they had been during the Great Depression. Like postwar literature, however, some films protested social conditions or reflected the bewilderment many people felt with modern life.

Science and technology. After the Soviets launched *Sputnik*, the first artificial space satellite, in 1957, the United States placed a new emphasis on science and mathematics at all levels of schooling. Nations in Western Europe responded to the Soviet challenge by increasing technical colleges. The result of this increased

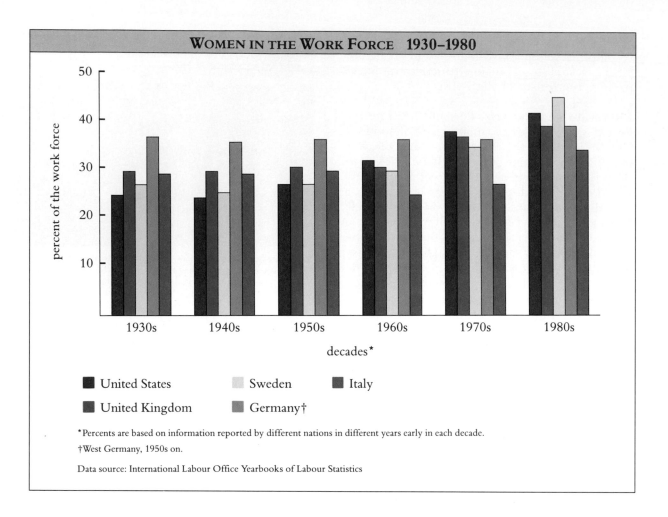

WOMEN IN THE WORK FORCE 1930–1980

percent of the work force

decades*

■ United States □ Sweden ■ Italy
■ United Kingdom ■ Germany†

*Percents are based on information reported by different nations in different years early in each decade.
†West Germany, 1950s on.

Data source: International Labour Office Yearbooks of Labour Statistics

interest was a spectacular rate of growth in technological and scientific knowledge.

The American space program benefited the most from this accelerated growth and in 1969 successfully landed astronauts on the moon and returned them safely to earth. By the early 1980s, the program also developed the first reusable spacecraft to carry astronauts and materials back and forth between the earth and orbiting space stations and to launch satellites.

New technology generated by the space program was applied to the development of products for ordinary use. For example, microchips, first developed for satellites, made it possible to design personal computers so small that they could be easily carried from place to place.

New technology can also pose new problems. For example, to provide inexpensive energy, nations built many nuclear power plants in the 1960s and 1970s. However, disposal of deadly radioactive wastes produced in the power plants and accidental releases of radioactivity are hazards of nuclear power production.

Other advances in science have raised questions about how societies adapt to change. For example, with advances in medical technology, a society must decide how to pay for expensive new techniques.

SOCIAL CHANGES IN EASTERN EUROPE

Like Western nations, Eastern nations also became industrial, urban, and relatively prosperous. However, society in the East has been influenced as much by Communist teachings as by industrial and urban growth.

Role of women. Communist teachings, which stress the equality of the sexes, led to expanded roles for women. Even before World War II, women were an integral part of the work force. In the Soviet Union during the war, women stepped into the jobs of men who went to battle. High casualties caused a shortage of workers, and many women remained in their wartime jobs well into the 1950s.

Although a vital part of the economy in the decades after the war, many women were confined to low-paying jobs. By 1974, about 60 million Soviet women held jobs outside the home. This number equaled about 85 percent of all working-age women, compared with about 40 percent in the Western nations.

Women in the Soviet Union performed heavy manual labor as well as office and professional work. Although many women worked in government, they seldom held powerful positions in the Communist party. Even in the 1980s, the upper levels of the Communist party have been reserved exclusively for men.

Literature and the arts. Communist governments have long influenced literature and art in Eastern Europe. Socialist realism in art was first introduced in the Soviet Union in the 1920s, after the Communist revolution. Paintings and sculpture portrayed those who worked for the good of the state—the industrial laborers, collective farmers, students, and soldiers—as healthy and happy heroes.

The thaw of the 1950s under Khrushchev had a profound effect on artists and intellectuals. In the satellite nations, art began to reflect the renewed sense of nationalism that accompanied the uprisings in Poland and Hungary in 1956. Yet those uprisings led to another tightening of restrictions by the Soviets and to stricter censorship.

By the mid-1960s, some artists chose to flee those restrictions and defect to the West. In part, these artists moved to the West because of the lack of an audience for their works, since the state dictates what may be performed and published in Eastern Europe and buys most of the art works, at a set price. In the mid-1980s, however, as a result of *glasnost*—the new Soviet policy of openness—censorship decreased, allowing artists to express new ideas more freely than in the past.

SECTION REVIEW

1. Define *high-tech* and *popular culture*.

2. Why did Western nations attract a new flood of immigrants in the 1970s?

3. Describe how the roles of women in both Eastern Europe and the West changed after World War II.

4. Compare the influences that have shaped the works of postwar artists and writers in Eastern Europe and in the West.

Analysis. Compare the Western tradition of individualism with the Communist philosophy that puts the needs of the state—the society as a whole—above individual freedoms. For both traditions, show how historical developments helped shape attitudes and values that support the present system.

Data Search. Compare the information on Great Britain, the United States, and the Soviet Union in the appropriate chart on page 834 to determine which country in 1988 had **(a)** the highest population density, **(b)** the highest percentage of industrial workers, **(c)** the highest ratio of physicians to population, and **(d)** the highest per capita income.

HISTORY IN FOCUS

The United States and Canada remained politically and economically stable during the Second World War and were able to focus on expanding their economies in the postwar years. Increasing affluence led to changes in society and culture. Advances in science and technology abounded, and the American economy began to shift from heavy manufacturing to service industries.

In the postwar years, Western Europe saw changes in government from totalitarian regimes and military rule to socialist democracies and other forms of constitutional government. Inasmuch as each nation has its own political history—many have been dictatorships—each has taken its own path to political and economic stability.

In 1989, great upheaval in Eastern Europe speeded the region's independence from the Soviet Union. New leaders in the Soviet Union developed warmer relations with the West and less restrictive policies at home than earlier Soviet leaders had. The Soviet leadership's new policy of openness has been welcomed by both Soviet citizens and people around the world. The 1990s will continue to be a time of change as communism is cast aside or radically changed, and the new regimes take their place on the world stage.

SUMMARY

- After World War II, the United States and the Soviet Union became the world's two most powerful nations. They began an ideological struggle known as the cold war.

- Western Europe remained politically stable and democratic. With American aid, it quickly recovered from the war and entered a new era of prosperity that lasted until high oil prices led to a worldwide business slowdown in the 1970s. Governments then started to limit social welfare programs.

- Fear of communism in the United States led the government to intervene diplomatically, economically, and militarily in the affairs of nations around the world. At home, the civil rights movement ended legal segregation against blacks and spurred demands for equal treatment by other groups. As women gained more education and entered the work force in record numbers, they too demanded equal rights and more equitable pay.

- Canada's economy grew rapidly. The government tried to limit American investment and to give more rights to the French-speaking minority.

- Eastern European nations became satellites of the Soviet Union. After Stalin's death, repression eased somewhat, but uprisings against Soviet control in Poland, Hungary, and Czechoslovakia were quickly put down.

- Different ideologies in the East and West produced different cultures. Rising affluence affected society in the West. In the Communist bloc a new middle class arose, made up of Communist party officials. Both East and West made great advances in science and technology.

VOCABULARY REVIEW

Match each numbered term with the lettered term most closely related to it. Then explain how the terms in each pair are related.

1. civil rights   (a) cold war
2. containment   (b) peaceful coexistence
3. détente   (c) constitution

CHAPTER REVIEW

1. (a) What policies did the Soviet Union follow in Eastern Europe after World War II? **(b)** How did President Truman respond to these Soviet policies? **(c)** What are NATO and the Warsaw Pact?

2. (a) Why was Berlin a source of cold-war tensions? **(b)** How did events in Cuba contribute to a heightening of world tensions? **(c)** How have relations between the United States and the Soviet Union changed since 1979?

3. (a) What are the Benelux nations? How did they serve as a model for other European nations? **(b)** What part did they play in furthering European economic cooperation? **(c)** What is the European Economic Community and what are its goals?

4. What changes in social welfare policies occurred in Western Europe after the war?

5. (a) Why did the United States become involved in a war in Vietnam? **(b)** What impact did the Vietnam War have on politics in the United States?

6. (a) Why did President Nixon seek to open relations with China in the 1970s? **(b)** What foreign policy successes did Nixon achieve?

7. (a) What changes did Khrushchev make in Soviet policies that had been in place since Stalin's time? **(b)** How did Brezhnev's policies differ from Khrushchev's? **(c)** Did political and economic conditions in the Soviet Union change substantially under Gorbachev? Explain your answer.

8. (a) How were economic policies established in Eastern Europe after World War II? **(b)** What were the aims of these policies? **(c)** How did Eastern European nations show dissatisfaction with Soviet policies?

9. (a) What has caused increased cross-cultural contacts among nations since World War II? **(b)** What evidence of cross-cultural interchange can be found in music?

10. (a) How do the roles of women in society differ between Eastern and Western nations? **(b)** How does the new policy of openness benefit Soviet society?

THINKING CRITICALLY: ACTIVITIES

1. Select members of the class to act as representatives from the Soviet Union and its satellite nations. Soviet and Eastern European representatives discuss whether the relationship is an advantage or disadvantage for Eastern Europe.

2. Much of postwar military policy has hinged on a balance of nuclear power between the United States and the Soviet Union. Collect newspaper articles and then write a brief report on this topic: Is nuclear disarmament desirable?

3. Divide into groups of four or five to discuss specific environmental and economic problems, such as international trade deficits. Have a representative from each group present conclusions and possible solutions for these problems.

APPLYING SOCIAL STUDIES SKILLS

Analyzing statistical tables. Look carefully at the following table and answer the questions.

AMERICAN LIVING STANDARDS 1900 AND 1970		
	% of all families: 1900	% of poor families: 1970
Running water	24	98
Refrigeration	18	99
Flush toilets	15	99
Electricity	3	99
Central heating	1	58
Automobiles	1	41

Data source: *The American Economy*, by Stanley Lebergott. Princeton, 1976.

1. What do the numbers represent?

2. Which items did more than 90 percent of poor families have in 1970? Which items did less than 50 percent have?

3. Which item shows the greatest percentage increase between 1900 and 1970? The smallest?

4. Briefly summarize what this table shows.

APPLYING THINKING SKILLS

Identifying evidence. Below is an excerpt from a speech delivered by Winston Churchill in 1946 at Westminster College in Missouri. Analyze it to determine what evidence Churchill provided that is relevant to his claim. Then answer the questions that follow the excerpt.

It is my duty . . . to place before you certain facts about the present position in Europe. . . . From Stettin in the Baltic to Trieste in the Adriatic, an iron curtain has descended across the Continent. Behind that line lie all the capitals of the ancient states of central and eastern Europe. Warsaw, Berlin, Prague, Vienna, Budapest, Belgrade, Bucharest, and Sofia; all these famous cities and the populations around them lie in what I might call the Soviet sphere and all are subject . . . to a very high and increasing measure of control from Moscow. Athens alone, with its immortal glories, is free to decide its future. . . . The Russian-dominated Polish government has been encouraged to make enormous and wrongful inroads upon Germany, and mass expulsions of millions of Germans on a scale grievous and undreamed of are now taking place. . . .

. . . Police governments are prevailing in nearly every case, and so far, except in Czechoslovakia, there is no true democracy. . . . Whatever conclusions may be drawn from these facts . . . this is certainly not the liberated Europe we fought to build up. Nor is it one which contains the essentials of permanent peace. . . .

If the Western democracies stand together in strict adherence to the principles of the United Nations Charter, their influence for furthering those principles will be immense and no one is likely to molest them. If, however, they become divided or falter in their duty, and if these all-important years are allowed to slip away, then indeed catastrophe may overwhelm us all.

From Winston Churchill's "iron curtain" speech, published in *Vital Speeches of the Day*, March 15, 1946.

1. Define the term *evidence*.

2. Why is it important to search for evidence that is relevant to a claim?

3. Identify Churchill's claim in the first paragraph and three pieces of evidence supporting that claim.

CHAPTER THIRTY-THREE

TENSIONS IN THE MIDDLE EAST

1945–PRESENT

American President Jimmy Carter addressing the Israeli parliament, 1979.

During its long history, the Middle East has been a crossroads for trade and cultural diffusion, a cradle of religions, and a center of cultural development. After most countries of the Middle East and neighboring North Africa achieved their independence in the two decades following World War II, the region once again assumed a central role in world history. As new political boundaries left the peoples of this region more divided than ever before, old rivalries resurfaced to fuel new tensions. Traditional ways began to clash with modern, while the superpowers—the United States and the Soviet Union—competed for influence within the region. The Middle East and North Africa quickly became a center of world conflict.

33–1
THE ORIGINS OF CONFLICT

READ TO FIND OUT

—what religious and ethnic groups inhabit the Middle East and North Africa.
—how countries under French and British mandate achieved independence.
—how Israel was created.
—how nations of North Africa obtained self-rule.

World War II signaled the end of European rule in the Middle East. A few countries on the eastern and southern fringes of Arabia did not achieve formal independence until about two decades after the war. However, the years immediately following 1945 saw important countries of the Middle East break away from direct foreign control to join others that had gained independence after World War I. As new political boundaries were drawn and a Jewish nation was created in Palestine, the seeds of future conflict were sown.

The nations of North Africa threw off colonial rule between 1951 and 1962. Although not as divided politically as the nations of the Middle East, the North African nations shared problems common to new nations in the postwar era. North Africans were also closely tied to the peoples of the Middle East and their conflicts. The people of North Africa shared the common culture and religion of Islam, and for some, a common Arab identity. Since World War II, the term *Middle East* has increasingly come to include North Africa.

THE LEGACY OF THE PAST

At the crossroads of three continents, the peoples of the Middle East have since ancient times played important roles as merchants, scientists, and artisans. They have played key roles in the birth and spread of major religions. They have both conquered and been conquered. Modern inhabitants of this region have inherited a past

TIMELINE

1945	
	Syria becomes independent
	League of Arab Nations established
	Lebanon becomes independent
1950	
	State of Israel proclaimed
	Shah of Iran restored to throne
	Egypt becomes a republic
1955	
	Nasser becomes Egypt's leader
	Egypt nationalizes the Suez Canal
1960	
	OPEC formed
	PLO formed
1965	
	Six-Day War
	Qadhafi becomes ruler of Libya
1970	
	Yom Kippur War
	OPEC oil embargo
1975	
	Egyptian-Israeli peace treaty
	Islamic revolution in Iran
1980	
	Israeli invasion of Lebanon
	Iran-Iraq War
1985	

Muslim pilgrims pray at the Kaaba, the holiest shrine of Islam, in the city of Mecca in Saudi Arabia. Every Muslim must, if possible, make at least one pilgrimage to Mecca.

of conflict and memories of repression, forced migration, and foreign rule. Yet, many peoples have been brought together by common culture and language, and by the religion of Islam.

Diverse peoples and religions. The people of the Middle East and North Africa who embrace Islam are ethnically diverse. They include Arabs in the heartland of the Middle East, Berbers in North Africa, Turks in Asia Minor, and Persians. Tensions have flared between these peoples for centuries. The Arabs and Persians, for example, have maintained separate civilizations and cultures and an intense rivalry since ancient times. Often one people has dominated others, as when the Ottoman Turks ruled many Arab and Berber lands from about 1500 to 1917.

Although Islam has tended to bring some unity to these peoples, there are significant divisions within Islam. In the 600s, a major split occurred between the Sunnis and Shiites who disagreed on who should lead the Muslim community. Although most Arabs, Berbers, and Turks are Sunnis, and most Persians are Shiites, this division also crosses ethnic lines.

Besides Muslims, large numbers of Jews and Christians call the Middle East and North Africa home. Jews and Christians regard Jerusalem as a holy city. However, Jerusalem and the surrounding lands of Palestine have also been inhabited since ancient times by Arabs, many of whom became Muslims. Muslims also consider Jerusalem a holy city.

Foreign rule. In addition to the conflicts caused by these religious and ethnic divisions, the Middle East and North Africa have been affected by their recent history of foreign rule. During the centuries of Ottoman control before World War I, the needs of non-Turkish people living within the empire were given little attention. The Ottoman Turks made up the ruling

RESEARCHING CURRENT EVENTS

INTRODUCING THE SKILL

One reason for studying world history is to gain the knowledge needed to understand and analyze current events around the world. Knowledge of current events is essential for making informed judgments as a voter and is useful in many types of jobs. Much of our information about current events comes from newspapers. Most libraries subscribe to local newspapers and to widely circulated newspapers such as the *New York Times* and the *Wall Street Journal*. The tools for researching current events are in the reference section of your library.

EXPLAINING THE SKILL

To find information on current events quickly, you have to know where to look. Your choices will depend in part on what your library has available. Three common references for locating information found in newspapers are *Facts on File, National Newspaper Index,* and printed indexes for specific newspapers.

A. *Facts on File* is a large, looseleaf binder containing weekly summaries of world news on various subjects, such as *Israel* or *Palestinians.* Each fact-filled summary is based on articles in more than 50 foreign and American newspapers. Summaries of the most recent news are added to the binder each week. At the end of each year, all the weekly summaries are published in a bound book titled *Facts on File Yearbook.*

Instructions on how to use *Facts on File* are at the front of each binder. At the back of each year's binder, you will find both a blue and a yellow index. A new yellow index comes out every three months and lists all topics covered since the year began. Blue indexes come out twice a month and list the most recent articles. Check both indexes when using *Facts on File.*

B. *National Newspaper Index* lists recent articles in five major newspapers: the *New York Times, Wall Street Journal, Christian Science Monitor, Los Angeles Times,* and *Washington Post.* The index is on microfilm, and some libraries also have it in computer files.

National Newspaper Index lists subjects in alphabetical order. Under each subject heading, articles are in reverse chronological order, with the most recent article listed first. Listings go back for approximately three years. The index gives each article's title, author, and date; the name of the newspaper; and the article's location in the newspaper.

C. Libraries may also have printed indexes for specific newspapers. The most widely used printed index is *The New York Times Index,* which has yearly listings of *New York Times* articles going back to 1851. Indexes are for a number of other major city newspapers, including the *Houston Post, Detroit News, Chicago Tribune, Los Angeles Times, Denver Post, San Francisco Chronicle, Boston Globe,* and *The Atlanta Constitution.* Indexes are also printed for *The Wall Street Journal, Christian Science Monitor,* and *USA Today.*

Printed indexes list subjects in alphabetical order and give each article's title, author, date, and location. The most important articles are briefly summarized. Under each subject heading, articles are in chronological order, with the earliest listed first. Under a particular subject heading, such as *Egypt,* you may be referred to other headings.

Annual hardcover volumes of newspaper indexes are updated with paperback volumes that come out once or twice a month and list the most recent articles. At the front or back of each volume, you will find instructions on how to use the index and a list of the abbreviations used in the index.

REVIEWING THE SKILL

What do each of the following sources offer researchers looking for information on current events?

1. *Facts on File.*
2. *National Newspaper Index.*
3. Printed newspaper indexes.

class, which bred resentment among non-Turks. Moreover, the long decline of Ottoman power, which had begun in the late 1500s, brought political disorder and economic stagnation to much of the region.

Colonial rule in North Africa and the Middle East, lasting from the early nineteenth century to after World War II in some countries, also had important effects. Foreign control bred nationalist movements and a desire among many leaders for what they believed to be the benefits of westernization. When peoples of the Middle East and North Africa began to win their independence, the newly established countries largely followed the European model of the nation-state and began to modernize.

Several Middle Eastern nations achieved independence before the end of World War II and became the leading nations of the region in the postwar period. Egypt won partial self-rule from the British in 1922; Arabia became an independent kingdom called Saudi Arabia between 1916 and 1932; and Iraq achieved independence in 1932. Defeated in World War I, the Ottoman Empire was dismantled, and its heartland—Turkey—became an independent nation in 1923. Persia gradually shook off British and Russian control after World War I and became Iran.

Other countries of the Middle East, which had been Ottoman territories, were made mandates of Great Britain or France by the League of Nations after the war. France received Syria and Lebanon, and Great Britain took over control of Palestine.

SELF-RULE IN THE MIDDLE EAST

After World War II, Syria, Lebanon, and Palestine threw off foreign rule. These countries lay between the eastern shores of the Mediterranean and the independent nations of Saudi Arabia and Iraq.

The French mandates were controlled by France's military between the wars. In Syria, most people were against French rule, and the years of French control were full of uprisings and French reprisals. France, which was in a weak position at the end of World War II, gave in to Syrian demands for self-rule, and Syria became independent in 1946. France finally withdrew all of its troops from Syria by the end of that year.

In contrast, French rule in Lebanon was welcomed by its Christian population which feared Muslim control of the government. Despite the religious divisions in this small country, the period between the two world wars was characterized by peaceful growth. After 1936, the Lebanese began to demand independence, and the last French troops left an independent Lebanon in 1946.

South of Syria and Lebanon, Britain had split its mandate of Palestine into two countries, using the Jordan River as a dividing line. On the river's eastern side was Trans-Jordan, which means "across the Jordan." In 1921, the British created Trans-Jordan in order to protect their claims to oil deposits in Iraq and their access to the Suez Canal. Thus Trans-Jordan had no history of cultural unity or recognized geographical borders. In 1946, however, the British granted the people of this region independence because they had supported the Allies during World War II.

THE CREATION OF ISRAEL

The lands on the western side of the Jordan River also became independent after World War II, but, in a way, that event would cause lasting conflict. After 1946, this small area, called Palestine during the period of the British mandate, became the object of a bitter struggle between Jews and Palestinian Arabs. Both groups claimed that the land of Palestine was theirs.

Since the late 1800s, Jews all over the world had been calling for the establishment of a Jewish homeland in Palestine, the site of a Jewish state destroyed by the Roman Empire in A.D. 66. In 1917, during World War I, Britain announced in the Balfour Declaration that it favored the creation of a "national home for Jewish people." This home should be created without prejudicing the "civil and religious rights of existing non-Jewish communities in Palestine."

The Holocaust in Europe before and during World War II strengthened Zionism, the movement for a Jewish state. Many Jews had immigrated to Palestine during the 1930s, and Hitler's persecution had created an even stronger desire for a Jewish nation among the survivors of the Holocaust. At the same time, many world leaders were in sympathy with the Zionist cause.

Arabs living in Palestine, however, opposed both increased Jewish immigration and any plan for the creation of a Jewish nation. They feared they would lose the right to live on lands they had inhabited for thousands of years. As violence between the two groups increased, Britain's plan for shared rule between Arabs and the growing number of Jews was soundly rejected by Arabs. Unable to keep order in the region, Britain turned over the problem of administration of the area to the United Nations in 1947 and announced that a year later it would withdraw all its troops from Palestine.

As the British prepared to withdraw, the United Nations drew up a plan to divide Palestine into two independent states, one Jewish and the other Arab. This plan was rejected by the Arabs in Palestine, who outnumbered Jews by about two to one. When the British forces withdrew in 1948, however, the Jewish leader David Ben-Gurion proclaimed the independent state of Israel.

Arab-Israeli war. Refusing to recognize the new nation, Egypt, Trans-Jordan, Lebanon, Syria, and Iraq sent troops to invade Israel in support of the Palestinian Arabs. In what they called the "war of survival," the Jews gained in more than a year of fighting even more territory than had been called for under the plan established by the United Nations.

In 1949, an armistice was signed, but fighting did not completely end, and no agreement was reached about Israel's borders. Most of Palestine became the state of Israel. The West Bank—the area on the west bank of the Jordan River that was to become a Palestinian state under the UN plan—was joined with Trans-Jordan, which became known simply as Jordan. Jerusalem was also split into Israeli and Jordanian sections.

As a result of the creation of Israel and the Arab-Israeli war, about 700,000 Palestinian Arabs became refugees, fleeing to Jordan, Syria, Lebanon, and parts of Egypt. From these lands, Palestinians organized to launch raids against Israel.

Growth after independence. After independence, Israel developed quickly into a strong and modern nation. Its first leaders were President Chaim Weizmann (VĪTS-mahn) and Prime Minister David Ben-Gurion. More Jewish im-

migrants poured in from many countries, including Arab ones. Many people settled on a type of collective farm called a *kibbutz* (kih-BOOTS). Using ancient water-saving ideas and modern technology, Israeli farmers turned desert areas into thriving farms.

Other immigrants, many of them highly skilled and educated Europeans and Americans, settled in cities, and Israel developed numerous modern industries. Israel also received loans and gifts from the United States government and other donors worldwide. Israel's quick and successful growth and modernization contributed even more to Arab-Israeli hostility, which would continue to fuel Middle Eastern conflict.

THE RISE OF EGYPT

Although Egypt had been formally independent since 1922, nationalists resented the control that the British government had retained in the country. Following World War II, Britain still had a military base at Suez, owned most of the Suez Canal, and heavily influenced Egypt's monarch, King Farouk (fuh-ROOK). Nationalists believed this British influence held back Egypt's development.

In 1952, nationalist army officers ousted the king. The following year they abolished the monarchy and made Egypt a republic. By 1954, a strong-willed leader named Gamal Abdel Nasser (NAS-uhr) had become Egypt's prime minister. Nasser set out to reform Egypt's poverty-ridden society, free Egypt of British influence, and establish himself as a leader of the Arab world.

NEW NATIONS OF NORTH AFRICA

Soon after most Middle Eastern nations gained independence, North African countries began to achieve self-rule. Each nation's struggle for independence differed considerably depending on which European power had ruled it and for how long.

Libya was the first nation to throw off colonial rule. It had been controlled first by the Ottoman Empire, then by Italy, a nation defeated in World War II. As a result of the treaties ending the war, France and Britain had been given temporary control over Libya. In 1949, the United Nations declared that Libya would be independent within two years.

Egyptian police try to clear a path for President Nasser in April 1956. Nasser's guiding principles of nationalism and Arab unity made him popular throughout the Middle East.

Libya's independence in 1951 generated agitation for self-rule in other North African countries controlled by France. In both Morocco—which had been independent for 11 centuries before French occupation—and Tunisia, widespread riots broke out between 1951 and 1954. The French finally pulled out of both countries in 1956.

The French were more reluctant to give up control of Algeria, which they considered to be a province of France. Algeria had been a French colony since 1830. The French had poured millions of dollars into the colony, and nearly one million French people lived there.

Algerian nationalists declared open war against France in 1954, and bitter fighting dragged on for seven and a half years at a cost of more than one million lives. Finally in 1962, France negotiated an armistice with the nationalists, and Algeria gained its independence. Algerians joined other North Africans and Middle Easterners in facing the difficult challenges of the modern world.

SECTION REVIEW

1. Name the major ethnic groups of the Middle East and North Africa, along with the areas in which they live.

2. How did Syria, Lebanon, and Trans-Jordan achieve independence?

3. Describe how the independent state of Israel was created.

4. How did Libya, Morocco, Tunisia, and Algeria gain their independence?

Evaluation. Did Britain make the best decision in turning over administration of Palestine to the United Nations? Explain your answer, giving supporting evidence.

33-2
THE CHALLENGE OF MODERNIZATION

READ TO FIND OUT

—what the terms *concessions* and *cartel* mean.
—why the superpowers tried to gain influence in the Middle East.
—what caused the Suez crisis of 1956.
—how nations tried to overcome barriers to modernization.
—what political changes resulted from attempts to achieve economic growth.

Once most of the nations of the Middle East and North Africa had achieved independence, the struggle against imperialism gave way to new issues and to intensified conflict within the region. As French and British influence declined, the world's new superpowers, the United States and the Soviet Union, began to compete for allies among the region's new nations.

During the 1950s and 1960s, the Middle East gained international importance because of its strategic location near the Soviet Union and because of its new prize—oil. At the same time, leaders' efforts to modernize their nations brought new and difficult challenges.

THE NEW IMPORTANCE OF OIL

After World War II, Middle Eastern oil became increasingly important to the industrialized nations, which were rebuilding factories, roads, and railways following the destruction of the war. Oil production rose in the Middle East, and conflicts between nations and corporations from all over the world developed over control of oil deposits and oil wealth.

In 1908, oil had been discovered in Persia—the country that is now called Iran. Between the two world wars, foreign corporations, mostly British and American, had acquired from Middle Eastern governments the rights to use their land for oil production. These rights were called *concessions*.

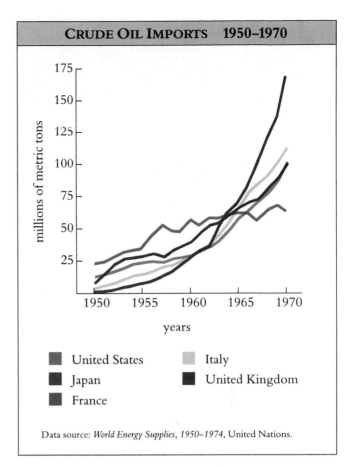

CRUDE OIL IMPORTS 1950–1970

millions of metric tons / years

- United States
- Japan
- France
- Italy
- United Kingdom

Data source: *World Energy Supplies, 1950–1974*, United Nations.

During the 1930s, huge oil fields were discovered—mainly in Saudi Arabia and Iran. Foreign oil companies, however, gained control of most of this oil through concessions. The foreign companies had little difficulty in acquiring these concessions because most governments they dealt with were weak and poor.

When oil became the region's major item of trade after World War II, nationalists began to challenge foreign control of oil deposits. As nations acquired independence and greater strength, they tried to change the terms of the concessions to gain greater profits from oil.

In 1951, a new nationalist government in Iran nationalized, or declared to be the property of the nation, all foreign oil operations within the country. A British blockade and efforts organized by the United States Central Intelligence Agency (CIA), however, helped depose this government and restore power to the shah, or traditional monarch of Iran, Muhammad Riza Pahlavi (PAH-luh-VEE). Shah Pahlavi signed an agreement by which Iran gained some power over its oil production and oil income.

Tankers carry oil from the oil-rich nations of the Middle East to the United States and other industrialized nations. The hum of industry is sustained by this precious natural resource.

The Iranian attempt to nationalize its oil industry signaled the beginning of greater negotiating power for Middle Eastern countries. As they obtained changes in the concessions, they gained more control over oil resources and larger oil profits.

WORLD POLITICS AND THE MIDDLE EAST

As oil made the Middle East increasingly important economically to industrialized nations, the cold war made the Middle East an area of crucial strategic importance. The United States feared territorial expansion by the USSR, which bordered the Middle Eastern nations of Turkey and Iran. The USSR, on the other hand, wanted to counter the greater political and economic influence gained in the area by Western European nations and the United States since the turn of the century.

Taking advantage of the political instability following World War II, the Soviet Union put pressure on the governments of Iran and Turkey to give up some of their territory. Guided by the Truman Doctrine, the United States responded by providing aid to these and other friendly governments, setting up military bases in the region, and signing economic agreements with friendly Middle Eastern countries.

Unsuccessful in gaining territory or influence in Iran or Turkey, the USSR challenged Western influence in the Middle East by seeking an arms agreement with Egypt. In 1955, Egypt's leader,

Nasser, accepted the offer of Soviet arms, in part to bolster his forces against a growing Israeli military financed by the United States.

Fearing that Egypt might become a Soviet ally, the United States and its allies responded by offering to help Nasser build a huge dam at Aswan on the Nile River. Such a dam was a keystone of Nasser's development plan for Egypt. This offer, however, was withdrawn when Nasser seemed to drift toward the Soviet camp. In July 1956, Nasser responded to the withdrawal of the American offer by nationalizing the Suez Canal, which was owned mostly by French and British companies.

The Suez crisis. Egypt's takeover of the canal sparked a second Arab-Israeli war. This time, however, nations outside the Middle East were drawn into the conflict, demonstrating how deeply tied to world politics the Middle East had become.

European leaders feared that Egyptian control of the Suez Canal would threaten their oil supply from the Middle East, which passed by ship through the canal. Knowing that Israel sought retaliation for Arab raids from within Egyptian territory and that Egypt had banned Israeli ships from the canal, France and Britain secretly encouraged Israel to attack Egypt.

In October 1956, Israel invaded the Gaza Strip, a small Mediterranean coastal area held by Egypt since the 1949 war. Israeli forces quickly defeated the Egyptians there and moved on toward the canal through the Sinai Peninsula, the Egyptian territory bordering Israel to the southwest. At the same time, France and Britain sent paratroopers and ships to seize the canal. For a time, it seemed the Suez crisis would explode into another global conflict, as the USSR hinted its intention of joining Egypt in the fighting.

After the United Nations finally demanded a ceasefire and the United States and Soviet Union strongly protested the invasion, France, Britain, and Israel withdrew. United Nations troops were sent to the Sinai Peninsula as a peacekeeping force, and the canal was reopened in 1957 to all ships except those of Israel.

As a result of the war, Arab-Israeli hostility intensified. Soviet influence in the Middle East increased as Arab nations turned away from Western nations, which had supported Israel and seemed hostile to Arab nationalism. Many

SAUDI ARABIA: MODERNIZATION AND TRADITION

For hundreds of years, life in the area now known as Saudi Arabia remained unchanged. Nomadic Bedouin tribes herded their camels, goats, and sheep from oasis to oasis. Everyday life was ruled by the religion that had been born there—Islam.

However, as the twentieth century began, a strong leader—ibn-Saud (sah-OOD)—emerged to draw the Bedouin together as one nation. Then, in the 1930s, oil was discovered and Saudi Arabia was transformed.

Money from the sale of oil made the ruling Saud family very rich, and they plowed a great deal of their wealth into the modernization of Saudi Arabia. This process of modernization has been very rapid in the last 25 years. Riyadh (rih-YAHD)—the country's capital—quickly grew from a small oasis town into a huge commercial center with a population of more than one million people.

Many Saudis have moved from their mud and adobe homes to brick houses with running water, electricity, and electrical appliances and gadgets such as refrigerators and video recorders. Almost every city-dweller owns at least one car.

Although signs of modernization can be found everywhere, the traditional ways of life are still apparent. In Riyadh, for example, old adobe houses butt up against skyscrapers of concrete and steel. For sport, Bedouin traders still keep camels—as well as a truck or car.

Saudi women have made tremendous strides under the various modernization programs. Before World War II, few Saudi women went to school. In recent years, however, hundreds of women have graduated from college with advanced degrees. Nevertheless, these women are limited in what they can do with their education, for Islamic law requires the strict segregation of the sexes. Saudi women are not permitted to drive. When traveling on public transportation, they must use seats that have been screened off from the rest of the vehicle. Women may work only where they will not come into contact with male strangers.

Saudi rulers have tried to balance the old and the new. They feel that they must modernize Saudi Arabia so that their people can enjoy a decent standard of living. Saudi rulers claim, however, that the changes that are introduced will not threaten the country's Islamic heritage.

Arab nations developed closer ties with the USSR, and Egypt built its dam with financing from the Soviets rather than the Americans.

EFFORTS TO BUILD ARAB UNITY

Although Arab nations accepted Soviet aid and arms, most preferred not to become Soviet allies, but to remain neutral. Arab unity and neutrality had been aims of Arab nations since 1945, when most had joined together to form a loose organization called the League of Arab Nations.

Following the Suez crisis, the movement calling for Arab unity, called Pan-Arabism, was revived in an effort to strengthen the region's independence from superpower influence. Arab nations were also drawn together by their common opposition to Israel.

Nasser used his growing power to take leadership of the Pan-Arab movement. Through his efforts, Syria and Egypt merged in 1958 to become the United Arab Republic. In the same year, Nasser's major opposition in the Arab world, the monarchy in Iraq, was overthrown by pro-Nasser Iraqi army officers. The new rulers set up a one-party government similar to Egypt's and ended Iraq's tie with the West.

Nasser's power, however, declined after 1958, and Syria broke away from the United Arab Republic in 1961. Although Pan-Arabism was weakened, Arab states remained largely neutral, and opposing political forces achieved an uneasy balance.

MODERNIZATION

In the 1950s and 1960s, governments in the Middle East and North Africa gave high priority to improving agriculture and expanding industry. Although many countries had only recently gained independence, the nations of the region in general did not face economic problems as overwhelming as those of other regions of the world, such as sub-Saharan Africa and Latin America. Many nations, especially Iran, Iraq, Saudi Arabia, and Libya, had the good fortune to possess valuable oil resources. Other nations, such as Egypt and Turkey, had begun to achieve economic growth after World War I.

Despite these advantages, most nations faced barriers to economic expansion. Among the most important were poverty, unequal distribution of land, lack of a skilled labor force, and strong beliefs in traditional ways of life.

To improve agriculture, most leaders began to break up the vast estates owned by only a few wealthy families and redistribute the land among peasants. Nasser, for example, had divided up 500,000 acres (200,000 hectares) of land in Egypt by 1957. Leaders also built irrigation projects and acquired tractors, fertilizers, and new varieties of seeds.

In the effort to build new industries, some nations such as Turkey relied on foreign loans and aid. These nations took advantage of the desire of the superpowers to gain influence in the region through financial assistance. Much of Turkey's program of industrialization, for instance, was financed with funds provided by the United States.

In oil-rich nations, the profits from oil production were channeled into industrial development. This pattern was particularly evident in Iran and Saudi Arabia.

Social effects of modernization. Along with industrial development came the construction of new hospitals, roads, and schools. Cities grew quickly, attracting former farmers, people from small villages, and nomads. Better educational opportunities increased the number of technicians, engineers, and teachers. Slowly many Middle Eastern and North African countries began to overcome the barriers to modernization. Yet, many people remained poor and illiterate.

Moreover, modernization itself caused additional problems. Cities could not accommodate the huge numbers of people attracted to them. Population growth began to outpace increases in food production.

Many of the demands of modernization and city life also challenged traditional values. Islamic beliefs, for instance, tended to shield women from public display. Yet, economic growth required that women as well as men become doctors, bankers, technicians, and factory workers. Many women also wanted greater freedom to perform new kinds of work. The changes in women's roles caused tremendous disruption of family life and social structure.

POLITICAL RESPONSES TO MODERNIZATION

Throughout much of the Middle East and North Africa, the desire to expand industry and promote growth led to important political changes. Within many nations, the most important of these changes was a trend toward authoritarian government.

Many leaders felt that the political challenges of rapid modernization required strong leadership and government control. By the end of the 1960s, countries such as Egypt that had begun self-rule with republican forms of government had drifted toward domination by one ruler. In other nations, the traditional monarch had assumed greater control and authority.

In Iran, for example, modernization and repressive rule were closely connected. After Shah Pahlavi had been restored to his traditional throne in 1953, he began to promote economic growth. In 1963, he launched a program in which he pledged to raise the standard of living of all his subjects. Although highways and schools were built, some land was redistributed to the landless, and national income rose, the country remained very poor overall.

In the meantime, the shah ruled with absolute power. He ignored the Iranian constitution, outlawed opposition, and silenced enemies with a ruthless secret police force trained by the United States CIA.

Despite this trend toward authoritarian rule, Turkey, Israel, and Lebanon kept republican forms of government. Unlike the conservative monarchies in other nations, these countries stressed reform and close ties with the West.

In this photograph, taken in 1986, veiled women offer a used radio for sale. Some Middle Eastern women still follow the ancient tradition of wearing a veil for reasons of modesty.

THE FORMATION OF OPEC

In addition to using authoritarian rule to promote their goals, the leaders of oil-producing countries such as Iran took an important step to increase their income from oil. In 1960, the Persian Gulf nations of Iran, Iraq, Kuwait, and Saudi Arabia joined the Latin American nation of Venezuela to form the Organization of Petroleum Exporting Countries (OPEC). Eight other nations joined OPEC in the 1960s and 1970s, including Libya, Algeria, and the African nation of Nigeria.

OPEC was designed to give these countries more power to control the price of oil. OPEC is an example of a *cartel*, an organization formed to regulate the production and control the price of a product produced by its members. As OPEC members began to control a large percentage of the world's oil, oil-consuming nations were forced to pay the price for oil determined by the OPEC nations.

SECTION REVIEW

1. Define *concessions* and *cartel*.

2. Why did the Middle East seem important to the superpowers?

3. What reasons did Israel have for attacking Egypt in 1956?

4. Describe how Middle Eastern and North African nations attempted to modernize.

5. How did modernization affect government in the Middle East and North Africa?

Analysis. What motives did the superpowers have for offering aid to Middle Eastern nations?

Data Search. Refer to the appropriate charts on pages 831 and 834 to identify **(a)** the first and second largest producers of crude oil in the Middle East in 1986, **(b)** three Middle Eastern countries that are at least 90 percent Muslim, and **(c)** the per capita income in Saudi Arabia compared with that of the United States for the year 1988.

33–3
CENTER OF WORLD CONFLICT

READ TO FIND OUT

—what the terms *embargo* and *sanctions* mean.
—what caused the Six-Day War.
—how relations between Egypt and Israel improved.
—what two major factions fought in Lebanon.
—what caused the Islamic revolution in Iran.

Soldiers are a common sight on the streets of Israel. Because of Arab-Israeli strife, Israelis live in a state of preparedness for war.

Beginning in the late 1960s, tensions developing in the Middle East since World War II erupted into a series of often violent conflicts. Arab-Israeli hostilities flared into outright war twice more after 1956, while civil wars arose out of religious and political differences in Lebanon and Iran. Furthermore, Iraq and Iran clashed in open warfare throughout the 1980s.

These conflicts commanded the attention of many other nations of the world, especially the superpowers, which relied on Middle East oil and considered the region to have growing strategic importance. These nations and others became involved in Middle Eastern conflicts in the roles of peace negotiators and suppliers of arms, economic aid, and military forces.

ARAB-ISRAELI CONFLICT

During the 1960s, Israel and its Arab neighbors had built up their military forces. Palestinian refugees also organized commando groups, or small fighting units, to strike across Israel's borders in an attempt to win back what had been their homeland. In 1964, many different groups of Palestinians united in an organization called the Palestine Liberation Organization (PLO). Attacks and counterattacks kept tensions at a constant boil.

The Six-Day War. In 1967, Egyptian president Nasser, wanting to continue as unofficial leader of the Arab world, decided to act in support of the Palestinian cause. He expelled the UN peacekeeping forces that had been supervising a buffer zone between his country and Israel. Nasser then ordered Egyptian and Syrian troops to mass at Israel's southern and northern frontiers. Jordan also massed troops along its western border with Israel. Meanwhile Egypt blocked Israel's access to the Indian Ocean through the Gulf of Aqaba (AH-kah-BAH).

Israel decided to act quickly in response to this threat, and on June 5, Israeli troops attacked the Egyptian, Syrian, and Jordanian forces. In this short-lived conflict called the Six-Day War, Israel won a major victory, seizing Egypt's Sinai Peninsula, Syria's Golan Heights, and Jordan's West Bank. Israel also annexed the Jordanian half of Jerusalem.

The Six-Day War was followed by a bitter unofficial war. Israel refused to discuss returning the occupied territories unless the Arabs agreed to recognize Israel's right to exist and to sign a peace treaty with Israel. Meanwhile, Palestinian guerrilla groups such as the PLO raided Israeli communities and hijacked airliners, and Israel retaliated by bombing Egyptian cities. Israel received more support from the United States, and the USSR aided Syria and Egypt.

GOLDA MEIR

One day in 1903, five-year-old Golda Mabovitch watched in terror as her father nailed wooden planks across the doors and windows of their house in the Russian city of Kiev. He was preparing the house for a *pogrom* (PŌ-grahm)—an organized attack on Jews.

While she sat on the stairs waiting for the attack, the frightened little girl resolved to do all she could to make the lives of her fellow Jews free from such fear. Years later, she would fulfill this resolution by helping to found the modern state of Israel.

Because of crushing poverty and the constant fear of pogroms, the Mabovitch family left Kiev in 1906 to seek a better life in Milwaukee, Wisconsin. As a teenager in the United States, Golda Mabovitch became very interested in Zionism. In 1921, she left the United States for Palestine to begin working toward the goal of establishing an independent Jewish state.

Once in Palestine, Mabovitch became increasingly involved in Zionist politics. She also joined the Haganah—the underground Jewish defense army—and was a key organizer of its plans for the illegal immigration of European Jews to Palestine.

When Israel became an independent nation in 1948, Mabovitch signed Israel's declaration of independence along with 25 other prominent Israeli leaders, and became the new state's ambassador to Moscow. In 1949, she was elected to the Knesset—the Israeli parliament.

Mabovitch adopted a Hebrew form of her name—Meir (may-EER)—in the 1950s, and approached her government responsibilities with great enthusiasm and unflagging vigor. Her dedication and down-to-earth attitude toward life made her very popular with the Israeli people, who called her "our Golda."

After serving as Minister of Foreign Affairs, Meir retired from the government in 1966. Three years later, however, she was called back to head the government after the death of Prime Minister Levi Eshkol. As prime minister, Meir hoped to ensure the security of Israel through a peace treaty with the Arab nations. However, this hope was shattered when Egypt and Syria attacked Israel in 1973. Because she felt responsible for the Israeli army's lack of preparation for this attack and for Israel's heavy early losses, Meir resigned in 1974.

Golda Meir died from leukemia in 1978 at the age of eighty. She left instructions that no monuments were to be erected in her memory, but she lives on in the minds of millions of people as a symbol of modern Israel.

Nasser's death in 1970 did little to soothe hostilities because his successor, Anwar Sadat (suh-DAHT), carried on Nasser's policies. Sadat, however, did end Egypt's close ties with the Soviet Union, sending home Soviet military advisors in 1972.

The Yom Kippur War. In October 1973, Anwar Sadat launched a fourth Arab-Israeli war. By attacking on the holiest Jewish day of Yom Kippur, Syria and Egypt gained an early advantage. However, with vital supplies provided by the United States, Israel shortly turned the tide of battle and encircled a large Egyptian force in the Sinai Desert. Although Israel secured a military advantage, it suffered heavy casualties. The war, which became known as the Yom Kippur War, or October War, ended after several weeks of fighting.

During the Yom Kippur War, the Arab nations of OPEC decided to use their economic power to weaken Israel and protest Western aid to Israel. The OPEC members temporarily reduced oil production, causing prices to soar. They also refused to sell oil to the United States and any other supporters of Israel.

This oil *embargo*, or restriction of trade, had deeply felt effects all over the world, creating oil shortages and a recession. The embargo demonstrated both the power of Arab nations to fix oil prices and the reliance of industrialized nations on outside sources of energy.

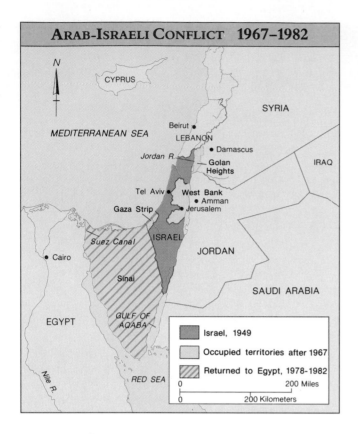

ARAB-ISRAELI CONFLICT 1967–1982

N

CYPRUS

SYRIA

MEDITERRANEAN SEA

Beirut

LEBANON

Jordan R.

Damascus

Golan
Heights

IRAQ

Tel Aviv

West Bank

Gaza Strip

Amman

Jerusalem

ISRAEL

Suez Canal

JORDAN

Cairo

Sinai

SAUDI ARABIA

EGYPT

GULF OF
AQABA

Nile R.

RED SEA

Israel, 1949

Occupied territories after 1967

Returned to Egypt, 1978-1982

0   200 Miles

0   200 Kilometers

Negotiations. After the Yom Kippur War, the United States saw a chance to get Arab and Israeli leaders to the negotiating table. American leaders wanted to help build stability in the Middle East by easing Arab-Israeli tensions and to prevent any further cut-offs in oil supply. Secretary of State Henry Kissinger shuttled back and forth from one Middle Eastern capital to another. His energetic "shuttle diplomacy" paid off. Tensions eased as Israel pulled back some of its troops and the United States began an extensive program of aid to Egypt.

A further breakthrough came in 1977, when Egypt's President Sadat made a dramatic visit to Israel. The next year, American President Jimmy Carter invited Sadat and Israeli Prime Minister Menachem Begin (BAY-gihn) to Camp David, Maryland, for peace talks. Out of those talks came the Camp David Accords, laying the basis for an Egyptian-Israeli peace treaty that was signed in 1979. Egypt became the first Arab nation to grant diplomatic recognition to Israel. In return, Israel handed back almost all of the Sinai Peninsula. This treaty between two nations that had fought four wars in 25 years was seen as an historic event.

Israel and the Palestinians. Although relations between Egypt and Israel improved, those between Israel and the rest of the Arab world soon grew worse. Palestinian leaders denounced Sadat for dealing with Israel, saying such cooperation weakened Arab unity. Palestinians were also angry that Israel still occupied the West Bank, where the Palestinians hoped to establish an independent state, and the Gaza Strip.

Chances of the Palestinians reaching that goal seemed to diminish during the 1970s and 1980s. Israel established scores of Jewish settlements in the occupied West Bank and harshly quelled Palestinian uprisings against Israeli rule.

Intifada. In December 1987, after a clash between Palestinian protestors and Israeli troops in Gaza, the PLO called a strike: all Palestinian businesses would close at noon every day, causing hardship for the Israeli people who relied on goods from Arab shops. The Palestinians maintained that this strike, called the *Intifada* (an Arabic word meaning "uprising"), would continue until the occupation of the West Bank and Gaza was over. The issue of a homeland for Palestinians remained unresolved.

CONFLICT IN LEBANON

After the Yom Kippur War, tensions between Arabs and Israelis increased in the border area between Israel and its small neighbor to the north, Lebanon. These tensions resulted in a Lebanese civil war and an Israeli invasion.

The population of Lebanon is composed mainly of Muslims and Christians. Each main religion is also divided into sects—Sunni and Shiite Muslims, and Maronite, Greek Orthodox and other Christians. Before Lebanon became independent in 1944, its leaders agreed on how the separate groups should share power. Christians, who outnumbered Mulsims, wielded the most power in the government.

Civil wars. For a time, the system worked well, and Lebanon's capital of Beirut became a bustling center of Middle Eastern trade. However, the delicate balance broke down after Palestinian refugees flooded Lebanon. The refugees, who were mostly Muslims, tipped the population balance to the Muslim side. In 1958, a civil war erupted, but American troops, sent at Lebanon's request, restored order.

After nearly two decades of unrest, full-scale civil war broke out between right-wing Arab Christians, who opposed the Palestinian presence, and leftist Arab Muslims, who supported them. Palestinians in turn aided the Muslim forces, prompting Lebanon's eastern neighbor, Syria, to intervene on the rightists' behalf. Syrians feared that a Muslim victory might invite an Israeli invasion of their country. Syria helped restore some order in Lebanon in 1976, but warfare between Lebanese Maronites and Muslims remained commonplace.

Israeli invasion. Palestinians remained in Lebanon despite its civil war. Hoping to smash the PLO and destroy Syrian missile sites in Lebanon, Israel invaded in June 1982.

Israeli planes destroyed the missile sites, while Israeli troops swept north and occupied the capital of Beirut, where PLO leader Yasir Arafat (AR-uh-faht) had his headquarters. According to an agreement, Arafat and many of his followers retreated to new camps in Tunisia, far from Israeli borders.

Israel's invasion seemed to be a success, but it added to Lebanon's chaos and made new enemies for Israel. After a massacre of Palestinians by members of the Christian militia in Beirut, American, French, British, and Italian troops arrived to act as a multinational buffer force. They became the targets of terrorist attacks by Muslims who resented what they saw as American support for the Christians. In October 1983, a bombing killed at least 237 American and 31 French troops.

Israel withdrew its troops in 1985. However, Lebanon remained chaotic as civil war and violence continued into the late 1980s.

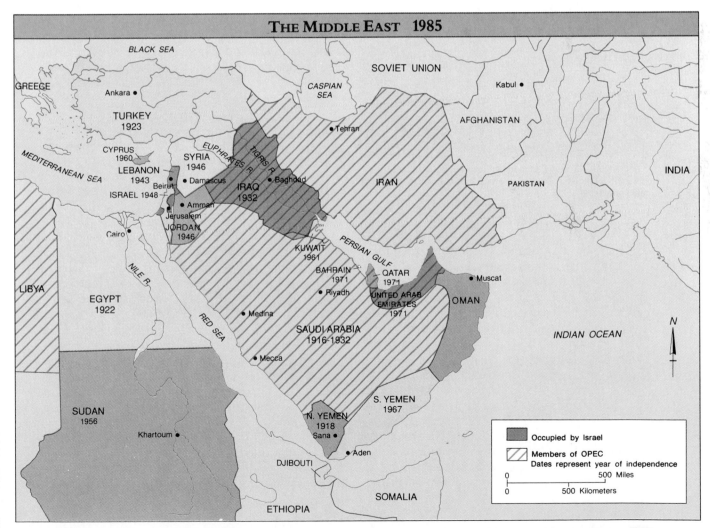

THE MIDDLE EAST 1985

Zealous Iranians raise a portrait of Ayatollah Khomeini, Iran's powerful religious leader from the Islamic revolution in 1979 until his death in 1989.

REVOLUTION IN IRAN

As Arab-Israeli conflicts continued to create turmoil in the countries surrounding Israel, tensions were building in Middle Eastern countries outside the Arab world. In the late 1970s, Iran entered the international political spotlight.

The reforms and modernization initiated by Shah Pahlavi in Iran during the 1950s and 1960s had brought great change to the country. Women had gained new rights, including the right to vote. Oil wealth had helped to build new industries and a modern army, but many Muslims criticized the shah for undermining Islamic traditions and introducing Western ways that they claimed led to moral corruption.

Riots and mass demonstrations began in 1978, as Islamic leaders pressed for an Islamic revolution. Led by Ruhollah Khomeini (hoh-MAY-nee), the revolutionaries succeeded in deposing the shah in 1979. A repressive Islamic government took power after crushing both the liberals and moderates who had helped to overthrow the shah.

Rule under the ayatollah. Known by his religious title of *ayatollah* (ī-uh-TŌ-luh), Khomeini sought to banish Western influences and restore traditional Islamic culture. Under the new constitution, which affirmed traditional Islamic values, Iran would have both a political leader and a religious leader, but the religious leader would be the final authority.

Many supporters of the Islamic revolution bitterly resented American support of the shah. When the shah flew to the United States for medical treatment late in 1979, Iranian mobs stormed the American embassy in Tehran.

For more than a year, Iranian militants held hostage 53 Americans. Americans charged the Iranian government with violation of international law. Iranians released embassy documents that they claimed showed massive American interference in Iranian affairs. The hostages were finally released in January 1981.

WAR BETWEEN IRAN AND IRAQ

When he took power in Iran, the Ayatollah Khomeini sought to arouse support for an Islamic revolution in neighboring Iraq, where a slight majority of the people are also Shiite Muslims. Traditionally, power in Iraq had been held by a Sunni Muslim minority.

Angered by Khomeini's attempt to cause unrest, Iraqi leaders sent troops to invade Iran in September 1980. The Iranians drove the Iraqis back across the border and the war entered a stalemate, with the two sides divided over many issues, including a border dispute.

The Iraqi-Iranian war—also called the Gulf War—took a high toll in human lives and resulted in great damage to cities and oil facilities in both countries. Finally, in August 1988, Iran and Iraq agreed to accept a UN resolution calling for the two countries to end hostilities and begin peace talks.

In June the following year the ailing Khomeini died. Iran had a new religious leader and a new political leader, but other nations expected little immediate change in Iran's policies.

OPERATION DESERT SHIELD

A new crisis arose in August 1990, when Iraqi President Saddam Hussein sent 100,000 troops into oil-rich Kuwait claiming that this small country was really a part of Iraq. According to the United Nations, the invasion jeopardized the security and stability of the Persian Gulf, threatening the economies of oil-dependent countries around the world. Within a week, the U.N. Security Council voted 13-0 to impose economic and military sanctions, or blockades, against Iraq unless Hussein immediately withdrew his troops from Kuwait. The blockade kept food and other supplies from being sent into Iraq and prohibited Iraq from shipping oil and other exports through the Persian Gulf. But Hussein ignored the United Nations' demands and, in retaliation, detained all foreigners who were in Iraq.

Within the next few weeks, the United States, Egypt, Great Britain, Syria, Saudi Arabia, and France sent more than 450,000 troops to the Persian Gulf to carry out a military mission called *Operation Desert Shield*. The Security Council gave Hussein until January 15, 1991, to release all hostages and comply with the U.N. resolution, or military force would be used. Just before Christmas, Hussein allowed his "guests" to return to their homelands; but diplomatic efforts to avoid another costly war in the Middle East were growing dimmer.

LIBYA AND QADHAFI

International conflicts also centered on North Africa. Perhaps the most controversial conflict involved Libya, a former Italian colony with large reserves of oil.

After army officers overthrew Libya's king in 1969, a new ruler, Colonel Muammar Qadhafi (kah-DAH-fee), took power. Like Khomeini in Iran, Qadhafi sought to make Libya a model Islamic state, with strict laws based on the Koran.

Qadhafi denounced both communism and capitalism, and declared his support for revolutionary movements in Arab, African, and European countries. The United States and other nations blamed Qadhafi for acts of terrorism around the world. In 1986, the United States retaliated for the Libyan bombing of a dance hall in West Germany by bombing Qadhafi's headquarters in Libya itself. Qadhafi thus became a symbol for terrorism.

SECTION REVIEW

1. Define *embargo* and *sanctions*.

2. Describe the events leading up to the Six-Day War.

3. How did Egypt and Israel reach agreements after the Yom Kippur War?

4. Describe the opposing sides in the Lebanese civil war and the issue over which they fought.

5. What were the major causes of Iran's Islamic revolution?

Evaluation. On the whole, did Egypt's peace treaty with Israel contribute to or detract from Middle Eastern peace? Explain your answer.

HISTORY IN FOCUS

The problems confronting the Middle East and North Africa are rooted deep in historical conflicts about which people feel very strongly. The issues have no easy solutions. They become more complicated, in fact, as the regions develop even tighter connections to the economy and political struggles of the rest of the world.

The Palestinian question is perhaps the most important of many unresolved issues. Out of 3.5 million Palestinians, one-third live in exile, mostly in squalid refugee camps. Most Palestinians seek an internationally recognized homeland in the Israeli-occupied territory of the West Bank. Israel, however, sees this territory as necessary to its defense against hostile Arab neighbors.

At the same time, modernization and oil revenues have transformed the Middle East and North Africa. Several nations, most notably Saudi Arabia, have used their tremendous wealth from oil to build factories, cities, hotels, airports, and roads. In only decades, cultures dominated by age-old traditions seem to have been completely altered. And yet much of the change remains on the surface. Islamic traditions, the formation of OPEC, and opposition to Western influence all demonstrate the desire of many Middle Easterners and North Americans for political and cultural independence from the rest of the world. Far from becoming similar to the Western nations, the nations of the Middle East and North Africa want to keep their traditions and find their own solutions to modern problems.

SUMMARY

- Although many people in the Middle East and North Africa share a common Islamic heritage, important ethnic and religious differences have caused rivalries and tensions in the region.

- World War II spelled the decline of European rule in the Middle East and North Africa, although several nations had already gained their independence. Israel emerged as an independent Jewish state in 1948, and in 1954 Nasser took power in Egypt. North African states won their independence in the 1950s and 1960s.

- Massive oil deposits and the cold war sparked superpower interest in the Middle East, prompting new developments in the region. Iran attempted to nationalize its oil industry in 1951. Four years later Egypt seized the Suez Canal, previously under foreign control. Pan-Arabism reemerged under Nasser's leadership.

- Most Middle Eastern and North African countries modernized in the 1950s and 1960s, which created many problems, including a clash with traditional Islamic values. Political changes also took place, most notably a drift toward authoritarian rule. OPEC was formed in 1960.

- Conflict and upheaval have shaken the region since the 1960s. Events include two Arab-Israeli wars, an oil embargo, civil war in Lebanon, revolution in Iran, and the war between Iraq and Iran.

VOCABULARY REVIEW

Match each numbered vocabulary term with the appropriate person or organization. Then explain the connection between that person or organization and the vocabulary term.

Example: *Zionism* could be associated with *Ben-Gurion* because he was a leader of the Jewish state of Israel.

1. concessions	(a) Saddam Hussein
2. embargo	(b) the shah
3. sanctions	(c) OPEC

CHAPTER REVIEW

1. (a) Describe one ethnic rivalry in the Middle East. (b) Name at least three religious groups that reside there. (c) Why were the Ottoman Turks resented?

2. (a) Compare the effects of Ottoman and European control in the Middle East and North Africa. (b) List four Middle Eastern nations that gained independence before World War II, along with the date each achieved self-rule.

3. (a) How and why was the response to French rule different in Syria and Lebanon? (b) Contrast the independence of the two former British mandates in the Middle East. (c) What problems resulted for both Jews and Palestinians from the creation of the independent state of Israel?

4. (a) What factors helped determine the nature of the North African independence movements? (b) Why was Libya's independence especially significant? (c) What made the Algerian struggle for independence different from that of other North African countries?

5. (a) How did foreign companies gain control over Middle Eastern oil in the 1930s? (b) Why did nations of the Middle East begin to challenge foreign control of oil? (c) Explain the origins of the Organization of Petroleum Exporting Nations (OPEC) and the cause and significance of the oil embargo.

6. (a) Describe the actions taken by the superpowers to increase their power in the Middle East. (b) How did the cold war help provoke the Suez crisis? What was the result?

7. Compare the causes and effects of the four Arab-Israeli wars.

8. (a) List four barriers to Middle Eastern development and three problems that have resulted from modernization. (b) How has development caused political change?

9. (a) Contrast Nasser and Shah Pahlavi. (b) Compare Khomeini and Qadhafi. (c) Explain the significance of the PLO and Yasir Arafat.

10. (a) Describe Lebanon's system of power sharing and why it broke down. (b) Explain the circumstances and results of Israel's invasion of Lebanon.

THINKING CRITICALLY: ACTIVITIES

1. Imagine that you are a reporter assigned to write an editorial on President Nasser's nationalization of the Suez Canal. Comment on the reasons for his action and whether it will strengthen Egypt and promote Arab unity.

2. Choose a partner to discuss the Israeli-Palestinian question. One of you should take the role of an Israeli; the other, a leader of the PLO. Discuss the following question: Why do both Jews and Arabs feel a "right" to the land making up Israel?

3. Divide into groups of four or five and discuss the following questions: Why is Lebanon the scene of so much violence? What might be done to resolve the problems there?

APPLYING SOCIAL STUDIES SKILLS

Researching current events. For each of the research tasks described below, choose the most appropriate source that would help you find the information you need.

(a) *Facts on File*

(b) *National Newspaper Index*

(c) *The New York Times Index*

1. You want to read a summary of major political developments in Israel the past month.

2. You are looking for news reports written when Israel became a state in 1948.

3. You want to compare how two or three major newspapers are covering developments relating to Islamic fundamentalism.

4. You would like a summary of last week's political developments in Iran.

5. You are curious to see what the *Wall Street Journal* has written recently on the future of OPEC.

6. You want to read some articles written in 1978 about the Camp David Accords between Egypt and Israel.

7. You want to locate articles about the Palestine Liberation Organization in several newspapers over the past two years.

8. You would like a summary of political developments in Lebanon over the past year.

APPLYING THINKING SKILLS

Identifying cause-effect relationships. Review the procedure described on page 139. Then identify any cause-effect relationships in the events listed below. Next, arrange the events to show how they are related. Finally, answer the questions that follow.

Israeli forces attack Arab forces in the Six-Day War.

European Jews who survived the Holocaust seek a place of refuge.

The Palestine Liberation Organization is formed in 1964.

Nineteenth-century Zionists call for establishment of a Jewish homeland in Palestine.

In 1947, the United Nations votes to divide Palestine in order to create a Jewish and an Arab state.

Egyptian and Syrian forces attack Israel in the Yom Kippur War.

In 1948, hundreds of thousands of Palestinian Arabs flee from land gained by Israel in war with Arabs.

Arabs block Israeli access to the Indian Ocean (1967).

The state of Israel is proclaimed by David Ben-Gurion.

The Balfour Declaration is made in 1917.

Tensions arise in 1967 over Jewish settlements on the West Bank.

Arab forces attack Israel in 1948.

1. Define the terms *cause* and *effect*.

2. Why is it important to be cautious when identifying cause-effect relationships?

3. Put the above events in chronological order. Refer to your text if necessary.

4. What are the immediate and the underlying causes of the establishment of the independent state of Israel?

5. Identify and explain three other cause-effect relationships in the above events.

6. Briefly summarize why there are continuing conflicts between the Arabs and the Israelis.

CHAPTER THIRTY-FOUR

CHALLENGES FOR SUB-SAHARAN AFRICA AND LATIN AMERICA

1945–PRESENT

Modern embroidered wall hanging. Isaac Ojo Fajana, Nigeria.

Latin American nations had declared their independence from Spain in the 1800s and had developed a strong sense of nationalism before World War II. Accordingly, their political systems and economic patterns were more firmly established than those of sub-Saharan Africa, where most nations became independent in the years after World War II.

Sub-Saharan Africa and Latin America shared experiences in the postwar years. The population of each region grew rapidly after the war, particularly in cities. This growth led to tremendous pressures on government services and housing. In addition, the economy of each region depended on exports to industrialized nations. While economic dependency was a major theme in Latin America during these years, Africa's energy was focused on nation building.

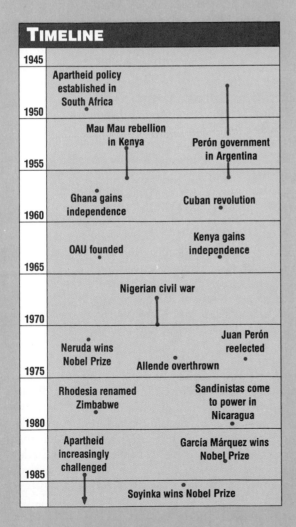

TIMELINE		
1945		
1950	Apartheid policy established in South Africa	
1955	Mau Mau rebellion in Kenya	Perón government in Argentina
1960	Ghana gains independence	Cuban revolution
1965	OAU founded	Kenya gains independence
1970	Nigerian civil war	
1975	Neruda wins Nobel Prize	Juan Perón reelected
	Allende overthrown	
1980	Rhodesia renamed Zimbabwe	Sandinistas come to power in Nicaragua
1985	Apartheid increasingly challenged	García Márquez wins Nobel Prize
	Soyinka wins Nobel Prize	

34–1
AFRICAN INDEPENDENCE

READ TO FIND OUT

—what the terms *apartheid*, *desertification*, and *coups* mean.
—what patterns African independence movements followed.
—who led Africa's nationalist movements.
—how South African whites excluded nonwhites from full participation in society.

After 1945, European colonial powers, exhausted by two world wars, were losing the military and economic strength needed to rule their overseas territories. At the same time, the African participation in the war stirred up feelings of nationalism within the continent. The example of Mohandas Gandhi's nonviolent protests in India encouraged African nationalists to organize efforts for their own independence.

In many of the new African nations, the new leaders often did not have the training needed for government service. Therefore, stable governments were difficult to establish. In addition, the boundaries of the new nations had been drawn in the 1800s when the continent of Africa had been carved up by rival imperialist powers. These borders often placed many different ethnic groups within one nation, while splitting up members of the same group among several nations.

GROWTH OF AFRICAN NATIONALISM

The roots of the African independence movement go back well before World War II. For example, the African National Congress, a black political party, had been founded in South Africa in 1912. Between the two world wars the number of African nationalists grew as they started newspapers and magazines to spread their message. Like the African "local elite" that developed in the 1700s and 1800s, these early nationalists were middle-class. Many of them had been educated in the United States and

Europe. These educated Africans had little contact with the millions of people in the villages and countryside of Africa.

Many Africans knew of the successful independence movements in Asia, where by the late 1940s, India, Indonesia, Ceylon, and Burma won independence. With these examples to inspire them, African nationalist movements gained strength.

Having fought World War II in the name of freedom and self-determination, the Western nations could not ignore African nationalism. The colonial powers, however, saw themselves as a "civilizing" force for backward peoples. The British, for example, planned to extend self-rule gradually to their colonies over a period of 50 years or more, allowing for a smooth transition to independence. African nationalists, however, had a different timetable. Discontented after years of colonial rule, they blamed the colonial powers for unemployment, high prices, and other social and economic ills.

STRUGGLES FOR INDEPENDENCE

Independence came to African nations in one of two ways, peacefully or violently. British colonies in West Africa, for example, had few white settlers, and the move toward self-rule tended to go smoothly. In contrast, in East Africa, where large numbers of white settlers owned farms and businesses, the transition was violent. Whites fought against any changes that would take away certain privileges granted only to them.

Peaceful transitions. In 1947, a group of African lawyers and businesspeople formed the first nationalist movement in the British West African colony of Gold Coast—now Ghana. Called the United Gold Coast Convention, the movement worked to increase African influence in the local legislative councils that advised the British governor. The Convention, therefore, hired Kwame Nkrumah (en-KROO-mah), a political activist who had studied in the United States. A tireless campaigner and a fiery speaker, Nkrumah developed a large following, and in 1949 he formed his own political party. Its slogan was "Self-Government NOW."

An admirer of Gandhi, Nkrumah called for nonviolent protests such as strikes and boycotts against British rule. Jailed on charges of sedi-

tion, or treason against the state, Nkrumah and his followers became heroes for many Africans. Despite the strong British opposition, Nkrumah's party won 34 of 38 open seats in a new legislative assembly in 1951. Faced with such strong support for the jailed leader, the British freed Nkrumah and asked him to form a new government.

The Gold Coast lived under limited self-rule for the next six years, until the British fully withdrew in 1957. The peaceful transition to independence made Ghana a model for independence movements in other British colonies in Africa.

As in some of Britain's colonies, the transition to independence in most of the French African colonies was peaceful. In the early 1950s, as France fought in Algeria, concern grew that violence would spread south to the other French colonies. To ward off riots and violent protests, Charles de Gaulle, when forming the Fifth Republic in 1958, gave the territories a choice. The first option was having limited self-rule within the Franco-African community. In this case, countries would receive French economic aid in return for French control of their financial and foreign affairs. The second option was having immediate and full political freedom without French economic aid.

Out of the 12 French territories in Africa, only Guinea (GIH-nee), under the leadership of Sékou Touré (too-RAY), voted for full independence. Touré was a militant nationalist. Meeting with de Gaulle before the vote, Touré told him "We prefer poverty in freedom to riches in slavery." After the people of Guinea voted for independence, a furious de Gaulle ordered French officials to withdraw from the territory at once. Having thrown off French rule, Touré became a hero for other African nationalists. Encouraged by Guinea's success, within two years the other French colonies also chose independence.

Violent transitions. Not all countries, however, moved to political independence without bloodshed. In Kenya, a British colony in East Africa, whites owned most of the country's good farm land, while millions of Africans toiled on the poor plots that were left over. Although only 30,000 in number, whites in Kenya also firmly controlled the government and prevented any increase in African political or

RECOGNIZING POINT OF VIEW

A point of view is the position or set of concerns from which a person sees, considers, or presents an event, idea, or condition. People's points of view are reflected in what they focus on when talking or writing about a subject. A farmer and a city dweller may describe the same rural scene differently because they differ in their knowledge of, and interest in, rural life. In trying to build a complete, objective understanding of some event, idea, or condition, you should examine various discussions of it by people with different points of view.

EXPLAINING THE SKILL

A point of view is like a telescope. It focuses the viewer's attention only on certain aspects of what is being observed, while omitting or blurring other aspects. An author's point of view frequently limits what he or she writes about, resulting in an incomplete picture of the subject.

As noted on pages 436 and 437, to identify a point of view you first have to identify the subject. Then identify what the author emphasizes most, ignores, or gives only brief attention to. Look for "loaded" words, value judgments, and unstated assumptions that indicate the author's feelings about the subject. In this way, you can identify the concerns, beliefs, and interests that make up the author's point of view.

APPLYING THE SKILL

The following excerpt is from a speech by Patrice Lumumba, the first prime minister of Zaire. The speech was delivered on June 30, 1960, the day Zaire—then known as Congo—gained its independence from Belgium. Examine the excerpt to determine Lumumba's point of view.

Our lot was eighty years of colonial rule; our wounds are still too fresh and painful to be driven from our memory.

We have known tiring labor exacted in exchange for salary which did not allow us to satisfy our hunger, to clothe and lodge ourselves decently, or raise our children like loved beings.

We have known . . . insults [and] blows which we had to endure morning, noon, and night because we were "Negroes."

We have known that our lands were despoiled in the name of supposedly legal texts which recognized only the law of the stronger.

We have known that the law was never the same depending on whether it concerned a white or a Negro: accommodating for one group, it was cruel and inhuman for the other.

We have known the atrocious sufferings of those banished for political opinions or religious beliefs; exiled in their own countries, their end was truly worse than death itself.

We have known there were magnificent houses for whites in the cities and tumble-down straw huts for the Negroes, that a Negro was not admitted in movie houses or restaurants, or stores labeled "European". . . .

All that, my brothers, we have profoundly suffered. . . .

From A.P. Merriam, *Congo: Background to Conflict*. Evanston: Northwestern University Press, 1961.

MAKING MEANING

Answer the following:

1. Lumumba's point of view is (a) anti-government, (b) pro-colonialism, (c) anti-European.

2. Lumumba's point of view is *least* revealed by (a) the aspects of colonialism he emphasizes, (b) his choice of words, (c) his unstated assumptions.

3. Most of the words used by Lumumba (a) are neutral in meaning, (b) indicate how Africans suffered, (c) show contempt for the life styles of Europeans.

4. Lumumba's speech indicates his concern about (a) revenge, (b) equal treatment of people, (c) maintaining law and order.

REVIEWING THE SKILL

5. Define the term *point of view*.

6. What is a procedure you can follow to recognize an author's point of view?

economic power. The Kikuyu (kih-KOO-yoo)—Kenya's largest African ethnic group—under the leadership of Jomo Kenyatta, demanded a redistribution of the colony's farm land, claiming as their own much of the land owned by white colonists.

Kenyatta, who had spent 17 years in London working with anticolonial groups, proved to be an able leader. He had also studied in Moscow and had written a book, *Facing Mount Kenya*, about the Kikuyu. In 1947, a year after Kenyatta returned to Kenya, he became head of the Kenya African Union, a political group organized to oppose British control.

In the late 1940s, a secret group that favored violent revolution against British rule formed under the name Mau Mau. Although Kenyatta condemned the Mau Mau, the British incorrectly accused him of directing it. For this alleged activity, he was imprisoned in 1953. The Mau Mau's violent attacks continued.

Realizing that a white minority could not continue to rule a black majority intent on gaining political freedom, the British began to include more Africans in government. In 1963, the Kenya African National Union (KANU), a political party which had Kenyatta's support, won a national election, and Kenya became independent. Kenyatta, whom the British had released from prison, was elected Kenya's first prime minister.

Violence in Zimbabwe. After World War II, the British created the Central African Federation, made up of the colonies of Northern and Southern Rhodesia and Nyasaland. Southern Rhodesia, however, had a strong white minority that tightly controlled the colonial government. African leaders in Northern Rhodesia and Nyasaland feared that the Central African Federation would be controlled by Southern Rhodesian whites. These leaders agitated for independence. In 1963, Britain dissolved the Central African Federation, and in 1964 Nyasaland gained independence as Malawi and Northern Rhodesia as Zambia.

In Southern Rhodesia itself, discontent with white minority rule grew under the leadership of African Joshua Nkomo. Opposing Nkomo's nationalists was the white Rhodesian Front party, led by Ian Smith. Tension in Southern Rhodesia turned to violence in 1963 as Nkomo's supporters began to agitate for indepen-

dence and an African voice in government. To prevent the black majority from gaining power, Smith declared Southern Rhodesia independent from Britain in 1965 and set up a state divided on rigid racial lines. In reaction, African nationalists began a ten-year-long guerrilla war against Smith's government which eventually led to majority rule in 1978. Under African leadership, the nation was renamed Zimbabwe (zihm-BAH-bway).

RACIAL TENSION IN SOUTH AFRICA

The Union of South Africa, the country at the southern tip of the continent, achieved self-rule from Great Britain in 1910 and became fully independent by 1934. The nation, however, remained a part of the British Commonwealth. Minerals, especially gold, made South Africa the richest nation on the continent. Although foreign investors developed the country's mines and industries, prosperity did not reach the black population. Indeed, state laws prevented blacks from taking high-paying jobs.

In 1948, just as independence movements were developing throughout Africa, a right-wing white party took power in South Africa. Under new leadership, the South African government established a policy called *apartheid* (ah-PAHRT-hayt). This policy divides schools, workplaces, housing—indeed, the whole nation—by strict racial laws to keep races from mixing in any way.

The new government recognized four categories of race: white, black, people of mixed ancestry called coloreds, and Asian. Under apartheid laws, all nonwhites had to carry passes and show them on demand to any police officer. Only whites could vote, and men and women could marry only within their own racial group.

Because Great Britain strongly opposed the policy of apartheid, South Africa withdrew from the British Commonwealth in 1961, changing its name to the Republic of South Africa. Apartheid laws were then strengthened rather than relaxed. South Africa found itself diplomatically isolated as more and more countries broke relations because of the government's racial policies.

The struggle against apartheid. In the wake of international condemnation for the apartheid system, black Africans in South Africa joined nationalist movements that called for a revolution against the white minority. To control these movements, the government restricted the number of blacks living in urban areas, where blacks could more easily organize against the government.

Blacks were now forced to live in several Bantustans, or Bantu states. These were tribal areas that had been given some self-rule but were not fully free from South African control. White officials also banned black nationalist organizations and arrested their leaders. The nonviolent, multiracial African National Congress, the largest nationalist movement in South Africa, was banned in 1960 and its leader, Nelson Mandela, was sentenced to life in prison. From bases in neighboring black nations, the African

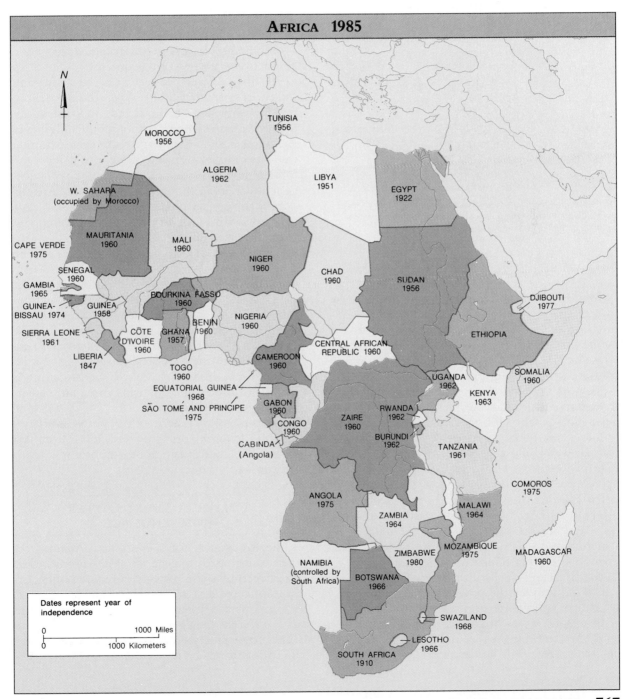

AFRICA 1985

MOROCCO 1956

TUNISIA 1956

ALGERIA 1962

LIBYA 1951

EGYPT 1922

W. SAHARA (occupied by Morocco)

MAURITANIA 1960

MALI 1960

NIGER 1960

CHAD 1960

SUDAN 1956

CAPE VERDE 1975

SENEGAL 1960

GAMBIA 1965

GUINEA-BISSAU 1974

GUINEA 1958

BOURKINA FASSO 1960

BENIN 1960

NIGERIA 1960

DJIBOUTI 1977

SIERRA LEONE 1961

CÔTE D'IVOIRE 1960

GHANA 1957

CENTRAL AFRICAN REPUBLIC 1960

ETHIOPIA

LIBERIA 1847

TOGO 1960

CAMEROON 1960

SOMALIA 1960

EQUATORIAL GUINEA 1968

UGANDA 1962

KENYA 1963

SÃO TOMÉ AND PRINCIPE 1975

GABON 1960

CONGO 1960

ZAIRE 1960

RWANDA 1962

CABINDA (Angola)

BURUNDI 1962

TANZANIA 1961

COMOROS 1975

ANGOLA 1975

ZAMBIA 1964

MALAWI 1964

MOZAMBIQUE 1975

MADAGASCAR 1960

NAMIBIA (controlled by South Africa)

ZIMBABWE 1980

BOTSWANA 1966

SWAZILAND 1968

LESOTHO 1966

SOUTH AFRICA 1910

Dates represent year of independence

0   1000 Miles

0   1000 Kilometers

This footbridge, with separate lanes for whites and nonwhites, vividly illustrates how the policy of apartheid affects even the simplest activities in the daily lives of South Africans.

National Congress began guerrilla warfare against the government in the 1970s.

Mandela's wife, Winnie, continued the fight to end apartheid after her husband's imprisonment. In the 1970s, she became a central figure in the struggle for a black-ruled South Africa after she was banished to an all-black township for her role in a 1976 uprising.

Responding to growing unrest, white leaders eased some apartheid laws. The government legalized black labor unions and announced plans to allow interracial marriages. A new constitution in 1984 allowed coloreds and Asians to vote in elections. However, blacks, who made up 67 percent of the population, still could not vote. Furious that they had been excluded, blacks responded to the new constitution with riots and strikes which resulted in much destruction and many deaths. Protests became so great in 1985 that South African president P. W. Botha (BŌ-tah) declared a state of emergency, which gave police the power to arrest hundreds of African nationalists and black union leaders.

In response to South Africa's civil strife, many Western businesses and universities gave up their financial holdings in the country.

In 1989 Botha was replaced by F.W. de Klerk, who pledged change through negotiation with the black population. In February 1990, Nelson Mandela was released from prison after almost three decades. Representing the African National Congress, Mandela met with de Klerk to discuss a peaceful negotiation process.

ECONOMIC CHALLENGES

The stability of each new African government depended in part on how well it met its nation's economic needs. Although the new nations had economic problems, they all struggled to become competitive in the world economy.

At first, African leaders believed only rapid industrial growth would make the economies strong, so they nationalized industries and formed state-owned corporations. However, lacking skilled managers and technicians, many of the new companies failed or went in debt.

The new governments also tended to neglect agriculture, even though four out of five Africans depended on farming. The agricultural crisis grew to serious proportions as the African population dramatically expanded.

To produce more food, in some areas farmers overused land for grazing and planting. They planted in drier areas or on hills, causing erosion. Forests were cut down for use as fuel. All of these factors combined to cause *desertification*, or the transformation of useful land into desert. Droughts led to a further loss of vegetation. Lack of fertile land caused food shortages. In the mid-1980s, food shortages reached a crisis point in many nations—especially in Ethiopia, where millions of people starved.

In an attempt to deal with the food shortages, African governments imported food from the West. The increase in food imports left many African nations deeply in debt.

POLITICAL TRENDS AFTER INDEPENDENCE

In the 1960s and 1970s, most new African nations developed one-party political systems. Defenders of such systems compared them to traditional village councils, in which informal discussions led to agreements. Ideally, people with different views would compete within the single party but would follow the decisions of the majority.

Political instability, however, was frequent. *Coups* (KOOZ), or sudden changes in government by force of arms, often occurred in response to corruption and mismanaged economies. Coup leaders claimed that the only way to gain honest, efficient government was through temporary military rule. Often, however, these military regimes were also corrupt.

An exception was the reign of General Eyadema, who took power in Togo in 1967. He overcame ethnic divisions that had caused instability. His government, though authoritarian, was free of corruption, and his economic policies were generally successful.

Idi Amin led a military coup in Uganda in 1971 that had far different results, however. Amin promised free elections but never kept this promise. Instead, he built up the army and established a brutal dictatorship. Opposition to Amin's rule brought bloody reprisals. Nevertheless, opposition grew, and in 1979 his government was toppled.

Political instability was also often caused by competing ethnic groups. Nigeria, for example, was home to the Hausa and Fulani peoples in the north, most of whom were Muslims, and the Yoruba in the southwest and Ibo in the southeast, two groups influenced by Christian ideas. After the British withdrew in 1960, tensions grew as these groups competed for political and economic power. After bloody conflicts throughout 1966, the Ibo region—Biafra—declared its independence in 1967.

More than two years of civil war followed. Because Nigeria considered the war an internal dispute, it refused to allow foreign nations to ship food to the war-devastated Ibo regions. As a result, disease and starvation killed about two million Biafrans. In 1970, Biafra surrendered and rejoined Nigeria.

A similar division occurred in Zaire, which gained independence from Belgium in 1960. Political loyalties were divided among rival leaders. Civil war erupted when Zairian troops rebelled against Belgian officers still in Zaire's army. When the copper-rich Katanga province, later known as the Shaba Region, broke away from the government, Zaire seemed to be dissolving. United States, Belgium, and Soviet interest in Zaire added to the tension.

Only after years of turmoil did Zaire become stable. A military leader, Mobutu Sese Seko, seized power in 1965. His authoritarian rule suppressed dissent among his opponents. Meanwhile, an improved economy enabled him to keep power.

Despite one-party rule and serious economic problems, other African nations have also been stable. Senegal, for example, has remained peaceful since achieving independence. In 1980, the man who led Senegal to independence, Sedar Senghor, became the first leader of an

Many African nations must rely on outside aid in times of natural disaster, such as the prolonged drought and invasions by crop-destroying locusts in the northeastern region during the 1980s. However, internal disputes and civil wars may hamper relief efforts, as was the case in Biafra in the 1970s.

independent African nation to turn over the government to a successor peacefully. Senghor's successor, Abdou Diouf, extended political rights. Kenya, Cote d'Ivoire (formerly Ivory Coast), and Zimbabwe have all also made slow, but steady economic and political progress.

INTERNATIONAL RELATIONS

African nations have pursued a policy of neutrality in East-West disputes. However, African nations accepted aid from both Western and Communist countries. At the same time, Africans strongly opposed Western intervention in African affairs as a continuation of colonial rule. In the 1950s, for instance, Africans protested against French efforts to crush the Algerian independence movement, and in the 1970s, they objected to Western trade with white-ruled Rhodesia.

To provide a unified voice for Africa in international affairs, the Organization of African Unity (OAU) was founded in 1963. Within Africa, the OAU supported liberation movements, such as that of Angola against Portugal. Nevertheless, the OAU became deeply divided over disputes that arose between new nations.

More important than the OAU as a voice for Africa on the international stage is the General Assembly of the United Nations. The 54 nations of Africa make up the largest voting bloc in the General Assembly and thus wield great influence. The African bloc voted together on such issues as opposition to colonial rule and actions against South Africa. Through the United Nations and the OAU, many of the young nations of sub-Saharan Africa have become very influential in world affairs.

SECTION REVIEW

1. Define *apartheid, desertification,* and *coups.*

2. Explain how the independence movements in Ghana and Kenya differed.

3. What roles did Nkrumah and Kenyatta play in African nationalist movements?

4. What methods did South Africa adopt to fight black nationalist movements?

Evaluation. Think about problems facing new nations in Africa. How would you approach such issues as desertification? Explain.

34–2
THE CULTURE OF SUB-SAHARAN AFRICA

READ TO FIND OUT

—what the term *negritude* means.
—how city life affected traditional African social structures.
—how African writers responded to independence.

Independence has had great impact on African culture and society. Economic development has changed the way people live, and contact with cultures in other parts of the world has influenced African thought.

FAMILY LIFE

Between 1960 and 1979, Africa's population grew by 63 percent, to a total of 344 million people. By the early 1980s, the population was growing by one million per month—faster than any other region on earth. Much of this growth could be attributed to better medical care which resulted in both a rise in the average life expectancy and a decline in the death rate among children. Rapid population growth has been a major factor in urbanization, the movement of people from the countryside to the cities. By 1980, one African in five lived in an urban area. Population growth and urbanization have altered traditional patterns of family life.

The family had been the foundation of traditional African society. Family members provided each other with work, and the most distant relative could be counted on to lend assistance in hard times. Many family members left their villages for the cities, however, changing both the role of the family and family structure. People have become increasingly involved in society as individuals, not simply as members of a family.

Within the context of the extended family, precolonial African societies had been struc-

This decorative cement screen at a Nigerian gasoline station combines ancient designs with new materials. The art reflects how today's Africa retains elements of tradition.

tured by sex and age. Men and women performed traditional roles and elders governed the group. The elders lived within the group, not set apart, and generally were not richer than the rest of the people. With independence, however, a new African elite developed as the role of the traditional chiefs passed to well-paid civil servants, politicians, businesspeople, and military officers.

By the 1970s, a new class structure developed. In the cities, the new upper class was composed of professionals, and political and military leaders, whose children received the best education and were groomed to take their own place in society. Children of middle-class clerks, shopkeepers, and craftspeople lack such opportunities. Meanwhile, in rural and urban areas alike, poor people have remained poor, unable to afford the "New Africa."

Opportunities for African women. In many areas of Africa, women traditionally did much of the farming and ran most local markets. As more and more men flocked to the cities, women continued to play an important role in rural villages. In the mid-1980s, they had complete responsibility for their families, which still included growing the food.

At the same time, urbanization and economic development led to new opportunities for women in the cities. In addition to job opportunities, many women found that they could wield political power. Angie Brooks of Liberia, for example, was the first woman to serve as president of the United Nations General Assembly. Annie Jiagge (jee-AH-gee) of Ghana chaired the United Nations Commission on the Status of Women. These women, and a growing number of others, served in their respective national governments as well.

LITERATURE

African literature has ancient roots, going back to traditional poems, myths, and oral history. After independence, more African writers began writing in French, English, and Portuguese as well as in African languages such as Swahili, Zulu, and Yoruba. Many African works have been written in the European languages their authors were educated in, but the subject matter has been African experiences.

The French had ignored African culture and had tried to replace it with French culture. In response, Leopold Senghor and other African writers popularized the idea of *negritude*, or blackness. Although they wrote in French, they praised African achievements and revived pride in African history and culture. Negritude sparked a revolution in French West African culture, not only in art and literature but also in history, religion, and anthropology. Senghor, a distinguished poet, served as president of Senegal from 1960 to 1981.

THE GROWTH AND CHALLENGE OF AFRICAN LITERATURE

Lord, harken to my voice. LET IT RAIN. It rains
And you have opened from your arms of thunder
   the cataracts of forgiveness.
Rain on New York, on Ndiongolar on Ndialakhar
Rain on Moscow on Pompidou, on Paris and
   suburbs, on Melbourne on Messina on Morzine
Rain on India, China . . .
Rain on the Sahara and on the Middle West, on
   the desert on the wheatlands and the ricelands
On straw heads and wool heads.
And life is born again color of whatever is.

          —from *Nocturnes*, by Leopold Senghor (1971).

In the cultural revolution that accompanied African independence, the voice of poet Leopold Senghor led the way in washing out colonialism and advancing the African literary voice. Unlike other written literatures, which developed gradually over centuries, African literature has experienced a dramatic burst of creative growth within the past 40 years. Increasing numbers of African writers have produced a flood of poems, plays, novels, and short stories in dozens of African languages, as well as in French, English, and Portuguese.

Most African authors write in their own language, and few of their works are being translated. Therefore, authors who wish to convey their experiences to non-Africans generally feel compelled to write in European languages. Reflecting the frustration of many of these writers, Leopold Senghor asks his readers, "Do you not feel my suffering and despair, which is beyond compare, to be forced to express in French this heart which comes from Senegal?"

Even when authors write in European languages, their works may reach only a few readers. This is largely because many works have not been collected and preserved in libraries. For instance, only a few issues remain of an African literary magazine published in French during the 1920s. One of these issues contains a chapter of a novel by Massyla Diop. This one chapter is all that survives of his novel.

So that a similar fate does not befall recent authors, more of their works must be collected, preserved, and translated for present and future generations. Only then can their voices be increasingly heard both within and beyond Africa. As Nigerian writer Chinua Achebe has noted, African authors must be able to share with the world the "great depth and value and beauty" of their cultures.

The British had not left their African colonies with the same sense of rootlessness as the French had. Yet, independent English-speaking Africans have not found the same comfort in the past as French-speaking Africans. Literary themes in former British colonies tended to treat the tensions between tradition and change and the political and social problems that followed independence rather than pride in an African past. In Nigeria, Wole Soyinka, a poet and novelist, wrote in English of the "been-to's"— those Africans who had studied in England and then returned home full of idealistic plans for improving their nations. In 1986, Soyinka won the Nobel Prize for literature.

ART AND MUSIC

Art in Africa has always been part of everyday life, and as such has been featured in celebrations, structures, utensils, and fabrics. Traditional art has continued to flourish after independence. With increased cross-cultural contacts, however, African art has continued to be influenced by Western art. The abstract sculpture of Vincent Kofi of Ghana, for instance, reflects his awareness of both European art, about which he had studied, and Akan civilization, of which he was a part. In Nigeria, Jimoh Buraimoh created new art forms by using traditional beads on hardboard.

Music, too, has continued to be an important part of daily life in Africa, one that fulfills the need of rituals and social life. Urbanization, the changing social relationships of modern society, and the development of industry and technology have all influenced African music. In the cities, music and dance clubs have sprung up, playing a wide variety of popular music from Ghana, Nigeria, Europe, and the United States. African songs have blended complex traditional rhythms with pounding electronic sounds. Indeed, in music more than any other medium, tradition and modernization have been joined to create a new art form.

SECTION REVIEW

1. Define *negritude*.

2. What effects has urbanization had on African family life?

3. How have African writers responded to independence?

Analysis. In what ways has African culture since 1945 reflected both tradition and change?

34–3
THE ECONOMY AND POLITICS OF LATIN AMERICA

READ TO FIND OUT

—what the term *import-substitution* means.

—how industrialization affected Latin American nations after World War II.

—what role class interests played in Latin American politics.

—how revolutionary governments emerged in some countries.

—what role the United States played in Latin American affairs.

Economic development in Latin America went ahead unevenly in the different nations in the region after World War II. New

industry added to the wealth of the upper classes without improving life for urban and rural workers, and conflicting class interests aggravated by economic problems led to political instability in many nations.

ECONOMIC DIFFICULTIES AFTER WORLD WAR II

Before World War II, the economies of the Latin American nations had developed by producing food and raw materials for export to the industrialized nations in return for mass-produced consumer goods. When nations like Brazil began to industrialize during World War II, they produced items for their home markets rather than for European or North American consumers. Despite an increase in industrial output in some areas of Latin America, most countries continued to rely on natural resources or agriculture for economic stability.

Problems with agricultural developments. During World War II, Latin Americans had helped feed the Allied armies, exporting tons of beef, grains, and other raw materials. After the war, however, the demand for those products declined, and the Latin American nations struggled to reorganize their economies to fit into the postwar international commerce. Most countries concentrated on a single crop or industry. Honduras grew bananas, Chile mined copper, Colombia and Guatemala exported coffee, and Panama relied on the canal.

Such single-product economies left the Latin American nations especially vulnerable to changes in the world market. Colombia and Guatemala, for example, could be economically destroyed by a small drop in the world demand for coffee, while a fall in copper prices could drive Chile to the brink of a depression. This concentration of the national economies on export products also hurt food production for the home market. For example, Costa Rica had an economy based on agriculture, yet because it focused on export crops, it had to import food.

Industrial development. Latin American nations such as Brazil and Mexico had begun to industrialize in the 1930s and 1940s. In these years, they had set out to build *import-substitution* industries, or industries that would produce goods such as cars or airplanes that were ordinarily imported from foreign industrial nations.

Both Brazil and Mexico increased their industrial strength after World War II. Brazil even became an exporter of cars. However, the demand for manufactured products within Latin America leveled off because most people could not afford to purchase the items produced. With this decline in the new industrial economies, many Latin Americans, including most Brazilians, found themselves still working in agriculture.

With such deep-rooted economic difficulties, Latin American nations could not support long-term industrial growth on their own. Economic expansion depended, in large part, on foreign investment, especially from the United States. Latin American governments at first encouraged such investment, seeing it as a way to benefit quickly from the advanced technology of the industrial nations.

Soon, however, the governments in Latin America discovered that foreign investors, not Latin Americans, collected most of the profits from the industries they financed. Feeling cheated by capitalist investors, many Latin Americans became more anti-American as executives of large corporations in the United States became wealthy at the expense of the Latin Americans.

Land reform. In most Latin American nations the problems of economic development were heightened by the patterns of land ownership. Huge estates owned by the very wealthy stood in sharp contrast to the tiny plots belonging to the peasantry.

In the late 1960s, 17 percent of the landowners in Latin America held 90 percent of the land, while 83 percent of the people lived and worked the other 10 percent. In Brazil, for instance, 1 percent of the population owned 43 percent of the agricultural land while millions of rural workers owned none. Moreover, because foreign countries could pay more money than could most Latin Americans for such cash crops as bananas and coffee, large landowners preferred to produce crops for export rather than food crops for local consumption.

Resulting from this unequal division of land were widespread poverty and hunger in the countryside and expensive food in the cities. To make up for the shortages, governments imported food. In the 1940s, for instance, Chile had grown enough food to export a surplus, but as more and more of the nation's resources became concentrated in export industries in the 1960s and 1970s, food made up 25 percent of Chile's imports. In short, the little money that countries saved by developing import-substitution industries was lost owing to a need for increased food imports.

Some nations saw the disparity between a few wealthy property owners and millions of landless peasants as a basic problem in their economic structure. Accordingly, some countries tried different programs of land reform aimed at breaking up large estates into small plots and redistributing the land to the lower classes. While such programs gave peasants a chance to make a living by raising their own crops, the efficiency of the large farm system was lost.

Some nations tried using land not previously cultivated for agriculture. Much of the land that had not been used before, however, was poor and not fit for farming.

Large landowners naturally objected to having their holdings reduced to small plots. In Guatemala, American fruit companies—which controlled huge banana plantations—fiercely resisted land redistribution until, at their urging, the United States supported the overthrow of the left-wing governments that had called for land reform in the first place.

CONFLICTING CLASS INTERESTS

Just as in sub-Saharan Africa, when industries and cities grew in Latin America so did an educated urban middle class of professionals, merchants, and civil servants. Political reforms after World War II gave members of this class the right to vote and generally won their loyalty to the government. Along with the upper class, the new middle class wanted the development of an urban consumer economy, with shops and services. The middle class was less interested in spending government funds on the problems of illiteracy and unemployment that led to lower-class poverty.

Another group, the urban industrial workers, sought to maintain the economic and social gains they had made in the first burst of industrialization. They wielded political influence through strong unions and advocated laws that would provide for a minimum daily wage and

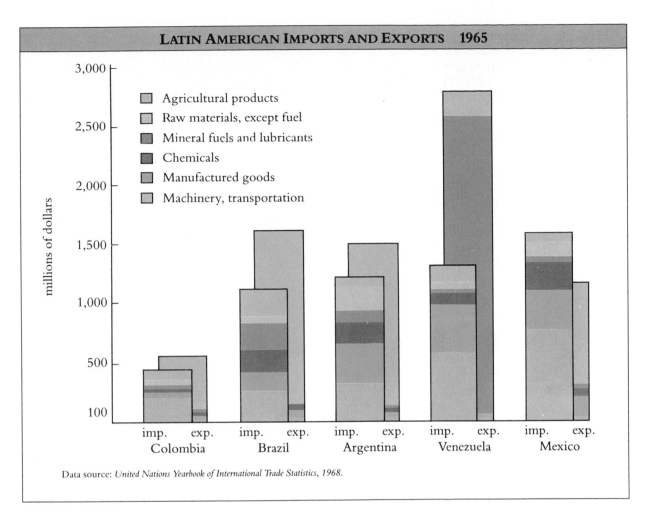

LATIN AMERICAN IMPORTS AND EXPORTS   1965

Legend:
- Agricultural products
- Raw materials, except fuel
- Mineral fuels and lubricants
- Chemicals
- Manufactured goods
- Machinery, transportation

y-axis: millions of dollars (100, 500, 1,000, 1,500, 2,000, 2,500, 3,000)

x-axis categories: imp. / exp. for Colombia, Brazil, Argentina, Venezuela, Mexico

Data source: *United Nations Yearbook of International Trade Statistics, 1968.*

other protections against exploitation at the hands of management. Whereas the middle and upper classes did not see a need for government funding of social programs, the industrial workers—frequently hit by economic hardship—were strong advocates of such programs.

These conflicting class interests resulted in political instability, as different groups were seldom able to unite in support of one party or candidate. Civilian governments seemed unable to answer the needs of one group without causing additional conflict for another.

THE INSTABILITY OF DEMOCRACY

In the 1940s and 1950s, the middle class and urban industrial workers in Latin America demonstrated their growing strength in free elections. This political participation seemed to indicate that democratic forms of government were taking hold throughout Latin America.

Such democratic trends were not deep-rooted, however. Latin American governments most often acted to preserve their own power, hesitating at extensive land reform and trying to control the labor unions. Moreover, the Latin American middle class had little intent of changing society, and in times of crisis, it tended to follow the lead of the upper class. In the 1960s, as industrialization slowed and unemployment and unrest grew, several Latin American nations such as Brazil, Argentina, and Chile came under authoritarian rule.

There were, however, exceptions. Costa Rica, a nation of small coffee farms, had developed a middle-class society and democratic traditions before World War II. In 1948, President José Figueres Ferrer (feh-REHR) disbanded the army, declaring Costa Rica neutral in all international affairs. Without an expensive military system to support, the country concentrated on subsidizing social services.

A stable democratic system had been established in Mexico by the late 1930s. A strong government party consistently won national offices, though other parties fielded candidates. Not all Mexicans were content, however, and in 1968, left-wing Mexican students protested government policies. Government troops, however, quickly suppressed the protests.

MILITARY GOVERNMENTS

Civilian governments such as those in Chile and Panama had to deal with the problem of controlling the power of the military. With the exception of Costa Rica, Latin American nations strengthened their armies after World War II as government leaders depended on the military more and more to quiet the voice of opposition. Military leaders thus gained influence over governments and competed for political power.

As in Africa, military governments sometimes took complete power, claiming that civilian governments had mismanaged the economy. Military governments tended to protect the privileged and to suppress all dissent. Brutal repression of opposition in Guatemala and Chile led to international concern over human rights violations in the 1970s and 1980s.

In Argentina, military regimes have played a major political role. In the 1940s, Juan Perón (peh-RŌN), an army colonel, gained the support of industrial workers and city residents. He won election as president in 1946 and 1951. At first, he raised wages and reduced foreign economic influence. Lower class support gave Perón the political power he needed to become a dictator and choke dissent. His economic policies reflected a view that popular support, rather than military force, was the key to maintaining political power.

As world prices for Argentine wheat and beef dropped in the early 1950s, Perón was forced to change his economic policies. He froze wages and sharply reduced state welfare programs. Growing dissatisfaction with his regime led to a military coup in 1955.

After 18 years of military rule, the Argentines again turned to Perón and elected him president in 1973. When Perón died the next year, he was succeeded by his wife, Isabel Perón. The policies of the Peróns, however, could not cope with runaway inflation and the growth of strong opposition among the middle class. Again the military intervened and overthrew Isabel Perón in 1976.

In the early 1980s, the new military rule brought the harshest repression Argentina had known since the early nineteenth century. "Death squads" sent out by the government murdered thousands of people suspected of dissent. The Argentine people, however, would put up with only so much tyranny. When the British soundly defeated the Argentine forces in a short war over control of the Falkland Islands, the discredited military rulers gave up power and Raúl Alfonsín (ahl-fōn-SEEN), a moderate civilian candidate, won the presidency.

REVOLUTIONARY GOVERNMENTS

Desperate poverty and flagrant misrule led to armed revolts in nations such as Cuba in 1959 and Nicaragua in 1979. People had become dissatisfied with low standards of living, repressive governments, and lack of services such as education and health care. In both Cuba and Nicaragua, dictators ruled so badly that they finally lost the support of even their most loyal followers. The Soviet Union provided economic and military support to help establish Marxist governments in both countries. Cuba, in turn, provided aid to revolutionaries in Nicaragua and other Latin American countries, as well as in Ethiopia and other African nations.

Cuba. In Cuba a revolution led by Fidel Castro ended the harsh dictatorship of Fulgencio Batista in 1959. Castro at first called for democracy and social justice. He also quickly nationalized the sugar industry, most of which had been been owned by investors from the United States. Castro also set up Soviet-style collective farms, and he limited private land ownership to 167 acres (67 hectares).

Fearing that Cuba was drifting toward communism, the United States objected to Castro's policies and began a trade embargo against Cuba. The Soviet Union responded by sending aid to Cuba and buying up Cuban sugar, which the United States had stopped importing.

During the 1960s, Cuba developed along Soviet lines and followed Soviet foreign policies. Castro held no elections, repressed opposition, and took all power for himself. Meanwhile,

The Communist guerrillas in this photograph have just captured a town in El Salvador. These guerrillas are typical of the thousands of young men and women who left their homes to fight in Central America's civil wars in the 1980s.

Cuba made great strides in medical care and education. Poverty-stricken urban and rural workers felt that they had a government that worked for them, but many members of the discontented middle class left Cuba for the United States soon after Castro's revolution.

By the mid-1980s, Castro's Cuba had built up industry, but the island's economy still depended largely on sugar exports. Although the standard of living had greatly improved for many, since most Cuban trade was with Eastern European nations, Cubans still lacked a variety of consumer goods that could be found in many other Latin American countries.

Nicaragua. In the 1960s and 1970s, Nicaragua underwent years of guerrilla warfare resulting in the overthrow of the repressive dictatorship of Anastasio Somoza (sō-MŌ-sah). In 1979 the Sandinista Front for the National Liberation, named after a guerrilla fighter of the 1930s, Augusto Sandino, took power from the Somoza family, which had ruled since 1936.

The Sandinistas, as the new leaders called themselves, began land reform by establishing some peasant-run collective farms. The new government leaders nationalized some industries but left local markets and small shops in private hands. The Sandinistas' goals were to build a socialist-capitalist economy and to follow a foreign policy of nonalignment. In 1984, the Sandinistas—led by Daniel Ortega—held elections, which they won, and in 1986 a new constitution was approved.

Like Fidel Castro in Cuba, the Sandinistas gave hope to rural and urban workers who had been ignored—or worse, repressed—by earlier governments. Students began teaching peasants to read. Free medical care greatly reduced the infant death rate, winning Ortega's government more grateful supporters.

However, critics of the Sandinistas pointed to their control of dissent and of trade unions. The Sandinistas also faced armed opposition from Nicaraguan rebels known as *contras* (CŌN-trahs). These rebels received support from the United States, which feared that the Sandinistas were leading Nicaragua toward communism.

Meanwhile, with the economy weakened by civil war, more Nicaraguans became discontented with the Sandinistas. In February 1990, a national election resulted in a surprise victory by Ortega's opponent, Violeta Chamorro. With the country's pressing problems, though, she had little time to enjoy her victory. The key question became: could her government strengthen the economy?

FOREIGN INVOLVEMENT IN LATIN AMERICA

Foreign nations have played a large part in Latin American politics. The foreign nation most actively involved has been the United States. Fearing the spread of Soviet-style communism, the United States government generally supported authoritarian regimes as long as they were anti-Communist.

United States intervention against Communist regimes has not been limited to Cuba and Nicaragua. In 1965, United States troops prevented a Communist-supported president from taking office in the Dominican Republic. In 1973, American support aided in the overthrow of the left-wing government of Salvador Allende (ay-EHN-day) in Chile. United States forces overthrew the Marxist regime of the Caribbean island of Grenada in 1983. In explaining the intervention in Grenada, the United States government stated that the island's political turmoil endangered the lives of Americans living there.

The policy of continued American intervention has brought strong objections from many Latin American leaders, especially since the 1970s. Most Latin Americans have admired the technological success of the United States, enjoyed its culture, and appreciated its economic aid. However, they have opposed American intervention in their region and have tried to reduce their financial and political dependency on the United States. In the 1980s, many Latin American countries have turned to Europe, to the Eastern bloc, and to Japan in an effort to get out from under the shadow of the United States.

SECTION REVIEW

1. Define *import-substitution*.

2. How did industrialization affect nations like Mexico and Brazil?

3. How did the middle class and the industrial workers influence politics in Latin America?

4. Why did revolutionary governments emerge in Cuba and Nicaragua?

5. How did the United States interfere in Latin American national politics?

Evaluation. Compare the problems or issues confronting Latin America in the postwar era with Latin American problems and issues of concern in the nineteenth century. How much progress has Latin America made in 150 years?

Data Search. Refer to the appropriate charts on page 834 to **(a)** identify Argentina's and Brazil's major partners in export trade in 1988 and **(b)** compare the United States with Guatemala in terms of per capita income, life expectancy, and literacy rate in 1988.

34–4
LATIN AMERICAN CULTURE

READ TO FIND OUT

—what the term *machismo* means.
—why people flocked to Latin American cities in the years after World War II.
—who were some of the leading Latin American writers of the postwar years.

Changes in Latin American society and culture after World War II were linked to economic and political developments. As cities have grown, poverty has become more visible and protest has been easier to organize.

The traditional Latin American concept of *machismo*, or belief in masculine strength and supremacy, has remained strong since World War II. Yet, other hallmarks of Latin American society and culture, such as the role of the Catholic Church in daily life, have diminished.

Outside contact has changed Latin American culture. Not only have popular music and movies become available from the United States and other nations, but Latin American writers and musicians have gained international audiences.

URBANIZATION THROUGHOUT LATIN AMERICA

By the mid-1980s, the developing nations of Latin America were more urbanized than those in Africa and southern Asia. Four of the world's 10 cities with populations of over 10 million are in Latin America. The largest, Mexico City, had a population of about 18 million in 1985. Even in Central America, where the majority of the people still live in rural areas, more than 40 percent lived in cities by 1970.

As in Africa, people who have been unable to make a living in rural areas have moved to the cities, seeking jobs and services, such as health care, that will provide them with a better life. As more infants have survived through better health care, urban populations have grown more quickly than rural populations.

The skyscrapers of São Paulo, the industrial center of Brazil, stand in sharp contrast to the squatter settlements, called *favelas*, in the foreground. Relatively high wages draw rural workers to the city, but insufficient low-cost housing forces millions of people to seek shelter in the favelas.

Although the cities have supplied better health care, they have been unable to provide enough jobs for their growing populations. Economic development in Latin America has not advanced rapidly enough to supply jobs to all those who want them. Meanwhile, employed workers have usually accepted low pay and poor working conditions because if they were to strike, thousands of unemployed people would quickly replace them. As food has grown more expensive in the cities because of shortages and inflation, hunger and malnutrition have haunted the urban poor.

Even if people can find work in the city, they cannot afford to live there, and governments cannot meet the need for low-cost housing. Squatter settlements have quickly grown on unoccupied land, sometimes within a matter of days as people claim little plots for themselves. These settlements ring the broad avenues and shining skyscrapers of the great cities of Latin America with acres of shacks made from cardboard, plastic sheeting, tin, and wood. The squatter settlements have no running water, sewers, or electricity. Today, about 40 percent of the people in the capital cities of Latin America live in such settlements, which continue to grow rapidly.

Disillusionment with economic and political opportunities has affected the major cultural institution in Latin America—the Catholic Church. In some nations, like Mexico and Panama, the Church has become weak, almost insignificant. However, in other nations, such as Peru and Nicaragua, a new movement within Catholicism emerged in the 1960s to confront political and social repression. This movement, called liberation theology, mixes traditional Christian values with Marxist views of economic and social equality.

EXPANDING ROLE OF WOMEN

Despite the traditional view that women should stay at home, changes in roles for women have occurred in Latin America. Women in some Latin American nations had won the right to vote in the 1930s, starting a trend that continued after World War II. The women's vote was a strong part of the Peronist movement in Argentina, and in Chile women helped elect a socialist government. In some Latin American countries, such as Brazil, Argentina, and Colombia, women have been appointed to government positions.

Educational opportunities have opened for women since World War II. With more education, more and more women are working as teachers and in business. Prejudice against them in business, however, has remained strong. Women often have not received equal pay for equal work and have seldom won promotions to high-level executive positions.

In the large cities of Latin America, middle-class women have enjoyed much the same freedoms in social and working life as women in Europe and the United States. However, the feminist movement in Latin America has received less attention than similar movements in the United States and Europe.

LITERATURE AND THE ARTS

As an educated middle class has grown in Latin America since World War II, citizens of the middle class have wanted to read literature by their own writers. Latin American writers have been strongly influenced by surrealism and by the stream-of-consciousness technique pioneered by the Irish writer James Joyce. Yet in their poetry, stories, and novels, Latin American literary figures have developed a vision and a voice uniquely their own.

Several authors who began writing before World War II have become internationally known. These include the Chilean poet Pablo Neruda, who won the Nobel Prize for literature in 1971. His poems range from political commentaries to love sonnets.

Another towering figure in modern Latin American literature is Gabriel García Márquez of Colombia, who won the Nobel Prize for literature in 1982. Through novels like *One Hundred Years of Solitude*, García Márquez makes social and political statements about Latin American problems such as repression and poverty.

Both Brazil and Mexico have led the way in modern Latin American architecture. In the 1950s, Brazilian leaders built a new capital city called Brasília. Architect Lúcio Costa designed

---

ECHOES OF THE PAST

ANA FIGUEROA: "ON MISUNDERSTANDING GOOD NEIGHBORS"

Ana Figueroa, who lived from 1907 to 1970, was one of Chile's most significant leaders in education and diplomacy. In 1947, after visiting a number of high schools in the United States, she wrote an article titled "On Misunderstanding Good Neighbors." Below is an excerpt from that article.

At the beginning of my visits, I was somewhat surprised when pupils in the last year of high school asked me about the geographical location of Chile. Full of curiosity, they asked me to give them a description of the "typical costume" used in that country, inquired whether Chilean women also wear the large Mexican "sombrero," and whether I had dressed in European fashion for the first time when I came to the United States. Later, when teachers of Spanish asked me whether the language spoken in Chile was Portuguese or French, I found that I need not have wondered at the questions put to me by the children.

The means of communication and transportation between countries have been advanced so rapidly by technology that it is urgent that the peoples of a world, which is becoming geographically smaller, understand and respect each other. [However] in the majority of secondary schools that I visited, especially in the West, the rooms in which Spanish is taught are profusely decorated with posters printed to attract tourists to Mexico showing the Indian man dressed in multicolored costumes and the Indian woman with a large hencoop lifting a big basket of fruit to her head. A picture that I saw hundreds of times shows a Mexican Indian sleeping cuddled up close to an enormous cactus and practically lost under a large sombrero. I was not surprised, then, when teachers asked me how I could get used to doing without my "siesta."

On the basis of some 35 [movies] that I have seen about Latin America produced in the United States, I have reached the following conclusions: All of them show the typical and picturesque, which actually does not exist in our countries: the Indian stretched on the ground asleep; great gun fights in bars; and children dragging themselves along on the floor surrounded by a swarm of flies.

And now we might ask ourselves just what do South Americans know about the English-speaking peoples and the North Americans: We are no better informed. Of the culture and civilization of the United States we believe what the movies tell us: it is the country of chewing gum and divorce, of Chicago gangsters, and of cowboys in Texas.

Abridged from Ana Figueroa, "On Misunderstanding Good Neighbors." *School and Society*, 66:90–92 (August 2, 1947).

For questions on Echoes of the Past, see "Analyzing Primary Sources" on page 819.

Diego Rivera's mural *Fruit from the Tree of Life* decorates the Ministry of Education building in Chapingo, Mexico. Many works by Mexican artists have nationalistic themes.

the city in the shape of a bird with outstretched wings, a great achievement in modern architecture.

Contemporary Mexican architecture often reflects both modern style and nationalist feeling. Shapes of some buildings echo ancient structures. Mexican muralists have decorated the exteriors of some of these buildings with powerful Indian themes relating to the interaction between people and nature.

The cultural variety among the nations of Latin America has perhaps been best reflected in the variety of its music, which ranges from classical compositions in the European style to ancient Indian melodies. A spirit of nationalism in the 1950s and 1960s led Chilean poets and musicians to collect rural folk songs and dances. A mixture of folk and popular music, known as *nueva canción*—Spanish for "new song"— became the music of protest in the universities. Chilean musicians supported the socialist candidate, Salvador Allende, in the 1970 elections. When he was overthrown and killed by the

military in 1973, musicians and artists were tortured and imprisoned. *Nueva canción* then became the music of exile and resistance.

SECTION REVIEW

1. Define *machismo*.

2. What forces drove rural peasants to the cities and what problems did they encounter there?

3. What themes did Latin American writers stress in their works?

Analysis. Using examples from both postwar Latin America and sub-Saharan Africa, discuss how writers, artists, and musicians make political statements about society and culture. How might their works influence the course of events?

HISTORY IN FOCUS

As sub-Saharan Africa and Latin America move toward the twenty-first century, serious problems loom on their respective horizons. In Africa, overpopulation, food shortages, and diseases threaten the lives of hundreds of millions of people. With few economic resources, African governments were poorly equipped to handle these problems. Accordingly, many African nations must continue to look to the United States, Europe, and the Soviet Union for massive amounts of aid in the form of food, medicine, and technology.

In Latin America—especially in Mexico— overpopulation is also a problem, though not as serious as in Africa. The biggest problem facing Latin America is foreign debts. To pay for industrial expansion, as well as basic social services, most Latin American nations have taken out huge loans from North American and European banks, with Brazil, Mexico, and Argentina each owing about $100 billion. Monthly payments on these loans drain the Latin American economies of all surplus capital, making investment in industry and social programs nearly impossible.

In both Africa and Latin America, these problems are creating political instability as people increasingly turn their anger toward their governments. This political instability, of course, makes it more difficult than ever before to make headway against the crises facing these regions.

SUMMARY

- After World War II, nations of sub-Saharan Africa and Latin America struggled against political and economic control by industrialized nations of the West. Latin American nations had declared their independence in the 1800s, but most African nations gained their independence after the war.

- Both regions industrialized rapidly after the war but still depended on the export of food and raw materials to industrialized nations. The economies of many nations were vulnerable because they relied on production of a single crop or mineral. In both regions, populations grew rapidly and cities expanded as people left farms to seek a better life.

- In sub-Saharan Africa, some nations suffered from desertification, which led to severe food shortages. Stable governments proved difficult to establish as different groups competed for power. Despite difficulties, a growing nationalist spirit raised the interest of Africans in their native cultures. Greater cross-cultural contact spread African culture to the West and brought new elements to African art, music, and literature.

- A few wealthy owners controlled most of the land in Latin America. Poverty among farm workers limited the market for domestically manufactured goods. The military held a strong influence over many governments. In several nations, repression of dissent contributed to social unrest and revolutions.

- In Latin America, urbanization brought new opportunities for women. Latin American writers and artists gained recognition.

VOCABULARY REVIEW

Match each numbered term with the lettered term most closely related to it. Then explain how the terms in each pair are related.

1. import-substitution   (a) blackness
2. negritude   (b) industry
3. desertification   (c) division
4. apartheid   (d) agriculture
5. machismo   (e) masculine

CHAPTER REVIEW

1. (a) What factors contributed to the growth of an independence movement in Africa after World War II? (b) How did attitudes toward independence differ in France and Great Britain?

2. (a) What have been the major economic problems African nations have faced since independence? (b) What problems in self-government have these nations faced?

3. (a) Why have populations of African cities grown so rapidly since 1945? (b) What effects has this growth had on society? (c) How was the impact of urbanization similar in Africa and Latin America?

4. (a) How does South Africa's government differ from those of other African nations? (b) With what measures does the South African government control its black population? (c) How have black South Africans responded to these measures?

5. How did economic and political changes in sub-Saharan African society affect the opportunities available to African women?

6. How could reliance on a single major export crop harm the economy of a Latin American nation?

7. (a) What factors led to revolutions in Cuba and Nicaragua? (b) What was the outcome of those revolutions?

8. (a) List some of the major issues treated by African writers in recent years. (b) What elements influenced Latin American writers?

9. How have African and Latin American nations attempted to deal with the influence of nations from outside their regions?

10. (a) How did ethnic conflict contribute to political instability in some African nations? (b) How did class divisions lead to social unrest in some Latin American nations?

THINKING CRITICALLY: ACTIVITIES

1. Divide into groups of four or five to discuss the following question: Should the United States intervene in a Latin American nation to prevent a possible Communist takeover?

2. Have members of the class assume roles as representatives from nations of either sub-Saharan Africa or Latin America. Then discuss how the nations of the region might work together to improve economic conditions.

3. Imagine that you are a large landowner in Latin America. Argue against a program of land reform. Now take the viewpoint of a landless peasant and argue for breaking up large estates.

APPLYING SOCIAL STUDIES SKILLS

Evaluating secondary sources. Review page 402. Then evaluate the following excerpts.

> The glorious battle of May 5, 1862, may be viewed from at least three standpoints: that of the facts and circumstances of this major event; that of the developments of which it was the outcome; and that of its consequence . . . .
>
> In his report, Mexican General Ignacio Zaragoza describes the scene with conciseness:
>
> > But I was unable to counterattack after the battle, for, although routed, the French forces were still stronger than my own; I therefore ordered C. General Díaz to disengage . . . . The French army fought bravely; the attack was a gross blunder by its Commander in Chief . . . . I can state with pride that at no time . . . did the Mexican army turn its back to the enemy.
>
> . . . In a proclamation addressed to his [defeated] soldiers, [French General Lorencez] stated:
>
> > . . . you had been told a hundred times that the City of Puebla . . . would warmly welcome you . . . . With the trust inspired by those deceitful assurances we advanced on Puebla.
>
> . . . Why is it that we Mexicans attach such signal importance to the Battle of the Fifth of May . . . ? Among the reasons . . . are, I think, the following:
>
> > The defeat of the French . . . raised the morale of the nation . . . was a splendid affirmation of the principle of nonintervention [and] gave strength to the Republican Party and its vigorous leader, Benito Juárez, to continue the struggle . . . .

From Rafael de la Colina, "The Glorious Fifth of May." *Américas,* Vol. 31, No. 5 (May 1979), pp. 40-44.

1. Why is this article a secondary source?

2. What primary sources does it include?

3. According to the author, what were the reasons for the victory? What were the effects?

4. Does this article include opinion? Explain.

APPLYING THINKING SKILLS

Recognizing point of view. The following statements were made by two different South Africans in the early 1960s. Analyze each to determine its author's point of view.

> There is no place for [the Bantu] in the European community [in South Africa] above the level of certain forms of labor. Within his own community, however, all doors are open. . . . Until now he has been subject to a system which drew him away from his own community and misled him by showing him the green pastures of European society in which he is not allowed to graze. . . . What is the use of teaching a Bantu child mathematics when it cannot use it in practice? . . . That is absurd. Education is not, after all, something that hangs in the air. Education must train and teach people in accordance with their opportunities in life. . . . Native education should be controlled in accordance with the policy of the State.

Abridged from a statement by former South African Prime Minister Hendrik Verwoerd, as quoted in the film *Last Grave at Dimbaza.*

> The [Nobel Peace] award could not be for me alone, nor for just South Africa, but for Africa as a whole. Ours is a continent in revolution against oppression. . . .
>
> How great is the paradox and how much greater the honor that an award in support of peace and brotherhood should come to one who is a citizen of a country where the brotherhood of man is an illegal doctrine. Outlawed, banned, censured, proscribed, and prohibited; where to work, talk, or campaign for the realization in fact and deed of the brotherhood of man is hazardous, punished with banishment or confinement without trial or imprisonment: where effective democratic channels to peaceful settlement of the race problem have never existed these 300 years, and where white minority power rests on the most heavily armed military machine in Africa.
>
> This is South Africa.

Abridged from "The Dignity of Man": The 1961 Nobel Peace Prize Acceptance Speech by Albert Luthuli, published in the *New York Times.*

1. What can you look for to detect an author's point of view?

2. What is at least one unstated assumption in each of the above statements?

3. What is the point of view in each statement?

CHAPTER THIRTY-FIVE

A NEW AGE FOR ASIA

1945–PRESENT

1960s. Mixed media on ceramic mural, Tadanori Yokoo, Japan, 1986.

The face of Asia changed significantly after 1945. When colonial powers withdrew from almost all their outposts, more than a dozen new nations gained independence. Social change swept across the region, sometimes by force.

After 1945, agricultural methods changed dramatically and new industries sprang up, vastly improving the living standards of many—but not all—Asians. Nations such as Japan, South Korea, Taiwan and Pakistan prospered, while other countries such as Bangladesh and Laos remained desperately poor.

In this time of rapid change, the Asian nations that thrived were those that successfully combined old and new—ancient traditions and modern ideas. Although some nations are still torn by internal differences, others have achieved economic and political stability.

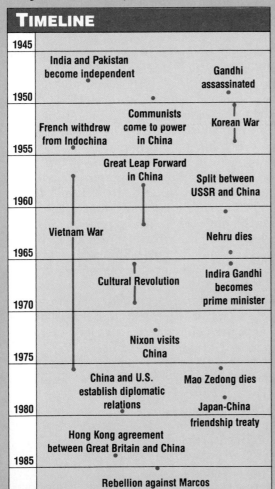

TIMELINE

1945	
	India and Pakistan become independent · Gandhi assassinated
1950	
	French withdrew from Indochina · Communists come to power in China · Korean War
1955	
	Great Leap Forward in China · Split between USSR and China
1960	
	Vietnam War · Nehru dies
1965	
	Cultural Revolution · Indira Gandhi becomes prime minister
1970	
	Nixon visits China
1975	
	China and U.S. establish diplomatic relations · Mao Zedong dies
1980	
	Japan-China friendship treaty · Hong Kong agreement between Great Britain and China
1985	
	Rebellion against Marcos

35–1
INDEPENDENCE FOR SOUTH ASIA

READ TO FIND OUT

—what the term *partition* means.
—how India split into separate nations upon gaining independence.
—why hostility remained between India and Pakistan.
—what factors led to the formation of Bangladesh.

The British held tenaciously to the Indian subcontinent during World War II, using India as a base for military operations against the Japanese in neighboring Burma. Although the subcontinent was still united under British rule after the war, religious splits among Indian nationalists were widening and demands for independence were increasing.

INDIA: INDEPENDENCE AND DIVISION

After World War I, India began to demand independence from British rule. In 1919, Mohandas K. Gandhi, leader of India's major political party, the Indian National Congress, developed his campaign of passive resistance and civil disobedience—the refusal on principle to obey a law.

However, discord between castes and between Hindus and Muslims created rifts in the independence movement. The Indian National Congress favored a centralized, independent India. In 1940, a rival nationalist group, the Muslim League, demanded *partition*, or division, of India into two separate nations, one for Hindus and the other for Muslims. This partition would formalize the serious split between India's two major religious groups.

When World War II ended, Britain offered independence to India whenever the Indian leaders could form a government. Britain's decision to free the colony was hastened by its need to spare its treasury the costs associated with governing such a vast, faraway possession.

In this photograph, taken in 1966, Indira Gandhi celebrates her appointment as prime minister of India. A graduate of Britain's Oxford University, Gandhi had taken part in India's independence movement. She had also served as an adviser to her father, Jawaharlal Nehru, India's first prime minister, and had acted as minister of information and broadcasting.

A decision on a form of government was not reached, however, because Hindu and Muslim Indian leaders could not settle their differences. Instead, they and the British leaders agreed to a partition. Thus, independence, which came in August 1947, created two nations—India and Pakistan. India's large Hindu majority occupied most of the subcontinent. Pakistan, where Muslims predominated, was made up of two parts—West Pakistan, to the northwest of India, and East Pakistan, to the northeast. One third of the Muslim population remained in India.

Violence after independence. After partition, millions of Hindus found themselves within the borders of Pakistan, while millions of Muslims lived in the new India. Masses of people boarded trains or set out on foot to seek a new home with people of their own religion. Bloody riots and massacres broke out as fear and hatred spread.

Among the victims was Gandhi himself, who had spoken out for reconciliation between Hindus and Muslims. Extremists considered Gandhi a traitor to his fellow Hindus, and in 1948, a young Hindu fanatic assassinated him.

STRUGGLE FOR STABILITY

In an attempt to bring the nation's many peoples together, India's leaders created a federal republic with 22 states—later 25—based on cultural diversity. A constitution, which was adopted in 1950, made India a parliamentary democracy in the British style. It proclaimed freedom of worship and barred discrimination based on sex, caste, religion, or race.

Gandhi's successor as head of the National Congress, Jawaharlal Nehru (NAY-roo), became the nation's first prime minister. Serving in this position from 1950 until 1964, Nehru helped to set India on a path of democratic socialism and industrial growth.

In 1966, Nehru's daughter, Indira Gandhi, became prime minister. Although she carried on many of Nehru's policies and seemed to inherit his popularity, her troubles grew. In the 1970s, drought caused widespread hunger, and rising oil prices hurt the Indian economy. She also faced political problems. In 1974, after charges of election fraud, a court ordered Gandhi to be excluded from parliament for six years.

Gandhi responded immediately by declaring a constitutional state of emergency, censoring the press, and jailing many opponents. In response to her policies and tactics, however, voters removed Gandhi from office in 1977. This was a stunning achievement for a young democracy. For the next three years, a coalition of small parties governed India.

In 1980, after a split in the National Congress party, Gandhi made a dramatic comeback. She regained power as the head of a new party named Congress-I, the I standing for Indira.

More troubled times followed, however, when India's Sikhs demanded greater autonomy

DETERMINING THE CREDIBILITY OF A SOURCE

One way to determine the probable accuracy of a claim is to determine the credibility of the source that makes the claim. A credible source is one that consistently provides accurate information. For example, you can generally rely on encyclopedias to be credible sources because their articles are written by experts. However, many sources are written by authors who have not yet established their reputations as experts on the subjects they write about. Therefore, you may have to determine the credibility of these sources before accepting them as accurate.

EXPLAINING THE SKILL

As noted on pages 286 and 287, one way to determine a source's credibility is to compare its information with information in sources already known to be credible. Another way is to determine if the author has expertise in the subject and a reputation for accuracy, and to determine whether the author has any conflict of interest regarding the subject.

When determining a source's credibility, you should identify the author's intended audience and his or her purpose in writing the source. Generally, sources written for private use, such as diaries, may be more credible than those intended to please particular types of readers. Information about an author's purpose is sometimes found in the source itself, in critical reviews of the source, or in books containing information about the author.

There is no absolute guarantee of credibility in any source. Even authors who have reputations as experts may sometimes give inaccurate information. Also, an author may be credible on one subject but not on another. Therefore, a good rule to follow is to consult several sources when seeking information on any subject.

APPLYING THE SKILL

Read the following descriptions of several sources relating to Jawaharlal Nehru. Determine which source would be most credible on the subject of Nehru's views about Gandhi and India's independence. Then answer the questions.

A. A statement by Nehru to newspaper reporters on January 12, 1928, in which he responded to unnamed critics of an independence resolution he had introduced to the Indian National Congress. In the statement, Nehru explained that the resolution sought independence but did not rule out any future alliance with Great Britain.

B. A personal letter from Nehru to Mohandas Gandhi objecting to Gandhi's public criticism of Nehru's independence resolution. In the letter, written on January 17, 1928, Nehru explained how he and Gandhi differed on the resolution and other issues, and chastised Gandhi repeatedly for putting the Congress in an embarrassing position.

C. A letter from Nehru to the editor of an Indian newspaper, in which Nehru complained about being accused of criticizing Mohandas Gandhi. In the letter, Nehru called the accusation a "monstrous notion." He also praised Gandhi as the "supreme example of latter-day India."

MAKING MEANING

1. Which source would probably be most credible on the given subject? **(a)** source A, **(b)** source B, **(c)** source C. Explain why.

2. Probably the main purpose of Nehru's statement to the reporters was to **(a)** refute the critics, **(b)** win the support of the critics, **(c)** demonstrate his leadership.

3. Which would be *most* useful in checking the credibility of Nehru's letter to Gandhi? **(a)** a newspaper history of the relationship between Nehru and Gandhi, **(b)** letters from Gandhi to Nehru around the time of Nehru's letter, **(c)** Nehru's autobiography. Explain why.

REVIEWING THE SKILL

4. What makes a source credible?
5. What are two ways to determine the credibility of a source?
6. In what ways might a source's purpose and intended audience affect its credibility?

for Punjab—the Indian state where most of the members of this religious minority lived. When Sikh militants began a campaign of terror, Gandhi ordered troops to storm the holiest of all Sikh shrines in Amritsar, where armed Sikhs were headquartered. About 800 Sikhs were killed in the attack. Retaliation came four months later, in October 1984, when two Sikhs who were serving as the prime minister's bodyguards assassinated her. In the days that followed, anti-Sikh riots swept throughout India, and hundreds of Sikhs were killed by outraged Hindus.

Leaders of the Congress-I party immediately chose Rajiv Gandhi, Indira's son, to replace her. After winning an early election, he set to work to try to ease Hindu-Sikh tensions and to turn India's energies to economic growth.

Economic growth. Despite nagging political problems, in the four decades since independence, India has built a wide variety of modern industries. India's factories turn out automobiles, aircraft, satellites, computers, and nuclear reactors. Its textile industry exports cloth and clothing throughout the world.

Improvements in agriculture have contributed greatly to India's economic growth. Expanded irrigation and mechanization have enabled more land to be cultivated, and increased use of fertilizers has improved crop yields. By the 1980s, India was self-sufficient in food and even had surplus crops to export to other nations.

Domestic problems. In spite of economic growth, several problems plague India. These problems include rapid population growth, high rates of illiteracy, and continued caste and sex discrimination. In addition, thousands of homeless people, who have no jobs or other means of providing food and shelter, live on the streets in the large cities.

Even though India produces adequate amounts of food, many people cannot afford to buy it. Distribution from the agricultural regions to other parts of this vast land is also a major obstacle in feeding India's people. Meanwhile, India has been trying for decades, with some success, to curb its rate of population increase. Even so, the nation's population reached 804 million by the late 1980s.

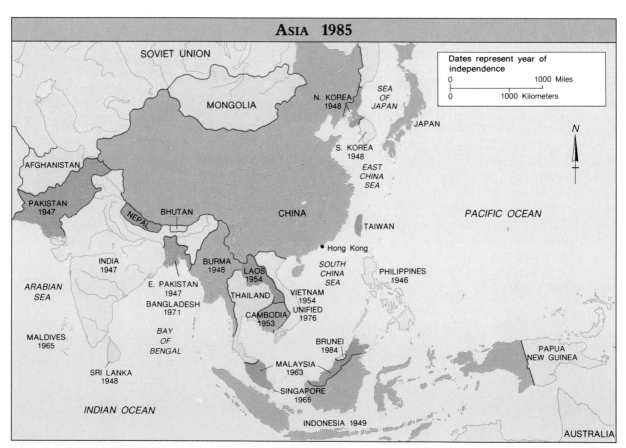

ASIA 1985

Foreign policy. India has also had problems with its neighbor Pakistan. Hostility between India and Pakistan flared into war on three occasions—in 1947, 1965, and 1971. The source of the first two disputes was control of a northern border region known as Kashmir. A further source of dispute was India's support for rebels in a 1971 civil war in Pakistan.

India's relations with other nations have been generally friendly. In the 1950s, India's leaders played a prominent role in organizing the non-aligned movement—neutral countries that are not aligned with either the Communist bloc or the West. For a time, India enjoyed friendly relations with China, but a brief border war between the two nations in 1962 cooled that friendship. However, in the 1970s and 1980s, India has made efforts to improve relations with China.

INDIAN SOCIETY AND CULTURE

Today, India is a land of sharp contrasts: rural and urban, traditional and modern, poor and rich. It is a place where one can see sari-clad women at a construction site carrying pots of fresh mortar on their heads, or a young upper-class woman in jeans driving through a village where some wives are never permitted to leave their houses. It is easy to see why India has been described as a nation living in several centuries at once.

Although India's constitution guarantees equality for all, the caste system is still the dominant force in rural areas, where more than 70 percent of the nation's people live. However, education has tended to blur class lines among Indians who work in the cities; and in housing areas that have grown up around industrial cities, members of different castes live together.

People from the upper and middle classes may have a Western education and work in a profession, a high-tech industry such as computer software, or other business. In contrast, the uneducated rural population is almost universally destined to have a difficult life, just trying to survive. Most Indians are engaged in agriculture, but conditions are so poor in some regions that crops yield barely enough to feed the family. To help these people escape a life of poverty, the government has set aside a number of jobs that can be filled only by members of the lowest class.

This hand-painted billboard advertises an Indian movie. Centered in Calcutta and Bombay, India's film industry boasts 60 major studios and distributes more than 300 features per year.

Despite grinding poverty, Indian culture continues to flourish. Music and dance are important parts of Hindu custom, and decorative arts abound. India's movie industry—the world's largest—has a wide audience throughout the nation. Modern Indian music, art, and literature reflect not only the country's richly diverse cultural heritage but also the Western influence of the recent past. In turn, Indian art and music have been embraced by the West and were especially popular among young people in the 1960s and 1970s. This exchange and blending of diverse ideas—political, economic, and cultural—has been a major factor in India's cultural success.

PAKISTAN AND BANGLADESH

Between West and East Pakistan, which had gained their independence in 1947, lay 1,000 miles (1,600 kilometers) of Indian territory. West Pakistan was lightly settled. Its area included both high mountains and the rich agricultural area of the Indus River system. In contrast, East Pakistan was densely settled, rainy, and flat. Its people were poorer and less educated than the people of West Pakistan. The religion of Islam was one of the few elements uniting the two sections of Pakistan.

After independence, Pakistan tried to work out a blend of democratic and Islamic traditions. Democracy lasted until a military takeover in 1958. The East Pakistanis, however, felt that they were being oppressed by the West Pakistanis, who dominated political life. An attempt in 1970 to restore civilian rule ended in disaster, and conflict between East and West Pakistan led to civil war in 1971.

Aided by Indian troops, the East Pakistanis won independence, forming the new nation of Bangladesh. Burdened by poverty, Bangladesh struggled to install democracy, but by the late 1980s, it was still under military rule.

In Pakistan, civilian rule was reestablished in the 1970s, but in 1977 the military again seized power. Although a civilian was elected prime minister in 1985, the military kept control of the government. Pakistan's economy grew between 1977 and 1987. In November 1988, Bhutto was elected prime minister, marking a peaceful transition to civilian rule.

TROUBLE IN SRI LANKA

Formerly known as Ceylon, this island off India's southeast coast gained independence from Britain in 1948 and adopted the name Sri Lanka (sree LAHN-kuh) in 1972. The government of Sri Lanka is democratic, and the main political parties favor a form of socialism.

Divisions between ethnic groups have been the source of violent conflict since the 1970s. The majority of the island's inhabitants practice Buddhism, although a second, smaller group, called the Tamils, follow the Hindu religion. Tamils seeking a separate state began using guerrilla warfare in the early 1970s to force the government to give in to their demands. By the late 1980s, clashes had increased and the conflict showed little sign of resolution.

SECTION REVIEW

1. Define *partition*.

2. Why was the British colony of India divided into two separate nations in 1947?

3. What issues have been responsible for hostilities between India and Pakistan?

4. Why did Bangladesh secede from Pakistan?

Analysis. How do the problems India's leaders face differ from those of other large nations such as the United States or the Soviet Union?

Data Search. Refer to the appropriate charts on page 834 to identify **(a)** India's major partners in export trade and **(b)** the population density, per capita income, and life expectancy in Bangladesh in 1988.

35–2
CONFLICT IN EAST ASIA

READ TO FIND OUT

—how the Great Leap Forward affected China.
—how Deng Xiaoping changed Mao's policies.
—how China's foreign relations changed.
—how the prodemocracy movement ended.
—why war broke out in Korea.

Both China and Korea became involved in civil warfare almost as soon as World War II ended. As Communists took control from the Nationalists in China and grew stronger in Korea, attempts to make drastic changes in traditional society resulted in a great clash of ideologies.

TURMOIL IN CHINA

Since the 1920s, China had been torn by war, first civil war and then the struggle against Japan. For a time, the Nationalists led by Chiang Kai-shek and the Communists led by Mao Zedong buried their differences to concentrate on fighting the Japanese. When the war with Japan ended, the Nationalist party was still in power in China, but Mao's Communists controlled much of the north. In 1946, civil war resumed.

The Nationalists received aid from the United States, and American officials tried without success to persuade Chiang to curb corruption in his government. Angered by this corruption, many urban Chinese turned against their leader. The Communists, meanwhile, won the support of many country people with promises of reforms that would eliminate the landlord class. By 1949, the Communist armies had swept Chiang's government from power.

Thousands of Nationalists—including Chiang—now fled to the island of Taiwan, off the coast of China. The transplanted government continued to rule in the name of the Republic of China. With American support, the Taiwan government held China's seat in the UN for the next two decades.

After defeating the Nationalists in 1949, Mao established the People's Republic of China, with its capital at Beijing (Peking).* Power was held by the Communist party, with Mao at the helm, and the Chinese Communists set up government institutions like those of the Soviets.

Mao wanted to eliminate the ancient system in which landlords had exploited farmers. Under Mao's government, all the nation's economic resources would be owned by the people and controlled by the government, and all citizens would work for the common good. The end of capitalism and imperialism would mark the beginning of a new way of life in China.

Mao's dream was ambitious, but he had strong popular support. In addition, a program of "reeducation" convinced many opponents to become followers; resisters were jailed or killed.

ECONOMIC AND SOCIAL REFORM

Under Mao, the Communist party proposed social and economic reforms designed to convert China from a land of rich landowners and peasant farmers into a modern industrial nation. The Communists declared that they would abolish social classes in favor of full equality.

Through a disruptive and at times brutal campaign, Mao's government destroyed the landlord class. Agricultural reform went through several stages. At first, landless farmers received land of their own. Then the state encouraged the creation of farm cooperatives, pooling the lands and efforts of many families.

Between 1953 and 1958, China's five-year plan stressed the rapid buildup of heavy industry. The state took over businesses, until by 1956 all private industry had disappeared.

In 1956, feeling confident that the people agreed with them, Communist officials asked for comments on their progress. In what was known as the Hundred Flowers campaign, party leaders invited criticism, saying: "Let a hundred flowers bloom together, let the hundred schools of thought contend [disagree]." The people's negative response startled the authorities. Mao and his supporters had no idea there was so much disagreement about communism or the rapid pace of reform.

*As of January 1, 1979, the People's Republic of China began using Pinyin—a new system of translating Chinese words into the Roman alphabet. Words in Pinyin spelling are used in the text, with the old system of translation in parentheses.

The Great Leap Forward. In 1958, Communist leaders launched what they called the Great Leap Forward. They urged people to work longer hours than ever—even to make steel in their spare time by melting iron ore in "backyard furnaces." If iron ore was unavailable, people were expected to melt down tools, pots, and other iron objects. Officials also sent bureaucrats, educators, and other professionals from urban areas to the countryside to do manual labor and "learn from the masses."

The new economic policy also included the formation of large units called communes, which incorporated agriculture and industry and were supposed to be self-sufficient. Some communes had as many as 5,000 families and provided schooling and child care.

The Great Leap Forward did not last long, however. People resisted communal living. Many also complained about the long hours and hard work, which had not increased productivity. In fact, the new policies, combined with a few years of bad weather, caused shortages of food and industrial products. By the early 1960s, party leaders concluded that they had made a mistake and decided to pursue a slower, more orderly plan of development.

The Cultural Revolution. Debate within the party continued, however, on the proper way to develop industrial might. Some leaders wanted to focus on steady economic growth, relying on the willingness of the people to keep production high. Other leaders, including Mao, thought China's revolution was losing its spirit. These leaders argued that growth depended on teaching a new generation about the hardships of the past and inspiring them to build a better society. To achieve this goal, Mao launched in 1966 a movement he called the Great Proletarian Cultural Revolution.

Mao's apparent intention was to stir revolutionary enthusiasm among young people and party officials, but the situation quickly got out of hand. Mao closed the high schools and universities. Rallying to Mao's cry for support, students by the millions joined military-style groups called the Red Guards, organized by Mao's wife, Jiang Qing (jee-AHNG CHING). The Red Guards surged through the country, denouncing "the Four Olds"—old ideas, culture, customs, and habits. Red Guards beat up party officials, destroyed "bad" books, and

Bearing oversized images of Mao Zedong, Red Guards parade through Beijing (Peking) streets during the Great Proletarian Cultural Revolution, which lasted from 1966 to 1969. Mao urged his followers to action by proclaiming, "We are not only able to destroy the old world, we are able to build a new world instead."

disrupted factories. Fighting broke out as troops were called on to control Red Guard disturbances.

In addition, many people who were deemed to be enemies of the revolution were jailed, put under house arrest, or killed. Thousands of people, including party officials and educated citizens with ties to the West, were silenced.

By 1969, Mao and other officials managed to tame the revolution that they had helped launch, but its effects lasted for years. Rival factions continued to struggle for control of the Communist party. After Mao died in 1976, the leaders who shared his emphasis on revolutionary struggle—the legendary Gang of Four, which included Jiang Qing—slipped from power.

A NEW DIRECTION FOR CHINA

Deng Xiaoping (DUNG SHŌ-PING), who became China's leader in the late 1970s, reversed many of Mao's policies. Deng introduced economic reforms and sought to expand China's ties with the outside world. He led a drive to loosen the government's control over China's economy. Small private businesses reappeared, and China welcomed foreign investments. In many rural areas, communes and cooperatives gave way to large farms run by groups of farmers or to small family farms. Some party officials argued that China was on the way to restoring capitalism, but Deng insisted that this was not his goal. Basic industries remained under state ownership.

Deng also tackled the problem of China's growing population. According to government policy, the ideal family is to consist of one child. Late marriage is encouraged and family-planning services are freely available for married couples. Although China's population surpassed a billion in the mid-1980s, the nation's rate of population growth slowed to the official goal of 1 percent.

As the rate of population growth slowed and industrialization increased, China seemed to be accepting some limited capitalism. By the 1980s, Chinese leaders encouraged consumer goods, Western-style hotels and restaurants, and tourists. However, change comes slowly in such a vast land, and China still struggles with a low standard of living.

FOREIGN POLICY

China's relations with the Soviet Union underwent a startling reversal in the 1950s. The Soviets had been supportive of the Chinese Communists in their struggle against the Nationalists, but by the mid-1950s relations between the two countries had begun to cool. China's leaders saw the Soviets drifting away from Marxism and disagreed with the Soviet policy of peaceful coexistence with the West. These differences finally resulted in a split between the world's two largest Communist nations in 1960, when the Soviets abruptly cut off aid to China.

After the split, China openly competed with the Soviet Union for leadership of Communist movements in other countries. China also stepped up its drive to become a leader of the developing nations, offering foreign aid to many countries, especially in Africa.

Not until the 1980s did relations with the Soviets improve. Soviet and Chinese officials held a series of meetings to discuss such matters as trade and withdrawal of troops from border areas. As a sign of warming relations, Soviet premier Mikhail Gorbachev traveled to Beijing in May 1989 to meet with Deng Xiaoping and other Chinese leaders, the first such high level meeting between the two powers in 30 years.

Relations with the United States. For many years China and the United States maintained an icy distance, especially after Chinese Communists fought American troops in the Korean War. Relations remained cool in the 1960s, when China backed the United States' opponents in the Vietnam War. During the 1970s, however, American-Chinese relations improved as Soviet-Chinese relations worsened. China needed a powerful friend—and the United States was eager to widen the gap between Soviets and Chinese. The result was the historic visit to China by President Richard Nixon in 1972, which paved the way for better relations between the two nations. Late in 1978, the United States formally recognized the government of the People's Republic of China.

Agreement with Britain. Relations between China and Great Britain also improved. In 1984, China reached agreement with Britain on the future of the British colony of Hong Kong, which China had given to Britain in the 1840s in the settlement of the Opium Wars. According to the agreement, China will resume control over Hong Kong when Britain's lease on the entire colony runs out in 1997. China promised, however, to leave the colony's capitalist economy in place for another 50 years.

THE PRODEMOCRACY MOVEMENT

Efforts to improve China's economy resulted in industrial growth, but also led to rising prices and grain shortages as farmers turned to more profitable activities. Many Chinese expressed discontent with the shortages and rising cost of living, prompting China's leaders to slow economic reform and tighten political control—the "new authoritarianism."

The stricter measures were challenged by intellectuals and organized students. The earlier economic freedoms had induced these people to seek greater political freedoms, also. Early in 1989, student groups staged peaceful prodemocracy demonstrations in Beijing's Tienamen Square, China's symbolic seat of power. Joined by thousands of workers, the students demanded rights granted in China's constitution but not in practice, such as freedom of the press and freedom of assembly. Afraid that such rallies might spread, government leaders agreed to meet with student leaders. However, the students felt that the officials did not really listen and planned another demonstration for May 4.

Bearing posters with slogans like "Down with Corruption" and "Give Us Democracy or Give Us Death," 100,000 students again marched on Tienamen Square in May to begin a demonstration that would last for weeks. People in other cities staged similar demonstrations. These protests continued during the visit of Mikhail Gorbachev, greatly embarrassing Chinese leaders.

On May 20 the Chinese government declared martial law. Some 200,000 soldiers massed on the outskirts of the city. For days government officials were silent while behind the scenes factions that included the moderate Zhao Ziyang (JOW ZEE-YAHNG) and the stricter Li Peng disagreed over how to handle the protest. The hardest among them won out.

On June 4, troops entered the city. In the night, tanks rolled through the student encampment in the darkened square. After several days of fighting, 5,000 people were dead, 10,000 more were injured, and thousands were arrested. The government had smashed the prodemocracy movement. As the government moved to strengthen its control, the rest of the world wondered if Chinese leaders could long continue their policy of economic reform without also permitting political reform.

TAIWAN: A THRIVING ISLAND NATION

Communists and Nationalists agree that Taiwan is part of China. Since 1949, the Nationalist government on Taiwan and the Communist government on the mainland have both claimed to represent all of China.

During and after the Chinese civil war—the United States gave military assistance to the Nationalists and almost went to war in the mid-1950s to prevent Communist China from taking Taiwan by force. Taiwan kept China's seat in the United Nations until 1971, when it was replaced by the People's Republic of China.

In 1979, the United States gave full diplomatic recognition to Communist China and severed formal ties with Taiwan. The Americans promised, however, to help .repel any Communist attack on the island. Communist leaders have sought, without success, to interest the Nationalists in peaceful reunification.

Economic stability. The Nationalists have ruled Taiwan by authoritarian methods, while promoting agricultural reform and industrial growth. Taiwan has built a vigorous industrial economy, and its 18 million people have a standard of living far above that of the people in the rest of China. This island nation produces clothing and a variety of other consumer goods for export. In addition, low labor costs have attracted many Western businesses.

DISUNITY IN KOREA

After World War II, the Soviet Union and the United States occupied Korea—held by the Japanese during the war—and established governments there. The Soviet Union occupied the part north of the 38th parallel, and the United States occupied the southern part.

When the time came for the United Nations to supervise elections that would reunite the country, the Soviets refused access to the northern sector. Elections were held in South Korea, however, and it became the Republic of Korea in 1948, with Syngman Rhee as president. In North Korea, the Soviets responded by setting up the Democratic People's Republic of Korea headed by President Kim Il Sung.

The Korean War. Two years later, in June 1950, North Korea invaded South Korea in an

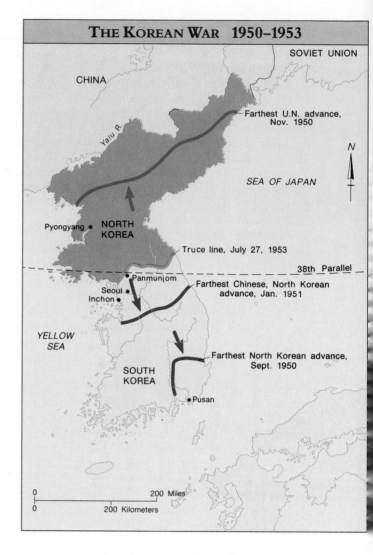

THE KOREAN WAR 1950–1953

attempt to unite the peninsula under Communist rule. The United Nations called on member nations to provide military aid to the South. The United Nations forces assisting South Korea included troops from the United States.

For weeks, the UN forces, commanded by American General Douglas MacArthur, were driven south. However, a successful amphibious attack behind enemy lines at Inchon turned the tide of battle. UN forces pushed the North Koreans northward and then crossed the 38th parallel in pursuit, driving toward the Yalu River, the border between North Korea and China.

In November 1950, Chinese troops poured across the border and drove the UN forces southward. By March 1951, however, the UN forces had fought their way back to about the 38th parallel, where the war deadlocked.

In May 1987, students at more than thirty universities throughout South Korea gathered to demand democratic political reforms from the government of President Chun Doo Hwan. Protests often erupted into violence as South Korean police and students clashed.

To win the war, MacArthur insisted on invading China. The United States and the United Nations, however, believed that such actions might lead to a third world war, and President Harry Truman removed MacArthur from his command.

Truce negotiations began in July 1951 but were not completed for two more years. The 1953 truce that ended the fighting reestablished the original border between the two nations, but North and South Korea remained enemies. Because of the continued threat of invasion, the United States kept troops in South Korea.

ECONOMIC AND POLITICAL CHANGES IN SOUTH KOREA

After the Korean War, South Korea built up its industry, mixing state ownership and private enterprise. By the mid-1980s, the nation was a major steel producer with a thriving auto industry. South Korea's economic growth rate was among the highest in the world by the 1980s, rivaling that of Japan.

Politically, the decades following the Korean War have been a time of tension for South Korea. The authoritarian rule of Syngman Rhee ended after riots in 1960 forced his resignation. A military takeover the following year blocked efforts to build democracy. Beginning in 1961, General Park Chung Hee ruled South Korea as a police state for 18 years before being assassinated in 1979. Still another military leader,

Chun Doo Hwan, took power in 1980, despite American objections to his dictatorship.

Student demonstrations calling for an end to military rule and for a democratic government erupted and were met with police violence. When Chun chose his own successor in 1987 instead of allowing free elections, violent clashes broke out between police and thousands of students and other protesters. Fearful that unchecked violence would disrupt plans for the 1988 Olympic Games to be held in South Korea, the Chun regime agreed to free elections and an end to the military dictatorship.

After a turbulent campaign, the ruling party's candidate, Roh Tae Woo (NOH TAY OO), was elected president in late 1987. Roh has set South Korea on a more democratic course. Political opposition, suppressed under Chun, has been allowed under the new government.

SECTION REVIEW

1. How did the Great Leap Forward affect China's economic and political life?

2. How did Deng Xiaoping reverse Mao Zedong's policies?

3. Describe China's changing relations with the two superpowers and with Taiwan.

4. What caused the Korean War?

Analysis. Why did Chinese Communist leaders in the late 1980s allow more economic freedom in their nation? Describe the results.

35–3
JAPAN: AN ECONOMIC SUCCESS STORY

READ TO FIND OUT

—how occupation by American troops changed Japan.

—how Japan attained economic success after the 1950s.

—why Japanese-American trade relations have provoked controversy.

—how some other nations in Asia have gained economic prosperity.

Japan emerged from World War II a defeated nation occupied by American forces. Within a few years, however, a new Japan began to appear, boasting democratic institutions and a vigorous economy. Japan allied itself with its former enemy, the United States, and by the 1980s was an economic giant.

POSTWAR CHANGES

After Japan's surrender in 1945, American troops, led by General Douglas MacArthur, occupied the country. Through these occupying forces, American leaders intended to rid Japan of its militaristic leaders and traditions. They also wanted to shape a democratic Japan with close ties to the United States.

In 1947, under General MacArthur's direction, Japan adopted a new constitution that implemented much of the American program by prohibiting the nation from maintaining a military force. The emperor, no longer considered divine, was given only a ceremonial role. Power now lay in the hands of a revised parliament, called the Diet, which had two elected houses. In contrast to prewar years, voters now included women. In addition, a bill of rights guaranteed freedom of speech, freedom of religion, and equality of the sexes.

Japan also changed its system of education, increasing compulsory schooling from six years to nine. New textbooks stressed democratic values in place of traditional ones. However, exams remained highly competitive, with students studying for long hours to attain the high scores necessary for admittance to the nation's growing colleges and universities.

Japan—where industrialization had begun almost a century earlier—rebuilt its economy, with both management and technical assistance from the United States. An agricultural reform program broke up large landholdings. Japan's landowning class expanded to include many small farmers, who became major supporters of the government. As a result of pressure from some Americans, the large, family-owned businesses called *zaibatsu* were also broken up. The effect of that action was limited, however, as Japanese business leaders—many from the original zaibatsu families—created massive new companies.

Restoration of independence. The Korean War, which had begun in 1950, revived Japan's economy and hastened the end of the American occupation. The United States bought large quantities of war goods from Japanese manufacturers and shifted many of its troops from Japan to Korea.

In 1951, Japan worked out a peace treaty with the United States and 47 other nations. The treaty took effect the following year, formally ending the American occupation and restoring Japan's independence.

Also that year, Japan signed a defense treaty with the United States whereby the United States agreed to defend Japan in return for the right to have American military bases on Japanese soil.

ECONOMIC RECOVERY

The 1950s saw the beginning of an economic boom for Japan. Industry grew rapidly, agricultural output rose, and the standard of living increased sharply. In the 1950s and 1960s, the annual growth in Japan's economic output averaged about 10 percent, one of the highest growth rates in the world.

There were many reasons for Japan's economic success. One was its stable political climate. Although many parties competed for votes, the Liberal Democratic party controlled the national government. Big businesses and

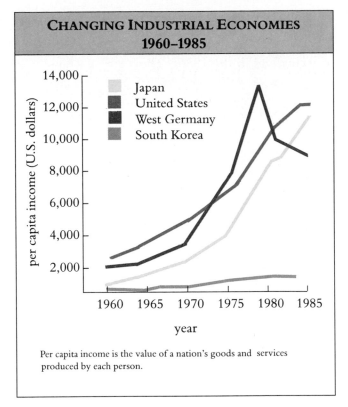

CHANGING INDUSTRIAL ECONOMIES 1960–1985

Japan
United States
West Germany
South Korea

per capita income (U.S. dollars)

14,000
12,000
10,000
8,000
6,000
4,000
2,000

1960 1965 1970 1975 1980 1985

year

Per capita income is the value of a nation's goods and services produced by each person.

small farmers alike enthusiastically supported this party.

Another reason for economic growth was close cooperation between privately owned businesses and the government. As a result, the government frequently influenced business decisions by funneling bank loans to the industries it considered most likely to help boost the national economy.

Many other factors also contributed to economic growth. By holding down military spending, keeping wages relatively low, and encouraging people to place money in savings accounts, Japan managed to accumulate large amounts of capital for investment. Moreover, relatively low tariffs in other countries helped Japan to build up its exports. Through money from exports, Japan was able to pay for imports—raw materials that it lacked and food crops that could not be grown on the limited farm land in Japan.

In addition to raw materials and food, technology was another key import. Japanese firms bought technical information and up-to-date machinery from other countries and put them to work in Japanese factories. So efficiently did the Japanese use this technology that soon they

were turning out high-quality goods, such as cars and television sets, for prices that producers in other nations could not match. Japanese exports boomed, and brisk sales brought in more money that could be invested in still further expansion.

By the mid-1970s, Japan's gross national product (GNP)—the total value of the annual production of its goods and services—was exceeded only by that of the United States. By the 1980s, Japan's per capita income had passed that of all but the most prosperous countries of Western Europe and North America.

FOREIGN POLICY

Japan and the United States have been steady allies through the postwar years. The two countries revised their defense treaty in 1960, giving Japan more responsibility for its own defense. Although leftist parties attacked the pact, claiming that it represented a return to the militarism that had led to the war, most Japanese seemed to accept Japan's continued close ties to the United States.

Japan followed the American lead in snubbing the Communist government in China for many years, but in the 1970s Japan and China began a lively trade. The two nations signed a treaty of peace and friendship in 1978.

Trade relations. Despite their close cooperation, Japan and the United States did not always see eye to eye. In fact, trade relations were a major source of friction between Japan and most other industrial nations. In the 1970s, Japan regularly exported more to the West than it bought in return, and in the mid-1980s the trade gap grew wider. In the United States, the auto and steel industries were particularly hurt by less expensive imports from Japan. Thousands of Americans lost jobs, and hundreds of businesses closed.

Many nations claimed that Japan was using unfair trade rules and high tariffs. For instance, in the 1970s Japan forbade the import of American rice, even though rice from the United States would be less expensive for Japanese consumers. High tariffs on other agricultural products also made trading with Japan difficult. The European Common Market joined the United States in protesting what it, too, saw as unfair restrictions on imports. Japanese leaders, how-

A Kyoto woman in the 1980s performs the tea ceremony, following a ritual more than 500 years old. The goal of the ceremony is to achieve tranquility by focusing on the preparation and serving of tea.

ever, argued that Japan had relatively few trade barriers.

Americans urged new tariffs and other trade barriers as a means of putting pressure on Japan to change its trade policies. For example, in the late 1980s some American companies accused Japanese firms of unfair pricing of computer chips and urged increased tariffs as retaliation. These trade disputes were a serious concern for Japanese leaders, who saw attacks against Japanese exports as a threat to Japan's prosperity.

A CHANGING SOCIETY

American influence—especially in the area of culture—has remained strong in Japan since the American occupation ended in 1952. Many Japanese learn English and eat American instead of traditional foods.

Many older Japanese are disturbed by the "Westernization" of Japan. They believe that Japan's strength lies in a strong sense of unity and national identity. The willingness to work together for common goals and to put the needs of the nation—or of the company or certain other groups—above individual needs has long been acknowledged as a key factor in Japan's success. Now, however, the elders claim that young people are becoming more individualistic and less willing to sacrifice for any but their own wants and needs. The younger generation is seen as giving up age-old customs, such as the tea ceremony, in favor of such modern pleasures as television and comic books.

As in the West, many women in Japan now work outside the home. This break with tradition indicates the view that many Japanese have of themselves in the 1980s. They live in a rapidly changing world and believe that they are simply keeping up with the times—not forsaking their heritage.

Another response to the increasing Western influence in Japan is a new emphasis on nationalism. Some Japanese people want to reclaim what they lost in the postwar years: the pure Japanese spirit, or national soul. These nationalists favor rejection—not assimilation—of foreign ideas and culture, and want a return to traditional Japanese values and unity.

Other observers of modern Japanese society maintain that tradition is still an important part of Japanese life, despite outward appearances. For example, Japan's rich cultural heritage is widely evident in the use of traditional themes and procedures in present-day crafts, arts, literature, and architecture.

PROSPEROUS MARKET ECONOMIES

Japan's economic success—mirrored in Taiwan, South Korea, Hong Kong, and Singapore—was the beginning of a new trend in the world economy of increased trade among the Pacific Rim, or nations that border the Pacific Ocean. The Asian nations of the Pacific Rim have thriving market economies based on exports of manufactured goods. Specializing in mass-produced items such as televisions, cars, and radios, these nations have become the world's major producers of high-tech products.

The economic prosperity resulting from this thriving export trade has greatly raised the standard of living in these countries, moving them out of the category of developing nations. Indeed, Japan—the most economically powerful nation in the region—is often referred to as a member of the industrialized West.

A major reason the Asian Pacific Rim has been able to compete successfully with American and European industries is the lower cost of labor in Asia. While assembly-line workers in auto plants in the United States earn as much as $20 per hour, South Koreans working in the same capacity earn less than $10 per day. Because lower wages make Asian products cheaper than American ones, these foreign goods are popular with consumers in the West.

1. What changes did the American occupation bring to Japan?

2. Describe three major reasons for Japan's economic success in the postwar years.

3. Why have recent Japanese-American trade relations stirred controversy?

4. How have the Asian nations of the Pacific Rim been able to achieve economic success?

Analysis. Why is it so important for nations to keep a balance between imports and exports?

Data Search. Refer to the appropriate chart on page 834 to compare Japan's gross national product in 1988 with that of West Germany and the United States.

35-4
TRANSITIONS IN SOUTHEAST ASIA

READ TO FIND OUT

—why the American role in Vietnam changed.
—how the Vietnam War ended.
—what happened in Cambodia after the Khmer Rouge took over.
—what caused turmoil in the Philippines.

Colonial powers ruled most of Southeast Asia until World War II. The only independent nation was Siam, renamed Thailand in 1939. After the war, nationalist forces gained strength throughout Southeast Asia and made plans for achieving independence. Some of the new nations, such as the Philippines and Singapore, attained political stability and economic success. Others—especially Vietnam and Cambodia—were exploited by authoritarian heads of state and even now remain desperately poor.

VIETNAM: WAR AND REUNIFICATION

Before World War II, Vietnam was part of French Indochina, along with what are now Laos and Cambodia. The French had controlled the Indochinese peninsula since the early 1900s and had a strong influence on the region's culture, especially in the cities.

During World War II, Vietnamese Communist leader Ho Chi Minh (HŌ CHEE MIN)—who had been educated in France—organized an independence movement called the Viet Minh. At the war's end, Ho set up an independent government in the northern city of Hanoi.

France sought to bring Ho's government under the control of the French Union, which offered limited self-rule. To this end, the French established a second Vietnamese government in the southern city of Saigon. In 1946, when Ho continued to insist on full independence, war broke out between the Viet Minh and the French.

The key battle occurred in 1954 at Dien Bien Phu (DYEN BYEN FOO), where the Viet Minh besieged and captured a French fort. After the defeat, France withdrew from Vietnam, and the country was temporarily split into two independent halves, which were to be united by elections in 1956. A Communist government ruled the north and a non-Communist government ran the south.

American leaders thought Ho Chi Minh was a Soviet puppet and feared that Communist control would spread from country to country in Asia. Accordingly, the American government gave strong support to the South Vietnamese president, Ngo Dinh Diem (NŌ DIN ZIM).

After Diem refused to hold elections in 1956, Communist-led South Vietnamese—called the

A computer operator patterns knitwear made by machine. American and European clothiers often buy Asian clothing, produced inexpensively, to sell under their own labels.

Viet Cong by the government—launched a guerrilla war against Diem. In 1959, North Vietnam began to supply major assistance to the guerrillas in the south.

American involvement. The United States stepped up involvement in Vietnam. Disenchanted with Diem's repressive rule, American leaders secretly encouraged a military coup in 1963. The plotters seized power and killed Diem. Slowly at first and then more rapidly, the United States poured huge numbers of troops into Vietnam. In 1960, there were only 600 American military advisors in the country, but by 1968 half a million Americans were fighting the Viet Cong. The United States also trained and supplied a large South Vietnamese army.

As the war dragged on, fighting spilled over into neighboring Cambodia and Laos. After President Nixon took office in 1969, the United States pulled out some of its troops while stepping up air attacks. Peace talks, begun in 1968, finally led to a cease-fire in 1973. Fighting resumed, however, once the American troops left. Two years later, in 1975, North Vietnamese and Viet Cong troops captured Saigon, which then was renamed Ho Chi Minh City, and took over South Vietnam's government.

Postwar developments. Hundreds of thousands of people fled South Vietnam after the Communist takeover. Many were professionals and merchants who feared the changes a Communist regime would bring. Some went by land, but others—called boat people—braved the seas in fragile boats. Numerous people lost their lives in their attempt to gain freedom. By the late 1980s, thousands of the survivors remained in refugee camps in Thailand and Malaysia. More than 700,000 Indochinese refugees had settled in the United States, and others found homes in Canada and Western Europe.

In 1976, Communist leaders reunited the two parts of Vietnam and renamed it the Socialist Republic of Vietnam. Sharp differences between north and south remained, however. In the north, almost all farms were large collectives and most businesses were government-owned. Failing to impose rigid central planning on the south, government leaders allowed most farms there to remain in private hands.

In the late 1980s, Vietnam still maintained an army of more than a million soldiers, largely

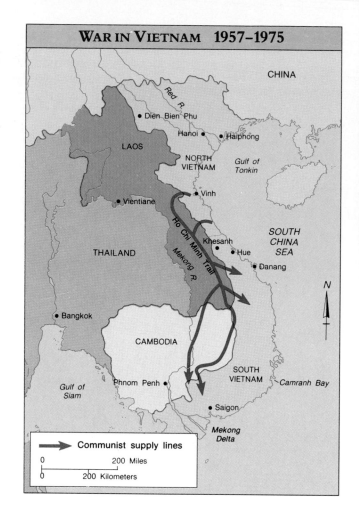

with aid from the Soviet Union. The drain on its economy has been tremendous, and living standards have suffered. High inflation, massive unemployment, and shortages of food and other goods continue to plague the nation.

LAOS AND CAMBODIA

Established as an independent nation in 1954, Laos suffered from the civil strife that swept French Indochina in the early years after independence. In 1975, Laos became a Communist nation. In time, fearful of Chinese aggression across the border, Laos allied itself with Vietnam and allowed Vietnamese troops to be stationed in Laos.

Like Laos, Cambodia—which had gained independence in 1953—was once part of French Indochina. During the Vietnam War, the Cambodian ruler, Prince Norodom Sihanouk (SEE-hah-nook), had tried to isolate his country from the conflict. However, North Vietnamese and Viet Cong forces set up bases inside Cambodia and established supply routes through regions bordering South Vietnam.

In 1969, American planes began large-scale bombing in Cambodia to disrupt the flow of supplies. The following year, Cambodian General Lon Nol led a military takeover and set up a new regime. Ground fighting spread from Vietnam into Cambodia, as the new military government allowed American and South Vietnamese troops to pursue the Communist forces into Cambodia.

Settling in China, Prince Sihanouk threw his support to a group of Communist rebels called Khmer (KMER) Rouge, who had been trying to take over Cambodia. In 1975, after the United States had withdrawn from Vietnam, the Khmer Rouge toppled Lon Nol and installed a Communist government.

Pol Pot, the Khmer Rouge leader, imposed a rule of terror. He ordered people to abandon cities and become farmers. Many starved or died of exhaustion on mass marches to the countryside. The Khmer Rouge executed many others, especially political and military leaders, as well as educators and other professionals. More than 2 million of Cambodia's 8 million people died under Pol Pot's rule.

Pol Pot had bitter differences with the Communist leaders of Vietnam. Moreover, traditional rivalries had divided the people of the two countries for centuries. Vietnamese troops invaded Cambodia in 1978, then ousted Pol Pot early in 1979 and helped a rival Cambodian Communist leader—Heng Samrin—take over, renaming the country the People's Republic of Kampuchea (kahm-poo-CHEE-ah).

Although Pol Pot's brutality earned wide condemnation, many nations also denounced the Vietnamese invasion. The United Nations General Assembly refused to recognize the new regime. Vietnamese troops remained in Cambodia to defend Heng Samrin against the Khmer Rouge and other rebel forces. In 1989, the Vietnamese withdrew from Cambodia, but fears that the Khmer Rouge will return to power make the future of the nation uncertain.

THAILAND

Thailand—originally Siam—has always been an independent nation, although it was occupied by Japanese troops during World War II. Concerned by the Communist victory in China in 1949, Thai leaders allied their nation with the United States.

When the Vietnam War ended, large numbers of Vietnamese, Laotians, and Cambodians sought refuge in non-Communist Thailand. Thousands were still living in camps along Thailand's borders in the late 1980s.

Unlike its Communist neighbors, Thailand is a thriving nation with a free-enterprise economy. Although military leaders have had a strong influence in most postwar governments, the 1978 constitution called for a gradual phase-out of the military's role in politics.

THE PHILIPPINES

Spain occupied the Philippines until 1898, when the United States won the Spanish-American War and took over the islands. In 1934, after 36 years of rule, the United States promised to move the Philippines toward independence. A Japanese invasion during World War II forced delays, but in 1946, the United States handed power to a new Philippine republic.

For many years, the Philippines had a vigorous democracy. The nation's leaders began land reforms and rapidly built up industry. In the 1950s, the military put down a rebellion by Communist-led guerrillas called Huks.

Nonetheless, social tensions built up. Farmers complained about large corporations taking over their lands, and business owners complained of widespread corruption. Guerrilla warfare spread, this time by the New People's Army (NPA), the military wing of the Philippines' Communist party.

The Marcos regime. Ferdinand Marcos, elected president in 1965 and 1969, declared martial law—rule by the military—in 1972 in order to stop the uprisings. He ordered hundreds of his political opponents arrested but made little progress in fighting the guerrillas.

One jailed Marcos opponent, Benigno Aquino (buh-NIG-no uh-KEE-no), had his wife, Corazon, carry anti-government messages to the outside world. Freed after eight years of imprisonment, Aquino left the Philippines and went into exile in the United States.

Although he ended martial law in 1981, Marcos remained in power. Then, economic

JIM THOMPSON

As a young boy growing up in Greenville, Connecticut, James H. "Jim" Thompson found his grandfather's stories of life as a diplomat in Thailand spellbinding. Later, during World War II, Thompson parachuted into Thailand as an agent for the Office of Strategic Services (OSS)—the forerunner of the Central Intelligence Agency (CIA)—and became even more fascinated by the country. His fascination would lead him to revive a dying ancient art and turn it into a twentieth-century enterprise, patterned after American businesses.

After the war ended, Thompson settled in the Thai capital, Bangkok. On one of his many trips into the country, Thompson came across a family weaving silk. Knowledge of this traditional craft had been passed down from generation to generation. Now, however, modern clothing was replacing traditional dress, and inexpensive manufactured clothes were being imported into Thailand. With no market for their silks, weavers were turning to more profitable trades.

Thompson was convinced that there was a world market for a fabric with such intricate designs and vivid colors. In 1948, he sought out the last of the weavers and organized the Thai Silk Company, a corporation that was 51 percent Thai-owned. He provided the weavers with new colorfast dyes and scoured Thai museums for traditional designs they could use.

In the beginning, business was slow. Then Thai silk was used to make costumes for the 1956 movie *The King and I,* and sales soared. By the mid-1960s, the Thai Silk Company employed 4,000 weavers and was exporting more than $1.5 million worth of silk each year.

Thompson was pleased when many Thai businesspeople entered the silk business. Soon dozens of companies were competing in this profitable market, providing work for thousands of people and bringing money into the Thai treasury. Thompson's success also caught the attention of other Asian nations. Burma, Malaysia, and Singapore all sought his advice.

In March 1967, on the way to answer a request from the government of Singapore, Thompson stopped at a mountain resort in Malaysia. On March 26, he set off for a walk in the jungle-clad hills. However, he never returned. Local guides, Malaysian troops, and even American helicopter teams failed to find a trace of him. What happened to Thompson remains a mystery. However, the Thai silk industry he helped to develop continues to flourish more than twenty years after his disappearance.

---

conditions worsened and discontent spread. Anti-Marcos demonstrations reached a fever pitch in 1983 when Aquino was assassinated as he left the plane that brought him back to the Philippines. Some anti-Marcos feeling was also directed at the United States, which backed President Marcos despite his tactics.

Rise of Corazon Aquino. With the economy in a shambles and Marcos's health in question, the future of the Philippines seemed doubtful. Then Corazon Aquino, still in mourning, announced that she would challenge Marcos in the February 1986 presidential election. Aquino, who rallied support from the millions of people who were dissatisfied with Marcos, won a majority of the votes. However, Marcos,

struggling to maintain power, had the National Assembly declare him the winner. Aquino immediately protested, calling the election a fraud. She encouraged nonviolent strikes and boycotts to force Marcos from office.

Soon violence broke out between soldiers loyal to Marcos and those who favored Aquino. Shortly thereafter, pressured by the United States, Marcos resigned. Aquino then formed a new democratic government with close ties to the United States and set about rebuilding the nation. In 1987, voters approved a new constitution and reelected President Aquino in free elections. Although Aquino's government was periodically shaken by ambitious military leaders seeking to overthrow it, by the end of the year, she remained in control of the nation.

Campaigning in 1986, Corazon Aquino and her vice-presidential running mate, Salvador Laurel, gained enormous popular support.

INDONESIA, MALAYSIA, AND SINGAPORE

Indonesia won independence from the Netherlands in 1949. Its first president, a nationalist named Sukarno, had led the fight for freedom for the colony known as the Dutch East Indies. Sukarno formed close ties with China and won support from the Indonesian Communist party.

A power struggle in 1965 led to Sukarno's downfall. The army smashed an apparent Communist coup attempt and took over the government. The new military ruler, General Suharto, sought aid from the United States and other Western nations, banned the Communist party, and welcomed foreign investment.

Indonesia became a major oil producer, built up its industry, and slowly raised its standard of living. By the late 1980s, however, Suharto's authoritarian rule was troubled by unrest. Nevertheless, he remained in control.

Neighboring Malaysia was formed in 1963 when Singapore, Malaya, and two other former British colonies united. Half of Malaysia's people are Malays. Chinese make up a third of the population, and Indians, one tenth. Cultural differences have led to friction between the Malays, who control the government, and the Chinese, who control much of the nation's wealth.

Since the 1970s, tension between Malays, and the Chinese and Indian minorities, has sometimes resulted in violence. Despite this ongoing problem, by the late 1980s, Malaysia had developed the most democratic government in Southeast Asia, and economic growth had resulted in an expanding middle class.

Tensions between Malays and Chinese led to Singapore's withdrawal from the Malaysian nation in 1965. Under a conservative and authoritarian government, Singapore built a strong capitalist economy. Often considered part of the Pacific Rim, Singapore became a center of banking, insurance, and light manufacturing. By the late 1980s, Singapore had a thriving high-tech industry as well.

SECTION REVIEW

1. How did the role of the United States in Vietnam change after 1954?

2. How did the Vietnam War end?

3. Describe what happened in Cambodia after the Khmer Rouge seized power.

4. Describe Corazon Aquino's rise to power.

Analysis. Discuss to what extent the following statement is valid: Since World War II, tensions in Southeast Asia have been based mainly on conflicts between the Communists and the non-Communists.

HISTORY IN FOCUS

Weakened by World War II, colonial empires in Asia crumbled when nationalist movements applied pressure for independence. As colonial powers withdrew or were driven out, struggles among native groups for political control often erupted in bloody violence. Millions of Asians died in such strife, and millions more succumbed to disease and starvation.

Communism spread in Asia when Communists supported movements for independence. Some of Asia's fiercest struggles took place where Communist and anti-Communist forces wrestled for power. This rivalry resulted in two major conflicts—the Korean War and the Vietnam War—as well as numerous lesser clashes.

Nevertheless, the future of Asian nations has never seemed brighter. Agricultural reforms and the growth of industry have increased trade. Many Asian nations—especially those of the Pacific Rim—have developed sound economies.

This economic transformation has led to an expanded role for Asia in world affairs. Never before has any non-Western region exercised the influence over world economy, culture, and society that Asia wields in the 1980s.

CHAPTER SURVEY

SUMMARY

- After World War II, Asia underwent great change: colonies gained their independence, revolutions took place, wars and ethnic violence broke out, and the superpowers spread their influence throughout the area.

- With independence in 1947, the Indian subcontinent split into India and Pakistan. In 1971, war erupted between these two nations. East Pakistan—with India's support—split off from Pakistan and became Bangladesh.

- Communists under Mao Zedong took power in China in 1949, sparking a process of radical change. Later, China adopted more moderate policies and renewed ties with the West. In Taiwan, the Nationalists set up a separate Chinese state with a capitalist economic system.

- After World War II, Korea was divided into two nations. The Korean War, lasting from 1950 to 1953, ended in an uneasy truce. South Korea's economy boomed, but under repressive governments.

- Japan emerged from American occupation with a democratic system and a growing economy and soon became one of the world's economic powers. In the 1980s, trade disputes damaged relations between Japan and the United States.

- Southeast Asia has experienced conflict and turmoil since 1945, especially in Vietnam and Cambodia. Communism and capitalism are both firmly entrenched in the region. In 1986, Filipinos overthrew the dictatorship of Ferdinand Marcos.

VOCABULARY REVIEW

From the list below, select the three words whose meanings relate to the underlined vocabulary term and explain the relationships.

partition

(a) paternalistic   (d) division
(b) unity   (e) disagreement
(c) factions   (f) authoritarian

CHAPTER REVIEW

1. (a) Give three examples of ethnic or nationalist disputes in Asia since 1945. **(b)** Compare India's problem involving the Sikh minority with disputes that led to the formation of Bangladesh.

2. (a) Explain the differences among the foreign policies of India, Japan, and China. **(b)** Give an example of the influence of the superpowers on the Indian subcontinent, in Southeast Asia, and in China.

3. Explain how each of the following countries was divided, and describe the results of each division: India, Pakistan, China, Korea.

4. Compare the reasons for, and the results of, the following wars: **(a)** the civil wars in Bangladesh and China; **(b)** the Korean and Vietnam wars.

5. (a) Explain the difficult choice made by the Vietnamese boat people. **(b)** Why were there refugees along the Thai border?

6. (a) Describe the political systems of China, India, and Japan. **(b)** In what ways were China's Cultural Revolution and the Pol Pot regime in Cambodia similar?

7. Compare the following heads of government: **(a)** Mao and Pol Pot; **(b)** Marcos and Aquino.

8. (a) List the Southeast Asian states that are Communist and those that are capitalist. Then describe their general policies. **(b)** Since 1945, has the political and economic development of Southeast Asia been more like that of China, or more like that of the Indian subcontinent? Explain your answer.

9. (a) Contrast the economic basis of China with that of Taiwan. **(b)** Compare the shifts in economic policy in China and Vietnam. **(c)** How has agrarian reform differed in India, China, and Japan? **(d)** How are the economies of the Pacific Rim countries similar?

10. (a) How have social and cultural changes been evident in India, China, and Japan since 1945? Why have these changes occurred? **(b)** How has cultural continuity been evident in these countries?

THINKING CRITICALLY: ACTIVITIES

1. Imagine that you are a South Korean political leader. Write a letter to your people stating your opinion regarding whether South Korea should establish a true democracy.

2. Imagine that you are the prime minister of Japan. Prepare a speech for the people of the United States, giving your analysis of the economic relationship between the two countries and how current problems can be solved.

3. Divide into groups to discuss how the Vietnam War is still affecting Americans. What are some signs of these effects? Consider attitudes that you have heard people express, as well as recent events or incidents related to Vietnam.

APPLYING SOCIAL STUDIES SKILLS

Analyzing graphs. Look at this graph and answer the questions below.

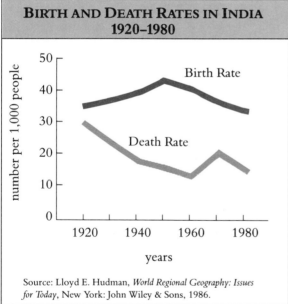

BIRTH AND DEATH RATES IN INDIA 1920–1980

Source: Lloyd E. Hudman, *World Regional Geography: Issues for Today*, New York: John Wiley & Sons, 1986.

1. What happened to the birth and death rates in India between 1920 and 1960? Between 1960 and 1980?

2. What effect do you think these trends had on the size of India's population?

3. What do the trends shown on this graph suggest about India's future population?

APPLYING THINKING SKILLS

Determining the credibility of a source. Read the following descriptions of sources dealing with the subject of the Communists' rise to power in China. Rank the sources according to their credibility on this subject, beginning with the most credible source. Then answer the questions that follow the descriptions.

A. A book written in 1950 by an American student of East Asian affairs. The author spent a year in China from 1948 to 1949 on a Fulbright Scholarship, a prestigious award given by the United States government. He offered his account as a "fragmentary record of a crucial year in Chinese history—1949."

B. A book written in 1969 and titled *To Change China*. The book traces the developments that brought about the Communists' rise to power in 1949. The author, a professor of history at Yale University, has had numerous fellowships to study in eastern Asia and was a winner of the honored Guggenheim Fellowship in scholarly study. He has served as chairperson of the Council of East Asian Studies and is the author of five widely acclaimed books on China.

C. A book published in 1964 and titled *How To Be A Good Communist*. The book was written by a Chinese Communist labor leader who played an active role in organizing Chinese laborers to support communism in the 1920s and 1930s. A close associate of Communist leader Mao Zedong, this person eventually was the leader of China from 1959 to 1968. He was later expelled from the Communist party and arrested in 1971 during the Cultural Revolution.

1. Define the term *credibility.*
2. What makes a source credible?
3. When is it important to try to determine the credibility of a source? Why is it important?
4. Of the above sources, which one is likely to be *least* credible on the given subject? Explain.
5. Of the above sources, which one is likely to be *most* credible on the given subject? Explain.
6. Suppose you had to explain to an eighth grader how to determine the credibility of a source. What specific directions would you give?

CHAPTER THIRTY-SIX

TOWARD THE TWENTY-FIRST CENTURY

Redbal, 1980. Computer painting, David Em, United States, 1980.

A study of history both brings us to the present and points us toward the future. By understanding history, we are better prepared to face the issues of today and tomorrow simply because we are able to draw upon centuries of human experience. Events and themes from distant ages can provide examples and possible solutions to issues facing the world as it moves toward the twenty-first century.

At the same time, however, it is important to remember that history does not simply "repeat itself." Indeed, the issues facing today's leaders are in many ways different from those of the past because today's world is far different from that which has existed through the centuries.

New connections among the world's peoples have been forged in the last half of the twentieth century, producing many similarities in outlook and behavior. Technological innovation in transportation and communication have led to stronger international relationships than in previous eras. Such connections have made it possible for different regions of the world to share ideas more easily.

In such a world, it is important to develop a global perspective—a way of looking at the world that takes into account both connections and differences among the world's peoples. Through a global perspective, we see that innovation as well as tradition has a place in the world.

Such international understanding can provide society with new strengths to solve some of the pressing problems that face humankind. Widespread hunger, overpopulation, international health problems, the destruction of the environment, and the threat of global nuclear destruction are problems that cross national borders and cultural divisions. Accordingly, these problems must all be addressed by the world community as a whole.

The fact that history has often shown humankind to be more receptive to confrontation than cooperation casts a shadow across the future. At the same time, however, people today are equipped with more resources than ever to meet the challenges of tomorrow.

TRADITIONS AND NEW DIRECTIONS

READ TO FIND OUT

—what the terms *multinational corporations* and *terrorism* mean.
—how the conquest of distance has made the world a smaller place.
—how nations have become economically dependent on each other.
—why cross-cultural friction has become a major problem facing some societies.
—why wars today are far more dangerous than wars in the past.
—how terrorism has become a political tool.
—why human rights issues are a major concern to many people.

GLOBAL CONNECTIONS

Today, rapid travel and instantaneous communications link distant regions of the globe. Because technology has made it possible to travel thousands of miles in just a few hours and to communicate information around the world within a few seconds, in some respects today's world is as small as a town in medieval Europe. At the same time, however, computers, data processing systems, and other technological innovations have made even the smallest twentieth-century city far more complex than the whole of medieval society.

The conquest of distance. Much of human history has revolved around the question of travel and commerce between far distant regions. Goods such as tea or pepper that are produced in Asia, for instance, have always been in high demand in Europe. Shorter trade routes and faster and better means of travel have been sought after for thousands of years. This effort—still under way today—might be called the "conquest of distance."

A thousand years ago, Muslim trading ships linked the Middle East and Europe with North Africa, India, and Asia. Voyages were slow and dangerous, but such voyages brought into contact people who lived very different lives. Information, new ideas, and culture, as well as commercial goods, were exchanged.

Five hundred years later, new ship designs and navigational instruments such as the compass allowed sea voyages across vast distances. A new age of European exploration and conquest began as Portugal, Spain, France, Holland, and England set up their colonies in the New World. By the 1700s, European merchants were carrying on vigorous trade around the world. Still, however, global connections were checked by distance. Even in the early nineteenth century, travel between Australia and Europe—on slow-moving sailing ships—required more than a year.

Industrialization furthered the conquest of distance. Steam engines provided steady, efficient power which freed ships from dependence on the wind, and telegraph lines allowed people to communicate within hours instead of months. Land transportation also benefited greatly from industrialization, with railroads moving goods across countries at 60 miles (90 kilometers) per hour, and automobiles providing many people with a degree of mobility never before imagined. With the invention of airplanes, people circled the planet in just over a day. Today, travelers fly on supersonic airplanes, whizzing from New York to London in just three hours.

Revolution in communication. The revolution in long-distance communication has been linked directly to developments in transportation. In the sixteenth century, for example, letters between Spain and its colonies in the New World could move only as fast as the sailing ships that served to connect the Eastern and Western hemispheres. Later, however, technological advances freed communication from transportation. Late nineteenth-century inventions, such as radios and telephones, made it possible to communicate to any part of the world in seconds. Beginning in the mid-twentieth century, new computers and satellites increased the range of possibilities for long-distance communication.

Rapid communications have given local events new significance and worldwide impact. Millions of people around the world quickly learn of events once known in only one area of the world. The news of the 1985 earthquake disaster in Mexico City, for example, was instantly communicated around the world. Because of this global communication network,

lifesaving aid from Europe and the United States was flowing to the stricken people within one day.

The new network of instantaneous communication means that no nation is truly remote from another. People have begun to perceive that problems in a distant area can have a local impact.

A global economy. A technological world requires the mobilization of a great array of economic resources to maintain itself. This need has created strong connections between economic activities in distant parts of the world—so many, in fact, that economists now speak of the existence of a global economy. For instance, one observer has noted that "coal from West Virginia runs Japanese factories that use Australian iron ore to make steel for cars that are shipped on Panamanian freighters powered by Persian Gulf oil to be sold in Florida."

As the global economy has developed, nations have become less self-sufficient. Both developed and developing nations rely on one another for raw materials or manufactured goods. The Soviet Union, for example, purchases wheat from nations such as the United States and Argentina, while the United States imports coffee from Brazil and Colombia, and electronics equipment from Japan. Such international trade often creates strong economic links between nations, as well as economic disputes over tariffs and import quotas, or limits.

In helping to create a global economy, many companies throughout the world have become *multinational corporations*. These corporations have headquarters in one country, while managing branches or operations in many different countries. Multinational corporations must make economic decisions on a worldwide basis. Many of the world's large oil companies, for example, have operations in oil-producing Middle Eastern nations. These companies have also invested in operations in the oil-consuming United States and Western Europe. As a result of such increasing international economic ties, economic decisions are often global in impact. The closing of one factory, for instance, can affect the economies of several nations.

A new level of cultural diffusion. These economic linkages have heightened cultural diffusion. Western styles of dress, for example, are

IDENTIFYING UNSTATED ASSUMPTIONS

An unstated assumption is something that a writer or speaker presumes to be true but does not actually write or say. For example, suppose someone claims: "Jane finally got an afternoon job. Now she can buy that car she has wanted for so long." The claim that Jane can buy the car is partly based on the unstated assumption that she will have the job long enough to earn the necessary money.

Many accounts you hear or read contain unstated assumptions. You need to identify these assumptions and judge their accuracy before accepting as true what the author has actually stated.

EXPLAINING THE SKILL

Unstated assumptions are often hidden ideas that link an author's claim and the stated reasons supporting that claim. As noted in the procedure described on pages 384 and 385, identifying unstated assumptions involves searching for the author's claims, which sometimes follow words such as *thus, therefore, so,* and *consequently.*

After identifying a claim, look for any stated reasons given in support of the claim. Then ask, "What else must I presume to be true if I am to accept what the author has said here?" What you uncover will probably be some unstated assumptions. Be especially aware of any claim supported by only one stated reason. Such a claim is probably based mainly on unstated assumptions.

APPLYING THE SKILL

Helmut Schmidt, a former West German chancellor, made these remarks in 1982. Identify any of his unstated assumptions.

> I will be 82 in the year 2000, and I think I can look as far as that. . . . There will be no world war because the responsibility of governments and the awareness of the danger of war are much greater nowadays than they have ever been in the first three quarters of the twentieth century. And they will . . . have arms reductions and arms control.

Secondly, as in the past, also in the future there will be ups and downs in the economic well-being of . . . governments. . . . But I think we will again learn to overcome our structural economic deficiencies.

This leads me to the third aspect, which might in the end be the prevailing one. When this century started, we had quite a few less than two billion people on the earth. At the end of the century, the number will have more than tripled to . . . six billion people. . . . If you want not only to feed but to give a fair standard of living to four billion people today, try to do this for six billion people within the next 18 years or so. . . . Mankind will have to learn during the last 20 years of this century . . . to set the goal for stabilization of global population.

From Helmut Schmidt, in *The New York Times* (January 3, 1982).

MAKING MEANING

1. One assumption that Schmidt makes in the first paragraph is that **(a)** he will not live past the year 2000, **(b)** before World War II, leaders did not fear war, **(c)** arms control will prevent another world war.

2. One of the sentences that gives a clue to the above assumption is **(a)** paragraph 1, sentence 3; **(b)** paragraph 1, sentence 1; **(c)** paragraph 2, sentence 1.

3. An unstated assumption in the final paragraph is that **(a)** there are not enough natural resources to provide a fair standard of living for 6 billion people, **(b)** stabilization of global population can be easily accomplished, **(c)** economic deficiencies result in small populations.

4. What does Schmidt consider to be the most serious challenge facing humankind? **(a)** world war, **(b)** economic trends, **(c)** rapidly growing world population.

REVIEWING THE SKILL

5. What is an unstated assumption?
6. What is one procedure you can use to find unstated assumptions?
7. Why is it worthwhile to search for unstated assumptions?

Disney characters Mickey and Minnie Mouse appeal to people in many lands. This kimono-clad pair resides in Disneyland, opened in Tokyo in 1983. A Disneyland is also planned near Paris.

now seen almost everywhere in the world, even in nations such as India and Japan which have their own strong traditional styles. Similarly, American and British television programs are shown in almost every country, and Western music can be heard on every continent.

Asian, African, Latin American, and other cultures have also greatly influenced society in the West. African art forms, for example, have played a critical role in shaping contemporary painting and sculpture, while Latin American and Asian foods have significantly influenced what Westerners eat. Japanese production methods stressing efficiency have revolutionized modern industry throughout the world.

THE DIVERSE WORLD

The growing contacts among peoples of the world, and the interaction of different cultures, might give the impression of a "shrinking" world. Nevertheless, cultural diversity and dif-ferent world outlooks persist and continue to have a significant impact on events.

In some regions of the world, the sudden close interaction of different cultures and traditions has caused friction—even violence—to develop. Such conflict has erupted because forces of change or modernization are often seen as a new variation of Western imperialism, and thus a threat to cultural and social traditions. In other areas, however, people from different cultures live side by side, taking pride in their own traditions. At the same time, these diverse peoples take the opportunity to learn about and enjoy the cultures of their neighbors.

Gap between rich and poor. The gulf between the economies of rich, developed nations like the United States, Germany, Sweden, or Japan and poor, developing nations of Latin America, Asia, and Africa is enormous. For example, in the mid-1980s, per capita annual income in the northern European nation of Sweden was nearly 14 times that of the Central American nation of Guatemala. Accordingly, while most Swedes live in pleasant homes and enjoy the conveniences of modern luxuries, many Guatemalans live in squalid grass huts, wondering where they will get tomorrow's food. Sweden is wealthy enough to provide a free college education for all of its youth, but in Guatemala much of the population will never learn to read or write.

Guatemala is not an isolated case. In many nations, basic needs such as food, shelter, and health care are not guaranteed. In 1987, in Africa—especially in Ethiopia and the Sudan, where the effects of a 17-year-long drought combined with large-scale desertification—13 million people face immediate starvation. Another 140 million Africans live in areas that are threatened by famine. Feeding these people has become the primary concern of many African governments, most of which are unable to muster the financial and social resources to handle the problem without massive international aid.

Clash of values. The great wealth of the industrialized nations of Europe, North America, and Asia has led to the development of a society very receptive to change. New technological innovations, such as compact disc players, video cassette recorders, and home computers, are available to most Western consumers, and breakthroughs in medical technology have led to better health and longer lives.

While frequent technological "miracles" have made Western society receptive to change, other societies view such alterations in the basic fabric of society differently. In many non-Western nations, modernization is seen as Westernization. In the case of Iran, Westernization has led to social upheaval, with traditional Islamic culture pitted against modern Western attitudes.

During the 1960s and 1970s Iran's leader, Shah Muhammad Riza Pahlavi, launched vast modernization programs—much as Kemal Ataturk had done in Turkey after World War I. Along with social and political unrest caused by dictatorial rule, the Shah brought Iran modern hospitals, and efficient communication and transportation networks. However, with modernization came an influx of Western ideas that disrupted traditional society.

Conservative Islamic leaders reacted strongly to changes such as the liberation of women from traditional subservient roles and the introduction of modern popular music. In 1978, these Islamic leaders launched a revolution against the Shah's regime that led to the reestablishment of the more traditional Islamic state that exists today.

ISSUES FOR THE FUTURE

Technological changes and the interrelationships of distant regions of the modern world have created an ever-increasing number of problems that affect most of the world's nations and peoples. Situations that affect health and the environment, and, of course, the threat of war, are global issues that must be addressed by the world community as a whole.

New threats to health. Starvation in Africa remains one of the most pressing problems affecting world health. Meanwhile, new threats have appeared in recent years. Just as the black plague had a great impact on medieval Europe, a new disease called Acquired Immune Deficiency Syndrome (AIDS) seems poised to deliver a terrible blow to civilization.

The disease is spread primarily through sexual activity with persons carrying the AIDS virus, contaminated blood transfusions, and intravenous drug abuse. The AIDS virus has infected millions of people in Africa and in the Western world since first discovered in 1981. In some cities, such as New York and San Francisco, AIDS has become the principal cause of death in people under the age of fifty.

Traditional Muslim women of Iran go about their everyday chores, left. Across the continent, in Hong Kong, Asian women perform their daily tasks at a modern assembly plant. In diverse cultures, the influence of tradition on daily life varies.

Ever-increasing demands for energy have led people to seek alternative sources. On these breezy hills in northern California, people have attempted to harness the wind as a source of power. When the wind blows over the rolling hills, the sleek, modern propeller-type wheels turn at a high rate of speed, generating electricity. This windfarm sells the electricity to a large power company.

The problem posed by AIDS highlights the close relationships among modern nations. Researchers in France, Britain, West Germany, Africa, and the United States are cooperating in an effort to find a cure for the disease.

Challenges to the environment. Closely related to health questions are environmental questions. Industrialization and a global economy have created both a growing demand for natural resources and a vast amount of waste such as noxious chemicals and garbage. Pollution and depletion of natural resources are creating an environmental crisis.

In the interconnected modern world, people are discovering the global effects of pollution. The spectacular accident at the Soviet nuclear power plant at Chernobyl in 1986 is one example of how the use of new sources of energy can have disastrous effects beyond the borders of any one nation. An explosion and fire at the Chernobyl plant caused massive releases of radiation, contaminating not only the nearby area but neighboring countries. Radioactive particles also spread throughout the world.

In the Chernobyl accident, 31 people died. In addition, scientists predict that 2,000 West Germans who live far from the disaster will die prematurely from cancer because of the radiation leak. Some experts estimate that worldwide as many as 40,000 cancer fatalities in the future might be traced to Chernobyl.

No nuclear disasters on the scale of Chernobyl have occurred in other parts of the world, but different forms of pollution threaten lives every day. The discovery of growing numbers of contaminated water supplies demonstrates that industries can no longer simply bury their wastes or dump them into lakes, rivers, and oceans without causing permanent damage to the environment and to people who live nearby.

Industries must also take action to prevent air pollution that results in acid rain—rain or snow that has been polluted by chemicals discharged into the air by coal-burning power plants and factories and then carried by the wind. A major concern in the United States, Canada, and northern Europe, acid rain has damaged vegetation, fish, and water supplies far from the source of the pollutants.

The environment of the earth is much like a huge, complex organism. Each species lost from the world and every new chemical introduced into the air, soil, or water alters the environment and produces effects that are not only difficult to forecast but can also be irreversible. With this realization have come efforts from industry, government, and concerned citizen groups to combat these threats.

The possibility of war. Besides the problems civilization faces from threats to health and the environment, the possibility of nuclear war hangs over the head of humankind. The twentieth

PLACE: THE GROWTH OF CITIES

O my city which exists no longer,
O my city attacked and destroyed!

This touching lament was uttered 4,000 years ago when Ur, one of the first cities to rise out of the dust on the Mesopotamian plain, was ravaged by war. Then, as now, cities inspired love, awe, and at times, despair.

Cities are unique places. While almost all landscapes have been altered somewhat by people, city landscapes have been affected the most. Cities are also the most densely populated places. With 18 million people, Mexico City, along with the area nearby, ranks as the world's largest urban region today.

The Spanish founded the city in the early 1500s on the rubble of Tenochtitlán, center of the Aztec empire. Spanish colonists laid out the city in precise rectangular blocks arranged outward from a grand plaza, the center of city life.

Over the centuries, Mexico City remained compact, and all parts were within easy reach on foot or on horseback. However, the city began to expand rapidly during the late 1800s, when Mexico began to industrialize. People had to settle farther and farther from the center of the city, and horse-drawn trams carried them downtown. However, since tram service was slow and unreliable, people still settled as close to the central city as they could.

The introduction of trolley and rail lines in the early 1900s accelerated urban growth. The trolleys allowed people to travel from the outskirts, where land was cheap, to the center of the city for work or business. The city's shape changed as residential areas formed along the trolley and rail lines that extended outward from the city's core, like the rays of a star.

In the 1940s, many factories sprang up. A new bus service allowed people to live even farther from the downtown district. As country people rushed to the city for a chance to work at the new factories, urban settlement spread outside the city boundaries.

Because of economic distress in the 1970s, even more Mexican citizens poured into Mexico City seeking work. The population leaped by an astonishing 70 percent in the 1970s, making Mexico City the fastest growing urban area in the world. With a thousand people moving to the area each day, a severe shortage of housing arose. Many people had to live in shacks built of wood scraps, cardboard, and tin. The swift, enormous rise in population also placed a great strain on other city services.

Many other cities in Latin America and throughout the developing world have experienced similar rapid growth, outstripping the ability of city government to provide adequate housing, jobs, transportation, and services. To prevent the destruction of modern cities, this time not by war, but by overcrowding, congested traffic, unemployment, poverty, substandard housing, and choking pollution, officials from different nations have shared ideas about managing rapid growth. Citizens too have worked to preserve their cities. With success, the lament of Ur will not also become the lament of the twenty-first century city.

1. How have various modes of transportation influenced Mexico City's size and shape?

2. What has been a major cause of the city's rapid population growth?

3. List five problems of rapid urban growth.

THE LATIN AMERICAN CITY

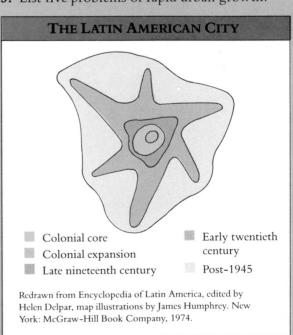

- ▨ Colonial core
- ▨ Colonial expansion
- ▨ Late nineteenth century
- ▨ Early twentieth century
- ▨ Post-1945

Redrawn from Encyclopedia of Latin America, edited by Helen Delpar, map illustrations by James Humphrey. New York: McGraw-Hill Book Company, 1974.

century has been the most violent period in human history, and recent innovations in war technology have made modern conflicts not just societal crises, but natural disasters as well.

Since 1945, when the United States dropped two atomic bombs on Japan, the world has lived under the threat of nuclear holocaust. By the late 1980s, the United States, the Soviet Union, Great Britain, France, India, and the People's Republic of China all had nuclear weapons. In addition, Israel, Pakistan, and South Africa had the proven capability to develop their own atomic bombs in the near future.

A conflict involving any of these nations threatens to develop into a nuclear exchange that could render the planet a radioactive desert. Never before in human history has the chance of war carried with it the possibility of the elimination of all life as we know it. The different political systems, needs, and goals of the world's societies mean that working together to prevent nuclear war remains a large problem. Positive action to prevent nuclear war has resulted in talks and treaties, and closer cooperation between potential enemies, such as the United States and the Soviet Union.

Terrorism. Tensions among nations in the 1970s and 1980s have led to incidents of *terrorism*, or the systematic use of violence to intimidate people or their governments for political ends. Groups often use terrorism when they see no other way to achieve their goals.

Terrorism has occurred all over the globe. In the mid-1980s, terrorists seized foreigners, particularly in Western Europe and the Middle East, in order to publicize political demands. Groups seeking political ends have murdered diplomats, hijacked airplanes, and bombed crowded public buildings. Because terrorism provides small groups or nations with a means of striking successfully at major world powers such as the United States, such attacks have become more frequent in recent years.

The population explosion. Another problem facing many nations is overpopulation. The dramatic increase in the number of people in many poorer countries could be one of the worst problems facing society today.

During the 1970s, some nations introduced birth control measures and other incentives to lower birth rates. By the mid-1980s, the rate of population growth in such nations as China and Japan had decreased. Nevertheless, in developing countries such as Kenya and Bangladesh, populations continue to grow at a fast rate. In 1986, the total world population grew by 220,000 people per day. Of this number, 90 percent were in developing nations. In 1987, the world's population moved beyond the 5 billion mark.

In contrast to developing nations, most Western nations were concerned about the dramatic drop in birth rates since the 1960s. Low birth rates and improved health care led to an increase in the average age and in the number of elderly people in the population. These changes raised questions about how societies with a large elderly population could meet the medical and other costs associated with aging.

Poverty. A gap between rich and poor exists among nations and among groups within nations. Even wealthy industrialized nations such as the United States and Great Britain have large populations of poor people. In the United States, Great Britain and the Soviet Union, many poor people are members of minority groups that have been denied economic opportunities because of discrimination.

The poverty in other nations is often so severe that it causes political unrest. In countries such as El Salvador and Nicaragua in Central America, poor peasants organized to overthrow governments controlled by a few wealthy landowners. Often people in such countries see revolution as their only hope for economic relief.

Human rights. Many people in the modern world are concerned with issues of human rights. Advocates of human rights point out that adequate food and shelter, basic medical care, and freedom from torture and political persecution are basic rights to which every person is entitled. As a result, these advocates speak out against political systems that fail to recognize such rights. To bring international pressure for change, organizations such as Amnesty International identify those governments that are violating human rights.

Human rights violations are frequent in developing nations, where grinding poverty and inadequate resources strain social and political systems. However, human rights are also vio-

In 1985, performers from many nations staged the Live Aid Concert, which raised $71.5 million for famine relief in Africa. Broadcast from London and Philadelphia, the concert was seen by a billion and a half people. The aid reached Africans through Red Cross centers such as this one (right).

lated in some modern, industrialized nations. In the Soviet Union, for example, political dissidents are imprisoned. New laws created by the white minority government of South Africa have caused intense suffering among blacks, who have virtually no political or human rights.

The whole issue of human rights is tied to the question of a balance between the rights of the individual and the role of the state. In most Western societies, individual freedom is considered sacred, while in many Communist nations the good of society in general is seen as more important than the rights of any single person.

LOOKING TO THE FUTURE

In a world of both continuing traditions and rapid change, we constantly ask ourselves where events are leading civilization. In tomorrow's world, new ideas and technologies will continue to develop. Change will come more rapidly than ever before, and societies will need to adjust to an increasingly complex world.

However, over the centuries, patterns of continuity have been woven. These deeply rooted traditions will help to guide and support the many diverse travelers of the twenty-first century.

SECTION REVIEW

1. Define *multinational corporations* and *terrorism*.

2. What have been some important changes that have occurred because of the conquest of distance?

3. Why have nations become economically dependent on each other?

4. Why do some cultures react strongly against modernization?

5. What are some of the dangers of a nuclear conflict?

6. Why has terrorism become a useful tool to advance political goals?

7. In what ways do governments suppress human rights?

Evaluation. Has terrorism been an effective means of pressuring governments to meet demands? To support your conclusion, cite current examples of terrorism and describe the results.

Data Search. Refer to the appropriate chart on page 835 to identify **(a)** the populations of India, China, Mexico, the United States, and the Soviet Union in 1988 and **(b)** the annual percent change in the populations of China, Japan, Kenya, and Bangladesh.

SUMMARY

- Over a thousand years ago, when the first Arab ships sailed on voyages that linked continents, new contacts between distant regions made the world seem a smaller place. The twentieth century hastened this process with technological innovations such as airplanes, communication satellites, and computers.

- These new communications links brought world attention to situations that had once been known only within a small radius from the point of origin. The new links also increased economic ties among nations and diffused elements of different cultures throughout the world.

- In spite of these new ties, the peoples of the world remained diverse. Many societies have kept traditional cultures, religions, and forms of government, while others have been more open to change. Tension over issues of tradition and change has often led to conflict.

- Issues that people in these many societies have to face as the future becomes the present include new threats to health, challenges to the environment, the possibility of nuclear war, terrorism, overpopulation, a growing gap between the rich and poor, and abuses of human rights.

VOCABULARY REVIEW

For each underlined vocabulary term, select the two words or phrases from the accompanying list whose meanings relate to the term. Then explain the relationships.

1. multinational corporations
   (a) discrimination   (c) world economy
   (b) economic ties   (d) human rights

2. terrorism
   (a) political goals   (c) violence
   (b) diplomacy   (d) nuclear war

EXPLORING ISSUES

1. Act as a representative from the Soviet Union, East Germany, West Germany, Sweden, or Poland, and ask four other members of the class to represent the other nations. Discuss any changes in nuclear energy policies you think should be made as a result of the Chernobyl incident. You may want to write a letter to the appropriate United Nations delegate stating your recommendations for policy changes.

2. Study the problem posed by acid rain. You may want to write to an environmental group such as the Environmental Protection Agency in Washington, D.C., for information on the following: the areas of the world that are most affected; the effect acid rain has had on the state where you live; action governments have taken to solve problems relating to acid rain; and ways the environment might be affected in the future if pollution is not kept under control. With the information you gather, make a poster that will illustrate your point of view about acid rain.

3. Select a class member to debate the future of nuclear arms policy. One person should represent the Soviet Union; the other, the United States. Discuss the following issues: efforts that should be made to prevent nuclear war and how conflict in "hot spots" such as Central America and the Middle East—regions in which the Soviets and the Americans find themselves on opposing sides in the conflicts—can be prevented from escalating into global conflict.

4. Over the course of centuries, civilization has experienced remarkable changes. Write an essay, poem, or short story that describes a society of the twenty-first century. Include how governments, industries, and cultures might be structured and how this futuristic society will deal with such problems as international conflicts and challenges to the environment.

THINKING CRITICALLY: ACTIVITIES

1. Go to the library and look up credible newspaper and magazine articles dealing with AIDS to answer the following questions. How is AIDS spread? How can people keep from getting AIDS? How does AIDS affect the health of people who have the disease? What social issues are raised by the AIDS epidemic in the United States? Using the information you have gath-

ered, create a brochure or pamphlet that will educate those who are uninformed about the disease.

2. Reread the subsection entitled "The Conquest of Distance." Note how a single aspect of modern-day society—transportation—is treated in a broad historical context. Refer to earlier chapters in the book and any outside sources to write short essays placing each of the following topics in historical context: medicine, libraries, energy, and music.

3. In the late 1980s, many nations throughout the world were either engaged in conflict or were unstable. For example, Iran and Iraq were fighting a war. Also, South Korea was unstable as the people there fought for democratic rights. Select one nation that is currently involved in a conflict and one that is undergoing political unrest. If you have difficulty identifying particular nations, refer to newspapers and news magazines. Then, using the textbook as an historical sourcebook, and magazine and newspaper articles for current information, analyze the problems confronting the nations you have selected. Attempt to place late twentieth-century problems in an historical perspective. Present your analysis to the class.

APPLYING SOCIAL STUDIES SKILLS

Researching information in periodicals. See page 580 to review the use of the *Reader's Guide*. Now suppose that you are doing a report on recent efforts to control the nuclear arms race. In the *Reader's Guide* you find the following headings:

Arms control *See* Disarmament
Arms race *See* Nuclear weapons
Arms trade *See* Munitions—
  Export-import trade

Under one heading is the following entry:
  Why the Soviets want an arms-control agreement, and why they want it now. E. V. Rostow. *Commentary* 83:19-26 F '87

1. Which heading was the most appropriate one to look under first? Explain.
2. Identify where the article appeared (magazine title, date, and pages).

APPLYING THINKING SKILLS

Identifying unstated assumptions. Analyze the following observations by Jawaharlal Nehru to identify any unstated assumptions.

> The past brings us . . . all that we have today of culture, civilization, science, our knowledge of some aspects of the truth . . . . We acknowledge our obligation to the past . . . . We owe a duty to the future also . . . . For the past is past, . . . the future is yet to come, and perhaps we may be able to shape it a little . . . . The future hides many aspects of the truth and invites us to search for them. But often the past is jealous of the future and holds us in a terrible grip, and we have to struggle with it to get free and advance towards the future.
>
> History, it is said, has many lessons to teach us; and there is another saying that history never repeats itself . . . . We cannot learn anything from it by . . . expecting it to repeat itself . . . but we can learn something by prying behind it and trying to discover the forces that move it . . . .
>
> History teaches us of growth and progress and of the possibility of an infinite advance for man . . . . It is easy to admire the beauties of the universe and to live in a world of thought and imagination. But to try to escape in this way from the unhappiness of others, caring little what happens to them, is no sign of courage . . . . Thought, in order to justify itself, must lead to action . . . . People avoid action often because action means risk and danger. Danger seems terrible from a distance; it is not so bad if you have a close look at it . . . .
>
> All of us have our choice of living in the valleys below, with their unhealthy mists and fogs, but giving a measure of bodily security; or of climbing the high mountains, with risk and danger for companions, to breathe the pure air above, and take joy in the distant views, and welcome the rising sun.

From Jawaharlal Nehru, *Nehru on World History*. New York: The John Day Company, 1960.

1. What is a claim Nehru makes about the past? About the future? What information does he give to support each claim?
2. Identify one unstated assumption. Explain how it was evident in the account.

UNIT REVIEW

1. (a) Explain why independence movements in Asia and Africa gained strength after World War II. **(b)** Explain why some independence movements were nonviolent and some were violent. Give two examples of each.

2. (a) Discuss two factors that have hindered the growth of many nations' economies since 1945. **(b)** Discuss two factors that have improved some nations' economies.

3. (a) Why has the Soviet Union been able to strongly influence Eastern Europe since World War II? Identify two specific instances of this influence. **(b)** Why has the United States been able to influence the governments and economies of many developing nations since 1945? Identify two specific instances of this influence.

4. (a) Trace the major developments in postwar relations between the United States and the Soviet Union. **(b)** Discuss how the superpower rivalry has affected other nations.

5. (a) Give an example of a nation or region in which religion has significantly influenced politics since World War II. Explain why. **(b)** Give an example of a nation or region in which religion has had little influence on politics. Explain why.

6. (a) Discuss at least two factors that have contributed to stable governments in some nations since 1945. Identify at least two nations as specific examples. **(b)** Discuss at least two factors that have contributed to political instability in some nations. Identify at least two nations as specific examples.

7. (a) Briefly describe the functions of each of the following organizations: OAU, NATO, OPEC, COMECON, Warsaw Pact, Arab League, EEC, the Commonwealth. **(b)** Discuss the effects of United Nations involvement in at least two crises.

8. (a) In what ways have women's opportunities generally improved since World War II? **(b)** What factors have limited women's opportunities in some nations? Explain. **(c)** Identify two other human rights issues. Explain how each issue has been evident in two or more nations or regions.

9. (a) Discuss how Western cultural influence is evident in Asia, Africa, the Middle East, and Latin America. **(b)** Give at least two specific examples of non-Western influence on Western culture. **(c)** Discuss how efforts to preserve cultural heritage are evident in Asia, Africa, the Middle East, and Latin America.

10. Discuss how the following· products of technology have influenced the postwar world: **(a)** nuclear arms, **(b)** airplanes, **(c)** computers.

RELATING PAST TO PRESENT

1. Discuss how both cultural diversity and cultural diffusion have been evident in the United States from 1945 to the present. Give at least four specific examples of each, including some current examples from within your community. For example, a past example of cultural diffusion was the influence of black rhythm-and-blues music on the development of rock music. A current example of cultural diversity might be a performance featuring traditional Mexican and Native American dances.

2. Explain how the United States' dependence on oil imports has been evident since 1945 and how it has affected our foreign policy. Has this dependence increased since World War II, or has it decreased? Explain why.

3. Much of the current conflict in the Middle East is rooted in Arab-Israeli tensions. Discuss the origin of these tensions and trace the major developments that have fueled them since 1945.

PROJECTS AND ACTIVITIES

1. Prepare a collage to illustrate the global impact of an issue such as arms control. Include items relating to the issue, such as newspaper or magazine clippings. Explain to the class the significance of each item you have included.

2. Dividing into groups of four or five, discuss the major events in chapters 32 through 35, selecting the five most important events in each chapter. Then, after discussing the global impact of these 20 events, list what your group considers to be the five most significant ones. Explain your group's choices and compare them with those of other groups.

3. Form groups of four or five, with each group choosing a different nation, such as the USSR, Mexico, Iran, Kenya, India, France, Japan, or China. Then do the following: **(a)** Research how the people of that nation and the people of the United States generally perceive each other. Refer to sources such as newspaper or magazine articles and statements by tourists or political leaders. **(b)** Discuss the reasons for these perceptions. Be sure to consider how cultural differences affect people's ideas and attitudes. **(c)** Evaluate the accuracy of these perceptions by using information from your textbook, other written resources, and your own experience. Present your group's findings to the class.

ANALYZING PRIMARY SOURCES

Refer to "Echoes of the Past" on page 780 to answer the following questions.

1. What main point does the author make about many students and teachers in the United States? What examples does she give to support her point?

2. The author states that American movies show "typical" scenes from Latin America. What meaning of the word *typical* is she using here? Explain your answer.

3. The author states that advances in communication and transportation make it urgent for the peoples of the world to understand each other. What do you think is her reasoning?

4. For what audience is this article intended: Latin American readers, readers in the United States, or both? Explain your answer.

5. Discuss the appropriateness of the article's title.

GEOGRAPHY REVIEW

Place. Divide into groups of four or five to study your town or city, or if you live in the countryside, a nearby town or city of more than 2,500 people. Do research to create a map of the location you chose that includes the following features: town or city boundaries, built-up areas that are associated with the town or city but lie outside its boundaries, federal highways, state highways, expressways or other main roads, navigable rivers or canals, railroad lines, airports, the central business district, and major secondary business districts, if any.

Then, analyze the growth of the town or city by answering the following questions.

1. How many square miles (kilometers) lie within the town or city boundaries?

2. What was the population within the town or city boundaries in 1900? 1940? 1970? What is the population today?

3. Is the urban area densely or sparsely populated? For comparison, New York City has more than 23,000 people per square mile (2.59 square kilometers), while Anchorage has fewer than 200.

4. Compare the locations of the central business district and the oldest part of town.

5. How have transportation routes affected urban growth? Consider the locations of major transportation routes and business districts, and the shape of the city.

6. From local news sources and from conversations with citizens, determine what special challenges the town or city faces as a result of population growth or loss.

SUGGESTED READINGS

Clayre, Alasdair. *The Heart of the Dragon.* Boston: Houghton Mifflin Company, 1985. A portrait of life in past and present China.

Fitzgerald, Frances. *Fire in the Lake: The Vietnamese and Americans in Vietnam.* Boston: Little, Brown & Co., 1972. An account of American involvement in Vietnam.

Ribaroff, Margaret. *Mexico and the United States Today: Issues Between Neighbors.* Danbury, CT: Franklin Watts, Inc., 1985. A survey of the issues, differences, and common interests between the two countries.

Rushdie, Salman. *Midnight's Children.* New York: Knopf, 1981. A fascinating novel set in postcolonial India.

Smith, Hedrick. *The Russians.* New York: Times Books, 1983. A firsthand look at the daily lives of the Russian people.

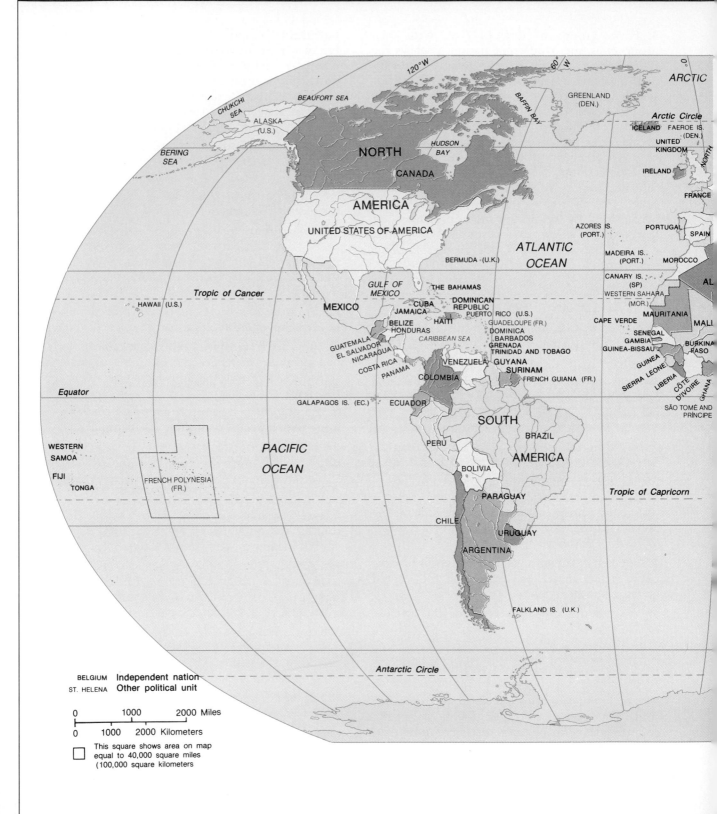

ARCTIC

120°W
60°W
0°

CHUKCHI
SEA
BEAUFORT SEA
BAFFIN BAY

ALASKA
(U.S.)

GREENLAND
(DEN.)

Arctic Circle

ICELAND FAEROE IS.
(DEN.)
UNITED
KINGDOM

BERING
SEA

NORTH

HUDSON
BAY

IRELAND

NORTH

CANADA

FRANCE

AMERICA

UNITED STATES OF AMERICA

ATLANTIC
OCEAN

AZORES IS.
(PORT.)

PORTUGAL

SPAIN

BERMUDA (U.K.)

MADEIRA IS.
(PORT.)
MOROCCO

Tropic of Cancer

CANARY IS.
(SP)
WESTERN SAHARA
(MOR.)

AL

HAWAII (U.S.)

GULF OF
MEXICO

THE BAHAMAS

MEXICO

CUBA
JAMAICA

DOMINICAN
REPUBLIC
PUERTO RICO (U.S.)

CAPE VERDE

MAURITANIA

MALI

BELIZE
HONDURAS

HAITI

GUADELOUPE (FR.)
DOMINICA
BARBADOS
GRENADA
TRINIDAD AND TOBAGO

SENEGAL
GAMBIA
GUINEA-BISSAU

BURKINA
FASO

GUATEMALA
EL SALVADOR
NICARAGUA

CARIBBEAN SEA

GUINEA

COSTA RICA
PANAMA

VENEZUELA GUYANA
SURINAM

SIERRA LEONE
LIBERIA

CÔTE
D'IVOIRE

GHANA

COLOMBIA

FRENCH GUIANA (FR.)

Equator

GALAPAGOS IS. (EC.)

ECUADOR

SÃO TOMÉ AND
PRÍNCIPE

SOUTH

PERU

BRAZIL

WESTERN
SAMOA

PACIFIC
OCEAN

AMERICA

FIJI

FRENCH POLYNESIA
(FR.)

BOLIVIA

TONGA

PARAGUAY

Tropic of Capricorn

CHILE

URUGUAY

ARGENTINA

FALKLAND IS. (U.K.)

Antarctic Circle

BELGIUM Independent nation
ST. HELENA Other political unit

0   1000   2000 Miles

0   1000   2000 Kilometers

This square shows area on map
equal to 40,000 square miles
(100,000 square kilometers

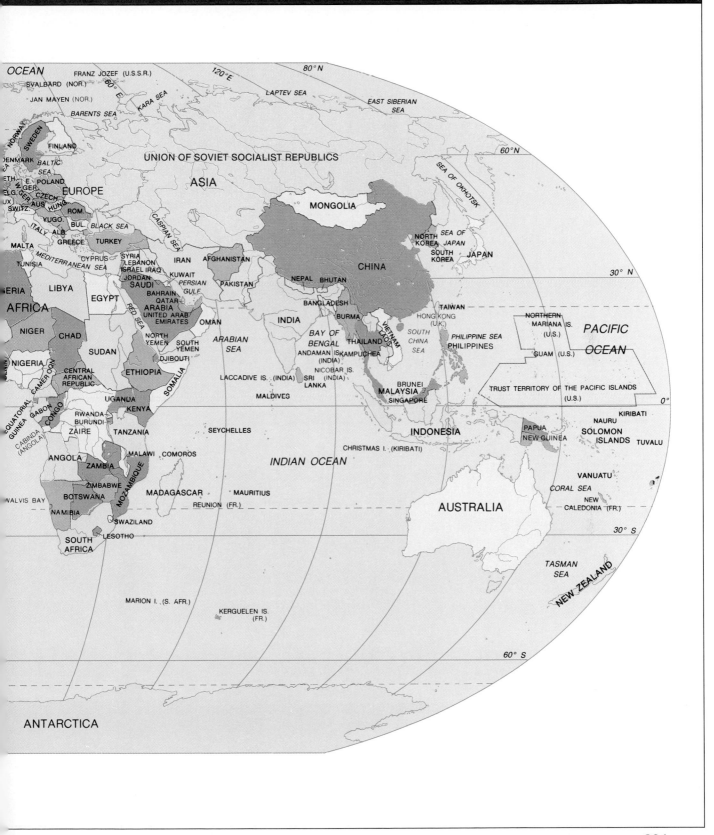

SOUTH AMERICA

CENTRAL
AMERICA

CARIBBEAN SEA

GULF OF VENEZUELA · Point Gallianas

GULF OF
DARIEN

10°
North latitude

• Maracaibo
LAKE
MARACAIBO

★ Caracas
· Valencia

Orinoco River

Georgetown
★ Paramibo
FRENCH
SURINAM GUIANA · Cayenne

River

• Medelin

· Bogota

LLANOS

VENEZUELA

GUYANA

GUIANA
HIGHLANDS

Magdalena River

· Cali

★ Quito
ECUADOR

Japura River

Equator

GALAPAGOS
ISLANDS

0°

• Guayaquil

GULF OF GUAYAQUIL

Manaus •

Amazon River

• Belem

Point Parinas
Point Aguja

SELVAS

· Fortaleza

Cape Sao Roque

Purus River

PERU

A
N
D
E
S

10°
South latitude

· Recife

★ Lima

LAKE
TITICACA

BRAZIL

M
O
U
N
T
A
I
N
S

BOLIVIA

★ La Paz
LAKE
POOPO

★ Sucre

Pilcomayo

Sao Francisco River

· Salvador

★ Brasilia

MATO GROSSO
PLATEAU

Goiania •
BRAZILIAN
HIGHLANDS

· Belo Horizonte

Paraguay River

20°

ATACAMA
DESERT

GRAN CHACO

PARAGUAY

★ Mt. Ojos
del Salado
22,590 ft.
(6,885 m.)

River

· Asuncion

Parana River

Rio de Janeiro •
Santo Andre · · Duque de Caxias
· Nova Iguacu Cape Frio
★ Sao Paulo
· Curitaba

Tropic of Capricorn

Uruguay

River

· Porto Alegre

ARGENTINA

· Cordoba

CHILE ★ Mt. Aconcagua
22,834 ft (6,960 m)
· Rosario
Rio de la Plata

LAKE
MIRIM

URUGUAY
★ Montevideo

30°

Santiago ★

Mt. Tupungato
22,310 ft.
(6,800 m.)

PAMPAS

★ Buenos Aires

Rio Negro

BAHIA BLANCA

PACIFIC OCEAN

ATLANTIC OCEAN

GULF OF SAN MATIAS

VALDES PENINSULA
-131 ft.
(-40 m.)

CHILEAN
ARCHIPELAGO

PATAGONIAN PLATEAU

40°

GULF OF
SAN JORGE

West longitude

★ Stanley
FALKLAND
ISLANDS
(U.K.)

Strait of
Magellan

TIERRA DEL FUEGO
Cape Horn

50°

Drake Passage

Meters	Feet	
3 050	10,000	
1 525	5,000	
610	2,000	
305	1,000	
0	0	
Below Sea Level		

CITIES
★ National Capital
• 5,000,000 population and over
• 1,000,000 - 4,999,999
• 500,000 - 999,999
• Less than 500,000

0   500   1000 Miles

0   500   1000 Kilometers

100°   90°   80°   70°   60°   50°   40°   30°   20°

Meters	Feet
3 050	10,000
1 525	5,000
610	2,000
305	1,000
0	0

Below
Sea Level

CITIES

★ National Capital

● 5,000,000 population and over

● 1,000,000 - 4,999,999

● 500,000 - 999,999

· Less than 500,000

0 ——————— 500 Miles

0 ——————— 500 Kilometers

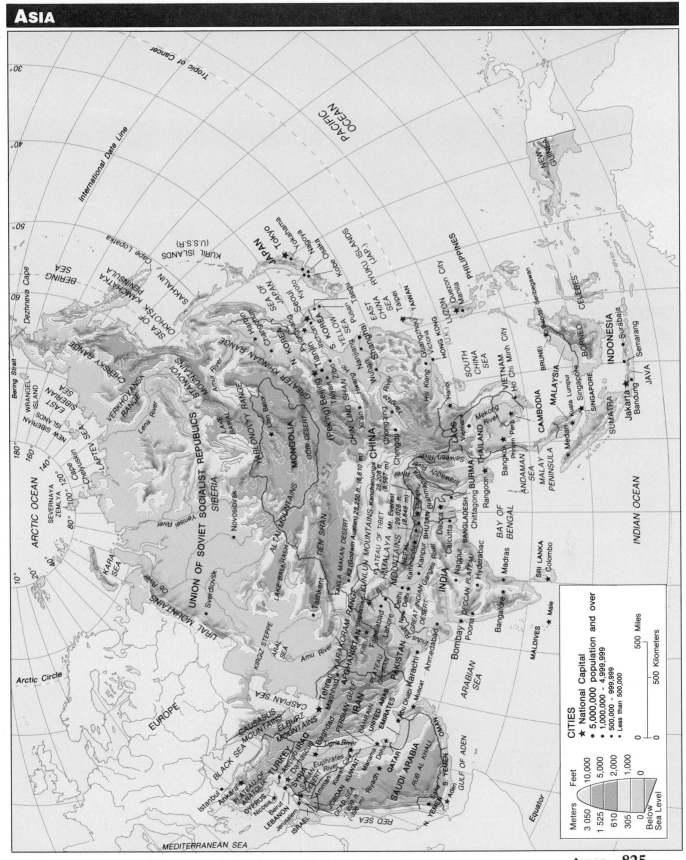

ASIA

Tropic of Cancer

International Date Line

PACIFIC OCEAN

NEW GUINEA

KURIL ISLANDS (U.S.S.R.)
Cape Lopatka
KAMCHATKA PENINSULA
SEA OF OKHOTSK
SAKHALIN

BERING SEA
Dezhneva Cape
Bering Strait

RYUKYU ISLANDS (JAP.)

JAPAN
TOKYO
Yokohama
Nagoya
Osaka
Kobe
Kyoto

PHILIPPINES
LUZON
Quezon City
Manila

CHERSKIY RANGE

Cape Chelyuskin
SEVERNAYA ZEMLYA

ARCTIC OCEAN

NEW SIBERIAN ISLANDS
EAST SIBERIAN SEA
WRANGEL ISLAND

LAPTEV SEA
VERKHOYANSK RANGE
STANOVOY MOUNTAINS
Lena River
YABLONOVY MOUNTAINS

Amur River

N. KOREA
Seoul
PYONGYANG
Inchon
S. KOREA
Pusan Taegu

Harbin
Changchun
GREATER KHINGAN RANGE

Ulan Bator

MONGOLIA

GOBI DESERT

Beijing (Peking)
Tianjin
Taiyuan Zibo
Jinan

YELLOW SEA

EAST CHINA SEA
Shanghai
TAIWAN
Taipei

Hwang Ho

KARA SEA

Novosibirsk

Sverdlovsk

URAL MOUNTAINS

UNION OF SOVIET SOCIALIST REPUBLICS

SIBERIA

LAKE BAIKAL

ALTAI MOUNTAINS

TIEN SHAN

TAKLA MAKAN DESERT

CHIN LING SHAN
Xian
Nanjing
Wuhan
Chongqing
Chengdu
Yangtze River

CHINA

HONG KONG (U.K.)
Victoria
Guangzhou
Hsi Kiang

SOUTH CHINA SEA

VIETNAM
Hanoi
Ho Chi Minh City

BRUNEI
MALAYSIA
Kuala Lumpur
SINGAPORE
Singapore

CELEBES

BORNEO

INDONESIA
Bandar Seribegawan
Surabaja
Semarang

JAVA
Jakarta
Bandung

SUMATRA
Medan

CAMBODIA
Phnom Penh

LAOS
Vientiane

THAILAND
Bangkok

BURMA
Rangoon

Salween River
Mekong River
Irrawaddy River

ARAL SEA
KIRGIZ STEPPE
Tashkent

Amu River

PLATEAU OF TIBET

KUNLUN MOUNTAINS

HIMALAYA

Mt. Everest 29,028 ft. (8,848 m)
Kanchenjunga 28,208 ft. (8,597 m)

K-2 (Godwin Austen) 28,250 ft. (8,610 m)

KARAKORAM RANGE

NEPAL
Kathmandu
BHUTAN
Thimphu

BANGLADESH
Dacca
Chittagong

BAY OF BENGAL

ANDAMAN SEA

MALAY PENINSULA

Brahmaputra River
Ganges River

Calcutta

INDIA
Nagpur
Hyderabad
DECCAN PLATEAU
Madras
Bangalore

SRI LANKA
Colombo

INDIAN OCEAN

MALDIVES
Male

AFGHANISTAN
Kabul
Fyzabad

PAKISTAN
Islamabad
Lahore
New Delhi
Delhi
Kanpur

GREAT INDIAN DESERT
Indus River

Faisalabad
Ahmedabad

Bombay
Poona

ARABIAN SEA

Karachi

IRAN
Tehran
Mashhad

PLATEAU OF IRAN

ELBURZ MOUNTAINS

CASPIAN SEA

CAUCASUS MOUNTAINS

EUROPE

Ob River

Muscat
OMAN

UNITED ARAB EMIRATES
Abu Dhabi

QATAR
Doha

BAHRAIN
Manama

SAUDI ARABIA
Riyadh

RUB AL KHALI

PERSIAN GULF

IRAQ
Baghdad
Tigris River
Euphrates River

Kuwait City
KUWAIT

BLACK SEA

TURKEY
Ankara
Istanbul

ANATOLIA
PLATEAU OF ANATOLIA

CYPRUS
Nicosia

SYRIA
Damascus
Aleppo

LEBANON
Beirut
ISRAEL
Jerusalem
JORDAN
Amman

DEAD SEA 1,286 ft. (-392 m)

SYRIAN DESERT

N. YEMEN
Sanaa
S. YEMEN
Aden

GULF OF ADEN

RED SEA

Equator

MEDITERRANEAN SEA

Arctic Circle

Meters	Feet
3 050	10,000
1 525	5,000
610	2,000
305	1,000
0	0
Below Sea Level	

CITIES
★ National Capital
● 5,000,000 population and over
● 1,000,000 - 4,999,999
● 500,000 - 999,999
• Less than 500,000

500 Miles
500 Kilometers

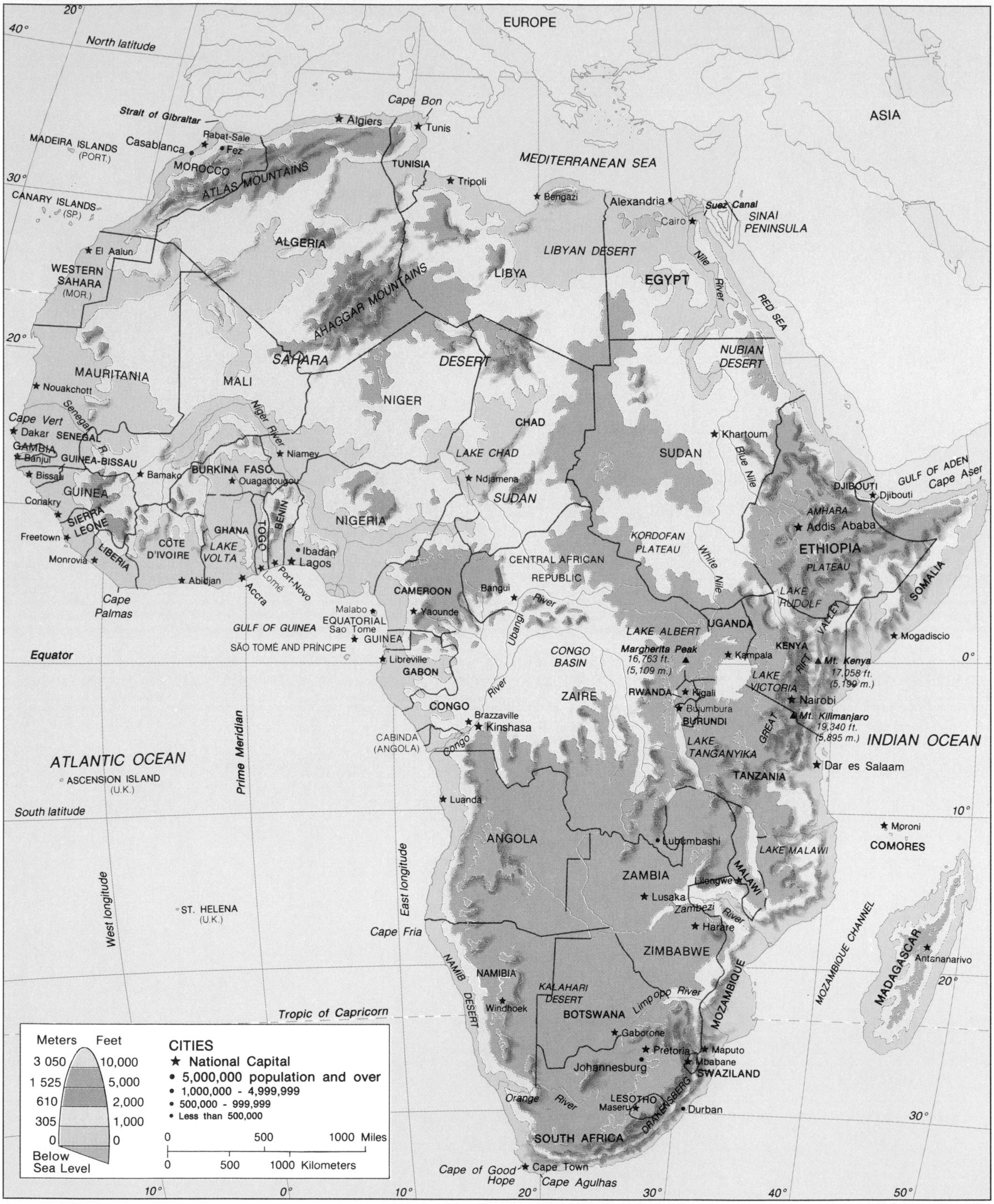

EUROPE

ASIA

MEDITERRANEAN SEA

Strait of Gibraltar
Cape Bon
★ Algiers
★ Tunis
MADEIRA ISLANDS (PORT.)
Casablanca
Rabat-Sale
• Fez
MOROCCO
ATLAS MOUNTAINS
TUNISIA
★ Tripoli
Bengazi •
Alexandria •
Cairo ★
Suez Canal
SINAI PENINSULA

CANARY ISLANDS (SP.)
★ El Aaiun
WESTERN SAHARA (MOR.)
ALGERIA
LIBYA
LIBYAN DESERT
EGYPT

AHAGGAR MOUNTAINS
SAHARA DESERT
NUBIAN DESERT

Nile River
RED SEA

★ Nouakchott
MAURITANIA
MALI
NIGER
CHAD
★ Khartoum
SUDAN

Cape Vert
★ Dakar SENEGAL
Senegal R.
Niger River
Niamey ★
LAKE CHAD
Blue Nile
GULF OF ADEN
Cape Aser

GAMBIA
★ Banjul
GUINEA-BISSAU
• Bissau
BURKINA FASO
Bamako •
★ Ouagadougou
★ Ndjamena
SUDAN
KORDOFAN PLATEAU
White Nile
DJIBOUTI
Djibouti •

GUINEA
• Conakry
SIERRA LEONE
Freetown •
GHANA
CÔTE D'IVOIRE
LAKE VOLTA
TOGO
BENIN
NIGERIA
• Ibadan
• Lagos
Port-Novo
AMHARA
★ Addis Ababa
ETHIOPIA
PLATEAU
SOMALIA

LIBERIA
Monrovia •
★ Abidjan
Accra
Lomé
CENTRAL AFRICAN REPUBLIC
• Bangui
LAKE RUDOLF

Cape Palmas
Malabo •
EQUATORIAL GUINEA
Sao Tome
SÃO TOMÉ AND PRÍNCIPE
• Yaounde
CAMEROON
Ubangi River
Congo River
LAKE ALBERT
Margherita Peak 16,763 ft. (5,109 m.)
UGANDA
★ Kampala
KENYA
★ Mt. Kenya 17,058 ft. (5,199 m.)
• Mogadiscio

GULF OF GUINEA
• Libreville
GABON
CONGO BASIN
ZAIRE
RWANDA ★ Kigali
★ Bujumbura
BURUNDI
LAKE VICTORIA
★ Nairobi
GREAT RIFT VALLEY
Mt. Kilimanjaro 19,340 ft. (5,895 m.)
INDIAN OCEAN

Equator

Prime Meridian

CONGO
Brazzaville •
★ Kinshasa
CABINDA (ANGOLA)
Congo River
LAKE TANGANYIKA
TANZANIA
• Dar es Salaam

ATLANTIC OCEAN
° ASCENSION ISLAND (U.K.)

South latitude

★ Luanda
ANGOLA
• Lubumbashi
★ Moroni
COMORES

West longitude
East longitude
° ST. HELENA (U.K.)
ZAMBIA
LAKE MALAWI
MALAWI
Lilongwe ★
★ Lusaka
Zambezi River
MOZAMBIQUE

Cape Fria
ZIMBABWE
★ Harare
MADAGASCAR CHANNEL
★ Antananarivo
MADAGASCAR

Tropic of Capricorn
NAMIB DESERT
NAMIBIA
KALAHARI DESERT
Windhoek ★
BOTSWANA
Limpopo River
MOZAMBIQUE

Orange River
★ Gaborone
• Johannesburg
Pretoria ★
★ Maputo
Mbabane ★
SWAZILAND

LESOTHO
Maseru ★
DRAKENSBERG
• Durban

SOUTH AFRICA
Cape of Good Hope
★ Cape Town
Cape Agulhas

Meters	Feet
3 050	10,000
1 525	5,000
610	2,000
305	1,000
0	0
Below Sea Level	

CITIES
★ National Capital
• 5,000,000 population and over
• 1,000,000 - 4,999,999
• 500,000 - 999,999
• Less than 500,000

0   500   1000 Miles
0   500   1000 Kilometers

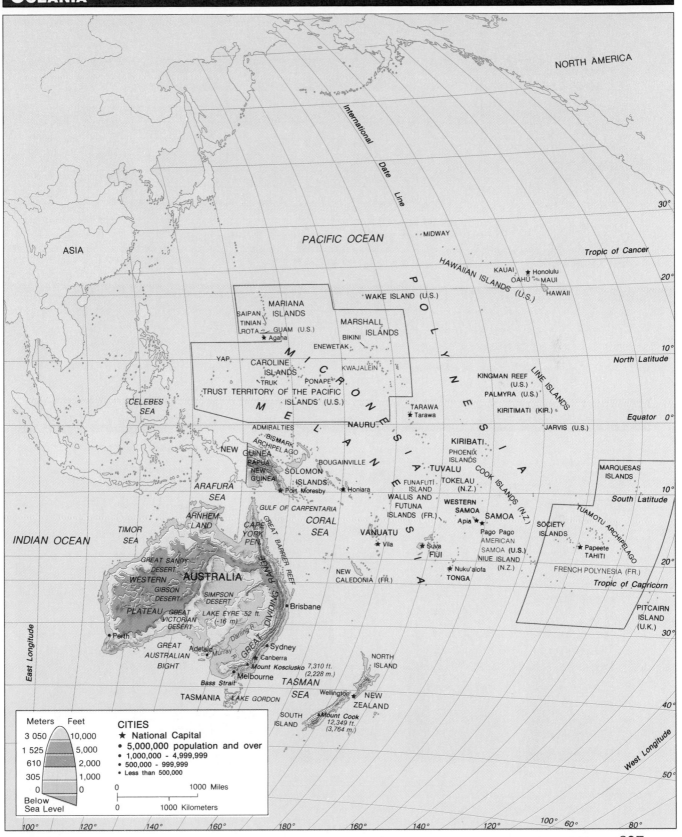

NORTH AMERICA

ASIA

PACIFIC OCEAN

International Date Line

• MIDWAY

Tropic of Cancer

HAWAIIAN ISLANDS (U.S.)

KAUAI
OAHU ★ Honolulu
MAUI
HAWAII

WAKE ISLAND (U.S.)

30°

20°

MARIANA ISLANDS
SAIPAN
TINIAN
ROTA • GUAM (U.S.)
★ Agaña

MARSHALL ISLANDS
BIKINI
ENEWETAK

P O L Y N E S I A

North Latitude 10°

YAP
CAROLINE ISLANDS
TRUK •
PONAPE •

KWAJALEIN

M I C R O N E S I A

TRUST TERRITORY OF THE PACIFIC ISLANDS (U.S.)

KINGMAN REEF (U.S.)
PALMYRA (U.S.)
KIRITIMATI (KIR.)

LINE ISLANDS

CELEBES SEA

TARAWA
★ Tarawa

NAURU •

JARVIS (U.S.)

Equator 0°

ADMIRALTIES

BISMARK ARCHIPELAGO

NEW GUINEA
PAPUA NEW GUINEA
• Port Moresby

BOUGAINVILLE

SOLOMON ISLANDS
★ Honiara

KIRIBATI
PHOENIX ISLANDS

TUVALU
FUNAFUTI ISLAND
TOKELAU (N.Z.)
WALLIS AND FUTUNA ISLANDS (FR.)

COOK ISLANDS (N.Z.)

MARQUESAS ISLANDS

South Latitude 10°

ARAFURA SEA

INDIAN OCEAN

TIMOR SEA

ARNHEM LAND

CAPE YORK PEN.

GULF OF CARPENTARIA

CORAL SEA

VANUATU
★ Vila

FIJI
★ Suva

WESTERN SAMOA
Apia ★

SAMOA
AMERICAN SAMOA (U.S.)
Pago Pago

NIUE ISLAND (N.Z.)

SOCIETY ISLANDS

TUAMOTU ARCHIPELAGO

★ Papeete
TAHITI

FRENCH POLYNESIA (FR.)

20°

GREAT SANDY DESERT
GIBSON DESERT
WESTERN PLATEAU
GREAT VICTORIAN DESERT
• Perth

AUSTRALIA

SIMPSON DESERT
LAKE EYRE -52 ft. (-16 m)

GREAT BARRIER REEF

GREAT DIVIDING RANGE

• Brisbane

NEW CALEDONIA (FR.)

TONGA
★ Nuku'alofa

Tropic of Capricorn

PITCAIRN ISLAND (U.K.)

30°

GREAT AUSTRALIAN BIGHT

Adelaid
Murray R.
Darling R.

• Sydney
Canberra
Mount Kosciusko 7,310 ft. (2,228 m.)
Melbourne

NORTH ISLAND

BASS STRAIT
TASMANIA
LAKE GORDON

TASMAN SEA

Wellington ★
NEW ZEALAND

SOUTH ISLAND
Mount Cook 12,349 ft. (3,764 m.)

40°

East Longitude

West Longitude

50°

Meters	Feet
3 050	10,000
1 525	5,000
610	2,000
305	1,000
0	0
Below Sea Level	

CITIES
★ National Capital
• 5,000,000 population and over
• 1,000,000 - 4,999,999
• 500,000 - 999,999
• Less than 500,000

0   1000 Miles

0   1000 Kilometers

100°   120°   140°   160°   180°   160°   140°   120°   100°   60°   80°

Centers of Plant and Animal Domestication

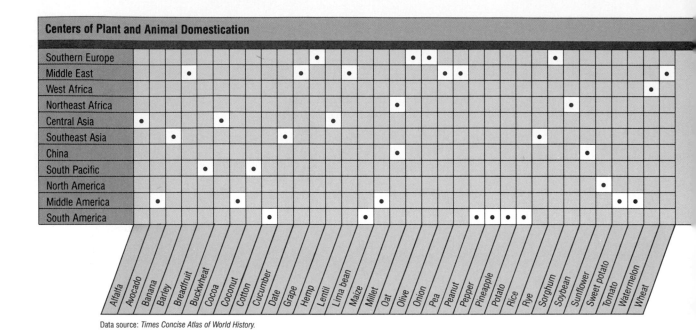

Region	Alfalfa	Avocado	Banana	Barley	Breadfruit	Buckwheat	Cocoa	Coconut	Cotton	Cucumber	Date	Grape	Hemp	Lentil	Lima bean	Maize	Millet	Oat	Olive	Onion	Pea	Peanut	Pepper	Pineapple	Potato	Rice	Rye	Sorghum	Soybean	Sunflower	Sweet potato	Tomato	Watermelon	Wheat
Southern Europe												●						●	●								●							
Middle East				●								●		●						●	●													●
West Africa																																	●	
Northeast Africa																		●										●						
Central Asia	●					●							●																					
Southeast Asia			●							●																●								
China																	●												●					
South Pacific					●			●																										
North America																														●				
Middle America		●							●							●							●									●	●	
South America									●						●							●	●	●	●									

Data source: *Times Concise Atlas of World History.*

Regional Economies 500 B.C.–A.D. 1

Legend

Agriculture   Hunting   Urban Life   Trade

The bar graph below indicates the relative role each factor played in the region's economy.

Region

Mesopotamia Persia   Egypt   Greece Asia Minor   Italy North Africa   Northern Europe

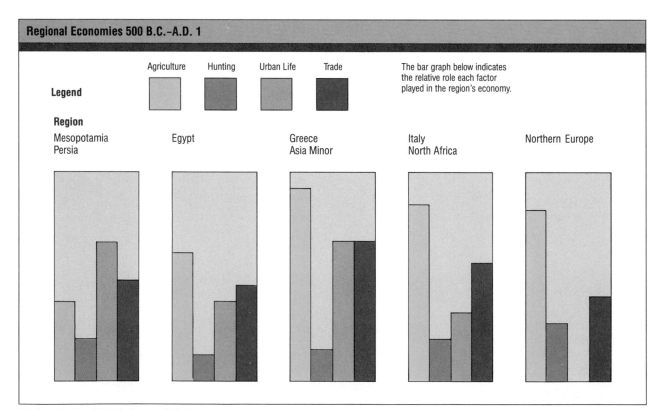

Data Source: *The Atlas of Early Man*, by Jacquetta Hawkes.

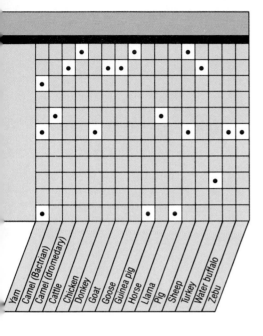

| | Yam | Camel (Bactrian) | Camel (dromedary) | Cattle | Chicken | Donkey | Goat | Goose | Guinea pig | Horse | Llama | Pig | Sheep | Turkey | Water buffalo | Zebu |

Life Expectancy 700 B.C.–A.D. 1983

Region	Year	Age
Greece	700 B.C.	18
Rome	50 B.C.	22
England	1500	33
U.S.	1790	33.5
U.S.	1850	40.0
U.S.	1900	47.3
U.S.	1910	50.0
U.S.	1920	54.1
U.S.	1930	59.7
U.S.	1940	62.9
U.S.	1950	68.2
Spain	1970	72.5
Japan	1978	73.7
U.S.	1980	73.0
U.S.	1983	73.9

Data source: WGBH Educational Foundation.

Architecture 3000–2000 B.C.
(materials in use)

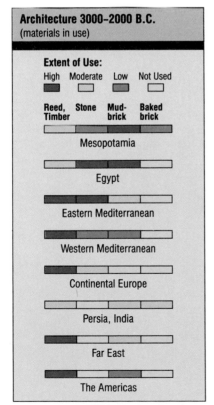

Extent of Use: High, Moderate, Low, Not Used

Reed, Timber — Stone — Mud-brick — Baked brick

Mesopotamia
Egypt
Eastern Mediterranean
Western Mediterranean
Continental Europe
Persia, India
Far East
The Americas

Data source: *The Atlas of Early Man*, by Jacquetta Hawkes.

Technology 2000–1000 B.C.
(materials in use)

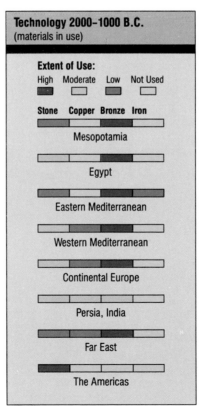

Extent of Use: High, Moderate, Low, Not Used

Stone — Copper — Bronze — Iron

Mesopotamia
Egypt
Eastern Mediterranean
Western Mediterranean
Continental Europe
Persia, India
Far East
The Americas

Data source: *The Atlas of Early Man*, by Jacquetta Hawkes.

World Religions A.D. 1–500

Region	Buddhism	Taoism	Shintoism	Zoroastrianism	Hinduism	Judaism	Christianity
Asia Minor				•		•	•
England				•			•
China	•	•					
Gaul (France)				•			•
Greece				•		•	•
India	•				•		•
Italy				•		•	•
Japan	•		•				
Persia				•		•	•

Data source: *The Times Concise Atlas of World History*, Hammond, 1982.

Major Exports A.D. 700

Region	Resources
Asia Minor	silk, slaves, grain, spices
China	copper, tea, silk, paper, wool, porcelain
Egypt	slaves, grain, gold, silver, jewelry, leather
England	tin, fish, weapons, coal
Gaul (France)	slaves, grain, wool, oil, silver
Germany	copper, tin, honey, silver, wine
India	tin, mercury, glass, gold, spices
Italy	grain, wool, oil
Persia	sugar, slaves, grain, jewelry, leather
Russia	copper, fish, furs, honey, grain, timber, silver, wine, jewelry
Spain	copper, sugar, salt, slaves, weapons, silver, wine

(Resource columns, left to right: copper, tea, silk, tin, fish, furs, horses, sugar, salt, slaves, mercury, honey, paper, grain, wool, oil, timber, weapons, glass, gold, silver, wine, linen, jewelry, leather, coal, porcelain, spices)

Data source: *Penguin Atlas of Medieval History*, Penguin Books, 1967.

Indo-European Language Family

Branch	Examples
Germanic	English, German, Dutch, Danish, Norwegian, Swedish
Romance	French, Spanish, Portuguese, Italian, Romanian
Slavic	Russian, Ukranian, Polish, Czech, Bulgarian, Latvian
Indo-Iranian	Hindustani, Bengali, Persian
Celtic	Irish, Scots Gaelic, Welsh
Albanian	
Armenian	

Data source: *World Book*

Land Ownership by Women in Medieval Europe A.D. 701–1200

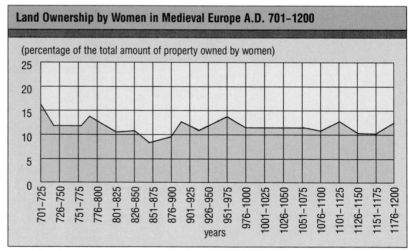

(percentage of the total amount of property owned by women)

years

From David Herlihy, "Land, Family, and Women in Continental Europe, 701–1200," *Traditio*, Vol. 18, p. 109. New York: Fordham University Press, 1962. © 1962 by David Herlihy.

Impact of the Black Death 1347–1350 (approximate population)

City	Avignon (France)	Barcelona (Spain)	Bristol (England)	Florence (Italy)	London (England)	Milan (Italy)	Montpellier (France)	Nuremberg (Germany)	Winchester (England)
Before	46,000	50,000	11,000	80,000	50,000	88,000	40,000	18,000	7,000
After	23,000	28,000	7,000	20,000	28,000	75,000	23,000	16,000	3,000

Data source: *The Black Death*, by Robert Gottfried. London: Collier-Macmillan, 1983.

Spread of Islam A.D. 610-1989

Region	Approximate Year Islam Introduced	Approximate Percentage of Muslims at Last Census
China	1500	5%
Egypt	656	90%
Ethiopia	1250	31%
India	711	11%
Iran	656	98%
Libya	750	97%
Mali	1200	90%
Morocco	750	99%
Pakistan	750	97%
USSR	1500	11%
Saudi Arabia	610	99%
Spain	750	1%
Syria	656	90%

Data source: *Islam in the World*, by M. Rusven. Oxford University Press, 1984, *Encyclopedia Britannica 1989 Book of the Year*.

Population of China A.D. 2-1988

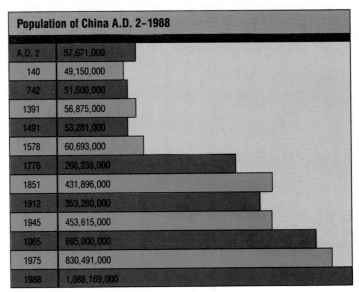

A.D. 2	57,671,000
140	49,150,000
742	51,500,000
1391	56,875,000
1491	53,281,000
1578	60,693,000
1776	268,238,000
1851	431,896,000
1912	353,260,000
1945	453,615,000
1965	695,000,000
1975	830,491,000
1988	1,088,169,000

Data source: *World Book Encyclopedia*, 1989.

Population Growth 1650-1850

Country	1650	1700	1750	1800	1850
Australia	200,000	200,000	250,000	250,000	600,000
Egypt	4,000,000	4,500,000	4,000,000	3,500,000	5,500,000
France	19,000,000	19,300,000	22,000,000	27,000,000	36,000,000
Germany	11,500,000	12,500,000	15,700,000	18,500,000	27,000,000
Great Britain and Ireland	8,250,000	8,940,000	10,475,000	15,960,000	28,000,000
Holland	1,900,000	1,900,000	1,950,000	2,078,000	3,000,000
Italy	11,000,000	13,000,000	15,500,000	18,500,000	25,000,000
Japan	25,000,000	29,000,000	29,000,000	28,000,000	32,000,000
Korea	5,000,000	6,250,000	7,000,000	7,500,000	9,000,000
Portugal	1,750,000	2,000,000	2,250,000	2,750,000	3,500,000
Russia	17,000,000	20,000,000	26,000,000	36,000,000	60,000,000
Spain	7,700,000	7,500,000	9,300,000	11,500,000	15,000,000
United States	850,000	1,000,000	2,000,000	6,000,000	24,000,000

Data sources: *Atlas of World Population History*, Penguin, 1978 and *European Political Facts*, 1984.

Slave Economies of the Western Hemisphere 1451–1870
(estimated slave imports)

	1451–1600	1601–1700	1701–1810	1811–1870
Brazil	60,000	580,000	2,000,000	1,000,000
Spanish America (including Cuba)	100,000	325,000	600,000	600,000
British West Indies	*	275,000	1,380,000	*
French West Indies	*	150,000	1,350,000	100,000
British North America and United States	*	*	320,000	80,000

*figure not available

Data source: *Rand McNally Historical Atlas of the World*.

Urbanization in Europe and the United States 1800–1890
(percentage of population in towns of over 10,000)

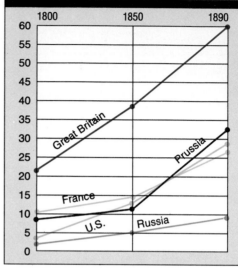

Data source: *Outline Atlas of World History*, by R. Sellman. St. Martin's Press, 1970.

Literacy in England by Occupational Group 1754–1844

	1754–1784 Sample Size	1754–1784 %	1785–1814 Sample Size	1785–1814 %	1815–1844 Sample Size	1815–1844 %
Gentry and professionals	68	99	170	99	204	97
Officials	20	99	43	95	94	98
Retail workers	19	95	94	90	150	95
Yeomen and farmers	97	81	262	82	315	83
Textile workers	41	80	83	61	38	84
Transport workers	154	69	462	62	549	70
Armed forces (non-officers)	180	59	773	49	122	68
Construction and mining workers	146	49	352	53	499	62
Servants	192	41	596	35	1,632	34
Total population		64%		61%		65%

Data source: *Literacy and Social Development in the West*, edited by Harvey Graff. Cambridge University Press, 1981.

Emigration 1846–1932

Country of Emigration	Total (in thousands)
Austria-Hungary	5,196
France	519
Germany	4,889
Great Britain and Ireland	18,020
Holland	224
Italy	10,092
Japan	518
Russia	2,253
Spain	4,653

Data source: Carr-Saunders, *World Population*.

Immigration 1821–1932

Country of Immigration	Period	Total (in thousands)
Argentina	1856–1932	6,405
Australia	1861–1932	2,913
Brazil	1821–1932	4,431
Canada	1821–1932	5,206
South Africa	1881–1932	852
United States	1821–1932	34,244

Data source: Carr-Saunders, *World Population*.

Balance of World Trade 1860–1913 (in millions of U.S. dollars)

			Europe	North America	South America	Asia	Africa	Total
Great Britain	1860	imports	419	252	96	143	80	990
		exports	358	132	74	139	36	739
	1913	imports	1,548	848	393	458	220	3,457
		exports	917	265	272	620	248	2,322
United States	1860	imports	217	*	80	29	*	326
		exports	249	*	46	11	*	306
	1913	imports	893	199	381	298	26	1,797
		exports	1,479	469	294	140	29	2,411
France	1860	imports	234	47	41	16	34	372
		exports	293	49	53	3	45	443
	1913	imports	880	187	183	192	148	1,590
		exports	937	89	94	36	181	1,337
Germany	1913	imports	1,402	423	290	250	118	2,483
		exports	1,828	184	183	130	50	2,375

*figure not available
Data source: *The Times Concise Atlas of World History.*

Major Raw Materials Exported to Europe 1880–1900

	Argentina	Australia	Belgian Congo	Brazil	Canada	Ceylon	China	Egypt	India	Japan	Malaya	Mexico	New Zealand	Peru	South Africa	United States	Venezuela
grain					•											•	
meat	•	•											•				•
tea						•	•		•								
cotton				•				•	•						•		
silk							•			•							
rubber			•	•							•						
copper			•											•			
wool	•	•															
diamonds															•		
silver												•					
cane sugar				•								•		•			
gold		•			•										•		
tin					•						•						
dairy produce		•			•								•				

Data source: *The Times Concise Atlas of World History.*

Military Casualties: World Wars I and II

Nation	World War I 1914–1918	World War II 1939–1945
Austria-Hungary	1,050,000	*
China	*	2,200,000
France	1,500,000	211,000
Germany	1,950,000	2,850,000
Great Britain	1,000,000	398,000
Italy	533,000	78,000
Japan	2,000	1,510,000
Ottoman Empire	325,000	*
United States	116,000	293,000
USSR (Russia)	1,700,000	7,500,000

*figure not available
Data sources: *Times Concise Atlas of World History*; *World Atlas of Military History*, by Arthur Banks. New York: Hippocrene Books, 1978.

Percentage of Labor Force Unemployed in Four Nations 1923–1938

Year	United Kingdom	Germany	Sweden	United States
1923	11.3	9.6	*	3.2
1926	12.7	18.0	12.2	1.9
1929	11.0	13.1	11.2	3.2
1932	22.5	30.1	22.8	23.6
1935	16.4	11.6	16.1	20.1
1938	13.3	2.1	10.9	19.0

*figure not available
Data sources: *Historical Statistics of the United States*; *European Historical Statistics*, Mitchell.

Economic and Social Statistics for Selected Nations 1988

	United States	United Kingdom	USSR	China	Bangladesh	Saudi Arabia	Guatemala
Population (in millions)	246.1	57.0	285.8	1,088.2	107.8	12.9	8.7
Population density (per square mile)	67	605	33	294	1,938	15	207
Per capita income	$16,444	$7,216	$4,200	$258	$151	$11,500	$1,000
Life expectancy (males/females)	72/79	72/77	65/74	68/71	51/50	55/58	58/62
Physicians (per 100,000 people)	239	150	437	138	17	106	44
Literacy rate	99%	99%	99%	75%	33%	57%	55%
Labor force in agriculture	3%	2%	19%	61%	58%	14%	57%
Labor force in industry	21%	22%	33%	19%	9%	15%	11%
Telephones (per 100 people)	76.9	52.6	11.1	0.7	0.2	11.7	1.6

Data sources: *Encyclopedia Britannica 1989 Book of the Year, World Almanac, 1990.*

Leading Crude Petroleum Producers 1986
(thousands of metric tons per average calendar month)*

	1970	1980	1986
Canada	5,033	5,866	6,008
China	1,991	8,825	10,883
Iran	15,941	6,075	7,783
Mexico	1,791	8,325	10,516
Nigeria	4,516	8,683	6,006
Saudi Arabia	15,700	41,325	20,975
United Kingdom	833	6,575	10,100
U.S.	39,608	35,350	35,683
USSR	29,417	50,267	51,250
Venezuela	16,192	9,566	7,833

Data source: *Statistical Abstract of the United States*, 1984 and 1989.

Gross National Product, Total Exports, and Major Export Trade Partners of Selected Nations 1988

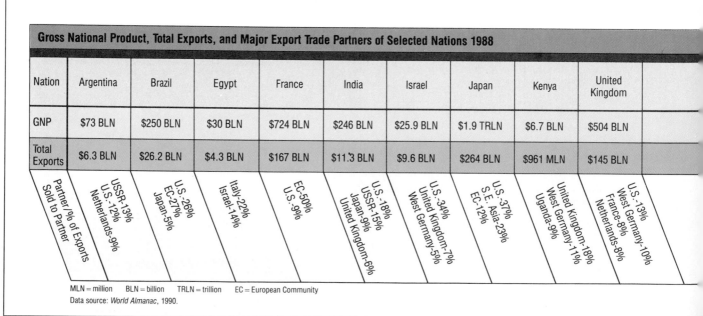

Nation	Argentina	Brazil	Egypt	France	India	Israel	Japan	Kenya	United Kingdom	
GNP	$73 BLN	$250 BLN	$30 BLN	$724 BLN	$246 BLN	$25.9 BLN	$1.9 TRLN	$6.7 BLN	$504 BLN	
Total Exports	$6.3 BLN	$26.2 BLN	$4.3 BLN	$167 BLN	$11.3 BLN	$9.6 BLN	$264 BLN	$961 MLN	$145 BLN	
Partner/% of Exports Sold to Partner	USSR-13% U.S.-12% Netherlands-9%	U.S.-26% EC-27% Japan-5%	Italy-22% Israel-14%	EC-50% U.S.-9%	U.S.-18% USSR-15% Japan-9% United Kingdom-6%	U.S.-34% United Kingdom-7% West Germany-5%	U.S.-37% S.E. Asia-23% EC-12%	United Kingdom-18% West Germany-11% Uganda-9%	U.S.-13% West Germany-10% France-8% Netherlands-8%	

MLN = million   BLN = billion   TRLN = trillion   EC = European Community

Data source: *World Almanac*, 1990.

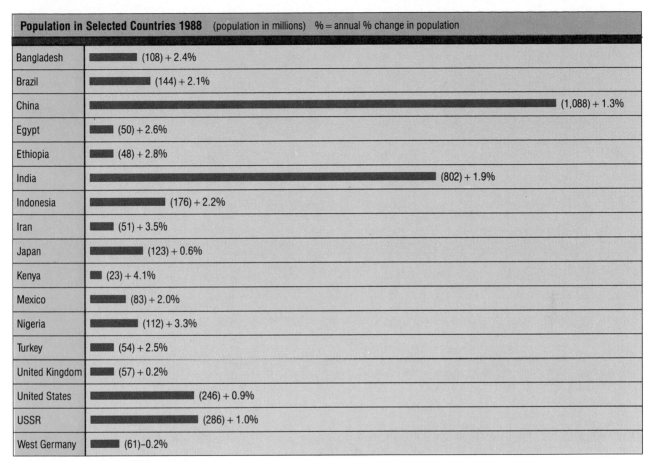

Population in Selected Countries 1988   (population in millions)   % = annual % change in population

Bangladesh	(108) + 2.4%
Brazil	(144) + 2.1%
China	(1,088) + 1.3%
Egypt	(50) + 2.6%
Ethiopia	(48) + 2.8%
India	(802) + 1.9%
Indonesia	(176) + 2.2%
Iran	(51) + 3.5%
Japan	(123) + 0.6%
Kenya	(23) + 4.1%
Mexico	(83) + 2.0%
Nigeria	(112) + 3.3%
Turkey	(54) + 2.5%
United Kingdom	(57) + 0.2%
United States	(246) + 0.9%
USSR	(286) + 1.0%
West Germany	(61) –0.2%

Data source: *Encyclopedia Britannica 1989 Book of the Year*.

	United States	USSR	West Germany
	$4.5 TRLN	$2.3 TRLN	$898 BLN
	$321 BLN	$86.9 BLN	$323 BLN
	Canada-22% Japan-10% Mexico-6% United Kingdom-5%	East Germany-10% Poland-8% Bulgaria-8%	France-14% Netherlands-8% Italy-8% Belgium-7%

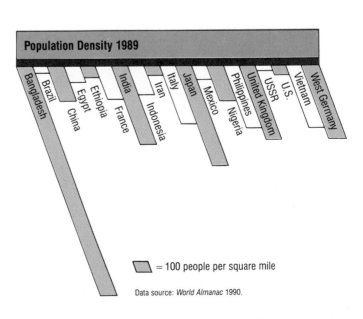

Population Density 1989

☐ = 100 people per square mile

Data source: *World Almanac* 1990.

Life Expectancy at Birth in Selected Nations Mid–1980s

Nation	Male	Female
Afghanistan	42.5	40.8
Argentina	66.8	73.2
Brazil	62.3	67.6
Burma	51.9	55.0
Cuba	71.0	74.0
Denmark	71.5	77.5
El Salvador	62.6	66.3
France	71.3	79.5
Iceland	73.5	79.5
India	56.7	57.6
Iran	58.0	58.3
Lebanon	65.0	68.9
Nigeria	48.3	51.7
United States	71.5	78.5

Data Source: *World Almanac, 1989*.

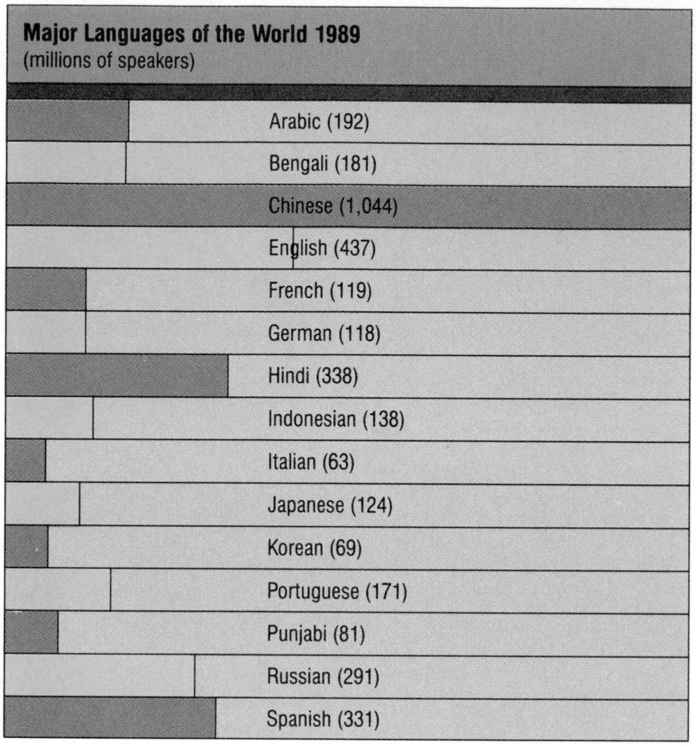

Major Languages of the World 1989
(millions of speakers)

- Arabic (192)
- Bengali (181)
- Chinese (1,044)
- English (437)
- French (119)
- German (118)
- Hindi (338)
- Indonesian (138)
- Italian (63)
- Japanese (124)
- Korean (69)
- Portuguese (171)
- Punjabi (81)
- Russian (291)
- Spanish (331)

Data Source: *World Almanac 1990*.

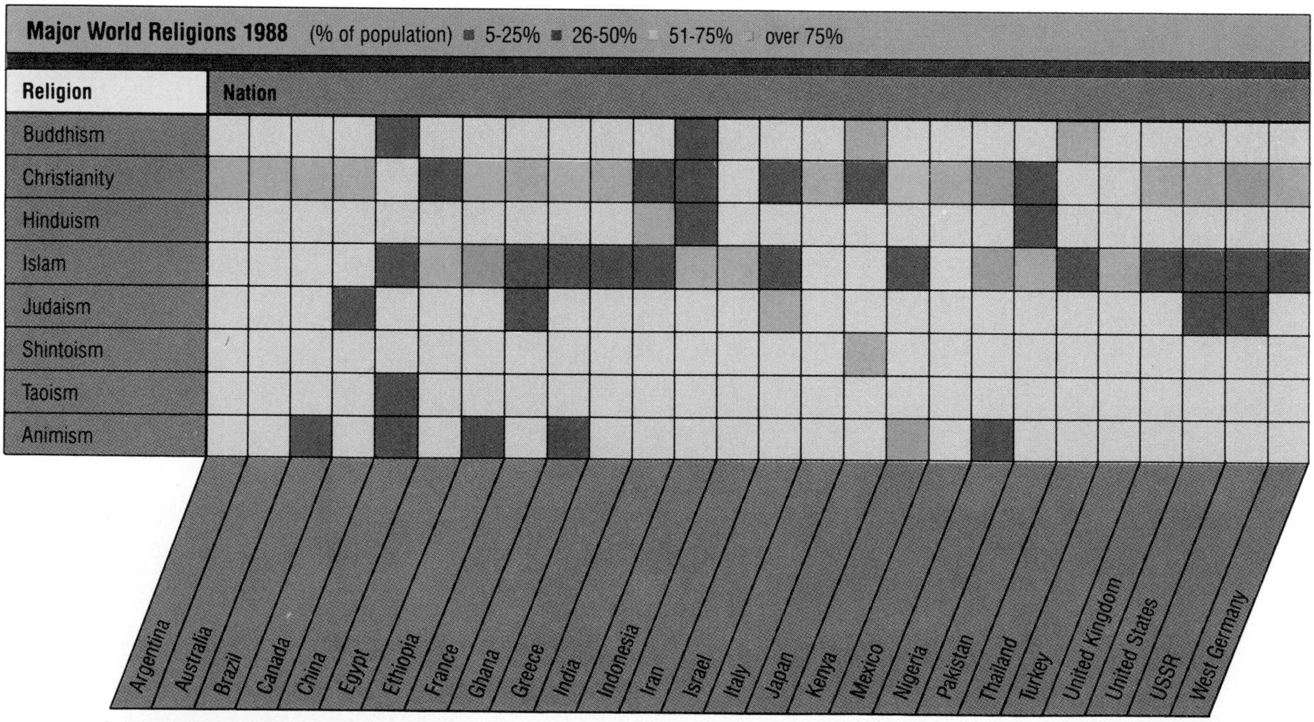

Major World Religions 1988
(% of population) ■ 5-25% ■ 26-50% □ 51-75% ▨ over 75%

Religion	Argentina	Australia	Brazil	Canada	China	Egypt	Ethiopia	France	Ghana	Greece	India	Indonesia	Iran	Israel	Italy	Japan	Kenya	Mexico	Nigeria	Pakistan	Thailand	Turkey	United Kingdom	United States	USSR	West Germany
Buddhism																										
Christianity																										
Hinduism																										
Islam																										
Judaism																										
Shintoism																										
Taoism																										
Animism																										

Data source: *Encyclopedia Britannica 1989 Book of the Year*.

Defense Budgets of Selected Nations 1985–1988

(percentage of GNP spent on defense)

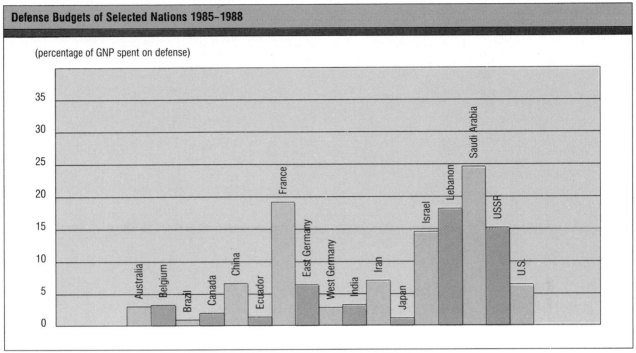

Data source: *World Almanac*, 1990.

Per Capita Income in Selected Nations mid-1980s

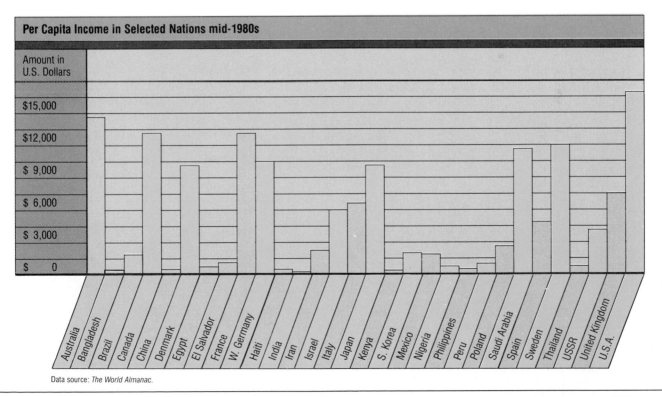

Data source: *The World Almanac*.

TIMETABLE OF WORLD HISTORY

	PREHISTORY	3000 B.C.	2000 B.C.	1000 B.C.	A.D. 1
EUROPE	• **30,000 B.C.** Richest period of paleolithic culture of Cro-Magnon hunters • **25,000 B.C.** Cro-Magnon cave paintings • **18,000 B.C.** Bone sewing needles used in France • **9000 B.C.** Dog domesticated	• **3000** Farming settlements established throughout Europe • **2900** Neolithic culture at its peak in Danube region • **2000** Scandinavians begin burying their dead in graves • **2000** Barbarians colonize Greece	• **2000** Minoan civilization flourishes • **1900** Stonehenge built in southern England • **1400** Mycenaeans become dominant force in Mediterranean region • **1100** Iron being used in Austria	• **800** Etruscans in Italy • **750** Greek city-states • **700** *Iliad* and *Odyessy* • **509** Roman republic • **508** Greek democracy • **469–322** Height of Greek philosophy • **336–323** Reign of Alexander the Great • **46** Julius Caesar crowned dictator	• **1–180** Pax Romana: Peace and prosperity in Roman Empire • **14** Death of Augustus • **79** Mt. Vesuvius eruption buries Pompeii and Herculaneum • **79–84** Romans conquer England
AFRICA	• **5000 B.C.** Agriculture introduced into Africa • **4500 B.C.** Honeybee domesticated • **4000 B.C.** Sahara begins to turn into a desert	• **3000** Beehive-shaped huts built in Central Africa • **3000** Migration of Saharan peoples to West Africa	• **2000** Development of Kushite culture	• **700** Kushites gain control of Upper Egypt • **250** Kush becomes most powerful empire in Africa	• **50** Axum becomes a major trade center
THE AMERICAS	• **10,500 B.C.** Humans reach southern South America • **3500 B.C.** Potatoes grown in South America • **3372 B.C.** First date in Mayan chronology	• **2500** Maize cultivated • **2200** Peruvians grow beans, cotton, chili, squash	• **1500** Chiapa de Carzo: earliest known settlement in Mexico • **1200** Olmecs build first planned city in Central America	• **1000** Olmecs raise pyramid at La Venta, southeastern Mexico • **900** Gold ornaments buried in northern Peru: earliest known metalwork in Americas • **900–200** Chavin culture controls northern Peru • **100** Olmec civilization vanishes	
MIDDLE EAST	• **8000 B.C.** Sheep domesticated in Iran • **8000 B.C.** Jericho settled: oldest known city • **7000 B.C.** Wheat cultivated • **3500 B.C.** Wheeled vehicles used in Sumer • **3500 B.C.** Cuneiform writing in Sumer	• **3000** Sumerian civilization flourishes • **3000** Egyptians develop earliest known numerals and hieroglyphic script • **2700–2200** Old Kingdom in Egypt • **2650** Egyptians erect first pyramid, begin writing on papyrus	• **2000–1800** Middle Kingdom in Egypt • **c.1800** Hebrews establish Judaism • **1695** Code of Hammurabi • **1570–1100** New Kingdom in Egypt • **1300** Assyrians conquer Babylon • **1100–800** Phoenicians create seafaring empire in Mediterranean	• **1000** Israelites unify under King David • **900** Assyrians conquer eastern Mediterranean • **700** Assyrians assume control over Egypt • **600** Babylon becomes most sophisticated city of ancient world • **550** Cyrus founds Persian Empire	• **1** Birth of Jesus Christ • **33** Jesus Christ, hailed as the Messiah by his followers, is crucified by the Romans • **47–65** Paul, disciple of Christ, begins his missionary journeys • **66–70** Revolt in Judea against Romans
ASIA	• **24,000 B.C.** Earliest known rafts used in southeastern Asia • **4000 B.C.** Collapsible huts built in Central Asia	• **2700** Legendary beginning of Chinese silk making • **2500** Indus Valley civilization; Harappa and Mohenjo-daro become major centers • **2100** Chinese musicians use bamboo pipes; artisans begin making painted pottery	• **2000** Elephants and chickens domesticated • **1800** Rice cultivated • **1500–800** Early Vedic Age in India • **1500–1027** Shang Dynasty • **1500–1000** Development of Chinese writing • **1400** Horses domesticated • **1027–256** Chou Dynasty	• **1000** Invention of silk looms in China • **1000** Caste system develops in India • **400** Development of Buddhism in India • **221–207** Ch'in Dynasty: Great Wall built • **202–A.D. 220** Han Dynasty: civil service established • **150** Confucianism and Taoism evolve in China	• **25** Chinese begin making paper, porcelain • **c.50** Buddhism introduced to China • **50** Chinese drive invading Huns toward Western Asia • **50–250** Kushan Dynasty of northern India

Europe includes Western and Eastern Europe.
Africa includes sub-Saharan Africa.
The Americas include North America and South America.
Middle East includes North Africa and Southwest Asia.
Asia includes East Asia, South Asia, and Southeast Asia.

A.D. 100	A.D. 200	A.D. 300	A.D. 400	A.D. 500
• **122–127** Hadrian's Wall built in England • **150** Latin translation of the Bible from Greek • **160** Stoicism becomes a dominant force in Roman society • **160** Greek physician Galen uses plant juices as medicines • **161–180** Reign of Marcus Aurelius	• **212** Emperor Caracalla gives Roman citizenship to most of the inhabitants of the Empire • **285** Roman Empire: divided into East (under Diocletian) and West (under Maximian)	• **313** Edict of Milan • **324–337** Constantine reigns, reuniting the Roman Empire • **325** Council of Nicaea • **341** Ulfilas invents Gothic alphabet used for Biblical translations • **379–85** Papal power gains strength: Christianity becomes official religion of Roman Empire	• **407** Roman troops leave England • **431** First Christian mission in Ireland • **433** Attila the Hun advances west, invades Italy • **476** Rome falls to Germanic barbarians	• **500–600** Anglo-Saxons continue setting up kingdoms in England • **500s** Byzantine Empire invaded by Huns, Bulgars, and Slavs • **527–565** Reign of Justinian • **533** Justinian's Code • **533** St. Columba develops monasticism in Ireland • **590–604** Pope Gregory I
• **100** Beginning of Bantu migrations • **100** Axum expands to become an empire		• **300** Christianity begins to spread throughout the kingdom of Axum • **c.320** King Ezana becomes first Christian ruler of Axum • **325** Axum conquers Kush • **300s** Kushites spread iron-smelting techniques to other sub-Saharan peoples		• **500** Christianity begins to spread throughout Nubian kingdoms
• **c.150** Mayan monuments erected		• **c.300** Great cult center of Teotihuacán develops in Mexico • **c.300** Mayan civilization develops cities throughout southern Mexico, Guatemala, and Honduras	• **400s** Teotihuacán influence extends into Mayan region • **400s** Teotihuacán orange pottery common throughout most of Mexico	• **500s** Mayan hieroglyphic-dated monuments in Guatemala, Yucatan, Honduras
• **135** Rome destroys Judea, forcing Jewish population abroad in The Diaspora			• **409** Persia permits Christians freedom of worship	• **500s** Pre-Islamic poetry flourishes in Arabia • **570** The prophet Muhammad is born in Mecca, Arabia
	• **200** Most of Japan is split into small states • **220** Han Dynasty falls: China fragments into three competing dynasties (Wu, Wei, and Shu)	• **320** Chandragupta I founds the Gupta Dynasty: Golden Age of India • **c.350** Tea-drinking in China • **360–390** Japanese establish footholds in Korea • **c.370** Yamato becomes leading kingdom in Japan and adopts Chinese writing	• **400** Aryabhata, Indian mathematician, conducts experiments to prove that the earth rotates • **478** Shinto shrines appear in Japan	• **550–557** Northern Ch'i Dynasty flourishes in China • **552** Buddhism officially introduced in Japan; Japanese emperor embraces Buddhism (587) • **589** China is reunited under the Sui Dynasty, first time since A.D. 220

	A.D. 600	A.D. 700	A.D. 800	A.D. 900
EUROPE	• **600s** Benedictine monasteries throughout Europe • **610–641** Heraclius rules Byzantine Empire • **627** Edwin becomes the first Christian king of Northumbria • **660** Caedmon, first known English poet, enters monastery	• **711–715** Muslim conquest of Spain • **717** Charles Martel reunites the Frankish kingdom • **726** Byzantine Emperor Leo III forbids image worship • **731** Pope Gregory III excommunicates iconoclasts • **768–814** Age of Charlemagne	• **800s** Feudalism emerges in France • **825** First law school established at Pavia, Italy • **837–840** Muslims invade Italy, crush revolt in Spain • **850** Ireland: Danes establish towns of Dublin and Limerick • **850** University of Constantinople founded • **860** Jews settle in Germany • **860–90** Magyars invade Italy	• **900** First medical school opens in Salerno, Italy • **900s** Byzantines invade Persia and Egypt • **900s** Magyars settle in Hungary • **962** Otto the Great crowned Holy Roman Emperor • **988** Prince Vladimir converts to Christianity, leading to general conversion of Russian people
AFRICA	• **c.600** Emergence of kingdom of Ghana	• **700s** Islam spreads to sub-Saharan kingdoms	• **800s** Hausa and Yoruba states evolve in northern and western Nigeria • **800s** Bantu-speaking chiefdoms emerge in what is now Zaire • **800s** Kanem Empire emerges in central Sudan region	• **900s** Ghana Empire at its peak
THE AMERICAS	• **680** Native Americans build temple mounds in what is now southeastern United States	• **700s** Pueblo culture succeeds basketmaker culture in what is now the southwestern United States	• **800–1100** Tiahuanaco culture, named for a ceremonial center in Bolivia, thrives	• **c.900** Toltecs, led by the Nahua Indians, enter Valley of Mexico • **980** Tula becomes center of the Toltec Empire
MIDDLE EAST	• **612** Muhammad founds Islam • **622** The Hejira • **633–644** Omar expands Islamic Empire beyond Arabian Peninsula, conquering Syria, Persia, and Egypt • **640–710** Conquest of North Africa by the Arabs • **650** Windmills being used in Persia • **661** Umayyad Dynasty rules Islamic Empire from Damascus	• **c.700** Arabs and Berbers make peace in North Africa; Berbers align themselves with Muslim Arabs • **750** Abbasid Dynasty replaces Umayyad Dynasty • **794** Paper manufacturing in Baghdad	• **820** Arab caliph Al-Mamun founds center for classical and oriental studies at Baghdad; Arab culture at its zenith	• **968–1171** Fatimid Dynasty in Egypt • **969** Cairo founded
ASIA	• **604** Indian mathematicians are using a decimal system • **618** T'ang Dynasty replaces the Sui in China, establishing a form of centralized government that will last until 1912 • **647** Fall of the Gupta Empire • **650** China establishes cultural links with India and Persia	• **c.700** Sumatra develops into a major trading center • **700s** Age of great poetry in China • **710** Nara becomes Japan's first permanent capital	• **800s** Japanese culture begins to develop independent of China • **841–846** Christians persecuted in China under Taoist emperor Wu Tsung • **c.850** Hinduism replacing Buddhism in northern India	• **c.900** Most of Polynesia, except New Zealand, is peopled • **c.910** "Kokinshu" anthology of Japanese verse affirms independence from China • **960** Sung Dynasty founded in China; great cultural advances follow, largely based on printing • **967–1068** Fujiwara clan dominates Japan

Europe includes Western and Eastern Europe.
Africa includes sub-Saharan Africa.
The Americas include North American and South America.
Middle East includes North Africa and Southwest Asia.
Asia includes East Asia, South Asia, and Southeast Asia.

A.D. 1000	A.D. 1100	A.D. 1200	A.D. 1300
• **1000s** Spain is divided by civil war between Muslims • **1030** Italian monk Guido devises modern musical notation • **c.1030** Romanesque architecture emerging throughout Europe • **1036–54** Reign of Yaroslav • **1054** Schism between Roman Catholic and Orthodox Churches • **1066** Norman conquest of England • **1096** First Crusade reaches Constantinople	• **1116–1120** England at war with France over Normandy • **1126** First artesian well produces water in France • **1147** Portuguese capture Lisbon from the Muslims • **1167** Oxford University founded • **1196** Height of papal political power under Pope Innocent III	• **1215** The Magna Carta • **1233** Pope Gregory IX initiates the Inquisition • **1237–1240** Mongols conquer Russia • **1240** Alexander Nevsky defeats Swedes at Neva River • **1289** Wood block printing in Italy	• **1308** "Babylonian Captivity" of Church • **1337** England and France begin Hundred Years' War • **1341–47** Civil war in the Byzantine Empire • **1348–52** Bubonic plague, the "Black Death," wipes out one third of Europe's population • **1382** First English translation of the Bible • **1387** Chaucer's *Canterbury Tales*
• **1000** Yoruba city-state of Ife founded • **1000** East African trading states well established • **1000s** Decline of Ghana • **1000s** Expansion of trade across Sahara • **1000–1500** Kanem Empire expands in the region of Lake Chad and eventually includes the plain of Bornu	• **1100** Kanem Empire well established as an Islamic state • **1100s** Development of Yoruba city-states of Benin and Oyo	• **1235** Kingdom of Mali established as Muslim state • **1200s** Mali controls gold and salt trade throughout much of West Africa	• **c.1300** Stone buildings constructed in Great Zimbabwe • **1300s** Timbuktu well established as a center of Muslim scholarship • **1300s** Bronze casting introduced to Benin from Ife • **1312–1337** Height of Mali Empire under Mansa Musa • **1352** Ibn Batuta writes description of Mali Empire
• **1002** Viking Leif Ericson discovers North America • **1003** First Norse settlement in North America; disappears in 1006 • **c.1050** Many of the classic Mayan cities have been abandoned • **c.1050** Mississippian culture developing in North America	• **1100–1400** Height of Hohokam culture in what is now the southwestern United States • **1130** Chimu culture in coastal Peru; based on urban centers in irrigated valleys • **1165** Toltec capital of Tula destroyed by Chichimec invaders	• **c.1200** Aztecs conquer Toltecs • **c.1200** First Inca emperor	• **1325** Aztecs found Tenochtitlán (Mexico City)
• **c.1000** Persian poet Firdausi completes the epic *Book of Kings* • **1055** Seljuk Turks conquer Baghdad	• **1150** Normans are driven out of North Africa by the Berbers		• **1390s** Ottoman Turks invade eastern Europe
• **1000** Polynesians colonize New Zealand • **1020** Japanese writer Murasaki Shikibu completes her novel *Tale of the Genji* • **1050** In China, compasses are being used, and movable type is being developed	• **1126** Jürchen tribes overrun Northern China: end of Northern Sung Dynasty • **1160** Chinese are using explosives in warfare • **1175** Indian girls are forbidden by law to marry below their own caste • **1184–1333** Kamakura period in Japan	• **1206** Delhi Sultanate established in India • **1210** Mongols attack northern China • **1227** Genghis Khan dies, leaving Mongol Empire to his sons • **1231** Mongols invade Korea • **1271** Kublai Khan founds Yuan Dynasty in China • **1280** Marco Polo visits China	• **1300** Mongols invade India • **1304** Delhi Sultanate resists further Mongol invasion • **1331** Emperor Daigo II restores imperial power in Japan • **1368** Beginning of Ming Dynasty in China • **1392** Li Dynasty begins in Korea, lasting until 1910

	1400	1500	1550	1600
EUROPE	• **1414** Medici family become bankers to papacy • **1420–80** Early Italian Renaissance • **1431** Joan of Arc executed • **1434** Printing press developed in Germany • **1455–85** War of the Roses • **1462–1505** Reign of Ivan the Great in Russia • **1481** Spanish Inquisition begins • **1494** Treaty of Tordesillas	• **1500–1549** High Renaissance painting: Leonardo, Holbein, Michelangelo, Raphael, Bosch • **1517** Martin Luther launches the Reformation • **1533** Henry VIII of England breaks from Roman Church • **1533–84** Reign of Ivan the Terrible, first Russian czar • **1540** Jesuit order founded • **1543** Experiments of Copernicus	• **1558** Church of England established; Elizabeth I crowned • **1562** Dutch revolt against Spanish rule • **1577** Francis Drake begins voyage around the world • **1580–1599** Literature: Montaigne, Cervantes, Shakespeare, Marlowe • **1588** Spanish Armada defeated • **1590** Science: Galileo, Bacon	• **1602** Kepler's laws of planetary motion • **1610** Civil war in Russia • **1616** Physician William Harvey discovers blood circulation • **1624** Cardinal Richelieu becomes Chief Minister of France • **1630** Thirty Years' War begins • **1641** Dutch take control of East Indies trade
AFRICA	• **1400s** Mali absorbed into Songhai Empire • **1400s** Benin and Oyo expand to become large kingdoms • **1400s** Kongo Kingdom flourishes, developing into the largest state in West Central Africa • **1460–1478** Portuguese navigators explore African coast and inland	• **1500** Timbuktu reaches height as center of culture and learning • **c.1500** Portuguese establish trading posts in East Africa • **1500–1528** Height of Songhai Empire under Askia Muhammad • **1500** First African slaves transported to West Indies • **1590s** Moroccans overthrow Songhai	• **1550–1800** Expansion of Atlantic slave trade • **1570** Kanem-Bornu Empire reaches its height	
THE AMERICAS	• **1438** Inca Empire expands in Peru under Pachacutec • **1440** Moctezuma I becomes Aztec king • **1492–1502** Christopher Columbus, sponsored by Isabella of Spain, explores the Caribbean islands • **1497** Explorer Cabot makes British claim on North America • **1499** Vespucci explores South American coast	• **1500** Cabral claims Brazil for Portugal • **1518** Cortés conquers the Aztecs • **1520** Moctezuma II is killed • **1522** Spanish explorers reach Peru • **1524** Spaniards subdue Mexico, Salvador, and Honduras • **1532** Pizarro in Peru • **1534–1536** Cartier in Canada	• **1570** Iroquois League formed • **1597** England begins transporting convicts to its colonies	• **1607** Jamestown Colony founded • **1609** Champlain founds Quebec • **1612** Tobacco plantations in Virginia • **1626** Dutch purchase Manhattan from Native Americans • **1632** English settle in Massachusetts Bay Colony • **1636** Harvard College established in Massachusetts
MIDDLE EAST	• **1453** Byzantine Empire falls to Ottoman Turks	• **1502–1736** Safawid Dynasty • **1520–1566** Reign of Ottoman sultan Suleiman • **1537** War between Ottoman Empire and Venice	• **1566–1574** Selim II's reign over Ottoman Empire • **1571** Battle of Lepanto: Ottoman fleet defeated by Europeans	• **1612** Persia makes peace with the Ottoman Empire
ASIA	• **1408** Chinese naval mission visits Sri Lanka • **1424** Muslim trade expands to East Indies; natives convert to Islam • **1446** Japanese *No* drama perfected	• **1521** Ferdinand Magellan explores the Philippines • **1526** Mogul Empire established in India • **1549** First Christian mission in Japan	• **1556** Akbar becomes Mogul ruler of India • **1557** Portuguese settlement of Macao in China • **1560** Spanish colonize the Philippines • **1597** Hideyoshi bans Christian missionaries in Japan, launches invasion of Korea	• **1600s** English establish colonies in India • **1603** Tokugawa shogunate established in Japan (lasts until 1868) • **1627** Manchus occupy Korea • **1636** Japanese citizens forbidden to leave country • **1639** Portuguese expelled from Japan; 37,000 Christians killed by Tokugawa government • **1644–1912** Ch'ing Dynasty

Europe includes Western and Eastern Europe.
Africa includes sub-Saharan Africa.
The Americas include North America and South America.
Middle East includes North Africa and Southwest Asia.
Asia includes East Asia, South Asia, and Southeast Asia.

1650	1700	1750	1800
• **1650** Charles I executed; monarchy replaced by Commonwealth government under Oliver Cromwell • **1652–1715** Reign of Louis XIV in France • **1670** Restoration of monarchy in England • **1689–1725** Reign of Peter the Great in Russia • **1687** Newton's law of gravitation • **1688** Bill of Rights in England	• **1700s** Beginning of the Industrial Revolution/Age of Enlightenment • **1700–1714** War of the Spanish Succession • **1701–1745** Music: Bach, Handel • **1740–1780** Reign of Maria Theresa in Austria • **1740–1846** Reign of Frederick the Great in Prussia • **1740–1748** War of the Austrian Succession	• **1730–1790** Philosophy: Hume, Diderot, Montesquieu, Voltaire • **1756** Seven Years' War begins • **1762** Rousseau's *Social Contract* • **1762–1796** Reign of Catherine the Great in Russia • **1765** Watt develops steam engine • **1783–1799** Music: Mozart, Beethoven • **1789** French Revolution • **1792** Gas lights in England • **1793** Reign of Terror in France • **1799** Napoleon becomes dictator	• **1800s** Age of Imperialism • **1804** Napoleon crowns himself Emperor; Napoleonic Code • **1812** Napoleon invades Russia • **1814–1815** Congress of Vienna • **1829** Braille alphabet invented • **1833** Factory Act regulates working hours of British children • **1837–1901** Reign of Victoria • **1845** Potato blight in Ireland • **1848** *Communist Manifesto*
• **1652** Dutch settlers found Cape Town in South Africa • **1660** Bambara kingdoms along Niger River • **1680** The Akan people of West Africa form Asante confederation	• **1700s** Expansion of Asante power in West Africa	• **1758** Britain founds Sierra Leone as a haven for former slaves	• **1815** Britain acquires Cape Colony, South Africa • **1822** American colonization society founds Liberia: colony for freed American slaves • **1837** Boers begin to occupy Zululand in South Africa • **1841** Livingstone begins missionary work in southern Africa
• **1654** Brazilians revolt against the Dutch • **1659** Puritans persecute Quakers • **1660** Navigation Act: England prohibits free trade between colonies and other nations • **1682** LaSalle claims Louisiana for France	• **1712** Slave revolt in New York Colony • **1716** Settlement of Shenandoah Valley • **1727** Brazil's first coffee plantation • **1729** Benjamin Franklin begins publishing "Philadelphia Gazette"	• **1754–1763** French and Indian War • **1764–1765** Stamp Act, Sugar Act • **1773** Boston Tea Party • **1775** American Revolution begins • **1776** Declaration of Independence • **1776** De Anza reaches San Francisco • **1783** Treaty of Paris ends Revolutionary War • **1787** U.S. Constitution drafted • **1793** Whitney's cotton gin	• **1804–1806** Lewis and Clark explore Western United States • **1807** Fulton's steamboat • **1808** United States bans import of slaves from Africa • **1810** Simón Bolívar leads Venezuelan revolt; other revolts follow in Mexico, Chile • **1812–1815** War of 1812 • **1822** Brazilian Independence • **1823** Monroe Doctrine • **1824** Mexico becomes a republic
	• **1705** Husseinite Dynasty established in Tunis	• **1768** Turkey declares war on Russia	• **1802** British and French troops evacuate Egypt • **1805–1848** Reign of Mehemet Ali in Egypt • **1847** French take control of Algeria
• **1658** Aurangzeb becomes Mogul ruler • **1661–1722** Reign of K'ang-hsi: Manchus conquer all of China	• **1709** Afghan state wins independence from Persia • **1736–1795** Height of Ch'ing Dynasty under Emperor Ch'ien-lung	• **1765** Chinese invade Burma • **1769** Famine kills one third of the population of Bengal, India	• **1825** Javanese revolt against Dutch rule • **1829** Western Australia colonized by British settlers • **1839–1842** Opium War; Chinese ports opened to foreign trade • **1842** Hong Kong becomes British territory • **1845** British suppress Sikhs in India

	1850	1900	1950	2000
EUROPE	• 1851 Crystal Palace exhibition in London • 1852–1870 Second French Empire • 1854–1856 Crimean War • 1854 Florence Nightingale pioneers modern nursing • 1855–1899 Literature: Baudelaire, Ibsen, Tolstoy, Dostoevsky, Shaw, Zola • 1859 Darwin's *Origin of Species* • 1860–1899 Music: Wagner, Brahms, Tchaikovsky • 1875–1890 Art: Impressionism • 1885 Pasteur's rabies vaccination	• 1901 Freud's *Psychotherapy of Everyday Life* • 1905 Einstein's theory of relativity • 1914–1918 World War I • 1917–1918 Bolshevik Revolution in Russia • 1921 Irish Free State formed • 1922 Mussolini assumes control in Italy • 1933 Hitler becomes German chancellor • 1936–1939 Spanish Civil War • 1938 Germany annexes Austria • 1939–1945 World War II • 1947 Marshall Plan established	• 1955 Warsaw Pact • 1956 Revolutions in Hungary and Poland • 1957 USSR launches *Sputnik* • 1957 Common Market founded in Europe • 1961 Berlin Wall built • 1968 Soviets invade Czechoslovakia • 1975 Helsinki Accords • 1975 Franco dies • 1980 Strikes in Poland • 1985 Gorbachev: *Glasnost* in USSR	
AFRICA	• 1873 The Asante fight British troops in West Africa • 1875 Stanley explores Congo River • 1879 Zulu War begins • 1884 Sudanese defeat British at Khartoum • 1684–1885 Belgium takes control of Congo • 1889 Italy claims Ethiopia as an Italian protectorate • 1896 Italian invaders are defeated by Ethiopians • 1899–1902 Boer War	• 1910 British South African colonies unite	• 1952–1956 Mau-Mau rebellion in Kenya • 1957 Ghana gains independence under leadership of Kwame Nkrumah • 1960 French colonies assert independence • 1960 African National Congress banned; Nelson Mandela imprisoned for life • 1963 Organization of African Unity founded; Kenya gains independence • 1978 Rhodesia renamed Zimbabwe • 1980s Apartheid laws increasingly challenged in Republic of South Africa	
THE AMERICAS	• 1851 Harriet B. Stowe: *Uncle Tom's Cabin* • 1859 John Brown's attack on Harper's Ferry • 1861–1865 Civil War in United States • 1862 Lincoln's Emancipation Proclamation • 1867 Canada becomes a British dominion • 1879 Edison invents incandescent lamp • 1884 Boston and New York City are connected by telephone • 1888 Eastman produces Kodak camera box • 1888 Serfdom ends in Brazil • 1896 Henry Ford makes his first car • 1898 Spanish-American War	• 1910 Mexican Revolution • 1914 Panama canal completed • 1917 United States enters World War I • 1927 First full-length film with sound • 1929 Stock market crash: beginning of the Great Depression • 1933 Roosevelt implements the New Deal • 1941 United States enters World War II • 1943–1955 Peron dominates Argentina • 1945 United States drops atomic bombs on Japan • 1946 United Nations founded	• 1959 Cuban Revolution • 1962 Cuban missile crisis • 1966 National Organization of Women founded • 1968 Martin Luther King assassinated • 1969 U.S. astronauts walk on moon • 1972 U.S. and USSR sign SALT I treaty • 1979 Sandinista government deposes Somoza in Nicaragua • 1983 Civilian rule restored in Argentina • 1985 Nuclear arms reduction talks resume between United States and USSR • 1987 Intermediate-range Nuclear Forces (INF) Treaty	
MIDDLE EAST	• 1869 Suez Canal completed • 1879 Britain and France resume joint control over Egypt • 1881 Tunisia becomes French protectorate	• 1914 Egypt declared British protectorate • 1917 Balfour Declaration favors establishment of Jewish homeland • 1925 Arabs revolt against French in Syria • 1945 Syria becomes independent • 1945 League of Arab Nations established • 1946 Lebanon becomes independent • 1948 Israel founded; first Arab-Israeli war	• 1954 Nasser becomes leader of Egypt • 1956 Egypt nationalizes Suez Canal • 1960 OPEC formed • 1964 PLO formed • 1967 Six-Day War • 1973 Yom Kippur War; OPEC oil embargo • 1975 Civil war begins in Lebanon • 1978 Camp David Accords between Egypt and Israel • 1979 Iranian Revolution: Shah deposed • 1980 Beginning of Iraqi-Iranian War • 1981 Anwar Sadat of Egypt assassinated	
ASIA	• 1852 Taiping Rebellion in China • 1872 Philippine rebellion against Spanish rule • 1877 Queen Victoria proclaimed Empress of India • 1882 Repressive measures taken against Jews in Russia • 1887 France creates Union of Indochina • 1889 Japan establishes a parliament • 1894 Japan declares war on Russia • 1898 United States organizes overthrow of Hawaii's monarchy, annexes the islands	• 1901 Boxer Rebellion • 1904–1905 Russo-Japanese War • 1910 Japan annexes Korea • 1912 Republic established in China • 1921 Chinese Communist party founded • 1922 Gandhi imprisoned by British • 1927 Stalin assumes control over Russia; Trotsky expelled • 1931 Japanese invade Manchuria • 1941 Japanese attack Pearl Harbor • 1947 India becomes independent • 1949 People's Republic of China established	• 1950 North Korea invades South Korea • 1954 French withdraw from Indochina • 1957–1975 Vietnam War • 1966–1969 Cultural Revolution in China • 1971 Bangladesh declares independence • 1979 China and United States establish full diplomatic relations • 1979 USSR invades Afghanistan • 1986 Rebellion in Philippines: Aquino succeeds Marcos as national leader	

Europe includes Western and Eastern Europe.
Africa includes sub-Saharan Africa.
The Americas include North America and South America.
Middle East includes North Africa and Southwest Asia.
Asia includes East Asia, South Asia, and Southeast Asia.

Certain words in the Glossary and in the text have been respelled as an aid to pronunciation. A key to pronouncing the respelled words follows.

The words in the Glossary are defined to clarify their meaning in the text. The page numbers given after the definitions refer to the places in the text where the words first appear. Occasionally, a vocabulary term is used again later in the book in a way different from the definition given. In these cases, a second definition is provided along with the page number identifying where the second usage first appears. The words selected for definition in the Glossary are important in world history.

PRONUNCIATION KEY

Like certain other words in this book, the name *Sophocles* has been respelled to indicate its pronunciation: SOF-uh-KLEEZ. The large capital letters mean that the first syllable should be spoken with a major stress. The small capital letters mean that the third syllable should be spoken with a minor stress. The vowel sounds shown by the letters *o*, *uh*, and *ee* correspond to the vowel sounds in the pronunciation key.

Pronounce

a	as in	hat	j		jet
ah		father	ng		ring
ar		tar	o		frog
ay		say	ō, oh		no
ayr		air	oo		soon
e, eh		hen	or		for
ee		bee	ow		plow
eer		deer	oy		boy
er		her	sh		she
ew		new	th		thick
g		go	u, uh		sun
i, ih		him	z		zebra
ī		kite	zh		measure

abolitionists: opponents of slavery (page 567)

absolutism: a system of government in which a monarch is the only source of power, controlling all functions of the state (page 381)

Agricultural Revolution: a turning point in history when people began to grow their own food instead of relying on hunting and gathering (page 10)

ancestor worship: the practice of honoring the wisdom and guidance of ancestors (page 58)

animistic: reflecting a belief that spirits or deities inhabit natural elements, such as sand, rocks, and plants (page 290)

anthropologists: scientists who study human beings and how they live in groups (page 6)

apartheid: a policy that divides schools, workplaces, and housing by strict laws to keep races from mixing in any way (page 766)

apostles: followers of a teacher; the name that Jesus gave to his followers (page 141)

appeasement: a policy of giving in to the demands of an aggressor to avoid war (page 693)

archaeologists: scientists who specialize in searching for clues about how human beings lived in the past (page 6)

aristocrats: members of the old, landowning noble families who made up the most powerful social class (page 78)

artifacts: small movable objects made by human hand that are clues to past cultures (page 6)

artisans: people who make and sell tools, clothing, and other items (page 14)

assimilation: the absorption of a people into the culture of another nation (page 582)

bakufu: a form of military government in Japan made up of a group of military leaders headed by the shogun (page 294)

balance of power: the prevention of any one nation from becoming too powerful (page 386)

barter: a system of payment in which goods or work of equal value are exchanged (page 24)

Bedouins: nomadic Arab herders living in tribes ruled by an elected chief (page 254)

blitzkrieg: a German word meaning "lightning war" that describes a surprise attack (page 693)

bourgeoisie: members of the European middle class (page 368)

boyars: Russian landed nobles and wealthy merchants (page 194)

boycott: a form of protest in which people refuse to buy goods (page 601)

buffer state: a neutral zone (page 561)

bureaucracy: a system set up to carry out the affairs of government through departments managed by appointed officials (page 163)

canton: a local district in Switzerland (page 342)

capital: large pools of money available to invest in business ventures (page 366)

capitalism: economic system in which persons invest money in the means of production or distribution, hoping to gain a profit, and businesses compete freely for markets (page 366); an economic system that is based on the idea of free enterprise (page 481)

cartel: an organization formed to regulate the production and to control the price of a product that is produced by its members (page 753)

cash crops: crops grown for the world market, not for local consumption (page 584)

caste system: a system of social classes in which members' social life is restricted to the class into which they were born (page 159)

cataracts: steep rapids (page 30)

caudillismo: a leadership style in Latin America; ruling by force (page 560)

chivalry: a code of conduct for knights and nobles that developed in the 1100s (page 239)

citizen: a resident of a Greek city-state granted definite rights and responsibilities by that city-state (page 76)

city-states: political units, each consisting of a city and its surrounding farm land dotted with villages (page 21)

civil rights: rights guaranteed to all people by their nation's laws and constitution (page 728)

civil service: a system of hiring government workers by examination (page 163)

civilization: a society in which a high level of art, technology, and government has been achieved (page 13)

cold war: a state of tension and hostility between two world powers (page 717)

commons: grazing lands and forests around the villages of a manor which were shared by everyone (page 214)

communism: a final stage of socialism in which there would be no social classes, cooperation would replace competition, and everyone's needs would be met equally (page 494); a system in which all the nation's economic resources are owned by the people and controlled by the government (page 791)

concessions: rights acquired from a government to use land for oil production (page 749)

conquistadors: Spanish explorers sent by their monarch to discover and conquer new lands and peoples (page 356)

conscription: the drafting of eligible persons into military service (page 460)

conservatism: a political philosophy of absolutist rule by aristocrats (page 516)

consul: a person who looks after a nation's citizens and commercial interests in a foreign country (page 607)

containment: a policy of the United States to halt the spread of Communist influence (page 718)

corporation: an economic unit, formed by law to act as a single "person," whose main purpose is to provide capital and a pool of management talent (page 481)

coups: sudden changes in government by force of arms (page 769)

covenant: a solemn agreement (page 39)

creoles: people born in the Latin American colonies of European parents (page 359)

cubism: a school of art having a complicated, careful way of looking at objects and influenced by photography and movies (page 664)

cultural bridge: a link between two civilizations (page 73)

cultural diffusion: the sharing and blending of ideas and customs between groups of people (page 15)

culture: the way of life of a people, including their arts, beliefs, inventions, traditions, and language (page 3)

culture areas: the nine major groups of native North American peoples defined by anthropologists according to geographical area (page 313)

cuneiform: Sumerian writing, made by pressing a reed tool with a wedge-shaped tip into wet clay tablets which harden to form a permanent record (page 25)

czar: Russian word for "emperor" (page 389)

decentralized government: rule based on the power of local leaders who are not controlled by a strong higher authority (page 203)

deities: gods and goddesses who controlled the lives of human beings (page 12)

delta: an area of land formed from sand and soil deposited by a river (page 20)

democracy: a form of government in which the people hold the power to rule (page 78)

dependency: a situation in which a nation's economy is strongly influenced by foreign nations (page 571)

depression: a widespread decline in economic activity (page 653)

desertification: the transformation of useful land into desert (page 768)

détente: lessening of tensions (page 722)

direct democracy: a democracy in which every citizen participates in political decision making (page 80)

dissidents: Soviet citizens who are outspoken critics of the Soviet system (page 723)

division of labor: organization of the manufacturing process into separate jobs (page 483)

dogma: established teachings (page 343)

domestic system: a manufacturing system that organized people to work at home and sell their products to a manufacturer (page 367)

domesticate: to tame animals for human use (page 12)

domino theory: the idea that when one country's government falls to communism, the neighboring countries' governments would then topple—like a row of dominoes (page 720)

dynasty: series of rulers from the same family (page 31)

economic sanctions: rules forbidding trade with a nation (page 690)

embargo: restriction of trade (page 755)

empire: a government uniting different territories and peoples under one ruler (page 21)

enclosure movement: fencing in of land traditionally available for common use (page 472)

enlightened despotism: a political philosophy that proposed rule by a monarch whose decisions were based on rational thought rather than tradition or whim (page 439)

entente: a friendly understanding between nations (page 552)

entrepreneurs: people who risk organizing a business to make a profit (page 225)

epic: a story-length poem (page 74)

Epicureanism: the belief that pleasure is the highest good (page 103)

ethical monotheism: a doctrine that associates an emphasis on ethical behavior with the belief in one god (page 41)

ethics: a code of conduct (page 41)

evolution: the idea that all forms of life have developed from earlier, simpler forms through natural selection (page 503)

evolved: developed over time by gradual changes (page 4)

extended family: several generations of family members living in the same household, with other family members living nearby (page 53)

extraterritoriality: the exemption of foreigners from the authority of local officials (page 602)

fascism: a form of totalitarianism in which the state assumes supreme power through the rule of a nationalist dictator (page 676)

feudal monarchies: governments in which monarchs rule over kingdoms unified by feudal ties (page 230)

feudalism: a political system based on small, local units controlled by lords bound by an oath of loyalty to a monarch (page 215)

fief: lands granted to vassals in return for loyalty and military service to a more powerful lord (page 215)

forum: the public square in an ancient Roman city (page 113)

fossils: the remains or impressions of human, animal, or plant life preserved in rock (page 6)

free enterprise: the freedom to do business in a competitive market with little regulation or interference by government (page 481)

frescoes: paintings on wet plaster (page 72)

friars: Franciscan monks who traveled from town to town preaching (page 235)

genocide: the attempt to kill an entire ethnic group (page 698)

guerrilla warfare: a type of warfare using hit-and-run tactics (page 541)

guild: an alliance of merchants or artisans (page 226)

haiku: a form of Japanese poetry containing 17 syllables in 3 lines (page 405)

hellenization: the spreading of Greek influence (page 100)

heresy: a belief opposed to established church teachings (page 184)

hieroglyphics: Egyptian writing that combined pictures or symbols for ideas and words with those for sounds (page 35)

high-tech: technology that is very specialized and complex (page 737)

Holocaust: the mass killing of 6 million Jews by the Nazis (page 698); total destruction of life (page 814)

humanism: a way of thinking that focuses upon the concerns of humankind (page 329)

iconoclasts: people who oppose the use of religious images or icons (page 184)

icons: images of religious figures (page 182)

ideology: the official political philosophy of a state (page 673)

imperialism: a policy used by strong countries to gain social, political, and economic control over weaker countries (page 542)

import-substitution: the domestic production of industrial goods that are usually imported from foreign industrial nations (page 773)

impressionism: a nineteenth-century movement in painting in which artists rejected traditional realistic styles and tried instead to capture impressions of fleeting moments by using patches of color (page 500)

individualistic: a point of view focusing on the happiness of the individual, not on the welfare or good of society (page 104)

industrialization: the shift in manufacturing from handwork done in homes by individual artisans to production of goods using power-driven machines in factories (page 471)

isolationism: a government policy of non-involvement in foreign affairs (page 639)

jihad: a righteous struggle on behalf of Islam; a holy war (page 255)

joint-stock company: a business organization formed to raise capital by the scale of shares in the organization to investors (page 367)

kabuki: a type of Japanese theater that features popular drama with a mixture of older, stylized acting and dancing traditions (page 405)

karma: the belief that one's actions determine how one's soul will be reborn (page 54)

kowtow: the act of kneeling and touching the ground with one's forehead to show submission to the Chinese monarch (page 397)

laissez faire: the policy of letting business operate without government regulation (page 489)

landed aristocracy: nobles who owned land (page 453)

latifundia: large Roman estates composed of a number of small farms (page 123)

limited constitutional monarchy: a system of government in which the power of a monarch is limited by a constitution (page 381)

lineage: a direct line of relationship to a particular ancestor (page 308)

machismo: the traditional Latin American belief in masculine strength (page 778)

mandate: an order or command from a higher authority (page 61); a former colonial territory placed under the protection of the League of Nations after World War I (page 639)

manorialism: an economic and social system based on self-sufficient estates made up of small villages and farms (page 214)

martyrs: people who choose to die rather than to give up their beliefs (page 143)

Marxism: a form of socialism in which all land and all means of production are owned by the workers (page 494)

mass communication: methods of communication such as newspapers, radio, and magazines designed to reach large numbers of people (page 669)

mass production: the manufacture of products using standard parts (page 478)

mechanistic world view: the belief that the universe is like a machine (page 433)

mercantilism: the theory that a nation is strengthened by government control of its economic interests (page 367)

mercenaries: paid soldiers from other lands (page 121)

mestizos: the offspring of Native American and Spanish or Portuguese parents (page 359)

migrate: to move from place to place (page 4)

militarism: a policy of reliance on military power in government (page 386)

minimum wage: the lowest amount that a worker can be paid (page 524)

mobilize: to organize resources for combat (page 627)

monarchy: a system of government in which a king or queen has total power (page 78)

monasteries: residences isolated from the outside world where Christians called monks lived, worked, and practiced their faith (page 147)

monopoly: exclusive control of the sale and price of a certain product or service (page 365)

monotheism: belief in one god (page 33)

monsoon: a seasonal wind (page 48)

mosaics: pictures or designs made of bits of stone, glass, and enamel (page 180)

mosques: places for Islamic worship (page 256)

mulattoes: people born of European and black parents (page 359)

multinational corporations: companies with their headquarters in one nation and branches or operations in many nations (page 808)

mystic: one who believes that spiritual truths can be learned through contemplation and faith rather than human reason (page 235)

Napoleonic Code: a series of laws written by Napoleon that guaranteed the equality of all citizens before the law (page 463)

nationalism: the love of one's nation (page 461); the desire for and support of independence for one's nation (page 655)

negritude: effort to emphasize the culture and achievements of black Africans (page 771)

nomads: people who move from place to place in search of food (page 8)

objectivity: the use of reason, without emotion, intuition, or appeal to supernatural forces (page 431)

oligarchy: a form of government in which a few rule over many (page 78)

papyrus: a paper made by the Egyptians from reeds that grew along the Nile (page 35)

partisans: resistance fighters in a conquered nation (page 697)

partition: division of one nation into separate nations (page 785)

paternalism: the attitude of colonial administrators that they should behave toward those governed as parents behave toward children (page 582)

patriarchal: reflecting the belief that the oldest male is the head of the family and that male family elders are heads of the tribe (page 52)

patricians: the Roman upper class of wealthy landowners (page 114)

patrons: people who support and encourage some person or institution (page 330)

peaceful coexistence: a policy between nations of maintaining peaceful relations and not interfering in each other's affairs (page 720)

pharaoh: a title given to rulers of ancient Egypt (page 31)

philosophy: the study of knowledge, ideas, and ethics (page 86)

plebeians: Roman citizens who were farmers, merchants, laborers, or artisans (page 114)

polis: an ancient Greek city-state (page 76)

polytheism: belief in many deities (page 24)

popular culture: entertainment that appeals to a mass audience (page 737)

potlatches: great feasts held by Native Americans of the northwestern coastal area (page 314)

predestination: the Christian doctrine that God has already determined everything that will happen, including who will have eternal life and who will be condemned (page 342)

prehistory: the extremely long period before writing was invented (page 3)

primogeniture: the practice of limiting the inheritance of family property to the oldest son (page 461)

principalities: territories, each of which is governed by a ruler whose rank is less than king or queen (page 61)

proletariat: the working class (page 494)

propaganda: the spreading of ideas to promote a given cause or damage an opposing cause (page 629)

prophets: persons believed to speak with divine guidance (page 41)

protectorates: countries under the protection and control of stronger nations (page 546)

rationality: the belief that the use of reason is the key to gaining knowledge (page 431)

Realpolitik: a political strategy in which whatever means necessary are used to achieve practical goals (page 538)

Reconstruction: a period of federal military occupation of the South following the Civil War in the United States (page 567)

reich: the name for the German Empire unified under Kaiser Wilhelm (page 539); name for Germany under the Nazis (page 680)

reparations: payments for damages caused by war (page 637)

republic: a form of government run by representatives elected by the citizens (page 114)

Romance languages: the Latin-based languages, which include French, Italian, Portuguese, Romanian, and Spanish (page 130)

Romanticism: an artistic movement of the late 1700s and early 1800s that emphasized simplicity and naturalness, creativity, freedom of expression, emotion, and individualism (page 495)

samurai: in feudal Japan, a warrior class whose duty it was to serve the lords (page 294)

sanctions: a blockade, an action usually taken by several nations together to force a country to obey a law (page 759)

savanna: a type of flat, tropical grassland dotted with trees (page 301)

scholasticism: a philosophy in which human reason and faith are compatible (page 237)

scientific method: a method of gathering and interpreting information that follows a fixed pattern of research (page 431)

secular: nonreligious (page 340)

serfs: peasants who work the lands and are tied to the service of the lord of a manor (page 214)

shareholders: people who have bought stock in a company (page 367)

shogun: title given to military rulers of Japan from the late 1100s to 1868 (page 294)

shogunate: Japanese military government from the late 1100s to the mid-1800s (page 294)

silt: fine soil carried by water (page 20)

social Darwinism: a social theory stressing "survival of the fittest" as a way to explain social and economic conditions (page 506)

socialism: a social theory in which the means of production—factories, machines, and land—are controlled or owned by government or society rather than by individuals (page 492)

society: human beings living together in a community (page 6)

solidarity: unity of purpose among union members (page 523)

soviets: small councils formed in Russia in which political and economic problems are discussed (page 644)

spheres of influence: areas in which an imperialist nation maintains sole investment or trading rights (page 546)

steppes: vast plains of Central Asia (page 15)

stock: shares in a company that are sold to individual investors (page 367)

Stoicism: a philosophy teaching that fate or destiny controls the outcome of events in each person's life (page 103)

strike: a protest in which workers stop work until employers meet their demands (page 484)

subcontinent: the large land mass of India separated from Asia by the Himalayas (page 47)

suffrage: the right to vote (page 524)

surrealism: a twentieth-century movement in art which attempted to express subconscious thoughts and emotions (page 664)

technology: methods for solving practical problems (page 8)

temperance: moderation, particularly in the use of alcoholic beverages (page 525)

terrorism: the systematic use of violence to intimidate people or their governments for political ends (page 814)

theology: religious belief system (page 206)

theory of relativity: a theory of physics stating that space and time are not fixed, and that the speed of light is the only constant (page 502)

tithe: payment of 10 percent of one's income to the Church (page 208)

totalitarianism: a system of government in which the state completely controls individuals' lives by demanding that they serve only the interests and goals of the state (page 669)

treaty port: a port that must be kept open for foreign trade (page 602)

tribe: an organized group believed to be descendants of a common ancestor (page 39)

tribute: wealth sent from one ruler or nation to another as a sign the other is supreme (page 28)

tundra: frozen plain where the ground under the surface never thaws (page 4)

turning point: a decisive change (page 10)

unions: associations of workers formed to protect their rights and interests (page 484)

urban: having to do with cities (page 14)

vassals: a lesser class of nobles in the feudal system who were given land by more powerful lords, such as counts and dukes, in return for loyalty and military service (page 215)

veto power: the right to cast a negative vote prohibiting action on an issue (page 708)

viceroy: a colonial governor representing the ruler of another nation (page 357)

war communism: Lenin's economic policy during the Russian civil war, in which the government took over factories and outlawed labor strikes (page 646)

welfare state: a nation in which the government takes responsibility for the basic needs of each citizen (page 725)

ziggurat: a grand, pyramidlike temple built in the center of each Sumerian city (page 24)

Zionism: the belief that an independent Jewish state should be established in Palestine (page 656)

Italicized page numbers preceded by an *f* or an *m* indicate a special feature (f) or a map (m). **Boldface** page numbers indicate pages on which glossary terms first appear.

Atomic bomb, 704–06, *f706*, 709, 710, 717, 814
Atomic energy. *See* Nuclear energy
Atoms, 501, 502
Augustine, St., 147, 236
Augustus, 126–29, 138
Aurangzeb (ruler), 409–10
Auschwitz, 698
Australia, 6, *f291*, 701; British expansion in, 615; and World War I, 630
Austria, 374, 392, *m638*, 639; Congress of Vienna, 511–12, *m513*; Crimean War, 537; depression in, 654; First Coalition, 460; Franco-Prussian War, 539–40; Hapsburgs in, 374, 387–88; Hitler annexes, *m692*, 692, *m709*, 710; and imperialist expansion, 552; invades France, 459, 460; partition of Poland, 391; post World War I, 650; post World War II, 707; revolution of 1848, 520; Second Coalition, 462, 464; Seven Weeks' War, *m539*, 539; Seven Years' War, 389; socialism in, 523; Third Coalition, 464; Treaty of Utrecht, 387–88; unification of German states, 536, 538–39, *m539*; unification of Italy, 540–41; War of the Austrian Succession, 388
Austria-Hungary, 646; militarism in, 624; Triple Alliance, 623; in World War I, 623, 624, *m625*, 625–27, 633–34, 636, *m638*, 638, 639, 640
Austrian Hapsburgs, 374, 387–88
Averroës, 237, 269
Avicenna, *f271*
Axis Powers, 693–98, 699, 703–05, 710
Axum Empire, Africa, 301–02, *m303*
Aztec, *m315*, 316–18; Spanish conquest of, 356

Babylon, 26, *m27*, 29, 101; Babylonia, 26–28, *m27*; Alexander the Great conquers, *m99*, 99
Babylonian Captivity, 242–

43, 340
Bach, J. S., 441
Bacon, Francis, 369, 431, 432, 444
Bacon, Roger, 237
Baghdad, 269; Abbasid Dynasty in, *m260*, 261; Seljuk Turks in, 262
Balance of power, **386–89**, 643, 727
Balboa, Vasco Núñez de, 352–53, 356
Balfour Declaration, 656
Balkans, 71, 72, *m73*, 73, 76, *m112*, 112, 145, 202, 203, 517; European imperialism in, 552; and Ottoman Empire, *m262*, 263; Pan-Slavism in, 552, 625–27, 640; Russian interest in, 589, 624–26; in World War I, *m625*, 625–27, 640
Baltic states, 696
Balzac, Honoré de, 497
Bangladesh, 785, 790, 804
Banking, 367. *See also* Commercial Revolution
Bantu migrations, 304
Baroque music, 440–41
Barter system, 24, 43
Batista, Fulgencio, 777
Bedouins, 253–54, 256, *f751*
Beethoven, Ludwig van, 496
Beijing, 791. *See also* Peking
Beirut, Lebanon, *m38*, 38, *m757*, 757
Belgium, 375, *m377*, 647, 706; African colonies, 579, *m581*, *m767*, 769–70; Congress of Vienna, 512, *m513*; and imperialist expansion, 545; industrialization in, 476; labor movement in, 484–85; and Nazi Germany, *m692*, 695, *m702*, 702–03; rebellion in, 518; and Romans, 126; World War I, 629–30, *m630*, *m633*, *m638*, 638–39
Benelux Economic Union, 724. *See also* Belgium, Netherlands, Luxembourg
Bengal, 413, 601
Ben-Gurion, David, 747
Benin, *m303*, *f307*, 307, 309, *m415*, 415–16, 417

Bentham, Jeremy, 492
Berbers, 259, 264, 591, 593, 744
Berlin, 695, 703; airlift in, 718–19; bombing of, 696, *m702*
Berlin Conference, 545–46, 581
Berlin, Congress of, 552
Berlin Wall, *m709*, 722
Bernard of Clairvaux, 235
Bernini, Gianlorenzo, 441
Bessemer, Henry, 474
Bethlehem, 141, *m143*
Bhagavad-Gita, 159
Bhutto, Benazir, 790
Biafra, 769
Bible, 41–42, 141, 334, 335, 340; and Martin Luther, *f339*, 339
Bismarck, Otto von, 538–41, 545, 546–48, 554
Black Death, 188, 221, 240–42, *f241*, *m241*, 243, 245, 246
Black Sea: and Byzantine Empire, 177–78, 188; and early Russia, 190, *m194*; and Europe, 201, *m202*; and Greek colonies, *m77*, 77; and medieval trade, *m224*, *m225*; and Persians, *m42*, 42; Russian access to, 517, 589, 625; in World War I, 630
Blacks: civil rights in U.S., 728–29, 740; and jazz, 308, 319, 661; and slavery, 358–59, 370, 525, 558, 560, 566–68, 571, 573, 578; in South Africa, 766–68
Boccaccio, Giovanni, 329
Boer War, 550–51
Boers, 417, 579
Bohemia, 377, 378, 387, 520, 624
Boleyn, Anne, 342–43
Bolívar, Simón, 559, 574
Bolivia, *m558*, *m559*, 559, 561
Bolshevik Revolution, 644–46, 665, 666. *See also* Russia
Bonaparte, Louis Napoleon. *See* Napoleon III
Bonaparte, Napoleon, 462–68, *f464*, 511, 512, 517, 528, 590
Boniface VIII, 208, 242

Borgia, Cesare, 330
Botha, P. W., 768
Bourgeoisie, **368**, 494, 513
Boxer Rebellion, 604–05
Boyars, 194, 196
Brahmans, 53, 156, 158, 159
Brazil, *f355*, *m558*, *m559*, 570, 660, 775; early land claims, 352, 354; independence in, 562; industrialization in, 773–74; slavery in, 358, 571; imperialism in, 352, 571
Brecht, Bertolt, 661, 64
Brezhnev, Leonid, 731–32
Britain, *m123*, *m128*, 202; invasion of Germanic tribes, 203; and Romans, 126, 127
British East India Company, 597–601, *m599*, 602, 616
British Empire. *See* Great Britain
Bronze, 33; Benin, *f307*, 309; Bronze Age, 14; in China, 58, 62, 63; Indus Valley, 50; Minoan, 73
Brunelleschi, Filippo, 330, *f331*
Brutus, Marcus Junius, 126
Bubonic plague, 240–42, *f241*. *See also* Black Death
Buchenwald, 698
Buddha, 156–157, *f157*, 160, 167
Buddhism: in Burma, Cambodia, and Ceylon, 157, *m158*; in China, 157, *m158*, 167, 170, 277, 281, 285; in India, 156–58, *f157*, *m158*, 160; in Japan, 157, 292–93, 295, 296; in Korea, 157; in Malaysia, 157, *m158*; in Sri Lanka, 790
Bulgaria, 188; communism in, 718, 730–33; World War I in, *m625*, 625–26; World War II in, 696, *m709*
Bureaucracy, **163**; in African colonies, 582; in China, 163–65, 166, 279, 280, 382, 398; in France, 382–83; in Russia, 390. *See also* Civil service system
Burma, 397; British imperialism in, 614;

(continued)

Mongol Empire, 283–85, *m284*, 296; nationalism in, 658–59, 666; and Open Door policy, 793; Opium Wars, 602–03, 793; Period of the Warring States, 161, 165, 168; post World War I, 658–59; post World War II, 790–94; prehistoric cities, 13; prodemocracy movement, 793; Red Guards, 792; relations with U.S., 793; relations with USSR, 397, 729, 731, 793; revolution of 1911, 605–06; Shang Dynasty, 55, 57–59, *m60*, 60, 64; Sino-Japanese War, 610; Six Dynasties period, 165; social class in, 61–62, 791; Sui Dynasty, 275–76, 296; Sung Dynasty, *m278*, 278–79, 281, 282, 283, 289, 296; T'ang Dynasty, 276–83, *m278*, 295, 296; Taiping Rebellion, 603; Taiwan, *m604*, 605–06, 790–91, 793–94; trade with Alexandrian Empire, 102; trade with Japan, 606; trade with Middle East, *f168*, 168; trade with Roman Empire, 129; treaty with Russia, 390; unification of, 275; and Vietnam War, 800; war with Japan, 604; Yuan Dynasty, 284–85, 296

Chinampas, 318

Chinese civilization, 47, 54–63, *f63*, *m55*, *m60*, 63, 64, 369; art, 169, 277, 281–82, 289, 295; achievements, 62, 63, 265, 268–69, 277, 279–80, 282, 289, 295, 334, 350; Confucianism in, 165–66, 169, 170, 281, 285, 292; education in, 277; family life, 58, 62, 280; influence on Japan, 276, 289–90, 292; literature, 281–82, 289, 295; music, 266; philosophy, 281; porcelain, 282, *f288*; religion in, 157, 165–66, 167, 170, 277, 281, 285, 289, 292, 295, 296;

slavery in, 280; Taoism in, 166; view of Europeans, 395–96; women in, 62, 277, 280; writing, 59, 63

Ch'ing Dynasty, 396–401, *m397*, 420, 601–06, 616, 658

Chivalry, **239**

Chou Dynasty, 59, *m60*, 60–63, 64, 169

Christian Church: Byzantine, 178, 179, 180–82, 184, 188, 192–93, 195, 196, 197, 198; Crusades, 188, 194, 197, 223–24, *m224*, 246, 257, 259, 262, 349, 589; early church, *f7*, 142, *m143*, 146–47, 149; Eastern Orthodox, 590; and Franks, 205, 207–12; role of priests in, 213; in Roman Empire, 150; structure of, 146–47. *See also* Protestant Church, Roman Catholic Church

Christian Holy Land. *See* Palestine

Christianity, 281, 285, 302, 308; in Africa, 579, 584, 585; and Byzantine Church, 178, 179, 180–82, 184, 188, 192–93, 195, 196, 197, 198; and colonies in New World, 349, 351; and Constantine, 146; and imperialism, 544; in Japan, 354, 404–05; in Kievan Russia, 192–93; in Middle Ages, 235; in Middle East, 146, 156–57, 744; origins of, 141–42, *m143*; and religious intolerance, 207; in Roman Empire, 140, 141–47; spread of, *m143*, 143, 145, 146–47, 149; women in, 207

Chu Hsi, 281, 289

Chu Yuan-Chang. *See* T'ai Tsu

Chun Doo Hwan, 795

Church of England, 342–43, *m344*, 346, 379

Churchill, Winston, 695–96, 700, 703, 704, 707, 718

Cicero, 138

Cities, 494, 507, 508; in Alexandrian Empire, 103;

in China, 280; growth of during Industrial Revolution, 472, 482; in Middle Ages, 221, 222–23, 226, 231, 245; in Middle East, 752; prehistoric, *f13*, 13, 16; in Roman Empire, 129; in twenty-first century, *f813*

Citizenship, 76–77, 79–80, 120, 126

City-states: in ancient Greece, 76–85, 92, 95–96, 120, 131; Hellenic, 92; Phoenician, 38; Roman, 113; Sumerian, 20–27

Civil disobedience, 658, 785

Civil rights movement, in U.S., 525, 728, 740. *See also* Blacks, Human rights

Civil service system: in China, **163**–65, 166, 277, 279, 280, 382, 398. *See also* Bureaucracy

Civil war. *See* individual countries

Civilization, **13**; development of, 3, 47, 51, 54, 63, 153; Greek influence on, 114, 131, 135, 136, 137, 138, 140; prehistoric, 12–15; Sumerian city-states, *m20*, 20–27; *See also* individual regions

Class. *See* Social class, Middle class, Working class

Claudius (ruler), 127–28

Cleisthenes, 79, 80

Clemenceau, Georges, 637

Cleopatra, 101, 126

Clive, Robert, 413

Clovis, 203–05

Cluny, 212–13

Code of Hammurabi, 27

Code of Ur-Nammu, 21, 27

Codes of law, 44; in ancient Greece, 79–80; in China, 162; in England, 231, *f232*, 234; Hammurabi, 27; Hebrew, 39–40, 41–42; Justinian, 179; Napoleonic, 463, 465, 468; Roman, 129–30, 131; Ur-Nammu, 21, 27

Cold war, **717**–18, 741

Coleridge, Samuel Taylor, 496

Collective bargaining, 485

Collective farms, 672–73, 731, 732

Colombia, *m558*, *m559*, 559, 561, 572, 773; imperialism in, 570–71

Colonialism. *See* Imperialism

Colonies, 391; in Africa, 351–52, 364, 365, 370, 577–88, *m578*, *m581*, *f585*, 591–92, 593, 594; in America, *m365*, 447–52, *m448*, *m451*, 451, 455, 468; ancient Greek, *m77*, 77–78, 113, 131; British, 360–64, *m365*, 535–36: Dutch, *m365*, 365; and European imperialism, 542–53, 577–82; French, 364–65, *m365*, 558; Portuguese, 354, *m357*; slavery in, 358; Spanish, 354–58, *m357*, 557–58

Columbus, Christopher, *f351*, 351–52

COMECON (Council for Mutual Economic Assistance), 719

Commercial Revolution, 366–67, 370, 427

Commodus (Roman ruler), 128–129, 144

Common law, 234, 379, 381. *See also* Law

Common Market, 724, 727

Commonwealth, 379, 380, 724, 729; South Africa in, 766

Communalism, in medieval society, 214

Communards, 527

Commune, Paris, 459, 486, 527

Communications: advances in during Industrial Revolution, 474–75; cross-cultural, 737; mass, 669, 685; Reuters news service, *f526*; twentieth-century innovations, 807, 808, 816

Communism, **494**, 707; Brezhnev Doctrine, 731, 733; in China, 658–59, 689–90, 729, 790–93, 804; in Czechoslovakia, 718; in Eastern Europe, 717–19, 731–33, 739; Eurocommunism, 727;

(continued)

Imperialism *(continued)*
European expansion in Africa, 577–88, *m578*, *m581*, *f585*, 593, 594, 763–70; European expansion in Latin America, 557–64; European expansion in Middle East, 589–93; and World War I, 637
Import-substitution industry, **773**–74
Impressionism, *f498*, 500, 508
Inca Empire, *f318*, 318–19, 356
Inchon, South Korea, 794
India: Age of Invasions, 154–55; agriculture in, 788, 789; British East India Company in, 364, 597–601, *m599*, 602, 616; British rule in, 412–13, *m599*, 599–601, 616; Buddhism in, 156–58, *f157*, *m158*, 160; classical, 153–61, *m155*; Delhi sultans, 407; Dravidians, 52, 54, 154; early civilizations, 13, 47–54, *m48*, *m49*; economic growth in, 788–89; European imperialism in, 544, 597–601, 616, 657–58, 666; geography of, 47–48, *m48*; Gupta Empire, 155; Hindus in, 156, *m158*, 158–59, *f159*, 597, 598, 600, 601, 658, 785–86; independence in, 601, 725, 764, 785–90, *m788*; Indian Councils Act of 1892, 600–01; Indian National Congress, 600–01, 785, 786; Kushan Empire, 155, 163; Maurya Empire, 153–54, 155; Moguls, 407–13, *m410*, 420, 597, 598; Muslims in, *m265*, 265–66, 597, 600, 601, 658, 785–86, 789; nationalism in, 600–01, 616, 657–58, 666; partition, 601, 785–86, 804; population growth in, 788; and Portuguese trade, 354; relations with Pakistan, 786, 789–90, 804; Sepoy Rebellion, 599, 616; Sikhs in, 787–88; social change in, 598,

599; Vedic Age, 52–54; World War I, 630; World War II, 785
Indian Civil Service, 599
Indian civilization, 47–54, *m48*, 63, 64; achievements, 160–61; caste system in, 53, 159–60, 170, 407, 658, 788, 789; Classical Age, 153–61, *m155*, 170; education in, 598; modern culture, 789; Mogul culture, 407, *f408*; women in, 598
Indian National Congress, 600–01, 785, 786
Indochina, 545, 615. *See also* French Indochina
Indonesia, 611, 803; Buddhism in, 157, *m158*; independence movement in, *m612*, 615, 764; Islam in, 266; prehistory, 6, 8; trade with India, 160
Indus River, India, 47, *m48*, *m49*, *m99*, 99, 153, 160, 265
Indus Valley civilization, *m49*, 49–50, 63, 64
Indus-Ganges Plain, 47, *m48*
Industrial Age, 511–20, 521
Industrial Revolution, 443, 471–86, *m477*, *f490*, 651; children in, 472–73, 485; creative effects of, 495–501, 507, 508; effects on science, 501–08; and growth of middle class, 513; role in imperialist expansion, 542–44; second revolution, 542; social effects of, 489–94; technological advances, 472–86, 507, 548; women in, 472–73, 485
Industrialization, **471**, 808; economic theories of, 491–92; in Europe, 476–77, *m477*, 489–94, 507, 508, 511, 521–25; and growth of working class, 522–23; and reform, 485, 492; and labor unions, 523; and social conflict, 511–20; in U.S., 477–78, 521–25, 567; in USSR, 672–73
Industry: assembly line, 478; cartels, 753; in China, 791; corporations,

481, 486, 808; cottage system, 472; domestic system, 367, 486; and entrepreneurs, 472; expansion of business, 491–94; factories, 269, 472–74, 478, 483–85; import-substitution industry, 773–74; "iron law of wages," 491–92; labor unions in, 523, 527, 528; in Latin America, 660, 773–74; law of competition, 491; in Middle Ages, 225; oil, *f568*, 808; post World War II, 735; steel, 473; textile, 471, 472, 478, 485; woolen, 367
INF (Intermediate-range Nuclear Forces) Treaty, 723, 724
Innocent III, 233–34, 345
Inquisition, 233, 343, 374, 430–31
Intolerable Acts, 449, 450
Inventions, 434; airplane, 808, 816; aqueducts, 136, *f137*; arch, 136; armor, 28; astrolabe, 270; atom bomb, 704, 705–06, *f706*; automobile, 808; battering ram, 28; bellows, 167; bronze, 14, 25, 58; cannon, 245; compass, magnetic, 282, 350, 808; computer, 738, 807; concrete, 136; cotton gin, 472, 478; decimal system, 160; dome, vaulted, 136; engine, internal combustion, 480; engine, steam, 473, 808; flying shuttle, 472; horse collar, padded, 222; inoculation, 160; iron, 27, 160; irrigation, 25, *f137*; Linotype machine, 480; longbow, 244; microscope, 432; paper, 168; papyrus, 35–37; plow, 222, 478; potter's wheel, 14, 25; printing, block, 282; printing press, 429; pulley, 168; radar, 695; reaper, mechanical, 478; rudder, 282; ruler, 50; screw propeller, 107; seismograph, 168–69; silk, *f57*; spinning jenny,

472; steam locomotive, 475; steamboat, 474; steam-powered loom, 472; steel, 167; suspension bridge, 168; telegraph, 475, *f526*; telescope, 430; television, 737, 810; three-field system, 222; triangular sail, 350; tubular screw, 107; type, movable, 282, 334, 346; umbrella, 167; water frame, 472; waterwheel, 136; wheel, 14, 25; wheelbarrow, 167; X-ray, 502
Investiture, lay, 233
Ionia, 76, 84, 86
Iran, 655, *m656*, 746, 754; agriculture, 10; Iran-Iraq War, *m757*, 758–59, 760; Islamic fundamentalism in, 811; oil in, 749–50, 752, 758; in OPEC, 753; revolution in, 758, 760; USSR pressure on, 750; women in, 758. *See also* Persia
Iraq, 638, 655, *m656*, 746, 751; agriculture, 10; and creation of Israel, 747; early civilizations, 19, *m20*; Iran-Iraq War, *m757*, 758–59, 760; oil in, 752; in OPEC, 753
Ireland, 661, 724; independence in, 649; strife in, 725–26
Irish Free State, 649
Iron, 27, 28, 160, 301, 473–74
Iron curtain, 718
Iroquois League, 314
Isabella, 351, 373–74
Islam, 183, *m260*, 281, 285, 303, 304, 308; in Africa, 264–65, 413–14, *m415*; in Arabia, 253–59; and Byzantine Empire, 184, 257, 259; and Crusades, 188, 194, 197, 223–24, *m224*, 246, 257, 262, 349, 589; founding of, 253–59, 272; fundamentalism in, 758, 759, 811; in Ghana, *m260*, 264; in India, *m260*, *m265*, 265–66, 597, 600, 601, 785–86, 789; in Indonesia, *m260*, 260; Islamic Empire, 257, 259–63, 272; Koran, 255,

Mozart, Wolfgang, 441
Muckrakers, 525–26
Muhammad, 254–56, 257–59, 270, 272
Muhammad, Askia, 414
Mulattoes, **359**, 560
Murals, 664, 781
Muscovy, 195–97
Music: in Africa, 772–73; Baroque, 440–41; during Enlightenment, 441; jazz, 308, 319, 661; in Latin America, 781; medieval, 238; post World War II, 737; realism and naturalism in, 497–500; during Renaissance, *f332*; Romantic, 495
Muslim League, 601, 785
Muslims, 253, 259, 369; in Africa, *m260*, 264–65, 585; and Christians, 207, 374; and Crusades, 223–24; in India, *m265*, 265–66, 597, 600, 601, 658, 785–86; influence on European thought, 428; influence on Mogul art and literature, 407, *f408*; invade Byzantine Empire, *m180*, 183, 184; invade Gaul, 207; invade Italy, 212, *m213*; in Lebanon, 746; in Moorish Spain, 263–64, *f271*; in Pakistan, 787, *m788*, 789–90; scientific achievements, 236, 264, 270, *f271*; Shiite, 257, 259, 272, 744, 756–57, 758; in Southeast Asia, *m266*, 266, *m268*, 611; Sunni, 257, 259, 272, 744, 756–57, 758; trade routes, 267–68, *m268*. *See also* Arabs, Islam, Middle East
Mussolini, Benito, 675–77, 679, 686, 690, 691, 692, 695, 696, 701
Mutsuhito, Crown Prince. *See* Meiji
Mwenemutapa, 417
Mycenae, *m73*, 73–76, 92; and Trojan War, 74
Mythology, 81–82, *f83*

Nagasaki, 704, 705
Napoleon Bonaparte. *See* Bonaparte, Napoleon
Napoleon III, 526–27, 535, 536, 537, 540–41, 554,

562–64
Napoleonic Code, 463, 465, 468
Napoleonic Empire, 462–67, *m465*
Nara, Japan, 292–93
Nasser, Gamal Abdel, 747, 750, 751, 752, 754–55, 760
Nation-states, 373–92, 553
National Assembly (France), 455, 458, 519, 527
National Congress party (India), 657–58
National Organization for Women (NOW), 728
National People's party. *See* Kuomintang
National Socialist German Workers' party. *See* Nazi party
Nationalism, 234, 379, 461, 465, 466, 489, 512, 516, 517, 520, 538, 540–41, 553; in Africa, 656–57, 763–70, 782; in China, 658–59; and creative expression, 495–97; in eastern Europe, 552, 623; in German states, 538; in India, 600–02, 616, 657–58, 785; in Italy, 675–77; in Japan, 683–84; in Latin America, 659–60, 773, 781; in Middle East, 655–56, *m656*, 746; in Nazi Germany, 678–82; post World War I, 655–60; and resistance to European imperialism, 593, 594; in Spain, 691
Nationalist party (Germany), 679–80
Nationalist party (Taiwan), 790–91, 793–94, 804
Native Americans, 351, 359, 361, 729; and Christianity, 357; enslavement of, 354, 357–58, 370; in Latin America, 315–19, *m315*, 320; in North America, 311–14, 320
NATO, 718–19
Naturalism, 500, 501
Navajo, 314
Navigation, 282, 350, 428
Nazareth, 141
Nazi party, 678–82, 685, 686; and persecution of Jews, 681–82;

propaganda, 681, *f682*
Neanderthals, 8–9, 16
Nebuchadnezzar, 29, 40
Negritude, **771**
Nehru, Jawaharlal, 786
Neoclassical art and literature, 441–42
Neo-Confucianism, 281, 289, 296
Neolithic Age, 7, 10–12, 16
Nero, 127–28, 143
Neruda, Pablo, 780
Nerva (Roman ruler), 128
Netherlands, 373, 374, 392, 460; Congress of Vienna, 518; invasion by Nazi Germany, 695; Renaissance in, 335; revolt against Spanish rule, 375; and trade, 365, 367, 368, 370, 375, 405, 406, 411, 417, 606, 607, 612
Nevsky, Alexander, 195
New Deal, 653–54
New Economic Policy (NEP), 670
New Granada, 557, 560
New Kingdom, 33, *f36*
New People's Army (NPA), 801
New Stone Age, 7, 10–12, 16
New Testament, 141, 147
New World, 352–53, 354–70; goods from, 368–69; slavery in, 358; treasure, 354, 356, 360, 361, 376. *See also* Americas and individual countries
New York Stock Exchange, 651–53
New Zealand, 615
Newcomen, Thomas, 473
Newspapers, 439, *f526*
Newton, Isaac, 432, 444, 501, 502
Ngo Dinh Diem (ruler), 799–800
Nicaragua, *m558*, *m559*, 561, 572, 777
Nicene Creed, 147
Nicholas I (czar), 518, 537
Nicholas II (czar), 552, 624, 634, 643–44, 645, 666
Niger River, 300, 303, 304
Nigeria, *m767*, 769–70
Nightingale, Florence, 537
Nile River, 19–20, *m20*, *m38*, 39, *m99*, 99, *m300*, 300, 750; valley, *m30*, 30–37, 301

Nineteenth Amendment, 525
Ninety-Five Theses, *f339*, 340
Nineveh, 28
Nixon, Richard M., 729, 793, 800
Nkomo, Joshua, 766
Nkrumah, Kwame, 764, 766
NKVD (secret police), 675
No plays, 405
Nobunaga, Oda, 401, 404
Nomadic peoples: art of, *f191*; Bedouin, 253–54, 256, *f751*; central Asian, 194; farming tools of, 222; Germanic tribes, 203; Magyars, 212; in Manchuria, 279; Middle Eastern, 19; migration to North America, 311–12; Mongols, 283–85, 296; steppes, *f190*, 190; Stone Age, 8, 9; Turks, 276
Normandy, 212, 231, 702
Normans, 188, 212
North Africa, 111, 112, 545, 589; agriculture, 752; European imperialism in, 551, 591–92, 593, 594, 746, 743; Islam in, 259, 261, 263–64, 271, 744, 760; modernization in, 749–53, 759, 760; nationalism in, 656; and Ottoman Empire, 263; Punic Wars, 121–22; self-rule in, 743, 747–48, 760; World War II in, 696, 701, 710
North America, 299, 349, *m448*, *m451*; colonies in, 352–58, 360–61, 364, *m365*, 365, 391; early cultures, 312–14, 319, 320; French and Indian War, 389, 448, 449; Huguenot migration to, 382; Industrial Revolution in, 477–80; revolution in 447–52, *m448*, *m451*, 468; slavery in, 361; War of the Austrian Succession, 388. *See also* Americas, Canada, New World, United States
North Atlantic Treaty Organization. *See* NATO
North Korea, 720, *m794*, 794, 795. *See also* Korea

Religion *(continued)*
346; in China, 58, 62–63, 165–67, 277; Christianity, 140, 141–43, 145, 146–47, 302, 308; Confucianism, 165–66, 167, 170, 281, 285, 292; in early Russia, 192–93; Hinduism, 156, *m158*, 158–59, *f159*, 170; in India, 156–59, *m158*, *f159*; Islam, 183, 184, 253–72, 281, 285, 303, 304, 308; in Japan, 295; Judaism, 39, 40–41, 141, 142, 281, 302, 308; in Latin America, 359; Lutheranism, 339–40; in Mogul Empire, 409–10, 420; monotheism, 33, 41; neo-Confucianism, 281, 289, 296; in Persian Empire, 43; polytheism, 24, 81–82; prehistoric, *f13*, 13–14; in Roman Empire, 119, 140, 141–43, 145, 146–47, 150; and Scientific Revolution, 429–31, 433; Shintoism, 290–92, 295; Stone Age, 12; Sumerian, 24; Taoism, 166, 167, 170, 281, 285; Zen, 295; Zoroastrianism, 43, 105, 281. *See also* Roman Catholic Church
Renaissance, 327–38, *f332*, 345, 346, 349, 373, 427, 429
Renoir, Auguste, 500
Reparations, **637**, 639, 647, 707
Republic, **114**
Republic of China, 605–06. *See also* China, Taiwan
Republic of Ireland, 649
Republic of Korea. *See* South Korea
Republic of South Africa. *See* South Africa
Restoration, in England, 380
Reuters News Service, *f526*
Revolutions of 1848, 518–20, 526–27, 528
Revolutions of 1830, 517–18, 527, 528
Rhine River, 126, 148, 203
Rhineland, 512, 691, 710
Rhodes, Cecil, 545
Rhodesia, 587, 766, *m767*. *See also* Zimbabwe

Ricardo, David, 491–92
Richard III (England), 242
Richelieu, Cardinal, 378
Richthofen, von, Baron Manfred, 630
Rickenbacker, Eddie, 630
Rig Veda, 53, 54
Rivera, Diego, 664
Roads, 28, 43, *f125*, 129, 136, 162, 284, 474, *f490*
Robespierre, Maximilien, 459, 460–61
Rockefeller, John D., *f568*
Rococo, 441
Rodin, Auguste, 498, 500
Roentgen, Wilhelm, 502
Roh Tae Woo, 795
Roman Catholic Church, 188, 192, *m344*; Babylonian Captivity, 242–43, 340; Catholic Reformation, 327, 343–44, 345, 346; corruption in, 243–44; and Crusades, 188, 223–24, *m224*; early, 142, 146–47, 149; and Enlightenment, 442, 444; and Frankish kingdom, 205, 207–12, 218; and French Revolution, 452–53, 455, 458, 464; Great Schism in, 243–44, 340; Henry VIII breaks with, 342–43, 379; and Holy Roman Empire, 232–33; iconoclasm controversy, 184, 208; Inquisition, 233, 343, 430; in Latin America, 357, 359; and liberation theology, 779; in medieval politics, 208, 230–31, 233, 246; medieval revival of learning, 235, 246; in Middle East, 744; in New World, 357–58; in Philippines, 612; and Protestant Reformation, 338–45, *f339*, *m344*, 345, 346; reform in, 212–13, 218; during Renaissance, 334, 335, 338–39; and Scientific Revolution, 429–30; split from Byzantine Church, 180, 184, 195, 198, 205–06, 208, 223; taxes, 233; and witch craze, 344–45
Roman civilization, 107, 111–49, *m112*, *m123*, *m128*; achievements,

135–40, 150; agriculture, 221–22; army in, 120, 121, *f122*, 124, 126, 127, 129; cities in, 129; Eastern Roman Empire, 145–46, 147, 149, 178, 198; fall of, 177, 183, 201, 203, 214, 327; Germanic tribes invade, 144, 145, 147–48, *m148*, 149; influence on Africa, 301, 302; influence of ancient Greeks on, 113, 122, 131, 135, 136, 137, 138, 140, 149; influence of on Renaissance, 328, 329, 330, 346; law in, 129–30; and oppression of Jews, 141; religion in, 140, 150; slavery in, 131, 137, 146, 149; social reforms, 124, 126; and spread of Christianity, 141–43, *m143*, 145–47, 150; system of roads, *f125*, 129, 136; and trade, 129, 160, *f168*, 168
Roman Empire, 120, 127–32, *m128. See also* Roman civilization
Roman law, 179, 197, 328
Roman Republic, 111–26, *m112*, *m123*, 132. *See also* Roman civilization
Romance languages, 113, **130**, 149
Romanesque architecture, 238
Romania, 552, 625; communism in, 718; post World War I, 649–50; Soviet influence in, 730–33; World War II in, 696
Romanov Dynasty, 389–91
Romanticism, 442, 489, **495**–97, 508
Rome: Christianity in, 142–43, 144; early history, 112–13; founder of, 138; geography of, 111–12, *f125*, 131; Papal States, 206, 208; during Renaissance, 332; and unification of Italy, 540–41. *See also* Roman Catholic Church, Roman civilization, Roman Empire, Roman Republic
Rome, Bishop of, 184. *See also* Italy, Papacy, and individual popes by name
Roosevelt, Franklin D.,

653–54, 660, 696, 699, 700, 702, 703, 704, 707
Roosevelt, Theodore, 572
Rosas, Juan Manuel de, 560–61
Rosetta Stone, *f35*
Rothko, Mark, 737
Roundheads, 379
Rousseau, Jean Jacques, 435–38, 442
Roy, Ram Mohan, 598, 600
Rubber, 543
Rubens, Peter Paul, 441
Rudder, 282, 350
Rurik Dynasty, 389
Russia, 177, 190, 198, 202, *m390*; absolutism in, 389–91, 392; and Aegean port, 552; Bolshevik (October) Revolution, 634, 644–46, 665, 666; border disputes with China, *m397*, 397; Byzantine influence on, 188, 189, 192–93, 196, 197; civil war in, 645–46, 665; Communist party in, 645, 646, 670–75, 686; Congress of Berlin, 552; Congress of Vienna, 511–12, *m513*; Crimean War, 537, 589, 590; Crusades, 194; feudalism in, 391–92; free election in, 645; geography of, 189, *m202*, *f671*; and Greek war of independence, 517; Imperial Russia, 644; and imperialist expansion, 552, 548; Kievan Russia, 190–95, *m194*; militarism in, 624–25; Mongols in, 195, 196, 197, 389; Muscovy, 195–97; 1905 revolt, 643; 1917 revolution in, 633–34, 639, 640, 643–44, 666; and Ottoman Empire, 391, 589; post World War I, 643–44; Red Army, 645–46, 705, 709; Romanov Dynasty, 634; Russo-Turkish War of 1877–1878, 552, 589; Second Coalition, 462, 464; sphere of influence in China, *m604*, 604; Third Coalition, 464; trade with Japan, 607; Treaty of Portsmouth, 610; treaty with China,

390; treaty with Napoleon, 465; treaty with Persia, 592–93; Triple Entente, 623; war with Japan, 610, 643; and warm water port, 625; White Army, 645–46, 669, 670; and World War I, 623, 624–25, 626, 627, 629–30, 633–35. *See also* Union of Soviet Socialist Republics

Russian Orthodox Church, 390

Russo-Japanese War, 610

Rutherford, Ernest, 502

Sadat, Anwar, 755-56

Sahara Desert, 19, 299, 300

Saigon, Vietnam, 799. *See also* Ho Chi Minh City

St. Lawrence River, 364

St. Peter's Church, 332, 340

St. Petersburg, 390

Salamis, 85, 86

Salons, 439-40

SALT I, II, 722-23

Samurai, **294**, 295, 404, 406, 608

Sanctions, **758**

Sandinistas, 777

San Martín, José de, 559-60, 574

Sankore Mosque, 414

Sanskrit, 54

Santa Anna, Antonio López de, 561

Santander, Francisco de Paula, 561

Sappho, 88

Sardinia, 460, 540-41, *m541*

Sargon (Sumerian king), 21, 26

Satrapy, 42

Saudi Arabia, *m656*, 746; formation of, 656; modernization, *f751*, 752; oil in, 656, 749, *f751*, 752, 759; in OPEC, 753; women in, *f751*

Saul (Hebrew ruler), 40

Savanna, **301**

Saxons, 203

Scandinavia, 192, 202, 203, 206, 212

Schiller, Friedrich von, 495

Schleswig, 538-39

Schlieffen plan, 629-31

Schliemann, Heinrich, 88

Scholasticism, 236–**37**, 340

Schubert, Franz, 496

Schumann, Robert, 496

Science: in ancient Greece, 87, 91, 92, 105–07, 108; in ancient Rome, 135–36, 137–38; in early American cultures, 315, 316; and Industrial Revolution, 501–08; in Islamic civilization, 236, 264, 270, *f271*; medieval, 237; post World War II, 737, 739, 740; and Scientific Revolution, 427–33, 443, 444

Scientific method, 87, **431**, 444

Scientific Revolution, 427–33, 443, 444

Scientific socialism, 492–93

"Scorched-earth" policy, 466, 696–97

Scotland, 379, 381, 492

Scott, Sir Walter, 495–96

Scribes, *f35*

Sculpture: in Africa, *f307*, 309; in ancient Greece, 91, 92; in Armory Show, *f662–63*; in China, 169; medieval, 238; post World War I, 664; post World War II, 737; realistic, 498, 500; in Renaissance, *f331*, 332; in Roman Empire, 137

Second Balkan War, 626

Second Coalition, 462, 464

Second Continental Congress, 450, 452

Second Empire, France, 526–27

Second Estate, 453, 454–55

Second French Republic, 527

Seismograph, 168–69

Seko, Mobutu Sese, 770

Selassie, Haile, 690

Seleucid Dynasty, 101

Seleucus, 101

Self-government, 447

Seljuk Turks, 188, 223, 262

Semitic peoples, 38, 39–42, 253, 301. *See also* Arabs, Hebrews, Jews

Senate, Roman, 114, 118

Seneca, 314

Senegal, 545, 587

Senegal River, 302

Senghor, Leopold, 771

Sepoy Rebellion, 599, 616

Sepoys, 597, 599

Serbia, 552; Black Hand in, 626; First Balkan War, *m625*, 625–26; post World War I, 638; Second Balkan War, 626; start of World War I, 626–27, 640

Serfdom, 388, 439, 467

Serfs, **214**, 226, 227

Seven Weeks' War, 539

Seven Years' War, 389

Shah Jahan (Mogul ruler), 409

Shakespeare, William, 338, 369

Shang Dynasty, 57–59, *m60*, 60, 61, 64, 161

Shareholders, **367**, 481

Sheik, 254

Shelley, Percy Bysshe, *f490*, 496

Shih Huang Ti (Ch'in ruler), 161, 162, 166

Shiite Muslims, 257, 259, 272, 744, 756–57, 758

Shintoism, 290–92, 295

Shogun, **294**, 295

Shogunate, **294**

Shoin, Yoshida, *f608*

Shotoku Taishi (Soga ruler), 292

Shozan, Sakuma, *f608*

Siam, 597, 614, 799. *See also* Thailand

Siberia, 311, 644, *f671*

Sicily, 107, 111, 113; ancient Greek colony, 77; and Islamic Empire, 260; Punic Wars, 121; revolution of 1848, 519–20; slave revolt, 123

Siddhartha Gautama. *See* Buddha

Sihanouk, Norodom, 800–801

Sikhs, 410, 787–88

Silk industry, *f57*, 58, 182, *f802*

Silk Road, 163, *f168*, 277

Sinai Desert, 39, 755

Sinai Peninsula, 39, 751

Singapore, 611, 614, 798–99, 803

Sino-Japanese War, 604

Sistine Chapel, 332

Six Dynasties Period, 165, 167, 170

Six-Day War, 754, *m756*. *See also* Arab-Israeli conflicts

Slater, Samuel, 477-78

Slave trade, 160; in Africa, 413, 414, 416, 417–19, 420; decline of, 578; impact of on Africa, 418–19, 578–79; in Roman Empire, 160

Slavery, 359, 361, 370, 434, 461; abolitionism, 578; and Africa, 358, 370, 577, 578–79; in Alexandrian Empire, 102; in American colonies, 448; in ancient Egypt, 34; in ancient Greece, 77, 78, 79, 80; in ancient Rome, 114, 118, 122, 123, 131, 137, 146, 149; in Brazil, 571; in Byzantine Empire, 182; in China, 167; in Code of Hammurabi, 27; compared with serfdom, 214; in Islam, 267; in Latin America, 357, 358–59, 370, 558, 560, 561, 573; and Native Americans, 313, 314, 316, 318, 354, 358, 370; in U.S., 525, 566–68; views of, 417–18

Slavs, 190, 191, 198, 590, 624; and Byzantine Empire, 183, 184, 188, 189, 192; and Nazis, 697–98; invade Europe, 212; Pan-Slavic movement, 552, 625–27, 640; post World War I, 649–50

Smallpox, 160, 507

Smith, Adam, 491, 492, 508

Smith, Ian, 766

Social class: in Africa, 414–15, 771; in Americas, 313, 314, 315, 316, 319, 448; in ancient Egypt, 34; in ancient Greece, 77, 78, 80; in ancient Rome, 114, 118, 124, 138, 149; in Aryan society, 53; caste system in India, 159–60, 170, 407, 788, 789; in China, 57–58, 61–62, 167, 170, 277, 791; and economic theory, 489–94; and Enlightenment, 435–38, 439; in Europe, 212, 221, 231, 327–28, 435–38, 439, 511, 512–16, 527, 528; and feudalism, 215–17; and French

(continued)

Tz'u Hsi (Manchu empress), 604–05

U-boats, 632, 635
Uganda, Africa, *m767*, 769
Ulyanov, Vladimir Ilyich. *See* Lenin
Umayyad Dynasty, 257, 259–60, 261, 262, 263–64, 272
Union of Soviet Socialist Republics: agriculture in, 670, 672–73; arts in, 739; Bolsheviks, 644; Brezhnev Doctrine, 731, 733; builds Berlin Wall, 722; Catholic Church in, 732; Chernobyl, 812; cold war with U.S., 717–18, 740; collective farms, 731, 732; Communist party in, 670–75, 686, 720, 730–33, 740; Cuban missile crisis, 722–23, 731; de-Stalinization, 731; dissidents in, 723, 730, 731, 732; doctrine of peaceful coexistence, 720; five-year plans, 672–73, 730, 732; *glasnost*, 732, 739, 740; industrialization in, 672–73; influence in Eastern Europe, 730–34, 739; influence in Middle East, 749, 750–51, 754–55, *m757*, 759, 760; invades Afghanistan, 723; invades Baltic states, 696; invades Czechoslovakia, 733, 740; invades Poland, 695; Jewish emigration from, 731, 732; in Korea, *m794*, 794; Nazi Germany invades, 695–97, 701, *m702*, 718; New Economic Policy, 670; nuclear arms race with U.S., 719–20, 722–24; *perestroika*, 732; post World War II, 705, *m709*, 709, 710; purges in, 675; relations with China, 729, 731, 793; relations with Cuba, 776; relations with Latin America, 777–78, 781; relations with Poland, 733–34; relations with West, 717–24, 731; repression in, 730, 731, 732, 733; satellite nations, 718, 720, 722, 730–734, 739, 740; *Sputnik*, 738; Vietnam War, 800–01; Warsaw Pact, 719, 733; women, 739; World War II, 691, *m692*, 692, 695, 696–97, 699, 700–01, *m702*, 703, 705, 707, 709, 710
Unions, **484**, 485, 486; growth of, 523, 527, 528. *See also* Labor unions
United Kingdom, 649, 725. *See also* Great Britain
United Nations, 707–08, 710, 750, 754, 770, 794; and creation of Israel, 747; in Korean War, 794; in Middle East and North Africa, 747
United States, *m448*, *m451*; American Revolution, 447–52, *m448*, *m451*; antiwar movement, 728–29; atomic bomb, 704, 705–06, *f706*, 709, 710, 717; Bay of Pigs, 722; Berlin airlift, 718–19; Camp David Accords, 756; civil rights struggle in, 728, 740; Civil War, 525, 557, 574; cold war, 717–18, 740; Constitution, *f232*, 435, 452, 468, 567; containment policy, 719; Cuban missile crisis, 722–23; Declaration of Independence, 451; education in, 728, 737; Emancipation Proclamation, 567; French and Indian War, 389, *m448*, 448, *m451*; Good Neighbor policy, 660, *f780*; Great Depression, 654–55, 666, 727; industrialization in, 568, 573; influence in Middle East, 749, 750–51, 754–58, 759, 760; in Iran, 758; isolationism in, 700, 708; Jacksonian Era, 525; Japan attacks Pearl Harbor, 699–700; and Korea, 794–95; and Korean War, *m794*, 794–95; labor movement in, 484–85; in Latin America, 570–72, 573, 574, 659–60, 774, 776–78, 781; League of Nations, 637–39, 640;

in Lebanon, 756–57; Lend-Lease Act, 696; liberal reforms in, 521, 525–26, 527, 528; Marshall Plan, 718; Mexican War, 564–66, *m566*; Monroe Doctrine, 571–72, 574; New Deal, 653–54; Nineteenth Amendment, 525; Nixon's foreign policy, 729; nuclear arms race with USSR, 719–24, *f723*; occupation of Japan, 796; Panama Canal, 572; in Philippines, 614–15, 801–02; post World War I, 648, 650–51, 661, 665, 666; post World War II, 705, 708, 709, 710, 727–29, 739; Progressive Era, 525–26; Reconstruction, 567–68, 574; relations with USSR, 717–24; Roosevelt Corollary, 572; Sherman Antitrust Act, 481; slavery in, 525, 566–68; space program, 738; Spanish-American War, 572, 574, 801; stock market crash, 651–53; territorial expansion, 564–69, *m566*; Thirteenth Amendment, 525; Treaty of Guadalupe Hidalgo, 566; Treaty of Versailles, 637–39, *m638*; Truman Doctrine, 750; Vietnam War, 720, 729, 799–800, *m801*, 803; War of 1812, 564; women's rights movement in, 735–37; woman suffrage, 525; World War I, 623, 632, *f634*, 635–39, 640; World War II, 691, 692, 696, 698–704
Universities, 236, 237, 246, 269, 304
Untouchables, 658
Upanishads, 54, 64, 158
Ur, 21, 39, *f813*
Ural Mountains, 189, 195, 201, 390, *f671*
Ur-Nammu, 21
Urban II (pope), 223
Urbanization, *f813*. *See also* Cities
Uruguay, *m558*, *m559*, 561, 570
Utilitarianism, 492

Utopian socialism, 492–93, 523
Vaccination, 507
Vaisya, 159
Van Gogh. *See* Gogh, Vincent van
Vargas, Getúlio, 660
Vassals, **215**–16
Vatican City, 332
V-E Day, 703
Vedas, 53–54, 64, 158, 160
Vedic Age, 52–54, 64
Venezuela, *m558*, *m559*, 559, 561; imperialism in, 570–71; in OPEC, 753
Venice, 188; Crusades, 224; trade routes, 224, *m225*
Verdi, Giuseppe, 496
Verdun, battle of, 631
Verrazano, Giovanni da, 364
Versailles, 382, 455
Vesalius, Andreas, 432
Vespucci, Amerigo, 352, *f355*
Veto power, **708**
Viceroy, **357**
Vichy government, 695
Victor Emmanuel II, 540
Victor Emmanuel III, 677
Victoria (queen of England), *f474*, 535, *f537*, 554, *f588*, 599
Victorian Age, 535–36
Vienna, 703; Congress of, 511–12
Viet Cong, 800, 801
Viet Minh, 799
Vietnam, 397, 611; communism in, 720, 799–800, *m800*; French imperialism in, 612–14; war in, 720, 728–29, 793, 800–01, *m801*, 803
Vietnam War, 720, 728–29, 737, 793, 799–800, *m800*, 803
Vikings, 192, 349; invade Europe, 212, *m213*, 214, 215, 218, 221
Virgil, 138
Vishnu, 158
Visigoths, 207; in Iberian Peninsula, 203; and Islamic Empire, 259
Vizier, 31
V-J Day, 704
Vladimir I, 192–93, 194
Vladivostok, 610
Volga River, 190, 203
Voltaire, 435, 439, 493
Vote. *See* Suffrage

Wagner, Otto, 664
Wagner, Richard, 496
Wales, 379, 381
Walpole, Sir Robert, 381
Wang An-shih (Sung ruler), 279
Wang Mang (Han ruler), 165
Wangara, Africa, 302, 303
War communism, 646, 670
War of 1812, 564
War of the Austrian Succession, 388, 412–13
Wars of the Roses, 245
War of the Spanish Succession, 387
Warfare: chemical, 630; effects of World War II on, 705–06; guerrilla, **541**, 800; nuclear, 704, 705–06, *f706*, 709, 710, 717, 719–20, 722–24; trench warfare, 630, *f631*
Warsaw (Poland), 693, 705
Warsaw Pact, 719, 732
Washington, George, 451
Washington Naval Conference, 683
Water frame, 472
Waterloo, battle of, *f464*, 466, 512
Waterwheel, 137, 473
Watt, James, 473
Weaponry, 27–28, 538, 545; Amorite, 33; atom bomb, 704, 705–06, *f706*, 709, 710, 717, 719–20, 722–24; battering ram, 28; cannon, 188; cavalry, 28; longbow, 244; machine gun, 577; medieval, 244, 245; musket, 414; prehistoric, 9; World War I, 629, 630–32; World War II, 705–06
Weimar Republic, 647, 678, 679, 681
Weizmann, Chaim, 747
Welfare state, 725
West Africa, *m581*, 587; and English East India Company, 364; independence movements in, 764. *See also* Africa
West Bank, 754, 756, 759
West Berlin, 733
West Germany: Berlin airlift, 718–19; Berlin Wall, 722; Common Market, 724; economic success in, 733; European

Coal and Steel Community, 724; post World War II, 727. *See also* East Germany, Germany
West Pakistan, 78. *See also* Pakistan
Western Europe. *See* Europe
Wheel, 14, 15, 25, 50
Wheelbarrow, 167
Whigs, 524
White Army (Russia), 669, 670, 705
White Lotus Society, 400
Whitney, Eli, 472, 478
Wilhelm II. *See* Kaiser Wilhelm II
William I (Prussia), 538, 539. *See also* Kaiser Wilhelm
William IV (England), *f474*
William of Orange, 381
William the Conqueror, 231
Wilson, Woodrow, 573, 632, 636–37, 639, 651
Wittenberg, Germany, 340
Wollstonecraft, Mary, 440
Women, 444; in Africa, 308, 771, 782; in ancient Egypt, 34; in ancient Greece, 77, 80; in Aryan society, 53; in Babylonia, 27; in Byzantine Empire, 179; in China, 62, 277, 280; and Christianity, 145; in Code of Hammurabi, 27; in Eastern Europe, 739; during Enlightenment, 430–40; in European religion, 345; in French Revolution, 458; in guilds, 226; in India, 598; and Industrial Revolution, 472–73, 481, 485; in Iran, 758; in Islam, 256, *f751*, 752; in Japan, 796, 798; in Latin America, 779, 782; in medieval literature, 240; in medieval society, 207, 214–15; in Napoleonic Code, 463; in Native American culture, 314; post World War I, 661; post World War II, 717, 729, 734, 735–37, 740; during Reformation, 345; in Roman Republic, 118; in Saudi Arabia, *f751*; in

steppe nomad tribes, *f190*; in Sumer, 25; in USSR, 738–39; in war, 244; and witches, 345; in World War I, *f634*; in World War II, 708. *See also* Women's rights movement
Women's rights movement, 440, 525, 735, 737, 779
Wordsworth, William, 496
Workers, 242, 246, 483–85
Working class, 485, 486; conflict with middle class, 522–23; in France, 518–19; in Industrial Revolution, 481, 482, 489; in Marxist theory, 393–94; rise of, 511, 527, 528
World War I: American entry into, 635; American women in, *f634*; Balkan crisis, 625–27; battles and campaigns of, 627–36, *m630*, *m633*; causes of, 623–27; Central Powers, 627–36, 640, 655, 658; cultural effects of, 660–65, 666; effects of on Europe, 675–82, 686; League of Nations, 637–39, 640; peace settlements in, 636–39; postwar period, 643–65, *m638*, 666; and Russian Revolution, 633–35, 640; Treaty of Versailles, 647; weaponry in, 629, 630–32
World War II: Axis Powers, 693–98, 703, 704, 705, 710; battles and campaigns, 700–04, *m702*; beginning of, 690, 693; effects of, 705–10; German military expansion during, 689, 691–97; U.S. enters, 700; weaponry, 704, *f706*
Wright, Frank Lloyd, 664
Writing, in ancient Egypt, *f35*, 35–37; in China, 59, 63; in early American cultures, 315, 316, 320; in early civilizations, 13, 14–15; in Indus Valley, 49–50, 160; in Japan, 292; in Persia, 42; in Phoenicia, 38; in Sumer, 25, 44
Wu Chao (China), 276

Wu Ti (Han ruler), 162–163, 165
Wycliffe, John, 243, 340, 342

Xavier, Francis, 354
Xerxes I (Persian ruler), 43, 84–85
X-ray, 502

Yaa Asantewa, *f588*
Yahweh, 39, 40–41
Yalta, 703, 707
Yamato clan, 290, 296
Yang Ti (Sui ruler), 275–76
Yangtze River, China, 56, 161, 275
Yaroslav (Russia), 194, 198
Yom Kippur War, *f755*, 755–56, *m756*
Yoritomo (shogun), 294, 295
Yorktown, Virginia, 451
Yoruba tribe, 415
Yu the Great (Hsia king), 60
Yuan Dynasty, 284–85, 296
Yuan Shih-kai, 606, 658
Yucatán Peninsula, 315
Yugoslavia, 190, 647; communism in, 718; economic success in, 734; formation of, 638; Soviet influence in, 730–34; World War II in, 696, *m702*, 703
Yung Lo (Ming ruler), 285–89

Zaibatsu, 608, 684, 796
Zaire, *m767*, 769–70
Zama, battle of, 121–22
Zambezi River, 300, 304
Zanzibar, 264
Zealots, 141
Zen, 295
Zeno, 103, 138
Zero, concept of, 160
Zeus, 82, 90, 119
Zhao Ziyang, 793
Ziggurat, **24**
Zimbabwe, *m303*, 304, 320; independence movement in, 766
Zionism, **656**, 746–47, *f755*; and Balfour Declaration, 656
Zola, Emile, 500
Zoroastrianism, 43, 105, 277, 281
Zulu, 551
Zwingli, Ulrich, 341–42

"Heji Monogatari Emaki" 13th century, Kamakura period, paper handscroll with ink and colors, Museum of Fine Arts, Boston, Fenollosa-Weld collection.

Chapter 14 298 (detail) Mural from Bonampak, Chiapas, Mexico, National Museum of Anthropology, Mexico City/Norman Prince. 301 Mike Yamashita/Woodfin Camp. 302 Michael Holford. 307 (top, center left and center) Museum of Mankind (The British Museum)/Michael Holford. 307 (bottom left) Museum für Völkerkunde, Berlin/Bridgeman Art Library/Art Resource. 307 (bottom right) Lee Boltin. 308 Lee Boltin. 311 Harald Sund/Image Bank. 313 Harald Sund. 316 Volkland Museum, Vienna/Robert Harding Picture Library. 319 Loren McIntire/Woodfin Camp.

Unit V: 324 Piccolomini Library, Siena Cathedral/Erich Lessing/Magnum (and detail on p. ix).

Chapter 15 326 Scala/Art Resource. 328 (detail) "Guidoriccio da Fogliano" by Simone Martini, Palazzo, Siena/Scala/Art Resource. 331 (top, center left and bottom right) Scala/Art Resource. 331 (center right) Museo dell'Opera/Scala/Art Resource. 331 (bottom left) Giraudon. 331 (bottom center) Erich Lessing/Magnum. 333 Vatican, Rome/Scala/Art Resource. 334 Erich Lessing/Magnum. 335 Picture Archive. 341 "The Prediction of Martin Luther" by Lucas Cranach the Elder, Church of Saint Mary, Wittenberg/Jurgens/Giraudon. 343 "The Procession of the League, Place de Grive," France 1590, Musée Carnavalet/Lauros/Giraudon. 345 National Gallery, London/Erich Lessing/Magnum.

Chapter 16 348 (detail) Kunsthistorisches Museum, Vienna. 350 The New York Public Library, Map Division, Astor Lenox and Tilden Foundations. 352 "Savages of the Streights of Magellan" from *Voyage to the Pacific Ocean*, fol 89, Bibliothèque du Histoire Marine, Vincenns/J.E. Bulloz. 356 from *Ceremonias y Ritos del los Indos de Mechuacan*, 1540–1, Library of Escoriale, Spain/Michael Holford. 358 Museo de America, Madrid/George Rainbird/Robert Harding Picture Library. 361 Maryland Historical Society. 364 from *Voyage to the Pacific Ocean*, fol 148, Bibliothèque du Histoire Marine, Vincenns/J.E. Bulloz. 367 "The Forge" by Louis LeNain, Louvre/J.E. Bulloz.

Chapter 17 372 National Gallery of Art, Washington; Andrew W. Mellon Fund. 375 Kunsthistorisches Museum, Vienna/Erich Lessing/Magnum. 376 "The Armada Portrait" by George Gower, c. 1588, Woburn Abbey/*Newsweek* Books. 378 Louvre/J.E. Bulloz. 381 Duke of St. Albans/Robert Harding Picture Library. 382 "Louis XIV in Front of the Grotto of Thetis" by an anonymous French artist. Musée de Versailles/*Newsweek* Books. 387 Aldenburg-Iconographish Bureau/W.K. Steffan/Robert Harding Picture Library. 388 Mansell. 391 from *L'Imagerie Populaire Russe*, Prints Division, The New York Public Library.

Chapter 18 394 Namban screen by Kano Naizen, 17th century, Kobe City Museum/*Newsweek* Books. 398 Private Collection/*Newsweek* Books. 399 Mansell. 400 Bitong brushholder by Wu Zhifan, Palace Museum, Peking/Wan-go H.C. Weng. 403 Copy of scroll by an unknown artist of the Edo period, University of Tokyo/Laurie Platt Winfrey. 404 Museum of Fine Arts, Boston, Bigelow Collection. 406 Harald Sund. 408 Cleveland Museum of Art, gift of Mrs. A. Dean Perry. 410 Scala/Art Resource. 412 Victoria and Albert Museum/Michael Holford. 414 Robert Harding Picture Library. 416 Museum of Mankind (The British Museum)/Michael Holford. 417 Nail Figure from the Western Kongo, Mayombe, Yombe, 1875–1900, wood with screws, nails, blades, cowrie shell and other materials, 46", 76.79 © 1987 Detroit Institute of Arts, Founders Society purchase, Eleanor Clay Ford Fund for African Art. 418 National Maritime Museum Neg. No. CT A1818.

Unit VI: 424 National Gallery of Art, Washington. Widener Collection (and detail on p. ix).

Chapter 19 426 National Gallery of Art, Washington, Ailsa Mellon Bruce Fund. 428 Metropolitan Museum of Art, gift of Mr. and Mrs. Charles Wrightsman, 1978 (1978.517). 430 (right) Documentation Photographique de la Réunion des Musées Nationaux. 432 J.E. Bulloz.

434 Pascal Soalhat. 435 Louvre/J.E. Bulloz. 441 Lauros/Giraudon/Art Resource. 442 National Gallery of Art, Washington, Samuel H. Kress Collection.

Chapter 20 446 Musée Carnavalet/Giraudon/Art Resource. 449 Museum of the City of New York. 450 "Surrender of Cornwallis at Yorktown" by John Trumbull, 1787, American 1756–1843, oil on canvas, 13 7/8 x 21", 48.217 © 1987 Detroit Institute of Arts, gift of Dexter M. Ferry, Jr. 453 Musée Carnavalet/Giraudon/Art Resource. 454 Louvre/Giraudon/Art Resource. 458 Bettmann Archive. 460 Musée Carnavalet/Pascal Soalhat. 461 "Execution, Place de la Revolution," Musée Carnavalet/J.E. Bulloz. 462 Louvre/J.E. Bulloz. 463 Musée Legion d'Honneur/J.E. Bulloz. 466 Metropolitan Museum of Art, Schiff Fund, 1922, 22.60.25(15). 467 Bibliothèque Nationale, Paris/Robert Harding Picture Library.

Chapter 21 470 National Gallery of Art, Washington, Chester Dale Collection. 473 Tate Gallery. 475 Engraving by J. Pass, published by J. Wilkes, Radio Times Picture Library/Bettmann Archive. 478 Giraudon/Art Resource. 482 Musée de l'Annonciade, St. Tropez/Laurie Platt Winfrey. 483 "Poverty" by Kathe Kollwitz (1867–1945), lithograph, National Gallery of Art, Washington, Rosenwald Collection.

Chapter 22 488 National Gallery of Art, Washington, gift of Helen Farr Sloan. 490 BBC Hulton/Bettmann Archive. 491 "La Bourse," by Edgar Degas, Pascal Soalhat. 493 Brown Brothers. 494 Ullstein Bilderdienst. 496 © M/C City A.G./Robert Harding Picture Library. 497 J.E. Bulloz. 498 (top) Philadelphia Museum of Art, Mr. and Mrs. Carroll S. Tyson Collection. 498 (center left) Metropolitan Museum of Art, purchased with special contributions and purchase funds given or bequeathed by Friends of the Museum, 1967. (67.241). 498 (center right) National Gallery of Art, Washington, Ailsa Mellon Bruce Collection. 498 (bottom) Jeu de Paume, Paris/Art Resource. 499 (top left) "Street in Tahiti" by Paul Gauguin, French, 1848–1903, 1891, oil on canvas, 45 1/2" x 34 7/8", Toledo Museum of Art, Toledo, Ohio, gift of Edward Drummond Libbey. 499 (top right) Musée Municipal de Pau, France, purchased by the City through the Noulibos bequest, 1878/D. Sorbe. 499 (center) "The Gardener" by Paul Cezanne, Tate Gallery/John Webb/Robert Harding Picture Library. 499 (bottom left) State Museum Kroller-Muller, Otterlo, The Netherlands. 499 (bottom right) National Gallery of Art, Washington, Chester Dale Collection. 500 BBC Hulton Picture Library/Bettmann Archive. 501 Rodin Museum, Paris/Art Resource. 502 BBC Hulton Picture Library/Bettmann Archive. 503 The Eurynome Hermit, from monograph of Trochilidae by John Gould, Rainbird/Robert Harding Picture Library. 506 The University Museum, Philadelphia

Chapter 23 510 Kunsthalle, Hamburg/Ralph Kleinhempel/Robert Harding Picture Library. 516 "Battle of Navarin" by Garneray, Versailles/J.E. Bulloz. 518 Musée Carnavalet/J.E. Bulloz. 519 Mansell. 521 Ullstein Bilderdienst. 523 National Gallery of Art/Rosenwald Collection. 524 BBC Hulton Picture Library/Bettmann Archive. 525 F.B. Johnson/Library of Congress.

Unit VII: 532 Japan Folk-Craft Museum (and detail on p. x).

Chapter 24 534 Metropolitan Museum of Art, New York, gift of the estate of Mrs. Edward Robinson, 52.126.6. 536 (left) Bettmann Archive. 536 (right) John Hillelson Agency. 540 Mansell. 542 Popperfoto. 543 BBC Hulton Picture Library/Bettmann Archive. 544 Brown Brothers. 545 Ullstein Bilderdienst. 547 (top) Erich Lessing/Magnum. 547 (center left) The Metropolitan Museum of Art, H.O. Havemeyer Collection. 547 (center right) Museum of Fine Arts, Boston, Ernest Wadsworth Longfellow Fund. 547 (bottom left) Fogg Art Museum, Harvard University, Massachusetts. 547 (bottom center) Columbia University, New York, Engel Collection, Rare Book and Manuscript Library. 547 (bottom right) Metropolitan Museum of Art. 550 Ullstein Bilderdienst. 551 (left) Mansell. 551 (right) John Hillelson Agency.

Chapter 25 556 Museo Nacional de Arte Moderno, Mexico City/Laurie Platt Winfrey. 560 Bettmann Archive. 561 Laurie Platt Winfrey. 562 Laurie Platt Winfrey. 565 National Museum of American Art,

Smithsonian Institution. **567** Brady Collection, Library of Congress. **569** Mansell. **570** Ullstein Bilderdienst. **572** Brown Brothers.

Chapter 26   576 Compiegne/J.E. Bulloz. **579** Ullstein Bilderdienst. **582** Ullstein Bilderdienst. **584** John Hilleslon Agency. **586** (top left) Horniman Museum/Robert Harding Picture Library. **586** (top right) The Royal Museum of Fine Arts, Copenhagen. **586** (center left) Musée Picasso, Paris/Art Resource. **586** (center right) Mask by an anonymous artist of the Fang people, 19th century, Africa, wood, kaolin, 1983.24 © Detroit Institute of Arts, Founders Society Purchase, New Endowment Fund, General Endowment Fund, Benson and Edith Ford Fund, Henry Ford II Fund, Conrad H. Smith Fund. **586** (bottom left) Museum of Mankind (The British Museum)/Michael Holford. **586** (bottom right) "Actor's Mask" by Paul Klee, 1924, oil on canvas mounted on board, 14 1/2 x 13 1/2"; Sydney and Harriet Janis Collection, gift to The Museum of Modern Art, New York. **591** Popperfoto.

Chapter 27   596 India Office Library/*Newsweek* Books. **598** John Hilleslon Agency. **600** John Hilleslon Agency. **602** Popperfoto. **603** Popperfoto. **605** (left) Popperfoto. **605** (right) John Hilleslon Agency. **607** Victoria and Albert Museum/Michael Holford. **609** (top) "Ho-tarugari" by Eishosai Chōki, Honolulu Academy of Arts, James A. Michener Collection. **609** (center left) Metropolitan Museum of Art, 16.2.9. **609** (center right) Metropolitan Museum of Art, anonymous gift in memory of Horace Havemeyer, 1971.185. **609** (bottom left) Hotel de Chanaleilles/Scala/Art Resource. **609** (bottom right) Freer Gallery of Art, Smithsonian Institution, Washington, D.C., Acq. no. 92123. **610** Brown Brothers. **611** BBC Hulton Picture Library/Bettmann Archive. **614** John Hilleslon Agency.

Unit VIII: 620 "Guernica" by Pablo Picasso, 1937, oil on canvas, 137 1/2 x 306", The Prado Museum, Madrid/Giraudon/Art Resource LA 17080, SPADEM/ARS (and detail on p. xi).

Chapter 28   622 "The Assault, Verdun" by H. de Groux, 1916, Musée des Deux Guerres Mondiales, Paris/Hubert Josse. **624** "HMS Dreadnought" by Frank Wood, National Maritime Museum, Greenwich, England/Michael Holford. **626** Bettmann Archive. **628** Courtesy Meehan Military Posters. **629** Culver Pictures. **631** Granger Collection. **635** Bettmann Archive. **636** "Allies Day, May 1917" by Childe Hassam, 1917, oil on canvas, 36 3/4 x 30 1/4", National Gallery of Art, Washington, Gift of Ethelyn McKinney in memory of her brother, Glenn Ford McKinney. **637** Bettmann Archive.

Chapter 29   642 (South Wall detail) "Detroit Industry" by Diego M. Rivera, 1932–33, fresco, © 1987 The Detroit Institute of Arts, Founders Society Purchase, Edsel B. Ford Fund and Gift of Edsel B. Ford. **644** Sovfoto. **645** Anne S.K. Brown Military Collection/*Newsweek* Books. **646** Culver Pictures. **647** Culver Pictures. **648** UPI/Bettmann Newsphotos. **650** Poster by Alphonse Mucha, 1928. Photo by David Brinson, courtesy Gunn Brinson. **651** Granger Collection. **652** Culver Pictures. **653** "Bread Line—No One has Starved" by Reginald Marsh, 1932, etching, Museum of the City of New York. **655** Historical Pictures Service, Inc. **657** UPI/Bettmann Newsphotos. **659** Bettmann Archive. **661** Culver Pictures. **662** (top) "Armory Show Poster," 1913, Hirshhorn Museum and Sculpture Garden, Smithsonian Institution, Washington. **662** (center) "Horse" by Raymond Duchamp-Villon, 1914 (cast 1954–1963), bronze, Hirshhorn Museum and Sculpture Garden, Smithsonian Institution, Washington, Gift of Joseph H. Hirshhorn, 1966. **662** (bottom) "Garden of Love (Improvisation No. 27)" by Wassily Kandinsky, 1912, oil on canvas, The Metropolitan Museum of Art, The Alfred Stieglitz Collection, 1949 (49.70.1). **663** (top left) "The Red Studio" by Henri Matisse, 1911, oil on canvas, 71 1/4" x 7' 2 1/4", Collection, The Museum of Modern Art, New York, Mrs. Simon Guggenheim Fund. **663** (top right) "Mlle. Pogany" Version 1 by Constantin Brancusi, 1913 after a marble of 1912, bronze 17 1/4" high, Collection, The Museum of Modern Art, New York, acquired through the Lillie P. Bliss Bequest. **663** (bottom right) "Portrait of Chess Players" by Marcel Duchamp, 1911, oil on canvas, 39 5/8 x 39 3/4", Philadelphia Museum of Art: The Louise and Walter Arensberg Collec-

tion. **663** (bottom left) "Woman with Mustard Pot" by Pablo Picasso, 1910, oil on canvas, Collection Haags Gemeentemuseum, The Hague, The Netherlands. **664** "In Vaudeville" by Charles Demuth, 1918, watercolor on paper, 12 3/4" x 8", Philadelphia Museum of Art/A.E. Gallatin Collection. **667** Library of Congress.

Chapter 30   668 Bettmann Archive. **670** Popperfoto. **671** Howard Sochurek/Woodfin Camp. **673** Sovfoto. **675** "I and the Village" by Marc Chagall, 1924, oil on canvas, Philadelphia Museum of Art, given by Mr. and Mrs. Rodolphe M. de Schauensee. **676** AP/Wide World Photos. **679** Granger Collection. **681** (top) Ernst Haas/Magnum. **681** (bottom) Bettmann Archive. **685** Historical Pictures Service, Inc.

Chapter 31   688 "Liberation" by Ben Shahn, 1945, tempera on cardboard, mounted on composition board, 29 3/4 x 40", Collection, The Museum of Modern Art, New York, James Thrall Soby Bequest. **690** Eastfoto. **691** UPI/Bettmann Newsphotos. **695** Granger Collection. **697** AP/Wide World Photos. **698** AP/Wide World Photos. **701** Historical Pictures Service, Inc. **703** Granger Collection. **705** Granger Collection. **707** UPI/Bettmann Newsphotos. **711** "The Isolationist" by Albert Hirschfeld from *New Masses*, June 21, 1938, © Al Hirschfeld. Drawing reproduced by special arrangement with Hirschfeld's exclusive representative, The Margo Feiden Galleries Ltd., New York.

Unit IX: 714 "Mahoning" by Franz Kline, 1956, oil on canvas, 80 x 100", Collection of Whitney Museum of American Art, purchase, with funds from The Friends of the Whitney Museum of American Art, Acq. #57.10, Photo: Steven Sloman (and detail on p. xii).

Chapter 32   716 Roger Malloch/Magnum. **719** AP/Wide World Photos. **720** AP/Wide World Photos. **722** Andrew St. George/ Magnum. **725** Peter Marlow/Magnum. **729** UPI/Bettmann Newsphotos. **731** Martti Kainulainen Lehtikuva/Woodfin Camp. **734** Wallis/SIPA Press. **736** (top right) "Marilyn Monroe" by Willem de Kooning, 1954, oil on canvas, 50 × 30", Collection Neuberger Museum, State University of New York at Purchase, gift of Roy R. Neuberger. **736** (center right) "Magenta, Black, Green on Orange" by Mark Rothko, 1949, oil on canvas, 7'1 3/8" × 65", Collection, The museum of Modern Art, New York. Bequest of Mrs. Mark Rothko through The Mark Rothko Foundation, Inc. **736** (bottom left) "Convergence" by Jackson Pollock, 1952, oil on canvas, 93 1/2 × 155", Albright-Knox Art Gallery, Buffalo, New York, Gift of Seymour H. Knox, 1956. **736** (top left) "Black Widow" by Alexander Calder, 1959, Standing stabile, painted sheet steel, 7'8" × 14'3" × 7'5", Collection, The Museum of Modern Art, New York, Mrs. Simon Guggenheim Fund. **737** Dirck Halstead/Liaison.

Chapter 33   742 Micha Bar Am/Magnum. **744** Abbas/Magnum. **748** AP/Wide World Photos. **750** Bruno Barbey/Magnum. **753** Abbas/ Magnum. **754** Cornell Capa/Magnum. **758** Abbas/Magnum.

Chapter 34   762 Nigerian Wall Hanging by Isaac Ojo Fajana, embroidery on cloth, 57 x 69", Collection Mbari Art West/Richard Wolford. **768** Andrew Bailey/Camera Press Ltd. **769** John Chiasson/ Gamma-Liaison. **771** Marc and Evelyne Bernheim/Woodfin Camp. **777** C. Steele-Perkins/Magnum. **779** Pascal Maitre/Gamma-Liaison. **781** (detail of mural) "Blessed Fruit of Knowledge" by Diego Rivera, 1926, Ministry of Education, Mexico City/Laurie Platt Winfrey, Inc.

Chapter 35   784 "1960s" by Tadanori Yokoo, 1986, mixed media on ceramic, 240 x 240 cm, Collection of the artist. **786** Marilyn Silverstone/Magnum. **789** Bruno Barbey/Magnum. **792** Harry Redl/Black Star. **795** Philip J. Griffiths/Magnum. **798** (top) D.E. Cox/FPG Int. **798** (bottom) Philip J. Griffiths/Magnum. **802** James Nachtwey/Magnum.

Chapter 36   806 "Redbal," 1980 © David Em, 1980, computer painting. **810** Graig Davis/Black Star. **811** (left) Gilles Peress/Magnum. **811** (right) Lincoln Potter/Gamma Liaison. **812** James Sugar/Black Star. **815** (left) George De Keerle/Gamma-Liaison. **815** (right) F. Scianna/ Magnum.

Skills Bank   920 Jerry Doyle *Philadelphia Record*.

CONTENTS

To the Student

Thinking skills and social studies skills lessons are provided throughout your textbook. The lessons will help you develop basic skills to improve your understanding of history. These same basic skills can be applied to many other subjects, as well as to situations in your everyday life. Additional skills lessons in this section will further expand your ability to process and interpret information. Skills practices are included to give you an opportunity to try out your skills, which will develop and grow as the year passes.

USING THE SKILLS BANK

On the practice pages of this Skills Bank, you will be asked to analyze and interpret various pieces of information related to information in the chapters of the text. Each problem requires that you apply a particular skill. Developing these skills is important because using them can be a lifelong habit. They can be applied to any source of information, such as other books, magazines, newspapers, and radio and television broadcasts. Some of these important skills in locating and understanding information are:

- Identifying social studies and other special terms

- Figuring out the word meaning from context clues

- Figuring out the word meaning from structural analysis

- Identifying the main idea

- Identifying the important, or supporting, details

- Identifying the sequence of events

- Distinguishing between facts and opinions

- Identifying cause and effect

- Drawing logical conclusions

- Making accurate generalizations

- Identifying the author's point of view

- Identifying the author's purpose

- Selecting references

- Using reference sources

- Using graphic sources

Skills that help you communicate what you have learned, as well as your own ideas, are also important. To communicate information and ideas, you will need to develop the following writing and speaking skills:

- Spelling commonly used words correctly

- Using standard punctuation

- Using standard capitalization

- Using English correctly

- Forming complete and correct sentences

- Describing objects or events

- Narrating a sequence of events

- Comparing objects, events, or ideas

- Taking a stand and supporting the choice with evidence

- Persuading others to choose one thing or action over another

Writing in the Social Studies

To write a social studies paper, first decide what you want to say, then how you want to say it. Learning a way to approach this task may eliminate unnecessary work.

Much of the work takes place before you actually begin to write the paper itself. The effort you put into getting ready will help focus your thoughts, making your finished product clearer.

Preparing to Write

The first step in approaching your paper is choosing your subject, or topic. The next step is determining the purpose. What do you plan to show about the main subject, problem, or issue? Once you have decided what you plan to show, write a sentence stating your main idea. This statement provides the core around which to organize, and eventually write, your paper.

Using your statement of purpose, you can now write an outline for the paper. Identify some supporting ideas, each of which would make a good topic for a paragraph. For each of these ideas, outline some supporting details. A thorough outline will give shape, direction, and purpose to your writing.

Writing the Paper

One format for papers consists of an introductory paragraph, three supporting paragraphs, and a concluding paragraph. Using this format can help you systematically approach your paper. Alter the format to suit your needs and the desired length of your paper.

The introductory paragraph contains the statement of purpose, or thesis statement, and also lets the reader know what to expect from the following paragraphs. One effective way to create interest and draw the reader in is to begin with a general statement and work toward more specific statements. By putting your thesis at the end of the paragraph you create a springboard effect, propelling your reader into the body of the paper.

Each body paragraph should have a clearly stated main idea that supports the thesis. In each body paragraph, back the main idea up with some details, examples, explanations, evidence, or definitions. In this way, the body paragraphs become the building blocks of an effective paper. If you first outline your ideas in a clear order, each of your paragraphs should lead logically to the next. You may choose to reorganize the sequence of your paragraphs to help your paper flow from one point to the next.

The general purpose of your concluding paragraph is to summarize your thesis and the supporting ideas. There are many ways to conclude a paper, but they all give the reader a sense of coming to an end. Your conclusion should confirm that what you set out to say in your introduction, you accomplished in the body of your paper. Avoid introducing any new information that might confuse your reader about your purpose. Vague generalities, trite phrases, or speculation unrelated to your topic give an unsatisfying end to even the best-written paper.

Revising

Allowing yourself time to rework your paper will improve your writing and show you what areas to concentrate on next time you write. Consider asking another student to read your paper to make sure your ideas come across clearly. Here are some questions that will help you evaluate your paper yourself.

- Does the opening paragraph make your reader want to know more?
- Do your ideas flow logically from general to specific?
- Is the purpose focused and clearly stated?
- Do you give your reader a clear idea of what to expect from the body of the paper?
- Does each paragraph support your purpose?
- Does each paragraph have a clearly-stated main idea?
- Are the details, descriptions, etc. in each paragraph strongly linked to the main idea and therefore to the purpose of the paper?
- Is there a logical transition from one paragraph to the next?
- Does your conclusion relate directly to what you set out to say in your paper? Does it have unity with your purpose?
- Does the final paragraph give the reader a satisfying sense of coming to a conclusion?

FOUR KINDS OF SOCIAL STUDIES WRITING

Social studies papers fall into various categories depending on the purpose and goal of the paper. When writing, consider the purpose and goal as well as the audience and point of view.

THE DESCRIPTIVE COMPOSITION

Directions for a descriptive composition often ask you to "describe" or "tell what you see." Start by listing descriptive details you might include. Then you can select what to emphasize. For example, in describing de Groux's *Assault on Verdun* on page 622, you might choose to focus on how de Groux uses color to convey the horror and senseless destruction of World War I.

Keep in mind the overall impression you wish to put across and choose language which supports your purpose. Although some words have similar meanings, one word might be more effective than another. A thesaurus may help you find just the word you want.

After completing your paper you are ready to evaluate and revise. Ask yourself these questions. Is the description appropriate for your purpose, audience, and point of view? Does your choice of words contribute to the overall impression you wish to convey? Do you describe each feature fully before moving on to the next?

THE NARRATIVE COMPOSITION

An assignment for a narrative composition asks you to tell how something was done, tell the events leading to a point in history, or describe causes of a situation or occurrence. First, list the specific steps or stages you plan to include. Then list details for each paragraph. For example, consider an assignment to tell how the events of the first stage of the French Revolution led to the second stage. You might choose three events as your three main ideas, then list the supporting details for each.

Ask yourself these questions. Do the steps proceed logically? Is each step or idea linked to the main topic and to the steps that precede and follow it? Are these steps well-supported and cause/effect relationships clear? Do you describe each step fully before moving on to the next? Does your conclusion bring these elements together with your stated purpose?

THE COMPARATIVE COMPOSITION

A comparative composition assignment asks you to "compare and contrast" or "give advantages and disadvantages of." Defining the categories or ideas to be discussed and listing similarities and differences are key steps in organizing your paper. Consider an assignment to compare totalitarian rule under Mussolini and under Hitler. First, list similarities and differences and then decide how to categorize them. You might choose to compare three aspects of their rules, such as political goals, economic goals, and means of preserving power. Then write a body paragraph for each aspect. Clearly defining the aspects and listing similarities and differences will give your writing purpose.

After you have written your paper, ask yourself these questions. For each point you make, do you discuss both objects of comparison? Within each paragraph, do you stick to the aspect being discussed? Are your comparisons well-supported?

THE PERSUASIVE COMPOSITION

An assignment for a persuasive composition asks you to "convince," "persuade," or "make an argument for," or "make a decision and give reasons." Your goal is to persuade your audience to a particular point of view or course of action. First, choose a topic and define your purpose, or thesis. Next, gather evidence to support your position. Keep in mind your audience. What arguments will be most convincing to them? Anticipate objections and try to address those issues. Organize your arguments and supporting details. Be sure you have enough evidence to make a convincing case before you begin to write.

In writing your paper, keep in mind your overall purpose with each supporting paragraph. Each point should build on the last and be solidly supported by facts, examples, reasons, etc. Avoid generalizations that you cannot back with evidence. Be sure your tone and approach are appropriate to your audience. Refer to the questions on page 882 to help you evaluate your work.

FINDING THE MAIN IDEA

To make sense out of a reading selection, you will need to identify the main idea. First find the general topic, such as airplanes, prehistoric beasts, or ways to cross Arctic ice. The general topic is not the main idea, however. The main idea is what the author is trying to say about the topic—the author's message.

To find the main idea, look at each paragraph. Note what the details say about the topic. For each paragraph, write a one-sentence summary. Finally, write a single sentence that covers all of the other sentences you wrote.

For example, suppose you summarize the paragraphs in a reading selection on ancient civilizations with these sentences: In Egypt, farming villages sprang up along the Nile River; India's earliest civilization arose along the Indus River; the first Mesopotamian cities grew along the Tigris and Euphrates rivers. The main idea of the selection might be that early civilizations sprang up mainly near rivers.

Sometimes, you will find details or whole paragraphs that seem to contradict the main idea. These may represent exceptions that are probably not so great as to change the main idea. In this case, when you express the author's main idea, write a two-part sentence using phrases such as "Even though . . . " or "Despite the fact that . . . " to explain the contradiction.

APPLYING THE SKILL

Read the following selection through quickly and identify its topic. Then look at each paragraph more closely. Decide what the main idea of each paragraph is. Then combine the main ideas for the paragraphs into a main idea for the whole selection.

One advantage of the city was personal safety. One band of nomads might easily be destroyed by another. A small settlement—simply because it was a nonmoving target—was even more vulnerable. But a city of several thousand people could stand up to any but the most powerful enemy. Even natural disasters such as floods were less likely to overwhelm a city, protected by its many resources.

Perhaps more important in the long run than personal safety was the city's promise of personal fulfillment. The man—and woman—of the city could take one of many jobs. The city, in fact, depended on variety. Its concentration of numbers was possible only because the people who lived in it carried out special duties that were supported by the larger society of which the city was a part. No longer did every man have to be a hunter or a farmer, every woman a mother and housekeeper. In even the very first cities, there were also goods to be made, trade to carry out, shrines to be cared for, and construction projects to be finished.

Adapted from Dora Jane Hamblin, *The First Cities*. (Amsterdam: Time-Life Books, 1973, pp. 9-10).

MAKING MEANING

Answer on your own paper.

1. The topic of this selection is **(a)** everyday life in cities, **(b)** the difference between cities and settlements, **(c)** trade in cities, **(d)** why people came to cities.

2. The main idea of the first paragraph is **(a)** cities were attractive because they offered personal safety, **(b)** cities could survive natural disasters because of their many resources, **(c)** nomads in bands were safer than people in cities, **(d)** people formed small settlements before they formed cities.

3. The main idea of the second paragraph is **(a)** people in cities performed many different jobs, **(b)** people came to cities to find personal fulfillment, **(c)** people came to cities because they didn't want to be hunters, **(d)** early societies allowed people to have special duties.

4. The main idea of the whole selection is **(a)** people came to cities for protection, **(b)** people formed cities when they no longer needed to hunt or farm, **(c)** the chance of doing work they liked, as well as safety, brought people to cities, **(d)** people found cities a secure place because everyone did the same kind of work.

REVIEWING THE SKILL

5. What is a main idea? How is it different from other ideas or information in a selection?
6. How do you find the main idea of a paragraph?
7. How do you find the main idea of a reading selection?

IDENTIFYING SPECIFIC DETAILS

Paying attention to details can help you understand an author's ideas. Details complete the picture and support the main idea. For example, if the main idea of a written account is that Roman roads were built to carry heavy traffic, the account will be more convincing if it also goes on to say that the roads were built of heavy stones set over several layers of gravel.

Details are specific pieces of information such as people, places, things, times, or amounts. Details provide answers to "who," "what," "when," "where," "why," "how," or "how many" questions. Asking and answering such questions can help you remember details and understand how they are related.

Classifying, or grouping into categories, is another way to understand how details combine to form complete ideas. Details can be grouped according to features they share. For example, China and India can both be placed in the category "Asian Civilizations."

The categories you choose will depend on your purpose for classifying. If your purpose is to learn about inventions of ancient civilizations, the category "Architecture" might be helpful, but the category "Literature" would not. After classifying the details, determine how the groupings relate to the main idea.

APPLYING THE SKILL

The excerpt below describes the sporting events in the ancient Greek Olympic games. Write at least three questions that can be answered by details in the passage. Then classify the sporting events into at least three groups. In addition, identify the main idea of the selection, expressed in the first paragraph. Then write a sentence using your three groups to back up the main idea.

> Shortly after 500 B.C. the program of sports in the Olympic Games reached its more or less final form. There were three days of major competition given over to about a dozen different events. It most likely started with the most spectacular, the chariot race. Then came the horse race.
>
> The chariot and horse races were the showiest events. But the crowd's favorites tended to be the body-contact sports. These were wrestling, boxing, and the pancratium (a combination of the

two). The first Olympic event to be recorded was a straight run the length of the course, in effect a 200-meter dash. Soon a second race was introduced: down the course and back, a 400-meter dash. A long-distance run was added of nearly 4,800 meters. Later there was even a dash in which contestants ran in armor. These were the only track events; the marathon in today's games is a modern idea. The field events were three: broad jump, discus throw, javelin throw. They were always part of a curious mix called the "pentathlon" or "five-contest": the jump, discus, and javelin followed by a 200-meter dash and a wrestling match. If a man took three of the five he was the winner.

Adapted from Lionel Casson, "The First Olympics: Competing for the Greater Glory of Zeus" (*Smithsonian*, June 1984, pp.68-69).

MAKING MEANING

1. Which event probably began an Olympic contest? **(a)** the pentathlon, **(b)** a 200-meter dash, **(c)** a chariot race, **(d)** a wrestling match.

2. How many events were in the pentathlon? **(a)** four, **(b)** five, **(c)** six, **(d)** seven.

3. Which of the following would fit in the category "Track Events in the Ancient Olympic Games" **(a)** wrestling, **(b)** javelin throwing, **(c)** the marathon race, **(d)** the 200-meter dash.

4. Which of the following categories would allow you to put chariot races and horse races together and separate them from other Olympic events? **(a)** "Events Involving Horses," **(b)** "Events Involving Vehicles," **(c)** "Events Held Outside," **(d)** "Events Using a Track."

5. The chariot and horse races could be placed in one category, and the various dashes could be placed in another. These two groups could be most usefully combined in a broader category labeled **(a)** "Races," **(b)** "Body-contact Sports," **(c)** "Olympic Events," **(d)** "Pentathlon."

REVIEWING THE SKILL

Answer on your own paper.

6. Give two examples of questions that can be answered by details.

7. Define the term *classifying*.

8. What determines the categories you choose when you classify details?

IDENTIFYING AUTHOR'S POINT OF VIEW AND PURPOSE

An author's *point of view* is made up of the author's background, feelings, interests, and beliefs. For example, in the 1500s, a Roman Catholic priest describing the selling of indulgences would have had a very different point of view from a follower of Martin Luther.

An author's *purpose* is often closely related to the author's point of view. For example, material written to amuse readers may reflect the author's point of view that the things being written about are funny or foolish.

Sometimes the author's purpose is clearly stated. Often, however, the purpose is implied, or shown indirectly. In that case, you will need to look for clues to the author's purpose.

First, knowing the intended audience can help you decide the writer's purpose. Second, identifying opinions and beliefs in the writing can help you determine its purpose. Notice whether or not the author uses words meant to provoke strong emotions, such as *barbarians* or *peace*. Ask yourself what emotions the author is appealing to. Finally, if the writing seems to be factual, figure out what claims or arguments the facts are supposed to support. These claims will show the author's purpose.

APPLYING THE SKILL

Antonio de Mendoza, the first viceroy of the Spanish settlements in Mexico, wrote instructions to Fray (Friar) Marcos de Niza, who was to lead a scouting party into the American Southwest in 1539. On a sheet of paper list words and phrases in the selection that give clues to Mendoza's point of view and purpose.

> You must take great care to observe the people. Note if they be many or few, if they are scattered or in communities. Report the quality and fertility of the land. Describe the climate, the trees and plants, and domestic and wild animals which may be present. Tell of the type of ground, if rough or flat. Say whether the rivers are large or small. Describe the minerals and metals which are there. Of the objects of which you can send or bring specimens, do so, in order that His Majesty may be advised of everything.
>
> And if God, Our Lord, is so pleased that you find some large settlement, where it appears to you there is an advantageous place to found a monastery and to send friars to undertake the conversion, you shall send such information with all secrecy. Then whatever is necessary may be done without commotion. Remember that in bringing peace to the country beyond, we look to the service of Our Lord and the good of all the inhabitants.
>
> You shall, in my name, take possession of all the land for His Majesty. . . .

Adapted from Udall, "Coronado in History" (*Arizona Highways*, April 1984, pp. 7-8).

MAKING MEANING

Answer the following questions.

1. Mendoza's point of view is that of a **(a)** government official, **(b)** religious leader, **(c)** king, **(d)** explorer.

2. Mendoza's main purpose in having Fray Marcos gather information was probably to **(a)** find new ways to convert the Indians to Christianity, **(b)** find new lands and wealth to tell the king about, **(c)** make a scientific study of the land and people of the Southwest, **(d)** find new places for Spanish farmers to settle.

3. The most likely reason why Mendoza wanted Fray Marcos to keep his information secret is that Mendoza **(a)** didn't want to frighten the Indians, **(b)** didn't want anyone to get excited about Fray Marcos's discoveries, **(c)** wanted to keep the Spaniards from visiting the new land, **(d)** wanted to be the first to tell the king about whatever Fray Marcos found.

4. Your conclusions about Mendoza's point of view and purpose might lead you to question his statement that **(a)** he wanted Fray Marcos to take great care in observing the people and land, **(b)** he wanted Fray Marcos to send his information secretly, **(c)** his *main* goal was to serve the Lord and see to the good of all the inhabitants, **(d)** he wanted Fray Marcos to take possession of the land in his name.

REVIEWING THE SKILL

Answer on your own paper.

5. What is an author's point of view? What can it tell you?

6. What things in a reading selection can give you clues to an author's purpose?

DRAWING LOGICAL CONCLUSIONS

Once you have read through a selection and evaluated it by applying such thinking skills as detecting bias and distinguishing facts from opinions, you are ready for a final step—drawing conclusions. You may need to draw logical conclusions to determine unstated causes or effects, predict what will happen next, make comparisons, make judgments, or arrive at a generalization, or general rule, that is supported by specific details. Most writers do not spell out everything they expect a reader to understand. To reach a conclusion, you must examine information in the passage and then make logical guesses about what is not stated. For example, if a writer describes soldiers leaving a town and then describes wounded soldiers returning, you can conclude that a battle must have taken place in between these two events.

When drawing a conclusion from a reading selection, carefully study facts and reasons given in the selection. Your conclusion is likely to be inaccurate if it is not supported by information in the selection. Decide whether the selection provides enough information, as well as whether the information is sound. In the example above, for instance, you could conclude that a battle had taken place, but from the evidence given you could not guess whether the city's soldiers had won or lost the battle. Combine the evidence in the selection with what you know from other reading or your own experience to draw a reasonable conclusion. For instance, you know that battles are the most likely places for soldiers to be wounded.

APPLYING THE SKILL

The following selection was written by Baroness Friederike von Riedesel during the American Revolutionary War. On your paper write at least two conclusions that you can logically draw from the selection.

In the beginning all went well. We cherished the sweet hope of a sure victory, and of coming into the "promised land." When we passed the Hudson River and (British) General Burgoyne said, "The English never lose ground," our spirits were greatly exhilarated.

But that which displeased me was, that the wives of all the officers belonging to the expedi-tion knew beforehand everything that was to happen. And this seemed the more strange to me as I had seen, when in the armies of the Duke Ferdinand, during the Seven Years' War, with how much secrecy everything was conducted. But here, on the contrary, the Americans were apprised beforehand of all our intentions, so that at every place where we came they already waited for us. This circumstance hurt us exceedingly.

On the ninth, we spent the whole day in a pouring rain, ready to march at a moment's warning. The savages had lost their courage. They were seen in all directions going home. The slightest reverse of fortune discouraged them, especially if there was nothing to plunder.

Adapted from account quoted in Richard M. Dorson, ed., *America Rebels* (New York: Pantheon Books, 1953, pp. 193, 199).

MAKING MEANING

Answer the following questions.

1. The Baroness probably **(a)** supported the British side in the war, **(b)** supported the American side in the war, **(c)** was opposed to the war, **(d)** did not have strong feelings about the war.

2. The sentence that provides the best evidence for the conclusion you drew in question 1 is **(a)** In the beginning all went well. **(b)** When General Burgoyne said, "The English never lose ground," our spirits were greatly exhilarated. **(c)** The wives belonging to the expedition knew beforehand everything that was to happen. **(d)** We spent the whole day in a pouring rain, ready to march at a moment's warning.

3. The Baroness apparently thought that **(a)** the British troops should go home, **(b)** the British troops should plunder, **(c)** the war should be conducted with more secrecy, **(d)** the war should be conducted with less secrecy.

4. The "savages" the Baroness referred to were probably **(a)** Indians, **(b)** German troops, **(c)** American troops, **(d)** British troops.

REVIEWING THE SKILL

5. What kinds of conclusions can you draw from a reading selection?

6. On what should you base these conclusions?

7. How can you try to make sure your conclusion is accurate?

MAKING ACCURATE GENERALIZATIONS

Generalizations, either those made by authors or those that you make yourself, can help you understand relationships. You are making a generalization when you look over a group of facts or details to see what they have in common and then state a general idea that applies to the group overall. Examples of generalizations are "Most Britons were satisfied with their country's government during the Victorian period" and "Overall, industrialization improved the standard of living in Europe." A generalization may be valid even though there are exceptions to it.

Generalizations often are signaled by such words as *most*, *few*, and *usually*. Generalizations that use words such as *always*, *every*, *none*, or *never* are invalid, because most generalizations have some exceptions. When evaluating a generalization, examine available facts or examples to see whether they support the generalization. You can also make your own generalizations. Look for things that most of the facts on a certain subject have in common. Try to state the common feature or features.

APPLYING THE SKILL

The following selection describes working conditions for British ironworkers and miners in the late eighteenth century. On a sheet of paper, list each generalization you find. In addition, use facts in the selection to make at least one generalization of your own. Write down the generalizations, listing the facts that support each.

> Work for the men in the forges and blast furnaces was tough and hard. Many of the men were highly skilled and worked very long hours. Blast furnacemen worked twelve-hour shifts from six till six and they had to work seven days a week to keep the furnaces in continuous blast. On Sundays the shifts changed over so the men who had done the day shift had to do the night shift as well. This meant that on alternate Sundays the men worked twenty-four hours. Forge workers also worked a twelve-hour day. Puddling, especially, was very hard work and the working life of a puddler was said to be over by the time he reached forty.
>
> Mining was well paid too but it was very tiring. Some miners worked twelve-hour shifts and others only six- or eight-hour shifts. Although long-wall mining was safer than the old methods there were still frequent accidents and the health of most miners was permanently damaged by the time they were fifty because of the damp and bad air in the mines.

From Christine Vialls, *The Industrial Revolution Begins* (Minneapolis: Lerner Publications, 1982, pp. 29-30).

MAKING MEANING

1. In the selection, a stated generalization supported by facts is **(a)** Work for the men in the forges and blast furnaces was tough and hard. **(b)** Many of the men were highly skilled. **(c)** Blast furnacemen worked twelve-hour shifts from six till six. **(d)** Mining was well paid.

2. A fact that supports the generalization you chose is **(a)** Work in the forges and blast furnaces was tough and hard. **(b)** Many of the men were highly skilled. **(c)** Blast furnacemen worked twelve-hour shifts from six till six. **(d)** Some miners worked twelve-hour shifts.

3. An unstated generalization supported by facts in the second paragraph is **(a)** Mining attracted few workers. **(b)** Miners worked longer hours than ironworkers. **(c)** Mining was a relatively safe occupation. **(d)** Mining was a relatively dangerous occupation.

4. A fact supporting the generalization you chose for question 3 is **(a)** Mining was well paid. **(b)** Some miners worked twelve-hour shifts. **(c)** Long-wall mining was safer than the old methods. **(d)** The health of most miners was permanently damaged by the age of fifty.

5. The generalization best supported by the whole selection is **(a)** Both ironworkers and miners were well paid. **(b)** Both ironworkers and miners worked extremely long hours. **(c)** Both ironworkers and miners had hard but healthy lives. **(d)** Both ironworkers and miners were worse off than most other workers.

REVIEWING THE SKILL

6. What is a generalization?

7. How can you identify a generalization stated by an author? How can you evaluate an author's generalization?

8. How can you make a generalization of your own from facts in your reading?

SELECTING REFERENCES

When you are researching a problem in social studies, you may use several kinds of reference tools. You need to know what each tool does and how to use it in order to do your research quickly and accurately. The following five reference tools are especially likely to be useful in social studies research.

Atlas. An atlas is a book of maps. The maps may show physical characteristics such as terrain and climate, human characteristics such as cities and political boundaries, or both. A historical atlas shows areas of settlement, political boundaries, trade routes, and other human characteristics of the world as they were at different times in the past.

Almanac. An almanac contains an assortment of data—facts, statistics, lists of events—about different parts of the world. Almanacs are published yearly, so they are a good source of up-to-date information. Many almanacs also have some kinds of historical information.

Biographical Dictionary. A biographical dictionary gives brief descriptions of the lives of famous people. It tells facts such as the places and dates of the people's births and deaths. It also describes the people's major achievements. Information is arranged in alphabetical order by last names.

Reader's Guide to Periodical Literature. *Reader's Guide* lists articles that appear in major magazines. The listings are arranged in alphabetical order. You may look up an article by the last name of the author, the title of the article, or the subject of the article. Each listing gives the name, date, and page numbers of the magazine in which the article appeared.

National Newspaper Index. This index lists recent articles in five major national newspapers: the *New York Times, Wall Street Journal, Christian Science Monitor, Los Angeles Times,* and *Washington Post.* Titles of articles and general subjects are listed together in alphabetical order. Articles are also listed under general subject headings, with the most recent article listed first. The *Newspaper Index* is on microfilm.

APPLYING THE SKILL

Decide three to five names, titles, general subject areas, or other words you would try looking up to find each of the kinds of information described below. List these words and phrases on your paper.
1. background information on the leaders of the Mexican Revolution
2. the colonies established in Africa by European powers between 1850 and 1914
3. a magazine article on the modernization of Japan in the nineteenth century
4. a brief description of Nigeria, including its current population, major exports, and government leaders
5. a *New York Times* article on the growth of export industries in China

MAKING MEANING

Answer the following questions.
1. The best reference to use for item 1 is **(a)** an almanac, **(b)** an atlas, **(c)** a biographical dictionary, **(d)** *Reader's Guide.*
2. The best reference to use for item 2 is **(a)** an almanac, **(b)** an atlas, **(c)** a biographical dictionary, **(d)** *National Newspaper Index.*
3. The best reference to use for item 3 is **(a)** an almanac, **(b)** an atlas, **(c)** a biographical dictionary, **(d)** *Reader's Guide.*
4. The best reference to use for item 4 is **(a)** an almanac, **(b)** an atlas, **(c)** *Reader's Guide,* **(d)** *National Newspaper Index.*
5. The best reference to use for item 5 is **(a)** an almanac, **(b)** a biographical dictionary, **(c)** *Reader's Guide,* **(d)** *National Newspaper Index.*
6. The best reference to use for item 6 is **(a)** an almanac, **(b)** a biographical dictionary, **(c)** *Reader's Guide,* **(d)** *National Newspaper Index.*

REVIEWING THE SKILL

Answer on your own paper.
7. Briefly describe the kind of information each of the following references contains and tell how to use it.
a. an atlas, **b.** a biographical dictionary, **c.** an almanac, **d.** *Reader's Guide to Periodical Literature,* **e.** *National Newspaper Index*

IDENTIFYING WORD MEANING

In your reading of books, magazines, and newspaper articles you may often encounter words whose meaning you do not know. Looking the words up in a dictionary is one good way to find out their meanings, of course. Even if you don't have a dictionary handy, though, you can often make a good guess about the meaning of an unfamiliar word.

One way to figure out the meaning of an unknown word is to look at the *context* of the word. A word's context is its surroundings—the other words in the sentence and the other sentences in the paragraph. The context often contains clues such as a synonym (a word with about the same meaning as the unknown word), an antonym (a word with a meaning opposite to that of the unknown word), a definition, or an example of the idea the unknown word represents. Try to find these clues in the context and use them to help you guess the meaning of the unknown word.

For example, from context clues in the following sentence, you can guess that agronomists are people who have something to do with crop production: "Although none of them has actually been on the moon, these *agronomists* are hard at work determining what crops could be grown there."

Sometimes the word itself may contain clues that can help you guess its meaning. Look at the word carefully to see whether any part of it is familiar. Some words are made up of a base word joined with one or more prefixes (syllables added at the beginning of the base word) or suffixes (syllables added at the end of the base word). *Pre-*, *re-*, *sub-*, and *un-* are common prefixes. *-Tion*, *-ism*, *-ate*, and *-ize* are common suffixes.

If you know the meaning of a base word and of the prefixes or suffixes attached to it, you can usually work out the meaning of the complete word.

For example, *form* means "to shape or to make something." *Re-* means "again," and *-er* means "a person who has something to do with" whatever the base word refers to. *Re-* plus *form* plus *-er*—reformer—is a person who reshapes something. When you work out the meaning of a word by examining the word's parts this way, you are using *structural analysis*.

APPLYING THE SKILL

The following news story from *Newsweek* describes a flood in Bangladesh. Use context clues and structural analysis to work out the meanings of the italicized words. Write your guesses on your own paper.

> It was the wrath of Allah, some Muslims said in Dacca last week. Indeed, it seemed that nothing less than divine *retribution* could explain Bangladesh's bad luck. For the second straight year, unusually heavy flood waters poured out of the Himalayan foothills. They swept into the 50,000-square-mile *alluvial* plain, breaking down dikes and barriers. At one point, three fourths of the country was *submerged*. Officially, nearly 800 people died. Other estimates counted 1,500 fatalities. Water-carried diseases hit more than 100,000, officials said. About 30 million Bangladeshis were homeless or stranded. Hunger was everywhere.
>
> If nothing else, the disaster called attention to the need for flood control in the Bangladesh delta, a *confluence* of rivers beginning in India and Nepal. A system of upstream dams and reservoirs would need the cooperation of both countries along with China, however. It would also need more planning than has been seen in a region that falls from one crisis to another.

Adapted from "Bangladesh: The Water This Time" (*Newsweek*, September 19, 1988, p. 32).

MAKING MEANING

1. A synonym for *retribution* that appears in the word's context is **(a)** wrath, **(b)** Allah, **(c)** divine, **(d)** luck.
2. An *alluvial* plain is a plain found **(a)** in the mountains, **(b)** under water, **(c)** around a river, **(d)** behind dikes and barriers.
3. The prefix *sub-* in *submerged* means **(a)** over, **(b)** under, **(c)** behind, **(d)** again.
4. *Confluence* means **(a)** a delta, **(b)** a large river, **(c)** a flood, **(d)** a place where rivers join.

REVIEWING THE SKILL

5. Name two kinds of context clues that can help you work out the meaning of a word.
6. Explain how you can work out a word's meaning by examining the parts of the word.

CHAPTER ONE SKILLS PRACTICE

Identifying Social Studies Terms

1. Read the sentence. Then choose the meaning of the underlined word.

The development of human <u>culture</u> began about two million years ago.

a. education and good taste
b. cells grown in a nutrient liquid
c. farming
d. way of life of a people

Read the following selection and answer question 2.

Scientists called one early type of people *Homo erectus*. *Homo* means "human." *Erectus* means "one who walks upright." *Homo erectus* lived on earth for about a million years, from 1.5 million years ago to about 300,000 years ago.

These prehistoric hunters made tools. At sites where *Homo erectus* once camped, scientists have found scrapers, choppers, and hammers chipped from stones. Thousands of stone hand axes have been found throughout Europe and Asia. These axes are carefully formed. They all have the same design, showing that *Homo erectus* could pass skills and learning from one group to another.

Remains of firepits at some sites show that these early people knew how to control and use fire as long as 500,000 years ago. They probably first learned to capture fire started by lightning, volcanoes, and other forces of nature. They may have carried fire from place to place as live coals or slowly burning torches.

Once people controlled fire, they could eat more kinds of food. By using fire for cooking, they made meats and other foods more tender. Campfires also protected people by frightening away wild animals. Thus, the campfire, with its warm glow, became an important center of group life.

Identifying the Main Idea

2. Which of the following is the best statement of the main idea of this selection?

a. *Homo erectus* hunters could control fire.
b. *Homo erectus* hunters used stones as tools but did not shape them.
c. *Homo erectus* hunters could control their environment in important ways.
d. *Homo erectus* hunters were more advanced than the humans who came before them.

Read the following selection and answer question 3.

Finds in shelters dating from about 25,000 years ago to about 20,000 years ago show a system for preparing skins and sewing clothing.

The skins of animals were first scraped with flint blades. Knives were used to cut the leather made from the skins. The leather pieces were sewn together with thread made of reindeer tendons or taken from the manes or tails of horses. Needles were made of bone, ivory, or reindeer horn. Clothing from this time was probably much like that of the Eskimos. Some pieces had bone buttons with holes. The buttons were often decorated with engraving. A recent find shows this skin clothing quite well: an animal skin opened over a rich vest, worked in the same red color as its background. A nearby headdress was decorated with hanging olives.

Adapted from Raymond Lantier, *Man Before History* (New York: Walker & Company, 1965).

Identifying Specific Details

3. According to this selection, what were prehistoric needles made from?

a. reindeer tendons
b. bone, ivory, or reindeer horn
c. flint
d. slivers of copper or iron

WRITING ACTIVITY

Assume that you are a museum director preparing an exhibit on early peoples. Classify the following artifacts according to which display you would plan to put them in—the exhibit on early nomads or the exhibit on the first settled peoples: a red pottery bowl containing petrified seeds, a wooden plow, a spearthrower, a scrap of woven cloth, a stone scraper, a stone tablet with symbols scratched on it, fragments of a skin-covered tent, a sunbaked brick, a carved antler harpoon. Write a description of the two exhibits and briefly summarize the differences between the earlier and the later artifacts.

CHAPTER TWO SKILLS PRACTICE

Study the following map and then answer questions 1 and 2.

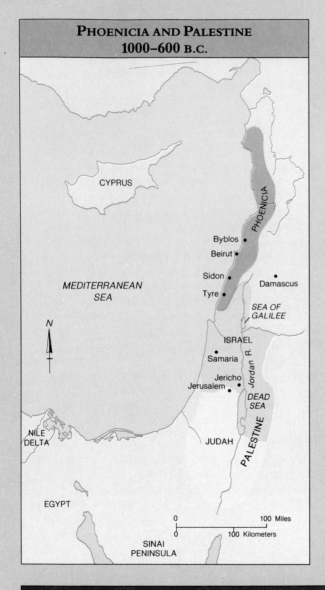

PHOENICIA AND PALESTINE
1000–600 B.C.

CYPRUS

MEDITERRANEAN
SEA

PHOENICIA

Byblos
Beirut
Sidon
Tyre

Damascus

SEA OF
GALILEE

N

ISRAEL

Samaria

Jericho
Jerusalem

Jordan R.

DEAD
SEA

NILE
DELTA

JUDAH

PALESTINE

EGYPT

0   100 Miles
0   100 Kilometers

SINAI
PENINSULA

Using Graphic Sources
1. According to this map, where was Israel located in ancient times?
a. north of Judah
b. east of Phoenicia
c. north of Phoenicia
d. south of Judah

Using Graphic Sources
2. Judging from the map, which of the following regions probably carried on the most trade in the Mediterranean Sea?
a. Palestine
b. Phoenicia
c. Israel
d. Judah

Identifying Social Studies Terms
3. Read the sentence. Then choose the meaning of the underlined word.

Sargon created the world's first empire.

a. ruler of a very large territory
b. government uniting many territories and peoples under one ruler
c. referee at a sporting event
d. very large palace

Read the following selection and answer question 4.

The Egyptians believed in many deities. However, Amenhotep came to worship only the sun god Aton, "the sole god, beside whom there is no other." Amenhotep was perhaps the earliest supporter of monotheism.

Identifying Word Meaning from Context
4. What is the best meaning of monotheism as used above?
a. belief in a sun god
b. belief in many gods and goddesses
c. belief in one god
d. belief in supernatural powers

WRITING ACTIVITY
Ancient Beersheba lay southwest of Jerusalem, at the edge of the desert. Study the ruins of this village, shown in an aerial view on page 41. Then write a description of Beersheba as it might have looked to a merchant traveling the trade route from Egypt to Palestine. Consider how the village would have looked to you as you approached it from a distance, and what the entrance to the village, as well as its buildings might have been like. (To locate Jerusalem, the Sinai, ancient trade routes, and the desert areas, refer to the maps on pages 20, 30, and 38.)

CHAPTER THREE SKILLS PRACTICE

Identifying Word Meaning from Structural Analysis

1. What is the best definition of the following word?

subcontinent

a. a piece of land that is almost a continent
b. land under a continent
c. part of a continent
d. large land mass surrounded by water

Read the following selection and answer question 2.

Sanskrit, the classical language of India, is related to almost all the languages of Europe, including English. The Sanskrit word "Arya," or "Aryan" is the name of the people who began to conquer India about 1500 B.C. Most ancient Indian literature was written in the Aryan tongue, Sanskrit, and Hindi, modern India's national language, is written in characters derived from Sanskrit.

Sanskrit is a branch of a linguistic tree known as Indo-European. The trunk of the tree was a common tongue probably spoken in the region northwest of the Black Sea about 2500 B.C. After the people living in this region migrated in different directions, the tree branched into different but related languages. "Iran," the modern name for Persia, for example, resembles the Sanskrit "Arya." In Celtic the word was transformed into "Erin," which in English became "Ireland."

Adapted from Lucille Schulberg, *Historic India* (New York: Time Inc., 1968).

Identifying the Main Idea

2. Which of the following is the best statement of the main idea of this selection?
a. Indo-European is the base of the classical language of India and most of the languages of Europe.
b. Sanskrit is the base of the classical language of India and most of the languages of Europe.
c. The Aryans conquered most of Europe.
d. Indo-European is widely spoken today.

Use the following timeline to answer question 3.

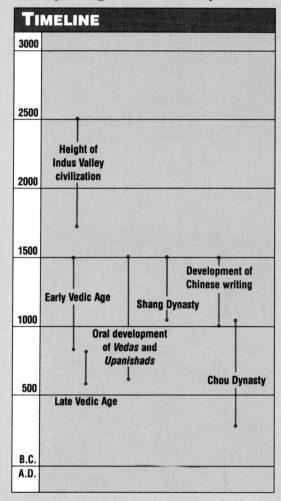

Using Graphic Sources

3. According to the timeline, when did Chinese writing develop?
a. at the same time as the Early Vedic Age
b. during the Chou Dynasty
c. at the same time as the Late Vedic Age
d. after the oral development of the *Vedas* and the *Upanishads*

WRITING ACTIVITY

You are an anthropologist studying Indus Valley civilization. Considering what you know about the life of the people in Harappa and Mohenjo-daro, write an article on how you think their government probably was organized. What issues might a government official have had to face? (Refer to pages 49–51.)

CHAPTER FOUR SKILLS PRACTICE

Study the following map and then answer questions 1 and 2.

Using Graphic Sources

1. Judging from this map, where were most Greek colonies established?
   a. along coastlines
   b. on islands
   c. in mountain regions
   d. on inland rivers

Using Graphic Sources

2. Where are most of the trade routes shown on the map?
   a. along rivers
   b. across the Mediterranean Sea or Black Sea
   c. inside Greece
   d. in Africa

Identifying Social Studies Terms

3. Read the sentence. Then choose the meaning of the underlined word.

   A Greek <u>citizen</u> often spent time debating important issues.

   a. person who lives in a city
   b. member of a legislative body
   c. person granted definite political rights and responsibilities
   d. slave or poor person

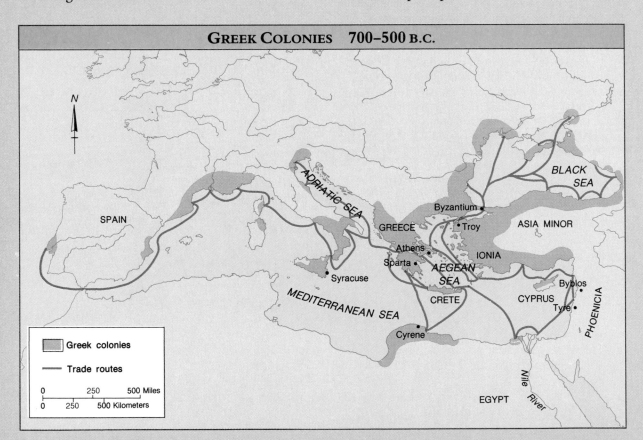

GREEK COLONIES   700–500 B.C.

- ▨ Greek colonies
- — Trade routes

0   250   500 Miles
0   250   500 Kilometers

SPAIN · ADRIATIC SEA · GREECE · Byzantium · Troy · ASIA MINOR · BLACK SEA · Athens · Sparta · IONIA · AEGEAN SEA · Syracuse · MEDITERRANEAN SEA · CRETE · CYPRUS · Byblos · Tyre · PHOENICIA · Cyrene · EGYPT · Nile River

---

WRITING ACTIVITY

Imagine that you are an opponent of Cleisthenes, living during his rule. Describe Cleisthenes's reforms and tell why you are against them. (Refer to page 79.)

CHAPTER FIVE SKILLS PRACTICE

Read the following selection and answer questions 1 and 2.

Manolis Andronicos, flashlight in hand, peeked into a room that had been closed for over 2300 years. When he looked at the stone door leading to the antechamber, he found that the door was carved but unfinished. "But then I saw the vases. On one side, silver vessels and goblets. On the other side the bronze and gold arms—helmet, shield."

The first day in the tomb, the archaeologists just looked, touching nothing. The second day they took pictures and made drawings, but everything was left as it was.

In the center of the room stood a white marble coffin. When it was opened, the archaeologists saw a pile of bones and teeth and a delicate crown of oak leaves and acorns, carefully fashioned from gold.

Newspaper headlines announced that the tomb of Philip of Macedon, father of Alexander the Great, had been found. As yet, though, there was no proof of this. Then Andronicos took a powerful flashlight and examined the tomb again. Among the rubble he found several small ivory heads. The fifth one was of a man with a luxuriant beard and world-weary eyes—the face of Philip, familiar from hundreds of ancient coins.

Adapted from "Splendor and Mystery of Philip's Tomb," *San Francisco Examiner & Chronicle Sunday Punch*, January 8, 1978, pp. 2, 5.

Identifying Specific Details

1. What did Andronicos find that suggested that this was Philip's tomb?

a. newspaper headlines

b. an ivory head that looked like Philip's head on ancient coins

c. a pile of bones and teeth

d. Philip's name carved on the coffin

Drawing Logical Conclusions

2. What would the place where they were found suggest about the pile of bones and teeth?

a. They belonged to the person who was buried in the tomb.

b. They belonged to animals that wandered in during the centuries.

c. They belonged to a servant of the king.

d. They were put there to scare away intruders.

Read the following selection and answer question 3.

As a result of Alexander's conquests and policies, there was a remarkable blending of Persian and Greek cultures. This sharing of ideas and traditions took place on a much larger scale and in a shorter time than ever before.

To spread Greek influence, Alexander encouraged Greeks to settle in all parts of the empire. He established seventy new cities for his Greek and Macedonian followers. These cities had a Greek form of government. Later, many of the Greek settlers married local people. This naturally led to widespread sharing of ideas and customs. Even the style of sculpture in faraway India was influenced by Greek art.

To help bring Persian culture to Greece and Macedonia, Alexander arranged the marriage of thousands of his men to Persian women at Susa. In a separate ceremony, eighty of his officers married the daughters of Persian nobles. He himself married the daughter of the dead Persian king, Darius. Alexander also brought Persian soldiers into his army, wore Persian clothes, and followed many Persian customs.

Identifying the Main Idea

3. Which of the following is the best statement of the main idea of this selection?

a. There was much friendship between Greeks and Persians in Alexander's empire.

b. Most people in Greece and Macedonia lived in large, prosperous cities.

c. Alexander took many steps to combine Greek and Persian cultures.

d. The Greeks had an important influence on the culture of India.

WRITING ACTIVITY

Imagine that you are a Hellenistic philosopher transported to the United States today. When you report back to the Alexandrian court, will you say Americans seem more Epicurean or more Stoic? Describe what you saw in American culture that brought you to your conclusion. (Refer to page 103.)

CHAPTER SIX SKILLS PRACTICE

Read the following selection and answer question 1.

The wealthy landowners made up about 10 percent of Rome's population, not including slaves. The remaining 90 percent, the plebeians, were nearly excluded from political life. Plebeians faced many restrictions.

Identifying Word Meaning from Context

1. Which of the following is the best definition of plebeians as used above?
a. professional soldiers
b. consuls, senators, and other government officials
c. slaves and hired workers
d. farmers, merchants, laborers, and other citizens of modest means

Identifying Social Studies Terms

2. Read the sentence. Then choose the meaning of the underlined word.

Rome was a republic until the time of Octavian.

a. government ruled by an emperor or an empress
b. government run by representatives elected by the citizens
c. a small city-state
d. government ruled directly by the people

Read the following selection and answer questions 3 and 4.

In the days of Augustus, about a million people lived in Rome. Most of them were jammed in stuffy apartments. (The air smelled so bad that Pliny suggested covering up the smell by burning bread.) People complained about the lack of houses, high rents, and prices. Traffic blocked the streets. The air was often polluted. Robbers made the streets dangerous.

When ways of farming changed, more farming families had to move to the city. To try to keep order, the government set up a civil service with tax collectors, police, fire wardens, building inspectors, and public health officers.

Adapted from Moses Hadas, *Imperial Rome* (New York: Time Inc., 1965).

Identifying Cause and Effect

3. According to this selection, what was one reason why more people moved to Rome?
a. There were good jobs in the city.
b. The city walls offered protection from enemies.
c. Food prices were low in the city.
d. Changes in farming methods forced many families to leave their farms.

Drawing Logical Conclusions

4. Which of the following conclusions can most reasonably be drawn from this selection?
a. There were no advantages to living in Rome.
b. Crowding helped cause many of Rome's problems.
c. The government was successful in solving Rome's problems.
d. Rome provided cheap housing for many people.

Identifying Social Studies Terms

5. Read the sentence. Then choose the meaning of the underlined word.

Many a strong young man decided to serve as a mercenary.

a. a slave trained for construction work
b. a person willing to die rather than deny a religious belief
c. a soldier paid to fight in a foreign army
d. a merchant who provides military goods

WRITING ACTIVITY

Describe the theatrical troupe mosaic pictured on page 117. Write as if you are the archaeologist who first discovered the mosaic.

CHAPTER SEVEN SKILLS PRACTICE

Read the following selection and answer question 1.

The Church fathers lived, worked, and practiced their faith in remote monasteries. During the A.D. 300s, monasteries became centers of Christian thought. As the Roman Empire continued to decline, monks living in monasteries collected and copied all the classical literature of Greece and Rome they could find. After the collapse of the empire, the monks helped to preserve the culture and achievements of the Romans.

Identifying Word Meaning from Context
1. Which of the following is the best definition of monasteries as used above?
a. large city churches
b. residences devoted to the practice of religion apart from the world
c. universities
d. castles or fortresses

Read the following selection and answer questions 2 and 3.

By the third century A.D., the Romans were using the arch and the vaulted dome. These innovations enabled the Romans to build much larger buildings than the Greeks.

The Romans also developed technology useful outside of architecture. One of their most important inventions was the waterwheel, or water-powered mill. This was the first new way of harnessing a natural source of power since the invention of the sail.

The Romans were not very interested in developing new technology to grow more food or to make things more efficiently or quickly. Part of this lack of innovative spirit can be traced to the importance of slave labor. Since slaves did all the work, Romans did not feel a need to make their work easier.

Technology was seen as a way to make the army stronger or to provide the people with things they needed such as water, but not to increase production. If the Romans needed to grow more food, they brought in more slaves to work in the fields.

Identifying the Main Idea
2. Which of the following best describes the main idea of this selection?
a. The Romans used technology mainly for the military and for public works.
b. The Romans had little interest in technology.
c. Rome borrowed most of its technology from the earlier Greek culture.
d. Technology helped Roman slaves be more productive.

Drawing Logical Conclusions
3. What would have been likely to happen to Roman technology if slaves had been scarcer or more expensive?
a. The Romans would not have used waterwheels.
b. The Romans would have developed more machines to help with farming and manufacturing.
c. Technology would have been too expensive for anyone except the army.
d. The Romans would have lost their interest in technology.

Identifying Social Studies Terms
4. Read the sentence. Then choose the meaning of the underlined word.

Many people secretly admired the courage of the martyrs.

a. famous preachers
b. soldiers who fight in enemy territory
c. people who die for their beliefs
d. spies

WRITING ACTIVITY
Describe the spread of Christianity in the first century. Include how it spread, who spread it, where it spread to, and who converted to Christianity. (Refer to pages 142–143.)

CHAPTER EIGHT SKILLS PRACTICE

In the Bhagavad-Gita, *Lord Krishna spoke to the warrior Arjuna before a great battle. Read the following selection and answer question 1.*

The Spirit, which moves through all that we see, is not perishable. Nothing can destroy the Spirit.

Weapons cut It not, fire burns It not, water drenches It not, and wind dries It not.

Be not anxious about these armies. The spirit in man is not perishable.

You must look at your duty. Nothing can be more welcome to a soldier than a righteous war. Therefore to waver in your resolve is unworthy.

Look upon pleasure and pain, victory and defeat, with an equal eye. Make ready for the combat, and you will commit no sin.

Reprinted by permission of Faber & Faber, Ltd. from *The Geeta: The Gospel of the Lord Shri Krishna*, trans. by Shri Purohit Swami, copyright 1935.

Identifying Author's Purpose

1. Based on this selection, what is Krishna's main purpose in speaking to Arjuna?
a. to glorify war
b. to get Arjuna to give up violence
c. to encourage Arjuna to do his duty and be at peace with himself
d. to explain how some wars can be right

Read the following selection and answer question 2.

The Han Dynasty ruled their empire with the aid of a vast <u>bureaucracy</u>, a system set up to carry out the affairs of government through departments managed by appointed officials. Each department had a chief minister and many minor officials.

Identifying Word Meaning from Context

2. Which of the following is the best definition of bureaucracy as used above?
a. a large group of office buildings
b. the structure of departments and officials that carry out government policy

c. a form of government
d. an important government official who has many assistants.

Read the following selection and answer questions 3 and 4.

The people are the most important part in government; the ruler is least important.

If the people have plenty, their prince will not be left to want alone. If the people are in need, their prince will not be able to enjoy plenty alone.

When rulers love to observe the rules of proper conduct, the people respond readily to the calls upon them for service.

The ruler must first possess in himself the qualities that he requires of the people; and must be free from the qualities that he requires the people to give up.

Adapted from M.M. Dawson, *The Ethics of Confucius* (New York: G.P. Putnam's Sons, 1915).

Identifying Author's Purpose

3. What was the author's purpose in writing this selection?
a. to describe the ideal form of government
b. to show rulers how to govern well
c. to prove that democracy is better than monarchy
d. to encourage people to be good citizens

Identifying the Main Idea

4. Which of the following is the best statement of the main idea of this selection?
a. Most rulers treat their people well.
b. Rulers have a right to expect good conduct from the people.
c. The personal conduct of the ruler is not as important as the qualities of the people.
d. A ruler's success depends on being concerned about the people's happiness and on giving them a good example.

WRITING ACTIVITY

Imagine that you are an Indian merchant carrying the word of Buddhism to China along with your wares. Explain how you got from your home near the Ganges River to the Chinese city of Chang-an. (Refer to the maps on pages 48, 158, and 163, as well as the map of Asia on page 825.)

CHAPTER NINE SKILLS PRACTICE

Read the following selection and answer question 1.

Constantinople is a busy city, and merchants journey to it from every country by sea or land, and there is none like it in the world except Baghdad, the great city of Islam. In Constantinople is the church of Santa Sophia, and the seat of the Pope of the Greeks, since the Greeks do not obey the Pope of Rome. There are also churches according to the number of the days of the year. A quantity of wealth beyond description is brought hither year by year as tribute, and the like of this wealth is not to be found in any other church in the world. And in this church there are pillars of gold and silver, and lamps of silver and gold more than a man can count.

The Greek inhabitants are very rich in gold and precious stones, and they go clothed in garments of silk with gold embroidery, and they ride horses, and look like princes. Indeed, the land is very rich in all cloth stuffs, and in bread, meat, and wine.

Adapted from Benjamin of Tudela, *Itinerary*, trans. Marcus Nathan Alder (London: Oxford University Press, 1907).

Distinguishing Between Facts and Opinions

1. Which of the following is a FACT presented in the selection?
   a. The church of Santa Sophia is the largest church in Constantinople.
   b. The church of Santa Sophia contains lamps of gold and silver.
   c. Material for clothing is plentiful in Constantinople, but food is not.
   d. The Greek inhabitants of Constantinople look like princes.

Read the following selection and answer questions 2 and 3.

Steppe nomads were skilled warriors. However, they spent much of their time looking for fresh grazing land for their livestock. Some of these livestock gave the nomads a staple diet of goat's milk, beef, and mutton. Livestock also provided wool and leather for clothing.

The nomads' most important animal, however, was the one that kept them so mobile—the horse. Without horses, the nomads could not have controlled large herds of livestock or hunted fast-moving game such as elk. The nomads were on horseback most of their waking hours. They often ate their meals perched on a saddle.

A life of almost constant movement required clothing fit for riding, such as close-fitting trousers tucked into soft high boots. The nomadic life also required that each family's possessions be limited to what could be carried in a covered wagon. Perhaps the most important of these possessions was the collapsible felt tent. When the nomads set up camp, thick rugs made the tents comfortable inside. Dyed animal skins decorated the tent walls.

Identifying Specific Details

2. According to this selection, what were steppe nomads' tents made from?
   a. leather
   b. heavy woven cloth
   c. silk
   d. felt

Drawing Logical Conclusions

3. Which of the following conclusions can most reasonably be drawn from this selection?
   a. A steppe nomad would welcome the gift of a fine horse.
   b. A steppe nomad would welcome the gift of a large house.
   c. A steppe nomad would welcome the gift of a gold necklace.
   d. A steppe nomad would welcome the gift of fertile farm land.

WRITING ACTIVITY
Refugee groups fled the Mongol invasion of Russia in the 1200s. As a member of such a group fleeing north from their home along the Don River, decide whether to settle in Moscow or continue on toward Novgorod. Write a speech to convince the other members of the group that you have made the best choice. (Refer to pages 195–196.)

CHAPTER TEN SKILLS PRACTICE

Identifying Word Meaning from Structural Analysis

1. What is the best definition of the following word?

decentralized

a. lacking a center or single focus
b. broken into many pieces
c. having a central location
d. uncertain

Read the following selection and answer questions 2 and 3.

One task of farm women in Iceland went on all the year round: the making of woolen cloth. First, the wool was carded [combed] and cleaned of its grease. Then it was spun on a distaff [spinning staff] and spindle. The distaff was held in the crook of the left arm. The spindle, weighted at one end by a disk of stone, was set spinning by the right hand. The spindle sank slowly to the floor, drawing the wool out to a thread. This thread would be wound up. Then the process would be repeated until a large ball of yarn had been made. One great advantage of this way of spinning was that it could be practiced while standing or walking.

Weaving was done on an upright loom leaned against a wall, working from the top down. There were two sets of warp [vertical] threads, held taut by stones hanging from them. Horizontal rods controlled the warp threads' positions as the woof threads were slipped through. The woof was then pushed up with a wooden or whale-bone "sword."

Adapted from Jacqueline Simpson, *Everyday Life in the Viking Age* (New York: Dorset Press, 1987).

Identifying the Sequence of Events

2. According to this selection, what did a woman do immediately after she let her spindle sink to the floor?

a. She carded the wool and cleaned it of its grease.
b. She pushed the woof threads upward.
c. She dyed the yarn.
d. She wound up the thread.

Identifying Specific Details

3. According to this selection, which of the following is used in weaving?

a. a loom
b. a distaff
c. a spindle
d. a needle

Identifying Social Studies Terms

4. Read the sentence. Then choose the meaning of the underlined word.

Everyone on the manor shared the commons.

a. ordinary people
b. grazing lands and forests used by a group
c. towns
d. entrances to a village

Read the following selection and answer question 5.

In order to set up a more independent Roman church, Pope Gregory I helped create a theology that was separate from that of the Byzantine Church. For instance, he worked out the idea of purgatory as a place one goes for purification before being let into heaven. The Byzantine Church had no such belief.

Identifying Word Meaning from Context

5. What is the best meaning of theology as used above?

a. god
b. system of religious beliefs
c. study of ancient Church documents
d. a religious belief

WRITING ACTIVITY

You are a monk in a Cluniac monastery. Write a letter to the pope telling him what changes you think are needed in the Church and why. (Refer to pages 212–213.)

CHAPTER ELEVEN SKILLS PRACTICE

Read the following selection and answer question 1.

King Henry II of England, who ruled from 1154 to 1189, took important steps that led to what is today known as trial by jury. To rule his kingdom more effectively, Henry ordered local sheriffs to represent him in disputes over the ownership of land. Twelve trusted citizens who knew something about the case were to act as witnesses. The sheriff decided the case based on what the witnesses said.

Gradually, practices changed. Instead of serving as witnesses, 12 citizens were chosen to act as jurors, judging the case. In 1215, the Magna Carta stated that no person "shall be taken or imprisoned except by the lawful judgment of his peers," or equals.

Today, the trial jury is usually made up of 12 men and women. They hear from witnesses for both sides of a dispute. After thinking about all the evidence, the jury decides if the accused is guilty.

Identifying Specific Details

1. According to this selection, which detail supports the idea that trials during Henry II's reign were fair?

a. Decisions in trials were made by the local sheriff.

b. Twelve trusted citizens who knew about the case were witnesses.

c. Decisions in trials were made by twelve jurors.

d. Today's trial jury is usually made up of twelve men and women.

Read the following selection and answer questions 2 and 3.

How did a master glassmaker make a stained glass window? Using a small sketch, the glass painter made a full-size drawing of the window on a whitened table top. This "cartoon" included all the details of heads, hands, and drapery. Different colors were indicated by letters. Having chosen a colored sheet of glass, the painter laid it over the drawing. Each individual piece was made by drawing a red-hot iron round the shape required, after starting a crack by dropping water or—more probably—spitting on it. The resulting rough piece was then cut away round the edges with a notched iron until the shape and size were correct.

When all the shapes had been cut, they were laid out over the drawing. Then the painter traced the details of the design onto the surface of the glass. He used an enamel made from copper or iron oxide. The pieces of glass were then fired in a simple oven or kiln.

Finally the glassmaker joined all the pieces together by means of thin strips of lead. He smeared the joints with resin. Then he soldered them together to make the window.

Adapted from John Baker, *English Stained Glass of the Medieval Period* (London: Thames & Hudson Ltd., 1978).

Identifying the Sequence of Events

2. According to this selection, what did the glassmaker do immediately before cutting the first piece of glass?

a. He fired the glass in a kiln.

b. He made a small sketch of the design of the window.

c. He made a full-sized drawing of the window.

d. He colored the pieces of glass.

Identifying Cause and Effect

3. Why did the glassmaker fire the pieces of glass in a kiln?

a. to make the enameled details permanent

b. to cut the glass

c. to join the glass pieces together

d. to color the glass

WRITING ACTIVITY

Write a speech for the leader of the English nobles to give to the greater and lesser lords, knights, clergy, and representatives of townspeople gathered for the first parliament in the 1260s. Keep in mind that he is seeking to gain support against the king. (Refer to page 234.)

CHAPTER TWELVE SKILLS PRACTICE

Read the following selection and answer question 1.

The faithful built <u>mosques</u> where people could pray under the guidance of a prayer leader or imam. Scholars called ulama, who were educated in Islamic faith and laws, also became important in Islamic society.

Identifying Word Meaning from Context

1. What is the best meaning of <u>mosques</u> as used above?

a. tombs
b. ceremonial masks
c. places of worship
d. universities

Read the following selection and answer question 2.

Most of the time Muslim rulers in Spain let people practice other religions. Because of this, Arabic, Jewish, and Christian influences came together to build a vital civilization.

Cultural life centered in the famous and beautiful cities of Cordova, Toledo, and Granada. Mosques and palaces filled the cities, which had public sewers and lighted streets. People enjoyed the feast days of both Islam and Christianity. They sang the romantic songs written by Moorish musicians. The universities of Seville, Granada, and Cordova became centers of intellectual life.

Spanish Jews played a special part in science and learning during Muslim times. Able to work with many languages, they translated Greek works on philosophy and medicine into Arabic. As Islamic scientific knowledge grew, Jews translated information from Arabic into Latin and other European languages.

Identifying the Main Idea

2. Which of the following is the best statement of the main idea of this selection?

a. The cities of Muslim Spain had many modern public facilities.

b. Arabs, Jews, and Christians lived together in Muslim Spain.

c. Religious tolerance in Muslim Spain encouraged the growth of a rich and diverse civilization.

d. Spain was troubled by deep-rooted religious conflicts.

Read the following selection and answer question 3.

In the sultan Suleiman's court not one man owed his position to anything but his own merits and bravery. No one is distinguished from the rest by his birth, and honor is paid to each man based on the kind of work he does and the office he holds. Because of this there is no fighting for higher position or rank, every man having a suitable position.

The Sultan himself assigns to all their duties and offices. In doing so, he pays no attention to wealth or empty claims of rank, and he is not moved by any influence or popularity a candidate may have. He only considers merit.

Those who hold the highest offices under the Sultan are very often the sons of shepherds and herdsmen. Far from being ashamed of their birth, they often boast about it. They do not believe that good qualities can be given by birth or handed down by inheritance.

Adapted from Antony Bridge, *Suleiman the Magnificent: Scourge of Heaven* (London: Grafton Books, 1983). Reprinted by permission of Grafton Books.

Making Accurate Generalizations

3. According to this selection, what in general was considered when someone applied for a job at Suleiman's court?

a. amount of education
b. recommendations from influential or popular people
c. ability and personal qualities
d. the nobility of the person's family

WRITING ACTIVITY

You are a Hindu living in India under the Delhi Sultanate in the 1300s. Explain why you decided to convert to Islam. (Refer to page 265.)

CHAPTER THIRTEEN SKILLS PRACTICE

Like Marco Polo before him, the friar Odoric tells of the marvelous road and communication system in China. Read the following selection and answer questions 1 and 2.

The emperor has caused certain inns to be built along the highways. There all things that a traveler might need during a journey are kept.

If any news happens in any part of his empire, and he happens to be far away from that place, the news will be brought quickly to the emperor. Messengers on horses or camels ride post to him. When they and their beasts are weary, they blow their horn. At the noise of it the next inn likewise provides a horse and a man, who takes the letter from him that is weary, and runs to another inn. And so by many inns, and many posts, the report which ordinarily could scarcely come in thirty days, is in one natural day brought to the emperor.

Adapted from Malcolm Ross Macdonald, *Beyond the Horizon: Encyclopedia of Discovery and Exploration*, Vol. 2. (London: Aldus Books, 1981).

Identifying Author's Purpose
1. Which is the most likely reason why Odoric made this speech?
a. to describe what he had seen in his travels
b. to persuade others to take the same trip he had taken
c. to argue in favor of the emperor
d. to analyze the efficiency of the Chinese postal service

Drawing Logical Conclusions
2. Which of the following conclusions can reasonably be drawn from this selection?
a. Chinese messengers could ride faster than messengers in other lands.
b. China provided for all of its people's needs.
c. The Chinese communication system was designed to deliver messages as quickly as possible.
d. Most people in China could travel easily.

Read the following selection and answer question 3.

Strikingly different from other kinds of Buddhism was Zen, a mystical sect that reached Japan from China. It won great influence with the Kamakura military rulers because of its discipline.

The main idea of Zen is sudden enlightenment, in which a person learns that what had seemed to be real about life is an illusion. Enlightenment was held to be beyond all price, more valuable than any teaching. Some compared it to speaking directly to the soul of Buddha.

Zen taught that enlightenment may come in a flash after great mental and physical discipline. During this effort, the mind is not supposed to be thinking in the ordinary way. Instead, it is given what seems to be a ridiculous idea, such as "listen to the sound when one hand is clapped." Sometimes the Zen master would help jolt the student's mind into enlightenment by shouting in his ear or beating him with a stick.

Adapted from Jonathan Norton Leonard, *Early Japan* (New York: Time Inc., 1968).

Making Accurate Generalizations
3. In general, how did Zen masters try to bring enlightenment?
a. through religious teachings
b. by urging students to perform good works
c. by praying to the soul of the Buddha
d. through discipline and mental exercises

Read the following selection and answer question 4.

Samurai were bound to defend their daimyo. Awarded land in return for valiant service, some samurai themselves became feudal lords.

Identifying Word Meaning from Context
4. Which of the following is the best definition of samurai as used above?
a. mercenary
b. warrior who serves a lord
c. tenant farmer
d. high government official

WRITING ACTIVITY
Describe the detail of the *Tale of the Heiji War Scroll*, pictured on page 294. Tell how it reflects aspects of society in feudal Japan.

CHAPTER FOURTEEN SKILLS PRACTICE

Read the following selection and answer questions 1 and 2.

Like other archaeologists, I have always been skeptical of the term "lost" for cities or civilizations. Most often, even the most remote ruins are well known to the people living nearby. Not so with many of the Classic Maya cities: in the end, they were covered up by the very jungle that had sheltered them.

Classic Maya civilization was truly lost until the beginning of the 19th century. Around that time, news of crumbling jungle cities began to appear in little known books. Thus was born the air of mystery that always seems to be associated with the Maya.

In 1822, Henry Berthoud of London published the *Description of the Ruins of an Ancient City, Discovered Near Palenque*. This book was the story of Antonio del Rio, a captain who had been sent in 1786 by the Spanish king to search the ruins for treasure. Del Rio and 79 Maya Indians had broken apart Palenque with crowbars and pickaxes.

"In the end," recalled Captain Antonio del Rio, "there remained no window or doorway blocked up, no wall that was not thrown down, no room, corridor, hall, tower, or underground passage that was not dug out from two to three yards deep."

Adapted from George E. Stuart and Gene S. Stuart, *The Mysterious Maya* (Washington, D.C.: National Geographic Society, 1977).

Distinguishing Between Facts and Opinions

1. Which of the following is an OPINION expressed by the author of this selection?

a. The jungle quickly hides Maya ruins.

b. Del Rio's book describing the Palenque ruins was published in 1822.

c. Del Rio explored the ruins near Palenque carefully.

d. The term "lost" is often wrongly applied to ancient civilizations.

Identifying Specific Details

2. Why did del Rio go to the Palenque ruins?

a. to look for treasure for Spain

b. to search for lost civilizations

c. to prepare for an archaeological expedition

d. to rebuild the Maya city

Read the following selection and answer question 3.

By 1000 B.C., Egyptian power had waned, and around 700 B.C., the Kushites gained control of upper Egypt. About 70 years later, however, the Kushites were overthrown by invading Assyrians from the east. The Kushites, who used weapons of copper and bronze, could not withstand the superior iron weaponry of the Assyrians.

The Kushites retreated south. Although they had been defeated, they had gained a valuable skill from the Assyrians: the secret of smelting iron. Equipped with the iron hoe and iron spear, the Kushites improved their agriculture, strengthened their army, and developed into a major commercial power. They began to trade not only in Africa but in Arabia, India, and possibly in China. The first iron makers in Africa, the Kushites developed the first civilization in sub-Saharan Africa.

The Kushites built their capital, Meroë, between the Nile and Atbara rivers. This region was rich with iron deposits and with forests that provided wood to fuel iron furnaces. Meroë soon became a crossroads for trade in northeastern Africa.

Identifying Cause and Effect

3. According to this selection, what key event led to the development of the first civilization in sub-Saharan Africa?

a. The Assyrians discovered iron in Egypt.

b. The Kushites built a capital near the Nile.

c. The Egyptians traded with Arabia, India, and possibly China.

d. The Kushites were defeated by the Assyrians, but learned about iron from them.

WRITING ACTIVITY

Compare the early African empires of East Africa to those of western Africa. Remember to discuss religion, trade, and the influence of geography on culture. (Refer to pages 301–303.)

CHAPTER FIFTEEN SKILLS PRACTICE

Identifying Word Meaning from Structural Analysis

1. What is the best definition of the following word?

humanism

a. the way human beings think
b. way of thinking that focuses on the affairs of human beings
c. way of thinking that stresses being kind to others
d. way of thinking that says men are more important than women

Read the following selection and answer question 2.

The impact of Luther's work was enormous. Along with the turmoil and conflict accompanying such a clash of deeply felt beliefs, the Reformation spread rapidly.

Several religious factors explained why Luther's ideas became widely accepted. First, some people had lost respect for the Roman Catholic Church during the Babylonian Captivity and the Great Schism. Second, early religious reformers such as John Wycliffe had already planted seeds of doubt about church practices. Third, many Christians felt that the views of the scholastics and Thomas Aquinas were too unemotional. Martin Luther's appeal to faith attracted them.

Other reasons were political. The Great Schism had ended in 1417, and Rome had again become the center of the Church. In countries such as England, Denmark, Sweden, and Germany, however, strong princes and national monarchs had gained power while feudalism declined. These rulers no longer wished to bow to the authority of the Church.

Still other reasons were economic. By the 1500s, the Church owned a great deal of land. In Germany, for example, the Church may have owned as much as one-third of the land. The Church paid no taxes on the land, however. Thus, a heavier tax burden fell on other landowners.

Also, the Church itself had the power to collect taxes from every household. Many people felt that their lands were being drained of wealth, which was flowing to Rome.

Some European rulers also were eager to keep revenues within their own borders. A break with the Church would give these rulers the opportunity to seize Church lands and collect taxes on them.

Identifying the Main Idea

2. Which of the following is the best statement of the main idea of this selection?
a. Political and economic as well as religious reasons explained why Luther's ideas spread widely.
b. Strong princes and monarchs discouraged the spread of Luther's ideas.
c. Several religious factors helped Luther's ideas become popular.
d. To combat the spread of Luther's ideas, the Roman Catholic Church began its own reforms.

Read the following selection and answer question 3.

Wealthy merchant princes, kings, and popes were often patrons of Renaissance art. They sponsored the artists whose work graced public buildings, palaces, private homes, and cathedrals. Thanks to their patrons, the best-known artists had everything they needed to work and live comfortable lives.

Identifying Word Meaning from Context

3. Which is the best meaning of patrons as used above?
a. fathers
b. people who support and encourage a person or institution
c. buyers
d. people who collect fine art

WRITING ACTIVITY

Describe Giotto's *Lamentation of the Dead Christ*, pictured on page 331. Tell how it reflects Renaissance thinking and ideals. (Refer to pages 328–333.)

CHAPTER SIXTEEN SKILLS PRACTICE

Use the following selection from the Index to answer question 1.

Latfundias, 123, 123
Latin, 130, 132, 149, 206
Latin America, agriculture in, 562, 660, 773, 782; arts in, 359, 664, 665, 780-81, 782; authoritarian governments in 560-61, 774-75, 776, 777; colonies in, 354-59, 369, 370; communism in, 777, 778; culture, 778-81, 782; economic development in, 773-74; European imperialism in, 570-72, 573, 574, 577, 593; independence in, 773, 781. . . .
Latium, 112
Latvia, 638, 695

Using Reference Sources

1. On which pages would you find information about colonies in Latin America?
a. 560-61, 774-75, 776, 777
b. 354-59, 369, 370
c. 777, 778
d. 638, 695

The following account was written by a Spanish historian and priest, Fray Diego Duran. In fact, one of Cortés's generals, not Cortés, planned and carried out the massacre Duran describes. Read the account and answer questions 2 and 3.

Every day the Indians came out to dance in preparation for their religious feast. Cortés asked Moctezuma to order that all the sovereigns and lords of the provinces gather to dance in the courtyard, together with the bravest men. All this was a cunning plan to massacre the Indians.

When the feast day came, the Aztecs, unsuspecting, came out to worship their idol and to show the grandeur of Mexico. Cortés commanded ten of his men to go where the Indians were beating drums, where the most important lords had gathered. The soldiers were told to kill the drummer and all those around him. In this way the preachers of the Gospel of Jesus Christ

attacked the unfortunate Indians. The Indians carried nothing in their hands but flowers and feathers. All of them were killed.

Many other cruelties were committed by Cortés's men, always believing that they were serving God. All of the above things I found in certain writings. This was the most terrible act ever committed in this land: the end of the flower and nobility of Mexico.

Adapted from Fray Diego Duran, *The History of the Indies of New Spain*, trans. with notes by Doris Heyden and Fernando Horcasitas. (London: Cassell, 1964), pp. 297–299.

Identifying Author's Point of View

2. What is the most likely reason why the author wrote this selection?
a. to praise the Spanish
b. to criticize the Spanish
c. to praise the Indians
d. to criticize the Indians

Distinguishing Between Facts and Opinions

3. Which of the following is an OPINION presented in the selection?
a. This was the most terrible act ever committed in this land.
b. Many other brave acts were committed by Cortés's men, who were serving God.
c. The Indians carried nothing but feathers and flowers.
d. The Indians were a peaceful people.

Identifying Social Studies Terms

4. Read the sentence. Then choose the meaning of the underlined word.

Beginning in the 1400s, some companies sold stock to people willing to invest money.

a. cattle
b. supplies of goods
c. shares in a business
d. family groups

WRITING ACTIVITY

In the role of an official of the Dutch East India Company in the mid-1600s, you have made the decision to set up a supply station—Cape Town—at the southern tip of Africa. Write a letter to your superiors proposing such a supply station and defending your decision. (Refer to page 365.)

CHAPTER SEVENTEEN SKILLS PRACTICE

The following speech was made by King James I to Parliament in 1610. Read the selection and answer questions 1 and 2.

The state of Monarchy is the supremest thing upon earth. Kings are not only God's lieutenants upon earth and sit upon God's throne. Even by God himself, kings are called gods. In the Scriptures kings are called gods, and their power is compared to the Divine power. Kings are also compared to the fathers of families, for a king is truly father of his country, the political father of his people.

As for the fathers of families, they had long ago the power of life and death over their children or family.

Now a father may dispose of his inheritance to his children at his pleasure. He may even disinherit the eldest and prefer the youngest. He may make them beggars or rich at his pleasure; send them away from him or place them in favor again. So may the King do with his subjects.

It is sedition [rebellion] in subjects to dispute what a king may do in the height of his power. Still, just kings will ever be willing to declare what they will do, if they will not incur the curse of God. I will not be content that my power be disputed upon, but I shall ever be willing to make the reason appear of all my doings, and rule my actions according to my laws.

Adapted from King James I, *Works* (1616).

Identifying Author's Point of View

1. What is the most likely reason why James made this speech?

a. to explain some of his actions to Parliament

b. to assure Parliament members that he was willing to listen to their opinions

c. to warn Parliament members not to disagree with him

d. to remind Parliament that he was head of the Anglican church

Drawing Logical Conclusions

2. Which of the following conclusions can most reasonably be drawn from this selection?

a. James believed that kings were just like other human beings.

b. James believed that kings were truly gods.

c. James believed that kings should decide how much money each subject had.

d. James believed that God gave kings the right to do anything they pleased.

Read the following selection and answer question 3.

Ivan the Terrible increased the power of the Russian monarch during his rule between 1533 and 1584. As a symbol of his power, Ivan the Terrible began the practice of formally calling himself czar. This Russian word came from the Latin word "caesar," the title that had been given to Roman emperors.

Identifying Word Meaning from Context

3. Which of the following is the best definition of czar as used above?

a. emperor

b. god

c. prince

d. servant of the people

Identifying Word Meaning from Structural Analysis

4. What is the best definition of the following word?

militarism

a. belief that all adult males should be soldiers

b. belief in a democracy in which each adult citizen has a vote

c. reliance on the power of arms

d. belief that military officers should control a country's government

---

WRITING ACTIVITY

You are a French aristocrat who opposes Louis XIV. Write a letter to an aristocrat in Louis's court explaining why he or she should consider leaving Versailles. (Refer to pages 382-383.)

CHAPTER EIGHTEEN SKILLS PRACTICE

Read the following selection and answer questions 1 and 2.

Let's go to a Kabuki performance. We have come a little early. As there is no curtain in this theater, we can see the design of the popular Japanese stage. It is a platform stage, a simple place for acting. From the front of the stage a long, narrow runway extends through the audience to the back of the hall. We take seats near this. Many of the actors will make their entrances and exits almost above our heads.

We try to follow the story through its pantomime. Japanese acting is highly formalized, a kind of slow ballet. It is made up of many conventional gestures and still poses. When an actor wants to emphasize a special point, he strikes a rigid, fixed pose, with eyes wide open and staring. This is called a *Mie*. To leave no chance that the audience might overlook this important stance, the assistant stage manager claps wooden blocks together loudly.

Adapted from Edmund Fuller, *A Pageant of the Theatre* (New York: Thomas Y. Crowell, 1965).

Identifying Author's Point of View

1. What is the most likely reason why the author wrote this article?

a. to teach Japanese actors how to perform a Kabuki play

b. to tell people who have never seen a Kabuki play what one is like

c. to explain the details of Kabuki to people who have seen some Kabuki plays

d. to compare European and Japanese plays

Making Accurate Generalizations

2. Which of the following generalizations can most reasonably be made from this selection?

a. The acting style in Kabuki plays is realistic.

b. Kabuki plays are boring.

c. The acting style in Kabuki is not realistic.

d. Acting in Kabuki plays requires great skill.

Read the following slave song and answer question 3.

Where are we going? Where are we going?
Where are we going, Rubee?
Help us, save us, make us free,
Send our freedom papers down from thee!
Here the Ghiblee wind is blowing,
Strange and large the world is growing!
Tell us, Rubee, where are we going?
Where are we going, Rubee?

Bornu! Bornu! Where is Bornu?
Where are we going, Rubee?
Bornu-land was rich and good,
Wells of water, fields of food;
Bornu-land we see no longer,
Here we thirst, and here we hunger,
Here the Moor man smites in anger;
Where are we going, Rubee?

Where are we going? Where are we going?
Hear us, save us, Rubee!
Moons of marches from our eyes
Bornu-land behind us lies;
Hot the desert wind is blowing,
Wild the waves of sand are flowing!
Hear us! tell us, Where are we going?
Where are we going, Rubee?

From Louis Daniel Hutchinson, *Out of Africa* (Washington, D.C.: Smithsonian Institution Press, 1979).

Identifying Author's Point of View

3. What feelings are expressed most strongly in this song?

a. fear and misery

b. curiosity and excitement

c. anger

d. pleasure

WRITING ACTIVITY

You are a member of the samurai class in the late 1700s in Tokugawa Japan. Write a letter to the Tokugawa ruler arguing against the seclusion policy and urging him to open up contact with the West. (Refer to pages 404–406.)

CHAPTER NINETEEN SKILLS PRACTICE

Identifying Word Meaning from Structural Analysis

1. What is the best definition of the following word?

mechanistic

a. person who repairs machines
b. having machine-like qualities
c. having a highly developed industry
d. rational and objective

The following selection is Voltaire's reply to the question of what makes something or someone beautiful. Read the selection and answer questions 2 and 3.

Ask a toad what beauty is. He will answer you that it is his toad wife with two great round eyes issuing from her head, a wide, flat mouth, a yellow belly, a brown back. Ask the devil. He will tell you that beauty is a pair of horns, four claws, and a tail. Finally, if you consult the philosophers, they will answer you with gibberish: they will insist on something following the model of essential beauty.

After much reflection, a philosopher came to the conclusion that beauty is often very relative, just as what is decent in Japan is indecent in Rome, and what is fashionable in Paris is not fashionable in Peking; and he saved himself the trouble of writing a long treatise on beauty.

There are actions which the whole world finds beautiful. A friend gives his life for his friend. Algonquin [an American Indian], Frenchman, Chinaman will all agree that this is very beautiful, that these actions give them pleasure, that they admire them.

Adapted from Ben Ray Redman, ed., *The Portable Voltaire* (New York: Viking Press, 1968).

Identifying Author's Purpose

2. What is the author's main purpose in writing this selection?

a. to propose a standard of beauty for people in all cultures
b. to prove that toads are beautiful
c. to use humor to suggest that standards of beauty are relative
d. to describe standards of beauty in different cultures

Identifying Specific Details

3. Which of the following does Voltaire say is considered to be beautiful by many different people?
a. a toad
b. people who do good things for others
c. whatever is fashionable
d. the action of giving your life for your friend

Read the following selection and answer question 4.

Descartes attacked the authority of ancient learning even more strongly than had Bacon. Vowing "never to accept anything for true which I did not clearly know to be such," Descartes emphasized the importance of doubting and questioning.

He promoted the deductive approach of the ancient Greeks. Descartes's strong belief in the importance of doubt, however, set him apart from the Greeks. Descartes became one of the foremost advocates of rationality during the seventeenth century.

Identifying Word Meaning from Context

4. Which of the following is the best definition of rationality as used above?
a. belief arrived at through faith
b. scientific accuracy
c. belief in the value and use of reason for gaining knowledge
d. a limited supply

WRITING ACTIVITY

Compare the political ideas of Thomas Hobbes and John Locke. In your opinion, which man's ideas best describe modern thinking? Be sure to support your position with evidence. (Refer to pages 434–435.)

CHAPTER TWENTY SKILLS PRACTICE

Read the following selection and answer question 1.

George Washington was, on the face of it, an unlikely person to lead a revolution. At 43, he was rather far from being a young hothead. (Yet he was a bit younger than the average of revolutionary leaders from the 13 colonies, which was 47.6 years.)

Moreover, in 1776, George Washington was one of the richest men in America. He owned 12,463 acres of the best Virginia soil and claimed 24,100 acres of wild western land along the Kanawha and Ohio rivers. Back home on his plantation, Mount Vernon, he hunted in a black velvet cap with a silk band and handsome silver buckle. He wore a coat of scarlet cloth and gold lace. He owned 130 horses, 135 slaves, and earned as much as 3,213 pounds sterling (over $160,000) a year from his farms.

Adapted from Thomas Fleming, "America 1776," *Reader's Digest*, July 1976, p. 51.

Distinguishing Between Facts and Opinions

1. Which of the following is an OPINION presented in this selection?

a. Washington did not appear to be the type of person you would expect to lead a revolution.

b. In 1776, Washington was one of the richest people in America.

c. The average American revolutionary leader was somewhat older than Washington.

d. Washington owned a considerable amount of property.

Read the following selection and answer questions 2 and 3.

Historians have debated Napoleon's role as the heir of the French Revolution. He said that he was acting in its spirit, but he removed many of its gains. He used secret police and censorship to put down people who did not agree with him. He was the source of authority and made all the laws. However, he chose people for civil and military offices according to talent rather than birth. Although France under Napoleon was not a free or parliamentary society, people were treated the same by the law.

Napoleon took advantage of some changes made by the revolution to set up a government more powerful than that of the old king. He built up French nationalism and used the excitement of military victory to win the support of the people. With the power of aristocrats, clergy, guilds, and most local authorities weakened or destroyed, it was easy for him to add to the power of the central government, including its police power. Although Napoleon kept important parts of the French Revolution, at the same time he was in many ways like a modern dictator.

Identifying the Main Idea

2. Which of the following is the best statement of the main idea of this selection?

a. Napoleon became an absolute ruler like previous French kings.

b. Napoleon strengthened local government in many ways.

c. Napoleon destroyed the power of the aristocrats and clergy.

d. Napoleon kept some ideas of justice and equality but ruled like a dictator.

Drawing Logical Conclusions

3. Based on this selection, which of the following people would be most likely to benefit from Napoleon's policies?

a. a poor but intelligent person looking for a government job

b. a writer whose book criticized the government

c. a wealthy bishop

d. the head of a powerful guild

WRITING ACTIVITY

In what ways could Napoleon be seen as being true to the ideals of the French Revolution? In what ways could he be said to have betrayed these ideals? (Refer to pages 452–467.)

CHAPTER TWENTY-ONE SKILLS PRACTICE

Study the graph below and answer questions 1 and 2.

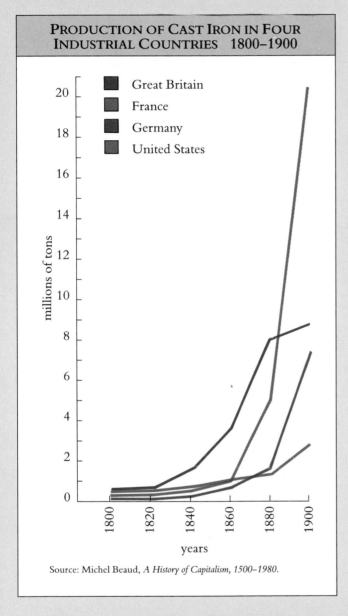

PRODUCTION OF CAST IRON IN FOUR INDUSTRIAL COUNTRIES   1800–1900

■ Great Britain
■ France
■ Germany
■ United States

millions of tons

20
18
16
14
12
10
8
6
4
2
0

1800   1820   1840   1860   1880   1900

years

Source: Michel Beaud, *A History of Capitalism, 1500–1980.*

Using Graphic Sources
1. Which of the four countries produced the most cast iron in 1860?
a. the United States
b. Great Britain
c. Germany
d. France

Using Graphic Sources
2. Which country's production of cast iron increased the most between the years 1800 and 1900?
a. the United States
b. Great Britain
c. Germany
d. France

Identifying Word Meaning from Structural Analysis
3. What is the best definition of the following word?

industrialization

a. development of natural resources
b. large factories
c. increase in dangerous particles in the atmosphere
d. use of machines and factories in manufacturing

Identifying Social Studies Terms
4. Read the sentence. Then choose the meaning of the underlined term.

Mass production has reduced the cost of many kinds of goods.

a. a literary or artistic work
b. manufacture of products using standard parts
c. an exaggerated action
d. distribution of goods

WRITING ACTIVITY
You are an American factory worker with four children in the mid-1800s. An accident has left you unable to work. Write a letter to a relative in England explaining your situation. What rights and benefits do you have? What are your options? What will you do? (Refer to pages 482–485.)

CHAPTER TWENTY-TWO SKILLS PRACTICE

Identifying Social Studies Terms
1. Read the sentence. Then choose the meaning of the underlined word.

Marx said that <u>communism</u> was the final stage of society.

a. system without social classes where everyone's needs were to be met equally
b. society in which no one would have to work
c. an early form of socialism
d. the system of free enterprise and competition

Read the following selection and answer questions 2 and 3.

British economist Thomas Malthus linked the size of population with levels of poverty. People multiply, Malthus pointed out, but the food supply does not grow as rapidly. If population continued to grow at the same rate, people would have less and less to eat. Eventually, there would be a food shortage. The poor, who could not pay for food, would be the ones to go hungry.

David Ricardo, also an English economist, described how, as population grew, the number of workers also grew. As more workers competed for jobs, wages would fall. People would be willing to work for less money, since even a small income was better than none.

Faced with poverty, workers would have smaller families, eventually reducing the number of workers. As the labor supply decreased, employers would have to pay higher wages to attract workers from a smaller labor pool. In time, however, the cycle would be repeated.

Making Accurate Generalizations
2. What do Malthus and Ricardo have in common?
a. They deal with the labor market.
b. They are both basically optimistic.
c. They both believe that population will continue to increase without limit.

d. They both consider population to be an important factor in economics.

Drawing Logical Conclusions
3. How is the problem that Malthus describes likely to be affected by improvements in farm machines and the use of fertilizer?
a. The population will level off.
b. More people will starve, reducing the population.
c. The food supply will be more likely to keep up with growth in population.
d. The food supply will stay about the same.

Identifying Word Meaning from Structural Analysis
4. What is the best definition of the following word?

socialism

a. ability to get along with others
b. concern for the needs of the individual
c. theory that society should own or control the means of production
d. a labor movement

Read the following selection and answer question 5.

Marx sided with the <u>proletariat</u>. He argued that labor is the most important factor in production and that the real value of goods is the amount of labor used in producing them. A worker should be paid the full value of the labor that goes into a job.

Identifying Word Meaning from Context
5. Which of the following is the best definition of <u>proletariat</u> as used above?
a. union hall
b. working class
c. capitalists
d. skilled workers

WRITING ACTIVITY

Imagine that you live in the late 1800s. Choose the role of either a social reformer who opposes social Darwinism or a member of the middle class who supports this view. Write a newspaper editorial defending your position. (Refer to page 506.)

CHAPTER TWENTY-THREE SKILLS PRACTICE

Identifying Word Meaning from Structural Analysis

1. What is the best definition of the following word?

conservatism

a. movement to preserve the natural environment

b. belief in traditional institutions such as monarchy

c. movement to protect and extend the rights of workers

d. an absolute ruler

Read the following selection and answer questions 2 and 3.

Another powerful force of change in the nineteenth century was nationalism. At this time, nationalism meant more than love of one's country. It also meant a desire for independence. Many groups, united by a common language and culture, did not have a country to call their own. Instead, like the Greeks under Ottoman rule, these Europeans were living within another country's borders.

Other cultural groups with a common heritage were scattered among several independent states. This was true in the German states, where many wanted a united German nation. Thus, nationalism was a movement for both national independence and national unity.

Nationalism, like liberalism, often led people to oppose aristocratic rule. However, nationalism also came into conflict with liberalism. Often liberals wanted a government that united the entire nation, but ethnic minorities within a country wanted their own independent nations. Depending on circumstances, liberalism became an important force in some countries, while nationalism dominated the politics of others.

Identifying Specific Details

2. According to this selection, which group of people was scattered among many independent states?

a. Ottoman Turks

b. Germans

c. Italians

d. Greeks

Drawing Logical Conclusions

3. For which of the following goals would nationalists and liberals most likely have worked together?

a. to unite many small states into a large nation

b. to support a powerful but fair ruler

c. to help a minority group form its own state

d. to oppose a ruler who treats an ethnic minority unfairly

Identifying Social Studies Terms

4. Read the sentence. Then choose the meaning of the underlined term.

In 1912, Parliament established a minimum wage.

a. lowest amount a worker can be paid

b. highest amount a worker can be paid

c. average amount a worker can be paid

d. required amount a worker must be paid

Identifying Word Meaning from Structural Analysis

5. What is the best definition of the following word?

solidarity

a. heaviness

b. desire to be apart or live alone

c. unity of purpose among union members

d. feeling of belonging to a group

WRITING ACTIVITY

Write a speech for Prince Metternich to deliver to the Congress of Vienna. Metternich hopes to convince the other delegates to oppose liberals and revolutionaries. (Refer to pages 512–513 and 516–520.)

CHAPTER TWENTY-FOUR SKILLS PRACTICE

Study the following table and answer question 1.

CAUSES OF DEATH IN NINETEENTH-CENTURY WARS		
War	**Killed or Died of Wounds** (per thousand troops)	**Died of Disease** (per thousand troops)
Napoleonic (1805–1815)	35	270
Crimean (1854–1856)	35	190
U.S. Civil War (1861–1865)	20	71
Boer (1899–1901)	17	30

Data source: *Encyclopedia Britannica*, 1981 ed., V. 11, p. 79.

Using Graphic Sources

1. Which of the following conclusions is supported by this table?
a. Disease killed far more soldiers than wounds in nineteenth-century wars.
b. Wounds killed far more soldiers than disease in nineteenth-century wars.
c. Disease and wounds killed about equal numbers of soldiers in nineteenth-century wars.
d. Far fewer soldiers died in nineteenth-century wars than in twentieth-century wars.

Identifying Word Meaning from Structural Analysis

2. What is the best definition of the following word?

imperialism

a. policy of absolute rule by an emperor
b. something belonging to an emperor
c. policy followed by strong countries to gain control over weak countries
d. way of giving orders to military troops

Winston Churchill, later the prime minister of Great Britain, wrote the following letter while he was a prisoner in South Africa during the Boer War. Read the letter and answer question 3.

> I have no doubt that the newspapers will have told the tale of the armored train. It was a very dangerous and feeble contrivance, and when it moved beyond the line of the cavalry patrols, it was almost entirely at the mercy of the enemy. I expect that the general's action in sending it out has been criticized; but critics should remember that it was very important to scout far to the front. The armored train could do this easily and quickly. It did so every day for two weeks. The advantage as well as the risk was great. The final loss of the train was the price we had to pay. We paid it willingly for good and accurate information that could not have been collected by any other means. So far as my opinion goes, no blame belongs to anyone. War means risk and danger. It is a great mistake to expect generals to fight without loss or raise an outcry over every small affair in which we have the disadvantage.

Adapted from Randolph S. Churchill, *Winston S. Churchill*, Companion Vol. I, Part 2 (Boston: Houghton Mifflin Company, 1967).

Identifying Cause and Effect

3. What probably happened to the armored train?
a. The British destroyed it.
b. The Boers destroyed it.
c. It broke down and could not be repaired.
d. It was taken out of action because it was no longer needed.

WRITING ACTIVITY

Explain how the ideas of nationalism, liberalism, and progress could be used by an imperialist of the late 1800s to support his or her activities. (Refer to pages 489, 491, and 542-546.)

CHAPTER TWENTY-FIVE SKILLS PRACTICE

Identifying Social Studies Terms

1. Read the sentence. Then choose the meaning of the underlined word.

Sharp disagreement between slave owners and <u>abolitionists</u> helped to bring about the American Civil War.

a. northerners
b. slaves
c. people who wanted to outlaw slavery
d. people who wanted to outlaw drinking of alcohol

Read the following selection and answer questions 2 and 3.

Foreign investment in Latin America went on at a high level in the 1800s. Latin America still was mostly a supplier of raw materials to the industrial nations. Because of their greater economic power, Great Britain, France, Germany, and the United States were able to set the prices on Latin American products. With large loan payments to make to foreign investors, Latin American countries had to sell their products at these prices. Latin America, therefore, had no control over its exports.

Foreign investors were also able to set the terms of investment. For example, railroads in Latin America were not built to join important cities. Instead, they were laid to make it easier for industrial nations to get hold of the continent's natural resources. In the same way, ports were improved because they were needed by the export trade. Hospitals and schools, however, were left half-built.

Making Accurate Generalizations

2. Which of the following generalizations can most reasonably be made from this selection?
a. Foreign investment greatly benefited Latin America.

b. Foreign investment benefited the investors more than it benefited Latin America.
c. Foreign investment benefited the investors and Latin America about equally.
d. Foreign investment did not benefit Latin America at all.

Drawing Logical Conclusions

3. Which of the following most probably would have been built by foreign investment in Latin America?
a. housing for poor people
b. a road between two large cities
c. a road between a gold mining area and a port
d. a library

Read the following selection and answer question 4.

After independence, Latin America continued to be divided along rather rigid racial and social lines. Creoles remained at the top of the social ladder. They made up about 20 percent of the population and held most of the land in large estates. As people of mixed European and Indian heritage, the mestizos ranked below the creoles in social standing. Just as during the colonial centuries, the mulattoes were below the mestizos, while Indians and blacks remained at the bottom of the social scale. Most blacks remained in slavery. However, a few were freed as a result of service in the revolutionary armies.

Making Accurate Generalizations

4. Based on this selection, what generally determined a person's social status in Latin America?
a. language
b. racial background
c. religion
d. whether the person was native born

WRITING ACTIVITY

Describe the painting *Revolutionists*, pictured on page 556. How does it support ideas presented in the chapter?

CHAPTER TWENTY-SIX SKILLS PRACTICE

Read the following selection and answer question 1.

European administrators of African colonies thought of themselves as parents and the Africans as children. They set up rules of behavior based on this paternalism. By seizing African land, disregarding traditional rule, and destroying traditional ways of making a living, Europeans made Africans feel more and more helpless.

Identifying Word Meaning from Context

1. Which of the following is the best definition of paternalism as used above?

a. attitude that the people who govern are socially superior to the people being governed

b. attitude toward one's children

c. attitude toward people of another race

d. attitude that the people who govern are more mature and wise than the people who are being governed

Many Africans rebelled against head or hut taxes imposed by colonial governments. In this selection, Mary Kingsley, an Englishwoman who explored West Africa in the 1890s and studied African law, explains why. Read the selection and answer question 2.

A lesson in our misunderstanding of African law is before our eyes now in these disturbances connected with the enforcement of the hut tax on the natives of the Protectorate of the Colony of Sierra Leone. This tax of 5 shillings per hut is a heavy tax because the African's average wealth is no more than 1 pound [20 shillings] a year. This form of taxation is against the principles of African law. One of these principles is that the thing you pay anyone a regular fee for is not your own. It is a thing belonging to the person to whom you pay the fee. Therefore, if you have to pay the government a regular fee for your hut, it is not your hut. It is the property of the government. The fact that the government has neither taken this hut from you in war, bought it of you, nor had it given as a gift by you, the owner, vexes you "too much." It makes you, if you are any sort of a man, get a gun.

Adapted from Stephen Gwynn, *Life of Mary Kingsley* (London: Macmillan & Co., 1933).

Identifying Cause and Effect

2. According to this selection, what is the most important reason why Africans in Sierra Leone rebelled against the hut tax?

a. They did not want to support the colonial government.

b. They felt that the tax meant that the government had seized their property.

c. They could not afford to pay the tax.

d. They felt that only their chiefs had a right to collect hut taxes.

Use the following selection from Reader's Guide to Periodical Literature *to answer question 3.*

Africa   Climate

Grassland Today, Desert Tomorrow? S. Herkimer. map *Int Bull Meteorol* 94:28-9 Ap 18 '86

Colonial Period

Era of the "White Man's Burden." P. A. Walsh. il map *Nat Geog* 251:538-74 Jl '86

Indirect Rule: Success or Failure? W. Widdecombe. bibl *Jour Af Studies* 17:213-15 Ag '86

Rhodes, the Colossus. G. A. Meredith. il *Brit Hist Illus* 33:17-21 O '86

Using Reference Sources

3. In which magazine would you find an article about Cecil Rhodes, the founder of Rhodesia?

a. *International Bulletin of Meteorology*

b. *National Geographic*

c. *British History Illustrated*

d. *Journal of African Studies*

WRITING ACTIVITY
You are a member of the African local elite. Explain why you feel that Western values raise questions about European authority in Africa. (Refer to pages 587-588.)

CHAPTER TWENTY-SEVEN SKILLS PRACTICE

The following speech was given by Dadabhai Naoroji as president of the Indian National Congress in 1886. Read the selection and answer question 1.

It is under the civilizing rule of the Queen and people that we meet here together, hindered by none, and are freely allowed to speak our minds without the least fear or hesitation. Then I put the question plainly: Is this Congress a nursery for rebellion against the British government, or is it another stone in the foundation of the stability of that government? Were it not for the blessings of British rule I could not have come here without the least hesitation and without the least fear that my children might be robbed and killed in my absence.

Adapted from *Speeches and Writings of Dadabhai Naoroji*, 2nd ed. (Madras: G.A. Nateson and Co., n.d.)

Identifying Author's Purpose

1. What is the purpose of Dadabhai Naoroji's speech?
a. to summarize the history of India under British rule
b. to persuade the Congress to cooperate with British rule
c. to persuade the Congress to support the independence movement
d. to describe the journey from his home to the Congress

The following is part of the Chinese emperor's response to a British request to set up diplomatic relations with China in 1790. Read the selection and answer questions 2 and 3.

You, O King, have longed for the blessings of our civilization. In your eagerness to come into touch with our converting influence, you have sent an Embassy across the sea.

Our Celestial Empire has all things in abundance. It lacks no product within its own borders.

There was therefore no need to import the manufactures of outside barbarians in exchange for our own goods. However, the tea, silk, and porcelain which the Celestial Empire produces are necessities to European nations. Therefore, we have permitted foreign hongs [warehouses] to be set up in Canton, so that your wants might be supplied.

Your Ambassador has now put forth new requests which completely fail to understand the Throne's principle to "treat strangers with indulgence" and to exercise a pacifying control over barbarians the world over. Suppose other nations, following your bad example, wrongfully importune my ear with impossible requests. How can I treat them with easy indulgence?

Adapted from E. Backhouse and J. O. P. Bland, *Annals and Memoirs of the Court of Peking* (Boston: Houghton Mifflin Company, 1914).

Identifying Author's Point of View

2. Which of the following best describes the Chinese emperor's feelings about the British king?
a. The emperor feels greatly superior to the king.
b. The emperor feels humble and respectful toward the king.
c. The emperor feels that he and the king are equals.
d. The emperor feels that the king is a dangerous enemy.

Drawing Logical Conclusions

3. What will the emperor probably do about the British request?
a. He will accept it eagerly.
b. He will reject it.
c. He will accept it reluctantly in order to increase trade with the British.
d. He will use it as an excuse to declare war on Britain.

WRITING ACTIVITY

Late in 1853, the shogun asks you, as daimyo, for advice. His dilemma is whether to stick to his policy of isolation or to give in to Commodore Perry's demands for a treaty. Give some pros and cons for both courses of action and make your recommendation. (Refer to pages 606-607.)

CHAPTER TWENTY-EIGHT SKILLS PRACTICE

Identifying Social Studies Terms

1. Read the sentence. Then choose the meaning of the underlined word.

The government's <u>propaganda</u> campaign encouraged many people to contribute to the war effort.

a. ideas spread to support or oppose a cause
b. official newspaper
c. army recruiting agency
d. reports from the field

Study the following table and answer question 2.

STRENGTH OF THE GREAT POWERS 1914			
	Army (millions of soldiers)	*Battleships*	*Airplanes*
Germany	4.5	37	500
Austria-Hungary	2.5	14	100
Russia	5.5	8	500
France	4.0	24	500
Britain	0.8	69	250
Italy	2.0	9	150

Using Graphic Sources

2. Which of the following questions can be answered using information in this table?
a. Which nation had the most effective navy in 1914?
b. Which side had the advantage in number of troops available?
c. How important were airplanes in World War I?
d. How quickly could the Russians mobilize their forces?

Read the following selection and answer question 3.

The German plan called for a quick strike against France in the first weeks of the war. The Germans thought that because Russia was such a large country, more time would be needed to mobilize the czar's army than the French forces. Therefore, if Germany could knock France out of the war fast enough, Germany could then put its major forces in the east well before Russia could attack.

The quick destruction of France, however, meant that German troops had to march through Belgium, which had declared neutrality. Once through Belgium, the Germans could circle around French troops who were heading east, and attack from behind, cutting off any way of escape.

Britain, however, had promised to defend Belgian neutrality. Thus, a few days after the war began, Britain joined the Allies by declaring war against Germany. British and French troops slowed the German march through Belgium.

Identifying Cause and Effect

3. What caused problems for the German plan?
a. The French army escaped from the advancing Germans.
b. Russia mobilized much more quickly than the Germans had expected.
c. The United States declared war against Germany.
d. Britain entered the war and slowed down the German advance in Belgium.

Identifying Word Meaning from Structural Analysis

4. What is the best definition of the following word?

isolationism

a. independence
b. not being involved in foreign affairs
c. living on an island or faraway place
d. seeking peace by making treaties with other nations

WRITING ACTIVITY

Imagine that you are President Wilson. Write a speech to be delivered to the Senate promoting the League of Nations and urging approval of the Treaty of Versailles as well as American membership in the league. (Refer to pages 637 and 639.)

CHAPTER TWENTY-NINE SKILLS PRACTICE

Read the following selection and answer question 1.

In the cities of Russia, angry workers began to form soviets to discuss Russia's political and economic problems. Influenced by Marxism, many soviets moved beyond discussion and openly agitated for a restructuring of Russian society according to Marx's vision of a communist society. For the most part, however, the soviets were run by moderate socialists.

Identifying Word Meaning from Context

1. Which of the following is the best definition of soviets as used above?
a. Russian republics
b. councils of workers
c. Communist party meetings
d. factories owned by the workers

Read the following selection and answer question 2.

By the summer of 1929, prices had soared far above the stormy levels of last winter into the blue and cloudless heavens. All the old markers by which the price of a promising common stock could be measured had long since passed. If a stock once valued at 100 went to 300, what on earth was to prevent it from sailing on to 400? And why not ride with it for fifty or a hundred points, with Easy Street at the end of the journey?

By every rule of logic the situation had now become more perilous than ever. If inflation had been serious in 1927, it was far more serious in 1929, as the total of brokers' loans climbed toward six billions (it had been only three and a half billions at the end of 1927). If the price level had been extravagant in 1927 it was preposterous now. But the speculative memory was short. People were comforted by the fact that every crash of the past few years had been followed by a recovery that had ultimately brought prices to a new high point. The really wise man, it appeared, was he who "bought and held on."

Adapted from Frederick Lewis Allen, *Only Yesterday* (New York: Bonanza Books, 1986).

Identifying Author's Purpose

2. What is the author's main purpose in this selection?
a. to show how serious inflation had become by 1929
b. to describe the reckless attitude of stock investors in 1929
c. to analyze and predict stock prices
d. to describe the life of the average American in 1929

In the following interview in the 1960s, Dorothe Bernstein described the Great Depression. Read the selection and answer question 3.

I went into an orphan home in 1933. I was about ten. I had clean clothes all the time, and we had plenty to eat. We'd go through the park when we walked to school.

The men there waited for us to go through and hand them our lunches. If we had something they'd prepared at the home that we didn't like, we'd give them the little brown paper bags.

These were guys who didn't have work. Who'd probably work if there was work. I don't know how they got where they were going or where they ended up. They were nice men. You would never think that they would do you bodily harm. They weren't bums. These were hard luck guys.

People talk about the good old times. These can't be the good old times when men wanted to work and couldn't work.

Adapted from Studs Terkel, *Hard Times: An Oral History of the Great Depression* (New York: Avon Books, 1970).

Identifying Author's Point of View

3. How did Dorothe Bernstein feel about the men she met in the park?
a. She was afraid that they would harm her.
b. She looked down on them.
c. She respected them and felt sorry for them.
d. She thought that they were trying to avoid working.

WRITING ACTIVITY

Describe the painting *Portrait of Chess Players*, pictured on page 663. Tell how this cubist painting reflects cultural trends after World War I. (Refer to pages 660–665.)

CHAPTER THIRTY SKILLS PRACTICE

Look at the following cartoon and answer question 1.

Using Graphic Sources

1. According to cartoonist Jerry Doyle, when Japanese forces seized Manchuria in 1931, what did they destroy or violate?
a. the rights of American sailors
b. American naval bases in China
c. several international treaties
d. the civil rights of the Chinese

Read the following selection and answer question 2.

Like communist rule in Russia, Italian fascism gave supreme power to the state. The only political party allowed made up the government. The philosophies upon which these two kinds of totalitarianism were based, however, were different in many ways. While the philosophy of communism did not require totalitarian rule, fascism was based on the belief in a strong state. Fascists wanted Italians to concentrate on their own nation, while Marxist communism ignored national borders and was meant to start a worldwide movement.

The two philosophies also differed strongly in what they wanted for the economy. Communism opposed capitalism and promised a classless society. Fascism, on the other hand, supported capitalism and private ownership of factories and land. Fascism promised economic security by keeping the existing class structure.

Making Accurate Generalizations

2. Which of the following general ideas is supported by this selection?
a. Communists and fascists differed in philosophy even though they both wanted a strong state.
b. Communism and fascism had little in common.
c. Both communists and fascists tried to overthrow the class structure.
d. Fascism was more dangerous to world peace than was communism.

Read the following selection and answer question 3.

In 1929, Joseph Stalin emerged as the only leader of Russia. Under Stalin's rule, the Soviet government began to use even more control over its citizens. It became the first government to impose totalitarianism on its people.

Identifying Word Meaning from Context

3. Which of the following is the best definition of totalitarianism as used above?
a. system that looks at the world as a whole
b. rule by a monarch with limited powers
c. system in which the individual is forced to serve the interests and goals of the state
d. extensive system of bureaucracy

WRITING ACTIVITY

Both Stalin in Russia and Mussolini in Italy used propaganda and the mass media to gain support. How might the media campaigns of these two leaders have differed? Consider political and economic goals and the means by which they hoped to achieve them. (Refer to pages 669–677.)

CHAPTER THIRTY-ONE SKILLS PRACTICE

Identifying Social Studies Terms

1. Read the sentence. Then choose the meaning of the underlined word.

Many powerful, haunting books have been written about the Holocaust.

a. nuclear explosion
b. great battle where many people are killed
c. killing of millions of Jews and others by the Nazis
d. protest demonstration

Anne Frank wrote the following entry in her diary on June 6, 1944. Read the selection and then answer question 2.

"This is D-day," came the announcement over the English news and quite rightly, "this is the day." The invasion has begun!

Great commotion in the "Secret Annexe"! Would the long-awaited liberation that has been talked of so much, but which still seems too wonderful, too much like a fairy tale, ever come true? Could we be granted victory this year, 1944? We don't know yet, but hope is revived within us. It gives us fresh courage, and makes us strong again. Since we must put up bravely with all the fears, privations, and sufferings, the great thing now is to remain calm and steadfast.

The best part of the invasion is that I have the feeling that friends are coming. We have been oppressed by those terrible Germans for so long, they have had their knives so at our throats, that the thought of friends and delivery fills us with confidence!

I may yet be able to go back to school in September or October.

Adapted from *Anne Frank: The Diary of a Young Girl*, trans. by B.M. Mooyart. Copyright © 1970. Reprinted by permission of Doubleday.

Identifying Specific Details

2. According to her diary, why did Anne Frank feel that she might be able to go back to school soon?
a. All the German armies had surrendered to the Allies.
b. The schools were going to be reopened in the fall.
c. The Allied invasion had begun, and liberation might come soon.
d. Her family was planning to move back to the city.

Identifying Author's Point of View

3. Which of the following best describes Anne Frank's feelings in this selection?
a. She was relieved that her troubles soon would be over.
b. She was hopeful, but careful not to be too excited.
c. She was discouraged about the progress of the war.
d. She viewed events calmly, expressing little feeling.

Identifying Word Meaning from Structural Analysis

4. What is the best definition of the following word?

appeasement

a. policy of openness and friendliness toward other nations
b. use of demands and bluffing to gain concessions from other nations
c. policy of giving in to the demands of an aggressor to avoid war
d. money given to compensate for damages caused in a war

WRITING ACTIVITY

Imagine that you are President Truman the night before deciding to drop the first atomic bomb. Write a journal entry which shows your thinking. (Refer to pages 700–709.)

CHAPTER THIRTY-TWO SKILLS PRACTICE

Read the following selection and answer questions 1, 2, and 3.

The most dramatic measure of the Thatcher Revolution is unquestionably economy. Margaret Thatcher came into office in 1979 at the end of the "winter of discontent," when the seemingly all-powerful unions had brought Great Britain almost to a standstill.

The nation was fed up with second-class status, performance, service, and prospects. The time was ripe for change. What has happened in the past nine years is the very essence of Thatcherism.

Today Britain has a balanced budget, a feat President Reagan has yet to match.

In 1982, when the recession of the early Thatcher years was at its worst, unemployment was around 12 percent. Today it is at 8.7 percent and still falling. Critics point out, though, that it is still above the jobless rate in the United States, West Germany, and Japan. It is also two times the rate of 4.3 percent Thatcher inherited in 1979.

Britain's economic growth index (with 1980 standing for the base 100) stood at 99.7 percent in 1979. Last year it was 118.7, and it is still growing at a yearly rate of 4.5 percent. For eight years it has averaged a 3-percent increase. This is the fastest sustained rate of any European industrial country.

Adapted from Gilbert A. Lewthwaite, "Controversial Leader Transforms Britain," *Baltimore Sun*, reprinted in *San Francisco Chronicle*, July 13, 1988.

Making Accurate Generalizations
1. Which of the following generalizations can most reasonably be made from this selection?
a. Overall, Britain's economy has suffered under Margaret Thatcher.
b. Overall, Britain's economy has improved under Margaret Thatcher.
c. Overall, Britain's economy today is stronger than that of the United States.
d. Overall, Britain's economy has stayed about the same during the Thatcher years as it was before.

Identifying Specific Details
2. Which of the following statements supports the claim that Britain's economy has improved in some ways under Margaret Thatcher?
a. Margaret Thatcher came into office at the end of the "winter of discontent."
b. In 1982, British unemployment was around 12 percent, but today it is 8.7 percent.
c. Today's unemployment rate in Britain is twice what it was when Thatcher took office.
d. Britain's economic growth index stood at 99.7 percent in 1979.

Distinguishing Between Facts and Opinions
3. Which of the following is an OPINION presented in this selection?
a. Britain has a balanced budget.
b. Unemployment has doubled since 1979.
c. The time was ripe for change.
d. The economy has grown steadily.

Identifying Word Meaning from Structural Analysis
4. What is the best definition of the following word?

containment

a. restriction of the United States' influence to the Western Hemisphere
b. a policy of the United States to halt the spread of Communist influence
c. attractive packaging of political programs
d. a policy of reducing government spending

WRITING ACTIVITY
The Soviet-American arms race is based on the theory that a nation would be discouraged from starting a nuclear attack by knowing that its enemies would then be able to destroy it with nuclear weapons. Take a position opposing or defending this theory and write an editorial supporting your view. (Refer to pages 719-724.)

CHAPTER THIRTY-THREE SKILLS PRACTICE

Identifying Social Studies Terms

1. Read the sentence. Then choose the meaning of the underlined word.

Between the two world wars, many Middle Eastern countries granted oil concessions to foreign companies.

a. acts of giving up
b. admitting of points claimed in argument
c. meetings
d. grants of land for a particular use

Selecting References

2. Where should you look to find the titles of recent magazine articles on Saudi Arabia?
a. an almanac
b. an encyclopedia
c. *Reader's Guide to Periodical Literature*
d. a newspaper

Study the following selection from an almanac and answer question 3.

Republic of Lebanon

People: Population (1985 est.): 2,619,000. **Pop. Density**: 652 per sq. mi. **Urban** (1984): 64%. **Ethnic Groups:** Lebanese 82%, Armenians 5%, Palestinians 9%. **Languages:** Arabic (official), French, Armenian. **Religions:** Predominately Moslem 60%; Maronite Christian 25%; Greek Orthodox 7%; Druze 7%.

Geography: Area: 4,015 sq. mi., smaller than Connecticut. **Location:** On Eastern end of Mediterranean Sea. **Neighbors:** Syria on E. Israel on S. **Topography:** There is a narrow coastal strip, and two mountain ranges running N-S enclosing the fertile Beqaa Valley. The Litani R. runs S. through the valley, turning W. to empty into the Mediterranean. **Capital:** Beirut. **Cities** (1984 est): Beirut 1,100,000; Tripoli 240,000.

From *World Almanac and Book of Facts*, 1987.

Using Reference Sources

3. What is the population density of Lebanon?
a. 2,619,000
b. 652 per square mile
c. 82% Lebanese, 5% Armenians, 9% Palestinians
d. 4,015 square miles

Read the following selection and answer question 4.

The Organization of Petroleum Exporting Countries (OPEC) was formed in 1960. OPEC was designed to give its members more power to regulate the production and control the price of oil. As this cartel began to control a large percentage of the world's oil, oil-consuming nations were forced to pay the price for oil determined by the OPEC nations.

Identifying Word Meaning from Context

4. What is the best meaning of cartel as used above?
a. a small wagon
b. an organization for the protection of consumers
c. a group of companies involved in the same industry
d. an organization used by producers to control production and prices

Identifying Word Meaning from Structural Analysis

5. What is the best definition of the following term?

Islamic fundamentalism

a. strong Islamic beliefs
b. limited government
c. belief that traditional Islamic culture is the best basis of Islamic society
d. philosophy that seeks pleasure

WRITING ACTIVITY

In what ways could the revolution in Iran be viewed as a religious war? Imagine that you are an Iranian Shiite Muslim trying to arouse support for a revolution in Iraq. Explain why you think the religious reasons for revolution in your country apply to Iraq as well. (Refer to pages 758–759.)

CHAPTER THIRTY-FOUR SKILLS PRACTICE

Read the following selection and answer question 1.

In 1948, the South African government established a policy called apartheid. Under this policy, blacks and whites had to use separate schools, workplaces, and housing. Indeed, the races were kept separate in every possible way.

Identifying Word Meaning from Context

1. What is the best meaning of apartheid as used above?

a. a policy of racial hate

b. a policy enforcing government control by whites

c. a policy of sending blacks out of a country

d. a policy of keeping races from mixing

Read the following selection and answer questions 2 and 3.

Before conservation came to Kanyariri, Esther Wairimu was a tree killer.

Two days each week, the Kenyan woman trudged along the red dirt paths of her village with bundles of branches lashed to her back, scouring the hillsides for firewood. Along with her other jobs of hauling water, tending crops on her husband's six-acre farm, and cleaning house, Wairimu had ten children to cook for over an open hearth. This required a lot of firewood. No small tree was safe.

Then in 1982, a fledgling conservation project called the Green Belt Movement arrived in Kanyariri. It began a campaign to transform Wairimu, and others like her, from tree killers into tree planters.

"My neighbors joined the Green Belt and began to argue with me," Wairimu recalls. "They said if I planted my own trees I would not have to go looking all the time for firewood." And so when the time came for Wairimu to put in her rows of maize and beans, she planted trees as well. Now, five years later, her farm is a woodland.

From Maryanne Vollers, "Healing the Ravaged Land," *International Wildlife*, January-February 1988, p. 5.

Identifying Author's Point of View

2. Which of the following is the most likely reason why the author wrote this selection?

a. to scold women like Wairimu for cutting trees

b. to persuade people not to cook over open hearths

c. to show how people can get firewood without cutting down forests

d. to describe the daily life of a woman who lives in Kenya

Identifying Cause and Effect

3. Which of the following is the most likely effect of the actions of Wairimu and her neighbors?

a. More trees remain on the hillsides near the village.

b. Their children are healthier.

c. Their farms are larger.

d. The hillsides near their villages are more bare of trees.

Read the following selection and answer question 4.

Latin American nations such as Brazil and Mexico had begun to industrialize in the 1930s and 1940s. In these years, they had set out to build import-substitution industries to produce goods such as cars or airplanes.

Identifying Word Meaning from Context

4. What is the best meaning of import-substitution as used above?

a. finding simpler substitutes for expensive foreign goods

b. not allowing the import of goods from industrialized nations

c. a nation importing more than it exports

d. manufacturing goods at home that otherwise would have to be imported

WRITING ACTIVITY

You are a member of the middle class in Argentina under the Peróns' government in the mid-1970s. Explain your opposition to the policies of the Peróns. (Refer to pages 773-776.)

CHAPTER THIRTY-FIVE SKILLS PRACTICE

The following selection was written by an American who lived with his family on a commune in China in the early 1970s. Read the selection and answer questions 1 and 2.

We share a fair sampling of the work of the commune. We are finding muscles that we haven't known for years. We marvel at the strength and endurance of the men and women who work the fields. Their labor is continuous, graceful, and cheerful. It is accompanied by much talk and joking and music from the community loudspeaker. We especially respect their ability to squat on their heels for hours on end without becoming tired. We can last only about five minutes. In harvesting beans and picking rice seedlings, this is a distinct disadvantage.

Our reaction to this hard work after one week surprises us. We love it. We enjoy working with a group taking part in a mutual, productive effort. We also feel that the problems of the world have receded. What is really important is harvesting the wheat before the rains come, getting the vegetables watered before the drought hurts them, and increasing the happiness of our friends on the commune. In short, we are hooked. We have become emotionally attached to the commune.

Adapted from Arthur W. Galston, "Down on the Commune," in Alan Ternes, ed., *Ants, Indians, and Little Dinosaurs* (New York: Charles Scribner's Sons, 1975).

Identifying Specific Details

1. According to this selection, what seemed very important to the author after he had worked on the commune for a week?
a. becoming stronger
b. talk, joking, and music from the community loudspeaker
c. the problems of the world
d. harvesting the wheat before the rains come

Distinguishing Between Facts and Opinions

2. Which of the following is an OPINION presented in this selection?

a. Work of the commune members is continuous, exhausting, and depressing.
b. Work of the commune members is continuous, graceful, and cheerful.
c. Commune workers can squat on their heels for hours without becoming tired.
d. Commune farming is an efficient way of raising crops.

Study the following table and answer question 3.

TRADE BETWEEN THE UNITED STATES AND JAPAN			
	1980	1984	1985
Exports from U.S. to Japan in millions of dollars	20,790	23,575	22,631
Imports from Japan to U.S. in millions of dollars	30,701	57,135	68,783

Data source: *World Almanac and Book of Facts, 1987.*

Using Graphic Sources

3. Which conclusion about trade between the United States and Japan is best supported by this table?
a. Trade between the United States and Japan increased greatly.
b. Imports from Japan to the United States decreased.
c. The difference between the value of imports and the value of exports increased greatly.
d. Japanese products became increasingly better than United States products.

WRITING ACTIVITY

You are an economic analyst for a national news magazine. Write an article discussing some arguments for and against increased tariffs on Japanese goods. Then make your recommendation. (Refer to pages 797–798.)

CHAPTER THIRTY-SIX SKILLS PRACTICE

Read the following selection and answer question 1.

We should not stop or cut back help for the hungry in Asia. Instead, we should ship more fertilizers, chemicals, plows, tractors, and other things that can upgrade living standards. India is demonstrating what can be done with programs using new technology. Some model farming communities have made their food yield per acre grow by more than 200 percent. In light of these facts, nothing is more irresponsible than to say help by the outside world should be held back.

Famine in India and Bangladesh is a test of our capacity to respond to human beings. We can't ignore outstretched hands. If we do, we destroy the most important part of the American character—a feeling of identification with human beings wherever they are.

Adapted from Norman Cousins, "Of Life and Lifeboats," *Saturday Review*, March 8, 1975.

Identifying Author's Point of View

1. Which of the following best expresses the author's point of view?
a. People should be helped by giving them ways to help themselves.
b. Because the United States is a rich country, it should send money as well as food to poor countries.
c. It is a waste of money to help some people.
d. People in Asia do not need outside help because they can help themselves.

Identifying Word Meaning from Structural Analysis

2. What is the best definition of the following word?

terrorism

a. the state of being frightened
b. systematic use of violence to frighten people or governments
c. the use of violence to establish a communist government

d. a violent or frightening person

Read the following selection and answer question 3.

Each year, the amount of carbon dioxide in the atmosphere has risen. Carbon dioxide from the world's exhaust pipes, farms, and factories is warming the earth through a process called the greenhouse effect. Because of this tinkering with the atmosphere, scientists warn of a drastic increase in temperature through the next century. Probable effects include wetter tropics, stormier winters, and hotter and drier summers for regions in a wide band around the earth's middle.

Melting of ice near the poles may lead to a rise in sea level of more than three feet in the next half-century. The higher waters may wipe out areas like the Nile Delta and up to 20 percent of the overcrowded nation of Bangladesh. Along the coasts of the United States, homes may be flooded.

Increasing drought may push the main grain-growing regions northward to find water in little-used areas such as Siberia and Canada. With changes in crops, agriculture may be a net winner, but decades of adjustment could strain food production.

Widespread loss of wild species and forests may occur as natural ecosystems face rapid changes in temperature and rainfall.

Adapted from "Why the Earth's Climate is Changing Dramatically," *San Francisco Chronicle*, Aug. 8, 1988.

Drawing Logical Conclusions

3. Based on information in this selection, which of the following is most likely to reduce the greenhouse effect?
a. clearing away forests and jungle
b. building walls to keep the sea from flooding coastal towns
c. growing crops in northern regions
d. reducing the use of fuels that release carbon dioxide when burned

WRITING ACTIVITY
Choose an area of the world where a clash of values is occurring today. Using what you have learned about the history of the area, explain the historical roots of this clash. Have such clashes occurred in this area at other points in history? Give examples. (Refer to pages 810–811.)